Bridge

Techniques and Tips from the Masters—
4,249 Diagrammed Hands and Plays

Bridge

Techniques and Tips from the Masters— 4,249 Diagrammed Hands and Plays

Edited by Glorya Hale and Nancy Starr

By Tony Sowter, Freddie North, Brian Senior,
Sally Brock, Alan Mould, Robert Berthe & Norbert Lébely,
Raymond Brock, Mark Horton, and Barry Rigal

BLACK DOG
& LEVENTHAL
PUBLISHERS
NEW YORK

Compilation Copyright © 1998 by B. T. Batsford Publishing Ltd. and Black Dog & Leventhal Publishers, Inc.

This edition contains the texts of the original editions. They have been reorganized and reset for this volume.
This edition was originally published in separate volumes under the titles:
"Step-by-Step: Constructive Bidding" by Tony Sowter © 1994 by Tony Sowter
"Step-by-Step: Competitive Bidding" by Tony Sowter © 1996 by Tony Sowter
"Conventional Bidding Explained" by Freddie North © 1994 by Freddie North
"Raising Partner" by Brian Senior © 1994 by Brian Senior
"Step-by-Step: Overcalls" by Sally Brock © 1995 by Sally Brock
"Step-by-Step: Slam Bidding" by Alan Mould © 1995 by Alan Mould
"Cards at Play" by Freddie North © 1995 by Freddie North
"Step-by-Step: Card Play in Suits" by Brian Senior © 1994 by Brian Senior
"Step-by-Step: Card Play in No Trumps" by Robert Berthe and Norbert Lébely © 1981 by Robert Berthe and Norbert Lébely
"Planning the Defense" by Raymond Brock © 1996 by Raymond Brock
"Step-by-Step: Signaling" by Mark Horton © 1994 by Mark Horton
"Step-by-Step: Deceptive Declarer Play" by Barry Rigal © 1996 by Barry Rigal

Published by
Black Dog & Leventhal Publishers, Inc.
151 West 19th Street
New York, NY 10011

Distributed by
Workman Publishing Company
708 Broadway
New York, NY 10003

Printed and bound in the U.S.A.

ISBN: 1-57912-003-2

h g f e d c b a

Designed by Martin Lubin
Composition Tony Meisel
Production by Tim Stauffer

CONTENTS

INTRODUCTION

Bridge is played nearly everywhere in the world: casually in homes, on trains, and even on the Internet, as well as in American Contract Bridge League clubs. The ACBL is the organization which sanctions the thousands of club games and tournament events run annually in North America, and in many off-shore locales, and publishes a directory of affiliated duplicate bridge clubs that is more than one hundred pages long. It lists games that are held in hotels, store fronts, office buildings, on cruise ships, at military bases and in many other facilities. People who travel, or who have recently arrived in a community, can visit any of these clubs and play bridge with strangers who may soon become friends and partners. If you play bridge you can always have good company, and such is the fascination of the game that even after the play is completed, a discussion of the hands can continue endlessly.

Whether you are a "strictly social" or fiercely competitive bridge player, you are likely to be interested in improving your game. This book, a compilation of twelve volumes written by outstanding international players, presents a multitude of ways to help you do that by introducing you to the theories developed and systems played by many of the world's experts. You will also be shown hundreds of deals that illustrate skillful play. There is no attempt here to cover every system currently in vogue. Instead there are variations on the most reliable old favorites, including Blackwood and Stayman, some less widely known but highly effective methods, and a smorgasbord of devices with which even a seasoned player can add to his or her success in that special language of bridge known as bidding. In those cases where a method has different names in different parts of the world, the terminology most familiar to American players has been used. Some of the examples and analyses have been reshaped to make the text as accessible as possible to the average player in the United States, and some treatments that are too esoteric to be permitted in many competitions have been deleted.

The more experienced player will notice that systems bidding four-card major suits and weak no-trumps are included along with the more familiar five-card majors and 15-17 point no-trumps. Whether or not the examples and information conform to your personal style, there is much to be gained from examining what is played elsewhere. Fewer differences show up in the sections on defense and on the play of the hand. There you will find valuable direction no matter what system you favor, and there are many opportunities to learn how the world's best bridge players succeed—and fail—at tackling special problems.

You will notice a variety of styles in our authors' writing and may also discover that a method is so well respected or a subject so troublesome that more than one expert will explain it, although perhaps not in exactly the same way as his colleague. This should come as no surprise to most players who have participated in post-mortems that describe "my way, your way, and the right way."

Grammarians and feminists will note that bridge may be one of the last remaining bastions of chauvinist sexism and that the masculine pronoun is used throughout to include the feminine, except when describing hands of a player who is known to be female. Similarly, mathematicians may demand further proof that the percentages so often cited are accurate. And ethicists might be concerned (though entertained) at being taught how to deceive at cards.

This book is for every bridge player who keeps going back to the table no matter how often he or she loses. You are special warriors always ready for a new battle and a chance to try out a new weapon. You may be a brand new player or a seasoned Life Master, but whatever your level of expertise, and whether you browse in various chapters or read this volume from cover to cover, your game is bound to sharpen.

NANCY STARR
Norwalk, Connecticut

FOREWORD

Had it not been for a game of bridge that happened sixty-five years ago, this publishing house would probably never have been founded.

In 1933, an advertising man and a close friend of my father named Jack Goodman had a job interview with Max Schuster of the book publishing house Simon & Schuster. Schuster told Goodman that given the Depression there was no job available for him. During the interview, Schuster's partner Dick Simon came into the room and was briefly introduced to Goodman. Later Goodman and Simon met again in the elevator leaving the building and Simon asked Goodman whether he wanted to share a cab uptown.

"Sure," Goodman said, "I'm going uptown to play in the Vanderbilt Cup."

"Wow," Simon said, "I'm a big bridge fan. Can I come and kibitz?"

"Of course you can," Goodman said.

That evening, Jack Goodman and my father, Albert Rice Leventhal, played and won the Vanderbilt Cup.

Simon, always an enthusiastic and often an impulsive man said, "I like the way you guys play bridge. You'd be great working at Simon & Schuster."

Goodman took the offer immediately. A few months later, my father left his job in the newspaper business and joined S&S. Goodman spent the rest of his career at S&S where he became Editor-in-Chief. My father worked there for twenty-three years, ending up as Publisher and Executive Vice-President. He then worked for another twenty years elsewhere in the book business.

Goodman and Leventhal, and Simon and a woman named Lee Wright, another S&S employee, continued playing contract and duplicate bridge together for many, many years. They loved the game. They also loved publishing.

Sadly, I am not much of a bridge player, but I got my love of publishing from my father and from Jack, Dick and Lee.

As publisher of Black Dog & Leventhal, I'd like to dedicate this book to them and to that game in 1933.

J.P. Leventhal
New York

NOTE:
The hands are displayed in the text in their relative positions:

Top is North

Bottom is South

Left is West

Right is East

PART I

CONSTRUCTIVE BIDDING

by Tony Sowter

This first section of this book has been inspired by the countless hours that I have enjoyed both teaching and discussing the principles of natural bidding in my bridge classes. Unlike most bridge teachers, I cannot claim that I have spent many years introducing new players to the game, preferring, instead, to spend my time quenching the thirst of the many enthusiastic established players who want to improve their game. Unfortunately, all too often there are enormous gaps in these players' knowledge of basic bidding theory and, worse still, complete reliance on rules which were driven home in early lessons in order to get them started.

I hope that this section addresses most, if not all, of these issues in a way that helps you to understand the principles involved and to learn them. To this end, each chapter begins with a discussion of one or two major issues. Then you are faced with a series of bidding problems, which are intended to drive the point home as well as illustrate a few other principles that apply in each area.

To get the most out of this section, I urge you to force yourself to write your answers to each quiz on a separate piece of paper before reading the answers and explanations in the text. Equally important, if you are sharing this book with your partner, make sure that you answer the questions separately. By all means, compare notes afterwards, but rely on your own bidding judgement first.

Over the years I have played all kinds of systems, strong 1♣ systems, strong 2♣ systems, four card majors and five card majors, and even a variable forcing pass system at international level. I am most at home, however, playing a natural, four card major system.

Without doubt, in the world of bridge at the moment, five card majors hold sway. In the past twenty years, the theory of bidding after a five card major opening has advanced rapidly; however, whatever the advantage is of knowing that when partner opens 1♥ or 1♠ he has at least five of them, in my view it is largely negated by the need to open with either a prepared 1♣ or prepared 1♦ or even both.

While four card major systems do not suffer in quite the same way from this disadvantage, all too often four card major players fail to exploit the natural advantages of opening four card majors. In the competitive situation, however, it is a great advantage to be opening one of a major more frequently. It is a lot harder for your opponents to get into the bidding if you open 1♥ or 1♠ than if you open 1♣ or 1♦ and your opponents' problems are compounded if your partner can raise you as high and as frequently as possible.

Although this section is not about competitive bidding, to extract the maximum competitive advantage from playing four card majors, you need a sound basis to your system. I hope this will help to provide it for you.

Opening the Bidding

It may seem strange to start with an example; however, when the following deal occurred, it struck me as being an excellent illustration of one of the major problems encountered by many average players day after day.

Playing in a teams competition, you find yourself holding this hand:

> ♠ A K 5 2
> ♥ 10 6 4
> ♦ 8 2
> ♣ A Q 9 6

Partner opens 1♦ and naturally you bid 1♠. When your partner rebids 2♣ you face your first problem. You are far too strong to raise 2♣ to 3♣ since this is not forcing and you would probably feel a little uncomfortable jumping to 4♣, because this bypasses 3NT which could easily be the best game. On the other side of the coin, an immediate jump to 3NT suffers from the obvious flaw of having nothing resembling a stopper in the unbid suit.

Thirty years ago this hand would have posed a genuine problem, but these days most players have adopted a convention known as Fourth Suit Forcing, whereby a bid of the fourth suit (in this example 2♥) need not show any particular holding in the suit. It simply maintains fluidity in the sequence and forces partner to make another bid to try and describe his hand. So, in our example, you can elect to bid 2♥ and listen to what partner has to say.

In practice, over 2♥, opener bids 2♠. Now what?

Given that an immediate raise of 2♣ to 3♣ would have been non-forcing, most players have adopted the style that if they use Fourth Suit Forcing (FSF) and then support openers second suit, it is forcing and that would be a convenient method to use here. So you bid 3♣, giving partner yet another opportunity to describe his hand, and he obliges with 3NT. Now you have to decide what to do.

Just to remind you, so far the bidding has been:

Partner	You
1 ♦	1 ♠
2 ♣	2 ♥ (FSF)
2 ♠	3 ♣
3 NT	?

First of all, what is partner's shape? It is a strange sequence for partner has bid both minors, then he has supported spades and then showed something in hearts by bidding 3NT. After opening 1♦ and rebidding 2♣, you must surely expect him to hold five diamonds and four clubs, which leaves only four cards in the majors. Over your 2♥ bid, he did bid 2♠, but this need not promise three cards in that suit. The truth is that with 6-4 in the minors he would have bid 3♦ and with 5-5 or more he would have bid 3♣; and with a good holding in hearts he would have bid either 2NT with a minimum or jumped to 3NT with some extra values. So, he had little alternative but to bid 2♠ with any 2-2-5-4 shape without very good hearts. When he bid 3NT over 3♣ he merely confirmed that he did hold a 2-2-5-4 shape but with something approaching a stopper in hearts—he might have as little as Qx in hearts.

How strong is he? Well, his 2♣ rebid suggested that he was not in the maximum range for a one-opening and neither his 2♠ bid nor his 3NT bid suggested that he had anything more than a minimum opener. Just for example he might have either:

(a)	♠ Q 6	or	(b)	♠ Q 6
	♥ Q 5			♥ A 5
	♦ A K 7 5 3			♦ K Q 7 5 3
	♣ K 10 4 2			♣ K 10 4 2

even though I would personally feel more comfortable bidding 3♥ rather than 3NT holding the second example hand.

How will you fare in 3NT? In both cases the answer must be "very badly." If partner does have hand (a) you probably have nine top tricks, but unless you are lucky the opponents will take five heart tricks before you start. If partner has hand (b) you do have a definite heart trick, but you can only cash eight tricks without knocking out the ♦A. Whereupon the defense should have enough heart winners to beat the contract.

So, what is to be done? Does any other game contract look attractive?

Yes, given reasonable breaks you should be able to make eleven tricks in clubs facing either hand (a) or hand (b). You should lose just two hearts if partner has hand (a) and one heart and one diamond if he holds hand (b). So, the solution to your problem is not to pass 3NT but to bid 5♣.

It is all very easy when you come to think of it—the introduction of Fourth Suit Forcing gave you the time to let partner describe his hand and, having done so, you could almost picture his cards which allowed you to select a sensible final contract. However, to coin a common phrase—the operation was a success but the patient died, for my partner produced the following startling collection:

♠ Q J 6
♥ J 5 3
♦ A K Q J
♣ K J 10

and, needless to say, against 5♣, our opponents happily cashed three hearts.

So, why did my partner make that horrible 2♣ bid? Well, like many players he knew that he could have rebid 2NT to show a balanced hand of about this strength, but he didn't like to suggest playing in no trumps with such weak hearts.

Having bid 2♣ he then had to decide what to do over 2♥. Had he jumped to 3♠ to show three card support and extra values I would have expected a 3-1-5-4 shape, so he closed his eyes and hoped that I would bid again over 2♠. He had not reckoned with my "picturing" his hand so precisely.

That all very neatly brings us to my first rule of bidding which is simply:

"If you hold a balanced hand, bid it like a balanced hand."

4-3-3-3, 4-4-3-2 and 5-3-3-2 distributions account for approximately 48 percent of the total number of hands—if we can establish a straightforward method for dealing with all of these hands, then when opener starts bidding all the suits, as in the example, you should know that he possesses an unbalanced hand.

So, when you open the bidding, how should you plan to bid a balanced hand? Very simply, if the hand falls into your 1NT opening range then you should open 1NT with the possible exception of when you hold a rebiddable five card major. If you hold a hand outside your 1NT opening range and not sufficiently strong to open 2NT, then you should open one of a suit and rebid in no trumps at the appropriate level unless partner bids a suit which you can sensibly support.

There are no other possibilities!

Theorists may complain that, even playing a weak no trump, it is still considered normal to open 1♣ on a minimum strength opener with four clubs and four spades. After all, they will say, if partner responds in either red suit you can sensibly rebid 1♠. However, for the structure of bidding to be easy to follow, it is much better to know that if opener bids two suits he has a distributional hand—normally he will have five cards in the first suit bid and four cards in the second with the rare exception that he might have a 4-4-4-1 distribution. So, playing the weak no trump, it would be silly to consider opening anything other than 1NT holding a hand like:

♠ J 7 6 2
♥ K 5
♦ A J 6
♣ K J 7 4

In truth, I will admit that there are some minimum openers with just 4-4 in the black suits which I would open 1♣ like:

♠ K J 10 4
♥ 7 5
♦ 10 8 2
♣ A K Q 4

but when I have bid 1♣ followed by 1♠ I will expect my partner to bid his hand on the *assumption* that I have five clubs and four spades when I might have opened one spade with this hand.

I will always remember a hand that occurred in a major pairs tournament in France when I was playing with a young English international for the first time. I held:

♠ 7 5
♥ 4
♦ J 10 8 7 6 5
♣ A 10 4 2

My partner opened 1♣, I responded 1♦ and he bid 1♠. I gave preference to 2♣ and he bid 2NT which, given the limited nature of my bidding, must show in the region of eighteen points. What to do now? It seemed to me at the time that, weak though my hand was, it was very suitable to play in clubs; indeed if partner held prime cards like:

♠ A K 4 2
♥ A Q
♦ 4 2
♣ K Q 8 7 6

even 5♣ might be possible. Of course, he was not certain to hold such excellent cards so I decided to leave him a way out by jumping to 4♣. He passed—that was no surprise—but two down was something of a rude awakening. His hand was:

♠ A Q 4 2
♥ A K 5
♦ K 4
♣ Q 8 6 3

Had he opened 1♠, I would either have passed or bid 1NT. After 1♠-1NT the bidding would surely have progressed 2NT-3♦-Pass; a most sensible and successful contract.

If two good players can generate such a mess by introducing two suits when they have a strong balanced hand, how much more important is it that the average club player expunges this dire habit from his vocabulary.

Regardless of the strength of your 1NT opener it should not be too difficult to produce an opening bid and rebid structure to cover all balanced hands.

BALANCED HANDS:
OPENING BID AND REBID STRUCTURE

Basic System: Acol Four Card Majors:
Weak No Trump (12-14)

Strength	Action
less than 12	Pass.
12-14	1NT. Exception: When you hold a rebiddable five card major you open the major.
15-17	Open one of a suit planning to rebid no trumps at minimum level. If partner bids your second suit you may raise to an appropriate level.

With two four card suits:
With both minors open 1♦.
With both majors open 1♥ (and raise a 1♠ response to 3♠).
With a major and a minor—open the major.

18-a bad 20	Open one of a suit and jump in no trumps.
A good 20-22	Open 2NT.
23-24	Open 2♣ and rebid in no trumps at minimum level.

BALANCED HANDS:
OPENING BID AND REBID STRUCTURE

Basic System: Acol Four Card Majors:
Strong No Trump (15-17)

Strength	Action
less than 12	Pass.
12-14	Open one of a suit planning to rebid no trumps at minimum level. If partner bids your second suit you may raise to an appropriate level.

With two four card suits:
With both minors open 1♦
With both majors open 1♥ (and raise a 1♠ response to 2♠).
With a major and a minor—open the major.

15-17	Open 1NT.
18- a bad 20	Open one of a suit and jump in no trumps.
A good 20-22	Open 2NT.
23-24	Open 2♣ and rebid in no trumps at minimum level.

Notes:

(i) A number of players might regard 16-18 as their chosen range for a strong no trump opening. This is highly inefficient as it results in a minimum no trump rebid covering a very wide range (i.e. 12-15) and a jump rebid catering just a nineteen point hand.

(ii) A number of leading tournament players have started playing a 14-16 1NT opening. In our approach this does have advantages with the weaker (more frequent) hands. For example, when partner responds at the two level it narrows the band of the 2NT rebid to just 12-13, which does make it easier for responder to guess what to do. The downside is that opener will be forced to jump to 3NT on a fairly wide range of 17-19 points.

Before going any further, a special request. Don't just skip to the page with all the answers on it, pick up a pen and a piece of paper and write down your answer to each question. The simple truth is that the best way of learning is to benefit from your own mistakes, so make sure you put yourself to the test before reading the answers. After all, there is no point in cheating yourself.

QUIZ

Suppose it is Neither Side Vulnerable and you are the dealer, what would you bid with each of the following hands? If you normally play a weak no trump showing 12-14 points consider the hands in the left-hand column. If you prefer to play a strong no trump showing 15-17 points then look at the hands on the right.

For Weak No Trump	**For Strong No Trump**
1. ♠ A K 10 6	♠ A Q 10 6
♥ A K Q 5	♥ A K 5 3
♦ J 7 2	♦ J 7 2
♣ 6 4	♣ 6 4
2. ♠ K 4 2	♠ A Q 2
♥ J 8 7 4 2	♥ J 8 7 4 2
♦ K J 2	♦ K 10 2
♣ A 5	♣ A Q
3. ♠ K Q 4 3	♠ K Q 4 3
♥ Q 6	♥ Q 6
♦ A J 5 2	♦ A J 5 2
♣ K J 3	♣ J 3 2
4. ♠ Q 10 7 2	♠ Q 10 7 2
♥ K 2	♥ K 2
♦ Q 5 3	♦ K 5 3
♣ A K 4 2	♣ A K 4 2

For Weak No Trump	**For Strong No Trump**
5. ♠ Q 5	♠ K 5
♥ J 5	♥ Q 5
♦ K Q 4 2	♦ K Q 4 2
♣ A J 7 4 2	♣ A J 7 4 2
6. ♠ A Q 7 5 2	♠ A Q 7 5 2
♥ A 10 6 4	♥ A 10 6 4
♦ 9 6 5	♦ 9 6 5
♣ 5	♣ 5
7. ♠ A 10 6 4	♠ A 10 6 4
♥ A Q 7 5 2	♥ A Q 7 5 2
♦ 9 6 5	♦ 9 6 5
♣ 5	♣ 5
8. ♠ A 4 2	♠ A 4 2
♥ A Q 9 6 5 2	♥ A Q 9 6 5 2
♦ 7 5	♦ 7 5
♣ 6 4	♣ 6 4
9. ♠ A 7 4 2	♠ A J 7 4
♥ K J 6 4	♥ K J 6 4
♦ A J 7 4	♦ A Q 7 4
♣ 2	♣ 2

10. ♠ A Q 10 4	♠ A Q 10 4
♥ 10 7 6 4	♥ 10 7 6 4
♦ A Q 7 4	♦ A Q 7 4
♣ 2	♣ 2

ANSWERS TO QUIZ

1. (a) Playing the weak no trump, what do you open with:
♠ A K 10 6
♥ A K Q 5
♦ J 7 2
♣ 6 4

(b) Playing the strong no trump, what do you open with:
♠ A Q 10 6
♥ A K 5 3
♦ J 7 2
♣ 6 4

Recommended bid: 1♥ **Recommended bid: 1♥**

With two good four card majors, it is tempting to open 1♠ intending to bid 2♥ on the next round. However, if you choose that route, partner will think that you have five spades and four hearts and you might find yourself given preference to a 4-2 fit. The solution is to bid 1♥ and rebid in no trumps at minimum level unless partner bids spades. If partner has a good hand with, say, five clubs and four spades he will respond 2♣; but you should still not miss your spade fit, because after you bid 2NT he should introduce spades at the three level. If partner turns out to be too weak to bid again after your 2NT rebid, he should not have responded 2♣, preferring to respond 1♠ instead.

2. (a) Playing the weak no trump, what do you open with:
♠ K 4 2
♥ J 8 7 4 2
♦ K J 2
♣ A 5

(b) Playing the strong no trump, what do you open with:
♠ A Q 2
♥ J 8 7 4 2
♦ K 10 2
♣ A Q

Recommended bid: 1NT Recommended bid: 1NT

Yes, I understand that it is tempting to open your five card major, but before you open the bidding you should always consider what you are going to bid on the second round. Over 1♥ – 2♣ you are really stuck for a rebid: you can bid 2♥, but don't be surprised if partner leaves you there with a singleton. The sensible approach is to disregard poor five card suits, treat them as if there were only four cards in the suit, and open 1NT.

3. (a) Playing the weak no trump, what do you open with:
♠ K Q 4 3
♥ Q 6
♦ A J 5 2
♣ K J 3

(b) Playing the strong no trump, what do you open with:
♠ K Q 4 3
♥ Q 6
♦ A J 5 2
♣ J 3 2

Recommended bid: 1♠ **Recommended bid: 1♠**

There is a view that with 4-4-3-2 hands with two non-touching suits outside the 1NT opening range, it is right to open the suit below the doubleton. The idea is that when responder bids the two card suit, opener bids his second suit and, if responder bids the three card suit, opener can support him. The thought of opening 1♦ and calmly raising 2♣ to 3♣ fills me with dismay.

For those who play the weak no trump, it is much better to say, "I have a balanced hand of 15-17 points with at least four spades," while opening 1♠ and rebidding 2NT showing a balanced 12-14 with a four card spade suit is a much better description if you play a strong no trump. On a good day, opening the major rather than the minor also leaves open the possibility of finding the 4-3 major fit when 3NT is wrong.

A number of players would choose to open this hand with a "short" 1♣, so that they could have a comfortable rebid at the one level. Playing the strong no trump, there is some case to open with a club on hands like these, indeed, without the proviso that a 2NT rebid should be 12-14 after responder introduces a new suit at the two level, it would be essential to open this hand 1♣. However, if you do adopt the short club style, you still have to decide whether to rebid 1NT to show the 12-14 points with or without four spades or to bid 1♠ to show at least four spades and at least three clubs!

How much more comfortable it is to play naturally: if responder is expected to have at least ten points to bid a new suit at the two level, then you can open 1♠ on hands like this and comfortably rebid 2NT over a response in a new suit at the two level.

4. **(a)** Playing the weak   **(b)** Playing the strong
     no trump,   no trump,
     what do you open with: what do you open with:

	(a)	(b)
♠	Q 10 7 2	Q 10 7 2
♥	K 2	K 2
♦	Q 5 3	K 5 3
♣	A K 4 2	A K 4 2

Recommended bid: 1NT   Recommended bid: 1NT

You have a balanced hand that falls within your 1NT opening range, and there is no good reason not to open 1NT, especially since your high card strength is well scattered. If you pack all your high cards into your two suits, with the clubs being better than the spades, I would have some sympathy with your treating the hand as a club/spade two suiter. However, you should remember that if you voluntarily bid two suits, your partner will expect you to have at least five cards in your first suit and four cards in the second, and he should bid accordingly.

So, weak no-trumpers might open 1♣ planning to rebid 1♠ with:

    ♠ A Q 6 5
    ♥ 6 5
    ♦ 7 6 5
    ♣ A Q J 5

rather than opening 1NT while strong no trump players might do the same with:

    ♠ A Q J 5
    ♥ 6 5
    ♦ 7 6 5
    ♣ A K J 5

However, you should remember that when partner puts you back into clubs with very marginal support, he was expecting you to have five of them.

5. **(a)** Playing the weak   **(b)** Playing the strong
     no trump,   no trump,
     what do you open with: what do you open with:

	(a)	(b)
♠	Q 5	K 5
♥	J 5	Q 5
♦	K Q 4 2	K Q 4 2
♣	A J 7 4 2	A J 7 4 2

Recommended Bid: 1NT   Recommended Bid: 1NT

Here once again you have a hand that falls into the range of your 1NT opening, but a 5-4-2-2 distribution is not usually regarded as balanced, so what are the alternatives? There are two—you could open with either 1♣ or 1♦, but before choosing either you should consider what you are going to do in the next round.

If you open 1♦ and partner responds in a major you are really forced into bidding your club suit. Nothing wrong with that, you might think, except that partner will think you have at least five diamonds and four clubs and, when he gives you preference to diamonds and puts two cards in both minors down in the dummy, you are likely to be at least marginally disappointed.

Alternatively, what is going to happen if you open 1♣ and partner responds in a major? You face an interesting choice of evils. You can either repeat your poor quality club suit when partner should expect less high card strength but a better suit or you can overbid by reversing into 2♦. If you choose the latter, remember that most partners would expect this bid to show in the region of seventeen points, so they will drive to game with a respectable eight count and, this time, it will be their turn to be disappointed with the dummy.

In any system there are always hands that don't fit well into any compartment. Clearly, any particular choice might work out well on any particular hand and you have to make a choice between less than perfect alternatives. Here the potential flaws in choosing to open either 1♣ or 1♦ make 1NT by far the most attractive choice. Admittedly, partner will not expect you to have a doubleton in *both* majors, but certainly he will not be at all surprised if you have a doubleton in *either* one.

6. (a) Playing the weak no trump, what do you open with:
- ♠ A Q 7 5 2
- ♥ A 10 6 4
- ♦ 9 6 5
- ♣ 5

Recommended Bid: 1♠

(b) Playing the strong no trump, what do you open with:
- ♠ A Q 7 5 2
- ♥ A 10 6 4
- ♦ 9 6 5
- ♣ 5

Recommended Bid: 1♠

Yes, I know that you only have ten high card points but this hand qualifies as a minimum opening bid. Indeed, it qualifies under the "Rule of 19" because it has ten high card points and nine cards in the two longest suits. Two aces provide the expected defensive strength and 5-4-3-1 shapes always tend to play well. Add to that the fact that you have both majors and can describe your hand quite well, by opening 1♠ and rebidding 2♥ with the expected 5-4 distribution.

On the minus side, it is possible that partner will drive too high with no fit for either of you suits, or if he has too many "wasted" values facing your singleton club; but against that you are likely to reach a thin game when you do have a fit and you are particularly well placed in any part-score battle. So open 1♠.

7. (a) Playing the weak no trump, what do you open with:
- ♠ A 10 6 4
- ♥ A Q 7 5 2
- ♦ 9 6 5
- ♣ 5

Recommended Bid: Pass

(b) Playing the strong no trump, what do you open with:
- ♠ A 10 6 4
- ♥ A Q 7 5 2
- ♦ 9 6 5
- ♣ 5

Recommended Bid: Pass

Curiously enough this hand also qualifies as an opening bid under the "Rule of 19": it has the same 5-4-3-1 distribution, the same pointage and the same two aces and both majors, but I would not recommend opening the bidding. Why not? Well, if you do open the bidding, you have no convenient way of describing your hand. If you opened 1♥ and partner responded 1♠ you would be delighted to support him, but if he responded 2♣ you would be forced to rebid your heart suit, which gives a rather poor description of the hand. Using two bids to describe nine of your cards is much more illuminating than using two bids just to convey that you have a five card suit—especially so when on many occasions your partner should expect you to have a six card suit to bid this way.

As a general rule, if you are the dealer, it is not worth opening light on any hand unless you can describe it well. If you play the weak no trump you should have something approximating to 12-14 balanced points when you open 1NT. Of course, there is room to upgrade a good-looking eleven point hand to twelve, but opening any old eleven point hand figures to be a losing policy in the long run. After all, your partner should bid as if you have guaranteed

twelve points and therefore you will get too high on many occasions.

With distributional hands it is much the same story. If you know you can describe your hand well on the first two rounds of the bidding then it is worth considering opening light, but otherwise don't bother. One final word of caution: be particularly wary of 4-4-4-1 shaped hands as experience suggests that unlike 5-4-3-1 shapes they don't play well *and* they always tend to be good in defense when the opponents play the hand, since most of the time their suits will not break well.

8. (a) Playing the weak no trump, what do you open with:
- ♠ A 4 2
- ♥ A Q 9 6 5 2
- ♦ 7 5
- ♣ 6 4

Recommended Bid: 1♥

(b) Playing the strong no trump, what do you open with:
- ♠ A 4 2
- ♥ A Q 9 6 5 2
- ♦ 7 5
- ♣ 6 4

Recommended Bid: 1♥

After all that, here is another routine opener. Once again this hand qualifies as an opening bid under the "Rule of 19" and we have no trouble describing this hand since we would plan to bid and rebid hearts. In fact, in terms of playing strength this hand is the broad equivalent of a hand with thirteen high card points and five hearts—and you would certainly open that! More specifically, consider the power of the sixth heart. Providing you play in hearts, or perhaps even in no trumps, you will expect to take one more trick with a six card suit than a five card suit. The pack comprises forty high card points and there are thirteen tricks, so on average for each three points you should take a trick. It's obvious really, that providing you can make use of the sixth heart, it can be assigned a value of three points.

9. (a) Playing the weak no trump, what do you open with:
- ♠ A 7 4 2
- ♥ K J 6 4
- ♦ A J 7 4
- ♣ 2

Recommended Bid: 1♥

(b) Playing the strong no trump, what do you open with:
- ♠ A J 7 4
- ♥ K J 6 4
- ♦ A Q 7 4
- ♣ 2

Recommended Bid: 1♥

We finally arrive at the scourge of our system. In general terms 4-4-4-1 hands do not qualify as balanced, so you cannot sensibly open with 1NT even if they are of the right strength, though occasionally you might be able to rebid in no trumps if partner responds in your singleton. They create a problem not only because without a five card suit they are poor in playing strength, but also because they are very difficult to describe. After all, if you open in one suit and then rebid in another, partner may expect you to have five cards in the first suit and four in the second—so in effect anything you do becomes a lie.

Until the early 1960's, all 4-4-4-1 hands tended to be opened with the suit below the singleton; however, at about that time, it was suggested that the particular distribution that we have here could be more sensibly opened with 1♥. The reason was simply that if you open 1♥ you can support spades if partner bids them and rebid 2♦ if partner happens to respond 2♣—so with this particular 4-4-4-1 hand the normal opening bid is certainly 1♥. At least, if you follow this style religiously you can be assured that if partner opens 1♠ and rebids in any other suit, then he must have five spades for there is no 4-4-4-1 type hand on which he would open 1♠.

This point of view became so popular that many players will tend to open a 1-4-4-4 hand with 1♦ following exactly the same principles. However I would argue that if the hearts are good you should open 1♥ and not 1♦—after all there is a large family of hands where 4♥ on a 4-3 fit may prove to be the only opening game and if you don't bid them right away you will never get to play in that strain.

Overall, the best advice I can give is:

(1) Remember that whatever you open you must make sure you have a reasonable rebid when partner responds in your short suit.

(2) Then choose the suits that best describe your hand.

For example, consider the next hand:

10. (a) Playing the weak no trump, what do you open with:
♠ A Q 10 4
♥ 10 7 6 4
♦ A Q 7 4
♣ 2

(b) Playing the strong no trump, what do you open with:
♠ A Q 10 4
♥ 10 7 6 4
♦ A K Q 7
♣ 2

Recommended Bid: 1♣   Recommended Bid: 1♣

These examples are obvious constructions to illustrate the principle. Opening this hand 1♥ planning to rebid 2♦ over a 2♣ response is tantamount to committing suicide. Remember that partner's actions will be strongly influenced by his expectation that you hold five cards in the first suit that you bid. Inviting preference on a doubleton when you hold four to the ten is no thing of beauty, and even jump support on king to three might be embarrassing.

With this kind of hand you need to back your eyesight with good common sense. Don't open 1♥, open 1♣, planning to rebid 2♦. Sure, you will still have one spade less than your partner will expect but at least, if he supports spades, it is likely to be a playable spot.

Alter the hand to something like:

♠ A 6 5 4
♥ Q 6 5 4
♦ A K J 5
♣ 5

and I would solve the problem by opening 1♦. If partner responds at the one level I would clearly have no problem, and if he inconveniently chooses to bid 2♣ I will rebid 2NT.

Admittedly, if I am playing the weak no trump, I am a point short but, as I suggested before, there are many hands that don't conform exactly to anything and then you will have to use your commonsense. In this case, by opening 1♦ you avoid all the pitfalls associated with suggesting that you hold a five card major, and give a good indication of what you would like your partner to lead should you end up defending the contract. So, I ask you: "Is owing your partner a point such a high price to pay?"

2
Chapter

The First Response

Let's start by asking what you would bid on both of the following hands in response to a 1♣ opening from your partner:

(a)	♠ 7 5	**(b)**	♠ A 5
	♥ K Q 7 5		♥ K Q 7 5
	♦ Q 8 5 4		♦ Q 8 5 4
	♣ 10 4 2		♣ K 10 2

The popular view of responding with two four card suits is that you should bid your lowest one, so on both of these hands I would expect most players to bid 1♦. The theoretical argument for bidding this way is simply that by responding in your lowest suit, it gives you the maximum chance of finding a 4-4 fit in either of your suits. If he has four hearts you would expect partner to rebid 1♥ and if he has four diamonds he should support you right away.

Certainly if opener has a weak hand with five clubs and four diamonds, you might miss your diamond fit by responding 1♥, though it is also true to say that, if partner has a good enough hand for you to make a game contact in diamonds facing hand (a), then he will be strong enough himself to reverse into 2♦ on the next round. Accordingly, you may not be totally surprised to hear that I believe that 1♥ is the right response in both cases! Let's look at each hand in turn.

Hand (a)

Notice that, while you have more than enough to make a response to 1♣, your expectation is that, unless partner shows substantial extra values, you are only going to make minimal noises on this hand. Whichever red suit you bid, if partner rebids 1♣ you are going to bid 1NT or give preference to 2♣, and if partner rebids 1NT or 2♣ you are going to pass. So first you should be planning to make just one voluntary bid and 1♥ gives a much better description of where your assets are than 1♦. In the long term, your partner will have a much better chance of judging what to do if you show him the assets you have rather than those you haven't.

There are a number of reasons for this:

1. If you respond 1♦ and find partner with three diamonds and a singleton heart in a strong distributional hand, he is likely to find your actual holdings most disappointing when he comes to rest in a high level club contract, but if he holds three hearts and a singleton diamond and you bid 1♥ he certainly won't be disappointed.

2. If the opponents enter the auction and partner decides to support you on a marginal hand, you will be much better off playing in your best suit than in your worst one.

3. Let's suppose that you do have a 4-4 heart fit and you respond 1♦ only to hear the next hand bid 1♠ or worse still 2♠. Are you still so confident that you are going to find your major suit fit?

4. Then suppose that your opponents actually have the effrontery to play the hand and your partner is on lead, is he supposed to find a heart lead when you have responded 1♠?

No, however I look at it, it is much better to bid a suit where you have values than one where you haven't. However, that is not the only reason for responding 1♥ on this type of hand. Let's suppose that partner has a hand something like:

♠ 9 4
♥ A 9 3
♦ A K 6
♣ A Q J 6 5

Now, where would you like to play this hand facing your motley collection, which if you remember is:

♠ 7 5
♥ K Q 7 5
♦ Q 8 5 4
♣ 10 4 2

Yes, that's right. The best game contract is undoubtedly 4♥!—a contract that is unlikely to be on the menu if you respond 1♦ but which you might just reach if you bid 1♥.

Whichever red suit you respond in, your partner is likely to rebid 2NT—showing a balanced 18-19, so you have the values to go on and with good hearts and three club card support a careful bidder might just continue with 3♦. Opener should now show his three card heart support and with only a small doubleton in spades you should really try a fourth suit 3♠, to try to see what partner chooses to do. Clearly, with no semblance of a spade stopper, he will want to play in either clubs or hearts.

I'm not pretending that such a sequence would be easy for most pairs to produce at the table, but if you don't respond 1♥ you have absolutely no chance of hitting the jackpot. Remember that with most balanced hands without a primary fit the most likely game destination is 3NT, but on many hands a good 4-3 fit in a major may be a sensible alternative. So apart from the maxim of bidding good suits before bad ones, also try to respond in a decent four card major suit rather than bidding a four card diamond suit.

Hand (b)

Quite clearly, the second example is a totally different kettle of fish. Partner has opened the bidding with 1♣ and you are looking at:

♠ A 5
♥ K Q 7 5
♦ Q 8 5 4
♣ K 10 2

First, facing even the most minimum opening bid, you must plan to be in game, but which one? The most likely destinations are 4♥, 5♣ and 3NT—so to describe our hand well, you need to show your heart suit and show a game-going hand with clubs at a low enough level to play in 3NT. The best start to this plan must be to bid your good major suit.

Furthermore, just as in the previous example, it will be difficult to get out of no trumps to either a 4-3 heart fit or to a 5-3 club fit when it is right, if you start by responding 1♦.

Let's consider what you would bid on the next round if partner rebids 1♠. First, if you have chosen to respond 1♦ on the first round, you have a game-going hand with very good hearts, so the normal bid would seem to be 3NT. Alternatively, if you start with 1♥ you have a much better choice on the next round. Admittedly, many players would still blast into 3NT, but those with a good understanding of Fourth Suit Forcing are likely to proceed with 2♦.

Note that if partner holds something like:

♠ K 9 8 7
♥ A 9 2
♦ 7
♣ A Q J 9 6

after the following bidding sequence:

1♣	1♦
1♠	3 NT
?	

he would have little option but to pass, but after:

1♣	1♥
1♠	2♦
?	

he has a comfortable jump to 3♥ available, and with opener painting a picture of a reasonable 4-3-1-5 hand it should not be impossible for you to recognize the considerable potential of the combined hands (note just how important it is to know that after 1♣–1♥–1♠ partner does have five clubs and four spades). The full sequence might be:

1♣	1♥
1♠	2♦
3♥	4♣
4 NT	5♦
6♣	Pass

Despite a combined holding of only twenty-eight high card points, the hands fit particularly well so that 6♣ is an excellent contract. By contrast note that when opener has a subsidiary fit for your diamond suit like:

♠ K 9 8 7
♥ 6
♦ A 9 2
♣ A Q J 9 6

then 6♣ is a terrible contract and 3NT, which we will reach regardless of whether we respond 1♦ or 1♥, is right.

Of course, there is a moral to the story: in response, don't start your campaign by bidding a bad four card suit when you have a good hand!

RESPONDING TO 1NT

So far, I have said nothing about an area of the game which many pairs devote a lot of time to developing, that is responding to 1NT. I am not going to say too much on this particular subject and far be it from me to try and stop players devoting many hours of their valuable time to honing up on their sophisticated methods. However, I firmly believe that in practice, all this wonderful machinery makes little contribution to improving their results at the table. Indeed, while Stayman in some form or other would be fairly high on my list of essential conventional aids, transfers in any one of their many guises would have very low priority. I have no intention of wasting too much space reploughing regularly tilled soil; however, whatever methods you employ there are some hand types which seem to be notoriously difficult to handle well. Let's consider an example:

♠ A Q 4 2	♠ K 10 5
♥ 7 5	♥ 8 4
♦ A 9 5 4	♦ K 8 2
♣ K 10 4	♣ A Q J 7 6 2

With West as dealer, picking a weak no trump, he has little option but to open 1NT and who could criticize East for simply raising to 3NT. Nobody would deny that East's hand is right for a raise to game, but barring miracles the opponents will take the first five heart tricks to beat the contract—and, what is worse, 4♠ and, for that matter, 5♣ are much better spots.

This situation is unsatisfactory yet it only takes a moment's consideration to find a fairly reliable way of bidding this pair of hands to the top spot. Let's suppose that East starts his campaign by using Stayman—yes, I know he doesn't actually have a four card major but bear with me for the moment. So, the auction starts:

1 NT	2♣
2♠	?

What should East do now? Well, I know what I want to bid, and that is 3♣ natural, forcing to game, but unsure of the final destination. Now, the whole auction should be:

1 NT	2♣
2♠	3♣
3♦	3♠
4♠	Pass

With nothing in hearts, but values in both the minors, West is careful to bid 3♦, showing where his outside values are. Again, with nothing in hearts, East takes the opportunity to show his three-card support for spades, and West completes the exercise by raising to game as his spades are quite good. With poorer spades and better diamonds, West might consider bidding 4♣ as 5♣ might then be a better spot than 4♠.

Without any doubt, adopting this free-wheeling exploratory style has been worth bushels of points over the years, especially in team play, and I would thoroughly recommend it.

Obviously, this would mean a total change of method if you still play that 2♣ Stayman followed by 3♣ is to play; however, you might like to consider whether the up side of being able to conduct natural exploratory auctions of the type shown in the example is more than adequate compensation for the rare hand when passing 1NT rather than running out into 3♣ proves to be a disaster.

Relaxing the requirement that a hand that uses Stayman *must* have a four card major is also a small price to pay. After all, the inference would still be that if responder rebids 2NT or 3NT after using Stayman, he must have at least one four card major.

If you already play an involved system of transfers, please consider how you would handle this type of hand. If the honest answer is "Probably, not very well," then consider using Stayman followed by three of either minor in this way. I firmly believe that you will find this a lot more beneficial than using a sequence like:

1 NT	2♣
2♠	3♣

to show an invitational strength hand with four hearts and at least five clubs—a method that seems quite popular in some transferring circles.

In each case, your partner opens 1♥, what do you respond?

1. ♠ Q 8 7 6 5
    ♥ A J 6
    ♦ K 5
    ♣ 10 4 2

2. ♠ J 8 7 6 5
    ♥ A J 6 2
    ♦ K 5
    ♣ 4 2

3. ♠ K 4 2
    ♥ K J 6
    ♦ K 10 8 2
    ♣ A 10 5

4. ♠ K 4 2
    ♥ K 6
    ♦ K 10 8 2
    ♣ A J 10 5

5. ♠ Q 8 7 2
    ♥ K 2
    ♦ 7 5
    ♣ K J 8 7 2

6. ♠ K J 8 7
    ♥ K 2
    ♦ 7 5
    ♣ K J 8 7 2

7. ♠ A 7
    ♥ A J 6 2
    ♦ 4 2
    ♣ K J 8 7 2

8. ♠ A 7 2
    ♥ A J 6 2
    ♦ K J
    ♣ J 7 4 2

ANSWERS TO QUIZ 2

In each case, your partner opens 1♥, what do you respond?

1. ♠ Q 8 7 6 5
    ♥ A J 6
    ♦ K 5
    ♣ 10 4 2

Recommended Bid: 1♠

We start with a relatively easy one. Even if partner has five hearts he may still have four spades, so your first move is to bid 1♠ before supporting hearts on the next round. If, for example, partner rebids 2♦ you are worth a limit raise to 3♥, showing three card support for partner's presumed five card suit and inviting him to press on to game with more than minimum values. Yes, when opener rebids 2♦, he should be expected to have five hearts because with a balanced hand of any strength he should have either opened in no trumps, rebid in no trumps or supported your 1♠ response.

2. ♠ J 8 7 6 5
    ♥ A J 6 2
    ♦ K 5
    ♣ 4 2

Recommended Bid: 3♥

This is similar to the last hand except that you are blessed with four card trump support for partner's major suit. If you introduce spades and then jump to 3♥ when partner rebids two of a minor (as you did on the last example), partner can only be certain of three card support. Therefore it is right to give him the good news right away by supporting hearts.

How many should you bid? In standard methods, the limit raise to 3♥ shows about 10-11 points and four card trump support. Here you only have nine high card points, but you have extra distributional values. The 5-4-2-2 shape is much better than the more normal 4-4-3-2 shape: in playing the hand partner should benefit from the extra ruffing value in the minor suits or the chance of establishing the spade suit.

If I were forced to select between the two alternatives of under bidding with just a simple raise to 2♥ or over bidding with a leap to game, I would prefer the latter on the basis that there are some fairly minimum opening hands where partner might pass 3♥ only to find that the hands fit rather well and the game may be made. For example, holding:

♠ K Q
♥ K 9 8 7 3
♦ A 7 4 2
♣ 8 7

partner will pass 3♥ and the game depends on little more than the hearts breaking evenly.

3.   ♠ K 4 2
     ♥ K J 6
     ♦ K 10 8 2
     ♣ A 10 5

Recommended Bid: 3NT

One of the most frequently misused bids in good standard Acol and in standard American bridge is the immediate response of 3NT after partner has opened with one of a major. Many players believe that this immediate 3NT response should simply mean that they wish to play in 3NT regardless—that is unless partner has sufficient values to explore a possible slam. The bid clearly shows a game-going balanced hand without the ability to bid the other major. But how many cards should it promise in a partner's suit—two or three?

I am a firm believer that over openings of one of a major the immediate jump responses of both 2NT and 3NT should *guarantee* three card support, and that both bids invite partner to help make the decision on what the contract should be. Consider the advantages. If he can be certain of three card support then he can judge whether to play in 3NT, remove to four of his major or, with a better hand, he can explore the slam possibilities with much greater safety knowing that he always has a safe haven in which to play.

Furthermore, if I am not allowed to respond 3NT on hands of this type, then what am I to bid? A 2♦ response to 1♥ normally shows five cards in the suit and when partner rebids his hearts I have little alternative but to raise him to game regardless. He may well be disappointed with my lack of ruffing values, but I can barely make a unilateral decision to play in 3NT after he has rebid his suit.

4.   ♠ K 4 2
     ♥ K 6
     ♦ K 10 8 2
     ♣ A J 10 5

Recommended Bid: 2♣

This is the reverse of the coin: a game-going hand, no spade suit and good cover in both minors—everybody's 3NT bid except that you do not have three card heart support. Notice that without three hearts you must hold either a five card suit or two four card suits, so what is the panic?

By bidding 2♣, you give yourselves the chance to find a fit in either minor and if partner does rebid 2♥ you can still bid 3NT on the next round.

5.   ♠ Q 8 7 2
     ♥ K 2
     ♦ 7 5
     ♣ K J 8 7 2

Recommended Bid: 1♠

Although you have nine points and a fair five card suit, the natural 2♣ bid risks losing a 4-4 spade fit. If opener holds five or six hearts and four spades without the strength to reverse, over 2♣ he will be endplayed into rebidding his hearts. Of course, you could continue by bidding spades yourself, but this would be an overbid taking you to at least 2NT facing any minimum opener. With a hand of this shape you should always bid 1♠ unless you are strong enough to bid both of your suits in natural order.

6.   ♠ K J 8 7
     ♥ K 2
     ♦ 7 5
     ♣ K J 8 7 2

Recommended Bid: 2♣

I have always found it strange that, when they have the strength to bid both their suits in the natural order, many players are seduced by the quality of their spades to bid them first. Curiously, starting with 1♠ on this hand is potentially much more damaging than responding with 2♣ on the previous hand. On hand five you would be a little unlucky to miss 4♠ by responding 2♣, but on this hand you will be in considerable difficulty if partner simply rebids his hearts. If you introduce your clubs at the three level you will be committed to playing in game, and partner will expect you to have five spades or a much stronger hand. No, if you do bid 1♠ on the first round your best continuation over a 2♥ rebid is to raise to 3♥, giving your partner to proceed to 4♥ with a good minimum opener. Of course, you might miss 3NT in this way, but at least you will not have put your head indiscriminately on the chopping block.

How much simpler it is to bid your suits in their natural order. Respond 2♣ and if partner rebids 2♥ introduce your spades. If opener rebids 2♦ instead you have a comfortable 2NT continuation.

7. ♠ A 7
♥ A J 6 2
♦ 4 2
♣ K J 8 7 2

Recommended Bid: 2♣

With a good opening bid and four card support for partner's major, it is quite clear that this hand belongs in at least game. However, rather than just raise to game, it may help partner to judge the slam prospects more clearly if you let him know that you have a reasonable club fit. By bidding 2♣ and then jumping to game in hearts if he rebids 2♦, you paint a good picture of your hand. Not quite strong enough to jump in clubs immediately, but good enough to consider a slam if the opener has some kind of fit in clubs.

For example, suppose that the opener holds:

♠ 9 7
♥ K Q 9 8 3
♦ A 9 8 7
♣ A Q

Facing a decent five card club suit and good hearts you can already "see" eleven tricks and presumably responder must have some other cards beside clubs and hearts. In essence I would believe it right to decide to bid 6♥ provided that partner can provide a spade control. To find out I would make a cuebid of 5♣ which in itself already suggests that I am looking for a spade control. If responder bids 5♦ I would sign off on 5♥. If he just bids 5♥ I will pass, but, hopefully, on this hand he will recognize the importance of his spade control and take the plunge to the six level.

8. ♠ A 7 2
♥ A J 6 2
♦ K J
♣ J 7 4 2

Recommended Bid: 4♦

This example is included because it is one of the few areas of the game where I believe some conventional aid is of particular use to the average player. If you bid 2♣ and follow it with 4♥ as you did on the previous example, partner will expect better clubs and may press on for the wrong reason. Equally with a pronounced shortage in clubs he is likely to pass on the reasonable assumption that you have wasted values in clubs. For example, holding:

♠ K Q 6
♥ K Q 8 7 2
♦ A 9 8 7
♣ 5

partner will pass, only to find that 6♥ is cold. (Notice that facing your previous hand 6♥ is terrible.)

Equally if you just raise 1♥ to 4♥ partner will not really know that you have so many high cards. After all, would you not raise 1♥ to 4♥ on something like:

♠ 7
♥ A J 6 4 3
♦ 10 4
♣ K Q 8 7 2

To cope with this problem, I would recommend that you play some form of Swiss to help distinguish between high card and distributional raises to four of either major.

There are lots of different varieties, some of which just employ the rarely used bids of 4♣ and 4♦ as immediate responses to one of a major, and some that use all the double jump bids in a new suit after the one of a major opening. For example, if you chose to jump to 3♠ to show a spade control plus good trump support you were already using a simple version of Swiss—and you had better have agreed this with your partner or else you might find yourself playing in spades!

For simplicity, I am going to recommend a variety of Swiss known in England as Fruit Machine, and elsewhere as Control Swiss.

The immediate response of 4♣ shows a high card raise to four of the major with one of three possibilities:

(a) Three aces.
(b) Two aces and the king of trumps.
(c) Two aces and a side-suit singleton.

If your partner needs to know which, he can proceed with a relay of 4♦ asking and then with:

(a) Three aces, you bid 4NT
(b) Two aces and the king of trumps, you bid four of the trump suit.
(c) Two aces and a side suit singleton, you bid your short suit.

The immediate jump to 4♦ shows a high-card raise to four of the major without the requirements to bid 4♣.

For players whose slam bidding is inexorably based on the use of Gerber, the sacrifice of the 4♣ bid to the virtues of Swiss may just be too much to bear. However, at the very least it does make good sense to adopt the 4♦ bid as an artificial forcing raise to game. The hands with good controls that fit into the 4♣ Swiss bids are more easily described in other ways.

If you want to play an even more modern Swiss variation, the idea of using Splinters might appeal. The idea is that an unnecessary jump in a new suit agrees partners suit and shows a shortage in the suit bid. So, for example, after a 1♥ opening you might bid an immediate 4♣ holding:

♠ A 6 5 4
♥ A Q 6 5
♦ Q 10 4 3
♣ 8

Clearly, this method is particularly good in helping partner to make an assessment of whether his hand is "working." For example, with:

♠ Q 8 2
♥ K J 10 8 7
♦ A 6
♣ K Q 6

opener does have more than a minimum opening bid, but slam prospects are poor as he only has ten points outside clubs and no particularly good distribution. He should sign off in 4♥.

Contrast this with:

♠ K Q 2
♥ K J 10 8 7
♦ A 6
♣ 6 5 3

However you look at it, this is a minimum opening hand, yet with no wasted values in clubs a heart slam is in the offing. Opposite your example splinter hand you would still need some good luck to make twelve tricks, but add the ♠J to either hand, or replace the ♦Q with the ♦K and the slam would be excellent. So clearly this opening hand should make a more encouraging bid than 4♥, the obvious choice being a cuebid of 4♦.

If you decide to play splinters the good news is that it is a method that is easily adaptable to other situations. For example, after:

| 1♠ | 2♥ |
| ? | |

bids of 4♣ and 4♦ can be used as splinters, showing a good heart raise with shortage in the suit bid. Similarly, after:

| 1♠ | 2♣ |
| 2♥ | ? |

a bid of 4♦ could be a splinter showing shortage in diamonds and four card heart support.

Of course, the bad news is that you still won't have solved the problem of what to do with a balanced raise to game with four card support. Some players have solved this problem by giving up the natural 3NT response and using 3NT to show a balanced high card raise to game. While this is probably the easiest option, there are some much more complicated arrangements available. For example, it is not difficult to devise a method whereby the lowest splinter bid, i.e. 3♠ over 1♥ or 4♣ over 1♠, is either a splinter or a balanced raise to game, with opener using the next step up as a relay to find out.

Whichever method you choose, I strongly recommend that you adopt some conventional aid to distinguish between high card and distributional raises to four of a major.

RESPONDER'S QUIZ 3
Your partner opens 1♠. What do you respond holding:

1. ♠ K 4 2
   ♥ Q 8 2
   ♦ K 10 4
   ♣ Q J 4

2. ♠ K 4 2
   ♥ K Q 8 4 2
   ♦ K 10
   ♣ Q J 4

3. ♠ K 4 2
   ♥ Q 7 6 2
   ♦ J 7 6
   ♣ Q 7 6

4. ♠ K 4 2
   ♥ K 7 2
   ♦ 7 6
   ♣ Q 7 6 2

5. ♠ K Q 4 2
   ♥ 8 7
   ♦ 5 3
   ♣ A K Q 7 2

6. ♠ K 2
   ♥ A J 2
   ♦ Q J 5
   ♣ A K 10 7 2

7. ♠ K 2
   ♥ K 5
   ♦ A K 10 7 2
   ♣ A J 7 2

8. ♠ K 4 2
   ♥ 8 7
   ♦ A K 10 7 2
   ♣ A K 5

ANSWERS TO RESPONDER'S QUIZ 3
Your partner opens 1♠, what do you respond holding:

1. ♠ K 4 2
   ♥ K Q 8 2
   ♦ K 10 4
   ♣ Q J 4

Recommended Bid: 3NT

If there was any doubt in your mind as to whether an immediate response of 3NT to an opening of one of a major should show two or three card support, this is the hand type that should resolve the issue. For an immediate response of 2♥ to 1♠ you are expected to have a five card heart suit, and certainly opener should be encouraged to support a 2♥ response with only three trumps. So with only four hearts and no other suit what are you expected to do? The only alternative to an immediate jump in no trumps is to enter the world of inventive bidding and make up a suit, the popular choice being to respond 2♣.

With a solid fourteen points opposite an opening bid you must be sure that you arrive in game so the only possible response is 3NT. Take away the ♠K and you would still have enough to bid 2NT—the same hand type but only invitational strength. Notice that with five spades and four hearts opener can comfortably remove 3NT to 4♥—giving you the choice of games. This would not be such a successful action if you could have a 2-3-4-4 shape.

2. ♠ K 4 2
   ♥ K Q 8 4 2
   ♦ K 10
   ♣ Q J 4

Recommended Bid: 2♥

This hand was initially included in my classes as a counter-balance to the last example. With five hearts and a game-going hand of no particular distinction it is totally normal just to bid 2♥. If partner rebids 2♠ you have a comfortable raise to 4♠ and if he rebids 2NT you raise to 3NT (probably via 3♠) regardless of whether his rebid is weak or strong.

Imagine my surprise when more than 40 percent of players in my classes have wanted to jump to 3♥ immediately. With no aces, a poor heart suit and only fourteen points, I can see no reason to be suggesting that you have an interest in anything higher than game, unless partner has such an interest himself. To jump the bidding in a new suit the normal expectation is a sixteen point hand with a good suit or some support for opener—and this hand does not qualify. If you do bid 3♥ on the first round and partner rebids 3♠ your choices are clear. You can either continue with 4♠, hoping that partner will not go on expecting a somewhat better hand, or you can bid 3NT, suggesting a balanced hand in the 16-18 point region.

3.　♠ K 4 2
　　♥ Q 7 6 2
　　♦ J 7 6
　　♣ Q 7 6

Recommended Bid: 1NT

An obvious 1NT bid, but 2♠ may work out well if partner has a 5-3-3-2 shape with insufficient strength to bid again over 1NT. Note that opener should bid his second suit with a 5-4 shape even if he has a very weak hand and he should rebid spades only if he has a six card suit.

4.　♠ K 4 2
　　♥ K 7 6 2
　　♦ 7 6
　　♣ Q 7 6 2

Recommended Bid: 2♠

Yes, you still have only eight points just like last time. However, the doubleton diamond promises the possibility of scoring a ruff playing in a spade contract, which should make the difference between supporting partner and bidding 1NT.

One of the greatest advantages of raising spades on a hand of this type is that it removes much of the pressure for partner to rebid his moth-eaten five card spade suit when you do actually respond 1NT. Occasionally his 2♠ rebid works well, especially if you have a hand like the one in this example and, unless you learn to bid 2♠ on hands like this, he will continue to bid 2♠ over 1NT regardless of the number of times he gets a bad result when you have a singleton or doubleton spade.

Certainly, over the years I have been surprised by a substantial minority who want to bid 2♣ rather than 2♠. They argue that with eight points and a partial fit for partner they are strong enough to bid at the two level. That may be so, but the choice of 2♣ reveals a lack of thought about what they intend to do on the next round.

For example, over 2♦ they propose to bid 2♠. Fair enough, but preference at the two level is consistent with holding just a doubleton spade. For example, what else can you do on:

♠ 4 2
♥ K 7 6 2
♦ 7 6
♣ K Q J 10 6

Notice that if opener holds:

♠ A Q 7 6 5
♥ Q 5
♦ A Q 5 3 2
♣ 5

he should pass the simple preference to 2♠ but make a game try after a simple raise to 2♠.

Even worse, if opener raises 2♣ to 3♣ they could be playing in a very inferior contract and even if he rebids 2NT showing a strong no trump responder will have to guess whether to drive on with 3♠ in case his partner has five spades or pass 2NT and hope that he hasn't.

Overall, it is much better to bid 2♠ right away; after all, if you had:

♠ Q 7 6 2
♥ K 7 6 2
♦ 7 6
♣ K 4 2

which is a better hand in support of spades, you would raise 1♠ to 2♠ without giving the matter any further consideration.

5.　♠ K Q 4 2
　　♥ 8 7
　　♦ 5 3
　　♣ A K Q 7 2

Recommended Bid: 3♣

While this hand may only be fourteen points in theory, it is worth a lot more in support of spades. Indeed 6♠ will roll opposite many a minimum opener including two aces (one of which is the ♠A) and some form of control in the remaining suit. For example:

♠ A 8 7 6 3
♥ A 9 4 2
♦ K 5
♣ J 4

would make the slam lay down even without a favorable diamond lead unless trumps are 4-0 or clubs are 5-1. Accordingly, it is nonsense to believe that treating this hand as a delayed game raise by responding 2♣ and jumping to 4♠ on the next round does it justice. Jump to 3♣ and raise spades on the next round.

6. ♠ K 2
♥ A J 2
♦ Q J 5
♣ A K 10 7 2

Recommended Bid: 3♣

Jump to 3♣, planning to rebid 3NT on the next round. The real problem with starting with a simple 2♣ bid is that you will have no sensible way to describe this hand next time. 2♣ followed by 3NT should not conceal a hand of better than about fifteen points, for you cannot expect opener to continue with a suitable thirteen or fourteen point hand for fear of getting too high.

Any other choice defies the imagination.

7. ♠ K 2
♥ K 5
♦ A K 10 7 2
♣ A J 7 2

Recommended Bid: 2♦

I would not be at all surprised if you also jumped to 3♦, but the problem with that should soon become clear. Let's suppose partner rebids 3♠. Now what are you going to do?

Obviously, you might well settle for 3NT—not a totally bad description of the hand, but you have not given yourself any chance of finding a possible club fit. Alternatively, if you continue with 4♣ you may come up smelling like a rose but you may also be heading for the stratosphere with no real fit. And are you sure that if opener rebids 4NT you will take it as natural and not Blackwood?

No, it is for this reason that most good players have adopted the view that it is ill-advised to jump in a new suit with a two-suited hand. The initial response of 2♦ should be

forcing and you plan to bid the clubs on the next round. You can show your general strength later after you have found out whether you have a fit.

8. ♠ K 4 2
♥ 8 7
♦ A K 10 7 2
♣ A K 5

Recommended Bid: 3♦

This hand illustrates the reverse of the coin. If we are not going to jump in a new suit with a two suiter what can a sequence such as 1♠-3♦-3♠-4♣ possibly show?

Happily the obvious conclusion is that it must show a hand with support for partner, with the 4♣ bid being a cuebid agreeing on spades in this case.

Overall, it is well worth noting the various types of hands on which it is sensible to make a jump response in a new suit. They are:

1. A hand such as Example 5, where you have an excellent suit of your own plus a good fit for your partner where you plan to jump in your suit and then support partner.

2. A hand of 16-18 points such as Example 6 with no particular fit for partner but good cover in both the other suits. Here you plan to jump in your suit and rebid 3NT.

3. A hand of 16+ points in value with at least three card support for partner where you will jump in your best suit and then bid another suit which will be a cuebid agreeing partner's first bid suit. Hand 8 is an excellent example.

4. A hand with a very good suit of your own—normally a one loser suit or better!—where you plan to rebid your own suit setting that suit as trumps and inviting your partner to cuebid.

Chapter 3

Opener's Rebid

Let's start by posing a straightforward question. Suppose you deal yourself the following reasonable collection:

♠ Q J 5
♥ A K 6 5
♦ Q J 8 7 2
♣ 5

You open the bidding with 1♦ and with the opposition silent your partner responds 1♠. What would your rebid be?

When I first set this question to one of my classes, I was confidently expecting that a large majority would bid 2♦ rather than elect for what I regard as an automatic raise to 2♠. You can only imagine my surprise when I found that about half of a class of some forty experienced players made neither of these choices, electing instead to show their second suit by "reversing" into 2♥. Most of the remaining players had chosen to rebid their diamond suit while just two or three rather hesitantly suggested that they might support their partner.

It was the ensuing discussion of this particular deal that drove home to me the message that many average players really do flounder like fish in the sea. After all, this is not an issue that has anything to do with learning a new system, or even a newfangled treatment: it is simply an application of the fundamental principles of bidding. I was horrified, but, on reflection, it was clear that this lack of understanding was primarily because, despite their many years of playing the game, most of my class had never been introduced to the ideas involved.

In the class there was one good, experienced tournament player who had already demonstrated a high level of card play yet not only did he bid 2♥ on this hand but he was still adamantly defending his choice a full hour later. Yes, of course he recognized that 2♥ was a reverse forcing his partner to the three level to give preference back to diamonds, and, of course, he recognized that this meant that a reverse promised a good hand, but somehow it would all come out in the wash when he showed his support for spades later. Far from it, for his stated intention to bid again

on the next round meant that by rebidding 2♥ he had effectively committed his side to game, opposite any minimum responding hand.

The very thought of voluntarily arriving in 3NT with a collection like:

♠ K 10 7 6   ♠ Q J 5
♥ 9 7 2   ♥ A K 6 5
♦ 6 3   ♦ Q J 8 7 2
♣ K 9 6 4   ♣ 5

or 4♠ with:

♠ K 10 7 6 3   ♠ Q J 5
♥ 9 7 2   ♥ A K 6 5
♦ 3   ♦ Q J 8 7 2
♣ K 9 6 4   ♣ 5

fills me with horror, but, curiously, in both cases I would not complain at having to play 2♠.

The simple truth is that with what is essentially a minimum opening hand you should strive to:

(a) Limit the strength of your hand as soon as possible—after all you have done your bit by opening the bidding.

(b) Support your partner if it is at all possible.

Of course, looking at the second of these pairs of hands, it should be immediately obvious why 2♠ is a far superior rebid to 2♦. Opposite a 2♦ rebid, the responding hand has little option but to pass and hope that opener manages to scramble a few tricks. Certainly he should not try to improve the contract by rebidding 2♠ lest his partner's spade support matches his own for diamonds and the 2♦ rebid could easily conceal a decent six card suit rather than the actual holding.

However, the "obvious" reason that 2♠ figures to be a sensible contract, while 2♦ will frequently be a poor spot, is really only part of the reason why opener should support his partner on this hand.

For the sake of example, suppose that the responder holds a much better hand, like:

♠ A 10 7 6 3
♥ Q J 2
♦ K 3
♣ K 9 6

then, facing a 2♦ rebid, won't he just jump to 3NT, although after a 2♠ rebid he would at least consider 4♠?

Alternatively, suppose the responder holds a more indeterminate hand like:

♠ A 10 7 6 3
♥ 9 4
♦ 10 4
♣ A J 6 4

Despite holding two aces most players would not consider making another bid if opener simply rebid 2♦, but after a raise to 2♠ the hand is worth a second look. Facing our example hand:

♠ Q J 5
♥ A K 6 5
♦ Q J 8 7 2
♣ 5

you can see that 4♠ is certainly quite a playable contract, but to get there responder really has to know just how much the lowly 3♠ is worth!

Very simply, playing in a diamond contract responder's fifth spade is most unlikely to take a trick, but playing with spades as trumps the fifth spade is almost certainly going to take a trick. It is well worth repeating that, because there are forty high card points in the pack, and thirteen tricks in a hand, on average you need about three points to make a trick. So, playing in spades, what is the value of that fifth spade? Yes, you've got it, once you know you have got a spade fit, that lowly 3♠ is worth about three points and, with twelve points facing an open bid, even the most conservative players would at least make a game try.

Put another way, your choice of rebid is most important in helping your partner to evaluate the combined potential of the two hands and, if you want to give him a chance of making a sensible decision, you must tell him that you have already located a playable fit. In this particular case, your 3-4-5-1 shape makes this hand attractive for playing in spades. Consequently, raising 1♠ to 2♠ to show a minimum opening with diamonds and spade support gives a much better picture than just repeating your diamonds.

Average club players are frequently amazed at how often expert players seem to reach good game contracts with little more than half the high cards in the pack. Without doubt

their success is based on their ability to identify the degree of fit on each hand quickly, and it is for this reason that it is essential to support your partner whenever you have support.

On a totally different theme, consider what you would do as opener with the following hand:

♠ Q 9 4
♥ K J 5 4 3
♦ –
♣ A K Q 7 4

There is no real problem on the first round. Your clubs might be much better than your hearts but it is much more important to get your five card major into the action rather than your five card minor, so you open 1♥. Now, suppose that your partner responds 1NT, what are you going to do next?

It is a popular misconception that just because you hold a good hand you should jump the bidding. In practice, your benchmark should be that if partner passes 2♣ will you be unhappy or, more specifically, if partner passes 2♣ are you likely to have missed a game contract?

Put in those terms, on this hand, the answer should be a categorical *no*—you will not have missed game if he passes 2♣.

First of all, which game do you have in mind? For 3NT, your partner will need a monster hand: he has to bolster the spade suit, stop the diamonds and convert your heart suit into a source of tricks. What about 4♥? Well, first, if he has three cards in hearts he will certainly strain to bid again over 2♣ even if it is only to put you back to 2♥. That leaves an outside possibility that he can fill the heart suit with a good doubleton and have sufficiently good spades. That is possible but not likely. Finally, how about 5♣? Again it is most unlikely that you can make eleven tricks in clubs without partner having sufficient to raise 2♣ to 3♣. So, at worst, by bidding 2♣ you give up a very slender chance of a game contract.

Now look at 3♣. How many times will your leap drive partner into a totally unmakeable game? Quite often, I would say.

No, 2♣ is the winner and, better still, if partner bids again you get a good chance to paint an accurate picture of your hand. For example, over preference to 2♥, you can make a further try via 2♠. Knowing of your shortness in diamonds, partner should downgrade cards in that suit and bid 3♥ or 4♥ accordingly.

Quiz 4

You open 1♥, your partner responds 1♠, what do you rebid holding:

1. ♠ A 4 2
   ♥ A K 10 7 2
   ♦ Q 10 2
   ♣ 5 4

2. ♠ A 4 2
   ♥ A K 10 7 2
   ♦ Q J 2
   ♣ A 5

3. ♠ Q 10 4 2
   ♥ A K Q 7 4
   ♦ 6 2
   ♣ A 5

4. ♠ Q 10 4 2
   ♥ A K Q 7 4
   ♦ 6 2
   ♣ A K

5. ♠ Q 10 4
   ♥ A Q J 7 4 2
   ♦ A J 3
   ♣ 2

Answers to Quiz 4

You open 1♥, your partner responds 1♠, what do you rebid holding:

1. ♠ A 4 2
   ♥ A K 10 7 2
   ♦ Q 10 2
   ♣ 5 4

Recommended Bid: 2♠

With a clearly rebiddable suit, both weak and strong no-trumpers open 1♥, expecting to pass a 1NT response or rebid their hearts after partner bids two of a minor. But what if he bids 1♠? If you stop to think about it, you have very good cards for playing in spades even if partner has only four cards in the suit. The ♥AK figure to score whatever suit is trumps and you have both control of the trump suit—the ♠A—and a possible ruffing value in clubs. Of course, partner might have four spades and three hearts when 2♥ will play better than 2♠, but he may also have five spades and only one heart, when 2♠ will play very well indeed and 2♥ may have no chance. On balance, I believe it right to support partner with three trumps to an honor and a ruffing value in a minimum opener, and accordingly I would rebid 2♠.

Putting it another way, 1♥ followed by 2♠ suggests a minimum opener with hearts and some spade support. 1♥ followed by 2♥ suggests a minimum opener with no spade support. Which is the more definitive description of your hand?

Playing a strong no trump there is a further option—you could bid 1NT to show your balanced minimum without support for spades. However, the prime nature of your cards still suggests that a 2♠ bid would be more descriptive. After all, if your partner has as little as:

♠ K Q 8 7 6
♥ 8 4
♦ K J 8 5
♣ 8 7

game in spades would be a fair proposition, but playing in hearts or no trumps you would be lucky to make more than eight tricks.

2. ♠ A 4 2
   ♥ A K 10 7 2
   ♦ Q J 2
   ♣ A 5

Recommended Bid: 2NT

The 2NT rebid should show a balanced hand of 18-19 points which may include either five hearts or three spades or both. Responder can still check back to look for an eight card major fit.

Almost inevitably, there will be some players who will look elsewhere. The hand is quite good in its support for spades, but a jump to 3♠ is reserved for hands with four card support that are not worth raising 1♠ to game, while a jump rebid in hearts shows a slightly weaker hand in overall high card strength but with a good six card heart suit. Meanwhile, some of those so-called scientific bidders are heading for trouble in another way: 2♦ could easily become the final contract with either 4♠ or 3NT makeable while the immediate jump to 3♦ is categorically game forcing facing any kind of hand. There are times when it can be sensible to invent a suit to bid but not when there is a fully descriptive bid available.

3. ♠ Q 10 4 2
   ♥ A K Q 7 4
   ♦ 6 2
   ♣ A 5

Recommended Bid: 3♠

With four card support and substantially better than a minimum opening, it is right to make the invitational limit raise to 3♠. In case of doubt, I would much prefer to take a shot at 4♠ than languish in 2♠.

4. ♠ Q 10 4 2
   ♥ A K Q 7 4
   ♦ 6 2
   ♣ A K

Recommended Bid: 4♣

Putting this example to my classes has always produced a very wide range of opinion but at least the majority have recognized that the hand belongs in game in spades. Quite a few players have always wanted to jump to 3♣, preparing to support spades on the next round, but jumping in clubs and then bidding spades is consistent with holding four clubs and only three spades —another fine example of bidding all the suits. This hand is much better than the previous example—a full trick better to be precise—and for game to have no reasonable play partner will have to be missing both the top two spade honors and the top two diamond honors. So, clearly, the hand is full value for a raise to game. But having said that it must be more helpful to partner to paint a more detailed picture of your hand if it is at all possible. By jumping to 4♣, which can barely be natural, you convey the message of a full weight raise to 4♠ including a club control. If partner has a diamond control, he might just be able to consider bidding a slam.

For example, partner might hold as little as:

    ♠ A K 9 7 5
    ♥ 8 6 2
    ♦ 5
    ♣ 9 7 4 2

and 6♠ is excellent but reverse his minor suit holdings and the slam has no chance. The *advance-cuebid* of 4♣ makes it easier to explore slam possibilities at both a lower and safer level.

5.   ♠ Q 10 4
     ♥ A Q J 7 4 2
     ♦ A J 3
     ♣ 2

Recommended Bid: 3♥

With only fourteen high card points, many players would not think of jumping to 3♥ on this type of hand; however, the hand is much improved by the subsidiary fit in spades. If partner has as little as:

    ♠ K J 6 5
    ♥ 9 3
    ♦ K 8 6 5
    ♣ 7 6 5

the heart game is excellent but turn the black suits around and even 2♥ is not certain to succeed.

QUIZ 5

On each of the following hands, you open 1♦ and your partner responds 1♠, what is your rebid?

1. ♠ A 5 3
    ♥ 7
    ♦ A J 10 6 5
    ♣ K 8 7 2

5. ♠ A 5 3
    ♥ A Q 7 2
    ♦ A K 10 6 5
    ♣ 7

2. ♠ A 5 3
    ♥ 7
    ♦ A K 10 6 5
    ♣ K 8 7 2

6. ♠ 7 5
    ♥ A K J 5
    ♦ A Q 6 4 3
    ♣ Q 5

3. ♠ A 5 3
    ♥ 7
    ♦ A K 10 6 5
    ♣ A Q 7 2

7. ♠ Q 5 3
    ♥ A J
    ♦ A K 10 6 5
    ♣ K Q 7

4. ♠ A Q 3
    ♥ 7
    ♦ A K 10 6 5
    ♣ A Q 7 2

8. ♠ 5
    ♥ A J 5
    ♦ A K Q 7 5 3
    ♣ K 10 4

ANSWERS TO QUIZ 5

On each of the following hands, you open 1♦ and your partner responds 1♠, what is your rebid?

1. ♠ A 5 3
    ♥ 7
    ♦ A J 10 6 5
    ♣ K 8 7 2

Recommended Bid: 2♠

When you opened 1♦, you might well have expected to hear a 1♥ response—in which case your natural rebid would have been 2♣, showing the expected 5-4 shape in your minors. You might be tempted to make exactly the same rebid here, however, this would not be the choice of most experts. They choose to rebid 2♠. Why?

It is quite acceptable to support partner at minimum level with only three trumps especially with a top honor in the trump suit and a singleton in a side suit. Indeed, with a minimum opener, it is your duty to support your partner if you can.

Let's put it another way. Suppose that you do decide to rebid 2♣ and your partner gives you preference to 2♦, wouldn't it be tempting to continue with 2♠? Surely, you will have described your shape, but you would also have contravened the principle of supporting as soon as possible with a minimum hand. Therefore your partner will expect you to have this shape *and* some extra values.

Hopefully, the whole picture will become clear when you consider the next three examples:

2. ♠ A 5 3
♥ 7
♦ A K 10 6 5
♣ K 8 7 2

Recommended Bid: 2♣

This time you have a rather better hand. Admittedly this is only two points more than the previous example, but now, if you rebid 2♣ and support spades on the next round, we will not only deliver the expected 3-1-5-4 shape but also the extra values consistent with volunteering to make three bids.

3. ♠ A 5 3
♥ 7
♦ A K 10 6 5
♣ A Q 7 2

Recommended Bid: 2♣

Many players would be tempted to jump to 3♣ on this hand because they have substantially more than a minimum opening. However in standard methods this jump into a new suit at the three level not only forces partner to bid again, it is forcing to game. Opposite a poor six or seven count trying for nine tricks in no trumps or ten in spades may well be too ambitious.

At least equally to a point, if you rebid 2♣ it is actually very difficult to construct a hand where game is a good prospect and partner won't bid again, even if all he can manage to do is give you preference back to 2♦.

In the previous example, you rebid 2♣ and then bid 2♠ over 2♦. In this case, you are clearly about one trick better, so, after preference to 2♦, you should jump to 3♠. Even this is not absolutely forcing, but it does show a hand of about this strength, too good to advance with just 2♠ but not quite strong enough to force to game, facing what might be a totally minimum responding hand. With such a good description of your hand, your partner ought to be able to judge what to do.

4. ♠ A Q 3
♥ 7
♦ A K 10 6 5
♣ A Q 7 2

Recommended Bid: 3♣

This hand is that little bit stronger again. With nineteen high card points you should have some prospect of making game even if partner is totally minimum. So, this time, jump to 3♣ immediately, forcing to game. Obviously, your plan should be to support spades on the next round which will complete an excellent picture of your hand.

As you can now see, these first four examples all feature hands with the same 3-1-5-4 shape but they vary in strength right through the spectrum from the minimum to the maximum for a one level opener. Notice that for each step up in strength there is a slightly stronger treatment available. In fact, even quite sophisticated strong club style bidders

might be surprised to see just how much definition is available sometimes in good old fashioned natural methods.

5. ♠ A 5 3
♥ A Q 7 2
♦ A K 10 6 5
♣ 7

Recommended Bid: 2♥

Here we have another hand with that attractive 5-4-3-1 shape, still with three card spade support, but this time with four hearts rather than four clubs. It is the same shape as the hand shown early in this chapter—the difference is that this hand is much stronger, certainly strong enough to bid 2♥, a reverse, planning to support spades on the next round.

The name "reverse" comes from the fact that you have bid your suits in such an order that partner will be forced a level higher just to put you back into our first bid suit. After 1♥–1♠–2♦ responder can give preference back to 2♥ without raising the level of the auction, but after 1♦–1♠–2♥ responder has to bid 3♦ to give preference. This simple fact is the reason why it is necessary to have a strong hand before reversing.

Although most experts play that a reverse bid is forcing for at least one round, there are those who play it non-forcing.

Since a reverse might conceal up to, say, twenty or twenty-one points and a shapely hand, passing a reverse is likely to be risky, certainly not a venture to be entered into without a full understanding of what you are doing. Having said that, I would still reserve the right to choose to pass the reverse bid despite those risks. Suppose, for example, you held:

♠ J 8 7 4 2
♥ J 9 3
♦ –
♣ Q 9 8 4 2

Partner opens 1♦ and it is over to you. Would you pass 1♦ and leave partner to his likely doom or take the risk of getting far too high by responding 1♠? Despite my lack of high card points, I would risk responding 1♠; after all, it is not that difficult to construct a hand where 4♠ is much more likely to make than 1♦! However, when I then hear my partner continue with 2♥ I would take the view that the time had come to risk a pass before we hit the stratosphere. Admittedly, we might still be lay down for 4♠ but it really isn't that likely and 2♥ figures to be a much, much better contract than 1♦.

6. ♠ 7 5
♥ A K J 5
♦ A Q 6 4 3
♣ Q 5

Recommended Bid: 1NT

Once again, we have five diamonds and four hearts and rather more than a minimum opening bid. So just like the last hand you could reverse into 2♥, but I would not recommend it. While many partnerships have a way for the responder to show a minimum hand after a reverse, in practice the 2♥ rebid figures to carry your side into game every time responder has a good seven or eight points.

So, is there any alternative? Yes, provided you are playing a weak no trump, you could rebid 1NT to show a balanced 15-17. This hand is not really balanced, but the ♣Q is likely to have more value in no trumps than in suit play, and there is no real risk of either missing a game or even a heart fit. If responder has four hearts, he must have at least five spades and after a 1NT rebid you can be confident that with that shape he will bid his hearts.

Clearly this option of rebidding 1NT is not available if you are playing a strong no trump. However, if you think ahead, you might have decided to open 1NT and not 1♦.

7.   ♠ Q 5 3
   ♥ A J
   ♦ A K 10 6 5
   ♣ K Q 7

Recommended Bid: 2NT

Back to a more mundane balanced hand. With nineteen high card points, were you still tempted to jump to 3NT? Remember, whether you are playing a range of 12-14 or 15-17 for your 1NT opener, a jump rebid of 2NT is plenty on this type of hand. Apart from the advantage of being able to stop out of game opposite a really weak hand, there is a much more significant advantage in that rebidding 2NT gives much more room to explore which game you want to play in. For example, suppose that partner actually holds:

   ♠ K J 8 7 6
   ♥ 9 7 2
   ♦ 4 2
   ♣ A 9 4

Clearly, if you have jumped to 3NT he will have a totally blind guess whether to continue with 4♠ or pass, and most players would choose the latter option. However, over the 2NT rebid there is room to explore to see whether the opener has three card spade support. If responder continues with 3♣ (showing where his outside values actually are) opener will bid 3♠ and responder has a comfortable raise to 4♠.

3NT will make most of the time, but, whenever the opponents lead hearts and a hand with five hearts also has the ♠A, 3NT will fail, while 4♠ will be a make most of the time.

8.   ♠ 5
   ♥ A J 5
   ♦ A K Q 7 5 3
   ♣ K 10 4

Recommended Bid: 3NT

Now this is a hand where many will be tempted to make a jump rebid in diamonds. I would much prefer to jump to 3NT on this kind of hand. With a couple of diamonds

opposite and some sort of spade stopper, nearly any other high card will give 3NT good play. ♠J10xx and the ♣A would be a particularly suitable holding but there is a myriad of hands where 3NT will be an excellent contract and partner will not be close to making another bid after a 3♦ bid.

Once again, you should appreciate the power of those long diamonds: the fifth and sixth cards in the suit may not have a value under the Milton Work Point Count, but they definitely have a value at the table where you expect they will make two tricks.

QUIZ 6
This time you open 1♠, and you hear your partner respond 2♥, what do you rebid now?

1.	♠ A Q J 7 5 ♥ Q 6 2 ♦ K 7 2 ♣ 6 4		4.	♠ A K Q 4 2 ♥ K 10 2 ♦ 10 7 3 ♣ A 5
2.	♠ A Q J 7 5 ♥ Q 6 2 ♦ A 7 4 2 ♣ 6		5.	♠ A K Q 7 4 ♥ A Q 7 4 ♦ 7 4 2 ♣ 6
3.	♠ K Q 10 9 4 2 ♥ J 5 ♦ A Q J 4 ♣ 7		6.	♠ A K Q 7 4 ♥ K 7 4 2 ♦ 7 5 ♣ K Q

ANSWERS TO QUIZ 6
This time you open 1♠, and you hear partner respond 2♥, what do you rebid now?

1.   ♠ A Q J 7 5
   ♥ Q 6 2
   ♦ K 7 2
   ♠ 6 4

Recommended Bid: 3♥

A boring minimum opening bid with a good five card spade suit and three card support for partner. A straightforward hand? Evidently not, for over the years well over half of players attending my courses have chosen to rebid their spades while about 40 percent have supported their partner, raising to 3♥. I won't dwell on the much more exotic choice of the missing 10 percent but concentrate on the major issue.

The response of 2♥ usually shows a five card suit, so as opener you have an obligation to announce your knowledge of an eight card fit immediately. If you rebid 2♠ you might get the chance to show your heart support on the next round, but there again you might not. Do you really want to insist on playing in 2♠ and find your partner with something like:

   ♠ 6
   ♥ K J 8 7 3 2
   ♦ A 4 3
   ♣ 9 7 5

With these cards 4♥ is basically dependent on the spade guess and your partner should leave you to suffer in 2♠. Of course, it is tempting to rebid those spades—after all you can actually see what you have in your own hand—but the art of good bidding is based on building the picture of the combined holdings of the two hands.

2. ♠ A Q J 7 5
    ♥ Q 6 2
    ♦ A 7 4 2
    ♣ 6

Recommended Bid: 4♥

Once again you have three card support for partner but, in reality, you have a much better hand than in the first example. Admittedly, you only have one more high card point but, in the overall context of the hand, the ♦A is worth a lot more than just one point more than the king and the singleton club gives you both additional control and ruffing value. Now why is the ♦A so much better than the king? It's not just that the ace is a sure trick, but rather that it is likely to give you more time to get the spades going before you lose any tricks in diamonds.

So, if this is a much better hand than the bare twelve count shown in the first example, you owe it to your partner to show him that you have extra values by jumping to 4♥ rather than making the same, tame 3♥ bid.

3. ♠ K Q 10 9 4 2
    ♥ J 5
    ♦ A Q J 4
    ♣ 7

Recommended Bid: 3♠

Here is a good hand for trapping overbidders who tend to bid 3♦ and underbidders who stolidly bid 2♠.

Let's start with the overbidders. You must remember that if you introduce a new suit at the three level, you have committed your side to playing to game. After all, even *you* would hesitate to criticize your partner for responding 2♥ on something like:

                ♠ 5 3
                ♥ K Q 9 8 7
                ♦ K 5 3
                ♣ K 6 4 2

Over 3♦ he is bound to bid 3NT—which has absolutely no chance on the marked club lead. Admittedly, 4♠ is much better than 3NT opposite this hand, but are you really going to remove 3NT to 4♠ and risk finding partner with a singleton or void spade?

Then the underbidders. If you just count your points you might think that you have little more than a minimum opener, but, be fair, you do have quite a good hand for playing in spades! If you content yourself with just 2♠ you can't really blame your partner for not moving on with a hand like:

                ♠ J 5
                ♥ K Q 9 8 7
                ♦ 10 5 3
                ♣ A 9 8

when 4♠ is virtually laydown. So what is to be done?

The simple solution is to jump to 3♠—a bid which is natural and invitational in traditional Acol methods. Notice that your hand has been improved by your partner's response of 2♥—with Jx in clubs and a singleton heart the hand would clearly not be worth a jump to 3♠.

The invitational jump rebid after a two level response is a bid that has been much maligned by the pseudo-scientists in recent years. Nobody argues against using the jump rebid in this manner after a one level response. On average, if you open 1♦ and jump to 3♦ after a response in one of the majors, you will be showing a good six card suit and about sixteen points. The pseudo-scientists will then argue that with sixteen points and a good six card suit you will normally want to go to game facing a two level response; thus, the jump rebid should be treated as forcing. That all sounds more than reasonable, but no one ever said that a jump rebid facing a two level response should show sixteen points in the first place. If a two level response shows more values than a one level response, it should follow that you need correspondingly less to make an invitational jump rebid after a two level response.

If you choose to play it as invitational in the traditional manner then you should be making the bid with hands like the one in the example. If you choose to play the bid as forcing then, clearly, you should have a better hand.

My view is that retaining the bid in its traditional manner, as non-forcing after a two level response, is particularly helpful in judging whether to stretch to good fitting, low point count games. On the stronger types you can normally make do, either by inventing a suit at the three level or by just blasting to game.

4. ♠ A K Q 4 2
    ♥ K 10 2
    ♦ 10 7 3
    ♣ A 5

Recommended Bid: 4♣

Very few players have any doubt that this hand is full value for a jump to 4♥. However, if you are going to jump to game on hand two, can't you find a way of getting the message through to partner that you actually have a very good raise to 4♥ and not just one based on a bit of good-looking distribution? After all, partner needs very little more than ♥AQxxx and the ♦A to give a heart slam good play, but you cannot afford to propel the auction higher than 4♥ on your own just in case the hands fit badly. Indeed, you might even struggle to make 4♥ if partner has three low diamonds as well.

So, what is to be done? The answer is to jump to 4♣, a cuebid to show control in clubs and a good raise to 4♥. Whatever else it may be, there is absolutely no need for this bid to be natural as you would rebid 3♣ (game forcing) with a strong hand with spades and clubs. Hence, the jump to 4♣ can be used to agree partner's suit and set the slam investigation rolling.

Think about it! What does it cost you? If your partner makes a return cuebid of 4♦, you can put the brakes on by signing off in 4♥. Partner should know that you have a good raise to 4♥ with a club control but you are not that good as you signed off over his 4♦ cuebid.

5. ♠ A K Q 7 4
   ♥ A Q 7 4
   ♦ 7 4 2
   ♣ 2

Recommended Bid: 4♣

While this hand has a point less in high cards, it has considerably more potential than the last example, the singleton club and the fourth trump combine to add enormous playing strength. Now you might be in the slam zone even if partner has a totally minimum 2♥ response. ♥Kxxxx and the ♦A will probably give you excellent play for twelve tricks. However, there is still plenty of room for partner to have a sound 2♥ response while your opponents have three cashing minor suit winners.

Once again, you should jump to 4♣ to show control of that suit and a good raise to 4♥. The only difference is that, this time, if partner cuebids 4♦ I would bid more than 4♥. (Playing standard Blackwood, I would settle for a 4♠ cuebid, and if I was fortunate enough to be playing Five Ace Blackwood, where the king of trumps counts as an ace, I would invest in 4NT.)

6. ♠ A K Q 7 4
   ♥ K 7 4 2
   ♦ 7 5
   ♣ K Q

Recommended Bid: 4♣

Once again you hold a very good raise to 4♥, and you would like to express your strength without propelling your side too high. My solution would be to bid 4♣ once again.

Now, the last three example hands combine well to illustrate two important principles:

1. There is no space in our methods to incorporate the Gerber 4♣ ace-asking convention when we are considering playing in a suit contract. Neither Gerber nor Blackwood will help you to locate distributional controls, i.e. singletons and voids, which are of great importance in suit contracts. Before pushing your side too high in the search for the slam bonus, it is essential to be able to establish that you at least have some form of control in all the side suits. The only sensible way of doing this is to adopt some form of cuebidding. Using the unnecessary jump to 4♣ as a cuebid is an essential part of your armory. To use a golfing analogy, there is not much point in carrying four different wooden clubs in your bag if it means that there is no room for a putter.

2. If you like your advance cuebids to guarantee the ace in the suit bid, or if you prefer to confine the use of one of these jumps to being a splinter, then I hope that these last three examples will help to persuade you to change your mind. Adopt a less rigorous style, use these bids to guarantee a control in the suit, any control—the ace or king, singleton or void. After all, there is nothing to stop you using Blackwood on the next round to make sure that you are not missing two aces. Indeed, it is the fact that Blackwood doesn't really interfere with cuebidding that makes Blackwood the popular choice of ace-asking convention among the experts.

Chapter 4

Responder's Rebid

Consider the following awkward hand:

♠ A J 4
♥ K J 10 7 4
♦ A J
♣ 6 5 2

1♦	1♥
1♠	?

With a solid fourteen points facing an opening bid it should be quite clear that you want to be in game, but which one?

First of all, given the information that you have so far, there is no certainty as to which strain you want to play in, let alone at what level. Let's consider some of the alternatives:

1. No Trumps
3NT may be the most likely destination, but there is no guarantee that your opponents will not be able to take the first five tricks, especially with the lead going through partner's club holding. Suppose that the whole layout is like this:

♠ K Q 6 5	♠ A J 4
♥ 6 5	♥ K J 10 7 4
♦ K Q 10 9 5	♦ A J
♣ K 7	♣ 6 5 2

Played from the West seat, 3NT would be very unlucky to go down. Since you have nine top tricks as soon as you get in, South would have to have the ♥A and North the ♣A, and North would have to find the inspired lead of a heart to put South in to lead a club through—a defense that is most unlikely.

2. Hearts
Of course, partner might still hold three card heart support, but, even if he only has a doubleton, 4♥ could still be the right destination. For example, suppose that your combined hands are:

♠ K 6 5 2	♠ A J 4
♥ Q 5	♥ K J 10 7 4
♦ K Q 10 9 5	♦ A J
♣ Q 7	♣ 6 5 2

Certainly, partner really does have a moth-eaten opener but, despite that, 4♥ is still a fair contract. If the opponents attack clubs early, all you will need to do is ruff the third round in the dummy. If the defense is less aggressive, you will be forced to play off three rounds of diamonds before drawing trumps. Of course, you may go down if diamonds are not 3-3, but all other game contracts are considerably worse.

3. Spades
Now suppose that your combined assets are:

♠ K Q 10 9	♠ A J 4
♥ A	♥ K J 10 7 4
♦ K 8 7 5 2	♦ A J
♣ 10 4 3	♣ 6 5 2

On this layout 3NT will fail more than half the time. You will go down either if the opponents take the first five club tricks or if the ♥Q doesn't drop doubleton and the diamond finesse is wrong. Meanwhile, all you need to make 4♠ is for neither opponent to hold a singleton or void in either red suit. Whatever they lead, you should be able to cash two hearts, two diamonds and ruff two of your diamonds with dummy's high trumps making ten tricks in all.

4. Diamonds
While this contract might be the furthest from your mind, once it transpires that partner has a six card diamond suit, playing in diamonds becomes a definite possibility. For example look at this layout:

♠ K 6 5 2	♠ A J 4
♥ A 5	♥ K J 10 7 4
♦ K Q 10 9 6 5	♦ A J
♣ 8	♣ 6 5 2

See how this hand will play in diamonds. Ruff the second club, cash the ♥A K and ruff a heart high. If the ♥Q was doubleton or hearts are 3-3, you will already be able to claim twelve tricks. Failing that, ruffing another heart and taking the spade finesse might still yield a small slam bonus and that is facing not that much more than a minimum opener.

All this proves nothing except that you do not really have any idea of the best final destination and you can't sensibly find out without having some way of getting partner to describe his hand further. After all, without some such device what are you going to bid? Today, a jump to either 3♥ or 3♠ would not be regarded as forcing and it should be fairly clear that it is a total guess if you just decide to bid a game. But there is an elegant and particularly useful solution.

The modern style is to play a bid of the fourth suit as forcing, saying: "At this stage, partner, I cannot make an accurate bid to describe my hand. Would you, please, describe your hand further and then I may be able to make a definitive bid on the next round." The bid of the fourth suit does not promise any particular holding in that suit.

Of all the conventional bids or treatments I have played, I would regard Fourth Suit Forcing (FSF) as the most important. Apart from giving an immediate solution to the problem of what you are going to bid on the example hand, it is a device that considerably broadens the scope and range of ways in which you can describe your own hand.

Let's consider how the auction might develop on each of the example hands:

1.
♠ K Q 6 5	♠ A J 4
♥ 6 5	♥ K J 10 7 4
♦ K Q 10 9 5	♦ A J
♣ K 7	♣ 6 5 2

1 ♦	1 ♥
1 ♠	2 ♣ (FSF)
2 NT	3 NT
Pass	

Having already shown an opening hand with five diamonds and four spades, West has an easy 2NT rebid after East uses Fourth Suit Forcing. Since East knows that his partner has a club stopper and at most two hearts and four spades, 3NT looks like the obvious contract for East to choose.

2.
♠ K 6 5 2	♠ A J 4
♥ Q 5	♥ K J 10 7 4
♦ K Q 10 9 5	♦ A J
♣♣ Q 7	♣ 6 5 2

1 ♦	1 ♥
1 ♠	2 ♣ (FSF)
2 ♦	2 ♥
3 ♥	4 ♥
Pass	

or

1 ♦	1 ♥
1 ♠	2 ♣ (FSF)
2 ♥	4 ♥
Pass	

West faces an interesting choice between 2♦ and 2♥ after East introduces Fourth Suit Forcing. While there is nothing

wrong with showing secondary support for hearts with just ♥Q5, the good texture of the diamond suit would persuade most players to rebid 2♦ at this stage. However, as you can see, you should end up in the right spot either way.

Notice that, after the 2♦ rebid, East has no need to jump the bidding since 2♥ should be forcing. With a weak hand he would not have used the fourth suit bid and, with only a reasonable five card suit, it would be very space consuming if he had to jump to 3♥ to explore the hand further. West eventually admits to holding some heart support by raising to 3♥ and East presses on to game.

If West admits to having some heart support right away, the sequence will be a lot shorter with East just settling for 4♥.

3.
♠ K Q 10 9	♠ A J 4
♥ A	♥ K J 10 7 4
♦ K 8 7 5 2	♦ A J
♣ 10 4 3	♣ 6 5 2

1 ♦	1 ♥
1 ♠	2 ♣ (FSF)
2 ♦	2 ♥
2 ♠	3 ♠
4 ♠	Pass

West really has no attractive bid after East uses Fourth Suit Forcing. He can barely bid no-trumps with no club stopper, spades without extra length or hearts with only a singleton. East's bid is still forcing, so West has to find yet another bid, but, now, he can emphasize the quality of his spades without any risk of East thinking he has a five card spade suit as clearly as he would have bid 2♠ in response to 2♣.

In a similar way, if East had four spades he would have supported West earlier so now he can bid 3♠ comfortably. With no really sensible alternative, West presses on to the spade game.

4.
♠ K 6 5 2	♠ A J 4
♥ A 5	♥ K J 10 7 4
♦ K Q 10 9 6 5	♦ A J
♣ 8	♣ 6 5

1 ♦	1 ♥
1 ♠	2 ♣ (FSF)
3 ♦	3 ♥
4 ♥	4NT
5 ♦	6 ♦
Pass	

Although the West hand has only twelve high card points, my feeling is that the most descriptive bid after the fourth suit 2♣ is 3♦. After all, on the last deal we saw that failing anything else, West would have to rebid 2♦, which means that 2♦ is essentially a nothing bid. This West hand has a very good diamond suit and is a bit better than minimum whichever way you look at it. You could either argue that the sixth diamond is likely to produce one more trick in the play compared with a five card suit or you could say that many players would still open this hand if the ♠K was replaced with just the ♠J, so you do have a couple of points more than you might have.

East has a slightly awkward rebid at this stage: clearly he has good enough diamond support to consider supporting his partner but, if West has a singleton heart and two clubs, 3NT might still be the only place to play, so East maintains his original intention to repeat his hearts in forcing to game fashion.

Now what should West do? With a singleton club and ♥A5 facing a possible six card suit, 4♥ must be a real possibility. Indeed, as West has already jumped to 3♦, if he now just raises to 4♥ East really should have a good picture of his hand. Clearly, West has shown a 4-2-6-1 distribution with good diamonds, and if East can picture the type of hand he should expect opposite then he could proceed with Blackwood, just to make sure that the partnership is not missing two aces before bidding the slam in diamonds.

All this may seem a little far-fetched, but it does illustrate the kind of descriptive bidding that should become available once you have become accustomed to the use of Fourth Suit Forcing. Quite clearly, regular partnerships will discuss the sequences that might follow Fourth Suit Forcing in some detail. However, at the very least, it gives you a way out of many impossible bidding situations.

Better still, the fourth suit provides a way of describing a whole new tier of hands. For example, suppose that when you bid 2♣ partner obliges by rebidding 2NT; then any suit bid you make at the three level must be forcing.

For example:

1♦	1♥		1♦	1♥
1♠	3♥		1♠	2♣ (FSF)
			2NT	3♥

non-forcing   *forcing*

1♦	1♥		1♦	1♥
1♠	3♦		1♠	2♣ (FSF)
			2NT	3♦

non-forcing   *forcing*

Now consider what you would do on the following hand:

> ♠ A 6
> ♥ K J 10 7 4
> ♦ A J
> ♣ J 6 5 2

1♦	1♥
1♠	?

This time, you have something of a club stopper in principle so, at least, you could take a shot at 3NT—but is there any guarantee that 3NT will be the right contract? I think not.

To start with, partner could possibly still have three card support, and even if he has only two hearts, 4♥ could easily be better than 3NT.

Suppose that opener holds:

> ♠ K Q J 5
> ♥ Q 5
> ♦ K Q 10 8 7
> ♣ 7 2

would you not prefer to play in 4♥? Certainly, 4♥ is not laydown, especially if the defenders are unkind enough to lead a low heart and duck the first round, but it is a lot better than playing in 3NT and watching the opponents take the first five tricks.

No, once you have decided to add Fourth Suit Forcing to your system, it is much better to employ it on this round and see what partner does before making a final decision. After all, you can always bid 3NT next. To bid 3NT directly over 1♠ should suggest a very good club holding—in principle, two club stoppers. To bid 3NT after using Fourth Suit Forcing suggests less good cover in the fourth suit.

Let's look at a different situation:

RESPONDING TO REVERSES

Consider the following situation:

1♥	1♠
2♥	?

What would you bid next holding either:

(a)	♠ K J 6 5	or	(b)	♠ K J 6 5
	♥ J 7 2			♥ 7 6 5
	♦ 7 6 5			♦ K 7 2
	♣ J 7 2			♣ K 7 2

The traditional view is that with hand (a) you should simply give preference to 3♣. This is a weak bid and despite the fact that the opener has shown a good hand by reversing, there is no compulsion for him to bid again after 3♣ unless he has noticeable extra values. Meanwhile, that creates a problem with hand (b) where the only real way ahead is to wheel out the fourth suit bid of 3♦ to create a forcing situation. Thereafter, on the next round, responder can reveal the reason for his enthusiasm should he wish to do so. For example, if opener bids 3NT, should responder call it a day and pass or should he press on with 4♣?

In fact, in past years, after:

1♣	1♠
2♥	?

bids of 2♠, 2NT and 3♣ were all regarded as natural and non-forcing and I have even heard some experts say that a jump to 3♠ should be treated the same way. Frankly, this just doesn't make sense any more.

Clearly, we need to have some way of putting the brakes on but, on many hands, our main interest will be in exploring which is the best game or even whether we have a slam. This is very difficult if the only real way to show any extra values is to introduce the fourth suit.

As a first step, I believe that it is essential to treat a return to opener's suit as showing at least three card support and game-going values, so that on hand (b) above you can bid 3♣ as a first move towards exploring the hand. That all sounds fine, but what are you going to bid with hand (a) if 3♣ is natural and forcing?

The answer is that you need to introduce some sort of artificial negative to help handle this situation. In my experience, the bid that most average players seem to consider playing this way is 2NT. I am not suggesting that this is necessarily the best solution, but it certainly goes a long way towards improving bidding structure. (In expert circles many players choose to use either the lowest available bid, or a rebid of responders suit in this way.)

See how the auction might develop opposite one example hand. Suppose opener holds:

♠ 8
♥ A K 8 2
♦ Q 8
♣ A Q J 10 6 4

Opposite hand (a) the whole auction ought to be:

1 ♣	1 ♠
2 ♥	2 NT (negative)
3 ♣	Pass

After the artificial 2NT negative, opener rebids his six card club suit and responder passes. With a game-going hand opposite a minimum responding hand opener would have to find a stronger action like introducing the fourth suit himself.

Opposite hand (b) the bidding might be:

1 ♣	1 ♠
2 ♥	3 ♣ (forcing)
3 ♦	3 NT
Pass	

Knowing of a club fit and game-going forcing values, opener explores the hand by introducing the fourth suit. Having already expressed the value of the hand and shown his club support, responder should have no qualms in bidding 3NT, a sensible final resting place.

Just because 2NT may be an artificial negative does not necessarily mean that you have to bid 2NT with all weak hands. After all, if the main feature of the responding hand is a reasonable five card spade suit, it would make a lot more sense to rebid 2♠ than 2NT. Opener can pass or raise or make another bid as appropriate.

However, this additional option would only be available if responder can rebid his suit at the two level, as a suit rebid at the three level should be treated as unconditionally forcing.

Finally, if opener makes a high level reverse, like:

1 ♥ 1 ♠	*or*	1 ♥ 2 ♦
3 ♣		3 ♣

it is already game forcing. Thereafter, all bids by responder are aimed at finding the best game or exploring for slam. Similarly, there is much less case for adopting the 2NT negative arrangement if the initial response was at the two level.

QUIZ 7
Consider what you would bid next in the following:

1.
♠ Q 7 2
♥ K 4 2
♦ 8 6
♣ K Q J 4 2

Partner	You
1 ♥	2 ♣
2 NT*	?

*2NT showed 15-17

2.
♠ Q 4 2
♥ A 7 6
♦ Q 8 4 2
♣ J 5 3

Partner	You
1 ♠	1 NT
2 NT	?

3.
♠ A 10 8 7 2
♥ K 7 2
♦ K 6
♣ 8 4 2

Partner	You
1 ♥	1 ♠
2 ♦	?

4.
♠ Q 10 9 7 2
♥ A Q 5
♦ 8 7
♣ K 4 2

Partner	You
1 ♥	1 ♠
1 NT*	?

*1NT showed 15-17

5.
♠ A J 7 4 2
♥ 8 6
♦ K J 5
♣ Q 10 5

Partner	You
1 ♥	1 ♠
2 ♣	?

6.
♠ A 10 5
♥ A J 7 4 2
♦ 10 7 5
♣ Q 5

Partner	You
1 ♣	1 ♥
1 ♠	?

7.
♠ A K 6 4 2
♥ 10 5
♦ 7 4 2
♣ A Q 10

Partner	You
1 ♥	1 ♠
2 ♥	?

8.
♠ A K 10 4 2
♥ J 5
♦ 7 4 2
♣ K 10 4

Partner	You
1 ♥	1 ♠
2 ♥	?

Consider what you would bid next in the following:

1.

♠ Q 7 2
♥ K 4 2
♦ 8 6
♣ K Q J 4 2

1 ♥	2 ♣
2 NT*	?

*Partner's 2NT showed 15-17

Recommended Bid: 3♥

This is a straightforward problem. Clearly you have enough for game but, if partner has five hearts, 4♥ is likely to be a better spot than 3NT, especially if his diamonds are not too strong. How can you find out?

The classic solution to this problem is to bid three of your partner's major to offer him a choice of games. If he holds five hearts you expect him to bid 4♥, if not he will bid 3NT.

Note that this type of sequence needs to be distinguished from the jump to three of partner's major when he has bid two suits. On a sequence like 1♠–2♣–2♦, the jump to 3♠ is purely invitational, but, on a sequence where partner rebids in no trumps, three of his suit has to be forcing. When you have bid three suits you can bid the fourth suit to create a forcing situation. When you have only bid two suits, you can't.

2.

♠ Q 4 2
♥ A 7 6
♦ Q 8 4 2
♣ J 5 3

1 ♠	1 NT
2 NT	?

Recommended Bid: 3♠

In practice this is a similar sequence to the first example. If you were minimum you would pass 2NT, but, as you are clearly maximum, you press on to game. Once you have decided to bid on, 3♠ offers a choice of games. As before, you expect your partner to bid 4♠ with a five card spade suit or 3NT with only four. He should not pass 3♠.

3.

♠ A 10 8 7 2
♥ K 7 2
♦ K 6
♣ 8 4 2

1 ♥	1 ♠
2 ♦	?

Recommended Bid: 3♥

Now that your partner has rebid 2♦ you know that he has five hearts and four diamonds at least, so your cards are really working. In fact, if your partner holds as little as:

♠ 6 4
♥ A Q 6 4 3
♦ A Q 7 5
♣ 9 5

4♥ is a fair contract that will succeed with no more than reasonable distributions. On the other hand, he could have:

♠ 6 4
♥ J 8 7 6 4
♦ A Q J 7
♣ K Q

and 4♥ is a very poor contract. So the right approach is to jump to 3♥ to invite partner to bid the game.

Notice that when you have already bid three suits, you do not need the jump in the opener's first suit to be forcing and offering a choice of games, because you can always create a forcing situation by bidding the fourth suit first.

4.

♠ Q 10 9 7 2
♥ A Q 5
♦ 8 7
♣ K 4 2

1 ♥	1 ♠
1 NT*	?

*Partner's 1NT shows 15-17

Recommended Bid: 3♥

As in the first two examples, this time you have enough to insist on game, but which one? If partner has five hearts, 4♥ should be right; if he has three spades, 4♠ should be right; and if he has neither, you will have to settle for 3NT.

As before, after the 1NT rebid the jump to 3♥ is forcing and offers a choice of games. With five hearts opener should press on to 4♥; without five hearts he should bid 3♠ with three spades or 3NT with only two spades.

3♣ is a possible but inferior alternative because at the very least it should locate a 5-3 spade fit. With a game-going hand with five spades but only two hearts, responder is a little stuck for a bid, since the immediate 3♠ rebid is consistent with an invitational strength hand with six spades. Accordingly, to find the 5-3 spade fit responder has to "invent" a suit at the three level to try to get preference to spades. Over the pseudo-natural 3♣ bid, opener should bid 3♠ with three or else make an alternative descriptive bid, provided that he does not go past 3NT. If his hearts are good and he is relatively weak in diamonds he may bid 3♥, so the 5-3 heart fit will not always be lost.

5.

♠ A J 7 4 2
♥ 8 6
♦ K J 5
♣ Q 10 5

1 ♥	1 ♠
2 ♣	?

Recommended Bid: 2NT

With good cover in the fourth suit it is right to bid no trumps yourself rather than pass the buck, and since partner has not guaranteed holding more than twelve high card points (and on a bad day he may have less!), there is no need to bid more than 2NT. This is a limit bid and, like all other limit bids, partner may pass or go on to game with a couple of points to spare.

6.
    ♠ A 10 5
    ♥ A J 7 4 2
    ♦ 10 7 5
    ♣ Q 5

1 ♣	1 ♥
1 ♠	?

Recommended Bid: 2♦

This time, without Fourth Suit Forcing you would really have a problem. You have an invitational strength hand without enough black cards to support either of partners suit in invitational manner. A jump to 3♣ would show invitational strength and three card support, while a jump to 3♠ would show the same sort of values but with four card spade support.

Once you have decided to adopt Fourth Suit Forcing you can solve this problem by bidding 2♦. Note that if your partner just bids 2NT you can pass for your 2♦ bid guaranteed at least invitational values, so with a good looking fourteen point hand with a good diamond holding your partner could, and should, have jumped to 3NT.

It might be worth noting at this stage that today, while some players choose to play Fourth Suit Forcing as game forcing, the traditional style is to regard the use of Fourth Suit Forcing at the one or two level as guaranteeing just invitational values, while using the fourth suit at the three level is forcing to game. Indeed, bidding any "new suit" at the three level should be regarded as game forcing.

7.
    ♠ A K 10 4 2
    ♥ 10 5
    ♦ 7 4 2
    ♣ A Q 10

1 ♥	1 ♠
2 ♥	?

Recommended Bid: 3♣

With a trim looking thirteen high card points facing an opening bid, it is fairly clear that you should play this hand in game, but if you had to choose which game to play in at this stage you could easily get it wrong. So bid 3♣ and see what partner has to say.

Note right away that if opener has five hearts and four clubs, you would have expected him to rebid 2♣ rather than 2♥, so there is no real danger of him supporting your "club suit" at this stage. Even if he does support clubs now he must have very good hearts, so you put him back to 4♥ in comfort.

Also note that over 3♣ opener has a wide choice of possible actions. He could repeat his hearts with a good suit (and you will have a comfortable raise to 4♥), he could support spades (and you will try 4♠) or with a good diamond holding he can bid 3NT. With none of these he can fall back on Fourth Suit Forcing by bidding 3♦.

8.
    ♠ A K 10 4 2
    ♥ J 5
    ♦ 7 4 2
    ♣ K 10 4

1 ♥	1 ♠
2 ♥	?

Recommended Bid: 3♥

While your hand does have some promising features, you really do not have enough to commit your side to game. But that doesn't mean that game can't be made. While 3♣ would indicate where your minor suit values actually are, it is an overbid because it is forcing to game. So what is to be done?

The choice lies between an invitational 2NT and an invitational raise to 3♥. Since partner should have either a six card suit or five good hearts, the raise to 3♥ seems to fit the bill.

QUIZ 8

On every one of the following examples, your partner opens 1♠, you respond 2♣ and partner rebids 2♥. What do you do next?

1.
    ♠ J 4
    ♥ Q 7 2
    ♦ Q 7 2
    ♣ A J 10 6 2

5.
    ♠ 7 2
    ♥ K J 6 2
    ♦ 8 4
    ♣ A J 10 6 4

2.
    ♠ Q 4
    ♥ J 4 2
    ♦ Q 7 4
    ♣ A K J 6 4

6.
    ♠ Q 4
    ♥ K J 6 2
    ♦ 8 4
    ♣ A J 10 6 4

3.
    ♠ Q 4
    ♥ J 4
    ♦ Q 10 7 4
    ♣ A K J 6 4

7.
    ♠ 7 4
    ♥ K J 6 2
    ♦ A 4
    ♣ A J 10 6 4

4.
    ♠ A J 3
    ♥ Q 4
    ♦ K 7 4
    ♣ A 10 9 6 5

8.
    ♠ K 4
    ♥ K J 6 2
    ♦ 8 4
    ♣ A Q J 10 4

On every one of the following examples, your partner opens 1♠, you respond 2♣ and partner rebids 2♥. What do you do next?

1. ♠ J 4
   ♥ Q 7 2
   ♦ Q 7 2
   ♣ A J 10 6 2

Recommended Bid: 2♠

This is a slightly awkward hand. Add the ♦J and most players would happily continue with 2NT, but as it is the hand is not quite strong enough to make an invitational bid in no-trumps and the diamond holding isn't really solid enough either. On the other hand, passing 2♥ would be a very dangerous position to take, since partner has anything in the region of fifteen or sixteen points your expectation would be that you should be in the game.

The answer here is to give false preference to 2♠—after all, your expectation is that opener has at least five spades and four hearts, so if he does pass 2♠ it should prove to be a playable spot. Meanwhile, the real hope is that partner will have sufficient values to drum up another bid so that we can reach game.

2. ♠ Q 4
   ♥ J 4 2
   ♦ Q 7 4
   ♣ A K J 6 4

Recommended Bid: 3♦

This time you clearly have sufficient values to expect to make game. Of course, many players would simply gamble out 3NT but, facing a small singleton diamond or even a doubleton, it is all too likely that 3NT is not the right spot. Once again, the solution is to fall back on 3♦, Fourth Suit Forcing. If opener rebids 3 ♥, showing at least 5-5 in the majors, you have an easy raise to 4♥, if opener rebids 3♠ suggesting a six card suit or stressing a good five carder then you raise to 4♠ and if opener bids 3NT you are happy to pass, and just as a useful bonus if he has ♦Kx you will be playing 3NT from the right side.

3. ♠ Q 4
   ♥ J 4
   ♦ Q 10 7 4
   ♣ A K J 6 4

Recommended Bid: 3NT

An easy one this time. With game-going values and a potential double-stopper in diamonds, you bid 3NT—what else?

4. ♠ A J 3
   ♥ J 4
   ♦ K 7 4
   ♣ A 10 9 6 5

Recommended Bid: 3♦

This is another game-going hand where you have a pretty good idea of where you want to play. Partner is known to have five spades so 4♠ looks like an excellent spot. Accordingly, many players would succumb to the temptation to play 4♠ immediately but, in my view, that would be a mistake.

If you remember, in Chapter 2, we introduced the concept of a Delayed Game Raise, so if you bid 4♠ now your partner will probably expect you to deliver a decent five card club suit and four card trump support. To avoid overexciting your partner, use 3♦ Fourth Suit Forcing again, planning to support spades on the next round.

Sometimes this style can yield a really unexpected bonus; for example consider this layout:

♠ K Q 7 5 2   ♠ A J 3
♥ A 10 9 5 4   ♥ Q 4
♦ A 5   ♦ K 7 4
♣ 7   ♣ A 10 9 6 5

The whole auction might even be:

1♠	2♣
2♥	3♦ (FSF)
3♥	3♠ (i)
4♦ (ii)	5♣ (iii)
5♥ (iv)	6♦ (v)
6♠ (vi)	Pass

(i) Opener's convenient 3♥ rebid left room for East to show his spade support at the three level.

(ii) With a fairly good hand West takes the opportunity to show some extra values by cuebidding 4♦.

(iii) All of a sudden this routine game-going hand looks a lot more interesting. If partner has 5-5 in the majors and the ♦A, then East already knows that there are no minor suit losers. Even if West has two small clubs, the ♦K will provide a discard. East should surely expect West to have some extra values for his mild slam try, and nine or ten points in the majors would still only give West thirteen or fourteen points. However, East has seven points in the majors himself—so at worst it would appear that East/West are missing only three or four points in the majors, and most of the time that will mean only one major suit loser. So, even without any more information, East should be able to determine that 6♠ is a likely final destination. In fact, it would not be ridiculous for East to bid the slam at this stage, but cuebidding 5♣ at least gives West a chance to back-pedal with poor holdings in the majors.

(iv) With no wasted values West cooperates with a further cuebid of 5♥.

(v) From East's point of view it is unclear that West would have bid any differently with:

♠ K Q 7 5 2
♥ A K J 5 2
♦ A 5
♣ 7

when the grand slam should be easy, so East makes a clear-cut grand slam try making yet another cuebid.

(vi) Without the ♥K West has little option but to sign off in 6♠.

I hope that the message is clear: in many situations Fourth Suit Forcing provides the extra space needed to really explore a hand.

5.　♠ 7 4
　　♥ K J 6 2
　　♦ 8 4
　　♣ A J 10 6 4

Recommended Bid: 3♥

While this is very much a minimum hand for a 2♣ response there is no question of passing the opener's 2♥ rebid. After all if partner holds as little as:

(a)　♠ A K 8 6 2
　　♥ A Q 5 3
　　♦ 6 5
　　♣ 5 3

game is excellent, but facing a rather less suitable hand:

(b)　♠ K J 9 8 6
　　♥ A 10 7 5
　　♦ K Q
　　♣ 5 3

even 3♥ is likely to prove to be a struggle. So, responder should raise to 3♥ and leave the final decision to opener.

Both hand (a) and hand (b) contain thirteen high card points but with hand (a) opener should accept the invitation, while with hand (b) he should most surely decline. The real difference is that hand (a) has good controls and crisp values with nothing really wasted in terms of playing in hearts, while hand (b) lacks top controls and has much slower values. The doubleton ♦KQ is a particularly poor holding: one quick loser but only one trick. Adding another diamond and taking away a club would leave West with a much better hand.

6.　♠ Q 4
　　♥ K J 6 2
　　♦ 8 4
　　♣ A J 10 6 4

Recommended Bid: 4♥

This is a much better hand. Notice that even facing hand (b) 4♥ depends on little more than finding the queen of trumps. The real difference is not just that the ♠Q is two more points but that the additional queen is known to be in a key suit. So responder should leave nothing to chance by raising to 4♥.

7.　♠ 7 4
　　♥ K J 6 2
　　♦ A 4
　　♣ A J 10 6 4

Recommended Bid: 4♦

It should be reasonably clear that this is a much better hand than our last example, and if that hand was worth a raise to game this hand has some considerable slam potential, but you would not want to get too high facing hand (b). Once again, we could use Fourth Suit Forcing and then support hearts to show a better game-going hand but there is a better approach with this type of hand. Jump to 4♦, an advance cuebid showing control in diamonds and a good raise to 4♥.

8.　♠ K 4
　　♥ K J 6 2
　　♦ 8 4
　　♣ A Q J 10 4

Recommended Bid: 3♦

This hand is by way of contrast with the last example. Once again you have a good enough hand to want to show a good raise to 4♥, but since you have no control in diamonds you cannot jump to 4♦. This time settle for bidding a fourth suit 3♦ planning to support hearts on the next round.

Quiz 9

First, consider your choice of action if the bidding has started:

1 ♦	1 ♠
2 ♥	?

1.　♠ K J 10 6 5　　　3.　♠ Q J 6 5
　　♥ Q 5　　　　　　　　♥ Q 5 2
　　♦ 7 5　　　　　　　　♦ 7 5
　　♣ J 9 5 2　　　　　　♣ K J 9 4

2.　♠ K J 10 6 5　　　4.　♠ Q J 6 5
　　♥ A 5　　　　　　　　♥ Q 5
　　♦ 7 5　　　　　　　　♦ 7 5
　　♣ J 6 5 2　　　　　　♣ J 10 7 6

Now suppose instead that the auction starts:

1 ♥	2 ♦
2 ♠	?

What would you bid with each of the following hands:

5.　♠ 7 5　　　　　　　7.　♠ K 5
　　♥ Q 6 5　　　　　　　♥ A Q 5
　　♦ K Q J 10 5　　　　♦ A J 10 5 4
　　♣ Q 5 2　　　　　　　♣ 7 5 3

6.　♠ K 5　　　　　　　8.　♠ K 5
　　♥ Q 6 5　　　　　　　♥ 7 5
　　♦ A J 10 5 4　　　　♦ A Q J 9 7 6
　　♣ 7 5 2　　　　　　　♣ J 7 5

ANSWERS TO QUIZ 9

First, consider your choice of action if the bidding has started:

1 ♦	1 ♠
2 ♥	?

1. ♠ K J 10 6 5
♥ Q 5
♦ 7 5
♣ J 9 5 2

Recommended Bid: 2♠

Without doubt the main feature of this hand is the good five card spade suit, so, without much more than you have already promised, just bid 2♠. If opener cannot drum up another bid you are unlikely to have missed a game and if he does bid again you should be reasonably well placed.

If partner continues with 2NT, 3♣, 3♦ or even 3♥, you would bid 3NT, comfortable in the knowledge that you have already shown a fair spade suit. If partner raises to 3♠, you have enough to continue to game; after all, you might bid exactly the same way without the ♥Q.

2. ♠ K J 10 6 5
♥ A 5
♦ 7 5
♣ J 6 5 2

Recommended Bid: 3♣

This time you have the same shape, but clearly you have enough values to commit your side to game. However, with such good spades and relatively poor clubs, it would be a mistake to just jump to 3NT. Bid 3♣, Fourth Suit Forcing, showing that you have game-going values, but asking your partner to continue describing his hand.

3. ♠ Q J 6 5
♥ Q 5 2
♦ 7 5
♣ K J 9 4

Recommended Bid: 3NT

With nine high card points facing a reverse, you should be confident of making a game on your combined assets and you have a pretty good idea of where you want to play. A jump to 3NT gives a good description of your hand.

4. ♠ Q J 6 5
♥ Q 5
♦ 7 5
♣ J 10 7 6

Recommended Bid: 2NT

Since partner could easily have nineteen or twenty points on this auction, you really have to drum up another bid. Try 2NT, then, if opener bids 3♦, you can sensibly pass. On the other hand, if he continues with either 3♣, Fourth Suit Forcing, or 3♠ you have a comfortable 3NT bid.

Now suppose instead that the auction starts:

1 ♥	2 ♦
2 ♠	?

What would you bid with each of the following hands:

5. ♠ 7 5
♥ Q 6 5
♦ K Q J 10 5
♣ Q 5 2

Recommended Bid: 3♥

With three card heart support, this hand is just a little too strong to raise to 2♥ on the first round, but in choosing to respond 2♦ you should always have been planning to support hearts on the next round. As opener's reverse guarantees a five card heart suit it seems obvious that responder should support hearts now. After the initial two level response, there is no question of 3♥ not being forcing, but, having supported hearts, you should be more than happy to pass if opener continues with 3NT.

6. ♠ K 5
♥ Q 6 5
♦ A J 10 5 4
♣ 7 5 2

Recommended Bid: 4♥

This hand has the same number of high card points and the same shape, but it has much greater playing potential, much better controls and rather more high card strength in partner's two suits. With this kind of hand, the recommended Acol style action is to jump to 4♥, to show a fairly minimum, but highly suitable, hand. The real issue is that with hands of this type you would feel unhappy if you bid 3♥ and partner just raised to 4♥, for 6♥ could easily be a good contract facing a fairly minimum reversing hand like:

♠ A 9 4 3
♥ A K 10 7 4 2
♦ K 7
♣ 8

but you wouldn't really want to bid on, just in case partner produces something like:

♠ Q J 9 4
♥ A K J 7 4
♦ K Q
♣ Q 5

With eighteen high card points this hand is full value for the reverse, but there are still three obvious top losers if you press on to the five level.

7. ♠ K 5
♥ A Q 5
♦ A J 10 5 4
♣ 7 5 3

Recommended Bid: 3♥

By way of contrast, this is an even stronger hand. This time, when partner simply raises your 3♥ to 4♥, you would feel confident that you have enough to risk pressing on to the five level. Personally, I would cuebid 4♠ in the hope of eliciting a club cuebid from opener.

8. ♠ K 5
    ♥ 7 5
    ♦ A Q J 9 7 6
    ♣ J 7 5

Recommended Bid: 3♦

Having already responded at the two level, there is no need to do more than repeat your diamonds to emphasize the quality of your suit. As you can see, opposite a good high card reverse such as:

♠ A 6 4 2
♥ A K 8 6 2
♦ K 2
♣ A 4

6♦ is the winning contract and opposite:

♠ A Q 6 4
♥ A K 8 6 2
♦ K 2
♣ 8 6

5♦ is undoubtedly the right place to play.

Part Score or Game

Most players do not experience too much difficulty learning the basic requirements for bidding and making game with two balanced hands. Indeed, one of the early lessons most players learn is that twenty-five high card points is enough to make game, and most no trump bidding is oriented to establishing whether or not the partnership holds this magic total of twenty-five points.

However you look at it, distributional hands are not so easy, but many players improve dramatically when they come to appreciate that the degree of fit is frequently more important than the point count. It is all very well learning to adjust the point count evaluation to allow for distributional features, but most of the time it is an appreciation of the *combined assets* of the two hands that is important and not an individual evaluation.

It is for this simple reason that I have placed so much emphasis on the importance of supporting partner when you have support. Unless he knows the extent of your support for his suit quickly, he will have no chance of applying sensible judgment in the bidding. Now, consider just how many tricks you will make from the following pair of hands:

♠ A 5 4 3 2	♠ K 8 7 6
♥ A 5	♥ 4 3 2
♦ A 4 3 2	♦ K 5
♣ 3 2	♣ 5 4 3 2

However you look at it, three unsupported aces and no singleton is not that much more than a minimum opening bid and just two kings is not the greatest responding hand. But if spades break 2-2 and the side suits break reasonably most players will soon manage ten tricks by ruffing two diamonds in the dummy.

This remarkable result is entirely due to the degree of fit—a nine card trump fit, no wasted values in the honor cards, and the very convenient diamond combination, effectively providing four tricks with the aid of two ruffs.

Now look at what happens if you move the responder's holdings around:

♠ A 5 4 3 2	♠ K 8 7 6
♥ A 5	♥ K 4
♦ A 4 3 2	♦ 7 6 5
♣ 3 2	♣ 7 6 5 4

Just switching the red suit holdings clearly costs a trick. Move the K 5 into the club suit and, if the ace of clubs is on the wrong side, the total trick count will be right back down to eight; indeed on a bad day when the trumps break 3-1 and the ♣A is wrong you will struggle to make even eight tricks.

So, while it is fairly clear that the total number of trumps is an important factor in determining how many tricks your side can take, it should also be clear that the location of both high cards and shortages is equally important. For example, consider the following pair of hands:

(a)	♠ A Q 7 6 5	*or*	**(b)**	♠ A Q 7 6 5
	♥ Q 5			♥ 7 5
	♦ A J 5 2			♦ A J 5 2
	♣ 7 5			♣ Q 5

You open 1♠ and let us suppose that your partner responds 2♣ but then jumps to 3♠ over your 2♦ rebid. What would you do next?

Of course, with only thirteen high card points and not particularly good distribution, you may be tempted to pass on both hands, but it is fairly clear that hand (b) is much better than hand (a), for while the ♥Q figures to be waste paper, the ♣Q is likely to be working hard for you. Your partner could easily have something like:

♠ K 4 2
♥ 9 8 2
♦ Q 6
♣ A J 8 6 4

Opposite hand (a) you have two certain heart losers and a club loser and then, even if the diamond finesse is right, you really have very poor prospects of disposing of your fourth diamond. While you can ruff the third round of the suit, you will need to find a very good lie of the cards to allow you to ruff the last diamond.

Meanwhile, prospects facing hand (b) are much better. If the club finesse is right, declarer will have the luxury of leading up to the ♦Q. Even if the ♦K is over the queen, he will then only need one diamond ruff in the dummy to make his contract. If the club finesse is wrong then declarer will need the diamond finesse to be right, but the club suit will provide a parking place for the fourth diamond.

Accordingly, it seems right to pass with hand (a) and press on to game with hand (b). Is this double dummy? No, I don't think so. It seems common sense to me to upgrade minor honor cards in the suit that partner has bid and downgrade minor honor cards in the unbid suit. In effect, hand (a) should be re-evaluated at about eleven high card points while hand (b) should be upgraded to about fourteen.

If the decision whether to continue to game depends on the mesh of high cards and distributional values, it seems sensible that you should use methods that help you to find this out whenever you can. One of the most obvious situations is after partner raises one of a major to two. All of which brings us to the subject of trial bids.

The idea is that if opener wants to make a game try, he bids the suit where he would most like his partner to be able to help him. Of course, responder is allowed to sign off with a totally minimum hand or bid the game with a maximum hand anyway, but on all the variety of hands that fall somewhere in between he should pay particular attention to his holding in the trial bid suit. He should upvalue his hand if he holds the ace or king of the suit or a singleton or doubleton, and downgrade his hand with holdings like three small. Qxx is clearly much better than three small, but it is still not a very good holding; certainly Qx would be much better.

It may seem fairly amazing that you are very close to having enough to make a game try with the hand this chapter started with, which was:

> ♠ A 5 4 3 2
> ♥ A 5
> ♦ A 4 3 2
> ♣ 3 2

Opposite the right six point hand, you have already established that game will have reasonable play. On balance, however, making a game try with this hand is a very aggressive action and my assessment would be that you would go down in either 3♠ or 4♠ slightly too often to make the adventure worthwhile. Make the hand just a little bit better and it would be a different story.

So with:

♠ A Q 4 3 2	*or*	♠ A 5 4 3 2	*or*	♠ A 5 4 3 2
♥ A 5		♥ A Q		♥ A 5
♦ A 4 3 2		♦ A 4 3 2		♦ A Q 3 2
♣ 3 2		♣ 3 2		♣ 3 2

I would make a game try by bidding 3♦ and I would expect my partner to bid 4♠ holding:

> ♠ K 8 7 6
> ♥ 4 3 2
> ♦ K 5
> ♣ 5 4 3 2

You can work out for yourself just how much better the game is with the addition of a working queen in opener's hand.

By the same token you can see that if the additional queen was in the club suit, the hand would not be worth making the game try.

Now, how would you tackle the following hand:

> ♠ A J 10 5 4
> ♥ 10 9 5
> ♦ A K Q 4
> ♣ 7

You open 1♠ and your partner raises to 2♠, what do you do now? 5-4-3-1 shape hands are always powerful, and you can see that, if partner has just an ace and the king of spades, 4♠ will have fair play, so a game try is called for—but what is that game try going to be?

If the idea is that partner should be able to upvalue his hand when he has a useful holding in the suit that you choose to bid, it should be patently obvious that it is a waste of breath to bid 3♦—for you really don't need any help in that suit. On the other hand, you would be pleased to find a doubleton heart in the dummy, so you should use 3♥ as your game try.

Now let's look at a slightly different situation. Suppose you find yourself looking at:

> ♠ A Q 7 6 4
> ♥ Q 5
> ♦ Q 6
> ♣ 10 7 6 2

Your partner opens 1♦, and you respond 1♠ which partner raises to 2♠. What are your thoughts now?

Many of the players I know would simply pass without giving the hand very much thought, but facing a hand like:

> ♠ K 8 5 2
> ♥ J 7 2
> ♦ A K 10 8 7
> ♣ 8

4♠ is excellent and you could barely blame the opener for not bidding more than 2♠.

Of course, this responding hand is a little deceptive. The spade holding is excellent and don't forget the power of that fifth trump: the ♥Q is a poor card which might be worth absolutely nothing but the ♦Q looks to be much more valuable as partner has bid the suit. If I was trying to value this hand in the terms of points alone I would add three points for the quality and length of the spades now that opener has supported that suit, deduct one or two for the poor heart holding and add one back on for the diamond holding. So however you look at it this responding hand is worth about twelve high card points and that should be enough to make a game try.

So, what are you going to bid? I would recommend that you bid 3♣ and treat it just like a trial bid. If opener is good for his bidding he might bid the game anyway, and if he is poor he might just go back to 3♠. However, with an in-between hand he should look at his holding in clubs to help him decide. On the example opening hand, opener only has eleven high card points, but with a singleton club opposite our length and four card trump support, when he might only have three, he should have no hesitation in accepting your game try.

Alter the opening hand so that he has a singleton heart and jack to three clubs, then he should definitely reject the game try.

QUIZ 10

You open 1♠ and your partner raises to 2♠. What do you do with each of the following hands?

1.   ♠ A Q 10 4 3
       ♥ K Q 5
       ♦ A 5 4 2
       ♣ 7

2.   ♠ A Q 10 7
       ♥ K Q 5
       ♦ A 5 4 2
       ♣ 7 5

3.   ♠ A Q 10 5
       ♥ K Q 5
       ♦ A 7 5
       ♣ K 4 2

4.   ♠ A 10 9 5 4 3
       ♥ K Q 5
       ♦ A 7 5
       ♣ 7

5.   ♠ A 10 9 5 4 3
       ♥ A Q J 4
       ♦ K 5
       ♣ 7

You open 1♠ and your partner raises to 2♠. What do you do with each of the following hands?

1.   ♠ A Q 10 4 3
       ♥ K Q 5
       ♦ A 5 4 2
       ♣ 7

Recommended Bid: 3 ♦

This is a good hand, well worth a game try, but to make 4♠ a good contract you would much prefer some help in diamonds to some wasted values in clubs. So bid 3♦.

2.   ♠ A Q 10 7
       ♥ K Q 5
       ♦ K J 4 2
       ♣ 7 5

Recommended Bid: Pass

Yes, you do have some extra values, but really no more than you have promised. After all, if you would have opened 1NT to show 12-14 balanced points then when you open 1♠ with only four spades, you must have at least fifteen points. In terms of playing strength, this hand is really no better than a 5-3-3-2 hand with twelve high card points, so you should pass.

3.   ♠ A Q 10 5
       ♥ K Q 5
       ♦ A 7 5
       ♣ K 4 2

Recommended Bid: 2NT

This is a rather better hand which should yield game if partner has seven or eight high card points. Bid 2NT to show a hand of about this strength, then leave the decision to partner; if he has a really weak hand he can still sign off in 3♠.

4.   ♠ A 10 9 5 4 3
       ♥ K Q 5
       ♦ A 7 5
       ♣ 7

Recommended Bid: 3♦

Only thirteen high card points but the sixth spade is certain to yield an extra trick. Bid 3♦ to help partner to judge whether to bid 4♠ or not.

5.   ♠ A 10 9 5 4 3
       ♥ A Q J 4
       ♦ K 5
       ♣ 7

Recommended Bid: 4♠

Despite the low point count this is a much better hand still. If spades break 2-2 you would have some play for game if all partner has is ♠Kxx. So don't make a game try with this hand; simply bid what you think you can make, 4♠.

This time you have the responding hand. What would you bid after the sequence:

1♠	2♠
3♦	?

1. ♠ K 7 6
    ♥ J 7 5 3
    ♦ 6 5
    ♣ Q 8 7 6

2. ♠ K 7 6
    ♥ J 7 5 3
    ♦ K 5
    ♣ J 8 7 6

3. ♠ K 7 6
    ♥ A J 7 5 3
    ♦ 7 6 5
    ♣ 8 6

4. ♠ K 8 7 6
    ♥ J 7 5
    ♦ 7 6 5
    ♣ Q 7 6

5. ♠ K 8 7 6
    ♥ A 7 5
    ♦ 7 6 5
    ♣ Q 7 6

6. ♠ K 8 7 6
    ♥ J 7 5
    ♦ Q 5
    ♣ 10 7 6 2

This time you have the responding hand. What would you bid after the sequence:

1♠	2♠
3♦	?

1. ♠ K 7 6
    ♥ J 7 5 3
    ♦ 6 5
    ♣ Q 8 7 6

Recommended Bid: 3♠

You have a totally minimum hand for your initial raise to 2♠. Despite the fact that you have a totally suitable diamond holding you should reject the game try since you only have three spades.

2. ♠ K 7 6
    ♥ J 7 5 3
    ♦ K 5
    ♣ J 8 7 6

Recommended Bid: 4♠

This time, although you only have three card spade support, you should bid 4♠ because your diamond holding could not really be more suitable and one of your outside jacks may make some contribution.

3. ♠ K 7 6
    ♥ A J 7 5 3
    ♦ 7 6 5
    ♣ 8 6

Recommended Bid: 3♥

With the king of trumps and an outside ace you have enough to accept the game try despite having the worst possible diamond holding. However, if the opener has three hearts, 4♥ might well be a better contract than 4♠, so bid 3♥ for the moment. If opener raises you to 4♥ that will be a sensible contract, if instead he bids 3♠ you can still raise him to game.

Notice that, despite having a five card heart suit, eight high card points and only three spades, it is right to support spades initially rather than bidding 2♥. The reason is that if you respond 2♥ and partner rebids 2♠ you will be committed to raising to 3♠ in order to show him any spade support—and this is clearly an overbid. It is much better to support spades right away hoping to get your hearts with the action later.

4. ♠ K 8 7 6
    ♥ J 7 5
    ♦ 7 6 5
    ♣ Q 7 6

Recommended Bid: 3♠

While now you have four card trump support you still have very much a minimum for your raise to 2 ♠ and your diamond holding really could not be worse. So just bid 3♠

---

and hope that you have enough for your partner to make it.

5. ♠ K 8 7 6
   ♥ A 7 5
   ♦ 7 6 5
   ♣ Q 7 6

Recommended Bid: 4♠

Despite the poor diamond holding, you have a maximum hand for your raise to 2♠. Once again, you have the advantage of holding two key cards so bid 4♠. Note that with only three card spade support and a maximum you could bid 3NT with good holdings in both unbid suits.

6. ♠ K 8 7 6
   ♥ J 7 5
   ♦ Q 5
   ♣ 10 7 6 2

Recommended Bid: 4♠

This time you are back to holding a minimum hand for your initial action, but the diamond holding is very suitable and since you hold four trumps, there is every prospect of ruffing two diamonds in your hand, so bid 4♠. Just see your prospects opposite either of the hands which you decided that you should bid 3♦ on in the first quiz, namely:

No 1.
         ♠ A Q 10 4 3   ♠ K 8 7 6
         ♥ K Q 5   ♥ J 7 5
         ♦ A 5 4 2   ♦ Q 5
         ♣ 7   ♣ 10 7 6 2

Here we have three obvious losers, but if the ♦K is right, there will be no difficulty making 4♠ unless the spades break 4-0. If the ♦K is wrong, we will need to be a bit more fortunate but if trumps are 2-2 it will be easy to ruff both losing diamonds in the dummy.

and No 4.
         ♠ A 10 9 5 4 3   ♠ K 8 7 6
         ♥ K Q 5   ♥ J 7 5
         ♦ A 7 5   ♦ Q 5
         ♣ 7   ♣ 10 7 6 2

With this combination you should have no difficulty making ten tricks with spades as trumps unless the spades break 3-0 or the defense take an immediate heart ruff.

QUIZ 12

This time you have a mixture of problems to consider. First consider what you would do in the following situation:

1 ♥	1 ♠
2 ♠	?

1. ♠ K Q 7 5 3   2. ♠ K Q 7 5 3
   ♥ Q 5   ♥ 7 5
   ♦ K 10 4 3   ♦ K 10 4 3
   ♣ 7 5   ♣ Q 5

Then, on each of the following hands what would you do after:

1 ♥	1 ♠
3 ♠	?

3. ♠ K Q 7 5   4. ♠ K Q 7 5
   ♥ Q 5   ♥ 7 5
   ♦ 7 5 3   ♦ 7 5 3
   ♣ 9 6 5 2   ♣ Q 6 5 2

Finally, what would you bid after the following sequences with this hand:

   ♠ K 5 4 3
   ♥ 6 4 2
   ♦ Q 8 6 4 2
   ♣ 5

5. | 1 ♠ | 2 ♠ |
   | 2 NT | ? |

6. | 1 ♠ | 2 ♠ |
   | 3 ♣ | ? |

7. | 1 ♠ | 2 ♠ |
   | 3 ♥ | ? |

This time you have a mixture of problems to consider. First consider what you would do in the following situation:

1 ♥	1 ♠
2 ♠	?

1. ♠ K Q 7 5 3
♥ Q 5
♦ K 10 4 3
♣ 7 5

Recommended Bid: 3♦

An aceless ten count looks like only a marginal candidate for making a game try except for two key attributes:

First, you should expect the fifth spade to be worth a playing trick, and then the ♥Q is well placed to fill a hole in partner's suit. If you add one point on for the well-placed queen, even rigid point counters will be making a game try.

2. ♠ K Q 7 5 3
♥ 7 5
♦ K 10 4 3
♣ Q 5

Recommended Bid: Pass

This time, a slightly different story. If you should add a point for a well-placed queen you should take one off for the poorly placed ♣Q on this hand.

Then consider what you would do after:

1 ♥	1 ♠
3 ♠	?

3. ♠ K Q 7 5
♥ Q 5
♦ 7 5 3
♣ 9 6 5 2

Recommended Bid: 4♠

In just the same way here, the well placed queen is well worth an additional point, so you should continue to game.

4. ♠ K Q 7 5
♥ 7 5
♦ 7 5 3
♣ Q 6 5 2

Recommended Bid: Pass

Just as before, deduct one point for the badly placed ♣Q and you are left with very much a minimum responding hand. If partner can't raise to game, why should you bid on?

Finally, suppose that you hold:

♠ K 5 4 3
♥ 6 4 2
♦ Q 8 6 4 2
♣ 5

then, what do you bid after:

5.

1 ♠	2 ♠
2 NT	?

Recommended Bid: 3♠

For partner 2NT bid, you should expect partner to hold in the region of a balanced eighteen point hand, something like:

♠ A 8 7 2
♥ K Q 5
♦ A J 7
♣ K J 4

As you can see, even with normal breaks 4♠ would be a real struggle, probably requiring king doubleton in diamonds onside and something favorable in hearts.

6.

1 ♠	2 ♠
3 ♣	?

Recommended Bid: 4♠

Despite your minimum it looks like you have just the right cards for partner. The singleton club is excellent when backed up with four trumps.

7.

1 ♠	2 ♠
3 ♥	?

Recommended Bid: 3♠

With partner looking for help in hearts, three small cards is the worst possible holding.

Chapter 9

Choosing The Best Game

In Chapter Four, we addressed the problem of the responder offering a choice of games and how he might fall back on Fourth Suit Forcing to start exploring to find the best game. In this chapter we take a further look at Fourth Suit Forcing and all of its ramifications.

First of all, let's suppose that you are fortunate enough to pick up:

♠ K 5
♥ 10 6
♦ K Q 10 2
♣ A K 6 4 2

Partner opens 1♠ and you respond 2♣ as we have already established that you don't jump in response with a two-suiter. Rather to your surprise your partner rebids 2♦. What is your best move?

Of course, it is easy to dream of slam, and most players that have attended my classes over the years have been eager to jump to four or even five diamonds. This is all very well, but while it is clear that you would like to show interest in a diamond slam, it is not at all clear that even 5♦ will be a good contract if partner has a minimum opening bid. Of course, you want to play in at least game, but couldn't 3NT or 4♠ be a more desirable spot than 5♦?

For example, suppose that the opener has:

♠ A Q J 7 5
♥ Q 7
♦ J 9 7 6
♣ Q 7

I would have to agree that this really isn't a great hand but I would be surprised if most experienced players passed with it. Looking at the combined holdings, 5♦ suffers from the obvious embarrassment of three top losers and you would expect the defense to take the first six tricks against 3NT. However, 4♠ is an excellent contract which should succeed unless either of the trumps break exceptionally badly or the defense are able to score a quick diamond ruff.

So, rather than leap into the stratosphere, you should start by

bidding 2♥, Fourth Suit Forcing, and listen to what partner has to say. Of course your plan is to support diamonds on the next round. If you had four card diamond support and only invitational values, you would have supported diamonds as soon as partner bid them, so using the fourth suit and then supporting diamonds is forcing to game. The real advantage comes because this gives your partner two further opportunities to say something about his hand before you really have to make any decision.

Let's consider how the auction might develop facing four different minimum opening hands. First:

(a)
♠ A J 10 7 5	♠ K 4
♥ Q 9 5	♥ 10 6
♦ A J 6 4	♦ K Q 10 2
♣ 5	♣ A K 6 4 2

The full sequence:

1 ♠	2 ♣
2 ♦	2 ♥ (FSF)
2 NT	3 ♦
3 ♠	4 ♠
Pass	

Having already shown five spades and four diamonds, opener shows his heart stopper but when responder shows his diamond support opener takes the opportunity to stress the quality of his spades. Having already got the rest of his hand off his chest, responder has a comfortable raise to 4♠.

(b)
♠ A Q 7 5 3	♠ K 4
♥ 8 7 2	♥ 10 6
♦ A J 9 4	♦ K Q 10 2
♣ 7	♣ A K 6 4 2

The full sequence:

1 ♦	2 ♥ (FSF)
2 ♠	3 ♦
3 ♥ (FSF)	3 ♠
4 ♠	Pass

With only three small hearts, opener is effectively forced into repeating his spades. Over 3♦, opener returns the compliment by using Fourth Suit Forcing himself, after all, 3NT could be the right contract if responder has any length in hearts. As it happens responder has no help there, but, at least, he can now show his modest spade support. After 3♠, opener raises to game.

(c)   ♠ Q 7 5 3 2   ♠ K 4
      ♥ A J 9   ♥ 10 6
      ♦ A J 6 4   ♦ K Q 10 2
      ♣ 5   ♣ A K 6 4 2

The full sequence:

1 ♠	2 ♣
2 ♦	2 ♥ (FSF)
2 NT	3 ♦
3 NT	Pass

With a good heart stop and poor spades in a minimum hand, opener responds 2NT to the fourth suit inquiry. When responder reveals his diamond support, opener stresses the good quality of his heart holding by rebidding 3NT. There is no reason for responder to bid on.

(d)   ♠ A J 5 3 2   ♠ K 4
      ♥ 7   ♥ 10 6
      ♦ A J 6 4   ♦ K Q 10 2
      ♣ Q 8 3   ♣ A K 6 4 2

The full sequence:

1 ♠	2 ♣
2 ♦	2 ♥ (FSF)
3 ♣	4 ♦
4 ♥	4 NT
5 ♥	6 ♦
Pass	

After Fourth Suit Forcing, West shows his club support. Since it is inconceivable that West has more than two hearts, this has the effect of persuading East that 3NT is off the menu. East makes his intentions clear by jumping to 4♦, committing his side to playing in a diamond game or slam.

West's choice of action over this is of considerable interest. Since it is possible that he might have bid 3♣ with honor doubleton in clubs, and therefore have two hearts, it seems to me that the most helpful action West could take at this stage is to cuebid 4♥. Confirmation of the hoped for 5-1-4-3 shape is really all East wanted to hear, so he checks for aces and bids the small slam. Notice that 6♦ is a better contract than 6♣ as, if the clubs fail to break, you can still fall back on the spade suit.

One of the noticeable aspects of the first three of these sequences is that, even after responder has shown his strong hand with four card diamond support, the bids below 3NT are aimed at finding the right game rather than being cuebids looking for slam. The same principle should be applied in other situations.

For example, consider your action with the following hand:

♠ Q J 5
♥ K Q 7 5
♦ K 6 5
♣ 8 7 2

after the auction starts:

| 1 ♦ | 1 ♥ |
| 3 ♦ | ? |

Since partner has shown extra values and a six card diamond suit by making a jump rebid, it is fairly clear that you have enough values to bid game. But which one?

In all fairness, you really do not know. Opener could easily have:

♠ 10 4
♥ A 4
♦ A Q J 9 7 2
♣ K Q 4

when everybody would want to play in 3NT, or he could have:

♠ A 10 4
♥ A 4 2
♦ A Q J 9 7 2
♣ 4

when you would much prefer to come to rest in 4♥, 5♦ or even 6♦ than play in 3NT and lose the first five club tricks.

So, what is to be done? With insufficient information to make an accurate decision yourself, you have to try and help partner. The way to do this is to show partner where your values lie. In this case, try bidding 3♠.

Note that this bid does not guarantee a four card spade suit and neither is there any legitimate reason for you to be showing five hearts. Pure and simple, you are inviting partner to bid 3NT with a suitable club holding. If he doesn't have a club stopper then he must bid something else.

Then, in a similar vein, consider:

♠ 7 5
♥ J 6 4
♦ K Q 10 4
♣ J 7 4 2

Partner opens 1♠ and, naturally enough, you respond 1NT. Now partner jumps to 3♣, what would you do next?

First, as a matter of system, partner's jump to 3♣ should show game-going values with at least five spades and at least four clubs, so we have to bid again. However, at this stage, once again, it is totally unclear which game is going to be best. It could easily be 3NT, 4♠, or 5♣, so what can you do to help partner?

Show him where your values are by bidding 3♦. With a good holding in hearts, he will undoubtedly bid 3NT, with good spades he will probably bid 3♠ and even if he raises diamonds you can go back to 5♣. Indeed, it will be the right contract if he has something like:

♠ A K 8 6 2
♥ 8
♦ A 5 3
♣ A K 9 6

QUIZ 13

For the first three problems, suppose that you hold the following attractive hand:

♠ 4
♥ 10 6 3
♦ K Q 10 2
♣ A K Q J 4

What do you bid, as responder, after the auction has started:

1.	1♠	2♣
	2♦	2♥ (FSF)
	2NT	3♦
	3♠	?

2.	1♠	2♣
	2♦	2♥ (FSF)
	2♠	3♦
	3♥	?

3.	1♠	2♣
	2♦	2♥ (FSF)
	2NT	3♦
	3NT	?

Now suppose that your partner opens 1♠, you respond 1♥ and partner jumps to 3♣. What do you bid next holding:

4.	♠ J 7 5	6.	♠ K 7 5
	♥ K J 7 5 4		♥ A J 4 2
	♦ A J 6		♦ Q J 5
	♣ 7 5		♣ 7 5

5.	♠ K 6 5	7.	♠ Q J 5
	♥ A Q 10 5 4		♥ A 8 5 3
	♦ 5 4 2		♦ 9 7 6 4
	♣ 7 5		♣ 7 5

You hold:

♠ 4
♥ 10 6 3
♦ K Q 10 2
♣ A K Q J 4

What do you bid after the following sequences?

1.	1♠	2♣
	2♦	2♥ (FSF)
	2NT	3♦
	3♠	?

Recommended Bid: 3NT

Having been through the Fourth Suit Forcing paraphernalia to show your forcing diamond raise, you are now faced with making a sensible decision. Opener has shown a heart stopper and then emphasized his spades. Obviously, you have no interest in playing in spades but, since partner is known to have a heart stopper, why should you look further than 3NT? After all, could you not have three potential heart losers playing in 5♦?

Strangely enough, partner's bidding is totally consistent with a hand shown earlier in this chapter, in example (a):

♠ A J 10 7 5
♥ Q 9 5
♦ A J 6 4
♣ 5

2.	1♠	2♣
	2♦	2♥ (FSF)
	2♠	3♦
	3♥	?

Recommended Bid: 3NT

On the previous round partner repeated his spades but now he has used Fourth Suit Forcing himself. Clearly he has heart length but no heart stopper as such, rather like the hand suggested in example (b):

♠ A Q 7 5 3
♥ 8 7 2
♦ A J 9 4
♣ 7

So, what should you bid over 3♥? You should bid 3NT. After all, it is much better to play in 3NT which will succeed as long as the opponents can't cash five heart tricks right away than in 5♦ which has three top losers.

3.	1♠	2♣
	2♦	2♥ (FSF)
	2NT	3♦
	3NT	?

Recommended Bid: Pass

This time partner has shown a heart stopper over your Fourth Suit Forcing and emphasized it by bidding 3NT over your 3♦. You have no excuse to bid again!

Now, what do you bid after:

> 1♣   1♥
> 3♣   ?

4.
> ♠ J 7 5
> ♥ K J 7 5 4
> ♦ A J 6
> ♣ 7 5

Recommended Bid: 3♦

After our previous discussion, it should seem obvious to bid 3♦, showing enough for game and a diamond stopper for no trump purposes. If opener has three hearts you expect him to bid 3♥. With a spade stopper, he can bid 3NT. Without either a spade stopper or three hearts, he will probably try a Fourth Suit Forcing 3♠ just to see what you will do next!

5.
> ♠ K 6 5
> ♥ A Q 10 5 4
> ♦ 5 4 2
> ♠ 7 5

Recommended Bid: 3♥

At first sight, it is tempting to bid 3♠ to show your no trump stopper but in my view this would be a mistake. The problem with 3♠ is that it doesn't show five hearts, so bid 3♥ to make this clear. If partner needs help in spades, he will surely bid a Fourth Suit Forcing 3♠ to give you another chance to bid 3NT.

6.
> ♠ K 7 5
> ♥ A J 4 2
> ♦ Q J 5
> ♣ 7 5

Recommended Bid: 3NT

An easy one here, plenty enough values for game and stoppers in both unbid suits. Bid 3NT.

7.
> ♠ Q J 5
> ♥ A 8 5 3
> ♦ 9 7 6 4
> ♣ 7 5

Recommended Bid: Pass

Of course, it is possible that you will make 3NT if you play in it, but there is no guarantee. With a minimum hand for responding 1♥, why should you feel that you have to make another bid?

The Slam Zone

If you have turned to this chapter in the hope of finding an instant panacea to solve all your problems in the slam zone, you will probably be sorely disappointed. While it is true to say that much of this chapter is designed to improve the tools that may help you to make the final decision, I believe that, for most players, the real barrier to improving their slam bidding is recognizing the combined potential of the two hands.

Unless the basic structure of your system is sound and you follow the principles expounded in the earlier chapters of this section, you will have great difficulty distinguishing between hands where it is a sensible investment to venture above game to explore the slam possibilities, and hands where the chances of slam are so remote that the risk of going down at the five level outweighs the potential gain of bidding a slam. By increasing the degree of definition in your sequences up to the game level, you should be able to reduce the risk of proceeding to the five level on the wrong hand significantly, while identifying hands on which you can explore that little bit further without passing your safety level.

Perhaps an example will help to illustrate exactly what I mean. Your partner opens 1♥, and you respond 1♠ looking at:

> ♠ A 10 8 7 6
> ♥ 7 5
> ♦ A Q 6 5
> ♣ 8 6

Rather to your surprise, partner leaps to 4♠, and it is up to you! However you look at it, this is a pretty good hand and with partner having in the region of seventeen points with four card spade support, it is tempting to press on with 5♦—but, in my view, if you trust your partner, you should pass. Why?

Well, would you blame your partner for raising to game with something like:

> ♠ K J 5 3
> ♥ A K Q J 4
> ♦ K 5
> ♣ 9 2

Over your 5♦, dependent on your style, he will either bid 5♠ directly, or 5♥, in which case he would pass your 5♠ bid since he doesn't have a club control. All very reasonable, except that after you have lost the first two club tricks you will need to guess the location of the spade queen right to make your contract. No matter how strong the vibes are, sometimes you will get it wrong.

Of course, you can claim that you were unlucky, and indeed in many ways you were. You were unlucky that partner's trumps weren't a bit better and you were unlucky that you failed to consider what alternative bids partner might have made instead of raising directly to 4♠.

Let's give partner nearly perfect cards, something along the lines of:

> ♠ K Q 5 3
> ♥ A K Q 4 2
> ♦ 7 5
> ♣ A 2

Now, 6♠ is excellent, but in all honesty your partner can't have that hand for he would have made an advance cuebid of 4♣ and not just raised you to 4♠. Alter the hand so that opener has a singleton in either minor and most of the hands that would have made the slam good would also qualify for a jump to 4♣ or 4♦. In fact, about the only way that partner can have enough to make the slam a good prospect without him being good enough to make a jump cuebid is if his hand includes the ♦K and the ♣A, when your ♦Q will provide a parking place for his losing club. Even then, he will need to have relatively weak hearts and good spades, something like:

> ♠ K Q J 3
> ♥ A 8 5 4 2
> ♦ K 5
> ♣ A 6

and many expert players would still jump to 4♣ with this. Remove the ♠J and the slam is nowhere near as attractive a contract.

Without any doubt, one of the great skills of bidding is to bear in mind not only the bids that your partner actually made, but also those that he might have made, but didn't.

CUEBIDDING

You open 1♠ and you hear your partner raise to 3♠, how do you proceed holding:

♠ K Q J 6 4 2
♥ A K J 4
♦ 7 5
♣ A

With partner showing four card spade support and about ten high card points, you will probably be feeling quite bullish, but unless your partner has at least second round control in diamonds you would certainly not want to get too high. In this situation the normal approach is to bid 4♣, a cuebid showing control in clubs. The idea is to find out if your partner can show a control in diamonds by cuebidding 4♦.

If partner owns the ♦A he is likely to cuebid 4♦, but what are you going to do if he just bids 4♠? Could your partner still have such a highly suitable hand as:

♠ A 9 8 3
♥ 7 6
♦ K Q 6
♣ J 7 5 2

when 6♠ is clearly an excellent contract?

In my view, even if you are a firm believer that a cuebid should normally show first round control, the answer should be no! Why is this?

The normal argument for refusing to cuebid a second round control in this type of situation is that "Partner will think I have the ace and so he may get too high." This is a fallacious position to adopt with this hand. Even though you do not have the ace of diamonds, you have adequate compensation in that you hold the ace of trumps; a card which by its very nature you cannot show by cuebidding. Put it another way, if your partner jumps to slam expecting that you will put the ♦A down in the dummy, he is unlikely to be disappointed when you produce the ♠A instead!

At the very least, if I can persuade the most conservative player that he should cuebid 4♦ with this hand, it will take a lot of pressure off his partner to make more than one slam try on the opening hand under discussion.

Once I persuade you that you really ought to cuebid with this hand it becomes clear that in the absence of a 4♦ cuebid from responder, opener should not proceed above 4♠.

How would you plan your campaign with the following hand?

♠ A Q 7 5 4
♥ A K Q 4
♦ Q 7 5
♣ 5

Once again, you open 1♠ and your partner raises to 3♠, what are you going to bid now?

Once again, you have a good hand and the traditional cuebidders might well issue a slam try by cuebidding 4♥. No doubt, they would expect their partner to cooperate by cuebidding 5♦ if he had a suitable hand such as:

(a) ♠ K 9 8 2
♥ 6 2
♦ A K 4 2
♣ 9 8 2

when 6♠ is virtually laydown but they would be most aggravated if he had the audacity to cuebid 5♣ on:

(b) ♠ K 9 8 2
♥ 6 2
♦ 9 8 2
♣ A K 4 2

when even 5♠ should go down. Obviously, apart from the switch round in the minors, hands (a) and (b) are identical, so how is responder to know which one is gold dust and which one is rhubarb?

To me, it is perfectly clear that opener should issue a slam try, but he should bid 4♣ and not the space-consuming 4♥. Admittedly, you do not have the ♣A or a void in clubs but you do have compensating top controls in the majors. If you cuebid 4♣ and partner bids 4♠ (which he would be forced to do with hand (b)) you should be 100% confident that you do not have a slam on. Obviously, responder would cuebid 4♦ with hand (a) but in addition he should cuebid 4♦ whenever he has second round control, providing he has a compensating first round control. In this case, as you hold the ♠A, it would have to be the ♣A.

BLACKWOOD

As you know Blackwood is the use of a bid of 4NT to ask for the number of aces partner holds. The responses follow the easy system that:

5♣ shows 0 or 4 aces
5♦ shows 1 ace
5♥ shows 2 aces
5♠ shows 3 aces

What is not quite so obvious is that Blackwood is principally a convention designed to keep you out of a slam missing two aces. The idea is that you should have already established that you intend to bid a slam before you use the convention. In other words, if you find that you are missing only one ace you are expected to be bidding a small slam. In particular, this means that before using Blackwood you should have a good expectation that you have all the suits controlled. Let's look at an example:

(a) ♠ A Q 9 7 6 4   **(b)** ♠ K Q 9 6 4
♥ A K Q 4 2   ♥ A K Q 5 3
♦ 5   ♦ 7 5
♣ 7   ♣ A

Once again, let's suppose that the auction starts with 1♠ from you, raised to 3♠ by partner. Both hands have enormous potential, and hand (a) is particularly suitable for Blackwood. If partner has no aces you would clearly settle for 5♠; if he has one ace you would bid 6♠, expecting that at worst it would depend on a spade guess; and, if he has two aces, you might just employ some further gadget to find out if he has the king of trumps before deciding whether to settle for just 6♠ or trying for a grand slam.

Hand (b) is nowhere near as suitable. If partner has no aces you will hope that 5♠ is not too high, and if he has two aces you should probably take a shot at the grand slam—which should have good play unless his red suit distribution is highly unfavorable. But what are you going to do if he only has one ace?

Obviously, partner could hold the ♠A and the ♦KQ, or the ♦AK when you would clearly want to be in 6♠; but equally he could hold the ♠A and the ♣KQ if you play in the slam. How do you find out? Certainly not by using Blackwood.

Cuebid 4♣ and, if partner cooperates by bidding 4♦, you can use Blackwood then in some safety.

Over the years there have been all sorts of variations made in the use of 4NT as an ace-asking convention. Roman Key Card Blackwood, which seems to be all the rage with most expert players these days, is the most useful of the variations.

ROMAN KEYCARD BLACKWOOD (RKCB)

The basis of Roman Keycard is that the king of trumps is regarded as a fifth ace. The additional feature is that possession of the trump queen or lack of it is also identified quickly. The basic responses to 4NT are:

5♣	=	0 or 3 out of five
5♦	=	1 or 4 out of five
5♥	=	2 or 5 without the trump queen
5♠	=	2 or 5 with the trump queen

Then, after the 5♣ and 5♦ responses, if the 4NT bidder wants to know about the queen of trumps, he can use the next step up (excluding the trump suit) as a relay to find out.

So, suppose that you pick up this collection:

♠ J 7 4 2
♥ A K
♦ K Q J 6 5
♣ A 5

and hear partner open 1♠. Obviously there is a case to go slowly, but with controls in all the outside suits and a good source of tricks on the side, it is tempting to launch into Blackwood immediately. So playing Keycard the auction starts:

1♠	4NT
5♣	5♦
?	

Notice that, while we have yet to support spades, on this type of direct sequence it is clear that spades must be regarded as the trump suit. Thus, in calculating how many aces he has, the opener will have to count the ♠K as an ace.

So we've already asked for aces and have found out that partner has zero or three out of five, and it would be a very bizarre hand if he actually had zero. So we know that partner has the ♠AK and the ♦A. Now, we ask for the queen of trumps by bidding 5♦.

How does the responder to Blackwood show whether he has the queen of trumps or not? At this stage opinions differ. However, in my view, it makes most sense to use the next step up to deny the queen of trumps. Then, any other bid shows the trump queen.

So, on our example hand, if partner bids anything other than 5♥ over 5♦ he must have the spade queen, and we can bid the grand slam in comfort.

But what if he doesn't have the queen of trumps but he does have a six card spade suit? Now, despite missing the queen, we would still want to be in 7♠.

Curiously enough, this really shouldn't be a problem for players of four card majors in this sequence. When we jumped to 4NT it was quite clear that spades were agreed as trumps immediately and, as the opener only guaranteed holding four spades when he opened 1♠, it should be clear to him that the 4NT response also showed 4 spades. Once the opener can be reasonably sure that his partner has four card support then, when responder asks him for the trump queen, if he holds AKxxxx he should use his judgment to say, yes he has it.

If the 4NT bidder continues with 5NT at any stage, he is guaranteeing that you have all the aces between you and inviting you to show any additional tricks that you might have.

Suppose you hold:

♠ K Q 7 6 5
♥ A 5
♦ K Q J 10
♣ 7 6

You open 1♠ and partner responds 3♣. You bid 3♦ and your partner bids 3♠. As it is most unlikely that partner has jumped the bidding on a queen high suit, you could use RKCB yourself if you really wanted to but you show unusual restraint by cuebidding 4♥. Partner takes control now by using RKCB himself. Over 4NT you respond 5♠ which shows possession of two out of five "aces" plus the queen of trumps, and partner then bids 5NT—what would you bid next?

Clearly partner is looking for a grand slam, and showing that he has the other three aces, so you know that you actually have three extra diamond tricks. So grasp the bull by the horns and bid the grand slam. The full deal turns out to be:

      ♠ K Q 7 6 5   ♠ A 9 8 2
      ♥ A 5   ♥ 8 3
      ♦ K Q J 10   ♦ A 5
      ♣ 7 6   ♣ A K 6 4 2

As you can see there is no problem in 7♠ unless spades break 4-0.

Some of my pupils have objected to this hand on the basis that, if partner was looking for the ♣K when he bid 5NT, he might be sorely disappointed but in my view they are ignoring an important principle of constructive bidding. If you held:

      ♠ K Q 7 6 5
      ♥ A 5
      ♦ K 7 6 5
      ♣ K 6

what should you bid, after the auction has started:

      1♠   3♣
      3♦   3♠
      ?

At the stage, where we bid 4♥ in the previous auction, if we decide to cuebid rather than leap into Blackwood, 4♣ is certainly the right bid. Why?

Very simply, partner has jumped in this suit and possession of the ♣K is likely to make a very great difference to his assessment of the combined playing strength of the two hands. Just consider how important the ♣K is if partner's holding is something like ♣ A Q J 5 4.

RAISES TO THE FIVE LEVEL

Have you ever considered what the following sequences mean?

(a) 1♠   3♠   (b) 1♠   3♠
     4♦   4♥   4♣   4♦
     5♠   4♥   4♠
                       5♠

In both sequences the opener has pressed on to 5♠, but the two 5♠ bids have totally different meanings.

Let's look at each sequence in turn:

On sequence (a), opener has cuebid in diamonds, heard a return cuebid in hearts and then jumped to 5♠. What is he doing?

The traditional interpretation of this sequence is that the opener is asking for a club control. Think about it! If opener had a club control, he would have either bid 4♣ two rounds earlier or he could bid 5♣ instead of 5♠ now. So, when there is one unbid suit, a jump to the five level in a major has come to be a request for partner to bid on to slam with a control in the unbid suit.

For the example sequence we are considering, the opener might have:

      ♠ A K 7 6 4 3
      ♥ 5
      ♦ A K Q 5
      ♣ 7 5

Now let's consider sequence (b). This time opener has cuebid in both clubs and hearts, while responder has made a return cuebid in diamonds before signing off in 4♥. So what does this raise to 5♠ mean?

This time, opener is asking the responder for good trumps. He might have:

      ♠ K 6 5 4 3
      ♥ A
      ♦ K 3
      ♣ A K Q 5 2

Expecting his partner to have the ♦A, opener wishes to play in slam providing responder has reasonable trumps, say ♠QJxx or better.

Now, before giving you the opportunity to test out these slam bidding tools, there is another area of bidding where playing standard methods, average players tend to get notoriously bad results. Of course, I refer to the Acol 2♣ opening, or more specifically the standard methods of responding to it. The discussion is included here because of the frequency of sequences that start with a 2♣ opening ending up in the Slam Zone.

OPENING 2♣

Unfortunately you don't pick up hands strong enough to open in 2♣ very often but, when you do, how often do you end up in a silly contract? Part of the reason for inefficiency in this area is a general lack of experience as to the best way to proceed but the main influence is the unwieldy methods that a standard system recommends in this area.

The general approach requires that responder has one and half honor tricks before he gives a positive response to a 2♣ opening, that is an ace and a king, three kings or a king/queen and a king; otherwise with the possible exception of a 2NT response he has to bid 2♦.

This has the effect of making responses other than 2♦ incredibly rare and it puts a lot of strain on the structure of bidding after the 2♦ response. As the 2NT rebid after a 2♦ response is non-forcing, the popular treatment of any balanced 25-26 count is to jump to 3NT on the second round of the bidding. While it makes sense to bid over this using the same general treatments that you might use over a 2NT rebid, the auction is already uncomfortably high. All in all, a rather silly approach on a selection of hands which have enormous slam-going potential.

In the early 1980s, a group of English players experimented with a totally different style of responding to 2♣. The idea was that all positive hands should respond 2♦, 2♥ was reserved for all hands with about 0-4 points and balanced hands in the 5-7 point range, while the other bids were used to deal with hands in the 5-7 point range. Certainly, it seemed to me that this was a step in the right direction but there is so much work involved in sorting out the fine tuning that such methods are unlikely to come into common usage.

For most fairly regular, but not too serious partnerships, let me make an alternative suggestion. Why not play the responses to 2♣ to show how many aces and kings the responding hand has in simple ascending order? For some years I have experimented with using this scheme:

> 2♦ = 0 controls (i.e. no ace or king)
> 2♥ = 1 control (i.e. one king)
> 2♠ = 2 controls (i.e. one ace or two kings)
> 2 NT = 3 controls (i.e. one ace and one king, or three kings)
> and so on.

Bids of 3♥ and higher could sensibly be used for other meanings as the chance of you ever having six controls facing a genuine 2♣ opening is very small indeed.

Obviously this system has the great merit of being very easy to learn, but is there anything to be gained by adopting it?

There is one obvious advantage and one that is somewhat less obvious. Let's start with the more obvious one, which is simply that there is a whole range of hands where being told just how many aces and kings partner holds can be useful. Let's look at one or two examples:

Suppose you pick up a hand like:

> ♠ A K Q J 5 4
> ♥ A Q 5
> ♦ A 5
> ♣ K Q

You open 2♣ and hear partner bid:

(a) 2♦ denying a single control

Your ambition is immediately limited to determining whether you are going to play in 4♠ or 3NT. Your likely plan will be to bid your spades and then rebid 3NT.

(b) 2♥ showing one control

As partner must have one of the red kings, you know immediately that 4♠ is safe. Your effort here will be to try and find out if partner has a reasonable suit of his own, as you have potential to make a slam in any of the other three suits. If the auction were to proceed something like:

2♣	2♥
2♠	3♣
3♠	4♣
?	

wouldn't you be thinking of playing in 6♣? Note that if you had rebid 3NT, in all probability partner would pass with ♣J10xxxx and the ♦K, yet 6♣ looks excellent.

Of course, partner might not have the ♥K and not the diamond king and then 6♣ would not be so good on a diamond lead. However, note that you can find out by bidding 4♦ yourself. If partner has the ♥K he will surely bid 4♥, and you will settle for 4♠; if he has the ♦K he will bid something else and you can bid 6♣ with some confidence.

(c) 2♠ showing two controls

Ironically you would now much prefer him to have both kings rather than the ♣A, but at least you can already be certain of ten tricks.

(d) 2NT showing three controls

Now you already know that he has the ♣A and a red king. If it's the ♦K you might have to settle for just twelve tricks but, if you find out that he has the ♥K instead, the grand slam should make barring ridiculous distributions.

As you can see, knowing how many controls partner has gives you a good idea of the range of possible contracts very early in the proceedings.

What about the second advantage? Consider, a more balanced hand, like:

> ♠ A Q J 4
> ♥ K Q 9 4
> ♦ A Q 4
> ♣ A K

the sort of hand that is all too regularly bid 2♣–2♦–3NT. Now, even adopting our new methods, we are in a similar position if partner responds 2♦ to our 2♣ opening, though my own preference would be to try 2♥ at this stage rather than 3NT. However, there are many responding hands that would have formerly been "negative" responses that will now respond 2♥ or even 2♠. In both of those situations it should be clear that a 2NT will now be forcing, which will allow the bidding to proceed at a conveniently lower level.

The opposite side of this coin means that with a hand like:

> ♠ K 5
> ♥ A 4
> ♦ K 5
> ♣ A K Q 7 6 5 2

I can start by opening 2♣ and if I get a response showing less than three controls I can simply gamble out 3NT.

I am not trying to suggest that this change in method will be a panacea for all ills, but I do believe that many players would find it well worth a try.

Quiz 14

It is all very well deciding to play Roman Keycard Blackwood but in practice far too many disasters occur because the players disagree as to whether a bid is Blackwood or not. Certainly, in some casual partnerships I have agreed with my partner that 4NT is always Blackwood unless or until we have specifically agreed that it isn't. At least in this text, we don't have to address the different ways in which 4NT might be used in a competitive sequence, but even so, it is well worth making sure that you are on the same wavelength as your partner in the more common 4NT situations.

So, this is a quiz with a difference. All you have to do is decide in each of the following sequences: what does 4NT mean?

1.	1 NT	4 NT
2.	1 NT	3 ♥
	4 ♣	4 NT
3.	2 NT	3 ♦ (Transfer)
	3 ♥	4 NT
4.	1 ♥	4 NT
5.	1 ♠	3 ♠
	4 ♣	4 ♥
	4 NT	
6.	1 ♠	2 ♣
	2 ♦	4 NT
7.	1 ♠	2 ♦
	3 ♣	4 NT
8.	1 ♠	3 ♦
	3 ♥	4 ♦
	4 NT	

Answers to Quiz 14

In each of the following sequences: what does 4NT mean?

1.

	1 NT	4 NT

We start with a situation where nearly all players are agreed that 4NT should be natural and invitational (and if you want to ask for aces you might use 4♣, Gerber). However, while that may be clear, it is nowhere near so certain if you introduce a Stayman response first. For example, suppose the bidding starts:

	1 NT	2 ♣
	2 ♠	4 NT

Is this Blackwood with spades agreed, or is it a balanced invitational strength hand with four hearts? My own inclination would be to the latter description but only because I would expect to be able to make a suitable advance cuebid in a minor on any hand where I might subsequently want to use Blackwood. If you play regularly with one player, do you know what your partner would mean if he bid this way?

2.

	1 NT	3 ♥
	4 ♣	4 NT

Now, what is going on here? Presumably the responder is showing a forcing hand with hearts and opener's 4♣ bid is a cuebid showing heart support, a club control and a maximum. As hearts are clearly agreed as trumps, 4NT must be Blackwood.

3.

	2 NT	3 ♦ (Transfer)
	3 ♥	4 NT

This sequence is totally different. By transferring into hearts and then bidding 4NT, responder is showing a five card heart suit in a balanced hand with slam invitational values. Except by special arrangement this is not Blackwood.

4.

	1 ♥	4 NT

Here, 4NT is Blackwood with hearts agreed by inference. Indeed, in this situation it is difficult to think of any sensible alternative meaning.

5.

	1 ♠	3 ♠
	4 ♣	4 ♥
	4 NT	

Another clear-cut sequence with spades agreed from the off. To me, it is quite clear that 4NT should be Blackwood especially given a fairly freewheeling style of cuebidding. However, I could introduce you to quite a few internationals who would prefer to play this as a quaint form of cuebid, maybe showing a further heart control. Frankly, for 99.9% of players, it is not worth looking further than Blackwood.

6.
    1♠   2♣
    2♦   4NT

On this sequence there is probably enough room for responder to develop his hand with either a natural type or a hand with four card diamond support as, if need be, he can toil through Fourth Suit Forcing. Having said that, most players would suggest that this should be Blackwood with opener's last bid suit, diamonds, agreed by inference.

7.
    1♠   2♦
    3♣   4NT

This one is as clear as mud. To me it seems obvious that 4NT should be natural and invitational. The sequence has already arrived at the three level, so there is insufficient space to develop and describe the responding hand. What are you supposed to do with a hand that feels too good for 3NT but not strong enough to sensibly try 6NT? Meanwhile, if instead you have the luxury of having four card club support you can proceed by raising to 4♣. Remember that partner's 3♣ bid was forcing to game.

8.
    1♠   3♦
    3♥   4♦
      4NT

Finally, an interesting one. Responder has shown a very good hand with a solid or near solid diamond suit and is inviting opener to cuebid. So, what is opener supposed to do with a 5-4-1-3 minimum hand with a club stopper other than bid 4NT?

QUIZ 15

First, let's take a look at the opener's hand. What would you do in each of the following situations?

1.
♠ K Q 8 7 6 3
♥ 5
♦ A K Q 5 4
♣ 8

1♠   3♠
?

2.
♠ K Q 6 4 3 2
♥ J 5 3
♦ A 5
♣ 7 5

1♠   3♣
3♠   4♥
4♠   5♠
?

3.
♠ K Q 5
♥ A K J 4 3 2
♦ A
♣ 8 4 2

1♥   3♥
?

4.
♠ A K 6 5 4
♥ A J 5 2
♦ 7 5
♣ K 5

1♠   2♣
2♥   4♦
?

5.
♠ A Q 10 5 4
♥ 6 4
♦ Q J 5 4
♣ A 5

1♠   2♥
2♠   3♦
?

6.
♠ K 5
♥ A K 6 4 2
♦ J 5 3
♣ A K 5

1♥   1♠
2 NT   3♥
?

7.
♠ A J 6 4 2
♥ Q 7 4 2
♦ K 4
♣ A 5

1♠   2♦
2♥   4 NT
5♠   5 NT
?

8.
♠ A K Q J 5
♥ K 5 2
♦ 7 5 3
♣ Q 7

1♠   3♣
3♠   3 NT
4♣   4♦
?

What would you do in each of the following situations?

1.
  ♠ K Q 8 7 6 3
  ♥ 5
  ♦ A K Q 5 4
  ♣ 8

 1 ♠ 3 ♠
 ?

Recommended Bid: 4♦

It is sorely tempting to blast into 4NT planning to bid 6♠ if partner shows two aces, and settling for 5♠ if he only has one. However, it is not clear how you explain your choice of action when partner's hand is:

  ♠ J 9 5 2
  ♥ K Q 4 2
  ♦ 7 2
  ♣ K Q 5

With eleven high card points and four card support you can barely blame him for raising you to 3♠. Curb your impetuosity and cuebid 4♦ and hope that with two aces partner is tempted into some forward move.

2.
  ♠ K Q 6 4 3 2
  ♥ J 5 3
  ♦ A 5
  ♣ 7 5

 1 ♠ 3 ♣
 3 ♠ 4 ♥
 4 ♠ 5 ♠
 ?

Recommended Bid: 6♦

This is a command sequence. Partner's 5♠ demands that you bid on to slam with any diamond control. With the king or a singleton, you should just bid the slam but with the ace you should cuebid it just in case partner is planning to bid a grand slam. Strangely enough, although you had very much a minimum opening bid, your hand has rapidly gained in stature. Now, if partner put me to the test by bidding 6♥ over 6♦, I would happily bid the grand slam in spades.

3.
  ♠ K Q 5
  ♥ A K J 4 3 2
  ♦ A
  ♣ 8 4 2

 1 ♥ 3 ♥
 ?

Recommended Bid: 3♠

Slam prospects on this hand largely depend on partner having a good club holding and little, if anything, wasted in diamonds. Bid 3♠ to leave space for partner to cuebid 4♣. If

he does you can continue with 4♦.

4.
  ♠ A K 6 5 4
  ♥ A J 5 2
  ♦ 7 5
  ♣ K 5

 1 ♠ 2 ♣
 2 ♥ 4 ♦
 ?

Recommended Bid: 4NT

What is going on here? Partner's jump to 4♦ is a cuebid agreeing hearts as trumps. While you only have fourteen high card points you really do have an excellent hand with excellent controls and what may prove to be the vital ♣K in partner's suit. Playing ordinary Blackwood, 4NT would not really help you very much, but RKCB gives you the opportunity to find out about the king and queen of trumps as well, so it's well-suited for this hand.

5.
  ♠ A Q 10 5 4
  ♥ 6 4
  ♦ Q J 5 4
  ♣ A

 1 ♠ 2 ♥
 2 ♠ 3 ♦
 ?

Recommended Bid: 4♣

As you have the ♣A you could bid 3NT here, however your cards look excellent for playing in diamonds. The low diamond honors will fill partner's suit admirably; indeed you have such good cards for diamonds that it is not that difficult to construct a hand where a diamond contract would be best, even if it turns out to be only a 4-3 fit. So it looks right to support diamonds, but we might as well take the opportunity to cuebid 4♣ on the way. Clearly this should show a good raise in diamonds with club control, limited by the fact that you rebid 2♠, and that is what you've got.

6.
  ♠ K 5
  ♥ A K 6 4 2
  ♦ J 5 3
  ♣ A K 5

 1 ♥ 1 ♠
 2 NT 3 ♥
 ?

Recommended Bid: 4♣

Partner's 3♥ is offering a choice between 4♥ and 3NT. As you have five hearts and rather poor diamonds, it is clear that you should prefer 4♥ but, with excellent high cards and a key card in partner's suit, take the opportunity to stress your suitability for hearts by cuebidding 4♣. Just occasionally, partner will have enough to be able to take advantage of this accurate description of your hand.

7.

     ♠ A J 6 4 2
     ♥ Q 7 4 2
     ♦ K 4
     ♣ A 5

1 ♠	2 ♦
2 ♥	4 NT (RKCB)
5 ♠	5 NT
?	

Recommended Bid: 6 ♦

Obviously your partner was pleased to hear your 2♥ rebid, as 4NT is Roman Keycard Blackwood with hearts as trumps. Your 5♠ response promised two out of the five aces plus the queen of hearts but now partner has bid 5NT to confirm that you have all the aces and ask you if you have anything extra. While you have given a fair description of your hand so far, you do have a very important card your partner doesn't know about yet, the ♦K. So bid 6♦ to identify this extra value.

8.

     ♠ A K Q J 5
     ♥ K 5 2
     ♦ 7 5 3
     ♣ Q 7

1 ♠	3 ♣
3 ♠	3 NT
4 ♣	4 ♦
?	

Recommended Bid: 4NT

You have followed a clever campaign so far. After the jump to 3♣ you had plenty in reserve for your 3♠ bid. When partner clarified his hand type by rebidding 3NT you made the clever move forward of supporting clubs. Now partner has cuebid in diamonds, you have sufficient cover to try RKCB with clubs agreed even though your final destination is likely to be 6♠.

QUIZ 16

This time switch seats to take the responding hand:

1.

  ♠ J 7 4 2   ♠ K 6 5
  ♥ 7 5   ♥ J 7 5 4
  ♦ K Q 5   ♦ K Q
  ♣ A 8 4 2   ♣ 8 5 4 2

| 1 ♠ | 3 ♠ | 2 ♠ (Strong) ? |
| 4 ♣ | ? | |

2.

  ♠ Q 10 5 4   ♠ 8 2
  ♥ K Q 5   ♥ K Q 8 7
  ♦ K 6 4 2   ♦ A 6
  ♣ 7 5   ♣ A 9 7 4 2

1 ♠	3 ♠	1 ♠	2 ♣
4 ♣	?	2 ♥	4 ♦
		4 NT	5 ♣
		5 ♦	?

3.

  ♠ Q 7 4 2   ♠ A J 5
  ♥ A J 6 5   ♥ 5 4 2
  ♦ 7 5   ♦ A K 6 4 2
  ♣ K 6 5   ♣ A 6

1 ♠	3 ♠	1 ♠	3 ♦
4 ♦	4 ♥	3 ♠	?
5 ♠	?		

4.

  ♠ J 7 6 4
  ♥ A Q 6 2
  ♦ K 5 2
  ♣ J 2

1 ♠	3 ♠
4 ♦	4 ♥
5 ♣	?

5.

  ♠ K Q 6
  ♥ 7 4
  ♦ A 6 3 2
  ♣ 7 6 3 2

2 ♠	3 ♠
4 ♣	4 ♦
4 ♥	?

ANSWERS TO QUIZ 16

This time switch seats to take the responding hand:

1.
    ♠ J 7 4 2
    ♥ 7 5
    ♦ K Q 5
    ♣ A 8 4 2

| 1 ♠ | 3 ♠ |
| 4 ♣ | ? |

Recommended Bid: 4♦

There is nothing to be afraid of here. You can afford to cuebid 4♦ because you have the compensating ♣A.

2.
    ♠ Q 10 5 4
    ♥ K Q 5
    ♦ K 6 4 2
    ♣ 7 5

| 1 ♠ | 3 ♠ |
| 4 ♣ | ? |

Recommended Bid: 4♠

With a very ordinary hand for the initial raise to 3♠ and no ace, cooperating by cuebidding 4♦ is a bit rich for me. Settle for 4♠ on the basis that you can own up to possession of the ♦K if partner does press on.

3.
    ♠ Q 7 4 2
    ♥ A J 6 5
    ♦ 7 5
    ♣ K 6 5

1 ♠	3 ♠
4 ♦	4 ♥
5 ♠	?

Recommended Bid: 6♠

Partner has highlighted the lack of club control. You have one, so you should press on with 6♠.

4.
    ♠ J 7 6 4
    ♥ A Q 6 2
    ♦ K 5 2
    ♣ J 2

1 ♠	3 ♠
4 ♦	4 ♥
5 ♣	?

Recommended Bid: 5♦

Partner's 5♣ bid almost invites you to show a diamond feature if you have one. You should cuebid the ♦K now.

5.
    ♠ K Q 6
    ♥ 7 4
    ♦ A 6 3 2
    ♣ 7 6 3 2

2 ♠ (Strong)	3 ♠
4 ♣	4 ♦
4 ♥	?

Recommended Bid: 5♠

You have shown support for spades and you have cuebid 4♦, but you could have less suitable cards for your initial raise to 3♠. Get the plus values of your hand off your chest now by jumping to 5♠.

6.
    ♠ K 6 5
    ♥ J 7 5 4
    ♦ K Q
    ♣ 8 5 4 2

| 2 ♠ | ? |

Recommended Bid: 3♠

While we are on the subject of strong twos, what would you respond with this hand? There are some old-fashioned textbooks which would claim that the immediate spade raise guarantees an ace; however, can anyone see a more sensible bid than 3♠ on this deal?

7.
    ♠ 8 2
    ♥ K Q 8 7
    ♦ A 6
    ♣ A 9 7 4 2

1 ♠	2 ♣
2 ♥	4 ♦
4 NT	5 ♣
5 ♦	?

Recommended Bid: 6♥

Partner is now checking on whether you hold the queen of hearts. As you do, you must respond positively but with nothing extra to add simply sign off in 6♥.

8.
    ♠ A J 5
    ♥ 5 4 2
    ♦ A K 6 4 2
    ♣ A 6

| 1 ♠ | 3 ♦ |
| 3 ♠ | ? |

Recommended Bid: 4♣

So you've already forced by jumping to 3♦ with this hand. When partner rebids his spades, cuebid 4♣ to show your club control on the way to 4♠.

By its very nature slam bidding is a vast subject. It is explored in greater detail in Part VI.

Chapter 8

Getting Into Action

It is curious that although there are a number of popular bidding systems and a vast range of not so popular ones, for most players all over the world the two main tools of defensive bidding are the simple overcall and the takeout double. Admittedly there are some variations in style, but the basic methods are the same for most good players.

THE SIMPLE OVERCALL

While bridge players are taught in their cradles that they need 12 or 13 High Card Points (HCP) to open the bidding, the same is not true of the simple overcall. To make an overcall, it is much more important to have a respectable suit than to have sufficient points to open the bidding.

Suppose, for example, that the dealer opens one diamond on your right, and you are looking at the following hand:

♠ K Q 10 4 2
♥ 4 2
♦ K 6 2
♣ 7 4 2

Although you have only eight HCP you have just about the perfect hand for a minimum one spade overcall at any vulnerability. Even facing minimal support in partner's hand you are likely to be able to scramble three or four spade tricks and a diamond. Given a reasonable suit, the point range for making a one level overcall is about 7 or 8 up to about 16 or 17.

This might seem like a very wide range but, when you stop and think about it, the normal range for an opening bid is about 12 to 20 and most players open 11 point hands with good intermediates or even shapely 10 point hands. Thus, the point range for an overcall is similar to that of an opening bid, albeit at a lower level.

THE TAKEOUT DOUBLE

The basic idea behind the takeout double is to show a hand of roughly opening bid strength with support for the other three suits. If your opponents open one diamond, the following hand is a good example of a minimum hand for making a takeout double.

(a) ♠ K 10 4 2
     ♥ A J 5
     ♦ 7 5
     ♣ K J 4 2

Four cards in both majors would be better and a singleton or void diamond would be better still. But at least this hand has reasonable support for all three other suits.

What would you do with the next three hands:

(b) ♠ K J 10 4 2   (c) ♠ K 10 4 2   (d) ♠ K 10 4 2
    ♥ A Q 10 5   ♥ A Q 4   ♥ A J 5
    ♦ 6   ♦ 6   ♦ J 7 5
    ♣ K 5 4   ♣ Q J 6 4 2   ♣ K J 4

On (b) while you clearly have opening bid values, shortage in diamonds and support for the other three suits, the modern view would be that you should overcall one spade rather than double. Suppose, for example, that your partner holds something like:

♠ A 7 5
♥ J 4
♦ 9 7 4 2
♣ Q J 6 2

If you double one diamond, what would you expect your partner to bid with this hand? Although 1NT would roughly describe his values he can barely risk making this response with nothing remotely resembling a diamond stopper and, while he has rather more than he might have, he is not really strong enough to jump to three clubs. So, in reality, your partner is going to respond two clubs if you make a takeout double. Yes, he is maximum for the bid, but unless you are strong enough to volunteer another bid he is most unlikely to miss a game.

Turning back to your hand, what can you do facing a two club response. Given that you can see partner's hand, you might think that you could bid two spades, but this would be taking the enormous risk that partner had virtually nothing for his two club response, say ♣ Q 9 7 5 2 and a bust, maybe even a singleton spade. Indeed, most players have adopted the view that if you double on the first round and then introduce a new suit later you should be showing considerable additional strength, say at least 17 points.

Certainly, the whole auction will be much smoother if you start by overcalling one spade. Partner will probably raise you to two spades and with the knowledge of an eight card fit you are now worth a game try.

To recap, if you start with a takeout double, the whole auction is likely to be:

1♦	Double	Pass	2♣
Pass	Pass	Pass	

If you start with an overcall of 1♠, the auction could be:

1♦	1♠	Pass	2♠
Pass	3♥	Pass	4♠
Pass	Pass	Pass	

In this case, the overcaller makes a long suit game try of three hearts, which his partner is happy to accept since his heart holding looks as if it will be useful. The heart jack is a useful filler facing many such different holdings as A Q 10 5, K Q 9 5, A 10 9 5, Q 10 9 5, K 10 8 7, and holding only two cards in the suit it might be possible to ruff either the third or fourth round of the suit.

Of course, the disadvantage of overcalling one spade when you have four hearts is that occasionally you might find it difficult to find a heart fit. But with the growing addiction to all types of competitive doubles there will frequently be an opportunity to get hearts back into the picture later.

Hand (c) is a totally different situation since your five card suit is a minor. Here making a takeout double seems to be a much better choice since it gets your fair holding in both majors into the picture immediately.

Hand (d) poses a different problem. There are many excellent players who would choose to make a takeout double with this hand. They would say that they have opening bid values and support for all the other suits, but, critically, they do not have a shortage in the opponents' suit so pass is a superior bid. The problem is a simple one. The lack of shortage in the opponents' suit makes this a much weaker hand from a playing strength point of view than the very first example (a). Look at both hands again:

(a)	♠ K 10 4 2	(d)	♠ K 10 4 2
	♥ A J 5		♥ A J 5
	♦ 7 5		♦ J 7 5
	♣ K J 4 2		♣ K J 4

Let's see just how we would do facing two possible responding hands. First, how will you fare in hearts facing:

♠ A 5
♥ K Q 10 7 2
♦ 10 8 2
♣ Q 8 6

Facing hand (a) which is worth making a takeout double, you should make 10 tricks in hearts barring very bad distribution. Facing hand (d) you have no play to make 10 tricks. So which is better , hand (a) or hand (d)? Then try:

♠ A Q 5
♥ K Q 10 9
♦ 10 8
♣ Q 8 6

Facing hand (a) four hearts is once again a good contract. If the opponents start with three rounds of diamonds you can ruff in the short trump hand and thereby can expect to make the contract except when trumps break 5-1 or worse. Your best approach is probably to try knocking out the ace of clubs while you still have another high trump in the dummy to deal with a fourth round of diamonds.

Facing hand (d), however, you will have no choice but to ruff the third round of diamonds in the long trump hand thereby reducing yourself to a 3-3 trump fit. If trumps break 4-2 you will have to be fortunate to make your contract. Once again, which is the better hand, hand (a) or hand (d)?

This is not to say that there are no hands where you should double one diamond with three small cards in the opponents' suit.

Improve the hand to:

♠ K 10 4 2
♥ A J 5
♦ J 7 5
♣ A K 4

then start with a takeout double. The additional strength compensates for the lack of shortage in diamonds.

Before continuing, it is well worth considering one other facet of the takeout double. Very simply, when you make a takeout double you expect your partner to respond. This means that you can plan to describe your hand using two bids not one.

A simple analogy might clarify this further. If you play Stayman, a response of two clubs to a 1NT opener is asking opener whether he has a four card major. However, since you know that partner must respond to your two club inquiry, you can plan to describe your hand by making another bid on the second round. For example, suppose the auction starts:

1 NT	Pass	2♣	Pass
2♦	Pass	3♥	

What does that jump to three hearts mean?

This is not such an easy question. Years ago, players would be divided by this question. Half tended to play the bid as forcing, showing five hearts and offering a choice of games, while the rest played the bid as natural, showing five cards and inviting opener to go on with a maximum. Since the advent of transfers, the possible meanings for this bid seem to have multiplied. Some players would use this bid to show a game-going hand with heart shortage, others would choose to use this bid to show an invitational hand with both majors. No doubt, there are many other alternatives.

The actual meaning of the bid is irrelevant. The point of the analogy is that when responder started his campaign with two clubs, it is quite possible that he was not at all interested in opener's response; he was just planning to describe his own hand by jumping to three hearts on the next round.

In the same way, when we start our campaign by making a takeout double, it may be that we are actually planning to complete the description of our hand on the second round. Suppose for example, you double on each of the following hands and partner responds one heart, what would you bid next?

	(a)		(b)	
	♠ K Q 7 5		♠ A Q 5	
	♥ 9 7 2		♥ K J 5	
	♦ 7		♦ A Q 5	
	♣ A K J 4		♣ K 10 9 5	

With hand (a) you could have started with a one spade overcall, but this really risks missing a game when partner has a suitable hand but is not really strong enough to respond to an overcall. For example, if partner has three small spades and the ace of hearts, four spades is not without play. Worse still, if partner only has only one or two spades he could easily have seven or eight points and not be able to respond to an overcall. Then it would come as no surprise if you could make 3NT.

Accordingly, your plan with this hand should be to double on the first round and then bid spades, showing a hand too strong to overcall one spade on the first round.

With hand (b) you could have bid 1NT on the first round, but by most players' standards you have at least one if not two points more than partner will expect. A better plan is to double on the first round planning to bid 1NT on your next turn to show a hand too good to overcall 1NT in the first place. Of course, if partner bids at the two level you will be forced to rebid 2NT instead.

The following table will give you a good idea how you should plan your campaign with most hands.

BALANCED HANDS
With Stopper in Opponent's Suit

General Strength	Plan of Action
Up to bad 15	Pass
15 1/2-18	Bid 1NT
19-21	Double then rebid no trumps at minimum level

With No Stopper in Opponent's Suit

General Strength	Plan of Action
Up to 14	Pass
15-16	Double and pass partner's response unless the response shows positive values.
17-18	Double and raise partner's simple response. Over any positive response you should have sufficient values to make a game.
19-21	Double and then cuebid in the opponent's suit over a simple response.
22+	Double, then cuebid and then bid on.

SINGLE-SUITED HANDS
Five Card Suit

General Strength	Plan of Action
Approx 8-16	Make a simple overcall at the one-level.
Approx 10-16	Make a simple overcall at the two-level, but this should show a good suit.
Approx 17-19	Double and then bid your suit on the next round
Approx 20-22	Double and then jump in a good suit or cuebid the opponents suit.

Six Card Suit

General Strength	Plan of Action
Approx 7-13	Make a simple overcall
Approx 14-17	Make a jump overcall
18-20	Double then jump in suit
Game-going	Double, then cuebid and then bid your suit

Longer Suits

General Strength	Plan of Action
	Immediate double-jump overcalls are weak.
	Jumps to game are to play but are normally of a pre-emptive type.
	A jump cuebid is asking for a stop in the opponent's suit—this is normally based on a long solid minor suit. Use of this treatment is a partnership agreement about which you should alert your opponents.
	A double jump cuebid (e.g. 1♥-4♥) should be a solid game bid in another suit. So with 7 or 8 playing tricks in spades you can bid 4♠ after opponents open 1♥ dependent on the prevailing vulnerability. With a stronger hand you can bid 4♥ over a 1♥ opener.

Please note however, that this is a modern treatment and not one to try out on an unsuspecting partner.

Two-Suited Hands

General Strength	Plan of Action
Approx 7-14	Make a simple overcall preparing to bid your other suit later. Thus with two five card majors bid 1♠ over a 1♦ opening and hope to bid hearts next time around.
Approx 15-18	Double, then bid one of your suits preparing to bid the other one next time around.
Game-going	Make an immediate cuebid. Note that while:

♠ A K Q 5 4
♥ A K Q 5 4
♦ 5
♣ 6 5

is technically only 18 HCPs it is worthy of an immediate cuebid if opponents open in either minor.

The Michaels cuebid, dealt with in other chapters and the Unusual No-Trump are two conventions frequently used by experienced players to show two-suited hands. The Michaels bid will indicate either both major suits, over a minor suit bid, or the other major and one of the minors over a major suit bid. The Unusual No-Trump, which is a jump to two no-trump over opponent's opener, usually shows both minor suits.

Three-Suited Hands Short
in the Opponent's Suit

Singleton/Void

General Strength	Plan of Action
10-12	Double and pass response (other than a cuebid!)
13-15	Double and raise partner's simple response.
16-18	Double and jump raise partners' major suit response or cuebid over a minor suit response.

Doubleton

General Strength	Plan of Action
12-14	Double and pass response.
15-17	Double and raise partner's simple response.
18-20	Double and jump raise partner's major suit response or cuebid over a minor suit response.

Hands With Good Length
in the Opponent's Suit

General Strength	Plan of Action
Up to 15 points	Pass
15+	Some hands may sensibly be treated as strong balanced hands so bid 1NT or double as appropriate.

Alternatively, you may pass and take action on the second round. For example, if you double on the second round it should show a penalty double of the suit opened. If both you and your partner pass on the first round, a bid of openers suit on the second round should be treated as natural.

Now after all that try the following quiz.

Quiz 17

It is your turn to speak after the dealer on your right has opened 1♦. What do you bid holding the following cards with Neither Side Vulnerable:

1. ♠ K J 10 4 2
    ♥ 6 4 2
    ♦ K 2
    ♣ 7 4 2

2. ♠ A K J 10 4
    ♥ 7 5
    ♦ 6 4 2
    ♣ A K Q

3. ♠ A K 10 9
    ♥ K Q 5 2
    ♦ 7
    ♣ K 7 4 2

4. ♠ K 10 4
    ♥ A J 5
    ♦ 7 5 2
    ♣ K J 4 2

5. ♠ A 5
    ♥ K J 5
    ♦ K 10 4
    ♣ K Q 7 5 2

6. ♠ A 5
    ♥ K J 5
    ♦ A Q 4
    ♣ K Q 7 5 2

7. ♠ K 10 4 2
    ♥ A Q J 5 2
    ♦ 7 5
    ♣ K 2

8. ♠ 5
    ♥ K J 2
    ♦ K Q 10 4 2
    ♣ A K 4 2

The dealer on your right opens one diamond. What do you bid with each of the following hands?

1. ♠ K J 10 4 2
   ♥ 6 4 2
   ♦ K 2
   ♣ 7 4 2

Recommended Bid: 1♠

While this hand is slightly weaker than our very first example, nearly every good tournament player would overcall one spade. Obviously, it is possible that partner might push the bidding up too high, expecting you to hold a little more, but the premium on getting into the bidding is exceptionally high. Even if all your partner can manage is a gentle raise to the two level, you will have made your opponents' task of finding their best contract considerably harder and, if your partner ends up on lead against your opponents' contract, you will be more than pleased when he leads a spade.

2. ♠ A K J 10 4
   ♥ 7 5
   ♦ 6 4 2
   ♣ A K Q

Recommended Bid: Double

While many players would overcall one spade on this hand and get away with it, it is not difficult to see that there are many hands where partner would pass your one spade overcall yet can produce enough bits and pieces for you to make game. After all, just give partner stops in both red suits and you are more than likely to make 3NT. With a one-suited hand with this much potential it is best to double on the first round planning to bid spades next time to show a hand that was too strong to overcall one spade immediately. Notice, too, that, whatever strength of jump overcalls you like to play, it is to be recommended that they should show a six card suit.

3. ♠ A K 10 9
   ♥ K Q 5 2
   ♦ 7
   ♣ K 7 4 2

Recommended Bid: Double

The ideal shape for a takeout double planning to raise partner if he responds one heart, one spade or two clubs.

4. ♠ K 10 4
   ♥ A J 5
   ♦ 7 5 2
   ♣ K J 4 2

Recommended Bid: Pass

While you could make a takeout double, partner is likely to expect you to have both opening bid values and a shortage

in the opponent's suit. There is no real rush to bid with hands of this type, if your left-hand opponent (LHO) passes, partner is still there and is certain to bid if there is any chance of you missing game.

5. ♠ A 5
   ♥ K J 5
   ♦ K 10 4
   ♣ K Q 7 5 2

Recommended Bid: 1NT

In most circles the 1NT overcall shows about 15-17 or 16-18 balanced HCP with a stopper in the opponent's suit. While this hand contains 16 HCP, the five card club suit gives additional playing strength so that the hand should be regarded as a maximum for a 1NT overcall.

6. ♠ A 5
   ♥ K J 5
   ♦ A Q 4
   ♣ K Q 7 5 2

Recommended Bid: Double

With 19 HCPs and a five card suit this hand is far too strong for an immediate 1NT overcall. Of course, you could try 2NT immediately, but, unfortunately, many players reserve that bid as unusual, showing at least 5-5 in the two lowest unbid suits. Clearly, it would be unfortunate if your partner drew that conclusion, so it is better to double, planning to bid no trumps at the lowest available level in the next round. Notice that if partner is able to respond at the one-level in either major, you will be able to rebid 1NT, thus showing this stronger type of hand without raising the level.

7. ♠ K 10 4 2
   ♥ A Q J 5 2
   ♦ 7 5
   ♣ K 2

Recommended Bid: 1♥

Holding support for both majors many players would be tempted to double, but whenever I do this my partner always bids clubs and, since then a bid of two hearts would show a considerably stronger hand, I am fixed into passing. It is much more comfortable to overcall one heart, which sets a firm rock to build on. If your partner is not able to support hearts you will hope that you have an opportunity to get your spades into the auction later. For example, if the auction proceeds:

1♦	1♥	2♦	Pass
Pass	?		

you might consider making a takeout double now. In itself, a secondary double of this type tends to show a good hand for making the initial overcall and doesn't guarantee four spades. You would certainly make such a double on a 3-5-2-3 shape, but partner should be aware that you might have four spades and he will strain to bid them if he can.

8. ♠ 5
♥ K J 2
♦ K Q 10 4 2
♣ A K 4 2

Recommended Bid: Pass

The only possible alternative is to overcall 1NT, but that may prove to be uncomfortable especially if your partner chooses to run out to spades. With such a very good holding in the opponent's suit it is usually best to pass on the first round, hoping to get into the action later. For example, if the auction proceeds:

1♦	Pass	1NT	Pass
Pass	?		

you can double to show a good hand with diamonds; after all, if you had any other type of good hand you would have bid on the first round. Alternatively, if the auction proceeds:

1♦	Pass	1♠	Pass
2♠	?		

you can double as a takeout of spades, but once again your partner should suspect that you have good diamonds since you must have some reason for not bidding at your first opportunity.

QUIZ 18

You hear a one spade opening from the dealer on your right. What would you bid with each of the following hands?

1. ♠ 7
♥ A J 7 5
♦ K 8 7 6
♣ K J 7 5

5. ♠ 7 5
♥ K 10 5
♦ K J 7
♣ K J 8 6 5

2. ♠ 7 5
♥ A Q 10 9 5
♦ K Q 10 5
♣ 8 5

6. ♠ 7
♥ K 3
♦ A Q J 7 2
♣ K 9 7 5 2

3. ♠ 7 5
♥ A J 5
♦ 10 7
♣ K J 8 6 5 2

7. ♠ 7
♥ 8 3
♦ K Q J 8 6
♣ Q J 10 6 5

4. ♠ 7 5
♥ Q 10 5
♦ A Q
♣ A K Q 10 6 5

8. ♠ 7 5 4
♥ K Q 10
♦ A Q 7
♣ A K Q 10

There is a one spade opening from the dealer on your right. What would you bid with each of the following hands?

1. ♠ 7
♥ A J 7 5
♦ K 8 7 6
♣ K J 7 5

Recommended Bid: Double

With opening bid values and the perfect shape, you have an easy takeout double.

2. ♠ 7 5
♥ A Q 10 9 5
♦ K J 10 5
♣ 8 5

Recommended Bid: 2♥

You have a good heart suit, and excellent playing strength despite your lack of HCP. Bidding two hearts points your side in the direction of the most likely game contract and takes valuable bidding space away from your opponents. The intermediate cards in both red suits give you a fair chance of avoiding an excessive penalty even if partner holds an unsuitable hand.

3. ♠ 7 5
♥ A J 5
♦ 10 7
♣ K J 8 6 5 2

Recommended Bid: 2♣

By and large the quality of your suit doesn't matter too much once you have a six card holding. The sixth card in the suit means that you will take an extra trick playing with your suit as trumps, so in many ways this hand is the equivalent of a 12 point hand with a good five card suit.

4. ♠ 7 5
♥ Q 10 5
♦ A Q
♣ A K Q 10 6 5

Recommended Bid: 3♠

Of course, you could just overcall two clubs, or if you are playing strong jump overcalls you could jump to three clubs. You might even double intending to bid clubs on the next round, but none of these bids really give a good description of the potential of your hand. Provided the club suit runs, and you can get to your partner's hand once to take the diamond finesse, you would expect to have eight playing tricks in your own hand.

All partner really needs to make 3NT is a spade stopper, so make a jump cuebid asking him to bid 3NT if he has one.

If partner doesn't have a spade stopper and no real prospects of making game he should bid four clubs on the basis that you would pass with a long club suit or convert to four diamonds with a long diamond suit.

Curiously, the jump cuebid is also likely to serve you well if your LHO decided to bid a lot of spades. Partner will know the approximate strength of your hand and that you have a long minor. He has a much better chance of making a sensible decision if the auction starts:

| | 1♠ | 3♠ | 4♠ | ? |

than if it starts:

| | 1♠ | Dble | 4♠ | ? |

5.   ♠ 7 5
    ♥ K 10 5
    ♦ K J 7
    ♣ K J 8 6 5

Recommended Bid: Pass

You have near opening bid values and a modest five card club suit, but overcalling two clubs on this hand would be far too rich even for aggressive tastes. Apart from the lack of quality in the club suit your outside holdings have little playing strength. Finally, you don't really want to suggest a club lead. Should the opponents come to rest in 3NT, you would be quite happy if partner wanted to lead either red suit.

6.   ♠ 7
    ♥ K 3
    ♦ A Q J 7 2
    ♣ K 9 7 5 2

Recommended Bid: 2♦

Did you decide that with 5-5 in the minors the time had come to bid the Unusual 2NT? Certainly, partner will expect you to be 5-5 in the minors, but this is completely the wrong type of hand for the bid. In principle, the Unusual 2NT should be reserved either for very strong hands when you have an inkling that the contract belongs to your side or a hand where you want to suggest that, if partner has a fit for one of your suits, you might have a profitable sacrifice available.

This hand is nowhere near strong enough to suggest that you should be making a five level minor suit contract. At the same time the defensive prospects are too good to wish to suggest to partner that he takes a save. It is not totally inconceivable that you have enough defense in your own hand to beat a game contract in either major, so don't encourage your partner to make a phantom sacrifice.

7.   ♠ 7
    ♥ 8 3
    ♦ K Q J 8 6
    ♣ Q J 10 6 5

Recommended Bid: 2NT

This hand represents the other side of the coin. If partner has a good fit for one of your suits, five of a minor could easily prove to be a profitable sacrifice and you have very poor defensive prospects in your own hand.

8.   ♠ 7 5 4
    ♥ K Q 10
    ♦ A Q 7
    ♣ A K Q 10

Recommended Bid: Double

A difficult hand type. You have far too much to pass on the first round, since partner can easily have enough for you to make game, but you have nowhere near the values required to bid if the opening bid is passed around to him. So double on the first round. If partner responds 1NT you should confidently raise him to 3NT. If he bids a suit at the two level try cuebidding the opponent's suit. This shows a very strong hand and asks partner to define his hand further.

For example, if partner has something like:

  ♠ Q J 6
  ♥ 8 3 2
  ♦ J 8 6 2
  ♣ 8 3 2

he will respond two diamonds to your takeout double, and when you cuebid two spades, he will bid 2NT, which you can pass. On the other hand, if he has somewhat more, a hand like:

  ♠ Q J 6
  ♥ 8 3 2
  ♦ K 8 6 4 2
  ♣ 8 3

then he should jump to 3NT knowing he is facing a very strong hand.

PART II

COMPETITIVE BIDDING
by Tony Sowter

Many thousands of bridge players, often of great experience, may have assimilated a variety of ideas on competitive bidding, but have never really reviewed this important area of the game in a comprehensive manner. It is at these players that this section of this book is targeted.

Most of the examples have been used in lectures and seminars aimed at improving the players' insight into the structure of competitive bidding, improving their judgement in these situations, and creating a framework of relatively straightforward methods designed to help them cope with the most common competitive situations, without the necessity of remembering all kinds of complicated conventions.

Almost all of these chapters open with a section that concentrates on one or two principles which are frequently misunderstood. Thereafter, the subject is developed through a series of bidding quizzes and answers. Read the opening section of each chapter before doing the quizzes, but then write down your answers to the questions before you look at the answers. This is particularly important; the best way to learn is to get your feet wet.

Answering questions in your head makes it all too easy to change your mind or even take the view that "Of course, I would have done that at the table." Writing the answers down is akin to making a real decision at the table. Better still, if you have a regular partner get him or her to write down the answers to each question, too. At least then, if you don't agree with the answers that are given, you can be sure that both of you are on the same wavelength. And if you can master all the areas covered in this section, you will have acquired sufficient insight to help you in almost every competitive situation.

Chapter 6

Responding to a Takeout Double

Suppose the auction starts:

| 1♦ | Dble | Pass | ? |

What would you bid holding:

> ♠ 7 5 2
> ♥ J 5 2
> ♦ J 9 4 3
> ♣ Q 7 2

Do not consider passing because you are unlikely to set one diamond doubled. One no-trump is a similarly dangerous bid and could cost you a substantial penalty.

If partner had opened either one heart or one spade you would have passed, so your only real option now is to bid one of the majors at minimum level. Since the expectation is that you will bid something in response to a takeout double, a bid at the one level in one of partner's suits has to be consistent with having no positive values. On this particular hand you have no reason to prefer to play in one major rather than the other so it seems logical to bid the lower. However, if you held three spades and only two hearts it would be clear to bid one spade.

Putting it round the other way, if your partner opens the bidding with one diamond then your weakest response is to pass. However, here your partner has doubled the opponent's opening bid of one diamond, so choosing to pass is a positive decision, suggesting that the best possible result for your side will be achieved by defending one diamond doubled.

Now let's suppose that you have a much better hand, like:

> ♠ A J 7 2
> ♥ K 10 7 5
> ♦ 7 5 4
> ♣ K 5

What are you going to do this time after your partner has doubled 1♦.

Let's suppose that partner really does have a 4-4-1-4 distribution with 12 points. Then, you have one loser in the

opponent's suit and 23 of the available 30 points in the other three suits. Thus at most you should be missing an ace and a king in the three suits outside diamonds. One loser in diamonds and at most two in the other suits suggests that you should have reasonable play for 10 tricks provided that you settle in an eight card trump fit.

This means that you have the values to respond either four hearts or four spades but since it is possible that partner does not hold four cards in both majors, it is difficult to decide which major suit game to bid. The answer is to enlist partner's help by bidding the opponent's suit.

Now, first and foremost, it should be clear that it would be nonsense for a two diamond response to show a desire actually to play in two diamonds. Certainly you can expect no help in diamonds from partner so you would need very good diamonds to have any chance of making eight tricks in diamonds and, in that case, you would do better to let your opponents struggle in one diamond doubled. After all +300 or +500 looks a lot healthier than either +40, the score you would get for making two diamonds playing rubber bridge, or +90, the score you would get playing duplicate bridge.

Accordingly, it should be clear that a cuebid of the opponent's suit, in this case two diamonds, can be used as an artificial bid suggesting that you have quite a good hand and asking the doubler to describe his hand more fully. On this deal, whichever major he bids, you will be happy to raise him to game.

The cuebid of the opponents' suit in response to a takeout double is normally taken as being forcing to suit agreement. Thus, if your partner bids two hearts in response to your cuebid, you can raise to three hearts, which partner is allowed to pass. This would be a reasonable choice of action holding a slightly weaker hand like:

> ♠ A J 7 2
> ♥ K J 6 5
> ♦ 7 5 2
> ♣ 8 6

Clearly you expect to have an eight card fit in at least one if not both of the majors. By cuebidding the opponents' suit you can make sure of finding a fit.

Quiz 19

Your LHO opens one diamond, partner doubles and RHO passes. With Neither Side Vulnerable, what would you bid with the following hands:

1. ♠ Q 10 7 5
    ♥ Q J 7 5
    ♦ 7 4 3
    ♣ 8 4

2. ♠ J 4 2
    ♥ Q 5
    ♦ Q 10 5 4
    ♣ K 8 7 2

3. ♠ A Q 7 2
    ♥ K 5
    ♦ 7 5 4 2
    ♣ 8 7 2

4. ♠ A 9 7 5 2
    ♥ K 5
    ♦ 7 5 4
    ♣ 8 7 2

5. ♠ A Q 7 5 2
    ♥ K 5
    ♦ 7 5 4 2
    ♣ 8 2

6. ♠ A J 5
    ♥ 7 5 2
    ♦ A 10 5
    ♣ K J 7 2

1. ♠ Q 10 7 5
    ♥ Q J 7 5
    ♦ 7 4 3
    ♣ 8 4

Recommended Bid: 1♠

This time you have some positive values but not such a good hand that you would wish to go jumping around. The bid of one spade is recommended because it is much better prepared than a one heart response. If you decide to bid again or, if partner forces you to, then you can bid your hearts in comfort. Notice that if you bid one heart on the first round and opener bids two diamonds then you might feel uncomfortable bidding two spades when the auction comes back to you. In particular, this might force your partner to put you back to three hearts on a minimum hand. By bidding spades first you can offer a choice of major suit contracts at the two level.

A further marginal consideration is a one spade response to a takeout double is slightly more encouraging than a one heart response inasmuch as you would bid one heart with a 3-3-4-3 Yarborough while, at the very least, one spade suggests that you prefer spades to hearts.

2. ♠ J 4 2
    ♥ Q 5
    ♦ Q 10 5 4
    ♣ K 8 7 2

Recommended Bid: 1NT

This is about the minimum that your partner should expect from you for a 1NT response. Facing a 4-4-1-4 12 point hand, you have half the high cards in the pack between you and you have a good expectation of at least one if not two stoppers in the diamond suit. Of course, two clubs may turn out to be a better contract but 1NT has the merit of getting over a general description of your hand and may enable partner to judge your prospects better than two clubs, which you might be forced to bid with fewer points. After all, what else could you sensibly respond with something like:

    ♠ 7 5
    ♥ 6 4
    ♦ 9 7 4 3 2
    ♣ Q J 5 3

3. ♠ A Q 7 2
    ♥ K 5
    ♦ 7 5 4 2
    ♣ 8 7 2

Recommended Bid: 2♠

One of the features of responding to a takeout double is that most of the responses take the form of being limit bids. If your partner opens the bidding with one diamond and you respond one heart the change of suit is forcing for one round unless you have already passed. However, when you respond one heart to a takeout double of one diamond, your bid is totally non-forcing; indeed the bid suggests that, unless partner has an exceptionally strong hand, you have no desire to play the hand in a contract any higher than one heart. Accordingly, when you have a reasonable fit for one of the suits that your partner is expected to hold, you must show some sign of life if you have anything approaching the values that might make a game facing a reasonable hand. Notice that:

♠ A Q 7 2   facing   ♠ K 8 5 2
♥ K 5   ♥ A 8 6 4
♦ 7 5 4 2   ♦ 8
♣ 8 7 2   ♣ K Q J 5

combine to give an excellent play for four spades yet the doubler has very little more than a minimum double and not enough to volunteer another bid facing an initial response of one spade.

So, our example hand is a pristine example of a very suitable hand to jump to two spades, a limit bid allowing partner to pass with an unsuitable minimum but to press on with anything extra. In terms of high card points most players would regard the jump to two of a major to show four card support and in the region of 8-10 HCP.

4.   ♠ A 9 7 5 2
      ♥ K 5
      ♦ 7 5 4
      ♣ 8 7 2

Recommended Bid: 2♠

In many ways this is a stronger hand in support of spades than the previous hand, example 3. In terms of high card points, this hand is the equivalent of a hand with only a four card spade suit but 10 HCP, and thus like the last hand fulfils the requirements for a jump to two spades. Indeed, this hand is a total maximum for the jump response.

If you wonder just how this peculiar arithmetic is generated, the answer is simply that playing in a contract with spades as trumps you would expect to take one more trick holding ♠ A 9 7 5 2 than you would if you only held ♠ A 9 7 5, so that lowly two of spades is clearly worth an extra trick. How

many points is an extra trick actually worth? Well, if high cards were the only determinant of trick taking potential then every deal comprises 13 tricks and there are 40 HCPs in the pack, so in broad equivalence a distributional trick has the same value as 3 HCP.

5.   ♠ A Q 7 5 2
      ♥ K 5
      ♦ 7 5 4 2
      ♣ 8 2

Recommended Bid: 2♦

Just as in example 4, you have a five card spade suit, so in support of spades the two of spades can be counted as an extra 3HCP. With the equivalent hand, 12 HCP and four spades, facing a takeout double of one diamond you should have good chances of making four spades. Of course, you could bid four spades immediately but this is not to be recommended since occasionally partner will not have the expected shape for his takeout double. No, the safest route is to cuebid two diamonds. If, as expected, partner bids two hearts you can bid two spades which is forcing for one round.

6.   ♠ A J 5
      ♥ 7 5 2
      ♦ A 10 5
      ♣ K J 7 2

Recommended Bid: 2♦

With this hand many players are tempted to leap to either 2NT or 3NT immediately, but in my view there is no need to panic. By bidding two diamonds to start with you leave open the possibility of arriving at a better contract while not closing the door on 3NT. If partner bids two hearts in response to your cuebid you could introduce your club suit on the next round and planning to bid 3NT next. After all, if your partner produces something like:

♠ K Q 7 6
♥ K Q J 4
♦ 6
♣ A Q 10 8

6♣ is likely to make while 3NT figures to finish one down.

Now consider what you would do on the following hands after partner has doubled a one diamond opening, but RHO has raised to three diamonds:

1. ♠ 7 5
   ♥ K Q 7 2
   ♦ 8 4 2
   ♣ Q 9 4 2

2. ♠ K 5
   ♥ K Q 7 2
   ♦ 8 4 2
   ♣ Q 9 4 2

3. ♠ A 4 3
   ♥ K 5 2
   ♦ 8 4 2
   ♣ K 9 4 2

4. ♠ A 4
   ♥ 8 5 2
   ♦ Q J 10 9
   ♣ J 7 4 2

5. ♠ K Q 4 2
   ♥ A J 7 5
   ♦ 8 4 2
   ♣ 9 4

6. ♠ A Q 4 2
   ♥ 9 4
   ♦ 8 4
   ♣ K Q 8 7 4

What you would bid on the following hands after partner has doubled a one diamond opening, but RHO has raised to three diamonds:

1. ♠ 7 5
   ♥ K Q 7 2
   ♦ 8 4 2
   ♣ Q 9 4 2

Recommended Bid: 3♥

Many players want to pass on this hand, allowing the opponents to steal the hand in three diamonds unless partner has sufficient extra values to bid again. To illustrate why it is usually right to compete the part-score by bidding three hearts, I can demonstrate the likely outcomes if partner turns up with the expected 12 or 13 high card points in a 4-4-1-4 shaped hand.

Suppose, for example, our combined hands are:

♠ 7 5	♠ K 9 6 2
♥ K Q 7 2	♥ A 9 8 3
♦ 8 4 2	♦ 7
♣ Q 9 4 2	♣ A J 7 3

Now if hearts break 3-2 and the ace of spades is in the opening bidder's hand, as you would expect, you should have little difficulty making nine tricks with hearts as trumps. You will probably make five hearts, one spade and three club tricks. Indeed, if things go well you could easily find yourself making 10 tricks and wondering why you didn't take a pot at game.

Meanwhile, if you allow the opponents to play in diamonds you will take two heart tricks, one spade and one or two club tricks depending on just who happens to hold the king of clubs.

Now, of course, I could make partner's hand less suitable for playing in hearts by giving him more strength in spades and only three hearts, but hopefully the point is clear that once you have an eight card fit it is highly advantageous to play the hand if partner has a singleton in their suit. Using the same approach as used in the earlier examples you could argue that you have one loser in diamonds and 19 of the available high card points in the other three suits. That translates to an expectation of losing just three tricks outside diamonds or four tricks in all.

2. ♠ K 5
   ♥ K Q 7 2
   ♦ 8 4 2
   ♣ Q 9 4 2

Recommended Bid: 4♥

Strangely enough, if it was right to bid three hearts on the last hand it should be clear that you have enough to bid four hearts on this one. Of course, there will be times when it is the wrong thing to do but bridge is a game of probabilities and opposite a minimum 4-4-1-4 hand like:

- ♠ A 7 5 2
- ♥ A 8 6 3
- ♦ 7
- ♣ K J 5 3

You should have no difficulty making ten tricks provided the rounded suits break evenly. However, you cannot really expect partner to raise you to game if you just bid three hearts.

3.
- ♠ A 4 3
- ♥ K 5 2
- ♦ 8 4 2
- ♣ K 9 4 2

Recommended Bid: Double

Without the aid of a so-called responsive double, this hand would be particularly hard to deal with. Of course, with four clubs you could settle for just bidding four clubs but most players would feel much happier if they could simply describe their hand as having the values to want to bid but no good suit to bid themselves. Accordingly, most tournament players choose to play a double as showing values and inviting partner to bid, rather than as the old-fashioned penalty double.

Apart from anything else the frequency of your holding sufficient trumps to extract a suitable penalty from the opponents when they have at least eight if not nine trumps between them is very low and, as you shall see, just because you can't double three diamonds for penalties immediately doesn't mean that you will never collect a doubled penalty.

4.
- ♠ A 4
- ♥ 8 5 2
- ♦ Q J 10 9
- ♣ J 7 4 2

Recommended Bid: Pass

This is the other side of the coin, the kind of hand where the enthusiastic rubber bridge player might want to express his opinion that the opponents' contract is going to yield a juicy penalty. Well, I'm sorry, if you are going to play responsive doubles, as most tournament players would recommend, you have to pass this hand. If partner has a minimum takeout double that will probably be the end of the story and unless your opponents have extreme distribution their contract will probably drift one or two down. However, on a really good day, partner might have the extra values required to double again and then you will be able to express your opinion by passing for penalties.

If you were tempted to bid 3NT on the first round you should bear in mind that facing a minimum takeout double

you will really be struggling for tricks unless partner produces a good club suit. Indeed if partner produces the 16+ points that you are likely to need to make 3NT he is certainly strong enough to make another bid if three diamonds is passed back to him. With a five card major he will bid it and then you can try 3NT, otherwise he should double again.

5.
- ♠ K Q 4 2
- ♥ A J 7 5
- ♦ 8 4 2
- ♣ 9 4

Recommended Bid: 4♦

With both four card majors, 10 HCP and a doubleton in the other suit outside diamonds, you should have every expectation of making game just as you had in example 2. The difference here is that by bidding four diamonds you give partner the opportunity to choose the contract. If he has four hearts he will probably bid four hearts but with only three hearts and four spades he will undoubtedly bid four spades.

In this position the cuebid should be assumed to be offering a choice between the majors initially. If responder has an even better hand he might choose to bid four diamonds first and then raise his partner's response.

6.
- ♠ A Q 4 2
- ♥ 9 4
- ♦ 8 4
- ♣ K Q 8 7 4

Recommended Bid: 4♦

Once again the recommended bid is a cuebid in the opponents' suit, even though initially partner will think that you have both majors. However, if he bids four hearts you will convert to four spades offering a choice between spades and clubs. Using the cuebid in this kind of situation gives you a much better chance of landing in a playable fit than having to choose between bidding four spades or five clubs on the first round.

To summarize, when partner makes a takeout double, remember that if you bid any suit other than the opponents' one, it is a limit bid. In effect, your partner has shown opening bid values with some support for any suit that you wish to bid.

If you have a five card suit add three points for your additional playing strength in that suit.

Remember that a cuebid of the opponents' suit is forcing to suit agreement. With four-card support for two of the unbid suits and about 10 HCP outside the opponents' suit, you should definitely start with a cuebid.

Responding to Overcalls

Suppose you pick up the following uninspiring collection:

♠ J 5 3
♥ 7 5
♦ 8 6 4 3
♣ A Q 6 3

The dealer on your left opens one diamond, your partner bids one spade, and the next hand passes. What would you do now?

While an overcall can be much weaker than an opening bid, it would be a mistake to pass with this hand, mainly because you have three card support for partner's expected five card suit. Indeed, for successful competitive bidding it is essential that, whenever you have adequate support for partner's suit, you raise him for both defensive and offensive reasons.

For example, if you give partner one of the first hands on which you recommended that he overcall 1♦ with 1♠:

♠ K Q 10 4 2
♥ 6 4 2
♦ K 2
♣ 7 4 2

even two spades will be a struggle. If the ace of diamonds is right and the king of clubs is wrong, which seems probable given the opening bid, then partner is quite likely to lose one spade, two hearts, one diamond, and a club, and he will have to hope that the defense don't religiously lead trumps every time they are in if he is going to be allowed to ruff his third losing heart. One or two down may not seem like an elegant result, but it is, perhaps, comforting to note that the opponents will have quite good play for four hearts, losing just one spade, one diamond, and one club.

Left to their own devices, it is quite likely that they would have found their heart fit quickly, but your partner's one spade overcall made it difficult for your RHO to bid hearts, and by raising to two spades you will make it much more difficult for the opener to introduce the suit.

On the other hand, you don't actually need partner to have that much to have good play for four spades. A hand like:

♠ A Q 10 4 2
♥ K J 4
♦ 4
♣ K 9 8 3

gives a good play for game.

The principle of supporting partner and cutting out the opponents' bidding space remains even if your RHO manages to drum up a bid on the first round. If, for example, the auction starts:

	1♦	1♠	Dble	?
or	1♦	1♠	2♦	?
or	1♦	1♠	2♣	?

it is clear that you should strain to bid two spades whenever you possibly can, just to make it harder for your opponents to explore their hands properly.

However, if the auction starts:

	1♦	1♠	2♥	?

a bid of two spades removes very little, if any, bidding space from your opponents and so the bid should suggest you are happy for partner to compete at a higher level.

Certainly, I would still bid two spades with the example hand:

♠ J 5 3
♥ 7 5
♦ 8 6 4 3
♣ A Q 6 3

but only because there is a whole range of hands where it will be right to compete as far as three spades, and if I don't give partner any clue that I have some values and at least three card support now, he will be stuck when the bidding comes back to him at a higher level.

For example, if he actually holds:

♠ K Q 10 4 2
♥ 6 4
♦ A 2
♣ K 7 4 2

you would like him to be able to compete to three spades if the opponents bid three hearts. Once you have shown three card support and a modicum of values, the security of knowing of the eight card fit should persuade partner to bid on with what is actually quite a good hand for his initial overcall.

While it is certainly true that supporting partner on nothing more than three card support must be the order of the day to maximize the obstructive effect of the overcall, it does avoid the question of what the overcaller's partner is supposed to do with a somewhat better hand, like:

♠ A 5 3
♥ 7 5
♦ 8 6 4 3
♣ A Q 6 3

after the auction has started:

1♦   1♠   Pass   ?

Clearly this is a much better hand than the previous example, but facing a typical minimum overcall:

♠ K Q 10 4 2
♥ 6 4 2
♦ K 2
♣ 7 4 2

you would certainly not want to come to rest at more than two spades, a contract that you will probably make with most of the opposing strength in the opener's hand and reasonable breaks.

This would be a problem except for the neat device called the "unassuming cuebid," which allows you to bid the opponents' suit at minimum level to show a "good raise" to the two level in partner's suit. So, in this case you would bid two diamonds to show a better than minimum raise in spades.

Notice that opposite the "quite good hand" for the initial overcall:

♠ K Q 10 4 2
♥ 6 4
♦ A 2
♣ K 7 4 2

your "good raise to two" hand yields a good play for game.

Now test out these ideas by trying the following quiz.

QUIZ 21

Suppose your LHO deals and opens 1♦, your partner overcalls 1♠, and there is a pass on your right. What would you do with Neither Side Vulnerable if you were holding:

1. ♠ J 5 3
    ♥ 7 5
    ♦ A 6 4 3
    ♣ J 10 5 3

2. ♠ A J 2
    ♥ 7 5
    ♦ 8 6 4 3
    ♣ A J 7 2

3. ♠ J 5 3
    ♥ K Q 10 4 2
    ♦ 6 4 3
    ♣ Q 5

4. ♠ 4
    ♥ K Q J 7 4 2
    ♦ 6 4
    ♣ A 7 4 2

5. ♠ 7 5
    ♥ K 4 2
    ♦ 10 4 2
    ♣ A J 7 4

6. ♠ J 5
    ♥ K 4 2
    ♦ Q 10 4 2
    ♣ A Q J 5

7. ♠ A 4 3
    ♥ 7 5
    ♦ 8 6 4 2
    ♣ A K J 2

8. ♠ J 4 3 2
    ♥ 7 5
    ♦ 8 6 4
    ♣ A Q 7 4

9. ♠ A 4 3 2
    ♥ 7 5
    ♦ 8 6 4
    ♣ A K 4 2

Suppose that your LHO deals and opens 1♦, your partner overcalls 1♠, and there is a pass on your right. What would you do with Neither Side Vulnerable holding:

1. ♠ J 5 3
   ♥ 7 5
   ♦ A 6 4 3
   ♣ J 10 5 3

Recommended Bid: 2♠

Once again you have three card support for partner and not a very good hand, but raising to two spades will maximize the opponents' difficulties and might enable partner to judge correctly later.

2. ♠ A J 2
   ♥ 7 5
   ♦ 8 6 4 3
   ♣ A J 7 2

Recommended Bid: 2♦

Still not a great hand, but much better than example 1. Cuebid the opponents' suit to show your extra values for a raise to two spades.

3. ♠ J 5 3
   ♥ K Q 10 4 2
   ♦ 6 4 3
   ♣ Q 5

Recommended Bid: 2♠

The key feature of this hand is the three card spade support. A bid of two hearts would show a good suit and, while it is non-forcing, it is encouraging. Basically it denies reasonable support for partner so he could easily pass leaving you to play in a 5-1 or 5-2 fit when you already *know* that you have at least eight spades. Support your partner first, then, if he goes on, you might get the opportunity to bid your hearts on the next round.

4. ♠ 4
   ♥ K Q J 7 4 2
   ♦ 6 4
   ♣ A 7 4 2

Recommended Bid: 2♥

This is the recommended hand type on which to bid two hearts. Clearly you have no interest in playing in a spade contract, but you would be happy to play in any number of hearts that partner raised you to. If you had an even stronger hand, say:

```
          ♠ 4
          ♥ A K Q J 7 4
          ♦ 6 4
          ♣ A 7 4 2
```

you could force partner to bid again by jumping to three hearts.

5. ♠ 7 5
   ♥ K 4 2
   ♦ Q 10 4 2
   ♣ A J 7 4

Recommended Bid: 1NT

We have already established that the normal range for a one spade overcall in terms of HCP is 8-16 while an opening bid carries a range more like 11-19 HCP. Notice that both are 8 point ranges, but the opening bid range is 3 points stronger. So, if you would normally respond 1NT to an opening bid with a range of say 6-9, it would be reasonable to respond 1NT to an overcall with a range that is three points higher, about 9-12. So bid just 1NT with this hand.

6. ♠ J 5
   ♥ K 4 2
   ♦ Q 10 4 2
   ♣ A Q J 5

Recommended Bid: 2NT

In a similar vein, don't press too hard with your opening bid since partner did not open the bidding: he made a simple overcall. 2NT should show a hand of about this strength. Indeed, notice that facing the example of a minimum spade overcall even 2NT is going to be more than something of a sweat.

```
    ♠ J 5           ♠ K Q 10 4 2
    ♥ K 4 2         ♥ 6 4 2
    ♦ Q 10 4 2      ♦ K 2
    ♣ A Q J 5       ♣ 7 4 2
```

After a diamond lead it only takes the defense to hold off the first round of spades for the dummy to be totally dead. You are favorite to make one spade, one heart, two diamonds and two or three clubs, but that still leaves you short of eight tricks.

7. ♠ A 4 3
   ♥ 7 5
   ♦ 8 6 4 2
   ♣ A K J 2

Recommended Bid: 2♦

This is an even stronger hand than example 2 with three card spade support. The right answer is: start with the same unassuming cuebid, but, if partner simply repeats his spades, you are worth a raise to three spades.

8. ♠ J 4 3 2
   ♥ 7 5
   ♦ 8 6 4
   ♣ A Q 7 4

Recommended Bid: 3♠

This time you have four card support for partner's suit, which in turn means that one of your opponents is much more likely to have a singleton or void. The fourth trump does provide extra playing strength while making it that much more likely that the opposition can make a contract somewhere. Accordingly, in the modern style it has become *de rigueur* to jump to three spades on this type of hand. There are those that play this type of jump as totally pre-emptive but, if that is a bit rich for your blood, this type of hand is ideal. So, basically, the jump to three spades should show a raise to two spades with four card support.

9. ♠ A 4 3 2
    ♥ 7 5
    ♦ 8 6 4
    ♣ A K 4 2

Recommended Bid: 3♦

While it might well be tempting to jump to four spades on this hand, it is not difficult to see that facing a standard minimum overcall:

            ♠ K Q 10 4 2
            ♥ 6 4 2
            ♦ K 2
            ♣ 7 4 2

four spades is no thing of beauty. So in reality hand 9 is nothing more than a sound high card raise to three spades albeit with four card support. Obviously you could deal with this in the same manner as hand 7 by making a cuebid and then raising to three spades. However, it is particularly helpful to know that the hand 7 route suggests only three-card support so I recommend that you play a jump cuebid in the opponents suit to show a high card raise to three in partner's suit but with four-card support.

QUIZ 22

Once again partner bids 1♠ after a 1♦ opening, but this time your RHO raises to 2♦. What do you do next with the following hands:

1. ♠ J 7 5
    ♥ 7 2
    ♦ 8 6 4 3
    ♣ A Q 6 3

2. ♠ 7 2
    ♥ K Q 10 5
    ♦ 6 4
    ♣ K J 9 6 3

3. ♠ J 7 5 2
    ♥ 7 2
    ♦ 6 4 3
    ♣ A Q 6 3

4. ♠ A J 4
    ♥ 7 2
    ♦ 8 6 4 2
    ♣ A K 7 2

Once again partner bids 1♠ after a 1♦ opening but this time your RHO raises to 2♦. What do you do next with the following hands:

1. ♠ J 7 5
    ♥ 7 2
    ♦ 8 6 4 3
    ♣ A Q 6 3

Recommended Bid: 2♠

Take the opportunity to show your three card spade support and modest values immediately. This is right both offensively and defensively. Your bid will reduce the space available to your opponents to explore their hand while making it easier for your partner to judge the combined potential of your sides' assets.

2. ♠ 7 2
    ♥ K Q 10 5
    ♦ 6 4
    ♣ K J 9 6 3

Recommended Bid: Double

This is an awkward hand. Without the two diamond raise you might have decided to keep the bidding open with a two club bid, just in case partner had club support or a secondary heart suit, even though your club suit really isn't that good. Now that possibility is not available to you but you would like to be able to show useful holdings in the two unbid suits in the hope that partner has a second suit. Fortunately that option is possible in the shape of a competitive double which by agreement shows values in the two unbid suits. Of course, choosing to use a double of a suit that has been bid and raised as competitive means that you are giving up the use of this bid as a penalty double. However, experience suggests that the frequency of a penalty double in this type of position is incredibly low and, even when you are able to make one, partner has an irritating habit of bidding on. In practice, if you do have a diamond stack then most of the time your best option will be to pass two diamonds in tempo, in the hope that partner will reopen with a takeout double.

Most expert players choose to play competitive doubles but it is something that you should remember to agree with your partner. In a similar way, most regular tournament players also play that a double is competitive if your RHO introduces a new suit. For example:

| 1♦ | 1♠ | 2♣ | Double |

Here the competitive double would suggest a hand with hearts and spade tolerance, whereas a bid of two hearts would tend to deny any spade support.

3. ♠ J 7 5 2
    ♥ 7 2
    ♦ 6 4 3
    ♣ A Q 6 3

Recommended Bid: 3♠

Here the extra trump gives your side extra playing strength and protection against a penalty double. However, in many ways, the extra trump also means that your opponents are much more likely to have a playable game contract as one of them is more likely to have a singleton spade. For sure you will be struggling to beat four hearts or, possibly even, five diamonds if partner has a minimum overcall.

If you feel that you need a rather better hand to jump to three spades, remember that you could always show a good raise to three spades by cuebidding three diamonds.

4. ♠ A J 4
    ♥ 7 2
    ♦ 8 6 4 2
    ♣ A K 7 2

Recommended Bid: 3♦

Despite only having three card spade support this time your hand is far too good for just bidding two spades and, as you have just seen a jump to three spades, really should be reserved for four card support, so what is to be done? Cuebid three diamonds to show a high-card raise to three spades.

This has the added advantage that, if the opponents do bid to game, your partner will expect you to have reasonable defense, so he is unlikely to sacrifice in five spades in front of you.

To summarize this chapter on responding to overcalls:

With three-card support for partner's suit:

Strength	Recommended Action
Good 5 to a poor 9	Make a simple raise, for example, raise a 1♠ overcall to 2♠ or 2♣ to 3♣
Good 9 to 11	Cuebid LHO's suit (an unassuming cuebid)
12-13	Cuebid LHO's suit and then raise if partner just rebids his suit. If the overcaller rebids a suit below his original suit give him jump preference, if the overcaller makes a rebid higher than his original suit bid game.
14+	Cuebid LHO's suit and then bid game or make a more descriptive bid.

With four-card support for partner's suit:

Strength	Recommended Action
Flat 5-7	Make a simple raise.
Distributional 5-7 or 8	Make a jump raise, for example, raise a 1♠ overcall to 3♠.

Strength	Recommended Action
9-12	Make a jump cuebid in LHO's suit
13+	Make sure that you reach game. Make a descriptive bid if you want partner to be able to judge what to do later. For example, you could start with a jump cuebid to show general high cards and then bid game in partner's suit or you can use a double jump in a new suit either as a splinter or as a cuebid.

With no support for partner's suit:

Strength	Recommended Action
0-8	Pass unless you have a very good suit of your own, say KQJxxx, when you bid the suit at minimum level.
9-12	With a decent stopper in the opponent's suit bid 1NT. Otherwise bid a decent suit if you have one. Sometimes you will have a difficult choice. For example, with two small cards in partner's suit, three small in the opponent's suit and two good four card suits and about 12 HCP you really do need to bid something. Brazen out 1NT if you have to. This type of hand is much easier when RHO has supported his partner because then you can make a Competitive Double. Facing a two level overcall, you should definitely strain to bid 2NT with hands of this strength including a stopper in the opponent's suit and a doubleton in partner's suit. If need be you can keep the auction open by supporting on honor doubleton, as to overcall at the two level partner is likely to have either a six-card suit or a good five card suit.
13-14	With a stopper in the opponent's suit you can jump in no trumps.
15+	Unless you have a total misfit you should be in game. A jump in a new suit shows a good suit and is forcing for one round.

Chapter 11

Bidding in the Balancing Seat

In this chapter we examine the extent to which tactics should be modified in the fourth seat when the partner of the opening bidder has been unable to drum up a response. Bidding in this situation is known as balancing or protective bidding.

For example, consider the following problem. You hear a one diamond opening on your left followed by two passes. What would you bid holding:

♠ K 7 4
♥ Q 8 3
♦ J 7 2
♣ A K 4 3

Believe it or not, nearly every good player would bid 1NT. In second seat the normal range for overcalling 1NT is something like a decent 15 to a poor 18. The basic philosophy for this is that if the opener has a minimum but sound opening bid of, say, 13 HCP and you have 15 HCP, this leaves 12 HCP split between your LHO and partner. If those points are evenly split, your partner will have 6 HCP giving your side the majority so that, on average, 1NT will be a sensible contract.

In a similar way let's look at the argument in the fourth seat. Suppose once again that the opener has a minimum but sound opener of 13 points and you have 13 points. That leaves 14 split between your partner and your right-hand opponent. If they are divided evenly that would mean 7 points each.

But, you have already heard your right-hand opponent pass his partner's opening bid, which normally means that he has a maximum of about 5 points. That would leave your partner with 9 and your side would comfortably have the majority of the points.

If the basis of argument is altered to look at the average strength of the hand held by each player, the same conclusion would apply. On average the opening bidder might have 14 or 15 points but, as his partner figures to only have 2 or 3, that leaves your side with the majority of the points.

Accordingly, it should be clear that you need rather less to bid 1NT with some safety in the fourth seat than you do in the second chair. Indeed this argument is so well-known that most good tournament players play a 1NT overcall in fourth chair to be approximately a weak no trump, about 12-14 HCP, though in practice many play a slightly wider range, perhaps 11-14 or even 11-15 HCP.

An alternative argument is that if partner holds a balanced hand of up to about 14 HCP, he would have been unable to make any sensible bid in second seat. Accordingly, when the opening bid is passed around to us, and we hold 11 HCP or more, it is quite possible that our side actually has enough strength to make a game in which case passing out one diamond, which may drift one or two down, is likely to be poor compensation. Hence, the idea of "protecting" our partner in the balancing seat.

Apart from a variation in strength, there is one other major difference between overcalling 1NT in second seat and bidding 1NT in the protective position. In second seat, you would really expect the 1NT bidder to have at least one stopper in the opener's suit, but it is not necessary when balancing. The reason for this is simply that you are hoping that partner, who was not able to bid on the first round, will come up with the goods. After all, you would be much better off with KQx in the opener's suit in dummy rather than in your own hand. Consider, two possible layouts:

(a)

```
                 K Q 5
  A J 10 7 4                  8 2
                 9 6 3
```

(b)

```
                    9 6 3
    A J 10 7 4                    8 2
                    K Q 5
```

In (a) you have two certain stoppers in opener's suit, but in (b) opener leads the jack and if you win the trick you will have to make sure that RHO never gets the lead to return his partner's suit.

So, in the balancing seat do not worry about your holding in opener's suit; if you have a balanced hand in the required range (11-15) just bid 1NT.

The corollary to this is that the strength required for most other actions is altered similarly. For example, if you hold a strong no trump, say 16-18 HCP, in the balancing seat, your plan of campaign should be to double first and then rebid in no trumps at minimum level. With slightly more than that, say 19 or 20, you can bid 2NT directly since there is little point in playing the Unusual 2NT convention in the balancing seat.

This idea extends way beyond no trump bidding. In the protective seat the minimum for a takeout double should be about 3 points less than in the second seat; say 8 or 9 points with a singleton in their suit. Therefore, if you double and then bid a suit, you are showing a good hand but you may be about 3 points weaker than you would be in second seat. For example, in Chapter Eight we decided that with:

```
    ♠ A K Q 7 5
    ♥ 9 7 2
    ♦ 7
    ♣ A K J 4
```

you would double an opening bid of one diamond, planning to bid your spades next. In the balancing chair, you could sensibly double the opening one diamond bid and bid your spades next holding a weaker hand like:

```
    ♠ A Q J 7 5
    ♥ 9 7 2
    ♦ 7
    ♣ A K 4 2
```

Similarly, if you would make a jump overcall in second seat with a decent six card suit and, say, 15 HCP, then in fourth seat you can make the same jump overcall with a decent six card suit and about 12 HCP.

Of course, if you can make a bid in the protective position with about 3 points less than you would have in second seat, your partner must bear this in mind when he comes to responding. In fact, the situation is as if the player in the balancing position has borrowed a king from his partner. The partner of the balancing player should always try to remember that his partner has already bid one of his kings.

Now, test yourself out on the following quiz:

QUIZ 23

Once again it is Neither Side Vulnerable and you hear 1♦ opened on your left. Both partner and your RHO decide to pass so it is you to bid looking at the following hands. Now decide what you are going to bid in each case.

1. ♠ J 7 4
   ♥ K 9 8
   ♦ Q 7
   ♣ K Q 10 4 3

2. ♠ K J 4
   ♥ Q 8 3
   ♦ A 7 2
   ♣ A K Q 4

3. ♠ K J 4 2
   ♥ A 10 5
   ♦ 7 2
   ♣ J 8 7 2

4. ♠ K J 7 2
   ♥ 7 3
   ♦ 8 4 2
   ♣ A J 6 2

5. ♠ 7 2
   ♥ Q 7 2
   ♦ K 10 7 5
   ♣ A 8 5 3

6. ♠ A Q 10 8 7 2
   ♥ 7 5
   ♦ 6 2
   ♣ A J 4

You hear 1♦ opened on your left. Both partner and your RHO decide to pass so it is you to bid looking at the following hands. Now decide what you are going to bid in each case.

1. ♠ J 7 4
    ♥ K 9 8
    ♦ Q 7
    ♣ K Q 10 4 3

Recommended Bid: 1NT

Admittedly you have a decent five card club suit, so you could balance with two clubs, but it is much more descriptive to bid 1NT. After all, you do have a balanced hand in the specified range. Furthermore, your diamond holding should be particularly persuasive for you to bid no trumps before your partner. Every time he plays in no trumps, the opening lead will go straight through your diamond holding, but if you play the hand the opening lead will come around to your queen.

2. ♠ K J 4
    ♥ Q 8 3
    ♦ A 7 2
    ♣ A K Q 4

Recommended Bid: 2NT

If the overcall of 1NT in fourth seat is limited to about 11-15 HCP, what is done with stronger balanced hands? With hands in the range of about 16-18 it is usual to double first and then bid no trumps at minimum level. With an even stronger hand, of say 19-20 HCP as shown in this example, you can bid 2NT right away and, if you are fortunate enough to be dealt even more than that, you can double first and then jump in no trumps.

One other point to notice is that in second seat an immediate jump to 2NT is usually used as the Unusual 2NT, showing at least 5-5 in the two lowest unbid suits. A large part of the reason for using this bid is to find a fit in one of those two suits, so that you can obstruct your opponents bidding or find a cheap sacrifice against their game level contract. Neither of these considerations bears much weight in fourth seat when your RHO has already illustrated the inability to respond to his partner's opening bid. Consequently, it is preferable to use the 2NT overcall as a natural bid in the balancing seat.

3. ♠ K J 4 2
    ♥ A 10 5
    ♦ 7 2
    ♣ J 8 7 2

Recommended Bid: Double

While you would not normally consider bidding in second seat, when the bidding is passed round to you in the fourth position you have a reasonable expectation that this hand belongs to you. That being the case you want to make the bid that describes your hand best. If you added a king to the strength of your hand you would just about have enough to make a takeout double in second seat, so double now and get over the message that you are short in your opponents' suit and have some support for the other three suits.

4. ♠ K J 7 2
    ♥ 7 3
    ♦ 8 4 2
    ♣ A J 6 2

Recommended Bid: 1♠

This time you would still like to bid since there is a reasonable expectation that it is your hand, even though it looks unlikely that you have a game on your way. However, you do not have the right shape to make a takeout double, so your best shot is to bid your decent four-card spade suit. Just about the worst that your partner can do to you is to jump all the way to 3NT, but to do that he will need a hand with two diamond stoppers and just a bit short of enough to have overcalled 1NT on the first round. Suppose he has something like:

    ♠ 8 5
    ♥ A Q J 2
    ♦ K J 3
    ♣ K Q 7 2

In normal circumstances you would think that 3NT is a very ambitious contract with only 23 HCP and no long suit, but in this case you already know that the majority of the opposition's points are likely to be in the opener's hand, so there must be a fair chance that the opener holds both the ace and queen of diamonds and the king of hearts. In that case your partner should be able to come to three heart tricks, with the aid of two finesses, two diamond tricks and four clubs, without any problem.

5. ♠ 7 2
    ♥ Q 7 2
    ♦ K 10 7 5
    ♣ A 8 5 3

Recommended Bid: Pass

While you have 9 HCP on this hand, too, you should not even consider bidding because, if partner had anything in the region of opening bid values with shortage in diamonds, he would already have taken some action. Alternatively, if he actually has some length in diamonds then it figures that your opponents are not playing in anything like their best spot. All too often players have protected with hands of this type, only to find their opponents bidding and making four spades when they could have left them floundering in 1♦.

6. ♠ A Q 10 8 7 2
    ♥ 7 5
    ♦ 6 2
    ♣ A J 4

Recommended Bid: 2♠

Quite clearly in fourth seat there is little point in employing weak jump overcalls which are principally used in second seat as a obstructive weapon. Here all the evidence indicates that your side has the majority of the points, so it is sensible to use a jump overcall as purely constructive.

This having been said, if you continue the philosophy of borrowing a king from your partner, then this hand would be the equivalent of a full-blooded strong jump overcall, so bid two spades.

Use a jump overcall in a suit in fourth seat to show a sound opening bid with a six card suit. With much more than this you would have to double first and then bid your suit.

QUIZ 24

You hear 1♦ opened on your right, you pass, LHO passes and your partner doubles. The opening bidder passes and it is your turn to bid holding:

1. ♠ Q 7 2
   ♥ Q 8 4
   ♦ K J 7
   ♣ A 9 4 2

2. ♠ A Q 7 2
   ♥ K 5
   ♦ 7 5 2
   ♣ Q 9 8 4

3. ♠ A Q 7 2
   ♥ K 5
   ♦ 7 5 2
   ♣ 9 8 7 2

You hear 1♦ opened on your right, you pass, LHO passes and your partner doubles. The opening bidder passes and it is your turn to bid holding:

1. ♠ Q 7 2
   ♥ Q 8 4
   ♦ K J 7
   ♣ A 9 4 2

Recommended Bid: 1NT

Don't crucify your partner for having the courage to protect you. Remember he has already "borrowed" three of your points. With 9 HCP facing an immediate takeout double you wouldn't dream of jumping to 2NT, so show the same restraint here. Settle for 1NT which you should be able to make opposite partner's 8 or 9 points. Remember if partner has upward of 13 HCPs he should bid again since he has much more than a minimum for a protective double.

2. ♠ A Q 7 2
   ♥ K 5
   ♦ 7 5 2
   ♣ Q 9 8 4

Recommended Bid: 2♠

Facing a second seat takeout double, this hand is good enough to drive to game, normally in spades. However in this situation partner has already bid 3 of your points so if you deduct 3 from your actual total of 11, you will see that you have just enough to jump to two spades, invitational.

3. ♠ A Q 7 2
   ♥ K 5
   ♦ 7 5 2
   ♣ 9 8 7 2

Recommended Bid: 1♠

Yes, facing a second seat takeout double, you would jump to two spades to show your 8-10 HCP with four card support for spades. However, remember now that partner can double in fourth seat with a lot less. To illustrate the point, what would you bid facing a second seat takeout double if you didn't have that king of hearts? That's right, just one spade.

QUIZ 25

This time look at the four example hands and decide what you would bid responsively in the following sequences:

(a)	1♥	1♠	Pass	?
(b)	1♥	Pass	Pass	1♠
	Pass	?		

Your hand is:

1. ♠ J 7 2
   ♥ A 5 4 2
   ♦ 7 5
   ♣ Q J 5 2

2. ♠ A J 7
   ♥ 6 4 2
   ♦ Q 10 4
   ♣ A 9 6 4

3. ♠ A J 7
   ♥ 6 4 2
   ♦ Q 10 4
   ♣ A Q 6 4

4. ♠ A 7
   ♥ K 9 2
   ♦ Q J 4 2
   ♣ K 6 4 2

ANSWERS TO QUIZ 25

This time what you would bid in two different situations.

(a)	1♥	1♠	Pass	?
(b)	1♥	Pass	Pass	1♠
	Pass	?		

1. ♠ J 7 2
   ♥ A 5 4 2
   ♦ 7 5
   ♣ Q J 5 2

Recommended Bids: (a) 2♠ (b) Pass

Facing the direct overcall, you have a full weight raise to two spades, three card support and a smattering of cards. Facing a protective double you still have three-card support but with three points transferred to your partner you really have a very weak hand. Remember as well that, facing the direct overcall, your bid has much more pre-emptive value than after your partner has balanced and the opening bidder has passed.

2. ♠ A J 7
   ♥ 6 4 2
   ♦ Q 10 4
   ♣ A 9 6 4

Recommended Bids: (a) 2♥ (b) 2♠

Facing the direct overcall, you have a very strong raise to two spades, comfortably strong enough to employ the Unassuming cuebid discussed in Chapter 10. Take away three points and you would have a comfortable raise to two spades, nothing more.

3. ♠ A J 7
   ♥ 6 4 2
   ♦ Q 10 4
   ♣ A Q 6 4

Recommended Bids: (a) 2♥ (then 3♠) (b) 2♥

Facing the direct overcall, you have a very good hand and would like to be in game unless partner is totally minimum for the overcall; so you start off with the Unassuming cuebid and when partner just bids two spades raise to three, a very strong invitation. Take away 3 points or so and you just have a very good raise to two spades, so facing a balancing overcall you should content yourself with just making the Unassuming cuebid.

4. ♠ A 7
    ♥ K 9 2
    ♦ Q J 4 2
    ♣ K 6 4 2

Recommended Bids: (a) 2NT (b) 1NT

Facing an opening bid you would have enough to drive to game but, remember, even a direct overcall can be made on three or four points less than an opening bid so 2NT is quite enough. Certainly, with opening bid values the overcaller should raise to game.

Facing a protective or balancing one spade overcall, you should be even more cautious, so 1NT is quite enough.

To summarize, when a one level suit opening is passed around to you in the balancing seat, you should bid as if you were in the direct overcalling seat with 3 points more. So, for example, in broad terms, a 1NT overcall in second seat is strong whereas the 1NT overcall in fourth is weak.

When responding to partner's protective bid always bear in mind that partner has already bid 3 of your points.

12 Chapter

Dealing With Pre-Empts

Suppose that the hand on your right opens three diamonds, what would you bid with the following hand?

♠ 7 5
♥ K 8 4 2
♦ A Q
♣ K Q J 4 2

This hand has much better playing strength than defensive strength. Playing in 3NT opposite three small clubs, for example, you will make four club tricks providing clubs break 3-2. In defense, however, you can only expect to take one trick. Meanwhile, if clubs break 4-1 you can make three tricks in the suit playing the hand while you will probably not make any defending.

Of course, that is not the only consideration. There is little point in playing the hand if you expect to concede a large penalty, but on the expected diamond lead this hand will make six tricks facing a Yarborough. Give partner a suitable 8 point hand, like one with both major suit aces, then you have excellent prospects of making 3NT, so you should bid it.

The key to coping with opening pre-emptive bids success-fully is to make sensible assumptions about the likely strength of your partner's hand and to bid accordingly.

In the example above, let's give the opening bidder a sensible hand, say:

♠ Q 8 4
♥ 9 3
♦ K J 10 9 8 7 2
♣ 5

6 HCP in the opener's hand plus 15 in yours leaves 19 HCP between the remaining two hands. On average your partner will have 8 or 9 HCP— on a bad day less, on a good day more.

Of course, there are no guarantees of success, but surely you will not succeed unless you take risks. Therefore, as a working rule, I would suggest that you base your initial action over a three level opening on the assumption that

your partner actually has about 7 HCP.

What would you bid, for example, after a three diamond opening holding:

♠ 7 5
♥ A Q J 7 5 3
♦ 4
♣ A K 4 2

While this hand might only have 14 HCP, it has substantial playing value. Obviously something like ♥K 10 x and a doubleton club would be enough to make game a fair shot and it is absurd to think that partner will have any chance of choosing to raise three hearts to four hearts with such minimal values. Indeed, as already suggested, in this situation you should be assuming that partner has about 7 HCP anyway, so take the pressure off and bid what you think you can make, four hearts.

By the same token, if the player taking action over a pre-emptive opening is going to assume that his partner has about 7 points anyway, then, in deciding how to respond to an overcall of a pre-empt, you should make allowances for the fact that partner has already bid seven of your points.

For example, suppose that you hear an opening three diamond bid on your left and you hear partner overcall three spades, what would you bid with the following hands:

(a)   ♠ Q 7 2
      ♥ A 7 5 4
      ♦ 7 2
      ♣ J 10 8 7

(b)   ♠ Q 7 2
      ♥ A K 5 4
      ♦ 7 2
      ♣ J 10 8 7

(c)   ♠ K 7 4 2
      ♥ A 7 5 4 2
      ♦ 7 3 2
      ♣ 7

While hand (a) has adequate trump support, you have no more than expected. Of course, when partner bid three spades there was no guarantee that you had anything a hand as good as you actually have, but your partner would have played you for some values initially, so pass and hope to make a plus score.

Hand (b) is substantially better, in effect you have one more trick than partner could sensibly play you for, so you should risk raising to four spades.

Hand (c) is even more clear cut. Admittedly you only have 7 HCP, but you have good working cards, and the fourth trump combined with a side suit singleton makes your hand worth at least two more tricks than average. Once again, raise to four spades.

Weak Two Bids

While there are a number of specific defenses designed to cope with natural weak opening bids at the two level, the consensus is that it makes sense to treat opening weak two bids as if they were one level bids as far as possible.

Therefore, if your RHO opens a weak two spades showing something like 5-9 HCP and a six-card spade suit, double should be for takeout and both 2NT and 3NT should be natural along with bids of three clubs, three diamonds, or three hearts. A useful addition to this is that jumps to four of a minor can sensibly be used to show that minor and the other major leaving the immediate cuebid (in this case three spades) available to ask for a stopper in the opponents' suit.

This is all fine, but the real problem comes not in the choice of initial action but in the cramping of space for the responder. Consider, for example, the following pair of hands:

(a)	♠ 7 5 3	(b)	♠ 7 5 3
	♥ 6 4		♥ A 4
	♦ J 5 2		♦ J 5 2
	♣ Q 8 7 5 3		♣ K Q 8 7 5

Facing a takeout double of one spade, you would happily respond two clubs on (a) and jump to 3♣ on (b).

Facing a takeout double of two spades, if you have to bid three clubs with hand (a) you would want to bid four clubs with hand (b), but, unfortunately, this will take you past the possible destination of 3NT.

So, what is to be done? A neat solution to this problem has recently become popular. In responding to a takeout double of a weak two, use 2NT as an artificial negative limited, say, to a maximum of 7 points. Then, with hand (a) you would respond 2NT as a negative and with hand (b) you can safely bid three clubs, constructive but not forcing.

Since the negative does not promise a stopper in the opponents suit it would be normal for the takeout doubler to remove the double to a suit at the three level and, unless he has an exceptional hand, you would expect him to bid three clubs. With hand (a) you would be happy to pass, but with a

five card diamond suit, instead of clubs, you would convert to three diamonds.

Multi-Colored 2♦

The multi-colored 2♦, which originated in England and is often played in tournaments in the United States, poses slightly different problems for defenders. In this method, an opening bid of two diamonds includes a number of possibilities: a weak two bid in either major, a strong 2NT opener type, and either a strong two bid in either minor or a very strong three-suited hand.

The first and most important rule of defending against it is that the strong hands have a much lower frequency than the weak hands, so if one of your opponents opens a Multi, you should assume that he actually has a weak two bid in either major until it is proved otherwise. In practical terms, this means that you should lean in favor of getting into the bidding in any case of doubt.

While there are any number of different defenses available to counter the Multi, it is important that you can get into the auction quickly to find a fit in the "other" major if one exists. In my view, it is essential to be able to overcall immediately in either major suit to show at least five cards in the suit and near opening values. In addition, in order to be able to find a 4-4 fit it is important to be able to make a takeout double of their suit at a suitably low level.

Perhaps the most dangerous position that arises occasionally when your opponents open a Multi is that the hand facing the two diamond opening gets to respond two spades. This usually means that if opener has spades, two spades will be high enough, but if opener has hearts he should choose between three and four hearts. In the final of the Gold Cup in the early seventies I was faced with the sequence:

Opener	Me	LHO	Partner
2♦	Pass	2♠	Pass
4♥	?		

Holding a balanced 13 point hand with four spades, I felt that there was little I could do. Unfortunately, when the auction reverted to my partner, he felt the same way and we found that we had allowed our opponents to steal the contract in four hearts undoubled when we had a 4-4- spade fit and a combined 26 HCP.

It was at this stage that I decided that it was essential to be able to double a two spade bid in this situation to show some spades and, as a result, I came up with the following defensive suggestion:

In both second and fourth seats, keep all immediate suit bids as natural. Then, a double can be used as a takeout of hearts or a good hand and 2NT can be used as a takeout of spades. The 2NT bid should always be shape suitable. In other words, it should always promise a hand with relative shortage in spades whereas the double can be more flexible. For example:

(a) ♠ A Q 5 4 (b) ♠ 6 5 (c) ♠ K J 5
♥ 6 5 ♥ A Q 5 4 ♥ A J 5
♦ K J 6 5 ♦ K J 6 5 ♦ A K 6 5
♣ A 5 4 ♣ A 5 4 ♣ Q 7 5

In second seat, 2♦ is opened on your right, you double with hands (a) and (c) and bid 2NT on (b). Of course, with hand (c) you would plan to bid the appropriate number of no trumps on the next round.

In fourth seat, after either 2♦-Pass-2♥ or 2♦-Pass-2♠, once again, you double with either hand (a) or hand (c) and bid 2NT with hand (b).

Overall, once you have got used to the idea, this seems to deal with the most dangerous situations and, since the same method is used on both sides of the table, it is quite easy to remember the convention.

QUIZ 26

RHO opens 3♦, what would you bid with the following hands?

1. ♠ K 7 5 2
   ♥ Q J 7 2
   ♦ 4
   ♣ A J 5 3

2. ♠ 5
   ♥ K Q 10 4 2
   ♦ 7 5 3
   ♣ A Q 6 2

3. ♠ K 7 2
   ♥ A Q 6 3
   ♦ K 4 3
   ♣ K Q 5

4. ♠ K 7 2
   ♥ Q 6 4 3
   ♦ K 4 3
   ♣ K Q 5

5. ♠ K Q 10 4 2
   ♥ A Q J 4 2
   ♦ 4
   ♣ 5 3

6. ♠ K 7 2
   ♥ 6 3
   ♦ K 4
   ♣ A Q J 10 6 5

RHO opens 3♦, what would you bid with the following hands?

1. ♠ K 7 5 2
   ♥ Q J 7 2
   ♦ 4
   ♣ A J 5 3

Recommended Bid: Double

Since you have the right shape and close to an opening bid, it is clear that you should double with this hand. It is a fundamental principle of defending against almost any specialized bid that the hand with shape should strain to take action, almost independent of strength. For example, if you don't bid, what would you expect your partner to bid in fourth seat with:

♠ A Q 8 4
♥ K 8 3
♦ 8 7 5
♣ K 10 6

Surely he is going to pass, yet 4♠ is laydown if spades are 3-2 and still has fair chances if spades are 4-1.

2. ♠ 5
   ♥ K Q 10 4 2
   ♦ 7 5 3
   ♣ A Q 6 2

Recommended Bid: 3♥

No one would hesitate to bid one heart over one diamond, so you should have no hesitation bidding three hearts over three diamonds. Partner should expect you to have bid a substantial portion of his values already.

3. ♠ K 7 2
   ♥ A Q 6 3
   ♦ K 4 3
   ♣ K Q 5

Recommended Bid: 3NT

With 17 high card points and a diamond stopper, it is difficult to avoid trying 3NT on this hand, especially since you expect partner to have 7 or 8 points anyway. However, I still prefer the bid on the hand with which this chapter began, where we had offensive strength and much less defensive strength than we have here.

4. ♠ K 7 2
   ♥ Q 6 4 3
   ♦ K 4 3
   ♣ K Q 5

Recommended Bid: Pass

Admittedly, you have an opening bid, but with no source of tricks neither a takeout double nor 3NT should have much appeal. After all, if you give partner a fairly nondescript 7 or 8 count, say:

♠ A 8 5 4
♥ K 7 2
♦ J 5
♣ 10 8 7 6

you are unlikely to make more than about five tricks playing in 3NT.

5. ♠ K Q 10 4 2
♥ A Q J 4 2
♦ 4
♣ 5 3

Recommended Bid: 4♦

Without the aid of the cuebid, this kind of hand can be a nightmare. If you overcall three spades, you find that partner passes holding a singleton spade and four hearts headed by the king. If you try three hearts partner puts his hand down, including four spades to the ace and a singleton heart. Alternatively, if you double first you are left with an insuperable problem when partner bids any number of clubs.

It is better to risk overbidding the hand a little to insure that your side ends up playing in the right strain. Your cuebid should be taken to show a two-suiter and initially partner should assume that you have both majors. A sequence like:

| 3 ♦ | 4 ♦ | Pass | 4 ♥ |
| Pass | 4 ♠ | | |

should suggest a good two-suiter with spades and clubs. Without the strength of hand required, partner might have bid three spades and if he had hearts he would have passed responder's preference to four hearts.

6. ♠ K 7 2
♥ 6 3
♦ K 4
♣ A Q J 10 6 5

Recommended Bid: 3NT

Of course, with a decent six card suit, you could settle for just bidding four clubs, but 3NT has a much larger upside. Find partner with a few right cards and you will collect the game bonus for your enterprise.

Quiz 27

You hear a three diamond opening on your left, partner doubles for takeout, and the next hand passes. What would you bid with the following hands?

1. ♠ A Q 6 3
♥ K 9 6 4
♦ 7 5 3
♣ Q 6

2. ♠ 10 6 3
♥ A 5
♦ K 5
♣ K 9 8 7 4 2

3. ♠ Q 9 3
♥ A 5 3
♦ Q 10 5 2
♣ K 6 4

You hear a three diamond opening on your left, partner doubles for takeout, and the next hand passes. What would you bid with the following hands?

1. ♠ A Q 6 3
   ♥ K 9 6 4
   ♦ 7 5 3
   ♣ Q 6

Recommended Bid: 4♦

With near opening bid values you have enough to play in game. Four diamonds is a more flexible call than guessing to bid either four hearts or four spades. While you expect your partner to have both majors there is no point in punishing him for making a double on a 3-4-2-4 shape. By cuebidding in your opponent's suit you are offering a choice of games and, once again, partner should assume initially that you have both majors.

2. ♠ 10 6 3
   ♥ A 5
   ♦ K 5
   ♣ K 9 8 7 4 2

Recommended Bid: 3NT

This is an interesting deal. There is no guarantee that you will make game but the fifth and sixth clubs add enormous playing strength to your hand. Facing a classic minimum for the double like:

> ♠ A 7 5 2
> ♥ K 8 7 6
> ♦ 6
> ♣ A 10 6 5

you would like to play 3NT, whereas opposite:

> ♠ A K 7 5
> ♥ K 8 7 6 2
> ♦ 6
> ♣ Q J 5

you would much prefer to play in five clubs. Unfortunately, there is no legitimate way of finding out what your partner's club holding actually is, so you have to make a decision. My view would be to take a gamble on the club suit running rather than hoping that you didn't have three quick losers in five clubs.

3. ♠ Q 9 3
   ♥ A 5 3
   ♦ Q 10 5 2
   ♣ K 6 4

Recommended Bid: Pass

Of course, 3NT is a live possibility, but you have no definite source of tricks and if partner only produces a 4-4-1-4 11 or 12 count, you will be way short of values. Go for the sure-looking plus. After all, if you can make 3NT without your partner having a long suit to run, how many tricks do you think your opponents will make in three diamonds doubled?

To summarize, when choosing your initial action over a weak three-level opening assume that your partner has about 7 HCP, and then bid to the limit on that assumption.

Strain to bid when you have shortage in the opponents' suit.

In responding to your partner's actions after a pre-emptive opening by your opponents, remember that your partner should already have bid 7 of your HCP.

Handling
Other Openings

DEFENDING AGAINST 1 NT

Tactical considerations play a major part in defending against a 1NT opening. When playing team or rubber bridge it takes several small gains to make up for one large penalty when you choose the wrong moment to compete.

At pairs, however, you will find that most of the time your opponents will do fairly well if they are left to play in 1NT especially with Neither Side Vulnerable. For example, if you collect +50 or +100 in defense you are likely to be able to make +110 or better if you can locate your best fit. Similarly, if your opponents are going to record +90 in 1NT then you can afford to go one down in any contract.

Of course, if you want to bid after your opponents open 1NT you do have to come in at the two-level. If you have a six card suit it is usuallly safe to bid it. If you overcall on a mediocre five card suit, however, the risk of running into a penalty double is considerably increased. On the other hand, if you can find something of a fit with your partner there is much less risk of being doubled. It is for this reason that a whole myriad of conventional defenses to 1NT openings have been developed. In most cases, the conventions are structured around the principle that it is important to be able to overcall naturally in a major suit, but much less important to be able to do so in a minor so that overcalls of both two clubs and two diamonds can easily be used conventionally.

I am not at all averse to playing an uncomplicated game. Indeed, on many occasions, I have enjoyed telling my opponents that when we overcall their 1NT opening we are using the BIYFLI (bid if you feel like it) convention. In reality, however, even if you are loath to subject your memory banks to too much pressure, I would strongly advise you to use a simple convention like Landy, that allows you to get into the action with a major two-suiter. This is important because overcalling in one of your suits only to find that you had an excellent fit in the other is particularly galling.

With a major-minor two-suiter, you may frequently get a reasonable score playing in the major, even if more tricks

are available in the minor. For example, making nine tricks with spades as trumps scores +140 at duplicate bridge; to beat this score playing in either clubs or diamonds you would have to make eleven tricks. The same consideration does not apply when the choice is between playing in hearts and spades. In other words, if you are going to play a conventional defense to 1NT, it is particularly important that it helps you to play in the best major suit fit.

Whatever conventional defense you choose, it is important that you work out some agreements as to how the bidding should continue thereafter. There are many possible conventional defenses to 1NT. Let us consider some of them, starting with Landy.

So far, all you know is that an overcall of two clubs shows both majors. How should you respond? The normal structure is:

Pass To play based on a long club suit in a weak hand.

2♦ Asks the overcaller to bid his longest or his best major. This is normally used by responder when he has equal length in the majors, but it can also be used as the first step in developing the auction.

2♥ To play.

2♠ To play.

2NT Natural, encouraging but not forcing.

3♣ In original Landy this was the forcing response and some players still play it that way. However, since you can develop a forcing auction by going through two diamonds, it is not unreasonable to play three clubs as natural, constructive, but not forcing.

3♦ Natural, encouraging, but not forcing.

3♥/3♠ Invitational.

While this tabulation might look slightly daunting, keep in mind that with the exception of the two diamond response all the responses are natural and non-forcing. The simplicity of the Landy convention has made it very popular.

Revised Landy adds the ability for the overcaller to show a hand with both minor suits:

2♣ shows both minors
2♦ shows both majors

There are, however, more comprehensive conventions which cover a greater variety of two-suited hands.

Brozel, a competitive system developed by New Jersey expert Bernard Zeller with Lucille Brown, uses a double over opponent's 1NT bid to show a one-suited hand. If partner prefers to play in the long suit, he bids two clubs which may be passed (if the long suit is clubs) or pulled to the real suit. Other hands are described as follows:

2♣ shows clubs and hearts
2♦ shows diamonds and hearts
2♥ shows hearts and spades
2♠ shows spades and a minor (partner bids 2 NT to ask for the minor
2NT shows clubs and diamonds
3♣, 3♦, 3♥ and 3♠ originally were used to show three-suited hands with a void or singleton in the bid suit, but are more frequently used today as natural suit bids.

For many years, Astro has been the convention of choice for many when competing against an opponent's 1NT opening bid. Invented by American experts Paul Allinger, Roger Stern, and Lawrence Rosler (and named by combining the first letters of their last names) Astro affords the opportunity to enter the bidding and find a fit with partner holding a two-suited hand and roughly 9 to 15 points.

2♣ shows hearts plus a minor and at least a five-four shape
2♦ shows spades and another suit, which could be hearts, and again at least 5-4 shape

With either bid, there is a "known major."

These are the responses to an Astro overcall of opponent's NT:

1. Pass shows at least six-card length in the minor suit bid and no game interest; a raise in the Astro bid would show a very good six-card suit and is invitational to game.

2. Two of the known major shows at least three cards in the suit and is not forcing.

3. Cheapest step (or relay) response, such as 2♦ over 2♣ and 2♥ over 2♦, denies three cards in the known major. The Astro bidder can pass if the relay is his second suit or bid his five-card suit which responder can pass with a doubleton. Responder can also bid 2NT over this to request Astro bidder's other suit, which obviously is a minor since he did not pass 2♥.

4. 2♠ over 2♣ or 3♣ over 2♦ shows a very long suit and no interest in the known major. This bid is, of course, not forcing.

5. 2 NT is the only forcing response to Astro and requires a near-opening hand. It shows interest in game and requests that partner bid his or her second suit.

6. Any jump bid is natural and invites to game, including a jump to three in the known major.

Landy, Astro and Brozel are sanctioned in all nearly all competitions and one of them should suit your taste. It is, however, worthwhile to mention that many experts play that all bids over opponent's NT opening are natural and show a six or seven card suit with appropriate strength. If your bids over 1NT are natural, 2NT would usually show at least 5-5 in the minor suits.

DEFENSES AGAINST STRONG ONE CLUB OPENINGS

As a general rule, strong club systems tend to be much more accurate than so-called natural systems. They are, however, much more susceptible to intervention. Accordingly, if your right-hand opponent opens with a Strong Club, your prime concern should be to interject some bid on the first round as often as possible.

Even if you have no intention of getting embroiled in learning any more conventions and wish to stick to natural methods, you should at least experiment by making very light overcalls. If you can find a partner with enough of a fit to raise the ante, you will soon find your opponents struggling. However, having said that, defending against a Strong Club with totally natural methods is like playing a full round of golf with just a putter. No matter how well you putt, you might regret having no other clubs in your bag.

Before we suggest any conventional defenses, the first club you should make sure is in your bag is the weak jump overcall. Obviously, when the hand on your right is advertising 16+ points, you are unlikely to have a hand worthy of a strong jump overcall and, even if you do, there is no need for you to act immediately. Indeed it is a basic tenet of defending against a Strong Club opening that you should interfere right away with weak hands and pass, planning to come in later, if you have a hand with genuine ambition.

Just like defending against 1NT, you are much more likely to find a fit if you adopt some sort of conventional defense where you can show two suits with one bid. Then, with any kind of fit your partner should attempt to jump the bidding as high as possible, to try to give the opponents a clue as to what it is best for them to do.

At the very least, you should consider assigning conventional meanings to bids that you are unlikely to use in a natural sense over a Strong Club—the most obvious being 1NT and Double. For example, it would be ridiculous to enter the auction with a strong no trump overcall when the hand on your right has already announced that it has at least 16 points. You and your partner are most unlikely to have game, so all you are doing is giving the partner of the opener an easy opportunity to double.

If you want to play a very simple defense, you would use a double to show the major suits and 1NT to show the minors. An equally easy system uses a bid of 2♣ to show the black suits and 2♦ to show the red suits.

A slightly more advanced defensive system uses the following bids over RHO's Strong Club:

Double of 1♣ shows clubs

Double of any other one level bid or of 2♣ (weak bids) are regular take-out doubles

2♣ shows both major suits, as would 2♦ over 1♦ (Michaels-type bids)

1NT shows the minors

All other bids are natural, and you should certainly incorporate a weak jump overcall into the plan.

Keep in mind that any of the two-suited bids will also tell the opponents exactly what you have. Furthermore, very experienced Strong Club players will have their own defenses in place to counteract interference and minimize their loss of bidding space.

It is also a good idea to pay careful attention to the vulnerability when deciding just how aggressively to butt into the auction.

QUIZ 28

Suppose that your right-hand opponent opens 1NT (say 12-14) with Neither Side Vulnerable, what would you bid on the following hands assuming that you have agreed to play Astro.

1. ♠ K J 6 5
   ♥ 6 5
   ♦ K Q 10 9 6 5
   ♣ 7

2. ♠ K 10 6 5 2
   ♥ K J 7 6
   ♦ 8 7 4
   ♣ 7

3. ♠ K J 7 5
   ♥ Q 7 6 5
   ♦ Q 7 5 4
   ♣ 8

4. ♠ K J 10 8 7 6
   ♥ Q 7 4 3
   ♦ A 5
   ♣ 7

5. ♠ 7
   ♥ K J 10 6 5
   ♦ Q 7 6
   ♣ A J 7 5

6. ♠ K Q 10 9 5
   ♥ A Q J 7 5 4
   ♦ 7 2
   ♣ -

Suppose that you right-hand opponent opens 1NT (say 12-14) with no one vulnerable, what would you bid on the following hands assuming that you have agreed to play Astro.

1. ♠ K J 6 5
   ♥ 6 5
   ♦ 7
   ♣ K Q 10 9 6 5

Recommended Bid: 2♦

A good hand for Astro since it allows you to get both of your suits into the action. If partner bids two hearts, denying three spades, you will bid your club suit, but if he bids two spades you should probably let him play there.

2. ♠ K 10 6 5 2
   ♥ K J 7 6
   ♦ 8 7 4
   ♣ 7

Recommended Bid: 2♦

In my view this is about the minimum you might have for a two diamond overcall. It is worthy of note that in general terms 5-4-3-1 shape hands tend to play very well so the playing strength of this hand is much higher than its point count, especially if you find that you have a reasonable fit.

Your initial overcall shows spades and any other suit. If partner responds two hearts, denying three spades, you will pass. It will be a very bad day if you find that partner has only one spade and two hearts! Admittedly, two spades could easily be a better contract, but at least if partner does not have a spade fit the play in two hearts might not be so bad.

3. ♠ K J 7 5
   ♥ K 7 6 5
   ♦ J 7 5 4
   ♣ 8

Recommended Bid: Pass

While you have one point more than in the previous example you have considerably less playing stength. Furthermore, you are very poorly placed if partner doesn't have a fit in your suits. If you must bid on this type of hand you would be better off using a convention that showed both majors immediately, but even then it would be my view that coming in is a more dubious proposition.

4. ♠ K J 10 8 7 6
   ♥ Q 7 4 3
   ♦ A 5
   ♣ 7

Recommended Bid: 2♠

Even though you have both majors it is usually best to play in your good six card major. Of course, occasionally you will find that partner has four or even five card support for your second suit and not enough to bid over two spades, but that will be far outweighed by the frequency of you playing in a 4-3 heart fit if you start by bidding two diamonds.

5. ♠ K Q 10 9 5
 ♥ A Q J 7 5 4
 ♦ 7 2
 ♣ -

Recommended Bid 2♦

Start off by showing your spade suit. If partner bids two hearts denying three spades you are strong enough to try three hearts. Partner should recognize that you must have a very good hand since with less you would have passed two hearts.

If partner responds two spades, my own view would be to bid game. And since partner would tend to pass a jump to four hearts with three spades and two hearts my feeling is that you should just bid four spades. Notice that just raising to the three level would be something of an underbid since the game has reasonable play if partner has ♠J 8 4 and a bust.

Quiz 29

Now suppose that you hear a weak 1NT (12-14) opened on your left, and partner overcalls two clubs, Astro, showing hearts and a minor suit. What would you bid on each of the following:

1. ♠ A Q 4
 ♥ Q 8 7
 ♦ 9 5 3
 ♣ Q 8 6 4

2. ♠ A 4 3
 ♥ A 9 8 4
 ♦ 9 3
 ♣ Q 8 6 4

3. ♠ A 4 3
 ♥ A Q 4
 ♦ A 5 3
 ♣ Q 8 6 4

4. ♠ Q 4 3
 ♥ 8 4
 ♦ K 5 3 2
 ♣ Q 8 6 4

5. ♠ A Q 4
 ♥ 8 4
 ♦ A 5 3 2
 ♣ Q 8 6 4

6. ♠ Q 4
 ♥ 8 4
 ♦ J 5 3
 ♣ Q 10 9 8 6 4

Suppose that you hear a weak 1NT (12-14) opened on your left, and partner overcalls two clubs, Astro, showing hearts and a minor suit. What would you bid on each of the following:

1. ♠ A Q 4
 ♥ Q 8 7
 ♦ 9 5 3
 ♣ Q 8 6 4

Recommended Bid: 2♥

Yes, you have ten high card points and three card heart support, but if partner is going to overcall on a shapely 5-4-3-1 seven or eight count you should have no ambition of playing any higher than two hearts. Indeed it is well worth considering how you might fare facing:

(a) ♠ 8 7 4 and (b) ♠ 7
 ♥ K J 7 6 ♥ K J 10 6 5
 ♦ K 10 6 5 2 ♦ Q 7 6
 ♣ 7 ♣ A J 7 5

Playing in a 4-3 fit facing hand (a), you will need a lot of luck to make two hearts, but one down and maybe even two down will score well as they should be making at least 1NT. Facing hand (b) you will fare much better making nine or ten tricks if the cards lie well, but in practice you would expect your opponents to be bidding spades.

2. ♠ A 4 3
 ♥ A 9 8 4
 ♦ 9 3
 ♣ Q 8 6 4

Recommended Bid: 3♥

With four card support for partner's known major suit you can afford to be a little bit more aggressive. After all, if partner has a very weak hand there is a fair chance that your opponents will be able to get back into the auction and find a fit if you just bid two hearts. Notice here that even facing hand (a) you have a reasonably good chance of making nine tricks. With hand (b) it is quite clear that partner will accept your game try, but you should be able to make four hearts if either the hearts or the clubs behave well.

3. ♠ A 4 3
 ♥ A Q 4
 ♦ A 5 3
 ♣ Q 8 6 4

Recommended Bid: 2NT

With three aces in your 16 point hand and good three card heart support you should expect to have some play for game. The 2NT bid asks partner to bid his second suit and you will choose the contract on the next round. If partner bids three diamonds, showing a five card diamond suit, I would be tempted to have a shot at 3NT and, if he bids three clubs to show a five card club suit, five clubs looks to be best.

Note that with example hand (b) he will bid three clubs, you will raise to four hearts and that contract is likely to make with an overtrick. Admittedly six clubs is a fair contract played by your hand, but that would be a most unlikely contract to reach.

4. ♠ Q 4 3
   ♥ 8 4
   ♦ K 5 4 2
   ♣ Q 8 6 4

Recommended Bid: 2♦

This is an artificial response which denies three hearts. Partner may pass if his second suit is diamonds. With hand (a) the overcaller will pass and you will be delighted. With hand (b) overcaller will rebid two hearts and knowing that he must now have five hearts you will be content to pass.

5. ♠ A Q 4
   ♥ 8 4
   ♦ A 5 4 2
   ♣ Q 8 6 4

Recommended Bid: 2♦

Although you have a much better hand with some prospects of making game, my own view is that you should still bid two diamonds, rather than the more aggressive alternative of 2NT. The advantage should be clear facing hand (a) when partner will bid three diamonds. You might raise this to four diamonds but even this will be something of a struggle facing example (a).

I would reserve the immediate response of 2NT for a hand of opening bid strength with a source of tricks of my own. Something like:

   ♠ K 10 6
   ♥ 8 4
   ♦ K Q J 9 4
   ♣ A J 4

If partner rebids two hearts as he will with hand (b) my view is that you would do best to pass. However if you do continue with 2NT then partner should bid his minor suit.

6. ♠ Q 4
   ♥ 8 4
   ♦ J 5 4
   ♣ Q 10 9 8 6 4

Recommended Bid: Pass

Unless partner has a rock crusher, prospects in anything other than two clubs are pretty remote. Pass while the going is good.

To summarize this chapter:

Defending Against 1NT

Even if you want to keep your methods as simple as possible, it is well worth taking aboard a conventional bid to show both majors.

Whatever defensive methods you employ, the hand with the appropriate shape must be allowed to take action without his partner punishing him for his enterprise. In other words, there is little you can sensibly do with a flat 12 point hand if the opponents bid 1NT, but your partner might be able to contest the part score with a distributional 8 or 9 count.

Defending Against Strong Club Openings

If you are playing against competent opponents playing strong club methods, there is a fair chance that they will be able to bid the spots off the front of the cards. Accordingly, it is worth taking the occasional risk to disrupt their bidding by making a light overcall.

Chapter 14

Your Opponent's Overcall

Let's start by concentrating on just one question. Your partner opens one diamond, you hear a one spade overcall on your right and it is your turn to bid, looking at:

♠ 7 5 3
♥ J 10 9 5
♦ K 5
♣ K 10 5 3

Well, what would you bid?

In traditional methods you are totally stuck. Double would be for penalties. 1NT would be fine except that you have nothing remotely resembling a spade stopper, and, since introducing a new suit at the two level is forcing for one round, both two clubs and two hearts overstate your values and suggest longer suits. So, unless you are brave enough to support your partner on a doubleton, you are left with little alternative but to pass.

Now this doesn't have to be the end of the world. If your left-hand opponent is kind enough to pass there is nothing to stop your partner bidding again. He should be aware that that you might have some values but not have anything you can bid. So far, so good — certainly, if your side has enough to make a game you are likely to get another chance to show your values. However, all too often your opponents are not so kind and if LHO raises to two spades (or even three spades) your side may be struggling.

Of course, this problem only arises when the overcall has cut out your natural response, in this case one heart. These difficulties were so great that the "Sputnik" double was invented in the 1950s.

A Sputnik double of one spade in this situation meant that you would have responded one heart had you been allowed to and that you were not suitable to bid two hearts now. In fact the Sputnik double is a specific example of a broader category of doubles known as "negative" doubles. Positive doubles are for penalties so negative doubles are for takeout.

While the modern vogue is for doubles to be for takeout in nearly all overcall situations, even the most staid experts have come around to the view that using the double for takeout is particularly appropriate after you open one of a minor and the opponents overcall one spade. Most would agree with employing negative doubles over jump overcalls too.

Once again, consider what you would bid after partner opens one diamond and there is a one spade overcall. This time your hand is:

♠ 7 5
♥ A 7 5
♦ K Q 7 5
♣ A 7 5 2

In traditional methods, the immediate cuebid just showed a game-going hand with no obvious alternative bid. However, the advent of the negative double has significantly reduced the number of hand types that might need to use the cuebid.

If you had five hearts or five clubs and a good hand you would bid that suit. With a balanced hand with four hearts you would double. With a good spade holding you would bid no trumps. This leaves two principal hand types. First, a good hand with four card support for partner, like the example hand shown above, and, alternatively, a balanced hand without four hearts.

For example, what are you going to bid with:

(a) ♠ 7 5 2
♥ A 5 2
♦ Q 6 5
♣ Q 7 5 3

or somewhat stronger:

(b) ♠ 7 5 2
♥ A J 2
♦ K J 6
♣ K J 5 3

On (a), whatever the meaning of the cuebid, the hand is not strong enough to contemplate using it. If the double of one spade is supposed to show four hearts then that is out and, although you have eight high card points, the hand is not really strong enough to bid two clubs. That leaves you with the only sensible choice: two diamonds.

Hand (b) is a different kettle of fish. The hand is far too good just to raise to two diamonds. So what is to be done? The old-fashioned approach to this hand would be to cuebid two spades just to show a game-going hand and, while this is a perfectly playable style, I believe that you are better off starting with a double. While it is true that initially partner will think that you have four hearts, you have a strong enough hand to correct that impression later.

For example, if the auction develops:

1♦	1♠	Dble	3♠
4♥	Pass	?	

I, for one, would expect my partner to have five diamonds and four hearts and, while four hearts might prove to be an awkward spot especially if partner is forced to ruff spades, five or even six diamonds looks to be sensible.

For example, the layout might be:

♠ 9 8	♠ 7 5 2
♥ K 8 6 4	♥ A J 2
♦ A Q 10 8 7	♦ K J 6
♣ A Q	♣ K J 5 3

Playing in four hearts, West ruffs the third round of spades and his best chance is to take the heart finesse. If the finesse is successful, he can cash the ace of trumps, a couple of clubs and then play on diamonds. When either opponent ruffs, declarer should be able to cope with any return. If the heart finesse loses, declarer should still prevail if hearts are 3-3.

So four hearts has reasonable play, but that doesn't compare with five diamonds which is laydown on anything but the most bizarre distribution.

So, rather than adopt the rule that the first round double after a one of a minor opening and a spade overcall guarantees four hearts, I would recommend the slightly more flexible rule that the double shows either four hearts or a hand that is strong enough to control the auction.

The real bonus of this is that the immediate cuebid can be reserved for good hands with genuine diamond support. So two spades is my recommended bid with the example hand:

- ♠ 7 5
- ♥ A 7 5
- ♦ K Q 7 5
- ♣ A 7 5 2

An interesting highly modern treatment has been built on the back of this arrangement. If you are a traditionalist you would assume that the cuebid has to show a game-going hand, but quite a number of leading tournament players have adopted the style that the cuebid should show a good raise to the three-level or better. This allows the immediate jump to three diamonds to be made on a weaker hand. While some

players like to treat this immediate jump as entirely pre-emptive I would suggest that you play it as a good raise to two diamonds. Thus after a one diamond opening from partner and a one spade overcall, you would raise immediately to three diamonds holding something like:

- ♠ 7 5 3
- ♥ 7 5
- ♦ K Q 6 5
- ♣ K 8 6 5

whereas you would cuebid two spades with:

- ♠ 7 5 3
- ♥ 7 5
- ♦ A Q 6 5
- ♣ A 10 5 4

QUIZ 30

Assuming that you have elected to play negative doubles, what would you bid after 1♦-1♠ on each of the following hands:

1. ♠ A Q 3
   ♥ 8 6 5
   ♦ K 8 6
   ♣ Q 10 5 2

2. ♠ 7 5 3
   ♥ Q 9 6 5
   ♦ Q 7 5
   ♣ A 7 5

3. ♠ 7 5 3
   ♥ A Q 10 5
   ♦ K 5
   ♣ A 7 5 2

4. ♠ 6 4
   ♥ Q 10 8 7 5 3
   ♦ 5
   ♣ K 7 5 2

5. ♠ 6 4
   ♥ K J 10 5 4
   ♦ A 8 6
   ♣ K 5 2

6. ♠ K J 10 5 4
   ♥ A 5 4
   ♦ 8 6
   ♣ Q 7 5

7. ♠ 6
   ♥ K 7 5 2
   ♦ A 5
   ♣ K Q 10 5 3 2

1. ♠ A Q 3
   ♥ 8 6 5
   ♦ K 8 6
   ♣ Q 10 5 2

Recommended Bid: 2NT

No problem with this hand. You have the values for a limit bid of 2NT with a double-stopper in the opponent's suit, so why not bid naturally?

2. ♠ 7 5 3
   ♥ Q 9 6 5
   ♦ Q 7 5
   ♣ A 7 5

Recommended Bid: Double

The classic conditions to make a negative double. You would have bid one heart had the bothersome opponent on your right not bid one spade. So double now to show four hearts and enough to compete at the two level.

3. ♠ 7 5 3
   ♥ A Q 10 5
   ♦ K 5
   ♣ A 7 5 2

Recommended Bid: Double

Once again you have four hearts in a balanced hand so start off with a negative (takeout) double since you should be able to get over your additional strength later. For example, if partner just rebids two diamonds you can continue with a cuebid of two spades to show that you have a good hand and ask him to bid something sensible like 2NT with a spade stopper.

4. ♠ 6 4
   ♥ Q 10 8 7 5 3
   ♦ 5
   ♣ K 7 5 2

Recommended Bid: Double

Clearly this hand is not strong enough to bid two hearts (forcing for one round) so double first and, for example, if partner rebids his diamonds you can then bid two hearts. Two further points are worth making.

(i) The additional length in hearts makes up for any shortage in strength. My own view is that you should not be too hidebound by points in this situation, but with a flat hand, say, 3-4-3-3 you might expect a minimum of about 8 HCP for the negative double. Alter the hand shape to 2-4-3-4 and I would certainly double on a decent 6 HCP hand (note that I would not ascribe any value to minor honors in spades).

(ii) Some players prefer the alternative style of immediate suit bids being non-forcing. Surely, it would be convenient to be able to bid two hearts (non-forcing) on this hand. However, the more traditional view that an immediate change of suit should be forcing for one round is preferable, for two reasons:

(a) Since it is what most players usually play, it is much easier for most players to remember.

(b) In high level auctions, you are much better placed having introduced your suit early when you have a good hand, rather than having to introduce a new suit at the five level, for example. Of course, there are good hands for both methods but, on balance, I believe that the stronger hands are the most important.

5. ♠ 6 4
   ♥ K J 10 5 4
   ♦ A 8 6
   ♣ K 5 2

Recommended Bid: 2♥

Two hearts, which is natural and forcing for one round, describes the hand well, a five card heart suit and at least ten high card points. It may also be worth noting that with a good six-card heart suit I would stretch to bid two hearts immediately knowing that I could rebid hearts on the next round, non-forcing, to show an invitational strength hand. A good example might be:

          ♠ 4
          ♥ K Q 10 8 7 5
          ♦ 5 3
          ♣ K 7 5 2

6. ♠ K J 10 5 4
   ♥ A 5 4
   ♦ 8 6
   ♣ Q 7 5

Recommended Bid: Pass

You would like to double one spade for penalties but unfortunately you have just agreed to play double for takeout. So, what is to be done? The answer is that you should pass in the expectation that your partner will have a shortage in spades and that he will be able to double for takeout when the bidding reverts to him. Indeed, your expectation should be that opener will double the overcall on every hand with shortage in spades that he might have been prepared to stand a penalty double from you.

Note that your pass is not absolutely forcing and so is not strictly alertable. If your partner happened to have three or four spades, there is absolutely no compulsion for him to bid again. It is only when he is short in the opponents' suit when you expect him to take further action.

7. ♠ 6
   ♥ K 7 5 2
   ♦ A 5
   ♣ K Q 10 5 3 2

Recommended Bid: 2♣

I do not believe that it is imperative to double on the first round just because you have four hearts, especially when you have a more descriptive bid available. Here, with a good club suit and good controls including a singleton spade, it makes much more sense to start off with two clubs. If your left-hand opponent bids two spades and partner passes you can still bid three hearts on the next round. If your left-hand opponent is more aggressive and tries three spades then, if that is passed back to you, you can either bid four hearts or double for takeout.

QUIZ 31

Most tournament players play negative doubles in all simple overcall positions, so this time your partner opens one club and RHO bids one heart. What would you bid holding the following hands?

1. ♠ 7 5
   ♥ 9 7 4 2
   ♦ A 10 6 5
   ♣ K 9 4

2. ♠ Q 7
   ♥ K J 4
   ♦ Q 10 7 5 4
   ♣ J 9 4

3. ♠ J 9 6 5
   ♥ 7 5 2
   ♦ K Q 7 5
   ♣ Q 6

4. ♠ K Q 10 5
   ♥ 7 5 2
   ♦ K 7 5
   ♣ 7 5 2

Now what would you bid on the following hands after partner opens 1♣ and RHO overcalls 1♦?

5. ♠ Q 8 5
   ♥ K J 9 5
   ♦ J 7 5 3
   ♣ 8 5

6. ♠ Q 8 5 4
   ♥ K J 9 5
   ♦ J 7 5
   ♣ 8 5

7. ♠ 9 7 5
   ♥ 7 5
   ♦ 10 7 5
   ♣ A Q 7 5 2

8. ♠ Q 7 5
   ♥ K 5
   ♦ 7 5 3
   ♣ A 10 6 4 3

Most tournament players play negative doubles in all simple overcall positions, so this time your partner opens one club and RHO bids one heart. What would you bid holding the following hands?

1. ♠ 7 5
   ♥ 9 7 4 2
   ♦ A 10 6 5
   ♣ K 9 4

Recommended Bid: 2♣

With only two spades a negative double would be risky, so support your partner. While many players really like to have four card support before supporting partner, the rough and tumble of the competitive auction frequently makes it necessary to support with only three trumps. If you pass on this round partner may be fixed when LHO supports hearts, and even if you are able to support clubs later he will not believe that you have as much as three card support with two key cards.

2. ♠ Q 7
   ♥ K J 4
   ♦ Q 10 7 5 4
   ♣ J 9 4

Recommended Bid: 1NT

Point count fanatics might want to bid two diamonds, but this bid leaves you very badly placed if partner is forced to rebid three clubs. Do you pass and hope that 3NT is not a spread, or do you gamble 3NT and hope that partner has the right cards to make it? No, the crucial factor in this hand is the potential double heart stopper. Get that message across by bidding 1NT immediately.

3. ♠ J 9 6 5
   ♥ 7 5 2
   ♦ K Q 7 5
   ♣ Q 6

Recommended Bid: Double

Before the advent of negative doubles, everybody would have bid one spade on this hand. No disaster, but not very comfortable when LHO bids two hearts and partner competes with two spades on some 3-2-3-5 distribution. So most modern tournament players would make a negative double.

4. ♠ K Q 10 5
   ♥ 7 5 2
   ♦ K 7 5
   ♣ 7 5 2

Recommended Bid: 1♠

There is a popular school of thought that suggests that if the double of one heart shows four spades, then a free bid of one spade should guarantee five cards in the suit. Of course, that is a very playable style; however, I prefer to bid one spade on any hand where I am happy for partner to support me with only three cards in the suit. In practice the minimum quality suit on which I would venture one spade would be Q10xx.

The advantage of this style is that it is no longer necessary to retain the restriction that the negative double should promise four spades. For example, what would you bid with this hand:

♠ K J 4
♥ 8 4 2
♦ Q 8 5 4 2
♣ Q 7

If you play that one spade shows five spades then your choice is between passing, which could leave partner stranded when LHO raises hearts, and making a negative double when partner will expect you to have four spades.

If you adopt my recommended more free-wheeling style there is a lot less risk if you make a takeout double with this hand. Partner will be expecting your spades to be no better than Q9xx, so, if he bids spades, he will probably not be too disappointed with your actual holding.

Now what would you bid on the following hands after partner opens 1♣ and RHO overcalls 1♦?

5.   ♠ Q 8 5
    ♥ K J 9 5
    ♦ J 7 5 3
    ♣ 8 5

Recommended Bid: 1♥

No need to do anything special. Partner will expect you to have both majors if you produce a negative double.

6.   ♠ Q 8 5 4
    ♥ K J 9 5
    ♦ J 7 5
    ♣ 8 5

Recommended Bid: Double

This is the ideal hand for a negative double. If you bid one heart partner will have no idea that you have four spades as well. That will not matter if your LHO passes, but if LHO ups the ante by raising to either two or three diamonds, you may have great difficulty locating a spade fit.

7.   ♠ 9 7 5
    ♥ 7 5
    ♦ 10 7 5
    ♣ A Q 7 5 2

Recommended Bid: 3♣

Early in this chapter I recommended that you adopt the style where an immediate cuebid shows a high card raise to three of partner's suit, so that the immediate jump can be reserved for sound raises to the two level with four card support. Here is an excellent example: admittedly you only have six high card points, but they are all in partner's suit and the fifth club is a bonus.

8.   ♠ Q 7 5
    ♥ K 5
    ♦ 7 5 3
    ♣ A 10 6 4 3

Recommended Bid: 2♥

Here is a full-blooded raise to 3♣, so cuebid 2♥.

QUIZ 32

This time your partner opens 1♥ and RHO ventures 2♣. What do you bid with each of the following hands:

1.   ♠ K Q 10 9 6
    ♥ Q 5
    ♦ A 6 3
    ♣ 9 5 4

2.   ♠ K J 10 4
    ♥ Q 5
    ♦ K 9 6 5
    ♣ 9 5 4

3.   ♠ K 7 5
    ♥ Q 7 4
    ♦ A Q 10 6 5
    ♣ 9 5

4.   ♠ 9 7 5
    ♥ Q 7 4
    ♦ A Q 10 6 5
    ♣ 9 5

Now suppose that you open 1♥, LHO overcalls 2♣, partner doubles and RHO passes. What do you do with the following hands:

5.   ♠ A Q 6 5
    ♥ A K J 10 2
    ♦ 10 4
    ♣ 6 2

6.   ♠ A Q 6
    ♥ A K J 10 2
    ♦ K 10 4
    ♣ 9 5

Finally, suppose that you open 1♠, and LHO overcalls 2♣ which is passed back to you, what would you bid holding:

7.   ♠ K J 7 5 3
    ♥ A Q 5
    ♦ K 5 4
    ♣ 9 5

8.   ♠ K J 7 5 3
    ♥ K 3
    ♦ A Q 5
    ♣ 9 5 4

This time your partner opens 1♥ and RHO ventures 2♣. What do you bid with each of the following hands:

1. ♠ K Q 10 9 6
   ♥ Q 5
   ♦ A 6 3
   ♣ 9 5 4

Recommended Bid: 2♠

No problem here. You have a decent five card spade suit and the values to push up to 2NT or the three level, so bid a natural two spades which most players play as forcing for just one round. This means that if, for example, partner bids just three hearts you are allowed to pass.

2. ♠ K J 10 4
   ♥ Q 5
   ♦ K 9 6 5
   ♣ 9 5 4

Recommended Bid: Double

You have the values to compete at the two level with good holdings in both unbid suits, so a negative double is just right.

3. ♠ K 7 5
   ♥ Q 7 4
   ♦ A Q 10 6 5
   ♣ 9 5

Recommended Bid: 2♦

Once again you have a good hand. In particular here you would bid two diamonds this time and support hearts on the next round to show three card support and near game-going values.

4. ♠ 9 7 5
   ♥ Q 7 4
   ♦ A Q 10 6 5
   ♣ 9 5

Recommended Bid: 2♥

With the same shape as in the previous example, but a weaker hand, it would be a mistake to bid two diamonds this time. The problem is that if you bid two diamonds initially, you are not strong enough to volunteer heart support later. Accordingly, it is much better to limit the hand and show the heart support right away by bidding two hearts, bearing in mind that you might get the opportunity to show the diamonds later. For example, compare these two sequences:

(a) 1♥   2♣   2♥   3♣
    Pass Pass 3♦

(b) 1♥   2♣   2♦   3♣
    Pass Pass 3♥

In (a) responder has limited his hand by bidding just two hearts. When he later bids diamonds he is clearly contesting the part score and suggesting diamonds as an alternative spot to play.

In (b) responder's two diamond bid is unlimited so you would expect at least invitational values for his three heart bid on the second round.

Now suppose that you open 1♥, LHO overcalls 2♣, partner doubles and RHO passes. What do you do with the following hands:

5. ♠ A Q 6 5
   ♥ A K J 10 2
   ♦ 10 4
   ♣ 6 2

Recommended Bid: 3♠

You would expect partner to have 8 or 9 points and four spades for his negative double. Since you have a better than minimum opener with four card spade support and nothing wasted you should jump to 3♠ to invite game.

For example, your partner might hold either of the following hands:

(a) ♠ K 9 8 2
    ♥ Q 6
    ♦ A 7 5 2
    ♣ 8 5 3

If you just bid two spades there is no reason for partner to bid again, yet you will find that most of the time you will make 11 tricks. On the other hand, if you bid three spades, partner should accept the invitation, not because he has a surfeit of points but because the values he does have are very well placed — reasonable trumps, a useful card in your suit and an outside ace. You can see the power of that card. You won't lose a single diamond trick unless the trumps break 4-1.

On the other hand:

(b) ♠ J 9 8 2
    ♥ 6 3
    ♦ K Q J 5
    ♣ Q 5 3

With this hand, it should be clear that partner will reject your invitation to game. He has poor trumps, nothing useful in hearts and no outside ace, though he still has enough to double two clubs initially. While you would prefer to be allowed to play two spades, three spades should make most of the time losing two clubs, one diamond and one spade.

6. ♠ A Q 6
   ♥ A K J 10 2
   ♦ K 10 4
   ♣ 9 5

Recommended Bid: 3♣

You have a good hand and facing 8 or 9 points, suggested by the two level negative double, you would expect to make a game; the problem is which one is best. Give partner the good news that you expect your side to make game and ask him to describe his hand further by cuebidding the opponents' suit. Your basic plan is to raise three hearts to four hearts, raise three spades to four spades or pass if partner bids 3NT.

Finally, suppose that you open 1♠, LHO overcalls 2♣ which is passed back to you, what would you bid holding:

7. ♠ K J 7 5 3
    ♥ A Q 5
    ♦ K 5 4
    ♣ 9 5

Recommended Bid: Double

With relative shortage in clubs and a sound opening bid your suspicion is that partner might have a penalty double of two clubs. While your double is for takeout, partner will clearly pass if he would have doubled two clubs for penalties were he not playing negative doubles.

If partner does shift to either red suit you can be certain that he has a weak hand since he did not bid over two clubs immediately. At least you have reasonable support for whichever suit he bids.

8. ♠ K J 7 5 3
    ♥ K 3
    ♦ A Q 5
    ♣ 9 5 4

Recommended Bid: Pass

While you are under considerable pressure as opener to reopen in case partner has a penalty double, you should not do so when you have reasonable length in the opponents' suit. The more cards you have in the suit the less likely it is that partner has a penalty double, and even if he does there is no guarantee that if they are doubled the opponents won't manage to run out to a better spot. No, the chances are that partner does not have a penalty double and therefore has a weak hand. Pass now while the going is good.

Now, suppose it is Neither Side Vulnerable, your partner opens 1♦ and RHO jumps to 2♠, what would you do next on each of the following:

1. ♠ 7 5
    ♥ A 5
    ♦ 8 6 3
    ♣ A K Q 8 5 3

2. ♠ A 5 2
    ♥ Q J 7 5
    ♦ 8 5
    ♣ K 8 5 4

3. ♠ 7 5 3
    ♥ A 7 3
    ♦ K 6 2
    ♣ K J 8 5

4. ♠ 7 5
    ♥ K J 10 6 5
    ♦ A 7 2
    ♣ Q 8 3

5. ♠ 7 5 2
    ♥ A 6
    ♦ Q 10 5 4
    ♣ Q 9 6 5

6. ♠ 7 5
    ♥ A 8 4
    ♦ K Q 7 2
    ♣ K 8 4 2

7. ♠ Q 10 7 6
    ♥ A 7 3
    ♦ A 5
    ♣ 8 5 3 2

8. ♠ Q 10 4
    ♥ K 6 2
    ♦ 6 5
    ♣ K Q 10 6 3

Answers to Quiz 33

Your partner opens 1♦ at Neither Side Vulnerable and RHO jumps to 2♠, what would you do next on each of the following:

1.   ♠ 7 5
    ♥ A 5
    ♦ 8 6 3
    ♣ A K Q 8 5 3

Recommended Bid: 3♣

An easy example to start with. Three clubs is natural and game-forcing and if partner just rebids his diamonds you have a comfortable cuebid of three spades on the next round to see if he can bid 3NT.

2.   ♠ A 5 2
    ♥ Q J 7 5
    ♦ 8 5
    ♣ K 8 5 4

Recommended Bid: Double

You have the ideal shape for a negative double and just about the values to compete to the three level. If partner bids three clubs, three diamonds or even three hearts you should pass. If he bids three spades you have an obvious 3NT bid.

3.   ♠ 7 5 3
    ♥ A 7 3
    ♦ K 6 2
    ♣ K J 8 5

Recommended Bid: Double

This time you have a point extra, but a less suitable shape. There is still no sensible alternative to double. If partner bids three hearts you have to plan to go back to four diamonds. If partner bids four hearts you can still go back to five diamonds.

4.   ♠ 7 5
    ♥ K J 10 6 5
    ♦ A 7 2
    ♣ Q 8 3

Recommended Bid: Double

You are not strong enough to force to game by bidding three hearts, so make a negative double and hope to be able to bid your hearts next time.

5.   ♠ 7 5 2
    ♥ A 6
    ♦ Q 10 5 4
    ♣ Q 9 6 5

Recommended Bid: 3♦

Admittedly, if the opponents hadn't got into the auction, you would not really consider raising a one diamond opener to three diamonds, but in competitive situations you should always push a little when you have an undisclosed fit. While it is true that, if you pass, partner may well take a further action, the real problem will arise if the next hand raises the ante by bidding either three or four spades. So, show your support while you can.

6.   ♠ 7 5
    ♥ A 8 4
    ♦ K Q 7 2
    ♣ K 8 4 2

Recommended Bid: 3♠

While there is no guarantee that you will make game, especially if partner has two small spades as well, you have the values to bid at least four diamonds. Of course, if partner can bid 3NT you will be content to play there. Because you have not made a negative double partner should expect you to have good diamond support.

7.   ♠ Q 10 7 6
    ♥ A 7 3
    ♦ A 5
    ♣ 8 5 3 2

Recommended Bid: Pass

While you have just about the values to bid 2NT in the hope that partner can raise to 3NT, your pristine defensive values should suggest that if you can make 3NT then your opponents are unlikely to fare too well in two spades. Pass in the expectation that your partner will double for takeout with short spades which you will be able to convert to a penalty double by passing next time round.

8.   ♠ Q 10 4
    ♥ K 6 2
    ♦ 6 5
    ♣ K Q 10 6 3

Recommended Bid: 2NT

In the last example you had four obvious defensive tricks against a two spade contract. This time you can only be confident of making about two tricks so it would be very dangerous to risk passing a reopening double from partner. On the other hand, your long club suit suggests that you might be able to make a fair few tricks in a no trump contract. You are not strong enough to drive to game by bidding three clubs, but you have enough to bid 2NT, invitational.

When you open the bidding in a suit and the opponents overcall in a suit, a double is most usefully used as negative, for takeout. This should apply unless the overcall is at game level or at the maximum level decided between you and your partner. Many people play that a double is negative only through a three spade bid by opponent.

At the one-level, a free bid immediately after the overcall should show a suit of decent quality. The recommended minimum standard is Q10xx. Unless you have already passed, a new suit bid by you should be treated as forcing for one round.

If partner opens with one of a minor and RHO overcalls one spade, then a double should guarantee either four hearts or a hand strong enough to control the auction.

If partner opens one of a minor and RHO overcalls one heart, then a double should deny holding a spade suit as good as Q10xx.

It is also recommended that a cuebid in the opponents' suit should show a high card raise to the three level in partner's suit so that an immediate jump to three of partner's suit can be used to show a good raise to the two level with four card support.

Opponents Make a Takeout Double

With your side vulnerable, your partner deals and opens one diamond and your RHO doubles. How would you plan your campaign holding:

♠ 5
♥ K Q 10 5 3
♦ A 10 5
♣ K J 5 3

In traditional methods, a change of suit would be natural and non-forcing, so, with sufficient values to force to game, a bid of one heart would be unacceptable here. That leaves two possibilities.

First, a jump to two hearts which could easily be interpreted as showing a better heart suit or just a better hand. Alternatively redouble, which is used to show a hand of 9+ points and to create a forcing situation.

In the absence of other methods, my experience is that most players would think that the choice of redouble is totally clear cut. In a sense, they are right. Quite clearly, this hand qualifies as being strong enough for a redouble. However, in my view, redoubling on this type of hand shows a lack of foresight about the problems that are likely to lay ahead.

Suppose, for example, that you choose to redouble and your LHO jumps to two spades. With nothing to say, your partner passes and, rather inconveniently, your RHO raises to three spades. Well, what are you going to do?

The limitations of traditional methods are now exposed. Your expectation is that you can make game, but you have absolutely no idea where to play.

At the prevailing vulnerability, it is unlikely that you will want to sit back and try to take a penalty from three spades doubled. Especially since it is all too likely that your RHO is short in diamonds and your LHO is short in either hearts or clubs, which suggests that they might make a lot of tricks without having many high card values. No, you will want to play in game, whether 3NT, four hearts or five of a minor. Indeed, if partner has a couple of aces and a decent diamond suit, a small slam is not beyond the realms of possibility.

Let's look at a few possibilities. For example, partner might have any of the following:

(a)   ♠ K 4 2
      ♥ 6 4
      ♦ K Q J 4
      ♣ A Q 4 2

With this hand both 3NT and five clubs look like a good places to play, but five diamonds and four hearts both look distinctly shaky.

(b)   ♠ Q 4
      ♥ 6 4
      ♦ K Q 8 6 4 2
      ♣ A Q 2

Now five diamonds is the only sensible place to play.

(c)   ♠ Q J
      ♥ J 6 4
      ♦ K Q 6 4 2
      ♣ A Q 4

While five diamonds is clearly playable, you would much prefer to play in four hearts since there is a strong possibility that in five diamonds you will either have a natural diamond loser or you will suffer a heart ruff. Indeed improve partner's hand slightly to:

(d)   ♠ 6 4
      ♥ A J 4
      ♦ K Q J 4 2
      ♣ A 4 2

and you would want to play in a small slam in either red suit.

Having decided that there are so many possibilities that you haven't got a clue what to do and having complete faith in your basic partnership arrangements, you might decide to pass rather than commit yourself at this stage. After all, partner should know that your redouble has created a forcing situation and so he will be forced to dredge out some sort of bid which might help you with your decision. After all, if he rebids four clubs you have a comfortable raise to game. Indeed you might even cuebid four spades on the way and if he rebids four diamonds you can raise to game in the same way. However, whatever you do at this stage you will be conscious that you have not really started to describe your hand and, if the final contract is somewhat less than optimum, it will be your responsibility.

If I were forced to play traditional methods in this situation, I would much prefer to start off with a jump to two hearts. While there is some risk that my partner would think I had a better hand, at least I could formulate a sensible overall plan for describing my hand.

I would be able to introduce my clubs on the second round of the auction and then support diamonds. At least then partner should know that there was a likelihood of my delivering a game-going hand with hearts, clubs and some diamond support, with a strong likelihood of my holding shortage in spades, enough information for him to make an informed decision.

Now, I could improve my chances of success by discussing with my partner that a jump shift after a takeout double might be slightly shaded. However, I would undoubtedly prefer to scrap traditional methods and play that a change of suit (after partner has opened and RHO has made a takeout double) should be natural and forcing rather than natural and non-forcing. At least if I can bid one heart on the first round, I have begun to describe the key features of my hand, and, just as important, I have a much better chance of establishing whether partner has any degree of heart support at a much earlier stage.

Once again let's suppose that the opponents are equally awkward so that the auction proceeds:

Partner	RHO	You	LHO
1♦	Dble	1♥	2♠
Pass	3♠	?	

Now, while you might be missing out on 3NT on rare occasions, you can bid four clubs, planning to pass a simple preference to 4♥ or raise a diamond rebid to game showing additional strength on the way by cuebidding four spades.

Just in case all this is not sufficient to convince you to take up the modern style of bidding after the opponents make a takeout double, consider what you would do with a slightly weaker hand of the same shape and you might not be convinced that game would be such an excellent proposition, say:

♠ 5
♥ K Q 10 5 3
♦ A 10 5
♣ J 7 5 3

After:

Partner	RHO	You	LHO
1♦	Dble	Rdbl	2♠
Pass	3♠	?	

You are in a terrible mess. If you pass the buck to partner whatever he bids you will have no real idea of what to do next and, while you could be totally laydown for four hearts, emerging from the thickets at this stage with a bid of four hearts could easily lead to you conceding a substantial penalty.

However, after:

Partner	RHO	You	LHO
1♦	Dble	1♥	2♠
Pass	3♠	?	

you are much better placed. Indeed, you have a choice of three plausible actions.

(1) You could plan to bid the hand in similar fashion to the previous example. You bid four clubs, pass a conversion to four hearts and probably guess to raise a four diamond rebid to game. While this might work out well, you are likely to be getting a bit too high, especially if partner has some wasted values in spades.

(2) You could bid four diamonds. This has the merit of being non-forcing and, in reality, gives partner the option of passing, pressing on to five diamonds or putting you back to four hearts. My view is that this is a much more disciplined and better approach than (1) but not quite as flexible as the following suggestion:

(3) You could double. This should show extra values and be positively for takeout. Essentially, you are announcing the values to compete at the four level in whatever strain your partner cares to pick. A double in this position does not guarantee that you have a 1-5-3-4 shape. Certainly, you should also double with a 2-5-2-4 shape and enough values to bid at the four level or even a 2-5-3-3 shape. Obviously with three hearts your partner can bid four hearts and if partner bids either four clubs or four diamonds you can pass. The corollary of this is that if he has some undisclosed values he can jump to game in either minor himself.

Apart from all this, your delayed double allows your partner two additional, important choices. For example, with a long diamond suit and a spade stopper, he might well elect to play in 3NT. And with a balanced type hand with short hearts and good spades he may elect to settle for collecting a penalty from three spades doubled.

Now, try the following quiz:

At Both Sides Vulnerable, your partner opens one club and RHO makes a takeout double. What do you bid with the following hands:

1. ♠ 7 3
   ♥ Q 7 5 2
   ♦ J 7 5 3
   ♣ K 7 3

2. ♠ 7 3
   ♥ A 7 5 2
   ♦ K 4 2
   ♣ K J 7 3

3. ♠ 7 3
   ♥ 7 5 3
   ♦ K 7 5 3
   ♣ K J 7 3

4. ♠ K J 10 4
   ♥ Q 10 5 2
   ♦ A J 7 2
   ♣ 7

5. ♠ K J 5
   ♥ Q 7 3
   ♦ J 6 5 3
   ♣ J 7 3

6. ♠ K J 7
   ♥ Q 10 5
   ♦ A 10 7 3
   ♣ 7 5 3

7. ♠ 7 3
   ♥ K Q 10 7 5
   ♦ J 7 5 3
   ♣ Q 3

8. ♠ 7 3
   ♥ K Q 10 7 5
   ♦ J 5 3
   ♣ Q 7 5

At Both Sides Vulnerable, your partner opens one club and RHO makes a takeout double. What do you bid with the following hands:

1. ♠ 7 3
   ♥ Q 7 5 2
   ♦ J 7 5 3
   ♣ K 7 3

Recommended Bid: 2♣

If RHO had passed you would probably have responded in one of the red suits, according to taste. However, since your RHO has probably got length in both majors, there is little point in mentioning a poor four card suit at this stage. Much better to tell partner of your reasonable support for his suit so that he can judge better what to do on the next round and, meanwhile, you make it that much harder for your LHO who will have to bid at the two level if he wants to get into the action.

2. ♠ 7 3
   ♥ A 7 5 2
   ♦ K 4 2
   ♣ K J 7 3

Recommended Bid: 2NT

This hand clearly qualifies as a good high card raise to three clubs. In recent years it has become the norm to use the jump to 2NT after your RHO doubles to show a good raise to three in partner's suit, the corollary being that the direct jump to three in partner's suit can be used on a weaker hand. The basic philosophy is that with a hand that would have bid 2NT without the double, you should redouble, so the 2NT bid is not needed in its natural sense.

3. ♠ 7 3
   ♥ 7 5 3
   ♦ K 7 5 3
   ♣ K J 7 3

Recommended Bid: 3♣

This is the other side of the coin. Normally you should respond two clubs (not one diamond) so now with four card support and a fair raise to two you can afford to jump to three clubs. If this takes you too high, then rest assured that the opponents will be able to make a fair number of tricks in their best contract.

4. ♠ K J 10 4
   ♥ Q 10 5 2
   ♦ A J 7 2
   ♣ 7

Recommended Bid: Redouble

This is just about the ideal hand for an initial redouble — a shortage in partner's suit and good holdings elsewhere. Your redouble not only carries the message of 9+ points, but also a suggestion that you might be prepared to punish the opponents for straying into the auction. Suppose LHO bids one spade, then, if partner passes, he is showing sound opening bid values and you would not be totally averse to doubling one spade for penalties. If partner's opening is principally based on distributional values he should issue a warning by bidding in front of you.

5. ♠ K J 5
♥ Q 7 3
♦ J 7 5 3
♣ J 7 3

Recommended Bid: 1NT

You are not strong enough to redouble, but you have a fair smattering of values. Passing to await developments could prove to be very difficult if the opponents arrive in two of a major quickly. Avoid this problem by expressing your hand type and limiting your values by bidding 1NT showing a balanced hand of about 7-8.

6. ♠ K J 7
♥ Q 10 5
♦ A 10 7 3
♣ 7 5 3

Recommended Bid: Redouble

This time you have a better hand, comfortably enough to redouble. You plan to limit your hand on the next round by rebidding no trumps at minimum level.

7. ♠ 7 3
♥ K Q 10 5 3
♦ J 7 5 3
♣ Q 3

Recommended Bid: 1♥

This time you have a decent heart suit, so bid it.

8. ♠ 7 3
♥ K Q 10 7 5
♦ J 5 3
♣ Q 7 5

Recommended Bid: 2♥

Somewhat more controversial. In simple terms, once you have decided that a change of suit should be forcing for one round, the need for the traditional strong jump response diminishes. As a result, many players have agreed to play the jump to two of a suit as weak rather like weak two opening or a weak jump overcall. That is all very well, but hands where you happen to hold K Q J 10 6 5 in a suit implied by your RHO do not come along very often. So it seems sensible to consider an alternative.

In my view, it is much better to use the bid as a mini-fit-showing jump. I like to play that this shows a good five card suit plus at least three card support for partner. This has two principal advantages:

1. If partner has no fit for your suit he is quite likely to have extra length in own first bid suit. Thus your known, three-card support provides something of a safety net.

2. If partner does have some sort of fit for your suit, then he can judge to raise the level as high and as quickly as possible.

To summarize, when opponents make a take out double:

Strength	Recommended Action
5-bad 9	Bid a decent suit at the one-level, raise partner one level with three-card support, make a jump raise with four-card support or bid 1NT with scattered values and no real support for partner.
	With a decent five card suit and three card support for partner jump in your suit.
Good 9-11	With four card support bid 2NT to show a high card raise to three in partner's suit.
	With a good suit of your own, bid it.
	With no good suit and not four-card support, redouble.
12+	With four card support for partner, you can either bid a good suit of your own (forcing for one round) or you can show a balanced type by starting with 2NT and then bidding on if partner signs off at the three level or you can use your favorite methods for showing a raise to game be it via splinter bids or cuebids.
	Without four-card support, bid a good suit of your own or redouble.

At the European Championships

It is all very well discussing methods in abstract, but what really matters is what happens at the table. In this chapter, we have a look at eight deals from the 1995 European Championships which were played at Vilamoura in Portugal.

Let's start by watching some of the women at work:

Deal 1. Germany versus Great Britain

Both Sides Vulnerable. Dealer West.

```
              ♠ K
              ♥ Q 7 6 2
              ♦ 10 3 2
              ♣ Q 10 8 7 2
♠ J 9 7                        ♠ A Q 4 2
♥ J                            ♥ 10 9
♦ A J 9 7 6                    ♦ K Q 8 5 4
♣ A J 5 4                      ♣ 6 3
              ♠ 10 8 6 5 3
              ♥ A K 8 5 4 3
              ♦ -
              ♣ K 9
```

Open Room:

West	North	East	South
Davies	*Zenkel*	*Smith*	*von Arnim*
1♦	Pass	1♠	2♥
2♠	3♣	4♦	Pass
4♥	Pass	4♠	Pass
5♣	Pass	5♦	All Pass

Closed Room:

West	North	East	South
Moegel	*Handley*	*Caesar*	*Landy*
1♦	Pass	1♠	2♥
Dble	4♥	All Pass	

Superficially, the two auctions appear to have started identically, but Moegel's one diamond was Precision and therefore did not guarantee a diamond suit. Even still, Zenkel's three club effort, which was supposed to show both

clubs and hearts, left plenty of room for Smith to show both her diamond support and her strength, whereas Handley's jump to game left East with a decision to make at the five level.

As it turned out there was little to the play of either contract and Great Britain gained an impressive 15 IMPs.

When you have good support for partner, try to bid directly to the limit of the hand. This is especially true when one of the opponents has made an artificial bid which may conceal a number of alternatives.

Deal 2. Italy versus Sweden

Both Sides Vulnerable. Dealer East.

```
              ♠ 8 6 4
              ♥ J 9 7 2
              ♦ 6 5 2
              ♣ Q 7 4
♠ 7 2                          ♠ A 9
♥ 6 5 3                        ♥ K Q 10 4
♦ Q 8                          ♦ A 10 9 7 3
♣ 10 9 8 6 3 2                 ♣ K 5
              ♠ K Q J 10 5 3
              ♥ A 8
              ♦ K J 4
              ♣ A J
```

Open Room:

West	North	East	South
Rovera	*Midskog*	*Gianardi*	*Langstrom*
-	-	1♦	Dble
Pass	1♥	Pass	3NT
All Pass			

Closed Room:

West	North	East	South
Swanstrom	*Rosetta*	*Flodqvist*	*De Lucchi*
-	-	1♦	Dble
Pass	1♥	Pass	2♠
Pass	3♠	All Pass	

While three spades made easily enough, +140 did not compare favorably with +600 in the Open Room. Superficially, this looks like an excellent return for Langstrom's bold 3NT rebid.

However, it seems to me that the problem in the Open Room did not arise as a direct result of the strong two spade rebid. Indeed, North did well to dredge up a raise, but then South failed to take advantage. 3NT looks like the obvious continuation, offering a choice of games.

Deal 3. France versus Poland

North/South Vulnerable. Dealer South.

```
              ♠ 9 8 6 2
              ♥ 4
              ♦ Q J 10
              ♣ A Q 8 7 2
♠ A K 10 4                   ♠ Q J 5
♥ Q 3                        ♥ A 10 6
♦ 7 3                        ♦ A K 9 8 5 2
♣ K J 9 6 4                  ♣ 10
              ♠ 7 3
              ♥ K J 9 8 7 5 2
              ♦ 6 4
              ♣ 5 3
```

Open Room:

West	North	East	South
Saul	*Haras'z*	*Bessis*	*Janczewska*
-	-	-	Pass
1♣	Pass	1♦	2♥
Pass	Pass	Dble	Pass
2♠	Pass	3♦	All Pass

Closed Room:

West	North	East	South
Banasz'z	*Willard*	*Krogulska*	*Cronier*
-	-	-	2♥
Dble	Pass	3♥	Pass
4♣	Pass	4♦	Pass
4♠	Pass	5♦	Pass
Pass	Dble	5♠	Pass
Pass	Dble	5NT	Pass
Pass	Dble	All Pass	

With 27 high card points between them, good cover in all four suits and a good diamond suit, you would expect most East/West pairs to arrive in game, probably 3NT, but failing that either four spades or five diamonds both of which are likely to be made. So, while the actual action at the table yielded 10 IMPs to France, the eventual European champions, you might not be over-impressed by the bidding at either table. It all goes to show what the effect of pre-emptive bidding can be.

In the Open Room, South didn't make an opening pre-emptive bid, but her subsequent jump overcall still created mayhem in the French ranks. With a minimum opener, West left the question of further action to East and her double was clearly takeout oriented. When she followed with three diamonds on the next round there can be no doubt that she intended this as forcing since she had not rebid three diamonds on the previous round. However, obviously, her partner was not on the same wavelength.

While +130 may not seem to be a result designed to set the world on fire, it was quite sufficient for the French to gain 10 IMPs after the inelegant performance put up by the Poles in the other room. Certainly, Cronier's weak two bid found Banaszkiewicz with an awkward hand. Quite clearly the hand isn't ideal for a takeout double, but the club suit is really not good enough to bid at the three level and passing could lead to even greater problems on subsequent rounds. The next three rounds of bidding were really quite sensible. East's cuebid of three hearts was clearly a good starting point to show her strong hand and the next two rounds clarified her good diamond suit.

While five diamonds is not the best spot, it is clearly playable, and on the actual lie of the cards there is no defense to beat it. However, when North doubled, East ran and the resultant 5NT finished two down when declarer tried a long-shot to make it.

This hand serves to illustrate a number of points. Like it or not, pre-emptive openings and overcalls are popular because they make it much more difficult to bid the opposing hands accurately. No doubt, if North/South were not allowed to bid on this hand, both East/West pairs would have sailed into 3NT, but comparatively low-level interference created insuperable difficulties for two quality pairs. Furthermore, no doubt, if both pairs had discussed their methods in these types of auction previously neither accident would have happened. If such modest pre-emption can create such chaos in a European championship just imagine the effect in your local bridge club.

Then, consider:

Deal 4. Israel versus Germany

East/West Vulnerable. Dealer East.

```
              ♠ -
              ♥ A 8 3
              ♦ K Q 10 7 6 5 2
              ♣ Q 8 4
♠ K Q J 10 4 2               ♠ A 9 8 6
♥ K Q                        ♥ 7
♦ J                          ♦ 9 8 4
♣ 7 6 3 2                    ♣ A K J 9 5
              ♠ 7 5 3
              ♥ J 10 9 6 5 4 2
              ♦ A 3
              ♣ 10
```

Open Room:

West	North	East	South
Nehmert	*Saxon*	*Rauscheid*	*Dan*
-	-	1♣	2♥
Dble	4♥	Pass	Pass
4♠	5♥	6♠	All Pass

Closed Room:

West	North	East	South
Porat-Levit	*Caesar*	*Zur-Alba*	*Moegel*
-	-	1♣	2♦*
2♠	3♦	4♠	Pass
Pass	5♥	Pass	Pass
5♠	Pass	Pass	6♥
Dble	All Pass		

In the Open Room, North's non-descriptive leap to four hearts put East under some pressure, but I doubt whether this would have been as effective had West been able to bid a forcing two spades on the first round, which would have left East with an easy four spade rebid. As it was, West had to double first to create a forcing situation, which left East in the dark after the jump to four hearts. East found the obvious way to express her suitability later. However, an alternative approach which is popular among the leading tournament players might have been better.

If Rauscheid had passed five hearts back round to West and then pulled West's likely double out to five spades, this would have implied high suitability for a slam. This is an arrangement that most players would find useful: in a forcing pass situation, passing and then pulling the double is more encouraging than bidding immediately.

The jump to two diamonds in the Closed Room showed hearts, so, effectively, the auctions started the same way. Caesar showed her diamonds and then bid five hearts, which made it easy for Moegel to decide to save over five spades. A good solid result for the German North/South pair but it was still 5 IMPs away. If you are not that impressed with the German East/West result, just bear in mind that it is much easier looking at all four hands in a textbook and, just a few months later, this pair played a major role in winning the World Ladies Teams Championship for Germany.

Now for a look at some examples from the Open Championship:

Deal 5. Greece versus Ireland

East/West Vulnerable. Dealer South.

```
                ♠ A 8 3
                ♥ 10 4
                ♦ A Q 8 6
                ♣ A 10 6 2
♠ Q 7 4                      ♠ J 10 9 6 5 2
♥ 9 8                        ♥ A K Q 6
♦ J 9 7 4 2                  ♦ -
♣ K 9 7                      ♣ Q J 4
                ♠ K
                ♥ J 7 5 3 2
                ♦ K 10 5 3
                ♣ 8 5 3
```

Open Room:

West	North	East	South
Milne	*Kap'nidis*	*MacHale*	*Liarakos*
-	-	-	Pass
Pass	1♣	1♠	Dble
2♠	2NT	4♠	Pass
Pass	Dble	All Pass	

Closed Room:

West	North	East	South
Yialrakis	*Timlin*	*Michalap's*	*Walsh*
Pass	1♣	1♠	Dble
Pass	2♦	2♠	3♦
All Pass			

Milne's skimpy raise to two spades was the key factor in Ireland's 14 IMP gain. Notice that knowledge of three card support and a few scattered values opposite was all MacHale needed to bounce to four spades and a few seconds later he had scored +790. Meanwhile, in the other room, West's failure to support his partner's overcall backfired when, with five diamonds in his own hand, he elected to defend three diamonds. -110.

The disruptive effect of getting into the bidding, even against the best players, is well illustrated by this fairly extreme example:

Deal 6. Poland versus Netherlands

North/South Vulnerable. Dealer West.

```
              ♠ K 9 7 3
              ♥ Q J 6 3
              ♦ 9 8 2
              ♣ 7 6
♠ 6 2                        ♠ Q J 4
♥ 10 7                       ♥ A 9 5 4 2
♦ Q J 6 3                    ♦ A 7 5 4
♣ J 10 5 4 3                 ♣ 9
              ♠ A 10 8 5
              ♥ K 8
              ♦ K 10
              ♣ A K Q 8 2
```

In the Closed Room, Jansen/Westerhof had no difficulty getting to the normal contract of four spades. This proved to be elusive in the Open Room when Westra took advantage of the favorable vulnerability to open two clubs which the Dutch play as either strong and artificial or any random weak hand which doesn't fit into any other opening. Leufkens responded two hearts and, for Poland, Lasocki made a takeout double and Gawrys bid two spades.

Now one might have thought that the spade fit had been discovered, but obviously there would be quite a few hands where Gawrys would have been forced to bid two spades on just a three card suit, so Lasocki showed a good hand by bidding three clubs. Naturally, with a good holding in the suit which his partner had made a takeout double, Gawrys bid 3NT which became the final contract; one down when the Dutch defended accurately.

At this time, Gawrys/Lasocki had established themselves as just about the best pair in Europe. As far as I can see, on this deal they did nothing wrong, yet they lost 12 IMPs. While there are very few competitions where the extreme methods used here by the Dutch are allowed, the hand does convey a real message about the effect of using up your opponents' bidding space.

Now look at the last board from the same match:

Deal 7. Poland versus Netherlands

Neither Side Vulnerable. Dealer West.

```
              ♠ J
              ♥ A K Q 7
              ♦ 4 3
              ♣ K Q J 9 6 5
♠ 9 6                        ♠ A Q 10 8 7 5
♥ 10 4 3                     ♥ 6
♦ K Q J 7 6 5 2              ♦ A 9 8
♣ 7                          ♣ 10 8 2
              ♠ K 4 3 2
              ♥ J 9 8 5 2
              ♦ 10
              ♣ A 4 3
```

Open Room:

West	North	East	South
Kirchoff	*Gawrys*	*Maas*	*Lasocki*
3♦	4♣	4♠	Dble
Pass	Pass	5♦	Pass
Pass	5♥	All Pass	

Closed Room:

West	North	East	South
Zmudzinski	*Westra*	*Balicki*	*Leufkens*
3♦	Dble	Rdbl	4♦
Dble	4♥	5♦	Dble
All Pass			

In the Closed Room, Westra's choice to make a takeout double with only one spade worked well enough. Leufkens made a cuebid to suggest holding both majors and the heart fit was duly located. However, when East took the save in five diamonds it seemed normal to double.

In the Open Room, Gawrys showed real class. Having started with a natural four clubs rather than a takeout double, he heard his partner double four spades but pass five diamonds, so he drew the "obvious" conclusion that his partner must have hearts. Five hearts was laydown and Poland gained 8 IMPs, winning the match by 27 IMPs.

Having admired Gawrys' judgement on this hand it is worth speculating what might have happened had Anton Maas jumped straight to five diamonds instead of introducing his spade suit. Lasocki would have had little alternative but to make a value showing double and, while Gawrys might have preferred the look of his hand for playing rather than defending, my guess is that he would have passed the double as he wouldn't be sure that his partner didn't have relatively more in spades.

Finally, consider the following remarkable deal:

Deal 8. Denmark versus Croatia

East/West Vulnerable. Dealer East.

```
                    ♠ Q 4 3
                    ♥ 10
                    ♦ K Q J 8 7 6 3
                    ♣ J 5
     ♠ A K 6                      ♠ J 5
     ♥ A K J 9 4                  ♥ Q 8 3
     ♦ 10                         ♦ A 9 2
     ♣ A 10 8 3                   ♣ K Q 7 6 4
                    ♠ 10 9 8 7 2
                    ♥ 7 6 5 2
                    ♦ 5 4
                    ♣ 9 2
```

Open Room:

West	North	East	South
G. Lanza	Christ'sen	V. Lanza	Blakset
-	-	1♦	Pass
1♥	3♦	Pass	Pass
4NT	Pass	5♦	Pass
5NT	Pass	6♦	Pass
7♣	All Pass		

Closed Room:

West	North	East	South
P. Schaltz	Spiljak	D. Schaltz	Vukelic
-	-	1♣	Pass
1♥	5♦	Pass	Pass
6♣	All Pass		

In the Open Room, the one diamond opener was Precision style, natural, a weak no trump or some semi-balanced hand with clubs. When East passed the three diamond overcall, it seems likely that West took the view that East's opening was unlikely to contain either a diamond suit or too many wasted values in the suit. West asked for aces and kings and then took the plunge, bidding the grand slam.

In the Closed Room, the Danes were effectively fixed by North's imaginative leap to five diamonds, which took nearly all of their bidding space, not to speak of denying them the opportunity to ask for aces.

An excellent example of the maxim "Bid as much as you dare!"

PART III

CONVENTIONAL BIDDING EXPLAINED

by Freddie North

In my experience of teaching and writing about bridge, I have become increasingly aware of the desire of improving and aspiring players to know something about the popular conventions, and how best to use them. Therefore in this section I have endeavored to introduce many of the more popular conventions, and useful tactics in defense so you can equip yourself to face the world and do battle on more equitable terms than might otherwise be the case.

Many of the finest players in the world have found it unnecessary to use a multiplicity of conventions. Gabriel Chagas and Marcelo Branco from Brazil, the four French world champions, Paul Chemla, Michel Perron, Alain Levy and Herve Mouiel are a few names that spring readily to mind, not to mention former world champions like Bobby Slavenburg and Hans Kreyns from the mid-sixties. But to look at the modern convention cards of some players you would be excused for mildly raising your eyebrows at the conglomeration of gadgetry. Having said that, there is no doubt that by attaching some useful conventions to your repertoire and by understanding the everyday language of bridge— the encouraging sequences, the sign-offs and the nuances—your game will surely improve immeasurably.

I have given a Star Rating to each convention. Five stars is a strong recommendation that you study the subject well. One star suggests that you can probably live without it, or at least postpone study until a later date, while the in-between stars reflect the importance of the subject as I see it.

Chapter 17

Hand Evaluation

When you first pick up your hand, you need easily memorizable rules of thumb to help you make a working assessment of the hand's potential. Your assessment may change as the auction develops, but initially you require a broadly accurate estimate of your strength. To achieve this you need a good understanding of the Milton Work Point-Count.

THE MILTON WORK POINT-COUNT
Star Rating: *****

While countries around the world may have different mother tongues and different currencies, bridge is fortunate to enjoy a language that everybody speaks, a common currency that everyone understands. It's called the point-count, publicized by Milton Work.

> Ace = 4
> King = 3
> Queen = 2
> Jack = 1

Although there are a number of anomalies, this simple formula proved so popular that its universal adoption was virtually guaranteed, and yet, paradoxically, it is because of this simplistic valuation that an inherent danger lurks. The danger is that while experts know how to adjust the points with pluses or minuses as the auction develops, or even before it starts, many less experienced players rely almost religiously on the basic point-count, just as though it were some omnipotent dogma that must never be questioned or altered.

The number of points for No trump opening varies with the system played. Many players open 1NT with 12-14 points non-vulnerable, and with 15-17 points vulnerable. A variety of styles are discussed here.

Generally, the point-count for no trump contracts on balanced hands works out fairly well. Sometimes, however, it is necessary to adopt a practical approach. Suppose you play a 12-14 point no trump opening bid, with a 15-16 point rebid, and hold the following hands:

(a)	♠ K Q 3	(b)	♠ K Q 10
	♥ Q 6 5		♥ A 9
	♦ K Q 4		♦ 10 9 8
	♣ K 7 6 3		♣ A J 10 9 6

The point-count fanatic, with his 15 points on (a), would undoubtedly open one club and show his "extra strength" by rebidding 1NT. On (b), since he has only 14 points, he would probably open 1NT, feeling confident that he was playing according to the system (12-14 points equals a 1NT opening bid).

Actually, the opposite approach is much more realistic. Hand (a), with its balanced shape and lack of intermediate cards like tens and nines, should be downgraded to a 1NT opening bid, while hand (b), with its exceptional intermediates and five-card suit, should be upgraded to a 1NT rebid. It is worth every one of the 15-16 points that the rebid will advertise.

This first example shows how intermediates or lack of them can influence an opening bid. What about a response to a 1NT opening (12-14)? Most textbooks tell you to raise 1NT to 2NT on 11-12 points. Sound enough in basic form, but dangerous if the point-count adherent sticks slavishly to his points. Partner opens 1NT (12-14). You hold:

(a)	♠ Q J 4	(b)	♠ A 10 8
	♥ K 6 3		♥ K 9
	♦ K 4 3		♦ A 10 8 3
	♣ Q 7 4 2		♣ 10 8 5 3
(c)	♠ A 10 8	(d)	♠ 8 3
	♥ K 9		♥ A 7 5
	♦ A J 10 8 3		♦ Q 10 4
	♣ 10 9 7		♣ A J 10 9 8 6

What would you bid in each case after your partner opens 1NT and the next hand passes?

(a) I remember taking part in a seminar with Jeremy Flint when we put up a hand similar to this and posed the same question. The overwhelming answer was 2NT. "Eleven points are eleven points, aren't they?" seemed to be the mood of the class. It took us longer on this question than any other to persuade our audience that "Pass" was the right bid. With such an empty 11 points, and the worst possible shape, there is little merit in suggesting game. It is much better to downgrade the hand by a point when, of course, you have a comfortable pass.

(b) Now you are on firm ground for a raise to 2NT. The intermediates are excellent and the two four-card suits offer additional scope.

(c) You have 12 HCPs (high-card points), so should you raise to 2NT? No, you should not! This hand needs upgrading to a good 13+ and you should bid a confident 3NT.

(d) This time you have only 11 HCPs. This, again, is a case for upgrading. The six-card suit with good intermediates does not lend itself to planting the decision in partner's lap. Best to bid 3NT and hope it keeps fine. It will, most of the time.

Your opening bid of 2NT is based on 20-22 points. What would you open on the following hands?

(a) ♠ A 10 6   (b) ♠ A 10 6
     ♥ A 10 9 8 3   ♥ A K 10 9 8
     ♦ A J   ♦ A J
     ♣ A Q 10   ♣ A Q 10

(a) You have 19 HCPs, but what a 19! With all four aces you should always add one extra point (the ace is slightly undervalued at four points). That brings you to 20 points, plus a five-card suit and good tenaces. It all adds up to a sound 2NT opening.

(b) You have 22 HCPs, so do you have a maximum 2NT opening? No, you are too good. The four aces (plus one point) and a fine five-card suit makes the hand worth a 2♣ opening with a rebid of 2NT over a 2♦ response. Advertising 23-24 points is more accurate valuation than announcing 20-22.

There is another situation in which it is necessary to consider the suitability of the points, rather than their number. Most players know how to apply distributional aids, but are less proficient when it comes to upgrading or downgrading their high cards. When the high cards are together in the long suit the hand becomes attractive to play.

         ♠ A Q 9 7 5
         ♥ A 10 8 4 3
         ♦ 6 5
         ♣ 4

This hand may contain only 10 HCPs, but all experienced players will surely open it with one spade. The honor cards are well placed with the length, and justice will never be done to it if the holder passes.

By contrast, consider the same 10 points in this setting:

         ♠ 9 7 5 4 3
         ♥ A 8 5 4 3
         ♦ A 10
         ♣ Q

With the rearrangement of the top cards, the hand becomes unattractive to open. Best to pass and listen.

When the honor cards are in the short suits, defense is more likely to appeal than offense.

(a) ♠ A J   (b) ♠ A J 8 3
    ♥ J 8 7 3   ♥ J 7
    ♦ A Q   ♦ 4 3
    ♣ J 8 7 5 4   ♣ A Q J 8 5

Both hands contain the same number of points, but while (b) is a clear-cut opening of one club, with an easy rebid of one spade, (a), with the honor cards in the short suits, is a hand full of misgivings—unless defending at a conveniently high level when it would probably be superior to (b). Undoubtedly you must open hand (a) and, despite the slightly off-beat shape, my strong preference is for 1NT—often a good opening when the long suits are weak and the short suits contain tenaces and honors that need protecting.

Although the next two hands also contain the same number of points, (a) is likely to be superior to (b).

(a)   ♠ A K 8 6 4 (b) ♠ A K 8 6 4
      ♥ K Q 7   ♥ K Q
      ♦ Q J 4   ♦ Q 7 4
      ♣ 7 5   ♣ J 7 5

King-queen doubletons, singleton honors, and unsupported honors, like Qxx or Jxx, should be regarded as minus values unless they are known to blend with partner's suit. On the other hand, tens added to honor cards, as in Q10x, QJ10, KQ10, A10x, J10x, may make a significant difference to the combined values and, therefore, must be looked on favorably.

With only the opposition vulnerable, your right-hand opponent bids one heart. You hold one of the following hands:

(a)   ♠ Q 7   (b) ♠ 5 3
      ♥ Q 6 4   ♥ 6 4
      ♦ A J 8 6 4   ♦ A K J 10 8 6
      ♣ K J 6   ♣ 8 6 4

Well, are you going to intervene? If you do, would you prefer hand (a) or hand (b)?

I don't see this as a contest, and perhaps you feel the same, but the point-count addict will be far more tempted to bid on (a), the 13-point hand, than on (b) with a mere 8 points. Nothing would induce me to bid on hand (a). The suit is too fragile, and if I am doubled there is no escape. It could cost a fortune in a most doubtful cause. We have "soft," potentially defensive points which might be enough to defeat them in a game contract, so why offer them a luscious alternative? Players who bid on hands like this, for one reason or another, do often come out unscathed, but, apart from the fact that even on a good day there is little to be achieved by such bids, when the ax does fall the carnage will not be pretty.

Hand (b) is quite a different matter. If they double 2♦, which in any case seems improbable, good luck to them! Your defensive values are slight and your playing tricks sound. I very much doubt if they will get value for money. Furthermore, if partner is on lead you want him to play a diamond.

It is interesting to compare the reactions of the two South players in a team match when holding these cards and with both sides vulnerable:

♠ A Q J 10 8	West	North	East	South
♥ A K 5	Pass	Pass	Pass	1♠
♦ K 6 4	2♦	2♠	Pass	?
♣ 9 8				

The bidding started similarly at both tables:

The first South bid a confident 4♠. The second South was inclined to devalue his ♦K and contented himself with a game-try of 3♦. North converted to 3♠ which became the final contract.

This is how they got on:

Both Sides Vulnerable. Dealer West.

```
              ♠ K 9 5
              ♥ Q J 8 7
              ♦ 10 3
              ♣ 6 4 3 2
♠ 7 4                        ♠ 6 3 2
♥ 9 6                        ♥ 10 4 3 2
♦ A Q 9 8 7 5                ♦ J 2
♣ Q 10 5                     ♣ A K J 7
              ♠ A Q J 10 8
              ♥ A K 5
              ♦ K 6 4
              ♣ 9 8
```

Contract: 3♠ by South. Lead: ♥9

It was the second South who was successful—he didn't just count his points but reassessed them—since nine tricks proved to be the limit of the hand.

Calculating the true value of the points can be such a difficult task because a hand can appreciate in value, or slump significantly, rather like a volatile share on the stock market. Let's see what you make of this situation. Everyone is vulnerable and you hold:

```
              ♠ 10 8 6 3
              ♥ K J 5
              ♦ 10 7 6 3
              ♣ J 10
```

Your partner opens 1♣ (natural) and you dredge up 1♠. He now rebids 2♥ (forcing for one round). For better or for worse, you continue with 2NT, which gets 4♥ from your partner. Would you do any more?

This was the full deal:

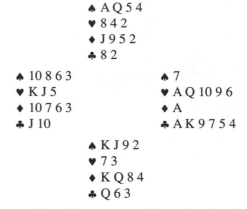

```
              ♠ A Q 5 4
              ♥ 8 4 2
              ♦ J 9 5 2
              ♣ 8 2
♠ 10 8 6 3                   ♠ 7
♥ K J 5                      ♥ A Q 10 9 6
♦ 10 7 6 3                   ♦ A
♣ J 10                       ♣ A K 9 7 5 4
              ♠ K J 9 2
              ♥ 7 3
              ♦ K Q 8 4
              ♣ Q 6 3
```

The player in the West seat advanced to 5♥, feeling that the doubleton ♣J10 plus good hearts might be enough for slam. How right she was! I was glad to be given a further opportunity and the decision to bid six was easy enough. So, too, was the play.

West's bid of 5♥ seems a very fine effort, upgrading a poor hand to its full potential and refusing to be intimidated by the shortage of points.

To summarize:

1. While distribution will always be a strong factor, intermediate cards like tens and nines, and even eights, add substantially to the value of a hand.

   Case for upgrading:

2. Aces are slightly undervalued and a hand improves with the addition of aces. Add one point if holding all four aces.

   Case for upgrading:

3. An aceless hand can prove to be the downfall of an otherwise sound contract, especially in no trumps when the opponents start with their long suit and then have the aces to get the lead.

   Case for downgrading:

4. Depending on the bidding, some unsupported honor cards should be upgraded if they blend with partner's hand, or appear to lie favorably. If they are badly placed, however, a downward adjustment may be necessary.

   Case for upgrading or downgrading:

5. Singleton honors, unsupported honor cards, and all "soft" points, like K, Q, J, KQ, QJ, Jx, Qxx, and Jxx, should be regarded in a possible minus light.

Case for downgrading:

6. If the high cards are in your long suit, the playing potential is high.

Case for upgrading when you are hoping to play:

7. If the high cards are in short suits, the defensive potential is good.

Case for upgrading if you are going to defend:

8. When considering an intervention—especially at favorable vulnerability—it is the quality of your suit rather than x number of points that really matters. Not having the odd Qx on the side may be an asset when you bid. With defensive values and a doubtful suit—err on the side of caution and downgrade the hand. With a good suit, especially a good six-carder, it's often right to bid.

The next most popular method of hand evaluation is of enormous value in assessing the worth of distributional hands. The Losing Trick Count is an invaluable tool.

THE LOSING TRICK COUNT

Star Rating: **

The Losing Trick Count (LTC) is a method of hand valuation that is especially useful (I am tempted to say only useful), when a fit has been located. While no trump type hands that are balanced in nature lend themselves ideally to a point-count method of calculation, the same cannot be said of strongly distributional hands that incorporate a good fit.

The LTC is based on the premise that each hand has a maximum of twelve losers, the ace, king, and queen in each suit (cards beyond three in a suit do not count as losers), so that the maximum number of losers between your hand and partner's is 24. Therefore, by deducting the actual number of losers that you and your partner have from the key figure of 24, you arrive at the number of tricks you can expect to make. There cannot be more losers in a suit than there are cards. Thus, x and xx represent one and two losers respectively.

A minimum opening hand usually consists of seven losers. Here is an example:

♠ 8 4	♠ K Q	**West**	**East**
♥ A K 7 5 3	♥ Q 10 8 4	1♥	4♥
♦ K 8 2	♦ Q J 5 3	Pass	
♣ A 7 4	♣ K 9 2		

West has seven losers (two in spades, one in hearts, two in diamonds, and two in clubs). East also has seven losers (one in spades, two each in hearts, diamonds, and clubs). Total is 14. Deduct from 24 and you get the answer 10. That is the number of tricks you would expect to make providing there are normal breaks and your finesses are right half the time.

A more shapely example:

♠ 2	♠ J 5	**West**	**East**
♥ A K 9 6 4 3	♥ J 10 7 2	1♥	3♥
♦ A 10 6 5	♦ 8 4	4♥	Pass
♣ 5 3	♣ A K 10 6 4		

Opener has only six losers, despite his lack of high-card points, so, when responder raises to 3♥ (eight losers), he bids the game.

We have seen that with seven losers and a fit responder raises to game (1♥–4♥). Let us see how lesser and better values fit into the scenario.

Responder raises opener's suit

Opener	Responder	Responder's losers	Responder's points inc. distribution
1♠	2♠	Usually 9 (maybe 10)	6-9
1♠	3♠	Usually 8	10-12
1♠	4♠	Usually 7	13-14

If responder has fewer losers, six or five, he will usually be able to proceed by another route.

Opener raises responder's suit

Opener	Responder	Opener's losers	Opener's points inc. distribution
1♦	1♠		
2♠		Usually 7 (maybe 6)	13-15
1♦	1♠		
3♠		Usually 6 (maybe 5)	16-18
1♦	1♠		
4♠		Usually 5	19-20

If opener has less than five losers, he will usually be able to proceed by a different route. This may also apply to some hands with five losers, where a jump cuebid or splinter would be more appropriate than a direct raise.

So, is it really just a case of putting a coin into the slot machine and punching out a ticket that tells you precisely what you can make? No, of course it is not as easy as that. What the LTC will do is to point you in the right direction. Then it will be up to you to assess fitting cards, wastage, controls, and so forth. But at least you will have some solid data on which to base your decisions.

The following combinations are worthy of study.

x or xx	Clearly one or two losers respectively.
Qx	This holding counts as two losers, but obviously must be afforded a plus value (unless the opposition have bid the suit) since opposite AKx, KJx, AJx, Kx etc., it may be invaluable.
AJx or KJx	Although there are two losers in each case the presence of the jack must warrant a plus value.

K or **Q**	If this singleton honor is in partner's suit it is certainly not correct to view it as one loser. A strong plus value.
J10x	This holding may well be better than xxx and warrants a plus in partner's suit.
AJ10	This combination should be counted as only one loser unless partner is known to be short in the suit.
Qxx	This holding calls for special treatment. To count it as two losers is an oversimplification. It is better to think of it as two and a half losers.

Now consider:

(a) AKJ   AQJ   AQ10   AKJ10   AQJ10
(b) AKx   AQx   AQx   AKJx   AQJx

Although at a basic level there is one loser in each of these combinations, the presence of the jack or ten adds considerable playing strength. Count a plus value if you hold any of the combinations denoted (a). In the last two examples in (b) the jack has already provided a plus value, but clearly adding the ten makes for an even stronger combination.

When to deduct a loser
1. Deduct a loser when you strike an extra rich trump fit, usually five or six cards in partner's suit.
2. Deduct a loser with hands rich in aces and kings—especially aces.

♠ A J 9 6
♥ A 8 4
♦ A K J 10 7
♣ 3

You open 1♦ and hear partner bid 1♠. It would now be appropriate to treat this as a five-loser hand, not six.

Even when the LTC tells you that you can make a slam, it is always necessary to check up on controls. Suppose you are West and hold:

♠ A Q 10 7 5 4
♥ A 6
♦ Q
♣ K Q 9 5

You open 1♠, which partner raises to 4♠. That looks promising. Partner is showing you seven losers and you have only four. That suggests a grand slam—if all the controls are present. Cautiously you trot out Blackwood and receive the disappointing reply of 5♣. There is nothing to do but to retreat to 5♠, and, when dummy goes down, you are at least thankful that you didn't get a rush of blood to the head!

These are the two hands:

♠ A Q 10 7 5 4   ♠ K J 8 6 2
♥ A 6   ♥ K 4
♦ Q   ♦ K J 7 5
♣ K Q 9 5   ♣ 3 2

The other side of the coin is when you pick up a hand like this:

♠ K 10 8 7 3
♥ A 4
♦ Q 5
♣ J 9 7 3

East, your partner, opens the bidding with 1♦. You respond 1♠, which East raises to 3♠. How would you react to that?

Without any cultured adjustment, West has eight losers plain and simple. East has shown six losers, which means that West should make ten tricks in spades—all things being equal. Is there a case for being more ambitious? If you count your points, no. If, however, you make allowances for the possibility of right cards (RCS—Right Cards Syndrome) then you might perhaps permit yourself one try. After all, you have counted two losers for the ♦Q5, which, in view of East's opening bid, may be unduly cautious, if not downright unimaginative. So you make your try with 4♥. Partner bids 5♦ and you pull down the shutters with 5♠, feeling confident that you have left nothing unbid. Partner does not share your feelings, however, and continues to 6♠.

The two hands:

♠ K 10 8 7 3   ♠ A Q 5 4
♥ A 4   ♥ 5 3 2
♦ Q 5   ♦ A K J 10 3
♣ J 9 7 3   ♣ 4

Although, perhaps, balanced hands with quite a few points may be slightly undervalued by LTC, and shapely features exaggerated a little, the salutary warning on the one hand, and the enthusiastic suggestion on the other, will often guide LTC adherents to the right contract.

Let us see.

♠ A K 9 7 4	♠ Q J 8 5	**West**	**East**
♥ A 8 3	♥ Q 6 4	1♠	2♠
♦ J 7 5	♦ A 6 2	Pass	
♣ K 8	♣ J 7 4		

Despite the relatively high point count, East can do no more than raise his partner to two spades (nine losers). With seven losers himself, West is not tempted to proceed. So the partnership stays on firm ground.

Then, there is the situation in which the shapely element is allowed full rein:

♠ K 9 8 6 5 3	♠ Q J 7 2	**West**	**East**
♥ A	♥ 8 7 3	1♠	3♠(i)
♦ A 4	♦ K Q 9 6 5	4♣(ii)	4♦(iii)
♣ A 7 6 2	♣ 8	4♥(iv)	5♣(v)
		6♠	

(i) East has seven losers, but the point-count is low in an aceless hand so he is content to raise to three spades.

ii) West's controls could hardly be better. It wouldn't be outrageous to jump to 6♠ immediately (five losers minus one for aces = four, plus eight losers makes twelve. 24 – 12 = 12 tricks), but he settles for the cuebid.

(iii) East does not want to sign off so he compromises with 4♦.

(iv) and (v) are cuebids and West settles happily for the small slam.

Success on a joint holding of 23 points can't be too bad.

This is a hand from the 1989 European Championships, which occurred in the Women's Series, Germany versus Netherlands:

East/West Vulnerable. Dealer West.

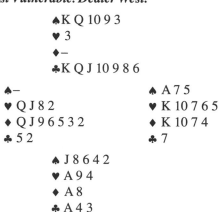

In one room, without opposition bidding, the North/South pair bid smoothly to six spades. There was plenty of time and all the relevant questions got answered.

In the other room this was the bidding:

West	North	East	South
Pass	1♣	1♥	1♠
4♥	4♠	All Pass	

Of course, 12 tricks were made without pausing for breath, but what about that bidding sequence? On this occasion the East/West bidding took up a lot of space and left little room for maneuver. East/West were vulnerable and were presumably not bidding on peanuts. Even so, North had only three losers and wouldn't be completely happy about bidding four spades. Still, if South were minimum and unsuitable then the five level might be too high.

How about South? She has eight losers, it is true, but an opening bid and three aces plus five trumps seems to suggest suitable cards (RCS again). Ardent fans of LTC might proceed via five clubs, but any move would obviously hit the jackpot.

Perhaps this brings us back to where we came in. All your guides and props can steer you in the right direction, but in the final analysis it comes down to your own judgment.

18

Chapter

Bidding To Game

TRIAL BIDS

Star Rating: ****

After partner has raised your major suit to the two level (1♥–2♥) do you ever wonder whether you should play it safe and pass, jump to game and hope for the best, or perhaps just continue with your suit to the three level (1♥–2♥–3♥) and hope partner can sort it out? And if you are the partner trying to sort it out do you ever wonder what to do? There is an (almost) magic formula that can save you many a headache in the future.

Suppose you open 1♥ holding:

        ♠ 8 4
        ♥ A Q J 6 5
        ♦ A 8 5 4
        ♣ A 3

Your partner raises to 2♥ and RHO passes. What would you do now?

Clearly you have some hope of making game if your partner holds the right cards—and very little hope if he holds the wrong ones. If you simply raise the ante to 3♥, how is partner to know whether he has what you require, or whether his values are largely wasted? Playing trial bids you don't bid 3♥ and you've no need to guess; you just bid three in the suit where you want help, in this case 3♦.

So, a trial bid is a change of suit after a major suit has been raised to the two level. Although, perhaps, a trial bid is more likely to be initiated by the opener (1♠–2♠–3♦), responder can also initiate a trial bid; for example after 1♣–1♥ –2♥ he might bid 2♠.

The trial bid is an invitation to game in the agreed major suit. It consists of three or more cards (usually three or four) in the suit where help is most wanted. For example, 1♠–2♠–3♦ means: "I am interested in four spades, and need help in diamonds." Always choose a weak suit for your trial bid, typically a suit with two or three losers. If there are two trial suits from which to choose, go for the weaker. If the suits are equal, select the cheaper. Don't make a trial bid in a suit with only one loser.

When to Make a Trial Bid

After 1♥–2♥, or 1♠–2♠, opener makes a trial bid on a hand where he can't quite be sure whether a game is on or not; this will usually be a hand with about 16-18 points (including distributional points) or a hand with six losers. If opener has seven losers, about 12-15 points, it will usually be right to pass, but if he has only five losers, about 19-20 points including distributional points, he will be able to bid game without searching for more information.

Responder's raise to the two level in partner's major (1♠–2♠) shows about nine losers—sometimes eight, sometimes ten.

After responder has been raised to the two level in his major (1♦–1♠ –2♠) he may make a trial bid with about 10-12 points—again, including distribution. This will usually mean about seven to eight losers. It is true that opener will more often than not have seven losers, but he may have something extra—six losers with a minimum point count— or, even more pertinent, his values may be just where they are needed. That is what trial bids are all about. Are partner's goodies in the right place to eliminate enough of your losers?

Sometimes responder—and occasionally opener—may envisage a slam after his suit has been raised to the two level. When this happens he can then use a trial bid to discover whether partner can help in the trial suit. Depending on the reply the trial bidder continues to game or to slam.

Replying to the Trial Bid – the (Almost) Magic Formula

If you have no losers in the trial suit - jump to game in the agreed major.

If you have one loser in the trial suit - jump to game in the agreed major.

If you have two losers in the trial suit - jump to game in the agreed major if maximum. Sign off in three of the agreed major if minimum.

If you have three losers in the trial suit - sign off in three of the agreed major, even when maximum.

Let us look at some hands.

Both Sides Vulnerable. Dealer South.

♠ 9 7 6 3		**South**	**North**
♥ K 9 7 4		1♥	2♥
♦ K 6		3♦	4♥
♣ 7 6 2		Pass	

♠ A K Q	♠ J 10 5 2
♥ 10 8 3	♥ 2
♦ J 7	♦ Q 10 9 3 2
♣ J 9 8 5 4	♣ K Q 10

♠ 8 4
♥ A Q J 6 5
♦ A 8 5 4
♣ A 3

When North raises opener's 1♥ to 2♥, South is in a dilemma. His hand is worth about 17 points (15 + 1 point for each doubleton after trump agreement) and he has exactly six losers. North is likely to have about nine losers which in isolation suggests a part score, not game. However, if North can help in diamonds the "right cards syndrome" may bridge the gap. So South introduces a trial bid with 3♦ and North, employing the (almost) magic formula, jumps to game since he has only one loser in the trial suit (Ax, Kx, or x count as one loser).

The play is easy. West leads three top spades and declarer ruffs the third round. Now all he has to do is insure that he ruffs his two losing diamonds in dummy before drawing all the trumps. The easiest plan is to cash the ♦A and ♦K and ruff a diamond. Return to hand with a high trump and ruff a second diamond. The rest is plain sailing.

Neither Side Vulnerable. Dealer South.

♠ Q 8 7 4		**South**	**North**
♥ K Q 7		1♠	2♠
♦ Q 8 7		3♣	3♠
♣ 10 5 3		Pass	

♠ 5 2	♠ 9 3
♥ J 9 6 5 3	♥ A 10 8 4
♦ J 2	♦ 9 6 5 3
♣ A K 8 7	♣ Q 9 2

♠ A K J 10 6
♥ 2
♦ A K 10 4
♣ J 6 4

After 1♠–2♠ South has every reason to be interested in game. Sixteen HCPs plus two for distribution give him a total of eighteen points and, of course, he has a six-loser hand. The doubt lies in just where North's high cards are situated. The trial bid of 3♣ soon gets the thumbs down (North has three losers in clubs) and the partnership stays in a safe part score. Interchange North's club and heart holding

and the (almost) magic formula would dictate that North rebid 4♠, which would then be easy.

Two suited hands that fit well always play for a lot of tricks. Consider:

Both Sides Vulnerable. Dealer South.

♠ 10 8 6 5		**South**	**North**
♥ Q 8 5 4		1♥	2♥
♦ K Q 5		3♦	4♥
♣ 8 6		6♥	Pass

♠ K J 3 2	♠ A Q 9 4
♥ 9 6	♥ 7 2
♦ 10 6	♦ 7 4 2
♣ K Q 10 4 2	♣ 9 7 5 3

♠ 7
♥ A K J 10 3
♦ A J 9 8 3
♣ A J

South realized that he had plenty of ammunition for a direct jump to game after North's raise to 2♥. Before committing himself to a modest game contract, however, he decided to try the effect of a trial bid of 3♦. North's jump to 4♥ got South's adrenaline going and he decided to risk the slam. In the event twelve tricks were virtually lay-down (five hearts, five diamonds, one club, and one club ruff in dummy).

Although the cards lay poorly on the next hand, North/South bid and made a thin game. which was not duplicated in the other room.

East/West Vulnerable. IMPs. Dealer West.

♠ K 10 5 2		**South**	**North**
♥ 7		–	1♦
♦ A J 10 9 4		1♠	2♠
♣ K 10 4		3♥	4♠

♠ Q J 7	♠ 9	Pass
♥ K Q J 8	♥ 10 9 4 3 2	
♦ 8 7	♦ K Q 5	
♣ 7 6 3 2	♣ A 9 8 5	

♠ A 8 6 4 3
♥ A 6 5
♦ 6 5 2
♣ Q J

North had nothing to spare when he opened the bidding with 1♦ and raised his partner's 1♠ to 2♠. However, South had the points to make an effort although he was quite heavy with losers. Nevertheless, he decided to make a trial bid with 3♥ and then the (almost) magic formula was applied by North—one loser in hearts meant a jump to game in the agreed major —and so they arrived.

Even with both diamonds offside and the spades failing to break, South was not severely tested. He won the opening heart lead, ruffed a heart, played a club to his queen, East ducking, and ruffed his last heart. Now the ♠K and ♠A were followed by the ♣J to establish a diamond discard. So the opponents made just one spade, one club, and one diamond.

There are two final points to consider. What do these sequences mean?

(i)	1♥	2♥	or 1♠	2♠
	2NT			2NT
(ii)	1♥	2♥	or 1♠	2♠
	3♥			3♠

(i) The first is fairly easy. It is a trial bid on a balanced hand of about 17-18 points. Something like this:

♠ A Q 10 6
♥ K J 5
♦ A J 10 3
♣ Q 10 4

Partner can pass, raise, sign off in 3♠, or jump to 4♠.

(ii) Interpretation of this sequence depends on partnership agreement. In some circles it will have a natural meaning: "I am interested in game but have no particular suit that I want to introduce as a trial bid. If you are maximum, go to game. If you are minimum, pass." That is a perfectly playable arrangement. Indeed, suppose you hold:

♠ Q J 10 8 4
♥ K J 10
♦ A K 5
♣ K 6

and open 1♠, which partner raises to 2♠. What now? Playing three spades as a general try you are in business. Partner can assess his hand fairly accurately. That, very briefly, is the case for the constructive raise.

The alternative treatment of 1♥–2♥–3♥ or 1♠–2♠–3♠ is based on a weak hand. The thinking is this: "If I pass after this sequence (1♥–2♥) my left-hand opponent is almost certain to re-open, and since we have a fit and are not very strong, they are sure to find a playable spot—perhaps even make game—so I will do my best to make life difficult for them. Even if I end up one over the top it may still be a good result."

Here is an example:

♠ 5		♠ Q 7 4	**West**	**East**
♥ A J 9 8 6 4		♥ K 7 5 2	1♥	2♥
♦ K Q 10		♦ 9 8 4 3	3♥	Pass
♣ J 7 4		♣ Q 8		

I am biased about the merits of these two treatments. I prefer the latter, which budgets for weak hands with a fit. Strong hands will often look after themselves while weak hands need wrapping up. Sometimes even camouflaging. So, is it to be the heavy artillery or the machine gun? While I have made it clear that I prefer the machine gun (one, two, three—shut them up), other views must be respected.

All I suggest is that you discuss it with your partner so you both know what you are doing and that you understand why all good players acknowledge that trial bids are invaluable.

THE DELAYED GAME RAISE
Star Rating: **

In the early days of bridge players' lives it is never easy to get him or her to support their partners. The natural instinct is to paint pretty little pictures and let the future take care of itself (with ♠xx, ♥Qxxx, ♦AQJxx, ♣xx they will almost all bid 2♦ over partner's 1♥, instead of raising to 3♥.) Then, just as you've got the player to raise major suits quantitatively, without stopping to pick the flowers or paint pretty pictures, you start introducing hands where it is clearly advantageous to do just that. All very confusing.

What it boils down to is this: There are five main types of reply you can make when you have length and values in partner's major suit:

(1) Raise partner quantitatively: 1♠–2♠; 1♠–3♠; 1♠–4♠.

(2) Show your own suit first and then leap to game on the next round:

(a)	1♥	1♠
	1NT	4♥
(b)	1♥	2♣
	2NT	4♥
(c)	1♥	2♣
	2♦	4♥

(3) Jump in a new suit and support partner on the next round:

(a)	1♥	2♠
	3♣	3♥
(b)	1♠	3♦
	3♥	3♠
(c)	1♥	3♣
	3NT	4♥
(d)	1♥	2♠
	3♥	4♥

(4) Use Swiss. (See Chapter 20)

(5) Use a Splinter Bid. (See Chapter 20)

Let us try to differentiate between the first three replies. Partner opens one heart and you hold:

(a)	♠ 4	**(b)**	♠ A 10 8	**(c)**	♠ A 10
	♥ K 10 9 6 4		♥ K J 8 3		♥ K J 8 3
	♦ K J 8 7 5		♦ K J 10 6 5		♦ A K J 10 4
	♣ 6 3		♣ 8		♣ 8 4

With hand (a) you may or may not make four hearts, but it is certainly in your interests to get there as quickly as possible. If your opponents now want to start bidding they can do so at the four level. It is by no means uncommon in these situations to find that while your partner succeeds in making 4♥, the opponents could have made 4♠. Even if 4♥ goes down it may well be in a good cause for at least you have crowded the auction and made it difficult for the opposition to get together. So, you can see, this is no occasion to paint pretty pictures.

Hand (b) is a very different proposition. Although anything is possible, you have no reason to fear the opposition. It is most unlikely that you will be outbid, so this is the moment to start painting a pretty picture. Bid 2♦ with the intention of leaping to 4♥ on the next round. This is called a Delayed Game Raise, DGR for short.

Hand (c) is much too strong for a DGR so you should jump to 3♦ and then support hearts on the next round. Plenty of time to stop and pick the flowers!

Having shown you a few hands where you want to be in game (at least) opposite partner's opening bid of one of a major, yet requiring a different treatment in each case, I now want to concentrate on the DGR.

A DGR hand will have at least four-card support for partner's major. It will have adequate values to go to game and will have sufficient high cards so that you do not fear the opposition. Ideally, it will contain a secondary suit of some substance, and in terms of general acceptability it lies between the hand that raises directly to game and the hand that forces and then supports.

Partner opens 1♥ and you hold:

(a) ♠ K 9
♥ Q 10 9 7
♦ A Q J 7 4
♣ 8 6

Respond 2♦. A fairly typical Delayed Game Raise.

(b) ♠ A 10 6
♥ K J 8 4
♦ 5 2
♣ K Q 7 4

Respond 2♣. A fairly typical Delayed Game Raise.

(c) ♠ K Q
♥ A 10 9 4
♦ 9 6 4 2
♣ K Q 10

Your hand is too strong in top cards to bid four hearts immediately, but the diamonds are too weak to mention. Compromise with two clubs where at least you have some values.

Partner opens 1♠ and you hold:

(a) ♠ K 10 8 2
♥ A K Q J
♦ 6
♣ 9 7 6 4

Respond 2♥. You don't need five since you are eventually going to play in spades. Partner would get the wrong impression if you bid 2♣ and would tend to devalue his

hand with, say, a singleton club.

(b) ♠ A Q 8 5
♥ 4
♦ K Q J 7 5
♣ 6 4 2

Respond 2♦. A textbook Delayed Game Raise.

(c) ♠ K J 7 4
♥ 8 5 4
♦ K Q J 7
♣ 4 2

Respond 3♠. You are not strong enough for 4♠ and therefore must not consider a Delayed Game Raise.

You will notice, perhaps, that in all these examples of the DGR I have avoided having two or more aces in the responding hands. That is because the Swiss convention is all about game-going hands with aces in response to partner's major. Both conventions, the DGR and Swiss, can be used by responder without necessarily clashing, but if I am forced to choose between the two I would invariably give preference to Swiss. If you don't play Swiss there is no reason to restrict the number of aces in responder's hand. Let's look at some hands.

Neither Side Vulnerable. Dealer West.

```
              ♠ A K 10 9 6 4
              ♥ –
              ♦ Q 10 3 2
              ♣ 9 7 2
♠ 8                          ♠ J 7 5
♥ A K 9 7 4                  ♥ Q 8 5 3
♦ A J 8 5                    ♦ K
♣ K 5 4                      ♣ A Q J 10 6
              ♠ Q 3 2
              ♥ J 10 6 2
              ♦ 9 7 6 4
              ♣ 8 3
```

West	North	East	South
1♥	1♠	2♣	Pass
2♦	Pass	4♥	Pass
4♠	Pass	5♣	Pass
5♦	Pass	6♥	All Pass

Although many Easts would "read" West as probably 5-4 in the red suits and would therefore jump to four hearts with any three-card support, West reasoned that his partner had DGR values because he had eschewed a 2♠ inquiry over 2♦ (a bridge player's thinking as opposed to a scientist's assumption). In any case, the top cards in the red suits, the club fit, and singleton spade all suggested further investigation. The three cuebids that followed confirmed the controls and decided East on the final slam target.

North led the two top spades and the moment of truth arrived as West trumped the second round. Remembering his lessons on precaution plays, West led the ♥7 to dummy's

♥Q and was able to pick up all South's trumps without loss. The point is this: If North holds all four trumps nothing can be done to avoid the loss of one trump trick, but if South holds them it is essential to play to the single honor first. Give East the ♥10 instead of a small one and then declarer must first cash one of the top honors from his own hand.

It sometimes happens that opener rebids his own major suit, thus thwarting responder's plan to paint a DGR picture with his first rebid. If the bidding starts 1♥–2♦–2♥ responder would raise to 4♥ with something like this:

                    ♠ 7 5
                    ♥ 10 6 4
                    ♦ A K J 8 4 2
                    ♣ K J

Even if he has DGR values it often won't matter because if partner can only rebid his suit at the lowest level nothing will be missed. But suppose instead he holds a highly suitable DGR hand:

                    ♠ 7
                    ♥ K 10 6 4
                    ♦ A K J 10 5
                    ♣ Q 10 3

Would he make the same rebid of 4♥? Let's see how East coped with a similar situation on the following hand:

Both Sides Vulnerable. Dealer South.

			West	East
♠ 2			1♥	2♦
♥ A J 10 5 3 2			2♥	3♣
♦ 8 6			3♦	4♠
♣ J 9 4 2			5♣	5♥

♠ A K 9 7 5 4		♠ Q J 8 3	6♠	Pass
♥ 8 6		♥ 7		
♦ Q 9 4		♦ A K 10 7 3		
♣ A 5		♣ K 8 3		

                    ♠ 10 6
                    ♥ K Q 9 4
                    ♦ J 5 2
                    ♣ Q 10 7 6

East started on an informative DGR sequence with his bid of 2♦, intending to leap to 4♠ on the next round. However, when West rebid 2♠ East decided on a different tack. 3♣ was forcing (a new suit at the three level) and provided just the opportunity he was looking for when West rebid 3♦. The leap to game now instead of on the previous round made West realize that he might have the right cards for slam. The heart cuebid over 5♣ reinforced this impression so West bid the slam which turned out to be lay-down.

When you have a misfit with partner's first suit it is generally wise to undervalue your hand somewhat, unless there are strong redeeming features.

West thought he had these features on the following hand:

North/South Vulnerable. Dealer West.

			West	East
♠ 9			1♠	2♣
♥ J 10 9			2♦	4♠
♦ K J 10 7 5			5♥	6♠
♣ K 6 3 2			Pass	

♠ A J 7 6 5		♠ K 8 4 3		
♥ A 6		♥ Q 5 4		
♦ A 9 8 6 4		♦ 3		
♣ 5		♣ A Q J 10 4		

                    ♠ Q 10 2
                    ♥ K 8 7 3 2
                    ♦ Q 2
                    ♣ 9 8 7

Despite his singleton club, West liked his shape and three aces and decided the best "urge" was 5♥. East did not take much urging. He could either sign off in 5♠ or bid the slam. With nothing to be ashamed of, he went for gold.

North led the ♥J, covered by the queen, king, and ace. West realized he had plenty on his plate and would need a little luck if he were to be successful. The first move was a club to the ♣A, followed by the ♣Q for a ruffing finesse. North won, but West was able to discard his losing heart and now, hopefully, there were three discards for declarer's losing diamonds, and the fourth could be trumped in dummy. The heart continuation was ruffed leaving just the problem of how to play the trump suit. West could not afford a wrong guess. A spade to the ♠K caught the ♠9 from North and the ♠2 from South. On the next spade from dummy South played the ♠10 and there was an agonizing trance before West guessed correctly by playing the ♠J. With one singleton in dummy and one in his own hand, declarer thought that North might perhaps have one as well—and so it proved. West made five spades, four clubs, the two red aces, and a diamond ruff, totaling twelve tricks.

Despite West's success on this hand, it is generally right to view misfits pessimistically, while taking an optimistic view of hands that knit well together.

FOURTH SUIT FORCING
Star Rating: ***

Ask a bridge expert what he considers the most useful contribution to bidding theory in the last thirty to forty years, and, as likely as not, he will answer "Fourth Suit Forcing." Indeed, so useful is this development, and so efficient its application, that one cannot help wondering how the good bidders of the pre-FSF era ever managed without it. Good judgment, good bridge sense, or just a nose for diagnosing the problem? Whatever it was, they did pretty well, but no one would deny that they would have done even better with the addition of FSF to their armory.

This is a typical problem. You are East and hold:

	West	East
♠ A 9 3		
♥ K J 10 7 4	1♦	1♥
♦ A Q	1♠	?
♣ 6 3 2		

You now have an almost insoluble problem—unless you are playing FSF. You have the points to go to game, but which game? Four hearts, four spades, 3NT, five diamonds? Bids like 3♥, 3♠, and 3♦ are all non-forcing so they must be discarded. 3♣ would be forcing, of course, but it certainly wouldn't be descriptive. The answer is to use a bid at the lowest level in the one remaining unbid suit as an artificial forcing bid. Since the other three suits have been bid by your side, you can see why this convention is called fourth suit forcing. This bid asks partner for further clarification. It is forcing and does not guarantee any strength in the suit at all. After all, if your clubs were strong in the above hand (interchange the clubs and diamonds, for example) you would rebid 3NT, since you would have no reason to ask any further questions.

It might be helpful to look at a few possible hands that West might hold consistent with the bidding (1♦-1♥-1♠-2♣) so far.

(a) ♠ K 7 5 4	(b) ♠ K Q 5 4	(c) ♠ K Q 5 4
♥ 6 3	♥ A Q 2	♥ A
♦ K J 10 5 3	♦ K J 5 3 2	♦ K J 10 5 3 2
♣ A Q	♣ 8	♣ 8 4

On hand (a) West will rebid 2NT and East will continue to 3NT. If the West hand were a little stronger, say the ♥Q instead of a small one, West would go direct to 3NT himself.

On hand (b) West will rebid 3♥ and that should pave the way to the small slam in hearts. With a minimum hand, say ♥QJ2 instead of ♥AQ2, West should rebid 2♥, which will lead to a final contract of 4♥.

On hand (c) West will rebid his diamonds leading to a final contract of 5♦.

Notice how easy it is to head in the right direction after the fourth suit has been introduced; guesswork is almost completely eliminated. Although responder is more likely to want to use FSF than opener, the bid is nevertheless available to both partners.

Suppose as West you deal and hold:

	West	East
♠ K J 4		
♥ A K 9 7 5	1♥	2♣
♦ 8 6 3	2♥	2♠
♣ A 4	?	

Now, surely, your best bid is 3♦ — the fourth suit asking for further clarification. Certainly you can't bid 3NT with three small diamonds (although East might be happy to do so) and it would be premature to be too demonstrative about the other three suits. However, let's concentrate on responder's FSF bid since that is probably where the bulk of the action lies.

There are a number of questions that need answering.

> **(a)** How strong do you have to be to introduce a FSF bid?
> **(b)** Which replies by partner are still forcing?
> **(c)** When should you avoid a FSF bid?

(a) Obviously if responder has game-going values he is on firm ground when demanding further information. Also, when just short of an opening bid himself, say about 11-12 points or even a promising 10 count, he may be best served by inquiring further.

(b) If the FSF bid is made at the three level this creates a game-forcing situation. If it is made at the two level, opener's minimum rebid can be passed. For example:

West	East
1♦	1♥
1♠	2♣ (FSF)
?	

Now rebids of 2♦, 2♥, or 2NT are all non-forcing (2♠ would be forcing) so clearly opener should avoid making a minimum reply to FSF with 15 or more points. Any jump bid after FSF is forcing to game. Any further bid responder makes short of game, however, is still forcing.

For example:

West	East
1♥	1♠
2♣	2♦ (FSF)
2♥	3♣
?	

This last bid is still forcing. With a weaker hand East would simply have raised 2♣ to 3♣ without using the FSF bid of 2♦.

(c) Never use FSF if you have a natural clear cut bid that you can make instead. Study these examples. You hold as East:

(1) ♠ A J 7 4 2	West	East
♥ K J 10	1♥	1♠
♦ 8 6 4 2	2♣	?
♣ 5		

Bid 3♥. A jump preference, limit bid.

(2) ♠ A J 10	West	East
♥ K Q 10 4	1♦	1♥
♦ 7 2	2♣	?
♣ Q J 5 3		

Bid 3NT. You have enough information.

(3) ♠ A J 9 7 4 3	West	East
♥ Q 5	1♦	1♠
♦ K 10 9 6	2♥	?
♣ Q J 5 3		

Bid 4♦. This bid is forcing and paves the way for further investigation. It would be pointless, and confusing, to introduce the fourth suit.

(4)
		West	East
♠	Q 6 4		
♥	A Q 6	1♠	2♦
♦	K 9 5 3	2♥	?
♣	A 7 2		

Here there is no obvious bid to make; you do need more information. So bid 3♣, FSF, you will see what actually happened later.

Action by Opener After Partner Bids the Fourth Suit

You hold as West:

(a)
		West	East
♠	Q J 10 5		
♥	6	1♦	1♥
♦	A Q J 7 4	1♠	2♣
♣	K 10 5	?	

Bid 2NT. You have a club stop and you are minimum. With, say, the ♠A instead of the ♠Q you would bid 3NT.

(b)
		West	East
♠	K J 5		
♥	A K 8 4 3	1♥	1♠
♦	5	2♣	2♦
♣	A J 10 5	?	

Bid 3♠—forcing to game. With a small spade instead of the ♠K you would bid 2♠.

(c)
		West	East
♠	A K 8 4		
♥	3	1♦	1♥
♦	A K J 10 6 3	1♠	2♣
♣	8 2	?	

Jump to 3♦—forcing to game.

(d)
		West	East
♠	A 10 8 6		
♥	A K 7 4	1♣	1♦
♦	–	1♥	1♠
♣	K Q J 8 6	?	

Raise to 3♠—forcing to game. Although you have the values to bid 4♠ it would be dangerous to do so because East might not have a spade suit.

Let us look at some full hands:

Neither Side Vulnerable. Rubber Bridge. Dealer North.

		North	South
♠	K 6		
♥	A K 7 6 4	1♥	1♠
♦	7 5	2♣	3NT
♣	K 8 7 5		

♠ 10 3		♠ J 9 8 4 2
♥ Q 10 8		♥ J 9
♦ K 10 8 3		♦ Q 9 6
♣ J 9 6 2		♣ 10 3

♠	A Q 7 5
♥	5 3 2
♦	J 4 2
♣	A Q 4

Hardly a cultured sequence, but nevertheless not too divorced from the real world of rubber bridge where sometimes sophistication is almost regarded as a dirty word.

West led the ♦3 and declarer used a fair portion of his good luck when the suit divided 4-4. However, he wasn't out of the woods yet. East won the fourth diamond and switched to a spade. Declarer won in dummy, tried the clubs, and when they didn't break he cashed his spade winners. On the ♠Q West was squeezed. He had to retain the ♣J so he parted with the ♥8. Dummy's club, having done its work, was discarded, and the ♥A, K, and 7 took the last three tricks.

So, to make his contract of 3NT, South not only had to be lucky with the diamond break, he also had to play well, in that he had to judge the right squeeze to play for. With the use of FSF North/South would have sailed to their right contract of 4♥ and made (at least) ten tricks without difficulty.

North	South
1♥	1♠
2♣	2♦
2♥	4♥

2♦, the fourth suit, asks for clarification and 2♥ denies a diamond stopper or three spades. 2♥ is the least helpful bid that North can make; nevertheless it is steeped in truth, and South responds accordingly. East, who hopefully is tuned into the bidding, should lead the ♦A, in which case the defense will make two diamonds and a trump. Playing pairs, North/South would be extremely grateful that they had FSF in their armory of bids.

This last hand demonstrates a further extension of the FSF principle. Remember, you held the following hand as responder in c (iv):

		West	East
♠	Q 6 4		
♥	A Q 6	1♠	2♦
♦	K 9 5 3	2♥	?
♣	A 7 2		

4♠ would not be right since that would show a DGR, and although East could have responded 3NT immediately, showing his hand type and point count (13-15), it is too late for that now. However, the fourth suit (3♣) is available. By this time East knows that he wants to play in spades and after the fourth suit there are two likely ways of continuing: (1) by jumping to 4♠ on the next round to indicate that he has completed his story, or (2) bidding spades without a jump so as to leave room for an exchange of cuebids.

Switching you to the North position for convenience. This was the hand:

			South	North
♠ Q 6 4			1♠	2♦
♥ A Q 6			2♥	3♣
♦ K 9 5 3			3♦	3♠
♣ A 7 2			4♣	6♠
♠ 9 8 7 2		♠ 5	Pass	
♥ 5 2		♥ K 9 8 3		
♦ 10 4		♦ J 8 7 2		
♣ K Q 10 9 6		♣ J 8 4 3		
	♠ A K J 10 3			
	♥ J 10 7 4			
	♦ A Q 6			
	♣ 5			

There was no problem in the play, twelve tricks being an easy make, but the declarer at this table was happier than his opposite number. At the other table the final contract rested in 4♠ after a less informative sequence.

Chapter 19

Bidding to Slam

Slams are one of the most exciting aspects of bridge. Bidding a hand to the six level, or, even better, to seven, and then garnering the requisite number of tricks is one of a bridge player's greatest thrills. Unfortunately, there is a downside. G oing down in a high-level contract is an enormous gift to the opposition and can hurt your own chances of winning. It is an area where all players can improve their performance overnight. This chapter aims to show you some of the tricks of the trade.

CUEBIDDING

Star Rating:*****

A cuebid is one of the most useful gadgets in the whole field of bidding and while it is worshipped by experts, to the extent that most would willingly forego almost anything else provided they were allowed to retain their favorite toy, the novice is deeply suspicious of having anything to do with it.

When does a cuebid occur?

A cuebid occurs after suit agreement, invariably at the three or four level, but sometimes at the five level. A new suit, after such agreement, is a cuebid showing slam interest and control of the suit mentioned:

(a)	1♥	3♥	(b)	1♣	1♠
	4♣	3♠		4♦	
(c)	2♥	3♥	(d)	1♦	1♠
	3♥	4♠		5♣	
(e)	1NT				
	4♦				

The last bid in every sequence is a cuebid. In the sequence 1NT-3♥-4♦ the bid of 4♦ shows the ♦A and agrees hearts by inference—opener could hardly want to play in his diamond suit.

What does a cuebid show?

Initially a cuebid shows first-round control—an ace or void—outside the trump suit. Subsequently, a cuebid shows second-round control—a king or singleton—outside the trump suit.

A cuebidder always bids his controls up-the-line, the cheapest first:

West	East
1♥	3♥
4♣	

West's bid of 4♣ denies the ♠A. Equally, should East continue with 4♠ he would be denying the ♦A.

What is the purpose of a cuebid?

A cuebid shows interest in slam, reveals controls and invites partner to cuebid in reply. By pinpointing specific controls a partnership can either stay at a safe level or continue to an excellent slam.

When does the cuebidding end?

A return to the agreed trump suit signifies that that player has no more to show. Otherwise cuebidding continues until one of the partners can tell whether to bid a small slam, a grand slam or reject a slam completely. Don't continue cuebidding if you know that a small slam offers good prospects but a grand slam is impossible. Just bid the small slam. But, if further information is required that could lead to seven—keep cuebidding.

Why bother with cuebids, why not just use Blackwood?

Many hands are just not suitable for a Blackwood 4NT inquiry. In particular, hands that contain voids or hands with only small cards (no ace or king) in a side-suit do not lend themselves to Blackwood. Blackwood is fine if all you want to know is the number of aces and kings held by partner. When you wish to discover specific controls and shortages then cuebids are the answer.

When is a new suit after (major) suit agreement not a cuebid?

(i) When a major suit is raised to the two level a change of suit is a trial bid, not a cuebid, e.g. 1♥- 2♣-3♦. Opener's bid of 3♦ is a trial bid for game in hearts.

(ii) When partner raises your minor suit, bids at the three level should be treated as stoppers for 3NT, not cuebids, e.g. 1♥-2♣-3♣; if responder continues with 3♦ or 3♠ he may be showing just a stopper in the suit bid. In certain circumstances this will enable opener to bid 3NT.

Look at the system at work. Suppose as West you hold:

> ♠ A Q J 7 5 3
> ♥ -
> ♦ J 10 9 8
> ♣ A K J

You open the bidding with 1♠. Your partner raises you to 3♠. What now? 4♠ might be enough, yet 6♠ might be cold. Blackwood won't solve your problem if partner tells you he holds one ace, because you won't know whether it is the ♥A or ♦A. Indeed, the five level might even be too high. However, you are now well into cuebids so you rebid 4♣— your lowest first-round control outside the trump suit. If your partner continues with 4♥ or 4♠ you will call it a day and settle for game, but if he shows you the ♦A that is quite a different matter.

Here is your hand again, opposite two possible hands that your partner, East, might hold:

West	(a) East	(a) West	East
♠ A Q J 7 5 3	♠ K 10 6 4	1♠	3♠
♥ -	♥ A Q 10 8	4♣	4♥
♦ J 10 9 8	♦ 7 5 3	4♠	
♣ A K J	♣ Q 9		
	(b) East	(b) West	East
	♠ K 10 6 4	1♠	3♠
	♥ 10 8 4	4♣	4♦
	♦ A Q 7 5	4♥	4♠
	♣ Q 9	6♠	

When East holds hand (a) the bidding stops in 4♠—just in time. The news that East holds the ♥A (he has denied the ♦A because he has to bid up-the-line, lowest control first) is bad medicine and West will want to close the auction with almost indecent haste.

When East holds hand (b) he is able to cuebid 4♦ over 4♣ and that is really exciting news for West. Caught up in the euphoria of the moment, West continues with 4♥, although it is almost impossible for East to have the right cards for a grand slam (remember he made the limit bid of 3♠ over 1♠). Maybe West visualizes something like ♠Kxxx ♥xxxxx ♦AK ♣xx. However, East has to sign off in 4♠. But West already knows that the small slam must be heavy odds so heads right there to close the auction. Maybe West was lucky to find the ♦Q in the East hand, but even without this card the small slam is still a tremendous bet. There are no red-blooded bridge players who would not wish to be in a small slam if success depended on nothing worse than losing only one trick in a suit consisting of J1098 opposite Axxx—in isolation a 76 percent chance.

Once more you are West and hold:

West	(a) East	(b) East
♠ A Q	♠ K J 9	♠ K J 9
♥ A K 8 4 3	♥ Q J 10 7 2	♥ Q J 10 7
♦ 6 5	♦ J 10	♦ A J 10 4
♣ K Q 9 3	♣ A J 4	♣ J 4

You open 1♥ and on both hands (a) and (b) East raises you to 4♥. Glancing across to East we see that each hand contains thirteen points, but whereas (a) has five trumps (b) has only four. Nevertheless, with hand (a) there is no play for 6♥. With hand (b), however, 6♥ is virtually ironclad. So how should the bidding go? First you must dismiss any idea of Blackwood. The reply won't help you.

Then you launch yourself into a cuebidding sequence:

(a)	West	East	(b)	West	East
	1♥	4♥		1♥	4♥
	4♠	5♣		4♠	5♦
	5♥			6♥	

West makes his first move with 4♠, cuebidding the ♠A and inviting a cuebid in return. With hand (a) East obliges with 5♣, but without diamond control himself West has to sign off in 5♥. With hand (b) East denies the ♣A when he responds 5♦. This is exactly what West wants to hear. With all suits controlled and expecting sufficient tricks on the bidding he has no hesitation in contracting for the small slam.

Study the following hands and sequences with West as dealer.

♠ A K J 9 6	♠ Q 10 8 4	West	East
♥ 4	♥ 10 5 3	1♠	3♠
♦ A K Q 9 2	♦ J 8	4♦	5♣
♣ 8 3	♣ A K 6 5	6♠	

West knows there are plenty of tricks available, but cannot be sure about club control. Blackwood would not solve his problem, but a cuebid and return cuebid provide the answer.

♠ Q 10 8 5	♠ A K 9 7 6 2	West	East
♥ K Q J 7 2	♥ A 4	1♥	1♠
♦ A Q	♦ J 8 5 3	3♠	4♥
♣ Q 9	♣ 2	5♦	6♠

Once East knows about diamond control he is not concerned that the ♣A is missing. The bidding indicates that there should be enough tricks available.

♠ A 10 7 5	♠ -	West	East
♥ A 6 3	♥ 7 4	1NT	3♦
♦ 8 4	♦ A K Q 10 7 5	3NT	4♣
♣ A 9 8 7	♣ K J 10 6 3	4♥	6♣

The 4♥ bid clearly shows the ♥A, and a liking for clubs. That is all East needs to know. If a small slam with 13 points opposite a weak no trump shocks you, reflect that all thirteen tricks will be made if the ♣Q comes down!

		West	East
♠ A Q J 10 8 7	♠ K 9 5	2♠	3♠
♥ A 4	♥ K Q 10 7	4♣	4♦
♦ 7 5	♦ A J 10 3	4♥	5♥
♣ A K 4	♣ 8 5	6♣	7♠

Having agreed the trump suit East/West set out on a cuebidding sequence. 4♣, 4♦ and 4♥ are all first-round controls. Now 5♥ and 6♣ (this last bid guarantees a small slam and shows interest in the grand) are second-round controls. At this point East is fairly sure he can count thirteen tricks so he bids the grand slam.

		North	South
♠ A J 9 8 6		Pass	1♦
♥ A 8 7 5		2♠(i)	3♣(ii)
♦ 9 7 4 2		3♥(ii)	4♥(iii)
♣ -		4♠(ii)	5♥(iii)
♠ Q 3 2	♠ K 10 7 4	6♣(iv)	7♦(v)
♥ J 9 4 3	♥ 10 2		
♦ 8	♦ Q 5		
♣ K Q 10 8 6	♣ J 9 5 3 2		
♠ 5			
♥ K Q 6			
♦ A K J 10 6 3			
♣ A 7 4			

(i) The jump bid after passing is universally recognized in good circles as natural but with partner's suit in this case diamonds. Without a fit you don't jump.

(ii) Cuebids showing first-round control.

(iii) Cuebid showing second- and third-round control of hearts.

(iv) Actually a first-round control, but North has only now been able to get the information across.

(v) Everything seems to be wrapped up so let's go for the jackpot.

As you can see, the grand slam is virtually lay-down, but the bidding . . . that was quite something.

This final hand almost ended in disaster since North/South stretched themselves to the limit—and perhaps a bit beyond!

East/West Vulnerable. IMPs. Dealer North.

	♠ K Q 7 5	
	♥ A K 8 4 2	
	♦ -	
	♣ 7 5 4 2	
♠ 3		♠ 8 4
♥ J 7		♥ Q 10 5
♦ A K J 10 7 5 2		♦ Q 9 4 3
♣ Q 10 8		♣ J 9 6 3
	♠ A J 10 9 6 2	
	♥ 9 6 3	
	♦ 8 6	
	♣ A K	

West	North	East	South
-	1♥	Pass	1♠
2♦	3♠	Pass	4♣
Pass	4♦	Pass	5♣
Pass	5♥	Pass	6♣
Pass	6♥	Pass	7♠

Once spades were agreed South cuebid his club controls while North showed first-round controls in diamonds and hearts. No doubt South hoped his partner held the ♥Q instead of the ♠Q, however, it does seem that South was rather optimistic (three small cards in partner's suit is not ideal) but, in fact, he made his contract.

It won't come as a surprise to know that the grand slam was not bid in the other room. However, it is no good criticizing South too much, since his card play easily justified his bidding. The ♦A was led and ruffed in dummy. At first sight, prospects did not look good; it appeared that declarer must lose a trick in hearts. However, two rounds of spades were followed by the ♣A and a second diamond ruff. Declarer returned to hand with the ♣K and continued playing spades to reach the following position:

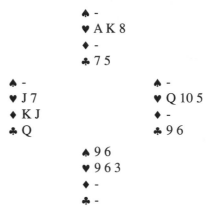

When the ♠9 was played West discarded a diamond and dummy the ♥8, but East was not happy. If he discarded a heart, the ♥AK would leave the South hand high; while, if he discarded a club, declarer had only to ruff one club to make the dummy high.

It is true that cuebids alone cannot take all the credit for the happy outcome on this hand. A little luck and skillful declarer play certainly helped. Still, without the use of cuebids, there must be some doubt about arriving in the small slam, let alone the ambitious grand. Long live cuebids!

ROMAN KEY CARD BLACKWOOD
Star Rating: ****

Most bridge players are reared on a few simple conventions and it would be fair to assume that one of these is Blackwood, perhaps the easiest and most popular convention in the world. Conceived by the American Master, Easley Blackwood of Indianapolis in 1933, it is still going strong. It is remarkable that his original idea has required little doctoring over the passing years. Perhaps the most significant improvement was to count the king of trumps as a fifth "ace" and amend the responses to incorporate this feature. Although standard Blackwood is still played in many circles, a new and increasingly popular version is the choice of many experts. This is Roman Key Card Blackwood.

RKCB recognizes the vital role played by the king and queen of trumps and this is reflected in the schedule of responses to 4NT. Initially the responses are geared to the four aces and the king of trumps, thus there are five key cards involved (the queen of trumps enters the stage later on, as an accessory).

These are the responses to partner's 4NT inquiry:

> 5♣=0 or 3 key cards
> 5♦=1 or 4 key cards
> 5♥=2 or 5 key cards without the trump queen
> 5♠=2 or 5 key cards with the trump queen

If you think there might be some ambiguity over the dual role that these responses embrace—forget it! The previous bidding will always make the situation clear, but if by some odd quirk of fate you are uncertain, assume partner has the weaker version. If it happens to be the stronger one he will continue bidding when it is his next turn to speak. It has never been my experience to witness a competent pair have a misunderstanding in this area.

As with all forms of slam investigation, it is necessary to have first agreed on a satisfactory trump suit, and then to make sure that partner's reply to your 4NT inquiry will not prove an embarrassment. If it might, then maybe you should curb your enthusiasm and proceed in a different way.

Over the responses of 5♣ and 5♦ (4NT-5♣/5♦) you can check on the trump queen by bidding the next suit up—excluding the trump suit. If the responder does not hold the trump queen he must sign off in the agreed trump suit. Holding the trump queen he may cuebid an outside king or bid 5NT.

After using 4NT you may then ask for kings (excluding the trump king, of course) by bidding 5NT. This reply should be based on the ladder principle as used in basic Blackwood, (6♣=0, 6♦=1, etc.). Please note that the bid of 5NT guarantees that all five key cards are held by the partnership.

What happens when the responder to 4NT has a useful void, that is not a void in partner's suit? There are a number of different ideas but I suggest the following: Make the same bid as you would normally, but now make it at the six level providing that this bid is not higher than the agreed trump suit, otherwise respond six of the agreed trump suit. Obviously some discretion is required in this area.

Let us look at an example:

♠ K 8	♠ A 6 4 2
♥ Q J 10 8	♥ A K 9 6 4 2
♦ 10 2	♦ -
♣ A K Q 10 6	♣ 9 4 2

West	North	East	South
1♣	1♦	1♥	2♦
3♥	Pass	3♠(I)	Pass
4♣(i)	Pass	4♦(I)	Pass
4NT(ii)	Pass	6♣(iii)	Pass
7♥(iv)	All Pass		

(i) Cuebids.

(ii) RKCB.

(iii) 0 or 3 keycards (it can't be nil), plus a useful void.

(iv) The grand slam must surely be icy.

In general terms, if two key cards are missing you should sign off at the five level. If only one key card is missing, a small slam should be worth bidding. If there are no key cards missing then a grand slam could be the answer, but you may still want to check up on the queen of trumps or a side suit king. You now have the machinery, so let's see it in operation:

♠ A J 9 6 4	♠ K Q 8 3	West	East
♥ A Q 5	♥ K 9 2	1♠	4♠
♦ K Q 8 3	♦ 7 4	4NT(i)	5♠(ii)
♣ 6	♣ A J 8 2	6♠(iii)	

After a natural opening bid and response West senses that there may well be a slam. The 4NT (i) RKCB inquiry reveals a great deal of information. 5♠ (ii) says "I have two key cards, plus the queen of trumps." West now knows that one key-card is missing, but decides the small slam (iii) should be a good bet. It is:

♠ A 8	♠ K 6 3	West	East
♥ K Q 8 4	♥ A J 10 7 3	1♣	1♥
♦ K 3	♦ A 6 4	3♥	4NT(i)
♣ A 9 8 6 4	♣ K 7	5♣(ii)	5♦(iii)
		6♦(iv)	7♥(v)

The promising start encourages East to trot out his toy, RKCB (i), although it wouldn't have been wrong to have exchanged a couple of cuebids first (4♦-4♠). Notice how the reply 5♣ (ii) simply cannot be ambiguous. Nil or three key cards. Yes, of course it has to be three, immediately identifiable as the black-suit aces and the king of hearts. 5♦ (iii) asks for the queen of trumps. West has got it (iv) (without it he would have to sign off in 5♥) so he shows the ♦K as well. He could also reply 5NT (yes, I have the trump queen and a side-suit king too) if a response at the six level looked dangerous (the ♠K, for example). Perhaps East cannot immediately underwrite the grand slam (v) but it certainly looks a good odds-on chance.

		West	East
♠ K J 8 2	♠ A Q 9 6 4	1♦	1♠
♥ 7 5	♥ K 3	2♠	3♣(i)
♦ A K J 3 2	♦ Q 10	4♠(ii)	4NT(iii)
♣ 8 6	♣ A 5 4 2	5♥(iv)	6♠(v)

When West raised to 2♠, East thought he would try to glean a little more information. 3♣ (i) looked like a trial bid for game to West who responded positively by jumping to 4♠ (ii). East was now sufficiently encouraged to try 4NT (iii), RKCB. 5♥ (iv) showed two key-cards and, of course, denied the queen of trumps. East decided to risk the slam (v) and as soon as he saw dummy he was glad he had done so.

Roman Key Card Blackwood has a lot going for it. In a sophisticated world where technology is always advancing even Blackwood can become more streamlined, more vibrant.

5NT GRAND SLAM ASKING BID

Star Rating: ***

The original 5NT asking bid, invented by Ely and Josephine Culbertson, was simplicity itself. It asked a straightforward question and received an uncomplicated answer.

The 5NT Question: Have you two of the top three honors (AKQ) in our agreed trump suit?

The Reply: With two of the three, bid seven in the agreed trump suit. With only one, or fewer, bid six in the agreed trump suit.

Here is an example from yesteryear:

		West	East
♠ K Q 8 5	♠ A J 7 6 4	1♥	2♠
♥ Q J 10 7 4	♥ A K	3♠	4♣
♦ A J 8	♦ K 5 2	4♦	5NT
♣ 6	♣ A 9 3	7♠	

Using cuebids to check that there were no outside losers, East then jumped to 5NT to find out about the K♠ and Q♠. West had them both so bid the grand slam. Missing one of these honors he would have replied 6♠ which would have become the final contract.

Note that the 5NT Grand Slam Force (GSF) can only be used when it is not preceded by 4NT (4NT followed by 5NT is Blackwood asking for kings). The GSF should not be used until it is ascertained that there are no outside losers.

In most rubber-bridge circles this method is still used today. However, it is not accurate enough for most progressive partnerships and, indeed, there is plenty of room for improvement. When one considers learning new conventions it is sensible to adopt a system which is efficient yet does not test the memory too severely especially since the use of the GSF is not an everyday occurrence.

One invaluable addition is to use the response of 6♣ (to 5NT, the GSF) to indicate Axxxx or Kxxxx in the agreed trump suit. This would cover almost 80 or 90 percent of grand slams that would otherwise be impossible to bid with accuracy under traditional methods.

Study the following:

		West	East
♠ A 10	♠ K 8 3	1♥	3♥
♥ A 10 8 6 4	♥ K 7 5 3 2	3♠(i)	4♣(i)
♦ A K Q 7 2	♦ 8 4	4♦(i)	4♠(ii)
♣ 4	♣ A 7 3	5NT(iii)	6♣(iv)
		7♥(v)	

(i)   Cuebids, all showing first-round control.

(ii) Second-round control of spades.

(iii) The Grand Slam Trump Asking Bid, or GSF for short.

(iv) This has to be Kxxxx as West has the ace himself.

(v) West knows that the grand slam is about 78 percent. Good enough odds to have a go. With the ♥J instead of the ♥10 the odds would improve to about 89 percent.

To make life as easy and comfortable as possible, we can retain the response of seven to show two of the top three honors, and the response of six to show none where the agreed trump suit is a major, but to show one or none where it is a minor.

In every case, except where clubs is the agreed trump suit, the response of six clubs shows Axxxx or Kxxxx. This is how the responses work:

The replies to 5NT (GSF) when the trump suit is clubs:
7♣	=	Two of the top three honors
6♣	=	One or none of the top three honors

The replies to 5NT (GSF) when the trump suit is diamonds:
7♦	=	Two of the top three honors
6♦	=	One or none of the three top honors
6♣	=	Axxxx or Kxxxx in diamonds

The replies to 5NT (GSF) when the trump suit is hearts:
7♥	=	Two of the top three honors
6♥	=	None of the top three honors
6♦	=	One of the top three honors with a maximum of four trumps, or Qxxxx, unless the bidding indicates differently (a pre-empt, for example)
6♣	=	Axxxx or Kxxxx in hearts

The replies to 5NT (GSF) when the trump suit is spades:
7♠	=	Two of the top three honors
6♠	=	None of the top three honors
6♥	=	One of the top three honors with a maximum of four trumps, unless the bidding indicates differently (a pre-empt, for example)
6♦	=	Qxxxx in spades
6♣	=	Axxxx or Kxxxx in spades

With a little more room to move when the agreed trump suit is a major it is possible to get some extra information across.

This is especially true when spades are going to be trumps since you can now show one of the top three honors with four trumps. Also queen to five and then ace or king to five.

All valuable data which is fairly easily assimilated as the bids of seven and six of the agreed trump suit and 6♣ (except where clubs are going to be trumps) are constant throughout.

Because of the popularity of Roman Key Card Blackwood, which accounts for the AKQ of trumps, the GSF is used much less these days. However, that is not to say that you can dispose of it entirely when you have adopted RKCB. There are moments when you will still have to rely on it. For example, when holding a void the 4NT inquiry is often less than completely satisfactory, and in some cuebidding sequences you may have to pass the 4NT level before you can decide how best to progress.

The following hands illustrate these points.

♠ K Q	♠ A 8 6 4	West	East
♥ K Q 8 4	♥ A J 9 7 5 3	1♦	1♥
♦ A Q 10 6 3	♦ K J 5	4♥	4♠
♣ 10 5	♣ -	5♦	5NT
		7♥	

Over West's rebid of 4♥ it would be foolish for East to bid 4NT because he wouldn't know whether West held the ♦A or the ♣A. The cuebid of 4♠ gets the reply of 5♦ (the ♦A) and now 5NT (GSF) asks about the top three honors. Holding both the king and queen West is only too happy to bid 7♥.

♠ 4	♠ A 5 2
♥ K J 10 9 8 6 5	♥ A Q 4
♦ J 7	♦ -
♣ A 4 2	♣ K Q 10 8 7 5 4

West	North	East	South
3♥	3♠	4♠	Pass
5♣	Pass	5NT	Pass
6♦	Pass	7♥	All Pass

4♠ agrees hearts as the trump suit and when West is able to cuebid the ♣A East's only concern is whether he holds the ♥K as well. 5NT asks the question and the reply of 5♦ confirms one of the top three honors. Obviously, in this case the number of cards in the trump suit does not apply because of West's pre-empt.

♠ K Q 7	♠ A 10 4
♥ A 9 7 4	♥ K 10 8 6 5
♦ 4	♦ A 3
♣ K Q J 8 5	♣ A 6 4

West	North	East	South
1♣	3♦	3♥	5♦
5♥	Pass	5NT	Pass
6♦	Pass	6♥	

From East's point of view 7♥ might be cold if West has both the ♥A and ♥Q. However, the reply to 5NT confirms that this is not the case so East subsides in 6♥.

20 Chapter

Getting to Better Slams

Cuebidding, Roman Key Card Blackwood, and the Grand Slam Force can improve your slam bidding overnight. This chapter features four more conventions commonly in play in tournament bridge which will help you become even more effective. The language of bidding is a restricted one, and each pair should work hard to increase their understanding. In the finely tuned area of slams the need for accuracy is paramount. Bidding good slams and staying out of bad slams is what it is all about. Here are four more conventional aides.

SWISS

Star Rating: ****

The Swiss convention consists of a jump to 4♣ or 4♦ by responder to an opening bid of 1♥ or 1♠. The idea is to differentiate between game-going hands that are shapely but lack aces (1♥-4♥ or 1♠-4♠), and hands that are rich in aces and therefore may have slam potential.

Suppose your partner opens the bidding with 1♥ and you hold either of the following hands:

(a) ♠ 4 (b) ♠ A 8 3
     ♥ K 10 9 6 4   ♥ Q J 10 6 4
     ♦ K Q 8 7 5   ♦ 6
     ♣ 6 3   ♣ A 8 7 4

By all usual methods of valuation you are worth a raise to game. But how is partner to know that on hand (a) you are all shape and hope, while on (b) your controls are eye-catching and there is a positive spring in your step?

The Swiss idea (it originated in Switzerland in the first place, hence the name) was to use the response of 4♣ or 4♦ (to one of a major) to indicate the more promising type of hand with an emphasis on controls. It is a kind of advanced announcement that responder is suitable for slam purposes should that suggestion appeal to opener in any way. The loss of the direct minor suit responses (1♥/1♠-4♣/4♦), on a frequency basis alone, was minimal. After all, how often do you want to respond four of a minor in the natural sense?

Certainly not frequently enough to regret discarding it for a far more useful purpose. Using the Swiss convention then, the direct major suit game raise (1♥/1♠-4♥/4♠) denies the qualifications attributed to Swiss.

Although Swiss is played in a number of different ways this is the method I suggest you adopt.

West opens 1♥ or 1♠. East responds 4♣.

The response of 4♣ shows game-going values in partner's major, 13-15 points including distributional points, four trumps or more, of course, plus one of the following conditions:

(1) Three aces
(2) Two aces and a singleton
(3) Two aces and the king of trumps

Should opener wish to inquire further, he now bids 4♦ over 4♣ and responder continues as follows:

(1) 4NT - three aces
(2) Bid the suit with the singleton - two aces and a singleton
(3) Reverts to four of the trump suit - two aces and the king of trumps

Note that with two aces, a singleton, and the king of trumps, responder shows the singleton first.

West opens 1♥ or 1♠. East responds 4♦.

The response of 4♦ also shows game-going values in partner's major, 13-15 points including distributional points, four trumps or more, and two aces. But this bid denies the other requirements of the 4♣ bid (no singleton, third ace, or trump king). Valuable negative information, perhaps, while still retaining the emphasis on aces.

Let us see Swiss at work:

West	(a) East	(b) East	(c) East
♠ A K J 9 6	♠ Q 10 8 4	♠ Q 10 8 4	♠ 10 8 7 5
♥ J 10 8 5	♥ 6	♥ A 9 6 4	♥ A 6
♦ K Q	♦ A 10 7 5	♦ 5	♦ A J 7 5
♣ K 4	♣ A Q 8 3	♣ A Q J 3	♣ A 8 3

West opens 1♠ and in each case East responds 4♣. So East has either two aces and a singleton or three aces. The third qualification—two aces and the king of trumps—is negated by West's own trump holding. West continues with 4♦—clarification please. On hand (a) East replies 4♥. That is exactly what West wanted to hear—a singleton heart—and so he bids a confident 6♠. On (b) East replies 5♦. That is bad news. A singleton diamond opposite the bare KQ does nothing for West's slam prospects so he signs off in 5♠. On (c) East replies 4NT—three aces—so there is no clearcut answer. There might be two heart losers, or one heart and one spade, or perhaps just one heart. West might try a cuebid of 5♣, hoping that East could show a doubleton or some other feature, but obviously East's options will be limited. In the actual example East would continue with 5♥, leaving West the final decision. If West's spades were headed by the AKQ, instead of the AKJ, he would be able to bid the slam with confidence.

The following hands are worth further study:

♠ K 7 5	♠ A 8 3	West	East
♥ A K 10 8 2	♥ Q J 9 6 4	1♥	4♣
♦ A 9 7 4	♦ 6	4♦	5♦
♣ 5	♣ A 8 7 4	6♥	

With only 14 HCPs, West has no qualms about bidding the slam.

♠ 6	♠ A J 8 4	West	East
♥ A Q J 9 7 3	♥ K 10 8 6	1♥	4♣
♦ K 10	♦ A J 7 4	4♦	5♣
♣ A 8 4 2	♣ 5	5♠	7♥

After a promising start West inquires with 4♦ and East shows a singleton club. West can virtually count twelve tricks so he now makes a grand slam try with 5♠. East realizes that the king of trumps must be the card his partner wants for thirteen tricks, so he bids a confident 7♥.

Suppose in response to the same hand East held only three spades and a doubleton club so that the two hands looked like this:

♠ 6	♠ A J 4	West	East
♥ A Q J 9 7 3	♥ K 10 8 6	1♥	4♣
♦ K 10	♦ A J 7 4	4♦	4♥
♣ A 8 4 2	♣ 7 5	6♥	

Now there would be no temptation for West to proceed beyond 6♥.

Here is another example of complete trust after the initial, more or less automatic, exchanges have been made:

♠ A Q 9 8 6 5	♠ K J 10 3	West	East
♥ A K Q	♥ 8 6 2	1♠	4♣
♦ 7 5 4	♦ A	4♦	5♦
♣ 3	♣ A 9 7 4 3	5♥	6♠
		7♠	

The bids up to 5♦ are routine, East showing two aces and a singleton diamond which, of course, has to be the ace. West

then makes a cuebid of 5♥. With the king of trumps not yet accounted for East jumps to 6♠. West interprets this development correctly and bids the lay down grand slam.

The response of 4♦ (1♥/1♠-4♦), while encouraging in one sense (two aces), offers a salutary warning against expecting too much:

♠ Q 6 3	♠ A J 10	West	East
♥ A Q J 8 6	♥ 10 9 7 5	1♥	4♦
♦ K Q J	♦ 7 3	4♥	
♣ 10 5	♣ A K J 6		

Knowing that one ace and the ♥K are missing West is not tempted to be ambitious.

♠ A Q 7 4	♠ K 5	West	East
♥ A K 10 8 4	♥ Q 9 7 5	1♥	4♦
♦ K 6	♦ A 8 5 3	4NT(i)	5♦(ii)
♣ 8 3	♣ A 6 4	6♥	

(i) How many kings?
(ii) One

West's bid of 4NT asks for kings—aces are already known—and when East shows one king the small slam seems to be a reasonable proposition.

Of course, there will be many occasions when the opener will not want to make further inquiries after the bidding has started 1♥/1♠-4♣.

♠ 7 4
♥ A 9 8 6 4
♦ A K 5
♣ Q 6 3

West opens 1♥ and hears 4♣ from his partner. Having no further ambitions he will sign off in 4♥.

It is important to remember that the 4♣ or 4♦ response to 1♥ or 1♠ should be limited, in that it does not contain forcing values. 13-15 points, including distribution, is about right. Suppose you hold ♠AK1093, ♥KQ72, ♦8, ♣A83 and hear partner bid 1♥—what is your response? With 16 HCPs plus two distributional points for the singleton diamond you are much too strong for Swiss. Your best bid is 2♠, a game force.

SPLINTER BIDS

Star Rating: **

A Splinter Bid is an unusual jump in a new suit which guarantees a fit for partner's last named suit (at least four card support) and shows a singleton or void in the suit in which the jump is made. Game is confirmed and a slam is suggested if partner is suitable.

You will notice that there is some similarity between Splinter Bids and Swiss in that the objectives, and to some extent the qualifications, occupy common ground. The main difference is that Swiss is primarily harnessed to aces, while Splinter Bids are concerned with singletons (the singleton may be an ace) and voids. The last bid in each of the following is a Splinter:

    (a) 1♥-3♠
    (b) 1♣-1♥-4♦
    (c) 1♠-2♦-4♣
    (d) 1♠-2♣-2♥-4♦
    (e) 1♠- 4♥ (be sure that your partner is on the same wavelength as you for this one)
    (f) 1♠-4♣
    (g) 1♥-4♦

If you play Swiss you might prefer to reserve (f) and (g) for the Swiss convention only. If you don't play Swiss then these sequences, 1♥/1♠-4♣/4♦, fall neatly into the Splinter Bid category.

In general, any jump during the auction when a lower level bid, or lower level jump bid, would be forcing, should be considered a Splinter Bid. A repeat bid in the Splinter suit confirms either the singleton ace or a void. Otherwise new suits are cuebids while 4NT is Blackwood.

How strong should you be to initiate a Splinter Bid?
If you are responder you require at least four card support for partner's suit (usually a major) and the equivalent of a minimum opening bid, about 13-15 points including distributional points, or six or seven losers. If you have more points or only five losers you will probably be too strong for a Splinter and should be considering a jump bid in a new suit. Let's look at some examples. Partner opens 1♥ and you hold.

(a)	♠ K Q 10 6 4	(b)	♠ 9 6 4
	♥ A Q 10 5		♥ K J 10 5 3
	♦ 4		♦ 4
	♣ J 9 7		♣ A 6 4 2
	Bid 4 ♦		Bid 3♥

(c)	♠ A 7 6	(d)	♠ 6
	♥ K Q 10 5		♥ K Q 10 5
	♦ 4		♦ A Q 10 9
	♣ A K J 10 4		♣ J 10 6 4
	Bid 3♣		Bid 3♠

(a) and (d) are natural Splinter hands. (b) is too weak for a Splinter so you just make the normal limit raise to 3♥. (c) is too strong for a Splinter Bid. It is best to force at once.

If you are the opener and strong enough to jump to game in responder's suit (1♦-1♥-4♥), that is, you hold 19+ points and no more than five losers, you should prefer a Splinter Bid whenever that is available. You open 1♦ and your partner responds 1♥. You hold:

(a)	♠ K Q 6	(b)	♠ 8
	♥ A Q 10 5		♥ K Q 7 5
	♦ A K J 10 4		♦ A K Q 10 5
	♣ -		♣ A 4 3
	Bid 4♣		Bid 3♦

(c)	♠ A J 9	(d)	♠ A
	♥ Q J 8 4		♥ K Q 9 2
	♦ A K J 9 7 3		♦ K Q J 10 5
	♣ -		♣ Q 10 5
	Bid 4♣		Bid 3♠

Object of Splinter Bids
The idea is to explore for slam, trying to discover if there is perhaps a super fit which sometimes will enable it to be bid on quite minimum high cards. Equally important is the other side of the coin—Splinter Bids may help you to stay out of a poor slam that might otherwise be bid on general values. Let's look at the system at work.

Both Sides Vulnerable. IMPs. Dealer West.

♠ Q J 5	♠ A 4
♥ A Q 9 6	♥ K J 10 7 5
♦ A K Q 10 4	♦ 8 5 3
♣ 7	♣ 9 6 4

In the open room the bidding was of a fairly pedestrian nature. West opened 1♦, East responded 1♥, and West raised to 4♥, where the matter rested.

In the closed room, after a similar start, 1♦-1♥, West rebid 4♣ a Splinter Bid agreeing hearts and showing a singleton or void club. East gave his next bid a little thought. Having no wastage in clubs was good news, but three little cards in partner's first suit is always an unattractive holding when considering slam and East was well aware of the dangers. On the other hand, he did have good trumps and an ace. In any case, a cuebid would not necessarily commit him to slam so he ventured 4♠. This was all West wanted to hear and he bid a confident 6♥.

Although South held some promising cards on the next deal, North's rebid started the alarm bells ringing.

Neither Side Vulnerable. Pairs. Dealer North.

	♠ A J 4	
	♥ K Q 10 3	
	♦ 8	
	♣ A Q J 9 6	
♠ 10 9 8 6		♠ K 7 2
♥ 4		♥ 7 6 2
♦ A 9 4		♦ Q 7 6 3 2
♣ K 10 7 5 3		♣ 8 2
	♠ Q 5 3	
	♥ A J 9 8 3	
	♦ K J 10 5	
	♣ 4	

North opened 1♣ and then rebid 4♦ over 1♥. Tempting though it was, South decided that the hands were too ill-fitting to go slamming and shut up shop with a bid of 4♥. This turned out to be a wise decision because a spade was led and there was no way he could make more than eleven tricks. (+ 450) on the score sheet was a pleasing sight.

The next hand was played in a Swiss Teams event. One North counted his points and allowed them to control his destiny.

Let's see what the other North did:

```
            ♠ K J 9 5
            ♥ K Q 7 4
            ♦ J 10 6 4 3
            ♣ -
♠ 2                         ♠ 7 4 3
♥ 8 5 2                     ♥ J 10 9 3
♦ A 9 7 2                   ♦ 8 5
♣ K Q 8 6 4                 ♣ A J 9 3
            ♠ A Q 10 8 6
            ♥ A 6
            ♦ K Q
            ♣ 10 7 5 2
```

At the first table the bidding was 1♠-4♠ and North thought he had been very forward in bidding 4♠, not 3♠—"Only 10 points, partner."

At the opposite table this was the auction:

South	North
1♠	4♣
4♥	5♣
5♦	5♥
6♠	Pass

4♣ was a splinter agreeing spades. 4♥ was a cuebid, denying the ♦A, and 5♣ confirmed a void or the singleton ♣A. 5♦ showed second round control in diamonds and 5♥ the same in hearts. That was enough for South to bid a confident 6♠.

Twelve tricks were made at both tables.

DOPI

**Star Rating: ** ✱✱

You and your partner have agreed a suit while your opponents have been active in the bidding, and then your partner pops the question via Blackwood 4NT, "How many aces have you?" Nothing too demanding so far. But then it happens—your RHO bids one more of his wretched suit and you are suddenly confronted with a problem. How are you to tell partner what he wants to know when the opposition have taken up your space? Unfortunately, in bridge your opponents are completely within their rights to impede you, take your ground, and do their very best to insure that at all times you get anything but a clear run. To counter this impertinent intrusion into the nice conversation you were having with your partner you need a bit of sophistication. Not a lot, but just enough to swing the pendulum back in your favor. Although there are a number of different methods available, by far the simplest and most popular is DOPI.

DOPI works like this (remember, over your partner's 4NT bid RHO has come in with, say, 5♥):

With no ace:	Double. That is the DO (Double = 0)
With one ace:	Pass. That is the PI (Pass = 1)
With two aces:	Bid the next suit up. If you've remembered the first bit this and the last case follow along logically.
With three aces:	Bid two suits up.

Thinking about all that for a moment, the worst type of hand you can have for partner for slam purposes is some aceless wonder, so double seems eminently sensible anyway. With one ace that may be good news or bad news, but by passing you will keep partner fully informed and then he can make his own arrangements. With two or three aces that must be good news, so you can afford to get busy.

Let's look at a few sequences. You are West.

1.
```
♠ A Q J 9 6   West   North   East   South
♥ 7 5         1♠     2♥      3♥     4♥
♦ K Q 6 3     Pass   Pass    4NT    5♥
♣ Q 6         ?
```
Pass, this shows one ace.

2.
```
♠ K Q 10 9 5   West   North   East   South
♥ 2            1♠     2♥      3♦     3♥
♦ K J 9 6      4♦     Pass    4NT    5♥
♣ K J 10       ?
```
Double, this denies an ace.

3.
```
♠ A Q 10 9 7   West   North   East   South
♥ 6 3          -      -       -      1♥
♦ A Q 4 2      1♠     4♥      4NT    5♥
♣ 6 4          ?
```
Bid 5♠ showing two aces.

4.
```
♠ 2            West   North   East   South
♥ A 10 9 6 3   1♥     1♠      3♦     3♠
♦ A 5 3        Pass   4♠      4NT    5♠
♣ A J 8 5      ?
```
Bid 6♣ showing three aces. 5NT would show two aces.

Let us look at two of the hands in more depth. On hand 2, DOPI helped East/West to judge correctly at the five level.

```
            ♠ 7
            ♥ K Q J 10 7 6
            ♦ 5 3
            ♣ A 9 8 7
♠ K Q 10 9 5                ♠ A J 6
♥ 2                         ♥ 4
♦ K J 9 6                   ♦ A Q 10 8 4 2
♣ K J 10                    ♣ Q 5 4
            ♠ 8 4 3 2
            ♥ A 9 8 5 3
            ♦ 7
            ♣ 7 3 2
```

West	North	East	South
1♠	2♥	3♦	3♥
4♦	4♥	4NT	5♥
Double	Pass	5♠	All Pass

Warned that there were two aces missing (West's double denies an ace), East's only decision was whether to take a penalty or play in 5♠. In settling for the spade game he judged it right since 5♥ and goes only two down whereas West had no difficulty in landing eleven tricks.

On hand 3, DOPI was used in bidding a good slam.

```
              ♠ 8
              ♥ K J 7 4
              ♦ J 10 9 8 7 6 3
              ♣ 3
♠ A Q 10 9 7              ♠ K J 5 4 3
♥ 6 3                     ♥ 2
♦ A Q 4 2                 ♦ 5
♣ 6 4                     ♣ A K J 10 7 2
              ♠ 6 2
              ♥ A Q 10 9 8 5
              ♦ K
              ♣ Q 9 8 5
```

West	North	East	South
-	-	-	1♥
1♠	4♥	4NT	5♥
5♠	Pass	6♠	All Pass

Over the nuisance bid of 5♥, West showed his two aces by bidding one suit up. This was exactly what East wanted to hear and he set course accordingly. The play of the hand presented no problems for West, although North/South were not too happy about their decision to defend. 7♥ should cost no more than 1100.

Notice how in each case East/West were not inhibited in any way by the opposition barrage. DOPI solved their problems and left the headaches with North/South.

There are other methods that may be used in this situation. DOPI has the merit of being simple and very effective.

RAISES TO FIVE OF A MAJOR

Star Rating: *

In an era when bidding was less sophisticated and less meaningful than it is today, free raises to the five level in a major suit were often regarded as being synonymous with an acute attack of buck passing. Bid one more and the slam fails—it's your fault. Chicken out and pass when the slam makes—it's still your fault. A convenient, if not particularly efficient, route for those players who never admit to making a mistake. Fortunately, methods have improved considerably so that bridge-players today are able to clarify the meaning of such bids so that ambiguity is minimized.

Remember that a raise to five of a major is a slam try only when the bid is "voluntary" and is made when it was possible to bid or pass four of that major.

Suppose you hold, as West:

```
♠ -
♥ A K 9 4 3
♦ 8 5
♣ A K 9 7 6 2
```

Your partner, East, opens 1♠. You reply 2♣ and, to your surprise, you hear partner rebid 2♥. What next? Yes, the correct bid is now 5♥, meaning bid six if you control diamonds. East's hand might be one of the following:

(a)
```
♠ A K J 6 4
♥ Q J 8 7 5
♦ 7
♣ 8 3
```
(b)
```
♠ A K J 10 8
♥ Q J 10 7
♦ Q 7
♣ Q J
```
(c)
```
♠ A K J 10 8
♥ Q J 10 7
♦ A 7
♣ 8 3
```
(d)
```
♠ K Q 9 6 4
♥ Q J 10 7
♦ K 7
♣ Q 3
```

(a) On this hand 6♥ should be an easy make, and East, following instructions, should bid it:

West	East
-	1♠
2♣	2♥
5♥	6♥
Pass	

(b) On the second hand there is no play for a slam, if a diamond is led, and East should pass:

West	East
-	1♠
2♣	2♥
5♥	Pass

(c) On the third hand East has first round control of the suit his partner is querying, so he bids 6♦, paving the way for a possible grand slam:

West	East
-	1♠
2♣	2♥
5♥	6♦

(d) On the fourth hand East has an aceless minimum, but his partner is not asking him about his overall strength, or the number of aces he holds. He is inquiring solely about diamond control. East has it and should bid 6♥:

West	East
-	1♠
2♣	2♥
5♥	6♥
Pass	

So we can lay down the rules for Case 1.

Case 1

When three suits have been bid and partner goes freely to five of the agreed major bid six if you control the unbid suit (that is, not two losers), or cuebid the suit if you have first round control in it.

Let us look at another example. This time West bids first and might hold any of the three following hands:

(a)	♠ K J 8 6	(b) ♠ K J 8 6	(c) ♠ K J 8 6
	♥ 5 3	♥ 5 3	♥ 5 3
	♦ A K Q 9 7	♦ A K J 9 7 3	♦ A K 10 7 3
	♣ Q 6	♣ 6	♣ A 6

Opposite East holds:

	West	East
♠ A Q 9 5	1♦	1♥
♥ A K 10 8 6 4 2	1♠	5♠
♦ -	?	
♣ 10 3		

(a) West cannot control the club suit, so should pass 5♠.

(b) With a singleton club, West must bid the slam—6♠.

(c) With the ♣A, West should bid 6♣. This may lead to a grand slam.

Case 2

When the opponents bid a suit and then you or your partner bid freely to five of your agreed major—bid six if you control their suit.

♠ A K J 9 7 5	♠ Q 10 8 4
♥ 6 4	♥ 7 2
♦ A Q 10 8	♦ K J 3
♣ A	♣ K J 10 6

West	North	East	South
1♠	4♥	4♠	Pass
5♠	All Pass		

Although East/West have tricks to spare in the minors and in the trump suit, they cannot get away from two losing hearts. However, West's message is completely unequivocal, and East has no option but to pass 5♠. With a singleton heart he would, of course, bid the slam.

♠ 8	♠ 7 3
♥ A Q J 8 7 6	♥ K 10 9
♦ 7 3	♦ A K J 10 8 4
♣ K Q J 5	♣ A 6

West	North	East	South
1♥	1♠	2♦	2♠
3♥	3♠	5♥	Pass
6♥	All Pass		

In this example East asks the question "Do you control the enemy suit?" West does, so he bids the slam.

The last case is when you are looking for "good" trumps in partner's hand. That is to say "good" in relation to the bidding. Suppose you open 1♠ as West, partner raises to 4♠, and you hold:

♠ Q 9 8 7 5
♥ A K J 8 2
♦ A 5
♣ A

Now for slam purposes, it seems likely that everything will hinge on the quality of East's spades. For example, East could easily hold any of the following hands:

(a) ♠ J 10 6 4 2	(b) ♠ K J 6 4 2	(c) ♠ A J 10 6
♥ 7	♥ 7	♥ Q 7 5
♦ K Q 8 4 3	♦ K J 8 4 3	♦ 8 3
♣ K 6	♣ 6 5	♣ K Q 8 6

To find out about the trumps, West continues by bidding 5♠ (1♠-4♠-5♠). On (a) East will pass, but on (b) and (c) he will continue to 6♠.

So these are the rules for Case 3:

Case 3

When only one major suit has been bid against silent opposition, a continuation to the five level asks about the quality of partner's trumps. If good in relation to the bidding, go to six, if not pass.

A common situation arises after an opening bid of 1NT. West opens 1NT (12-14) and East holds:

	West	East
♠ Q 10 8 6 4	1NT	3♠
♥ A 7	4♠	5♠
♦ A J 10	?	
♣ A K J		

West could hold any of these hands:

(a) ♠ J 9 7 5	(b) ♠ K 5 2	(c) ♠ A K 5	(d) ♠ A J 9 5
♥ K Q J	♥ K Q 10 5	♥ K 10 5	♥ K Q 10
♦ K Q 9	♦ K 9	♦ K 9 6 2	♦ K 9 6 2
♣ Q 10 8	♣ Q 10 8 6	♣ 10 8 6	♣ 10 6

On (a) West should pass 5♠, but on (c) and (d) he should convert to 6♠. Hand (b) is more debatable, which only goes to prove that there will never be an automatic answer all the time. Nevertheless, my feeling is that West should pass. On the given layout, that is likely to be the right decision, as indeed it might be most of the time.

Now let us consider this sequence:

West	East
1NT	3♠
4♣	5♠

In effect the only suit bid is spades, because West's rebid of 4♣ agrees spades and shows the ♣A on the way for no extra cost. West might hold any of the following hands:

(a) ♠ K J 9 6	(b) ♠ J 9 6	(c) ♠ K J 6
♥ Q 6 3	♥ J 5	♥ A J 10 6
♦ A 6 4	♦ A K 10 3	♦ 9 6 4
♣ A 10 4	♣ A 10 4 2	♣ A 9 4

On (a) and (c) West should be happy to continue to the slam but on (b) he should pass 5♠.

Now let's look at some hands from competition.

Suppose that, playing in a teams competition, you hold the following hand as East, vulnerable against not.

♠ A Q 9 6 3 2
♥ 8 4
♦ A K 2
♣ A 4

You open the bidding with 1♠, South comes in with 4♥ and West bids 4♠ which is passed to you. Would you bid any more? If you did go on, what would you say?

At one table East tried 5♣ but then passed when his partner converted to 5♠. At the opposite table, East tried the effect of a raise to 5♠ and although his partner was clearly reluctant to increase the commitment, discipline won the day and he did bid 6♠. These were the two hands:

♠ K 10 7 5   ♠ A Q 9 6 3 2
♥ 10   ♥ 8 4
♦ J 9 8 3   ♦ A K 2
♣ K J 6 2   ♣ A 4

At least East/West proved that they were on the same wavelength although perhaps the final contract was no thing of great beauty. The ♥A was led followed by the king which was ruffed in dummy. Superficially it seemed that success would depend on the ♦Q falling in two rounds or the ♣Q being with South.

Anyway, trumps were drawn in two rounds and then the ♦AK brought only small cards from the defenders. This was the moment of truth. After a small trance, declarer decided to abandon the soft option of the club finesse and go for the minor suit squeeze. After all, North was marked with length in the minors so clearly the squeeze was the better mathematical chance.

This was the three card ending.

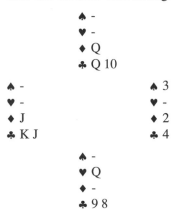

On the ♠3, South discarded the ♥Q, trying hard to look like a player who was hanging on to the guarded ♣Q. Dummy parted with the ♦J and North did his best by playing the ♣10 smoothly. But East was not to be denied his moment of glory—he played a club to the king and it was all over.

The next example hand occurred in the Women's section of the 1989 European Championships, Great Britain versus Netherlands.

South deals Both Sides Vulnerable, and West holds:

♠ -
♥ J 7 6 4 3
♦ A 7 5 3
♣ A K Q J

There is no opposition bidding and West opens 1♥ which East raises to 3♥. How should West proceed?

With the opposition remaining ominously silent, there must be some fear that East has wasted honors in spades. Length in spades won't matter, but high cards might if that means that East's trumps are somewhat anemic at the top. Still, the jump to 5♥, asking for the quality of East's trumps, has much to commend it and, as it happens, would have struck gold. In fact West decided on a cuebid of 5♣. East signed off in 5♥, which became the final contract.

Here are the East/West hands:

♠ -   ♠ 8 5 3 2
♥ J 7 6 4 3 ♥ A Q 10 5
♦ A 7 5 3   ♦ K 10 8
♣ A K Q J   ♣ 7 3

As the ♥K was held by North, all thirteen tricks rolled in without the slightest difficulty.

Chapter 21

Balanced Hand Bidding

STAYMAN

Star Rating: *****

Stayman, a conventional gadget used to locate a major suit fit (usually 4-4), after a 1NT or 2NT opening, is named after the famous American player Sam Stayman. The following discussion and examples assume a weak 1NT opening of 12-14 points. Stayman is equally effective if you play strong NT openings with 15-17 points. In the case of strong NT, responder will need the holdings described, but can bid with 3-4 fewer points in each case.

Opener bids 1NT (12-14)

When responder wants to ask "Have you a four card major?" the question is posed by bidding 2♣ (1NT-2♣).

Opener has three possible replies:

   2 ♦ - No four card major.
   2 ♥ - Four hearts, may also have four spades.
   2 ♠ - Four spades. Denies four hearts.

Possible action by responder on receiving opener's reply:

1. He can sign off in two of his five card major. To follow this route responder should be at least 5-4 in the majors.

2. He can sign off in 3♣. This will usually be a six-card club suit and insufficient values to be interested in game.

3. He can pass if a fit has been found.

4. He can invite game (so his bid is not forcing) with 2NT, 3♥, or 3♠.

5. He can bid game in the agreed suit or raise to 3NT.

These are the holdings when responder can inquire with Stayman:

1. With game-going values and at least one four-card major, 13+ points (10+ opposite 15-17 point NT).

2. With values to raise to 2NT and at least one four-card major, 11-12 points (8-9 opposite strong NT).

3. With a five-card major, but not enough points to insist on game, perhaps with a 5-4-3-1 shape, 11 points (8 opposite strong NT).

4. With five-four in the majors, 0+ points.

5. With a 4-4-5-0 shape, 0+ points.

In all five cases responder can cope with any reply by opener to his 2♣ inquiry. This is the essential test when considering the use of Stayman. If the reply to No. 4 is 2♦, responder signs off in two of his five-card suit, and if the same reply is made in No 5, responder passes.

The opening bid is 1NT (12-14)

Consider what responder should bid holding:

(a)	(b)	(c)
♠ A J 9 6	♠ 8 3	♠ J 6
♥ K 10 7 5	♥ A Q 7 5	♥ A K 7 5
♦ A J 6	♦ K Q 7 5 4	♦ K 10 8 4
♣ 8 4	♣ K 4	♣10 7 5
2♣	2♣	2♣

(d)	(e)
♠ Q 8 5 3	♠ 7 3
♥ A J 9 5	♥ 4
♦ 8 3	♦ J 10 9 8
♣ J 7 5	♣ K 10 9 8 6 3
Pass	2♣
(responder should bid 2♣ opposite 15-17 NT)	

(a) and (b) may play better in a major suit game if a 4-4 fit can be found. Failing that, responder will settle for 3NT. (c) Responder will raise 2♥ to 3♥ or bid 2NT over anything else (invitational, just as though the bidding had gone 1NT 2NT). (d) Responder cannot cope with a response of 2♦, so he must pass. (e) The intention here is to bid 3♣ (sign off) over any response.

(f) ♠ J 9 5 3   (g) ♠ 10 9 7 5 3 (h) ♠ 10 8 4 2
    ♥ K J 9 6 5   ♥ 8 6 4 2   ♥ A 8 6 3
    ♦ 7 5 4   ♦ 3   ♦ J 10 7 5 4
    ♣ 2   ♣ 10 5 2   ♣ -
    2♣   2♣   2♣

(i) ♠ 9 7 5 4 3   (j) ♠ 8 3
    ♥ 10 8 4 3 2   ♥ A Q 10 7 4
    ♦ 8 6 3   ♦ K Q 10
    ♣ -   ♣ A 6 3
    2♣   3♥

Because the shape allows responder to deal with any reply by opener, 2♣ is best in every case except (j). If a fit is not found the responder signs off, 2♥_ with (f), and 2♠_ with _(g). With (h) he passes any reply and with (i) has a choice between 2H and 2S. On (j) there is no point in asking about four card majors; better to bid naturally, showing the five-card major, unless you are playing transfer bids, which are discussed later in this chapter.

Let's see the convention at work:

Opener	Responder	Opener	Responder
♠ Q 9 3	♠ A J 10	1 NT	2♣
♥ A 10 8 6	♥ K Q 9 5	2♥	4♥
♦ A 6	♦ 10 7		
♣ Q J 10 5	♣ K 9 6 3		

3NT would fail on a diamond lead, but Stayman steers the bidding to 4♥.

Opener	Responder	Opener	Responder
♠ A J 9 6	♠ K Q 8 3	1NT	2♣
♥ K J 8 4	♥ A 5	2♥	3NT
♦ Q 6	♦ K J 10 7 5	4♠	
♣ Q 10 5	♣ 7 2		

When responder makes it clear that it is not the heart suit that interests him, he must have spades. Opener duly converts 3NT to 4♠—the best spot.

Opener	Responder	Opener	Responder
♠ Q 10 6	♠ 8	1NT	2♣
♥ A 9 5	♥ K J 10 6 4	2♦	3♥
♦ K 8 3	♦ A Q 7 5	4♥	
♣ A 10 9 4	♣ J 7 5		

Responder's bid of 3♥ (after 2♣, Stayman) is non-forcing but as opener seems to have suitable cards he continues to game.

Stayman works just as efficiently over 2NT. The asking bid, "Have you a four-card major?" is posed by responding 3♣ (2NT-3♣). Opener replies as for 1NT but, of course, at one level higher.

Opener	Responder	Opener	Responder
♠ A 10 3	♠ K 7 5 3	2NT	3♣
♥ A K 8 3	♥ Q 10 5 2	3♥	4♥
♦ K Q J 7	♦ 10 6 3		
♣ A 6	♣ J 5		

3NT would be hazardous with the club weakness, but 4♥ is sound.

Stayman still applies after a 2♣ opening and 2NT rebid (2♣-2♦-2NT). Here is an example:

Opener	Responder	Opener	Responder
♠ K Q 10 4	♠ J 9 7 5	2♣	2♦
♥ A K 10 3	♥ 8 4	2NT	3♣
♦ Q J	♦ K 9 7 5	3♥	3NT
♣ A 8	♣ 6 4 3	4♠	

Opener shows a balanced 23-24 points with his 2NT rebid and responder applies Stayman. Hearts is not the suit responder was after, so he has to bid 3NT on the third round. However, opener is still there and happily converts to 4♠ knowing that that is where there must be a fit.

Although rather rare, the same machinery can operate when the rebid is 3NT instead of 2NT (2♣-2♦-3NT).

Opener	Responder	Opener	Responder
♠ A K Q J	♠ 9 8 6 3	2♣	2♦
♥ A J 8	♥ Q 5 4 2	3NT	4♣
♦ K Q J 10	♦ 7 4 3 2	4♠	Pass
♣ K Q	♣ 10		

With two four-card majors responder decides to try Stayman, although there is some risk in this sequence. If a fit is not found the final contract will have to be 4NT, which might be dangerously high. However, all is well when opener bids 4♠—the best game contract.

It is worth noting that if the opposition intervene with a bid or a double, Stayman does not apply, that is:

West	North	East	South
1NT	2♦	?	

A bid of the opponent's suit (3♦ in this case) takes the place of Stayman.

West	North	East	South
1NT	Double	2♣	

East's bid of 2♣ is natural, not Stayman.

Apart from Blackwood, Stayman is the most universally played convention in the world. You cannot afford to be without it.

TRANSFERS

Star Rating: ****

Back in the late fifties, before Transfers had fully developed, the basic idea behind them was to allow the strong hand to become declarer, thus protecting the tenaces and delicate holdings like Kx from the opening lead. (On this basis alone surely everyone should play Transfers at least over 2NT.)

However advantageous it may be for the opening hand to play the contract, the real merit of Transfers lies in the additional information that they can convey. It would be neat and tidy if I could lay down a universal procedure that everyone plays, but unfortunately there are a number of variations. Anyway, I will give you a playable method with as few complexities as possible. Initially, let us consider Transfers that you can use after your partner has opened 1NT or 2NT.

Transfer Responses to 1NT (12-14)

2♣ is still your usual Stayman bid.
2♦ is a Transfer to 2♥.
2♥ is a Transfer to 2♠.
2♠ is a Transfer to 2NT if opener is minimum, otherwise he starts bidding his four card suits in ascending order.
2NT is a Transfer to 3♣

If you are playing 15-17 points NT, the same principles apply, but remember that the chances for game are excellent with a combined point count of 25 or more.

The Response of 2♦ to 1NT

Responder guarantees at least five hearts and requires opener to rebid 2♥. There the contract may rest, just as though you had signed off yourself, or you may continue with a number of informative bids that may invite your partner's further cooperation. Let us consider some hands. Remember, your partner has opened 1NT and you have replied 2♦.

Responder holds:

1. ♠ 7 6 3   1 NT   2 ♦
   ♥ Q 10 7 4 2   2 ♥   ?
   ♦ 5
   ♣ A 9 6 4

Pass. Arranging for partner to play in 2♥ is surely the best you can do so pass his forced rebid.

2. ♠ A J 3   1NT   2♦
   ♥ Q 10 7 4 2   2 ♥   ?
   ♦ 5 3
   ♣ A 9 6

Bid 2NT. This is your normal try for game, but in the process you have been able to tell partner that you have five hearts. (Opener will now pass, raise to 3NT or bid 3♥ or 4♥ with three card support or better.)

3. ♠ A J 3   1NT   2 ♦
   ♥ K Q 10 7 4   2 ♥   ?
   ♦ 5 3
   ♣ A 9 6

You are now a little stronger, so bid 3NT showing values to go to game plus a five-card heart suit. (Opener will either pass, convert to 4♥ or, if especially suitable, cuebid a minor suit ace en route to a heart contract.)

4. ♠ A 6   1NT   2♦
   ♥ A J 9 7 4 3   2 ♥   ?
   ♦ J 10 8
   ♣ 5 3

You are worth a try without insisting. Raise to 3♥. Partner already knows that you have five, so your raise shows six.

He should pass or raise to 4♥.

5. ♠ A K   1NT   2♦
   ♥ A 9 7 4 3 2   2 ♥   ?
   ♦ Q J 10
   ♣ 5 3

You must now be in game so bid 4♥. You could have bid this over 1NT, but since you lack tenaces it may be advantageous for partner to play the hand.

6. ♠ 6 3   1NT   2♦
   ♥ A K 7 4 3   2 ♥   ?
   ♦ A 10
   ♣ K Q 10 5

This time anything from 3NT to 6♣ is possible—so bid 3♣. There are various opinions, but I would play this bid as forcing to game and how high you get will depend on the subsequent exchange of information, but 3NT from the opener will close the auction.

The Response of 2♥ to 1NT

Responder now guarantees at least five spades and requires opener to bid 2♠. The procedure is then similar to that described already.

The Response of 2♠ to 1NT

The response of 2♠ should ostensibly be reserved for hands strong enough to investigate for slam, but without a five-card suit. This game forcing bid initiates a sequence in which both players name their four-card suits in ascending order until either a fit is found or 3NT is reached.

But, if opener's 1NT is minimum he must rebid 2NT over 2♠ and then responder starts the action of bidding his four-card suits. This proviso allows an important adjunct because responder can also use the 2♠ response on an 11-12 point balanced hand without a four-card major. If opener rebids 2NT responder passes. If opener starts bidding his four-card suits (so he is maximum) responder shuts up shop with 3NT.

We had better look at some examples.

1. Responder holds:

   ♠ A 7   1NT   2♠
   ♥ Q 10 3   2NT   ?
   ♦ K Q 10 4
   ♣ 9 7 6 5

Pass. Partner is minimum. Had partner started bidding his four- card suits, responder would have closed the auction with 3NT.

2.
Opener	Responder	Opener	Responder
♠ A 4	♠ K Q 8 5	1NT	2♠
♥ Q J 4	♥ A K 6	3♣	3♦
♦ K 10 7 5	♦ Q J 9 8	4♦	4♥
♣ K 10 6 5	♣ A 7	4♠	5♣
		6♦	Pass

Responder knows that his partner is maximum (the pluses come from the two tens and the two four-card suits) with four clubs and four diamonds. 4♥, 4♠, and 5♣ are all cuebids and 6♦ is the natural outcome. The extra trick by ruffing makes the slam an excellent proposition whereas a no trump contract would have to be fortunate to make more than eleven tricks, Traditional methods via Stayman would uncover a 4-4 major fit, but not a minor fit.

3.	Opener	Responder	Opener	Responder
	♣ K 10 5	♠ A Q 6	1NT	2♠
	♥ A 8 6 3	♥ K 7	2NT	3♣
	♦ Q 8	♦ A K 9 2	4♣	4♦
	♣ K 10 7 5	♣ A 8 6 4	4♥	6♣

Although opener shows a minimum hand, responder is anxious to locate a fit which he finds when opener makes his third bid. The 4♣ bid is worth noting, since with no four-card suit other than clubs opener would rebid 3NT over 3♣. With normal breaks 6♣ will succeed while 6NT would be poor.

The Response of 2NT to 1NT
This bid requests partner to bid 3♣ so that responder can sign off in 3♣ or 3♦, indicating at least a six-card suit.

Responder holds:

1.	♠ 6	1NT	2NT
	♥ A 8 4	3♣	?
	♦ 10 7 5		
	♣ Q J 10 9 7 4		

Pass. You may or may not make this contract, but (a) it is likely to be best, (b) the lead will come up to partner, (c) the 2NT bid has taken away some of the enemy's bidding space.

2.	♠ 7 4	1NT	2NT
	♥ -	3♣	?
	♦ K J 10 9 7 4 2		
	♣ 10 8 7 4		

Bid 3♦. Traditional methods would allow you to bid 2♦ immediately, but it is unlikely that you would be allowed to play there. If you hold the contract in 3♦ you may well feel satisfied whatever the result.

Although responder's 2NT bid (1NT-2NT) ostensibly suggests a weak minor suit with the intention of playing in 3♣ (the forced rebid) or 3♦, there is a further extension which can be invaluable when the right hands come along. Suppose you hold:

> ♠ K Q 10
> ♥ 5
> ♦ A 10 7
> ♣ A Q 10 7 6 4

and hear your partner open 1NT. Without much enthusiasm you respond 2NT and partner dutifully rebids 3♥. You now make the (apparently) strange bid of 3♥. In fact this bid shows a singleton heart plus a long minor (usually six cards). Although partner does not yet know your minor suit the fact that you have been able to indicate your singleton is

more than a little encouraging when the two hands are like this:

Responder	Opener	Responder	Opener
♠ K Q 10	♠ A 9 6 3	-	1 NT
♥ 5	♥ J 10 8	2 NT	3♣
♦ A 10 7	♦ K J 5	3♥	3♠
♣ A Q 10 7 6 4	♣ K J 3	4♣	4♠
		6♣	Pass

With an unsuitable hand opener would sign off over 3♥ with 3NT, but with little wasted in hearts, and good minors, he is only too happy to cooperate. 3♠ awaits further details, 4♣ names the suit and 4♠ is a cuebid. Trusting partner for the promised suitable hand, responder bids what he thinks he can make—6♣. The contract is not a lay down, but it is one you would want to be in. Make the opener's hand a fraction more suitable,

> ♠ A J 6 3
> ♥ J 10 8
> ♦ K J 5
> ♣ K 9 3

and twelve tricks are virtually guaranteed.

Before we go on to look at Transfers over 2NT, let me make one point clear. If the opposition interfere with a double, Transfers (and Stayman, too, for that matter) are out. Partner's bid is an attempt to escape into his long suit. This is no time for painting pretty pictures.

Transfer Responses to 2NT (20-22)
All the old arguments now apply with even greater vigor—it is wise to arrange for the strong hand to play the contract and get the lead up to, rather than through, the tenace holdings—but even so the extra dimension in bidding is often invaluable.

> 3♣ is still Stayman in the normal way
> 3♦ is a Transfer to 3♥
> 3♥ is a Transfer to 3♠

3♥ means I would have bid 3♦ had we not been playing Tranfers. (Some pairs play 3♠ as a minor suit slam sugges-tion. However, I feel it is more straightforward to use 3♠ as a diamond hand and then if you have clubs as well bid clubs on the next round. If you have clubs only you start with 3♣ and then bid 4♣ on the next round.)

The Response of 3♦ to 2NT

Responder guarantees at least five hearts and requests opener to rebid 3♥. Opener may break the Transfer if particularly suitable (for example, 2NT-3♦-3♠), but this is very much the exception rather than the rule.

Responder holds:

1.	♠ 8 4	2 NT	3 ♦
	♥ K J 10 5 4	3♥	?
	♦ Q J 5		
	♣ 7 5 4		

Bid 3NT. This gives opener the choice between 3NT and 4♥.

2.

♠ 8 4	2 NT	3 ♦
♥ K J 10 5 4 3	3 ♥	?
♦ Q J 5		
♣ 7 5		

Bid 4♥. With one more heart than already advertised and no ambitions above game level — raise to 4♥.

3.

♠ 8 4	2 NT	3 ♦
♥ K J 10 5 4	3 ♠	?
♦ A Q 8		
♣ 7 5 4		

Bid 4 ♦. Partner has refused the Transfer so he must be very suitable, perhaps ♠AKx, ♥Axxxx, ♦Kx, ♣KQJ. Bid 4♦, cuebidding your ace.

4.

♠ 8	2 NT	3 ♦
♥ K J 10 5 4	3 ♥	?
♦ Q 7 5		
♣ A J 10 6		

Bid 4♣. Partner can still sign off in 4♥, but his hand might be something like ♠QJx, ♥Ax, ♦AKJx, ♣KQ9x, when 6♣ would be a good spot.

The Response of 3♥ to 2NT

Responder now guarantees at least five spades and requires opener to rebid 3♠. The procedure is then similar to that described on page XXXXX

The Response of 3♠ to 2NT

This response is played in a number of different ways, but a simple and effective method is to treat it as a hand that would have replied 3♦ had you not been playing transfers. Look at the system in action on some difficult hands.

1.

♠ K J 5	♠ 8 4	West	East
♥ A K 6 4	♥ 5 3	2NT	3♠
♦ K Q 8 4	♦ A J 10 7 5	4♦	5♣
♣ A J	♣ K Q 8 2	6♦	Pass

After the first response there may be more than one route to 6♦, but it is essential for West to play the contract to protect his spade holding. The final contract is almost watertight. Declarer expects to make five diamonds, four clubs (discarding two spades), two hearts and one spade ruff.

2.

♠ K J 10	♠ 7 5 4	West	East
♥ K Q 8	♥ 5	2NT	3♠
♦ K 4 2	♦ A Q J 10 7 3	3NT	Pass
♣ A K J 7	♣ Q 6 4		

With only one ace and a minimum hand West signs off in 3NT. If West is only slightly better, say the ♠A instead of the ♠K (♠AJ10), then the ideal contract is unquestionably 6♦ by West. With the amended holding 6♦ by East would be in jeopardy on a spade lead while 6NT would leave West short of a trick on the same lead.

3.

♠ A J 10	♠ K 7 4 3	West	East
♥ Q J	♥ 4 3	2NT	3♠
♦ K 10 7 4	♦ A Q J 9 3	4♦	4♠
♣ A K Q 10	♣ J 8	5♣	5♦
		Pass	

East's initial reaction is that 6♦, played by his partner, might be a good spot, so he sets the ball rolling with 3♠. West is quite happy with this development and duly bids 4♦, but it then becomes obvious that the heart holding is extremely delicate and 5♦ is the limit of the hand. At least they avoided the trap of playing in 3NT. A slight alteration to the West hand, with the points remaining the same, would make 6♦ by West virtually impregnable—give him ♥Kx instead of ♥QJ.

Here are some general notes and reminders:

1. By playing Transfers over 1NT all you give up is the weakness takeout bid of 2♠. Not a great sacrifice for so much in return.

2. If the opponents double a 1NT bid all conventional aids like Stayman and Transfers are abandoned in order to allow responder to escape into any long suit.

3. With the use of Stayman and Transfers the immediate responses of 3♣, 3♦, 3♥ and 3♠ are going free. What should you do with them? Should they be weak (semi preemptive), invitational or strong? This is very much a matter for individual partnership preference. Twist my arm, and I would vote for strong—a good suit, slam suggestion.

4. Although I have dealt with Transfers only over a direct opening of 1NT or 2NT, it certainly makes sense to extend their use to analogous situations. For example (a) 2♣-2♦-2NT (b) 2♣-2♦-3NT, and perhaps after the overcall of 1NT. However, if you are experimenting with transfers insure that your partner is on the same wavelength.

BARON 2NT

Star Rating: *

When your partner opens the bidding and you have a strong hand, it is a moment to savor. Game will be on almost for certain. A small slam is possible. A grand slam—well, maybe. But one thing is for sure, good cards come your way only now and again, so when you strike lucky you want to have the machinery and the know-how to get the maximum reward with the minimum risk.

Say partner opens 1♥ and you hold:

(a) ♠ 8 6	**(b)** ♠ A K Q 10 8 6 5
♥ K J 10 6	♥ 6
♦ A K J 9 7	♦ A K 4
♣ A 10	♣ 9 3
(c) ♠ A Q 10 7 4	**(d)** ♠ A K 7 4 3
♥ 6 3	♥ 8
♦ K	♦ A Q 10 7
♣ A K J 6 5	♣ K Q 5

There is a certain basic procedure that should be followed when responding to your partner with a strong hand (16+ HCPs). With a fit in partner's suit, or a very powerful one suited hand, force at once—otherwise rebids will become extremely difficult. With a two suited misfit, don't force. Bid your suits naturally and await developments. With a three suited misfit, never force. You need time to develop the hand.

Thus, on hand (a) you should respond 3♦, on (b) 2♠ and on (c) and (d) 1♠. You are in a partnership that has agreed to play strong jump shifts.

So what has all this to do with the Baron 2NT? Not a lot, it sets the scene to take you on to another hand:

(e)   ♠ A J 6
      ♥ Q 10 5
      ♦ A Q J
      ♣ Q J 9 7

This hand does not fall into any of the categories we have discussed so far. In fact, if partner opens one of anything, it is not going to be easy to get your values as well as your hand type across to partner. You are too strong for an immediate or subsequent bid of 3NT, and too balanced to be involved in a number of suit bids. So there is a problem, but this problem quickly disappears if you are playing the Baron 2NT response, which shows 16+ points balanced.

The Baron 2NT (a response to partner's opening in one of a suit)

The response of 2NT shows 16+ HCPs. The upper range is unlimited. The hand must be balanced, with no five card suit, so the shape will be 4-3-3-3 or 4-4-3-2. The following hands are all typical 2NT responses:

(1)	(2)	(3)	(4)
♠ A J 10 7	♠ K 10	♠ Q 10 7	♠ A 6
♥ K Q	♥ A Q 5	♥ A 8 4	♥ K Q J 5
♦ Q 10 9 6	♦ K Q 8 2	♦ A J 9 6	♦ A J 10
♣ A Q 5	♣ K Q 7 5	♣ K Q 7	♣ A J 7 5

Playing this convention, all you have to give up is the natural response of 2NT which you would normally play as showing about 11 points—surely not too great a hardship. In any case, this restriction only applies if you have not yet passed. Passed hands automatically revert to their ordinary meaning since there is no way they could qualify for the 16+ HCP response.

Opener's Reaction to the Response of 2NT (1♣/1♦/1♥/1♠ - 2NT)

The basic idea is to bid as naturally as possible, but a reverse bid shows four cards in both suits:

1♥	2NT	3♠
1♦	2NT	3♥
1♣	2NT	3♦

So with five four in two suits opener must rebid the five card suit if it is lower ranking. This procedure facilitates the quest to locate a suitable fit. For example, let us say that the opener holds five diamonds and four hearts and the bidding starts 1♦-2NT. Now nothing is lost by rebidding 3♦. If responder has four hearts he will bid them over 3♦. Equally illuminating is when the bidding starts 1♥-2NT-3♠. Opener has four hearts and four spades. Clearly, when opener's suit lengths are 5-4, with the higher-ranking suit being the longer, he rebids naturally:

1♠	2NT	3♥
1♥	2NT	3♦
1♦	2NT	3♣

No trump rebids by opener should be informative and limited. Assuming the system plays a weak no trump opening (12-14) with a stronger rebid (15-16), the rebid of 3NT over 2NT should also show 15-16 HCPs. Carrying this principle one step further, the rebid of 4NT (1♦-2NT-4NT) shows 17-18 HCPs and, of course, is forcing to at least a small slam (17 HCPs + 16 HCPs = 33 = small slam target).

Let us look at some hands.

♠ A J 6	South	North
♥ Q 10 5	1♥	2NT
♦ A Q J	3NT	4NT
♣ Q J 9 7	6NT	Pass

♠ K 7 2		♠ 10 9 5 3
♥ J 9 8 6		♥ 4 3
♦ 10 9 8 6 3		♦ 4 2
♣ 8		♣ K 6 5 4 2

	♠ Q 8 4
	♥ A K 7 2
	♦ K 7 5
	♣ A 10 3

South's 3NT rebid showed 15-16 HCPs. North knew that the combined count was not less than 32, but he needed South to be maximum for the small slam to be a fair bet. 4NT expressed these feelings admirably. Looking at the four hands, we can see the good news and bad news just about level out. The black kings are well placed, but neither clubs nor hearts break and there is duplication in diamonds. Anyway, West led the ♦ 10 which was won in dummy. The ♣ Q won the second trick and was followed by a club to the ♣ 10, revealing the position. West threw a diamond. A spade to dummy's ♠ J held, and the ♣ A forced another diamond from West. Two top diamonds filled in a few more details and it only remained to try the hearts before executing the coup de grâce. This was the position, with South to lead, after the first ten tricks had fallen to declarer:

```
         ♠ A 6
         ♥ -
         ♦ -
         ♣ J
♠ K 7              ♠ 10 9
♥ J                ♥ -
♦ -                ♦ -
♣ -                ♣ K
         ♠ Q 8
         ♥ 7
         ♦ -
         ♣ -
```

West's hand was like an open book. South graciously gave him his ♠J, but West could not avoid conceding two spade tricks in return.

The next hand was bid and played in competent style:

```
         ♠ A K 5            South    North
         ♥ K 8 4 3          1♥       2NT
         ♦ A K 8            3♥       4♥
         ♣ J 10 4           5♣       5♦
♠ 10 9 8 6    ♠ 7 4 3       5♥       6♥
♥ 10          ♥ 7 5 2       Pass
♦ J 9 6 5 3   ♦ Q 10 7
♣ K Q 5       ♣ 8 7 3 2
         ♠ Q J 2
         ♥ A Q J 9 6
         ♦ 4 2
         ♣ A 9 6
```

The bidding was straightforward after North's response of 2NT (Baron). 3♥ showed five hearts, and 5♣ and 5♦ were cuebids. As South did not have spade control, he had to sign off in 5♥, but North not only had the spades bottled up, he also had something in reserve. Although 6♥ is completely cold as the cards lie, declarer needs to know exactly what he is doing before relinquishing the lead at the critical moment. The ♠10 was led. Declarer drew trumps, ruffed the third round of diamonds and cashed his spade winners, being careful to leave the lead in dummy. The ♣J was then run to West's ♣Q, leaving him in an unenviable position. If he returned a club, there would be no more club losers, while if he played anything else the ruff and discard would do just as well.

On my last hand it seemed that North/South had bitten off rather more than they could chew, but fortunately their guardian angel was on duty.

```
         ♠ 6                North    South
         ♥ A K 6 5 3        1♥       2NT(i)
         ♦ K J 7 6          3♦(ii)   4♣(iii)
         ♣ K 4 3            4♥(iii)  4♠(iii)
♠ K Q 10 8 5  ♠ J 7 4 3     5♣(iv)   5♥(v)
♥ 8 2         ♥ J 10 9 7    5NT(vi)  7♦(vii)
♦ 8 5 3 2     ♦ 10
♣ 10 7        ♣ Q J 8 5
         ♠ A 9 2
         ♥ Q 4
         ♦ A Q 9 4
         ♣ A 9 6 2
```

(i)   Baron showing 16+ points.
(ii) North rebids 3♦ in the normal way because his suit lengths are in natural order.
(iii) Cuebids. South's 4♣ must agree diamonds because he cannot have a five card suit and he certainly would not want to show a four card suit. To agree hearts he would have bid 3♥.
(iv) Second round club control.
(v)   A vital filler.
(vi) Grand Slam Force. Bid seven with two of top three trumps.
(vii) Trusting and obedient.

Getting to the grand slam was one thing, making it was something else. On top there are four diamonds, one spade, two spade ruffs, three hearts and two clubs, a total of twelve tricks. The red suits broke poorly; diamonds 3-2 would have made it easy for declarer to set up the fifth heart. Then West led the ♠K. Declarer won and ruffed a spade. The ♦K drew East's ten and a diamond to the the nine confirmed the break. A second spade ruff was followed by a heart to the queen and the ♦A, leaving:

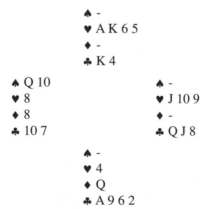

```
         ♠ -
         ♥ A K 6 5
         ♦ -
         ♣ K 4
♠ Q 10        ♠ -
♥ 8           ♥ J 10 9
♦ 8           ♦ -
♣ 10 7        ♣ Q J 8
         ♠ -
         ♥ 4
         ♦ Q
         ♣ A 9 6 2
```

When the last trump was drawn, dummy threw the ♥5, but East was in dire trouble. He was squeezed. In practice, he threw the ♣8, but it really did not matter. Whatever he did was going to be wrong and declarer was not going to be denied his moment of glory.

There is no doubt that the Baron 2NT is a useful and exciting convention to play. It fills an awkward gap in a natural system and is therefore to be thoroughly recommended.

22 Chapter

Doubles

NEGATIVE OR SPUTNIK DOUBLES

Star Rating: Played on a mini scale: *****
Played extensively: ***

"How did Sputnik get into the act?" you might well ask. Sputnik, a Soviet earth satellite, means (well, roughly, anyway) "travelling companion" and that seems to have nothing to do with doubles in any shape or form. But in the late fifties Alvin Roth of New York, one of the great theorists of our time, conceived the idea that when the opposition intervened at a low level there was more to be gained by using a double for takeout, or in a negative sense, than for punitive purposes as in standard methods. And what better name for this brainchild than Sputnik, because at that time there was much talk about the first Soviet Sputnik circling the skies. So we have Sputnik Doubles and Negative Doubles meaning one and the same thing, although perhaps Negative Doubles is the term most commonly used today. Such Doubles are usually made on fairly balanced hands and are especially useful when playing five card majors, although this is by no means a prerequisite.

Let's see the idea in action. Your partner, West, opens 1♣ and North intervenes with 1♠. You are East and hold:

> ♠ 10 5 4
> ♥ K 10 8 6
> ♦ A 9 7 4
> ♣ 8 3

In standard methods, where a Double would now be for penalties, you have no choice but to pass. Playing Negative Doubles you are on firm ground. You double, showing the values to respond at the one level (6 or 7+ points), a guarantee of four cards in the unbid major and some support for any unbid suit—in this case diamonds.

After a Negative Double the opener should support the major suit shown by the Double whenever he has them. He raises quantitively, always allowing for his partner's bid to have been made on minimum values:

West	West	North	East	South
♠ Q 3	1♣	1♠	Double	Pass
♥ Q 7 5 3	2♥			
♦ Q 8				
♣ A K 10 9 8				

Replace the ♦8 with the ♦K and the rebid should be 3♥. Make the hand stronger still, replacing the ♥3 with the ♥A while still retaining the king of diamonds, and the rebid should be 4♥.

All West's rebids are non-forcing (remember, he can rebid no trumps quantitatively, rebid his own suit or another suit at minimum level), so if he wants the auction to continue he must cuebid the suit in which the opponents have over-called. Of course, East may not be minimum at all. He may have quite a good hand (11+ points) in which case he will express the fact by continuing the dialogue.

Sputnik Doubles work just as effectively when an opponent intervenes at the two level. However, the doubler will now have to be a little stronger. Nine plus points is about right.

Your partner, West, opens 1♦ and North bids 2♠. East holds:

> ♠ 7 5
> ♥ A Q 8 3
> ♦ 7 5 2
> ♣ K 10 7 4

A negative double says it all.

Equally, when major suits have been bid, a Negative Double should show support for the minors. West opens 1♥ and North comes in with 1♠. Now when East doubles he is showing support for both diamonds and clubs. The double can be made on about seven plus points, but if the sequence has started 1♠–2♥–Double, then the doubler should hold nine plus points.

There seems little point in using a Negative Double to show spades in the sequence 1♣/1♦–1♥–? when you can quite easily bid the suit yourself (some players double to show four spades and bid the suit to show five). Another idea is for the Negative Double to deny four spades and show four or five cards in the other minor, perhaps with insufficient values to introduce the suit at the two level.

West	North
1♦	1♥

East holds:

(a) ♠ 7 4	(b) ♠ 8 6 3	(c) ♠ 10 6 3	(d) ♠ 10 6
♥ 8 7 5 3	♥ 7 5 3 2	♥ 8 5	♥ 9 7 4
♦ K 6	♦ K 9	♦ Q 8 5	♦ Q 10 6
♣ A 10 7 4 2	♣ K J 10 7	♣ A Q 5 4 2	♣ A J 10 7 5

Double in each case.

With the following hands you should bid naturally:

(a) ♠ K 10 6 3	(b) ♠ J 10 6	(c) ♠ 8 6	(d) ♠ Q J 6
♥ 8 7 4 2	♥ A J 9	♥ 10 7 4 3	♥ 7 5 3
♦ Q 10 6	♦ 10 6 3	♦ K 10 7 5	♦ K 6
♣ Q 3	♣ K 5 3 2	♣ A 7 2	♣ A Q J 10 7
Bid 1♠	Bid 1NT	Bid 2♦	Bid 2♣

Perhaps you are beginning to think that the Negative Double is the panacea for all opposition intervention and, indeed, that is the way many tournament players see it, extending its use to the three and even four level. While I don't want to dampen the enthusiasm of those who want to go all the way with their toy, I should point out that it is essential to agree the level at which your Negative Double ends and your Penalty Double begins.

Rubber bridge players who worry that their juicy penalties may one day be taken from them, as Negative Doubles gain popularity, can take solace from the tournament players who would no doubt claim that they actually have their cake and eat it too.

What happens is this. Whenever possible the opener is expected to re-open with a double after his partner has passed, often on values that would give traditionalists an acute feeling of unilateralism. As West you hold:

> ♠ A K J 5 3
> ♥ 6
> ♦ K J 9 7
> ♣ 9 7 4

You open 1♠, North bids 2♥, East and South pass … and you? You double, of course! The idea is that with values South would have bid whereas East may have been unable to do so. East is supposed to hold something like:

> ♠ 4 2
> ♥ K J 9 8 4
> ♦ A 3 2
> ♣ Q 10 5

and naturally passes your re-opening Double with confidence. When it works like this, Negative Doublers certainly have the best of all worlds.

If you are new to Negative Doubles and want to start practicing them, without putting the whole machinery into operation at once, you might like to begin like this:

Partner bids	Next player bids	You bid
1♣ or 1♦	1♥	?

Double denies four spades and shows the other minor (four or five cards) with 6 to a poor 9 points.

1♣ or 1♦	1♠	?

Double shows four hearts, tolerance for the other minor and 6+ points. Also five hearts with 6 to a poor 9 points.

1♥	1♠	?

Double shows 6+ points with both minors.

One of a suit (say 1♥) Two of a suit (say 2♦)?

Double is for penalty.

This mini approach, where doubles at the two level and above are penalties, will allow you to familiarize yourself with the machinery. Most experienced players, however, play that doubles are negative through the three level. You might adopt this method when you are more comfortable with negative doubles.

COMPETITIVE DOUBLES

Star Rating: **

A Competitive Double, as the name implies, is a Double used in a competitive situation, primarily for takeout, that asks partner to re-assess in light of information expressed by the Double. This double might also be described as a Cooperative Takeout Double which expresses the user's doubt as to what action to take and asks partner's help in determining the final contract.

As with most forms of negative Double the maximum benefit is derived during low level exchanges and especially, but not exclusively, when the opponents have supported each other in the same suit. Here are some of the most useful ways in which the Competitive Double can be used.

Partner (East) overcalls—opponents agree a suit.

(a) West	West	North	East	South
♠ 7		1♣	1♠	2♣
♥ A J 8 5 3	?			
♦ K J 6 4 2				
♣ 8 4				

(b) West	West	North	East	South
♠ A Q 7 4 2		1♥	2♦	2♥
♥ 8	?			
♦ 10 4				
♣ Q 10 9 8 5				

(c) West	West	North	East	South
♠ A 10 9 7 6		1♦	2♣	2♦
♥ K Q 10 8 4	?			
♦ 10				
♣ 10 4				

In each case West should double, showing length in the unbid suits. There would be little mileage in playing such Doubles for penalty so it is only sensible to employ them in a more useful role—defined as Competitive Doubles. Of course, all partnerships should agree on the level to which their Competitive Double applies. Up to 3♥ may be a reasonable compromise, but a number of tournament players take them even further.

There are so many situations in which a Competitive Double can be invaluable that it is hardly surprising that so many tournament players have adopted this gadget and use it extensively. Perhaps, like all good conventions, it is over-used. What you need to ask yourself is this: "If I am going to adopt a Competitive Double in situation X, am I going to lose out by discarding a penalty Double?" Where the opponents have bid and supported one another, one seldom loses by preferring a Competitive Double.

Playing pairs you hold as West: The bidding proceeds like this:

♠ A 8 3	West	North	East	South
♥ K 9 5	–	–	1♥	1♠
♦ Q J 7 5	2♥	2♠	Pass	Pass
♣ 6 3 2	?			

Maybe 2♥ would not have been your choice on the first round, but it is probably as good, or as bad, as anything else. Anyway, what are you going to do now? Playing Competitive Doubles you have an easy decision. Double and leave it to partner. You are showing him a maximum with only three hearts—with four you could continue to 3♥ yourself. Hopefully he will be able to arrive at the right answer. In a slightly different setting you might make the same Competitive Double and find partner only too delighted to pass for penalties once you show something extra.

Now let's look at another situation:

(a)
West	West	North	East	South
♠ Q 8		1♥	1♠	2♦
♥ A 4	?			
♦ 8 7 3				
♣ K 10 9 8 6 3				

(b)
West	West	North	East	South
♠ J 6 3		1♣	1♦	1♠
♥ K 10 9 8 6	?			
♦ K 4				
♣ Q 10 4				

(c)
West	West	North	East	South
♠ A J 10 7 4	–	1♦	1♥	2♣
♥ J 10	?			
♦ 7 5 4				
♣ K 10 7				

In each case West should double. When three suits have been bid, Double by the fourth player (Competitive) shows interest in the unbid suit and tolerance for partner's suit. Although the urge to play Competitive Doubles in the above

three situations may not be as strong as when the opponents support one another, nevertheless it is almost certainly the most beneficial arrangement. It is also worth remembering that the penalty element may not have disappeared entirely. With a suitable hand partner may opt to pass, or wield the axe should his RHO rebid his first suit.

Using Competitive Doubles, responder is well placed in this sort of situation:

West	North	East	South
1♣	Pass	1♠	2♦
Pass	Pass	?	

East holds:

♠ K 10 6 4 3	or	♠ K 10 6 4 3
♥ A J 5		♥ A 8 5 4
♦ 8 4		♦ 8
♣ Q 7 2		♣ 7 3 2

A bid of 2♥ by East should be reserved for a "playing" hand, maybe 5-5 in the majors. However, by doubling he gets the message across that he has enough high cards to want to compete. Opener now a decision; he can introduce a new suit, rebid his own suit, support partner's suit or pass hoping to collect a penalty.

There is yet another way in which a Competitive Double can come to your rescue. This is when you use it as a game try. This form of Competitive Double does not rate highly in the frequency stakes, but when it does occur it can be worth a million dollars. Give it the five star treatment for there is no way that it can cost.

Suppose you are West and hold: You open 1♥ and then the bidding proceeds like this:

♠	A Q 7				
♥	A J 10 8 4	West	North	East	South
♦	8	1♥	2♦	2♥	3♦
♣	A 6 5 3	?			

Do you see what has happened? There is no room for you to make a game try. If the opposition had not been so busy (1♥–Pass–2♥–Pass) you would probably have bid 3♣ over 2♥, urging partner to 4♥ with a suitable hand and help in clubs. That would have been neat and tidy. Of course, you could now bid 3♥ but that is exactly the bid you would make when you wanted to buy the contract at the lowest level possible. And how is partner to distinguish between "I want to play in 3♥ so for goodness sake don't bid on" and: "This is a game try—I want you to bid 4♥ if you are maximum and suitable?" The answer is—he does not have to. Using Competitive Doubles, you now double over 3♦. That is your game try. Thus when you advance to 3♥ in the sequence given the message is unequivocal. You wish to play there and partner is expected to pass.

Suppose you opt for the Competitive Double, as indeed you would on the above hand, partner will usually convert to 3♥ or 4♥, depending on suitability. However, a new option has been created. Perhaps East holds a hand like this:

♠ K 5
♥ 9 7 6 3
♦ K J 10 7
♣ 8 4 2

in which case he will happily pass your (takeout) double and play for penalties. Let's look at a hand:

```
              ♠ 7 4
              ♥ A K J 9 6
              ♦ 10 9 7
              ♣ K 8 5
♠ A K 10 9 8              ♠ Q J 6
♥ 2                       ♥ Q 10 8
♦ A K 5 2                 ♦ Q 8 3
♣ J 10 9                  ♣ 6 4 3 2
              ♠ 5 3 2
              ♥ 7 5 4 3
              ♦ J 6 4
              ♣ A Q 7
```

There was some spirited bidding on this hand from a large pairs competition with plus scores going both ways. 3♠ just made was good for East/West while 4♠ resulted in a plus for North/South. One East/West pair playing Competitive Doubles judged most successfully when, with Neither Side Vulnerable the bidding went like this:

West	North	East	South
1♠	2♥	2♠	3♥
Double	All Pass		

East reasoned that they were unlikely to make 4♠ but that his ♥Q108 might produce an unexpected trick so a pass had much to commend it. How right he was! Collecting two spades, three diamonds and one heart for a score of +300 was not difficult. Maybe they were a little lucky because with a slight alteration in the minor suits North would have gone only one down, but then West might well have had trouble in making more than eight tricks in spades. Anyway, in the event the defenders were very happy with both their gadget and the result!

Naturally, if you play Competitive Doubles then you have to give up the immediate penalty Double in all those situations where Competitive Doubles apply. But as you have seen, we have been able to use the Competitive Double as a game try—leaving partner with the option of transferring into a penalty Double if that suits him best. We have been able to contest the bidding at a low level in comparative safety (after partner has overcalled) because we have been able to show both our suits without bidding higher or taking a unilateral view. And where three suits have been bid we've been able to show interest in the fourth suit and tolerance for partner's suit. When responding with two suits, yet not strong enough to bid the second one after interference, we've still found a way of getting our message across. Finally, we were in a position to show a maximum raise to

the two level with only three trumps and an urge to do something more. All that can't really be bad!

RESPONSIVE DOUBLES
Star Rating: ***

Superficially, Responsive Doubles, originated by Dr. F. Feilding-Reid of Florida, give the immediate impression of passing the buck, or suffering an acute attack of indecision. North opens the bidding with one of a suit, East doubles for takeout, South raises his partner's suit and now West doubles for takeout. West's bid is a Responsive Double.

This has been the bidding so far:

West	North	East	South
–	1♥	Double	2♥
Double			

There are two sound reasons for using a Responsive Double:

1. Hands suitable for penalizing the opponents at a low level when they have agreed a suit are rare.

2. The responder to a takeout Double does not always have a clear-cut choice. Suppose West holds the following hand and the bidding has proceeded as above, but it is still West to call:

♠ 7 4
♥ 10 8 3
♦ K 10 7 5
♣ A 10 6 4

Should West bid 3♣ or 3♦? In an ideal world it probably wouldn't matter much because East would have four cards in each minor, something like:

♠ A J 8 3
♥ 6
♦ A 9 6 3
♣ K 8 7 5

However, in real life partner will sometimes have less than an ideal holding in one of the minors while being well stocked in the other, say:

♠ A J 8 3
♥ 6 2
♦ A Q 9 6
♣ K 7 5

It may now be crucial to locate the best fit and that is exactly what a Responsive Double sets out to do.

Responsive Doubles are usually played at the two and three level when there is no clear-cut decision to make. Strength should be appropriate for play at the level to which the responsive doubler invites his partner to bid (minimum, usually 6-9 points).

More often than not the responsive doubler will be denying a five card suit, and his suit lengths—those that he is offering—will be roughly the same. If it were otherwise he would hardly have a problem which needs further clarification. Where a major suit has been bid a Responsive Double (1♥–Double–2♥–Double) should deny four cards in the other major. Where a minor suit has been bid a Responsive Double normally shows four cards in both majors.

Let's look at some hands.

```
              ♠ 9 8 2
              ♥ Q 2
              ♦ J 9 5 3 2
              ♣ K 10 8
 ♠ K Q 7 5              ♠ J 10 4 3
 ♥ A 5 3               ♥ K 10 7 6
 ♦ 10                  ♦ 7 6
 ♣ A J 7 4 3           ♣ Q 9 2
              ♠ A 6
              ♥ J 9 8 4
              ♦ A K Q 8 4
              ♣ 6 5
```

Playing rubber bridge, after an initial pass by East, South opened 1♦, West doubled for takeout and North raised to 2♦. This was the moment of truth for East. Playing normal rubber bridge restricted conventions, his choice was limited to two of a major or pass. Not unreasonably, he chose 2♥. South bid one more diamond and West one more heart and that was where the matter rested. Final contract, 3♥ by East. Although East put up a spirited struggle he could not avoid the loss of five tricks (one spade, two hearts and one in each minor). Of course, it was obvious that a spade contract would have fared very much better, nine tricks being easy and ten a possibility. Had Responsive Doubles been permitted, then East could have doubled over Two Diamonds and the spade fit would have emerged.

This was a hand from a pairs tournament:

```
              ♠ K 7 5 3
              ♥ 6 2
              ♦ A 9 4
              ♣ 10 9 6 3
 ♠ 6                   ♠ 9 2
 ♥ A Q 7 5             ♥ 9 4 3
 ♦ K J 8 7 6           ♦ Q 10 5 3
 ♣ K 8 7              ♣ A Q 5 2
              ♠ A Q J 10 8 4
              ♥ K J 10 8
              ♦ 2
              ♣ J 4
```

As so often happens in pairs events, especially those of a not very high standard, the results were extremely varied. North/South achieved a good score when they were allowed to play in 3♠—just making. East/West did well when given the chance to double 4♠, but 4♦ just made was also well rewarded. The East/Wests who did really badly were those who played in 4♣. After 1♠–Double, North bid either 2♠ or 3♠, depending on style, and East was in the hot seat. Those Easts who were playing Responsive Doubles were com-

pletely at ease. They doubled and the right spot was soon found (South 3♠–West 4♦–All Pass). But spare a thought for those unfortunate Easts who had to guess whether to pass, or bid 3♣ or 4♣ depending on the level of North's raise.

Against a contract of 4♣ the defense was unrelenting. South led his singleton diamond to his partner's ace. The nine of diamonds was returned (McKenney suit preference lead asking for a spade back) and ruffed, and then a second diamond ruff was obtained when South underled his ace of spades for partner to win the king. The defense still had to score one heart and one natural trump trick for three down—instead of making ten tricks in diamonds!

Just in case you think it is all one-way traffic, there will be occasions when you will undoubtedly wish that you were not playing Responsive Doubles.

This is what you hold as West: The bidding starts:

♠ 8 6 3	**West**	**North**	**East**	**South**
♥ Q J 10 8	–	1♥	Double	3♥
♦ A 9 5 ?				
♣ 10 5 2				

Of course, you would dearly like to double for penalties … but you can't. It's tough, but you must pass. As with any conventional bid it is difficult to have the best of all worlds all the time. What matters is that you obtain sensible results most of the time; besides, on a good day your partner might double again, and then you'll certainly know what to do. Hopefully you've passed at normal tempo so that there is no question of an ethical problem.

LIGHTNER DOUBLES

Star Rating: ***

The opponents have just bid an uncontested small slam in a suit and with your two aces, or one ace and some other goodies, you think you may beat it. Do you double? If you do you are laying heavy odds on your judgment being right. After all, you are unlikely to gain more than an extra 50 points (or 100 vulnerable), but your loss can be several times that amount—quite apart from the risk of a redouble. Serious-minded bridge players are left in no doubt that it is both wrong and unprofitable to double a freely bid slam in a suit because you hold two aces, or because you hold a few values that might result in the contract going one down.

This brings us to the Lightner Double, invented by Theodore Lightner of New York as long ago as 1929. His idea was this: If competent opponents bid freely to a slam—not as a sacrifice but with obvious expectations of making it—it is fair to assume that they will fulfil their contract or go one down so there is little to be gained by a penalty Double. Therefore a Double by the hand not on lead should have a conventional meaning—"Partner, please find an unusual lead." The most frequent reason for this is that the doubler is void of a suit and wishes to score an immediate ruff.

The Lightner Double automatically bars the lead of any suit bid by the defense in a normal competitive sequence or, of course, a trump. If the opposition have bid three suits a defender should not double if he wants the lead of the unbid suit. Many players insist on the lead of dummy's first bid side suit or, if dummy has failed to bid a side suit, the first bid side suit by declarer. However, in the final analysis the player on lead must find something unusual and naturally he will look favorably on a long suit of his own that perhaps partner will be able to ruff. If in doubt play dummy's first bid side suit.

Let's look at a hand:

```
              ♠ K Q 6 5
              ♥ A K J 10 9
              ♦ Q 6
              ♣ 8 7
♠ 8 2                       ♠ 7 4 3
♥ 8 6 5 4 2                 ♥ —
♦ 10 9 8 7                  ♦ A K J 5 3 2
♣ 5 3                      ♣ 9 6 4 2
              ♠ A J 10 9
              ♥ Q 7 3
              ♦ 4
              ♣ A K Q J 10
```

West	North	East	South
—	—	—	1♣
Pass	1♥	2♦	2♠
Pass	5♠	Pass	6♠
Pass	Pass	Double	All Pass

Whether East bids 2♦ or not makes little difference. His final Double says it all. Lead something unusual, not my suit (if he has bid) and not the unbid suit (if he hasn't). Playing the Lightner Double, West won't have to be a genius to find a heart lead (dummy's first bid suit, by the way). It is worth noting that the East/West gain was not just an extra 50 for one down doubled, although that is what will appear on the scoresheet, but in reality 1080 (500 for slam, 300 for game, 180 for 6♠ plus 100 penalty) because without East's Double West would no doubt have led the ♦ 10 and the slam would have succeeded.

On the next hand East took steps to insure that he got the right lead by paving the way early on. At least this avoided any ambiguity.

Both Sides Vulnerable. Dealer South.

```
              ♠ —
              ♥ K 9 7 5 4
              ♦ A K Q J 7
              ♣ Q 9 4
♠ K Q 10 8 6 4             ♠ J 9 7 5 3 2
♥ —                        ♥ A 2
♦ 8 4                      ♦ 10 9 5 3 2
♣ J 8 7 5 2               ♣ —
              ♠ A
              ♥ Q J 10 8 6 3
              ♦ 6
              ♣ A K 10 6 3
```

West	North	East	South
—	—	—	1♥
1♠	3♦	4♣	Double
Pass	Pass	4♠	Pass
Pass	5♠	Pass	6♥
Pass	Pass	Double	All Pass

On a spade lead declarer would have made his contract in comfort but West was in no doubt about what was required of him and dutifully led a club. Once East had scored his ruff the defense had no further interest except for the ace of trumps, but they had every reason to feel pleased with their result. In fact 6♠ would have been remarkably cheap but who wants a cheap save when the alternative is a plus score?

Of course, on this occasion East did not bid clubs "in a normal competitive sequence," so there was no question of excluding that suit. On the contrary, he went out of his way to make it crystal clear that West should lead a club. Let us suppose that East, instead of bidding 4♣, bid 4♠ and that North/South continued directly to 6♥. Now when East doubles West may ponder over his lead. Something unusual, not a spade. So what? Dummy's first suit was diamonds, but can East really want a diamond lead? With only two in his own hand that seems most improbable, so no doubt West will arrive at the right conclusion. However, East's antics, designed to make life easy for partner, are worth noting.

This concluding hand contains an ominous warning for the unwary:

```
              ♠ 3
              ♥ Q J 8
              ♦ A K 10 8 4
              ♣ K 10 7 4
♠ 7 5 2                    ♠ 8 6 4
♥ K 4                      ♥ 9 7 5 3 2
♦ Q J 9 6 5 3 2            ♦ —
♣ 8                       ♣ Q J 9 6 3
              ♠ A K Q J 10 9
              ♥ A 10 6
              ♦ 7
              ♣ A 5 2
```

West	North	East	South
–	1♦	Pass	2♠
Pass	3♣	Pass	3♠
Pass	3NT	Pass	6♠
Pass	Pass	?	

You are East. Are you tempted to double? Of course you would like a diamond lead and it seems quite likely that partner has got a trick somewhere, but what about your defense to 6NT? Not good, and that's an understatement. Don't forget the opposition also know what you are up to when you double. On this occasion no trumps have already been suggested once and South will surely move to 6NT if you warn him of the impending danger. So, grit your teeth, pass and hope partner will find the right lead. They do sometimes.

STRIPED-TAIL APE DOUBLE

Star Rating: *

The Striped-tail Ape Double is not an everyday occurrence, and thus you may have to wait a while before you have the opportunity to practice this exciting coup. So, if you'll excuse the mixed metaphor, a rare bird it may be, but what a plumage when you see it in full flight! Let me set the scene. With North/South vulnerable, North opens the bidding with 1♦. East, your partner, bids 1♠ and South shows his muscles with 2♠. You, West, hold this unappetizing collection:

> ♠ Q 10 9 5 4 2
> ♥ 7 5 3
> ♦ 6
> ♣ 8 4 2

What is the best thing to do? Rightly or wrongly, you bid 4♠. This brings 4NT from North, a pass from East and 5♦ from South.

It's back to you:

West	North	East	South
–	1♦	1♠	2♠
4♠	4NT	Pass	5♦
?			

Suppose you double. Yes, I know it is for penalties and you have not a hope of defeating them, but as a result of your apparent eccentric optimism one of two things is likely to happen: (a) North passes, hardly able to believe his good fortune or (b) North, who is not the kind of person to be intimidated or short changed, redoubles. That is your cue to retreat to 5♠, or, in other words, flee like a Striped-Tail Ape!

This is the full hand:

> ♠ J
> ♥ K Q 2
> ♦ A Q 10 9 7 3
> ♣ A Q 6

> ♠ Q 10 9 5 4 2   ♠ A K 8 7 6
> ♥ 7 5 3   ♥ 10 9 8
> ♦ 6   ♦ 4
> ♣ 8 4 2   ♣ 9 7 5 3

> ♠ 3
> ♥ A J 6 4
> ♦ K J 8 5 2
> ♣ K J 10

The mathematics (duplicate scoring) are interesting:

5♦, doubled and made + 1 =	950
6♦ bid and made =	1370
5♠, doubled – 5 =	1100

You can see from this example that the best result obtainable on this particular hand is the first one—a swing of 9 IMPs when the other pair in your team bid to 6♦.

So the Striped-Tail Ape Double (usually of game) is an inhibitory shock tactic maneuver made when a player feels sure his opponents are going to bid and make a slam; the doubled contract with overtricks scoring less than bidding a successful slam. If the opposition redouble then the doubler flees like a Striped-Tail Ape to his own comparatively safe haven.

Does this gambit work? In theory, in a tough and enlightened world of seasoned players, there is no very good reason for such tactics to cause more than a ripple. But bridge has a strong emotional and psychological side. These very elements sometimes play funny tricks which defy all logical explanation—even at exalted levels.

In the 1969 British Trials for the European Championships the following hand gave the spectators and journalists a considerable amount of pleasure. Although personally involved my memory of the exact details was a little hazy, so I must acknowledge with thanks the amusing account related by Terence Reese in his entertaining book Bridge at the Top.

North/South Vulnerable. IMPs. Dealer South.

```
                  ♠ Q J 10 9 6 5 3
                  ♥ A 4
                  ♦ A Q J
                  ♣ 9
  ♠ A                            ♠ 8 7 2
  ♥ Q 10 8 7 5 3                 ♥ K J 9 2
  ♦ 8 7                          ♦ 10 9 5
  ♣ J 10 4 2                     ♣ 8 6 3
                  ♠ K 4
                  ♥ 6
                  ♦ K 6 4 3 2
                  ♣ A K Q 7 5
```

South opened 1♦, West (Freddie North) bid 3♥ and North, who appears to have a number of options, may well have hit the nail on the head when he bid 5♠. East (John Pugh) was reasonably certain that the opposition could make a slam so he doubled 5♠! Everyone passed, perhaps in various degrees of happiness and doubt, and North duly collected his twelve tricks for a score of 1050. So far so good, Pugh had produced the striped-tail ape at just the right moment and it only remained for our other pair, Nico Gardener and Tony Priday, to bid the slam for a nice swing (+1430).

Unfortunately, the Gardener/Priday wires got crossed because they reached 7♠, doubled. So the expected swing occurred—but not in the direction generally anticipated! Boris Schapiro, who had been kibitzing, lived up to his name of the Joker when he later announced to a crowded room "Priday and Gardener were unlucky on one hand. They bid a grand slam and the ace of trumps was on the wrong side. Bad luck. Could happen to anyone!"

Despite this unfortunate setback (the operation was a success, but the patient died) the Striped-Tail Ape Double has a definite place in your tool kit, but don't expect to reach for it too often.

Chapter 23

Competitive Bidding

In the modern game, competition is fierce. The opposition are always making nuisances of themselves. Intervening where previously they would have left well alone. If they are going to butt in, we will need counter measures. The take-out double is a big help, but there are other aids that can be adopted. We will look at some of these in this chapter. If the opposition are going to be so inconsiderate that they meddle in our auctions, then the least we can do is return the compliment. We will look at some tools that may prove useful in that respect, too.

THE LEBENSOHL CONVENTION

Star Rating: **

The Lebensohl Convention is designed to allow you greater accuracy and expression after your right-hand opponent (RHO) intervenes over your partner's 1NT opening bid (1NT–2♥–?). Before we look at the benefits that derive from Lebensohl, let us first look at standard methods.

Partner, North, opens 1NT and East overcalls in a suit. Options available to South under standard methods:

(a) 2NT does not promise a stopper in East's suit, just the number of points necessary for the bid.

(b) 3NT does not promise a stopper in East's suit, just the number of points necessary for the bid.

(c) A suit bid at the lowest level shows length, but is non-forcing (e.g. 1NT–2♥–3♦).

(d) A jump bid is forcing to game (e.g. 1NT–2♦–3♠).

(e) A cuebid in East's suit takes the place of Stayman. 1NT–2♥–3♥ would show four spades and values for game, while 1NT–2♦–3♦ would guarantee at least one four card major and values for game.

(f) Double is for penalties.

That is certainly a playable method and, is very widely used, although sophistication is limited and from time to time guesswork will be at a premium.

The Lebensohl Convention, invented by George Boehm of New York, was designed to give greater definition to responder's hand after partner opens 1NT and RHO intervenes. The mechanism varies somewhat depending on whether the overcall is made at the two level or three level and also whether it shows one suit or two. The cornerstone of this convention is that responder's bid of 2NT (1NT–2♥–2NT) is artificial and requires the opener to reply 3♣. Responder can now pass 3♣, if that is where he wants to play, or bid his suit, which is non-forcing. It follows that suit bids at the three level, without using the Lebensohl 2NT, are forcing. (1NT–2♠–3♦ is forcing.)

As with all gadgets, if a specific bid is harnessed to a conventional meaning, you can no longer use that bid in its natural sense. So if you play Lebensohl you have to forgo the natural limit raise of 2NT. If that, quite understandably, perturbs you, all is not lost. You can use a Double (1NT–2♥–Double) as your 2NT limit raise. Superficially, that might seem like a poor exchange since you can no longer penalize RHO for an indiscretion, but closer examination refutes this argument. There are bound to be hands where, pre-Lebensohl, you would have made a quantitative raise to 2NT only to find that partner, now aware of your limited wealth, would have liked to take a penalty. Now with Lebensohl in your armory your Double, although not penalty oriented, gives partner that option.

Before I summarize the responses over both one-suited and two-suited overcalls, there are two more important bids to remember.

2NT (Lebensohl) followed by 3NT over partner's 3♣ shows a stop in the enemy suit:

1NT	2♠	2NT	Pass
3♣	Pass	3NT	Pass

while a direct jump to 3NT:

1NT	2♠	3NT	Pass

denies a stopper in their suit.

Partner, North, opens 1NT and East overcalls with a natural

bid of 2♥. South's actions summarized:

1NT	2♥	?

2♠   Natural, competitive and non-forcing.

3♣   Natural and forcing.

3♦   Natural and forcing.

3♠   Natural and forcing.

3♥   Stayman (showing four spades, no stopper in opposition suit, forcing to game).

2NT   Followed by 3♥ over 3♣, Stayman (four spades) with a stopper in their suit.

2NT   Followed by 3NT promises stopper in their suit.

1NT	2♥	2NT	Pass
3♣	Pass	3NT	

3NT   No stopper in enemy suit.

1NT	2♥	3NT	Pass

Double   A natural raise to 2NT (occasionally South may double on a stronger hand, in which case South can control the subsequent auction). Partner can always "convert" to a penalty double by passing if that seems desirable.

Cuebids and jump bids short of game are, of course, forcing.

Partner, North, opens 1NT and East overcalls at the three level. South's actions summarized.

1NT	3 any	?

A suit bid at the three level is forcing to game.

Double: This bid is negative and promises support for any suit not shown by the overcall. It is not necessarily forcing to game.

Partner, North, opens 1NT and East overcalls conventionally, showing two suits (say 2♣, Landy, showing the majors). South's actions summarized:

1NT	2♣ (majors)	?

Double   Penalty oriented in at least one of the suits shown by the overcall.

2♦   A two-level bid in a suit not shown by the overcall is non-forcing.

3♣   Forcing to game.

3♦   Forcing to game.

2♥   A cuebid in the lower of the two suits shown by the overcall (spades and hearts) is not forcing to game.

2♠   A cuebid in the higher of the two suits shown by the overcall is game forcing.

2NT   Requests partner to bid 3♣. South can now pass 3♣ or bid three of his suit which is non-forcing. If South bids 3NT over 3♣ he shows stops in both suits shown by the overcall.

3NT   South may have a stop in one of the suits shown by the over-call, but denies stops in both.

A conventional overcall identifying one suit only (Astro, for example, where 2♦ shows spades and another suit) is handled as follows:

Double   Suggests the values to double 2♠.

2♠   Shows values in the other three suits.

2NT and other bids are used in the same sense as in the above examples.

Let us look at a few hands:

North opens 1NT (12-14 points), East overcalls 2♦), natural. South holds:

(a) ♠ A J 10 7 4
♥ K 5
♦ 6 4
♣ 9 7 6 3
Bid 2♠

(b) ♠ A J 10 7 4
♥ K 5
♦ 6 4
♣ A J 9 7
Bid 3♠

(c) ♠ A J 10 4
♥ K J 9 7
♦ 6 4
♣ A J 9
Bid 3♦

(d) ♠ A J 10 4
♥ K J 9 7
♦ A 10
♣ 9 7 3
Bid 2NT
then 3♦ over 3♣

(e) ♠ A 7 4
♥ K J 7
♦ 6 4
♣ K Q 10 7 3
Bid 3NT

(f) ♠ A 7 4
♥ 7 5
♦ K J 4
♣ K Q 10 7 3
Bid 2NT
then 3NT over 3♣

(g) ♠ A 7 4
♥ Q 10 8
♦ K 4 2
♣ Q 10 7 5
Double

(h) ♠ 7 4
♥ K 8 4
♦ 4 2
♣ K Q 9 7 5 3
Bid 2NT

Bids in (a) and (b) are natural, (a) being competitive and non-forcing in the usual way, and (b) being forcing as in standard methods. (c) This is Stayman promising at least one four-card major without a stopper in the opposition suit. (d) This requests partner to bid 3♣ and then, when South continues with 3♦, this becomes Stayman plus a stopper in the enemy suit. In (e) this shows the values for 3NT without a stop. In (f) you are showing the values for game plus a stopper. By doubling in (g) you show a natural raise to 2NT. (h) When partner bids 3♣, as requested, South passes.

North opens 1NT (12-14 points) and East overcalls with an artificial bid of 2♣ which shows the majors.

South holds:

(a) ♠ A 10 9 6
♥ K 6
♦ A 7 5 4
♣ J 6 2
Double

(b) ♠ 9
♥ A 6 3
♦ K Q 10 7 4 2
♣ A 7 5
Bid 3♦

(c) ♠ K 6
♥ 10
♦ K 10 7 3 2
♣ Q J 9 7 4
Bid 2♥

(d) ♠ J 4
♥ 10 5
♦ A Q J 5 3
♣ K Q J 10
Bid 2♠

(e) ♠ K 6
♥ 10 5 3
♦ A Q 7 5
♣ K J 10 7
Bid 3NT

(f) ♠ K 6
♥ Q J 5
♦ A 10 7 4 2
♣ K 9 5
Bid 2NT
then 3NT over 3♣

(a) The double shows that South is willing to double at least one of the major suits for penalties. (b) This bid is forcing to game. (c) This is a non-game-going competitive bid with support for the unbid suits. (d) This shows values for game and support for the unbid suits. (e) Denies a stopper in both majors, but may have a stopper in one of them. (f) Requests partner to bid 3♣, and then 3NT confirms a stopper in both majors. It is time to look at some complete deals:

Both Sides Vulnerable. Pairs. Dealer North.

```
              ♠ K J 5
              ♥ A Q 7 4
              ♦ K 6 3
              ♣ 9 8 5
♠ 10 9 6 4 2              ♠ A 3
♥ 3                      ♥ K J 10 9 8 6
♦ J 10 8                 ♦ 9 5 2
♣ A 6 3 2                ♣ K 7
              ♠ Q 8 7
              ♥ 5 2
              ♦ A Q 7 4
              ♣ Q J 10 4
```

At most tables North became the declarer in 2NT, just made after a heart lead. The popular bidding sequence was:

West	North	East	South
–	1NT	2♥	2NT
All Pass			

At one table where Lebensohl was employed by the North/South pair the bidding started the same way, 1NT–2♥, but then South doubled—showing the values to raise to 2NT. North happily passed, converting South's "raise" into a penalty double. Neither the lead nor the defense made a lot of difference because there was no way declarer could avoid losing the obvious six tricks, three diamonds, one spade and two hearts. Plus 200 earned a barrelful of matchpoints.

Neither Side Vulnerable. IMPs. Dealer North.

```
              ♠ A 7 3 2
              ♥ 9 8 4
              ♦ K 6
              ♣ A Q 8 4
♠ J 6                    ♠ K Q 10 9 8 5
♥ J 10 6 5 2             ♥ A Q 7
♦ J 10 7 4              ♦ 8 2
♣ 9 5                   ♣ 7 3
              ♠ 4
              ♥ K 3
              ♦ A Q 9 5 3
              ♣ K J 10 6 2
```

At one table this was the bidding:

West	North	East	South
–	1NT	2♠	3♠
Pass	3NT	All Pass	

The ♠K was led and North made just nine tricks for a score of 400.

At the opposite table North/South were playing Lebensohl:

West	North	East	South
–	1NT	2♠	3♦
Pass	3NT	Pass	4♣
Pass	4♠	Pass	6♣
All Pass			

As 3♦ was forcing South had plenty of time to show his suits. He reckoned that if North was unsuitable for a minor-suit contract he could always sign off in 4NT, which he (South) would pass. However, far from being unsuitable, North liked what he saw and signalled the good news with a cuebid in the enemy suit. Two long suits that fit together well invariably play for more tricks than the point count would seem to indicate, so South decided to take his chance in the slam. As it happened 6♣ was virtually ironclad, earning a score of 920 and a swing of 11 IMPs.

Lebensohl had played its part in achieving a fine score and there is little doubt that it is a useful gadget to have in your armory. But it does tax the memory rather more than most bidding aids. You may have noticed!

UNASSUMING CUEBIDS

Star Rating: *

How closely can you define your values when your partner makes an overcall and you wish to support him? Suppose you are East and hold:

```
♠ K 10 4
♥ A 6
♦ 10 6 5 3
♣ K J 9 3
```

The bidding starts like this:

West	North	East	South
–	–	–	1♦
1♠	Pass	?	

You have quite a respectable hand, with handsome support for spades, but how can this information be conveyed to partner without, on the one hand going too high, while, on the other, failing to impress him sufficiently, with the result that game is missed? Perhaps you decide on a value bid of 3♠ only to find that this is the full hand:

♠ 9 2
♥ Q 10 8 7 4
♦ 2
♣ 10 7 6 4 2

♠ A Q J 8 6 3   ♠ K 10 4
♥ 9 5 2   ♥ A 6
♦ 9 8 7   ♦ 10 6 5 3
♣ Q   ♣ K J 9 3

♠ 7 5
♥ K J 3
♦ A K Q J 4
♣ A 8 5

Unfortunately, eight tricks in spades is your limit, and, to make matters worse, North/South can't make any contract above the two level. So, perhaps you should have bid only 2♠—but then, if we rearrange the West hand slightly, giving it just two more points, the ♣A instead of the ♣Q and the ♣7 instead of the ♦7, would West not be sorely tempted to pass 2♠? Pity, because now ten tricks are icy. However, do not worry because help is at hand with the Unassuming Cuebid, a device that is employed to contend with these very problems.

In the old traditional way, a cuebid in the opposition suit was game-forcing, showing not only a powerful hand but, in all probability, strong support for partner's suit. When you play Unassuming Cuebids, which are similar to the Invitational Cuebids very popular among experts, you do not forgo this feature—you adopt another as well. The new feature, which takes priority initially, denotes sound support for partner, as opposed to mainly distributional values. About 11+, or perhaps a good 10, are the minimum points associated with an Unassuming Cuebid. The corollary is that direct raises, to whatever level, are based on distributional, rather than high-card strength.

Here is another idea that helps to streamline your responses. After partner's overcall you respond 2NT:

1♦   1♠   Pass   2NT

That is fairly normal showing about 12-13 points, but when you precede your 2NT bid with an Unassuming Cuebid:

1♦   1♠   Pass   2♦
Pass   2♠   Pas s   2NT

you should then show 14-15 points. Let's look at some examples:

South opens 1♦, West bids 1♠, North passes and East holds:

(a)   ♠ Q J 9
        ♥ J 6 4
        ♦ 10 6
        ♣ K J 8 5 3

Raise to 2♠. You are not good enough for an Unassuming Cuebid.

(b)   ♠ K 10 7 4
        ♥ J 6
        ♦ 9 4
        ♣ K Q 7 6 4

Raise to 3♠. With mainly distributional values, a limit raise is best.

(c)   ♠ Q J 9
        ♥ K Q 8
        ♦ 7 4
        ♣ A 10 8 6 4

Bid 2♦. With good top cards and sound support in partner's suit you start with an Unassuming Cuebid which is forcing to agreement.

(d)   ♠ A Q 8 4
        ♥ A 5
        ♦ 7 4 3
        ♣ A K 10 9

Bid 2♦. Again an Unassuming Cuebid, but this time you will not let the bidding stop short of game.

(e)   ♠ 10 6 3
        ♥ A J 9
        ♦ K J 6
        ♣ K J 10 9

Bid 2NT. A fairly normal response indicating 12-13 points and a balanced hand with either a doubleton or three small spades.

(f)   ♠ 10 6 3
        ♥ A Q 9 7
        ♦ K Q 10
        ♣ K J 9

Bid 2♦. You start with an Unassuming Cuebid and intend to follow it with 2NT showing 14-15 points.

Perhaps the third player makes a low-level bid. That need not disrupt your responses.

South opens 1♦, West bids 1♥, North 1♠ and East holds:

(a)   ♠ A 10 4 3
        ♥ K J 5
        ♦ J 6
        ♣ Q J 9 5

Bid 2♦. With so much bidding going on, it is quite likely that a part score will be your limit, but you have the right values for an Unassuming Cuebid so you should certainly make it.

(b)   ♠ 10 4
        ♥ Q 8 5 3
        ♦ A 10 5 4
        ♣ 8 6 3

Raise to 2♥. At favorable vulnerability it might be tempting to increase the ante by bidding 3♥, but partner would expect a little more, say:

(c) ♠ 10
    ♥ K 8 5 3
    ♦ A 10 5 4
    ♣ J 10 8 4

Raise to 3♥.

(d) ♠ K 10 4 3
    ♥ J 6
    ♦ A K 5
    ♣ Q 10 6 4

Bid 2NT. This describes your hand well, both in points and distribution.

(e) ♠ K J 7 3
    ♥ J 6
    ♦ A K 5
    ♣ Q 10 9 7

Bid 2♦. If West continues with 2♥, rebid 2NT showing the balanced nature of your hand plus the point count (14-15).

Overcaller's Reaction to the Unassuming Cuebid

(a) With a minimum hand, overcaller rebids his suit at the lowest level.

(b) With additional values, he makes a jump bid in his suit or bids a second suit.

(c) With game-going values, he bids game or cuebids opponent's suit.

South opens 1♣, West bids 1♠, North passes, East bids 2♣, what do you do as West holding:

(a) ♠ A Q 10 8 6 4
    ♥ 7 5 3
    ♦ J 9 7
    ♣ 4

Rebid 2♠. You are minimum and have no ambitions beyond a part score.

(b) ♠ A K 10 8 6
    ♥ K J 4
    ♦ Q 10
    ♣ 8 6 3

Rebid 3♠. With one more heart and one less club you would rebid 2♥.

(c) ♠ A Q 10 9 7 4
    ♥ K 7
    ♦ Q J 10 7
    ♣ 7

Rebid 4♠. There should be few problems.

(d) ♠ K J 7 5 4 3
    ♥ K Q
    ♦ 7 5
    ♣ A 7 4

Rebid 3♣. With the right cards in partner's hand a slam is a possibility.

Here is a hand that occurred in a local club duplicate.

    ♠ 8 6 2
    ♥ J
    ♦ A K 8 6
    ♣ A 8 5 4 2

♠ A 4   ♠ 9 5 3
♥ K 7 6 5 3   ♥ A Q 8
♦ 10 7 4   ♦ Q 5 2
♣ 10 9 6   ♣ K Q J 7

    ♠ K Q J 10 7
    ♥ 10 9 4 2
    ♦ J 9 3
    ♣ 3

The bidding might make purists wince but these things happen:

West	North	East	South
–	–	1♣	1♠
2♥	3♥	Double	3♠
All Pass			

The ♠A and another spade would have defeated the contract but, not unreasonably, West led the ♣10. Declarer won in dummy and played a heart to East's ♥A. Now the ♠A and a second spade cut down dummy's ruffing power, but declarer was still able to obtain one heart ruff and then exit with a low diamond. East went in with the ♦Q, and cashed the ♥Q, but that was the end of the defense. 3♠ just made. Note how North, with an Unassuming Cuebid, was able to get his values over to partner without rocking the boat.

The Unassuming Cuebid paves the way for an exchange of information at a relatively low level. This can be invaluable in competitive auctions.

BALANCING

Star Rating: ***

Balancing is a most important ingredient of good bridge and unless you are tactically well-equipped in this department you will be unable to cope effectively with many everyday situations.

The purpose of a Balancing Bid

When the opposition are about to buy at a low level, partner having passed, for example:

West	North	East	South
1♦	Pass	Pass	?

or

West	North	East	South
–	–	1♥	Pass
2♥	Pass	Pass	?

it is often in one's interests to contest the auction, sometimes on quite modest values. The idea is either to buy for your own side or to push the opponents over the top.

Why is it necessary to balance?

If the bidding is about to die at a low level in the opposition's best suit/fit, it is not unusual for your partner to have some fair values, although he has not so far felt able to bid. When you now enter the fray you are protecting his pass, or, balancing. This absolves partner from entering the auction on unsuitable hands when his side may be totally outgunned.

Before we start to define our various bids in the balancing seat, let us make quite sure what it is we expect from our partner.

1. We expect partner to make an overcall on a respectable suit—length and quality of suit being more important than a high number of points. Of course, the vulnerability and the level at which partner can enter the auction are very relevant.

2. We expect partner to use an informatory (take-out) double on suitable hands that have adequate support for unbid suits, especially unbid majors.

3. We expect partner to overcall 1NT on a strong balanced hand; with about 16-18 points and the bid suit stopped.

4. We expect partner to take appropriate action on strongly distributional hands that call for a systemic bid (like Unusual no-trumps, pre-empts, or Michaels Cuebid).

So it seems that our partner's biggest "problem" will be on hands where he would have opened the bidding comfortably enough, but because the opposition have got there first, he is left without a sensible bid to make. This is not really a problem at all, since it is almost always right to pass and rely on partner to balance, if that seems the right thing for him to do.

Suppose RHO opens 1♥ and you hold:

(a)	♠ A 4	(b)	♠ 8 6	(c)	♠ Q 6 5 4	(d)	♠ J 3
	♥ K J 7 3		♥ A J 9 6 4		♥ K J 9 2		♥ Q 7 4
	♦ K 10 6 2		♦ K Q 5 2		♦ 7		♦ A Q 8 6
	♣ Q 8 2		♣ A 6		♣ A Q J 5		♣ K Q 5 4

You should, of course, pass in each case. Indeed, pass has so much going for it that any alternative action can hardly be regarded as a serious contender.

If there are still any doubts about passing on modest balanced hands after RHO has opened the bidding, consider three common situations. East opens one of a suit on 13 points, South passes on 13 balanced points. This leaves 14 points at large.

Case 1: West holds all, or nearly all, the missing points, so North is marked with a worthless hand. East/West bid to game and would no doubt have done so whether South had spoken or not. The difference is that South has given nothing away and furthermore did not offer the opposition the chance of a juicy double, should they have preferred that option. In defense South knows more or less what to expect from his partner. East/West must proceed in the dark.

Conclusion: *South was right not to interfere.*

Case 2: North holds all, or nearly all, the missing points, thus when West has to pass his partner's opening bid North enters the auction. Now there is nothing to stop North/South arriving in their optimum contract.

Conclusion: South has lost nothing by passing in second position.

Case 3: The missing 14 points are approximately equally shared between the West and North players. It is now anyone's guess as to which side can make a contract. Quite often whoever plays it goes down, but in any case the bidding is likely to stop at a low level, which will give North/South another chance to assess their prospects.

Conclusion: A gray area, but no serious disadvantage occasioned by South's pass.

The overall conclusion therefore is that the second player, South in my examples, stands to lose little and gain a lot by passing on moderate balanced hands when RHO opens the bidding. This brings us to the fourth player, North, who is in the balancing position.

Action to be taken by the player in the Balancing Position

West	North	East	South
–	–	1♦	Pass
Pass?			

1. Bid 2NT on a strong balanced hand, 19-21 points (some play 20-22).

2. Bid 1NT on a weak balanced hand, 11-13 points. Popular ranges vary here, but perhaps it is easy to remember that your 3 point range starts at 1 point less than your 1NT opening (12-14), which, incidentally, is in line with your balancing bid of 2NT which also starts at 1 point less that your normal opening bid of 2NT (20-22).

3. Make a jump bid in a suit with a sound opening bid and a six card suit.

4. Bid a respectable suit if you have 10-12 points.

5. Bid two of opponent's suit on strong two-suiters.

6. Double on all other strong hands not necessarily ideal in shape, but too powerful to approach in any other way. Also double on ideal shapely hands with about 11+ points.

You are North in the following examples. The bidding proceeds:

West	North	East	South
–	–	1♥	Pass
Pass	?		

(a)	♠ A Q 10	(b)	♠ A 6
	♥ K J 6		♥ Q J 10 6
	♦ K 10 9 4		♦ A 10 7 5
	♣ A Q J		♣ 10 7 4
	Bid 2NT		Bid 1NT

(c)
♠ A 10 6 3
♥ K 6 3
♦ K Q 10
♣ A J 9

Double, then consider bidding 2NT over partner's two of a minor.

(d)
♠ A 6
♥ 8 6 3
♦ A J 7 5
♣ K 9 5 4

Bid 1NT. Don't let the three small hearts worry you. The missing honors are even better placed when they are in partner's hand.

(e) ♠ A K J 9 6	**(f)** ♠ A K J 9 8 6	**(g)** ♠ K Q 9 8 7 5
♥ 8 6 3	♥ 6 3	♥ 8
♦ Q J 9	♦ Q J 9	♦ –
♣ 5 3	♣ K 3	♣ A K J 10 8 6
Bid 1♠	Bid 2♠	Bid 2♥

(h) ♠ K 6	***(i)*** ♠ A Q 6	***(j)*** ♠ K 8 6 3	***(k)*** ♠ Q
♥ A Q 10	♥ 8 6	♥ 6	♥ A 8 5
♦ K Q 9 5	♦ A K J 9 5	♦ A K 9 5	♦ A Q J 10 5
♣ J 10 6 5	♣ 10 9 6	♣ J 10 9 4	♣ K Q 10 8

* Double in each case. A balancing double covers a wide range of hands.

As with the use of most conventional gadgets, common sense should always prevail in questionable circumstances. For example, with no one vulnerable West opens 1♣ which is passed to you in the South seat. You hold:

♠ 6
♥ A 6 4
♦ K Q 8 3
♣ K J 10 9 7

You have the values to protect, but wait a minute. Where have all the spades gone? Your partner did not overcall, so they have probably got a fit. If you disturb one club you may find yourself trying to defend 4♠. This is no time for heroics—pass.

This hand occurred in a teams event. You might like to consider the problem from the West position. This is what you hold as West at game to your side, dealer South:

♠ J 10 7 6
♥ Q
♦ K J 10 3
♣ K 10 9 2

South opens 1♥, you pass, North raises to 2♥, East passes and South, after giving it a little thought, also passes. It is now up to you. I can hear you saying, "Well, what do you want from me? Of course I pass."

No doubt you are right, but this is a tight match. You are fighting for every point and every point is vital so, against your better judgment perhaps, you double. North quickly raises to 3♥, East passes and South now bids 4♥. Everyone passes and with a sinking feeling that on this occasion your judgment, at best, is questionable and at worst certifiable, you lead the ♠J. The sight of dummy does nothing to restore your faith in the righteous! This is what you see:

♠ Q 3
♥ A 10 9 4 3
♦ Q 8 5 2
♣ J 7

♠ J 10 7 6
♥ Q
♦ K J 10 3
♣ K 10 9 2

"What was that two-heart bid?" you mutter to yourself. "He must have thought he was playing with his grandmother. Surely anyone with red blood in his veins bids 3♥."

The ♠J is covered by dummy's ♠Q, partner's ♠K and declarer's ♠A. Trumps are drawn in two rounds ending in dummy, and then the ♠3 is led. Partner plays the ♠8, declarer the ♠9 and you win with the ♠10. How do you continue? In fact, partner has told you. This was the full hand:

	♠ Q 3	
	♥ A 10 9 4 3	
	♦ Q 8 5 2	
	♣ J 7	
♠ J 10 7 6		♠ K 8 5 4 2
♥ Q		♥ 5 2
♦ K J 10 3		♦ A 9 6
♣ K 10 9 2		♣ 6 5 4
	♠ A 9	
	♥ K J 8 7 6	
	♦ 7 4	
	♣ A Q 8 3	

That ♠8 was a most thoughtful play—a McKenney suit preference signal asking for a diamond, not a club. A club switch sees declarer home. A diamond switch and the contract has to go down one.

Seldom has plus 50 looked so handsome on the scoresheet. Faith is restored in almost everything and balancing is even more firmly established in the bidding repertoire. Of course, if you don't want to live quite so dangerously as this last example would seem to suggest, there are still plenty of opportunities for Balancing which are of a less flamboyant, more mundane nature. They, too, can be both profitable and enjoyable.

MICHAELS CUEBID

Star Rating: **

My early experiences of playing with team-mates who were using Michaels Cuebids were memorable, if not exactly favorable. Going through the score card there would be a pregnant pause over a figure of, say, minus 800 and then later on minus 1100.

"What happened there?" I would ask. The reply began to have a familiar ring about it. "Ah, well you see that was a Michaels Cuebid."

I like to think I nodded gravely, smiled sympathetically and continued discreetly to the next hand, but of course it is always possible that my memory is somewhat clouded with the passing of time!

That may not sound like a very auspicious start for a gadget that is said to now officially be part of Acol in the '90s but—to use a driving term as an analogy—it's not really the car that kills, it's the driver. However, it must be admitted that a Michaels Cuebid is a highly explosive and volatile gadget, so it is essential to use it with care.

The basic structure of Michaels Cuebid

By cuebidding the opponent's suit directly, you show a two-suited hand as follows:

| 1♣ | 2♣ | or | 1♦ | 2♦ |

Shows at least 5-4, preferably 5-5 in the major suits.

| 1♥ | 2♥ | or | 1♠ | 2♠ |

Shows at least five of the unbid major and a five card or longer minor suit.

The sixty-four thousand dollar question is, "How strong should the cuebidder be?" It is certainly advisable for regular partnerships to discuss this point, although it has been suggested that a Michaels Cuebid should be "weak, pre-emptive and shapely." This would seem to leave an uncomfortable void for the stronger hands.

Obviously, vulnerability will play a vital part in deciding the partnership action and, while there is considerable scope for obstructive interference at favorable vulnerability, one would require a more freakish distribution, or a stronger version, before taking action at unfavorable vulnerability.

You will notice that, over one of a minor, a Michaels Cuebid can be made with 5-4 in the majors, although 5-5 is certainly preferable. If you are only 5-4, then it is advisable to insure there is some substance in these suits, especially in the four-card suit. For example:

> ♠ A Q 10 8
> ♥ K Q 10 8 7
> ♦ 8
> ♣ 10 7 4

would be acceptable, but:

> ♠ Q 7 5 4
> ♥ K J 5 4 3
> ♦ 8
> ♣ K J 4

would be decidedly risky.

I am loath to prescribe a minimum point count because distribution, intermediate and working cards, together with vulnerability, play such an important part. However, I suppose 6 or 7 points would be acceptable if all other factors are in your favor, otherwise 8-12 points would be normal in the weak pre-emptive version. Let us look at some examples:

Not vulnerable versus vulnerable: East opens 1♥, South holds:

> ♠ A J 10 9 6
> ♥ 4
> ♦ 6 3
> ♣ Q 10 9 8 5

Bid 2♥. You have the equipment.

East opens 1♥, South holds, vulnerable versus not vulnerable:

> ♠ A J 10 9 6
> ♥ 4
> ♦ 6
> ♣ Q J 10 9 8 6

Bid 2♥. Despite adverse conditions and a comparatively low point count, the shape and intermediates are such that only the faint-hearted would miss this opportunity.

East opens 1♥, South holds at equal vulnerability:

> ♠ K Q 10 7 4
> ♥ 4 3
> ♦ A J 10 7 6
> ♣ 3

Bid 2♥. This would be a fairly normal hand for unleashing your missile.

East opens 1♥, South holds at any vulnerability:

> ♠ Q 9 6 5 4
> ♥ 4 3
> ♦ 6
> ♣ K J 6 4 3

Pass. A good pass at any vulnerability.

It is always tempting to play around with a new toy but, if you are going to avoid those pregnant pauses as you announce minus 800 or minus 1100, it is wise to keep your Michaels Cuebid up to strength commensurate with the vulnerability. In its weak form, a Michaels Cuebid is an obstructive weapon, so clearly some risks are justified, just as they are with all pre-emptive bids. But unless you enjoy living dangerously, it is sensible to consider the risk of a misfit. If you open the bidding with 3♥ on:

♠ 4
♥ K Q J 10 9 7 6
♦ J 10 6
♣ 8 4

you can be fairly sure you will take six tricks, misfit or not, so your liability can be measured.

If you overcall 1♠ with 2♠ on:

♠ 4
♥ K Q 9 7 5
♦ A 9 7 4 3
♣ 8 6

you are entering an unknown area. Your liabilities will very much depend on partner's shape and high cards. If he is with you in one of the red suits then no doubt you have done the right thing, but if he is short in the red suits you may be in for an uncomfortable ride, eventually conceding a sizeable penalty, possibly in a doubtful cause. Such are the hazards of Michaels Cuebids.

Now let's look on the positive side. There is plenty going for us, and on a good day even miracles can happen. Remember too, that most experts give this conventional gadget the thumbs up and they would not do so unless they were reasonably confident of an overall gain. So our thanks to the late Mr. M. Michaels of Miami Beach for an interesting and provocative convention.

Before we go on to look at some hands, let's analyze partner's reaction to our Michaels Cuebid.

Partner's reaction to our Michaels Cuebid

1. He should bid the full value of his hand if there is a known fit, sometimes making an advance sacrifice to pressurize the opponents.

2. If he cannot support the major he can bid 2NT to ask his partner to name his minor suit. If 2NT is not available because of opposition bidding, then a cuebid in the opponent's suit will serve the same purpose.

With Both Sides Vulnerable, West opens 1♦, North bids 2♦ and East passes, South holds:

(a) ♠ K J 9 5
♥ A 10
♦ 7 6 4
♣ A K J 10

Bid 3♦. You are rather too good to shut up shop with 4♠. If North holds a singleton diamond a slam is a live possibility.

(b) ♠ K 9 7 5 4
♥ A 10
♦ 7 6 4 3
♣ J 4

Bid 4♠. You may or may not succeed but tactically this bid is sound enough.

(c) ♠ 7 5
♥ K 8 4
♦ J 10 9 6
♣ Q 10 8 4

Bid 2♥. There is no other choice. Since both suits are known 2NT would be natural, but this is not the hand for that bid.

Both sides vulnerable West opens 1♥, North bids 2♥ and East passes.

(d) ♠ 7 5
♥ A 8 6 3
♦ Q 9
♣ J 9 7 4 2

Bid 2NT. If partner's second suit is clubs you may have a good sacrifice, if it is diamonds you should pass 3♦.

(e) ♠ Q J 7 5
♥ J 8 6 3
♦ A K 7
♣ 4 2

Bid 3♠. The full value of the hand in the known fit.

With East/West vulnerable, West opens 1♠, North bids 2♠ and East raises to 3♠. South holds:

(f) ♠ 8 2
♥ 5
♦ Q 10 8 6 4
♣ K Q 9 7 3

Bid 4♠. You want to know partner's minor suit. Maybe there is a cheap save available.

This hand featured some ambitious bidding which was rewarded by a slight slip in defense.

Both Sides Vulnerable. Dealer North.

```
              ♠ Q 10 7 5 4
              ♥ –
              ♦ K 8 6 2
              ♣ A 8 6 3
♠ 8 2                       ♠ A K J 9 6
♥ Q 6 5 4 3                 ♥ A 8 2
♦ 9 3                       ♦ J 4
♣ Q 10 5 2                  ♣ K J 7
              ♠ 3
              ♥ K J 10 9 7
              ♦ A Q 10 7 5
              ♣ 9 4
```

West	North	East	South
–	Pass	1♠	2♠ (*)
Pass	2NT	Double	3♦
Pass	4♦	Pass	5♦
Pass	Pass	Double	All Pass

(*) Michaels Cuebid

Although East/West have slightly more in high cards than North/South, it is the latter who have the all-important fit, nicely located by a Michaels Cuebid. Clearly, 5♦ was going to be no pushover and the really critical point arrived at trick two. The ♠8 was led, covered by the ♠10 and ♠J, and now the spotlight fell on East. Had he switched to a club—and there is certainly a strong case for this—the contract would have failed. In fact he tried to cash the ♠A. Declarer ruffed and ran the ♥9 to East's ♥A, discarding a club from dummy when West played low. Now the club switch was won by the ♣A and two rounds of trumps gave South the lead to continue hearts. A second club was discarded on the ♥K, the ♥Q was ruffed out and dummy's last club disappeared on declarer's last heart. The rest of the tricks were made on a cross-ruff. Contract just made.

So Michaels Cuebid performed really well, albeit with a little luck in running.

This last hand illustrates the now familiar theme that shape is so very much more important than points.

North/South Vulnerable. Pairs. Dealer North.

```
              ♠ Q 5 4 2
              ♥ K 9 7 2
              ♦ 5 3
              ♣ A J 6
♠ 10 8 6 3                    ♠ A K J 9 7
♥ Q 5                         ♥ 4
♦ K Q 10 8 4                  ♦ A J 9 7
♣ 8 2                         ♣ Q 9 3
              ♠ —
              ♥ A J 10 8 6 3
              ♦ 6 2
              ♣ K 10 7 5 4
```

West	North	East	South
–	Pass	1♠	2♠ (*)
3♠	4♥	4♠	5♥
Pass	Pass	Double	All Pass

(*) Michaels Cuebid

East's double looks very ill-judged. He would have done much better to follow the policy of bidding one for the road—or would he? It is OK if East/West buy, then 5♠ will go quietly one down, but what happens if North/South also bid one for the road and continue to 6♥? On this sequence East would surely cash his ♦A and with the South hand on the table the defense can hardly go wrong, but you never know.

Against 5♥ doubled, East led his ♠A and declarer saw at once that locating the ♣Q was going to be worth a million dollars. It was fair to presume that the ♦A and ♦K were split (with both honors East would surely have led a diamond), but of course it was impossible to get even an approximate count of the hand. Certainly, East was short in hearts, but then he probably had more spades than West.

Perhaps the deciding factor for North was East's aggressive bidding, so, having ruffed the spade and drawn trumps, he played the ♣A and ♣J. East ducked smoothly, but declarer had made up his mind and let the ♣J run. A few seconds later he collected all thirteen tricks.

This time Michaels Cuebid played a rather less dynamic role in the bidding because most Souths would come in with their heart suit over 1♠. Nevertheless, it was the second suit which did so much damage and that, of course, is a key feature of the Michaels Cuebid.

To conclude, the following is a brief summary of the pros and cons of using the Michaels Cuebid.

For

Even used with care this is not a gadget to be tucked away in the closet and just trotted out on special occasions. It is an everyday weapon, obstructive, pre-emptive and at moments quite devastating. It provokes action, creates swings and, used in conjunction with the Unusual 2NT (this shows length in the two lowest-ranking unbid suits), makes you well-equipped to compete. With a little help from the opposition, almost unbelievable results are achieved.

Against

As with all bids showing weak distributional hands, a great deal of information passes into enemy hands. This does not enhance your defensive prospects when they buy the contract. With a misfit, the Michaels missile can behave like a boomerang and come zooming back to the sender with unpleasant consequences. 800s and 1100s come suddenly to mind. Then, having given over the immediate cuebid of the enemy suit to weak pre-emptive hands, strong two-suiters:

```
♠ A Q J 9 7 4
♥ —
♦ K Q J 10 6
♣ A Q
```

and exceptionally powerful one-suited hands are difficult to bid with any degree of accuracy. No doubt one has to fall back on the informatory double, but that is an improvisation which clearly has defects. Of course, the pro Michaels Cuebid fans would argue that these very strong hands occur only once in a blue moon. No doubt that is right but they are certainly difficult to bid without proper equipment when that blue moon emerges.

Let's hope your misfits are travelling companions of the blue moon!

MULTI TWO DIAMONDS
Star rating: ***

One of the most useful conventions to arrive on the bridge scene in comparatively modern times must surely be the "Multi." The brainchild of the late Jeremy Flint and expounded in depth in a number of publications by Terence Reese, the Multi has captured the imagination of players all over the world. Hardly surprising perhaps, when one considers the scope enjoyed by this gadget, embracing as it does weak hands, strong hands and almost unbiddable hands.

Although there are a number of versions of the Multi in circulation, there is one balanced, sensible and eminently playable method.

The opening bid of 2♦ covers three distinctly different types of hand:

- **(i)** A weak two in either major, 6-10 points.
- **(ii)** A strong two in either minor.
- **(iii)** A balanced hand of 23-24 points.

Let us look at some typical hands in each category.

(i) A Weak Two in either major:

(a) ♠K Q 10 8 6 4	**(b)** ♠ 3 2	**(c)** ♠ 2
♥ 6	♥ A Q J 9 7 5	♥ K Q J 10 8 4
♦ K 9 6	♦ 10 9 8 7	♦ 8 3 2
♣ 7 4 2	♣ 6	♣ K J 7

The opening bid in each case is 2♦. At the first opportunity opener will indicate a weak two in his long suit. A respectable six-card is the hallmark of this gambit.

(ii) A Strong Two in either minor:

(a) ♠ 3	**(b)** ♠ A 10 7	**(c)** ♠ 4
♥ A 7 4	♥ A	♥ A K
♦ A K Q J 9 5	♦ K Q 9	♦ A 3 2
♣ A J 6	♣ A Q J 10 7 4	♣ K Q J 10 9 7 4

The opening bid in each case is 2♦. As soon as possible, opener will indicate that this time he has a hand of power and quality with 8-9 playing tricks, with hand (a) he will rebid diamonds and with (b) and (c) clubs.

You will notice one important development here. In traditional Acol there is no way to show a powerful hand with 8-9 playing tricks when the main suit is clubs. You simply have to improvise, but when you play the Multi this problem is overcome.

(iii) A Balanced hand of 23-24 points:

(a) ♠ A K 10	**(b)** ♠ A 6 3	**(c)** ♠ A K J
♥ K Q J	♥ Q 10 9 4	♥ A Q 8
♦ A J 9 5	♦ A K J	♦ K 6 4
♣ K Q J	♣ A K Q	♣ A Q 10 6 5

As before, the opening bid in each case is 2♦. But now opener intends to rebid no trumps at the first opportunity which will inform his partner that he has a hand of this nature.

Although the 23-24 point count for the strong balanced version of the Multi is not universally played, I strongly advise it because it creates an important advantage in another area. In traditional bidding the sequence 2♣–2♦–2NT may be non-forcing because opener is showing 23-24 points and if partner has nothing, or almost nothing, there is no virtue in stretching for an improbable game. Thus if

opener has 25+ he has to rebid 3NT himself (2♣–2♦–3NT). But if your balanced version of the Multi shows 23-24 points (you open 2♦ and rebid 2NT) it follows that the sequence 2♣–2♦–2NT must be forcing as it now shows 25+. This development is an obvious advantage as you have more bidding space and it is no longer incumbent on you to jump about like a kangaroo with the bare minimum point count necessary for game.

Responder's initial reaction to opener's Multi 2♦

Responder should always assume, until advised otherwise, that opener has a weak two in one of the majors. On this basis, if he is content to play in a low-level contract he responds as follows:

- **2♥** – if opener has a weak two in hearts he will pass.
- **2♠** – if opener has a weak two in spades he will pass, but if his suit is hearts he will bid 3♥ with a minimum and 4♥ with a maximum.

When responder is strong and wishes to discover his partner's type of hand he bids 2NT—a forcing relay.

Any response at the three level is natural and forcing.

The most likely bid for responder to make is 2♥ (2♦–2♥) which covers all weak hands and would be the equivalent of passing a weak 2♥ opening.

Perhaps the response of 2♠ (2♦–2♠) may sound slightly strange because in fact it shows support for hearts. Of course, if opener has a weak two in spades he passes and, as already indicated, with a weak two in hearts he rebids his suit at the three or four level depending on strength.

Opener's rebid when responder inquires with 2NT (2♦–2NT)

With a weak two in the majors, he rebids like this:

- **3♥** – lower range weak two in hearts.
- **3♠** – lower range weak two in spades.
- **3♣** – upper range weak two in hearts.
- **3♦** – upper range weak two in spades.

With a 23-24 point balanced hand he rebids 3NT.

With a strong two in clubs or diamonds he must rebid four of his minor.

Opener's Rebid on strong hands when Responder bids 2♥ (2♦–2♥)

With a strong two in clubs or diamonds he rebids three of his minor. With a worthless hand responder can then pass.

With a 23-24 point balanced hand he rebids 2NT. Again, with a worthless hand responder can pass.

Let's look at some examples.

The bidding starts: West 2♦–East 2♥. West holds:

(a)	♠ A Q J 9 7 6
	♥ 6
	♦ 10 8 7 5
	♣ 4 2

Rebid 2♠ showing a weak two in spades. Interchange the major suits and you would then pass 2♥.

(b) ♠ A Q 10 8
　　　♥ K J 9
　　　♦ A K J
　　　♣ A J 10

Rebid 2NT showing a balanced 23-24 points.

(c) ♠ A J
　　　♥ 6
　　　♦ A K Q J 9 7
　　　♣ A 6 5 2

Rebid 3♦ showing a typical strong 2♦ opening with 8-9 playing tricks. Interchange the minor suits and you would rebid 3♣.

The bidding starts: West 2♦–East 2♠. West holds:

(a) ♠ A K J 9 7 6
　　　♥ 6
　　　♦ 7 5 3
　　　♣ 5 4 2

Pass. Partner is not interested in playing higher than 2♠.

(b) ♠ K 4
　　　♥ Q J 10 9 6 4
　　　♦ 10 5 3
　　　♣ 8 2

Rebid 3♥. You are in the lower range.

(c) ♠ A 4
　　　♥ K Q 10 9 6 4
　　　♦ 7 5 3
　　　♣ 8 2

Rebid 4♥. You are now in the upper range.

The bidding starts: West 2♦ – East 2NT. West holds:

(a) ♠ K J 10 8 7 5
　　　♥ 4 2
　　　♦ Q J 7
　　　♣ 8 6

Rebid 3♠. You have a weak two in the lower range.

(b) ♠ A Q J 10 8 7
　　　♥ 4 2
　　　♦ Q J 4
　　　♣ 6 4

Rebid 3♦ showing a weak two in spades in the upper range.

(c) ♠ 6
　　　♥ Q J 9 8 6 5
　　　♦ A 3 2
　　　♣ 8 6 4

Rebid 3♥. You have a weak two in the lower range.

(d) ♠ 6
　　　♥ A K J 9 6 3
　　　♦ J 10 7 5
　　　♣ 4 2

Rebid 3♣ showing a weak two in hearts in the upper range.

(e) ♠ K J 7
　　　♥ A Q J
　　　♦ A K J 7
　　　♣ A 6 4

Rebid 3NT showing 23-24 balanced points.

(f) ♠ 6
　　　♥ Q 10 8
　　　♦ A K Q J 7 4
　　　♣ A K 10

Rebid 4♦ showing a strong two in diamonds. Interchange the minor suits and you would rebid 4♣ showing a similar hand with clubs.

The bidding starts: West 2♦ – East 3♣/3♦/3♥/3♠

1.	♠ 7 4 3	♠ A Q	**West**	**East**
	♥ A Q J 10 7 4	♥ 6	2♦	3♦
	♦ J 10	♦ A K Q 8 6 2	3♥	3NT
	♣ 5 2	♣ K J 10 9	Pass	

When East discovers that West has a weak two in hearts—as expected—he subsides in 3NT.

2.	♠ 2	♠ A Q J 9 5	**West**	**East**
	♥ A K 10 9 6 4	♥ 7	2♦	3♠
	♦ 10 9 6 4	♦ K Q J	3NT(*)	Pass
	♣ 6 2	♣ K Q J 10		

(*) West must have a weak two in hearts.

3.	♠ K Q 10 9 7 4	♠ A J 6	**West**	**East**
	♥ J 9 7	♥ Q	2♦	3♣
	♦ K 4	♦ A 6	3♠	4NT
	♣ 8 4	♣ A K J 10 9 6 2	5♣	6♠
			Pass	

East was pleasantly surprised to hear West's rebid and immediately set course for slam. West denied an ace but East was quite happy with 6♠—an easy make.

One don't

Don't open 2♦ with a weak two, when you have four cards in the other major, for example:

　　　♠ A 10 9 6
　　　♥ K J 10 9 7 4
　　　♦ 7
　　　♣ 3 2

It is best to pass and await developments. The danger of employing the Multi is that you might play in 2♥ with 4♠ laydown.

Here is an exciting hand involving the Multi, which was played in a head-to-head teams match.

```
              ♠ A Q J 5 3
              ♥ 6
              ♦ Q 8 6 2
              ♣ Q 9 4
♠ 9 7                        ♠ 8 2
♥ K Q 9 7 4 3                ♥ A 10 8
♦ A 9 3                      ♦ K J 10 5 4
♣ 6 2                        ♣ K J 3
              ♠ K 10 6 4
              ♥ J 5 2
              ♦ 7
              ♣ A 10 8 7 5
```

In Room 1 this was the bidding:

West	North	East	South
–	–	–	Pass
Pass	1♠	2♦	4♠
All Pass			

South was a player not renowned for underbidding so his jump to game was fairly typical. In any case, it is hard to grumble with success as, right or wrong, West was silenced. A diamond and a heart were taken by the defense and the second heart was ruffed. Trumps were drawn in two rounds and then the ♣Q found the ♣K at home. So declarer lost three tricks: one heart, one diamond and one club.

In Room 2 the bidding took a very different course:

West	North	East	South
–	–	–	Pass
2♦	Pass	2♠	Pass
4♥	All Pass		

2♦ was the Multi and 2♠ showed willingness to play there if that was partner's suit. At the same time East's bid showed heart support and left partner to say whether he was maximum or minimum, if indeed he had a weak two in hearts. West was maximum, so he duly bid game.

With very little to guide him North's lead was something of a guess. In fact if West plays the minor suits to advantage ten tricks will roll in no matter what the defense scheme up. In practice, West was not severely tested when the ♦2 hit the table. Trumps were drawn and the run of the diamond suit provided eleven tricks, declarer ditching two spades. Then a right guess in clubs brought the total to twelve. Plus 620 in one room and plus 680 in the other gave one of the teams a swing of 16 IMPs—a result you dream about.

The Multi is something I can recommend with considerable confidence. It is fun to play and it has its moments!

PART IV

RAISING PARTNER

by Brian Senior

Partner bids a suit—whether as an opening bid, an overcall, or in response to one of your bids, is unimportant—what do you suppose he would most like to hear from you? The answer is, of course, that what he would most like is for you to support his suit. After all, one of the main purposes of the auction is to try to find a trump suit with which both partners are happy. That done, you can then decide at what level to play – part score, game, small, or even grand, slam. So if during the auction you find yourself with a close decision between two or more possible bids and one option is to raise partner's suit, that is probably the best choice since it will both make partner happy and, more to the point, create a sound base for the subsequent auction.

For the beginner, raising partner is relatively straightforward, being simply a matter of counting his points and deciding how high to raise; the more he has the more he bids. What he is doing is making a limit bid, that is, he adds his point count to the minimum number promised by partner's bidding to date and raises to the limit of what the partnership should be able to make with that combined strength. It is then up to partner to judge whether or not he has sufficient extra undisclosed values to justify bidding higher.

Players have to start somewhere, of course, and the basic concept of the limit bid is fundamental to any sensible structure for bidding. As experience is gained, however, players begin to realize that it is not just the number of high cards held which is important, but also their nature and how the two hands fit together. Simple limit bids, while still being valuable, often prove to be inadequate, particularly on big hands where slam may be in the picture. A little sophistication like "delayed game raise" and the Swiss convention, begin to be added to the player's methods.

As we progress up the tournament ladder, we discover more and more situations in which it could be beneficial to add a conventional aid to our basic bidding structure. We find that these conventional aids do indeed exist and are available for our use. Indeed, there is quite a staggering array from which to choose and it would be quite impossible to use them all.

My aim in this section is to look at all the main situations in which you might want to raise partner or where he has already raised your suit. Although simple limit bids will be mentioned, I do not intend to waste any time on them. Anyone who is not fully conversant with their use should really study a book on natural bidding before moving on to this one. Neither is it my intention to attempt to produce an encyclopædia of bidding conventions, so do not expect to find a comprehesive coverage of every artificial aid in use today. I could, for example, come up with a dozen different versions of the Swiss convention if I put my mind to it, but what would be the point? Though all have their good and bad points, they are fundamentally just variations on the same basic idea.

There are three important points I would like to make now and which you will find are repeated at regular intervals throughout this section. I emphasize them because there are many players who think that every problem situation in the bidding can be overcome if only they can find the right convention to solve it. If they play all the right conventions, they are sure to become winners. Alas, this is simply not true.

First, and most important, any convention is only an aid to judgment. Without the judgment to know when to use a particular convention and when not, or how to use the information given by partner's bid, your results will not improve to any great extent however sophisticated your bidding methods. Indeed, the more complex the methods, the more dramatic can be the disasters if they are misused.

Second, every time you add a conventional call to your armory, you lose the natural meaning of the same call. For example, if you agree to play a 3NT response to a 1♥ opening as a balanced raise to 4♥, you lose the ability to bid 3NT to play. When deciding whether or not a new convention is a good idea, you must consider both the benefits *and* the cost of using it. You need to ask yourself these questions:

> How big a problem currently exists?
> How frequently does it occur?
> How effectively does the proposed new convention handle the problem?
> Are there any alternative solutions and, if so, how effective might they be?
> How frequently does the natural meaning of this call come up?
> If you take up the new convention, is there a good alternative way of bidding a hand which would otherwise have made a natural use of the call in question, or have you merely transferred your problem?
> Only by careful examination of the answers to these questions can you assess the true costs and benefits of the new convention.

Third, it is frequently overlooked that each new piece of artificiality added to a player's methods is one more tiny strain on his or her memory. Of course, *you* would never forget the system, but it only takes partner to cause one disaster by a lapse of memory and it will take a long time for a player to feel comfortable using that particular convention. And even if neither of you ever forgets your system, if it is very complex it is still more tiring to play than is a simple style, and may leave you with less energy to devote to other areas of your performance.

Although you should always keep these in mind, there are many situations in which conventions are a genuine aid to accurate bidding and there are many excellent conventions in existence. I hope that this section will be a source of ideas of what is available and will help you to decide what will be most helpful to you. Don't forget that these methods can never be a substitute for good judgment: they are an aid to it.

24

Chapter

The Uncontested Auction

PARTNER OPENS ONE OF A MAJOR

Unless otherwise stated, I will assume that we are playing four card major suit openings. Most of what I have to say, however, is equally valid when playing five card majors.

The basic bidding structure is founded on the principle that, if a satisfactory trump fit is present, four of a major is the most desirable game contract. Normally, an eight card or better trump fit is deemed to be sufficient, and certainly so if both partners hold at least four cards in the trump suit. It follows then that if responder has four card support for opener's major he should raise it immediately. The only exception is when he is too strong to simply raise to game and chooses an indirect route to keep a possible slam in the picture. Even with only three card support, it can often be correct to give an immediate raise, though this is usually restricted to raises to the two level only. For example, when partner opens 1♠, it is surely better to bid 2♠ rather than 1NT with:

> ♠ Q 7 3
> ♥ 6
> ♦ K J 4 2
> ♣ 9 8 6 4 2

If partner is very strong, he has plenty of time to check to make sure that you have sufficient trump support before committing himself to 4♠, while if his strength is more limited your ability to ruff hearts could be crucial to the success of any part score contract.

While the precise values required may vary slightly according to a particular partnership's opening bid style (light, middle-of-the-road, conservative), these are roughly the point counts required for an immediate raise in a natural bidding system.

1M – 2M	=	6–9 points
1M – 3M	=	10–12 points
1M – 4M	=	13–15 points

Of course, these ranges are for the total point counts, not just high card points. It should be clear that distribution is also a significant factor, so that:

(a)	♠ Q 6 4 3	(b)	♠ Q 6 4 3
	♥ 8		♥ K 8 3
	♦ A Q 6		♦ A Q 6
	♣ 10 9 8 5 3		♣ 10 9 8

are roughly equivalent in value opposite a 1♠ opening. Indeed, were I forced to choose, I would prefer to hold (a) rather than (b).

If you are an aficionado of the losing trick count, you will, of course, agree, saying that (a) is a seven-loser hand while (b) has eight losers. Very true. You might also go on to say therefore that (a) should raise 1♠ to 4♠ while (b) should only bid 3♠; the idea of the losing trick count in this situation is that responder subtracts his losers from the magic number of eleven and raises to that level.

The losing trick count is at least as good a way, and probably better, of deciding how high to go when raising partner's suit, as is simply counting points. My personal judgment, however, tells me that (a) is only worth a raise to 3♠ and not 4♠. Actually, opposite a minimum opening, one which would pass a raise to 3♠, game prospects are likely to be decided by how many of partner's values are wasted opposite your heart shortage.

For the moment, however, there is a larger and more fundamental problem to consider. While the limit raises to the two and three levels work reasonably well, the game raise, 1 Major– 4 Major, to show 13–15 points, is extremely cumbersome, leaving as it does so little room to investigate slam possibilities when opener is strong. For this reason, most experienced players now play this immediate game raise as being more pre-emptive in nature. So 1♠–4♠ would be more like:

(a)	♠ J 9 8 7 5		(b)	♠ Q J 10 4
	♥ 6 2	*or*		♥ 8
	♦ K Q 8 5 4			♦ Q J 10 7 4 3
	♣ 6			♣ Q 2

rather than:

	(c)	♠ Q 10 9 4		(d)	♠ Q 10 9 4
		♥ A 3	or		♥ K 8 3
		♦ A Q J 5 2			♦ A Q 6 2
		♣ 7 3			♣ K 7

With (a) and (b) you have a known trump fit but, unless partner's hand is exceptional, there is little hope of a slam. It is still possible, however, that your opponents have a contract if they can get together, and an immediate jump to game is the most likely way to prevent them from doing so. Conversely, with (c) and (d), there is little danger from the opponents but every prospect of greater things if partner is strong. This is the time to look for a slower approach to give room to explore more fully.

THE DELAYED GAME RAISE

Where responder has not only four card support for his partner, but also a good suit of his own, it may well be that this second suit will be the key to the partnership's slam prospects.

Take example (c):

♠ Q 10 9 4
♥ A 3
♦ A Q J 5 2
♣ 7 3

When partner opens 1♠, it must be correct to show the excellent diamond suit, not because you think diamonds may be a better trump suit than spades—you always intend to support spades eventually—but because the diamonds are a potential source of tricks for slam purposes. Give partner something like:

♠ A K J 4
♥ 7 6 2
♦ K 8 3
♣ A 8 2

and slam is almost cold. Swap round his red suits, however, and slam is a much poorer proposition, requiring both the diamond finesse and a 3–2 break in at least one of the key suits. How is opener to appreciate that the king of diamonds is worth so much more than the king of hearts, or indeed clubs, unless you bid diamonds?

So with hand (c), you respond 2♦. Now what?

(i) If partner rebids 2NT, as he would with the example above, you jump to 4♠. Since he has done nothing to indicate possession of a fifth spade, you must have four card support to bid this way. So why not raise immediately? The only sensible explanation is that you were too strong to do so and are making a delayed game raise

But, of course, partner will not always rebid 2NT. What about other possible continuations?

(ii) Suppose his rebid is 2♠. 1♠–2♦–2♠–4♠ does not sound like anything special, and indeed it is not, merely showing a hand which wants to play in 4♠ now that partner has repeated his suit. If you feel that you are too strong to simply bid 4♠ over 2♠, you must find another forcing bid to keep the ball rolling. If your agreement is that a jump to 4♥ would be a cuebid here—a perfectly reasonable agreement as it is not needed in a natural sense—then it would fit the bill with our example hand. Otherwise, you would have to invent a new suit at the three level—presumably 3♥—and hope to be able to describe your hand later.

(iii) If partner's rebid is game forcing, 1♠–2♦–3♣ or 1♠–2♣–3♥, then you could agree that 4♠ from you would now be a delayed game raise, because with any other hand with spade support you could bid a forcing 3♠.

(iv) What if partner raises your suit, 1♠–2♦–3♦? Now it depends what your agreement is regarding a return to partner's suit, i.e. 1♠–2♦–3♦–3♠. We will be looking at this type of sequence in more detail later but, for the moment, we can say that if 3♠ would be forcing then a jump to 4♠ can be a delayed game raise; if our agreement is that 3♠ is not forcing then 4♠ would have to be just to play and with a hand too good for that we would again have to invent another suit—again, presumably, 3♥.

(v) The most contentious sequence is this one: 1♠–2♦–2♥–4♠. Is this a delayed game raise? There was a time when it undoubtedly was played as such. That was in the bad old days when it was considered quite proper to open 1♠ and rebid 2♥ with 4–4 in the two suits. It followed that responder still needed four card support to be able to jump to 4♠ so, following our previous argument, had to have a delayed game raise.

But modern players do not bid this way with 4–4 in the majors. For them, the sequence above guarantees five spades and it is quite possible for responder to want to play in 4♠ when he has only three card support. For me, therefore, a 4♠ bid is simply to play, for example:

♠ K 7 3
♥ A 2
♦ K Q 8 6 4
♣ 7 3 2

and not a delayed game raise. With the stronger hand, I would use fourth suit forcing and then support spades. The traditionalists would reverse these two sequences, and use jumping to 4♠ immediately as a delayed game raise. Which way you play these two sequences is a matter for partnership agreement. I would suggest, however, that partner's response to the fourth suit bid is going to give you extra information. It makes more sense to get this when you don't know where you are going (with the stronger hand) than when you do (when you know you intend to play in 4♠).

Swiss

As I mentioned in the introduction, there are many different versions of the Swiss convention. What they all have in common is that they utilize bids which are of little value in a natural sense to show good high-card raises to four of partner's major.

Hand (d):

> ♠ Q 10 9 4
> ♥ K 8 3
> ♦ A Q 6 2
> ♣ K 7

is a good example of the sort of hand for which Swiss was invented, a hand too good simply to raise to 4♠, but with no suit worthy of a delayed game raise.

In most forms of Swiss, there are just two artificial bids. These are immediate responses of 4♣ and 4♦ to an opening bid of one of a major.

1. Trump Swiss

One of the simplest forms of Swiss attempts to help opener by distinguishing between weak and strong trump holdings in responder's hand. Both 4♣ and 4♦ show sound opening values, around 13–16 high card points (HCP), but 4♦ shows at least two of the top three trump honors while 4♣ denies two top honors (some people reverse the meanings of the two bids). So in response to a 1♠ opening:

> (a) ♠ Q 10 9 4
> ♥ K 8 3
> ♦ A Q 6 2
> ♣ K 7

would bid 4♣, while:

> (b) ♠ K Q 10 9
> ♥ K 8 3
> ♦ A Q 6 2
> ♣ 7 4

would bid 4♦.

This distinction could be particularly useful to an opener with a strong hand but a weak trump holding.

2. Control Swiss

Perhaps the most popular form of Swiss among today's tournament players is what is known in the United States as Control Swiss and in Europe as Fruit-Machine Swiss. In this version, 4♣ shows either three aces, or two aces and the king of trumps, or two aces and an unknown singleton, while 4♦ shows a good raise but denies any of the above. Over 4♣, opener can bid 4♦ to ask which type responder holds. This is where the European name comes from. Initially there are three possibilities and, with an extra spin, opener can find out which it is.

In response to opener's 4♦ asking bid responder bids 4NT to show three aces, bids the trump suit with the king of trumps, and bids the suit of his singleton if he has one. For example:

1♠–4♣–4♦–

4♥/5♣/5♦	= Two aces plus a singleton in the bid suit
4♠	= Two aces plus the king of spades
4NT	= Three aces

Of course, if opener has no interest in slam he has no need to ask, simply signing off in the agreed trump suit.

For me, this is an improvement on Trump Swiss, because it is more specific and the ability to show a singleton can often be very useful.

3. Super Swiss

This is perhaps the most elaborate convention actually to go under the name of Swiss. The inventor realized the importance of being able to show short suits, but also wanted a way to cater to balanced high card raises to game. He, or she, used four artificial responses to do this.

1♠–3NT	= A good raise to 4♠ with any void
4♣	= A good raise to 4♠ with any singleton
4♦	= A good raise to 4♠ with poor trumps
4♥	= A good raise to 4♠ with good trumps

1♥–3♠	= A good raise to 4♥ with any void
3NT	= A good raise to 4♥ with any singleton
4♣	= A good raise to 4♥ with poor trumps
4♦	= A good raise to 4♥ with good trumps

(In another version of the convention, the highest two responses show and deny respectively two or more aces.)

After a singleton or void showing response, opener can make the cheapest available bid to ask for the shortage, if he is interested. The big drawback with this is that sometimes the response takes the partnership to the five level when responder has the wrong shortage. This, in my view, makes Super Swiss of dubious value. Control Swiss, of course, suffers from the same defect.

Splinter Bids

Any version of Swiss is probably better than nothing, but all have their defects. A much better idea is to play splinter bids. A splinter bid is a double jump-shift (1♠–4♣/♦/♥, 1♥–3♠/4♣/♦), and shows four card support for opener's major, opening values, and a singleton or void in the bid suit. A typical example for 1♠–4♦ might be:

> (a) ♠ A J 7 6
> ♥ K Q 5 2
> ♦ 8
> ♣ Q 8 5 3

When we were looking at delayed game raises, we saw that bidding a long suit could help partner to judge that his high cards in that suit would be worth more than their normal face value. Splinter bids are, in a sense, the reverse of the same coin. They work by showing partner where your shortage is and he can now judge that his high cards in that suit, with the exception of the ace, are unlikely to pull their weight. On the other hand, a holding of three or four small cards opposite partner's shortage would be very good because nothing would be wasted.

Take our example sequence, 1♠–4♦. If opener holds something like:

♠ K Q 9 8 3
♥ A J
♦ 7 6 4 2
♣ A 9

he can see that the hands will fit very well. Not only does responder have nothing in diamonds, but he must have about a dozen points in the other three suits, which will fit well with opener's hand.

The auction might proceed:

West	East
1♠	4♦
4♥(*)	4♠
5♣(*)	5♥(*)
6♠	Pass

(*) Cuebid

Now, give opener a different hand simply by reversing his minor suits:

♠ K Q 9 8 3
♥ A J
♦ A 9
♣ 7 6 4 2

This time, though he has no wasted values in diamonds, he will not be nearly so enthusiastic. Although his hand is not a terrible one, he will realize that if responder is short in diamonds he must have length in both clubs and hearts. Four small clubs will take quite a bit of covering. Nonetheless, opener is worth one try, after all:

(b) ♠ A 7 4 2   **(c)** ♠ A 7 4 2
♥ K 8 6 3   *or*   ♥ K Q 6 3
♦ 8   ♦ 8
♣ K Q J 5   ♣ A 8 5 3

would be enough for slam. This time, however, if responder could only sign off in this sequence:1♠–4♦–4♥–4♠, opener would give up on a slam and pass. This is where judgment comes in again. Responder should appreciate that both hands (b) and (c) are significantly better than hand (a), where the ♣Q may be of little value, and so should sign off in 4♠ over 4♥ with (a), but make a return cuebid with either (b) or (c).

Finally, suppose opener has wasted values opposite the splinter bid, for example:

♠ K 9 8 5 3
♥ A 7 4
♦ K Q 6
♣ Q 5

With 5 of his 14 HCP of very dubious value, opener should simply bid 4♠ over 4♦. Though again his hand is not a terrible one, responder will need a very good hand to make slam a good bet.

I would recommend the use of splinter bids to all regular partnerships. Let's look at a few possible problem areas.

(1.) First, which bids are actually splinter bids? 4♣ and 4♦ responses to one of a major are pretty clear, but there are those who insist on keeping 1♥–3♠ and 1♠–4♥ as natural. I would encourage you not to do this in your regular partnership, as I am convinced that splinters are more valuable than the natural uses of these two sequences. After all, do you really need to make a pre-emptive bid when your partner opens the bidding and your side holds both majors?

If you agree to play splinters with a stranger, however, it does no harm to check on his views. Firmly ingrained in my memory is a board from the final of The Hubert Phillips Bowl, the EBU's national pivot mixed teams championship. One of our pairs bid 1♠–4♥–Pass. They were lucky, the missing trumps broke evenly. Unfortunately, the break was 6–6! Instead of scoring +1430 in 6♠, our intrepid heroes scored -600 in 4♥. This would have been a disaster at any form of scoring, but this competition works on aggregate scoring not IMPs, so we had lost 2030 points on one deal. In case you were wondering, the story did have a happy ending as we won the match—but after this board we needed some luck!

(2.) Second, you need to consider how strong responder should be to use a splinter bid. While your judgment should be affected by such things as the number of trumps you hold and how good your controls are, you should usually be somewhere around the 11–14 HCP range. Once you get above that range, you get awkward hands where you have, perhaps, an ace to spare for your initial action and are tempted to go on even though opener signs off. Be honest now, you might be tempted to have one more try after 1♠–4♦–4♠ with say:

♠ K Q 4 2
♥ A Q J 6
♦ 3
♣ K 8 6 4

Yet, if partner has a minimum with wasted diamond values, 5♠ may be too high. Better with such a hand to go slowly and hope to get a feel for partner's hand-type without having to risk the five level.

What you could do, however, is to say that eventually a hand can be so strong that you can justify going to the five level even opposite a sign-off. Say:

♠ A K 4 2
♥ J 7 6 3
♦ 8
♣ A K Q J

It would not be unreasonable to bid this: 1♠–4♦–4♠–5♣ and see if partner can cuebid 5♥.

If you like this idea then you are saying that a splinter bid has two possible ranges, usually 11–14, occasionally 18+, but you don't splinter with 15–17.

(3.) Consider that, when partner hears you make a splinter bid, he is going to assume that you have a small singleton and evaluate his hand accordingly. If he has say, AQx, he will judge the ace to be valuable but probably not the queen, while holdings like KQx, KJx and QJx will be judged to be very poor.

But each of those holdings could be very useful if facing a singleton honor:

(a) AQx – K
(b) KQx – A
(c) KJx – Q
(d) QJx – K

The point I am making, is that to splinter in a suit where you hold a singleton ace, king or queen is likely to be self-defeating, because partner will devalue precisely the sort of holding which is actually ideal and gives your singleton honor some real value as well. Very occasionally, you will find that you simply have no alternative to a splinter with a singleton honor, but you should be aware of the risk that you take and avoid it whenever possible.

(4.) A splinter bid shows either a singleton or a void. If you splinter then bid the same suit again, you show that you actually have a void. For example: 1♠–4♦–4♥–5♦ with:

♠ A J 6 3
♥ K 8 4 2
♦ –
♣ Q J 9 6 3

Note, however, that had opener signed off over 4♦, you would have passed. If he makes a slam try, you are strong enough to cooperate because of your void, but you are certainly not strong enough to drive to the five level yourself.

(5.) A matter which requires fine judgment is what to do if you have both a singleton *and* a good suit of your own. Partner opens 1♠ and you hold:

(a)	♠ K 7 6 3	(b)	♠ K 7 6 3	(c)	♠ K 7 6 3
	♥ 8		♥ 8		♥ 8
	♦ Q 9 7 4 2		♦ A Q J 9 7		♦ K Q 9 7 2
	♣ A K J		♣ K 8 3		♣ A J 3

Do you splinter, or do you use the delayed game raise? In my experience a lot of players get hooked on splinter bids and use them too often. Splinters help partner to judge how much of his hand is wasted opposite your shortage, but to make a slam you also need to have twelve tricks, and your side suit could be a source of five of those twelve if partner has suitable fitting cards for you. Looking at the above examples, (b) should clearly bid 2♦, not 4♥, since you only

need partner to hold one card—the king—to make your diamonds solid and you want him to value that card highly. (a) is a clear splinter. True, you have a five card suit, but partner needs a very good holding to allow you to make many tricks from it. (c) is a little less clear but, even opposite as little as ace doubleton, there is a chance of running the diamonds so I would bid 2♦.

Am I now depriving you of the chance to use splinter bids just when you most want to?

No, because this is a situation where you can have the best of both worlds: bid your suit, then make a delayed splinter bid. 1♠–2♦–2♠–4♥ and 1♠–2♦–2NT–4♥ are both splinter bids in support of spades. This is more useful than using 4♥ as a general cuebid, helping partner's judgment much more.

If partner bids 1♠–2♦–3♣ or 1♠–2♦–3♦ you can simply agree spades by bidding 3♠, forcing—4♥ in these sequences would agree clubs and diamonds respectively—and take it from there.

Finally, if he bids 1♠–2♦–2♥ that is bad news, as he is likely to have wasted values in hearts. Clearly, you cannot bid 4♥ as a splinter bid, but you can bid 3♣ and see what he does next. 1♠–2♦–2♥–3♣–3NT–4♠ would show a hand too good for 4♠ on the previous round, though admittedly it would not pinpoint the heart singleton. Still, with partner unable to give any sort of help in diamonds, slam is looking quite unlikely anyway.

Mini-Splinters

Do you remember this hand?

♠ Q 6 4 3
♥ 8
♦ A Q 6
♣ 10 9 8 5 3

I said that, ideally, I would like to raise my partner's 1♠ opening bid to 3♠ but show my heart singleton on the way to help him judge whether or not to go on to game. If you have been persuaded of the benefits of splinter bids, you may now agree with me—but splinter bids are made at the four level, aren't they?

It is true that a normal splinter bid commits the user to game, but this is where mini-splinters come in. Where a splinter bid is a double jump shift, a mini-splinter is a simple jump shift, i.e. 1♠–3♣/♦/♥; 1♥–2♠/3♣/♦, and it shows game invitational strength with four card support for partner plus a singleton in the suit bid.

As you can see, this is perfect for the example hand, 1♠–3♥ getting everything across in one bid. Suppose partner holds:

(a)	♠ A K 7 5 2	(b)	♠ A K 7 5 2
	♥ J 5 3		♥ K 1 5
	♦ K 4 2		♦ 4 2
	♣ Q 7		♣ Q 7 3

Facing a normal limit response, 1♠–3♠, he should pass with either of these hands because he has very little to spare for his opening bid. Facing a mini-splinter response of 3♥, however, he can judge to bid game with (a) but sign off in 3♠ with (b). In both cases, he can see the possibility of ruffing two hearts in the dummy; the difference is that in (a) all his high cards are working opposite partner's length, while in (b) the king of hearts is likely to be wasted.

The other benefit of mini-splinters is that when responder makes a simple limit raise, 1♠–3♠ or 1♥–3♥, he is known not to have a short suit, because he didn't show it, so again opener has more information than when playing standard methods.

The benefits of mini-splinters are clear; what about the disadvantages? The obvious one is that using mini-splinters deprives you of the natural strong jump shift. How serious this is depends on your personal style. Modern experts seem to use the strong jump shift very rarely, generally preferring to explore slowly with good hands. For them, losing the strong jump shift altogether is not such a high price to pay. If, on the other hand, you like to jump shift quite often, then the loss will be much more serious for you and you should think very hard before experimenting with mini-splinters.

Even if you don't jump shift very much, you should still consider whether mini-splinters are the best use for these sequences. Another possibility, which would occur more frequently than the traditional strong jump shift, might be, for example, to play weak jump shifts. Now a jump shift shows a hand similar to one which would have opened with a weak two bid. 1♥–2♠ might be:

♠ K J 10 7 5 3		♠ A K J 7 5 3
♥ 6 2	rather than	♥ A 6
♦ Q 6		♦ A 6
♣ 8 5 3		♣ J 5 3

The other weakness of any method which involves bidding short suits is that you make it very easy for your opponents to compete—they can simply double the splinter to show an interest in the suit without having to take the risk of actually bidding it. This could be particularly significant where your trump suit is hearts and the splinter is in spades. Despite these problems, I quite like mini-splinters. Whether or not to bid a major suit game is part of the real "bread and butter" of the game and as such anything which makes the judgment easier should be welcomed. Meanwhile, big hands usually can be developed more slowly.

BALANCED AND SEMI-BALANCED GAME RAISES

You have seen how to raise to game when you have both trump support for partner and a good suit of your own (the delayed game raise), and you have seen what to do when holding a shortage (splinter bids), but apart from Swiss you have not seen any way of showing a good but balanced raise to game—and, of course, you can't play both Swiss and splinters. The most common solution for the casual partnership is to play that a response of 3NT to an opening bid of one of a major shows four card support, around 13–16 HCP, but no singleton or void. This has the merit of simplicity but, like Swiss, it is a little cumbersome, taking up quite a lot of space without giving a specific message. Nonetheless, unless you want to take on another significant piece of system, it is as good a solution as any. If your memory is not yet completely overloaded, however, there is something better.

Jacoby 2NT

Delayed game raises and splinter bids work well because, in each case, responder has a specific feature which he wants to describe to his partner. Good hands which do not have any special feature to show may do better to ask partner to describe his hand instead. This is the idea of the Jacoby 2NT response to one of a major, which simply shows support for opener and at least game values, but denies the ability to make a more descriptive bid. After 1♥/♠–2NT, opener gives more information about his hand.

As with most popular conventions which have been around for a while, there are now several modifications to the basic idea in use. The one described here comes from Chip Martel, a multiple world champion. It has the merit of being relatively simple.

1♠– 2NT		
3♣	=	Minimum strength, any distribution
3♦	=	Extra values, diamond shortage
3♥	=	Extra values, heart shortage
3♠	=	Extra values, club shortage
3NT	=	Extra values, balanced hand
4♣/♦/♥	=	Extra values, five cards in bid suit

If responder is still interested in slam, even opposite a minimum opening, he can use a 3♦ asking bid over 3♣. In response, opener bids three of the agreed trump suit with a balanced hand or bids the suit of his singleton or void. Though these are not part of the basic convention, there are also spare bids available which may be used to show two-suiters.

Suppose that responder holds something like:

♠ A Q 7 2
♥ 8 6 3
♦ K J 4 2
♣ Q J

(i) After 1♠–2NT–3♣ he will sign off in 4♠ as it is hard to visualize a slam opposite a minimum opener.

(ii) Also, 1♠–2NT–3♦/♥ would discourage him as he has wasted values opposite opener's singleton. Having already shown opening values, he would sign off in 4♠ and leave any further move to the opener.

(iii) And after 1♠–2NT–3NT he would sign off as he is completely minimum for his 2NT response.

(iv) 1♠–2NT–3♥ would be excellent news, showing, as it does, extra values and a shortage in hearts. With nothing wasted, responder should have high hopes of a slam. Best is a quiet 3♠ to leave room for opener to cuebid.

(v) 1♠–2NT–4♣/♦ are both good news because partner has a two-suiter and you have useful honors in his second suit, but:

(vi) 1♠–2NT–4♥ is disappointing. True, partner has both a two-suiter and extra values, but you have the worst possible holding in his side suit—neither a fitting honor card nor the ability to ruff—and some of your minor suit strength will be wasted opposite his shortage.

It will not have escaped your attention that if opener is 5–5 he must also have a short suit. Which should he show in response to 2NT? He is in a similar position to a responder who has to judge whether to show his own suit via a delayed game raise or make a splinter bid, except that here the balance should swing more towards showing the second suit if in any doubt. For example:

(a)	(b)	(c)
♠ A Q 7 3 2	♠ A Q 7 3 2	♠ A Q 7 3 2
♥ J 2	♥ A 4	♥ A K
♦ A Q J 4 3	♦ K J 5 3 2	♦ J 7 5 3 2
♣ 5	♣ 6	♣ 6

(a) is clear cut. The diamond suit well worth showing, so rebid 4♦.

The diamond suit in (b) would be completely minimum for a delayed game raise, but here it is more important to show it than to show the singleton. After all, diamonds could be a valuable source of tricks if partner has any fitting honor cards and, because he knows you are at least 5–5, he knows you have a short suit somewhere.

With (c), I would bid 3♠, showing the club shortage. True, you have a second five card suit, but it is very weak and you will need partner to have a very suitable holding if it is to be of any value. Better to let him judge how much wastage he has in clubs rather than bid diamonds and encourage him to look with favor on some holding like king to three—a disaster if you reach a slam.

1 Major – 3 Major Pre-emptive

If the bidding commences 1♥/1♠–Double, we are all familiar with the idea that a jump to three of partner's suit is pre-emptive while sound raises go via 2NT. Whether the second hand doubles, it is guaranteed that, if we have a good fit in one suit, then our opponents will have a fit in another suit. And the weaker we are, the more likely it is that they will wish to compete if we let them. Why not, then, play that 1M–Pass–3M is also pre-emptive, thereby making it much harder for them?

You will have to take the vulnerability into account, of course, but basically there is nothing new here, you simply bid here as you already are doing if right-hand-opponent (RHO) doubles.

But what do I do when I have a normal limit raise to three of partner's major, I hear you ask?

One reason for my choice of the Martel version of the

Jacoby 2NT response was that it includes a response to show a minimum opening. Although it is normal to play the 2NT bid as game forcing, it doesn't take much to modify it so that it can also be used on hands worth a limit raise to three of partner's major. Actually, it is not such a bad yardstick by which opener can judge whether or not he has extra values. If he would have passed a limit raise, he treats his hand as a minimum and rebids 3♣, over which responder can bid three of the agreed major as a sign-off. If, on the other hand, opener would have bid on over a limit raise, he says his hand has extra values and bids accordingly. There is a small price to pay. Opener has to be a little more careful about bidding on in a sequence like: 1♠–2NT–3♥–4♠ since responder could have either a minimum (or unsuitable) game raise or merely a limit raise with which he was only ever interested in game. If responder makes the mark time bid of 3♠ rather than 4♠ whenever he sees any slam prospects at all, however, when he does bid 4♠ instead this will be quite a severe dampener on opener's ambitions so it should be quite rare for him to take the partnership too high.

Bergen Major Suit Raises

Marty Bergen, a leading American expert, uses another system which includes pre-emptive raises. The system assumes five card major suit openings. 1M–2M shows 6–9 points and precisely three card support. Hands with four card or longer support are shown by jumping to the three level, as follows:

1♠–3♣	=	7–10, four card support
3♦	=	10–12, four card support
3♥	=	Game values, singleton or void in an unspecified suit
3♠	=	0–6, four card support
1♥–3♣	=	7–10, four card support
3♦	=	10–12, four card support
3♥	=	0–6, four card support
3♠	=	Game values, singleton or void somewhere

If opener wishes to know what shortage his partner holds after 1♠–3♥ or 1♥–3♠, he makes the cheapest available bid to inquire:

1♠–3♥		
3♠–3NT	=	Short hearts
4♣	=	Short clubs
4♦	=	Short diamonds
1♥–3♠		
3NT–4♣	=	Short clubs
4♦	=	Short diamonds
4♥	=	Short spades

Relative to standard methods, Bergen raises have the advantage of both a pre-emptive raise and two different strengths of invitational raise. They work well in conjunction with a Jacoby 2NT response and, because limit raises are taken care of elsewhere, allow this to be played in its traditional game forcing style.

1♠–3♥ and 1♥–3♠ are used for splinter raises and have a tactical edge over traditional splinters in that opener need only ask for the shortage when he has slam interest, leaving him the option of simply bidding game and leaving the opening leader in the dark.

The negative side is, of course, that you lose all the three level jump shifts so have to find a different way of handling whatever sort of hand you currently show by that route. My own preference would be to play mini-splinters, pre-emptive raises, and Martel-Jacoby 2NT to include the limit raise types—but there are enough perfectly sensible tactics available that I would prefer to have you make your own choices rather than try to persuade you all to play my way.

The Forcing No Trump

With the exception of 1M–2M, all the Bergen raises described above promise four card trump support, yet playing five card majors you will often want to raise with only three cards.

It is common, when playing five card majors, to play a 1NT response to 1M as forcing. It may seem that losing the option of playing in that beautiful little contract of 1NT is a high price to pay, but in truth it is not as big a loss as you might imagine and the forcing no trump does give responder many more options—in much the same way as do transfer bids over 1NT.

After 1♥/♠–1NT, opener makes the rebid which best describes his hand. Occasionally, since he has already shown a five card suit, it may be necessary to bid a three card minor rather than repeat the major with a 5–3–3–2 hand; for example:

(a)	♠ K J 7 5 3	(b)	♠ K J 7 5 3
	♥ A 6 4		♥ A Q 6
	♦ J 7		♦ A 7
	♣ K J 2		♣ K J 2

After 1♠–1NT, bid 2♣ with (a). Partner already knows you have five spades and will revert to that suit if he has any support for you. But with (b), your correct rebid is 2NT, just as it would be opposite a non-forcing 1NT response. You only have to bid a three card minor when you have no other descriptive bid available.

The forcing no trump means that all three card limit raises of partner's major can start off with 1NT. So with:

♠ K 7 3
♥ Q 6 4
♦ A 2
♣ Q 8 6 5 3

respond 1NT to either 1♥ or 1♠. If you bid 3♥ or 3♠ over partner's rebid, he will know you have three card support and 10–12 points. Remember that with less you would have raised to 2♥/♠ immediately. The forcing 1NT bid gives responder many more options than he has using standard methods. He can make any bid immediately or bid 1NT then

make the same bid on the next round; for example: (a) 1♠–4♣ or (b) 1♠–1NT–2♠–4♣. I don't want to go into a lot of detail here. If you play five card majors and a forcing no trump, you can create your own style easily enough. Just to give an idea, however, let me assume that you are a fan of splinter bids. You could agree that (a) and (b) showed two different strengths of hand with spade support and a shortage in clubs, say 11–14 and 15–17. Alternatively, one sequence could be used to show a singleton club, the other a void.

RESPONDING AS A PASSED HAND

In principle, there is no reason why you could not play exactly the same methods when responding to partner's third or fourth in hand opening bids as you do when he opens in first or second position. Of course, you will not often have a hand which is too strong for a direct raise to game, but it is possible. For example:

♠ K 9 7 5 3
♥ 7 5 3
♦ 8
♣ A K 4 2

Assuming that you would not open this hand, you are well worth a 4♦ splinter response to partner's third or fourth seat 1♠ bid. Indeed, turn the ♣K into the ♣Q and you would still splinter.

Mostly, however, as a passed hand, you will only really be concerned with inviting game and not slam, and should design your system to reflect this. Because you have already denied holding an opening bid, there is no longer the same conflict of interests where the meaning of a jump shift is concerned. Clearly you cannot hold a strong jump but equally, a hand suitable for a weak jump response would normally have opened with some sort of pre-empt, so you are free to play 1♠–3♣/♦/♥ and 1♥–2♠/3♣/♦ as major suit raises of some kind. The obvious use is as mini-splinters, as we saw earlier, a limit raise to the three level with a singleton in the bid suit. Now that there is no pressing need for the bids to mean anything else, it is surely right to use them in this way.

The alternative is to show sidesuit length rather than shortage. This is the traditional approach. A sequence like 1♠–3♣ shows the values for a 3♠ bid with spade support plus a club suit. The classic example would be something like:

♠ J 10 9 4
♥ 7 2
♦ 6 3
♣ A K 8 6 5

With a borderline hand, partner can look at his holding in your sidesuit and see how well the hands fit together. For example:

(a)	♠ A K Q 7 2	(b)	♠ A K Q 7 2
	♥ A 3		♥ A 3
	♦ 9 4 2		♦ Q 9 7
	♣ Q 9 7		♣ 9 4 2

If the auction went simply 1♠–3♠, no doubt we would all try 4♠ with either (a) or (b). But look at the difference after 1♠–3♣. Opener can almost write down his partner's hand and can see that with (a), 4♠ is likely to be almost laydown, while with (b) accurate defense will surely lead to defeat.

If responder actually jumped to 3♦ rather than 3♣, the reverse would, of course, be true. This time hand (b) fits the response well, hand (a) does not. Though these natural fit-showing jumps are undoubtedly the most common style in use today, I believe them to be a long way inferior to the use of mini-splinters. Their most serious defect is simply that hands suitable for their use occur so infrequently. Not only must you be 5–4, but your high cards must almost all be in two suits. To respond 3♣ to 1♠ with:

(a)	♠ A K Q 4		(b)	♠ J 7 6 2
	♥ 7 6	or		♥ K 4
	♦ 8 3			♦ A 7
	♣ 10 7 6 5 2			♣ J 9 7 3 2

hardly helps partner to judge how well the two hands will fit together. Also, even when the high cards are concentrated in the two suits, there is a big difference between:

(a)	♠ Q 10 9 4	(b)	♠ Q 10 9 4	(c)	♠ Q 10 9 4
	♥ 7 2		♥ 7		♥ 8 7 2
	♦ 8 6		♦ 8 6 2		♦ 6
	♣ A Q 10 9 7		♣ A Q 10 9 7		♣ A Q 10 9 7

The position of the singleton, if any, could be just as crucial to partner's judgment.

What about balanced raises? If you still play 1M–3M as a limit raise, you could also continue to do so after passing. There is still a good case for playing this as pre-emptive, however, because if you are weak the opposition might still wish to compete the part score. Pass–1♥/♠–2NT is little needed in a natural sense, as if you play a reasonably aggressive game most hands strong enough to respond 2NT now would have opened the bidding in the first place. Meanwhile, given that most players tend to shade their third-in-hand openings somewhat, to respond 2NT to one without having a fit for partner's suit is singularly ill-advised. Better to reserve the 2NT response to show a limit raise.

Actually, this has another benefit. After 1M–3M, partner has two options, to bid game or to pass. After 1M–2NT, however, he can make a game try by bidding a new suit to ask responder to bid game with a suitable holding in the suit and otherwise to sign-off.

For example, opener holds:

♠ A K 7 5 3

♥ K 4

♦ Q 6

♣ Q 9 5 2

and after Pass–1♠–2NT– is unsure about game, so bids 3♣. Responder holds:

(a)	♠ Q 10 9 4	(b)	♠ Q 10 9 4
	♥ A J 7 2		♥ A J 7 2
	♦ K 8		♦ 7 6 3
	♣ 7 6 3		♣ K 8

If opener has three or four cards in clubs and is looking for help in that suit, hand (a) looks very unsuitable while hand (b) looks ideal. Responder therefore bids 4♠ with (b) but only 3♠ with (a).

Drury

A very different approach to the problem of responding to a third or fourth seat opening of one of a major is supplied by the Drury convention. Rather than risk getting too high by making a limit raise when partner's opening bid may have been somewhat shaded, Drury uses an artificial 2♣ response to ask about the strength of opener's hand.

In the original version of Drury, opener rebid 2♦ to show a sub-minimum opening, otherwise made his natural rebid. Today, there are several versions of Drury in use; one, for example, reverses everything so that opener rebids 2♦ to show a sound opening, and rebids his suit with a weak hand. Anyway, the following is something close to "standard" Drury, if there is such a thing.

When you have support for partner's third or fourth in hand 1♥/♠ opening, you may:

(i) make your normal raise to 2♠ with up to about nine points;

(ii) with ten plus points bid 2 ♣ (Drury);

(iii) with less than ten points but both good support and a fair amount of shape, jump to the three level. Whether you simply make a limit raise or a mini-splinter is, of course, a matter for agreement.

Pass–1♠–2♣–?

(i) 2♦ = Opener's weakest rebid, showing a minimum or sub-minimum hand with which he sees no prospect of game opposite a passed hand. Responder normally converts to 2♠.

(ii) 2♥ = A sound opening with four hearts and, as such, a game try. Nonetheless, opener may now pass if responder merely goes back to 2♠, suggesting a minimum 2♣ bid.

(iii) 2♠ = Again, a sound opener and so a game try. It is not forcing, however, opener could have done more had he been confident of game opposite a minimum 2♣ response.

(iv) 2NT= Natural and forcing, at least strong no trump strength.

(v) 3♣/♦/♥ = Natural and a slam try, showing at least four cards in the bid suit.

(vi) 3♠ = A slam try, inviting a cuebid.

(vii) 3NT = Given that 2NT is forcing, this is redundant in a natural sense. Mike Lawrence has suggested that it could be used as Blackwood, thereby saving a level of bidding.

(viii) 4♣/♦/♥ = Splinter bids.

(ix) 4♠ = To play. Any hand which wants to play in game but has no slam interest.

A few examples may help those unfamiliar with this idea.

1.

West	East
♠ A J 7 3 2	♠ Q 9 8 4
♥ A K 6	♥ 7 4 3 2
♦ K 9 4	♦ J 8
♣ 10 8	♣ J 7

West	East
–	Pass
1♠	2♠
Pass	

When East raises quietly to 2♠, he is known not to be strong enough to use Drury so West passes 2♠.

2.

West	East
♠ A J 7 3 2	♠ K 9 8 4
♥ A K 6	♥ 7 4 3 2
♦ J 4 2	♦ A Q 8
♣ 10 8	♣ J 7

West	East
–	Pass
1♠	2♣
2♠	Pass

This time, East is just worth a Drury 2♣ response. West's 2♠ shows a second opening but East is minimum so passes.

3.

West	East
♠ A J 7 3 2	♠ K 9 8 4
♥ A K 6	♥ 7 4 3 2
♦ K 9 4	♦ A Q 8
♣ 10 8	♣ J 7

West	East
–	Pass
1♠	2♣
4♠	Pass

This time, West has enough for game opposite the Drury bid but has no interest in slam. He knows his partner has at least three card support so goes straight to 4♠.

4.

West	East
♠ A J 7 3 2	♠ K 9 8 4
♥ K Q 6	♥ 7 4 3 2
♦ 6 4 2	♦ A Q 8
♣ 10 8	♣ J 7

West	East
–	Pass
1♠	2♣
2♦	2♠
Pass	

West's 2♦ rebid shows a sub-minimum opening so East signs off in 2♠. Note that 3♠, the contract reached if Drury is not used, is in serious jeopardy.

So, is Drury a good idea? Certainly, it allows you sometimes to play a level lower than if you were not using it and that is no bad thing. The better the skill of your opposition, however, the less often you will be allowed to benefit from this. Simply, good opponents are unlikely to allow you to play peacefully in 2♥/♠ when you are known to have a fit but only limited values. Drury is not a bad idea, it just isn't quite as beneficial as some of its advocates might have you believe.

PARTNER OPENS ONE OF A MINOR

When partner opens one of a major, it is very unusual not to raise his suit if you have four card support. When partner opens one of a minor, you will quite often respond in a new suit, despite having support for him. This is because of the relative importance of major suit fits, whether it be to play in a higher scoring part score at matchpoint pairs, or because four of a major is easier to make than five of a minor at any form of scoring. Holding:

♠ Q 7 4 2
♥ A 3
♦ K 7 6 4
♣ J 8 5

for example, you would raise an opening bid of 1♠ immediately. If, on the other hand, the opening bid was 1♦, you would respond 1♠ rather than raise, despite your four card support.

With game values and four card support for partner's major suit opening, you will almost certainly make a bid which commits your side to playing with that suit as trumps. Even when you have no suit of your own to consider, you will rarely do the same thing with support for partner's minor suit opening. Unless you are very shapely, you will normally keep the bidding low and explore the possibility of playing in 3NT, settling for five of the minor only as a last resort.

Playing standard methods, this often involves inventing a suit, otherwise you have no way of making a forcing bid below the level of 3NT. For reasons of safety—you hardly want to hear partner leaping off into the stratosphere in support of your imaginary suit—it is usual to respond in the other minor. It would be quite normal to respond 1♦ to 1♣ with:

(a) ♠ A 7 4   **(b)** ♠ 7 4
     ♥ 8 6 3   or   ♥ A K Q
     ♦ K J 2   ♦ A 8 3
     ♣ A K 7 5   ♣ Q J 8 7 5

although personally I would have no violent objection to a 1♥ response on (b).

This is all very well, and a well-educated partner should always give you plenty of rope if you bid either 1♣–1♦ or 1♦–2♣ but later support his suit. But given the impressive array of artificial methods available when partner opens one of a major, surely we can come up with something a little better in this situation?

Of course, the answer is, yes we can. All the splinters, mini-splinters, and other techniques which I have advocated opposite a major suit can also be utilized opposite a minor if you so desire. While they take care of the distributional hands with which you are quite happy to support partner immediately, none of them does anything for the basic problem of how to handle a balanced hand like examples (a) and (b) above.

Minor Suit Swiss

One suggestion is that, just as you can use 4♣ and 4♦ responses to one of a major as Swiss, so you can use 1♣–3♦/♥/♠ and 1♦–3♥/♠ as Minor Suit Swiss. It will come as no surprise to hear that there are a number of different treatments in existence. Frankly, once you decide to use one of them, I doubt if it matters very much which one you choose. Possibilities are that each of the possible responses shows a different point range; that all show much the same strength and you respond in the lowest suit in which you have a stopper for no trump purposes; or that you bid a second suit, i.e. 1♦–3♥ shows game values, four hearts and at least four diamonds.

No doubt there are other possibilities. The trouble is that while the three level bids used are not particularly needed in a natural sense, they are extremely cumbersome. After all, you are trying to explore the possibility of playing in 3NT and these bids leave very little room to check that every suit is covered. So, while Minor Suit Swiss no doubt has its advocates within the expert community, personally, I would prefer to use these three level bids as splinters and stick to inventing a new suit to bid at a lower level when I want to keep 3NT in the picture.

Inverted Raises

The real solution to this problem is to play inverted minor suit raises. All this means is that 1m–3m becomes a weak bid and 1m–2m becomes a one round force, showing 10+ points, while awkward hands which don't quite fit into either category can always respond 1NT despite the four card support.

Our two example hands:

(a) ♠ A 7 4   **(b)** ♠ 7 4
     ♥ 8 6 3   ♥ A K Q
     ♦ K J 2   ♦ A 8 3
     ♣ A K 7 5   ♣ Q J 8 7 5

are solved simply by raising 1♣ to 2♣. This is forcing only as far as 3♣ (or 2NT if this would be a weak rebid in your system), but you can bid a new suit on the next round if you need to make another forcing bid to allow you to explore further. Because you have already supported clubs, partner will be under no illusions that you actually want to play in this second suit.

With a minimum single suited hand he re-raises to 3♣, non-forcing.

With a second suit he bids it. If responder now goes back to 3♣, he shows a minimum 2♣ response and it is non-forcing, otherwise he shows extra values. With a strong unbalanced hand, opener can jump in a new suit as a splinter bid, for example, 1♣–2♣–3♥ might be something like:

     ♠ A 7 6
     ♥ 8
     ♦ K Q 3
     ♣ K Q J 7 5 2

It is even more important to be able to make pre-emptive raises when your fit is in a minor suit because there is a real danger that your opponents will have a fit in a higher ranking suit and you want to make it as tough as possible for them to get together. Typical hands for 1♣–3♣ would be:

(a) ♠ 8   **(b)** ♠ 7
     ♥ 7 3 2   ♥ 10 6 5 3
     ♦ K 5 4 3   ♦ J 8 4 2
     ♣ Q 7 6 3 2   ♣ Q 9 7 3

Balanced hands which might have made a simple raise if playing standard methods should usually respond 1NT. For example bid 1♦–1NT with:

(c) ♠ Q 9 8   **(d)** ♠ 7 5 4
     ♥ 9 4   ♥ K 9 3
     ♦ K 7 6 3   ♦ A Q 6 2
     ♣ Q 4 3 2   ♣ 10 8 6

Actually, (c) is borderline between 1NT and 3♣, since your defense against a major suit contract is very poor. Add as little as the jack of hearts, however, and 1NT would be clearcut—just as it is with hand (d).

Inverted minor suit raises are an excellent idea. Relative to traditional limit raises, they improve both your constructive and competitive prospects and, unlike most conventions, they don't require you to lose the use of any natural bids.

THE LATER AUCTION

The Game Try

Good news. Partner has raised your opening bid of one of a major to the two level. Now what?

For the beginner, it is very simple. His partner has made a limit bid so he knows not only that the partnership has found a satisfactory trump suit, but also roughly what the combined assets of the two hands are. If he sees no prospect of game he passes, while, if he is confident that the partnership has the necessary values to make game a reasonable bet, he bids it. If he has an awkward hand where he is unsure whether or not game is worth bidding, he re-raises (1♥–2♥–3♥ or 1♠–2♠–3♠) to invite game, asking responder to bid game with a maximum but pass with a minimum. For example:

(a) ♠ Q J 6 4	(b) ♠ Q J 6 4
♥ A Q 3	♥ Q 6 3
♦ 7 4 2	♦ J 7 4
♣ 8 6 5	♣ 8 6 5

After 1♠–2♠–3♠, responder would bid 4♠ with hand (a) but pass with hand (b).

This is all very well, but it is an extremely cumbersome way of going about things. So often opener will have a distributional hand and the fate of a prospective game contract will be decided not so much by the volume of high cards in responder's hand as by their positions, that is, how well they fit together with opener's hand. For example, give opener:

♠ A K J 10 8
♥ 7
♦ Q 7 5 4
♣ A J 9

and responder:

(a) ♠ Q 7 6 5	(b) ♠ Q 7 6 5
♥ 8 3 2	♥ K J 6
♦ K J 6	♦ 8 3 2
♣ Q 3 2	♣ Q 3 2

Opener's hand is unchanged, while responder has exactly the same shape and high card values in each case, yet see the difference! Hand (a) makes game a near certainty, while even 3♠ will need some good fortune with hand (b).

If responder is simply to decide whether his hand is maximum or minimum for his previous bid, then clearly he will make the same decision with both hands (a) and (b). Equally clearly, this will result in one winning decision and one losing one. Surely it must be possible to devise something more accurate than this?

Of course, the answer is yes, and one of the earliest refinements most players make to their bidding methods as they pass beyond the beginner stage is to play some system of game tries in this situation. What has to be remembered is that you have already bid and raised a major suit so if you bid some other suit, there is no danger that partner will misunderstand your intentions. You may occasionally choose to play in no trump, but basically you have already agreed on a trump suit so any new suit you bid must be merely an attempt to help partner to judge how high to go in that suit.

Natural Game Tries

Most people begin by playing natural game tries, using which opener makes a natural descriptive bid to help responder to judge how well the two hands fit together. Returning to the earlier example:

♠ A K J 10 8
♥ 7
♦ Q 7 5 4
♣ A J 9

and responder:

(a) ♠ Q 7 6 5	(b) ♠ Q 7 6 5
♥ 8 3 2	♥ K J 6
♦ K J 6	♦ 8 3 2
♣ Q 3 2	♣ Q 3 2

Playing natural game tries opener's rebid after 1♠–2♠ would be 3♦. If all responder had been asked to do was to decide whether or not his hand was a maximum via 1♠–2♠–3♠, he would have had a tough decision. True, he holds 8HCPs, in the top half of his initial range of 6–9, but the unattractive shape and lack of aces or intermediate cards would tend to suggest a minimum. The 3♦ game try, however, solves his problem. Hand (a) now becomes a maximum as he has two honor cards in opener's sidesuit where they are likely to pull their weight. Hand (b), however, is just as clearly a minimum. Not only does it contain no help in diamonds, but surely opener will be short in either hearts or clubs and responder's high cards in that suit will be wasted.

The above examples are the kind of awkward middle of the range hands which game tries were designed to help with. A real maximum will accept the game try, however bad a holding it may have in partner's sidesuit. For example, after 1♠–2♠–3♥, with:

♠ Q 7 3 2
♥ 7 6 4
♦ A 10 5
♣ K 8 2

bid 4♠ despite the dreadful heart holding. True, there could be four top losers, but there is a fair chance that all your high cards will be working.

♠ J 7 3 2
♥ 7 6 4
♦ Q J 10
♣ K Q 6

is a much closer decision. There is a real danger that the minor suit values will not pull their weight in 4♠. At teams, where the odds favor bidding thin games, particularly vulnerable, I might try 3NT, suggesting a maximum with most of the strength in the minors and offering partner a choice of games. I would not be at all surprised to find that no game was making, however, and I would not criticize partner for signing off in 3♠—unless this proved to be a losing decision, of course. A real minimum will normally decline the game invitation, though responder might still accept with a really exceptional holding in the sidesuit. Again, the auction begins 1♠–2♠–3♥:

(a) ♠ 10 8 7 5   (b) ♠ K 8 7 5
    ♥ 6   ♥ K 2
    ♦ A 6 4 3   ♦ 9 6 4 3
    ♣ 9 8 7 2   ♣ 9 8 5

Both are worth a shot at game. Hand (a) will be able to ruff most of partner's losing hearts and has a sure trick in diamonds, while (b) has two well placed kings plus the potential to ruff hearts. Note that the non-specific 1♠–2♠–3♠ game try could never persuade either example to bid game, yet, opposite either (a) or (b), as little as:

♠ A Q 6 4 3
♥ A 8 4 3
♦ 7 2
♣ A 6

♣ makes 4♠ an excellent contract.

When responder is judging whether to accept the game try, he looks for two types of holding in opener's second suit, either fitting honor cards, or extreme shortage allied to an abundance of trumps. The other side of the coin is that he will look with disfavor on holdings like three or four small, which offer no help in the play.

It follows that opener has to use a little commonsense when selecting his game try.

(a) ♠ Q 7 5 4 2 (b) ♠ A 10 9 7 5 (c) ♠ A Q 10 9
    ♥ K 6 3   ♥ A 6 4   ♥ K 10 7
    ♦ 7   ♦ 8   ♦ A J
    ♣ A K Q J   ♣ K Q J 3 ♣ K J 10 4

After 1♠–2♠, to make a game try of 3♣ with any of the above hands would be extremely short-sighted. The club holdings in (a) and (b) are of a type which require no help from responder's hand and which will play very nicely opposite the sort of holding responder is most likely to have, three or four small, and which he will devalue opposite a 3♣ game try. On these two hands partner's heart holding is likely to be the key to a contract of 4♠, and the best game try is therefore 3♥, not 3♣. In other words, make your try in a suit where you have length *and* need help. Example (c) should try with 2NT. This shows a balanced hand and lets responder know that all his high cards are important whatever suit they may be in.

The sequences, 1♥–2♥–3♥ and 1♠–2♠–3♠ have become largely redundant as game tries, and many tournament pairs now prefer to use them pre-emptively. For example, bid 1♠–2♠–3♠ with:

(a) ♠ K J 10 9 7 4   (b) ♠ A K J 10 7 4
    ♥ A 8   ♥ 6
    ♦ Q J 3   ♦ Q J 3
    ♣ 7 2   ♣ 7 5 2

In neither case do you have any serious hope of making game. Probably, you will go down in 3♠ too. The problem is that you know that your side has a big trump fit but may be outgunned in terms of high cards. It may well be that your opponents have a game on in their trump suit and you can be pretty certain that if you pass over 2♠ they will come into the auction. By re-raising to 3♠ you try to make it sufficiently dangerous for them to join in that they decide to let you play the hand. Even when they have no game on, 3♠ down one will be no disaster since they are surely going to make a three level contract.

Short-Suit Game Tries

By now, I'm sure that you will have realized that there never is one version of anything. No sooner does somebody think of a new idea than somebody else wants to modify it. Let's go back to the original example;

♠ A K J 10 8
♥ 7
♦ Q 7 5 4
♣ A J 9

Instead of opener bidding his second suit as a game try, asking partner to judge how well the two hands fit together, it is just as reasonable an approach for opener to bid his short suit as the game try—as long as he has agreed this with his partner, of course.

Again reverting to our original examples:

(a) ♠ Q 7 6 5   (b) ♠ Q 7 6 5
    ♥ 8 3 2   ♥ K J 6
    ♦ K J 6   ♦ 8 3 2
    ♣ Q 3 2   ♣ Q 3 2

Suppose that 1♠–2♠–3♥ is a short-suit game try. Now, responder evaluates his hand in much the same way as when facing a splinter bid. In other words, he looks to see how many of his high card values are wasted opposite the shortage.

It should be clear that hand (a) is much more suitable than hand (b), since the latter's king and jack of hearts may be of no value, while in the former, nothing is wasted. Turn (b)'s hearts into A62, and now nothing is wasted. Probably the hand is still not as suitable as is (a), as it still contains much less help in opener's long suits, but it too should now accept the game try.

Two-Way Game Tries

Much of the time, it will matter very little which kind of game tries opener has at his disposal. Our basic example:

♠ A K J 10 8
♥ 7
♦ Q 7 5 4
♣ A J 9

can equally comfortably make a natural game try of 3♦ or a short-suit game try of 3♥. Occasionally, responder will have a hand with which he will accept one kind of invitation and decline the other, but the pluses and minuses of these variations will largely cancel each other out in the long run.

There are some hands, however, which do lend themselves better to one approach than the other.

	(a)		(b)
	♠ A Q 7 5 2		♠ Q 7 5 4 2
	♥ A J 4 3		♥ 7
	♦ A 2		♦ A K 4
	♣ 8 5		♣ K Q 10 2

With (a), a natural game try of 3♥ is clearly superior to a short-suit try with a hand which has no really short suit. Hand (b), on the other hand, is much better suited to a short-suit try of 3♥ than to a natural try of 3♣ or 3♦. Neither of these suits are ones which necessarily need a great deal of help from partner. Clearly, either hand will prove awkward to handle if you happen to be playing the "wrong" methods. For this reason, two-way game tries were invented, the idea being to give opener the best of both worlds. They work like this:

A new suit by opener after 1M–2M is a long-suit game try in the bid suit (except that 1♥–2♥–2NT is the long-suit try in spades), while if opener wants to make a short-suit game try he relays by making the next cheapest bid, i.e. 1♠–2♠–2NT or 1♥–2♥–2♠. This obliges responder to make the next cheapest bid in turn, i.e. 1♠–2♠–2NT–3♣ or 1♥–2♥–2♠–2NT, and now opener makes his short-suit try. If he now bids the agreed trump suit, it is a short-suit try in the suit which cannot be bid without forcing the partnership to game.

Sounds complicated? It's not quite as bad as it sounds. The full treatment is as follows:

1♠–2♠–3 ♣/♦/♥=		Natural long-suit game tries
1♠–2♠–2NT–3♣–		
	3♦ =	short-suit try in diamonds
	3♥ =	short-suit try in hearts
	3♠ =	short-suit try in clubs
1♥–2♥–3♣/♦ =		Natural long-suit game tries
1♥–2♥–2NT		Long-suit game try in spades
1♥–2♥–2♠–2NT–		
	3♣ =	short-suit try in clubs
	3♦ =	short-suit try in diamonds
	3♥ =	short-suit try in spades

The system works well enough and it is undoubtedly true that if you play one-way game tries, whether long or short, you will occasionally wish you were using the other kind. However, you do lose the ability to make a natural game try of 2NT with a balanced hand and, for me, that price is too high, particularly because there is also the extra strain on your memory.

Reverse Game Tries
The only problem with all the different types of game try we

have looked at so far is that opener has to give information away about his own hand to make the try, thereby helping the defense. Some devious soul came up with the idea that, instead of asking for help in a particular suit, opener should ask partner in which suits he would accept (or decline) a game invitation. This way, at least some of the time opener's hand would remain undisclosed.

Either long- or short-suit tries can be used, but the basic idea is that 1♠–2♠–2NT and 1♥–2♥–2♠ are asking bids. By agreement, responder now bids either the lowest suit in which he would accept a game invitation or the lowest suit in which he would decline the invitation (1♥–2♥–2♠–2NT meaning spades). Let's suppose we play the version where you bid the lowest suit in which you would decline a game try. Now:

1♠–2♠–2NT–
- 3♣ says you would decline a game try in clubs but says nothing about diamonds or hearts, so, if one of those suits is opener's, he now has to bid it to invite game.
- 3♦ means you would accept a try in clubs, decline one in diamonds, and are neutral about hearts.
- 3♥ says you would accept a try in either minor but not hearts
- 3♠ means you would refuse any game try.
- 4♠ means you would accept any game try.

This is best played in conjunction with two-way game tries, as otherwise it leaves the sequences:

1♠–2♠–3♣/♦/♥ and 1♥–2♥–2NT/3♣/♦ with no meaning. While seeing what the inventors were trying to do, I really don't think the benefits of this idea are sufficient to justify the extra strain on memory from its use.

The Slam Try
While it is possible to bid a slam after a 1M–2M start, it is unusual and I will not concern myself with such possibilities here. What is worth considering, however, is the situation after 1M–3M (limit).

Standard methods here seem to be that 3NT suggests an alternative contract, four of the major is to play, and if opener is interested in slam he either uses Blackwood or bids a new suit as a cuebid.

If you hold:

♠ K Q J 8 6
♥ 8
♦ 7 4
♣ A K Q J 5

then, after 1♠–3♠, a cuebid of 4♣ is the only sensible way forward. Slam is dependent on partner's holding two aces, but Blackwood will not solve the problem because it is also important which two aces he holds due to the diamond position. But many experts believe that it is important to be able to make natural slam tries in this situation. They argue that, just as with game tries, it will often be the degree of fit responder has for opener's sidesuit which will decide the fate of a slam and not merely his controls. They prefer to bid 1♠–3♠–4♣ with a hand like:

♠ K 10 9 7 4
♥ A
♦ A Q
♣ K J 8 7 5

concentrating partner's attention on his black suit holdings. After all, cuebidding will not easily convey that:

♠ A Q 6 5
♥ Q 6 4 2
♦ J 5
♣ Q 9 4

provides an excellent slam, while:

♠ 8 6 5 3
♥ K J 4 2
♦ K 5
♣ A 9 4

makes slam a dreadful proposition.

I think it is clear that you will sometimes have hands with which you want to cuebid, sometimes ones more suitable to a natural slam try. There is a solution and it is quite a simple one.

A new suit can be a natural slam try, asking responder to focus his attention particularly on that suit and the agreed trump suit. Just as when facing a cuebid, he can either sign off in four of the agreed trump suit with a disappointing hand or can cuebid if his hand encourages him to cooperate in the slam hunt. After 1♠–3♠–4♣, with:

♠ A Q 6 5
♥ Q 6 4 2
♦ J 5
♣ Q 9 4

responder loves his black suit holdings but has no side control to cuebid. A jump to 5♠ would get this message across to partner.

If the opener prefers to go the cuebidding route over 1M–3M, he bids 3NT. By agreement, this shows slam interest and asks responder to start cuebidding. Use of this bid also provides a negative inference that while the number and position of responder's controls may be very important to opener, there is no particular suit in which he is looking for fitting minor honor cards—otherwise he might have made a natural slam try.

This idea has the merit of simplicity, and it does tackle a genuine problem. The only price is the loss of a natural bid of 1M–3M–3NT. Whether you think that price is worth paying will depend on how often you normally use the bid, and that is partly a matter of system.

If you play a five card major system, then 1M–3M will usually mean you have at least a 5–4 fit, making 3NT an unlikely alternative contract.

If you play four card majors with a strong no trump, how often will you have a strong enough balanced hand to want to bid 1M–3M–3NT in a natural sense? With 12–14 you would now pass, while with 15–17 you would have opened 1NT. So you will need the natural 3NT bid very rarely. Only a four card major, weak no trump, system has a real problem here. Certainly, if you open 1♠ with:

♠ J 7 4 2
♥ A Q 6
♦ K J 5
♣ A J 10

you want to be able to bid 3NT over a raise to 3♠. While I am quite fond of such bids myself, you can just settle for the known 4–4 fit and hope for the best. Alternatively, some only open decent four card majors with strong hands so would solve the problem by opening this example 1♣. Probably, even in this system, the price is worth paying to improve the accuracy of your slam bidding. It is, however, much closer than in other systems.

Opener Raises Responder's Suit
After the auction commences 1♣/♦–1♥ or 1♣/♦/♥–1♠, most of the methods we have already discussed are still available if opener wishes to support his partner's suit. Since the basic principles are pretty much the same, I don't intend to go into much detail here except to mention a few points which need consideration. Really, you could work out for yourself which methods are no longer sensible. There is no problem with continuing to use either Swiss or splinter bids; sequences like 1♦–1♠–4♣ are hardly of much value in a natural sense. But you need to be careful about mini-splinters. Unless you happen to play new suit forcing, for example: 1♦–1♠–2♣, a playable style but hardly standard, you cannot afford to play 1♦–1♠–3♣ as a mini-splinter for the simple reason that you need such bids in a natural sense. On the other hand, most experts today would say that 1♦–1♠–2♥, or indeed any other reverse, should be forcing. If you have that agreement, then it is certainly possible to play 1♦–1♠–3♥ as a mini-splinter; for example:

♠ K 10 7 4
♥ 6
♦ A Q J 9 5
♣ A 8 3

In other words, as soon as a jump becomes an unnecessary one, i.e. a bid of the same suit at a lower level would have been forcing, it can be used as a splinter bid—or indeed for any other artificial purpose you prefer.

What about after a two level response, for example 1♥–2♣?

Mini-splinters are probably not such a great idea any more. If opener is too strong to make a simple raise, then you will usually want to end up in game, and mini-splinters are used to invite game. That does not mean that splinter bids are not a good idea. On the contrary, they can often make slam exploration much easier,

Okay, so what bids are available as splinter bids in this situation? Clearly, the double jump shift (1♠–2♣–4♦/♥, 1♥–2♣–4♦) is available, as always. Also, since a reverse is forcing (1♥–2♣–2♠), a jump reverse (1♥–2♣–3♠) is not needed as a natural bid so can be a splinter.

More controversially, what about a sequence like 1♥–2♣–3♦? But surely that is simply natural and forcing, something like:

♠ 6 3
♥ A K 10 5 3
♦ A K J 6
♣ Q 8

isn't it? Traditionally, yes, a jump in this situation showed a hand which was too strong to make a simple non-forcing bid. But the modern trend is for more and more partnerships to play 1♥–2♣–2♦ and similar sequences as forcing, the argument being that you hardly ever want to pass it so why not make it forcing and avoid having to use up valuable bidding space by jumping around every time you hold a decent hand.

However, it is certainly a reasonable argument and a playable style. If that is the way you play, then you need to assign a meaning to a jump shift like 1♥–2♣–3♦, and to say that this supports partner's suit in some way makes a lot of sense. You will have noticed that in certain situations it is possible to make an artificial raise of partner's suit in two different ways in the same suit; for example; both 1♥–2♣–3♦ and 1♥–2♣–4♦ can agree clubs and be forcing. To simply say that both are splinter bids and leave it at that would be foolish—what is the difference between them?

There are a number of possibilities and, while we will all have our own ideas as to which is most useful, the most important thing is to have some agreement with partner. You could play that 1♥–2♣–3♦ was a cuebid, supporting clubs and showing either ace or king of diamonds, while 1♥–2♣–4♦ was a splinter bid. Perhaps 1♥–2♣–3♦ could show a singleton and 1♥–2♣–4♦ a void. Or the two bids could show different strengths of hand, say 14-17 and 18+. In that case you might bid 1♥–2♣–3♦ with:

♠ A J 2
♥ A Q 10 5 3
♦ 6
♣ K J 7 4

but 1♥–2♣–4♦ with:

♠ A K 2
♥ A K 10 5 3
♦ 6
♣ K J 7 4

Both would be forcing to game, but the distinction would help responder to judge whether or not to look for a slam.

The other bids which are no longer available as ways of supporting partner are 2NT and 3NT. Unless you are willing to make major changes in your basic bidding structure, you need to be able to bid both of these naturally. It is possible to play, for example, 1♥–1♠–2NT as an artificial game force, catering to, among other things, various types of strong hands with spade support, but this requires a wide-ranging 1NT rebid to include up to a poor 19 count, and there are significant problems attendant to that idea. Better, I think, to keep things simple. That is not to say that you cannot occasionally rebid 2NT with genuine support for partner after he has responded at the two-level, though partner will initially assume that you do not like his suit. The difference is that a sequence like 1♠–2♥–2NT is best played as forcing, so you can afford to take certain liberties with it since you know that you will get another chance to complete your description. The logic for playing this 2NT rebid as forcing is even more compelling than in the situation we looked at a few minutes ago. Opener is showing 15+ and responder 9+; how can you really afford to pass? Meanwhile, playing the bid as forcing is a big aid to accurate bidding.

Take these examples after 1♠–2♥:

(a)   ♠ A Q 10 8 7   (b)   ♠ A Q 10 8 7
      ♥ K J 4 2   ♥ K J 4 2
      ♦ K 2   ♦ Q 6 2
      ♣ 8 3   ♣ 8

(c)   ♠ A Q 10 8 7   (d)   ♠ A Q 10 8 7
      ♥ K J 4 2   ♥ K J 4
      ♦ A J 2   ♦ A 8 2
      ♣ 3   ♣ K 3

Hands (a) and (b) can raise directly to 4♥. The point count may be a little low, but there is a known nine-card fit and no accurate way to invite game. Hand (c) is significantly stronger and can splinter; 4♣ is only a single jump, but it can be a splinter because 3♣ would be forcing. What about (d)? It is clearly worth a game bid and, with a known eight card fit, presumably that game should be 4♥. But if you simply bid 4♥, how is partner to know that you hold this hand rather than (a) or (b)? The answer is to bid 2NT instead, then bid 4♥ on the next round. Assuming that partner is on the same wavelength, he should now get the message that you have a good balanced raise to 4♥.

One more thought before we move on. There are, as ever, a number of different treatments in use in this area, but if 1♥–2♣–2NT is forcing, then a hand which definitely wants to play in 3NT can always bid 2NT and then 3NT on the next round. Why not then play 1♥–2♣–3NT as a good balanced hand with club support; for example:

♠ K J 4
♥ A Q 10 7
♦ K 8
♣ K J 4 2

After all, this kind of hand is quite unbiddable using standard methods.

Fourth Suit Forcing (FSF)

The use of a bid of the fourth suit as an artificial inquiry, rather than in a natural sense, is almost fundamental to accurate bidding. Yet for many people it is little more than a way to check whether partner has a stopper in the suit and can bid no trumps. This is a waste of a valuable tool, since FSF is capable of much more than that.

First, lets take this sequence: 1♦–1♥–1♠, and the following hands:

(a)	♠ K Q 7 4	(b)	♠ K Q 7 4
	♥ A J 6 3		♥ A J 10 9 8
	♦ 8 3 2		♦ 8 3
	♣ K 4		♣ A 4
(c)	♠ K Q 7 4	(d)	♠ K Q 7 4
	♥ A K J 10 8		♥ A J 10 9 8
	♦ 8 3 2		♦ A 8
	♣ 4		♣ 4 2

In their different ways, all these hands are worth a raise to at least 4♠, yet they are quite different and to bid 4♠ with all of them would make it very difficult for partner to know when to bid on towards slam and when not.

Fortunately, there are four different routes available to get to 4♠ without having to distort our hands in the process. The obvious way is simply to bid 4♠. This is a reasonable approach on hand (a), one which would need a very good hand opposite before slam became a possibility.

The other three routes are to bid 2♣, 3♣ and 4♣ respectively. 2♣ is Fourth Suit Forcing, and as such does not immediately promise spade support. We will return to that in a moment. For now, what matters is that 2♣ is forcing, neither 3♣ nor 4♣ is needed in a natural sense and so can be used as different types of spade raise. One possibility would be to use 3♣ as a mini-splinter and 4♣ as a splinter, but, perhaps better is to play both as game forcing with one showing a high card club control and the other a shortage.

So hand (b) bids 3♣, showing the ace or king of clubs and a hand too strong to just raise to 4♠, while hand (c) bids 4♣, showing the same strength but a singleton or void in clubs (i.e. a splinter). Which leaves only hand (d), still too strong to only raise to 4♠ but with no club control of any kind. The solution is to bid 2♣, which partner will take as FSF. Over his rebid, however, you jump in spades, thereby showing genuine spade support, a hand too good to bid 4♠ on the previous round, but no club control—simple! By taking three different routes with three different types of hand, you give partner much more information and help him to assess the prospects for slam.

The second way in which FSF can help you when you have support for partner is in this sort of situation:

1♥–1♠–2♣–?

(a)	♠ K Q 8 5 2	(b)	♠ K Q 8 2
	♥ 6 2		♥ 8 5 2
	♦ Q 9		♦ A 9
	♣ Q 7 6 4		♣ K Q 7 4
(c)	♠ K Q 8 5 2	(d)	♠ A K 10 9 8
	♥ A 5 2		♥ K J 6
	♦ 7 6 3		♦ 7 6 3
	♣ K 4		♣ K 4

Hand (a) is not a problem, you can simply raise to 3♣. What about hand (b), though? Clearly 3♣ is inadequate because you have ample values for game. A raise to 4♣, if played as forcing, as some do, would allow an intelligent decision between game and slam in clubs, however, it does commit us to clubs. Opposite:

```
♠ 7
♥ Q J 10 8 5
♦ K Q 7
♣ A J 10 3
```

we want to play in 3NT – not easy if we jump to 4♣.

While:

```
♠ 7
♥ K Q J 10 5
♦ J 7 3
♣ A J 10 3
```

makes 4♥ the only game with a real chance.

Meanwhile, now that partner's rebid suggests that he has five hearts, hand (c) is quite happy to raise to 4♥. With the excellent fit for both opener's suits, even an unlikely 4–3 fit should play well. Hand (d), however, is far too good to give up on slam so easily. What both hands (b) and (d) need is a way of raising one of opener's suits at a low level to leave room for further exploration without fear of being passed out. Again, FSF comes to the rescue. Any bid below game which could have been made immediately and been non-forcing, for example 1♥–1♠–2♣–3♣ or 1♥–1♠–2♣–3♥, becomes forcing if it is preceded by FSF. So:

(a)	1♥ –	1♠	(b)	1♥ –	1♠
	2♣ –	2♦		2♣ –	2♦
	Any–	3/4♣		Any	3♥

are forcing. If you have this agreement , our two problem hands are solved. Not only that, but partner's response to your fourth suit bid will give you extra information about his hand and sometimes solve your problem even more quickly.

It is very easy to be lazy and to miss the opportunity to make clear helpful bids which let partner know what is going on. Take this sequence:

1♥	–	1♠
2♣	–	2♦
2NT	–	?

Holding:

    ♠ K Q 8 5 2
    ♥ 6 2
    ♦ A 9
    ♣ K Q 7 4

it is very easy to make a forcing 3♣ bid, just to make quite sure that 3NT is actually the correct game, as you are beginning to suspect. It would also be quite easy to make the same 3♣ bid with:

    ♠ A K 8 5 2
    ♥ A 6
    ♦ 9 2
    ♣ A Q J 7

then sit back and feel satisfied that you have done everything that could be asked of you. 3♣ would be a mistake, however. With the first hand, all you are doing is investigating the best game and partner will be aware of that and will respond accordingly. With the second hand, however, you know what suit you wish to play in and your only concern is five, six or seven. If you want partner to look at his hand from the point of view of investigating slam, you need to tell him that this is what you have in mind. The way to do this is to jump to 4♣, clearly setting the trump suit and inviting him to cuebid. There is nothing wrong with using up bidding space if you have a clear message to impart and this is the best way to do so.

Delayed Support

We have touched upon a number of sequences where, for one reason or another, support for partner's suit is not given immediately. There are a few more which can cause difficulties—not so much because the sequences are particularly complex, but simply because two partners may not have discussed them sufficiently. Take this family of sequences:

(a) 1♥ – 1♠   (b) 1♠ – 2♥
    2♠ – 3♥   3♥ – 3♠

(c) 1♣ – 1♦   (d) 1♦ – 2♣
    2♦ – 3♣   3♣ – 3♦

(e) 1m – 1M   (f) 1M – 2m
    2M – 3m   3m – 3M

Many players have never really discussed the meaning of the last bid in each of these sequences. Of course, it is natural, but is it forcing? If you had only thirty seconds to discuss the matter, you would probably agree that it was safest to play them all the same way and that that way should be forcing. Yet, while that is by no means a foolish approach, the sequences are not all of an identical nature.

The question to ask is, what kind of hand might partner have to want to bid this way?

The easiest sequences are (c) and (d). If you remember, we decided that it was quite common to invent a bid in the other minor when partner opened 1♣/♦ and we had genuine

support for him and game-going values. It is easy to see that if we have done this, we will be strong enough to make a forcing bid. Also, hands of less than game-going strength will rarely bother to bid the other minor if they have support for opener's suit. So sequences (c) and (d) should be forcing.

Sequence (b) is also clear. Having found an eight card fit in one major, you have no reason to look elsewhere unless you have higher things in mind. A forcing 3♠ bid could be a very useful start to a slam hunt.

Sequence (f) is a little less clearcut. True, you have already found one fit, but it is in a minor and you might well need to explore an alternative contract both for game purposes—4♠ may make when 5♣ has the same three losers—and to get back to a higher scoring part score at pairs scoring. On a double fit hand in this kind of auction, I would recommend that (f) be played as forcing. If you pick up:

    ♠ K J 2
    ♥ 7 3
    ♦ Q 6 2
    ♣ A J 9 5 3

and hear 1♠–2♣–3♣, just accept that you will have to play in game—presumably partner will have five spades for this sequence. (a) and (e) are quite similar. It seems to me that you will often want to make a game try and showing the double fit may be the best way to do so. But it is not uncommon for opener's rebid to only contain three card support; for example:

(a) ♠ K J 4   (b) ♠ K 9 6
    ♥ A Q 7 6 2   ♥ 7
    ♦ K 6 3   ♦ Q 8 3 2
    ♣ 7 2   ♣ A K 8 7 5

(a) 1♥ – 1♠   (b) 1♣ – 1♠
    2♠   2♠

If you are going to get to game, there should be plenty of room to discover which is the better trump suit. Opener's first suit could also be the best place to play the part score when he rejects the game try. For example, responder holds:

(c) ♠ 10 8 7 5   (d) ♠ Q 7 5 2
    ♥ K 9 4   ♥ K J 8
    ♦ 7 2   ♦ K 5
    ♣ A K J 4   ♣ Q 9 3 2

Pair together hands (a) and (c) or (b) and (d) and in neither case would you wish to reach game. Equally, if you were opener after:

(a) 1♥ – 2♠ and (b) 1♣ – 1♠
    2♠ – 3♥   2♠ – 3♣

respectively, you would like to be able to decline the game invitation by passing rather than by going back to what could easily be a very weak 4–3 fit. So, in these sequences, where the second fit to be agreed could be far better than the first one, I think it best to play the final bids as natural, non-forcing, game tries.

Let us take one more look at sequences (b) and (f). We have agreed that these sequences are forcing. What, then, is the difference between:

1♠	– 2♥	and	1♠	– 2♥	
3♥	– 3♠		3♥	– 4♠?	

Is the jump to game stronger, perhaps even a delayed game raise, or does it just mean that you want to play in 4♠? The latter is called the Principle of Fast Arrival, and works on the theory that the quicker you get to a contract the less interest you have in alternatives. So, if you had slam interest, you would bid 3♠ to leave room to explore, while with no interest you just jump to game.

It certainly makes sense to leave more room on those hands where you have more interest in further exploration, but a bid which gives a clear description of your hand in one go, such as a delayed game raise, is also attractive. If you play 1♠–2♥–3♥–3♠ as the stronger of the two sequences, you will have to go this route both with a delayed game raise:

♠ K Q 4 2
♥ A K 10 8 6
♦ 7 4
♣ 6 2

and a hand with only three card spade support but slam interest:

♠ K J 4
♥ A K 10 8 6
♦ A 7 4
♣ 6 2

Sometimes, the fourth trump may be vital to partner. This is a difficult decision, and one where you should follow your own preference because there is certainly no unanimity in the expert community.

You Open One No Trump

1NT–2♣–2♥/♠–?

Responder can, of course, invite or bid game simply by raising opener's suit to the three and four levels respectively. What other options does he have? If the partnership is using traditional methods, simple Stayman and natural suit bids, the answer is—very few.

Splinter bids are possible:

1NT–2♣–2♠–4♣/♦/♥

and

1NT–2♣–2♥–4♣/♦

but there is a gap in the scheme because 1NT–2♣–2♥–3♠ is needed as a natural bid. Still, this takes care of hands like:

♠ A J 10 5
♥ A Q 6 4
♦ A J 5 3
♣ 7

After 1NT–2♣–2♥, you have an easy slam try via a 4♣ splinter. This will excite partner if he holds:

♠ K Q 7
♥ K 10 8 5
♦ K Q 6
♣ 8 4 2

but have the opposite effect if he has:

♠ K Q 7
♥ K 10 8 5
♦ 8 4 2
♣ K Q 6

But, if you agree to play splinter bids, how would a hand of this type proceed over 2♥?

♠ K 5
♥ A K 6 4
♦ 8 7 2
♣ A K J 4

It is easy to construct hands for opener which make 6♥ virtually solid, but others where even a five level contract is in jeopardy. Unless responder can jump to 4♣ as a cuebid, rather than specifically a splinter, he has no good way to proceed with this more balanced type of slam try. Nonetheless, I would encourage you to play these jumps as splinter bids and look elsewhere for a way of developing balanced slam tries. Splinter bids are just so useful as an aid to judging the value of a hand. You must, of course, agree with your partner that four clubs over an opening NT is not an ace-asking bid.

Stayman in Doubt

There is a solution to the problem discussed above—a rarely used convention known as Stayman in Doubt. The idea is that if you use Stayman with a 4–3–3–3 hand and partner bids your four card major, you still don't know which will be better, four of the major or 3NT. If partner is 4–4–3–2, then his shortage suggests there may be an advantage gained from playing in the major—especially if the doubleton is a weak one—while if he is also 4–3–3–3 there may be no reason at all to play a ten trick contract rather than the nine trick 3NT.

Stayman in Doubt uses this sequence: 1NT–2♣–2♥/♠–3♦ to ask opener to choose which game to play. If he is also 4–3–3–3, he bids 3NT; if he has a weakish doubleton, he bids four of the agreed major. For example:

Responder		Opener			
♠ A 8 7 4		(a)	♠ K 9 6 3	(b)	♠ K 9 6 3
♥ K 9 6			♥ A 10 4		♥ A 10 4
♦ J 5 3			♦ Q 9 4		♦ Q 9
♣ K Q 3			♣ A J 4		♣ A J 4 2

	1NT			1NT
2♣ –	2♠		2♣ –	2♠
3♦ –	3NT		3♦ –	4♠
Pass			Pass	

Traditionally, this idea has been used only to help choose the best game contract. There is no reason, however, why it cannot be given a dual function. Suppose that responder continues to bid 3♦ when he has the 4–3–3–3 hand and just wants opener to pick the right game, but also bids 3♦ with hands which want to explore the possibility of slam but cannot splinter. If the bidding goes:

INT   –   2♣
2♥/♠   –   3♦
3NT

then responder can make a cuebid of 4♣/♦/♥. This has to be a slam try as otherwise he would simply have passed 3NT.

If opener prefers 4♥/♠ to 3NT, he has to modify his response to 3♦. Instead of just bidding four of the major, he cuebids if his hand is suitable for slam and only bids four of the major with a poor hand. His other option would be to bid three of the agreed trump suit as a neutral bid, leaving responder to make the first move. This might be appropriate with a goodish hand but no obvious cuebid; for example:

♠ K Q 6 4
♥ K Q 6 4
♦ K 8 3
♣ 7 4

Whichever major has been agreed, this hand is quite promising if partner has a balanced slam try, but to make an immediate cuebid when holding no aces might be a little misleading.

1NT–Three of a Suit

There is little to be said here. I am sure that most players are quite familiar with the idea that in standard bridge a sequence such as 1NT–3♠ asks him to choose between 4♠ and 3NT. The only other thing to consider is that partner might actually have slam in mind and, if your hand is at all suitable, you should try to make a helpful bid for him.

(a)   ♠ Q 7 3   (b)   ♠ K Q 3
       ♥ Q 6   ♥ A 6
       ♦ K J 10 4   ♦ A J 10 4
       ♣ K J 9 6   ♣ 9 6 4 2

After 1NT–3♠, both of these hands would choose to support spades rather than revert to no trump. Hand (a) should raise to 4♠, having no reason to encourage partner to consider a slam. Hand (b), however, is about as good a hand as is possible, apart from the lack of a fourth trump, and, rather than a lazy raise to 4♠, should cuebid 4♦ in case partner is interested in more than just game.

This would be even clearer if you were playing a transfer system. For many pairs, hands with only game interest go through the two level transfer mechanism while a jump to the three level is reserved for hands with slam interest. But if the bidding goes 1NT–3♠–4♠, responder may not be strong enough to venture to the five level, so it is essential that opener shows his suitability, or otherwise, for slam.

The same considerations apply after a 2NT opening and response of 3♥/♠.

1NT–2♥/♠

If you play this as a natural 'weak' take-out, you may wonder what it has to do with raising partner. Consider, however, that if you have a good fit for responder's suit then your opponents will also have a fit somewhere. They know that they have a fair amount of strength between them, and are very likely to balance in the auction:

1NT   –   Pass   –   2♥   –   Pass
Pass   –   ?

If you hold something like:

(a)   ♠ A 6   (b)   ♠ A 6
       ♥ K Q 7 4   ♥ K Q 7 4
       ♦ J 8 3 2   ♦ A J 10 3
       ♣ Q 7 4   ♣ 8 7 6

you could just wait for them to bid, then compete with 3♥. The opposition will now be quite well placed to judge whether or not to compete further, however. Think how much more difficult it will be for them if you raise immediately over partner's 2♥ response. They will know you have a fit and that therefore they also have one, but it will be much harder for them to find it, and consequently more dangerous to try, if they have to start at the three level.

Actually, hand (b) is so good that there is a second reason to bid on; partner could easily have a hand where game is a good bet. Give him, for example:

(c)   ♠ 8 7 3   (d)   ♠ 8 7 3
       ♥ J 9 6 5 3 2   ♥ J 9 6 5 3 2
       ♦ K Q 4   ♦ 4
       ♣ 4   ♣ K Q 4

(c) makes 4♥ almost cold, while even a less well-fitting hand like (d) gives nearly a 50 percent chance. Unless he is guessing well, partner may not manage to bid game with either (c) or (d) after 1NT–2♥–3♥. After all, opener may actually have hand (a) rather than (b).

Opener can help him out a little. If he is raising purely competitively, as with hand (a), he can bid simply 1NT–2♥–3♥. If, on the other hand. he is interested in game, as with hand (b), he can show where his outside tricks lie, 1NT–2♥–3♦ with hand (b). This not only shows game interest, but also helps responder to judge how well his, perhaps meager, values are working. This particular sequence would encourage him with hand (c) but discourage him if he holds hand (d).

It would also be possible for opener to show his interest in game by bidding his shortage or weak suit. For example, 1NT–2♥–3♣ with:

♠ A J 10
♥ A Q 7 4
♦ K 9 5 3
♣ 8 2

As usual with this kind of bid, responder judges how much he has wasted opposite the weakness. My view is that this is less useful than showing sidesuit length and strength. Also, from a competitive point of view, remember that the hand could still belong to your opponents. If you bid a weakness, you give them a very safe and easy way into the auction—they can double—while bidding a long sidesuit does not make it as easy for them.

1NT–2♦/♥ (Transfer) –?

All of this is just as relevant after partner's transfer response. With only two or three card support opener should just complete the transfer. With four card support he should normally break the transfer. There are various approaches that are used, but basically he should jump to three of partner's suit pre-emptively or bid anything else if he wants to encourage partner to bid game (of course, partner may have always intended to bid game no matter what opener did).

There is one more consideration here. Whether or not he is interested in game, responder may simply want to be dummy, believing it better to have the opening lead come up to the no trump hand. In that case, opener's breaking the transfer will have cut across his intentions. It is possible to play a bid of the suit immediately below the agreed trump suit as a re-transfer, like:

1NT	–	2♦	or	1NT	–	2♦
3♣	–	3♦		3♦	–	4♦

requests partner to bid hearts. You have to agree this, of course; it is no good assuming that just because a stranger agrees to play transfers with you he will automatically also be playing re-transfers. Actually, he probably won't be. Although they are a sound idea, only the most serious tournament player tends to bother with them.

1NT–Pass–2♦/♥ (Transfer) – Double

Although up to now we have been discussing the uncontested auction, this seems the most sensible place to mention this competitive situation.

When partner's transfer response is doubled, whether this double shows a strong hand or merely length in the transfer suit, most people play very simply. If they have three cards in partner's suit they complete the transfer, while with two they pass and a redouble shows length and strength in the suit doubled. If responder is strong enough to bid or invite game, we will have no problem in basically ignoring the double and continuing with our normal auction. There is a real danger, however, that this is going to develop into a competitive part score auction. If so, you should try to find an auction which is a little more helpful to partner. My suggestion is that with four card support you break the transfer as if the double had not occurred. By all means pass with only a doubleton, but the time when partner really needs help in judging whether to compete is likely to be when you have three card support.

| **(a)** | 1NT | – | Pass | – | 2♦ | – | Dble |
| | 2♥ | | | | | | |

| **(b)** | 1NT | – | Pass | – | 2♦ | – | Dble |
| | Rdbl | | | | | | |

Use sequence (a) to show a minimum with three card heart support and sequence (b) a maximum with three card support. Now you can leave it up to partner to make any later decision. Isn't that better than having to guess yourself whether or not to compete to 3♥ with:

> ♠ A 8 5 2
> ♥ K Q 3
> ♦ Q 7
> ♣ K 10 6 4

after:

1NT	–	Pass	–	2♦	–	Dble
2♥	–	3♦	–	Pass	–	Pass
?						

You should also consider this sequence: 1NT–Pass–2♦ (transfer)–2♥. The 2♥ bid is normally played as a takeout of hearts. You are quite likely to be in a competitive part score sequence and you should help partner to judge whether to compete.

With four card support you should bid as always. The question is, what should be the difference between pass and double? There are two possibilities. One is to play that pass shows two hearts, double shows three; the other is that pass shows either two hearts or perhaps three in a bad hand with which you do not wish to encourage partner to compete, double shows three card support and a suitable hand for competition.

This is a difficult one, with only two calls available to show three types of hand. My inclination would be to use a kind of compromise between the two; double with most hands with three card support but reserve the right to pass with poor hands or ones which look particularly defensive in nature, usually due to having weak hearts or a surfeit of queens and jacks in the other suits.

You Open With a Strong Two Bid

Although strong two bids are not as popular in the United States as they once were, many experienced players still use them. When you have support for partner's strong two opening, it is one of the few situations where limit bids are not appropriate. Classically, a single raise, for example, 2♠–3♠ promises positive values including at least one ace, while a jump raise, 2♠–4♠ also promises positive values but denies an ace. Positive values are defined differently by different people, but usually means something like eight, or maybe a good 7+ HCP.

The idea is, of course, that aces are particularly important when slam is a possibility and this distinction can be of considerable help to opener in making his decision whether to bid on. Sensibly, the more encouraging response leaves more bidding space for further exploration. There is little new to be said about this situation, but most experts would agree that, while the jump raise should deny an ace, you should be a little more flexible with the single raise.

(a)   ♠ K Q 7   (b)   ♠ K 8 4 2
      ♥ K 8 5 2   ♥ K 3
      ♦ K 6 4 3   ♦ K Q J 6
      ♣ 9 2   ♣ 8 5 3

Both these hands are surely worth a raise of 2♠ to 3♠, despite the lack of an ace. Quite apart from their all round potential, both have key cards in the trump suit and it is generally recognized that these are every bit as important as outside aces.

One thing to remember is that both a single and a jump raise do promise positive values and partner will bid accordingly. If you hold:

♠ J 6 4 2
♥ 8
♦ 7 5 3 2
♣ J 7 6 5

and hear partner open 2♠, there is no question that you are worth a raise to 4♠, but you must make the negative response of 2NT first and only bid 4♠ on the next round. Just because a jump raise denies an ace does not mean that partner can never bid over it. If he does so here after 2♠–4♠, dummy is all too likely to prove a sorry disappointment to him.

2M–3M–?

The most common way for opener to investigate slam prospects here is through the use of cuebids. Just as over 1M–3M, however, there is a strong case for natural slam tries, inviting partner to pay particular attention to his holdings in your suits. For example, after 2♠–3♠, 4♦ is surely more useful than a 4♣ cuebid with:

♠ A K Q 10 9 7
♥ K 8
♦ K 10 6 4
♣ A

Opposite:

♠ J 6 4 2
♥ A 5 3
♦ Q 7
♣ K 9 6 4

6♠ is cold, yet opposite:

♠ J 6 4 2
♥ Q 7
♦ A 5 3
♣ K 9 6 4

it has only a very slim chance of success.

As over 1M–3M, the solution is to play new suit bids as natural and bid 3NT to ask partner to start cuebidding. Here the cost is virtually nil, since you are hardly likely to want to suggest an alternative contract of 3NT after the auction has begun 2M–3M.

THE JUMP SHIFT RESPONSE

In traditional Acol, England's equivalent of Standard American, a sequence like 2♠–4♣ or 2♥–3♠ was natural and showed a solid suit. As you can imagine, you could wait a very long time to hold a suitable hand for this response. I am sure that most experts today would use these jumps as splinter bids. I would agree with them.

There is one other possibility you might like to consider, however, and that is something called an Economical Jump. Suppose that partner opens an Acol 2♥ and you hold something like:

♠ 7 3
♥ K 10 5
♦ A Q 10 6 3
♣ 10 8 5

Clearly, you are worth a positive response and, equally clearly, your hearts are more than good enough for a raise to 3♥. The trouble with that is that you will never be able to show your diamond suit, and diamonds could be a very valuable source of tricks if partner holds the king. How is he to realize that the king of diamonds is so much more valuable than either black king if you don't bid the suit? After all:

♠ A 5
♥ A Q J 9 8 6
♦ K 8 5
♣ A 6

makes seven an excellent prospect, while:

♠ A K
♥ A Q J 9 8 6
♦ 8 5 2
♣ A 6

leaves even six a poor bet on a club lead.

So, what is the problem? You respond 3♦ to 2♥ and support the hearts later. That's fine if it goes 2♥–3♦–3NT–4♥, as you have clearly shown genuine heart support. But what about 2♥–3♦–3♥–4♥? Isn't that equally consistent with:

♠ 7 3
♥ 10 5
♦ A K Q 10 6
♣ 10 8 5 2

And so, the Economical Jump was born. A jump shift such as 2♥–4♦ shows a raise to 3♥ plus a decent sidesuit all in one bid. Your original hand:

♠ 7 3
♥ K 10 5
♦ A Q 10 6 3
♣ 10 8 5

is an excellent example.

This situation is a genuine problem, and the solution a good one. My preference is to stick to splinter bids because you are more likely to hold a singleton than a good five card suit with your trump support. I suppose that if you do play splinters you just have to cross your fingers and bid 2♥– 3♦–3♥–5♥ with your example hand.

YOU OPEN WITH A WEAK TWO BID

There are different styles of weak two openings. For some, a typical 2♠ bid would be:

(a)   ♠ K Q 10 8 7 5
     ♥ K 3
     ♦ 7 4 2
     ♣ J 6

while for others

(b)   ♠ Q J 9 5 2
     ♥ 8 3
     ♦ 7 4 2
     ♣ J 6 3

is quite normal—at least non-vulnerable.

If you are to judge intelligently how to proceed when partner opens with a weak two bid, you obviously have to take into account his style; is he more likely to have hand (a) or hand (b)?

The partnership style might affect not only the bids you make but also their meanings. Most experts would say that a response in a new suit (for example: 2♠–3♦) should be forcing, arguing that this makes constructive bidding far easier and, anyway, you rarely want to rescue a pre-empt into another suit. That certainly makes a lot of sense if the opening is likely to be of style (a), but it is easy to see that opposite style (b) there could often be a better part-score available and that the ability to bid a non-forcing 3♣/♦/♥ could be useful.

Is there, perhaps, a way of getting the best of both worlds; both forcing and non-forcing responses in a new suit? Well, yes, there is actually, but you have to work our way up to it. First let's take a quick look at the basic structure of responding to weak two bids. You have already seen that a change of suit is normally played as forcing; what about a raise?

2♥–3♥ or 2♠–3♠ is not invitational, opener is expected to pass. Depending on the vulnerability and general partnership style, 2♥–3♥ could be:

(a)   ♠ 8 6   (b)   ♠ 8 6 3
     ♥ Q 10 7   ♥ Q 10 7
     ♦ A K 7 4   ♦ Q 7 4
     ♣ Q 6 5 2   ♣ 8 6 5 2

With hand (a), you hope to make 3♥ and bid it immediately in case the hand belongs to your opponents—quite likely given your spade weakness—so to pass and then compete with 3♥ would leave them much better placed on the next

round. With (b), you might try 3♥ because the vulnerability made 4♥ too big a risk. You know the opposition own the hand and just want to pre-empt the auction as high as you dare.

A raise to game (2♥–4♥, 2♠–4♠) is a two-way bid. 2♥–4♥ would be appropriate with:

(c)   ♠ A K Q   (d)   ♠ J 3
     ♥ Q 7 4 3   ♥ Q 7 4 3
     ♦ K J 10 7 3   ♦ J 10 7 3 2
     ♣ K   ♣ Q 5

With (c), you are bidding game because you hope to make it but have no real slam interest, while with (d) you are bidding 4♥ as a pre-empt, knowing that the hand belongs to your opponents. Quite apart from the bidding space you take up, the two-way nature of the bid will sometimes make it seem too dangerous for your opponents to come into the auction when they should be doing so.

The standard way to invite game has always been through a 2NT forcing bid. There are several approaches in use today. The three most common responses are for opener to show a side shortage, a high card feature, or to show his overall strength and suit quality artificially. I will give you, briefly the meanings of rebids after 2♠–2NT in each case.

(a) Opener shows his shortage:

3♣	=	Club singleton or void
3♦	=	Diamond singleton or void
3♥	=	Heart singleton or void
3♠	=	No shortage, minimum
3NT=		No shortage, maximum

(b) Opener shows a high card feature

3♣	=	Hx(x) in clubs, not minimum
3♦	=	Hx(x) in diamonds, not minimum
3♥	=	Hx(x) in hearts, not minimum
3♠	=	Minimum
3NT=		Maximum with no one feature worth stressing (or perhaps, a maximum with only a five card suit, according to style).

(c) Opener shows his strength and suit quality

3♣	=	Minimum points, poor suit
3♦	=	Minimum points, good suit
3♥	=	Maximum points, poor suit
3♠	=	Maximum points, good suit
3NT=		AKQxxx

Method (a) is becoming increasingly popular among British experts. It relies, of course, on the assumption that responder, with an invitational strength hand, can judge how many of his values are wasted opposite the shortage. Since this is exactly the reason why we play splinter bids, you might expect me to agree with this approach. Actually, I don't. If we were always sure that our decision would simply be between 3♠ and 4♠, I would say that showing a singleton was the most useful thing opener could do to help partner to make his decision. But if we are also to consider *which* game to play, 4♠ or 3NT, for example, then showing a singleton is not necessarily best.

The partnership opening style is significant here. If the weak two always promises a decent six card suit, then the simple choice between 3♠ and 4♠ will be most important. If, on the other hand, you frequently open with a five card suit, then 3NT will be the right spot considerably more often— also, you will inevitably have a singleton to show a lot less often. To decide which is the best game, I believe that to show a high card feature is most useful.

The third style, showing points and suit quality, is the least precise as far as showing sidesuit features is concerned, but, the best when it comes to defining suit quality. Again, the definition of a good or poor suit will vary according to a partnership's expectation of what an average opening hand looks like. This information about suit quality also helps responder to select the right game contract.

Method (c) might also appeal to those who play very wide-range weak two bids. By dropping the 3NT response showing a solid suit (very rare) and moving all the other responses up one, you make room for a 3♣ bid to say that you have a truly disgusting opening which no sane human being would actually have made. So:

(a)	♠ K Q 10 8 7 5	(b)	♠ K Q 10 8 7 5	(c)	♠ Q J 9 5 2
	♥ K 3		♥ 7 3		♥ 8 3
	♦ 7 4 2		♦ 7 4 2		♦ 7 4 2
	♣ J 6		♣ J 6		♣ J 6 3

Hand (a) is a maximum with a good suit so under the modified scheme bids 3NT.

Hand (b) is a normal minimum, also with a good suit, so bids 3♥.

Hand (c) is a disgusting sub-minimum, and warns partner of this by bidding 3♣.

If responder's decision is actually between game and slam, he will often start with the 2NT inquiry. If he does so and then bids a new suit on the next round, it is a cuebid. For example:

        2♠   –   2NT
        3♠(*)   –   4♣
        (*) maximum, poor suit

might be:

                ♠ A K 6
                ♥ A 8
                ♦ Q 5 2
                ♣ A K J 7 3

Opposite:

                ♠ Q 10 7 5 3 2
                ♥ Q 7 3
                ♦ K 8
                ♣ Q 4

slam is almost certain, while opposite:

                ♠ Q 10 7 5 3 2
                ♥ K Q 7
                ♦ 8 3
                ♣ Q 4

there are two top losers.

Opener, being limited by his pre-emptive opening, should be very willing to cuebid even a second round control in this situation.

This gives responder two ways to make a slam try. With a semi-balanced hand he can go through the 2NT inquiry then cuebid, as above; with an unbalanced hand with support he can make an immediate splinter bid, 2♠–4♣/♦/♥.

What responder cannot do is bid a suit of his own and then support partner clearly and unambiguously to make a slam try. That is the kind of hand we have seen many times before where opener's degree of fit for responder's sidesuit could be critical for slam prospects. That is all going to change, however, thanks to:

TRANSFER RESPONSES TO WEAK TWO BIDS

A perfectly playable system would be:

2♥–2♠	=	Inquiry, with whatever responses you favor
2NT=		Transfer to clubs, weak or strong
3♣	=	Transfer to diamonds, weak or strong
3♦	=	Transfer to hearts, weak or strong
3♥	=	Pre-emptive
2♠–2NT=		Transfer to clubs, weak or strong
3♣	=	Transfer to diamonds, weak or strong
3♦	=	Transfer to hearts, weak or strong
3♥	=	Invitational raise to 3♠
3♠	=	Pre-emptive

Opener would be expected to simply complete the transfer, allowing responder to pass with a long suit and a weak hand or to bid on as a game forcing bid.

                ♠ A Q 7 2
                ♥ A Q 3
                ♦ 7
                ♣ A Q 10 6 4

could now bid 2♠–2NT (transfer)–3♣–3♠ (forcing), allowing partner to appreciate the importance of his club holding. True, an alternative approach would be for re-sponder to make an immediate splinter bid, but this would not help partner to appreciate that:

                ♠ K J 8 5 4 3
                ♥ 7 5 2
                ♦ 8 3
                ♣ K 5

makes slam very good, while:

    ♠ K J 8 5 4 3
    ♥ K 5
    ♦ 8 3
    ♣ 7 5 2

does not.

2♥–3♦, I have defined as a heart raise, either weak or strong. If you consider that we already have a pre-emptive raise of 2♥–3♥, and that slam tries which have no special feature to emphasize can start by using the 2♠ inquiry and then cuebid, this response may seem largely redundant. It need not be so, however.

One possibility is to play it as denying any of the top three heart honors. When you hold the weaker variety, it is quite possible that you will eventually be outbid and partner may end up leading. Life will be considerably easier for him if he knows that 2♥–3♥ promises a top honor while 2♥–3♦ denies one. Also, when you have the stronger type, if the bidding goes: 2♥–3♦–3♥–3♠ partner knows you are cuebidding, but also that he will need strong trumps because you have no top honors. If he has, say:

    ♠ K 3
    ♥ Q J 10 8 7 5
    ♦ K 6 4
    ♣ 8 2

a solid maximum, it will be very difficult for him not to drive you to slam without this information, particularly since your weak trumps suggest that you will have plenty of controls to keep cuebidding.

2♠–3♥, however, has to be played differently. As this sequence does not include an artificial inquiry bid in response to a 2♠ opening, you need a bid to take care of the game invitational hand-types, and 3♥ allows for these.

Alternative Transfer Methods

The above method is excellent for slam exploration. It also allows a rescue into a new suit—a significant consideration if you play a random style of opening two bid. The downside is that while 2♥–2♠ is available as an artificial inquiry bid to handle invitational hands, after a 2♠ opening there is only a general, unspecific raise via 3♥. If you believe that knowing when to bid game is important—as I do—then you might prefer this alternative.

Very simply, instead of playing the transfer bids as either weak or strong, play them as at least invitational. Now opener only completes the transfer with a minimum and otherwise makes a descriptive bid. A hand like:

    ♠ A J 4
    ♥ K 10 2
    ♦ A K 10 8 5
    ♣ 7 3

can bid: 2♠–3♣–3♦–3♠, an invitational raise to 3♠ with a diamond sidesuit.

A well-fitting minimum:

    ♠ K 10 8 7 6 3
    ♥ 8 6 4
    ♦ Q 9 2
    ♣ 6

can now go on to game, while:

    ♠ K 10 8 7 6 3
    ♥ 8 6 4
    ♦ 6
    ♣ Q 9 2

will pass.

The other possible solution is to change the method over 2♠ to include an artificial inquiry, although this loses one of the transfer bids.

2♠–2NT=	Artificial inquiry
3♣ =	Transfer to diamonds
3♦ =	Transfer to hearts
3♥ =	Transfer to spades, either weak or strong
3♠ =	Pre-emptive raise

You still have to decide whether to play the transfers as weak/strong or invitational plus, and what responses to play over the inquiry bid, but perhaps this compromise is actually the best method overall.

Competitive Auctions

Most bids can be used in exactly the same way over an opposing double as in an uncontested auction. You might like to consider, however, that 2♠–Dble–3♥ leaves the fourth player a very easy cuebid of 3♠, while a simple raise to 3♠ does not. Does this outweigh the benefits to your side gained from telling opener if it is safe to lead the suit? A close decision, so I will leave it to your judgment. It is worth considering, however, that even after 2♠–Dble–3♠, with no clear alternative they can use a responsive double.

Where the intervention is an overcall, it is awkward to play transfers because usually too many bids have been taken away. What you might like to consider, however, is that you will sometimes want to invite game in partner's suit while on other occasions you will merely wish to compete and have no desire to hear partner bidding on. One possible solution is to use a bid one below a raise to three of partner's suit as an artificial invitational raise. For example, after 2♠–3♣:

(a) ♠ K J 4	**(b)** ♠ K J 4
♥ A 8 5	♥ A Q 5
♦ K 10 7 3 2	♦ K Q 10 7 3
♣ 7 2	♣ 7 2

Hand (a) bids 3♠, purely competitive, while hand (b) bids 3♥, saying nothing about hearts but inviting game in spades.

Where the overcall is actually in the suit immediately below partner's, 2♠–3♥ or 2♥–3♦, a double can be used to invite game in the same way. In both cases, there is an obvious price to pay, but most of the time your side will belong in partner's suit so what level to play at is likely to be your most important decision.

YOU OPEN AT THE THREE LEVEL

There isn't much to be said about natural raises here. A raise to game is two way, either pre-emptive or with an expectation of making. Opposite a non-vulnerable 3♥ opening, for example, both:

(a) ♠ 7 5 2   (b) ♠ A 5 2
    ♥ Q J 6 4   ♥ Q J 6 4
    ♦ 8 3   ♦ A K
    ♣ K Q 5 2   ♣ Q 5 3 2

would raise to 4♥.

A raise to four of a minor (3♣–4♣; 3♦–4♦) is not a constructive move, being simply intended to make life more difficult for the opposition. It may be made with quite a reasonable hand where you suspect that your opponents are about to compete, but also with a desperately weak hand where you want to add to the pre-empt, but feel that five of a minor could be too expensive. Both of these hands might bid 3♣–4♣:

(c) ♠ A 8 4 3   (d) ♠ Q 7 4
    ♥ Q 6 4   ♥ J 5 2
    ♦ 7 2   ♦ 6 5 4 3
    ♣ A 6 4 2   ♣ J 7 3

I have even seen some imaginative souls make this raise without support for their partner's suit, hoping to make the opposition misjudge each other's length in the suit as well as taking away their bidding space. I would be the last person to try to discourage the use of imagination in the bidding, but there is quite an important principle involved here. A regular partnership should have an agreed philosophy as to who should be making the pressure bids, opener or responder. If opener generally sticks to a "sound and sensible" pre-empting style, then responder can in turn pre-empt to the limit or do whatever else takes his fancy, knowing that he can rely on partner's hand not to be too big a disappointment. If, on the other hand, the opening style is wild (or imaginative, if you prefer), then responder should bid soundly. Generally, having both partners "out of control" on the same board is a recipe for disaster.

RESPONDING IN A NEW SUIT

Traditionally, a change of suit response has been forcing, though some players today who like to indulge in ultra-weak pre-empts play it as merely constructive but non-forcing. I have always played that a new suit is natural until proven otherwise, although in practice it may be that an advance cuebid is the only sensible way to start a slam hunt. Many players, however, make a distinction between a response in a new major and in a new minor. For them 3♥–3♠ is natural, while 3♥–4♣/♦ is a cuebid in support of hearts.

Either method is perfectly playable, but there is another, more recently developed alternative, that is to have one artificial response as a slam try and leave everything else as natural.

Playing this system, 3♦/♥/♠–4♣ and 3♣–4♦ are artificial slam tries in support of opener's suit. A number of different types of responses are possible, depending on what you consider to be most important. If your opening pre-emptive style is sound, always promising a reasonable suit, then you might now have opener showing his number of either controls (ace = 2, king = 1) or key cards (all aces and KQ trumps) by step responses.

If your pre-emptive style is loose, you might prefer to show the quality of the trump suit—for slam purposes there is, after all, a difference between Q107643 and KQJ10873. Or you might like to divide your responses into: bad hand, average hand, good hand, within the context of your opening style. The important thing is to choose a system which fits your partnership style. It would be wrong to say that one method is right for everybody. It would be reasonable to assume that you cannot afford to go beyond game in the agreed trump suit unless opener has a reasonable hand, so the system you devise may have to vary according to which suit partner has opened. For example, after 3♦–4♣, you could play:

4♦ =	Terrible hand, even game may be too high (sorry!)	
4♥ =	Poor, but normal, opening	
4♠ =	Good or reasonable opening, poor trumps	
4NT=	Good or reasonable opening, poor trumps, no outside control	
5♣ =	Good opening, good trumps and one outside control	
5♦ =	Good opening, good trumps and two outside controls	

Which leaves room to ask for controls with 4NT over 4♥/♠. After 3♥–4♣, however, there are only two possible responses before you commit your side to the five level. Playing the above first method, you would have to drop the first step response (terrible hand) to avoid going beyond game with an unsuitable hand.

There are, as I have said, plenty of alternative schemes, for example: first step = zero key cards, second step = one key card, etc, and I am sure you can devise something which fits your needs. The general idea, however, seems a good one, because it takes away only one natural bid and that one is in a minor, relatively less important than a major.

Another fairly new idea is to play a next suit response to three of a minor (3♣–3♦; 3♦–3♥) as an artificial inquiry. This has not yet really caught on with great numbers of players, but it does make a fair degree of sense. The assumption behind this convention is that, more often than not, when responder is thinking of bidding on constructively over a 3♣/♦ opening, his first interest will be in whether

3NT is a playable contract. Unless he has a huge hand or an excellent fit for partner, this is likely to depend on the quality of opener's suit—the likely source of tricks in 3NT. If, for example, responder holds:

$$♠ J 8 5 3$$
$$♥ A K 7$$
$$♦ A J 10 4$$
$$♣ K 7$$

and partner opens 3♣; 3NT will be excellent opposite:

(a) ♠ 9 2
    ♥ 6 5
    ♦ 7 2
    ♣ A Q 10 8 6 4 3

but very poor opposite:

(b) ♠ A 2
    ♥ 6 5
    ♦ 7 2
    ♣ J 10 8 6 4 3 2

Playing traditional methods, responder would have to either pass or close his eyes and bid 3NT, each of which actions would be rewarded if partner turned up with one of (a) and (b) but look foolish opposite the other.

Suppose, however, that responder could bid 3♣–3♦ as an inquiry bid and settle for 4♣ if he didn't like what he heard? As always, other methods are possible but, because opener's suit quality will so often be the key issue, something similar to the following is recommended:

3♣–3♦–3♥ = Short hearts, poor clubs but some diamond support in case responder was caught with real diamonds

3♠	=	Good clubs
3NT	=	Poor clubs but some diamond support
4♣	=	Poor clubs and no diamond support
3♦–3♥–3♠	=	Good diamonds
3NT	=	Poor diamonds but some heart support
4♣	=	Short clubs, poor diamonds but some heart support
4♦	=	Poor diamonds and no heart support

Note that 3♠ is the bid to show a good suit, not 3NT. This is because it must be wrong to make the weak hand declarer in 3NT, so the sort of hand which suggests 3NT should be the final contract does not bid no trumps.

If responder goes back to four of the opener's suit it is to play if opener has shown a poor suit, for example 3♣–3♦–3NT–4♣. Presumably he was only interested in 3NT opposite a good suit (as in the earlier example). If opener has shown a good suit, 3♣–3♦–3♠–4♣, it does not make sense for responder to want to play in 4♣—what was he hoping for?—so presumably this must be a slam try and he is inviting opener to cuebid—probably a shortage, because he will rarely have a good suit *and* an ace or king outside, although it is possible.

Finally, a sequence like 3♣–3♦–any–4♦ shows that responder was not interested in clubs after all, and actually has a natural diamond bid. Whether this should be forcing, inviting opener to cooperate if at all suitable for a diamond slam, or non-forcing but still invitational to game, is for you to decide, but probably it doesn't matter all that much. Do you currently play the natural sequence 3♣–3♦–4♣–4♦ as forcing or non-forcing? Play this sequence the same way.

This seems to be another quite useful idea, helping to solve an awkward problem for responder. Particularly noteworthy is the fact that when he does not hold a good suit, opener's rebid differentiates between hands with and without support for the artificial relay suit. This means that responder can use the relay on all hands with which he would normally have used the bid in a natural sense and only rarely be any worse off. The "cost" of this convention is therefore very low.

Defending against Pre-empts

This is an area of bidding which has been covered pretty thoroughly elsewhere, so all I want to do is to give you one newish thought. Take the situation where your partner overcalls an opposing pre-empt, for example 3♥–3♠. If you are only interested in game, you have no problem, but what do you do if you have spade support and want to try for slam? People will tell you that 3♥–3♠–Pass–4♣ is a cuebid, something like:

(a) ♠ K 6 4 2	(b) ♠ K 6 4
♥ 7 3	♥ K 6
♦ K Q 5 4	♦ 10 7 5 4
♣ A J 3	♣ A K Q 3

But there is no reason why you should not actually hold:

(c) ♠ 7 3	(d) ♠ 7
♥ 8 5 4	♥ 8 5 4
♦ A 6	♦ A Q 6 4
♣ A K J 7 5 3	♣ A K J 10 5

where you need to be able to bid naturally to find the best game, or indeed slam. Anyone who insists that 4♣ is a cuebid will have great fun with hands (c) and (d).

My suggestion, played by a number of experts but not all that widely known, is that, unless subsequently clearly proven otherwise, a bid of a new suit should be natural. That is not to say that:

(e) ♠ K J 7 5
    ♥ 6 2
    ♦ 8 3
    ♣ A K Q J 4

cannot be bid:

3♥	–	3♠	–	Pass	–	4♣
Pass	–	4♦	–	Pass	–	5♠

Even the most obtuse of partners should be able to work out that sequence—clubs and spades but no red suit controls. With a spade raise and slam interest, simply cuebid the opponents' suit, for example:

$$3♥ \quad - \quad 3♠ \quad - \quad Pass \quad - \quad 4♥$$

This bid becomes much more useful if it is simply a general spade slam try rather than specifically a spade slam try with a heart control.

Now:

(a)	♠ K 6 4 2	(b)	♠ K 6 4	(f)	♠ K 6 4 2
	♥ 7 3		♥ K 6		♥ A 3
	♦ K Q 5 4		♦ 10 7 5 4		♦ K Q 5 4
	♣ A J 3		♣ A K Q 3		♣ J 7 3

all start the same way—4♥, while:

(c)	♠ 7 3	(d)	♠ 7	(e)	♠ K J 7 5
	♥ 8 5 4		♥ 8 5 4		♥ 6 2
	♦ A 6		♦ A Q 6 4		♦ 8 3
	♣ A K J 7 5 3		♣ A K J 10 5		♣ A K Q J 4

can bid a natural and unambiguous 4♣, though (e) will support spades vigorously on the next round.

After the general cuebid, there is still plenty of time to sort out possession of a heart control before committing to slam. The first concern is to discover whether partner is interested. Obviously, if he is not he simply returns to the agreed trump suit, if he is he cuebids or uses Blackwood.

All the above is equally valid when partner opens the bidding and the next hand makes a pre-emptive jump overcall. If 1♠–(3♥)–4♥ or 1♦–(3♠)–4♠ is not a general slam try, a good hand with no control in the opponents' suit has no intelligent bid. He might survive if he begins with a negative double (if available at this level), but with genuine support for partner it is dangerous—partner may pass the double—and there is no reason to think that the problem will be any easier on the next round, even if there is one.

25

Chapter

The Contested Auction

When discussing the uncontested auction, we tended to assume that the auction would continue to be uncontested and that we could afford to take our time about describing our hands. The only real concession we made to possible competition was to suggest that immediate raises of partner's suit to the three level should be pre-emptive.

It would be possible to play exactly the same method of limit raises and splinter bids, after either you or your opponents have overcalled in uncontested auctions. Indeed, that is exactly the way the average club pair plays. But, once the opposition have become involved in the auction, there must be a real danger that they will continue to be so. Delicate descriptive sequences become risky; perhaps an opposing pre-emptive raise will prevent you from completing the description and leave you with an awkward decision at an uncomfortably high level.

Looked at from another point of view, the weaker you are the more reason there is to support partner as vigorously as you can afford to do to prevent your opponents from having their own descriptive auctions.

If you want to put as much pressure as possible on your opponents and, at the same time, handle the pressure they put you under as well as possible, there are three vital rules to follow.

Rule Number One:
    Support with support. In other words, if you have support for partner's suit, show it immediately, don't mess around with other suits.

Rule Number Two:
    Show the level to which your hand is worth a raise immediately.

Rule Number Three:
    Raise as descriptively as possible to help partner to judge what to do if there is further competition.

Mainstream tournament methods can do a reasonably good job of accommodating rules one and two, but they are seriously deficient when it comes to rule three. This is an area at the forefront of modern system development, and more effective methods are available, though they are currently used only by a small proportion of even the expert community. I am going to split my discussion of the competitive auction into two parts. The first will deal with what I have described as mainstream tournament methods, the second with these newer ideas and the reason why they are necessary.

WELL-CHARTED WATERS
You Open and the Opposition Double for Takeout
Everyone is aware that this is a situation in which it pays to raise aggressively when holding support for partner's suit. The logic that, if we have a fit in one suit then the opposition will have a fit in another, is sound. It has become sufficiently established practice that you can assume, without discussion, that a stranger will make a simple raise on many hands with which he would have passed but for the double, make a jump raise with many hands worth only a simple raise, and respond 2NT to show a sound raise to the three level.

If it goes 1♥–(Dble)–?, you would bid 2♥ with:

                    ♠ 8 5 3
                    ♥ Q 7 6 4
                    ♦ 10 5 4 2
                    ♣ 7 6

a clear pass without the double; 3♥ with:

                    ♠ 8 5 3
                    ♥ Q 7 6 4
                    ♦ K Q 5 2
                    ♣ 7 6

only worth a simple raise without the double; and 2NT with:

                    ♠ 8 5 3
                    ♥ Q J 7 4
                    ♦ A K 5 2
                    ♣ 7 6

a normal limit raise to 3♥.

Actually, if you are lucky enough to avoid further competition, bidding 2NT rather than 3♥ when holding a limit raise allows greater accuracy in bidding games because it leaves opener room to bid a new suit as a game try if he so desires. To this basic plan can be added familiar ideas like splinter bids, mini-splinters, 3NT as a good raise to 4♥, indeed most of the methods we looked at in the uncontested auction. One idea to get away from is that you can start off with a redouble to show a good hand, even when holding primary support for partner's major suit. If you do so, vigorous competition by your opponents could leave you poorly placed. Remember, there is no sounder foundation for an intelligent auction than the shared knowledge of a good trump fit. Support with support and get to the level where you belong as quickly as possible

Common sense should tell us that the more trumps we hold between us, the higher we should be prepared to compete, as extra trumps not only provide extra playing strength but also tend to reduce our defensive potential. When it looks as though the deal is going to be a competitive one, it may help partner considerably to know how many trumps you have when you raise him. One idea is to play that 1♥–(Dble)–2♥ promises four card support while 1♥–(Dble)–2♣ is an artificial raise to 2♥ showing precisely three card support. A typical hand might be:

> ♠ 8 6
> ♥ Q 7 4
> ♦ K 5 4 2
> ♣ 9 7 6 3

If opener has a hand like:

> ♠ J 7
> ♥ K J 9 8 6
> ♦ A 7
> ♣ K 5 4 2

he might well be tempted to compete to 3♥ after 1♥–(Dble)–2♥–(2♠)–?, despite his minimum opening, because of the known nine card fit. After 1♥–(Dble)–2♣–(2♠)–?, however, he would know that there was only an eight card fit and so choose to pass.

Similarly, if playing a five card major system, 1♥–(Dble)–3♣ can be used as an artificial raise to 3♥ based on precisely three card heart support, again enabling partner to know immediately the number of trumps between the two hands.

One point I should make here is that there is nothing special about the bids of 2♣ and 3♣. Once you decide that the basic idea is a good one you can choose any bid to act as the artificial raise depending on what you think is least likely to be required in a natural sense. 1M–(Dble)–1NT/2♣/2♦ are all possible, as are 1M–(Dble)–3♣/♦. Probably, bids of the other major are more needed as natural bids than are the minor suits. If you are not a fan of mini-splinters and currently play bids in new suits, both with and without a jump, as natural, you might not want to lose both 2♣ and

3♣ responses to artificiality. The obvious solution would be to use 2♦ and 3♣ or, alternatively, 2♣ and 3♦ as the artificial raises. At least then you could still bid both suits naturally some of the time.

1X–Pass–1Y–Dble–?

Just because both partners have bid before the opponents double does not make a big difference to our situation. It is still just as important to raise pre-emptively if we are weak (within the context of our opening bid, of course) as the hand could still belong to our opponents. It makes sense to play that:

1♦–(Pass)–1♠–(Dble)–3/4♠ are weakish distributional raises.

For example:

> ♠ K Q 8 6   or   ♠ A 7 5 3
> ♥ 7 2   ♥ 5 2
> ♦ A K 7 5 3   ♦ K Q 10 9 7 6
> ♣ J 5   ♣ J

might bid 3♠ in this sequence while:

> ♠ A K 5 3
> ♥ 5 2
> ♦ K Q 10 9 7 6
> ♣ J

would raise all the way to 4♠.

1♦–(Pass)–1♠–(Dble)–2NT can be used to show a strong raise to 3♠:

> ♠ K Q 8 6   or   ♠ A K 8 6
> ♥ K 2   ♥ A J 3
> ♦ A K 7 5 3   ♦ K Q 10 5
> ♣ 7 5   ♣ 7 5

2NT is not needed in a natural sense, because a balanced 17-18 count without support for partner's suit will surely start off by redoubling.

Holding:

> ♠ 8 6
> ♥ K Q 8
> ♦ A K 7 5
> ♣ K Q 10 8

for example, you might well be interested in doubling whatever contract your opponents choose. If the auction proceeds in a way which suggests that there are no rich pickings available on defense, you can always show your strong balanced hand later.

If you are playing a weak no trump, four card major system, opener who has four card support for responder's suit, as above, will normally either be at least 5–4, be 4–4–4–1 with a shortage in one of the opponents' suits, or be strong and balanced.

The strong balanced hands will all raise via 2NT, while the distribution of the other two types is sufficient for the majority to give a pre-emptive raise to the three level. The exception would be a hand with much of the high card strength in the short suits. I hope that nobody doubts that:

♠ K Q 8 6
♥ 7 2
♦ A K 7 5 3
♣ J 5

is a far better hand in support of spades than is:

♠ Q 8 6 4
♥ Q 8
♦ Q J 7 5 3
♣ A Q

The latter might well only raise to 2♠ in the example sequence.

There are not many hands, however, with four card support, which do not justify a raise to the three level of one kind or another. This suggests that 1♦–(Pass)–1♠–(Dble)–2♠ is likely to deliver only three card spade support far more often than not. Remember, however, that opener cannot hold a minimum balanced hand, since he did not open 1NT, so he is quite likely to have a ruffing value somewhere.

Your basic system makes a big difference here. Playing a strong no trump, five card major system, as is standard in many countries, it would be quite normal for opener to hold:

♠ K J 7 4
♥ A 2
♦ A 8 6 4
♣ J 7 3

for the sequence 1♦–(Pass)–1♠–(Dble)–2♠, so the inference that this will tend to be based on only three card support is no longer valid—though it is still possible, of course, that opener's actual hand will be:

♠ K J 8
♥ 7
♦ A Q 9 6 3
♣ Q 7 4 3

You Open and the Opponents Overcall

If anything, the opposition is even better placed to compete when one of them overcalls than if they have started with a takeout double. They have actually laid claim to a suit, and if the overcaller's partner has support for this suit they will be very well placed to compete effectively. It becomes even more important, therefore, that if your side also has a fit we let partner in on the glad tidings without delay.

Most people stick to their tried and trusted methods here as though the overcall had not occurred. If they normally play limit raises, they stick with them, along with whatever else takes their fancy.

Even if you do not normally play pre-emptive raises, surely this is a good time to do so. You can afford to play 1♥–(1♠)–3♥ as pre-emptive because there is a very obvious bid

available to show a sound raise to 3♥, namely 1♥–(1♠)–2♠. There is no other hand-type with which you need to start with a cuebid. If you have a suit worth bidding, you simply bid it, just as you would have done without the overcall.

For example, with:

♠ 6 3 2
♥ K 8
♦ A 5 4
♣ A Q 10 7 4

bid 1♥–(1♠)–2♣.

Holding a game-going hand with no particular suit to bid; for example:

♠ J 3 2
♥ Q 8
♦ A Q 5 4
♣ A J 7 4

start with a negative double. You can always cuebid on the next round if you need to. Meanwhile, if there is no more competition from your opponents, you have actually saved a whole level of bidding, giving more room to explore the correct game at your leisure.

Some pairs treat this cuebid as being specifically a limit raise, others as at least a limit raise—in other words the latter would bid 1♥–(1♠)–2♠ with both of:

(a)	♠ 7 4	(b)	♠ 7 4
	♥ K J 5 3		♥ A Q 5 3
	♦ Q J 2		♦ K J 2
	♣ A 7 4 2		♣ A 7 4 2

intending to show their extra values later with hand (b). If you have paid attention to rule two: you would always show the level to which your hand is worth by a raise immediately.

One possibility is to use a bid of 2NT as an artificial game raise, just as was recommended in an uncontested auction. Given that there is no further opposition bidding, opener can now rebid in exactly the same way as he would have done had there been no overcall. Of course, this is wishful thinking. The better your fit the more likely it is that the opposition have also found a fit and will continue to interfere with your auction. This is precisely why there is danger in the ambiguity of the unlimited cuebid approach. If the bidding does go 1♥–(1♠)–2NT–(3/4♠), you may not be able to have the beautifully descriptive auction you had hoped for, but you will still be very glad that you have already shown your game values rather than merely at least a limit raise. The price you pay for using 2NT as an artificial raise is its loss as a natural bid. Now that the opposition have overcalled, this is more serious than in an uncontested auction, but fortunately there is another way to get there.

If you hold:

(a) ♠ A Q 7   **(b)** ♠ K J 8 3
     ♥ 10 7   ♥ 10 6 3
     ♦ J 9 8 4   ♦ K 9 8
     ♣ A 8 5 3   ♣ A 5 3

you can make a negative double then bid 2NT on the next round if it still seems appropriate. With your strength in the opponents' suit, you are not too worried if they compete to a level which makes this impossible.

Support Doubles

The meaning of a double in this kind of sequence: 1♦–(Pass)–1♥–(1♠)–Dble could vary. Traditionally, it was played for penalties, but today there are people who play it for takeout, or to show a strong balanced hand unsuitable for bidding no trump, and there are also players who use something called a "Support Double."

Support doubles only apply over simple overcalls, 1♦–(Pass)–1♥– (3♣)–Dble would not normally be played as a support double, and they show any strength of hand but precisely three card support for responder's suit. Once again, we are trying to tell partner exactly how big a trump fit our side possesses to help him to judge how far to compete. The corollary is, of course, that 1♦–(Pass)–1♥– (1♠/2♣)–2♥ guarantees four card support.

If the auction goes 1♦–(Pass)–1♥–(1♠)–Dble/2♥–(2♠)–?, responder holding:

     ♠ Q J 7
     ♥ A 8 6 4 3
     ♦ 8 2
     ♣ J 9 7

might now judge to compete to 3♥ opposite a 2♥ raise, knowing of a nine card fit, but take his chance against 2♠ opposite the three card support shown by a double.

I said that the support double showed any strength of hand with three card support. After 1♦–(Pass)–1♥–(1♠)–Dble, a minimum opener would only bid again if forced to do so, for example:

(a) ♠ A 4
     ♥ K J 8
     ♦ Q 10 7 5 3
     ♣ K 6 3

while, with extra values:

(b) ♠ A 4   **(c)** ♠ 4
     ♥ A Q 8   ♥ K J 8
     ♦ A J 7 5 3   ♦ A J 7 5 3
     ♣ K 6 3   ♣ A Q 6 3

he will bid again, often by way of a second, value-showing double, as with (b). Depending on your agreements regarding the second double, hand (c) might make a take-out double in:

| 1♦ | – | Pass | – | 1♥ | – | 1♠ |
| Dble | – | 2♠ | – | Pass | – | Pass |

or might bid out its shape via 3♣.

It is worth remembering that if you play a weak no trump, four card major system, opener cannot have a minimum balanced hand for his support double. Hand (a) would have opened 1NT. So the double will either include a ruffing value or be a strong no trump type. While support doubles are a reasonable option in any system, they are particularly valuable in a method where opener will frequently have a weak no trump type (a) when he doubles as he will then be able to show his support on hands whose playing strength, or rather lack of it, make an immediate raise a bit of an overbid.

Game Try Double

There is one more artificial double we need to take a quick look at. In an uncontested auction, 1M–2M, opener has a whole range of possible game tries available to him. Even in the contested auction, there is usually some free bid he can use. For example, if the auction is 1♠–(2♦)–2♠–(3♦), he can bid 3♠ when all he wants to do is to compete and use 3♥ as a game try. There is no room to direct partner's attention to any particular suit, all that is possible is to invite him to bid 3♠ with a minimum but 4♠ with a maximum; still, it is better than nothing.

If the auction is 1♠–(2♥)–2♠–(3♥) there is no room for a game try—unless you use double for that purpose. Game try doubles apply only in this situation, where the overcall is in the suit immediately below opener's. If opener holds:

     ♠ K J 10 8 5 3
     ♥ Q 3
     ♦ A Q 2
     ♣ Q 5

he can compete with 3♠, safe in the knowledge that partner will not go on to game. Holding:

     ♠ K J 10 8 5
     ♥ 3
     ♦ A Q 5 2
     ♣ K J 3

however, he wants partner to bid game with a suitable maximum—partner will know to devalue heart honors—so makes a game try double.

Defense to Two-suited Overcalls

If the auction begins 1M–(2NT[minors]), responder will frequently be in difficulties if using standard methods. After 1♥–(2NT)– he will sometimes wish to compete, holding:

(a) ♠ A J 4 2   **(b)** ♠ K J 10 8 7 5
     ♥ Q 8 7 5   ♥ A 4
     ♦ 7 5 3   ♦ 7 5 3
     ♣ 6 2   ♣ 6 2

with 3♥ and 3♠ respectively, and on other occasions will want to invite game with:

> ♠ A J 4 2
> ♥ Q 8 7 5
> ♦ K 10 8
> ♣ 6 2

or make a forcing bid in spades with:

> ♠ K J 10 8 7
> ♥ A 4 3
> ♦ A 10 8
> ♣ Q 2

The solution is to use the two cuebids of the overcaller's suits to help you out. Other systems are possible, but this is as simple as any:

1♥–(2NT)–3♣	=	At least a limit raise to 3♥
	3♦	=	Forcing with five plus spades
	3♥	=	Competitive in hearts, less than a limit raise
	3♠	=	Five plus spades but non-forcing
1♠–(2NT)–3♣	=	Five plus hearts, forcing
	3♦	=	At least a limit raise to 3♠
	3♥	=	Five plus hearts but non-forcing
	3♠	=	Four card support but less than a limit raise

With minor adjustments, this method can be used over any kind of two-suited overcall where the suits are known.

There is a case for inverting the meanings of 3♦ and 3♠ after a 1♥ opening. The advantage is that if opener hates spades he can now comfortably bid 3♥ over 3♦.

They Open the Bidding and You Overcall

Traditional methods of responding to partner's overcall used limit raises to invite game, just as over an opening bid, except that you needed to be a bit stronger because an overcall did not necessarily promise opening values, and a cuebid of the opponents' suit as a general game force.

Undoubtedly, the biggest single advance in this area was the invention of the unassuming cuebid. Playing unassuming cuebids, a bid of the opponents' suit becomes two-way, either a traditional game force or, far more frequently, merely a good raise of partner's overcall. This leaves immediate raises free to be more pre-emptive, getting in the way of the opposition's bidding. For example, 1♦–1♠– Pass–?

(a)	♠ K J 8	(b)	♠ K J 8
	♥ 7 2		♥ A 7 2
	♦ 10 9 6 3		♦ K 9 3
	♣ 8 5 4 2		♣ 8 5 4 2
(c)	♠ K J 8 3	(d)	♠ K J 8 3
	♥ 7		♥ 7
	♦ 10 9 3		♦ A 9 3
	♣ 10 8 5 4 2		♣ K 8 5 4 2

Non-vulnerable, hand (a) should raise to 2♠. You have no

interest in game unless partner has a very powerful overcall, but want to make things a little more difficult for your opponents. Meanwhile, hand (b), with which you could be interested in game, makes an unassuming cuebid of 2♦, though you will go no further than 2♠ unless partner shows some interest.

Hand (c) is worth a pre-emptive raise to 3♠. If you are allowed to play in 3♠, you will usually score well whether or not you fulfil your contract. With an excellent fit and all your values in partner's suit, the less tricks you make in 3♠, the more certain it is that your opponents could have made something their way had you given them room to investigate properly. Even when they bid over 3♠, because you have left them so little room to investigate the hand, they will sometimes play in the wrong contract.

Hand (d) is worth an invitational raise to 3♠, indeed, if you play a conservative overcalling style, you might even consider this to be worth a game raise. As always, considerations of partnership style should affect your judgment. A mini-splinter of 3♥ would fit the bill perfectly if you happened to have that agreement here. They are perfectly playable, but give a very easy way back into the auction for an opponent who can double to show length in the suit – something he is quite likely to have if you are looking at a singleton.

Many players would make an unassuming cuebid of 2♦ with hand (d), intending to raise to 3♠ on the next round. This follows rule one—support with support, but not rule two—raise to the limit your hand is worth immediately. If the auction goes:

| 1♦ – | 1♠ | – Pass – | 2♦ |
| 2♥ – | Pass | – 4♥ | – ? |

you will regret not having got your hand off your chest on the previous round. Sure, 4♠ rates to be the winning action more often than not, but there is nothing to stop partner having a defensively oriented hand with a couple of heart tricks. By failing to show your strength immediately, you have left yourself with a guess instead of partner with a reasonably informed decision. The solution, without having to consider any more new ideas, is simply to make your unassuming cuebid at the level to which you want to raise. So this hand bids 1♦–1♠–Pass–3♦ to show a constructive raise to 3♠. The sequence 1♦–1♠–Pass–2♦ becomes specifically a good raise to 2♠ or a traditional game force.

Responding to an Unassuming Cuebid

Initially, the overcaller assumes that the unassuming cuebid is based on a constructive raise of the suit rather than a game force, and bids accordingly. Partner can show the game force type by bidding a new suit or cuebidding again on the next round.

The weakest rebid the overcaller can make is to repeat his original suit as cheaply as possible. Any bid he makes above the next level of his first suit shows significant extra values and a willingness to at least invite game. A bid of a new suit below the next level of his first is a little more contentious. One school of thought says that the only weak rebid is to repeat the original suit, hence any new suit shows extra values whether it be above or below the level of the original suit. The other school says that such a bid is neutral as regards extra strength, it may or may not have any. They argue that, because they do not raise the level of the auction, they can afford to describe the shape of their hand. After all, there may sometimes be a better fit available in the second suit.

There is merit in both approaches and if you are already used to playing in a particular way there is no compelling reason to change. If, however, you are relatively new to unassuming cuebids, I would suggest that you keep all bids other than a return to the original trump suit as showing extra values.

So after:

1♦   –   1♠ –   Pass   –   2♦
Pass

2♥/3♣	=	Second suit, extra values
2♠	=	Minimum, not necessarily showing any extra length
2NT	=	Semi-balanced, good diamond holding, extra values
3♦	=	Usually semi-balanced, game values, diamonds not suitable for bidding no trump
3♠	=	Sixth spade, extra values, game invitation

As always, the definition of a hand with extra values will depend on the partnership's overcalling style. Suppose your idea of a minimum 1♠ overcall of 1♦ would be:

(a) ♠ A K J 8 3
     ♥ 6 4
     ♦ 10 7
     ♣ K 10 4 2

Now, to qualify as having significant extra values, you might need something like:

(b) ♠ A K J 8 3
     ♥ K 4
     ♦ 10 7
     ♣ K 10 4 2

So after:

1♦   –   1♠ –   Pass   –   2♦
Pass–   ?

hand (a), having nothing at all to spare, would rebid 2♠, while hand (b) could make the encouraging and descriptive call of 3♣.

Now suppose that you favor a much looser overcalling style so that:

(c) ♠ K J 10 8 3
     ♥ 6 4
     ♦ 10 7
     ♣ K 10 4 2

would be an automatic 1♠ overcall of 1♦.

Now you might well consider that:

(a) ♠ A K J 8 3
     ♥ 6 4
     ♦ 10 7
     ♣ K 10 4 2

had sufficient extra values to bid 3♣ rather than 2♠. Actually hand (a) is very minimum for any forward-going move—as you will appreciate if you consider the type of hand with which partner will have made the unassuming cuebid—but I'm sure you will see the point I am trying to make.

Suppose that partner makes an unassuming cuebid and the next hand either bids or doubles, for example:

1♦   –   1♠   –   Pass   –   2♦
Dble/2♥ –

It is easy to see that redouble/double should show strong hands, but which is stronger, a bid of 2♠ or a pass?

Perhaps you think this one is obvious; you pass because you have a minimum and bid again to show extra values. But the situation is not quite so straightforward. There is a plausible argument that had opener not made a positive rebid, our side was forced to at least 2♠. In that case, following the Principle of Fast Arrival, an immediate 2♠ bid should be the weakest option available to us. This approach has two plus features. First, the weaker we are, the more bidding space we want to take away from our opponents. Second, it is better to pass with the stronger hand because we are then happier to cooperate in the slightly unlikely event that partner wishes to play for a penalty against their contract.

In truth, the advantages of playing one style rather than the other are pretty slender. As always, the most important thing is to be on the same wavelength as partner.

Rosenkranz Doubles and Redoubles

Mexican expert, George Rosenkranz has suggested that to help the overcaller to decide whether to lead his suit in defense, his partner should use a double or redouble in certain circumstances to show a top honor in the overcaller's suit and a willingness to compete to the two level. Using this idea:

After:

1♦–1♠ –Dble (Negative)

    –Rdbl   shows the ace, king or queen of spades, doubleton or trebleton.

    –2♠   is a weak raise but denies a top honor.

    –2♦   is a normal unassuming cuebid. By agreement, this may either deny or be neutral about possession of a top spade honor.

Also, after:

1♦–1♠–2♣/♥

    –Dble   shows a top spade honor in a raise to 2♠

    –2♠   denies a top honor, as before

    –2♦   is an unassuming cuebid

While it is undoubtedly useful to know whether or not to lead your suit, and these bids help you with this decision, I don't really like Rosenkranz doubles and redoubles. First, you lose the natural meanings of the two calls, redouble to simply show a good hand and double as takeout. Second, double or redouble leaves the opposition more room to describe their hands than does a straightforward raise. This should, I think, be sufficient to dissuade you from adopting what looks, at first sight, to be quite a pretty idea.

Passed Hand Raises

Where a hand fails to take an easy opportunity to bid at the one level yet suddenly lurches into the auction with a bid of a new suit at a much higher level, consider the logic of the situation. Can this really be a natural bid?

Take these examples:

(a) 1♣ – Pass – 1♦ – 1♠
     3♣/♦ – 3♥

(b) Pass – 1♥ – 2♠(*) – 3♥
     4♣/♦

    (*)Weak

In sequence (a), how is it possible to have a heart suit worth a bid at the three level yet not worth a simple overcall? Equally, in sequence (b), how can you want to bid a new suit at the four level, facing a weak hand, when you could not open the bidding?

In both cases, the only rational explanation is that you actually have genuine support for partner's suit. The precise meaning of sequence (a) will depend on whether 3♥ was the only free bid below the next level of partner's suit.

If opener actually rebid 3♣, then you could bid 3♦ as an unassuming cuebid with, say:

(a) ♠ K J 8 5
     ♥ A 7 3
     ♦ 6
     ♣ Q 10 7 5 2

and 3♥ can still be a constructive raise to 3♠, but also emphasising heart values; perhaps:

(b) ♠ K J 8 5
     ♥ A Q J 3
     ♦ 6 4
     ♣ 7 5 2

If, on the other hand, opener's rebid was 3♦, then 3♥ is the only free bid below 3♠ and has to take care of all game try hands, including both (a) and (b).

Either way, the existence of a game invitational bid means that you can bid 3♠ in a purely competitive sense:

(c) ♠ K J 8 5 or (d) ♠ K J 8 5
     ♥ 7 6 2   ♥ Q 7 6
     ♦ 6   ♦ 6 4
     ♣ J 10 8 7 5   ♣ Q 8 5 2

Turning our attention to sequence (b):

  Pass – 1♥ – 2♠(*) – 3♥
  4♣/4♦
  (*) Weak

The most likely explanation for such a bid is that you are willing to play in 4♠ but are telling partner what to lead in case the opposition go on to 5♥.

A typical 4♣ bid might be:

(e) ♠ 10 8 5 4 or (f) ♠ Q 7 6 3
     ♥ 6 4   ♥ 9
     ♦ 10 8   ♦ 7 5 3 2
     ♣ A K J 7 5   ♣ K Q J 4

There is nothing conventional about these bids. If I sat down opposite a stranger who I knew to be a good player, and he made one of these bids, I would know what he was trying to do. Common sense dictates that while the precise details might vary from person to person, he *must* be showing support for my suit.

THE LAW OF TOTAL TRICKS

Your instincts, experience, judgment—call it what you will—tell you that the more trumps your partnership owns, the higher you should be willing to go in competition. You have looked at a number of ideas to help you judge the extent of your fit. Support doubles and artificial three card raises such as 1♥–Dble–2♣, are two examples.

The Law of Total Tricks confirms what you have always suspected, that the size of your trump fit is important, and seeks to quantify it. The law states that, in a competitive auction, if you add together the number of trumps held by each side in their best fit, the total will be equal to the total number of tricks the two sides can make if they play in those trump suits.

Say, for example, that North/South have a nine card spade fit and East/West a ten card club fit. The total trick expectation for this deal is nineteen (9+10). If North/South can make ten tricks, East/West should be able to make nine; if North/South can only make eight tricks, then East/West can make eleven.

Instinctively, this may feel wrong. Surely you will only discover during the play whether a finesse will succeed or fail, and this will clearly effect how many tricks you can make. Consider this deal, however:

```
                ♠ A K 7 4 2
                ♥ 9
                ♦ A Q J 5
                ♣ 6 4 2
♠ 9 6 3                        ♠ 5
♥ K 10 8 6                     ♥ A Q J 5 4
♦ K 6 3                        ♦ 10 9 4 2
♣ K 8 5                        ♣ A 7 3
                ♠ Q J 10 8
                ♥ 7 3 2
                ♦ 8 7
                ♣ Q J 10 9
```

Assuming perfect play and defense, North-South can make ten tricks in spades and East-West eight in hearts. Try interchanging the East-West hands so that the diamond finesse is no longer onside for North-South. Now North-South can take only nine tricks, but the ♦K is now onside for East-West so they can also make nine tricks. The total available tricks remains at eighteen, as expected.

The Law of Total Tricks cannot work miracles. It cannot tell you precisely how many tricks will be available on any given hand, only the average expectation. As you shall see later, there are a number of factors which can affect the accuracy of the law on any given deal, but even without making any adjustments to take these into account, the average deviation from the total trick expectation given by the law is only about half a trick per deal. Make these fine adjustments, and the deviation can be significantly reduced.

The law always assumes double dummy declarer play and defense from both sides. For example, declarer will always guess the position of a missing queen correctly. This is obviously not true in real life, but it has to be remembered that defense is significantly more difficult than declarer play. Defensive error will, in the long run, at least cancel out declarer's misguesses, bringing the number of tricks actually made back up to that expected. Again, I must stress that you have to take a long term view; you cannot expect these factors to balance out on every individual deal.

If you are going to use the law to help you with your competitive bidding judgment, you have to try to judge the number of trumps each side holds. It will not always be possible to be precise, but that need not matter as long as you are reasonably close. A reasonable rule of thumb where the high card strength seems to be roughly evenly divided between the two sides is to say that you should compete to the level of your fit, i.e. bid to the two level with eight combined trumps, the three level with nine trumps.

The number of trumps you hold is more important than your high card strength when you are judging whether to bid

again, a concept with which not everyone will be happy. Remember, however, that extra trump length will both increase your offensive and decrease your defensive potential, while increased high card strength will increase both your offense and defense. In other words, extra high cards not only increase the number of tricks you can make as declarer, but also increase the number of tricks you can make on defense. Let's look at an example. Say that both sides are vulnerable and we are playing against a pair who play five card majors, the auction goes:

West	North	East	South
1♥	1♠	2♥	2♠
3♥	?		

We hold:

	(a)	♠ K Q 9 6 4	(b)	♠ K Q J 9 6 4
		♥ A 6 3		♥ 7 6 3
		♦ A 8 5		♦ A 8 5
		♣ 6 2		♣ 6

With which hand should we be more inclined to bid on with 3♠?

The likelihood is that both East and South have three card support for their partner's major—no certainty, but a likelihood. West may have five hearts or may have six. When you hold hand (a), the total trick expectation for the deal is either sixteen (8+8) or seventeen (8+9). Let's suppose for the moment that West has only five hearts, giving a total trick expectation of sixteen.

(i) If we can make +140 in 3♠, West can only make seven tricks in 3♥ so we would score +200 by passing.

(ii) If we can make eight tricks in 3♠, −100, so does West in 3♥, so we could score +100 by passing.

(iii) When West is making 3♥, −140, we will be two down in 3♠, −200.

It doesn't matter how the sixteen tricks are divided, we always score better on defense. If West has a sixth heart, the trick expectation goes up to seventeen. It is true that if one side is making their three level contract and the other going one down, it could be correct for us to compete further. But this assumes that neither side will be doubled, turning the price for one down into a disastrous (or lucrative, depending on your point of view) −200. At pairs scoring, good players are very light on the trigger against vulnerable opponents. Here it may be that if you pass your partner can double to show a good 2♠ bid, or if you bid 3♠ either opponent may make a matchpoint double. In the short-term, it could be right to bid 3♠ with hand (a), but it has to be a loser in the long run—whenever West has only five hearts or whenever someone can scrape up a double.

If you hold hand (b), the total trick expectation is at least seventeen (9+8) and possibly eighteen (9+9). Now bidding on is much more attractive. Even with a trick expectation of seventeen, there are good chances to gain by turning +100 into +140 or −140 into −100. When the trick expectation rises to eighteen, the situation is even better as you may also be turning −140 into +140.

If neither side is vulnerable, the odds shift more in favor of bidding—as you would expect. The total trick expectation has not changed, of course, but now it is possible for either side to go two down undoubled or one down doubled, for −100, and make a profit whenever their opponents were going to make their contract. Perhaps, in these auctions where it is not really clear exactly how many trumps each side has, the best solution is to assume the larger number, and therefore the higher total trick expectation, when non-vulnerable, but make the opposite assumption when vulnerable. That way, when you are in doubt, you will be bidding more at the vulnerability where it generally pays to bid (non-vul) and passing more at the vulnerability where it pays to pass (vul). Don't forget though that it is not only your vulnerability but also that of your opponents which is important. The odds when one side is vulnerable and the other not are somewhere in between the odds for the two sets of equal vulnerabilities.

Perhaps you begin to see why a number of our competitive bidding tools were designed to differentiate between three and four card support for partner. They help him to judge the degree of fit and hence the total trick expectation for the deal.

Adjustments to the Law

Let's look at the factors which could affect the accuracy of the law on a deal.

Really, they are all a matter of how well the hands fit together. Firstly, consider these hands:

(a)	♠ A K 10 7 4	(b)	♠ Q J 9 5	(c)	♠ Q J 9 5
	♥ A 4 3		♥ 6		♥ Q 8 6 5
	♦ K J 7		♦ Q 8 6 5		♦ 6
	♣ 6 3		♣ A K 7 4		♣ A K 7 4

Opposite hand (a), hand (b) gives a very good chance indeed of twelve tricks, yet hand (c), which is identical except for the switching around of the red suits, will produce only about ten and a half tricks on average. The degree of sidesuit fit has made a one and a half trick difference to your trick expectation.

Suppose you looked at the same deal from the point of view of your opponents. Presumably, when you have hand (b), their best fit is in hearts; when you have hand (c) it is in diamonds. Hand (b) means they are missing A643 of their trump suit; hand (c) means they are missing KJ76. The chances are that they will lose the same number of trump tricks on average whichever hand you have, should they play the hand. So the total tricks actually available on the deal are certainly decided by your degree of fit and the number could easily vary by one or two tricks.

Or take these hands:

(d)	♠ A K 7 4	(e)	♠ Q J 10 8	(f)	♠ 9 6 3 2
	♥ 7 5		♥ 8 3 2		♥ Q J 2
	♦ Q 7 5 3		♦ K J 6		♦ K J 6
	♣ Q 8 3		♣ A 5 4		♣ A 5 4

If (d) and (e) play together in a spade contract, they will lose two heart tricks but no spades. (d) and (f), however, will also lose two hearts but also at least one spade trick. Meanwhile, suppose the opposing hands play in a heart contract. Chances are that when we hold (d) and (e) the opposition will lose two spade tricks but no heart; when we hold (d) and (f), however, they will still lose two spades but also a heart trick. Both sides make a trick less when we hold hands (d) and (f) than when we have hands (d) and (e), resulting in the total number of tricks made varying by two. Yet in each case, the two sides have the same length of trump fit and number of high cards.

The difference is in the "purity" of the trump suits. Just as in the previous example, where hand (a) had wasted values opposite (c) but not opposite (b), so here, when you put hands (d) and (e) together both sides' trump suits are pure; there are no losers in the suits and no high card values which may prove of use in defense but which are worthless to declarer. Conversely, put hands (d) and (f) together and both sides have a trump loser and wasted values which, while producing a defensive trick, do not add anything to declarer's playing strength.

The message is clear: if either or both sides can lay claim to a pure trump suit, the total expected tricks may be slightly higher than normal, while if both sides hold minor honors in their opponents' suits, the total trick expectation will be lowered.

This is where judgment comes into the game. Not only must you try to get an idea of the length of each side's trump fit, but you must also be on the lookout for these little plus and minus features. Playing standard Acol, four card majors, the bidding goes:

| | 1♥ | – | 2♣ | – | 2♥ | – | 3♣ |

(a)	♠ 7 5	(b)	♠ 7 5
	♥ A K Q 7 5		♥ J 10 7 5 3
	♦ K J 6 4		♦ A K Q 4
	♣ 3 2		♣ K 4
(c)	♠ 7 5	(d)	♠ 7 5
	♥ A K Q 7		♥ K 7 5 3
	♦ A Q 6 4		♦ A K Q 4
	♣ 7 3 2		♣ Q J 8

Hand (a) is an automatic 3♥ bid. You hope for a nine card fit and know that your fit, at least, is a pure one.

Hand (b) is less attractive because there is a danger that both sides will have very impure trump suits. Still, the likely nine card fit makes 3♥ correct.

Hand (c) can only expect an eight card fit, which suggests a pass, but it looks as though both trump suits may be very pure, so 3♥ is a reasonable shot, though not a guaranteed winner.

Hand (d) is a clear pass. You can hope for no more than an eight card fit and there is evidence that both sides may have seriously impure trump suits.

Note that this purity affects both sides. What is good news for you will also be good for your opponents, bad news for you, bad news for them as well. If your partner makes a splinter bid and you like the sound of it, presumably because you have no wastage in the suit, this will also be good news for your opponents, because it also means that one of their main suits is pure. If the auction was already competitive, don't be surprised if it continues to be so.

The other feature which can increase the total trick expectation markedly is when both sides have a double fit.

For example:

```
            ♠ A Q 7 5 2
            ♥ 9
            ♦ A J 8 4 3
            ♣ 6 3
♠ 6 4 3                    ♠ 8
♥ K J 6 4                  ♥ A Q 8 7 5 3
♦ 7                        ♦ 10 6 5
♣ A Q 10 9 7               ♣ K J 5
            ♠ K J 10 9
            ♥ 10 2
            ♦ K Q 9 2
            ♣ 8 4 2
```

North/South have nine spades and East/West ten hearts, giving a total trick expectation of nineteen—yet North/South are cold for 4♠ and East/West for 5♥, a total of twenty-one tricks.

It is true that by swapping one of East's small diamonds for one of West's small spades we could bring the number of available tricks down to the expected nineteen, but this would give a false picture. That would mean that all the short holdings were dividing as evenly as possible, which can happen but is not normal. Actually, the 3–1 breaks as in the diagram are more likely from a statistical point of view than 2–2 breaks. And if there were a void in any hand the total tricks available would rise still higher. So the discrepancy of two between the total tricks expected and the total tricks actually available is about average in the circumstances.

Why is there a discrepancy? Because each side has not just one but two pure suits plus a lot of distribution. Double fits are very dangerous, the most common reason for double game swings, when a team concedes –790 in 4♠ doubled at one table and –550 in 5♣ doubled at the other. Because they fit together so well, each side's values are working overtime. So the adjustments we have to make to the basic law are to

make allowances for:

(i) Hands where both sides have impure trump suits, a sign that the total trick expectation should be reduced.

(ii) Hands where both sides have exceptionally pure trump suits, a sign that the total trick expectation is likely to be exceeded.

(iii) Hands where both sides have a double fit, a sign that the total trick expectation may be two or even three tricks below the total tricks actually available.

Points (i) and (ii) are often something you can recognize just by looking at your own hand. But just because you know the danger does not mean partner will also know of it—his hand may be giving him a quite different message. Whenever possible, therefore, you should try to tell him what you suspect. Point (iii) is going to come into play largely on highly competitive auctions where the level of bidding will often rise very quickly. The kind of auction where following the three rules for competitive auctions will prove to be absolutely vital. If partner is to use the law effectively, or his judgment, then it becomes essential that you not only "support with support" and "raise immediately to the level your hand is worth", but also "raise as descriptively as possible." The subject of the final section of this book is how to design a system of support showing bids to allow you to follow all three rules at once and make your side's later decisions as straightforward as you can and your opponents' as difficult as possible.

COMPETITIVE RAISES – THE NEW WAVE

When planning any system, the first thing to consider is what kind of hands we want to be able to show. When raising partner, we would certainly like to be able to make both limit and pre-emptive raises to various levels; what else? It would be nice to be able to show a sidesuit singleton (a splinter or mini-splinter) and, mindful of the danger of double fit hands, also hands with a fair sidesuit. We should be very conscious that the purity of each side's holding in their main suit(s) can have a significant effect on the total trick expectation for the deal.

It would be nice, therefore, if we could differentiate between "pure" and "impure" hands when making a limit raise. Finally, on deals which may be only played at part score level, whatever our basic method (four or five card openings), we should strive to differentiate between hands with three and four card support for partner because this will affect the total trick expectation for the deal and so alter the winning action in many sequences.

That is what we would like to be able to do. Alas, there simply are not enough bids available to do all of these things, particularly in view of the likelihood of further competition from our opponents. Just what we can fit into our system will vary somewhat with different bidding situations, but some types of bid should be there whatever the situation.

The first thing to consider is that we do not have room to describe both hands with four card support for partner plus a singleton (splinters and mini-splinters) and hands with four card support for partner plus a useful sidesuit. Up to now, I have been a great advocate of the various kinds of splinter bid, but now we are taking part in a competitive auction it is time for a change.

First let me say that I still believe in splinter bids when we have a shortage in the opponents' suit.

For example, with:

(a) ♠ 7
     ♥ K J 8 5
     ♦ Q 10 6 4
     ♣ A Q 7 3

to bid 1♥–(1♠)–3♠ is obviously an ideal description of the hand.

Now switch the hand around so that we have:

(b) ♠ Q 10 6 4   (c) ♠ A Q 7 3
   ♥ K J 8 5   ♥ K J 8 5
   ♦ 7   ♦ Q 10 6 4
   ♣ A Q 7 3   ♣ 7

A splinter bid is still the ideal way to describe either of these hands, but how often will we actually hold a singleton in one of the unbid suits? Far less often, as I am sure you would agree. Also, when we have both length and strength in the overcaller's suit, this is the one time when we can afford to go slowly, ignoring our rules for supporting partner in competition. Why? Simply because there will not be any vigorous competition from our opponents or, if there is, we will certainly know what to do about it. No, while an immediate splinter bid would still be ideal with the above hands, it is unnecessary as we should have plenty of time to investigate the hand properly if we start with a quieter bid, a 2♠ cuebid to show a limit raise or better, for example. There is a better use for a jump to 4♣/♦ in this sort of sequence.

Fit-Showing Jumps

A fit-showing jump shows four card support for partner's suit, a reasonable five card sidesuit, and the offensive values to justify going to whatever level we bid at. The sidesuit should be of a type which will play very well for our side if partner has any fitting top honor cards, for example:

(a) A J 10 7 3   (b) K J 9 6 4

but not:

(c) Q 8 7 6 3   (d) A 9 5 4 2

The idea of the fit-showing jump is to tell partner immediately about both your suits and your offensive potential on the hand. It tells him not only that you have support for his suit, but also whether or not the sidesuits are a double fit on the deal, raising the total trick expectation, or a misfit, lowering the total trick count. Although you may well bid again in the auction, this will only be in limited ways; you have given partner the information to make an intelligent

decision and have relinquished the captaincy to him for the remainder of this deal.

I have twice mentioned our offensive potential, in other words, what your hand is worth if your side declares the final contract, but I have said nothing about defensive strength.

Take this sequence: 1♥–(2♠)–?

(a) ♠ 7 4   (b) ♠ 7 4
   ♥ A Q 6 4   ♥ Q 6 5 4 2
   ♦ 10 8   ♦ 8
   ♣ A J 10 7 3   ♣ A J 10 7 3

Both example hands have the offensive potential to go to the four level, but there is a big difference in their potential on defense. Nonetheless, both should make a fit jump of 4♣ rather than a pre-emptive raise to 4♥. You must always allow for the possibilities of a double fit and let partner know first about your hand-type, worrying about high card strength later.

If the auction continues 1♥–(2♠)–4♣–(4♠), partner will be very well placed to judge how well the hands fit together and it is that on which he will base his decision whether to compete further, not on whether he has extra high card strength.

Holding:

(c) ♠ 9 2   (d) ♠ A 9
   ♥ K J 10 7 3   ♥ K J 10 7 3
   ♦ A 7   ♦ K Q 9 5
   ♣ K Q 9 5   ♣ 8 2

it will not matter whether you hold hand (a) or hand (b). In each case it is right to bid on with (c) but to pass with (d).

Assuming a spade lead, you would go down in 5♥ if opener had hand (d), whether you held hand (a) or hand (b). Holding hands (b) and (d), you should be happy to defend 4♠. The sidesuit misfits mean that it will go down, but neither of us can be sure enough to double—though opener might well risk doing so, he could be wrong if responder held a singleton spade instead of a singleton diamond. With hands (a) and (d), however, we should only be happy if we double 4♠.

The double is responder's responsibility. His 4♣ bid showed his hand-type; now he gets the chance to show his high card strength, or defensive potential. With hand (b), he passes out 4♠, but with hand (a), he doubles. This in no way contradicts what I said earlier about having passed the captaincy over to partner; all the double does is to complete the description of the hand, just as, in a negative way, the final pass with hand (b) also completes the description of that hand.

The reason why it doesn't matter whether we hold (a) or (b) when we bid 4♣ is that, if partner discovers that there is a double fit, he can bid 5♥ as a two-way shot. If he holds hand (c), 5♥ will be making when you have hand (a). If, on the other hand, you have hand (b), 5♥ will be going down, but most of the time this will still be okay because 4♠ will be making.

I should mention that it is also possible to play the splinter bid in the opponents' suit as two-way.

For example:

(e) ♠ 7
   ♥ K Q 7 3
   ♦ K 6 5 3 2
   ♣ K J 4

(f) ♠ 6
   ♥ K J 7 3 2
   ♦ 10 8 6 5
   ♣ K 10 8

Once you decide that both hands are worth a raise to the four level, there is some sense in telling partner why. You could bid 1♥–(1♠)–3♠ with both (e) and (f) and, if there is further competition, double 4♠ with (e) but pass with (f). My feeling is that this is a less useful treatment than the two-way fit jump, as your high card strength is of more significance to partner in this situation where a double fit is less likely.

If you are to play any of these bids as two-way, you will occasionally make life a little more awkward for partner when he has both a fit and a strong hand and is considering slam possibilities.

While:

(a) ♠ 7 4
   ♥ A Q 6 4
   ♦ 10 8
   ♣ A J 10 7 3

(b) ♠ 8 3 2
   ♥ Q 6 5 4 2
   ♦ 8
   ♣ A J 10 7 3

may both have the offensive potential to bid 1♥–(2♠)–4♣, hand (a) is significantly more suitable for slam purposes. While we could just stick to our tried and tested slam bidding methods and rarely come to too much harm, one other possibility is to use the cheapest available bid, in this case 4♦, as an artificial slam try. This would simply ask responder what sort of 4♣ bid he had. With (b), responder signs off in 4♥, while with (a) he makes a more encouraging noise—perhaps 5♥ with this particular hand, but a cuebid on any hand with a side control to show.

While it may seem quite novel, there is actually nothing new about these general slam tries. If you play 4♣ and 4♦ openings as South African Texas (good 4♥/4♠ openings), you will be familiar with the idea that a one step response is an artificial slam try rather than a cuebid, while we have also looked at a cuebid of the opponents' suit such as (3♥)–3♠–(Pass)–4♥ being used as a general try.

Fit-showing jumps can also be used to invite game. 1♥–(1♠)–3♣/♦ may be used to show something like:

(a) ♠ 8 3
   ♥ K 8 6 3
   ♦ 7 6
   ♣ A J 10 8 5

(b) ♠ 8 3 2
   ♥ Q 7 6 3
   ♦ 7
   ♣ A J 9 8 5

Just as with mini-splinters, which I am suggesting they replace in competitive auctions, it is not only that they help

partner to judge accurately when they occur, but there are also the negative implications when they do not. In other words, by taking this hand-type out of your limit raise showing bid, you help to define that bid more narrowly.

Fit Non-Jumps

There are a number of situations where a new suit can be fit showing even without a jump. We have already seen:

  1♣   –   Pass   –   1♦   –   1♠
  3♣   –   3♥

where the logic was that a hand which was not worth a 1♥ overcall could not possibly be suddenly worth a natural 3♥ bid. 3♥ in this sequence cannot be a normal fit jump type, because such hands include a reasonable five card suit and would have overcalled 1♥, but it can still be a raise to 3♠ with heart values. Our example was something like:

    ♠ A J 7 3
    ♥ K Q J 4
    ♦ 7 3 2
    ♣ 8 6

There are other sequences, however, where a bid of a new suit can show the classic fit jump hand-type.

Take the sequence:

  Pass   –   Pass   –   1♥   –   2♦
  3♣

A hand including a suit worth bidding at the three level in a purely natural sense would surely have opened the bidding while lesser hands with a club suit would now be making a negative double. This leaves you free to use this kind of 3♣ bid as a fit non-jump:

For example:

    ♠ 10 3
    ♥ A 9 7 3
    ♦ J 6
    ♣ K J 9 5 4

3♣ is surely more helpful to partner than an undefined limit raise.

The last example was clear cut; sometimes it will be more a matter of frequency. How often will you need to bid 1♠–(3♦)–4♣ in a natural sense? Sure, this one is more contentious, but if you held:

    ♠ Q J 6 4
    ♥ 8 7
    ♦ 5 3
    ♣ A K J 8 5

wouldn't you like to be able to give partner the whole story in one bid?

Andrew Robson and Oliver Segal, the authors of *Partnership Bidding*, suggest the use of fit non-jumps in defense to certain two-suited overcalls. Take the auction: 1♥–2♥ (spades and a minor) –?

If your only way forward with:

♠ 7 6
♥ Q 9 6 3
♦ 5 4
♣ A Q 10 8 5

is a limit raise, say via a 2♠ cuebid, you will not be at all well placed if the next hand "raises" to 4♠. It will now be up to you to guess whether the deal is a double fit, when you probably want to bid on, or a misfit, when you certainly do not.

Although it is clear that you might, on occasion, wish to bid 3♣/♦ in a wholly natural sense, the suggestion is that fit auctions are so important that these bids are better employed as fit non-jumps, i.e. limit raises to 3♥ with a good sidesuit.

If you like the concept of fit non-jumps, no doubt you will be able to find further examples for yourself. If, on the other hand, this is all a bit rich for you, don't worry—you have plenty of company and can always restrict their use to those clear situations where the bid *cannot* be natural.

Other Types of Raises

Having taken out the limit and game raises with good sidesuits, all of which are now described by fit-showing jumps, that still leaves us with pre-emptive, limit, and strong game raises without a good sidesuit to describe.

The simplest system is to play that jumps in partner's suit are all pre-emptive, so:

(a) ♠ 7
♥ Q 7 4 2
♦ 8 5 3
♣ J 10 8 7 5

(b) ♠ 8 5
♥ K 6 5 3 2
♦ 7
♣ Q 10 6 5 4

Hand (a) would bid 1♥–(1♠)–3♥ and hand (b) 1♥–(1♠)–4♥. In neither case is the club suit of sufficient quality for a fit jump. Meanwhile, all limit raises or better can start with a 2♠ cuebid.

This simple system really doesn't have enough options in it. There are just too many different strengths and types of hand which we need to show. One possibility is to keep the cuebid as a limit raise and use 2NT as a game plus raise, thereby avoiding any ambiguity about hand strength. As mentioned earlier, a natural 2NT bid can make a negative double and then bid 2NT on the next round instead. That is an improvement on the first method, but one of the basic ideas of this new hyper-modern approach to competitive bidding is that it is hand-type and not strength which it is most important to define first.

Consider these hands:

(a) ♠ 7
♥ 8 7 6 5 3
♦ 10 5 4
♣ 7 6 3 2

(b) ♠ 7 5 2
♥ K Q 7 4
♦ 8
♣ 10 8 6 3 2

(c) ♠ 8 6
♥ A K J 4
♦ 8 7 4
♣ 6 5 4 3

(d) ♠ K 10 2
♥ K 9 7 5
♦ A 6
♣ 7 4 3 2

(e) ♠ Q J 4
♥ 10 7 6 5
♦ Q J 4
♣ K Q 3

(f) ♠ 7 5
♥ A Q 4 2
♦ 8 3
♣ K 9 7 6 5

(g) ♠ 8 6 3
♥ K Q 7 4
♦ 8
♣ A 9 8 6 5

(h) ♠ K J 7
♥ K 9 7 5
♦ A 6
♣ K 4 3 2

(i) ♠ Q J 4
♥ J 7 6 5
♦ A J 4
♣ K Q 3

(j) ♠ 7 5
♥ K Q 4 2
♦ A 8
♣ Q 10 7 6 5

All these hands might want to make either a limit or pre-emptive raise to the three or four level. Roughly speaking, hands (a) to (f) are worth a three level raise and hands (g) to (j) a four level raise. Yet look how different the hands are within each group. Is a division into two hand-types—pre-emptive or constructive—sufficient? Perhaps a better approach is to say that, instead of showing two different strengths of constructive raise, 2NT and the cuebid should be two different types of raises, both being of limit raise strength or better.

Remember that a factor which affects the total trick expectation on a deal is the purity or otherwise of each side's trump fit. The purer the combined trump holdings, the higher the total tricks available and the more likely it is that you should compete further. Conversely, the more impure the trump suits, the lower the total tricks available and the more likely you are to want to defend. A possible scheme then would be to play that a cuebid, 1♥–(1♠)–2♠ shows at least a limit raise with an impure hand and 1♥–(1♠)–2NT shows at least a limit raise and a pure hand.

There will, of course, be borderline hands on which you have to use your judgment, but you cannot expect miracles from any system. How would this method work with the example hands?

(a) ♠ 7
♥ 8 7 6 5 3
♦ 10 5 4
♣ 7 6 3 2

is, if anything, a pre-emptive raise to 3♥. I say, if anything, because, while you would clearly like to be able to bid 3♥ with this hand, it is significantly weaker than other hands with which you will also wish to bid 3♥. I would bid 3♥ with this hand, but worry that partner might expect more.

(b) ♠ 7 5 2
♥ K Q 7 4
♦ 8
♣ 10 8 6 3 2

is a clear pre-emptive 3♥ bid—reasonable offense, no defense.

(c) ♠ 8 6
♥ A K J 4
♦ 8 7 4
♣ 6 5 4 3

is also a pre-emptive 3♥ bid. The offense is a bit lacking, with no real distribution, but the purity of the trump holding and lack of defense suggest 3♥ rather than 2♥.

(d) ♠ K 10 2
♥ K 9 7 5
♦ A 6
♣ 7 4 3 2

(d) is a sound constructive raise to 3♥ and so must go via one of the limit plus raises. The lack of minor heart honors plus the spade holding suggest a defensive raise—2♠.

(e) ♠ Q J 4
♥ 10 7 6 5
♦ Q J 4
♣ K Q 3

(e) is about as revolting a constructive raise as we could imagine. All the warning signs are there, weak trumps, secondary honors in other suits including spades, no distribution—an extreme 2♠ type.

(f) ♠ 7 5
♥ A Q 4 2
♦ 8 3
♣ 9 7 6 5

(f) would have been a fit jump or non-jump hand had the clubs been better. As it is, it is a pure limit raise to 3♥ so bids 2NT.

(g) ♠ 8 6 3
♥ K Q 7 4
♦ 8
♣ A 9 8 6 5

(g) is either a pre-emptive jump to 4♥ or a pure constructive 4♥ hand. Had this been an uncontested auction, would you have raised to 4♥ or made a 4♦ splinter? If the latter, then in theory you should now be bidding 2NT. The problem with this is an auction which continues:

1♥	–	1♠	–	2NT	–	4♠
Pass	–	Pass	–	?		

Would you feel comfortable about showing your extra values with a double? I think not. Perhaps, with such a borderline hand, you would be better to raise straight to 4♥. If 4♠ comes back to you now, you can try a double to show a good defensive hand within the context of your 4♥ bid and partner will not be misled as to your hand-type.

(h) ♠ K J 7
♥ K 9 7 5
♦ A 6
♣ K 4 3 2

(h) is a constructive game raise but with two spade honors and no heart intermediates, it is a defensive one—bid 2♠.

(i) ♠ Q J 4
♥ J 7 6 5
♦ A J 4
♣ K Q 3

(i) is an extreme example of a defensive/impure game raise. As clear a 2♠ bid as you will see.

(j) ♠ 7 5
♥ K Q 4 2
♦ A 8
♣ Q 10 7 6 5

(j) would have been a fit jump with better clubs. As it is, it is best treated as a pure game raise—2NT.

In all cases, opener assumes that responder has only a three level limit raise initially. If he would be interested in a slam opposite a game plus raise, he should not bid a lazy 4♥, but should make some sort of cuebid to invite responder's cooperation. Where the opposition compete further, responder can show his extra values by doubling or by bidding again as seems appropriate. Remember though that partner already knows your hand-type. Don't bid again simply because your limit raise happens to be a pure one—didn't you show that already when you bid 2NT?—make sure you really do have something extra.

An Alternative Method

The split between cuebid and 2NT in the above auctions was decided by the degree of purity of responder's raise. This is one factor which affects the total tricks available on any deal. The other big factor is the actual number of trumps held by each side.

An alternative would be to play:

1♥–(1♠)–2NT	=	Limit raise plus with four trumps
2♠	=	Limit raise plus with only three trumps or possibly a very impure hand with four trumps.

If we played a five card major system, it would be easy enough to see that being able to differentiate between:

(a) ♠ 7 4	**(b)** ♠ 7 4
♥ K J 7 4	♥ K J 7
♦ K 6 3	♦ K 6 3 2
♣ K 10 8 5	♣ K J 8 5

could be very helpful to partner, aiding him in judging the total trick expectation for the deal. What about in a four card major system?

I am sure that most players would start off hand (b) with a negative double—after all, how can you possibly raise to the three level with only three card support. If the auction continues:

1♥	–	1♠	–	Dble	–	3/4♠
Pass–		Pass–		?		

you are not that well placed, as it will be hard for partner to expect you to have such a suitable hand for play in hearts. But if you can raise to the three level and at the same time show that you have only three card support, how can you get badly hurt? The situation is different if you play strong no trump and four card majors, but few readers will play that combination. If you play weak no trump, isn't opener marked with either five hearts or 15+HCP? In the former case you can afford to support him with only three cards, while with the latter you have game values between you and have plenty of time to explore the correct game. However the auction progresses, you are better placed than had you begun with an uninformative negative double.

You Open One of a Suit, They Make a Takeout Double

We looked at this situation in an earlier section, of course. Now that we have discovered fit jumps, I should say that there is a good case for playing:

1♥	–	Dble	–	2♠/3♣/♦
			–	3♠/4♣/♦

as fit jumps rather than splinter bids. After all, if you have support for partner, you know that the opposition are bound to have a fit also so the auction could easily become competitive.

Having also discovered the Law of Total Tricks, you should also now appreciate the importance of telling partner how many trumps you hold when you support him. There is no cuebid available as yet, but perhaps now those schemes for showing a three card raise; for example, 1♥–Dble–2♣ = 6–9 with three card support, begin to look more necessary.

One new way to handle this situation is to give up a natural 1NT bid and play transfer responses. So:

1♥–Double–1♠	=	Natural
1NT	=	Transfer to clubs – any strength
2♣	=	Transfer to diamonds – any strength
2♦	=	Transfer to hearts, at least three card support usually 6–9, but could be stronger in which case will raise to 3♥ next
2♥	=	Natural, weak four card raise – too balanced or impure for a 3♥ pre-empt

Responding to Partner's Overcall

If the sequence begins, 1♣–1♠–Pass–?, you can use all the same bids as if partner had opened the bidding and they had overcalled. You have already looked at fit jumps so the only other bids to check on are 2NT and the cuebids.

1♣–1♠–Pass–2♣ is simply a standard unassuming cuebid, showing a raise to 2♠ with three card support or perhaps a very impure hand with four spades.

Meanwhile, 2NT and 3♣ show limit plus raises, either with different numbers of trumps (four and three respectively), or 2NT a pure type and 3♣ impure. If you prefer the latter

version, then perhaps both should show four card support and limit raises with only three card support should begin with 2♣.

A sequence like:

1♣	–	1♠	–	Pass	–	2♣
Pass	–	2♠	–	Pass	–	3♠

would now show a three card limit raise.

Where the opposition have bid two suits, things may be easier.

For example, after:

1♣–(1♥)–1♠–2♣	=	Three card raise to 2♥
2♠	=	Three card raise to 3♥
2NT	=	Pure raise to 3♥ with four card support
3♣	=	Impure raise to 3♥ with four card support
3♦	=	Fit-jump
3♥	=	Pre-emptive
3♠/4♣	=	Splinter bids
4♦	=	Fit-jump
4♥	=	Pre-emptive

Raising a Weak Jump Overcall

When partner makes a weak jump overcall, it is far more likely that you are going to want to ask him about his hand than to describe your own if the third hand passes. 1♣–2♠–Pass–2NT is not some kind of spade raise. By far the simplest plan is to use 2NT here as an asking bid with exactly the same responses as if partner had opened with a weak two bid. Other responses are what you would expect them to be—3♠ is pre-emptive, 3♦/♥ natural and forcing, and 3♣ forcing and asking partner to bid 3NT with a club stopper and otherwise to make a descriptive rebid. They will be quite rare, but jumps to 4♣ are splinters and 4♦/♥ fit jumps.

If third hand makes a negative double, 1♣–2♠–Dble–? the chances are that unless you have spade support, you are going to end up on defense. A natural 3♦/♥ is quite an unlikely bid but, equally, to transfer captaincy to a hand which has made a weak jump overcall is not a normal thing to do, so fit non-jumps do not really apply either. Best is to play these bids as lead-directional, showing strength but not necessarily any real great length in the suit and a willingness to compete to 3♠. For example, bid 3♦ with:

♠ K 6 3
♥ 8 6 4 2
♦ K Q J 4
♣ J 8

Perhaps, this is as good a situation as any for the Rosenkranz Redouble, i.e. 1♣–2♠–Dble–Rdbl to show a top spade honor and encourage partner to lead that suit. Other strong hands can, after all, bid 2NT just as if the double had not occurred, or pass then make a penalty double on the next round, according to hand-type.

The Uncontested Auction

There is no reason at all why you cannot use fit jumps in uncontested auctions instead of splinters and mini-splinters.

However, if the auction remains uncontested, then splinters have two advantages over fit jumps. The first one is that splinter bids are more frequent. Any singleton will do, whereas to use a fit jump requires not only that you have a five card sidesuit, but also that most of your values are in the two suits. Secondly, splinter bids are good for hands which simply cannot be bid in any other descriptive way. At least when you hold a strong fit jump, you can use a delayed game raise sequence instead.

As for which is the bigger aid to judgment, it is hard to say. Certainly, fit jumps allow opener to judge how well he fits partner's sidesuit but, for game purposes, there is quite a difference between:

(a) 7 5 3   opposite (b) A J 10 6 2   and (c) K J 9 6 2

both of which would be acceptable suits for a fit jump. So while fit jumps may be very good at uncovering a necessary source of tricks for a slam, I am less convinced by their use to invite game, where merely holding length in responder's sidesuit will be good news if he holds (b) AJ1062, but you may need a fitting honor if instead he holds (c) KJ962.

Splinter bids, on the other hand, tell you whether or not you have wasted values opposite the shortage—A63 or 763 are good holdings for opener, KJ3 or AQ10 poor holdings—but they don't tell you if a particular honor card is working overtime. A fit jump can tell you that one of your KJ7 suits is a golden holding, while a splinter can merely tell you that one of those suits is wasted.

In a contested auction, the balance shifts somewhat. Your most likely singleton is in the suit your opponents are bidding—and partner hardly needs to hear a splinter bid to know to devalue any high cards he has there. Meanwhile, the dread double-fit hand looms and anything you can do to help your side to recognize this hand when it occurs has to be a good idea.

The proponents of fit jumps in the uncontested auction will argue, quite correctly, that just because one opponent has passed doesn't mean that the other one will also do so. If you have a fit for your partner, the opposition are sure to have a fit elsewhere so this is a "potentially contested auction," and you should utilize all the weapons you have at your disposal in a truly contested auction, just in case. They are right, of course, these are potentially contested auctions.

The odds are different, however. A contested auction will, by definition, always be contested, while a "potentially contested auction" will only sometimes be contested, often uncontested. It depends which of splinters and fit jumps really are the greater aid to judgment in uncontested auctions and how big an edge the winning method has. Is it sufficient to outweigh the edge fit jumps have when the auction does become contested?

Many people have their own personal view on the above question but I don't *know* the answer, and question whether anybody does. I leave you to make your own decision.

The purpose of any bidding convention is to be an aid to judgment. It can never simply replace judgment. Conventions should also be used in a disciplined fashion. Don't decide that, just this once, A9863 will be a good enough sidesuit for a fit jump. You could get lucky, but as soon as you start to bend the rules you take the risk that (a) you will help partner to misjudge rather than judge correctly and, (b) he will remember what you did and not trust you in the future, when you may be following the rules perfectly.

Usually, when you make a descriptive bid, you pass the captaincy of the hand to your partner. Sometimes, he will bring you back into the decision making, for example by initiating a cuebidding sequence. Other times, he will retain control to the end of the auction. A fit jump, for example, is designed to save your side a guess by giving your partner all the information he requires to make an intelligent and, hopefully, winning decision. To make such a descriptive bid and then to overrule partner is both stupid and insulting.

I have deliberately tried in this section simply to describe how a system works, not to produce a series of examples showing how wonderful it is. Of course, I could have created deals tailor-made for each and every one of the methods I have discussed. They would have proved nothing. *Any* method will work some of the time.

I have tried to give some feel for the plusses and minuses of playing each of the methods outlined. Often, these are only my personal prejudices, however, and, had someone else written this section, some of their conclusions would have been different from mine. Try to make up your own mind. Only remember, as I warned at the beginning, to consider not only the benefits of any new idea but also its costs.

Building an effective bidding system is both fascinating and challenging and requires work.

PART V

STEP-BY-STEP OVERCALLS
by Sally Brock

This section looks at the overcall, a fundamental tool of competitive bidding. The overcall involves four major steps.

The first step is to determine why you wish to enter the auction and what you are trying to achieve. Why not let your opponents get on with it particularly if it seems that you are outgunned?

The second step is to decide what you are going to bid. In this chapter we look at the requirements for such basic initiatives as the simple overcall, the jump overcall, the 1NT overcall and the take-out double. Also considered are bidding over one-level openings in a suit, 1NT openings, strong club openings and pre-emptive openings of various kinds.

Step three discusses your reaction to your partner's overcalls. Sometimes you may want to try to bid to your own best contract; at others you may simply want to make life as difficult as possible for your opponents.

The fourth and final step looks at what you do when your opponents continue to bid.

All the full-deal examples in this section come from real games. It is all too easy when writing about overcalls to give examples which are too pure. What is a minimum one spade overcall? Less than opening values with a good five-card suit.

Perhaps:

♠ K Q 10 9 5
♥ 6
♦ A 6 5 2
♣ 8 7 3

That is all very well, but in real life we are not dealt the perfect hand very often. In this section we consider what we do when the suit is not necessarily good and when the hand is not exactly what we would like. We consider the best option when none of the options is attractive.

And, as in any other area of bidding, there is not always a right answer. Much is a matter of opinion and style and it is often surprising how greatly the experts disagree. When I think an issue is clear-cut and one on which most experts would agree, I try to make this clear; where it is a matter of opinion I have tried to outline the various choices, particularly in the answers to the quizzes at the end of Chapters 27 and 28.

Most auctions are contested; about 75 percent have both sides taking part in one way or another. Your opponents will always try to make your life as difficult as possible and it is important to learn how to make their lives equally miserable.

Step One: Why Overcall ?

When you first pick up your hand, the odds are even as to which side has the balance of high cards and who can make the higher contract, whether it be part score, game or slam. Almost every player knows that to open the bidding (at the one level in any event) you need in the region of 12 high-card points (HCP) or more, i.e. a little more than your allotted average of 10. This is because if partner also has what is now his average—i.e. $40 - 12 = 28$ divided by $3 = 9\frac{1}{3}$—you will have the majority of the HCP, and therefore, all other things being equal, should be able to make more tricks than your opponents. In an uninterrupted auction you continue to exchange information before eventually coming to rest in a final contract. When you are given a "free run" your bidding should be reasonably accurate and you should usually land in a decent contract, particularly at higher levels.

Let's look at the other side of the coin. Your right-hand opponent (RHO) has opened the bidding at the one level, showing 12 or more HCP. It is now likely that *their* side has the balance of high cards and given a free run their bidding should be reasonably accurate and they should usually arrive at a decent contract, particularly at higher levels.

Your reasons for bidding have multiplied.

THE REASONS FOR OVERCALLING

1. Bidding your own cards to the right contract

This is always a good reason for bidding whether or not your opponents are also in the auction. When there is good reason to suppose that your side has the balance of high cards or particularly good distribution you should always bid in order to try to reach your own best contract, whether it be part score or game or, occasionally, slam.

East/West Vulnerable. Dealer South.

```
              ♠ J 8 7
              ♥ J 8
              ♦ Q 10 7 3
              ♣ Q 10 7 6
♠ A K 9 4 3              ♠ 10 6
♥ K 7 6 4               ♥ Q 5
♦ J 6 2                ♦ A K 9 8 5
♣ 2                    ♣ J 5 4 3
              ♠ Q 5 3
              ♥ A 10 9 3 2
              ♦ 4
              ♣ A K 9 8
```

This hand comes from a North American board-a-match event (a team event, but the scoring is like matchpoints), where it is crucial to score as large a plus (or as small a minus) as possible.

West	North	East	South
–	–	–	1♥
1♠	Dble(*)	2♦	3♣
3♦	All Pass		

(*) negative

Although North/South would not have succeeded in their three club contract, it was crucial for East/West to bid to their making diamond part score. Declarer had no difficulty in making ten tricks, alerted to the distribution of the trump suit by the bidding.

Once RHO has announced opening values, the chances are slim that your side has the 25 HCP or so that you need to make game without a fit. It is much more likely that you can make game because you have a good fit when you need less high cards. It is more likely that you have a good fit when you have good distribution, therefore the main criterion for bidding after an opposing opening bid is good distribution not simply high-card strength.

While bidding will help you to locate a fit and thus know when to be prepared to bid at a high level, it may also help you to identify lack of fit. The following deal comes from the 1994 European Mixed Teams Championship:

East/West Vulnerable. Dealer East.

```
              ♠ K Q 9 7 6
              ♥ 6 4
              ♦ J
              ♣ K 7 6 5 2
♠ A 2                        ♠ J 10 5 3
♥ Q J 10 9 8                 ♥ A K 5 2
♦ Q 9 7 2                    ♦ 10 5 4
♣ 10 3                       ♣ A 4
              ♠ 8 4
              ♥ 7 3
              ♦ A K 8 6 3
              ♣ Q J 9 8
```

Open Room:

West	North	East	South
–	–	1♣	1♦
1♥	1♠	2♥	Pass
4♥	All Pass		

Closed Room:

West	North	East	South
–	–	1♥	Pass
4♥	4♠	Dble	All Pass

In the closed room, the pre-emptive nature of East's one heart opening stopped South from overcalling her diamonds. When West jumped to four hearts North had to guess and he naturally chose to bid his spades. Four spades doubled went two down.

In the open room, South could overcall diamonds at the one level and even if West had jumped to four hearts, North would have been warned against bidding because of his singleton diamond. As it was, four hearts went one down. This deal is a good advertisement for four-card majors!

2. Trying to score as small a minus score as possible

If you can't bid your own cards to your best contract, then you must try to achieve as small a minus score as possible. Suppose your opponents can make two hearts. If you bid two spades you will still show a profit providing you do not lose more than 100. If you are vulnerable and go one down in two spades, the opponents need to double to make this a losing action.

Similarly, if your opponents can make game, you want to sacrifice whenever it costs less than their game.

North/South Vulnerable. Dealer East.

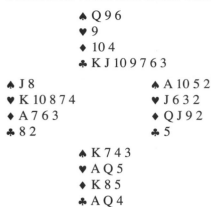

```
              ♠ Q 9 6
              ♥ 9
              ♦ 10 4
              ♣ K J 10 9 7 6 3
♠ J 8                        ♠ A 10 5 2
♥ K 10 8 7 4                 ♥ J 6 3 2
♦ A 7 6 3                    ♦ Q J 9 2
♣ 8 2                        ♣ 5
              ♠ K 7 4 3
              ♥ A Q 5
              ♦ K 8 5
              ♣ A Q 4
```

West	North	East	South
–	–	Pass	1♣
1♥	2♣(*)	3♣	3NT
Pass	Pass	4♥	4NT
Dble	All Pass		

(*) forcing

Many Wests passed with their minimal values and were soon on lead against 3NT. Nobody found the defense of a spade to the ace and the queen of diamonds switch. It was much easier to take four defensive tricks. Note that with some good guessing East/West may even make four hearts!

3. Making life difficult for your opponents

Even if your opponents have considerably more HCP than you do and if they can make a great many more tricks than you can, if you can get into the auction you can take away some of their bidding space. If your RHO opens one club his partner can respond anything from one diamond upwards; if, on the other hand, you intervene with one spade, he now can no longer bid one diamond, one heart or one spade. You have removed some of his bidding space, hopefully to your advantage.

Obviously, you have to be careful not to bid unless you have some playing strength or you will just be doubled and lose a large penalty, which may well score more than your opponents' best contract.

Perhaps the pros and cons of overcalling on marginal hands can be demonstrated by these two boards from the same match in the 1992 Junior European Championships. The North/South pair were Norway's Torp and Aaseng who had a reputation for living dangerously. They overcalled on both hands while their Swedish counterparts in the other room did not.

North/South Vulnerable. Dealer East.

```
              ♠ J 2
              ♥ Q J 9 8 4
              ♦ 8
              ♣ A Q 10 8 5
♠ A K 10 7 3              ♠ Q 9 8 4
♥ K 10 7 2               ♥ 6 3
♦ Q 4                    ♦ A 10 6
♣ K J                    ♣ 9 4 3 2
              ♠ 6 5
              ♥ A 5
              ♦ K J 9 7 5 3 2
              ♣ 7 6
```

Open Room:

West	North	East	South
	Torp		*Aaseng*
–	–	Pass	Pass
1♠	2♥	3♠	4♥
Dble	All Pass		

Closed Room:

West	North	East	South
–	–	Pass	Pass
1♠	Pass	2♠	3♦
3♥	Dble	3♠	All Pass

North did not play four hearts to best advantage and ended up down five for a 1400 penalty while his opponents could not even make game.

Both Sides Vulnerable. Dealer East.

```
              ♠ J 4
              ♥ A 9 6 3 2
              ♦ A J 8
              ♣ A 6 2
♠ 10 5 3 2               ♠ A K 9 8 6
♥ Q J                    ♥ –
♦ 9 4                    ♦ Q 10 6 5
♣ K J 8 5 4              ♣ Q 10 9 3
              ♠ Q 7
              ♥ K 10 8 7 5 4
              ♦ K 7 3 2
              ♣ 7
```

Open Room:

West	North	East	South
	Torp		*Aaseng*
–	–	1♠	2♥
2♠	3♠	Pass	4♥
All Pass			

Closed Room:

West	North	East	South
–	–	1♠	Pass
2♠	Pass	3♠	All Pass

This time four hearts made exactly while three spades made an overtrick when North/South did not find their club ruff.

The less information RHO has imparted with his opening bid, the more reason there is to live dangerously and bid on slender values. At the one extreme your opponent may have opened 1NT, informing his partner of his HCP strength and that he has a balanced hand . Any intervention by your side is unlikely to cause too much of a problem—his partner can double when he also is balanced, or bid a suit when he has some distribution. At the other end of the scale there is the strong club opening bid – all this has done is to inform the whole table that opener has an unspecified strong hand. This is surely the time to bid as much as possible, particularly when the vulnerability is favorable.

In uninterrupted auctions, most pairs have a reasonably good bidding system of which they are fairly confident. As soon as there is intervention they are on less firm ground. A top class pair may have a number of precise agreements when left to their own devices—relays, asking bids, etc.— but some of these have to go by the board in the face of heavy intervention. A weaker pair may suddenly have doubts when they are faced with a less familiar situation. For example, suppose a 1NT rebid shows 15-17 after, say, 1♦ – Pass – 1♥ – Pass, what about a 2NT rebid after 1♦ – 1♠ – 2♥ – Pass? Is this still strong? If so, what does opener do with a 4-1-4-4 12-count? If the 2NT rebid is weak then responder needed more to bid two hearts in the first place. Suddenly a number of awkward questions present themselves.

4. Helping with the opening lead

Okay, so your RHO has opened one club. You do not have a very good hand so you do not expect to make game. Even a low-level part score looks unappealing; your suit is diamonds so you cannot even take any bidding space away from your opponents. What other reason may there be for bidding? Well, it is unlikely that the final contract will be in clubs; it is much more likely to be in no trumps or a major and it may well be your left-hand opponent (LHO) who becomes declarer. In this eventuality it may well be a good idea to try to help partner with his opening lead.

The following hand comes from the 1994 Junior European Championships and resulted in a swing against the eventual winners, Great Britain:

North/South Vulnerable. Dealer East.

```
              ♠ K 8 3
              ♥ A 5 3 2
              ♦ 6
              ♣ J 9 7 5 4
♠ 6 2                        ♠ Q 7 4
♥ Q 6 4                      ♥ K J
♦ K 9 4 2                    ♦ A Q 8 7 5
♣ A K Q 8                    ♣ 10 3 2
              ♠ A J 10 9 5
              ♥ 10 9 8 7
              ♦ J 10 3
              ♣ 6
```

In the Open Room, the British South did not bid over East's one diamond opening. West jumped to 3NT and North, understandably, failed to lead a spade. 3NT made nine tricks.

In the Closed Room, East opened a weak 1NT which West raised directly to game. South found it easy to lead a spade and beat the contract by two.

Even if it turns out to be your opening lead you may be influenced by whether partner has supported your overcall.

These then are the main reasons for bidding when the opponents have opened. As in any other situation, you should never make a bid without having some idea about what you are trying to achieve. Every time you enter an auction after opponents have opened you should have at least one of these four aims in mind.

These are the good things that can happen; there is also a negative side.

THE DANGERS OF OVERCALLING

1. You may lose a sizable penalty

Just like Aaseng and Torp on the first of the two deals.

2. Your bidding may actually help the opponents

If your side bids and finds a fit, the opponents will know that they have no wasted cards in that suit, e.g. an opponent with, say, three small cards in a suit you have bid and supported enthusiastically will know that his partner probably only has a singleton. They will be able to value, say, a king sitting "over" one of your suits more highly than one sitting "under."

Both Sides Vulnerable. Dealer East.

```
              ♠ Q 8 7
              ♥ Q J 8
              ♦ K 4 3 2
              ♣ Q 9 6
♠ A J 10 6                   ♠ 9 3 2
♥ K 7 3                      ♥ A 10 9 6 5 2
♦ 10 7 6                     ♦ A Q J
♣ 8 4 2                      ♣ 5
              ♠ K 5 4
              ♥ 4
              ♦ 9 8 5
              ♣ A K J 10 7 3
```

West	North	East	South
–	–	1♥	2♣
2♥	3♣	3♥	Pass
4♥	All Pass		

East/West were playing a five-card major system so it was reasonable for West to support hearts immediately. Although East's three hearts was merely a competitive gesture, West pushed on to the good game, confident that his partner had some extra playing strength with no wasted club values. There is virtually no chance that East/West would have bid game if left to their own devices.

Here North/South's bidding was quite reasonable. South's overcall looks clear-cut and North has enough high cards to suggest that game is unlikely for his opponents. Nevertheless their actions did not turn out well.

3. You may help declarer in the play

If you bid and one of your opponents eventually becomes declarer, he may be able to use information in the play that you have given him in the bidding.

Look at Graham Kirby at work in this hand from the 1993 European Championships:

North/South Vulnerable. Dealer East.

```
              ♠ 3
              ♥ J 8 2
              ♦ 9 6
              ♣ Q J 10 9 8 4 3
♠ K 9 7                      ♠ A J 10 8 6 5
♥ 10 6                       ♥ A K Q 9 5
♦ A Q 8 5                    ♦ 7
♣ K 7 6 5                    ♣ 2
              ♠ Q 4 2
              ♥ 7 4 3
              ♦ K J 10 4 3 2
              ♣ A
```

West	North	East	South
Armstrong	*Perron*	*Kirby*	*Chemla*
–	–	1♣(*)	1♦
1NT	2♣	2♠	Pass
2NT	Pass	3♥	Pass
3♠	Pass	4♣	Pass
4♦	Pass	4♥	Pass
5♣	Pass	5♥	Pass
6♦	Pass	6♠	All Pass

(*) strong

South led the ace of clubs and switched to the three of hearts (playing 3rd and 5th leads). Kirby won in his hand, played a diamond to the ace and ruffed a diamond. He believed that the distribution was as it was so he cashed the ace of spades and played a spade to the nine. He soon claimed twelve tricks to land his slam.

The following deal is another example of brilliant declarer play inspired by the opponent's bidding:

Neither Side Vulnerable. Dealer East.

```
                    ♠ K 5
                    ♥ K Q 9 6 3
                    ♦ 4 2
                    ♣ A 9 7 3
  ♠ A Q 8 3 2                      ♠ 9 6
  ♥ J 7 4                          ♥ A 8 5
  ♦ A Q 7                          ♦ K 10 9 6 5 3
  ♣ Q J                            ♣ K 8
                    ♠ J 10 7 4
                    ♥ 10 2
                    ♦ J 8
                    ♣ 10 6 5 4 2
```

West	North	East	South
–	–	1♦	Pass
1♠	2♥	Pass	Pass
3♥	Pass	3NT	All Pass

3NT played by West would have been unbeatable, but it is hard to be too critical of East/West's bidding. South led the ten of hearts and declarer ducked two rounds before winning with the ace. He now ran six rounds of diamonds to reach the following end position:

```
                    ♠ K 5
                    ♥ K 6
                    ♦ –
                    ♣ A
  ♠ A Q 8                          ♠ 9 6
  ♥ –                              ♥ –
  ♦ –                              ♦ –
  ♣ Q                              ♣ K
                    ♠ J 10 7
                    ♥ –
                    ♦ –
                    ♣ 10
```

North has yet to make a discard and he is squeezed. He was a good player and although he discarded a small spade very smoothly, East played him for all the missing high cards—after all he had overcalled with only a five-card suit. Declarer dropped the king of spades and made his contract.

4. You may dissuade partner from making his natural, winning lead

If you bid with a poor suit partner may choose to lead that suit rather than make his natural opening lead which may have been more successful.

With all these disasters just waiting to happen, it is important that you have some good reasons for entering the auction—the good needs to outweigh the bad.

THE LAW OF TOTAL TRICKS

The Law of Total Tricks states that the sum of both sides' best fit added together equals the total number of tricks available on the hand.

That may be a succinct statement, but perhaps it is not very clear. Here is an example: suppose your side has a nine-card heart fit and the opponents have an eight-card spade fit, then the number of tricks they can make if they play in spades added to the number of tricks you can make if you play in hearts is 8 + 9 = 17. So, if in a competitive auction you are considering bidding three hearts over an opposing two spades you should do so. Most of the time both contracts will make, but if one of them goes one down then the other will make with an overtrick.

So, is this a magic formula which will tell you whether to bid in all circumstances? No, it is not, but it is surprisingly accurate and its application in competitive sequences will almost certainly improve your accuracy in these areas.

Of course, the main drawback with the law is that it is not always possible to judge how good a fit your own side has, let alone the opponents. However, there are some guidelines to help. More often than not, the opponents will have as good a fit as you do; nearly always their fit will only be one card more or less than yours. Therefore if you have a nine-card fit, usually they will also have a nine-card fit, but most often it will be eight or ten cards.

As long as you know how good your fit is, you can guess theirs with reasonable accuracy; alternatively, if you have a fair idea of their fit, you can guess at yours.

It is important that, as far as is possible, you structure your competitive bidding to make sure that you know the strength of your own fit. Only then can you guess at theirs and judge when to continue bidding in competitive sequences.

You will also see that when the opponents bid pre-emptively they are very likely to have a good fit, which means that your side also has a good fit, thus making it safer to bid, even with limited values.

Step Two: What to Overcall?

Whenever both sides are bidding there is always the possibility that one side or the other will find a fit and that the bidding may suddenly be bounced up a level or two. For that reason it is important to make as descriptive a bid as possible on the first round, hopefully enabling partner to judge accurately should he have to make a high-level decision when it is his turn. As the Law of Total Tricks suggests, it is more important to bid to the limit of your fit rather than the limit suggested by your high cards. It is more important to try to describe your distribution than your strength.

The rules are fairly straightforward: bid a suit when you have a suit, bid no trumps when you have a balanced hand, make a take-out double when you have the values to want to bid with support for all the other suits.

1NT OVERCALL

As described earlier, you needed 12 HCP to open because then, when partner has his share, you will have just over 21 HCP between you and could expect to make more tricks than your opponents.

However, when an opponent has shown 12 or 13 HCP, you need 15 for partner's average (6) to combine with yours to average 21. When you have less, there is no premium in bidding. Unless either side has a fit, if you are only going to make seven tricks, say, in 1NT, you might as well take them in defense as when playing the hand. It is only because the possibility of a game bonus exists that there is any point in choosing to declare no trumps rather than to defend.

A 1NT overcall in second seat shows a good 15 to 18 HCP and a balanced hand with at least one stopper in the suit opened.

In fourth position, i.e. after one of a suit followed by two passes, a 1NT bid can be much weaker. Now you are in a balancing position and, knowing that partner has some values, most pairs choose a wider range like 11-15.

If both opponents have bid, e.g. after 1♦ – Pass – 1♥, a 1NT

overcall needs to be stronger than in direct position because it is less likely that partner has any values. 17-19 would be a sensible range to adopt.

Bidding after partner's 1NT overcall is easy. Today most tournament players bid just as if they had opened 1NT. Most pairs have a well-defined method after a 1NT opening and still use it even when the 1NT bid is an overcall.

TAKEOUT DOUBLE

A takeout double is not really an overcall and is discussed in depth elsewhere in this book. It is mentioned here only to explain that there is a possible course of action on a hand that is not suitable for any other action.

A double of a one-level opening bid shows one of two hand-types:

1. Opening bid values with shortage in the suit opened (at most a doubleton) and support (at least three cards) for the other three suits.

2. A hand that is too strong for any other action, perhaps a balanced hand of 19 or more HCP, or a distributional hand with 18 or more HCP or the equivalent, too strong for an overcall.

A one-level overcall in a major should always be preferred to a takeout double, unless the hand is extremely strong. However, with 5-3-3-2 or 5-4-3-1 distribution with a five-card minor and shortage in the suit opened it would be normal to start with a takeout double on any hand with at least opening values.

TWO-SUITED OVERCALLS

The traditional meaning of a cuebid of the opponent's suit was a strong (virtually game-forcing) distributional hand. This could be single- or two-suited. Over the years, however, it was found that the frequency of such a bid was low and that it would be more useful if it described a more common hand-type.

Most tournament players use a direct cuebid to show a two-suiter, sometimes a specific two-suiter and sometimes to show the other major and an unspecified minor. This is allied to a 2NT overcall which shows the two lowest unbid suits. Some of the people who like a cuebid to show a specific two-suiter, also use a three club overcall to show a specific two-suiter.

In this part we will only consider Michaels cuebids allied to an unusual 2NT overcall. Thus:

Opening bid	1♣	1♦	1♥	1♠
The cuebid shows	Majors	Majors	Spades+ a minor	Hearts + a minor
2NT shows	Diamonds + Hearts	Clubs + Hearts	Minors	Minors

A Michaels cuebid, by definition, suggests that there is some wild distribution. If you have a fit and are not about to go for a significant penalty, then it is probable that your opponents also have a fit and might be about to make life difficult for you. It is essential that you know who has the balance of points. After a sequence such as:

West	North	East	South
1♥	2♥	4♥	

you need to know whether it is North or East who is light and distributional. Consequently, it is important to have fairly strict rules about the strength required for a Michaels cuebid. It should either be made with a weak hand (comparable to a weak jump overcall) or with significant extra values (always intending to make another bid). Making the cuebid on the in-between hands should be avoided.

Here are some examples of hands from world championship play where some expert players have used a two-suited overcall.

♠ A 9 4 3 2 With Both Sides Vulnerable, after a one heart
♥ 9 3 opening by East, both Souths cuebid
♦ - two hearts with this collection. Both major-suit
♣ J 9 8 6 5 3 games were making, so, to achieve par, East/ West had to be pushed to five hearts one down.

♠ A J 7 3 2 At favorable vulnerability, both Souths cuebid
♥ Q 9 6 5 4 two diamonds after East's one diamond
♦ - to opening. Four hearts was cold for North/South,
♣ 10 5 but both East/Wests bid on five diamonds. The British North doubled and collected 500, but the Americans at the other table pressed on to five hearts going down one.

♠ 10 9 5 4 2 Not many Souths cuebid two diamonds on this
♥ K J 8 5 4 hand, even at favorable vulnerability, but
♦ 9 4 those who did were soon in four spades and
♣ 3 then the best East/West could do was collect 300. The Souths who passed lost 660 to East/ West's 3NT.

Just as with any other overcall, there should always be a purpose behind bidding. A two-suited overcall is descriptive and gives away a great deal of information—to both sides. If your opponents end up as the declaring side they are likely to be helped in the play, so you need to have a real expectation of becoming the declaring side before using such a bid. Remember, there is no reason why you should not first bid one of the suits, intending to rebid the other on the next round.

♠ A Q J 9 5 With Both Sides Vulnerable, South overcalled
♥ 3 one spade after East's one diamond opening.
♦ 10 5 West made a negative double and North raised
♣ A J 10 7 5 to two spades. Now South made a game try of three clubs and eventually went on to four spades, a good sacrifice against four hearts.

♠ K After two passes, East opened one spade and
♥ A J 9 7 2 South chose to overcall two hearts at
♦ K 6 unfavorable vulnerability. This was partly
♣ J 10 9 8 4 because his hand was not really good enough to force his side to the three level, but also because he did not want to help his opponents either in the bidding or the play.

It is rarely a good idea to make a two-suited overcall with a six-card major and a five-card minor because partner is likely to give preference to the minor. It is usually better simply to overcall in the major, with a jump if appropriate. Even with both majors, when the spades are longer and stronger than the hearts it usually works better to overcall spades because, after a two-suited overcall, partner will give preference to hearts with equal length. In addition, partner is unlikely to underestimate the playing strength of the hand.

Consider the following deal:

Neither Side Vulnerable. Dealer West.

```
              ♠ K
              ♥ K Q 6
              ♦ 7 3 2
              ♣ A 9 7 4 3 2
♠ J 8 4 3                    ♠ A Q 10 7 6 5
♥ 9 8                        ♥ J 10 4 3 2
♦ K 10 8 6                   ♦ J
♣ J 10 8                     ♣ 6
              ♠ 9 2
              ♥ A 7 5
              ♦ A Q 9 5 4
              ♣ K Q 5
```

At one table East made a two-suited overcall after North's one club opening:

West	North	East	South
Pass	1♣	2♦(*)	3♦
Pass	3NT	All Pass	

(*) both majors

After South's natural three diamond call, North took a shot at 3NT and East, naturally enough, did not lead the ace of spades so declarer made eleven tricks.

At the other table East found a more sensible one spade overcall:

West	North	East	South
Pass	1♦	1♠	Double
2♠	3♣	4♠	4NT
Pass	5♦	Pass	6♦
All Pass			

North's one diamond opening was necessitated because of North/South's strong club system and South could not make a forcing bid in diamonds on the first round. Thereafter East/West took all the bidding space away and North/South misjudged to end up in the no-play slam.

JUMP CUEBID

For many years a jump cuebid was played as natural, but, as with a simple cuebid, hands that qualify for making such a bid are few and far between. Today a jump cuebid usually means partner is being asked to bid 3NT with a stopper in the opponent's suit. The hand will usually be based on a long solid suit with the other suits guarded. For example:

♠ K
♥ 9
♦ Q 9 8 6
♣ A K Q 10 8 6 2

A jump cuebid after RHO opened one heart led to partner declaring 3NT, which he was allowed to make; the five club contract reached in the other room had no play.

JUMP OVERCALLS

The strength of a jump overcall is a matter for partnership agreement and there are many differences of opinion, varying from weak through intermediate to strong. Often partnerships choose different strengths at the various vulnerabilities. Here we will be mainly concerned with weak jump overcalls. This is for several reasons:

1. Weak jump overcalls are currently in vogue among the world's top players.

2. Weak jump overcalls fit well with the philosophy that it is important to get into the auction as early and at as high a level as possible, in order to wreak maximum havoc when you have hands with good playing strength but limited defensive potential.

3. Weak jump overcalls are more limited because of the intermediate/strong single-suited hands that have to be dealt with in some other way – if you can cope with weak jump overcalls then there should be no problem in coping with their stronger cousins.

Although the jump overcall is referred to as "weak" it is not suicidal. Some people are afraid to play weak jump over-calls vulnerable because they have the idea that this means that they will go for large penalties when they overcall one

spade with three clubs on AQxxxx in clubs and nothing else! Well, if they made such an overcall they might well go for a large penalty! But the requirements for a weak jump overcall, just like any other pre-emptive bid, depend on the level at which it is made and the vulnerability. When the opponents are non-vulnerable, the worst that should happen is a 300 penalty; when they are vulnerable a 500 penalty is acceptable. Thus AQxxxx and nothing else would be fine for a two-level weak jump at favorable vulnerability, but would be completely absurd vulnerable at the three level.

Even if you choose to play weak jump overcalls throughout there are two situations when it is not sensible:

1. After a pre-emptive opening—"never pre-empt a pre-emptor!" After a weak bid it is probably your hand anyway so there is little to be gained by taking away your own bidding space. After a pre-empt all jumps should be strong.

2. In the balancing position—after an opening bid and two passes—it is unlikely that our opponents are going to want to do a great deal more bidding. In this situation it is best to play a jump overcall as intermediate, i.e. opening bid values with a good six-card suit—with a stronger hand double, with a weaker hand make a simple overcall.

Here are some examples of sensible weak jump overcalls at the various vulnerabilities:

♠ A Q 6 5 3 2
♥ 7 3
♦ 8 7 2
♣ 10 4

Bid two spades over one heart at favorable vulnerability. Vulnerable you would want better spade spot cards and preferably a singlton in an outside suit.

♠ 7 6
♥ 4
♦ K 10 8 3
♣ K Q J 9 8 4

Bid three clubs over one heart or one spade at all vulnerabilities except unfavorable four-card side-suit makes the hand quite powerful.

♠ 7
♥ A Q J 10 7 6 2
♦ K 7 6
♣ 8 2

Over a one spade opening bid, bid three hearts vulnerable or four hearts non-vulnerable.

The above hands all have fairly normal distribution and it is reasonably easy to calculate their playing strength. Sometimes the distribution is more extreme and you have to be more speculative:

♠ Q J 10 9 6 5
♥ 5
♦ A 10 7 6 3
♣ 8

Bid two spades over one club or one heart vulnerable, but non-vulnerable the good distribution should persuade you to try three spades.

There is a trend at the moment to devalue weak jump overcalls, particularly at favorable vulnerability. Some players would choose to overcall a weak two spades over an opening in another suit with a hand like:

♠ K J 10 9 7
♥ 4 3 2
♦ 7
♣ Q 10 7 6

There is no doubt that such actions can work well. However, where they tend to fail is not because they go for large penalties, but because partner misjudges and bids too much at high levels. He is trying to guess when to bid and when to defend and all he has to help him is the Law of Total Tricks. To use this successfully he has to make assumptions about the length of your suit. If you have a card less than he expects he is likely to make the wrong decision. Not only will he make the wrong decision this time but next time, when you have a six-card suit, he may undercompete because he is afraid that you have this hand.

My advice is that if you wish to make a weak jump overcall on this hand you need the agreement that such a bid *shows* only a five-card suit—with a "normal" weak jump you must overcall at the three level.

THE SIMPLE OVERCALL

At last we come to what is probably the most common action, the simple overcall. You have seen what it is not, now you need to look at what it is.

One-Level Overcalls

A simple overcall at the one level should not be taken very seriously, particularly if it is in spades and the opening bid is in a minor. Even in these days of negative doubles, opponents are usually inconvenienced by having some of their bidding space removed.

No partnership in the world bids as well when there is intervention as when they have a free run. The advent of negative doubles has made life a little easier but by no means solves all the problems. Different bidding systems are more susceptible to different types of intervention but here are some of the problems that can occur.

Let us first suppose that our opponents play a weak no trump and that they open a four-card major whenever they are outside their no trump range and have two four-card suits. First let us suppose that their agreement is that a negative double after 1♣/1♦ – 1♠ guarantees four hearts.

♠ 7 4 3	♠ A K 5
♥ A J 5	♥ 10 4 2
♦ K 10 6	♦ A Q 7 4
♣ 6 4 3 2	♣ Q 10 7

Without intervention East would open one diamond and West would respond 1NT and that would be the end. Look at the effect of a one spade overcall. What does West bid? 1NT without a spade stopper? Two clubs on such a dreadful four-card suit? Two diamonds with only three-card support? In truth, this last is probably the most sensible choice, but it does not result in a very sensible contract, particularly at matchpoint scoring.

Now let us suppose a negative double does not guarantee four hearts:

♠ 7 4 3	♠ 8
♥ A J 5 2	♥ K 10 6 3
♦ K 10 6	♦ A 8 7 3
♣ 6 4 3	♣ A Q 7 5

Without intervention East/West might happily bid 1♦ – 1♥ – 2♥. What if South overcalls one spade? West makes a negative double which does not guarantee four hearts. North bids two spades. What should East do? Bid three hearts and risk partner having your first example hand or pass and risk a negative part score swing when partner actually has this hand?

A weak no trump, four-card major system works well with this kind of hand (it does not fare so well in many other situations). With a strong no trump five-card major base, the problems are worse.

First, suppose that the negative double promises four hearts:

| ♠ 7 4 3 |
| ♥ A J 5 |
| ♦ 6 4 3 2 |
| ♣ K 10 6 |

Without intervention, 1♣ – 1NT is perfect. After a one spade overcall West has an even worse problem than before because the one club opening is frequently made on a three-card suit so he doesn't even have a raise to fall back on. He really has no option but to pass, but this can cause dreadful problems on the next round when his distribution will still be unprepossessing and he will worry about his undisclosed high cards.

So, let us suppose the negative double delivers no guarantees about heart length. What is opener to do after 1♣ – 1♠ – Double – Pass, with:

| ♠ A 10 5 |
| ♥ K Q 6 4 |
| ♦ 10 9 5 |
| ♣ A 9 4 |

Does he bid two hearts and find he is facing the example hand? Or does he bid 1NT and find you have:

| ♠ 7 4 |
| ♥ J 10 8 7 (5) |
| ♦ A J 4 (2) |
| ♣ Q 6 5 |

The overcaller's reasons for bidding are good ones, particularly when significant bidding space can be appropriated. You should always strain to bid spades, whatever the opening bid. There is a great premium on holding the highest-ranking suit. A spade sacrifice can be made at the same level as the heart game and forces the opponents to the five level if they decide to bid on.

If you are bidding spades over a minor it is more important to have a suit that you want led than if you bid over a one heart overcall. The final contract is likely to be in a major or no trumps and if you are leading it doesn't matter if you have overstated your suit.

If you had to put a point-count requirement on a one-level overcall, 8 HCP non-vulnerable and 10 vulnerable would be about right. That is what partner should assume you have if intending to bid without a fit. That is not to say that you cannot bid with less if you are taking away space and if you have good distribution and a good suit.

Here are some examples of one-level overcalls:

♠ K 6	Bid one diamond over one club at any
♥ A 5 4 3	vulnerability. Although, you are not
♥ A 5 4 3	depriving the opponents of any bidding
♦ A J 9 8 2	space, you have a fair suit and sufficient
♣ J 5	values to hope that your side can make
	something.

♠ 7 2	Bid one heart over one club or one
♥ K 8 7 6 4	diamond at any vulnerability. Although
♦ A 5 2	you would like the suit to be stronger you
♣ A 10	can't have everything and the overcall
	strength justifies an overcall.

♠ 10 7 4	You would not be ashamed of a one heart
♥ K Q 10 7 5	overcall at any vulnerability. In fact at the
♦ A 6 4 2	table, one heart was doubled and went 800
♣ 10	down, but the opponents could make a
	small slam in clubs.

♠ A J 9 8 3	Again, the suit is good and you would be
♥ 10 8 7 6	happy to overcall one spade over any
♦ 8 5	opening at any vulnerability.
♣ A 7	

♠ A 10 7 3 2	This is just about worth a one spade
♥ K 10 7 6	overcall, even vulnerable. Some experts
♦ J 5	believe in bidding even more friskily with
♣ Q 5	length in the opponent's suit. This is
	because there is more reason to push the
	opponents to too high a level if you think
	you can defeat the contract they eventu-
	ally reach.

These hands are not controversial. Most top players would overcall on all of them. Here are a few examples of one-level overcalls that would not receive universal approval, but nevertheless turned out to be winning actions:

Neither Side Vulnerable. Dealer North.

```
            ♠ 9
            ♥ J 6 4 3
            ♦ Q 5
            ♣ A K J 9 6 5
♠ K 7 3 2              ♠ Q 5 4
♥ –                    ♥ A 10 8 5 2
♦ A K 10 7 2           ♦ 9 6 4
♣ 8 7 4 2              ♣ 10 3
            ♠ A J 10 8 6
            ♥ K Q 9 7
            ♦ J 8 3
            ♣ Q
```

This deal cropped up in the Great Britain versus Japan match in the qualifying rounds of the 1991 World Championship. In the Closed Room North/South bid to four hearts. West cashed the ace and king of diamonds and switched to a spade to the queen and ace. The king of hearts was ducked and then declarer cashed the jack of diamonds, the queen of clubs and ruffed a spade. Then he played good clubs through East who discarded his remaining spade on the third club and ruffed the fourth. Declarer remained and ruffed his last spade with the jack of hearts. East had no answer to this so declarer ended up with +420. Nicely played by Roman Smolski.

This was the auction in the other room:

West	North	East	South
Kirby	**Hisatomi**	**Armstrong**	**Imakura**
Kirby	*Hisatomi*	*Armstrong*	*Imakura*
–	1♣	1♥	1♠
Pass	2♣	Pass	3NT
All Pass			

It would not normally be a good idea to overcall in the opponents' 4-4 fit and thus keep them out of that suit. However, Armstrong picked a good moment! West preferred to lead his own suit! On a diamond lead, 3NT had no chance.

Both Sides Vulnerable. Dealer North.

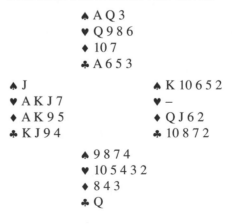

```
            ♠ A Q 3
            ♥ Q 9 8 6
            ♦ 10 7
            ♣ A 6 5 3
♠ J                    ♠ K 10 6 5 2
♥ A K J 7              ♥ –
♦ A K 9 5             ♦ Q J 6 2
♣ K J 9 4             ♣ 10 8 7 2
            ♠ 9 8 7 4
            ♥ 10 5 4 3 2
            ♦ 8 4 3
            ♣ Q
```

This deal is from the final of the 1993 European Women's Pairs. Many pairs had trouble because West had to find a way to bid her hand after North's one club opening was passed around to her. The eventual winners had no problems after East, Carla Arnolds, chose to overcall one spade. Maybe she bid to deprive her opponents of bidding space, but it turned out to be a good bid for an entirely different reason. Her partner, Bep Vriend, eventually became declarer in 3NT and made eleven tricks after a heart lead.

A one-level overcall should normally be made on a five-card (or longer) suit, but there are occasions when a good four-card suit is acceptable.

♠ A K J 4 ♥ A 6 3 2 ♦ 4 3 ♣ J 10 4	Double a one diamond opening (and perhaps one club also), but over a one heart opening one spade is the only option at any vulnerability.
♠ K Q J 9 ♥ 7 4 2 ♦ 8 6 3 ♣ 5 4 2	While not without risk, many aggressive experts would overcall one spade non-vulnerable over a minor-suit overcall. It is less sound after a one heart opening because you are more likely to be on lead and it uses up less bidding space.
♠ 6 4 ♥ A K J 9 ♦ Q 7 3 ♣ 7 4 3 2	After one of a minor risk one heart at any vulnerability. Partner is so likely to be on lead against a spade contract, it is worth the risk.
♠ 9 8 4 ♥ A K J 10 ♦ 9 3 ♣ A J 7 3	Even though the distribution is acceptable for a takeout double of one diamond, it often works better to overcall with such a good suit. When the deal occurred, those who doubled ended up in one spade on a 3-3 fit! (partner had a 3-2-5-3 Yarborough) and they lost a substantial penalty.
♠ 10 9 5 3 ♥ A K 10 7 ♦ K J 10 4 ♣ 2	At one table North passed over one diamond on the first round and later made a takeout double of clubs. However, his partner did not think he would have such a good hand and a good game was missed. At the other table an immediate one heart overcall worked much better.

Two-Level Overcalls

A two-level overcall, particularly in a minor, is a completely different kettle of fish. In the first place, if you look at it from your opponents' point of view, it is a much more attractive prospect to try to take a penalty at the two level rather than at the one level.

If the overcall is in a minor the most likely game for your side, even with a fit, is 3NT which partner is likely to bid with a partial fit and a stopper in the opponents' suit. It will come as a great disappointment to him if you do not have a decent six-card suit for him to run. If the overcall is in hearts over the opponent's spades much of the time when everyone has a fit they will bid four spades anyway and we need to have some expectation that either that contract will go down or that you can profitably bid on to the five level (either to make or to sacrifice)—otherwise all you have done is give declarer information.

A two-level overcall in a minor, especially vulnerable, should have a six-card suit most of the time. If there is only a five-card suit then there should be strong reasons for wishing to enter the auction. Perhaps the suit is so good that the lead-direction element is very strong; perhaps the hand is so good that you feel that game may be missed if you do not enter the auction on the first round. It is reasonable to stretch a little more when bidding hearts over spades—after all, if the opponents do not have a spade fit they may have a fit in a minor and you may be able to outbid them in hearts.

In terms of HCP, an overcall at the two level should show a couple of HCP more than a one-level overcall, i.e. about 10 points non-vulnerable and 12 vulnerable.

Here are some examples:

♠ 3 ♥ 7 2 ♦ A K J 10 4 2 ♣ K 7 3 2	This is a fine two diamond overcall in any situation. At this table North overcalled after two passes and his RHO opened one heart. His partner responded three clubs and he was happy to raise to the good game.
♠ A ♥ 10 4 2 ♦ Q 6 2 ♣ K J 10 8 4 3	With Both Sides Vulnerable, facing a passed partner, West overcalled two clubs over a one diamond opening. It was worth some risk to stop North responding in either major. In the event it was South who had an extremely strong hand and it would have mattered little what action West had taken.
♠ 10 6 ♥ A J 10 8 5 4 ♦ Q 5 2 ♣ A Q	With Both Sides Vulnerable, North is delighted to overcall two hearts after a one spade opening. It expresses his hand more accurately than a one heart overcall after one of a minor.

When you are considering bidding hearts over spades, it is not necessary to have such good playing strength. When a major-suit game is at stake it is acceptable to take greater risks.

♠ Q 10 3 ♥ A K Q 5 3 ♦ A 10 ♣ 9 6 5	With Neither Side Vulnerable, West's two heart overcall was passed out and made an overtrick for +140.
♠ K 9 ♥ K J 10 9 2 ♦ A 10 9 ♣ A 6 2	Again, a two heart overcall was chosen, vulnerable against not, because of the good five-card suit and all-round values.

♠ Q J 5 4	On the last two deals you might have
♥ K 9 6 5 2	preferred a 1NT overcall, but you chose
♦ K Q 5	two hearts because of the suit quality and
♣ A	relative weakness in spades. When the
	heart suit is very weak, but there is a good
	spade guard and the high-card points are
	sufficient, a 1NT overcall is a better
	choice.

♠ K J	This hand looks very unattractive for a
♥ Q 10 8 7 3	two heart overcall, but it was the action
♦ A 5	chosen by a Polish expert and led to a
♣ K 9 8 3	successful sacrifice.

Sometimes, the lesser evil is to overcall in a minor on only a five-card suit. This is usually when the hand is quite strong in terms of HCP.

♠ K J 6	This hand divided a bidding panel after a
♥ 7	one heart opening. Some experts feel very
♦ A K 9 5 3	strongly that they would like to have four
♣ A 10 9 2	spades to make a takeout double of one
	heart so chose two diamonds; others
	preferred a double.

♠ 3	At unfavorable vulnerability after a one
♥ A 9 5	diamond opening from RHO you have to
♦ K J 10 6	do something. A two club overcall looks
♣ A Q 10 8 7	the best option because there are two
	things wrong for 1NT—the hand is not
	really strong enough and there is a
	singleton spade. It is usually acceptable to
	make a bid that is flawed in one way but
	not in two.

The Upper Range of an Overcall

So, the minimum strength has been established for an overcall. What about the upper limit? Let's now assume that you hold a semi-balanced hand, say, 5-3-3-2, 6-3-2-2 or 5-4-3-1—obviously the HCP requirements can be lowered with more extreme distribution and greater playing strength.

Traditionally, a simple overcall showed a maximum of about 15 HCP, with more it was considered better to start with a takeout double and then rebid a five-card or longer suit, thus showing a hand too strong for an immediate overcall. There were several problems with this style: often the bidding was at an uncomfortably high level when it was next the doubler's turn to bid; he sometimes had to face the problem of his partner volunteering a suit in which he, the doubler, had no support. There were often difficult guesses to be made on the next round of the auction.

As is often the case, the pendulum has swung in the other direction and current practice in some expert circles is to almost dispense with an upper limit. The argument is that game is unlikely without a fit and partner will bid with a fit so why not start by bidding a good suit even on an extremely strong hand. The advent of negative doubles has meant that the opening bidder feels compelled to re-open the bidding when he is short (doubleton or less) in the suit overcalled, however weak the opening. This means that sometimes, even when your side can make game and were passing out a simple overcall, you may be rescued and given a second chance.

However, this style is not without its problems even if the first hurdle is negotiated successfully—i.e. not missing game immediately. The overcaller may wish to bid again on quite a wide range of hands. After, say, 1♠ – 2♥ – 2♠ – Pass – Pass, how do you distinguish between not wanting to sell out with a fairly ordinary overcall and a 19-count that still has game interest? You may find that you end up overbidding because you do not trust partner to realize just how good a hand you really have.

A reasonable compromise between the two styles is to allow the top limit for an overcall to be about 17 HCP. It is not so likely that you will miss a game when you make a simple overcall on such a hand; and it is not such a hardship to have to bid again at a high level after starting with a takeout double on an 18-count. Nevertheless you should still bear in mind that a double invites partner to bid a suit while an overcall shows your own suit, thus, after, say, a one heart opening it is more attractive to double with, say, a 3-1-3-6 distribution than with 1-3-3-6, whatever the strength of the hand.

♠ A K Q 7 5 4	South has about seven playing tricks and
♥ 7 3	is very strong for a simple overcall.
♦ A 10 6	Nevertheless, after a one heart opening it
♣ 5 2	is by far his best action. In the event
	partner responds two diamonds and it
	should be easy to reach four spades.

♠ 5 2	Although North has a full-weight 16-
♥ A K Q 6 4	count, after a one club opening it is much
♦ J 4	more sensible to start with a one heart
♣ A Q 4 3	overcall. After a one spade opening it
	would not be unreasonable to double,
	expecting to rebid two hearts if partner
	responded in a minor. The problem with
	this action would arise when East raised
	spades.

♠ A K 7 5	This time West has an extremely good
♥ A 10 9 6 5 3 2	hand and after South's one diamond
♦ A	opening it would not be totally unreason
♣ 10	able to bid four hearts. However, four
	spades could be a better game so to start
	with a simple one heart is best.

♠ A Q 8 3	Facing a passed partner, vulnerable
♥ 7	against not vulnerable, after a one heart
♦ 10 7	opening. North started with a quiet two
♣ A K Q 9 3 2	clubs. When his partner showed a few
	values he tried four spades before finally
	ending up in the club game.

Overcalling After Both Opponents Have Bid

So far we have only looked at overcalls in the direct position. In that situation only opener has begun to describe his hand and one of the reasons for bidding is to try stop responder from continuing the conversation. When you are considering bidding after both opponents have bid, there are two main reasons why you should be a little more circumspect:

1. Since they have both shown values it is less likely that you can make a contract.

2. Since they have both begun to describe their hands it is less likely that you can disrupt their communications.

Of course, it depends very much on what the response has been. Some responses make intervention more appropriate than others. If the response has been a change of suit, that response is forcing so that you know you will have a chance to bid on the next round; if their bidding looks like it is dying at a low level so that partner is marked with some values we can always bid later. If the response has been 1NT or a raise, it is quite likely that that will be the final contract unless you take action on this round. Let us look at the situations one at a time:

After a change of suit response

This is the least attractive occasion to bid. Both opponents have announced some values and there is no reason to suppose that they have a fit. All the bad things that can happen after overcalling in direct position are more likely to happen here. If responder has bid a new suit at the two level there is even more need for caution because their combined values are known to be higher. It is even more important that there is a good reason for bidding. At least one of the following reasons should apply:

1. You have good playing strength and hope that you might make a game or have a profitable sacrifice.

2. You can take away some of their bidding space. After 1♣ – Pass – 1♦, if you overcall one heart you do nothing to prevent them finding a spade fit, but if you overcall one spade you may make it difficult for them to find a heart fit.

3. You wish to direct the lead. Partner is likely to lead one of the unbid suits so there is less reason to bid with some strength in both unbid suits.

With reasonable values but little playing strength there may be the opportunity to bid on the next round when the opponents have limited their hands and the bidding is dying.

That is what North should have done on the next deal, but he preferred to intervene rashly and he got what he deserved.

East/West Vulnerable. Dealer East.

```
              ♠ 10 7 4
              ♥ A K 6 5 4
              ♦ J 5 2
              ♣ Q 7
  ♠ A 2                    ♠ K J 9 8 6
  ♥ 9 8                    ♥ Q 10 2
  ♦ K Q 10 7 6             ♦ A 3
  ♣ A 8 6 5                ♣ K J 3
              ♠ Q 5 3
              ♥ J 7 3
              ♦ 9 8 4
              ♣ 10 9 4 2
```

West	North	East	South
–	–	1♠	Pass
2♦	2♥	Pass	Pass
Dble	All Pass		

The defense took the first three diamond tricks, then two spades and a spade ruff, then two club tricks and East still had a trump trick to come: −800. In the other room North was silent and East/West bid to 3NT. An inspired South led the three of hearts (3rd and 5th) to the king and when North returned a low heart, East played the ten and so lost the first five tricks.

After a Raise

As always, once the opponents have found a fit there is a much greater likelihood that you have a fit. There is a much greater premium on bidding as the Law of Total Tricks comes into its own and you can bid to their level of your fit, expecting one contract or another (or even both) to make. The shorter you are in the opponents' suit, the more important it is to bid. After the sequence:

West	North	East	South
1♠	Pass	2♠	Pass
Pass	?		

partner is very likely to bid with minimal values, particularly non-vulnerable, but it is much easier for him to bid when he has shortage in the opponents' suit. Consider the following deals:

(a)
```
              ♠ J
              ♥ J 9 3
              ♦ K 10 5 3
              ♣ K Q 10 7 3
  ♠ A K Q 8 4              ♠ 10 9 5 2
  ♥ A 6                    ♥ 10 5 2
  ♦ Q 8 2                  ♦ J 9 7 4
  ♣ J 4 2                  ♣ A 9
              ♠ 7 6 3
              ♥ K Q 8 7 4
              ♦ A 6
              ♣ 8 6 5
```

(b)

```
          ♠ J 7 3
          ♥ J 9 3
          ♦ K 10 5 3
          ♣ K Q 3
♠ A K Q 8 4              ♠ 10 9 5 2
♥ A 6                    ♥ 10 5 2
♦ Q 8 2                  ♦ J 9 7 4
♣ J 4 2                  ♣ A 9
          ♠ 6
          ♥ K Q 8 7 4
          ♦ A 6
          ♣ 10 8 7 6 5
```

You do not really need to bid with the South hand on deal (a) because, since he is short in spades, partner will protect for you. Indeed, if you do bid you may find that partner raises when the opponents bid to three spades. On the second deal, on the other hand, if you do not bid immediately the opponents will probably buy the hand in two spades because it is not reasonable to expect partner to bid when two spades is passed around to him.

You do not have to change the hand around very much for a heart lead to be crucial to beat four spades:

```
          ♠ 8 4
          ♥ Q 9 3
          ♦ K 7 5 3
          ♣ K Q 3 2
♠ A K Q J 7 3           ♠ 10 9 5 2
♥ A 6                   ♥ 10 5 2
♦ Q 8 2                 ♦ 10 9 4
♣ 8 4                   ♣ A J 6
          ♠ 6
          ♥ K J 8 7 4
          ♦ A J 6
          ♣ 10 9 7 5
```

This is how the deal actually occurred. The Polish expert, Cezary Balicki, bid three hearts over two spades. Consequently, his partner led a heart against four spades. In the other room, where his partner did not bid, the unsuspecting North let the game through when he led a top club.

After a 1NT response

There is an enormous difference between a no trump response to a minor-suit opening and a no trump response to a major-suit opening.

After a major-suit opening, responder has announced that there is no fit as well as the fact that he is limited. This is quite a dangerous position in which to bid—the opponents may not have a fit and because one hand is limited it is quite easy for opener to know what to do.

After a minor-suit opening there very probably is a fit. Much depends on system, but suppose your opponents are playing a weak no trump and that when they are out of range for 1NT they open with the higher of two four-card suits

(except both majors). Now the one club opening is likely to be on a five-card suit and the 1NT response is likely to contain four-card support. Also, it is probable that neither opponent holds an outside four-card suit. This is almost like bidding after a raise. It is important to bid on this round of the auction because it is quite likely that opener will remove to two clubs and responder raise to three clubs before you get another chance. If opponents are playing a strong no trump system where the one club opening could be on a three-card suit, the inferences are not quite so strong. However, it is likely that the opponents have some degree of fit after 1♣ – Pass – 1NT or even 1♦ – Pass – 1NT.

So far we have only considered bidding after an opening one of a suit, but there are other opening bids we should consider:

THE OPPONENTS OPEN WITH A STRONG CLUB

When the opponents open with a strong club they are announcing to everyone at the table that they have a strong hand, but they impart no information about their distribution.

One of the main advantages of playing a strong club is that it keeps the bidding low on strong hands. If responder has sufficient values to make a positive response, they will be in a game-forcing auction by the time they are at the two level, sometimes even the one level. Accordingly, if they have done their homework properly, they should be able to bid game and slam hands more accurately than a pair using natural methods.

One of the main disadvantages of playing a strong club is that it is susceptible to intervention. You can enter the auction easily because the opening bid is so low; responder may well have his natural first response taken away from him. Better still, if your partner can raise you – to the two level when you have an eight-card fit, to the three-level when you have nine trumps—the opponents may well have to decide what to do at the three or four level when neither of them has bid a suit naturally. They will not guess right all of the time.

Neither Side Vulnerable. Dealer West.

```
          ♠ A 10 9 6 5
          ♥ A 7
          ♦ A J
          ♣ A 7 6 2
♠ 8 7 4                 ♠ 3 2
♥ J 8 4 2               ♥ K 10 9 6 5 3
♦ 7 6 2                 ♦ K Q 10 5
♣ Q J 8                 ♣ 3
          ♠ K Q J
          ♥ Q
          ♦ 9 8 4 3
          ♣ K 10 9 5 4
```

West	North	East	South
–	1♣(*)	3♥	Dble(**)
Pass	3♠	Pass	4♣
Pass	6♣	All Pass	

(*) strong
(**) takeout

Although six clubs is not such a bad contract, needing clubs 2-2 or East to have a singleton honor, it may not be the best contract because whenever six clubs makes so does seven spades. Perhaps South should have supported spades immediately (via a four heart cuebid) rather than introduce the club suit, but his choice was not unreasonable. East's intervention made life difficult and North/South got it wrong.

A recent addition to some bridge calendars is a match between two teams of experts, one of which is allowed to use whatever bidding methods it likes while the other is constrained to play natural methods with no conventions whatsoever. On the following deal, the Naturals North did not overcall over a Precision club whereas the Scientist in the other room overcalled over a natural one heart opening. Look at the full deal:

East/West Vulnerable. Dealer South.

```
            ♠ K 10 7 5 3
            ♥ K Q 2
            ♦ 10 6
            ♣ 9 6 5
♠ A 9                      ♠ 2
♥ 10 8 5 4                 ♥ A 6
♦ K Q J 7 4               ♦ A 9 8 5
♣ A K                     ♣ Q 8 7 4 3 2
            ♠ Q J 8 6 4
            ♥ J 9 7 3
            ♦ 3 2
            ♣ J 10
```

Jeff Meckstroth and Eric Rodwell, probably the pair with the most well-defined bidding system in the world, were allowed a free run after West's strong club opening. After five rounds of artificial bidding, they reached seven diamonds. There were no problems in the play.

This is what happened at the other table:

West	North	East	South
–	–	–	Pass
1♥	1♠	2♣	4♠
5♣	Pass	6♣	All Pass

West's opening bid looks a little strange, but remember that they were allowed no artificial conventions, including negative doubles. East/West had decided that whenever they held a four-card major they would open it, hoping that this would help them find their fits in competitive auctions. What were they to do after the spade barrage? They had to guess and did quite well to reach a small slam.

Neither Side Vulnerable. Dealer East.

```
            ♠ K J 10 2
            ♥ 10 4
            ♦ J 9 3 2
            ♣ 7 5 2
♠ A 5                      ♠ 9 7 4 3
♥ 8 6 3 2                  ♥ A Q J 9 7
♦ 6 5                     ♦ 10 7
♣ K J 9 6 4              ♣ 8 3
            ♠ Q 8 6
            ♥ K 5
            ♦ A K Q 8 4
            ♣ A Q 10
```

In one room North/South were playing natural methods and the bidding was:

West	North	East	South
–	–	Pass	1♦
Pass	1♠	Pass	2NT
Pass	3NT	All Pass	

West saw no reason not to lead a club and declarer made eleven tricks.

In the other room North/South were playing a strong club system:

West	North	East	South
–	–	Pass	1♣
Pass	1♦	1♥	2NT
3♥	3NT	All Pass	

Once East had been allowed to bid his hearts, North/South were in trouble. Their eventual 3NT contract went one down on a heart lead. Perhaps North should have preferred to double three hearts but, that only results in +100. The only game to have any chance as the cards lie is four spades on the 4-3 fit—very difficult to reach.

There are many artificial defenses against strong club systems in general use, but whatever you choose you should bid as often as possible, particularly when the vulnerability is favorable—obviously you have to exercise more restraint vulnerable against not. At favorable vulnerability you can start with a jump overcall on many hands that would only bid at the one-level after a natural one club (or maybe would not bid at all). A normal jump overcall can bid at the three level. It will be difficult for the opponents to penalize you when they know nothing about their partner's distribution.

The corollary of all this is: when you hold a good hand with reasonable playing strength you should start with a pass.

THE OPPONENTS OPEN WITH 1NT

This situation is almost the complete opposite to the last one. A strong club opener announces a good hand of unknown distribution, almost an invitation to intervene; a 1NT opener, on the other hand, announces a precisely defined collection of cards—the point count is known within a narrow range and the hand is known to be balanced. It is much more likely that the partner of a 1NT opener will guess correctly when faced with interference bidding.

Also, over a 1NT opening, if you are to intervene you must do so at the two level, while over a strong club you had most of the one level at your disposal. For these two reasons a little more caution is called for.

Nevertheless, as in any overcalling situation, the opponents will have to do a great deal more guessing if you intervene than if they are allowed a free run, so there are still great advantages to be gained from bidding. After all, suppose your partner opened 1NT (12-14) and the next hand overcalled two spades. What would you bid if you held:

    ♠ K 7 4
    ♥ A Q 10 6
    ♦ Q 7 5
    ♣ J 4 2

Do you double and find that this is the full deal:

    ♠ 10 2
    ♥ 9 8 3
    ♦ J 10 9 8 4
    ♣ 8 7 3

♠ K 7 4   ♠ J 3
♥ A Q 10 6   ♥ K J 7 2
♦ Q 7 5   ♦ A K 3 2
♣ J 4 2   ♣ Q 10 9

    ♠ A Q 9 8 6 5
    ♥ 5 4
    ♦ 6
    ♣ A K 6 5

Declarer will make his contract if he guesses spades correctly, but in any case will only go one down when your side can make four hearts.

So, should partner remove the double? But what if this is the full deal?

    ♠ 5
    ♥ Q 10 6 5 3
    ♦ 10 9 8
    ♣ K J 8 2

♠ A Q 9 4   ♠ J 3
♥ 9 4   ♥ K J 7 2
♦ 6 5   ♦ A K 3 2
♣ A 7 5 4 3   ♣ Q 10 9

    ♠ K 10 8 7 6 2
    ♥ A 8
    ♦ Q J 7 4
    ♣ 6

Here two spades goes down three while 3NT will go down

on a diamond lead.

So, perhaps you should not have doubled with the first hand? Maybe the full hand is:

    ♠ 2
    ♥ J 7 5 3
    ♦ 9 8 3 2
    ♣ 9 8 7 3

♠ K 7 4   ♠ J 10 8
♥ A Q 10 6   ♥ K 4
♦ Q 7 5   ♦ A J 10 6
♣ J 4 2   ♣ K Q 10 5

    ♠ A Q 9 6 5 3
    ♥ 9 8 2
    ♦ K 4
    ♣ A 6

Now two spades is booked to go two down with no game on for your side.

Although responder is better placed to guess what to do than he would be facing a less well-defined opening bid, he will still have to guess more often than if he was allowed a free run.

Again, in order to overcall it is more important to have good playing strength than a large number of high-card points—after all, with lots of points you would prefer to double and defeat their contract. A natural overcall in second seat, i.e. directly over the 1NT opening, should always show a decent six-card suit. There are many conventional defenses to 1NT in general use, some allowing bids to show two-suiters and some three-suiters. This increases significantly the chance of finding a playable fit.

It is not only the partner of the 1NT opener who can benefit from knowing his partner's hand. Suppose you play a common conventional defense to 1NT, Astro, which is popular in England, whereby a two club overcall shows hearts and another suit and two diamonds shows spades and another suit—at least nine cards are required in the two suits but the major may be only four cards. Further suppose that the bidding goes 1NT – Pass – Pass to you. What do you know about the hand?

This has actually been a very revealing auction, particularly if you are weak. You know:

1. Your side has at least 17 HCP between you (your right-hand opponent has not tried for game) and probably more.

2. If your partner had enough high cards to bid (say about 12 HCP vulnerable or 10 non-vulnerable) then you know he is balanced.

Suppose the bidding has gone 1NT – Pass – Pass, and you hold:

    ♠ Q J 9 7 3
    ♥ A 4 2
    ♦ 6

♣ 10 9 7 6

It is not so dangerous for you to bid two spades now, particularly non-vulnerable! You know partner has some scattered values and it is unlikely that he holds a singleton spade. Perhaps the full deal is:

```
              ♠ A 10 6
              ♥ J 9 7
              ♦ K J 8 3
              ♣ A 5 3
♠ Q J 9 7 3              ♠ K 5
♥ A 4 2                  ♥ K 8 5 3
♦ 6                      ♦ A 7 5 2
♣ 10 9 7 6              ♣ Q J 4
              ♠ 8 4 2
              ♥ Q 10 6
              ♦ Q 10 9 4
              ♣ K 8 2
```

Two spades looks set to make comfortably enough, perhaps with an overtrick. The fate of 1NT depends on partner's lead: a heart would kill your hand dead and even if you ducked we couldn't stop seven tricks; a diamond lead should lead to a one-trick defeat. At any vulnerability and form of scoring you would prefer to be in two spades.

There is more premium in bidding in fourth seat than second for several reasons:

1. It is safer when you know your opponents do not have game values.

2. You can often deduce that partner will have some degree of tolerance for your suit.

3. In second seat your alternative to bidding is to pass and lead fourth highest of your long suit against 1NT; in fourth seat your alternative is to pass and watch partner lead some other suit, probably only four cards in length, which is likely to be your short suit.

THE OPPONENTS OPEN WITH A PRE-EMPT

When your opponents open the bidding with a pre-emptive bid, i.e. anything from a weak two bid to five of a minor, they are announcing a hand weak in high cards but strong in playing strength. This is different to when they open 1NT and announce a hand of narrowly defined points and limited playing strength. When they opened 1NT you needed playing strength to enter the auction—someone needs some playing strength or you might as well defend! When they open a pre-empt they have shown a six- or seven-card suit. This already makes it likely that their side has a fit—if they have a seven-card suit and the other six cards are distributed evenly among the other three players, their side will have a nine-card fit. When they have a fit you have a fit so there is strong reason for you to consider entering the auction.

Many players are afraid to bid over an opposing pre-empt. They start to count the possible losers they could have if the next hand doubled with all the outstanding points and trumps. They worry about losing 1400 penalties and pass with good hands. They don't think about all the times their opponents will go a few down in their contract (or even make) when they had an easy game on. This might not result in a loss of 1400, but the missed opportunities soon add up. Although it is possible to lose a large penalty by coming in over an opposing pre-empt, it does not happen very often; it is much more likely that failure to bid will result in a missed game.

As over an opening one bid, there are two hand types of reasonable strength that it is not possible to bid with on the first round:

1. A hand with considerable length and strength in the suit opened.

2. A balanced hand in the 12-14 range (or even a little stronger after a pre-empt)—i.e. a hand that is not strong enough to overcall no trumps – there also might be problems with a stronger balanced hand with no stopper in the opponent's suit.

Your side needs roughly a combined 25 HCP to make a game. If these points are more or less evenly divided, someone has to make a bid. If partner has length and strength in the suit opened he will be hoping you have shortage and a hand suitable for a takeout double which he will pass. However, if partner has a weak no trump hand-type, he needs you to make a bid if you are to reach game. Therefore, you should not shy away from that overcall or takeout double. As usual it is easier to make game in no trumps or a major, so if you have opening values you should not be afraid to bid a decent five-card suit at the same level as the pre-empt. It may even be right to bid with less than opening values in case partner has a balanced 16-count without a guard in the opponent's suit. The problem is that he will not know that you have bid on so little. The chances are that when you were right to bid because you could make a part score, partner will raise and you will go down; when you can make a game he will place you with more and bid a slam. Here are some examples of overcalls after various pre-emptive openings:

```
♠ A J 9 6 5 3      ♠ K 7 4
♥ A 6 4            ♥ J 8 7 3 2
♦ K 4              ♦ –
♣ 10 6            ♣ A K J 8 7
```

It would be clear to overcall three spades on this weak hand after any pre-empt at any vulnerability. In the actual game neither side was vulnerable and South opened three diamonds. At one table North passed three spades, East cuebid four diamonds and then respected West's sign off in four spades. At the other table North jumped to five diamonds so now East guessed that there would be no diamond wastage and bid the slam. The slam was nowhere near as good a contract as East had hoped, but all was well when North turned up with ♣Qxx.

♠ Q J 10 8 5 3 ♠ 9 7 2
♥ A K ♥ 10 3
♦ 10 9 8 ♦ Q J 5 4 2
♣ 3 2 ♣ A K 7

With both sides vulnerable, East passed as dealer and South opened a weak two hearts. West made a rather minimum two spade overcall and then the auction took off. North jumped to four hearts and East tried four spades. When this was passed around to North, he doubled, but South moved to five hearts, thus swapping +500 for –500.

♠ K 10 9 8 7 6 5 4 ♠ Q J 3
♥ 10 5 ♥ A K 8
♦ 10 ♦ A Q 4 2
♣ K J ♣ A Q 10

With only North/South vulnerable, South opened three hearts. Although West had few high cards he could not really do other than overcall three spades and he found his partner with a real rock-crusher. Luckily, East remembered to use Blackwood before settling for a small slam.

♠ A 10 6 4 3 ♠ J 9
♥ K Q 9 4 3 ♥ A J 10
♦ 10 ♦ A K J 6 5 3
♣ K 8 ♣ 7 3

With neither side vulnerable, South opened three clubs, giving West an awkward decision. He did not feel that he was worth a four club cuebid which would show this major-suit distribution but would also overstate his values. Instead he chose a three spade overcall. East bid four diamonds and West four hearts. However, it was difficult for East to pass this because hc had no way of knowing that his partner was 5-5. He "corrected" to four spades which was unlucky to go two down when trumps broke 6-0! Eleven tricks could be made in hearts. As it turned out West would have done better to show his distribution and not bothered too much about his lack of high cards.

Quiz 35

1. What would you bid on the following hands after your RHO opens:

(a) 1♣ when he is vulnerable and you are not?
(b) 1♦ with neither side vulnerable?
(c) 1♥ with both sides vulnerable?
(d) 1♠ when you are vulnerable and he is not?

(i) ♠ A 10 6 5 (ii) ♠ K 4 (iii) ♠ K Q 8 4
♥ 8 ♥ K 9 6 4 2 ♥ A 5 4
♦ A J 4 ♦ 5 ♦ Q J 9 7 5 3
♣ A 10 9 6 4 ♣ K 7 5 3 2 ♣ –

(iv) ♠ J 6 2 (v) ♠ J (vi) ♠ J 6 3
♥ Q 8 5 ♥ A 8 2 ♥ A K 8 6 5 3 2
♦ A J ♦ A Q J 4 ♦ K
♣ K Q J 8 7 ♣ J 10 9 8 5 ♣ A K

2. What would you bid on the following hands after your RHO opens:

(a) 1♠ when he is vulnerable and you are not?
(b) 1♥ with neither side vulnerable?
(c) 1♦ with both sides vulnerable?
(d) 1♣ when you are vulnerable and he is not?

(i) ♠ A Q J 9 5 (ii) ♠ K 6 3 (iii) ♠ A K J 5
♥ K 5 ♥ Q 6 ♥ 7 5 2
♦ K 10 9 5 ♦ A J 7 ♦ Q 9 7 6 2
♣ A 6 ♣ Q J 9 7 6 ♣ 7

(iv) ♠ J 3 (v) ♠ J 10 6 4 3 (vi) ♠ K Q J 7 3 2
♥ 9 7 ♥ Q 6 ♥ Q J 10 6 5
♦ K 2 ♦ K 6 ♦ 5
♣ A J 9 8 7 5 3 ♣ A 9 4 2 ♣ K

3. What would you bid on the following hands after your RHO opens:

(a) 1♥ when he is vulnerable and you are not?
(b) 1♠ with neither side vulnerable?
(c) 1♣ with both sides vulnerable?
(d) 1♦ when you are vulnerable and he is not?

(i) ♠ J 9 5 (ii) ♠ 6 (iii) ♠ K J 5
♥ A Q 9 8 ♥ A 8 5 2 ♥ K 7 4 3 2
♦ 2 ♦ A 4 3 ♦ A Q 9
♣ 7 6 5 4 3 ♣ A K 10 6 5 ♣ K 6

(iv) ♠ A 10 9 5 4 (v) ♠ Q J 2 (vi) ♠ 5
♥ 8 7 3 ♥ A J 9 6 5 ♥ A Q J 10 4 3
♦ Q 6 ♦ K 10 7 3 ♦ A 5
♣ J 6 5 ♣ 2 ♣ 9 8 5 4

4. What would you bid on the following hands after your RHO opens:

(a) 1♦ when he is vulnerable and you are not?
(b) 1♣ with neither side vulnerable?
(c) 1♠ with both sides vulnerable?
(d) 1♥ when you are vulnerable and he is not?

(i) ♠ A Q 9 7 6 (ii) ♠ A Q 6 5 (iii) ♠ 3
♥ 9 5 ♥ Q 9 7 ♥ 7
♦ 6 ♦ A J 10 5 2 ♦ A J 9 6 3
♣ 7 6 5 3 2 ♣ Q ♣ A K 10 7 6 4

(iv) ♠ J 8 6 (v) ♠ 7 3 (vi) ♠ 9 7 3
♥ A 9 6 ♥ Q J 4 ♥ K J 8 7 5
♦ A J 10 5 3 2 ♦ A K Q 10 7 2 ♦ A J 4 3
♣ 3 ♣ K ♣ 3

5. What would you bid on the following hands, with neither side vulnerable after the following sequences:

(a) 1♥ – Pass – 1♠ – ?
(b) 1♦ – Pass – 2♣ – ?
(c) 1♣ – Pass – 1♥ – ?
(d) 1♠ – Pass – 2♦ – ?

(i) ♠ A 10 9 4 (ii) ♠ A K 10 9 5 (iii) ♠ 7
♥ A 9 6 5 4 3 ♥ A 7 ♥ A K 9 2
♦ 7 ♦ Q 9 2 ♦ 9 7 4
♣ 9 8 ♣ 8 7 2 ♣ Q J 8 6 2

(iv) ♠ Q 9   (v) ♠ Q   (vi) ♠ 9 6
♥ A   ♥ A K 10 9 8 7 3 ♥ A 10 4 3 2
♦ 10 9 3 2   ♦ 9 8   ♦ 6
♣ K Q 8 7 6 2   ♣ K 8 3   ♣ A Q 8 7 4

6. What would you bid on the following hands with both sides vulnerable after the following sequences:

(a) 1♣ – Pass – 1NT – ?
(b) 1♦ – Pass – 1NT – ?
(c) 1♥ – Pass – 1NT – ?
(d) 1♠ – Pass – 1NT – ?

(i)   ♠ A 6 3 2   (ii) ♠ A 10 8 7 4 (iii) ♠ J 9 5 2
♥ A 10 9 5 4   ♥ 9 3 2   ♥ A
♦ 4   ♦ A 10 3   ♦ A Q 6 4 3
♣ A 10 4   ♣ A J   ♣ Q J 8

(iv) ♠ A 4 2   (v) ♠ 7 6 5   (vi) ♠ –
♥ K J 4   ♥ Q 9 8 4 3 2   ♥ Q J 7 4 2
♦ K 10   ♦ K 10 7   ♦ K 10 8 6 2
♣ K 10 8 6 3   ♣ Q   ♣ A K 9

7. What would you bid on the following hands with neither side vulnerable after the following sequences:

(a) 1♣ – Pass – 2♣ – ?
(b) 1♦ – Pass – 2♦ – ?
(c) 1♥ – Pass – 2♥ – ?
(d) 1♠ – Pass – 2♠ – ?

(i)   ♠ Q 9 3   (ii) ♠ J 3   (iii) ♠ K Q 8 5
♥ 2   ♥ A K 9 3   ♥ J 10 8 6 4
♦ K 6 4   ♦ A 10 9 5 2   ♦ 10 8
♣ K J 9 7 5 4   ♣ A 2   ♣ K 6

(iv) ♠ 10 3 2   (v) ♠ J   (vi) ♠ 9 8 7 5 4
♥ A Q J 9 8 6   ♥ J 9 2   ♥ 7
♦ 7 4   ♦ J 8 5 2   ♦ A 4
♣ 3 2   ♣ A K 9 5 4   ♣ A K 9 4 2

1. (i)   ♠ A 10 6 5   (ii) ♠ K 4   (iii) ♠ K Q 8 4
     ♥ 8   ♥ K 9 6 4 2   ♥ A 5 4
     ♦ A J 4   ♦ 5   ♦ Q J 9 7 5 3
     ♣ A 10 9 6 4   ♣ K 7 5 3 2   ♣ –

   (iv) ♠ J 6 2   (v) ♠ J   (vi) ♠ J 6 3
     ♥ Q 8 5   ♥ A 8 2   ♥ A K 8 6 5 3 2
     ♦ A J   ♦ A Q J 4   ♦ K
     ♣ K Q J 8 7   ♣ J 10 9 8 5   ♣ A K

(a) What would you bid after your RHO opens 1♣ when he is vulnerable and you are not?

(i) Pass. It is always difficult to know what to do with length in the suit opened on your right. Some would choose a one spade overcall, but best is probably to pass for the time being—with any luck you will be able to make a takeout double of hearts on the next round.

(ii) One heart.

(iii) One diamond. Make a natural overcall on the first round and hope to double clubs for takeout next time.

(iv) Pass. Not quite strong enough for a 1NT overcall.

(v) One diamond. Some would prefer to pass and hope to bid later, but the trouble with that action is that the oponents are likely to be in spades and it is not entirely satisfactory to make a takeout double of spades without four hearts. With such a good suit it is sensible to get into the auction as quickly as possible.

(vi) One heart. You have sufficient defense not to fear the opponents bidding too high. It is silly to overcall four hearts with so many high cards because that contract is likely to go one or two down for no good reason. It is unlikely that one heart will be passed out when game is on.

(b) What would you bid after your RHO opens 1♦ with neither side vulnerable?

(i) Pass. The club suit is really not good enough to bid at the two level. If you really cannot bear to pass with such a good hand, a one spade overcall could work out well.

(ii) One heart. An unusual 2NT would be quite horrible on this hand with poor suit quality and an outside spade honor. You do not want to encourage partner to sacrifice.

(iii) Pass. With six cards in the opponent's suit it is surely best to pass to start with. On the next round you may be able to make a takeout double or bid diamonds naturally.

(iv) Pass. A close decision: not quite strong enough for 1NT; not quite enough playing strength for two clubs. No doubt many would disagree, but pass is best for the moment.

(v) Pass. Hope to bid next time.

(vi) One heart.

(c) What would you bid after your RHO opens 1♥ with both sides vulnerable?

(i) Double. A perfect takeout double.

(ii) Pass.

(iii) Two diamonds. It is more important to have length in the suit than top honors when considering a two-level overcall. This hand has great potential.

(iv) Pass.

(v) Pass.

(vi) Pass. Your opponents have warned you of a bad heart break. It is quite possible that you would like to compete in hearts and will be able to bid them naturally on the next round.

(d) What would you bid after your RHO opens 1♠ when you are vulnerable and he is not?

(i) Pass. Hope to bid on the next round.

(ii) Pass. Not enough for a Michaels cuebid, particularly at this vulnerability.

(iii) Two diamonds.

(iv) Pass. There is even less reason to bid when you are not taking away much of your opponents' bidding space.

(v) Double. Even without four hearts, it is better to make a takeout double than overcall with a poor five-card minor.

(vi) Two hearts. Again, there is no reason to get excited. Partner probably has few high cards and there is no reason to suppose you will make more than eight tricks.

2. (i) ♠ A Q J 9 5 (ii) ♠ K 6 3 (iii) ♠ A K J 5
        ♥ K 5   ♥ Q 6   ♥ 7 5 2
        ♦ K 10 9 5   ♦ A J 7   ♦ Q 9 7 6 2
        ♣ A 6   ♣ Q J 9 7 6   ♣ 7

    (iv) ♠ J 3   (v) ♠ J 10 6 4 3 (vi) ♠ K Q J 7 3 2
        ♥ 9 7   ♥ Q 6   ♥ Q J 10 6 5
        ♦ K 2   ♦ K 6   ♦ 5
        ♣ A J 9 8 7 5 3 ♣ A 9 4 2   ♣ K

(a) What would you bid after your RHO opens 1♠ when he is vulnerable and you are not?

(i) Pass. A 1NT overcall would be a good alternative, but at this vulnerability you may well be able to get a sizable penalty. Your LHO's most likely action is a 1NT response and, if it is passed around to you, you can double this for penalties. Even if one spade is passed out you can expect to score 200 or 300.

(ii) Pass. Insufficient playing strength for a two-level overcall.

(iii) Pass.

(iv) Three clubs. A little on the strong side for a weak jump overcall at favorable vulnerability but it doesn't hurt to have a little in hand for a change.

(v) Pass.

(vi) Pass. It may be appropriate to make a natural bid in spades on the next round.

(b) What would you bid after your RHO opens 1♥ with neither side vulnerable?

(i) One spade. This is a close decision between a natural overcall and a takeout double. It is right at the top of the range for an overcall and it would not be wrong to prefer to double first. However, it is unlikely that you would miss game by making a simple overcall and it often pays to bid your long suit first.

(ii) Pass. The best alternative would be a takeout double but it is best not to double with such minimum values without four spades. On the other hand, if you do double and end up defending, your ♥Qx is likely to make a trick because declarer will play you for shortage in hearts.

(iii) One spade. A good example of a four-card overcall.

(iv) Three clubs. Just about middle of the road with neither side vulnerable.

(v) One spade. Even with such a poor suit and despite taking away little space, this is just about worth a one spade overcall. It may well be right to compete for the part score or sacrifice in four spades over four hearts.

(vi) One spade. Some would prefer a jump overcall, but if partner has the expected heart shortage and some spade support he will raise anyway.

(c) What would you bid after your RHO opens 1♦ with both sides vulnerable?

(i) 1NT. This is a closer description of the hand than either a one spade overcall or a takeout double. It does not matter too much about the five-card spade suit—partner can still use Stayman to find out if you have a four-card major.

(ii) Pass. Certainly not enough for a vulnerable two-level overcall. Though non-vulnerable, the overcall would have some appeal over a one diamond opening simply because it cuts out both majors.

(iii) One spade. This cuts out the heart suit and is likely to find partner with some measure of support and diamond shortage.

(iv) Three clubs. A bit pushy vulnerable but worth the risk because of all the space it consumes.

(v) One spade. At least this time it cuts out the heart suit.

(vi) One spade. Tempting to bid two spades, but the hand is just a little too good with both sides vulnerable. A Michaels cuebid would not be a good idea because with equal length in the majors partner would give preference to hearts.

(d) What would you bid after your RHO opens 1♣ when you are vulnerable and he is not?

(i) One spade. Again double would be an acceptable alternative.

(ii) Pass.

(iii) One spade. It is more tempting to bid the robust four-card suit than the weak five-carder because it takes away more of the opponents' bidding space.

(iv) Pass. Even if there were a natural bid in clubs available, it would be unwise to do much bidding at this vulnerability with bad breaks expected.

(v) One spade.

(vi) Two spades. Here the temptation to make a jump overcall is too great. This hand has superb playing strength and limited high cards (the king of clubs is unlikely to be of use). It is much more likely to play well in spades than hearts and if you overcall two spades you keep your heart suit hidden from the opponents.

3. (i) ♠ J 9 5 (ii) ♠ 6 (iii) ♠ K J 5
   ♥ A Q 9 8 ♥ A 8 5 2 ♥ K 7 4 3 2
   ♦ 2 ♦ A 4 3 ♦ A Q 9
   ♣ 7 6 5 4 3 ♣ A K 10 6 5 ♣ K 6

   (iv) ♠ A 10 9 5 4 (v) ♠ Q J 2 (vi) ♠ 5
   ♥ 8 7 3 ♥ A J 9 6 5 ♥ A Q J 10 4 3
   ♦ Q 6 ♦ K 10 7 3 ♦ A 5
   ♣ J 6 5 ♣ 2 ♣ 9 8 5 4

(a) What would you bid after your RHO opens 1♥ when he is vulnerable and you are not?

(i) Pass.

(ii) Two clubs. Here the club suit and the overall strength is good enough to justify a two-level overcall. Still, there are those who would prefer to pass and hope to come in with a takeout double later. The trouble is that partner will not know you are so strong.

(iii) Pass. It is always difficult to know what to do with length in the opponent's suit. If you pass you can hope to make a penalty double later. A 1NT overcall would not be an unreasonable alternative.

(iv) One spade. Just about worth an overcall because of the possibility of a spade sacrifice.

(v) Pass.

(vi) Pass. There will probably be an opportunity to bid hearts naturally next time.

(b) What would you bid after your RHO opens 1♠ with neither side vulnerable?

(i) Pass.

(ii) Double. A perfect takeout double and also worth a raise if partner responds in clubs or hearts.

(iii) 1NT. This surely looks more like a balanced 15-17 than a two-heart overcall.

(iv) Pass.

(v) Two hearts. Here the heart suit is better and the hand is just worth a two heart overcall non-vulnerable. The 5-4-3-1

distribution is better than the balanced distribution of hand (iii).

(vi) Two hearts. A textbook two-level overcall.

(c) What would you bid after your RHO opens 1♣ with both sides vulnerable?

(i) One heart. This is very daring but is worth the risk because the chunky heart suit and the club length suggests that partner is likely to have some heart tolerance along with club shortage.

(ii) Pass. A 1NT overcall with a singleton spade is a possibility but could well lead to trouble. The heart suit is not really good enough for a four-card overcall. Hope to bid on the next round.

(iii) One heart. Top of the range for a simple overcall and preferable to 1NT because of only having a single club stopper.

(iv) One spade. Sub-minimum really but worth some risk because of taking so much space away and it is quite possible that a spade sacrifice would be a good idea.

(v) One heart. It is never (well, nearly never) a good idea to make a minimum takeout double in preference to a one-level overcall in a five-card major.

(vi) One heart. Too good for a weak jump overcall.

(d) What would you bid after your RHO opens 1♦ when you are vulnerable and he is not?

(i) Pass. The risk is not worth it now the vulnerability is unfavorable and the overcall would consume no space.

(ii) Two clubs. The best of a bad bunch.

(iii) 1NT. The double diamond stopper and poor quality of the heart suit make 1NT a better description than a heart overcall.

(iv) Pass. You have to draw the line somewhere!

(v) One heart.

(vi) Two hearts. The 6-4 distribution makes this hand worth a jump overcall at this vulnerability. However, many would prefer one heart and that would not be wrong.

4. (i) ♠ A Q 9 7 6 (ii) ♠ A Q 6 5 (iii) ♠ 3
   ♥ 9 5 ♥ Q 9 7 ♥ 7
   ♦ 6 ♦ A J 10 5 2 ♦ A J 9 6 3
   ♣ 7 6 5 3 2 ♣ Q ♣ A K 10 7 6 4

   (iv) ♠ J 8 6 (v) ♠ 7 3 (vi) ♠ 9 7 3
   ♥ A 9 6 ♥ Q J 4 ♥ K J 8 7 5
   ♦ A J 10 5 3 2 ♦ A K Q J 10 7 2 ♦ A J 4 3
   ♣ 3 ♣ K ♣ 3

(a) What would you bid after your RHO opens 1♦ when he is vulnerable and you are not?

(i) One spade. Two spades would appeal to the frisky because of the extra playing strength of the 5-5 distribution. A two-suited overcall would be a bad idea when the major is so much stronger than the minor.

(ii) One spade. A matter of style. Some would prefer to pass and hope to describe the hand later, perhaps with a penalty double which could turn out well at this vulnerability! However, this could get awkward. Suppose LHO responds one heart and RHO rebids 1NT. You can make a penalty double if you wish but then you have to lead.

(iii) Two clubs.

(iv) Pass.

(v) 3NT. But only because the diamonds are really solid! You cannot bid diamonds naturally on this round and could pass for the time being, but why not make everybody guess? You are at favorable vulnerability so you can always choose to run if you are doubled.

(vi) One heart. If you were facing a passed partner you could experiment with two hearts. The diamond length suggests that partner is quite likely to hold some heart tolerance along with diamond shortage. Also a diamond lead would probably be to your advantage.

(b) What would you bid after your RHO opens 1♣ with neither side vulnerable?

(i) One spade. Even two spades for the same reasons as above.

(ii) Double. With 5-4-3-1 distribution and a singleton in the suit opened, it is usually best to double when the five-card suit is a minor and to bid the suit when it is a major.

(iii) Pass. A one diamond overcall would not be a mistake but it might be difficult to know what to do on the next round—even if you can rebid clubs naturally, partner will keep giving you preference to diamonds. If you pass on this round you can hope to bid no trumps next time and partner will know you have both minors.

(iv) One diamond. A little too good for a jump overcall, but bid two diamonds facing a passed partner to try to stop the opponents finding a major-suit fit.

(v) 3NT. A bit on the risky side, but it makes them guess. You could choose three clubs to ask partner for a stopper, but singleton king is good enough facing half a stopper and your confident bidding may well stop your LHO leading a club anyway.

(vi) One heart.

(c) What would you bid after your RHO opens 1♠ with both sides vulnerable?

(i) Pass.

(ii) 1NT. A controversial suggestion on a hand where there is no right answer. Some would prefer a two diamond overcall even with a five-card suit and others would pass for the time being.

(iii) 2NT. For the minors. It is very likely that you will wish to press on to five of a minor over four of a major. It is good

that your clubs are stronger and longer than your diamonds because with equal length partner will choose clubs.

(iv) Two diamonds. The good suit makes this worth a two-level overcall even vulnerable.

(v) Three spades. Asking partner to bid 3NT with a spade stopper.

(vi) Pass. Not worth a two-level overcall, especially vulnerable.

(d) What would you bid after your RHO opens 1♥ when you are vulnerable and he is not?

(i) One spade. The extra playing strength of the 5-5 distribution makes this a good overcall even at adverse vulnerability.

(ii) One spade. Again this is a difficult choice and some would prefer 1NT, two diamonds or pass.

(iii) 2NT.

(iv) Two diamonds.

(v) 3NT.

(vi) Pass.

5. (i) ♠ A 10 9 4 (ii) ♠ A K 10 9 5 (iii) ♠ 7
     ♥ A 9 6 5 4 3   ♥ A 7   ♥ A K 9 2
     ♦ 7   ♦ Q 9 2   ♦ 9 7 4
     ♣ 9 8   ♣ 8 7 2   ♣ Q J 8 6 2

    (iv) ♠ Q 9   (v) ♠ Q   (vi) ♠ 9 6
     ♥ A   ♥ A K 10 9 8 7 3   ♥ A 10 4 3 2
     ♦ 10 9 3 2   ♦ 9 8   ♦ 6
     ♣ K Q 8 7 6 2 ♣ K 8 3   ♣ A Q 8 7 4

(a) What would you bid with neither side vulnerable after 1♥ – Pass – 1♠ – ?

(i) Pass. You have no sensible bid with length in both of the opponents' suits.

(ii) Pass. If your LHO rebids two hearts and this is passed to you, you can bid a natural two spades. If your LHO rebids 1NT and this is passed to you, you can make a penalty double, asking partner to lead a spade.

(iii) Pass.

(iv) Two clubs. A good suit is worth bidding, particularly with the 6-4 distribution. It would not be unreasonable to bid three clubs which might do more to suggest a sacrifice over four of a major.

(v) Pass. Most people would not play a two heart bid as natural in this sequence even if they wanted to bid it. Your LHO's opening bid has put you off a bit anyway. There is likely to be an opportunity to bid the suit on the next round.

(vi) Pass. It would be more attractive to bid with spade length rather than heart length—since it is, dummy is likely to be short in hearts but your RHO will be remaining. Some would risk a two club overcall for the lead and, indeed, it could work very well.

(b) What would you bid with neither side vulnerable after 1♦ – Pass – 2♣ – ?

(i) Two hearts. It looks right to bid this time with length in both of the unbid suits and it is better to bid the six-card suit than double. You are bidding because you hope there is a good fit and there is unlikely to be a good spade fit since partner has not overcalled.

(ii) Pass. The opponents are in a strong sequence and this hand does not have enough playing strength to risk bidding. Having said that, it could work well to bid two spades because it might help partner with his opening lead.

(iii) Pass.

(iv) Pass.

(v) Two hearts. No point in getting too excited. So far the opponents have shown good values and no fit. They probably have a 4-4 spade fit, but since that suit breaks 4-1 you do not mind too much if they find it. You have good defense and do not wish to do too much bidding unless partner can show some support.

(vi) Pass. You might risk two hearts if your hearts and clubs were exchanged.

(c) What would you bid with neither side vulnerable after 1♣ – Pass – 1♥ – ?

(i) Pass.

(ii) One spade. This is fine for a one-level overcall.

(iii) Pass.

(iv) Pass. A two club bid would not be played as natural by many players but you might bid clubs on the next round – if your LHO rebids 1NT and this is passed to you, for example. If the one club opening was prepared and your system allowed you to bid a natural two clubs, this would be a reasonable choice.

(v) Pass. You cannot bid the opponent's suit naturally but will almost certainly bid on the next round.

(vi) You have nothing to say when they bid both of your suits.

(d) What would you bid with neither side vulnerable after 1♠ – Pass – 2♦ – ?

(i) Two hearts. This is risky, but if your opponents end up in spades or no trumps you would very much prefer a heart lead.

(ii) Pass.

(iii) Double. Just about worth a takeout double non-vulnerable but this could work out badly if your opponents end up buying the hand because you will have told declarer about your distribution.

(iv) Three clubs. This would be too dangerous vulnerable but non-vulnerable it is worth the risk.

(v) Two hearts. You might even bid again if, for example,

your LHO's two spade or three diamond rebid is passed to you.

(vi) Double. This hand is more attractive for a double because of the 5-5 distribution.

6. (i)   ♠ A 6 3 2   (ii) ♠ A 10 8 7 4 (iii) ♠ J 9 5 2
         ♥ A 10 9 5 4   ♥ 9 3 2   ♥ A
         ♦ 4   ♦ A 10 3   ♦ A Q 6 4 3
         ♣ A 10 4   ♣ A J   ♣ Q J 8

    (iv) ♠ A 4 2   (v)   ♠ 7 6 5   (vi) ♠ –
         ♥ K J 4   ♥ Q 9 8 4 3 2   ♥ Q J 7 4 2
         ♦ K 10   ♦ K 10 7   ♦ K 10 8 6 2
         ♣ K 10 8 6 3   ♣ Q   ♣ A K 9

(a) What would you bid with both sides vulnerable after 1♣ – Pass – 1NT?

(i) Two clubs, for the majors. This is not so clear-cut because partner is likely to play you to be 5-5. However, the alternatives are also flawed. If you double (takeout of clubs) partner is likely to bid two diamonds and if you now bid two hearts he may think you are stronger. If you bid two hearts you may miss out on the spade fit. If you bid two clubs partner will choose hearts with equal length so you should always find your best fit. The danger is that partner bids too much, but that is unlikely after his pass of the one club opening.

(ii) Two spades. It sounds risky to bid such a weak suit at the two level vulnerable, but in truth you are almost in a balancing situation because your opponents probably have a club fit. That means you are very likely to have a fit, too, and that fit will usually be in your longest suit, spades.

(iii) Pass. It looks as if this is a better hand than the previous one but in a way it is much riskier because your RHO is more likely to have diamond length than spade length and your diamond spot cards are very small. If partner has some diamond support you are likely to do very well defending 1NT when you lead a diamond. Often in this kind of situation when you bid two diamonds you find that you have to play it like Garozzo to make 90 when you would have easily scored 100 or 200 simply by defending. The vulnerability makes defending most attractive—if you make and they go down you would rather score +100 than +90; if they make and you go down you would rather score -90 than -100.

(iv) Pass. Partner must have very little because he is marked with at most a singleton club.

(v) Two hearts. Partner probably has fair values, but was too balanced to bid. Your opponents must have some kind of club fit so two hearts should not fare too badly.

(vi) Pass. It is hard to believe that you really hold this hand. Who has the spades? Your opponents should have at most seven so partner has a very weak hand with a long spade suit. Not the time to be bidding.

(b) **What would you bid with both sides vulnerable after 1♦ – Pass – 1NT – ?**

(i) Double. Perfect takeout of diamonds and if partner does not know what to bid (say he is 3-3-4-3) he will choose your five-card suit.

(ii) Two spades.

(iii) Pass.

(iv) Pass. It is not worth the risk vulnerable. Not vulnerable, however, it may well be right to bid two clubs. Then if you make and they go down you score +90 instead of +50, whereas if you go down and they make you score –50 instead of –90.

(v) Two hearts.

(vi) Pass.

(c) **What would you bid with both sides vulnerable after 1♥ – Pass – 1NT – ?**

(i) Pass.

(ii) Two spades.

(iii) Double. The heart shortage makes the hand much more attractive. Partner can pass with heart length and you could take a sizable penalty.

(iv) Pass.

(v) Pass.

(vi) Pass.

(d) **What would you bid with both sides vulnerable after 1♠ – Pass – 1NT – ?**

(i) Pass. It is much more dangerous to bid suits below the level of the one opened than suits above. This is because your RHO has denied (in principle) four cards in a higher ranking suit than the one opened and it would be unlucky if your LHO had four cards in the suit you overcall.

(ii) Pass.

(iii) Pass. Two diamonds is very dangerous but might be worth the risk not vulnerable.

(iv) Pass.

(v) Pass.

(vi) Double. It is far from perfect to make a takeout double with a 5-5-3-0 distribution, but here it is the best available option. A two spade cuebid would force you too high and might miss a potential club fit.

7. (i) ♠ Q 9 3   (ii) ♠ J 3   (iii) ♠ K Q 8 5
    ♥ 2   ♥ A K 9 3   ♥ J 10 8 6 4
    ♦ K 6 4   ♦ A 10 9 5 2   ♦ 10 8
    ♣ K J 9 7 5 4 ♣ A 2   ♣ K 6

  (iv) ♠ 10 3 2 (v) ♠ J   (vi) ♠ 9 8 7 5 4
    ♥ A Q J 9 8 6 ♥ J 9 2   ♥ 7
    ♦ 7 4   ♦ J 8 5 2   ♦ A 4
    ♣ 3 2   ♣ A K 9 5 4 ♣ A K 9 4 2

a) **What would you bid with neither side vulnerable after 1♣ – Pass – 2♣ – ?**

(i) Pass. Let's hope partner re-opens with a double.

(ii) Two diamonds. You want to bid something and if you double partner is bound to bid spades. You probably have a fair diamond fit.

(iii) Double. If partner bids two diamonds you can correct to two hearts. Partner should now correct to two spades with preference for that suit. Because your opponents have shown a fit partner should realize that you are merely competing for the part score rather than showing a good hand.

(iv) Two hearts.

(v) Pass.

(vi) Pass. Partner almost certainly has some spade support and club shortage but if that is the case he will bid himself. If you bid in front of him he is likely to raise you too high.

(b) **What would you bid with neither side vulnerable after 1♦ – Pass – 2♦ – ?**

(i) Three clubs. Bid before they find out they have a heart fit.

(ii) Two hearts. You have a fit so partner must have heart length and diamond shortage. The trouble is that he probably has such a weak hand that he may not wish to bid when two diamonds is passed back to him.

(iii) Double. Partner will always prefer to bid a major than clubs. If he bids three clubs he will have at least a five-card suit.

(iv) Two hearts.

(v) Pass. No need to bid because partner is the one with the diamond shortage. If he protects with two spades bid three clubs because he will not have a very good suit or he would have bid on the first round.

(vi) Two spades. Prepared to bid three clubs if they double loudly!

(c) **What would you bid with neither side vulnerable after 1♥ – Pass – 2♥ – ?**

(i) Three clubs.

(ii) Three diamonds. Again, partner probably doesn't have enough to bid when two hearts is passed to him even with his singleton hearts. Non-vulnerable it pays to bid. If two hearts is going down, three diamonds is very likely to be making.

(iii) Pass. Partner is bound to bid if two hearts is passed to him.

(iv) Pass. Hope partner re-opens with a double.

(v) Pass. Again, partner is probably short enough in hearts to re-open.

(vi) Three clubs. This is difficult because you may well want to compete in spades. However, if you bid three clubs you can bid three spades on the next round if the opponents take the push to three hearts. If you start with two spades you are sunk if they press on to three hearts and partner will make the wrong lead.

(d) What would you bid with neither side vulnarable after 1♠ – Pass – 2♠?

(i)   Three clubs.

(ii) Double. If partner bids three clubs you can convert to three diamonds. Although your fit is most likely in diamonds, it is worth doubling because of the extra premium in finding a major-suit fit.

(iii) Pass. Partner will almost certainly re-open and then you can bid your hearts.

(iv) Pass. You have sufficient spade length to suppose that partner will re-open. If you bid three hearts now there is serious danger that he will bid on.

(v) Double. Here you must bid because you have the spade shortage. It is better to double even though you do not have four hearts. If partner has four hearts and a four-card minor, he should bid 2NT to suggest more than one place to play. You can then bid three clubs and he can pass or try three diamonds. You should still end up in your best fit.

(vi) Three clubs. While you know that partner will protect and you can then bid your clubs, here we do have a potentially good hand if partner has a good club fit. If partner has a singleton spade, good four or five-card club support and fair values, you want him to keep on bidding. Game is certainly not out of the question.

28

Chapter

What To Respond ?

So, you now know when you should bid and what you should bid, but you don't know what you should do when it is partner who bids. The requirements for an overcall are different to the requirements for an opening bid so it makes sense for the responding structure to be a little different.

The general rule is the same as for all bidding—bid up with a fit, otherwise be conservative. Once an opponent has shown opening values you are not very likely to have game on unless you have a fit.

RESPONDING TO A ONE-LEVEL OVERCALL
Responding Without a Fit

Change of suit response
A change of suit response is natural and constructive but non-forcing (although some expert pairs prefer to play it as forcing for one round). There is no need to "rescue" partner from his overcall. He should have a decent suit of his own and there is no guarantee that your long suit will play any better than his. If the opponents double for penalties (or pass and then pass a re-opening double), however, there may be reason to think again and remove to a good long suit of your own.

The values needed for a change of suit response are flexible. In principle, near opening values are needed, but it would be foolish to pass with a good suit and good playing strength and find that partner's overcall was passed out when there was a much better spot available. In practice, a long good suit and fair playing strength is sufficient to respond to partner's overcall.

Partner will bid again most of the time: he may bid another suit if he has one, he may raise with a fit, he may rebid in no trumps with a guard in the opponent's suit or he may cuebid the opponent's suit with extra values but no suitable natural bid. As always the auction should progress slowly until a fit is found.

Here are some example sequences:

Neither Side Vulnerable. Dealer East.

♠ A	♠ K Q J 10 8
♥ K Q 10 9 4	♥ 7 6
♦ A Q 9 7 5	♦ K 8 6
♣ 7 3	♣ 6 5 4

West	North	East	South
–	–	Pass	1♣
1♥	Pass	1♠	Pass
2♦	Pass	2♥	Pass
3♦	All Pass		

After West's one heart overcall, it would be foolish for East not to bid his strong spade suit, even without opening values. Although West has an extremely good one heart overcall, there is no need for him to jump around without a fit. East gave simple preference to hearts and West moved on with a non-forcing game try of three diamonds, describing his distribution and extra values. East had had enough, thankful to end up in a good part score.

Neither Side Vulnerable. Dealer South.

♠ K 10 7 6 4	♠ A 8
♥ K Q 4	♥ A 9
♦ 9 5	♦ 10 8 7 4
♣ J 5 3	♣ A K 10 9 6

West	North	East	South
–	–	–	1♥
1♠	Pass	2♣	All Pass

East had a very good hand when his partner overcalled one spade. However, without a fit, game is a long way off and there is not much premium in bidding thin non-vulnerable games, so he settled for a simple change of suit. Even though West had a fair fit for clubs, he was not quite worth a raise. A fair game was missed. Both hands were maximum for their actions and 3NT depended on bringing in the club suit for no loser (in this case playing South for queen singleton or doubleton, no doubt) or a diamond blockage to prevent the defenders taking four diamond tricks.

Both Sides Vulnerable. Dealer South.

	♠ A	♠ Q J 7 3	
	♥ K 10 7 6 5 2	♥ 9 3	
	♦ 5 3	♦ K 8 6	
	♣ A J 9 4	♣ K 10 7 5	

West	North	East	South
–	–	–	1♦
1♥	Pass	1♠	Pass
2♣	All Pass		

Here East had a tricky problem over his partner's one heart overcall. He was a little too good to pass and his diamond stopper not as robust as he would like to bid 1NT, consequently he chose temporizing one spade, usually showing a five-card suit. When his partner rebid two clubs he was delighted to pass.

Neither Sides Vulnerable. Dealer South.

	♠ A 7 4	♠ 9 8 6 2	
	♥ A K J 6 2	♥ Q 8	
	♦ J 10 2	♦ K 7	
	♣ 8 4	♣ A Q J 6 2	

West	North	East	South
–	–	–	1♦
1♥	Pass	2♣	Pass
2♦	Pass	2♥	All Pass

After his partner's one heart overcall, East had a fine hand for a two club response. West now had a tricky problem. He was too good to pass two clubs but had no suitable natural rebid. He chose to cuebid the opponent's suit to show extra values and this hand-type. Now East had a problem. He was not ashamed of his first bid, but his hand was too balanced to be well described by a jump. He downvalued his king of diamonds and chose the slight underbid of two hearts which his partner was happy to pass. Good judgment was well rewarded since only eight tricks could be made.

At the other table, East chose to rebid 2NT over two diamonds, which expressed his values slightly better but rather overstated the diamond stopper. This ended the auction and eight tricks were made here too.

Both Sides Vulnerable. Dealer South.

	♠ K 10 9	♠ A J 8 7 5	
	♥ K Q 10 9 7 3	♥ –	
	♦ 7	♦ A J 9 4	
	♣ 6 5 2	♣ A K 9 8	

West	North	East	South
–	–	–	1♣
1♥	Pass	1♠	Pass
2♠	Pass	4♠	All Pass

Here West had a sound, minimum one heart overcall (their system did not allow two hearts) and found his partner with an enormous hand. However, with a void heart and no good suit of his own, East contented himself with a quiet one spade. Although minimum, West had a fair fit for spades and

an outside singleton, so was worth a gentle raise. This was all East wanted to hear and he went right to game.

1NT response

A 1NT response to an overcall shows a slightly better hand than a 1NT response to an opening bid. This is logical since the overcall shows less high cards than an opening bid. A 1NT response to an overcall shows about 9-12 HCP with a good stopper in the suit opened. Partner can bid again over this 1NT response in much the same way as if he had opened the bidding, i.e. rebid a six-card suit, bid another lower-ranking suit without extra values, reverse with extra values, jump in a new suit to show 5-5 and considerable extra values, raise no trumps or, with extra values but no sensible alternative he can cuebid the opponent's suit.

Here are some example sequences:

Both Sides Vulnerable. Dealer South.

	♠ K J 7 6 2	♠ 9 8 4	
	♥ J	♥ K 7 6	
	♦ A Q J 9 3	♦ K 8 7	
	♣ Q 9	♣ K 10 5 2	

West	North	East	South
–	–	–	1♣
1♠	Pass	1NT	Pass
2♦	Pass	2♠	All Pass

Here East could have raised his partner's one spade overcall directly, but he preferred 1NT for two reasons. First, with no spade honor he did not want to suggest that his partner lead a spade should South become declarer. Second, with his unsupported kings, he did not really want to suggest that his partner should do very much more bidding. West had a good overcall but saw no reason to jump around and he settled for a simple rebid in his second suit and East gave preference to spades. West now had a close decision to make and took the conservative course because he imagined that his partner had only a doubleton spade; he also knew his partner did not have a great diamond fit, nor a good heart suit so it did not seem likely that either five diamonds or 3NT would be good. On this occasion he was well rewarded since eight tricks were the limit of the hand.

Neither Side Vulnerable. Dealer South.

	♠ K J 10 9 4	♠ 6 3	
	♥ A 4	♥ Q 9 8 5	
	♦ Q 9 2	♦ A K 10 7	
	♣ A 9 6	♣ 10 8 4	

West	North	East	South
–	–	–	1♥
1♠	Pass	1NT	Pass
2NT	All Pass		

East had a minimum 9 HCP for his 1NT response and so had no hesitation in passing his partner's invitational raise to 2NT.

East/West Vulnerable. Dealer South.

♠ K 8 7 5 3 2		♠ 10	
♥ Q 10 8 7		♥ A K J 3	
♦ A 8 3		♦ K 10 6	
♣ −		♣ 8 6 5 4 3	

West	North	East	South
–	–	–	1♣
1♠	Pass	1NT	Pass
2♥	Pass	4♥	All Pass

After West's one spade overcall East had an awkward choice of bid. He chose 1NT which expressed his length in clubs but not his strength! West quite rightly chose to rebid his second suit and East jumped to game. The reason he chose to bid game rather than invite was because he knew his partner would never believe that he did not have values in clubs. When you know partner will not make the right decision for the right reason because he could not possibly imagine the hand that you hold, you might as well make the decision for him.

North/South Vulnerable. Dealer South.

♠ A Q 10 9		♠ J 8 4	
♥ Q 3 2		♥ 10 9 6 5	
♦ K Q J 7 2		♦ A 4	
♣ 4		♣ A Q 10 7	

West	North	East	South
–	–	–	1♣
1♦	Pass	1NT	Pass
2♠	Pass	3NT	All Pass

Here West had a very good overcall and, after his partner's 1NT response, bid a higher-ranking suit, in this case spades, to show his extra values. East was maximum and had no fit, so jumped straight to 3NT.

Responding with a Fit

Raises of partner's suit

This is where the Law of Total Tricks really comes into its own. All raises of partner's overcall are by nature obstructive, i.e. they are based on fit rather than high cards. The greater the fit the more you should bid.

Most of the time partner will have a five-card suit for a one-level overcall and you should assume, until you hear otherwise, that this is the case. If you have three-card support then you have eight trumps and most of the time your opponents will have eight trumps. Therefore, most of the time, both sides will make a two-level contract, but when you cannot make your two-level contract they will usually make an overtrick in theirs. When you think you have eight trumps you should raise a one-level overcall to the two level.

When you have four-card support you will usually have nine trumps between you and most of the time the opponents will also have a nine-card fit. Frequently, both sides will be able to make a three-level contract but even if you go down they should make their contract, often with an overtrick. When

you think you have nine trumps you should raise a one-level overcall to the three level.

The same logic applies when you have five-card support. When you have ten trumps you should raise a one-level overcall to the four level.

Notice how conveniently it all works out. When people say "bid to the level of your fit" they mean that when you have eight trumps you should contract to make eight tricks, with nine trumps nine tricks and so on.

Here are some examples after a one spade overcall:

♠ K Q 5	♠ J 6 5 2	♠ J 10 8 7 2
♥ 10 9 8 5	♥ K 6	♥ 10 7
♦ 10 6 4 3	♦ K J 10 7 2	♦ A J
♣ Q 5	♣ 8 2	♣ J 5 4 3
Bid 2♠	Bid 3♠	Bid 4♠

Obviously this is a simplification. Occasionally, although you hold four-card support, a jump raise is inappropriate because you do not want to encourage partner to bid on, or, perhaps, because you have a strong holding in the opponent's suit or because you have a lot of "slow" cards, i.e. queens and jacks which are better for defensive purposes than for playing the hand, like these hands:

♠ J 6 4 2	or	♠ Q J 4 3
♥ A J 9 6		♥ Q 6 2
♦ J 9		♦ Q 7 5
♣ J 6 5		♣ J 3 2

How little, in terms of high cards, does one need to raise partner's overcall? Whenever making any bid in any situation you must have some idea of what you are trying to achieve. You should have one of several things in mind when you raise partner's overcall:

1. You should try to obstruct the opponents and make them guess. However, there is only some point in doing this if you think they may guess wrong. Suppose you hold:

| ♠ J 8 3 |
| ♥ 10 9 2 |
| ♦ Q J 9 5 4 |
| ♣ Q 5 |

and the bidding goes: 1♥ – 1♠ – Pass, if you bid two spades you know that opener will bid again. If you force him to bid at a higher level, he will still do so and now his partner will know he has a better hand and may choose to bid on more vigorously. You have no bad news for him—the more the opponents bid the more they are likely to make. All you are likely to achieve by bidding is to push them into game.

2. You should try to suggest the opening lead to partner. One reason for overcalling is to suggest an opening lead, but often, if the overcaller is the one on lead, he will only lead from a broken holding if he has been supported. Thus, after 1♥ – 1♠ – Pass, bid two spades with:

♠ A 6 4 but not with: ♠ 7 6 4
♥ 9 6   ♥ 9 6
♦ 7 6 4   ♦ A 6 4
♣ Q J 7 6 5   ♣ Q J 7 6 5

This aspect is really only relevant when considering a simple raise. The obstructive aspects of a jump raise are much more significant.

3. All jump raises should suggest that there is some prospect of a successful sacrifice.

Therefore, much depends on vulnerability. A sacrifice against an opposing game can afford to go two or three down (depending on vulnerability) if your opponents are vulnerable, but if they are non-vulnerable and you are vulnerable, one down is all you would want to lose. To a certain extent, partner should have taken this into account when deciding whether to overcall in the first place, but you also need to be a little more conservative at adverse vulnerability.

A simple raise is a little easier to define than a jump raise. All the following hands would be worth a raise of one spade to two spades after the sequence 1♥ – 1♠ – Pass:

♠ Q 9 3   ♠ K 5 3   ♠ K J 6
♥ 2   ♥ A 10 8 3   ♥ K 10 9
♦ K 6 4   ♦ 10 8 7 5 2   ♦ 8 4 3
♣ J 9 7 5 4   ♣ 10   ♣ J 9 7 6

♠ Q 8 3   ♠ 8 6 4 2   ♠ A 10 4
♥ A Q 7 3 2   ♥ A 5 2   ♥ 5
♦ Q 6 4   ♦ J 5 3   ♦ 10 9 8 6 3
♣ 8 6   ♣ J 3 2   ♣ 7 4 3 2

Here are some examples of when to make a jump raise:

♠ J 6 5 2   ♠ Q 4 3 2   ♠ K 10 9 5
♥ K 8 6 5 4   ♥ 9 8   ♥ 6
♦ 10 5   ♦ Q 10 9 6   ♦ Q 10 9 5
♣ A 3   ♣ 10 9 3   ♣ J 10 5 4

and when not to:

♠ 10 8 7 4   ♠ Q 6 4 3   ♠ K 7 5 2
♥ Q 7 4   ♥ K 10 8   ♥ Q J 5 3
♦ A J   ♦ K 8 4   ♦ Q J 7
♣ 6 5 4 2   ♣ 8 7 6   ♣ 9 2

So, what do you do when you hold a hand that is too strong to make a direct raise?

The Unassuming Cuebid
When you are too strong to make a simple raise of partner's overcall you can cuebid opener's suit instead. This bid of the opponent's suit shows one of two hand types:

1. A good simple raise or better of partner's suit.

2. Any hand that is too strong for any other action.

Many expert pairs prefer to use only the first interpretation. They feel that that is by far the most frequent hand-type and they are prepared to struggle along if by some remarkable chance they are dealt a hand that is too strong for any non-

forcing action—as established earlier, the chances of game without a fit are not very great once an opponent has shown opening values. Those who choose to play change of suit over an overcall as forcing can also restrict a cuebid to the fit-showing meaning. Whether both these options are allowed can affect the meaning of sequences such as:

West	North	East	South
1♥	1♠	Pass	2♥
Pass	2♠	Pass	3♦

If the cuebid need not show a fit for spades, this sequence is consistent with:

♠ 5
♥ A 6 5 2
♦ K Q J 10 5
♣ A K 6

However, if the cuebid guaranteed a spade fit, this sequence might show a hand like:

♠ A J 5
♥ 7 2
♦ A K J 5
♣ J 6 4 3

that is a further game try, showing values in the suit bid and asking partner to re-evaluate his hand.

In the past, the cuebid was the only way of showing a good raise in partner's suit and could be based on three-, four- or even five-card support. Today there are alternative ways of raising with four-card or longer support and the cuebid should be restricted to raises with three-card support (though the occasional unprepossessing hand with four-card support could be included, as with a simple raise).

Here are some example sequences:

Both Sides Vulnerable. Dealer South.

♠ J 10 6 4 3	♠ Q 9 8	West	North	East	South
♥ Q 6	♥ K 8 7 5	–	–	–	1♥
♦ K 6	♦ A 10 4 2	1♠	Pass	2♥	Pass
♣ A 9 4 2	♣ K 6	2♠	All Pass		

A normal, minimum unassuming cuebid shows about 10-13 HCP with three-card support for partner. In the light of that information West signed off in his suit and East had no reason to proceed.

Neither Side Vulnerable. Dealer South.

♠ Q J 10 3 2	♠ A 9 7	West	North	East	South
♥ A 7 5	♥ Q 9 8 6	–	–	–	1♥
♦ 9	♦ K 8 5	1♠	Pass	2♥	Pass
♣ A J 4 2	♣ K 6 4	3♣	Pass	3♠	All Pass

This time West was too good for a two spade sign-off and rebid his second suit at the three level. However, East was not encouraged—although he had 12 HCP, he had no ruffing value and his queen of hearts looked to be wasted. West had no reason to proceed after the sign-off. Had West's red suits been reversed he would have been more encouraged.

Neither Side Vulnerable. Dealer South.

		West	North	East	South
♠ A 10 9 5 4	♠ J 6 2				1♥
♥ A J 9	♥ Q 8 5	–	–	–	
♦ 9 6 2	♦ A 5	1♠	Pass	2♥	Pass
♣ A 6	♣ K Q J 8 7	2NT	Pass	3♣	Pass
		3♠	Pass	4♠	All Pass

Again West had a good overcall and made a natural 2NT rebid after East's cuebid. East had enough to proceed but was not sure whether 3NT or four spades would be the right game. He bid a natural three clubs to try to find out. When West rebid three spades there was the suggestion that he did not have very good diamonds and that the spade game would be better.

Both Sides Vulnerable. Dealer South.

		West	North	East	South
♠ K Q J 9 5 4	♠ 10 7 3				1♥
♥ A 4	♥ Q 10 5	–	–	–	
♦ 4	♦ A Q 9	1♠	Pass	2♥	Pass
♣ 10862	♣ A Q 4 3	3♠	Pass	4♠	All Pass

Here it was straightforward. Although West did not have that much in terms of high cards, he had an excellent six-card spade suit and good distribution. When his partner made an unassuming cuebid he jumped to three spades and his partner proceeded to game.

North/South Vulnerable. Dealer South.

		West	North	East	South
♠ A Q 7 4	♠ K 3				1♦
♥ 7 4 3	♥ A Q J 9	–	–	–	
♦ 9 8 7	♦ Q 10 6 4	1♠	Pass	2♦	Pass
♣ A 4 2	♣ J 8 5	2♠	Pass	2NT	All Pass

Here there is something different. West overcalled one spade on his fair four-card suit, hoping to make life difficult for his opponents. East had a tricky choice of bid for he was too good for 1NT but didn't want to punish his partner for an aggressive overcall. He settled for an unassuming cuebid, conscious that his partner would expect him to have three spades. West signed off quickly, by rebidding his suit—this does not promise any extra length. East felt he was too good to pass and proceeded with a natural 2NT, ending the auction.

Good raises with four-card support

There are several different ways to show good four-card (or longer) support for partner's one-level overcall. However, there are only a limited number of responses—2NT, a jump cuebid and a jump in another suit. Let's look at possible interpretations for all of these:

1. A 2NT response to a one-level overcall

Obviously this can be used as natural, just a shade stronger than a 1NT response, say 13-15 HCP. However, this is an infrequent hand-type, and when you do hold it the chances are partner has a very weak overcall anyway. Some pairs choose to manage without this natural bid and instead use it

to show a good four-card jump raise of partner's overcall—say 10-13 HCP. If you are still undecided whether to bid game, there is plenty of room for partner to bid a new suit naturally to ask you to evaluate our hand further. Here are some examples:

Neither Side Vulnerable. Dealer South.

		West	North	East	South
♠ Q J 6 3 2	♠ K 10 9 5				1♥
♥ A 7 3	♥ J 5	–	–	–	
♦ 5	♦ K 8 4 2	1♠	Pass	2NT	Pass
♣ K J 4 3	♣ A 10 8	3♣	Pass	4♠	All Pass

West had a reasonable overcall and, after his partner's 2NT response wished to invite game. He bid the suit where he wanted help—clubs. East had good help in clubs, a useful doubleton heart and good trumps so he accepted the invitation. Notice that the game depended only on guessing in clubs, despite the king of diamonds being wasted. Try changing one of East's trumps into a minor suit and consider the importance of that fourth trump.

Neither Side Vulnerable. Dealer South.

		West	North	East	South
♠ K Q 6 3 2	♠ J 10 5 4				1♥
♥ J 5	♥ A 9 4 3	–	–	–	
♦ 7 6 3	♦ K 2	1♠	Pass	2NT	Pass
♣ Q 10 4	♣ A J 8	3♠	All Pass		

This time, all West could do was sign off in three spades and East respected his decision. Note that much of the time declarer will go down in three spades.

2. A jump cuebid in response to a one-level overcall

Some pairs feel that a natural 2NT response is too valuable a bid in its natural sense to give up. They prefer to use a jump cuebid to convey the same message. It says nothing about the holding in the opponent's suit, merely shows a good four-card raise. One of the disadvantages of this treatment, as opposed to using 2NT to show the same hand-type, is that partner has less room to make a further game try, often no room at all.

If you use a 2NT bid to show a fit for partner, obviously there is no need for a jump cuebid to show the same thing. In that case you can use it to show a fit for partner and a singleton in the suit opened like:

Both Sides Vulnerable. Dealer South.

		West	North	East	South
♠ A Q 6 3	♠ K J 10 4				1♥
♥ 8 6 5	♥ 7	–	–	–	
♦ Q 8	♦ J 10 9 7 6	1♠	Pass	3♥	Pass
♣ A Q 10 3	♣ K 7 6	4♠	All Pass		

West chose a one spade overcall in preference to a takeout double because of his lack of diamond support. When East showed his four-card support and singleton heart West knew there was no heart wastage and, despite holding only four trumps, bid the thin game.

Neither Side Vulnerable. Dealer South.

♠ A K 8 5 4	♠ Q J 7 2	West	North	East	South
♥ 9 6 5	♥ 2	–	–	–	1♥
♦ –	♦ K J 7 4 3	1♠	Pass	3♥	Pass
♣ A K 7 6 4	♣ Q 9 2	4♣	Pass	4♠	Pass
		5♣	Pass	6♠	All Pass

East's singleton heart was music to West's ears. It was likely that slam was on, but he needed to find out about East's club holding. He made one slam try with four clubs and East signed off in four spades. Now West pressed on with five clubs, directing East's attention to that suit. With the club queen East bid the slam.

3. A jump in a new suit in response to a one-level overcall
The traditional meaning for such bids is that they should be natural and forcing. If a simple change of suit is not forcing, what do you do with a very strong hand? If you cannot jump in the suit you may have a problem, but these hands are very infrequent. If you are dealt such a hand you still have several alternatives: you can make a simple change of suit and hope partner does not pass (after all he will bid with a fit for you and if neither hand fits well the chances of a game making are reduced); you can jump to game in your suit; you can bid no trumps; if you have a doubleton honor in partner's suit you can perhaps risk starting with a cuebid.

If such bids are not natural and forcing, what other hand-type should they show? They show a fit for partner's overcall and either shortage or length in the bid suit, according to partnership agreement. (Though a two spade response to one heart would still be natural.)

The advantage of using the bids to show shortage is that the 2NT bid is now known not to contain a singleton. A hand is either balanced or it contains a singleton so there are no problems of judgment. Once partner knows of the singleton it is relatively easy for him to judge—obviously it is better if he holds length in the singleton suit with either no high cards or perhaps just the ace.

The other camp argues that the only singleton it is necessary to show immediately is one in the opponent's suit. Most of the time partner can guess whether shortage is held in that suit because of the opponents' bidding (or lack of it). They argue that it is more important to show where the high cards lie. These players argue for "fit jumps"—a jump in a new suit shows values in the suit bid (usually length as well) and primary support for partner. These players also argue that this treatment makes it easier for partner to know whether or not to sacrifice (or to bid on to make) at a high level. In the event that he decides to defend, his opening lead may have been made easier.

One of the drawbacks with this method is that it is often more difficult to apply. Let us look at some hands:

(a) ♠ K J 7 5	(b) ♠ K 8 7 5	(c) ♠ K 8 7 5
♥ 10 7	♥ 10 7	♥ A Q 4
♦ 6 4	♦ K 4	♦ 4
♣ K Q J 5 2	♣ A 10 5 4 2	♣ J 10 7 4 2

It is clear that hand (a) is a good example of a fit jump, but what about hand (b) or hand (c)?

It is also harder for the overcaller to judge. Suppose your RHO opens one heart, you overcall one spade and your partner jumps to three clubs. What do you bid with these hands:

(d) ♠ A Q 6 4 2	(e) ♠ A Q 6 4 2
♥ K 5 4	♥ A 6 4 2
♦ Q J 3 2	♦ 4
♣ 7	♣ 7 6 3

If you bid three spades on hand (d) that is fine if he has hand (a), but you will have missed game opposite hand (b). If you bid game with hand (e) you will be too high opposite hand (b) but OK facing hand (a). It is all very well to argue that you could bid three diamonds or three hearts to ask partner to judge further, but it is not clear that he will move with the right hand.

I hope I have presented the arguments fairly and it is up to each partnership to decide. What is crucially important is to know the strength of the trump fit, i.e. when there is a nine-card fit. The following combinations of these bids are all reasonable:

(i) 2NT = balanced + fit
All jumps show shortage

(ii) 2NT = fit
Jump cuebid shows shortage
Jump in a new suit shows values (usually length) + a fit

(iii) 2NT is natural
A jump cuebid shows any hand with a fit
Jumps in a new suit are natural and forcing or values + a fit

4. Higher jumps
Higher jumps (which are not game) all show shortage and a raise of the suit overcalled. They show greater playing strength than an ordinary jump—very often a fifth trump, like after 1♥ – 1♠ – Pass, bid four hearts with:

♠ A J 10 9 8	or	♠ A Q 9 7 4
♥ 6		♥ 6
♦ K 7 5 2		♦ J 10 6 3 2
♣ J 8 4		♣ 8 7

However, a word of caution. Whenever you choose to make a splinter-bid or a fit-showing jump in preference to raising partner you are giving your opponents more room. Consider the following two sequences:

(a)

West	North	East	South
–	–	–	1♥
1♠	Pass	4♠	

(b)

West	North	East	South
–	–	–	1♥
1♠	Pass	4♥	

On sequence (a), South can pass, double or bid at the five level. There is a great deal of guessing to be done and more often than not the four spade bid will buy the hand, perhaps doubled. Sequence (b) gives the opponents more space. Now South can double four hearts to suggest that his partner bids on, or he can pass and double for penalty. Had East bid four of a minor instead of four hearts, South would have had even more options.

It is important to be clear in your mind that you will gain more from making a more descriptive bid than will lose by allowing the opponents more room to describe their hands.

RESPONDING TO A TWO-LEVEL OVERCALL

The theory behind two-level overcalls is similar to one-level overcalls, but there are some significant differences:

1. There is less space to investigate the best game.

2. Partner will usually have a six-card suit so it is less important that you have a four-card fit.

3. Except for a two heart overcall over a one spade opening, you are dealing with minor suits where your first duty is to look for a no trump game.

Change of Suit Response

This is just the same as over a one-level overcall – natural but non-forcing. However, some people like to play that a new suit at the three level is forcing in competitive sequences just as it is when the opponents are silent.

A 2NT Response

This has to be natural after a two-level overcall. More often than not it will be made with a partial fit for the suit over-called. A much better hand is needed if there is no fit. Partner should usually either raise to 3NT or rebid his suit. Occasionally it may be more appropriate to bid a new suit. It is rarely right for the overcaller to pass—if it is not right to play in game it is usually better to have the security of a long trump suit like:

Both Sides Vulnerable. Dealer South.

♠ J 6	♠ A 9 8	West	North	East	South
♥ 6 4	♥ 9 3 2	–	–	–	1♠
♦ A 3	♦ Q 10 8 7	2♣	Pass	2NT	Pass
♣ K Q J 9 8 5 4	♣ A 6 2	3NT	All Pass		

East made an aggressive 2NT response to his partner's two club overcall and West went on to game. West expected his partner to have a club honor most of the time so he could count at least eight tricks plus a presumed trick in spades.

Neither Side Vulnerable. Dealer South.

♠ K J 3	♠ 10 9 5 2	West	North	East	South
♥ 10 4	♥ K 8 5 2	–	–	–	1♥
♦ 9 7	♦ A 8	2♣	Pass	2NT	Pass
♣ A J 9 6 5 4	♣ K 3 2	3♣	All Pass		

Here West had a minimum overcall, so signed off in three clubs. While it is true that 2NT may well make on a heart lead, on a diamond lead it will be one down even if the club suit comes in—and several down if there is a club loser. Three clubs needs the spade queen to be onside, even if the club suit comes in, but will rarely go more than two down.

Because it is seldom right for the overcaller to pass, many pairs like to play the bid as forcing. The advantage of playing 2NT as forcing is that it allows you to use it as the starting point on a number of stronger hands. For example:

Neither Side Vulnerable. Dealer South.

♠ 6 2	♠ K Q 3	West	North	East	South
♥ Q 3	♥ A K J 7 4	–	–	–	1♠
♦ K 6 4	♦ 7 2	2♣	Pass	2NT	Pass
♣ A J 10 7 4 3	♣ Q 6 2	3♣	Pass	3♥	Pass
		3NT	All Pass		

Here East had enough to insist on game after his partner's two club overcall, but which game? If he bid two hearts it would not be forcing and a jump to three hearts would not describe a hand that is so suitable for no trump play. Instead he started with a forcing 2NT and his partner signed off in three clubs. Now he bid three hearts, forcing, because it is a new suit at the three level, and his partner could choose between four hearts and 3NT. This time he chose 3NT but had he had the king of clubs instead of the king of diamonds he would have chosen four hearts.

A Cuebid

This is similar to a cuebid after a one-level overcall. However, when minor suits are involved its first message is to ask about the overcaller's suitability for a no trump game. The overcaller should strain to bid no trumps with a stopper in the opponent's suit, particularly when his own suit is strong, like:

Both Sides Vulnerable. Dealer South.

♠ K 8 7	♠ 6 4 3	West	North	East	South
♥ K Q 10	♥ 7 6 2	–	–	–	1♥
♦ K Q 10 8 4 2	♦ A J 6	2♦	Pass	2♥	Pass
♣ Q	♣ A K 7 6	3NT	All Pass		

With his maximum overcall and double heart stopper, West jumped to 3NT in response to his partner's two heart cuebid.

Neither Side Vulnerable. Dealer South.

♠ Q 9 8 5	♠ K J 7 4	West	North	East	South
♥ 9 3	♥ 7 6 2	–	–	–	1♥
♦ A Q 9 7 3 2	♦ K 4	2♦	Pass	2♥	Pass
♣ 6	♣ A 7 3 2	2♠	Pass	4♠	All Pass

Here West had a minimum overcall but showed his second suit in response to his partner's cuebid. East's jump to four spades was a slight overbid but showed good appreciation that every one of his cards was working.

RESPONDING TO A JUMP OVERCALL

The response structure to jump overcalls is not affected by the strength of the overcall, though obviously the values needed for any response depend on that strength.

A two-level jump overcall

It is normal to play change of suit as forcing after a jump overcall. This is because a jump overcall should always be made on a good suit and the range of the hand should be much more narrowly defined than for a simple overcall. Therefore, there is only any point in introducing a new suit to either help partner to judge or to suggest a different trump suit at game level. While a change of suit is always natural it could be used on a hand like:

```
        ♠ A 6
        ♥ 10 8 4
        ♦ A 3 2
        ♣ Q J 6 2
```

in a sequence like:

West	North	East	South
–	–	–	1♥
2♠	Pass	3♣	

With a borderline decision partner will sign off when he has no fit and bid more enthusiastically when the knowledge of your club values improves his hand.

A cuebid would have much the same meaning as over a simple overcall, but the problem with a cuebid, as mentioned earlier, is that it often leaves no room for partner to describe his hand. After, say, 1♥ – 2♠ – Pass – 3♥, partner can either bid three spades or commit your side to game. That is all very well if you have all around values and just want to know if he is minimum or maximum, but often you would like to know more about where his values lie.

For similar reasons, as over a two-level simple overcall, it makes a lot of sense to play 2NT as forcing after a two-level jump. However, in this instance it is better for it to be an inquiry rather than a natural bid. There are many possible methods of responding to such an inquiry, but one of the simplest and most useful is for the 2NT bid to ask partner if he has a singleton. With a singleton he bids it; without a singleton he signs off with a minimum, jumps to game with a maximum or bids 3NT with two of the top three honors.

On this hand from the 1991 Venice Cup it would have been easier for North to judge had she been playing such a method:

East/West Vulnerable. Dealer West.

```
                ♠ K 10 9 6 4 3
                ♥ A Q 8
                ♦ 2
                ♣ 9 8 2
♠ J 2                        ♠ Q 8 5
♥ 10 6 2                     ♥ K
♦ 8 7 5                      ♦ A Q J 10 9
♣ A K J 7 6                  ♣ 0 5 4 3
                ♠ A 7
                ♥ J 9 7 5 4 3
                ♦ K 6 4 3
                ♣ Q
```

At both tables South bid two hearts over East's one diamond opening. At one table West bid three diamonds, taking away North's space to make a game try (though perhaps that is what a double should mean in this situation). North chose the aggressive action and there they were.

In the other room, West passed two hearts and North was able to bid 2NT as a forcing game try. When her partner showed her a diamond honor (the correct response according to North/South's methods), North was discouraged. Had South been able to show her singleton club, North would surely have felt happy to bid the good game.

Here are some more examples:

Both Sides Vulnerable. Dealer South.

♠ 9 6 2	♠ A J 10 4 3	West	North	East	South
♥ K Q 9 8 6 4 3	♥ 8 5	–	–	–	1♣
♦ 5	♦ A K J	2♥	Pass	2NT	Pass
♣ 9 2	♣ 10 7 6	3♦	Pass	3♥	All Pass

The singleton diamond is of no use at all to East; had his partner shown a singleton club he would have bid the game.

Both Sides Vulnerable. Dealer South.

♠ K Q 10 9 4 2	♠ A 3	West	North	East	South
♥ 3	♥ A 9 2	–	–	–	1♥
♦ 9 8 6 2	♦ Q 5 4 3	2♠	Pass	2NT	Pass
♣ K 6	♣ A 10 5 3	3♥	Pass	4♠	All Pass

Here any singleton would have suited East. Only if his partner had signed off in three spades would he have stayed out of game.

A Three-Level Jump Overcall

Here there is very little room. Partner hoped to take bidding space from the opponents; instead he has taken it from you. You just have to guess the best you can. A cuebid asks partner to help you with this guess. He should bid 3NT with a stopper, otherwise he can sign off with a minimum or bid his side-suit values with a maximum.

For the purposes of this quiz, assume that we play that 2NT shows a good four-card raise, a jump cuebid is a splinter while other jumps are fit-showing.

1. What would you bid on the following hands after the sequences:

(a) 1♣ – 1♥ – Pass – ?
(b) 1♦ – 1♠ – Pass – ?
(c) 1♥ – 2♣ – Pass – ?
(d) 1♠ – 2♦ – Pass – ?

(i) ♠ 10 2
♥ A Q 5 3
♦ 10 8 4
♣ K J 7 2

(ii) ♠ Q 10 7 4
♥ A Q 5
♦ K J 6 5 4
♣ 3

(iii) ♠ A 10 9 4
♥ A 9 6 5 4 3
♦ 7
♣ 9 8

(iv) ♠ 4
♥ K 9 6 5 3 2
♦ A K J
♣ J 6 4

(v) ♠ A 8
♥ A K 10 4
♦ 10 8 7
♣ 10 8 7 4

(vi) ♠ K J 7 4 2
♥ K 10 8 5
♦ –
♣ K 5 3 2

2. What would you bid on the following hands after the sequences:

(a) 1♣ – 1♦ – Pass – ?
(b) 1♦ – 2♣ – Pass – ?
(c) 1♥ – 1♠ – Pass – ?
(d) 1♠ – 2♥ – Pass – ?

(i) ♠ Q 9 8 5
♥ 9 3
♦ A 9 7 3 2
♣ Q 6

(ii) ♠ A K 10 9 7
♥ 6 5 4
♦ K 8 3
♣ 5 3

(iii) ♠ J 8 3
♥ K 10 4 3
♦ Q 10 9
♣ K 7 2

(iv) ♠ 10 3 2
♥ 10 9 2
♦ K Q 10 5 3 2
♣ K

(v) ♠ A J 10 5 4 2
♥ 4
♦ 8 2
♣ K J 10 4

(vi) ♠ Q 10 9 7 6
♥ K 4
♦ J 8 7
♣ A Q 4

3. What would you bid on the following hands after the sequences:

(a) 1♥ – 1♠ – Pass – 1NT – Pass – ?
(b) 1♥ – 1♠ – Pass – 2♣ – Pass – ?
(c) 1♥ – 1♠ – Pass – 2♦ – Pass – ?
(d) 1♥ – 1♠ – Pass – 2♥ – Pass – ?

(i) ♠ K Q 9 7
♥ 6 2
♦ Q 10 8
♣ Q J 9 5

(ii) ♠ A K 6 5 3
♥ Q 7 4
♦ 4
♣ A K 5 4

(iii) ♠ A Q 10 8 4
♥ 10 9 6
♦ 10 4 3
♣ 7 5

(iv) ♠ A K 10 9 8 5
♥ A 9 7 4
♦ K 4
♣ Q

(v) ♠ A K J 5 4
♥ 7 6
♦ 8 3
♣ Q J 10 5

(vi) ♠ A 10 8 7 4
♥ 9 3 2
♦ A 10 3
♣ A J

4. What would you bid on the following hands after the sequences:

(a) 1♠ – 2♣ – Pass – 2♦ – Pass – ?
(b) 1♠ – 2♣ – Pass – 2♥ – Pass – ?
(c) 1♠ – 2♣ – Pass – 2♠ – Pass – ?
(d) 1♠ – 2♣ – Pass – 2NT – Pass – ?

(i) ♠ K 4 3
♥ 10 4
♦ 9 7
♣ A J 10 9 6 5

(ii) ♠ 10
♥ 5 4 3 2
♦ J 9
♣ A K Q J 4 2

(iii) ♠ 10 8 4
♥ A 6
♦ A J 3
♣ A K 10 6 2

(iv) ♠ K Q 8
♥ 9 6 2
♦ 10
♣ A Q 9 7 5 2

(v) ♠ 5 4
♥ K Q 6 2
♦ 9
♣ K J 8 6 5 3

(vi) ♠ Q 9 4 3
♥ 9
♦ 9 6
♣ A K 10 7 3 2

5. What would you bid on the following hands after the sequences with neither side vulnerable:

(a) 1♥ – 2♠ – Pass – 2NT – Pass – ?
(b) 1♥ – 2♠ – Pass – 3♣ – Pass – ?
(c) 1♥ – 2♠ – Pass – 3♦ – Pass – ?
(d) 1♥ – 2♠ – Pass – 3♥ – Pass – ?

(i) ♠ K 9 7 4 3 2
♥ 2
♦ J 10 8
♣ A 10 6

(ii) ♠ Q 8 6 5 4 3
♥ 10 4
♦ 10
♣ Q 10 7 2

(iii) ♠ A Q 9 7 3 2
♥ 8 3
♦ J 3
♣ 9 7 4

(iv) ♠ A 10 9 6 4 3
♥ 6
♦ K J 4 3
♣ 9 8

(v) ♠ K 10 9 8 7 3
♥ J 9 4
♦ 9 3
♣ 4 3

(vi) ♠ A Q 10 8 7
♥ –
♦ 7 6 3
♣ J 10 9 8 5

1. (i) ♠ 10 2 (ii) ♠ Q 10 7 4 (iii) ♠ A 10 9 4
        ♥ A Q 5 3   ♥ A Q 5   ♥ A 9 6 5 4 3
        ♦ 10 8 4   ♦ K J 6 5 4   ♦ 7
        ♣ K J 7 2   ♣ 3   ♣ 9 8

    (iv) ♠ 4   (v) ♠ A 8   (vi) ♠ K J 7 4 2
         ♥ K 9 6 5 3 2 ♥ A K 10 4   ♥ K 10 8 5
         ♦ A K J   ♦ 10 8 7   ♦ –
         ♣ J 6 4   ♣ 10 8 7 4   ♣ K 5 3 2

(a) What would you bid after the sequence 1♣ – 1♥ – Pass – ?

(i) Two clubs. A rare example of a simple cuebid with four-card support. Had the opening bid been one diamond you would have stretched to 2NT, but with your club values badly placed you will content yourself with an unassuming cuebid.

(ii) Two clubs. Intending to make one further try even after a sign-off from partner.

(iii) Four diamonds. Splinter bid. It is quite possible to envision a slam, opposite, say: ♠5 ♥KQ872 ♦A642 ♣K72. There may be slight worries that this might allow your opponents to find a minor-suit sacrifice, but that is not so likely when North has passed.

(iv) Three spades. Splinter bid. There is some risk that this may allow the opponent to find a spade fit, but you have such a good hand that you really must make some sort of try. Partner could easily have: ♠A653 ♥AJ1084 ♦Q53 ♣5.

(v) 2NT. A four-card limit raise.

(vi) Four diamonds. Again partner could have: ♠Q5 ♥AQ762 ♦J762 ♣A4.

(b) What would you bid after the sequence 1♦ – 1♠ – Pass – ?

(i) 1NT. A difficult choice with no spade support or diamond stopper. The hand looks too good to pass and at least 1NT may get you to clubs or hearts. At part score level it may not matter that you do not have a diamond stopper.

(ii) Four spades. While you certainly have a good hand and could make a four club splinter, your hand is not ideal. South will have diamond strength and length over you, so you will not be able to develop tricks in that suit and if you try to play on a cross-ruff you are likely to be overruffed.

(iii) Four diamonds. Even though you do not have anything like as many HCP as the last hand you are much more suitable for a spade slam. Partner may have: ♠KQ762 ♥K5 ♦9843 ♣A5.

(iv) Two hearts. A straightforward change of suit.

(v) Two diamonds. This is a similar problem to (i) and it would not be wrong to bid 1NT, but this time you have a high spade honor which should make you lean toward supporting partner. Partner will bid a four-card heart suit if he has one.

(vi) Four diamonds. Even more reason this time than before.

(c) What would you bid after the sequence 1♥ – 2♣ – Pass – ?

(i) 2NT. A good heart stopper and club support. What more could you want? If partner is minimum he will go back to three clubs.

(ii) 2NT. This is horrible. You do not have a club fit but you are too good to pass. Only when partner has a good hand is there a possibility of him having only five clubs, so if he returns to three clubs, it will be a 6-1 fit. Your alternative is two diamonds, but that seems inappropriate with a weak suit and good heart stopper.

(iii) Pass. There is nothing to say when the opponents have bid your best suit.

(iv) Two hearts. It looks strange to cuebid with such length in the opponent's suit, but you don't want to bid no trumps unless partner can bid spades. If partner rebids two spades you can bid 2NT otherwise you will play in clubs.

(v) 3NT. Although you only have 11 HCP you must bid more than 2NT because nine tricks will be cold if partner has AKxxxx in clubs and nothing else (provided the opponents cannot run the diamonds).

(vi) Two hearts. Again you cannot bid no trumps with such shortage in an unbid suit even if you do have a good heart holding. Bid two hearts for the time being and see what happens.

(d) What would you bid after the sequence 1♠ – 2♦ – Pass – ?

(i) Two spades. With all your values outside spades, this hand is a little good for a simple raise to three diamonds.

(ii) Two spades. Difficult. It could indeed be right to show your singleton and good hand by bidding four clubs but your major-suit holdings suggest that the opponents are not likely to do any more bidding and there is no need to cramp your own auction. It is easy enough to see that 3NT may be the right contract, opposite, say, ♠63 ♥82 ♦AQ10872 ♣KQ5, and you may be able to get there if you take things slowly.

(iii) Two hearts. Even though you do not have opening values, it would be silly not to bid your heart suit when you could easily have game on if partner has a fit.

(iv) Two hearts. You may get around to supporting diamonds later.

(v) Two spades. 2NT would not be wrong but you would prefer to have either a diamond honor or a second spade stopper. If partner signs off in three diamonds, that will probably be the right contract.

(vi) Pass. This is a dreadful bidding problem. It would be very undisciplined to bid 2NT with minimum values and a void in partner's suit – even if he doesn't rebid diamonds, the communication problems in 3NT will be terrible. Best to pass smoothly and hope someone bids again.

2. (i) ♠ Q 9 8 5   (ii) ♠ A K 10 9 7 (iii) ♠ J 8 3
     ♥ 9 3   ♥ 6 5 4   ♥ K 10 4 3
     ♦ A 9 7 3 2   ♦ K 8 3   ♦ Q 10 9
     ♣ Q 6   ♣ 5 3   ♣ K 7 2
 (iv) ♠ 10 3 2   (v) ♠ A J 10 5 4 2 (vi) ♠ Q 10 9 7 6
     ♥ 10 9 2   ♥ 4   ♥ K 4
     ♦ K Q 10 5 3 2 ♦ 8 2   ♦ J 8 7
     ♣ K   ♣ K J 10 4   ♣ A Q 4

(a) What would you bid after the sequence 1♣ – 1♦ – Pass – ?

(i) Three diamonds. Not enough to do anything more exciting with just two loose queens outside the trump suit.

(ii) One spade. No reason not to bid your good suit.

(iii) 1NT. Minimum but just about worth it, particularly as it stops South introducing a major.

(iv) Four diamonds. This kind of hand is very difficult and here it is a little unrealistic—at the table someone would surely have bid a major. When in doubt, bid to the level of the fit but be conservative when no one else looks interested.

(v) One spade.

(vi) One spade.

(b) What would you bid after the sequence 1♦ – 2♣ – Pass – ?

(i) Pass. No real reason to get involved. If you feel you must bid, raising partner to three clubs might work well—it is unlikely to come to harm and might make the opponents misjudge their fit.

(ii) Two spades. Again, no reason not to bid your good suit even at the two level.

(iii) Three clubs. Although you have a diamond stopper (of sorts) and a club honor you are not strong enough in outside tricks to bid 2NT. If partner has a good hand he can bid again and then you will bid no trumps.

(iv) Pass. Nothing to say with such length in their suit.

(v) Two spades. This hand has tremendous potential and you will probably bid clubs enthusiastically next time.

(vi) Two diamonds. It would not be wrong to bid two spades, but partner may pass when three clubs is a much better contract. With a poor suit and good support for partner, first show the support.

(c) What would you bid after the sequence 1♥ – 1♠ – Pass – ?

(i) Three spades. Just about maximum for three spades—any more and you would bid 2NT, not three diamonds with such a poor suit.

(ii) Four spades. Bid to the level of the fit.

(iii) 1NT. It would be a mistake to support spades immediately with such a balanced hand and chunky heart holding.

(iv) Two diamonds. Usually you would support partner immediately with three trumps, but here it seems a pity not to bid your good diamond suit. Whether partner has a fit for diamonds may well be the key to the hand and it is the suit you would like him to lead should South become declarer.

(v) Four hearts. This is very close between a four heart splinter and a simple four spades. Bidding four spades could miss slam when partner has something like ♠K8762 ♥872 ♦A6 ♣AQ5, but bidding four hearts could let the opponents back into the auction with a profitable sacrifice.

(vi) 2NT. With so many high cards there is no need to bounce too high. If partner cannot make any kind of try over 2NT, there is no need to bid game.

(d) What would you bid after the sequence 1♠ – 2♥ – Pass – ?

(i) Pass. Nothing to say.

(ii) 2NT. Not quite what partner will expect, but you have to do something and it seems more descriptive than a heart raise.

(iii) Three hearts. Not quite good enough for two spades. The four-card support is good, but the unsupported outside cards are poor. Remember, partner often only has a five-card suit for a two heart overcall.

(iv) Three hearts. You would like to be a passed hand because then you could bid three diamonds and partner would know that you would have to have a heart fit to bid a new suit at the three level on a weakish hand. As it is three diamonds would overstate your values and would not tell partner about your excellent suitability for playing in hearts.

(v) Pass. Again, with our main length in the opponent's suit there is nothing to say.

(vi) 2NT. Natural and very descriptive.

3. (i) ♠ K Q 9 7   (ii) ♠ A K 6 5 3 (iii) ♠ A Q 10 8 4
     ♥ 6 2   ♥ Q 7 4   ♥ 10 9 6
     ♦ Q 10 8   ♦ 4   ♦ 10 4 3
     ♣ Q J 9 5   ♣ A K 5 4   ♣ 7 5
 (iv) ♠ A K 10 9 8 5 (v) ♠ A K J 5 4 (vi) ♠ A 10 8 7 4
     ♥ A 9 7 4   ♥ 7 6   ♥ 9 3 2
     ♦ K 4   ♦ 8 3   ♦ A 10 3
     ♣ Q   ♣ Q J 10 5 ♣ A J

(a) What would you bid after the sequence 1♥ – 1♠ – Pass – 1NT – Pass – ?

(i) Pass. The one spade overcall was very aggressive in the first place; there is no need to bid again.

(ii) Two hearts. You have an excellent hand and should have enough for game opposite partner's 9-12. It would be wrong to bid three clubs for partner would think you had a second five-card suit. You could just settle for 3NT but partner may have diamond weakness and three-card spade support.

(iii) Pass. No reason to act on such a balanced hand. Hope partner is maximum or you may be doubled.

(iv) Two hearts. It would not be wrong simply to bid four spades but the hand could play better in 3NT and there is no hurry. If partner bids two spades over two hearts you can raise to game; if he bids 2NT we can bid a forcing three spades and offer him the choice.

(v) Two clubs. With a nice, crisp 5-4 hand, just bid your second suit.

(vi) 2NT. If partner is maximum you may well have game. This is a slightly aggressive action but you have good intermediate cards and often do not need quite so many points to make game when you have been told where most of them are.

(b) What would you bid after the sequence 1♥ – 1♠ – Pass – 2♣ – Pass – ?

(i) Three clubs. Pass would surely attract some sympathy, but if you are going to overcall on such hands you shouldn't be too frightened afterwards. You do have four-card support for partner so a gentle raise is in order.

(ii) Two hearts. You have a tremendous hand in support of partner's clubs. It would be nice to be able to make a three diamond splinter, but it is not clear that that is what three diamonds means. You could bid four diamonds, but that is very space-consuming. If you start with two hearts, you can see what partner has to say and if he rebids three clubs you can always bid four diamonds. You don't want to get too carried away because your heart holding is very unsatisfactory.

(iii) Pass.

(iv) Two hearts. The ubiquitous cuebid strikes again! This hand cannot be described by a jump in spades because of the length in hearts. Two hearts gives partner the chance to show a secondary spade fit or bid no trumps, either of which would make your life easier.

(v) Three clubs. I know this hand is considerably better than the first one, but game is unlikely unless partner can bid again.

(vi) Two hearts. Another cuebid, this time hoping partner can bid 2NT.

(c) What would you bid after the sequence 1♥ – 1♠ – Pass – 2♦ – Pass – ?

(i) Pass. This time only three-card support and discretion should be the better part of valor!

(ii) 2NT. It is rare to bid no trumps in this position with no fit for partner, particularly with an inadequate heart guard, but what else are you to do?

(iii) Pass.

(iv) Two hearts. Again, unsatisfactory to limit with a jump in spades because of the heart length and, this time, diamond fit.

(v) Pass. Hard to see game with no diamond fit and no heart guard.

(vi) Two hearts. Too good for a raise to three diamonds. Just hope partner can bid no trumps.

(d) What would you bid after the sequence 1♥ – 1♠ – Pass – 2♥ – Pass – ?

(i) Two spades. This sign off does not promise any extra length in the suit.

(ii) Three clubs. No need to jump around. Three clubs is forcing as far as three spades and may help partner choose the right game.

(iii) Two spades.

(iv) Three hearts. Most of the time four spades would be fine, but sometimes you may miss a slam.

(v) Two spades. Close, but even though this hand is a lot better than (iii), there are still a lot of losers. If partner proceeds you should accept his try.

(vi) Three diamonds. You are too good to sign off, but not quite good enough to insist on game. You bid your best side-suit and let partner decide.

4. (i) ♠ K 4 3   (ii) ♠ 10   (iii) ♠ 10 8 4
        ♥ 10 4   ♥ 5 4 3 2   ♥ A 6
        ♦ 9 7   ♦ J 9   ♦ A J 3
        ♣ A J 10 9 6 5   ♣ A K Q J 4 2   ♣ A K 10 6 2

    (iv) ♠ K Q 8   (v) ♠ 5 4   (vi) ♠ Q 9 4 3
        ♥ 9 6 2   ♥ K Q 6 2   ♥ 9
        ♦ 10   ♦ 9   ♦ 9 6
        ♣ A Q 9 7 5 2   ♣ K J 8 6 5 3   ♣ A K 10 7 3 2

(a) What would you bid after the sequence 1♠ – 2♣ – Pass – 2♦ – Pass – ?

(i) Pass. Nothing to say unless partner makes a forcing bid.

(ii) Three clubs. It is hard to see that it is wrong to play this hand in clubs—the shorter partner's clubs the more important it is that they should be trumps. Also, you are a little too good to pass two diamonds and this way you give partner another chance. The heart suit is really too weak to bid.

(iii) Two spades. If partner has a spade stopper, 3NT should be fine.

(iv) Three clubs. You are a little too good to pass two diamonds (and do not like to pass with a singleton) but should not strain to bid no trumps with no fit for partner.

(v) Two hearts. There is no reason not to introduce another suit—if it is below the level of the first suit it does not show any extra values.

(vi) Pass. A minimum with a doubleton in support of partner.

(b) What would you bid after the sequence 1♠ – 2♣ – Pass – 2♥ – Pass – ?

(i) Pass.

(ii) Four hearts. A very suitable hand in support of hearts. There is some case for a three spade splinter.

(iii) Two spades. You will probably end up in four hearts, but there is no law against partner having good spade guards.

(iv) Three hearts. This is a little conservative with three-card support and a singleton, but the queen of spades is likely to be wasted.

(v) Four hearts. Bid to the level of the fit. Even though you are quite weak you have an excellent fit and should let partner know.

(vi) Three clubs. You shouldn't let partner languish in what may be a 5-1 fit when you have such a good six-card suit.

(c) What would you bid after the sequence 1♠ – 2♣ – Pass – 2♠ – Pass – ?

(i) Three clubs. This is such a weak overcall that it is more prudent to sign off than show the spade stopper. If partner is very strong he can bid on and then you can bid 3NT.

(ii) Three clubs. Not enough extra for any real enthusiasm—remember when partner has a fit the queen and jack of clubs may be wasted.

(iii) Three spades. You don't know what partner is doing but you should tell him you have a good hand without a second suit and without a spade stopper.

(iv) 2NT. This time you can show your good stopper since you have quite a respectable hand.

(v) Three clubs. Minimum overcall. You cannot introduce a second suit above the level of the first unless you have significant extra values.

(vi) Three clubs. This is a close decision between a sign-off and 2NT. Although minimum, the hand is quite promising because of the good club suit so it may well work better to own up to the spade stopper on this round.

(d) What would you bid after the sequence 1♠ – 2♣ – Pass – 2NT – Pass – ?

(i) Three clubs. Minimum.

(ii) Three clubs. Partner will usually have a club fit so the fact that your clubs are solid is not so important.

(iii) 3NT. Your club length may be something of a disappointment, but you have good compensation elsewhere.

(iv) Three clubs. Again a close decision, but the club suit is not very good and the good spade holding implies that one of the red suits will be wide open.

(v) Three clubs. Minimum.

(vi) Three clubs. Minimum.

5. (i) ♠ K 9 7 4 3 2 (ii) ♠ Q 8 6 5 4 3 (iii) ♠ A Q 9 7 3 2
         ♥ 2   ♥ 10 4   ♥ 8 3
         ♦ J 10 8   ♦ 10   ♦ J 3
         ♣ A 10 6   ♣ Q 10 7 2   ♣ 9 7 4

(iv) ♠ A 10 9 6 4 3 (v) ♠ K 10 9 8 7 3 (vi) ♠ A Q 10 8 7
     ♥ 6   ♥ J 9 4   ♥ –
     ♦ K J 4 3   ♦ 9 3   ♦ 7 6 3
     ♣ 9 8   ♣ 4 3   ♣ J 10 9 8 5

(a) What would you bid after the sequence 1♥ – 2♠ – Pass – 2NT – Pass – with neither side vulnerable?

(i) Three hearts. No reason not to show your singleton.

(ii) Three spades. This really is sub-minimum with neither side vulnerable. Unless your partnership readily allows for such weak overcalls, it is better to sign off.

(iii) 3NT. This shows two of the top three honors and a balanced hand and lets partner decide the final contract.

(iv) Three hearts. A very good hand.

(v) Three spades. Minimum with no singleton.

(vi) Three hearts. It is quite enterprising to make a weak jump overcall with this hand because it has a great deal of playing strength even if there is only a five-card spade suit. It is important to follow it through, however, and show the shortage.

(b) What would you bid after the sequence 1♥ – 2♠ – Pass – 3♣ – Pass – with neither side vulnerable?

(i) Four clubs. It is not clear whether partner has a spade fit, but you have a good hand with a club fit so should simply raise partner.

(ii) Four clubs. Although you are (sub-)minimum you have an excellent club fit so you have no option but to raise partner.

(iii) Four clubs. Again, show partner your partial fit.

(iv) Three diamonds. Partner will not expect you to have a second suit, but he will expect you to have values in diamonds which is what you have.

(v) Three spades. No club fit, no enthusiasm for anything. You wish you could pass.

(vi) Four hearts. You must do something to show your enthusiasm. You have a fantastic hand with five-card club support and a void heart.

(c) What would you bid after the sequence 1♥ – 2♠ – Pass – 3♦ – Pass – with neither side vulnerable?

(i) Four diamonds.

(ii) Three spades. Sign-off.

(iii) Three spades. Sign-off. You have a much better hand than (ii), but it is hard to think of anything else to say. You do not have much of a diamond fit, nor an exceptionally good spade suit. It is best to go quietly until a fit is unearthed.

(iv) Four hearts. Again, an exceptional hand in support of partner—good four-card support, a singleton outside and the ace in your long suit. However, if he signs off in four spades you will respect his decision.

(v) Three spades. Sign-off.

(vi) Four diamonds. You greatly preferred clubs, but you do have a fair hand in support of diamonds.

(d) What would you bid after the sequence 1♥ – 2♠ – Pass – 3♥ – Pass – with neither side vulnerable?

(i) Four spades. Maximum.

(ii) Three spades. Minimum.

(iii) Three spades. Again, this is better than (ii), but is still not very exciting and it does not usually pay to push for thin non-vulnerable games.

(iv) Four spades. Maximum.

(v) Three spades. Minimum.

(vi) Four spades. Maximum. Even though you only have five spades you have terrific playing strength and must accept partner's invitation.

29

Chapter

29

When Opponents Keep Bidding

So far we have discussed why we want to bid, what we should bid and how the bidding should continue. But the assumption has been made that your opposition, having made their opening bid, have then kept quiet. This is actually quite a rare occurrence. Much more often they will continue to bid, making life difficult for you. The only reason that we have taken so much time and space discussing what to do in a free auction is because all the same principles apply and it is easier to discuss them without opposing bidding cluttering up the auction.

In this chapter we will look at the various situations that occur when opponents keep bidding and then at some examples from actual games.

The main consideration will be how to respond to partner's overcall when the next hand bids. Let's look at some examples.

RESPONDING TO PARTNER'S OVERCALL WHEN THE NEXT HAND BIDS
Responder doubles, 1♦ – 1♠ – Double

A penalty double

There is not a great deal to be said about bidding in this situation. If you are extremely short in partner's suit (like a singleton or void) there is a reasonable case for trying to rescue him from a one-level overcall since he probably only has a five-card suit. If his overcall was at the two-level or higher you would have a very good reason indeed for trying to rescue him. He has already shown a good suit and there is no reason to suppose he will have any support for your suit. All you will usually achieve is raising the level and increasing the penalty.

If you do decide to try to improve the situation you may have a long suit of our own, in which case you can simply bid it. However, sometimes you have length in both the unbid suits and would like partner to choose between them. Many years ago it was decided to use redouble for this purpose. After all, if you were to redouble with confidence

at such a low level, your opponents would only remove themselves to a safer spot. This is called an SOS redouble and it simply asks partner to choose between the remaining suits.

A negative double

This is by far the most common treatment in duplicate clubs and tournaments. The double is not for penalties, it merely shows values and a desire to compete, the precise requirements for the double depending on partnership agreement.

Your opponents have taken away none of your bidding space and all your bids mean just what they would have meant without the double. If anything you should raise partner a little more aggressively than previously because it is more likely that the opponents have the balance of high cards and you should do all you can to get in the way of their bidding before they get a chance to exchange precise information.

You have one bid available which you did not have before—redouble. The most common use of this bid is to show a hand which would have been difficult to bid without the double—reasonable values and tolerance but no real fit for partner, something like:

(a)		(b)	
♠	Q 4	♠	K 7 3
♥	K 10 7 6	♥	A 10 5
♦	A 5 4	♦	Q 9 7 3
♣	Q1052	♣	K43

Hand (a) would probably have bid 1NT without the double, but it would not have been really satisfactory because of the inadequate diamond guard. Hand (b) would have made a two diamond cuebid without the double but it is not really very suitable for play in spades and now that there is an alternative, it is better to redouble.

Whereas this use of a redouble is common in the United Kingdom, in the United States and some other countries a different treatment is more popular. The redouble is used to show support for partner that includes one of the top two honors; the corollary of this is that a single raise denies a top honor. When I was discussing single raises I noted that lead-direction was an important feature of such a raise, so here we have a method of distinguishing between lead-directing and non-lead-directing raises. That is obviously a great advantage of the method; the disadvantage is that you do not always deprive opponents of bidding space and therefore do not make life as difficult for them as you could.

Here is a problem for you, first in the bidding and then with the opening lead:

Both Sides Vulnerable. Dealer South.

West	North	East	South
–	–	–	1♦
1♥	Dble(*)	2♥	2♠
3♥	3♠	Pass	4♠
?			

(*) negative

West holds:

```
      ♠ A 4 2
      ♥ A Q 7 5 3
      ♦ 3
      ♣ J 10 8 6
```

I am sure everyone would pass. It looks as if North/South might have been pushed into game and it is not clear whether this is a good or bad thing to do. What would you lead? You might lead a diamond hoping to find partner with a quick entry, but it is always dangerous to lead a singleton when it is declarer's suit. If partner does not have a quick entry you might establish tricks for declarer. It could be right to lead a club, hoping to establish a trick in the suit and perhaps an entry to partner's hand so that he could lead a heart through declarer. Very difficult.

Mexico's Doctor George Rosenkranz is a strong advocate of using redouble to show a single raise with a top honor in the suit. When he held the hand the auction was:

West	North	East	South
–	–	–	1♦
1♥	Dble(*)	Rdble(**)	1♠
3♥	3♠	Pass	4♠
?			

(*) negative
(**) showing a top heart honor

He knew his partner had the king of hearts. He knew he could lead his singleton diamond, win the ace of spades, put partner in with the king of hearts and get a diamond ruff. It was reasonable to suppose there was at least one further defensive trick, perhaps two if his partner had as little as the jack of hearts. So he doubled four spades and led his diamond. This was the full deal:

```
              ♠ Q 10 7 5
              ♥ 10 6
              ♦ Q J 9 5
              ♣ A 7 4

   ♠ A 4 2                    ♠ 9 8
   ♥ A Q 7 5 3                ♥ K J 4 2
   ♦ 3                        ♦ 10 4 2
   ♣ J 10 8 6                 ♣ Q 5 3 2

              ♠ K J 6 3
              ♥ 9 8
              ♦ A K 8 7 6
              ♣ K 9
```

When East played back the ten of diamonds for his partner to ruff, West knew he could underlead his heart honors again to get another ruff. This led to an extremely useful 500 penalty.

Responder Bids a New Suit, 1♦ – 1♠ – 2♣

Competitive doubles
Most pairs play the two club bid in this position as forcing so there is little point in playing a double as penalty—all it will do is warn the opponents of bad breaks. A double can be put to a much more profitable use. What should we bid after the above sequence with:

(a)	♠ 6	(b)	♠ K 4	(c)	♠ K J 4
	♥ Q J 10 9 8 4		♥ K 10 7 6 3		♥ K Q 10 9 4
	♦ A 6 2		♦ 7 5 3		♦ 7 3
	♣ K 4 3		♣ A 4 3		♣ 8 6 4

You would bid two hearts with hands (a) and (b), but on (a) you would like partner to pass even if he is void, whereas on (b) you would be happy to hear him go back to two spades. On hand (c) you would no doubt choose to bid two spades, but would have liked to show your good heart suit as well.

A competitive double in this situation shows a heart suit with some spade support. It asks partner to choose between the two suits. You would expect him to bid a three-card heart suit, otherwise go back to two spades. To bid two hearts, on the other hand, shows a good suit and a hand that does not want to hear preference back to spades—either the hearts will be extremely good or the spade support nonexistent.

So, on the example hands you would double with both hand (b) and hand (c). With hand (b) you wish to offer partner a genuine choice; with hand (c) you would like him to know about your heart suit because it might help him to evaluate his hand or help him with the opening lead.

Raises
All direct raises are obstructive, just as before. However, there is a general principle to keep in mind. The more information the opponents have already exchanged, the less point there is in trying to disrupt them. They are more likely to guess accurately, particularly if you tell them where your values lie. After the auction 1♦ – 1♠ – Pass or 1♦ – 1♠ – Double, there is much greater reason to bid aggressively than after your given auction. That is not to say you should

not raise partner obstructively, just that you need a slightly better reason for doing so.

Cuebids

Now you have two cuebids to choose between. The lowest cuebid (here two diamonds) should be the one that shows three-card support and all three-level bids should show four-card support. Now both opponents have bid there is even less chance that you have any game on other than in spades (or occasionally hearts), so there is no reason for a natural 2NT.

So 2NT shows a balanced four-card raise, three clubs and three hearts both show shortage in that suit with four-card support and three diamonds shows values there, also with four-card support (though could still be played as natural and forcing if you prefer).

Responder Raises, 1♦ – 1♠ – 2♦

Responsive doubles

It is possible that you may want to make a penalty double in this situation, but it is rare for such a double to be profitable at such a low level when the opponents have found an eight-card fit. It is much more useful to play a double to show values in the outside suits with no clear bid to make. Here are some examples:

♠ K 4	♠ 6	♠ 7 3
♥ Q J 7 6 3	♥ K 10 9 7 6	♥ A Q 10 9
♦ 5 2	♦ 4	♦ 6 4 3
♣ A 10 6 3	♣ A J 10 9 6 4	♣ K J 10 8 4

The exact meaning of the double depends a little on the suits involved. As usual you concentrate more on the major suits. It might help if you look at how you expect partner to respond. If partner is minimum you do not expect him to bid above the level of his overcall. He should choose between rebidding his suit and bidding any new suit that is between their suit and his suit, i.e. here he should choose between spades and hearts, but if the opponents had been bidding clubs he could choose between spades and either red suit. He may bid a three-card suit provided it is below the level of his suit. If he wishes to show extra values he can bid a new four-card suit above the level of his first suit, rebid no trumps, jump in his first suit with six or cuebid the opponents's suit.

Here are some examples after the sequence: 1♦ – 1♠ – 2♦ – Double; Pass – ?

♠ K 10 9 4 3	♠ K Q 10 9 3	♠ A 10 9 3 2
♥ A 6 2	♥ 7	♥ K Q 10 2
♦ 7 5 3	♦ A 7 5 3	♦ 6
♣ A 4	♣ 7 4 3	♣ K 7 4
Bid 2♥	Bid 2♠	Bid 3♥

♠ A 10 9 3 2	♠ K Q 10 9 6	♠ K J 10 9 8 4
♥ K 7 4	♥ 7 3	♥ A 2
♦ 6	♦ A Q 4	♦ 7 5 3
♣ K Q 10 2	♣ K 10 3	♣ A 6
Bid 3♣	Bid 2NT	Bid 3♠

It is possible to use the responsive double a little like an unassuming cuebid. Suppose we hold:

♠ K 10 4
♥ A 6
♦ A 7 4 3
♣ 10 9 6 2

and the bidding goes: 1♦ – 1♠ – 2♦ – ? you are a little good for a simple two spades, but do not want to risk punishing partner by forcing him to the three level when he is minimum. Instead you start with a double and if he rebids two hearts you convert to two spades. You cannot come to any harm—whatever he bids you go back to spades. You can do this whatever suits are involved since you know that he will not go past the level of his suit without extra values.

You can also use a double when you have only one of the two missing suits and some tolerance for partner. Suppose the bidding goes 1♣ – 1♠ – 2♣ and you hold:

♠ K 4
♥ Q J 10 8 3
♦ 7 4 3
♣ A 6 2

Again you do not know whether to bid two hearts or two spades. What you can do is double. If partner bids two diamonds you convert to two hearts and he knows to choose between the majors.

Where there is no space at all, as after 1♥ – 1♠ – 2♥, double should be treated as an unassuming cuebid. You have seen that partner will not bid past the level of his own suit without extra values so there is no danger of getting too high.

If the opponents make a jump raise, the double keeps the same meaning, although obviously more playing strength is needed for such an action. However high responder raises, the meaning of double is basically unaffected, although it is much more likely to be passed the higher the level of the auction. A double of a game bid will be passed unless the overcaller has unusual playing strength.

Raises

Again, all raises are obstructive. A 2NT bid shows a good balanced raise; a three diamond cuebid shows shortage and jumps in hearts and clubs show values there with four-card support for spades.

Responder bids 1NT, e.g. 1♦ – 1♠ – 1NT

Double

Until recently double in this position was played as penalty but then players began to realize it didn't work very well because someone always bid over 1NT, either the opener or the overcaller, and it was rare to find a profitable penalty at such a low level. It was found to be much more useful to play a double as responsive, i.e. in principle showing the other two suits.

Raises

Again all raises are obstructive and a two diamond cuebid is available to show a good single raise. A jump to three diamonds would show shortage, whereas a jump in another suit would be a "fit raise."

THE OVERCALLER WANTS TO BID AGAIN OPPOSITE A SILENT PARTNER

There are two main situations when you may want to bid again despite partner's silence:

1. In a balancing position;

2. When you have significant extra values.

1. The overcaller bids again in a balancing situation

The whole subject of "balancing" or "protective bidding" is handled in detail in another section of this book. However, you have repeatedly seen that when opponents have a fit, so do you. It is bad practice to allow the opponents to play at a low level in their fit when you could make a contract at the same level in your fit. You want to bid even if you go down one. Perhaps they will misjudge by letting you play in a making contract or perhaps they will bid on and go down when, if they had left you alone, you would also have gone down. If you do not put your opponents to this sort of guess they will never guess wrong.

After an auction such as 1♦ – 1♠ – 2♦ – Pass – Pass it will rarely be right to pass. Partner has probably passed because he has no support for spades. Even if you do not have many extra values you should try to bid in this type of situation. Here are some examples:

(a) ♠ K 10 7 6 4 (b) ♠ A Q 7 4 2 (c) ♠ K J 10 7 6 4
   ♥ A Q 7 3   ♥ J 10 3   ♥ A 3
   ♦ 4   ♦ 5   ♦ 7 6
   ♣ 7 6 2   ♣ K 10 9 6   ♣ Q 6 3

With all these hands partner has probably passed because he has diamond length—he doesn't have a natural 2NT bid, remember. He is expecting you to bid again with shortage in diamonds. With hand (a) you simply bid your second suit to offer partner a choice. With hand (b) you do not have the values to bid three clubs, but a double implies more or less this distribution so partner can choose the trump suit. With hand (c) you rebid your own good six-card suit.

2. The overcaller bids again with extra values

There are many hands on which the overcaller would like to bid again because he has extra values, however it will not always be convenient for him to do so. You should always listen to the auction and to what the opponents tell you. It is much safer to bid on when the opponents have found a fit than when they have not.

Here are some examples of when a hand is worth another bid and when it is not:

Neither Side Vulnerable. Dealer South.

♠ A K 10 8 5 2	West	North	East	South
♥ K 3 2	–	–	–	1♥
♦ J 10	1♠	Pass	Pass	Dble
♣ 7 3	?			

This is a classic case of when you should keep your mouth firmly shut. Yes, I know, you had a hand which was too good for a weak jump overcall and you were always intending to overcall and then bid your suit again to show partner a decent hand with a good six-card suit, but you must listen to the bidding. Partner has not raised spades and the opener implied shortage when he re-opened with a double. Isn't it likely that North has most of the outstanding spades? In these days of negative doubles, defenders in North's position cannot double immediately, but have to pass and hope to pass partner's re-opening double. If you bid two spades here, you may well find that North will double, even happier to defend now you are at the two level. You should show some discretion here and pass for the time being; after all, if North removes the double you can always bid two spades on the next round.

North/South Vulnerable. Dealer South.

♠ K J 10 9 3	West	North	East	South
♥ Q J 9 4	–	–	–	1♣
♦ K 10 4	1♠	1NT	Pass	Pass
♣ 5	?			

When this hand occurred in a teams match, one West passed and one West bid two hearts. Both contracts made exactly, so bidding was worth 5 IMPs to the aggressive West's team. The full deal was:

         ♠ A Q 7 6
         ♥ 8 7
         ♦ 9 6 5 3 2
         ♣ K 7

♠ K J 10 9 3   ♠ 5 2
♥ Q J 9 4   ♥ A 5 3 2
♦ K 10 4   ♦ J 7
♣ 5   ♣ Q J 9 3 2

         ♠ 8 4
         ♥ K 10 6
         ♦ A Q 8
         ♣ A 10 8 6 4

Both Sides Vulnerable. Dealer South.

♠ K J 10 4 3	West	North	East	South
♥ 8	–	–	–	1♥
♦ K Q 5	1♠	3♥(*)	Pass	Pass
♣ A 10 5 2	?			

(*) pre-emptive

Here, you should make a re-opening double. You have a very respectable overcall and the opponents have found a good fit, almost certainly nine cards. On this occasion the full deal is:

	♠ A 7 6	
	♥ 10 7 5 4	
	♦ 10 6 3 2	
	♣ K 8	
♠ K J 10 4 3		♠ 9 8 5
♥ 8		♥ A Q 2
♦ K 7 5		♦ Q 4
♣ A J 10 5		♣ 9 7 6 4 2
	♠ Q 2	
	♥ K J 9 6 3	
	♦ A J 9 8	
	♣ Q 3	

You will make an overtrick in three spades, because of the favorable lie of the black suits. On the other hand, the opponents would also have made three hearts, losing just a trick in each suit.

Neither Side Vulnerable. Dealer South.

♠ 4 3	West	North	East	South
♥ A K 7 6 4	–	–	–	1♦
♦ K 2	1♥	1♠	Pass	2♦
♣ A J 7 4	?			

Here you are in quite a dangerous position because your opponents have not found a fit and North is unlimited. However, if you pass it is probable that two diamonds will become the final contract and bidding might have pushed them up a level. West has considerable extra values and also four cards in the unbid suit, clubs, so has a clear takeout double. When there is an unbid suit that is inconvenient to bid, like clubs here, a double tends to show four cards in that suit. If the minor suits were swapped, you would have been able to bid two diamonds, in which case a double would imply a 5-3-3-2 distribution with only three cards in the unbid suit.

Both Sides Vulnerable. Dealer South.

♠ A Q 7 5 4	West	North	East	South
♥ Q 7 2	–	–	–	1♥
♦ A J 9 5 2	1♠	1NT	Pass	2♣
♣ –	2♦	3♣	Pass	Pass
	?			

This is a difficult decision. The opponents have found a fit, albeit one that we know is breaking badly. It is very likely

that you have an eight-card fit in either diamonds or spades, but you also have good defense. I imagine that a panel of experts would disagree. My decision would be to double, offering partner the choice of defending when he has good clubs or, when his clubs are weak, showing some delayed support for one of my suits. However, this could easily backfire and see us losing 670.

THE BIDDING GETS HIGHER AND HIGHER

High-level bidding decisions are always difficult to judge. One of the worse things that can happen in bidding terms is to let the opponents bid and make game when you could have bid and made a game yourself. However, average players often use that as an excuse for persistent overbidding. They see the possibility of losing a large swing and prefer to settle for a small loss instead. This is not unreasonable as a philosophy, but it is important not to take it too far. If you find yourselves losing 5 IMPs or so every time there is a high-level bidding decision, then you are bidding too much.

You do have the Law of Total Tricks to help you. It is more reliable than the judgment of all but the very best players. Bidding to the limit of the fit is a good guideline.

The other thing to consider is whether you can help partner make the right decision. Consider the following bidding situation:

West	North	East	South
3♠	4♥	4♠	?

Suppose you, South, hold:

♠ 7 6 2
♥ K 5
♦ J 4 3
♣ A Q 10 9 2

You judge that you want to bid five hearts. If you simply bid five hearts all will be well provided East doesn't bid five spades. However, if he does bid five spades you will not know what to do next. If you pass (or double) partner will not know if he is supposed to bid on or not and if he passes he will probably lead a heart which could be bad for the defense. Why not bid five clubs instead? In the past this would have been interpreted as a slam try, but these days it is considered more important to try to judge whether to bid on or to defend. Now when East bids five spades you can pass happily and leave it up to partner. If he chooses to defend a club lead could well be best for the defense.

A word of warning. Care has to be exercised in the use of such bids. Consider the following auction:

West	North	East	South
1♥	1♠	4♣(*)	?

(*) splinter

Suppose you, South, hold:

     ♠ K J 10 3
     ♥ 5
     ♦ K J 9 8 4
     ♣ Q 10 4

Yes, you could bid four diamonds. It might help partner judge whether or not to sacrifice and it might help him find the right lead. But think what it will do for the opponents.

If East has a heart fit and is short in clubs, where do you think his other values are? Surely not in spades. He probably has the remaining diamond honors and you will be helping the opponents if you show them where the missing ones are. If you bid four spades West has to decide whether to pass, double or bid on. He would double with a bad hand, bid on with a very good hand and pass with a medium strength hand. If he passes East has then to decide. If, on the other hand, you bid four diamonds the opponents have more room to describe their hands to each other—West can bid freely without committing his side to the five level; if he passes or doubles, East can also bid freely without committing his side to a higher level. What a four diamond bid achieves is to commit us to bidding four spades while allowing the opponents to express a wider range of values without committing themselves to anything. You would need a very good reason indeed to make such a bid.

EXAMPLES FROM PLAY

In the first example, you see the overcaller make a game try in much the same way as he would if he had opened the bidding. However, whether his partner should accept the try depends upon the standard of the overcaller's card play!

1. Both Sides Vulnerable. Dealer West.

     ♠ A J 9 6 5
     ♥ A K 10 6 2
     ♦ –
     ♣ 8 7 5

♠ 2   ♠ Q 8 4 3
♥ Q 8   ♥ 9 5 4
♦ Q 10 5 3 2   ♦ A K 9 8
♣ A Q J 4 2   ♣ 6 3

     ♠ K 10 7
     ♥ J 7 3
     ♦ J 7 6 4
     ♣ K 10 9

Room 1:

West	North	East	South
1♦	1♠	2♦	2♠
3♦	3♥	Pass	3♠
All Pass			

Room 2:

West	North	East	South
1♦(*)	1♠	1NT	2♠
2NT(**)	3♥	Pass	4♠
Pass	Pass	Dble	All Pass

(*)   Precision
(**) Both minors

In both rooms, North's three heart bid was a game try, asking partner to revalue his hand. Here one could argue that both North/South pairs did well. In Room 1, South downgraded his balanced hand and his poor heart holding and signed off in three spades. His judgment was vindicated when he played trumps in normal fashion and made just nine tricks.

In Room 2 the bidding was much more revealing, even without East's final double. Here South reckoned that he would be able to pick up the spade suit without loss and then, hopefully, take a heart finesse through the opening bidder, so he jumped to game. He ruffed the diamond lead, cashed the ace of hearts, ran the jack of spades, played a spade to the ten, cashed the king of spades, played a heart to the ten, drew the last trumps and cashed his hearts for ten tricks, +590.

In the last example, it was arguable whether or not South overbid; here it is clear-cut.

2. Neither Side Vulnerable. Dealer East.

     ♠ K 5 4 2
     ♥ 10 9 8
     ♦ A K 10 4
     ♣ K 7

♠ J 9 8   ♠ A 7
♥ K 7   ♥ J 6 5
♦ Q 9 5 3   ♦ J 2
♣ Q 10 8 6   ♣ A J 9 5 3 2

     ♠ Q 10 6 3
     ♥ A Q 4 3 2
     ♦ 8 7 6
     ♣ 4

West	North	East	South
–	–	1♣	1♥
Dble	Rdble	2♣	2♠
Pass	4♠	All Pass	

South surely bid too much. North had shown about 11 or more HCP, without a particularly good heart fit. There was no reason to suppose that he had a fit for spades. Although North does not promise another bid with his redouble it is very unlikely that he will pass two clubs out. In this instance he would have bid a simple two hearts to end the auction.

In the next example there was too much bidding done by a balanced hand.

3. East/West Vulnerable. Dealer East.

```
              ♠ A J 8 2
              ♥ Q 10 2
              ♦ A 3 2
              ♣ J 3 2
♠ K 7                      ♠ 10 9 3
♥ J 8 3                    ♥ A 9 6 5 4
♦ Q 10 7 5 4               ♦ K
♣ K 9 7                    ♣ Q 10 6 5
              ♠ Q 6 5 4
              ♥ K 7
              ♦ J 9 8 6
              ♣ A 8 4
```

West	North	East	South
–	–	Pass	Pass
Pass	1♦	1♥	1♠
2♥	2♠	Pass	Pass
3♥	Pass	Pass	Dble
All Pass			

This is a good lesson in only bidding to the level of the fit. North chose to open his better minor in fourth seat and East made a normal but minimum one heart overcall. South bid his spades, West raised hearts and North raised spades. The bidding now came around to West who, for no good reason, went on to three hearts. South produced an aggressive double and that was –300. In addition, the defense has some chance of beating two spades—when declarer plays a trump to the jack, East should drop the nine or ten and declarer may well run the queen on the next round, thus losing a trump trick to go with a heart and two tricks in each minor.

In our next example, the overcaller gets the chance to make more than one game try before giving up.

4. East/West Vulnerable. Dealer East.

```
              ♠ A 9
              ♥ A K J 9 5 2
              ♦ Q 10 7
              ♣ 7 2
♠ 7 6 2                    ♠ K Q 10 4 3
♥ Q                        ♥ 10 7 6
♦ K J 6 4                  ♦ A 9 3
♣ K Q 10 9 6               ♣ J 8
              ♠ J 8 5
              ♥ 8 4 3
              ♦ 8 5 2
              ♣ A 5 4 3
```

Room 1:

West	North	East	South
–	–	Pass	Pass
1♣	1♥	1♠	2♥
Pass	2♠	Dble	Pass
Pass	3♦	Pass	3♥
All Pass			

Here it was West who opened with a sub-minimum one club in third seat and North made a full-weight one heart overcall. East bid his spade suit and South, rather aggressively, raised hearts. This does not seem to have a great deal to recommend it, with so few values, no heart honor and no ruffing value. North moved on with a game try of two spades. When there is a choice of try, as here, it usually works best to make the cheapest bid, leaving as much room as possible for investigation. East doubled and South passed.

This is an interesting situation and one which aspiring partnerships should discuss. North/South are forced as far as three hearts; there is no way that the bidding can stop below this level. What is South's weakest action after East's double? Some argue that the weakest action is to bid three hearts immediately, others say that a pass is always the weakest action. There are many similar situations so it is important for each partnership to have a rule that covers them all.

Here South's pass allowed North to make a further game try of three diamonds, which South declined, and North was sufficiently disciplined to let the auction drop, having described his hand well. That South would have done better not to raise hearts immediately is demonstrated by just how poor a contract three hearts is. It is lucky that there are only two losers in the red suits. North/South made +140.

Room 2:

West	North	East	South
–	–	Pass	Pass
Pass	1♥	1♠	Pass
2♠	3♥	Pass	Pass
3♠	All Pass		

At this table West passed in third seat and North opened the bidding with one heart. After the one spade overcall, this South did not raise hearts even after an opening bid. West raised to two spades and North bid his hearts again (though surely South would have done so had North passed). When three hearts was passed around to him, West opted to bid a third spade, despite having only three-card support. It may seem as if this refutes the Law of Total Tricks, but it was not unreasonable in view of his singleton heart and good playing strength in clubs. His judgment was vindicated when his partner, too, made nine tricks, +140, and a swing of 7 IMPs.

The decision of whether or not to overcall shows the fine line between the dangers in benefitting the opponents, perhaps by losing a large penalty or telling them where your cards are, and the advantages to your side. Wherever you draw the line there will always be examples where it would have worked better to take some other action. In the next example, according to our discussions, you would not have overcalled on North's hand and you would not have done as well as he did.

5. Both Sides Vulnerable. Dealer West.

```
                    ♠ 9 7 6
                    ♥ K Q 4
                    ♦ K 8 5 3
                    ♣ 10 9
♠ –                              ♠ K J 10 8 3 2
♥ A J 9 6 2                      ♥ 5 3
♦ 9 4                           ♦ Q 7 6
♣ K Q 8 7 5 2                   ♣ 6 3
                    ♠ A Q 5 4
                    ♥ 10 8 7
                    ♦ J 10 2
                    ♣ A J 4
```

Room 1:

West	North	East	South
1♥	2♦	2♠	Dble
3♣	3♦	Pass	3♠
Pass	3NT	All Pass	

Room 2:

West	North	East	South
1♥	Pass	1♠	Pass
2♣	Pass	2♠	All Pass

In our discussion of the requirements for a two-level overcall in a minor we decided that we should have a six-card suit most of the time, particularly when vulnerable. Thus, we would not advocate a two diamond overcall with that North hand. However, in Room 1, North not only overcalled two diamonds, but felt he had too much strength to pass on the next round after his partner's competitive double. After his three diamond rebid, South showed his spade stopper and North bid 3NT, a contract which could not be beaten on any defense.

In Room 2, North passed throughout! Two spades went three down for an 8 IMP swing.

The following hand is weak in a different way and here we would have overcalled:

6. North/South Vulnerable. Dealer East.

```
                    ♠ A K 9 5 4 2
                    ♥ 4 2
                    ♦ J 10
                    ♣ J 10 7
♠ Q 3                            ♠ J 8
♥ K 9 6 5                        ♥ Q J 8 7 3
♦ 7 3                           ♦ K 8 4
♣ K Q 9 6 4                     ♣ A 5 3
                    ♠ 10 7 6
                    ♥ A 10
                    ♦ A Q 9 6 5 2
                    ♣ 8 2
```

Room 1:

West	North	East	South
–	–	1♥	Pass
4♥	All Pass		

In this room neither North nor South dared enter the auction at unfavorable vulnerability so East played in four hearts going two down.

Room 2:

West	North	East	South
–	–	1♥	2♦
3♦	3♠	Pass	4♠
All Pass			

Here, South dared to overcall his diamonds—at least he had a good six-card suit. Now North was also more optimistic because of his partial diamond fit and bid three spades which South was happy to raise to game. On a heart lead, with the diamond finesse right, declarer made all thirteen tricks for 710.

On the next example the overcall is routine but West introduced a new suit into the auction on very few high cards and that worked well for his side.

7. Neither Side Vulnerable. Dealer South.

```
                    ♠ 10 5 2
                    ♥ K 10 8 4
                    ♦ A K 7 5
                    ♣ K 4
♠ J 9 6                          ♠ K 7 3
♥ J                              ♥ A 9 7 3 2
♦ Q 6                           ♦ J 4
♣ Q 10 9 7 6 5 2                ♣ A J 3
                    ♠ A Q 8 4
                    ♥ Q 6 5
                    ♦ 10 9 8 3 2
                    ♣ 8
```

West	North	East	South
–	–	–	Pass
Pass	1♦	1♥	Dble
2♣	Pass	3♣	3♦
All Pass			

Here North opened one diamond in third seat and East had a perfectly respectable one heart overcall. South might have done better to raise his partner's diamonds immediately, but he preferred to introduce his spades with a negative double. This gave West the chance to show his clubs—a reasonable bid despite the lack of high cards. East now raised to three clubs and South had to go to three diamonds, which went one down when East found the good opening lead of the ace of hearts. He then gave his partner a ruff, won the club switch, gave his partner another ruff and then sat back and waited for a spade trick.

Of course, when we have a good fit we don't need so many high cards to make game.

8. Neither Side Vulnerable. Dealer West.

```
            ♠ A J 8 6
            ♥ 3
            ♦ A K 10 8 3 2
            ♣ 7 6
♠ K Q 5 3                ♠ 7 4 2
♥ 10                     ♥ K Q 9 7 6
♦ 5 4                    ♦ J 9
♣ A Q 10 4 3 2           ♣ 9 8 5
            ♠ 10 9
            ♥ A J 8 5 4 2
            ♦ Q 7 6
            ♣ K J
```

West	North	East	South
1♣	1♦	1♥	2♥
3♣	3♠	Pass	3NT
All	Pass		

Here North/South managed to bid a good thin game—even if West does not lead a club at trick one, he may only have a singleton heart, as in this example, and be unable to reach his partner. This South was able to bid a natural two hearts on the first round which encouraged North into bidding an aggressive three spades when it was next his turn. South was delighted to bid 3NT with a club guard and a diamond fit.

But, if we don't have the high cards we do need the fit … or do we?

9. East/West Vulnerability. Dealer East.

```
            ♠ 5 4
            ♥ A 4
            ♦ 8 2
            ♣ A Q J 10 7 5 4
♠ Q 10 7                 ♠ K J 6
♥ K 7 6 5 2              ♥ 10 8
♦ A Q 7                  ♦ J 10 6 5 4 3
♣ 9 3                    ♣ K 8
            ♠ A 9 8 3 2
            ♥ Q J 9 3
            ♦ K 9
            ♣ 6 2
```

Room 1:

West	North	East	South
–	–	Pass	Pass
1♥	2♣	2♦	2♠
Pass	3♣	All Pass	

A sensible, controlled auction from North/South, ended in three clubs for a score of +110. North saw no reason to be particularly excited facing a passed partner.

Room 2:

West	North	East	South
–	–	Pass	Pass
1♥	2♣	2♦	Dble
Pass	2♥	Pass	2NT
Pass	3NT	All Pass	

Here, North was much more enthusiastic. To start with, South chose a competitive double rather than a simple bid in spades. The hand is not ideal for either action, the spades being a little inadequate to bid, but the club support being less than one would like for a double. This led North to suppose that South would have a club honor. Over the double, North showed his heart stopper and South rebid 2NT to show his diamond stopper. It is never right to play in precisely 2NT on this type of hand so North pushed on to game. On best defense this contract can go five down, but West led the queen of diamonds, which South won and played a club to the queen and king. East did not imagine that his partner would have the ace of diamonds so he thought he could see nine tricks for declarer—six clubs, two diamonds and the ace of hearts—so he switched to a spade!

Sometimes, it seems that your opponents can be talked out of anything

10. Both Sides Vulnerable. Dealer West.

```
                    ♠ 5
                    ♥ 9 4 3
                    ♦ J 8 6
                    ♣ K Q 9 5 3 2
♠ J 10 9 6 3 2                      ♠ –
♥ K 6                               ♥ A Q J 8 2
♦ A 7 3                             ♦ K 10 9 5 4 2
♣ 10 7                             ♣ A 8
                    ♠ A K Q 8 7 4
                    ♥ 10 7 5
                    ♦ Q
                    ♣ J 6 4
```

West	North	East	South
Pass	Pass	1♥	1♠
Pass	2♣	2♦	2♠
Dble	Pass	Pass	3♣
All	Pass		

East/West really let North/South off the hook here. First, East chose to open his five-card heart suit rather than his six-card diamond suit, never a good idea in my experience. South made a simple overcall when some would have preferred two spades, particularly facing a passed partner. West passed, hoping to be able to pass a re-opening double on the next round. North could not resist bidding his good club suit and East naturally bid his diamonds. Despite having good club support, South chose to first rebid his good spade suit and West was happy to double two spades. This caused South to reconsider and he removed himself to three club and, somewhat remarkably, this was passed out.

Note that East/West could have doubled and collected 500 or, perhaps more realistically, bid their own good six diamonds—even on a club lead, declarer can win, cash two top diamonds and play hearts, discarding dummy's club, thus making slam when diamonds are 3-1 or better and hearts 4-2 or better.

When there is a fit in two suits it is usually a good idea to do whatever you must to buy the contract. Even when you have done the wrong thing it is often difficult for the opponents to punish you.

11. North/South Vulnerable. Dealer South.

```
                    ♠ A Q 8 7 5 4
                    ♥ J
                    ♦ 10 9 2
                    ♣ J 8 5
♠ J 10                             ♠ K 3
♥ A 10 8 7 2                       ♥ 6 5 4 3
♦ A 8 7 5 4                        ♦ K Q J 3
♣ 10                               ♣ A 6 3
                    ♠ 9 6 2
                    ♥ K Q 9
                    ♦ 6
                    ♣ K Q 9 7 4 2
```

West	North	East	South
–	–	–	Pass
1♥	1♠	2♠	3♣
3♦	4♠	Dble	All Pass

West opened a light, distributional one heart in second position and North overcalled one spade (they were playing intermediate jump overcalls). East cuebid two spades, showing a limit raise or better in hearts. South, who had passed as dealer, took the opportunity to bid three clubs, implying a fit in spades. West bid his second suit as a game try and North jumped all the way to four spades. He had no idea who could make what but he did know that his side had good fits in both black suits; it seemed likely that his opponents would have fits in both red suits. In theory he did done the wrong thing—four spades can go for 800, losing three aces, two club ruffs and the king of spades—but in practice it is not so easy. In one room East/West pressed on to the five level because of the good diamond fit and went one down; in the other room the defense went astray and four spades went only one down.

Just because partner passes your overcall doesn't mean that you can't compete further.

12. Both Sides Vulnerable. Dealer South.

```
                    ♠ A 9 8 6 3
                    ♥ 9
                    ♦ K Q J 9
                    ♣ K Q 2
♠ K J 10                           ♠ Q 4
♥ A 8 4 2                          ♥ K J 6 5
♦ 6 4                              ♦ A 10 8 2
♣ A J 10 6                         ♣ 9 8 5
                    ♠ 7 5 2
                    ♥ Q 10 7 3
                    ♦ 7 5 3
                    ♣ 7 4 3
```

West	North	East	South
–	–	–	Pass
1♣	1♠	Dble	Pass
2♥	Dble	Pass	2♠
Pass	Pass	3♥	All Pass

North had an excellent overcall and was quite happy to double West's two heart rebid, suggesting four cards in the unbid suit, diamonds. When his partner showed delayed spade support, East/West had to choose between defending two spades, which is cold, or bidding on to three hearts. They chose the latter action and went one down. In the other room, North passed West's two hearts and that contract made for a 5 IMP swing.

13. Neither Side Vulnerable. Dealer South.

```
          ♠ A 4 2
          ♥ 6 4
          ♦ K 7 4 3
          ♣ A 10 9 3
♠ 10 9 6 5            ♠ Q
♥ K 3                ♥ A Q 9 8 2
♦ 9                  ♦ A J 10 8 2
♣ K Q 7 5 4 2        ♣ J 6
          ♠ K J 8 7 3
          ♥ J 10 7 5
          ♦ Q 6 5
          ♣ 8
```

Room 1:

West	North	East	South
–	–	–	Pass
Pass	1♣	1♥	1♠
Pass	Pass	2♦	Pass
2♥	2♠	Pass	Pass
3♣	All Pass		

Everyone's actions here seem reasonable. North opened one club in third seat and East had a fine one heart overcall. South bid his spades and North passed with his sub-minimum balanced opening. East competed further with two diamonds and West gave preference to hearts. North thought the time had come to support his partner's spades. West now assumed his partner would have a singleton spades and thus some club tolerance, so introduced his six-card suit. Three clubs became the final contract. The defense was accurate and this contract went one down for a satisfactory score for North/South who may or may not have made two spades.

In the other room there was more excitement:

Room 2:

West	North	East	South
–	–	–	Pass
Pass	1♦	1♥	1♠
2♣	Pass	Pass	2♦
Pass	Pass	3♣	Pass
Pass	Dble	Pass	3♦
4♣	Dble	All Pass	

This seems to be an example of how not to bid in a competitive situation! Everything seems reasonable until East's third bid, although perhaps North should have preferred to bid two spades rather than pass two diamonds. Then East, with AJ1082 of trumps and the ace in his long suit, in which partner was known not to have a fit, chose, not to defend, but to bid on with three clubs. North expressed his opinion about this with an aggressive penalty double which South, inexplicably chose to pull. North/South were now in serious trouble but West, understandably, did not realize his partner had such good defense against diamonds. Still, it is not usually a good idea to bid on in a suit in which you have been penalty doubled at a lower level. Again the defense was accurate and four clubs went two down, –300.

Of course, if our opponents have a fit, then you have a fit, even if you have not yet found it.

14. Both Sides Vulnerable. Dealer South.

```
          ♠ 6 4
          ♥ K Q 7 3 2
          ♦ J 2
          ♣ K J 9 3
♠ Q J 10 9 5         ♠ K 7
♥ 5                  ♥ 8 6
♦ K 10 9 7 5 3       ♦ A 8 6 4
♣ 6                  ♣ A 10 5 4 2
          ♠ A 8 3 2
          ♥ A J 10 9 4
          ♦ Q
          ♣ Q 8 7
```

West	North	East	South
–	–	–	1♥
1♠	2NT	Dble	4♥
5♦	Dble	All Pass	

Here West started by introducing his major, hoping to keep his diamonds up his sleeve for a while. North's 2NT showed a four-card heart raise and East's double was competitive, suggesting a wish to compete with values in the minors. South jumped to four hearts and West was happy to bid five diamonds, not knowing whether this or four hearts was making. In the event five diamonds made for a score of 750, while in the other room the defense went astray and let North/South make four hearts.

More often you find your fit immediately and then your only problem is to decide how high to bid.

15. Neither Side Vulnerable. Dealer North.

```
              ♠ K 4
              ♥ J 10 8 7
              ♦ A 9 2
              ♣ J 6 5 4
♠ A 10 8 6 2              ♠ Q J 7 5
♥ 3                      ♥ 9 6 5 4
♦ Q J 6                  ♦ K 4 3
♣ A 10 9 8               ♣ K Q
              ♠ 9 3
              ♥ A K Q 2
              ♦ 10 8 7 5
              ♣ 7 3 2
```

West	North	East	South
–	Pass	Pass	1♥
1♠	2NT(*)	3♥	Pass
4♠	All Pass		

(*) limit (as opposed to pre-emptive) raise

The action started when South chose to open his solid four-card heart suit in third position. West had a fine one spade overcall and North tried 2NT, showing a good raise to three hearts. This left East room to cuebid three hearts to show a good four-card raise and this was enough for West to bid the excellent game. Had North raised to three hearts instead, East could have doubled to show a good raise to three spades (a simple three spades would be merely competitive) but it would not have been so clear that he held four-card support.

16. Both Sides Vulnerable. Dealer East.

```
              ♠ J 9 7 5 4 3
              ♥ A K 4 3
              ♦ J 6
              ♣ 10
♠ K Q 10 8 6 2           ♠ A
♥ 2                      ♥ Q 7 5
♦ 7 4 3 2                ♦ 10 9 8
♣ Q 6                    ♣ A K J 9 7 2
              ♠ –
              ♥ J 10 9 8 6
              ♦ A K Q 5
              ♣ 8 5 4 3
```

West	North	East	South
–	–	1♣	1♥
1♠	2♠	3♣	3♦
3♠	4♥	All Pass	

After East's one club opening, South overcalled one heart, a very sensible bid despite the lack of top honors in the suit.

West showed his spades and North had a problem. With such extreme spade length he knew suits were breaking badly for his opponents so saw no need to bid too enthusiastically, risking a minus score when his partner was minimum. He contented himself with a two spade cuebid, showing a good four-card raise. When East rebid his clubs, South quite liked his hand with the concentration of honors in the unbid suit, so he bid three diamonds. After this it was easy for North to press on to the heart game over West's three spade bid. There were no problems in the play and four hearts made ten tricks.

17. East/West Vulnerable. Dealer South.

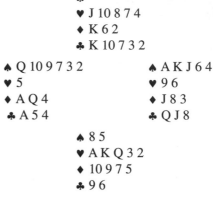

```
              ♠ –
              ♥ J 10 8 7 4
              ♦ K 6 2
              ♣ K 10 7 3 2
♠ Q 10 9 7 3 2           ♠ A K J 6 4
♥ 5                      ♥ 9 6
♦ A Q 4                  ♦ J 8 3
♣ A 5 4                  ♣ Q J 8
              ♠ 8 5
              ♥ A K Q 3 2
              ♦ 10 9 7 5
              ♣ 9 6
```

West	North	East	South
–	–	–	1♥
1♠	2♣	3♣	Pass
4♥	5♥	Dble	Pass
5♠	All Pass		

Here it seems that West misjudged a high-level competitive situation for no good reason. South started the ball rolling with a sub-standard one heart and West overcalled one spade. North decided to keep the bidding low by introducing his club suit rather than jumping in hearts. He knew that his opponents would bid more spades, however many hearts he bid so he hoped to learn more about the hand before making his final decision. East decided simply to show a four-card raise—although his spade support was wonderful, the rest of the hand was balanced and unattractive. From West's point of view, slam was possible and he chose to express this possibility with a jump to four hearts, showing his shortage there. North went on to five hearts as he had always intended. So far, East/West had done very well and, no doubt, West's previous four heart bid had created a forcing situation—i.e. East/West had to double their opponents or bid on. East judged well to suggest with his double that they had bid enough, that they would not make five spades. There does not seem to be any reason for West to overrule this decision as he has described his hand accurately, however overrule he did and lost 100 when he might have gained 100.

18. *Both Sides Vulnerable. Dealer North.*

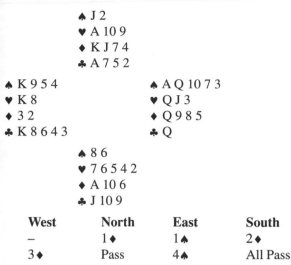

```
              ♠ J 2
              ♥ A 10 9
              ♦ K J 7 4
              ♣ A 7 5 2
♠ K 9 5 4               ♠ A Q 10 7 3
♥ K 8                   ♥ Q J 3
♦ 3 2                   ♦ Q 9 8 5
♣ K 8 6 4 3             ♣ Q
              ♠ 8 6
              ♥ 7 6 5 4 2
              ♦ A 10 6
              ♣ J 10 9
```

West	North	East	South
–	1♦	1♠	2♦
3♦	Pass	4♠	All Pass

This is a good example of why it is more efficient to use a 2NT bid as a game try in spades than a cuebid. Here West had a promising hand, definitely too good for a pre-emptive raise to three spades. His only way of expressing his good raise was to cuebid three diamonds. His partner also had a fair overcall, rather too many queens, but nevertheless a shapely 11-count with a good trump suit and one where the opponents' bidding suggested his partner was likely to have a singleton diamond. He could have made a three heart game try but it would have left West uncertain about what to do. How much better it would have been if West could have bid 2NT to show his good raise. Now East could have bid three diamonds to show his length there and West would have known that his king of clubs was likely to be wasted and that his diamond holding was probably unsuitable. He would have signed off in three spades and scored +140 instead of −100.

I hope that now you have a clearer idea of when and what to overcall and what to respond to your partner's overcalls, whether or not the opponents have bid further.

• Distribution and playing strength are much, much more important than high cards. When no one has a fit it doesn't matter very much whether you become the declaring or defending side; whichever you do is likely to lead to a similar score, either plus or minus. It is when both sides have a fit that it is vital to compete accurately.

• On many hands there is no right answer. Experts disagree among themselves and even when they agree it may work better to do something different. All you can do is develop a consistent style and expect to win points considerably more often than it loses them.

• When in doubt, err on the side of aggression in competitive situations. You will find that even when you have done the wrong thing, the opponents are more likely to rescue you by doing something else wrong themselves.

• It is very much easier to get these situations right when playing in a regular partnership and deciding the style of play you will adopt. Partnerships can agree on such things as the weakest overcall they would allow, the strongest overcall, when raises can be made on absolutely nothing and when they should be more constructive.

PART VI

SLAM BIDDING
by Alan Mould

This section is aimed at the majority of club and tournament players; in fact, at anyone who thinks their slam bidding could be improved, a category in which I include myself.

One of the many problems with slam bidding is that slam deals do not come up that often. It is rare to get more than a couple of slams in a single evening. By the time each one has come up you have forgotten anything you may have learned from the last one. Thus, while steadily improving in all other aspects of the game, a lot of players hardly improve their slam bidding at all.

You will find that many of the ideas in this section will require some discussion with your partner. However, much of it can be assumed as standard in the tournament world. If you sat opposite any reasonable partner you could wheel out many of the ideas in this book without discussion.

As far as possible, I have tried to give current standard thinking on slam bidding. Where there are alternatives, I have explained the merits of each. Where one method is almost universally played, I have attempted to explain why. It is not possible to play all the suggestions in this book simultaneously. Where alternative suggestions are made, you and your partner will need to decide which you prefer. Such discussions are often fruitful and yield additional partnership understanding.

This section is not about esoteric bidding methods and systems that will diagnose slams on four-two fits for you. There is much literature available on highly complex and artificial methods to bid good slams and avoid bad ones, but this book is not about system. Where necessary, the basic system I have assumed is the "standard" Acol system. That is, a weak NT, four card majors, light two over one responses, a 15-16 2NT rebid after a two level response and strong two bids. This is the standard system played by most club players in Britain. Apart from that, the only convention assumed is Blackwood. Of course, several slam bidding aids are introduced, but this is done gradually and each is carefully explained, in terms of its uses and its rationale.

The section will, however, help you to understand what is necessary for a slam to be present in the combined hands and how to find this out. It will not teach you how to be brilliant. Neither will it give you a foolproof method for bidding every slam. Nothing can do either of these things. But they are not necessary. Brilliance is very rarely necessary in bridge or in slam bidding. It is much more important to avoid messing up. Most slams need a sound knowledge of the types of hands that make a slam, allied to a clear understanding of the few simple tools used to help bid them. That is what I hope this section will provide.

30
Chapter

Trumps, Tricks and Controls

The Mathematics of Slam Bidding

No, don't skip this chapter! It's not going to get very hard—honest. All I wish to do is point out the odds required to bid a slam. Slam hands are particularly important at teams play where a vulnerable slam swing is 13 IMPs whereas at pairs it is just another hand. However, slams should not be ignored at pairs either. A top is a top whether got from squeezing out an overtrick in 1NT or bidding and making a slam.

These days, we are all taught that at teams you should bid 50 percent non-vulnerable games and 35 percent vulnerable games. These figures are simply derived from looking at the expected gain and comparing it with the expected loss. For example, if the question is whether you can make nine or ten tricks in a major suit vulnerable, then if you bid game and it makes you gain 10 IMPs (620 –170 = 450 which is 10 IMPs). If you bid game and it goes down you lose 6 IMPs (–100 –140 = –240 which is –6 IMPs). Thus you should bid vulnerable games if the odds are any better than 10 to 6 against; ie. 37.5 percent usually called 35 percent for convenience. This means that a vulnerable game that requires a three-two trump break and a finesse is just about okay (34 percent). In practice a lot of good players go around bidding vulnerable games on a wing and a prayer (sometimes no wings and several prayers). After all some get mis-defended and partners can hardly show off virtuoso dummy play in 2♥, can they? Very few freely bid games get doubled either, so they are pretty safe to bid.

To look at the odds necessary to bid slams we can do the same analysis of expected gains and losses. For small slams:

Non-Vulnerable

12 Tricks Made	980 –480	=	500	=	+11 IMPs
11 Tricks Made	–50 –450	=	–500	=	–11 IMPs

Vulnerable

12 Tricks Made	1430–680	=	750	=	+13 IMPs
11 Tricks Made	–100–650	=	–750	=	–13 IMPs

Thus the expected gain and loss are identical in each case and you should bid both non-vulnerable and vulnerable slams that are better than 50 percent. I should point out, I suppose, that I have assumed that the issue is a question of eleven tricks or twelve. These odds are often expressed as "You should bid a slam on a finesse." Personally I think this is misleading. But even if it is true then let us look at exactly what that means. For example, take these two hands:

♠ Q 6 4 2	♠ A K 8 7 3
♥ 7 6 5 2	♥ K Q J
♦ J 10 9	♦ A Q 5 2
♣ A J	♣ 4

This is not a slam on a finesse. It is considerably worse. For a start you need the trumps not to be four-nil. Okay you would be unlucky for this to happen, but it happens about 10 percent of the time. So your odds are already reduced to 45 percent.

Let's say I'm kind to you and add the ♠J instead of a small spade to one hand or the other. Personally I still wouldn't want to be in this slam. It is not against the rules for the hearts to break five-one. If the singleton is on lead, you will almost certainly go off and, as everybody has now learned to lead aggressively against slams, you will probably go down if the ace to five is on lead as the ace is quite likely to be led. What about if the diamonds are six-nil? Then you are going to get Lightner doubled, suffer a ruff on the opening lead and still have the ace of hearts and a diamond to lose for –500 or – 800.

Again you would be unlucky for this to happen but it all reduces the odds and you don't need many –500s to tilt the odds quite heavily against bidding slams. Notice that I have been kind to you on the hand above in that I have given you the ♦10 and ♦9. Without the ten in particular the slam is absolutely awful.

I've concentrated on this hand to try to convince you that a slam on a finesse may not be as easy as you think. I think you need better odds for a slam than that. The reasons include:

1. A slam depends on more than a finesse and you may be unable to determine these in advance. Among other things, you may need a trump break; you may need to ruff out a side suit which mustn't break too badly; you may suffer a ruff, or, perhaps a vital side suit might break badly.

2. You will get relatively few slams let through on the wrong lead. In general, leading against slams is much easier than leading against games. In addition, the auction often tips off the defenders to the killing lead.

3. You will make even fewer slams through mis-defense. Slams are much easier to defend against than games. For a start you're on lead less often and you have fewer high cards to worry about.

4. Teammates tend to get irritated about slams going down!

My advice then is to bid small slams which you are certain will be on a finesse at the worst (i.e. if partner puts down a completely unsuitable hand then it will be on a finesse). You might miss a few 55 percent slams like this, but you won't bid 40 percent slams and that will show a profit in the long run.

Now, what about grand slams? Superficially the analysis is similar:

Non-Vulnerable

| 13 Tricks Made | 1510–1010 | = | 500 | = | +11 IMPs |
| 12 Tricks Made | −50 −980 | = | −1030 | = | −14 IMPs |

Vulnerable

| 13 Tricks Made | 2210–1460 | = | 750 | = | +13 IMPs |
| 12 Tricks Made | −100–1430 | = | −1530 | = | −17 IMPs |

Thus non-vulnerable you should bid grand slams that are better than 11 to 14 on, i.e. 56 percent and vulnerable you should bid grand slams that are better than 13 to 17 on, i.e. just under 57 percent. However, things are not as simple as this. What happens if the opponents don't bid the small slam? You need to be absolutely certain that the opponents are going to bid the small slam for these odds to be correct and when are you going to be that certain? If the opponents don't bid the small slam you already have 11 or 13 IMPs in the bag for bidding that. You now need massive odds to bid the grand slam. If the grand slam makes you will gain an extra 3 or 4 IMPs and if the grand slam goes off you will lose 22 or 26 IMPs (the +11 or +13 you would have gained and the −11 or −13 you have lost)! You therefore need odds of at least 3 to 22 on, i.e. about 88 percent to bid a grand slam now! Even then is it worth it? Which would you rather have? If you were told that the opponents had stayed in game and you could have a certain 13 IMPs for bidding your cold small slam or bid a 90 percent grand slam which would you do? Even though it is mathematically incorrect I'd take my IMPs and run. What about, horror of horrors, if the opponents do not reach game? Do not tell me this is

impossible; there is at least one instance in world championship play where a pair were one off in a grand slam only to discover their opponents were playing a part score.

There has also been an occasion when a British pair played a laydown grand slam in game to gain 13 IMPs when their teammates where defending 2♣ on a three-two fit. Now the odds against bidding a grand slam rise even more since you are gaining 11 or 13 IMPs for just playing in game and 13 or 15 IMPs for playing in the small slam. In addition, even the kindliest of teammates tend to get a little irked when they have defended game with a slam cold and discover they have lost a double figure IMP swing. It tends to cheer up the opponents as well.

What odds you need to bid a grand slam are therefore difficult to determine since it depends on what contract your opponents are going to be in. The more likely they are to be in the small slam the happier you should be to be in the grand slam and vice versa. There are two rules of thumb about grand slams that are often bandied about. These are both based on experience rather than any rigorous mathematical background. One is to bid a grand slam if it is any better than 68 percent.

This happens to be the odds on a three-two break so the basic idea is that if you are playing a grand slam in a four-four trump fit and you need the trumps three-two and absolutely nothing else, then that is just about okay. Anything worse should be avoided. The other rule of thumb sometimes given is "Don't bid grand slams unless you can count fourteen tricks from both sides of the table!" I lean rather more to the second suggestion rather than the first. It is really a matter of your partnership's temperament and even more so that of your teammates. To a large extent it is also dependent on which you think is the stronger team. If you think yours is the stronger team you should be circumspect about bidding grand slams. Whereas if you think yours is the weaker team, you should bid grand slams more freely since there are going to be relatively few chances for you to gain IMPs.

So much for teams, what about bidding slams at pairs? Bidding slams at pairs is a high risk strategy. If it makes you will probably score 70 or 80 percent; if it fails you will score close to 0 percent. For this reason alone I would advise only bidding slams at pairs that you believe are considerably above 50 percent. If you assume you start with an average then you are usually gambling nearly all of the 50 percent of the matchpoints in order to gain 30 percent extra. Added to this is the problem that if you have an investigative auction that stops short of a slam then you have very often tipped off the best lead to an opponent and so may end up making one trick less than anybody else. This is irrelevant at teams. At pairs it is disastrous.

REQUIREMENTS FOR A SLAM

For a slam to make you require twelve tricks. To acquire twelve tricks you need trumps, tricks and controls.

Trumps

Unless you are contemplating playing in no trumps, the first thing you need for a slam to be successful is a trump suit which is good enough for slam purposes. This means that it has to play for no losers if there is an outside trick to lose or for one loser if the outside suits are completely solid. This may seem obvious, but it is surprising how often it is forgotten.

Personally, I never lead trumps against slams. Apart from the fact that it is usually too passive I have seen too many trump suits picked up for declarer by trump leads in slams.

Let's take as an example:

> ♠ Q 6 5 2
> ♥ A K 5
> ♦ K Q 9
> ♣ A Q 4

You decide that because of the flat shape and lack of intermediates you will not open this 2NT. Therefore, you open 1♠. Everybody in North America and most of Europe will laugh at you for this, but that is what your Acol system says, so that is what you open. Partner surprises you by bidding 3♠. Well, you obviously have a really great hand now, so you launch into Blackwood, find partner has one ace and confidently bid 6♠. Confident that is until the dummy comes down with:

> ♠ K 8 7 4
> ♥ Q J 7 2
> ♦ A J
> ♣ J 6 5

Partner is full value for 3♠ and yet this is a dreadful slam. You need Ax of trumps in one hand and the club finesse right, about 9 percent.

Let's give partner a much more suitable hand. How about:

> ♠ K 9 7 4 3
> ♥ 4 3
> ♦ A 6
> ♣ K 10 7 5

Now, partner has five good trumps and the vital king of clubs. Most players would consider this hand too good for 3♠, yet this is still only just about acceptable as a slam. You need to pick up the trump suit for one loser which is only 52.5 percent. While doing this you need to avoid a ruff. If the hand on lead has a singleton you are almost certain to go down. Yet I have given partner a great hand for you. Take away a trump from partner or the king of clubs and put them anywhere else and the slam is awful.

So, what went wrong?

The main problem is that your trumps are just too weak.

Partner must have absolutely great trumps to make a slam, and then won't be able to fill all the other holes. You shouldn't be worrying about a slam on this hand; you should be worrying about what the right game is. Personally I would bid 3NT to play and pass if partner converted back to 4♠. Say partner has:

> ♠ 10 7 4 3
> ♥ Q J 4 3
> ♦ A 7
> ♣ K J 2

You would be very unlucky to go off in 4♠ on this hand, but trumps have been known to be five-0 (or possibly three trump losers and a ruff). Why take the risk with ten ice-cold tricks in 3NT? The modernists will laugh at me for suggesting 3NT to play after 1♠ – 3♠ but if you open poor four card majors you have to be able to get into the right contract somehow.

Keep in mind that the slam possibilities are no better if you open the example hand 2NT, which is the likely American bid. The losers would be the same whether the final contract is in spades, hearts, or no trumps. There simply are not twelve tricks.

Tricks

The next requirement for a slam is to have enough tricks. Once you've managed to find a trump suit, you still need to generate twelve tricks. That is the other problem with the hand above. It has a lot of points but it hasn't got very many tricks. The real difficulty is that there are no long suits to develop. Once we've cashed our aces and kings and taken a couple of hopeful finesses we can pack up. Distributional hands are almost always better than flat hands as they contain greater potential for tricks. Instead of our flat 20 count let's try:

> ♠ A Q 10 7 6
> ♥ 4
> ♦ K Q J 5 2
> ♣ A 3

This is a much better hand for slam purposes. It is just possible that a grand slam is cold if partner holds ♠K, ♥A, ♦A and few enough clubs to discard them on the diamonds. Any two out of those three will make six laydown provided the defense cannot or do not set up a club trick. For example, partner might hold:

> ♠ K 8 4 2
> ♥ A 5 3 2
> ♦ 10 3
> ♣ Q 7 6

Not exactly overweight and yet you would be unlucky to fail. You will probably go down if the trumps are four-0 or the diamonds five-one. Otherwise you will only go down if they lead a club and the king is wrong. Add the ♣J and they can forget about leading clubs. What about:

♠ A 10 7 6 5 4
♥ 4
♦ A K 5 3
♣ A 7

This is a still better hand in some ways. Now the right six count in partner's hand will make the slam virtually cold (♠K, ♣K and a doubleton diamond). Yet now we only have a 15 count. Make the ace of clubs the king and we still have lively chances. OK we need two aces or one ace and the ♠K plus some diamond help. The first part of this we should be able to find out about. The problem is determining whether partner has the ♦Q or a doubleton.

What about:

♠ A Q 10 7 6
♥ A
♦ J 7 6 4 3
♣ K Q

Now this hand is nowhere near as good. For a slam to be possible you need partner to have two out of ♠K, ♦A and ♣A and good enough diamonds to avoid another loser in the suit. It is clear what the problem is on this hand. You have a weak side suit that is difficult to set up and lots of honors in your short suits that are not pulling their weight.

For there to be enough tricks in a slam you often need to set up a side suit. This consideration should apply when you are looking at your holding in partner's suit. Particularly if you are going to play in another suit the ease with which you can set up your partner's suit should be a big consideration.

Suppose you hold:

♠ 4
♥ K Q 8 6 5 4
♦ K 5
♣ A 10 7 6

Partner opens 1♦, you respond 1♥ and, to your surprise, partner bids 3♥. Now this is a great hand. Your ♦Kx are gold. Partner almost certainly has five diamonds. Either your king will make them solid or it will help to ruff them out. Say partner holds:

♠ 7 6
♥ A 10 3 2
♦ A Q J 7 6
♣ 8 2

This is barely an opening bid yet 6♥ requires only that diamonds break four-two or better. Now how about:

♠ 4
♥ K Q 8 6 5 4
♦ 9 4 3
♣ A K 6

This has the same number of points but is a much poorer hand for slam purposes. The three low diamonds mean that partner's diamonds need to be as good as AKQ to avoid a loser. Give partner a hand such as:

♠ Q 10 3
♥ A J 10 2
♦ A K 7 6 5
♣ 9

This time partner has the 3♥ bid and 6♥ has practically no play at all. Notice that if you make it two small diamonds and ♣AKxx then 6♥ is cold again.

Three small is just about the worst possible holding in partner's suit since it virtually always means there is a loser there. Ax or Kx are about the best holdings since either the suit will run or it can be ruffed out fairly easily. This is a rare example of honors in short suits being good.

Controls

Last, for a slam you need sufficient controls. You can have all the trumps and tricks in the world but if the opponents have two aces to cash or a cashing ace-king then most days of the week you will not make a slam, although you can even make some of these.

I emphasize that you should be thinking about the necessary controls for a slam last, not first. All the controls in the world will do you no good if you haven't got enough tricks. Take these hands for example:

♠ K 9 8   ♠ A Q 7
♥ A 9 2   ♥ K 6 5 4
♦ 8 6 5 3   ♦ A K 7
♣ A K 9   ♣ Q 7 6

They have all the controls and a combined 32 count yet it is impossible to make twelve tricks. We can all sit back smugly and say we would bid 1NT–3NT (or something like that) but say I add the ♠J and the ♣J instead of small cards to the hands. Now you have a combined 34 count and slam is still no play.

First, therefore, you need to decide if you have sufficient trumps and likely tricks for a slam. Only then should you worry about whether you have sufficient controls in the correct places. How you determine those controls is the subject of the following chapters.

What about no trump?

There are unquestionably some slams that are much better in no trumps than in a suit. You should think about playing in no trumps if:

    1. You are concerned that your trump suit may be a little weak.
    2. You are concerned about the possibility of an adverse ruff.
    3. You have a number of good suits between the two hands but no particular fit.
    4. You have the majority of high card points.

But be warned, it is not a panacea for solving the problems of bad slams (the only way to solve that problem is to stop bidding them). For it to be correct to play in no trumps you have to be able to make twelve (or thirteen) tricks without trumps and this may not be so easy. In particular you will need:

1. Sufficient positive controls (i.e. aces and kings) to insure that the opposition cannot run a suit. It is fine to have Axx opposite a singleton in a suit contract but it is a little embarrassing if they lead it against 6NT and you have an ace to knock out.

2. Sufficient tricks. In particular, if you are worried about your trump suit, you will have to be able to make sufficient tricks outside of it which usually means that a side suit will have to play for no losers. It is no good carefully avoiding 6♠ with Kxxx opposite Qxxx if you find that you have to play this suit for three tricks anyway.

My advice is not to worry too much about trying to bid the hands with bad trump suits to 6NT. Just play those in game and collect your 13 IMPs when the opposition bid silly slams. The two types of hands that I do think are worth worrying about are the ones where you are sure you have sufficient tricks and controls and the ones where you have lots of decent suits but no real fit. Take these three examples from play:

> ♠ K 9 7 4
> ♥ K Q J 4 2
> ♦ K
> ♣ A Q 6

This hand turned up in the Camrose Trials a few years ago. What do you do when partner opens 1♠? At three tables this hand discovered partner had five spades and then used Blackwood at some stage to discover partner had two aces. 6♠ was the result opposite:

> ♠ A J 8 3 2
> ♥ 10 6
> ♦ A 10 3
> ♣ K 7 2

The good news about this contract was that the trumps were four-0 onside, so could be picked up. The bad news was that the players on lead led the ♥A from ace to five and gave their partners' a ruff for one down. The only successful pair was able to determine that partner was balanced with five spades and had a club control, a diamond control and two aces. Thus partner had to have the ♣K, the ♦A and a major suit ace. This meant that every suit was double stopped and if the spades came in there were twelve tricks. So 6NT had to be as good as 6♠. Well done indeed, but note that the key was knowing that partner had the ♣K and ♦A rather than, say, a singleton club. Often you can work this out. For example, if partner shows a balanced hand at some point:

> ♠ 10 8 7 5
> ♥ Q 10 3 2
> ♦ A K
> ♣ Q 6 5

This hand came from a local league match. Partner opens 2♣ (Acol). Systemically you have to bid 2♦ and partner bids 2NT (23–24). Unless you have very sophisticated methods I am convinced that you should just bid 6NT. Yes, it is possible to construct hands where a grand slam is cold and possible to construct hands where a suit contract is better. But how are you going to tell? For a suit contract to be better partner needs excellent trumps and also a ruff has to be important for a twelfth trick. How likely is that to be the case? All the warning signs are there to suggest you should play in no trumps. You have lots of points (at least 34), bad suits and a heavy concentration of honors in short suits. So 6NT it is. Which shows what I know since partner held:

> ♠ A K Q J
> ♥ A K
> ♦ J 9 6 4
> ♣ A J 4

As you can see 6♠ is virtually cold whereas 6NT is poor and duly went down. However, what if we rearrange partner's hand so that there are not all those spade honors. How about:

> ♠ K Q 4 3
> ♥ A K J
> ♦ Q J 7 6
> ♣ A K

Now 6NT is cold whereas 6♠ needs the spades coming in for one loser and no ruff. And what about:

> ♠ A 7 6 2
> ♥ A K J
> ♦ Q J 7 6
> ♣ A K

Partner is now sub-minimum and yet 6NT is still cold whereas 6♠ has no chance.

The last pair of hands came up in the National Pairs final a couple of years ago.

> ♠ J   ♠ A K Q 8 6
> ♥ A K Q 8 7 6 ♥ 5
> ♦ K 9 6 5   ♦ Q 10 2
> ♣ Q 5   ♣ A K 6 4

I think these hands are very difficult to bid to the top spot. 6♥ is no good since you need the trumps three-three. All other suit contracts are clearly absurd. Yet 6NT is excellent. It is cold if either major suit breaks and even if that fails you can have a successful diamond position or a squeeze if you have managed to persuade the defense to take the ♦A on the first round. No solid trump suit but lots of good suits. What makes it particularly difficult of course is that the ♠J stiff improves the chances considerably since a four-three spade break will see you home.

What About 6NT at Pairs?

There are many players who want to gallop into 6NT every time a slam presents itself at pairs. I think this is a ridiculous policy. Bidding and making a slam at pairs is never below average and usually scores 70 or 80 percent. To bid 6NT means that you are gambling on gaining the extra 20 to 30 percent of the matchpoints at the risk of losing the 70 to 80 percent already in the bag. This means that you are laying odds of about four to one that you are correct. Are you that certain that 6NT is going to make? If it is one of the types of hands above when 6NT may well be a better contract, then go ahead and bid it. If you are sure you can count twelve tricks then go ahead and bid 6NT. If, for whatever reason, you think 6NT will be as good a contract as six of a suit then fine, bid it. But to play every slam at pairs in 6NT or even to try and play every slam at pairs in 6NT is just madness. Sure, you will get the occasional top when 6NT makes, but this will be outweighed by the bottoms when it doesn't. And remember you are laying odds of four to one against yourself.

Blackwood and All Those Things

Of all the conventions played in the world Blackwood and Stayman are the two most widely known and widely played. As with a lot of other conventions there are many different versions.

Let us start with the simplest version of Blackwood. That is, 4NT asks for aces and the responses are:

5♣ = 0 or 4 aces
5♦ = 1 ace
5♥ = 2 aces
5♠ = 3 aces

We are all aware that Blackwood is actually useless on certain hands. Notably, with a void there is no value in employing it since the information may be of no use to you. You have no way of telling whether one of partner's aces is opposite your void. In fact, Blackwood is actually inappropriate on many hands.

I was playing in a local duplicate recently. On the first board I picked up:

♠ K 8 7 4 3
♥ A K 5
♦ K 7
♣ A Q 5

A nice hand to begin with. I opened 1♠ and partner raised me to 3♠. This is a good hand. Surely there must be a slam if partner has an ace, so I bid 4NT, partner showed one ace and I bid 6♠. Partner put down:

♠ 9 6 5 2
♥ Q 7
♦ A Q 10 5
♣ K 6 4

I needed the trumps two-two with the ace onside and when that did not happen I was down one. On to the next hand where I picked up:

♠ K 8 7 4 3
♥ A K 5
♦ K 7
♣ A Q 5

These cards have been duplicated in a second board. No, no say my three opponents—left-hand opponent (LHO), right-hand opponent (RHO) and the one sitting opposite (IDIOT)—we all have different cards. How strange. I open 1♠ and partner bids 3♠. Curiouser and curiouser. Still I learned my lesson last time. I just bid 4♠, everybody passes. Partner tables:

♠ Q J 10 2
♥ 8 7
♦ A 8 5
♣ K 7 4 3

and I make twelve tricks in some comfort. Partner asks why I didn't use Blackwood and bid a slam!

Third board, and I'm pleased to see I have a different hand:

♠ A K Q 7 6
♥ Q 9 2
♦ A K 6 5
♣ 6

I open my usual 1♠ and partner again bids 3♠. This is getting monotonous. Still I bid Blackwood, partner shows one ace and I bid 6♠. LHO leads a heart and partner puts down:

♠ J 8 4 3
♥ J 7 3
♦ 10 8
♣ A K Q 2

I drop the ♥Q under RHO's ace but it does no good—he leads one back to his partner's king and I'm down one. Any other lead and I'd have made it. Why did partner have to have such heavy club values? Oh well, board four and I pick up:

♠ A K Q 7 6
♥ Q 9 2
♦ A K 6 5
♣ 6

What's going on here? This is the duplicate from Hell! I open 1♠ and not very much to my surprise partner bids 3♠.

I go quietly with 4♠, everybody passes and, not very much to my surprise partner, puts down:

♠ J 8 4 3
♥ A K 3
♦ Q 10 8
♣ J 9 2

and I make six easily. On to board five where I pick up:

♠ A K Q 7 6
♥ Q 9 2
♦ A K 6 5
♣ 6

just for a change. After I open 1♠ and partner bids the inevitable 3♠ I pause for thought. Surely these things are going in cycles so this must be a slam. I bid 4NT and partner shows two aces. Now I can bid 6♠ for sure. Everybody passes and partner puts down:

♠ J 8 4 3
♥ A 5 3
♦ 9 7 2
♣ A K 5

muttering that he downgraded the hand because of the flat shape. They lead a club. There are no miracles and I have to lose a heart and a diamond. Partner asks what on earth I was bidding slam on when it doesn't make after he puts down two aces and a king? I move on wearily to board six where inevitably I pick up:

♠ A 9 7 6 5
♥ A Q 5
♦ A J 4
♣ K 2

I open 1♠ (it begins to dawn on me that I always seem to be the dealer) and partner bids 3♠. I sigh and bid 4NT. Partner shows one ace and I bid 6♠. Partner puts down:

♠ K Q 4 3
♥ K 7 6
♦ 7 5 3
♣ A 7 5

Partner mutters that he downgraded it because of the flat shape. I mutter thanks and go down one when the diamond honors are not both onside. Partner starts saying something about how much does he need for a 3♠ bid, but I've already moved to the next table. On board seven I pick up:

♠ A 9 7 6 5
♥ A Q 5
♦ A J 4
♣ K 2

and after the inevitable start I bid 4NT. Partner shows no aces and so I subside in 5♠. Partner tables:

♠ K Q 4 3
♥ 10 7 4
♦ K 6
♣ Q J 10 6

As the opposition cannot lead hearts profitably I can set up the clubs for two discards and make six easily. I start to scream silently.

When Should You Use Blackwood?

Why did all of the hands above go wrong? Why could you make slam on some hands from partner and not on others, even though sometimes you had more aces?

The problem is that on all seven hands Blackwood is the wrong question to be asking partner. That is the key. Blackwood is a question. Blackwood does not say anything. It is a request for a very specific piece of information: the number of aces partner has. The clear implication of using Blackwood is that *all* you need to know is how many aces partner has. The implication is that given that one piece of additional information you can place the final contract with certainty.

So you had better be sure that the number of aces in partner's hand is really all you want to know. Because one thing is certain, if you do the wrong thing after using Blackwood you cannot blame it on the usual source of your disasters—that idiot opposite. All partner did was answer a simple question. Regrettably, the responsibility is yours. How about a couple of examples:

♠ K 8 7 6 5 4 3
♥ A K Q 5
♦ A
♣ 7

You open your usual 1♠ and partner bids 3♠. This is a great hand for Blackwood. If partner has one ace, at worst the slam will depend on picking up the spades if partner's spades are only jack high (a 52 percent chance); otherwise it seems to be cold. So you can confidently bid 4NT. If partner has one ace you can bid 6♠ and if partner has two aces you can bid 7♠. No problem. Now suppose you hold:

♠ Q 9 7 5 3
♥ A Q 8 6
♦ A K Q
♣ 5

After the inevitable 1♠ – 3♠ start, what now? Blackwood is absolutely useless to you on this hand as it will not tell you what you want to know. For 6♠ to be a good contract, certainly you need partner to have an ace but you also need partner to have some other specific cards. In particular you are desperately interested in the ♥K and some very good trumps. Blackwood will tell you none of these things. If you bid Blackwood now and partner shows one ace what are you going to do? If you bid 6♠ you know that dummy will produce:

♠ J 8 4 2
♥ 7 4 3
♦ J 5
♣ A K Q 8

Make partner's ace of clubs the ace of spades and you are

still in a very poor contract (you need ♠Kx or ♠K stiff onside and the ♥K onside). But if you just bid 5♠ now you can be equally sure he will put down:

♠ A K 4 2
♥ K 4
♦ 7 4 2
♣ 10 6 4 3

When 6♠ Is on Ice.

It is not a lot better if partner shows two aces. You are more likely to be able to make 6♠ now and you should bid it but partner could still produce:

♠ A 8 4 2
♥ 7 4 3
♦ 4 3 2
♣ A K 8

where the slam is just dreadful.

What are you going to do then? Launch into Blackwood, find one ace and then agonize over the response and finally bid 5♠? I suppose that will work sometimes. A good partner will never bid 6♠ over 5♠ whether you have paused or not. Remember the point about Blackwood is that you are in control. You have asked a question, partner has answered it and you have placed the final contract. The implication of your bidding 5♠ rather than 6♠ is that there are two aces off the contract. So partner can never raise to slam since logically you should be missing two aces.

The clear implication of all this is that every time partner shows enough aces for a slam you must bid a slam. Once you have used Blackwood, it is too late to start worrying about how good partner's trumps are or whether values are held opposite your singleton. You have already used up too much room to find out about all these other things anyway. You should have thought about this before using Blackwood, not after. That is the reason you will almost never find experts taking time over what to bid after a Blackwood response. If you ever watch experts playing a match they will often pause for long times when you are wondering what can they possibly be thinking about and they will certainly often pause for some time before deciding whether to use Blackwood, but they will virtually never pause after hearing the response. Before they bid 4NT they have checked that the number of aces partner held was all they needed to know.

Let's have a quick look at those hands from the duplicate from Hell. On the first one we picked up:

♠ K 8 7 4 3
♥ A K 5
♦ K 7
♣ A Q 5

and heard 1♠ – 3♠. Blackwood is the wrong bid on this one because you have considerable concern about trumps among other things and Blackwood will not tell you about those. On the second you held:

♠ A K Q 7 6
♥ Q 9 2
♦ A K 6 5
♣ 6

and again heard 1♠ – 3♠. Blackwood is no good here as you have an uncontrolled suit. Even when partner shows an ace you do not know whether you have two quick losers in hearts. If you like gambling on slams then go ahead and bid 6♠. Some days you will make and some days you will make it even when the ♥AK are in opponents' hands, but not very often. Everybody these days knows to lead very aggressively against slams and you are likely to get a lead from the ♥K or even the ♥A led.

Our third hand was:

♠ A 9 7 6 5
♥ A Q 5
♦ A J 4
♣ K 2

and we heard the inevitable 1♠ – 3♠ start. Personally I don't think this hand is worth any kind of slam try. I would just bid 4♠. You have to work hard to construct hands for partner that give the slam pretty good play; it requires a good mesh of minor honors. Blackwood certainly won't tell you that and not much else will either. So give up on the unlikely chance of partner having exactly the right cards for slam and settle for game.

What about 5NT?

What are the responses if you bid 4NT and then 5NT? Surprisingly there is no consensus on this. The simplest set of responses is to have the responses for kings exactly the same as the responses for aces, so:

6♣ = 0 or 4 kings
6♦ = 1 king
6♥ = 2 kings
6♠ = 3 kings

There are a number of possible alternatives though. However, whatever possibility you choose you must be certain of one fact. That is, to bid 5NT is a grand slam try. Therefore, in particular bidding 5NT to ask for kings guarantees that you hold all the aces between you. What this means is that partner is allowed to bid a grand slam directly. For example:

♠ 5
♥ 7 2
♦ A K Q J 8 5 3 2
♣ K 8

A fair hand and not made any worse when partner opens 1♠. You bid 3♦ and partner continues with 3♠. You bid 4♦ and partner surprises you by bidding 4NT which you play as Blackwood. You respond 5♦ and partner bids 5NT. Now the only sensible call in my view is to bid 7NT, put your cards away and get on with the next hand.

How can this not be completely cold? Partner has invited a

grand slam with no diamond honor. You have nine tricks for partner, partner's three aces make twelve so any king or even the ♣Q will provide thirteen tricks off the top.

So 5NT guarantees all the aces and shows some interest in playing a grand slam. Even if you have all the aces the rules of the game do not compel you to bid 5NT. Suppose you pick up:

> ♠ A 6
> ♥ K J 10 9 7 5 4
> ♦ K Q 5
> ♣ 8

and hear partner open 1NT(weak). Let's say you try a natural force of 3♥ and partner raises you to 4♥. That seems to clear up worries about trumps and you decide to let Blackwood do the talking. Blackwood reveals the somewhat surprising information that partner has three aces.

What now? 6♥ is obviously laydown and sometimes 7♥ will be back to back. More Blackwood won't help since partner can't have any kings with a weak NT opener. What will help is partner holding ♦AJxx or ♦Axxxx or even ♣Axxxx provided they are four-three.

How are you going to find this out, however? Certainly not from here. You would have needed to be playing some very sophisticated methods over 1NT that allowed you to discover partner's complete shape. Since that is beyond most of us, I suggest you give up on the grand slam and settle for 6♥.

I mentioned above that there is no universal method of playing responses to 5NT. Certainly just showing how many kings you have is the simplest, but there are a number of others.

Some people play that 5NT is the grand slam force in this position, so partner simply bids seven of the trump suit with two of the top three honors and six of the trump suit otherwise. Some people play that you show specific kings and sign off in six of the trump suit without any outside kings. Thus 6♣ shows the ♣K, 6♦ shows the ♦K but denies the ♣K, etc. This method is playable provided you know what to do if partner bids 6♣ and you are actually interested in the ♦K or the ♥K.

An alternative that seems more sensible to me is that partner should show the king they feel will be most important to you.

So if the auction has gone:

1♠	2♦
2♠	4NT
5♥	5NT

partner would show the ♦K as the first priority as that is clearly a very important card. Not having that card partner will show first the ♣K then the ♥K and sign off in 6♠ lacking any of these. This method does enable you to bid Blackwood with a hand such as:

> ♠ K Q J
> ♥ 6
> ♦ A Q J 7 5 3
> ♣ A 4 3

True, you might have forced with 3♦ on this hand, but the auction you have chosen has worked out very well. Blackwood has revealed that you hold all the aces and a small slam is surely safe. The card you would desperately like partner to hold is the ♦K and if partner does not hold this card you are very unlikely to have a solid play for thirteen tricks. Playing this method you can now try 5NT in comfort. If partner shows the ♦K you can bid 7NT and you can settle for 6♠ otherwise.

There is also a method that requires partner to use judgment. In this method when you bid 5NT you are essentially saying to partner "We have all the aces. I'm still interested in a grand slam. How about you?" If partner is hating the whole thing he signs off in six of the trump suit, but if partner fancies the hand he bids a grand slam. On in-between hands partner makes a bid that shows what he feels partner would most like to hear and the dialogue continues. Let us take the sequence we had above again:

1♠	2♦
2♠	4NT
5♥	5NT

If you hold:

> ♠ A 10 8 7 6 2
> ♥ A 8
> ♦ K 9 2
> ♣ 8 2

This is a really great hand. You have a sixth spade and the all-important ♦K. You should clearly bid a grand slam and should bid 7♦ to give partner a choice of contract (with slightly different hands for partner 7♦, 7♠ or 7NT could be correct).

If you hold:

> ♠ A 8 7 6 2
> ♥ A Q J
> ♦ –
> ♣ Q J 6 5 2

Now this, despite it having more shape and more values is a horrible hand. You have five weak spades and the void in diamonds is a real liability. You should sign off in 6♠ as fast as possible and hope it makes. If you don't believe this is a rotten hand try playing a grand slam opposite the responding hand I suggested above (and I've given partner a really good hand there). 6♠ is not cold. 7♠ is just awful. If you hold:

> ♠ A 10 8 5 4
> ♥ A 5 4
> ♦ Q 6
> ♣ K 4 2

Now this is very much an in-between hand. You only have 5♠ and they are not great. However the ♦Q is a very important card for partner so you are worth a try for the grand slam. I think you should bid 6♦ now rather than 6♣. Partner is much more likely to be interested in the ♦Q than the ♣K. You can imagine hearing 6♦ from you will cheer up a partner who holds ♦AKJxx or even ♦AKxxx immensely. If partner isn't interested in your diamond holding then you can ask partner why the suit was bid! How about:

> ♠ A 8 7 6 3 2
> ♥ A 5
> ♦ 4 3
> ♣ K Q 6

Again this is an in-between hand. You have six spades and the ♣KQ that should be good for some tricks. However your diamond holding is not great, so it certainly is not worth a grand slam bid. 6♣ is clearly in order particularly if partner can infer from this that you do not have a diamond honor (otherwise you would have bid 6♦ instead). Now partner knows that with:

> ♠ K Q J
> ♥ 2
> ♦ A K 7 6 5 4
> ♣ A 8 2

a grand ought to be easy enough, but with:

> ♠ K Q J
> ♥ 2
> ♦ A Q 8 7 6 5
> ♣ A 8 2

it is likely to be very chancey. Partner needs a singleton diamond to avoid a finesse and then you need some tricks. Finally how about:

> ♠ A J 10 9 6 5
> ♥ A Q
> ♦ 4 3 2
> ♣ K 3

This is a good hand apart from the awful diamond holding. Three small is the worst possible holding in partner's suit. I know pairs who have a rule that you always sign off with three small in partner's suit pretty much regardless of the rest of your hand. If you decide to take up this method of responding to 5NT that is something which your partnership needs to decide. I will merely repeat here that you should be very worried about grand slams (or small ones for that matter) when your holding in partner's suit is three small.

Which of these methods is best? Showing kings or trump honors has the merit of being simple, requiring no discussion and will simplify those hands where the number of kings or trump honors partner holds is all that matters. The other methods get steadily more complicated and require discussion and agreement with partner. The final method will, I feel, allow you to bid more good grand slams (and avoid more bad ones) with greater accuracy and does allow

you to get partner to tell you whether they can fill the gap in your suit. However, it is not a universal panacea. In the end you pays your money and takes your choice. That said, in Chapter 33 I'm going to try to persuade you to play a completely different version of Blackwood.

What About Voids?

What do you do when you're responding to Blackwood and you have a void? When it comes to Blackwood, voids are a pain in the neck and there is no easy answer. Just as you should never use Blackwood when you have a void, so it is that you should never have to respond to Blackwood when you have a void. The problem is that you have no idea whether or not your void is of any use to partner. If partner has three small in your void suit then it is magic but if he has KQ10x in the suit then it is terrible. If partner has the ace in your void suit then you are still going to need all the aces since your void is wasted as a first round control whereas if partner is lacking that ace it is potentially very useful. How can you cope with all this? One method that is quite widely played, though far from universal, is as follows:

> With none or one ace simply ignore the void.
> With two aces jump to the six level in your void *if* it is useful.
> With three or four aces ignore the void and hope to show it later.

It is important here to distinguish what is a useful void. Some voids you can tell from the bidding are not an asset. In particular you should never show a void in partner's suit. Unless partner has bid a very weak suit and you have loads of trumps between you, voids in partner's suits are a liability. Much better to have a void elsewhere.

The method suggested above will not solve all the problems and is hardly foolproof. For a start you should be a little worried about jumping in your void if it is above the trump suit, since it virtually commits you to a grand slam. However, it does work very well sometimes. Just don't expect to get all the hands right with voids opposite a Blackwood bid. That's not what Blackwood was designed for.

What About Gerber?

To those of you who don't play Gerber I say congratulations. To those of you who do, my advice is to give it up for a while and then forget to take it up again.

Gerber holds a unique place in bridge conventions. I can think of no other convention that is so universally ignored by experts and so universally played by club players. Expert players' convention cards (particularly those of a scientific bent) are bulging at the seams with transfers, reverse Lebensohl and weird and wonderful two bids. However, it would be quite rare to find Gerber anywhere mentioned on those convention cards. The reason is that we have already seen that hands on which it is sensible to use Blackwood are relatively rare and of a fairly specific nature. It is thus nonsense to have two bids (4♣ and 4NT) to ask for aces

when you don't very often want to do so in the first place!
4♣ is far too useful a bid either as natural or as a cuebid to
give up and use as Gerber instead. About the only place you
will find experts using 4♣ as Gerber is that some play that:

| 1NT | 4♣ |

is Gerber and if you wish to do that go ahead. Otherwise,
Gerber really is something that you don't need.

The Grand Slam Force

Apart from Blackwood the other very widely used slam
convention is the Grand Slam Force. In its simplest form
this is a jump to 5NT (or 5NT after 4NT if that is the way
you play) to ask how good partner's trumps are. Partner bids
seven of the trump suit (or preferably seven of an outside
control) with two of the top three honors and six of the
trump suit otherwise. This works extremely well on the
hands that come up where you want to know that partner has
exactly two of the top three honors. So if you are lucky
enough to hold:

> ♠ A K Q 7 5 3
> ♥ K J 10 5
> ♦ A 8 7
> ♣ A

and hear partner open 1♥ then go ahead and bid 5NT.

The problem with playing the grand slam force this way is
simply that the opportunities for it are all too rare. If the
hand is changed to:

> ♠ A K Q 7 5 3
> ♥ A Q 10 5
> ♦ A 8 7
> ♣ A

then all you care about is the ♥K and the grand slam force
will not allow you to find that out. With ♥AK53 all you
want is the ♥Q (partner could, after all, just about have
♥10xxxx). Even on the first hand if partner holds ace to six
hearts the grand will be cold and the grand slam force will
not tell you that either. Later I will be suggesting a very high
tech grand slam force that will cover all occasions, but for
the moment you can get much better (and therefore much
more frequent) use out of the grand slam force by allowing
more responses to cover various other possibilities. The
responses vary depending on what suit is trumps since you
have more room with some suits than others.

If spades are trumps then:

6♣	=	no top honors
6♦	=	the queen of trumps only
6♥	=	the ace or king of trumps only and no extra length
6♠	=	the ace or king of trumps only and extra length
7 any	=	two of the top three and an extra card in the suit bid

As you go down the suits from spades to clubs the responses
contract themselves, always starting from the bottom. So:

If hearts are trumps:

6♣	=	no top honors or the queen only
6♦	=	the ace or king of trumps only and no extra length
6♥	=	the ace or king of trumps only and extra length
6♠	=	two of the top three and an extra control in the suit bid
7 any	=	two of the top three and an extra control in the suit bid

If diamonds are trumps:

6♣	=	none or one top honor
6♦	=	the ace or king of trumps only and extra length
6♥	=	two of the top three and an extra control in the suit bid
Above	=	two of the top three and an extra control in the suit bid

If clubs are trumps:

> The standard grand slam force is used.

All this is not as difficult to remember as you might think.
Spades give you the most room and so you can distinguish
between the various cases (none at all, queen, ace or king,
ace or king with extra length). As you go down the suits
there is less room and you just collapse the responses from
the bottom until you finally arrived where you started with
clubs. If you decide to adopt this you will find that you can
use the grand slam force on many more hands and reach
good grands.

Other trump-asking bids

One of the problems with the grand slam force is that unless
you play 5NT after 4NT as asking for trump honors you
cannot use it after Blackwood. This is a pity because it is
often not until you have bid Blackwood that you know about
all the aces and are therefore interested in a grand slam. So
what do you do about trump honors after Blackwood? Later,
I am going to try and persuade you to use Roman Key Card
Blackwood, which largely solves the problem for you, but
you can still do something if you stick to ordinary
Blackwood.

A simple idea that works well is to play six of the suit below
trumps to say "Are your trumps better than you have already
shown?" There must, however, be no ambiguity here. If the
suit below trumps has been bid naturally then that is an
attempt to play there, so:

1♥	3♦
3♥	4NT
5♣	6♦

is a desire to play in diamonds. However:

1♠	3♦
3♠	4NT
5♣	6♥

cannot possibly be natural, so it asks if your trumps are
better than you have shown. By better than you have shown

means just that. If you have shown in the auction no more than a four card suit and you have AQxxx then you should bid a grand slam and should do so on AKxx probably as well. On the sequence given above you have promised at least a five card suit already, so Axxxx is certainly not enough and it is arguable than AQxxx is. However, Axxxxx certainly should be enough.

At the other extreme if the sequence is:

1♥	1♠
3♥	4NT
5♥	6♦

now you certainly should not bid a grand slam on ♥AQ10xxx or ♥AKxxxx since partner will be expecting at least this good a suit for a jump rebid. You either need solid heart or a seventh heart to contemplate bidding a grand in this case. Again this idea will not always get you to every grand slam, but it at least gives you a shot at some of them and that's better than nothing.

Now that we've had a discussion of Blackwood and some trump-asking bids, we will go on to discuss the other widely used slam bidding tool, that of cuebidding.

Cuebidding and All That Stuff

By now we have established that most slams cannot be bid sensibly just by using Blackwood. So what do we use instead? The most widely used slam bidding tool apart from Blackwood is cuebids.

The word "cuebid" is used in many different contexts in bridge. Here I am interested in bids made by our side which are definite slam tries and which are used to indicate a control (ace or king or void or singleton) in the suit bid. For a bid to be a cuebid in this sense it must be clear that:

1. The partnership is committed to game; and
2. the trump suit is known; and
3. there is a possibility of a slam.

Let's look at some sequences:

1♥	Pass	3♥	Pass
4♦			

4♦ is a cuebid because the partnership has been committed to game and trumps are clearly agreed.

1♠	Pass	2♥	Pass
3♦	Pass	4♣	

4♣ is not a cuebid. The partnership is definitely committed to game and very soon now it is going to have to work out what suit it is going to play in. However, at the moment no suit has been supported, let alone agreed, so 4♣ is not a cuebid.

1♠	Pass	2♠	Pass
3♦			

While a suit has been clearly agreed the partnership is not yet committed to game. 3♦ is just a trial bid normally showing length in diamonds.

1♥	1♠	2♥	Pass
2♠			

While this is a "cuebid of the opponents' suit" this is not a cuebid in the sense of showing a control for slam purposes. 2♠ is a request for more information and may not even be forcing to game. Partner might think that no trumps will play better and might be looking for a spade stopper.

1♥	1♠	2♥	2♠
3♠			

The opposition have been tiresome here with both of them bidding and partner has bid the opponents' suit at the three level. Now you are certainly committed to game and using 3♠ as a cuebid is extremely playable. However, it can equally well be argued that 3♠ here is just another strong bid asking for information and if you bid 3NT partner may be happy to pass. Serious partnerships will need to work out which method they think is best. For semi-serious or casual partnerships my advice is never to take a bid as a cuebid unless it clearly cannot be anything else; that is unless it definitely fulfills the rules for cuebids.

What Hands Should Make Cuebids?
What kind of hand should you make a cuebid on? First and foremost, you need to remember that a cuebid is a slam try. So, if you already have enough information from the auction to know that a slam is unlikely or impossible you should not cuebid. For example, suppose you pick up:

> ♠ J 7 5 3 2
> ♥ K Q 5
> ♦ Q 4
> ♣ A K Q

You open your inevitable 1♠ and hear partner bid 3♠. What next? Certainly, you should not be cuebidding on this hand. How can a slam be on? Partner needs good enough spades to hold you to only one trump loser and then both red aces as well. The right 13 count might make you a slam. Very likely for a three spade bid!

A cuebid both shows and asks for information. It shows a control in the suit you have bid and asks partner to co-operate by showing a control. Thus cuebids have a number of advantages over Blackwood which include:

1. They give information as well as ask for it, so that partner also has a hand in the decision.
2. You can discover specific controls from partner and vice versa (so at least if you bid missing an AK now you know that you are doing it. Regrettably you've

usually told the opponents as well).

3. You can often make slam tries below the game level and so stop at game when partner's hand is unsuitable.

Should You Bid First Round Controls Before Second Round Controls?

Consider this hand:

♠ A Q 7 5 3
♥ 7 5
♦ A K 7 5
♣ K Q

after our standard 1♠ – 3♠ start. Now this is clearly a hand with good slam potential (indeed it is possible to construct hands where a grand slam is playable – eg. ♠K1098 ♥A43 ♦106 ♣A1063) and a forward move is clearly in order. We now know that Blackwood is no good to us since that will not tell us if we have two heart losers. Thus a cuebid is in order. Should we bid 4♣ or 4♦? The answer to that question is "It depends on your style of cuebidding."

There are basically two styles of cuebidding widely used. In the more traditional style, first round controls are normally cuebid before second round controls. So on the example hand you would cuebid 4♦ and hope to hear 4♥ from partner. The alternative style is that you always bid the lowest control first regardless of whether it is first or second round. So on the example hand you would cuebid 4♣ and again hope to hear 4♥ from partner. This style was popularized by the Italian Blue Team and is thus usually known as Italian cuebidding. Since they won World Championships with monotonous regularity, people began to think there might be something in this freewheeling style of cuebidding and many pairs started to adopt it.

Which style is better? As with a lot of things in bridge there is no clear answer. Both styles have their advantages and disadvantages. Let's consider the freewheeling Italian style first. One of its great advantages is that it is often possible to identify that a vital control is missing very early on. Say you hold:

♠ A 9 8 7
♥ A K 8 4
♦ 10 5
♣ 7 4 2

and respond 3♠ to partner's 1♠ and partner continues with 4♦. You have a great hand for partner: two aces and a king and a potentially useful doubleton. Yet you should sign off in 4♠. Why? Because partner has denied a club control and you can "see" two club losers. An important corollary of this is that if you do cuebid 4♥ (or anything else) then you promise a club control as well as a heart control. Thus 4♥ would be correct on:

♠ A 9 8 7
♥ A 8 4 3
♦ 10 5
♣ K 7 4

Clever isn't it?! If the auction continued and you were called upon to cuebid again it would be correct to cuebid hearts again rather than clubs. Remember, you have already promised a club control, so there is nothing extra to show there whereas your heart control could have been first or second round control.

That seems to me to be the great advantage of this style of cuebidding. You can easily identify missing controls and there are inferences that partner must hold controls in suits you have missed out. This style makes the bidding of a number of slams where the presence of controls in all the suits is a key factor much easier. What then are its disadvantages? Well, there is the obvious one that people are always worried about: "Don't you end up in slams missing two aces?" The Italians were remarkably unbothered about it. "It can happen" they used to say with a Latin shrug. What this really meant was that their judgment was good enough to avoid it. All I can say is that it happens far less often than you might worry about. If there are two aces off sooner or later somebody becomes concerned that his hand isn't particularly good and he signs off. There is also Blackwood that can solve this problem for you and you can still use it after a couple of cuebids to make sure that you have enough aces.

There is a rather more subtle problem with the Italian cuebidding style. Sometimes it is difficult to know if your cards are of much use. Take our favorite bidding sequence of 1♠ – 3♠ and you hold:

♠ Q 9 8 7
♥ 10 5
♦ A 9 7
♣ K Q 10 9

Partner continues with 4♣, you bid 4♦ and partner bids 4♥. What now? If you could be sure partner had the ♣A then this is a good hand as your excellent clubs are going to provide tricks for partner. But what if partner has a singleton? Then you can consign your clubs to the waste-paper basket. Playing the Italian style of cuebidding it is impossible to tell.

This kind of problem is greatly simplified if you play the more traditional style of cuebidding. Here, when partner bids 4♣ you can be fairly sure that partner has the ♣A and your club values are working. Occasionally partner will have a void, but that is comparatively rare. I know partnerships that have a rule that you do not bid voids as your first cuebid precisely because partner mis-values holdings. While that is a bit unusual, it is certainly true that if partner bids 4♣ immediately then you can be 90 percent certain that your club holding represents some tricks and if partner bypasses 4♣ to begin and then cuebids 5♣, you can be 99 percent certain that partner has a singleton and your clubs are as useful as a bicycle is to a fish.

What are the advantages of the more traditional cuebidding style? Not surprisingly they are the exact reverse of the Italian style. You will find it difficult to bid slams with two aces missing (something teammates are often quietly grateful for). You will find it easier to evaluate your high cards in the knowledge that partner's cuebids normally show aces. Some pairs also tend to cuebid suits that they have values in and want help in first. This can work very well on certain hands. For example, suppose you pick up:

♠ A K 10 7 5
♥ 3
♦ A Q 9 7 4
♣ A 4

You open your usual 1♠ and hear partner's usual 3♠ response. Playing Italian cuebidding you have to bid 4♣, otherwise you have denied a club control. At least you will hear the vital diamond cuebid but the trouble is that this might be a singleton. If partner has a singleton diamond and all the other cards you need, you will have handling charges at the very least in 6♠ so it is not so attractive. Playing traditional cuebids you could bid 4♣ and if partner bids 4♥ you could continue with 5♦. However what is partner supposed to do then? How is partner supposed to know that the ♦K is gold and the ♣K or ♥K are pyrites? Pairs who believe in cuebids to show where you want help will argue that over 3♠ you should bid 4♦ and then continue with 5♣ so the sequence will go:

1♠	3♠
4♦	4♥
5♣	

Now partner will know that the ♦K is a very valuable card because you have chosen your cuebids in that order to put emphasis on the diamonds. Even if you do not like that idea, if you look at the sequence it is a sensible way to bid your hand, isn't it? You have organized your cuebids in such a way that partner will be constrained to show a diamond control and that is exactly what you want to hear. Yes, you could be unlucky and it still could be a singleton, but at least you have discovered whether or not partner has one. The problem with the other sequence:

1♠	3♠
4♣	4♥
5♦	

is that you had neatly organized your cuebids in such a way as to prevent partner from ever telling you the thing you most wanted to know.

This is another hidden advantage of the traditional cuebidding style. You have more scope to organize your cuebids to get the information you particularly want out of partner. The Italian cuebidding style forces your cuebids on

you in a particular order. In the traditional style if you miss out a suit and then cuebid it later, it generally shows a second round control. However, if you need specific information, you are free to organize your cuebidding to make it easy for partner to show you what you want.

If you decide upon a traditional style of cuebidding there is one point I cannot emphasize too strongly. Your cuebids need to be first round controls in principle only. It is completely unplayable to insist that all cuebids are first round controls. It makes a lot of hands unbiddable, particularly for the weaker, but suitable hand. A couple of examples should suffice to demonstrate what I mean. After the inevitable 1♠ – 3♠ start, partner bids 4♣ and you hold:

♠ A 10 7 6
♥ 9 6 4 2
♦ K Q 8
♣ Q 7

This is a good hand for partner. You have the ace of trumps, a king, queen and a potentially very useful ♣Q. You are clearly worth a move towards slam yourself. But if you play that absolutely all first time cuebids must be first round controls what are you supposed to do? Bid 4♠, lean across the table and say "That's a cuebid partner?" Bid Blackwood? No, the answer must be to allow you to bid 4♦, showing your control there. After all, what damage can come of it? Partner can find out how many aces you have with Blackwood, so that is no problem. What if partner leaps majestically to 6♠ over your 4♦ bid? Do you really think partner will mind about finding the ace of trumps rather than the ♦A in dummy. I think 4♦ is still the right bid after:

| 1♠ | 3♠ |
| 4♣ | |

on:

♠ K Q 7 6
♥ 7 5 3
♦ K Q J 8
♣ 7 5

and now you do not even have a compensating ace. However, you do have the KQ of trumps which should be of some use to partner and a very useful source of tricks in diamonds.

Don't get me wrong. I am not suggesting that you always bid kings if you haven't got any aces in a traditional cuebidding style. Far from it. Merely that if your hand is worth co-operating in a slam investigation and you haven't got an ace to bid then you should cuebid a king. If you hold:

♠ J 7 5 4
♥ K 4 3 2
♦ K Q
♣ J 7 6

and hear the auction:

1♠	3♠
4♣	?

then you definitely should not be bidding 4♦ or 4♥ on this hand. You have a bad hand. Do not give partner any encouragement at all. Partner needs much too good a hand to make a slam.

One more quick example. Say you hold your usual rubber bridge collection of:

♠ 8 7 5 2
♥ K 6 5
♦ K 9
♣ 10 8 6 3

and are pleasantly surprised to hear partner open with a strong 2♣. You respond 2♦, partner bids 2♥, you raise to 3♥ (stronger than bidding 4♥ of course) and partner bids 4♣. To recap, the auction has gone:

2♣	2♦
2♥	3♥
4♣	?

Not to bid 4♦ now is complete madness. How often are you going to have aces to cuebid after responding 2♦? Yet here you have a great hand for partner, king to three trumps and a doubleton king. You must be allowed to tell partner the good news.

To sum up then, each style of cuebidding has its advantages and disadvantages. For the remainder of this section I shall use a fairly traditional style of cuebidding because that is what most players do. If you sat down opposite a reasonable player for the first time he would not expect the sequence:

1♠	3♠
4♦	

to deny a club control. However, I repeat, there is certainly no expert consensus about which style is better; it is as much a matter of taste as anything else. Experiment with each of them if you like and see which gives you the better results.

While I say that it doesn't particularly matter which style of cuebidding you play, it is important that you are playing the same style as your partner. It is no good holding:

♠ A 9 8 7
♥ A K 8 4
♦ 10 5
♣ 7 4 2

and signing off in 4♠ after:

1♠	3♠
4♦	

"knowing" you have at least two club losers, only to discover partner has made what he considers to be a perfectly normal 4♦ bid holding:

♠ K Q 10 5 4 3
♥ Q 2
♦ A K Q 7
♣ 6

You have to agree on your style. Without discussion, most players would think that 4♦ was automatically the correct bid on this hand, but nevertheless it is something all partnerships should talk about.

Who is in Control of the Auction?
When you use Blackwood it is quite clear who is in control. You are. You have asked a question, partner will answer it (hopefully correctly) and you will place the final contract. However, cuebidding is a two-way process. Not only are you seeking information, you are also giving it. In particular, it is important for partnerships to answer the question "Do I have to cooperate with partner's cuebids even if I've got a lousy hand?"

The answer to these questions depends upon the level of the auction. Virtually without exception, good players will tell you that if partner has taken the auction above game level you have no choice. You must cuebid anything you have regardless of your hand.

Suppose you decide that you feel like opening 1♥ on:

♠ Q 7
♥ K 7 6 5 4
♦ J 8 7 6
♣ A 7

The light was bad; you thought your ♦6 was the ace; you thought you had seven hearts—any other excuse that you like. Partner bids 4♦—which you play as cuebid with heart support (see advance cuebids below). You try the "4♥. It's your lead" trick but partner, oblivious to all this, continues with 4♠. You may not like it but you've just got to grit your teeth and bid 5♣. If you bid 5♥ and all partner needs for the slam is a club control you will not be flavor of the month. After all, partner could have been dealt:

♠ A K 8 5
♥ A Q J 3 2
♦ A
♣ 10 6 5

Partner will not be interested in your excuses. All partner will say is that having organized cuebids to scream at you to bid a club control, you wouldn't do it. And partner is right. Partner has taken complete control of the auction and you have not done what you have been told to.

So, if partner has taken the bidding above game level you must co-operate and cuebid. The case when partner has made a cuebid below game level is very different and once again there is no universal expert view. Some pairs play that if you can cuebid yourself below game level it is mandatory to do so. In this style, a cuebid in response to partner's cuebid shows no extra values. It merely shows possession of the relevant control. So if you open 1♠ on:

    ♠ J 6 5 4 3 2
    ♥ A 4 3
    ♦ A 9
    ♣ 7 5

and hear partner bid 4♣ (a cuebid for spades) you must bid 4♦, otherwise partner will pass 4♠ on:

    ♠ A K 10 8
    ♥ K Q 7
    ♦ K 4 3
    ♣ A 7 5

and argue that you have denied both red aces.

The alternative style is to allow partner to sign off in game with a poor hand. In this style, if you had opened 1♥ on:

    ♠ Q 9 8
    ♥ Q 8 6 5 4
    ♦ A K 8
    ♣ J 7

and partner bids 4♣ you would sign off in 4♥. If partner continues with 4♠ you will admit to a diamond control by bidding 5♦. Notice that partner actually has discovered not only that you have a diamond control but also a rotten hand – otherwise you would have cuebid diamonds a round earlier. Again, it is a matter of preference, but I much prefer this style where I am allowed to sign off in game with a load of rubbish even if I could bid a control on the way. But it really is up to you.

Finally, if partner cuebids below game level and you take the bidding above game level, you should be showing substantial extra values since you are committing the partnership to the five level. So on:

    ♠ A K 6
    ♥ Q 8 6 4 2
    ♦ K J 8
    ♣ J 6

after 1♥ – 4♦ you wouldn't dream of bidding 4♠ since you are not good enough. Apart from anything else you can imagine hands for partner where there are two clubs and a trump off the contract. However with:

    ♠ A K 6
    ♥ A Q 8 6 4
    ♦ K J 8
    ♣ J 6

you are easily strong enough to bid 4♠ and will confidently bid a slam if partner can show a club control.

How Does All this Work in Practice
Let's look at some hands in practice and we might as well look at the ones we made such a mess of in the duplicate from Hell and see if we can do any better on them. On board one our hands were:

♠ K 8 7 4 3	♠ 9 6 5 2
♥ A K 5	♥ Q 7
♦ K 7	♦ A Q 10 5
♣ A Q 5	♣ K 6 4

and the auction began 1♠ – 3♠. If we assume our hand is worth a slam try we can cuebid 4♣, partner will cooperate with 4♦ and we continue with 4♥. My personal view is that East's awful trumps should suggest a signoff in 4♠ now and there the matter should rest. If partner takes a particularly rosy view and continues with 5♣, we will cuebid 5♦ and partner should sign off in 5♠. This is rather high on these hands (you would remember to duck the first round of trumps to cater for stiff ace offside wouldn't you?) but then partner has bid rather aggressively. So the recommended auction is:

1♠	3♠
4♣	4♦
4♥	4♠
Pass	

or, if partner is wearing rose-tinted spectacles:

1♠	3♠
4♣	4♦
4♥	5♣
5♦	5♠
Pass	

which is still a whole lot better than playing in 6♠.

On the second board the hands were:

♠ K 8 7 4 3	♠ Q J 10 2
♥ A K 5	♥ 8 7
♦ K 7	♦ A 8 5
♣ A Q 5	♣ K 7 4 3

Again the sequence will begin:

1♠	3♠
4♣	4♦
4♥	

and the slam may still be missed. Partner will have to view to make a second cuebid because of the reasonable trumps and good controls (for a 3♠ spade bid). Certainly this is a better hand to bid to the five level than the previous one and if partner does bid 5♣ we might bid the slam. However, this slam is a real "perfecto" because opener needs responder to have both good trumps and a doubleton heart. Otherwise, there is likely to be a late heart loser. Personally, I would shrug my shoulders about missing this one and get on with the next hand. (I did tell you that cuebids were not a universal panacea).

On the third board the two hands were:

♠ A K Q 7 6	♠ J 8 4 3
♥ Q 9 2	♥ J 7 3
♦ A K 6 5	♦ 10 8
♣ 6	♣ A K Q 2

This is a good hand for either cuebidding style. Playing traditional methods after 1♠ – 3♠ you continue with 4♦ and partner with poor trumps and no heart control should not take the bidding above game level. That should end the auction.

If you are playing the Italian style then the auction is even easier. It goes:

1♠	3♠
4♣	4♠(*)
Pass	

(*) denies a diamond or a heart control

Next board and the hands were:

♠ A K Q 7 6	♠ J 8 4 3
♥ Q 9 2	♥ A K 3
♦ A K 6 5	♦ Q 10 8
♣ 6	♣ J 9 2

Again this is a perfecto slam and I wouldn't expect to get to it every time. But you can get close after the start of:

1♠	3♠
4♦	4♥
5♣	

Now, if you adopt the suggestion that the first cuebid should show where your values are, then the responding hand is great and it should just drive to a slam (bidding 5♥ on the way in case a grand slam is on). If not, it is a bit more difficult and someone will have to take a good view. Responder should continue with 5♥ but then opener may be worried about the diamonds. After all, if responder has three small rather than Qxx, the slam is no play. If opener signs off in 5♠, responder knows that the ♦Q is good but may be worried about trumps. After all, partner does need ♠AKQxx or ♠AKxxxx to make the slam solid.

Board five and the hands were:

♠ A K Q 7 6	♠ J 8 4 3
♥ Q 9 2	♥ A 5 3
♦ A K 6 5	♦ 9 7 2
♣ 6	♣ A K 5

This is a difficult slam to avoid because of the presence of the three small diamonds in responder's hand. Give responder a doubleton diamond instead and there is no problem. I have a horrible feeling that a lot of pairs would bid it. In this case, it is definitely responder that has to judge well after the start of:

1♠	3♠
4♦	4♥
5♣	?

5♣ strongly suggests a singleton in partner's hand when you are looking at the AK. With weak trumps, the ♣AK not pulling their weight and no ruffing values, prudence really is the best course of action. If you are a dedicated point counter you will argue that you are maximum for your

bidding and hence there must be a play for a slam. However, before you go ahead and bid 6♠, try constructing hands for partner where slam is good on the assumption that he has a singleton club. Most of the time you will find partner needs ♠AKQ, the ♥K and the ♦AKQ. With that lot, partner should bid the slam anyway.

On to board six and the hands were:

♠ A 9 7 6 5	♠ K Q 4 3
♥ A Q 5	♥ K 7 6
♦ A J 4	♦ 7 5 3
♣ K 2	♣ A 7 5

and the auction starts with the usual 1♠ – 3♠. I've already said that I don't think this hand is worth a slam try at all. If you start cuebidding on this hand you are likely to get into trouble because partner will not let you off the hook easily. After 4♦ – 4♥ – 4♠, partner will certainly consider the hand good enough for 5♣, you will feel obliged to bid 5♥ and partner will bid 6♠. Unless responder can not only fill in the holes in the trump suit, but also provide a source of tricks like ♣QJ10x or ♥KJxx there just will be not enough tricks for a slam, despite all the controls in the world.

So there it is. We didn't do very well, did we? We didn't manage to bid all of the slams that were there or even most of them. But then this was the duplicate from Hell. However, I hope that you did notice that we bid very few bad slams. Similarly we arrived in a bad five level contract very rarely. The worst one we bid was 5♠ requiring the opposition not to take a heart ruff and even that could have been avoided with better judgment. That is one of the things you will find about the use of cuebidding. It will not enable you to bid every slam but it will enable you to stop bidding so many bad slams and bad five level contracts. That's got to be good, hasn't it?

Advance Cuebids

An advance cuebid is a bid that shows a control in the suit bid and supports partner's last suit by inference. It is the kind of clever thing experts are always doing. However, in this case it is a remarkably easy concept. The basic rule is that if a bid in a suit would be forcing then a jump in a suit is a cuebid supporting partner's last suit. The importance of this idea is that you can set trumps and issue a slam try without having to support partner explicitly. This is particularly important if you play that most raises at both the two and three level are non-forcing.

We have already seen a few advance cuebids. Bids such as:

| 1♠ | 4♣ | or | 1♥ | 4♦ |

were interpreted as cuebids with partner's suit agreed. Let's see why.

After say 1♠, 2♣ would have been forcing and 3♣ is a game force with clubs. So you do not need 4♣ for any natural purpose whatsoever. The person you're most likely to preempt is partner. So 4♣ is a cuebid supporting partner's suit.

Unless you have some other very specific agreement, all of these extra jumps in forcing positions should be played as cuebids.

So 1♥ – 3♠ is a cuebid (1♠ would be forcing, 2♠ game forcing, so 3♠ is a cuebid). Similarly, 1♣ – 3♦ or 1♦ – 3♠ or 1♦ – 4♣ are all cuebids.

However, a sequence such as 1♣ – 4♥ is best played as natural with a desire to play in 4♥. What about the sequence:

| 1♥ | 1♠ |
| 4♣ | ? |

In this case 2♣ may not be forcing, 3♣ is game forcing, so 4♣ is a cuebid for partner's suit. You would bid this way with, say:

♠ A Q 5 3
♥ A K 7 5 3
♦ 7
♣ A 9 2

This hand is worth bidding game opposite a 1♠ response and there are plenty of hands where a slam will be excellent. You should avoid a leap to 4♠. If you do bid 4♠, partner with at most one ace will almost never be able to proceed towards slam. After all, you could have a much weaker but more distributional hand like:

♠ A Q 5 3 2
♥ K Q 8 6 4 2
♦ 7
♣ 9

The solution to most of these problems is to make an advance cuebid on all hands that warrant it and then partner knows you have a good hand rather than just a highly distributional one.

Sequences for advance cuebids abound and you should make use of them. How about:

| 1♥ | 2♣ |
| 3♠ | |

2♠ should be forcing to game. (You have a reverse opposite a two level response. Even in non game-forcing two over one this must show at least about sixteen points opposite nine and that should be enough for game.) Thus 3♠ is a cuebid agreeing clubs. In a similar vein what about:

| 1♣ | 1♠ |
| 3♥ | |

Among expert players there is now an almost universal tendency to play reverses as forcing (indeed some play them as forcing to game!) and hence 3♥ can now be a cuebid supporting spades, which saves you having to leap all the way to the four level. Even if you do not want to play a reverse as forcing you still should really play 3♥ as supporting spades. Why have an entire bid just to show an extra king. If partner really does pass 2♥ you won't have missed

anything 95 percent of the time. The next offering is:

| 1♠ | 2♣ |
| 3♥ | |

What is 3♥? The answer to that depends on what 2♥ is. If you play the style where 2♥ is definitely non-forcing and is passed with some frequency, then you need 3♥ as a natural bid. However, now many experts treat such sequences as forcing. Consequently, they do not have to jump around to avoid partner passing and can develop the auction comfortably. It also means that jumps in new suits can be cuebids for partner's suit.

How about a more complicated sequence like:

| 1♠ | 2♣ |
| 2♦ | 3♥ |

Now 2♥ here would be fourth suit forcing and hence, as the name suggests, forcing. Thus 3♥ can and should be interpreted as a cuebid.

Another category of sequences that lend themselves very easily to advance cuebids is when you have opened or rebid no trumps. Let's say you hold:

♠ J 5 3 2
♥ K 7 5
♦ A 7
♣ A Q 7 6

and open a normal looking weak no trump. Partner bids 3♥ forcing and you happily raise to 4♥. Partner thinks about this and passes and proceeds to make twelve tricks, holding:

♠ 9
♥ A Q 10 9 8 2
♦ K J 4
♣ K J 3

You accuse partner of being chicken and ask what was wrong with Blackwood with all the suits controlled. However, understandably, partner was afraid of going down at the five level. Certainly, you can construct hands where you have no aces or only one ace but no trump king. The responsibility for missing this slam is unquestionably yours. You have a good hand for hearts and should cuebid 4♣ over partner's 3♥. This can hardly be natural, can it? Partner will now co-operate with 4♦ and this is more good news. If partner has diamond values your ♦A is a very valuable card. Indeed, I think you are now worth a cuebid above game level and should bid 5♦. Partner will know now that you do not have the ♠A or the ♠K. Why? Because you would have bid 3♠ over 3♥ with the ♠A (yes, 3♠ should be a cuebid as well) and you are likely to have bid 4♠ over 4♦ with the ♠K having already denied the ♠A. Partner should now be able to bid the slam knowing that you have few wasted values and that the trumps are going to be fine. I'm not saying that the auction is bound to go this smoothly, but at least you have given yourselves a chance to get there. Simply raising 3♥ to 4♥ gives the partnership no chance at all.

This is even more the case when you have opened 2NT. Say you hold:

  ♠ A Q 8 5
  ♥ A 5 3
  ♦ K 8
  ♣ A K J 8

Open 2NT (20-22) and partner bids 3♠ natural (or 3♥ transfer to spades). Do not just bid 4♠ on this mountain (or complete the transfer); make an advance cuebid of 4♣ instead. If you do not show partner when you have good support you will always leave partner guessing. How about:

  ♠ K Q 9 6 5
  ♥ A 8 7
  ♦ K 10 8
  ♣ K 5

You open 1♠ and rebid 2NT (15-16) over partner's 2♣ bid. Partner now bids 3♠. This is forcing and shows three card spade support, asking you to choose between 3NT and 4♠. With five good spades you naturally prefer spades so you bid 4♠, don't you? Shame on you! Don't forget that partner is unlimited at this point. Most of the time, I agree, partner will simply be asking you to choose between 3NT and 4♠, but just occasionally partner has a slam in mind and it is your obligation to show a good hand when you've got one. Here you have a great hand. Five good spades, ♥A, ♦K and the wonderful holding of ♣Kx. You should make an advance cuebid on this hand and in my view 4♣ is best.

Give partner a hand such as:

  ♠ A 10 2
  ♥ 4
  ♦ 7 6 2
  ♣ A Q J 8 4 3

Partner cannot possibly proceed over 4♠. With the wrong hand from you even 4♠ might have problems. Yet on this hand 6♠ is a great contract. You give yourselves a chance of reaching it if you bid 4♣ over 3♠ because partner can see a lot of tricks and has an easy return cuebid in hearts. Notice that when you bid 4♣ or anything else, apart from 3NT, you automatically promise five spades. Partner has, initially at least, asked you to choose between 3NT and 4♠. If you do not bid 3NT you have therefore chosen 4♠ and hence you must have five spades.

The point about all of these no trump hands is that the no trump hand is limited while the other hand is unlimited. The fact that your hand is limited enables you to make a lot of advance cuebids to help partner. The point is that you can do so without getting partner all excited that you have a really great hand. All you are saying when you make an advance cuebid with a limited hand is that within the limits you have already shown you have a good hand. In the example above if you had responded 2♣ on:

  ♠ 10 3 2
  ♥ K 7
  ♦ Q J 7
  ♣ A 9 6 4 2

and the auction had proceeded:

  1♠   2♣
  2NT 3♠
  4♣   ?

you know that there is no chance whatsoever of a slam being on and you can sign off quickly in 4♠.

Examples where you can happily cuebid in the knowledge that you have already limited your hand occur much more often than is realized. Look at:

  ♠ J 9 6 4
  ♥ 7 6 5
  ♦ K 7
  ♣ A 9 5 3

Partner opens 1♠ and you raise to 2♠ and partner now bids 3♦, a game try. You obviously should accept and could bid an easy 4♠. But you shouldn't! This is a marvelous hand and you should tell partner that with an advance cuebid of 4♣ and if partner bids 4♥ continue with 5♦. Most of the time this won't make any difference, but occasionally it will. Occasionally partner will be interested in a slam. Say partner held:

  ♠ A K Q 3 2
  ♥ 9
  ♦ A Q J 6 5
  ♣ 3 2

Partner wasn't thinking about a slam initially and might just have settled for game, thinking it would be on the diamond finesse at worst. But partner was careful and bid 3♦ as a game try, thinking you would be able to evaluate your hand. Now look at the difference. Partner can bid 4♥ and hear 5♦ from you. The sequence has gone:

  1♠   2♠
  3♦   4♣
  4♥   5♦
  ?

Now partner should know that you would not proceed above game without the ♣A (rather than say the ♣KQ) and the ♦K and can thus bid 6♠ to end a very satisfying auction.

If you have a partner who is prepared to make advance cuebids on hands like this you will find the bidding of a number of slams very much easier. You can also use game tries as sort of "advance slam tries" to try and direct partner's thoughts to the important suit for you. For example, consider:

  ♠ A Q
  ♥ A K 9 8 3 2
  ♦ A J 8 7
  ♣ 6

You open 1♥ and hear partner raise to 2♥. There could be a good slam here but the key will be partner's diamond holding. You could try an immediate cuebid of 3♠ (or even 4♣) to try to get a diamond cuebid out of partner, but even then you are still not sure whether you can proceed above the four level in safety. Provided you are playing with an intelligent partner, I suggest you start by making a game try of 3♦. If partner bids 3♥ you can clearly forget it and bid 4♥. If partner bids 4♥ you can forget it as well; partner should not have the ♣A and good enough diamonds to get you home in 6♥. But if partner bids 4♣ then you can start to think about it. Try 4♦ to cooperate (don't forget you have only shown a game try so far). If partner makes a cuebid above the game level you can confidently bid a slam and if partner signs off in 4♥ you have to decide whether to continue. I think you would be a little unlucky to go off at the five level, so you are worth one more effort. Notice how much more comfortable this is than the immediate cuebidding sequence.

Positive and Negative Controls

It can be difficult to tell if your cards are useful or not if you do not know whether partner has a positive control (ace or king) or a negative control (void or singleton). The obvious reason for this is that opposite positive cuebids you want values (KQ10x opposite a positive control is a great holding and xxx is awful) while opposite negative cuebids you do not want values (this time xxx is a great holding). For this reason it is now becoming more and more in vogue to try to distinguish between when your cuebids are negative and when they are positive.

To start with I want to make one point very clearly. Regardless of what cuebidding style you adopt, never, never make your first cuebid in partner's suit a negative cuebid. If you pick up:

> ♠ A Q 9 6 4
> ♥ K J 9 6 5
> ♦ K 6 4
> ♣ —

and hear the following auction:

| 1♣ | 1♠ |
| 3♠ | ? |

a slam seems extremely likely and you might just bid it. However, say you decide to get scientific. You cannot use Blackwood with the void so you try a cuebid. Do not bid 4♣. If looking at, say, ♣AQJxx partner will think you have shown the ♣K and will count five tricks. Actually there are probably two. Throughout this section I have stressed the need for tricks and for giving partner the most important information. Here, you have misled partner on both counts. Your first cuebid in partner's suit has to be a positive one, otherwise partner will frequently misjudge.

What about the hands where the negative control is of vital importance, say a void opposite partner's first suit of Jxxxx? My advice is forget them. These kinds of slams are notori-

ously difficult to bid accurately and, even if you do bid one, you may find you have a lot of work to do because you are likely to be short of tricks. Generally, you need a lot of trumps to make this kind of slam since you have to ruff out partner's five card suit. You will do much better if you stick to the first cuebid in partner's suit always being a positive one. I can assure you that if you can bid all the slams with five trump tricks, a running five card suit, an ace and a ruff, you will show a massive profit over the year.

All I want to do here is try to persuade you to play a style that as often as possible distinguishes between negative and positive controls. My suggestion is simply this: all jump cuebids are splinters. That is, a singleton (sometimes a void) in the suit bid. This is at least easy to remember and works surprisingly well. So the advance cuebids we started with, 1♠ – 4♦ or 1♥ – 4♣ are no longer just cuebids. They specifically show splinters. The great advantage of this method is that partner can tell immediately whether the hand fits well or not. He can sign off on quite good hands knowing that the fit is terrible and can proceed on quite moderate hands knowing that the fit is excellent.

Consider these two opening hands after the sequence 1♥ – 4♦:

> ♠ A 9 6 4
> ♥ K Q 10 7 5
> ♦ K Q 8
> ♣ 7

and:

> ♠ K Q 8
> ♥ K Q 10 7 5
> ♦ A 9 6 4
> ♣ 7

On the first hand your cards are lousy after partner's splinter. For a slam to be present you need two aces from partner and then still need to do something about your spades. Worse still, if you use Blackwood and find only one ace you could well be going down at the five level. Discretion is clearly the better part of valor here, so you bid a quiet 4♥.

What a difference changing round the pointed suits makes! As you can see, the second hand is great. You can cheerfully use Blackwood and bid a slam with a couple of aces opposite. If partner puts down as little as:

> ♠ J 10 4 3
> ♥ A J 9 2
> ♦ 8
> ♣ A 8 4 3

the slam is still extremely playable.

You might argue that on the hand above partner does not even have a slam try. Perhaps partner should just raise to game rather than try for the rainbow. Here again expert thinking will be very much against you. With a hand like this it is possible to make a slam if partner's cards fit well.

You will never find that out by bidding 4♥. After all, partner will pass 4♥ automatically with the ♠AK rather than the ♠KQ and then the slam is just a lay down. The current expert view is that these kinds of bids are not specifically slam tries. The bid shows "enough for game with a shortage in the suit bid." The really important point is that you have shown your shortage very precisely and hence partner can judge the degree of fit. Provided partner doesn't expect more than this, everything will be fine.

So what do you do if you've got a real slam try with a splinter? You make your splinter and when partner signs off you try again. So on:

　　　♠ A 10 4 3
　　　♥ A J 9 2
　　　♦ 8
　　　♣ A K 4 3

you splinter with 4♦ and continue over 4♥, probably with 4♠. Just occasionally you will get a minus score in 5♥. However, partner is going to find it extremely difficult to bid on over 4♦ with suitable hands. Thus on good hands you have to judge whether to go to the five level.

A standard rule for judging whether your hand is worth the five level or not is to ask yourself the question "Am I more likely to make a slam than go down at the five level?" Try constructing suitable and unsuitable hands for partner consistent with the bidding (remembering that partner may have cuebid on semi-suitable ones). If you can think of more unsuitable hands that go down at the five level than suitable ones that make a slam then put the brakes on. If it is the other way around go ahead and go to the five level. Occasionally, it means you will go down and partner and team-mates will be irritated. However, if you are sure that you were worth the five level then you have done the right thing.

Using the rule of "Am I more likely to go down at the five level than make a slam?":

　　　♠ A 10 4 3
　　　♥ A J 9 2
　　　♦ 8
　　　♣ A K 4 3

is clearly worth another bid. I have to construct a really horrible hand for partner to go down at the five level whereas there are plenty of hands that will make a slam. Of course, you will give up if partner bids 5♥, but you will expect that to make well over 95 percent of the time.

Before you go gaily tripping to the five level though, do remember that a lot of times partner could have cuebid with an intermediate hand and chose not to. Say we have this hand:

　　　♠ A K 8 7
　　　♥ A 9 4
　　　♦ K 10 6 5 4
　　　♣ 5

and respond 4♣ (splinter) to partner's 1♠ and partner bids 4♠. This is quite a nice hand and a slam could still be on opposite a minimum hand, say:

　　　♠ Q 9 6 5 4 3
　　　♥ Q 7
　　　♦ A Q 6
　　　♣ 7 2

This would produce an excellent slam and partner barely has an opening bid. Yet I suggest you pass 4♠. Partner had a chance to cuebid either red suit and declined to do so. Partner is not interested at all. Give partner the same hand with the minors reversed. Now you are quite likely to go down in 5♠ for a very silly result. If you allow partner to cuebid below game level on a hand with some mild interest you will avoid headaches like the one above. You can pass 4♠ in your sleep then.

So, to sum up: the modern tendency among experts is to play splinters that show no more than a raise to game and to allow cuebids below game level to show just mild interest.

What Do I Do Without a Splinter?

If you do not have a splinter you are balanced. A common toy is to play one bid to show a balanced raise to game. If you have a balanced hand worth 3NT you can always bid something else first and then 3NT later. So I suggest that you reserve an immediate jump to 3NT as a balanced hand, four card support for partner, about 12-15 points. It is non-forcing but is usually converted back to four of a major and passed over a minor. If it is bid over a minor then it should deny a biddable four card major. It is best to play the bid as limited because then partner has no headaches about what to do if you have a balanced 18 count. If you are lucky enough to pick up such a good hand with good support for partner you can usually find a way to bid it slowly and you are strong enough to control the auction. To recap, the scheme I am suggesting is:

Over 1♠:

3NT	=	balanced raise to game
4♣	=	splinter
4♦	=	splinter
4♥	=	splinter (some pairs play this as natural; however, for convenience of memory you might as well play them all as splinters unless you have strong views to the contrary)

Over 1♥:

3♠	=	splinter
3NT	=	balanced raise to game
4♣	=	splinter
4♦	=	splinter

Over 1♦:

3♥	=	splinter
3♠	=	splinter
3NT	=	balanced raise to game
4♣	=	splinter

Over 1♣:

3♦	=	splinter
3♥	=	splinter
3♠	=	splinter
3NT	=	balanced raise to bid

I think you should also play bids like:

1♥	1♠	or	1♥	2♣
4♣				3♠

as splinters. Obviously these bids show good hands, enough for game, but you will find that knowing your shortage is of great help to partner, who may well have the weaker hand, but can then judge how well the hands fit. So if partner holds:

> ♠ A 9 8 7
> ♥ 6 5
> ♦ K Q 9 2
> ♣ 8 6 5

after 1♥ – 1♠ – 4♣ partner knows this is good opposite club shortage and can easily afford to cuebid 4♦. Holding the same hand with the minors reversed partner knows this is a bad hand opposite club shortage and can sign off in 4♠ comfortably. Notice how much easier this is than if 4♣ is just any old cuebid when you don't know if your cards are working or not.

Again, what do you do if you don't have a splinter but enough for game? I suggest that after 1♥, 1♠ you just bid 4♠ and that you use it to show a balanced game raise. Partner actually needs quite a good hand opposite to make a slam and knowing of about 18-19 balanced opposite should press on with most of the right hands. This means that if you have a highly distributional raise such as the one offered earlier:

> ♠ A Q 5 3 2
> ♥ K Q 8 6 4 2
> ♦ 7
> ♣ 9

you either have to make a splinter on it which looks fine to me or you can bid 3♠. Strangely enough, this is perfectly safe. You know partner is going to bid again. Why? Because if partner doesn't this means that the opposition have remained silent throughout the auction with over half the pack between them and at most four spades. Unless the opposition have just arrived in coffins this never happens. If partner is then interested in a slam you can now bid your head off knowing that partner will never expect this much playing strength. Terence Reese was a great fan of making

early underbids so that you can then bid like a train later in the auction.

If you have a balanced hand with four card support for partner's minor after sequences such as 1♥ – 2♣ you have to find some other way to bid it. You could just bid four of partner's minor but this is a little dangerous since 3NT may be the only making game. Some partnerships have a toy to show this type of hand, some avoid the problem by always opening the minor and some ignore the problem by just bidding no trumps. It is a slight difficulty, but you will still be easily the winner in the long run by playing jump cuebids as splinters.

Finally, just to remain consistent I advocate that you play all the other advance cuebids we looked at earlier as splinters. So for example:

1♣	1♠	or	1♥	1♠
3♥	2♣			3♦

should be splinters. This method is not only efficient but is easy to remember.

Before leaving the area of splinters it is worth noting that you should try to avoid splintering with singleton honors, particularly singleton aces. Sometimes it is the only sensible bid on the hand and you have no alternative. Other times you can avoid it by bidding say a five card suit before supporting partner and that is preferable. The reason is two-fold. First it causes partner to mis-value his own honors. Partner will think KQ10x is a lousy holding but if you have stiff ace it is actually a good source of tricks. Similarly QJ10x will look dreadful to partner but will be three tricks if you have stiff A or K. The second reason is that partner will misplace your honors. If you splinter in a stiff ace and partner at some time bids Blackwood, partner will assume your ace is elsewhere and hence may think the hands fit rather better than they actually do. As I say, sometimes there is no other sensible bid, but, if possible, try to avoid it.

It is also worth avoiding splinters when you have a good five card (or longer) side suit. If you pick up:

> ♠ A 9 7 6
> ♥ 8 6 5
> ♦ 9
> ♣ A K Q 8 4

and hear partner open 1♠ it is folly to splinter with 4♦ in my opinion. The key to whether a slam is on may well be the fact that you have all these tricks in clubs and that is the most important feature of your hand to show. I would force with 3♣ on this hand and support spades next. Splinters with poor five card suits are fine, but with good ones you will find you start missing slams.

Of course, you are welcome to ignore all this and play what you like. However, before you consign it to the scrap heap why not give it a try? It is easy to remember and can be grafted on to any natural system. You may find that the use of splinters simplifies an awful lot of your slam bidding.

Doesn't All This Tell the Opposition What to Lead?

Well, yes it does. But then the whole of bidding does that. If you open 3NT blind on every hand you present the opposition with horrible lead problems, whereas if you bid three suits and come to rest in 3NT the opposition have a fair idea what to lead. Nevertheless, experience has shown that the latter is a winning strategy and the former a losing one. Similarly, all this advance cuebidding and splinters will sometimes tip off the opponents to the correct lead. Sometimes they will hear you cuebid every suit except one and so will lead that suit. Sometimes they will hear a splinter and lead a trump to protect their strong holding in the splinter suit. But if you are playing teams this rarely matters. It will only matter if the lead you have telegraphed will actually beat the contract. The odd overtrick is neither here nor there. Even if you have telegraphed the lead and it does beat the contract, teammates may have found the same lead. In practice all this stuff rarely costs more than an imp and that is a very small price to pay for bidding a lot more slams.

Even in pairs where every overtrick is vital I still think these are the correct tactics. Every so often it will cost an overtrick, most of the time it won't matter. Occasionally, you actually persuade the opposition to lead something else when it was correct to lead your cuebid suit. Again it is a small price to pay for bidding a higher percentage of good slams.

A Word of Warning

Finally a word of warning. I hope I have convinced you that cuebids and splinters are excellent ideas. However, that does not mean that you can lose sight of the basic requirements for a slam. In addition to controls, you need trumps and tricks. Many, many years ago partner and I agreed on spades and cuebid everything in sight at least twice. We had every side suit sewn up solid. Arriving in 6♠ the dummy presented a slight play problem as I wondered how to negotiate my ♠10xxx opposite partner's ♠9xxx for one loser! The opposition had played the sensible contract of 3NT and we deservedly lost a rich 13 IMPs.

Clever Blackwood and Other Things

When experts all over the world play different systems and different conventions, you can be sure that they all have their own merits and demerits. But when experts all over the world play the same convention you can be pretty sure that this is the best. That is the case with Roman Key Card Blackwood. Almost without exception now the expert community plays Roman Key Card Blackwood in some, if not all, slam bidding sequences. The most difficult part about it is the name and for that reason it is generally referred to as RKCB.

The first thing to know about RKCB is that there are five aces in responding to Blackwood. So what's the fifth one? The fifth ace is the king of trumps.

Which begs another question. What are trumps? You would rather like to know what trumps are as you use Blackwood. Generally, it is easy. If only one suit has been bid then that is assumed to be trumps. So in the auction:

1♠	4NT

4NT is RKCB with spades assumed to be trumps. If only one suit has been supported then that is obviously trumps. So in the auction:

1♠	2♥
3♥	4NT

4NT is RKCB with hearts agreed. If no suits have been supported then trumps are assumed to be the last suit bid by the partner of the 4NT bidder. So in the auction:

1♠	2♦
2♠	4NT

trumps are assumed to be spades and in the auction:

1♠	2♦
2♥	4NT

trumps are assumed to be hearts. That all seems straightforward. The only difficulties come when two suits have been bid and supported. Take for example:

1♠	2♥
3♥	3♠
4♠	4NT

or

1♠	2♥
3♥	3♠
4♥	4NT

or

1♦	1♠
2♠	3♦
4♠	4NT

What suit is trumps in any of these sequences? There are all kinds of ways of playing and you can have different rules in different situations if you like. However, for simplicity you might as well have one blanket rule and stick to it. It will avoid unfortunate problems. You can either play that trumps are always the last suit bid by the Blackwood bidder or that trumps are always the last suit bid by the responder to Blackwood. My personal preference is for the former but either will do provided you stick to it. In the first sequence I think that spades are clearly trumps. They have been bid, supported and raised. Apart from anything else, if partner wanted to bid 4NT with hearts as trumps, why didn't partner do it over 3♥ rather than muddy the waters with 3♠? That is the reason I think that spades should also be trumps in the second sequence. Okay, you have supported hearts and then gone back to them so you prefer hearts. You might argue that this will persuade partner that you had good heart support and therefore hearts should be trumps. However, if you decide to play that way then how is partner to get to bid 4NT with spades as trumps. I think it is more sensible to allow the Blackwood bidder to support your suit and then that will be trumps as far as Blackwood is concerned.

Thus, in the third sequence, I would argue that diamonds should be trumps. If partner was intending to bid RKCB and wanted spades to be trumps, why support diamonds? I repeat, however, that it is not particularly important one way or the other. What is important is that you and your partner agree.

What Are the Responses?

What are the responses when partner bids 4NT? As with so many conventions there are many different versions of RKCB. I will describe the one that is most commonly played. The responses are:

5♣	=	0 or 3 of the five aces
5♦	=	1 or 4 of the five aces
5♥	=	2 of the five aces and denies the queen of trumps
5♠	=	2 of the five aces and promises the queen of trumps

Notice first that there is no response for when you hold all five aces. So what are you supposed to bid if you hold all five aces? Think about it. What kind of a hand can partner have to use Blackwood and then decide whether to bid a slam or not without any of the four aces or the king of trumps? It means that you must have an earthquake and partner must have a pile of old garbage. So in this version of Blackwood, when you bid 4NT you are actually guaranteeing that you hold at least one of the five aces yourself. It is vital to remember this as it has some important consequences.

Notice that RKCB focuses not just on aces but strongly on the trump suit as well. Not only is the king of trumps counted as an ace but if you hold two aces you show whether or not you have the queen of trumps too. There is nothing special about holding two aces, the queen of trumps is always an important card and so the system always allows you to ask for it. Thus if the response is 5♣ or 5♦ then the next suit up which cannot be interpreted as a trump suit asks for the queen of trumps. So if the sequence is:

1♠	4NT
5♦	5♥ now asks for the ♠Q

and if the sequence is:

1♠	2♥
4♥	4NT
5♣	5♦ now asks for the ♥Q

Surprisingly, although everyone is agreed about how to ask for the queen of trumps there is no universal agreement about how to show it! Basically, one option is to bid the next suit up again to deny the queen of trumps and anything else to show it plus that feature. So, in this method:

1♠	4NT	
5♣	5♦	asks for the queen of trumps
	5♥	denies the ♠Q
	5♠	shows the ♠Q but denies any other useful feature
		All other bids would show the ♠Q plus a feature

The alternative to this is always to sign off in the trump suit when you do not have the queen of trumps and use anything else to show the queen of trumps plus that feature. In this method:

1♠	4NT	
5♣	5♦	asks for the queen of trumps
	5♥	shows the ♠Q and a ♥ feature
	5♠	denies the ♠Q
	5NT	shows the ♠Q but denies any other useful feature
		All other bids promise the ♠Q plus that feature

It does not particularly matter which of these methods you play provided you and your partner are on the same wavelength. I think it is slightly easier to remember to always sign off in the trump suit without the trump queen so that is the method I shall use from now on.

Just because partner responds 5♣ or 5♦ to your Blackwood there is no compulsion for you to ask for the queen of trumps. You may have already discovered that there are too many aces missing to go above the five level. However, if you continue to probe for a slam and you have not asked for the queen of trumps then the implication is that you are not interested in it. This means that either you are looking at it yourself or you have so many trumps that the possession of the queen is irrelevant. If you do not ask for the trump queen partner is entitled to assume that its presence is irrelevant, so if you end up playing a grand slam with a trump suit of Axxxx opposite Kxxx (or even worse Axxx opposite Kxxx) then you will have to take the blame.

So, RKCB concentrates very strongly on the solidity of the trump suit as well as on aces. This must be a positive move since a good trump suit is one of the prerequisites for a slam. RKCB's stress on the trump suit means that you are able to employ Blackwood on a number of hands that otherwise would not be suitable since you would be concerned about the quality of the trump suit.

Let's look at some hands and see how it works in practice. Firstly, you have the good fortune to pick up:

♠ A875
♥ AKQJ
♦ KQJ2
♣ Q

and hear partner open 1♠. You could now try a splinter, but since you will clearly go on over it and all you need are a couple of aces you might as well take the bull by the horns and bid 4NT. Partner responds 5♣ showing 0 or 3 aces. This is clearly three (go on, try finding an opening bid for partner with no aces). However, it is still possible to have a trump loser so you continue with 5♦. Partner shows the trump queen, but nothing else with 5NT. Now let's see, four spade tricks (minimum), four heart tricks, four diamond tricks and the ace of clubs; that would appear to be thirteen tricks, so you can bid 7NT with confidence.

As a sidelight on this hand you might be able to make 7NT but not 7♠ if partner does not have the ♠Q. Opener might have:

$$\spadesuit \text{ K 10 4 3 2}$$
$$\heartsuit \text{ 9 2}$$
$$\diamondsuit \text{ A 5 3}$$
$$\clubsuit \text{ A K 5}$$

Not very likely perhaps, but possible. After 5♠ denying the ♠Q you can still continue with 5NT. Whether you play this as asking for remaining kings or extra values or anything else is pretty irrelevant since the only extra value partner can hold is the ♣K and a bid of 6♣ will show it. If that happens you can again bid 7NT (2♠, 4♥, 4♦ and 3♣) and you have cleverly avoided a poor grand slam in spades. Of course, if you are really unlucky partner might have ♣AK stiff, but it is all but impossible to find that out. Now making a grand slam try when you already know there is a trick off the contract may seem very dangerous to you. I agree, it is, and usually I wouldn't advocate it at all. In this case though it is quite safe as you have such a powerful hand. Finally, before we move on, what if partner holds:

$$\spadesuit \text{ K 9 6 4 3 2}$$
$$\heartsuit \text{ 9 7 2}$$
$$\diamondsuit \text{ A 6}$$
$$\clubsuit \text{ A 9}$$

Now partner will deny the ♠Q and yet thirteen tricks are cold. Well, in my opinion partner shouldn't deny the ♠Q on this hand. Let's think about this. You have used RKCB immediately, so presumably you have four card spade support. You have then asked for the ♠Q. This means that a huge percentage of the time you have the ♠A (otherwise why are you bothering to ask for the ♠Q with an ace missing). But if you have ♠Axxx then this suit will now have no losers 78 percent of the time. Hence partner should show the ♠Q. What is the worst that can happen? You were not interested in a grand slam at all but were just checking as to whether the trumps were OK for a small slam. That might mean that we will end up playing a slam with ♠Kxxxxx opposite ♠xxxx. This needs the ♠A singleton or doubleton onside and so is 39 percent. If your trumps are even slightly better, say ♠Jxxx, the slam improves and if they are ♠J10xx the slam is flat out on a finesse. So, unless you have gone completely berserk you are most unlikely to end up in a slam that needs more than a finesse.

The point about ♠Kxxxxx is that you have considerably greater length in the trump suit than partner has any right to expect (especially playing four card majors). Thus the trump suit should be solid even without the queen of trumps. My advice is that you should show the queen of trumps even if you haven't got it when you have a trump suit two or more cards longer than you have promised. One extra card just isn't enough; for example, you don't want to end up playing 7♠ with ♠Kxxxx opposite ♠Axxx but ♠Kxxxxx opposite ♠Axxx is fine. Thus, if you play four card majors and

partner launches into RKCB, show the queen of trumps if you have six of them. If you open 1♥ and rebid 2♥ and partner then Blackwoods show the queen of trumps with ♥Axxxxx. After all, partner usually will have three of them and even I can play ace to seven opposite king to three for no losers most of the time. Be a little careful though. Say you open an Acol 2♠ strong and for some reason it is partner who ends up bidding Blackwood and then asks you for the trump queen. Now Acol Twos do not promise more than five cards, but most of the time you will have six of them. So I don't think you should show the ♠Q on ace to seven. After all, ♠Kx is quite adequate support for an Acol Two, particularly if the suit has been rebid. So because partner will assume a six card suit, most of the time I think you need an eight card suit to show the trump queen when you haven't got it.

You may think the one hand we have looked at so far is a little contrived. After all, how often do you pick up 22 points with primary support for partner's opening bid? However, I wanted to try to illustrate a couple of points, particularly the idea of showing the trump queen with extra length and also that you can ask for other features sometimes. Let's try some more examples and we may as well look at some hands from earlier. How about this one from chapter 30:

$$\spadesuit \text{ A Q 10 7 6}$$
$$\heartsuit \text{ 4}$$
$$\diamondsuit \text{ K Q J 5 2}$$
$$\clubsuit \text{ A 3 ?}$$

We opened 1♠ and partner raised us to 3♠. Now the ♦A and the ♠K will do very nicely for a slam and the ♥A and the ♠K or the red aces will be fine provided that the opponents cannot (or do not) set up a club trick. You could just give RKCB a blast and risk slam if partner has two aces. After all, even if partner doesn't have the right two aces for you the opponents do not have to lead a club or partner might have the ♣QJ (even the ♣Q will be good enough half the time) or partner might have the ♥AK to provide you with a pitch. Thus I have some sympathy with an immediate Blackwood. It is possible though that partner has no aces, in which case you could be rather embarrassingly down at the five level. You would be well advised then to try a cuebid first. Despite what I have said about some people's style to bid where they want help there is no doubt that the right bid here is 4♣. What do you most want to hear from partner? 4♦, correct. If you bid 4♣ and partner bids 4♠ you can now pass in comfort, since you know the red aces are off it (if partner has chosen to deny an ace—unlikely anyway—there still will not be a good slam since partner must have such a heap of garbage otherwise to do this). If partner bids 4♦ it is off to the races with RKCB and if partner bids 4♥ you have to decide what to do as now you know the ♦A is missing and a club lead may be embarrassing. Personally, I would bid my RKCB and have a go if partner showed two aces. Apart from all the holdings I mentioned above when a club lead does no damage, I am less likely to get a club lead now.

We have cuebid hearts and clubs so the most likely lead is a diamond. Failing that, the defense is reasonably likely to lead a heart. Leads to declarer's first cuebid, while not unknown, are relatively rare. So serendipitously I have arranged my bidding sequence to make the most damaging lead for us the least likely. I can live with that. Notice how smooth the auction has become because I could easily find out that the trumps were solid by the use of RKCB. The auction has been:

1♠	3♠
4♣	4♥
4NT	5♥ two aces, no queen of trumps
6♠	Pass

If you were playing ordinary Blackwood, partner would have shown one ace and you would have been worried about trumps. You would have had to invent some sort of bid to ask about partner's trumps. This is fine here since we can bid 5♥ and partner should figure out what that is supposed to mean. But why make yourself work so hard when a better form of Blackwood will solve the problem for you? Also, think what happens if the trump suit is hearts (just reverse your majors). Now the auction has gone:

1♥	3♥
4♣	4♦ (say)
4NT	5♦
?	

If you bid 5♥ you risk partner putting down ♥Kxxx when 6♥ is ice-cold, and if you bid 6♥ you risk partner putting down ♥xxxx when you need ♥Kx onside. Unless you really like playing roulette, I suggest you take up RKCB.

Before we leave this hand I would like to make one more point. There is a school of thought that preaches that if partner uses Blackwood after you have cuebid you should not count the ace you have already cuebid when responding to Blackwood. The argument goes that you have already shown this ace by cuebidding it and so you should not bid it again.

I think this is wrong and it certainly holds water only if your cuebids are always first round controls. I think you should always show all the aces you hold in response to Blackwood, regardless of whether you've cuebid them or not cuebid them.

How about this hand from Chapter 31:

♠ Q 9 7 5 3
♥ A Q 8 6
♦ A K Q
♣ 5

We opened 1♠ and partner raised us to 3♠. Blackwood wasn't the right bid and still isn't, but the hand is worth a slam try and I suggest you try 4♦. This will neatly push partner into bidding 4♥ on the ♥K with any suitable hand—which is exactly what you want. If partner bids 4♠ instead, give it up quickly! Let's say partner obliges with 4♥. Now

RKCB is a reasonable shot whereas ordinary Blackwood isn't. With ordinary Blackwood if partner shows one ace you are guessing about the trumps again and have to invent a bid.

With RKCB you are only going to bid a slam if partner shows two aces. At best partner will oblige with ♠AK. At worst partner will table ♠Kxxx and ♣A when you have still arrived in a 52 percent slam. Not so bad. Even if partner delivers only the ♠K, it is not impossible that partner will have the jack as well when all is fine; even the ten is a help and raises the percentage of the slam.

Finally, for the moment, let's say you respond 1♠ to partner's 1♥ on:

♠ J 8 7 3 2
♥ Q 7
♦ A 7 2
♣ A 7

Partner now leaps to 4♦ (splinter). This is a really good hand now (apart from the trumps) opposite diamond shortage and you wheel out Blackwood. Partner bids 5♣ (0 or 3) and again it is clear partner must have three. Most would now happily bid 6♠ and call it a day. But a grand slam is still possible if you can solidify the trumps. So you continue with 5♦ and partner produces 5♥. What's this? The sequence has gone:

1♥	1♠
4♦	4NT
5♣	5♦
5♥	?

According to our method partner has shown the ♠Q and a feature in hearts. Since partner has already shown the ♥A in response to Blackwood this would appear to be the ♥K. This gives partner:

♠ A K Q x
♥ A K x x x
♦ x
♣ Q x x

Okay, this is a good hand, but there was no choice except to open it 1♥, was there? Now opposite our

♠ J 8 7 3 2
♥ Q 7
♦ A 7 2
♣ A 7

7♠ seems to be excellent and we can bid it with confidence with two rounds of bidding to spare. Notice again the importance of being able to find out about the solidity of the trump suit.

The Importance of Blackwood Promising an Ace
Earlier I mentioned that when you bid RKCB you are promising an ace. Back in Chapter 31, we also decided that if you have enough aces for a slam you have to bid one after Blackwood. We can modify that slightly now in that we are

allowed to stop if we can identify that there is an ace and the trump queen missing. However, the basic rule still applies. That is, that with enough aces the partnership must bid a slam. This means that if partner bids Blackwood and you hold three or four aces, you are forced to bid a slam (partner holds at least one). Say you hold three aces, partner bids Blackwood, you bid 5♣ and partner signs off in the trump suit. Do not pass! You must bid a slam!

It is no use arguing now that you have shown your number of aces and partner has made the final decision. Perhaps partner should always be able to tell whether you have none or three, but occasionally a hand comes along where partner actually can't. If so partner is forced to guess whether to bid a slam. You might argue that this is a disaster anyway since you are likely to be going off at the five level anyway. But there are disasters and disasters. Going one off at the five level is nothing compared to bidding a grand slam off three aces (which is also almost certain to get doubled). You never know, the opposition may have found the hand as difficult as you and they may also be at the five level. There have been plenty of flat boards in international matches from five of a major off three bullets in both rooms. You sign off if you are even in the slightest doubt that partner may have the wrong number and partner with the larger number must go on. I repeat that with enough aces you have to bid a slam. Hence if partner bids Blackwood and you have three or four aces the question is a matter of six or seven not five or six.

While we are on the subject of continuing over partner's sign off you should not just raise partner to slam when you have the larger number of aces. You should always show any extra feature that you have not yet shown. This may enable partner to bid a grand slam that otherwise would have eluded you.

Let's take a couple of examples from actual play. On the first you hold:

♠ 6
♥ 7 4
♦ A K 6 5
♣ A 10 8 6 3 2

You open 1♣ and the auction rather tiresomely proceeds 1♠ – 2♦ – 3♠ back to you. Obviously, you have to support diamonds and so you bid 4♦. Partner now bids RKCB, you bid 5♣ and partner bids 5♦. The sequence has been:

1♣	1♠	2♦	3♠
4♦	Pass	4NT	Pass
5♣	Pass	5♦	Pass
?			

At the table the opener passed 5♦ in his sleep; but you must not pass. You have three aces and therefore you must bid a slam. You have nothing else to show and so bid 6♦. In this case partner genuinely could not tell which you had since his hand was:

♠ 8 7 2
♥ A Q
♦ J 10 9 8 5 3 2
♣ 5

While not guaranteed, partner was clearly bidding game and thought he could infer a singleton spade in your hand. He decided to take the risk on RKCB. If you had shown two aces with 5♥ and one of these turned out to be the ♦K then he would have been embarrassed. However, that hurdle was passed when you bid 5♣. Now, while it is likely that you hold three aces for this, regrettably it is not certain. You could hold the really helpful collection of:

♠ K
♥ K 4
♦ Q 7 6 4
♣ K Q J 8 7 2

You may not like it much but you are almost endplayed into 4♦ on this hand. However, partner was not worried because he knew that he could sign off and you would bid six with three aces. He's still waiting. Do not let him wait next time.

Our next offering was held by the American expert and former world champion Mike Lawrence. I've doctored his partner's hand very slightly, but that does not detract from the fine effort he made. He picked up:

♠ 9 5
♥ 10 8 7 6 4 2
♦ 5
♣ A 8 4 2

and heard his partner open 1♦. He responded 1♥ (yes, it is definitely right to respond on these hands) and heard his partner bid 4♣ (splinter). Lawrence realized the enormous potential of his ace to four clubs and the ten trumps between the hands. Lawrence bid Blackwood! Although one shouldn't bid Blackwood with an uncontrolled suit Lawrence decided to take the risk. To RKCB partner responded 5♦. Now it is indeed possible that partner holds only one ace. For example:

♠ K Q 2
♥ Q J 5 3
♦ A K Q J 2
♣ 5

would seem an exemplary 4♣ bid. So Lawrence beat a hasty retreat to 5♥. Partner continued with 5♠. So partner now had all four aces and was showing an extra card in spades. Not being interested, Lawrence signed off in 6♥ and there they were. Since partner held (in my example):

♠ A K 7 2
♥ A K 9 3
♦ A 10 6 3
♣ 5

as advertised, 6♥ was cold on the two-one ♥ break. (In case you are wondering about the opening bid, like most Americans they were playing five card majors, so 1♦ was the only choice on the hand.) I think this is a remarkable hand for demonstrating the power of both splinters and RKCB. Lawrence started with a four count; a hand that beginners of twenty years ago would have been taught to pass when partner opens 1♦. Yet Lawrence was able to bid his way to 6♥ on it.

Let's alter the cards in this hand slightly to look at other possibilities. Say Lawrence's hand was:

> ♠ Q 5
> ♥ 10 8 7 6 4 2
> ♦ 5
> ♣ A 8 4 2

Now over 5♠ Lawrence would have been able to bid a grand slam with complete certainly. How about giving Lawrence a better hand and his partner a worse one. Say:

> ♠ K Q ♠ A 9 7 5
> ♥ 10 8 7 6 4 2 ♥ A K 9 3
> ♦ 5 ♦ A J 6 3
> ♣ A 8 4 2 ♣ 5

Partner's splinter was decidedly aggressive now, but let's say he decided to make it.

Now the auction would be:

	1♦
1♥	4♣
4NT	5♦
5♥	6♥
7♥	Pass

Isn't that fun? The last three bids—5♥, 6♥, 7♥—sound like something you would hear in the nickel rubber game and yet it is all entirely logical once you accept that any responding hand with three or four aces must bid a slam.

Grand Slam Tries by "Signing Off"

Once you accept the idea that a hand with three or four aces in response to Blackwood always bids a slam then a whole new clever set of tricks opens up for you. You can now make grand slam tries by signing off in game! There are a number of hands (and a lot more than you realize once you get into this) where you can use Blackwood, hear a response, and from the auction know that partner has the higher number of aces. You can now sign off in the trump suit happy in the knowledge that partner must continue. Moreover, partner's continuation will show any extra feature. This might be music to your ears and so enable you to bid a grand slam.

The following example came up in actual play. You pick up:

> ♠ A 7 6 2
> ♥ K 5 2
> ♦ A Q 9 7 2
> ♣ K

Partner opens 1♥, you naturally respond 2♦ and partner raises you to 3♦. Now, whatever your views on whether this is right or wrong, this partnership virtually never raised minors on three card support, so you can be fairly well guaranteed of nine trumps, which simplifies things a bit.

This seems an eminently suitable hand for RKCB so you continue with 4NT and partner bids 5♣. Now partner must have three aces. Partner could not have an opener without any aces.

Would you open:

> ♠ K Q
> ♥ Q J 10 8 7
> ♦ J 10 8 3
> ♣ Q J

I certainly hope not. So partner has three aces and the small slam is cold. But the grand slam is far from out of the picture yet. You have a discard for your small heart on the ♣A, so that takes care of that. If partner has the ♠K then you should be able to ruff your spade losers (if partner has 3-4-5-1 pattern with a stiff ♣A that is incredibly unlucky) and if partner has the ♥Q then that is enough tricks anyway. There are other possibilities as well; ♣AQx will be enough for example. How do you get partner to tell you any of this? You sign off in 5♦ knowing partner must continue and give you some useful information. He might be a bit loath to show the ♥Q, but you still might be able to squeeze it out of him. At the table partner bid 5♠. This was enough and you closed the auction with 7♦. So the sequence has been:

	1♥
2♦	3♦
4NT	5♣
5♦	5♠
7♦	Pass

Partner tabled:

> ♠ 8
> ♥ A J 10 7 3
> ♦ K 6 4 3
> ♣ A 9 5

which goes fine with your hand which was:

> ♠ A 7 6 2
> ♥ K 5 2
> ♦ A Q 9 7 2
> ♣ K

You have arrived in an excellent grand slam that will make virtually every time the trumps are not four-0 and even sometimes when they are. What would your chances be of reaching this if you were not able to sign off in 5♦ and get partner to bid something sensible? Notice, partner made a good effort with 5♠ showing his extra feature with nothing much to spare for the opening bid.

Do not worry about pausing after the response to Blackwood either. Pausing in the auction is never a good idea and, if you can, you should keep all your bids in tempo. In particular you should always know where you are going when you bid Blackwood. But life is not always like that.

Sometimes you need to think, even after Blackwood. Earlier I told you that if you paused after Blackwood and then signed off and partner went on you would always get the score adjusted back. But that is not the same case as this. Here you have one response to show two different numbers of aces and your agreements are that partner must continue with the higher number of aces. So you put partner under no pressure by thinking. If you need to think and then feel that the right bid is to "sign off" go ahead and do so. Partner is under no ethical pressure at all.

What About Voids?

The news here with RKCB is no better than it was with ordinary Blackwood. No Blackwood system, no matter how sophisticated, will be able to cope with voids in the responding hand. It just is not designed for that. The best I can offer is that with one ace ignore the void; with two aces and a working void, jump to six of the void and with three or four aces ignore it for the moment and hope to work it out later. By the way, even with a useful void do not jump to six of a suit that is above the trump suit. If there is still an ace off the contract you may leave partner with nowhere to go.

What About 5NT?

As with 5NT after ordinary Blackwood there is no universally agreed method of responses over 5NT after 4NT RKCB. However, the same thing applies as with ordinary Blackwood. If you bid 4NT and then follow with 5NT you are guaranteeing that the partnership holds all of the (five) aces. Moreover in the case of RKCB you are also guaranteeing that you either have the queen of trumps yourself or that you do not care about it. So bidding 5NT after 4NT already conveys considerable information.

As for responses to 5NT you basically have the same set of options as you did over ordinary Blackwood that were outlined earlier. The only one that is clearly silly to play is that 5NT is a trump ask since RKCB has already sorted out the trump position for you. This leaves basically the options of simply showing kings, showing specific kings or allowing partner to use judgment to show the most important features. If you choose simply to show kings, then do remember that there are only three of them. The simplest set of responses, therefore, is to play:

6♣	=	0 kings
6♦	=	1 king
6♥	=	2 kings
6♠	=	3 kings

though some pairs combine the first and the last response so that 6♣ shows 0 or 3 kings. My own preference among the options is to allow partner freedom to sign off, bid a grand slam or show a useful feature. It seems to me that by the time you have identified all the aces and the KQ of trumps, then a grand slam will depend on the presence of certain key cards rather than just how many kings partner has. However, again it is not so important what you play as having a clear agreement with partner and a firm understanding of your methods.

All Slam Bidding Problems Solved?

Not at all. I believe RKCB is a significant improvement over ordinary Blackwood and so do most of the world's experts. That's why they play it and that's why I'm recommending it to you. However, do not think that it will solve all your slam bidding problems because it won't. Nothing will. RKCB is a big help but it does have some drawbacks and sometimes it simply won't get the job done. There are three drawbacks of RKCB that you may come across.

First, it does not work on those rare hands where you really are only interested in the number of real aces partner holds. I once picked up:

♠ 8
♥ A 7
♦ 9
♣ A K Q J 9 8 7 4 2

and heard partner open 1♠. What a great hand for Blackwood. Partner showed two aces and one king in response to 5NT and I bid 7NT and put my cards away. But you cannot do that with RKCB. If partner shows two aces you have no idea whether one of them is the ♠K. This means that on hands like this you have to pussyfoot around a bit and try to persuade partner that clubs, not spades, are trumps. Perhaps a force of 3♣ would be a good start. Nor can you launch into Blackwood, hear a discouraging response, bid a new suit like 5♥ in which you happen to have eight solid you haven't bothered telling partner about yet and expect partner to pass.

So on hands such as these you have to be a bit more delicate and insure that you bid your suits first of all so that partner will know that's where you want to play. However, that is really not such a great price to pay. How often do you really launch into Blackwood over partner's opening bid? When you do, how often do you really have a self-supporting suit rather than support for partner?

The second difficulty RKCB occasionally throws up is something often known as the "key card disaster." Let's say you pick up this good hand:

♠ 5
♥ J 10 7 6 4
♦ A K Q J 2
♣ K Q

and are somewhat surprised to hear partner open 1♥. Aces and trump honors seem to be what the hand is about so you emerge with 4NT. Partner bids 5♠, two aces and the queen of trumps. Not so bad unless one of the aces is the king of trumps. Now you have forced yourself into a position where you have to bid a slam knowing that there are two cashing aces off it. Even if partner is kind enough to produce two "real" aces then 6♥ is still on a finesse. This kind of problem can happen occasionally and it gets steadily worse as you go down the suits. It happens a lot less than you might worry about and is certainly no reason to give up

RKCB. However, it is worth considering whether any of partner's possible responses to RKCB could embarrass you.

The third problem with RKCB is that it does not work very well if trumps are a minor suit. This is by no means unique to RKCB. The problem is just as apparent with ordinary Blackwood. The reason, naturally enough, is that you have so much less room. If spades are trumps you can use RKCB quite happily knowing that no response partner can give will take you above the five level. If clubs are trumps the situation is very different. Every time partner has one or more aces the response will be 5♦ or higher and you are committed to a slam. There is no easy way around this. You simply have to be a lot more circumspect about using RKCB (or ordinary Blackwood for that matter) when trumps are a minor, particularly clubs.

Some expert pairs get around this problem by playing the suit above trumps as RKCB rather than 4NT. So if clubs are trumps then 4♦ is RKCB. This has the great advantage that partner always has a full set of responses before reaching five of the trump suit. However, it is not something I recommend to you without you being prepared to invest a lot of time in it. All the continuations need careful planning and when it is not clear what trumps are or the sequence has gone on for some time then the whole thing can get very murky with nobody sure which four level bids if any, are Blackwood. Unless you are prepared to devote a lot of effort to this I suggest you grin and bear the problems associated with using RKCB with minor suits as trumps.

The subject of RKCB is far from exhausted. There are all kinds of extra wrinkles you can introduce if you are so minded. For example, what do new suits at the six level mean, or can you find a sensible meaning for partner responding 5NT to 4NT? Anyone interested can find hours of harmless pleasure in a thorough study of RKCB.

Clever Trump Asking Bids

In Chapter 31 we looked at the Grand Slam Force and I tried to persuade you to play a somewhat more sophisticated set of responses to 5NT. If you do I think you will find your grand slams with poor trump suits diminish. I want to point out the kind of level of definition you can get to if you want.

RKCB or the Grand Slam Force will solve most of your trump problems for you, particularly if you play that you show the queen with two extra cards. But it will not manage all of them. Say you use the Grand Slam Force on AKxxx of trumps. Partner denies the queen and you settle for six only to find xxxxx in partner's hand. Situations like this have prompted some pairs to play a much more sophisticated set of responses to the Grand Slam Force whereby all the important categories can be distinguished. I include this to show you what can be done. It is not the first thing to worry about in your slam bidding armory, but if you use a complex Grand Slam Force it works well when it comes up.

There are many different versions. The one I am going to describe was developed by Alan Hudson of Manchester. In this system a bid of five of the suit above the trump suit is always the Grand Slam Force, rather than 5NT. So:

1♥	5♠
or	
1♦	3♦
5♥	
or	
1♣	1♠
5NT	

are all grand slam forces. This is to allow the complete set of responses no matter what the suit is. This Grand Slam Force can be played with a jump, during a cuebidding sequence or even after 4NT RKCB, provided you remember that five of the suit above the trump suit is always the Grand Slam Force. The responses to the Grand Slam Force are:

Step 1   shows two top honors or no top honors (but not AK to extra length nor neither to extra length)

Step 2   shows the ace or king (but not both) only

Step 3   shows the ace and king to extra length or neither to extra length

Step 4   shows the queen only

Anything at the seven level shows the ace, king and queen and an extra feature in the bid suit.

After steps 1 or 2 the next suit up is a relay. So after step 1 (none or two top honors) you relay and partner can then show:

Step 1   =   No honors

Step 2   =   Two honors no extra length

Any seven level bid = Two honors with extra length (but not AK) plus an additional feature in the suit bid.

After the original step 2 (A or K only) you can relay and partner shows:

Step 1   =   No extra length

Any seven level bid = Extra length plus an additional feature in the suit bid.

If you check through this carefully you will find that all the special cases are covered and you are able to identify whether trump suit is solid. As a quick example let's say partner opens 1♥ and you have an earthquake. A small slam is guaranteed and all you care about for the grand is that the jumps are solid opposite your ♥Kxxx. The sequence might go:

1♥	5♠(i)
6♣(ii)	6♦(iii)
7♥(iv)	

(i)   Grand Slam Force
(ii) Ace or king only
(iii) Relay
(iv) Extra length, no other feature.

And there you are.

Other Uses for 5NT

This is an area that you should think about as your partnership develops rather than at the start of your exploration of slam bidding techniques. However, I will mention briefly some modern ideas on the use of 5NT.

Even if you always play a jump to 5NT as the Grand Slam Force, opportunities to use it are rare. And it will only be of any value if there is definitely one and only one trump suit. But in many constructive sequences partners have supported each other's suits and it may then be unclear as to which suit the Grand Slam Force applies. For these and other reasons many pairs either do not use the Grand Slam Force at all or do so only in such specific circumstances as when there is only one possible trump suit. This leaves 5NT available to be used in another sense. The idea here is that you have a sequence where there are two, or even three, possible trump suits (maybe even no trumps are not out of the picture). You have got to the point where you are pretty sure that a slam is makable provided you pick the correct suit. Unfortunately, you do not know which the best suit is because it depends on partner's precise holdings. So you bid 5NT to say "I want to bid a slam, but I do not know which is the best trump suit. You choose." Hopefully, partner will then make the right decision.

A couple of examples should suffice. You pick up:

- ♠ K 9
- ♥ A K J 7 2
- ♦ A Q 9 2
- ♣ K 5

and hear partner open 1♣. You respond 1♥ and partner, not particularly to your surprise bids 2♣. Luckily you have agreed to play 2♦ forcing here so you can develop the hand slowly with that bid and this time, slightly to your surprise, partner raises you. A slam would appear to be very likely now and a sensible way forward seems to be to show your important club card with 4♣. Partner surprises you again by bidding 4♥ which you play as largely natural here (that is doubleton support). What now?

To recap, the sequence has been:

1♣	1♥
2♣	2♦
3♦	4♣
4♥	?

It looks as if partner has a 1-2-4-6 pattern (though 2-2-4-5 is possible) and a slam is highly likely. But in what? If partner has:

- ♠ 5
- ♥ Q 3
- ♦ J 7 6 5
- ♣ A Q J 9 3 2

then 6♣ is cold despite partner not having the world's greatest opening bid, while if partner holds:

- ♠ 5
- ♥ Q 6
- ♦ K J 4 3
- ♣ A J 9 4 3 2

then 6♦ is cold, while if partner holds:

- ♠ 5
- ♥ Q 6
- ♦ K 7 4 3
- ♣ A J 6 4 3 2

6♥ would appear to be best, while if partner holds:

- ♠ A
- ♥ 10 9
- ♦ K 7 4 3
- ♣ A 9 6 4 3 2

6NT is certainly best.

To solve this dilemma on your hand you now bid 5NT, asking partner to pick the best slam. With such good clubs 6♣ looks obvious on the first example and similarly 6♦ seems obvious on the second. Getting to 6♥ and 6NT on the last two look rather tougher, but at least you've given yourself a shot at it whereas before you had no real chance of reaching either of these contracts.

Do you remember this pair of hands from Chapter 30?

♠ A K Q 8 6	♠ J
♥ 5	♥ A K Q 8 7 6
♦ Q 10 2	♦ K 9 6 5
♣ A K 6 4	♣ Q 5

I said at the time that I thought this was a difficult pair of hands to bid, particularly since the only good slam is 6NT. However, playing 5NT (pick a slam) a reasonable auction might be:

1♠	2♥
3♣	3♥
3NT	4NT*
5NT**	6NT***

- * Natural. Worth a raise towards slam with all those tricks.

- ** Pick a slam. The heart shortage is a negative feature but we do have an 18 count with a good five card suit so we should accept. 5NT is chosen as spades are not yet out of the picture.

- *** If partner is not even prepared to suggest hearts over 4NT it does not look right to play in them, so 6NT.

As I say, while this is all the rage among the experts at the moment, it is another convention not to be adopted lightly. It does have significant advantages on certain hands, but it is something again that needs discussion with partner. You cannot start using 5NT, pick a slam, without clear understandings with partner; particularly if partner is going to take it as a grand slam force!

34

Chapter

Other Uses for 4NT and Other Slam Tries

It would be wonderful if every time we bid 4NT it was always RKCB. We could bid it whenever we wanted to and that would be the end of it. Regrettably life, or even bridge, is not that simple. Playing 4NT as RKCB in all sequences is just unworkable. Sometimes you need the bid for some other purpose. Certainly, I believe that you cannot bid sensibly without using 4NT as quantitative and 4NT as a sign off in certain sequences.

The biggest set of problems comes when partner has opened or rebid no trumps. In these cases you often want to invite a slam in no trumps based entirely on the point count of the two hands. We all know that with 33 points between two balanced hands we should be in 6NT and with 37 points we should be in 7NT. It doesn't always work, of course, and bidding challenges in magazines delight in having combined 33 counts where you cannot make more than ten tricks.

For the moment, however, let's concentrate on bidding 6NT when we have enough points between the combined hands. In theory this should be easy. Partner has opened or rebid no trumps to show a very specific range. We can add up the points and there you are. However, partner does have a three-point range for a 1NT or 2NT opening and usually the same (or more) for rebidding no trumps, so you really need to have a mechanism to ask if partner is minimum or maximum for the range. This kind of bid is known as a quantitative raise.

QUANTITATIVE 4NT

Thirty years ago the sequence:

    1NT   4NT

would have been Blackwood and no questions asked. Today even hardened rubber bridge players will play this as quantitative. 4NT asks partner to bid 6NT if maximum and pass if minimum. Assuming your partner opened a weak no trump, this means that you hold somewhere around a balanced 19-20 count. Very good 20 counts may just bid 6NT and to hell with it and very good 18 counts may get upgraded, I suppose. If partner is timid about bidding slams then you may be a bit more aggressive in your tries.

If partner happily accepts with most minimums however, you may have to rein yourself in a bit.

What are the responses to 1NT – 4NT? Well, most players will tell you that there are only two, pass and 6NT. But that is wasteful, isn't it? After all, there are nine other bids before 6NT, so why not make use of them? It would seem fairly obvious to play jumps to the six level in a suit to show a five card suit and a possible alternate place to play. So after 1NT – 4NT you would bid 6♦ on:

    ♠ K J 5
    ♥ A 4
    ♦ K Q 8 6 4
    ♣ 8 6 4

I think this is a clear cut acceptance. You have a 13 count with good controls and a good five card suit that should provide more tricks than partner can reasonably expect. So bid 6♦ to offer a choice of contracts. Partner can return to 6NT if that is preferred, but it is fairly easy to construct hands where 6♦ is laydown and 6NT is a struggle. So why not give partner the option? If you jump to six of a major then the quality of your five card suit will be limited by what you consider a reasonable hand for opening 1NT with a five card major. I know players, particularly strong no-trumpers, who are quite happy to open 1NT with ♠AKQJx. Personally, I think this is wrong and it is even worse playing a weak no trump. I'm quite happy to open 1NT on ♠Jxxxx but not ♠AQxxx. If you hold similar views then partner will be aware that if you jump to six of a major over 4NT then your suit will not be that great.

What about suits at the five level? There are various possibilities here. Some partnerships play that if you bid a suit at the five level you are accepting partner's quantitative raise and you then bid as if 4NT was Blackwood. 1NT – 4NT is not Blackwood, it is quantitative. But if you judge that you should continue then you show the number of aces you hold. This will occasionally enable you to play in 5NT when you have a combined 32 count and the missing eight points are exactly two bullets.

Some partnerships play that five level suits are an acceptance with a weak five card suit and six level suits are an acceptance with a decent five card suit. You can see that this will be important with some hands. Some partnerships play that five level suits are an acceptance and show decent four card suits. Again this may sometimes enable you to ferret out a slam in a good 4-4 fit at the eleventh hour. Finally some partnerships play that five level suits show values in the suit bid, probably but not necessarily four cards, and are a "semi-acceptance." That is, if partner's cards fit well then a slam will be bid, but it is still possible for the partnership to stop on the head of a pin in 5NT.

My least favorite is showing aces. For it to be right to show aces you have to have exactly a combined 32 count with two aces missing. This is extremely rare. It still won't solve the problem when you have a combined 33 count with the ace-king of one suit missing. In the end I'm sure it's better to shrug your shoulders about these and use the five level bids as something else. The slam is far more likely to make or fail on the degree of fit rather than whether you happen to have two aces off it.

Finally, what about 5NT over 4NT? 5NT really is a bid of exquisite torture. The only sensible meaning for it is to show a "semi-acceptance" hand and to force partner to make the last decision. I suggest you very rarely bid 5NT and, when you do, you have a very clear understanding of what it means. How about a 4-3-3-3 pattern with a poor four card suit and not quite enough at the top of the range to bid 6NT? At least that is fairly descriptive and gives partner a decent shot at getting it right.

I have said that almost without exception we all play that:

> 1NT   4NT

as quantitative. What about this sequence however:

> 1NT   2♣ (Stayman)
> 2♥   4NT

Are you sure you know what this means? Are you sure your partner will agree? My guess is you probably are sure and your partner will agree: it is Blackwood. That is the way most club players would interpret it and almost without exception not a single expert. I am going to try to convince you that 4NT here should definitely be played as natural and quantitative, inviting partner to bid 6NT. Say you hold:

> ♠ A K J 6
> ♥ K 4
> ♦ A Q 7 6
> ♣ Q J 2

Okay, maybe you could have just raised 1NT to 4NT quantitative, but you do have a very good four card major and it is likely that if opener has four spades, they will play better than no trumps. Thus you bid Stayman and partner bids 2♥. What now? Without a quantitative 4NT you are completely lost.

I have played against many club players who have had this sort of problem. The auction always tends to go the same way. They bid 2♣, partner bids 2♥ and then there is an agonized pause. Eventually they emerge either with 3NT that ends the auction or, more commonly, they try 4NT and partner happily shows aces, with 6NT the inevitable consequence. Sometimes partner has a good hand and this makes but more often that not it doesn't. Does this seem a sensible policy? Surely it must be better to be able to bid a quantitative 4NT and let partner judge whether to continue? And notice that you have given partner considerably more information than before. Partner knows that for this sequence you will have four reasonable spades. Isn't that a lot better than guessing to play in 3NT or 6NT at your second turn?

At least on the last hand you had a reasonable alternative of raising 1NT to 4NT directly. Let's say we make your ♥K the ♣K instead:

> ♠ A K J 6
> ♥ 4
> ♦ A Q 7 6
> ♣ K Q J 2

after your partner opens 1NT. A grand slam could be easily laydown here or you might not be able to make a slam at all depending on partner's holdings. Now a lot of pairs play highly sophisticated methods over 1NT and if you have a method to deal with very good 4-4-4-1 hands then good luck to you and your problems on this hand may be solved. But what if your methods are fairly straightforward? To raise 1NT to 4NT quantitative directly is absurd. It is a misdescription of your hand and could have partner passing minimums with slam laydown. So you start with 2♣ Stayman and partner bids 2♥. A quantitative 4NT is still not ideal, but if you are not allowed to bid that then what are you expected to do? Again if you bid 4NT and partner will interpret this as Blackwood then you have forced yourself to 6NT on what may easily be an ill-fitting 20 count. Remove the ♠J from your hand and you still have to bid like this; a small slam or even a grand slam could still be cold and yet now you have forced to 6NT on a mis-fitting 19 count opposite a weak no trump. That must be losing bridge.

Perhaps I still haven't convinced you. Perhaps you still feel that giving up 4NT as Blackwood when you want it to be is too high a price to pay. After all, if I reverse your majors on the first hand so that you now hold:

> ♠ K 4
> ♥ A K J 6
> ♦ A Q 7 6
> ♣ Q J 2

then you might think that 4NT (Blackwood) is the right bid after:

> 1NT   2♣
> 2♥   ?

I still don't think it is for a number of reasons, but it isn't a bad shot. However, you do not need to give up on Blackwood on this hand. If you are determined to drive to a slam opposite one ace you can still do so. All you have to do is make a cuebid first of all. Bid 4♦. Unless you have agreed another very special usage for this bid it should be a cuebid supporting hearts and partner should work that out even if you haven't discussed it. Partner will probably sign off in 4♥ at this point. Now you can bid 4NT. You have clearly agreed on hearts and so this must be Blackwood. Thus, you can have your cake and eat it in this case.

Let's look at some other sequences. Transfers over 1NT are now common at all levels of the game and I want to look at a couple of sequences involving them.

What do you think this sequence means:

| 1NT | 2♦ (transfer to hearts) |
| 2♥ | 3NT? |

We all know the answer. It is a raise to 3NT with five hearts, asking partner to choose the best game contract. What about:

| 1NT | 2♦ (transfer to hearts) |
| 2♥ | 4NT? |

You will not be surprised that I am firmly recommending that you play this sequence as quantitative and not Blackwood. It shows a 5-3-3-2 shape with about a 19-20 count, exactly like raising 1NT to 4NT directly except that partner now has the added information that you have five hearts.

In addition, many pairs play that on suitable holdings the 1NT opener can "break" the transfer. That is, instead of just bidding 2♥, with a good fit for hearts, the opener can bid a new suit or jump in ♥. Now if you bid 4NT, I agree that is definitely Blackwood. So, for example:

| 1NT | 2♦ (transfer to hearts) |
| 3♥ | 4NT |

is Blackwood. The difference in the two sequences is that you now have a definite fit and have agreed upon a suit, so it is logical for 4NT to be Blackwood (RKCB of course!). Also, your problems are solved on the 5-3-3-2 19 count. With partner showing a good fit you're just going to bid a slam, aren't you?

I hope you have been persuaded to play 4NT as quantitative in a lot of sequences after 1NT. I believe it is imperative to do so, but it is even more imperative to do so when partner opens 2NT. An opening bid of 2NT really does cramp you for room. There is simply not enough space to describe all the hands you want. Not to be able to use 4NT as a natural quantitative slam try is destructive. Again I would strongly advise you to play all sequences where a fit has not been clearly established as quantitative. We all play:

| 2NT | 4NT |

as quantitative but you should also play:

| 2NT | 3♠ (natural) |
| 3NT | 4NT |

or, if you are playing transfers:

| 2NT | 3♥ (transfer to spades) |
| 3♠ | 4NT |

as natural. If these sequences are not quantitative, how do you bid:

♠ A Q 8 6 5
♥ K Q 6
♦ 10 9 4
♣ 10 2

You bid your spades over 2NT and it is fine if partner supports them. Now you can bid 4NT, Blackwood, because there is a definite fit. But what if partner doesn't support them? Now you desperately want a bid that says bid 6NT if you are maximum and pass if you are minimum and that is exactly what a quantitative 4NT does. Playing it as Blackwood is like playing roulette.

I do not care what your methods are over 2NT, but unless a fit has been definitely established then 4NT should be quantitative and not Blackwood. So:

| 2NT | 3♣ |
| 3♠ | 4NT |

should show about a flat 11 count (usually with four hearts). And similarly:

2NT	3♣
3♥	3♠
3NT	4NT

should show a flat 11 count with four spades.

Of course, it does not make the slightest bit of difference what range you play 2NT as or if 2NT was bid after another opening bid. For example, in most standard systems the sequence:

| 2♣ | 2♦ |
| 2NT | |

shows a balanced 23-24. You should still play the same methods over all of these bids. In particular, unless a clear fit has been established 4NT should be interpreted as quantitative and not Blackwood.

Finally, it does not matter if partner has rebid no trumps rather than opened them.

What do you think this sequence means?

| 1♥ | 2♣ |
| 3NT | 4NT? |

Of course, it is quantitative. In traditional Acol this leap to 3NT covers a wide range. 2NT is traditionally played as 15-16 so 3NT has to be 17-19, even a poor 20. Unless you are allowed to make a quantitative 4NT what are you supposed to bid on an ordinary looking flat 14 count, say:

♠ A 6 5
♥ Q 8
♦ K 9 2
♣ K Q 10 6 5

Here 6NT could be on ice or 4NT could be the limit of the hand. Bidding Blackwood isn't going to help you. What you want to know is whether partner is maximum or minimum and the degree of fit for clubs. Unless you can bid a quantitative 4NT you are playing roulette again and the opposition do not even have to put up a stake. I also do not think it makes any difference at what level the no trumps come. If the sequence above had been:

1♥	2♣
2NT	4NT

then this should be quantitative. Partner's range is quite limited here (in traditional Acol it is 15-16) but it still makes sense for 4NT to be quantitative. Apart from anything else think about hands that would want to be Blackwood in this sequence? What have you got? If you have such a good club suit that you intend to play in it then why not force in it? If you have heart support then why not bid hearts to let partner in on the secret? No, 4NT should be natural and quantitative.

If a suit has been agreed then 4NT is certainly Blackwood. Do you remember a hand we held earlier?

♠ K Q 9 6 5
♥ A 8 7
♦ K 10 8
♣ K 5

The auction was:

1♠	2♣
2NT	3♠

and we made an advance cuebid of 4♣. If partner bids 4NT now that is Blackwood as spades have been clearly agreed. But if we held:

♠ K Q 9 6
♥ A 8 7
♦ K 10 8 5
♣ K 5

we would have bid 3NT over 3♠ since we only have four spades. Then a raise to 4NT should be quantitative because no fit has been established. Finally:

1♠	2♦
2♠	3♣
3NT	4NT

Yes, 4NT here should be quantitative. We have bid two suits and partner has shown little interest in either of them. We do not seem interested in partner's spades. If there is a slam surely no trumps is the most likely destination. No suit has been agreed. 4NT should definitely be quantitative here. The more so since opener has really quite a wide range, from a minimum opening bid with a heart stopper to an ill fitting

fourteen or fifteen count.

So, to recap, my strong advice is to play all bids of 4NT after partner has opened or rebid no trumps as natural and quantitative unless:

1. a fit has been definitely established
2. partner has gone out of the way to show a good suit of his own where he prefers to play.

4NT As a Sign Off
This is the other side of the coin. If you have opened or rebid no trumps and partner makes a four level slam try in a suit then it is essential to be able to sign off in 4NT. Take this hand and assume that you are playing traditional methods over 1NT with jumps to the three level natural and forcing:

♠ K J 7 2
♥ K Q J 5
♦ Q 5 3
♣ 7 5

The auction has proceeded:

1NT	3♣ (i)
3♥ (ii)	4♦ (iii)

  (i) natural and forcing
 (ii) natural (or 3NT if those are your methods)
(iii) natural

What now? You hate the whole thing. You've got just about the worst hand imaginable for partner and want the whole thing to end as soon as possible. Yet what can you do? You cannot raise diamonds and you might be concerned that partner will expect a bit better than seven five doubleton to bid 5♣. You cannot introduce spades or rebid hearts. The best solution is for partner to allow you to bid a natural and weak 4NT. 4NT in this case means "I have no fit for you. I don't like it. Please let me go!"

If you have a good hand for partner you can cuebid instead. So you would bid 4♠ on:

♠ A K 5 3
♥ K J 7 5
♦ 10 3
♣ Q 8 5

This may allow partner to bid Blackwood and anyway you have given a sensible description of your hand. It is also a lot more rational for partner to be bidding the Blackwood. It is usually right for the hand that is least known to use Blackwood, because if your hand is fairly closely described then it is entirely possible that all partner needs to know is the number of aces you hold. Whereas if partner can have a large number of possible hands, how can the number of aces be all you need to know? In this case you know that partner has a good hand with a lot of minor suit cards. Partner knows that you have a balanced 12-14 count, a heart suit, a fit for one suit and a spade cuebid. Who is in the better position to bid Blackwood?

Sequences in which opener wants to bid a sign off 4NT do not come up that often after opening 1NT but they are very frequent after a 2NT opening. Let's take a responding hand this time. Say you have the promising looking hand of:

♠ 9 7 3
♥ 9
♦ A K J 8 7 6
♣ 10 9 3

after partner has opened 2NT. This could very easily make 6♦ opposite a balanced 20-22 count so it must be correct to make a try for the slam. Suppose you try a natural 4♦. Partner now continues with 4NT. Get your dummy on the table quickly! You have to allow partner to bid a discouraging 4NT. If you do not, then what is your partner supposed to do with:

♠ A K 8 5
♥ K Q J 2
♦ 5 2
♣ A K J

Don't tell me you wouldn't open 2NT with a small doubleton because you know you would. What else are you going to open this hand? Anyway, what do you intend partner to bid now after 2NT, 4♦? Surely you would take 4♥ as a cuebid for diamonds, which is not quite what partner wants. Even if by some miracle you do think it is natural and now try and bid 4NT to play, do you think partner is going to think that is natural? And yet 4NT is much, much better than 5♦ and is where you want to play the hand.

This kind of sequence is one I have frequently encountered among club players. They bid 4♦ and partner bids 4NT. They happily show their ace and partner barks 5NT. Without a care in the world they continue with 6♦ and partner's 6NT ends the auction. This wanders a couple off with no particularly bad breaks for another bottom (or −11 IMPs). Next time partner has learned the lesson and raises to 5♦ instead. That either goes off or makes exactly for a bottom at pairs. Yet isn't it obvious that 4NT should be natural and discouraging? You have to allow partner one bid to say he does not like what is going on.

As before it is just the same if partner has managed to bid two suits. What about the sequence:

2NT   3♦ (natural)
3♥ (natural) 4♣ (natural)
4NT

This should be natural and discouraging. If you have a good hand for clubs, you can cuebid either major. So you can bid 4♥ comfortably on:

♠ A K J
♥ A K J 2
♦ Q 8
♣ K J 7 4

Indeed this hand is so good for a slam opposite partner's slam try that you are just going to bid it. If you have a good hand for diamonds (within the limits of not having supported them already of course) then you can easily just bid 4♦. Alternatively, you can even make a cuebid. Partner may think that you are supporting clubs, but it will do no harm because whatever level partner bids clubs at you can convert back to diamonds. So with:

♠ A K J
♥ A K J 2
♦ Q 8 4
♣ K J 7

bid 4♦ (or 4♥ according to preference). Note that even though you bid a natural 3♥ on the last round, 4♥ should be a cuebid here. The vital point is again that you must use 4NT as a discouraging noise in these sequences.

Finally in this section the same applies if you have rebid no trumps rather than opened them. In the sequence:

1♠   2♣
3NT   4♣ (natural of course)
4NT

4NT must be interpreted as a sign off. You have quite a wide range for 3NT. Partner has shown a slam try with a decent suit. With a poor club suit partner would just raise to 4NT, quantitative, remember. Any of 4♦, 4♥ and 4♠ from you would be a cuebid showing interest in the slam. You have to have a bid for when you have a minimum with two small clubs and wished somebody would stop rattling partner's cage. The only sensible bid for this is 4NT, sign off. Similarly, in the sequence:

1♠   2♦
3NT   4♣
4NT

4NT is again a sign off with no fit for partner. With a club fit, you could cuebid, with a diamond fit you could bid 4♦ or cuebid. 4NT shows a desire to see partner produce a pass card.

Most of the examples have concentrated on minor suits. That was deliberate since most of the occasions you wish to employ a discouraging 4NT are when partner is trying for a minor suit slam. If partner has a longer major and a minor then most of the time you can bail out in four of partner's major with a misfit and this will usually be a safe harbor. So on the sequence:

1♠   2♥
3NT   4♣
4♥

partner will know you only have a doubleton heart (you would have supported on three). Since you are trying to play there partner may manage to work out that you are not enamored of the way things are proceeding. That, however, doesn't alter the fact that 4NT in this sequence should still be natural and discouraging. 4NT looks the right bid after:

1♠	2♥
3NT	4♣
?	

on:

♠ A K J 6
♥ 3 2
♦ K Q J 6
♣ K 8 2

Assuming you play four-card majors and weak no trumps, you would open one spade and rebid 3NT. If you play mainly pairs you may have noticed how difficult it is to get to minor suit slams, particularly after one of you has bid no trumps. You are reluctant to leave the matchpoint heaven of no trumps in search of the Holy Grail and end up in the purgatory of five of a minor. While I'm not saying this will solve all your problems if you are clear that 4NT from partner will be a discouraging sign off, you can introduce your minor suit slam tries with considerably more comfort. If partner has a fit, fine, you will be able to bid some good minor suit slams. And if partner hasn't, partner can bid a discouraging 4NT and you are back in the right matchpoint contract. The only time that will be wrong is when exactly nine tricks are only available in no trumps. If you really have a slam try that is unlikely.

My second very strong recommendation in this chapter is that when partner has opened or rebid no trumps, you have continued to the four level and no fit has been established, then 4NT is natural and discouraging.

Those are the two uses of 4NT that I think you really need. Without a quantitative 4NT and a discouraging 4NT you are making a number of potential slams virtually unbiddable. The rest of the uses for 4NT are not in this category. Apart from the kind of sequences we have gone through, it is perfectly acceptable to play that all other 4NT bids are Blackwood. However, there are a number of other options that work very well and better than Blackwood in certain situations. I am not going to spend much time on them and again it is not something you should start your exploration of slam bidding techniques with. As you become more in tune with how to bid slams and what to do in various situations you may become dissatisfied at the way Blackwood works (or rather doesn't!) in certain circumstances. Then you might decide that the time has come to try one of these ideas.

The Encouraging 4NT

I mentioned in the last chapter that Blackwood does not work very well when the agreed suit is a minor, since there often will be too many responses to Blackwood that will embarrass you. For that reason some pairs simply give up entirely the idea of using Blackwood with a minor agreed. Instead, in a potential slam situation, they use 4NT to say "I have a good hand in context, partner" and five of the agreed minor to say "I have a bad hand in context, partner." (Some pairs reverse this so that 4NT is the discouraging bid and five of the minor encouraging. This is not particularly important.) Say the auction has gone:

1♣	2♠
3♣	4♥

and you play 4♥ as a splinter with clubs agreed in this sequence. Now this is an unfortunate sequence that partner has chosen because it has used up all the room in two bids. But let's assume partner is bidding sensibly and we have to find a bid. Now if we have:

♠ —
♥ K Q 10 6
♦ K Q 5
♣ J 9 7 6 5 2

we are feeling as sick as a dog and really wishing we hadn't listened to the whispers that told us to open this. 5♣ will drop out of your mouth. On the other hand, if we have:

♠ 10
♥ A 7 3
♦ K J 2
♣ Q J 9 8 6 3

this hand, although minimum, is taking on rather a rosy glow. ♥A opposite a singleton is good news, we have a diamond control, a potentially useful looking ♠10 and a perfectly reasonable six card club suit. A slam try is called for. The problem is we haven't got one. Partner is sure to interpret 4♠ because showing a high card which is not exactly what we want and Blackwood could well result in a slam with two aces off it. Would partner's bidding be so terrible on:

♠ A K J 9 6 4
♥ —
♦ Q 5
♣ K 10 7 4 2

So you are more or less constrained to bid 5♣ on the second hand, too. This is really rather irritating because you do not seem able to distinguish between a heap of old rope and quite a decent hand. Playing this gimmick of 4NT as a good hand and 5♣ as a bad hand solves the problem. You can bid 5♣ on the first and 4NT to show interest on the second and you stand a decent chance of getting to the correct contract in both cases. As with all conventions it doesn't always work but then what does? It is often more sensible for the hand with the long minor suit to be able to distinguish between good and bad hands by the use of 4NT. If you like it, try it but do make sure you agree carefully with your partner when it applies.

Jumps to Five of a Major

Another thorny area of bidding on which there is much confusion and no universal agreement is what jumps to five of an agreed major mean. You are having a sequence, wandering happily along, maybe a couple of cuebids, and suddenly partner leaps to five of the agreed trump suit. What does this mean? The answer to this question is bound up with what your other agreements are. You may well give different answers depending on what those agreements are.

First, I do not think that there is any blanket rule that will cover all situations. Many years ago, jumps to five of a major were always interpreted as "bid a slam with a control in the opponent's suit." In some sequences this is still the only sensible interpretation.

If the sequence goes:

2♥ (weak)   2♠   Pass   5♠

it is difficult to understand what this leap can be other than "bid six with a heart control." In such sequences it is essential that you bid 6♠ with second round heart control regardless of what you have overcalled on and bid something else with first round heart control. Either bid a feature at the six level or bid 6♥ with nothing else to show. Partner may need nothing other than first round heart control for a grand slam so you have to do your duty.

This method proved so popular that all jumps to five of a major were soon being interpreted in the same manner. In particular they were frequently employed to say "bid six with a control in the unbid suit." So in the sequence:

1♠	3♠
4♦	4♥
5♠	

or

1♠	2♠
3♥	3♠
4♦	5♠

both of these sequences would be interpreted as bid six with a club control. That is how it has remained for many pairs for many years.

My view is that sequences such as these hardly ever come up. Look at the second one in particular. It is absurd. How can a hand that refused a game try suddenly be issuing a slam force provided partner has a club control? Hands where you want to insist on a slam if partner has a particular control are fairly rare. And when one does come up there are often ways around it that are just as efficient.

Instead of this blanket rule about always asking for a control in the unbid suit I suggest that you adopt different meanings to jumps to five of a major depending on the sequence. A lot of the time, however, I think it is sensible to play a jump to five of the major to show exceptional trumps. Aces and kings you can show by cuebidding, but a hand with much better trumps that partner can reasonably expect is often difficult to express since you cannot cuebid in the trump suit.

Take the following hand for example:

♠ A K 9 7 2
♥ 10 7 2
♦ Q J 5
♣ 10 9

Partner opens 1♠ and you may well have simply jumped to game. However, lets say you elect to bid only 3♠ and partner now continues with 4♣. What do you suggest now? Surely ace king to five trumps must be of considerable value to partner who is busy making slam tries on a queen high suit. Yet you have no way to express these positive features since you have no cuebid to make. I suggest you jump to 5♠ here and that this shows exceptional trumps in context. Moreover, the lack of a cuebid should suggest to partner that you have no ace or king outside and so partner should be able to judge the better for it. After all, what on earth else can this jump mean here?

Similarly, say you hold:

♠ K Q 9 7 2
♥ 9 7 5
♦ A J 7
♣ 7 6

and have elected to raise partner's 1♠ to 3♠. Let us say the auction continues:

1♠	3♠
4♣	4♦
4♥	?

I think it is again clear to bid 5♠. You are very good for your 3♠ bid (many would say too good though I cannot think of a better bid) and should definitely go on after partner's two cuebids. Bid 5♠ to show very good trumps.

A style that was in fashion a few years ago was to play jumps to five of a major as two-way. They either showed good trumps and asked for good controls or they showed good controls and asked for good trumps. This has always seemed a sensible idea to me. If you are looking at a fistful of controls partner's jump to five of a major will reassure you about trump quality and if you are looking at a fistful of trumps partner's jump will reassure you about the outside controls. If by looking at your hand you cannot tell which partner has got then you know it is right to pass and expect to go off at the five level.

As an example of this style say partner opens 2NT. If you hold:

♠ K 7
♥ 8 7 4 3
♦ A 9 8 2
♣ A 8 5

you may well just raise to 4NT, quantitative, and I think that is a sensible idea. For the sake of argument let's say you decide to bid 3♣ and partner gives you a 3♥ bid. Now a slam is looking decidedly likely provided that the trumps are sufficiently robust. You could make a cuebid and then hope to get in Blackwood later (4NT now would not be Blackwood but quantitative remember) or make several cuebids and hope partner can bid the slam but there is much to be said for an immediate 5♥. If partner holds some such hand as:

♠ A10
♥ KQJ9
♦ KQ5
♣ KQ75

partner will know to bid the slam despite being minimum secure in the knowledge that you have good controls. On the other hand, if partner holds:

♠ A Q 2
♥ Q J 9 5
♦ K Q J
♣ K Q J

partner will know to pass the hand since the trumps are not good enough. Make the trumps as good as ♥A10652 and the same hand otherwise and we now have a 22 count with a five card suit for our 2NT opener and the slam is still lousy, requiring the trumps to be two two (40 percent). Add the ♥J to the hand so that the trumps are ♥AJ1065 and take away any black queen or jack and the slam is now excellent. So 5♥ is a bid that will get partner to focus on the right feature. There is no danger in 5♥. You would have to very unlucky for 5♥ to go down opposite any 2NT opening bid from partner.

Now let us instead give you a hand like:

♠ K 7
♥ A K J 7
♦ 9 8 5 2
♣ 8 7 5

and have the same sequence which if you remember was:

| 2NT | 3♣ |
| 3♥ | ? |

This time again a slam looks likely, but it will depend on partner holding enough aces and kings. Unless you can bid 5♥ on this hand you might as well give up now. You cannot bid 4NT as that is natural and you have nothing very sensible to cuebid. It must be right to bid 5♥ showing in this case excellent trumps and poor outside controls. This may well put partner's fears about the trumps to rest.

Give partner a hand with a five card major, like:

♠ A Q 9
♥ Q 8 6 5 2
♦ A 5
♣ A K 6

and partner can bid 6♥ easily despite the fact that this isn't even close to a 2NT opener. If partner has:

♠ A Q
♥ Q 8 6 5 2
♦ K Q 7
♣ A K Q

this is a horribly ill-fitting hand and yet the slam only depends on the location of the diamond ace. Finally 5♥ will score a real goal if partner has a hand such as:

♠ A Q 6
♥ 8 6 5 4 2
♦ A K Q
♣ A K

Unless you show really good trumps wild horses are not going to make partner bid a slam with that dreadful five card suit. But now partner can bid it expecting to lose only one trump trick.

Yet again this kind of idea is not something to throw into the auction undiscussed to see what partner makes of it. It should be used when the partnership frequently opens no trump when holding a five card major, or if you play five card Stayman over 2NT opening bids. Undiscussed jumps to five of a major are another way of torturing partner for past indiscretions. However, if you and your partner have discussed the situation then using a jump to five of a major to show good trumps, when that is the only possible explanation or as either good trumps or good controls, can solve a number of problems that otherwise would be real headaches.

Finally, sometimes it is sensible to play a jump to five of a major as a general slam try simply saying "I'm too good to bid four partner." These positions only occur when the opposition are messing around in your auction and they are up to quite high levels. Say you hold this hand:

♠ K Q 7 5
♥ 9 7
♦ K 6
♣ A K 9 7 4

and the auction proceeds:

| 3♥ | 3♠ | 4♥ | ? |

Absolutely wonderful! Maybe you should give up and bid 4♠ but that is really cowardly. A grand slam could be possible here. If you believe that all bids now promise spade support then that is fine and you can bid 5♣. But if you are one who would think that 5♣ is an attempt to make eleven tricks with clubs as trumps then that is out. You cannot bid 5♥ since that would show a heart control.

So what is left?

I suggest you try 5♠ as a general slam try. Unlike the old fashioned meaning, this is not a command to bid six with a heart control. Your 5♠ certainly denies a heart control so partner will need one of them but it also asks partner to assess the hand as well. So partner will pass with:

♠ A J 10 9 6 4 2
♥ Q 6
♦ A Q 8
♣ J

A good hand but no heart control. Partner will pass with:

♠ A J 10 6 4 2
♥ K
♦ Q J 10 7 3
♣ 5

A heart control but a heap of old rhubarb. Partner will bid 5♠ on:

♠ A J 10 6 4 2
♥ 5
♦ A Q 5 2
♣ 8 5

A heart control and a decent hand. And finally partner will bid 6♦ on:

♠ A J 10 6 4 2
♥ –
♦ A Q J 5 2
♣ Q 6

A first round heart control and first round diamond control. Then it is up to us to have the guts to bid 7♠. Clubs sewn up, a golden doubleton ♦K and good trumps. We really should bid seven.

This won't always work of course. You can never get all the hands right over pre-empts. That is why the tiresome opposition keep on pre-empting. But I think a "general slam try" jump to five of a major is a useful tool when you are cramped for space. By the way, do you know what 4NT would mean in the sequence given above? That kind of thing is what the next chapter is about.

Coping With Interference

So far we have concentrated on trying to get the best out of your partner. However, your opponents can make infernal nuisances of themselves at every stage of your auction from a one level overcall to bidding 7♠ over your cold 7♥. It is not the purpose of this section to discuss competitive methods.

However, I should say something about coping with intervention during your slam auctions. Since this is usually at the four or five level it generally means that the opponents have pre-empted to a high level. Thus I am going to confine myself to a discussion of how to defend against the opponents pre-empts at high levels. I am also going to assume that the opponents are pre-empting, you know this is the case, and the contract they are bidding is not making. Sometimes both sides have incredible freaks and slams can be made in either direction. Since I am going to suggest you double the opponents a lot of the time this is a less than winning policy on such hands! But freaks such as those are rare. When they do come up nothing except experience will help you to get them right. A well-established rule and one worth following is that if you think the hand is a complete freak always bid one more. You cannot always tell, however. One of the most famous hands of all time was dealt in Valkenburg in 1980 when the great American player Bob Hamman was on lead against 7♦ doubled with both major suit aces, having shown a massive major two suiter in the auction. Hamman led the wrong ace and the doubled grand came home. 7♠ would have cost 300. Let's leave those aside and deal with pre-empts that can be assumed to be sacrifices.

Pre-empts at the Three Level
Almost without exception every expert partnership in the world plays double of pre-empts for take out. It really is the best method. If you do not play it, try it for three months. You will probably find your results improve.

Pre-empts at the Four Level
The overriding consideration in defending against pre-empts, and particularly against high-level pre-empts, is to get a plus score. You should aim for "the best result possible and not the best possible result." High-level pre-empts take away a lot of room. It is no longer possible to explore properly. You have to make your best guess at the right outcome. In such situations you should always err on the side of caution. If there is a penalty available from their pre-empt and you might be able to make a game that scores more, but you are not sure, settle for the penalty. If partner bids game and you think there may be a slam on, but you're not sure, then pass and take the game rather than bid a dubious slam. As a partnership you need to allow great flexibility for each other to bid or double over pre-empts to try to get a plus score without punishing each other for enterprise. You should always err on the side of caution when bidding over pre-empts. Nothing encourages the opponents to pre-empt more than watching you get negative scores after they have done so. If they know that you are going to double them most of the time or bid a sensible game they will be a little more circumspect.

Apart from anything else, perfectly good contracts may well sink without trace by hitting the rocks of distribution. Take these two hands:

```
    ♠ A Q 4        ♠ K 6
    ♥ K 8          ♥ 9 4
    ♦ A Q 8 7 2    ♦ K 5 3
    ♣ K Q 4        ♣ A 8 7 3 2
```

Now this is a guaranteed 6♦ or 6♣ provided it is played by West. The contract appears to be on nothing more than the three-two trump break, a 68 percent chance. However, I wouldn't want to be in a slam if either opponent had opened 4♥. First, the hearts may well be eight-one, in which case you are off immediately. If you survive that, the trumps are now quite likely to be four-one and you are down again. On really bad days the pre-empter will have a void, use the Lightner double on you and it will go ruff, ♥A, heart ruff, ruff for -800. I would estimate that this slam is well under 50 percent after a 4♥ opener and I wouldn't want to be in it. Not that I would be, since my suggested auction would be:

4♥   Dble (take out)   All Pass

or if North had opened 4♥

4♥   Pass   Pass   Dble (take out)
All Pass

On very good days you will make a slam, but you probably won't. You will probably make 5♦ or 5♣ played by West, but how do you propose getting there? But you are always beating 4♥ doubled. Take what is available to you; the best result possible, not the best possible result.

How should you defend against the opponents' high-level pre-empts? Again, there is almost universal expert support for playing a double of 4♣, 4♦ or 4♥ as take out. There is a division of experts into those who play a double of 4♠ as take out (my preferred method) and those who play it as essentially for penalty. Let me emphasize first that even those who play it as penalty play it to show high cards, expecting partner to do the sensible thing. It would not be sensible to play any of these doubles as strictly penalty. Even against wild pre-empters (and there are plenty of those in the expert community) you will wait for the rest of your life to pick up a hand that beats a 4♠ opener in trump tricks. If you pick up:

♠ –
♥ 10 7 3
♦ 8 5 4
♣ A Q 10 9 6 4 3

and hear the auction:

4♠   Dble   Pass?

Do not pass! It is a common fallacy to think "I've got no spades therefore partner must have many." What is actually the case is that partner has a few and dummy has a few. Dummy's trumps will either score ruffs for declarer or help to neutralize partner's trumps. 4♠ doubled will not be down many with the hand you have and might even make. Meanwhile you could be cold for five or even six clubs. It is essential to bid 5♣ on this hand.

So if you play penalty doubles they are not always left in. Rather perversely, if you play take out doubles you should very often pass them out, despite not having much defense or very many trumps. This is particularly so if the option is to play something at the five level. Eleven tricks is an awful lot to make, particularly when the suits are not likely to be breaking well and you have to make your first guess at the trump suit at the five level. So you should pass a lot of partner's take out doubles out and accept the (hopeful) penalty rather than risk going off at the five level. The usual rule given in these sort of situations is "Don't pull the double to a minus score." This means that you should only bid if you expect to make your contract. Otherwise pass and accept the penalty. You may be able to make a higher score declaring, but you cannot tell, so take what is offered to you. Let us assume the auction has gone:

4♠   Dble   Pass   ?

and you play double for take out. On the hand above, which was:

♠ –
♥ 10 7 3
♦ 8 5 4
♣ A Q 10 9 6 4 3

you have an obvious 5♣ bid. True, you might make six, but you also might not. Take the fairly sure profit in 5♣. With:

♠ 9 7
♥ K 8 4
♦ 6 4 3
♣ A K 6 4 3

you would not find any expert who would do other than pass out 4♠ doubled despite holding AKxxx in one of the suits that partner has asked us to bid and an outside king. True, you may well make 5♣ but there are plenty of perfectly reasonable hands partner can have where you won't. Yet you know 4♠ doubled is going at least a couple down. Pass and take the money. With:

♠ 9 7
♥ 9 8 4
♦ 6 4 3
♣ K 8 6 4 3

you would again not find an expert who would do other than pass. This time 4♠ doubled may well make but what can you do about it? 5♣ is certainly going down, possibly a lot, probably doubled. For you to be able to make 5♣ partner needs a mountain and you will be raised to 6♣ anyway. You need a lot less from partner to beat 4♠ doubled; just four tricks. Even three tricks from partner will do if your ♣K turns out to be a trick. You are not likely to get a plus score from this hand but ask yourself which is more likely: that partner has a hand where you can beat 4♠ doubled or that partner has a hand that can make 5♣. The percentage must be to pass and hope.

The noticeable thing about the hands above is that almost all balanced hands, regardless of strength, will pass a takeout double. Conversely the more distributional you are the more you should be inclined to bid, more or less regardless of the point count. The first hand given is an obvious example, but it is usually right to bid on two suited hands of at least 5-5 as well. So again most experts would bid 4NT after the auction:

4♠   Dble   Pass   ?

holding:

♠ 9
♥ 10 8 7 6 4 3
♦ K J 9 8 4
♣ 8

4NT here shows any two-suited hand. If partner bids 5♣ we will bid 5♦ to show the red suits. Although this hand is considerably weaker than some of the others it is still right to bid. Quite often you can make a five level contract with even a minimum double from partner. When you cannot and are one or two down you quite often find that 4♠ doubled was cold. You are also less likely to get doubled as the opponents have fewer trumps between them. The only time it shows a big loss to pull on such hands is when both contracts go down two doubled, which is really not very likely.

Let's look at kinds of hands that should bid over pre-empts. Long experience has taught good players that it pays to be very aggressive in bidding over pre-empts. Some of the hands that the expert community considers it normal to bid on over four level pre-empts might shock you. A double of a 4♠ opener would be considered routine by most experts on:

    ♠ Q
    ♥ A Q J 2
    ♦ A Q 7 2
    ♣ J 7 5 2

Thus you have to be circumspect in bidding opposite a double if it can look like that, which is why so many of them get passed out. Let us examine our four sample hands opposite this potential double. First we held:

    ♠ –
    ♥ 10 7 3
    ♦ 8 5 4
    ♣ A Q 10 9 6 4 3

Here 5♣ is virtually cold and 6♣ is not unreasonable. Your RHO has been very timid holding a lot of spades. On the second hand we held:

    ♠ 9 7
    ♥ K 8 4
    ♦ 6 4 3
    ♣ A K 6 4 3

Here 5♣ is decidedly poor. You have a top spade loser, a trump loser unless they are two-two or stiff queen drops and a certain diamond loser unless the ♦K is correct, which is unlikely. It is not impossible that the clubs are four-0 either. Yet 4♠ is almost guaranteed down. On the odd occasions the opposition has so much distribution they make 4♠ doubled you certainly won't be making 5♣. Pass and take the penalty.

Our third hand was:

    ♠ 9 7
    ♥ 9 8 4
    ♦ 6 4 3
    ♣ K 8 6 4 3

Now 5♣ needs absolute miracles and is very likely to get doubled. 4♠ doubled will also probably make but it needs less good things for it to fail. One red king in declarer's hand and the clubs two-two, so that you have a club trick, could well be enough if you get around to your tricks in time. Anyway 4♠ doubled might well be cheaper than 5♣

doubled if the cards are really bad. Pass at least gives you a chance of a plus score, 5♣ doesn't.

Our final offering was:

    ♠ 9
    ♥ 10 8 7 6 4 3
    ♦ K J 9 8 4
    ♣ 8

On this we bid 4NT. Partner would respond 5♣, we would bid 5♦, showing both red suits, and there matters would rest, partner being content with diamonds. Now this isn't much of a contract either, needing the pre-empter to have the ♥K. But you will doubtless have observed that 4♠ doubled is cold if the pre-empter does not have the ♥K and will be cold if the diamonds are three-one. So we have either bid a making game ourselves or taken a very cheap save against theirs! You may think I have cheated on this hand by stuffing all of partner's points in our suits and to some extent you are right. But let's not be so generous. Try reversing partner's hearts and clubs (and altering the spots to be consistent) so that partner holds:

    ♠ 5
    ♥ J 9 5 2
    ♦ A Q 7 2
    ♣ A Q J 2

Now I hear you say, 5♦ is a lousy contract requiring the hearts two-two after the pre-empt. And so it is. But again 4♠ doubled is very likely to make. You will need two diamond tricks and two club tricks to beat 4♠ doubled and that is not very likely. To make it wrong to bid 4NT on this hand we have to give partner no diamond values at all. The lesson to be learned is that on highly distributional hands you should strain to bid and on balanced hands you should pass.

Just as expert players are very aggressive at doubling high-level pre-empts they are also very aggressive at bidding over them, particularly a major suit at the four level. This means that you should give partner significant latitude about how and if you continue. It is essential to allow partner to come in on distributional hands that are, in terms of point count, quite weak. Otherwise the pre-empters will rob you time after time. What would you bid on:

    ♠ 9 2
    ♥ A
    ♦ Q 9 8 4 3
    ♣ A Q 7 6 2

after the auction:

4♥	4♠	Pass	?

Now this is not a bad hand and a grand slam could be on. For example, partner could have:

    ♠ A K Q x x x x
    ♥ x x x
    ♦ A
    ♣ K x

Plenty of lesser hands will make a small slam. Yet most players passed. Several commented that they thought 4♠ might go down. Why did so many pass? Because they want to encourage their partners to bid 4♠ over 4♥ on:

♠ A K J x x x
♥ x x x
♦ K x
♣ x x

Here 4♠ is an eminently sound contract but you certainly wouldn't want to be playing 5♠, particularly not after a 4♥ opener. And if partner does not bid 4♠ immediately how do you intend to get to it? Presumably you're going to pass out 4♥. Or are you going to double 4♥ and pass 4♠? Sure!

The message therefore against high-level pre-empts is to try to bid the games and take the penalties. Let the slams go. It is no different if partner bids at the five level.

Say you hold:

♠ 9 3
♥ 7 6
♦ A J 8 5 4
♣ A 9 6 4

and the auction goes:

4♥	4NT	Pass	?

Partner's 4NT obviously shows the minors and you really have a very useful hand. AJxxx in one of partner's suits and Axxx in the other is not to be sneezed at, particularly when partner has forced you to bid at the five level. Yet, if this hand was given to an expert panel they would all bid 5♦. Some would certainly do so somewhat wistfully, but they would all bid 5♦. You simply cannot afford to bid anything else because you will then be punishing partner for competing on:

♠ 9 4
♥ A
♦ K Q 7 6 2
♣ K Q 8 5 2

where you notice exactly five of a minor is cold and it is not possible to get there otherwise.

As a final example take this hand from a local match. You open 1♦ holding:

♠ K 7
♥ 5
♦ A K J 10 6
♣ K Q J 7 6

and hear the auction proceed:

1♦	4♥	4♠	Pass
?			

Now this really is a rather good hand and far more than partner has any right to expect. Good suits, a singleton ♥ and Kx support for partner's freely bid suit at the four level. So how do you intend to proceed? The player at the table,

my partner, chose to pass and I agree with him. I held:

♠ A Q 9 8 6 5
♥ 9 7 3
♦ Q 9 2
♣ 8

and I just made 4♠ when the spades broke four-one. Not much of a 4♠ bid you might say but 4♠ is the only making game on the cards (the diamonds are also four-one and you lose control in 5♦). How are you going to get there unless you bid it now? And if partner goes on you are headed for a minus score. To bid these hands to 5♠ with no opposition bidding is pretty silly but most of the time you will get away with it unscathed. After a 4♥ overcall the spades will break four-one with monotonous regularity. In situations where the opposition have highly pre-empted you have to give partner a lot of leeway to lurch in with what he thinks might be the right game. You miss some slams playing this way but you do not get robbed by pre-empts so often.

Remember that when the opposition bounce high very early on in the auction, try to aim for a plus score, a penalty or game as appropriate. Sometimes you are a bit more fortunate in that you may know that you are in a potential slam situation and are making slam tries as the opposition is attempting to disrupt you with their high level pre-empts. Such situations, where it is a matter of judging whether to bid a slam or not, are the subject of the next section. Let's start from the top and work downwards to see if any sensible rules can be developed.

THE OPPONENTS SAVE AT THE SIX LEVEL ABOVE YOUR SUIT

It must have happened to you. You sail into 6♦ confident that you are going to make it and your opponents save in 6♠. Should you double them for their impudence or should you press on to the grand slam? The principles here are well established and agreed by almost all experts. First, if either partner thinks the grand slam is going to make then go ahead and bid it. If you were intending to bid seven anyway then you might as well do so. The only reason to be a little circumspect is that the cards are unlikely to be breaking very well. A grand slam on a three-two break may be just about okay in isolation, but if the opponents are up at the six level it is a lousy grand slam. You really do not expect your suits to be breaking three-two. Similarly, if you think you can make 6NT then go ahead and bid it but do be sure that you really can, otherwise you are liable to go down quite a lot if you are wrong.

Most hands do not fall into these categories however. On most hands you either do not feel you can make a grand slam or you are not sure and need to consult partner. The first set are fairly easy, you double the opponents. The ones where you need to consult partner are a bit more problematical and require some understandings.

In the immediate position, you pass with a first round control in the opponents' suit and some interest in a grand slam and double otherwise. I should emphasize that pass shows both of these things. Even if you have a first round control in their suit you do not have to pass. If your slam bid was a bit of a stretch anyway you do not want to encourage your partner to continue to a less than watertight grand slam, so you should double. The other side of the coin is that you should double even with a good hand for your auction if you lack a first round control in their suit. The only time you can risk a pass is if you are sure that partner must have a first round control. But if you pass without a first round control and you end up in a grand slam with the ace of the opponents' suit cashing, then you will have to take the blame.

What does partner do in the pass out seat? If you have passed, partner knows you have a reasonable hand for the bidding to date and a first round control in their suit. Partner will then need to make a judgment about whether the grand slam is a good bet or not. Partner either bids the grand slam or doubles.

If you have already doubled then partner knows that either you do not have a first round control or you do not have a good hand, or both. So before a grand slam can even be considered, partner needs a first round control in the opponents' suit. Lacking this partner is required to pass the double. Even with first round countrol, partner should consider very carefully to see if you really can make a grand slam. I strongly advise caution in these kinds of auctions. A vital minor honor card may be missing and the grand slam goes down; it may be a perfectly good grand slam but the extreme distribution ruins it; there may be an opening ruff; the opponents may have misjudged badly and their sacrifice goes for more than the value of your slam. There are so many ways to be right in doubling the opponents and only one way to be right in bidding seven—you've got to make it.

Finally, a forcing pass by partner does not in general invite 6NT. If you think that you have the tricks for 6NT and all of partner's cue bids are positive rather than negative controls, then go ahead and bid it. But you will need the stops in the opponents' suit. You cannot rely on partner for them despite the forcing pass promising first round control. Partner may have a void in the suit. Indeed, if the opponents are swinging suits around at the six level it is rather more likely that partner is void than that partner holds the ace. So. unless you know partner cannot be void do not assume that you can bid no trumps on the basis of partner's control in their suit. You may be sorely disappointed.

THE OPPONENTS SAVE AT THE FIVE OR SIX LEVEL BELOW YOUR SUIT

I've lumped these two together since the principles are very similar. I will start with the lower of them since that is the more common case. Lets take an auction where we really wish the opponents would leave us alone but they haven't.

2♥ (i)	2♠	3♦	4 ♥ (ii)
5♦ ?			

(i) weak
(ii) splinter

What are we expected to do here? Partner has some sort of mild slam try at least and the onus is on us to do something sensible. Essentially we have five options:

1. warn partner off when we think we cannot make a slam
2. bid 5♠ if we are sure we can make that but nothing else
3. bid a slam
4. invite a slam
5. pass the buck when we do not know what to do.

Taking each of these in turn, what about when we are sure that a slam cannot make? Well, double the opponents and take the profit. Say we have overcalled 2♠ on:

♠ A K 8 7 2
♥ K 9 5
♦ Q 4 2
♣ K 10 2

This is a perfectly respectable 2♠ overcall, yet we should now double the opponents at just under the speed of light. Partner will need an earthquake for us even to make 5♠ let alone six. We have nothing but wasted values such as the ♥K and the ♦Q that are likely to be valuable in defense and not far off useless in offense. It is important to remember that a double such as this is not a final command. Partner does not have to pass and it does not show 100 honors in trumps. True, partner will pass the huge majority of the time but it is not a command. A double like this one merely says that on the information so far gathered from the auction and looking at your hand your best judgment is that 5♦ doubled is your optimum result.

Moving on, you would bid 5♠ on hands that you are sure you are going to make 5♠. This is a relatively dangerous policy because you had better be right! Partners are easily irritated by people who bid one more in front of them and then go down one at the five level when the opponents' sacrifice was going for 300 or 500. It is a common fault of a number of players at most levels of the game to bid one more too often rather than take the sure profit. That is one of the upsides of taking saves; sometimes it is a good save, sometimes the opponents bid on to the five level and go down. I think it is reasonable to bid 5♠ on a hand such as:

♠ A J 9 7 5 3 2
♥ 8 5 3
♦ 9
♣ A 10

With partner's singleton heart all you need from partner is the ♣K or the ♦A. Even the ♣QJ will make the contract depend on a finesse and presumably partner has something for the splinter. What is also slightly worrying is that it is not clear that you are even going to beat 5♦! A spade trick hardly looks possible so partner will have to provide two defensive tricks to go with your ♣A. It must be right to press on to the five level on this hand. Some would argue that this hand is too good to bid 5♠ and you should make a forcing pass. They could well be right but you do need very specific cards from partner (♠K, ♦A and ♣A) to make a slam and it seems to me that there is too much danger of getting it wrong. Incidentally, change the hand round slightly and I do not think it is worth 5♠. If I had two small diamonds rather than a singleton I certainly would not bid 5♠. Two small is possibly the worst holding in the opponents' suit, particularly if they have bid it at quite high levels. The problem with two small is that partner is quite likely to have two small as well, so we immediately have two quick losers in their suit. Obviously a singleton is better but in many ways so is three small, since it increases the chances of partner having a singleton. So I would not bid 5♠ on:

♠ A J 9 7 5 3 2
♥ 8 5
♦ 9 3
♣ A 10

because I would be very worried about three quick red suit losers. This hand is a choice between a forcing pass and a double. I also wouldn't bid 5♠ with my rounded suits holdings reversed if, say I held:

♠ A J 9 7 5 3 2
♥ A 10
♦ 9
♣ 8 5 3

This is a bit more attractive but here there could easily be a diamond and two slow club losers off the contract. I wouldn't want to play 5♠ for example when partner held:

♠ K Q 10 5
♥ 3
♦ Q 6 2
♣ A J 7 6 4

and you can hardly argue that partner hasn't got enough to splinter. So be careful about bidding to the five level over the opponents' save. You need to be very right to do so.

Some players always double the opposition and take the money on the grounds that you can never get all of the five level decisions right and you should always aim for plus scores. That is quite a sensible policy but I don't see why you shouldn't bid on if you are sure that is the right thing to do. In particular, however, you need to be highly distributional. The more balanced you are the more you should double them. If you have overcalled 2♠ on a flat 19 count with ♠AKxxx do not for a second think about bidding 5♠ because "I was so much better than I might be so I had to bid it." Just double them. It is amazing how often 5♠ will go down when you are balanced, and, of course, the most points you have, the more they are likely to go down. Quite

often when you are actually making game, they will be going for more than the value of your game anyway. This is an application of the "Law of Total Tricks." It really works as well.

Let's get back to the sequence, which, if you remember, was:

2♥	2♠	3♦	4♥
5♦	?		

The third option you can take is to bid a slam yourself. Again you need to be very sure that this is the correct thing to do as otherwise you will not be a strong candidate for Most Popular Player of the Week. However, hands do come along where you can be reasonably sure of a slam. How about:

♠ A K 9 7 4 3
♥ A 8 4 3
♦ –
♣ A 8 5

Surely a slam is a reasonable shot on this lot? Many would argue that you are too strong and should be making a grand slam try. Maybe, but how you are supposed to get partner to envisage that ♣KQ and ♠Qxxx rather than ♠Jxxx are necessary, I don't know (you need the ♠Q since you have to ruff three hearts otherwise you are very likely to get one of them ruffed in front of dummy with the ♠Q). However, this is certainly a slam-going hand.

The final option is to pass. The pass again here is forcing since we have been making slam tries, so the assumption is that it is our hand. Thus partner must either bid or double. Sometimes the mesh of the cards and the distribution of the opponents' cards will mean that your options are to double their laydown contract or to bid on to the five level and go for 800 yourself. That is just unfortunate and experts accept the odd one of those with equanimity. It is worth it to add the extra clarity to all the other hands and give you more room to judge. You will obviously get it right more often if you can make the decision yourself when it is right to do so, or pass it to partner when you cannot make a sensible decision, in the knowledge that partner is not going to let them play undoubled.

The forcing pass is made on two kinds of hands. The first occurs when you do not know whether it is right to double the opponents or bid to the five level yourself. Essentially you are saying "Partner, I have reasonable expectation of making 5♠ but I cannot be sure. What do you think?" If partner doubles you will pass and if partner bids 5♠ that is OK. Note that pass is an invitation to partner to continue so you have to have some reasonable hopes of making 5♠. If you have overcalled on a heap of rhubarb you have to double and hope it goes down. That is much more likely than your being able to make 5♠. It is no good passing because you have garbage since it cannot get passed out anyway. You are likely to end up defending 5♦ doubled in any case, so you should double it yourself just in case when you pass partner does something stupid like bidding 5♠. So double after overcalling 2♠ on this hand:

♠ K Q 8 7 6
♥ Q 7 6
♦ J 7
♣ K J 6

True, you may well not beat it but you certainly won't be anywhere close to 5♠ which is the only alternative. However, pass on:

♠ A Q 9 7 6 4
♦ K 9 4
♦ A 5 3
♣ 9

Here you have quite lively chances of 5♠. Partner is likely to have a diamond singleton, so it looks like no more than the rounded aces off the contract at worst. However, partner will need two singletons, which is a little unlikely. The opponents have been known to bid like this with only eight diamonds and then you have a diamond loser. After all, the opponents do seem to have nine hearts between them. Your LHO may have done something clever and introduced diamond values rather than a long suit in order, later on, to judge the auction better. Why take the risk with 5♠? Make a forcing pass. With the hands where you can make 5♠ partner will surely continue. Partner may even be able to make another slam try on the way. And if partner doubles, that's fine, isn't it? You still might just about make 5♠ but surely this is going for a fair number? A likely spade trick, a likely heart trick, the diamond ace, a highly possible club ruff, a highly possible heart ruff and whatever partner can provide. It is not difficult to imagine this going for more than the value of your contract.

The final hand type is held when you pass and pull partner's double. The message you are now sending is roughly "I cannot decide what to do, you decide. Oh, you've decided to double them. In that case I will now bid 5♠." Since this is complete nonsense (or at best shows contempt for partner's judgment), this kind of sequence is used the world over as a slam try. Thus, this is the strongest sequence apart from bidding the slam yourself. It is stronger than an immediate 5♠. An immediate 5♠ simply says you are fairly sure you can make 5♠. To pass and pull partner's double is to say that you are sure you can make 5♠ and think you may be able to make six. Thus, passing and pulling to 5♠ may be done on a hand like:

♠ A K 9 6 3 2
♥ 7 6 2
♦ A K 6
♣ 7

Here you seem to need nothing at all from partner apart from the ♣A and the singleton heart already promised. But partner might not have the ♣A. Partners have an infuriating habit of holding ♣KQJ106 when you bid a slam like this.

The best solution is to pass, awaiting partner's expected double and then bid 5♠ as a slam try. I'm far from guaranteeing you will get to it now. After all, partner needs no more than ♠Qxxx and the ♣A and partner is certainly not going to bid it on that. But at least you've given yourself a chance. With a good hand partner may press on. It is always much, much better to miss a few slams when the opponents have pre-empted you than bid a number of non-making ones.

So passing and pulling partner's double is the strongest bid apart from bidding the slam yourself. Sometimes this is the only slam try you have. If the auction had gone slightly differently like:

2♥	2♠	3♦	4♥
5♥	?		

then the only way you can make a slam try is to pass and pull. If the opponents have not been irritating enough to bid the suit directly underneath you then you have some more options and can use them to help the partnership judge the availability or otherwise of a slam. On the original auction you could bid 5♥ directly, pass and bid 5♠ or pass and bid 5♥. If the opponents had conveniently bid clubs then you can bid 5♦, 5♥ or pass and bid each of these after partner's doubles. Experienced partnerships will be clear what each of these means. I suggest you just have a blanket rule that passing and then pulling is always stronger, so an immediate 5♦ (say) is not as strong as passing and then pulling partner's double to 5♦.

What if you pass intending to pull partner's double and he bids instead? Well, now you are quite well placed to bid a slam. You were intending to pull partner's expected double to 5♠ as a slam try and now partner has shown a better hand. A lot of the time, therefore, you will be raising to slam expecting to make it. You may possibly be worried about the lack of a vital control. In this respect partner should help you as much as possible. If partner is not going to double in the pass out seat, then on anything better than a minimum 5♠ bid partner should show a feature on the way to 5♠. This will usually be a control, but may be a reasonable suit as well. The suit the opponents have bid may make this impossible in which case the partnership will just have to use judgment.

If the opponents are saving at the five level above your suit or at the six level below your suit the principles are exactly the same. You have to decide whether to bid a slam or double the opponents. Since you are contracting for twelve tricks if you bid, a forcing pass should guarantee at least second round control in the opponents' suit unless partner has already promised a control. So, in the immediate position you have four basic options:

1. Double if you think you cannot make a slam.
2. Bid a slam if you think you think you can make it.
3. Make a forcing pass and accept partner's decision. The forcing pass shows at least second round control in the

opponents' suit unless partner has already shown a control.

4. Make a forcing pass and pull partner's double as a grand slam try. This should promise first round control in the opponents suit unless partner has already shown one.

In the pass out seat, if partner has passed you have to decide whether your hand is good enough to bid on to the six level or whether to double and take the sure profit. As always, unless you are sure a slam is a good bet, you should take the money. If partner has doubled you will need a very good hand to overrule partner's decision and bid a slam and you had better be right, otherwise partner will not be pleased. Don't forget that first of all you will need a control in the opponents' suit since partner will certainly double without one and you cannot rely on partner for it.

WHEN IS A PASS FORCING?

All this discussion about how to bid over the opponents' sacrifices is based on the assumption that you could make a forcing pass in second seat. "When is a pass forcing?" is a vexed question. Some experts seem to be playing more and more passes as forcing while others seem to play fewer and fewer as forcing. If you asked a hundred expert partnerships when a pass was forcing you might get a hundred different answers. Indeed you might even get different answers from the two members of the partnership! It is, however, essential that you have some rules for when a forcing pass occurs, otherwise you can pass with your grand slam try awaiting partner's double and suddenly discover that the auction has ended. These rules can be as complicated as you like and there are some partnerships who have very elaborate agreements about when a pass is forcing and when it is not. Unless you have the time and the inclination to do all the necessary work on this I suggest you have a much simpler system.

A pass is forcing whenever your side has bid a game and the auction is such that you expect to make it. So, in all the following sequences the final pass is forcing:

1♠	2♥	4♥ (*)	5♥
Pass			

*Splinter

1♥	1♠	4♣ (*)	4♠
Pass			

*Splinter

1♥	1♠	4♣ (*)	4♠
5♥	5♠	Pass	

*Splinter

1♠	Pass	3NT(*)	4♦
Pass			

*Balanced hand with four spades and 13-15 points

1♠	Pass	3NT(*)	4♦
4♠	5♦	Pass	

* Balanced hand with four spades and 13-15 points

1♠	4♥	5♥ (*)	6♥
Pass			

*Splinter

In all the above auctions, our partnership has bid game clearly expecting to make it. Occasionally we have shown genuine slam interest. At worst we have shown enough high cards for game. Thus in all these cases pass should be regarded as forcing. As I mentioned above, it won't always be correct (nothing can be in dealing with pre-empts). Sometimes the opponents will have so much distribution that your options are only conceding 5♥ doubled or going for 800 in 5♠ doubled. However, it will be correct most of the time and the forcing pass means that considerably greater clarity is added to the auctions, since the partner in second seat does not have to make a unilateral decision in fear that the auction will get passed out.

However, whenever we have bid game and the auction does not make it clear that we expect to make, a pass should not be forcing. So in each of the auctions below, the final pass is not forcing:

1♠	2♥	4♠	5♥
Pass			

1♠	4♥	4♠	5♥
Pass			

1♠	2♥	3♠	4♥
4♠	5♥	Pass	

1♦	4♥	4♠	5♥
Pass			

1♥	4♠	5♣	5♠
Pass			

1♥	2♠	3♣	4♠
5♣	5♠	Pass	

I don't think you should regard the final pass as forcing in any of these auctions. Perhaps I should emphasize at this point that this is my own view and many good players would disagree with me. There is little contention, I think, about the first three auctions. In the first one 4♠ is clearly pre-emptive and there is no reason why the final pass should be forcing. The onus is on partner with a good hand to bid or double (usually double) as appropriate. In the second auction the pre-empt has put the 4♠ bidder really under the gun.

4♠ would be bid on:

♠ K Q 6 3
♥ A 7 2
♦ A 8 4 2
♣ 8 6

but 4♠ could be bid by you as well when you hold:

♠ K Q 8 6 4
♥ 5
♦ 9 7 4 2
♣ 5 4 2

With such a wide range of potential hands, some of which contain no defense at all, it is nonsense to play pass as forcing. The 1♠ opener is expected to act with a good hand and with the better hands the 4♠ bidder is expected to bid (again usually double) in the pass out seat. The third auction is in many ways similar. Partner is often compelled to bid 4♠ on many very moderate hands. There is a great premium on bidding 4♠ over 4♥. It only needs one of the contracts to make for you to show a good profit; if both contracts make it is an enormous profit; and if both contracts go down one it is a small loss. For this reason good players will bid 4♠ on this sequence on any excuse (and sometimes less than that). It is, therefore, sensible not to play pass as forcing here. Either partner is expected to double now with reasonable defense.

The remaining three auctions are more contentious and many would argue that pass is forcing here. I disagree. In all the auctions again one member of the partnership has been put under enormous strain to act on any reasonable hand. In the fourth auction we have already seen that partner should bid 4♠, sometimes on a wing and a prayer, to get the suit in. The fifth auction is a little different; presumably you have some semblance of a hand for swinging in with 5♣. How-ever, 5♣ would seem to be eminently sensible on the auction with:

♠ –
♥ Q 5 2
♦ 5 2
♣ K Q J 10 9 8 4 2

and now you haven't a semblance of a defensive trick but need a very good hand from partner to make 6♣. Why should you be forced to double the opponents in a cold contract for no good reason? Finally in the last auction, partner is under great strain to support our suit which has been freely bid at the three level and will do so on good support and some distribution. I would expect partner to bid 5♣ on:

♠ 9
♥ K Q J 8 4
♦ J 9 2
♣ A K 8 7

and now see no reason why we have to double 5♠ to punish partner for his enterprise. The advocates of pass being forcing on these last three hands put forward the same arguments as I was quoting before. That is, rarely do you have no winning options and it adds clarity to your auctions to be able to make forcing passes. In these cases I am far from convinced.

Finally I will emphasize that it is the sound of the auction that makes the pass forcing or not and not what you have in your hand. It is no good on the auction:

1♠	4♥	4♠	5♥

to pass on your flat 19 count, saying that you had made a forcing pass since you expected to make 4♠. Partner doesn't know you have this much and is almost certain to pass out 5♥. You have to act on good hands in non-forcing pass auctions yourself.

There are some other commonly played rules about when a pass is forcing. You may find some of these more to your taste and you can use them or not as you see fit. Some partnerships play that pass is always forcing whenever you have bid game and are vulnerable, regardless of the auction as to how you got there. (Another version of this is to play pass as forcing only when you are vulnerable against not.) The argument here is that vulnerable (and particularly against non-vulnerable) partner will not be messing about at the four level on weak hands. A non-vulnerable partner might well bid 4♠ in the auction:

1♠	2♥	4♠

on:

♠ K Q 8 7 4
♥ 9 7 4 2
♦ 5 2
♣ 7 2

but partner would not be doing this vulnerable. The other side of this is that certain pairs play that pass is virtually never forcing when you are non-vulnerable (and particularly when non-vulnerable against vulnerable). This gives partner freedom to indulge in all sorts of pre-emptive and semi-pre-emptive maneuvers without fear of having to go around doubling cold contracts because forcing passes have been produced. Either or both of these systems has some merits and if they appeal to your partnership then adopt them. Once again it is not so much what you play that is important but the fact that both members of the partnership understand the methods and have a common agreement about what they are.

INTERVENTION OVER BLACKWOOD

This is something else the opponents will do from time to time just to annoy you. Sometimes they will have already been in your auction and are continuing bidding like:

1♠	2♥	3♣	3♥
4NT	5♥	?	

and sometimes they will be entering it for the first time such as:

1♠	Pass	4NT	5♦
?			

or even:

1♠	Pass	3♠	Pass
4NT	5♦	?	

is not unknown. How the opponents get into your Blackwood auction is not relevant. The important point is that they are there and you have to find a method of coping with it. The problem, of course, is that they have very inconveniently taken up some of your bidding room and you no longer have much scope to show the number of aces you have. To combat this there are a number of options available. It is sensible, in my opinion, to adopt different options depending on the level of the intervention since the higher the level of intervention, the steadily less room you have. It also makes a difference depending on whether you have decided to play RKCB or are sticking to ordinary Blackwood. I will deal briefly with each option in turn.

If you are sticking to ordinary Blackwood, let's say the opposition overcall 5♣ or 5♦. You no longer have these bids to show none or one ace but you can get around the problem easily by using pass and double instead. A common system is to use double as 0 aces as pass as 1 ace. With two aces you bid the first available step, with three aces the second step, etc. So in the sequence:

1♥	Pass	4NT	5♦
?			

then:

Dble	=	0 aces
Pass	=	1 ace
5♥	=	2 aces
5♠	=	3 aces
5NT	=	4 aces (not that this will ever happen!)

This system is known as DOPI (double 0, pass 1). The reversal of pass and double is known as DIPO (double 1, pass 0) and is equally common. Neither, as far as I can see, has any technical merit over the other. So you can show the number of aces you have conveniently and the important point is that the auction is taken to no higher level than it was before. Partner also has the option with either of the first two bids of ending the auction by doubling the opponents. If partner knows that there are not enough aces for a slam and judges that the five level may not be safe and/or the opposition are going for a fortune, then partner is at liberty to pass your double or double after your pass.

If the opponents are unkind enough to bid 5♥ or 5♠ then things are not as convenient for you. The method suggested above is not really practicable, since if the opponents overcall 5♠, for example, then you will have to bid 5NT on two aces and that may be too high. Thus a common approach is to use a system that never takes the bidding any higher. In this system you double with an odd number of aces (1 or 3) and pass with an even number of aces (0 or 2). This system is known as DOPE and its reversal DEPO (double even, pass odd) is equally common. The argument here is that most of the time partner can tell from the strength of your previous bids whether you are likely to hold the larger or the smaller number of aces and so can do the correct thing. If partner cannot tell then partner can settle for the penalty against the opponents' sacrifice. It will just be greater if you have two more aces than partner expects. You will notice that there is no bid for four aces. If you hold four aces you bid a slam! If it does not make you can ask partner how many aces you needed before a slam would make. Many people would argue that with three aces you should also be bidding a slam since there must be enough aces. If you agree with that view then the method of response can be easily modified so that:

Dble	=	1 ace
Pass	=	0 or 2 aces
1st step	=	3 aces
2nd step =		4 aces

Finally, if the opponents are inconsiderate enough to start overcalling at the six level it is relatively easy to play exactly the same system as over 5♥ and 5♠. Some pairs prefer to play forcing passes after intervention at the six level with no specific number of aces promised. In this system you bid a slam if you think you can make it, double if you don't think you can and pass if you are not sure. This is a matter for partnerships and it sensible to play whatever you feel most comfortable with.

If you have decided to take my suggestion and play RKCB then the situation is a little different. First, apart from the aces there is the queen of trumps to worry about. Second, there is the knowledge that partner holds at least one of the five aces and, therefore, you should always bid a slam if you hold at least three aces. As always there are several possible methods but a sensible one to me has always seemed to be as follows.

If the opponents overcall 5♣ or 5♦ then:

Double	=	0
Pass	=	1
1st step	=	2
2nd step	=	3
3rd step	=	4

If the opponents have overcalled 5♥ or 5♠ then:

Double	=	0 or 2
Pass	=	1
1st step	=	3
2nd step =		4

In all cases of both systems if partner bids the next suit up (provided that this is not a possible trump suit) then that asks for the queen of trumps. You show this in the usual way, signing off in the trump suit without it and bidding anything else with it.

Finally, if the opponents overcall at the six level you have the same options as before. That is, you can play the same system as above or you can revert to forcing passes.

THE OPPONENTS DOUBLE 4NT BLACKWOOD

The opponents doubling 4NT (Blackwood) is not something that should ever cause you any concern since it takes up no room and actually provides you with extra alternatives. However, it is something that some opponents will try from time to time just to try and sow a little confusion. And it is remarkable how often it works! A pair is happily employing Blackwood and suddenly somebody doubles 4NT. All logic now seems to disappear and either the pair miss a cold slam or they bid a slam off two aces. Yet this should never happen and can be easily prevented by a simple agreement about what to do over it. There are essentially three options.

The first is simply to ignore the double and just to make the same response as you were always going to. This has the merit of great simplicity and you should never get it wrong.

The second is to use the double to give you extra room to show the number of aces you have. If you are playing ordinary Blackwood then a common treatment here is called ROPI (redouble 0, pass 1).

Not surprisingly in this method

Rdble	=	0 aces,
Pass	=	1 ace
5♣	=	2 aces
5♦	=	3 aces

The reverse of this, RIPO (redouble = 1, pass = 0), is also common.

If you are using RKCB then a fairly common system is:

Pass	=	0 or 2 aces
Rdble	=	1 aces
5♣	=	3 aces
5♦	=	4 aces

with a bid of the next suit up (not a potential trump suit) to ask for the queen of trumps.

It is entirely possible to play that pass and redouble simply replace the first two bids, so:

Pass	=	0 or 3
Rdble	=	1 or 4
5♣	=	2 without the trump queen
5♦	=	2 with the trump queen

with 5♣ over either pass or redouble to ask for the trump queen.

The third option is to respond to 4NT as usual but to reserve a redouble of 4NT as an attempt to play there with a suitable hand. This can sometimes teach an injudicious opponent who has doubled 4NT on the off-chance you will get it wrong a real lesson. I once saw a pair who played this method duly redouble 4NT. This gave the opponents the options of conceding 4NT doubled double with two overtricks or going for 2,000 at the five level. At the end of the hand, the doubler's partner expressed his opinion of the double of 4NT in a full and frank manner, including a wide selection of adjectives.

4NT IN COMPETITION

Let's say I asked you a question: "What is the meaning of 4NT in each of these sequences?" and then "Would your partner agree?"

1♥	4♠	4NT	
1♠	4♥	4NT	
1♥	2♦	3♣	4♦
4NT			
1NT	3♦ (*)	4♠	4NT

(*) 2♦ was conventional so this is the lowest natural bid in diamonds

My guess is that both you and your partner know what 4NT is and you both agree. It is Blackwood. That is certainly a reasonable interpretation and unless and until you have discussions on the subject that is certainly how I suggest you play it. However, hands that want to use Blackwood on these kinds of auctions are really fairly rare. Don't forget that you need a hand that can be certain of a slam if partner holds enough aces and will need controls in all the suits (certainly in their suit) and sufficiently good trumps not to worry much about them. These hands occur only occasionally. As a result many expert partnerships are now finding alternative uses for 4NT in many competitive situations that come up much more often and are therefore more useful. Yet again there are several products on the market and you can pick those that appeal.

The first sequence probably lends itself to the greatest number of interpretations so let's start with that. First there are pairs that play this sort of sequence for the minors. The argument for this is along the lines of what are you supposed to do with:

```
♠ 5
♥ —
♦ K Q 8 6 4 3
♣ Q J 10 8 4 2
```

after:

1♠	4♥	?

It is almost certainly right to bid here but five of either minor is a real stab in the dark. If you play this for the minors you can also plan to wheel it out on less extreme distributions. For example:

```
♠ Q 6
♥ 9
♦ K Q 10 7 6
♣ K Q J 8 5
```

Unless 4NT is for the minors you have no option but to double here. Personally, I would double even if 4NT is for the minors but you can easily see how on some hands for partner 4NT would bring home the bacon. Using 4NT for the minors has applications in a number of other sequences. For example:

| 1♥ | 1♠ | 4♥ | 4NT |

With the devaluation of overcalls these days it is even less likely that you want 4NT as Blackwood. You will need most of the pack to be able to force to a slam opposite, say, a couple of aces. Thus using 4NT here for the minors is a sensible alternative.

The second option is to use 4NT as a "good raise" to five of partner's suit. The argument here is that after:

| 1♥ | 4♠ | ? |

you are more or less required to bid 5♥ with:

♠ 5
♥ A J 9 7 6 5
♦ 9 8 7 6
♣ 5 2

and also with:

♠ J 5
♥ A K 8 7 2
♦ A 10 9 6 5
♣ 8

Since partner has to allow for the first possibility he is virtually never in a position to bid a slam. So you distinguish between the five level bids by using five of the suit as purely competitive and 4NT as a good raise. In this method 4NT is, of course, only used in this way if the four level has been taken away by the overcall. The sequence:

| 1♠ | 4♥ | ? |

is quite different since 4♠ is available and 5♠ and 5♥ are available as slam tries. It would thus be more sensible to use 4NT as something else, say the minors as above.

The third option is to use 4NT as "two places to play." The argument for this option is that it gives you something to do with a hand like:

♠ 9
♥ K J 6
♦ K Q J 9 6 5
♣ 8 5 3

After:

| 1♥ | 4♠ | ? |

Unless you are playing this you have a pretty unpalatable choice between double and pass. The only other options are a pretty wild stab at 5♦ and an even wilder 5♥, which partner will really thank you with a balanced 15 count and playing four card majors. So in this method you bid 4NT showing two places to play. If partner bids 5♣ you bid 5♦ and partner will know you have diamonds with some heart support. If partner bids 5♦ you rest content. With the same hand with the minors reversed, you would pass 5♣ and convert 5♦ to 5♥.

Those then are the three basic options apart from Blackwood on this sequence. If any of them appeal then give them a try. My least favorite is the two places to play

method since it always seems to me that if partner does not have a fit for your suit, then you have done the wrong thing by bidding 4NT. Still, all the methods work well if the right hands come along and that really is the secret.

The second sequence, which, if you remember, was:

| 1♠ | 4♥ | 4NT |

has fewer possibilities. Since 4♠ is available you do not need it to show a good raise, nor do you need it to show two places to play one of which was spades. You would bid 4♠ on a partial fit and perhaps reconsider if somebody doubled in a voice of thunder. So really the only options in this case are Blackwood and the minors. Most (but by no means all) experts would plump for the minors.

The third sequence was:

| 1♥ | 2♦ | 3♣ | 4♦ |
| 4NT | | | |

Here again the possibilities are relatively few. Either it is Blackwood or it shows a "good raise" to 5♣, allowing you to distinguish between a competitive 5♣ and 5♣ with a decent hand.

Finally the last sequence was:

| 1NT | 3♦ | 4♠ | 4NT |

This sequence came up at the table. It really makes very little sense for it to be Blackwood. There would need to be a lot of points in the pack for the 4NT bidder to have a good enough hand to be using Blackwood. So either it shows a good raise, or the other two suits, or two places to play. That is really a matter for partnership discussion. However, since partner has shown a good suit with 3♦ it seems a little perverse to insist on playing in a different one. The player at the table had:

♠ —
♥ 10 7 2
♦ 10 8 7
♣ K Q J 9 6 3 2

The partnership was non-vulnerable against vulnerable so a save looked very reasonable (five of a minor could have been cold after all). To bid either 5♣ or 5♦ may have been to arrive in the wrong minor so he tried 4NT. With the clubs and hearts reversed he could have bid 4NT, intending to convert 5♣ to 5♦. This looks extremely sensible but you need to discuss it first.

Whether you decide to adopt any of the above suggestions for alternative uses for 4NT depends on your inclination and whether you are prepared to put in the amount of work to decide what the various categories of sequences mean. Until that time you are better off leaving them all as Blackwood and making the best of it. At least you won't have any silly misunderstandings. There are a number of sequences, however, where it makes no sense whatsoever for 4NT to be Blackwood. Therefore it must be something else. We have already seen a few of these when discussing defensive methods to high-level pre-empts. You and your partner should at least learn to recognize these and bid accordingly. A few examples:

> 4♠   4NT

Most people would get this one right. Whether you play a double of 4♠ as penalties or (as I prefer) take out, 4NT is definitely not Blackwood. It shows a two or possibly three-suited hand that wishes to compete. You respond 5♣ unless you cannot stand clubs in which case you respond 5♦. With better diamonds than clubs you can only afford to respond 5♦ if you are prepared to hear 5♥ from partner.

How about:

> 4♠   Dble   Pass   4NT

Again, whether you play double as penalties or take out here, it is logical nonsense to play this as Blackwood, so it must be some sort of two suited take out. Respond to it as before. If the opening bid had been 4♥ then 4NT must unequivocally show the minors now (else you would have tried 4♠). Similarly:

> 2♠(*)   Dble   4♠   4NT
> (*) weak

can only logically be played as take out.

Finally, what about the sequence:

> 1♥   4♠   Dble   Pass
> 4NT

Whether you play double as penalty or just showing "cards" in the modern style is irrelevant. The point is that it is very difficult to construct a hand that would open 1♥ and then want to bid Blackwood on this sequence. Also if we were two-suited we could just bid our second suit. Thus this sequence shows specifically a three-suited hand good enough that it thinks it can make a five level contract. You respond accordingly, playing in what you expect to be your best fit. Alter the sequence slightly so that it has gone:

> 1♦ 4♠ Dble   Pass
> 4NT

and 4NT will now show a three-suited hand or possibly a hand with five hearts and six diamonds that will be shown by converting the expected 5♣ response to 5♦.

I hope you have found this section useful and that your slam bidding will improve. I believe in the merits of certain of the conventions introduced, particularly RKCB and splinters. But if you disagree and find something else more to your taste, that is fine and I hope I have provided some sensible alternatives. If nothing else, I hope that your understanding of the requirements for a slam and your appreciation of how to go about finding out the necessary information have improved. If you get those right you can use just about any methods that take your fancy. Again it is not so important what you play as the fact that you and your partner understand it and agree on it.

PART VII

CARDS AT PLAY

by Freddie North

You can't be held entirely responsible for the bids your partner makes.

We all know that feeling when faced with some hideous contract that has resulted from less than inspired judgment by the person sitting opposite. Still, with the spotlight centered upon us, this can be a magical moment to draw from our reserves of know-how. The player who is familiar with the many techniques available will often be able to turn disaster into success and twist the bad breaks around to his favor.

Such are the thrusts and counter thrusts of top players, and the purpose of this section is to bring them out into the open, making less experienced players aware of the glittering array of tools which are at their disposal.

I have given a star rating for each chapter. Five stars is a very strong recommendation that you study the subject well. One star suggests that you can probably live without it, or at least, postpone serious contemplation until a later date, while the in-between stars reflect the importance of the subject as I see it.

Elimination

Star Rating: ★★★★★

Elimination is one of the most prolific and rewarding gambits in the whole field of card play technique. Never mind that the name sounds slightly reminiscent of a Mafia orgy, the fact remains that, correctly executed, the opposition are left without an escape route. The frequency is so high that you could reasonably expect this gambit to turn up at least once in most sessions of bridge. This makes a thorough understanding of the subject a must.

So what is Elimination? It is the process of removing safe cards of exit from the opponents' hands so that when they are allowed to regain the lead they have to make a play that is disadvantageous for their side. Very often this involves leading into your waiting tenace (perhaps AQ or KJx), or round to an unsupported honor (perhaps Kx) or conceding a ruff and discard.

Now, look at the following position. Spades are trumps. It is South to lead and make four out of the last five tricks.

```
              ♠ 5
              ♥ 6 4
              ♦ J
              ♣ K
  ♠ —                    ♠ —
  ♥ K 8                  ♥ J 10
  ♦ Q 5                  ♦ 9
  ♣ 7                    ♣ 10 5
              ♠ 8
              ♥ A Q
              ♦ 8
              ♣ 6
```

The complete novice would probably enter dummy with the ♣K and take the heart finesse. He makes only three tricks. The more experienced player might choose this moment to give West his ♦Q and wait for something to turn up. He will fare no better than the novice since West will simply exit safely with the ♣7. Yes, of course, the seasoned player will cash the ♣K before playing a diamond. With all safe exit

cards removed, West has an unenviable choice. He can play a heart into South's open jaws or another diamond, thereby conceding a ruff in one hand and a discard in the other.

Good players dislike guessing the position of a missing queen when the opponents can be forced to do the work for them.

Now, with a big clue in the preamble, see what you can make of the following hand:

```
              ♠ Q J 9 5
              ♥ A 10 6
              ♦ J 10 7
              ♣ K 5 3

              ♠ A K 10 7 4
              ♥ K J 8
              ♦ 4 2
              ♣ A 8 6
```

With plenty of values, South finds himself in 4♠. However, there are four possible losers so the contract needs some care. West starts with the ♦AK and then switches to the ♣J. How should South plan the play?

If you've decided, have a look at the full deal:

```
              ♠ Q J 9 5
              ♥ A 10 6
              ♦ J 10 7
              ♣ K 5 3
  ♠ 6 2                  ♠ 8 3
  ♥ Q 5 3                ♥ 9 7 4 2
  ♦ A K 9 6 5            ♦ Q 8 3
  ♣ J 10 9              ♣ Q 7 4 2
              ♠ A K 10 7 4
              ♥ K J 8
              ♦ 4 2
              ♣ A 8 6
```

With two losing diamonds and one losing club the contract appears to depend on the guess in hearts (who has the ♥Q?) However, declarer can avoid the guess as long as he extracts his opponents' safe cards of exit before relinquishing the lead.

Trick three is taken by either the ace or king of clubs. Two rounds of trumps finishing in the dummy enables declarer to ruff dummy's last diamond. It only remains to cash the other top club and exit with a third round to leave the defense helpless.

This is the position:

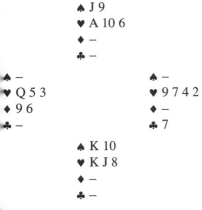

It does not matter which opponent is on lead—the result will be the same. If a minor-suit card is played, declarer ruffs in one hand and discards the losing heart from the other. If a heart is played, the queen will be trapped so there will be no loser in the suit.

At the time of relinquishing the lead, the presence of trumps in both hands is the key to success. The fact that North held the ♥10 was a big bonus, for that made the case watertight. But without dummy's ♥10 declarer should still play along the same elimination lines. Maybe West will have to win the third round of clubs, but even if East wins this trick the straightforward heart finesse has not gone away.

South was pleased with the auction on the following hand because the partnership had arrived in a 76 percent slam— good enough odds even for the ultra cautious:

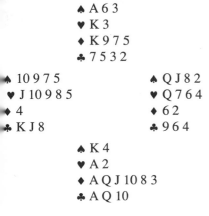

South	North
2♦	3♦
3♥	3♠
4♣	4♥
4♠	6♦
Pass	

After a natural two diamond opening and suit agreement, a series of cuebids led to the excellent slam. The ♥J was led.

South wasted little time in winning the jack of hearts with the ace, drawing trumps, entering dummy with the heart king and playing a low club to his ten. It only needed just one of the missing honors to be with East. Not too much to ask, surely? However, when the club queen lost to West's king, South complained bitterly about his bad luck. True, one could reasonably expect one of the club honors to be well placed, but no one should complain of bad luck after taking a 76 percent chance instead of investing in a certainty.

Before taking the club finesse, declarer should have played three rounds of spades. Now, this would have been the ending with dummy to play:

```
              ♠ —
              ♥ —
              ♦ K 9
              ♣ 7 5 3 2
    ♠ 10                    ♠ Q
    ♥ 10 9                  ♥ Q 6
    ♦ —                     ♦ —
    ♣ K J 8                 ♣ 9 6 4
              ♠ —
              ♥ —
              ♦ J 10 8
              ♣ A Q 10
```

A club from dummy to South's ten and West's jack gives the defense their first—and only—trick. What is West to do? Exit with a club into South's tenace (AQ) or concede a ruff and discard (ruff in dummy and discard the club queen). Any fair-minded person would be quite content to allow West a free choice! Now look at another slam hand that required just the right touch:

```
              ♠ A K 10 7
              ♥ A 9 2
              ♦ A K Q
              ♣ 5 3 2
    ♠ 8                     ♠ 6 3
    ♥ K Q J 8 6 5 4         ♥ 10 7
    ♦ 8 2                   ♦ J 10 9 7 6
    ♣ K J 6                 ♣ 10 9 8 7
              ♠ Q J 9 5 4 2
              ♥ 3
              ♦ 5 4 3
              ♣ A Q 4
```

Avoidance Play

Star Rating: ✶✶✶✶✶

An Avoidance Play is used to deprive a particular opponent from obtaining the lead. It is perhaps the commonest form of technical play, apart from the finesse, having an especially high frequency in no trump contracts.

The two main reasons for using avoidance technique are: (a) to prevent a defender who has established winners from gaining the lead—especially at no trumps. (b) To prevent a vulnerable suit holding from being attacked by the dangerous or wrong opponent.

Suppose the contract is 3NT and West leads the six of hearts to East's queen:

(a) ♥ 7 5 2   (b) ♥ 7 5 2

♥ K J 4   ♥ A J 4

Should you win the first trick or should you duck? Of course, it depends entirely on your overall strategy. If you duck, then West will become the dangerous hand. If you win, then East is the hand to be feared.

Often an unsupported king is an obvious target for attack—if the defense can get at it. Avoidance Play, which deprives the dangerous opponent from obtaining the lead, is the successful counter.

Let us look at some hands:

```
              ♠ A 6 2
              ♥ 6 3
              ♦ Q 10 7 5
              ♣ K 6 5 3
♠ K Q 10 9              ♠ J 7 5 4 3
♥ A Q J 7 5             ♥ 10 9 8 2
♦ 3                     ♦ J
♣ 9 8 7                 ♣ Q J 10
              ♠ 8
              ♥ K 4
              ♦ A K 9 8 6 4 2
              ♣ A 4 2
```

West opened the bidding with one heart and after a spirited auction South became declarer in five diamonds. The king of spades was led.

A thoughtless declarer would almost certainly call for the ace and only then start pondering his overall plan. Well, it is not hopeless. The ace of hearts is likely to be with West, but the clubs may divide 3-3 and does that not make eleven tricks? Seven diamonds, one spade and three clubs. There is just one small snag. East is going to win the third club and push through a heart. The solution is simple enough if you are familiar with Avoidance Plays. Duck the first spade! Later declarer discards a club on the ace of spades, plays the ace, king and another club, ruffing the third round, and then enjoys his discard on the thirteenth club without the dangerous hand (East) obtaining the lead.

A more sophisticated approach, but nevertheless employing the same basic technique, is required on the following hand:

```
              ♠ A K 6
              ♥ J 3
              ♦ A J 8 7 4
              ♣ K J 10

              ♠ 4
              ♥ K 5
              ♦ 5 3 2
              ♣ A Q 9 8 7 6 3
```

West	North	East	South
1♠	1NT	Pass	3NT
4♥	Pass	4♠	5♣
All Pass			

The queen of spades is led. What is your plan?

With ten tricks on top declarer has to find a way of manufacturing the eleventh. The king of hearts is a dead duck for sure, so the best prospect lies in establishing an extra trick from the diamond suit. But how can this be done without allowing East in to play a heart? Once again the solution is really quite simple once you think of it. Duck the queen of spades! Then discard two diamonds on the ace and king of spades. This Avoidance Play keeps West on lead and denies access to East, the danger hand.

The full deal:

```
                 ♠ A K 6
                 ♥ J 3
                 ♦ A J 8 7 4
                 ♣ K J 10
♠ Q J 10 8 7 2              ♠ 9 5 3
♥ A Q 10 9 7 6             ♥ 8 4 2
♦ 9                        ♦ K Q 10 6
♣ —                        ♣ 5 4 2
                 ♠ 4
                 ♥ K 5
                 ♦ 5 3 2
                 ♣ A Q 9 8 7 6 3
```

Let's say West continues with a second spade. Declarer discards a diamond, plays a third spade and discards a second diamond. Now the ace of diamonds and a diamond ruff. Two rounds of trumps, winning in dummy on each occasion and ruffing a diamond both times, enables declarer to set up a diamond in the following position with South to play:

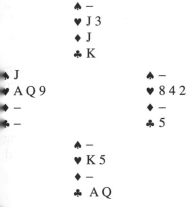

```
                 ♠ —
                 ♥ J 3
                 ♦ J
                 ♣ K
♠ J                        ♠ —
♥ A Q 9                    ♥ 8 4 2
♦ —                        ♦ —
♣ —                        ♣ 5
                 ♠ —
                 ♥ K 5
                 ♦ —
                 ♣ A Q
```

The queen of clubs is played to dummy's king and the jack of diamonds provides a discard for the five of hearts. Declarer loses just one spade and one heart.

To satisfy eagle-eyed analysts—yes, there is an alternative method of success, but this depends on West holding precisely one diamond. Eliminate the spades, throwing a diamond. Cash the ace of diamonds and play one round of trumps (in case). Now allow West to have his ace and queen of hearts. He will then have to concede a ruff and discard allowing declarer to pitch his third diamond.

Now let us look at two 3NT contracts where Avoidance Play is essential:

```
                 ♠ 8 3
                 ♥ 7 5 4
                 ♦ A Q 10 9 3
                 ♣ K Q 10
♠ Q 5                      ♠ J 10 9 7
♥ A 10 8 6 3              ♥ Q 9
♦ 7 5                      ♦ K 8 2
♣ 9 7 4 3                  ♣ 8 6 5 2
                 ♠ A K 6 4 2
                 ♥ K J 2
                 ♦ J 6 4
                 ♣ A J
```

West leads the six of hearts against 3NT and East contributes the queen. Declarer is immediately faced with the most critical decision of the hand. Should he win or should he duck? It is clear that the contract cannot succeed without bringing in the diamonds. If West holds the diamond king there will be plenty of tricks. But what happens when East has that card? Then, holding the hearts, West is the danger hand. So declarer must duck the queen of hearts to break communications between the defenders.

You will notice that if declarer takes the king of hearts at trick one the contract fails when East wins the king of diamonds and plays another heart. However, if the queen of hearts is allowed to hold the first trick, declarer cannot be prevented from taking ten tricks. The defense can establish their heart tricks, but West has no entry to cash them since East will not have a heart left after winning the king of diamonds.

It is worth comparing the last hand with the next one where West leads the five of diamonds against South's 3NT.

```
                 ♠ A 7 6 5 3
                 ♥ 9 8
                 ♦ 9 7 6
                 ♣ A Q J
♠ Q 10                     ♠ K 9 8 4
♥ Q 6 4                    ♥ 5 3 2
♦ A 10 8 5 3              ♦ Q 2
♣ 7 5 4                    ♣ 10 9 6 2
                 ♠ J 2
                 ♥ A K J 10 7
                 ♦ K J 4
                 ♣ K 8 3
```

The five of diamonds is covered by the six and queen and this time declarer notes that to succeed he will have to play on hearts, finessing through East for the queen. If South ducks the queen of diamonds, East will continue the suit and if West happens to have at least three hearts to the queen there will be no way for declarer to establish his heart tricks without letting West in to cash his diamonds. So, on this occasion, declarer should win the the opening lead with the king, enter dummy with a club and run the nine of hearts to West's queen. With the jack of diamonds still protected and no quick entry into the East hand, there is nothing West can do to jeopardize the contract.

The next hand needs careful timing. You might like to try it:

```
♠ Q J 3
♥ K 6 2
♦ 8 7 5
♣ K J 7 6

♠ A 7 6
♥ A 7 3
♦ A J 10
♣ Q 10 9 8
```

Once again, the contract is 3NT by South. West leads the four of spades and the queen from dummy holds the first trick. How do you plan to continue? Here is the full deal:

```
              ♠ Q J 3
              ♥ K 6 2
              ♦ 8 7 5
              ♣ K J 7 6

♠ K 10 8 4 2              ♠ 9 5
♥ 9 8 5                   ♥ Q J 10 4
♦ K 6 3                   ♦ Q 9 4 2
♣ 4 2                     ♣ A 5 3

              ♠ A 7 6
              ♥ A 7 3
              ♦ A J 10
              ♣ Q 10 9 8
```

It may seem natural to start on your long suit, knocking out the ace of clubs, but this would be quite wrong. It is essential to avoid East having the lead yet. Suppose you do play on clubs at trick two; an alert East will grab his ace and shoot through a spade to clear the suit. Now with only eight tricks on top you won't be able to avoid West getting in with the king of diamonds to take the setting tricks (three spades, one club and one diamond).

Since East is the danger hand and you need two diamond tricks, it is imperative to play on diamonds at trick two. A low diamond to the ten loses to the king but the safe hand is on lead. West cannot continue spades to advantage. This gives declarer time both to establish his clubs and take a second diamond finesse. He makes three tricks in clubs and two tricks in every other suit.

Here is another hand that you might like to try before seeing the full deal.

```
              ♠ A 10 8 6
              ♥ 5 2
              ♦ A K 8 5 4
              ♣ 6 4

              ♠ K J 9 5 3
              ♥ A 7
              ♦ Q J 7 6
              ♣ K 5
```

West	North	East	South
1♥	Pass	Pass	Dble
Pass	2♥	Dble	2♠
Pass	4♠	All Pass	

West leads the ♥K, on which East plays the ♥J. How would you play?

Declarer saw that he had plenty of tricks—provided he didn't lose four. The top priority was to avoid East obtaining the lead to play a club through declarer's king. So declarer's first avoidance play was to duck the king of hearts just in case West got the lead with the queen of spades and was able to underlead his queen of hearts to give East the lead. West continued hearts and South won with the ace perforce.

Now the next problem was how to tackle the trumps. Here again Avoidance Play dictated the terms: declarer could afford to lose a trump trick but not to East. So declarer played a spade to the ace and finessed the jack on the way back. That this finesse was successful and declarer made an overtrick was merely the icing on the cake. The important point was that the contract had never been placed in jeopardy.

Here is the full deal:

```
              ♠ A 10 8 6
              ♥ 5 2
              ♦ A K 8 5 4
              ♣ 6 4

♠ 4                      ♠ Q 7 2
♥ K Q 9 8 6              ♥ J 10 4 3
♦ 9 3 2                  ♦ 10
♣ A Q J 7               ♣ 10 9 8 3 2

              ♠ K J 9 5 3
              ♥ A 7
              ♦ Q J 7 6
              ♣ K 5
```

Notice that if declarer had played the trump suit in the "normal" way, by cashing the ace and king hoping for a 2-2 break or the queen dropping singleton, he would have failed since East would have been able to ruff a diamond and play a club through. If declarer's finesse had failed he would still have made the contract as West would have been unable to tackle the club suit with profit.

It would be easy to go wrong on the following hand if you had never seen this situation before:

```
        ♠ 2
        ♥ K J 2
        ♦ K J 5 3
        ♣ A J 10 6 3

        ♠ Q J 9 3
        ♥ A 6 5 3
        ♦ A 6
        ♣ Q 9 2
```

West leads the six of spades against your 3NT contract. East wins the first trick with the king of spades and returns the seven. What is your plan?

This is the full deal:

```
              ♠ 2
              ♥ K J 2
              ♦ K J 5 3
              ♣ A J 10 6 3
♠ A 10 8 6 4                ♠ K 7 5
♥ 9 7 4                     ♥ Q 10 8
♦ Q 8 7                     ♦ 10 9 4 2
♣ 7 5                       ♣ K 8 4
              ♠ Q J 9 3
              ♥ A 6 5 3
              ♦ A 6
              ♣ Q 9 2
```

If you put in the jack or queen of spades on the second round you are about to go down. West will duck and then when the club finesse loses East will play his last spade enabling his partner to take three more spade tricks. The simple solution is to contribute the nine of spades at trick two—a form of Avoidance Play. West can do no better than win with the ten, but then there is no way the defense can take more than three spades and one club.

Alter the hand round so that the North/South cards are distributed something like this:

```
        ♠ 2
        ♥ K J 5 3 2
        ♦ A K 6 3
        ♣ 10 9 2

        ♠ Q J 9 3
        ♥ A 6
        ♦ J 5
        ♣ A Q J 6 3
```

and it would be imperative for declarer to contribute the jack or queen of spades at trick two. The difference this time is that the East hand is no longer a danger since the club finesse will be taken through his hand around to West.

This hand introduces another element of Avoidance Play.

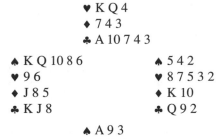

```
              ♠ J 7
              ♥ K Q 4
              ♦ 7 4 3
              ♣ A 10 7 4 3
♠ K Q 10 8 6               ♠ 5 4 2
♥ 9 6                      ♥ 8 7 5 3 2
♦ J 8 5                    ♦ K 10
♣ K J 8                    ♣ Q 9 2
              ♠ A 9 3
              ♥ A J 10
              ♦ A Q 9 6 2
              ♣ 6 5
```

West	North	East	South
Pass	Pass	Pass	1♦
1♠	2♣	Pass	2NT
Pass	3NT	All Pass	

West leads the ♠K. Plan the play.

Declarer wins the third round of spades and appreciates that his problem is to avoid West regaining the lead while at the same time bringing in the diamond suit for four tricks. To succeed, the king of diamonds will have to be with East, but there is more to it than that. The suit must be handled correctly otherwise West may be left with the master diamond.

A heart is played to the king and now a diamond from dummy gives East a choice. If he plays the king, South must duck. If he plays any other card, the queen wins and the process is repeated once more. Dummy is entered with a heart and another diamond is played. If the king appears, as will happen in the layout actually shown, it is allowed to hold. If on the other hand East plays low, South must take his ace and, assuming the suit breaks 3-2, play a third round which East will be forced to win. Thus declarer will make four diamonds, three hearts and the two black aces.

Avoidance Plays come under the general heading of timing and, as we all know, in every walk of life, those who perfect their timing techniques are valuable allies and formidable and difficult opponents.

Coups

The Bath Coup

Star Rating: ★★★★★

The Bath Coup is probably the oldest, best known and easiest coup to execute. It was well recognized in the days of whist, long before contract bridge became the most popular and sophisticated card game in the world.

The Official Encyclopedia of Bridge suggests that the name arises due to an association with the city of Bath. Maybe that was where the coup was first officially recorded. Whatever the reason for the name, I suspect many players have been on the receiving end, or have perhaps executed a Bath Coup, without being fully aware of its correct classification.

The mechanics of the Bath Coup are completely uncomplicated. Consider the following position:

```
            ♠ 6 5 4
♠ K Q 10 9 2        ♠ 8 7
            ♠ A J 3
```

West leads the king and South follows with the three. If West continues the suit West would be a victim of the Bath Coup. Declarer set the trap by ducking the first round, just as South would without the ace, or perhaps without the jack. It is then up to West, with any help East may provide, to determine the actual position.

A similar situation arises when the cards are divided like this:

```
            ♠ A 4 2
♠ K Q 10 8          ♠ 9 7 5
            ♠ J 6 3
```

The king is led and allowed to hold. East will do his best to discourage by following with the five. However, declarer should give West a little nudge in the wrong direction by playing the six. Maybe West will think that East is starting a high/low and blithely continue the suit.

As you've seen, in both cases there is nothing to be lost by ducking the opening lead and quite possibly something to be gained. Even if West does not walk into the Bath Coup by continuing the suit, West will have to switch and that may cost a valuable tempo, perhaps one from which there is no recovery. The following deal from rubber bridge illustrates the position:

```
            ♠ A Q 7 3
            ♥ K Q 10 5
            ♦ 8 6 2
            ♣ 10 2
♠ 8 2                    ♠ 5 4
♥ 7 4 3                  ♥ A 9 8 2
♦ K Q 10 9              ♦ 7 5 4
♣ J 9 7 5              ♣ A 8 6 4
            ♠ K J 10 9 6
            ♥ J 6
            ♦ A J 3
            ♣ K Q 3
```

South plays in four spades and West leads the diamond king. Clearly it is in South's interest to duck (Bath Coup). Should South fail to do so the contract will be defeated since the defense will come to two diamonds and two aces.

When the king of diamonds is allowed to hold, West has nowhere to go. West can't continue the suit to advantage, and a heart switch is no solution. A club to the ace is the best shot, but this simply provides a parking space for dummy's losing diamond on the third round of clubs.

Defending against no trump contracts, one should not fall foul of the Bath Coup since partner has a mandatory role to play. The standard lead from KQ10xx is the king and partner is duty bound to contribute the jack if he has it. Most experts today will lead the queen from a specific holding of KQ109, which requires partner to contribute the jack if he has it. This play enables even a four card suit to solidify in defense. Thus situations like the following are immediately identifiable:

(a)

          ♠ 6 3

♠ K Q 10 8 4   ♠ 9 7 5

          ♠ A J 2

(b)

          ♠ 6 3

♠ K Q 10 8 4   ♠ J 7 5

          ♠ A 9 2

In (a) East, perforce, will not play the jack, therefore South must have it.

In (b) East will follow with the jack and South's secret is out in the open.

Just look at the following hand where East was not versed in the niceties of the Bath Coup.

      ♠ A Q 7 5
      ♥ A K 7 3
      ♦ 6 4 3
      ♣ 3 2

♠ J 4   ♠ K 10 8 6
♥ 10 5 4   ♥ J 9 8 6
♦ Q 10 5   ♦ J 9
♣ K Q 10 8 6   ♣ J 7 5

      ♠ 9 3 2
      ♥ Q 2
      ♦ A K 8 7 2
      ♣ A 9 4

The bidding was straightforward enough. South opened a weak 1NT (12-14), North went through the Stayman routine and finding no joy settled for 3NT. West made the book lead of the king of clubs and you can see that there is no play for the contract. The club ace is knocked out and then West waits for his diamond trick. However, things did not work out like that. On the club king, East followed with the seven and South the four. Convinced that East could not hold the club jack, West switched to the jack of spades.

Declarer did not need any second chances going up with the ace of spades to establish the diamonds. In with the queen of diamonds, West played a second spade, ducked to East's ten, but nine tricks were now in sight. In fact East failed to cash his king of spades, switching to the jack of clubs instead. Subsequently East was squeezed in the majors so declarer made ten tricks.

"Partner, why didn't you throw your jack of clubs under the king?" demanded a frustrated West.

"I played an encouraging card—the seven—I thought you were sure to continue," replied East.

Well, there you have it. West, correctly, expected East to jettison the jack if he had it, and since no jack appeared West assumed that South must have it. On the other hand,

East saw no necessity to play the jack rather than encourage with the seven. The fallacy in East's argument is what would East play holding just the seven and five, or the nine and seven? Whichever it was, it would be impossible to avoid ambiguity using East's methods.

It is more difficult when the king is led against a suit contract. Remember, the standard lead against no trumps from KQ753 is the five, but against a suit contract it is the king. The priorities are quite different. Against a suit contract there is no certainty that the lead is from length thus partner may not be able to afford the jack. Indeed, unless he has the ten as well, or jack doubleton, he is unlikely to do so. Let us look at some examples:

(a)

          ♠ 9 7 4 2

♠ K Q 10   ♠ J 8 6 3

          ♠ A 5

West leads the king. Now clearly it would be unwise to contribute the jack for fear of establishing dummy's nine. Encourage with the six.

(b)

          ♠ 9 6 3

♠ K Q 7 5   ♠ J 8 4

          ♠ A 10 2

Again the king is led and you cannot afford the jack. Play the eight and if South ducks hope partner can read your signal.

Now two hands from actual play. The first was in matchpointed pairs:

      ♠ A Q 2
      ♥ A 3 2
      ♦ J 10 7 4
      ♣ 10 8 3

♠ 8 7 4   ♠ K 9 6 3
♥ K Q 10 9   ♥ 7 6 5
♦ 9 3   ♦ 6 5 2
♣ K 7 6 2   ♣ J 9 4

      ♠ J 10 5
      ♥ J 8 4
      ♦ A K Q 8
      ♣ A Q 5

The normal contract was 3NT by South. The heart king was led and this was the classical situation for declarer to duck in dummy and for East to deny the jack by failing to play it. West had to switch to a spade. East won and returned a heart. Those players who relied on the club finesse had to go one down. A better plan, as the cards lie, was to win the ace of hearts at trick three and cash the diamond and spade winners. With seven tricks in the bag, this was the position with dummy to play:

```
          ♠ —
          ♥ 3
          ♦ —
          ♣ 10 8 3
♠ —                    ♠ 9
♥ Q 10                 ♥ 6
♦ —                    ♦ —
♣ K 7                  ♣ J 9
          ♠ —
          ♥ J
          ♦ —
          ♣ A Q 5
```

The three of hearts was led allowing West to take his two winners, but then West had to lead a club into declarer's tenace.

This hand comes from rubber bridge.

```
          ♠ K Q J 7 5
          ♥ 7 5 4
          ♦ A J
          ♣ A K 6

          ♠ A 8 4
          ♥ K Q 10 8 2
          ♦ 8 4
          ♣ 10 9 2
```

North	South
1♠	1NT
2NT	3NT
Pass	

You lead the heart king against 3NT, declarer winning the ace and East following with the three. Your ace of spades is knocked out; perhaps you withhold this card until the third round but partner has to follow each time so can't contribute a useful discard. So what are you going to do now? Are you going to play your queen of hearts and hope to crash the jack, or try to find partner with an entry (king of diamonds perhaps) so that East can play a heart through declarer? Let's look at the evidence.

East did not contribute the jack of hearts on the first round so South is marked with this card. If South held ♥AJx why didn't South duck the first round? Then there is East's three of hearts. That would be consistent with an odd number of cards—most probably three. The picture that is emerging clearly shows declarer holding the ace-jack of hearts alone. So you cash the queen of hearts and your hopes are fulfilled.

The full deal:

```
          ♠ K Q J 7 5
          ♥ 7 5 4
          ♦ A J
          ♣ A K 6
♠ A 8 4                ♠ 9 6 2
♥ K Q 10 8 2           ♥ 9 6 3
♦ 8 4                  ♦ K Q 6 2
♣ 10 9 2               ♣ 7 5 4
          ♠ 10 3
          ♥ A J
          ♦ 10 9 7 5 3
          ♣ Q J 8 3
```

Although in negative form—just like the case where the dog failed to bark – knowledge of the Bath Coup helped West to solve the problem.

A Trump Coup (Grand Coup)

Star Rating: ★★★★

A Trump Coup occurs in the end-game when a defender's trumps are trapped yet there is no trump available to take the finesse. This necessitates the declarer disembarrassing himself of surplus trumps. Consider:

1.

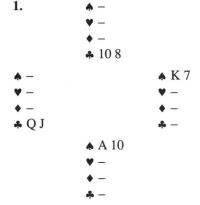

South plays in spades and dummy has the lead. In this example it doesn't matter what cards are left in dummy. The important point is that the lead is on the table and South is down to the same number of trumps as East. A club is led and East can retire.

2.

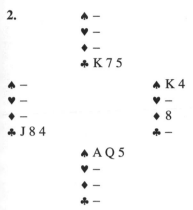

♠ –
♥ –
♦ –
♣ K 7 5

♠ –   ♠ K 4
♥ –   ♥ –
♦ –   ♦ 8
♣ J 8 4   ♣ –

♠ A Q 5
♥ –
♦ –
♣ –

In this example South has one more trump than East, so South can make only two out of the last three tricks. When a club is led East discards the diamond.

3.

♠ 10
♥ 4
♦ 6
♣ –

♠ –   ♠ J
♥ Q J 8   ♥ –
♦ –   ♦ J
♣ –   ♣ 10

♠ –
♥ K 10 9
♦ –
♣ –

Hearts are trumps—South to play. In this case it doesn't matter whether North or South is on lead. Declarer exits with the ♥10 and must make two out of the last three tricks.

4.

♠ 10
♥ 4
♦ 6
♣ 8

♠ –   ♠ J
♥ Q J 8   ♥ –
♦ –   ♦ J 10
♣ J   ♣ 10

♠ –
♥ K 10 9 6
♦ –
♣ –

Now declarer has left himself with one trump too many. If the lead were in dummy, declarer could ruff a club and then play as in example 3. As it is, with the lead in his own hand, South exits with the ♥10. West wins and plays the ♣J and then must make a second trump.

There is really very little difference between the Trump Coup and the Grand Coup, the mechanics being virtually the same.

The distinguishing feature of the Grand Coup is that it is necessary to trump winners to reduce to the right number of trumps for the end-game; this somewhat grandiose name emanates from the game of whist. Let's look at some hands:

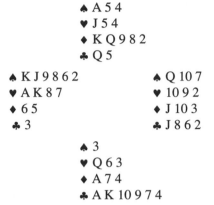

♠ A 5 4
♥ J 5 4
♦ K Q 9 8 2
♣ Q 5

♠ K J 9 8 6 2   ♠ Q 10 7
♥ A K 8 7   ♥ 10 9 2
♦ 6 5   ♦ J 10 3
♣ 3   ♣ J 8 6 2

♠ 3
♥ Q 6 3
♦ A 7 4
♣ A K 10 9 7 4

You play five clubs as South. West leads the ace-king and another heart. Although, in the event, 3NT would be a trouble-free contract, you are saddled with the perfectly reasonable alternative of five clubs. Without prior knowledge of the club break, you make the normal play of the queen of clubs followed by a club to your ace. It is at this point that your know-how about trump coups will be invaluable. You must reduce your trumps to the same number as East's and you must be in dummy at trick eleven.

So, the ace of spades and a spade ruff are followed by the king of diamonds and a second spade ruff. Now the ace and queen of diamonds (too bad if East has only two diamonds, then there is nothing you can do about it) gives dummy the lead with these cards remaining:

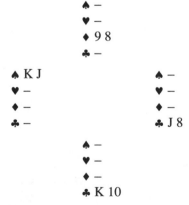

♠ –
♥ –
♦ 9 8
♣ –

♠ K J   ♠ –
♥ –   ♥ –
♦ –   ♦ –
♣ –   ♣ J 8

♠ –
♥ –
♦ –
♣ K 10

No doubt East has sensed his fate earlier than this, but in any case when a diamond is played from dummy East will have to give in.

On the next hand declarer will have to rely on the Grand Coup:

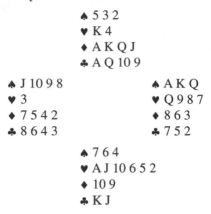

```
          ♠ 5 3 2
          ♥ K 4
          ♦ A K Q J
          ♣ A Q 10 9
♠ J 10 9 8              ♠ A K Q
♥ 3                    ♥ Q 9 8 7
♦ 7 5 4 2              ♦ 8 6 3
♣ 8 6 4 3              ♣ 7 5 2
          ♠ 7 6 4
          ♥ A J 10 6 5 2
          ♦ 10 9
          ♣ K J
```

South plays four hearts on the jack of spades lead. East cashes three top spades and exits safely with a diamond. Declarer plays the king of hearts and takes the heart finesse. Good news and bad news! The finesse is right, but the hearts don't break. Oh well, at least it is East who holds the protected queen. Had it been West, the contract would have been doomed.

Realizing the necessity for reducing his trumps to the same number as East's, declarer cashes the diamond king and ruffs the jack. The jack of clubs is overtaken with dummy's queen and the diamond queen is ruffed, East discarding a club. The hand has now been reduced to the following position:

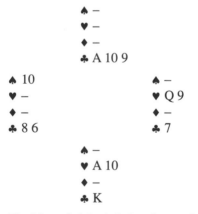

```
          ♠ –
          ♥ –
          ♦ –
          ♣ A 10 9
♠ 10                  ♠ –
♥ –                   ♥ Q 9
♦ –                   ♦ –
♣ 8 6                 ♣ 7
          ♠ –
          ♥ A 10
          ♦ –
          ♣ K
```

The king of clubs is led and overtaken with the ace. When East has to follow to the club the hand is over. East's ♥Q9 are caught under the ♥A10.

On the next hand declarer has to take precautions against the only possible danger. After a pre-emptive bid of three clubs by West, South ends up in 6♠.

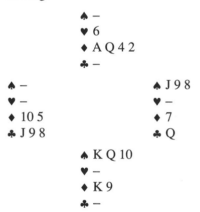

```
          ♠ A 7
          ♥ A 6 4 3 2
          ♦ A Q J 4 2
          ♣ 6
♠ –                    ♠ J 9 8 5
♥ 10 8 7              ♥ K Q J 5
♦ 10 5 3             ♦ 7 6
♣ A K J 9 8 4 2      ♣ Q 10 3
          ♠ K Q 10 6 4 3 2
          ♥ 9
          ♦ K 9 8
          ♣ 7 5
```

West leads the ace of clubs and continues with the king. Superficially it seems that declarer has no problems, for there are plenty of tricks. Of course, there is one possible danger—that East holds all the outstanding trumps. After West's barrage bid and play at trick two, forcing dummy to ruff, the possibility of a 4-0 trump break belies the normal mathematical odds. Taking all this into account, declarer wisely cashes the ace of hearts and ruffs a heart before tackling trumps. Now a spade to the ace reveals the bad split and highlights declarer's foresight. A second heart ruff is followed by a diamond to the jack and a third heart ruff, leaving:

```
          ♠ –
          ♥ 6
          ♦ A Q 4 2
          ♣ –
♠ –                    ♠ J 9 8
♥ –                   ♥ –
♦ 10 5               ♦ 7
♣ J 9 8              ♣ Q
          ♠ K Q 10
          ♥ –
          ♦ K 9
          ♣ –
```

The nine of diamonds to dummy's queen followed by the six of hearts leaves East without further resource.

If the declarer fails to see the danger and cashes the ace of spades at trick two, it will be impossible to finish in the right place at the right time for the end-play. Try it and you'll see. Inexperienced players simply hate trumping their good tricks, so it is very necessary for them to understand the mechanics of the Grand Coup if they are to succeed on hands like this.

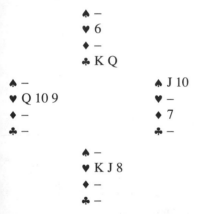

♠ 8 6
♥ 6 4 3
♦ A K 3
♣ A K Q J 10

♠ A K Q   ♠ J 10 9 7 3
♥ Q 10 9 7   ♥ —
♦ 10 9 8   ♦ 7 6 5 2
♣ 9 6 4   ♣ 8 7 5 2

♠ 5 4 2
♥ A K J 8 5 2
♦ Q J 4
♣ 3

North opened the bidding with one club and then had an awkward rebid over one heart. Eventually North settled for 2NT which South converted to four hearts. West led two top spades and then switched to the ten of diamonds. Everything looked plain sailing for declarer until East failed to follow to the first round of trumps. However, declarer was equal to the task, realizing that he would have to ruff two master clubs in order to shorten his trumps. The ace of clubs, club ruff, spade ruff, club ruff and two more diamonds left the following cards:

♠ —
♥ 6
♦ —
♣ K Q

♠ —   ♠ J 10
♥ Q 10 9   ♥ —
♦ —   ♦ 7
♣ —   ♣ —

♠ —
♥ K J 8
♦ —
♣ —

It did not matter in which hand declarer finished having reduced his trumps and stripped West of plain cards. Also, the trump in dummy was equally unimportant. West was simply thrown on lead by playing the eight of hearts and declarer had to make the last two. The next hand has an amusing side to it, as well as being an object lesson in the maxim "Silence is Golden."

♠ Q J 7 3
♥ A 8 3 2
♦ A J
♣ 5 4 3

♠ 9 8 4   ♠ 10 6 5 2
♥ —   ♥ K Q 6
♦ Q 9 7 4 3   ♦ 10 6 5
♣ Q J 10 9 8   ♣ 7 6 2

♠ A K
♥ J 10 9 7 5 4
♦ K 8 2
♣ A K

South opened the bidding with one heart, was raised to four, and having checked on aces bid six hearts.

West led the queen of clubs. The declarer was the late Kenneth Konstam, a former world champion, and as the dummy went down he had every reason to be pleased with what he saw. Indeed, the contract was a certainty as long as West held one heart—any heart. However, as soon as East saw the ace of hearts in the dummy he couldn't resist a little gloat. "This is one slam you won't make, Konnie," he remarked gleefully. Now East was no slouch at the game. He was an experienced old-timer who had made plenty of money at rubber bridge over the years, thus making his little speech all the more remarkable.

In the ordinary way declarer would have led the jack of hearts at trick two, from which point there would have been no recovery. But now, armed with details of the opponent's secret weapon (East must hold all the missing hearts for his remark to make sense), Konstam set about reducing his trumps to the same number as East—an essential requirement if East was to be end-played. After cashing the black suit aces and kings he led a diamond to dummy's jack. The finesse was obligatory otherwise dummy was short of an entry. When the jack of diamonds held a spade was ruffed, a diamond played to the ace and a second spade ruffed. Now the king of diamonds was trumped on the table—he still needed that entry—and dummy's last club trumped in hand, leaving the following position with dummy, declarer and East all down to three hearts each:

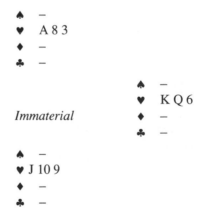

♠ —
♥ A 8 3
♦ —
♣ —

              ♠ —
              ♥ K Q 6
Immaterial   ♦ —
              ♣ —

♠ —
♥ J 10 9
♦ —
♣ —

Long before the jack of hearts was played and ducked in dummy East knew his fate and bitterly regretted his foolish outburst.

Is there a defense to the trump coup? Yes, sometimes. If you see that the declarer is trying to reduce trumps, or if you know that that is what he should be doing, don't lead cards for declarer to ruff. Instead, attack declarer's entries. Then he may not be able to reduce his trumps sufficiently.

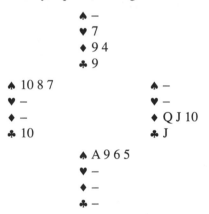

♠ 4
♥ K Q 7 4
♦ 9 4 3 2
♣ 9 6 3 2

♠ K 10 8 7   ♠ J
♥ A 6 3   ♥ 8 5 2
♦ 8 5   ♦ Q J 10 7 6
♣ A K Q 10   ♣ J875

♠ A Q 9 6 5 3 2
♥ J 10 9
♦ A K
♣ 4

West led two top clubs against South's contract of 3♠ doubled. South ruffed and led a heart to dummy's king followed by a spade to the jack, queen and king. It may seem convenient for West to play a third club—that is what happened at the table—but it is completely fatal. South ruffs, cashes the ace and king of diamonds and plays a second heart. West takes the ace and exits with a heart to dummy's queen, leaving:

♠ –
♥ 7
♦ 9 4
♣ 9

♠ 10 8 7   ♠ –
♥ –   ♥ –
♦ –   ♦ Q J 10
♣ 10   ♣ J

♠ A 9 6 5
♥ –
♦ –
♣ –

Declarer now ruffs a club and exits with a small spade. West has to lead away from the ♠108 into declarer's ♠A9. Had West read the script, he would have returned a heart at trick five, not another club, thus denying declarer the opportunity to reduce his trumps sufficiently for a successful end-game.

Finally, this is a hand played in the British trials some years ago:

♠ 8 6 2
♥ A 10 7
♦ A J 4
♣ A K J 5

♠ Q J 5 3   ♠ –
♥ J 5 2   ♥ K 9 8 6 4 3
♦ 10 9 8   ♦ 7 6 5 2
♣ 7 6 3   ♣ 10 9 4

♠ A K 10 9 7 4
♥ Q
♦ K Q 3
♣ Q 8 2

The popular contract was six spades by South—superficially an excellent spot. West led the ten of diamonds, won by the king and the bad news broke when East discarded the nine of hearts on the ace of spades. Realizing that he must reduce his trumps to the same number as West's, and also strip West of his remaining plain cards, declarer cashed the ace of hearts and ruffed a heart, entered dummy with a diamond and ruffed a second heart. Now three rounds of clubs followed by the diamond ace left:

♠ 8 6
♥ –
♦ –
♣ J

♠ Q J 5   ♠ –
♥ –   ♥ 8 6
♦ –   ♦ 7
♣ –   ♣ –

♠ K 10 9
♥ –
♦ –
♣ –

A spade to declarer's ten endplayed West.

If you found the mechanics of this last hand rather difficult, it may be comforting to know that two of the trialists actually conceded defeat as soon as they saw East show out on the first spade! Politely, that is called having a "Blind Spot."

MORTON'S FORK COUP

Star Rating: ★★★★

Some of the more exotic names ascribed to certain technical plays in bridge may leave you wondering if they really deserve their colorful labels. It was Aneurin Bevan who once accused Harold Macmillan of having an absolute genius for putting flamboyant labels on empty luggage. Perhaps Bevan was right, perhaps not. But certainly his accusation would not stand up in the case of the Morton's Fork Coup. It's a brilliant name to cover a reasonably common scenario. Suppose you are South in a spade contract. It is your lead, and you need to make six out of the last seven tricks:

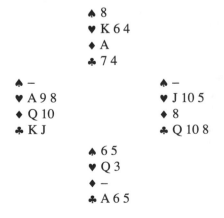

♠ 8
♥ K 6 4
♦ A
♣ 7 4

♠ –   ♠ –
♥ A 9 8   ♥ J 10 5
♦ Q 10   ♦ 8
♣ K J   ♣ Q 10 8

♠ 6 5
♥ Q 3
♦ –
♣ A 6 5

You play the one and only card that will see you home—the three of hearts. This places West in an unenviable position. If he goes up with the ace, there will be two discards in dummy for your two losing clubs. On the other hand, if West ducks, dummy's king wins and your losing heart disappears on the diamond ace. You concede a club trick and that is the only trick you lose. What a lovely situation to be in! Whatever your opponents do, you must win and they lose—and that is where the name comes in.

Cardinal John Morton was the notorious fifteenth-century chancellor to Henry VII, noted as a zealous collector of taxes. The cardinal worked on the principle that those who lived in lavish style could well afford to pay, while those who lived modestly must have plenty of money stashed away. In either case they became impaled on Morton's Fork. A less well known name for this play—which embraces a heads-I-win, tails-you-lose situation—is the Dilemma Coup, but perhaps you agree with me that Morton's Fork Coup sounds far more exotic and satisfying.

Let us look at some hands:

```
          ♠ Q 9 8
          ♥ —
          ♦ K Q 8 7 6 4
          ♣ 10 8 7 6

          ♠ K 2
          ♥ A 9 4
          ♦ A J 10 9 5
          ♣ A K J
```

West	North	East	South
–	Pass	Pass	1♦
Dble	5♦	Pass	6♦
All Pass			

West leads the king of hearts. How should South plan the play?

The doubler is marked with the ♥KQ, ♠A and quite likely the ♣Q as well, thus the scene is set for Morton's Fork Coup. One essential ingredient of this coup is to avoid taking a premature discard. First, a defender must be put on the rack to make the "wrong" decision, and only after that can the discard be taken. So declarer ruffs the heart in dummy, plays a diamond to his hand, both opponents following, and then plays the two of spades towards dummy. If West goes up with the ace, there will be a parking place for declarer's knave of clubs on dummy's queen of spades. If West ducks, the queen of spades wins, a club is played to the ace, the ace of hearts is cashed, dummy discarding a spade, and declarer's last heart is ruffed. Declarer now exits with a spade leaving this position:

```
          ♠ —
          ♥ —
          ♦ K Q 8
          ♣ 10 8 7
```

```
          ♠ —
          ♥ —
          ♦ J 10 9 5
          ♣ K J
```

West can make his own arrangements, but they are strictly limited to conceding a ruff and discard or leading into South's club tenace. Either way West is impaled on Morton's Fork.

My next hand was an exciting affair played in a pairs event:

```
          ♠ K 9 7
          ♥ K 9 6
          ♦ K 8 4
          ♣ A 9 7 5

♠ 4 3              ♠ Q
♥ 8 7 5 3 2        ♥ A J 10
♦ J 10 7 6         ♦ Q 5
♣ Q 2              ♣ K J 10 8 6 4 3

          ♠ A J 10 8 6 5 2
          ♥ Q 4
          ♦ A 9 3 2
          ♣ —
```

South arrived in the fair contract of six spades after East had opened one club. The queen of clubs was led and, again, one sees that declarer must not make the mistake of taking an early discard. So South plays low from dummy and ruffs in hand. The ace of spades is followed by a second spade to the king. Now a low heart puts the question to East: "To take or not to take?" If East takes, the king of hearts and ace of clubs will provide the necessary discards for declarer's two losing diamonds; if East ducks, dummy is re-entered with the king of diamonds and the four of hearts is discarded on the ace of clubs. Finally, one diamond is conceded and one ruffed in dummy. This way declarer makes seven spades, one heart, two diamonds, one club and one diamond ruff.

Some interesting points arose from the following hand which occurred in a straight teams match:

```
          ♠ 7 4 2
          ♥ K Q 7 4
          ♦ A J 3
          ♣ Q 6 2

          ♠ K 3
          ♥ A J 10 9 5
          ♦ K 10 9 2
          ♣ K 4
```

West	North	East	South
1♠	Pass	Pass	Dble
Pass	2♠	Pass	3♥
Pass	4♥	All Pass	

After West had opened 1♠, passed to South, both Souths became declarer in four hearts. The lead was the three of hearts.

Having found the trumps 2-2, how would you plan the play?

The first declarer took what he claimed to be "the odds play." Superficially, everything seemed to hinge on finding the diamond queen. West had opened the bidding, there were only fourteen points missing and most of these would be with West. Therefore this declarer played West for the missing diamond honor. Unlucky, for this was the full deal:

```
              ♠ 7 4 2
              ♥ K Q 7 4
              ♦ A J 3
              ♣ Q 6 2
♠ A Q J 10 5              ♠ 9 8 6
♥ 8 3                    ♥ 6 2
♦ 7 5                    ♦ Q 8 6 4
♣ A J 9 7                ♣ 10 8 5 3
              ♠ K 3
              ♥ A J 10 9 5
              ♦ K 10 9 2
              ♣ K 4
```

The second declarer thought about the problem more deeply than his counterpart and he realized that he could almost certainly make his contract regardless of the position of the queen of diamonds, provided he finessed through East. The fact that East held this vital card was a bonus. The ace of diamonds, knave of diamonds and a third diamond left this position:

```
              ♠ 7 4 2
              ♥ Q 7
              ♦ –
              ♣ Q 6 2
♠ A Q J 10               ♠ 9 8 6
♥ –                     ♥ –
♦ –                     ♦ Q
♣ A J 9 7                ♣ 10 8 5 3
              ♠ K 3
              ♥ 10 9 5
              ♦ K
              ♣ K 4
```

At this point South carefully refrained from cashing his fourth diamond but instead played the four of clubs. Poor West was caught on Morton's Fork and there was nothing he could do about it. He delayed the evil hour by ducking, but his respite was short-lived. The queen of clubs won, the seven of hearts was led to the nine and the king of diamonds was now cashed, dummy discarding a club. It only remained to play the king of clubs and claim eleven tricks, West making just the two black aces.

Now let us suppose that West really did have the queen of diamonds, and to make life easy for him we'll give him two small cards with his queen. So West makes the queen of diamonds at trick four and exits with a diamond (best). Now South wins in his own hand and plays in exactly the same way as in the eight card diagram above. The only difference

is that this time South will make just ten tricks, but his contract has never been in jeopardy.

It sometimes happens that you have the choice between taking two immediate discards or ruffing the opening lead. If the Morton's Fork Coup is in the offing there may be a big bonus for delaying the discards. The following hand illustrates the point.

```
              ♠ J 10 6 5 3
              ♥ A K 3
              ♦ K 6 2
              ♣ K 10
♠ 8                      ♠ 7 4
♥ Q J 10 9 7 6           ♥ 8 5 4 2
♦ Q 5                    ♦ J 10 4
♣ A 9 8 5                ♣ J 7 6 3
              ♠ A K Q 9 2
              ♥ –
              ♦ A 9 8 7 3
              ♣ Q 4 2
```

West	North	East	South
–	–	–	1♠
2♥	3♥	Pass	4♦
Pass	4♠	Pass	5♠
Pass	6♠	All Pass	

West leads the queen of hearts and declarer must resist the temptation of playing an honor from dummy. Instead, ruff in hand, draw trumps and play a small club towards the king. If West plays the club ace, dummy's losing diamond will disappear on the queen of clubs, and then the third round of diamonds can be trumped in dummy to set up the suit. If West ducks the club, the king wins and now the ace and king of hearts provide discards for declarer's remaining clubs. In this case declarer's only loser is a diamond.

If declarer takes the discards at once, instead of waiting to employ Morton's Fork, the contract will surely be defeated.

My last hand brings back pleasant memories of the Morton's Fork Coup. Again, it was a team-of-four match.

```
              ♠ A 8 6
              ♥ A 7 5
              ♦ A K 6
              ♣ K 7 4 3

              ♠ –
              ♥ K Q J 10 9 6 3
              ♦ J 10 5 3
              ♣ Q 6
```

West	North	East	South
–	1♣	Pass	4♥
Pass	6♥	All Pass	

North, my partner on this occasion, was Ian Panto, the whiz kid from Sussex and a great traveller in the fast lane. No doubt our auction lacked a modern scientific flavor, but at least it was succinct. This time there is no opposition bidding to assist us and the lead was an unhelpful knave of spades. So how would you plan to make your contract?

Obviously, if the queen of diamonds is right, there will be no problem. But we have all the ingredients of a Morton's Fork Coup, so we must try that first. The trouble is that we don't know who has the ace of clubs (or do we?) If East has it, we must play a low club from dummy towards the queen. But if West has it, then we must play the six of clubs towards dummy. Whichever line we adopt it is still essential to withhold the ace of spades for the moment and ruff the opening lead in hand.

When I said "This time there is no opposition bidding to assist us" this may have been slightly misleading because the very fact that East passed over one club provides a clue. The lead of the jack of spades, although unhelpful, strongly suggests that East has both the king and queen, and with so many spades missing maybe length too. Add the queen of diamonds and the ace of clubs and surely he would have found a bid at the one level. Conclusion: East does not hold the ace of clubs, West does. Time to look at the full hand:

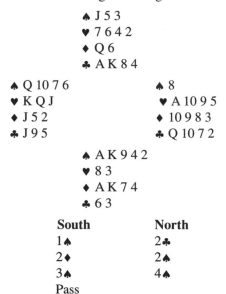

So, you ruff the spade lead, draw trumps ending in hand, and lead the six of clubs. If West wins, it is all over—there are two discards for your losing diamonds. However, West ducks and the king wins. Now you cash the spade ace and discard the club queen. At this point your contract is secure so it only remains to ruff a spade and take the diamond finesse for a possible overtrick.

Exciting stuff, I hope you agree, and well worth a little study.

COUP EN PASSANT

Star Rating: ★★★

A Coup en Passant—the name comes from the game of chess—is a play which enables a contestant to score a lower trump than that held by an opponent. The coup arises when a plain suit is led through the opponent holding the higher trump.

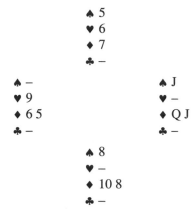

Spades are trumps. Dummy to play. The six of hearts is led and no matter what East plays, declarer must make the eight of spades en passant.

Let us look at some hands from actual play. The first comes from rubber bridge resulting in a rather amusing incident.

```
                ♠ J 5 3
                ♥ 7 6 4 2
                ♦ Q 6
                ♣ A K 8 4
♠ Q 10 7 6                  ♠ 8
♥ K Q J                     ♥ A 10 9 5
♦ J 5 2                     ♦ 10 9 8 3
♣ J 9 5                     ♣ Q 10 7 2
                ♠ A K 9 4 2
                ♥ 8 3
                ♦ A K 7 4
                ♣ 6 3
```

South	North
1♠	2♣
2♦	2♠
3♠	4♠
Pass	

West led the king of hearts and continued the suit, declarer ruffing the third round. Two top trumps signalled the bad break, but prospects improved when the ace and king of clubs and a club ruff gave declarer six tricks. South then cashed three rounds of diamonds.

It was at this point that West claimed the remainder of the tricks! This was the position with South to play:

```
              ♠ J
              ♥ —
              ♦ —
              ♣ 8
    ♠ Q 10
    ♥ —
    ♦ —              Immaterial
    ♣ —
              ♠ 9
              ♥ —
              ♦ 7
              ♣ —
```

"The rest must be mine," said West. "I can take both trump tricks."

"I think perhaps we should play on," replied South with a smile tabling the seven of diamonds.

The next hand was played in a multiple teams event and mostly resulted in minus scores for North/South.

```
              ♠ A K Q 3
              ♥ 7 4
              ♦ A 6 4 2
              ♣ J 8 3
  ♠ J 10 9 5             ♠ 8 7 4
  ♥ 5 3                  ♥ J 10 9 6
  ♦ Q 8                  ♦ J 10 9
  ♣ A K Q 10 7           ♣ 9 6 4
              ♠ 6 2
              ♥ A K Q 8 2
              ♦ K 7 5 3
              ♣ 5 2
```

Three no trumps and five diamonds were doomed from the start, and in four hearts there look to be four losers—two clubs, one diamond and one heart? At one table this was the bidding:

West	North	East	South
—	—	Pass	1♥
2♣	2♦	Pass	3♦
Pass	3♠	Pass	4♥
All Pass			

The defense started well by taking two clubs and switching to the spade jack. Declarer won, drew three rounds of hearts and then took two more spades and ruffed a club. Two top diamonds gave dummy the lead again leaving:

```
              ♠ 3
              ♥ —
              ♦ 6
              ♣ —
                        ♠ —
                        ♥ J
    Immaterial          ♦ J
                        ♣ —
              ♠ —
              ♥ 8
              ♦ 7
              ♣ —
```

When the three of spades was led declarer could not be prevented from making the tenth trick en passant with the eight of hearts. The next hand was played in a pairs event.

```
              ♠ A K 8 6 4
              ♥ K 8
              ♦ J 4 2
              ♣ Q 5 3
  ♠ Q J 10 9            ♠ 7 5 3
  ♥ 2                   ♥ J 10 7 5 4
  ♦ A K 10 7            ♦ 9 8 6
  ♣ J 9 6 4             ♣ 7 2
              ♠ 2
              ♥ A Q 9 6 3
              ♦ Q 5 3
              ♣ A K 10 8
```

At one table South came to rest in four hearts. West started with two top diamonds and continued with a third round. The two top hearts revealed the bad trump break but declarer found an effective counter. Two top spades and a spade ruff were followed by the ace and queen of clubs. With the lead in dummy and eight tricks already in the bag, the position was:

```
              ♠ 8 6
              ♥ —
              ♦ —
              ♣ 5
                        ♠ —
                        ♥ J 10 7
    Immaterial          ♦ —
                        ♣ —
              ♠ —
              ♥ Q 9
              ♦ —
              ♣ K
```

A spade was led and East had no satisfactory answer. East did his best by ruffing with the knave of hearts but declarer just discarded the king of clubs and waited for the two final tricks.

So, when you next run into a bad trump break resulting in one too many "inescapable" losers, give a little thought to our friend the Coup en Passant.

Scissors Coup

Star Rating: ✱✱✱

The Scissors Coup is a play that cuts the defenders' only line of communication, frequently to prevent an impending ruff. The following seven-card ending illustrates the point. Spades are trumps. West leads the two of hearts, South to make five tricks.

```
              ♠ 6 4
              ♥ A K
              ♦ A Q
              ♣ 8
    ♠ A 5               ♠ –
    ♥ 2                 ♥ Q 6 3
    ♦ K J               ♦ 8 7
    ♣ 7 4               ♣ A 9
              ♠ K Q J
              ♥ 9 5
              ♦ 4
              ♣ J
```

Unless South employs the Scissors Coup immediately, South will lose one spade, one club and a heart ruff, making only four tricks. To avert the ruff South cashes the ace of diamonds and follows it with the queen. When East plays a low diamond South discards the jack of clubs. West wins this trick and later the ace of spades, but the link has been severed, so East can never obtain the lead to give his partner a ruff.

A few hands may help you to recognize the position.

```
              ♠ A K J
              ♥ J 9 6 2
              ♦ A K Q J
              ♣ 6 3

              ♠ 7 5
              ♥ K Q 10 8 4
              ♦ 10 7 5 4
              ♣ 10 4
```

West	North	East	South
–	1♦	Pass	1♥
Dble	4♥	All Pass	

West leads the ace of clubs, East following with the queen. West then switches to the three of diamonds. How should declarer plan the play? This was the full deal:

```
              ♠ A K J
              ♥ J 9 6 2
              ♦ A K Q J
              ♣ 6 3
    ♠ Q 10 3 2           ♠ 9 8 6 4
    ♥ A 7 5             ♥ 3
    ♦ 3                 ♦ 9 8 6 2
    ♣ A K 8 5 2         ♣ Q J 9 7
              ♠ 7 5
              ♥ K Q 10 8 4
              ♦ 10 7 5 4
              ♣ 10 4
```

When East followed to the first trick with the queen of clubs—traditionally guaranteeing the jack—West switched to his singleton diamond, safe in the knowledge that there was likely to be an entry to the East hand. The defensive plan was straightforward enough. Win the ace of trumps, put partner on lead with the club jack and ruff the diamond return for one off. However, South was also in the game and sensed the impending danger. On the bidding West was marked with the ace of hearts, and most probably the spade queen, so South decided on an ingenious counter. After the ace of diamonds, declarer played dummy's ace, king and jack of spades, discarding the club on the third round. West won this trick with the queen but now the only line of contact with East had been cut (Scissors Coup), and the defense had to settle for just one more trick, the ace of trumps.

```
              ♠ Q 8 6
              ♥ A 8 7 6 4
              ♦ Q 6
              ♣ A K 10
    ♠ A 9 5             ♠ –
    ♥ 2                 ♥ J 10 9 5
    ♦ 9 7 5 4           ♦ A K J 10 8 3
    ♣ Q J 9 7 5         ♣ 8 6 3
              ♠ K J 10 7 4 3 2
              ♥ K Q 3
              ♦ 2
              ♣ 4 2
```

This hand was played in a local pairs event. At one table the bidding was:

West	North	East	South
–	1♥	2♦	2♠
4♦	Pass	Pass	4♠
Pass	Pass	5♦	Pass
Pass	5♠	All Pass	

Aggressive bidding by East/West pushed North/South to five spades. Superficially, this contract looks secure—at least until West leads the two of hearts, an obvious singleton. One diamond, one spade and a heart ruff would have been the inevitable outcome had South not been aware of the danger, and just as important, familiar with the antidote—the

Scissors Coup. Winning the heart in the closed hand, South immediately played the ace, king and ten of clubs. When West followed low to the third round declarer ditched his singleton diamond, and that was the end of the defense.

The following hand was also played at local club level.

```
                    ♠ J 9 7
                    ♥ 7 2
                    ♦ K J 6 4 2
                    ♣ A Q 10
    ♠ 4 2                          ♠ A 3
    ♥ K Q 10 9                     ♥ A J 8 6 4
    ♦ Q 7 3                        ♦ A 10 9 8 5
    ♣ 8 7 6 3                      ♣ 4
                    ♠ K Q 10 8 6 5
                    ♥ 5 3
                    ♦ –
                    ♣ K J 9 5 2
```

This was a fairly typical bidding sequence:

West	North	East	South
–	Pass	1♥	1♠
2♥	3♠	4♥	4♠
Pass	Pass	Dble	All Pass

They seem to have judged this well—or have they? Four hearts looks a warm favorite (only an inspired defense will crack it—a club lead and a diamond ruff, with a spade and diamond trick to come), while four spades can hardly be expensive—perhaps one down on a club ruff. Anyway, this is what happened at one table. West led the king of hearts, which East overtook with the ace to play his singleton club. Declarer won in dummy and tried the effect of the king of diamonds. East followed with the ace and South smartly discarded his second heart—the Scissors Coup again. With the communications neatly severed South only had to knock out the ace of trumps and draw the remainder as soon as he regained the lead. Plus 790 earned North/South a barrel-load of matchpoints.

My next hand comes from a teams-of-four match.

```
                    ♠ 10 5
                    ♥ J 9 7 5
                    ♦ A K Q J 10
                    ♣ A 2
    ♠ A K 7 3                      ♠ Q J 8 4 2
    ♥ 3                            ♥ K Q 2
    ♦ 9 7 5 4 3                    ♦ 8
    ♣ J 8 3                        ♣ Q 10 7 5
                    ♠ 9 6
                    ♥ A 10 8 6 4
                    ♦ 6 2
                    ♣ K 9 6 4
```

In one room the defense against four hearts by South left something to be desired. West cashed both top spades and switched to a club. Declarer won in dummy and ran the jack

of hearts, thus South lost just three tricks.

In the other room, where the defense was a little more imaginative, this was the bidding:

West	North	East	South
–	–	Pass	Pass
Pass	1♦	Dble	1♥
1♠	3♥	3♠	4♥
All Pass			

West started with the ace of spades and received the thumbs down (the two) from his partner. Interpreting the message correctly, West switched to a diamond. South viewed this as a very sinister development which was going to call for careful timing if he was going to avoid a diamond ruff as well as two spades and a trump. The first move was to cash the ace and king of clubs and ruff a club. Now the jack of hearts forced the queen and a fourth round of clubs was ducked to East, dummy discarding the ten of spades. This play—yes, the Scissors Coup again—left East powerless to take more than one additional trick, the king of hearts. No swing, but South in room two needed his wits about him to counter a strong defense.

The last hand illustrates the Scissors Coup in a slightly different way—not to stop a ruff, but to prevent a fragile holding from being attacked.

```
                    ♠ Q 9 7
                    ♥ A Q 10 9 3
                    ♦ A 6
                    ♣ 8 6 3
    ♠ A 5                          ♠ –
    ♥ K 8 7 4                      ♥ J 6 5
    ♦ Q 8 4 2                      ♦ K J 10 5 3
    ♣ A 10 5                       ♣ Q J 9 4 2
                    ♠ K J 10 8 6 4 3 2
                    ♥ 2
                    ♦ 9 7
                    ♣ K 7
```

West	North	East	South
1NT	Pass	2♦	3♠
Pass	4♠	All Pass	

West led the two of diamonds, and declarer saw the danger of losing one spade, one diamond and two clubs. It seemed probable that West held the ace of clubs, so a plan was needed to keep East off lead. The ace of diamonds and ace of hearts took the first two tricks and then came the key play—the queen of hearts, South discarding his second diamond. West won this trick and continued diamonds, ruffed by South. The contract was still far from secure, but a spade to dummy's nine, West electing to duck, and the ten of hearts covered by the jack was the answer for which declarer had hoped and planned. South ruffed this trick and exited with a spade. The best West could do now was to cash the ace of clubs—the defenders' third and last trick.

What is interesting about the Scissors Coup is that, while it is not particularly high on the frequency chart, it is often the only way to salvage an otherwise doomed contract from the jaws of defeat. Worth a little study.

THE DEVIL'S COUP

Star Rating: *

The Devil's Coup is not unlike a card trick where mysteriously a "certain" trump trick gets spirited away. Well, see what you think.

You and your partner hold these trumps between you:

Q6 *opposite* J52

If you don't do anything crazy are you not sure to make one trick? Well, it seems like it—but there are ways of making "certain" tricks disappear when the cards lie favorably. Just see what happened on the following hand:

```
              ♠ A 9
              ♥ K 9 3
              ♦ 9 7 4
              ♣ 9 6 5 4 3
♠ 7 5 3                    ♠ J 10 4 2
♥ Q 6                      ♥ J 5 2
♦ Q J 10                   ♦ A K 8 5 2
♣ A Q J 10 2               ♣ 8
              ♠ K Q 8 6
              ♥ A 10 8 7 4
              ♦ 6 3
              ♣ K 7
```

In Room 1, West opened the bidding with one no trump and was allowed to play there. North led a club and West had no difficulty taking nine tricks.

In Room 2, this was the bidding:

West	North	East	South
1♣	Pass	1♦	Double
2♦	Dble(*)	Pass	2♥
Pass	Pass	3♦	Pass
Pass	3♥	All Pass	

(*) Showing some values

The diamond queen was led and overtaken by East to play his singleton club. West cashed a second club, East discarding a diamond, and then continued with the jack and ten of diamonds, declarer ruffing the third round. Having lost four tricks already, declarer's prospects did not look too good. However, a spade was led to the ace and a club ruffed in hand, East mistakenly discarding his last diamond rather than a spade. The king and queen of spades were now cashed to leave the following position:

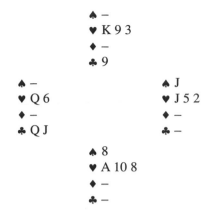

When the eight of spades was played West might have tried ruffing with the queen of hearts, but that would have left an easy finesse against East's jack. In fact West threw a club, dummy ruffed with the three of hearts and led the nine of clubs. Now East was under pressure—to ruff high or low. Not that it mattered, for declarer had already correctly assessed the position. In practice East ruffed low, South overruffed and drew trumps. Three hearts just made.

In this case South needed a little cooperation from East with discards, but frequently this is quite unnecessary, as we shall see on the next hand. From declarer's point of view the mechanics for success remain constant. Don't draw trumps. Cash your side winners and shorten your trumps. In the endgame you must not have more than three trumps and two is often better.

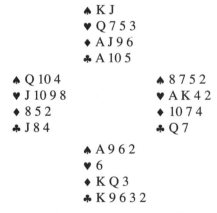

It is probably best to draw a veil over the bidding at one of the tables; suffice it to say that playing pairs, the North/South players needed a top, which may account for the ambitious final contract of six clubs by South.

Against six clubs West led the jack of hearts and continued the suit when the jack was allowed to hold. Declarer's prospects looked bleak, but South perked up considerably when everyone followed to the king and ace of spades, a spade ruff, a heart ruff, three rounds of diamonds and one more heart ruff. This left the following position with South to play:

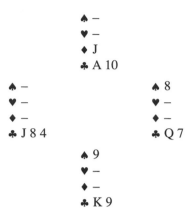

♠ —
♥ —
♦ J
♣ A 10

♠ —   ♠ 8
♥ —   ♥ —
♦ —   ♦ —
♣ J 8 4   ♣ Q 7

♠ 9
♥ —
♦ —
♣ K 9

The nine of spades was led placing West in an unenviable position. West tried ruffing with the jack but dummy simply overruffed and then picked up East's queen of trumps on the way back.

Well, we've now seen what to look for when trying to recognize a Devil's Coup. The trump holding will consist of eight cards missing the queen and jack and these honors will be split. Assuming that you don't intend to play for a doubleton QJ, or a singleton honor, you will have to embark on the Devil's Coup if you are to avoid losing a trump trick. Obviously you need the cards to be well placed for your purposes, but when up against it that is the very moment to make this assumption.

My last hand comes from the Aunt Agatha collection:

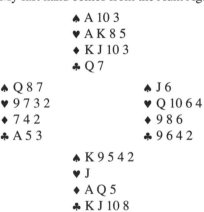

♠ A 10 3
♥ A K 8 5
♦ K J 10 3
♣ Q 7

♠ Q 8 7   ♠ J 6
♥ 9 7 3 2   ♥ Q 10 6 4
♦ 7 4 2   ♦ 9 8 6
♣ A 5 3   ♣ 9 6 4 2

♠ K 9 5 4 2
♥ J
♦ A Q 5
♣ K J 10 8

After a strong no trump opening by North (16-18 points), South bulldozed his way to six spades. West led the ace and another club, hoping that he might also make a trump trick. The ace of hearts and a heart ruff were followed by two more heart ruffs—dummy being entered each time with a diamond—which, of course, included the king of hearts. Now the ace of diamonds and king of clubs were cashed, dummy discarding the last diamond, to leave the following position. South to play having lost just one trick:

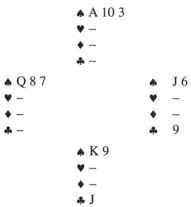

♠ A 10 3
♥ —
♦ —
♣ —

♠ Q 8 7   ♠ J 6
♥ —   ♥ —
♦ —   ♦ —
♣ —   ♣ 9

♠ K 9
♥ —
♦ —
♣ J

When the jack of clubs was played West could see that it was no use ruffing with a small trump, so he played the queen. Dummy won with the ace and now a straight finesse against the jack landed an exciting contract.

It would be wrong to suggest that the Devil's Coup is likely to be a frequent visitor to your bridge table. It won't be, but it is nice to know how to handle the situation when the occasion arises.

Smother Play

Star Rating: *

Having just explained the Devil's Coup, it seems logical to continue with Smother Play, because the two are closely related—both involve making an apparently certain trump trick disappear. Suppose this is the trump suit:

♠   A 5 4

♠   Q J 10 9 8

You lead the queen and it holds the trick, but when you follow with the jack, although it wins, East shows out. So this is now the position:

♠ A

♠ K 7   ♠ –

♠ 10 9 8

As things stand, you must lose a trick to the king, but suppose you are able to ruff once in your own hand and then throw the lead to East, yielding:

```
              ♠ A
              ♥ –
              ♦ 8
              ♣ –
♠ K 7                    ♠ –
♥ –                      ♥ 9
♦ –                      ♦ –
♣ –                      ♣ 9
              ♠ 10 9
              ♥ –
              ♦ –
              ♣ –
```

Whether East plays a heart or a club is immaterial; South ruffs and West's trump trick vanishes. West can choose the method of his demise either by underruffing, to no purpose, or by playing the king which is then smothered by the ace.

Here is another ending with just a little more work to do. This time hearts are trumps.

```
              ♠ A K 7
              ♥ A
              ♦ 3
              ♣ 7
♠ Q 8 6                  ♠ J 10 5 4
♥ K 7                    ♥ –
♦ –                      ♦ –
♣ 6                      ♣ J 9
              ♠ 9 3
              ♥ 10 9 6
              ♦ –
              ♣ 10
```

Declarer must cash the ace and king of spades and ruff a spade before exiting with his losing club. Once again West's king of trumps is smothered.

So, when it appears that you cannot trap a high trump because it is too well guarded, you need to reduce your trumps to the same number as your opponent, eliminate your side suits and then the defender who is void in trumps must be thrown in to apply the coup de grâce. It is essential that this defender is unable to play a suit held by the declaring side. If all this falls into place you can execute a Smother Play. Let's look at some hands:

Swiss Teams.

```
              ♠ A 8 4
              ♥ J 7 2
              ♦ 9 7 5 2
              ♣ A J 7
♠ K 6 5 2                ♠ 9
♥ A K 10                 ♥ Q 9 8 6 4
♦ 10 8 3                 ♦ Q J 6
♣ Q 10 9                 ♣ 6 5 3 2
              ♠ Q J 10 7 3
              ♥ 5 3
              ♦ A K 4
              ♣ K 8 4
```

At one table West opened 1NT, East removed to two hearts and, rather lamely, everyone passed. East collected seven tricks and was not too dismayed at conceding 50 points. At the other table the North/South players were considerably more aggressive:

West	North	East	South
1NT	Pass	2♥	2♠
Pass	3♠	Pass	4♠
All Pass			

Against four spades West started with three rounds of hearts, declarer ruffing the third round. The queen and jack of spades won the next two tricks, but it was somewhat disconcerting when East showed out on the second round. South's contract now appeared doomed. Two heart losers already, a certain trump and diamond loser, and the club position to resolve. However, declarer was not done yet. He cashed the ace of diamonds, everyone following with small cards, finessed the club successfully and played a diamond to the king. Two top clubs came next which left:

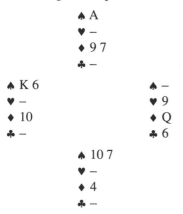

The scene was now set to play a diamond to East's queen. East's next card left his partner without further resource.

No doubt you've noticed that East might have risen to the occasion by unblocking his queen and jack of diamonds. That would have been excellent play on his part and would certainly have saved the day, but let's take nothing away from South's technique.

The next hand created quite a lot of discussion when played in a local pairs event:

```
            ♠ A K 5 2
            ♥ A K 5
            ♦ J 9 2
            ♣ J 10 8
♠ Q J 10 8              ♠ 9 6 3
♥ Q 8 7 4              ♥ 2
♦ 7 4                  ♦ Q 10 8 6 3
♣ 7 5 3                ♣ 9 6 4 2
            ♠ 7 4
            ♥ J 10 9 6 3
            ♦ A K 5
            ♣ A K Q
```

Six no trumps and six hearts were popular contracts, but those who made plus scores were mostly the unambitious players who settled in game. However, at one table, where the contract was six hearts, this is what happened.

West led the spade queen to dummy's ace. The heart ace was followed by the club ace and jack of hearts. West naturally refused to cover, and prospects looked poor. Two top diamonds confirmed declarer's fears that he had a loser in this suit as well. However, the king of spades and a spade ruff were followed by two more rounds of clubs to leave the following:

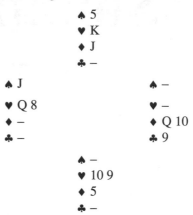

The five of diamonds was led and West could do no better than to discard his spade, leaving East to win his side's first trick. But now, no matter what East played, West's "sure" trump trick was smothered.

My final offering was played by my Aunt Agatha in a team match and, as indeed one might expect, there was something a little unusual about the hand.

```
            ♠ 7 4 2
            ♥ 9 2
            ♦ A 9 3
            ♣ J 7 6 4 3
♠ J 9 8 6              ♠ K Q 10 5 3
♥ 10 8 5              ♥ Q J 7 4 3
♦ K Q 6 4              ♦ –
♣ 9 8                  ♣ Q 10 5
            ♠ A
            ♥ A K 6
            ♦ J 10 8 7 5 2
            ♣ A K 2
```

Against Aunt Agatha's other pair, North/South played in the indifferent contract of 3NT, going one down after an initial spade lead. In Aunt Agatha's room this was the bidding:

West	North	East	South
Pass	Pass	Pass	1♦
Pass	2♦	Dble	5♦
Dble	All Pass		

The six of spades was led and although this contract can be made by a different and perhaps more straightforward route, this is how Aunt Agatha tackled it. At trick two she led a small diamond, and when West played small she called for the nine. A spade ruff followed by the ace and king of hearts, a heart ruff, a second spade ruff and then three rounds of clubs reduced the hand to this position with East to lead:

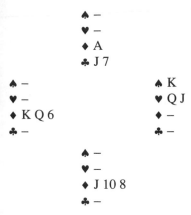

```
                    ♠ —
                    ♥ —
                    ♦ A
                    ♣ J 7
    ♠ —                         ♠ K
    ♥ —                         ♥ Q J
    ♦ K Q 6                     ♦ —
    ♣ —                         ♣ —
                    ♠ —
                    ♥ —
                    ♦ J 10 8
                    ♣ —
```

East had an unenviable choice of plays, but it didn't really matter. Whatever he selected would result in West's second "sure" trump trick disappearing into thin air.

The straightforward line is to play West for the two missing diamond honors. If he splits, take the heart ruff and concede one diamond and one club. If he refuses to split his honors on the first two rounds, turn your attention to clubs. Eventually you will be able to discard a losing heart on a good club. Whatever the merits of this strategy, it must be admitted that Aunt Agatha's solution was as effective as it was elegant.

Chapter 40

Deceptive Plays

Star Rating: ****

In falsecarding, declarer has the immediate advantage of no partner to consider. No one to mislead except the opposition, so there is no limit to the shenanigans available. The repertoire stretches from a tiny piece of deceit, hardly causing a ripple, to a massive psychological coup that results in much gnashing of teeth and one or two red faces as the enormity of the sting unfolds.

Let us start with the minnows. This is a side suit which offers little hope unless you can give the defense a nudge in the right direction—yours.

$$8\ 3\ 2$$
$$A\ K\ 10\ 6 \qquad J\ 9\ 5$$
$$Q\ 7\ 4$$

West leads the ace. East, of course, plays his lowest card, the five, since he has no reason to encourage continuation. However, you follow with the seven. West may now read his partner's five as the beginning of an echo—asking for continuation. If West does continue with the king, your little ruse has worked, for there was no other way that you were going to make your queen. If West refuses to accept the bait, nothing is lost.

The other side of the coin is when you do not wish the suit to be continued:

$$Q\ 10\ 7$$
$$A\ K\ 8\ 6\ 5 \qquad 4\ 3$$
$$J\ 9\ 2$$

Against a suit contract West leads the ace and East starts a high/low with the four. It would be suicidal for declarer to help East by playing the nine. West might well conclude that East had started life with the 4-2. So South follows with the two. West may wonder who has the three but, of course, it could be South. Hopefully West will now switch to another suit.

The rule in these cases is simple enough. If you want the suit continued, start an echo just as you would with your partner. If you don't want continuation, play your lowest card. But you sometimes have to choose your card carefully.

$$K\ 8\ 4\ 2$$
$$3 \qquad A\ Q\ 7\ 6\ 5$$
$$J\ 10\ 9$$

West leads the three of a suit bid by East and you can see that the defense can take the ace, queen and a ruff. However, if South follows with the ten this creates the possibility that West has led from J93. Note that neither the jack nor the nine will do for West would not lead low from either 1093 or J103.

Now suppose you want two tricks from this next combination of cards and there are no other entries to dummy; does it matter which card you play from the South hand?

$$K\ Q\ J\ 7\ 2$$
$$10\ 6\ 4 \qquad A\ 9\ 5$$
$$8\ 3$$

If you play the three, West will follow with his four (his lowest, showing an odd number of cards) and East will have no difficulty in holding off the first round and winning the second. But if you play the eight first, West's four could be the start of a high/low showing a doubleton. Declarer must arrange to continue the suit from dummy so that East cannot be sure of his partner's length. If East ducks again you have achieved your objective.

It is sometimes necessary to play twice from the concealed hand when the control card is on your left and you don't want it held up until the third round.

$$K\ Q\ J\ 3$$
$$A\ 9\ 5 \qquad 10\ 8\ 4$$
$$7\ 6\ 2$$

Here you lead the six to the king and East's four, return to hand and play the seven. If West decides that you had started with the bare 76 and East with 10842, then he will win the ace. Had you led the two originally the defense should not go wrong.

The tip to remember is to make the defender with the control card play to the second trick before his partner, so that the count has not yet been verified.

This is another situation where choice of card is important:

```
            7 4
10 8 6 5 3          J 9 2
            A K Q
```

The defense have not found the killing attack against your 3NT and when you lose the lead again you would like them to continue the suit. The correct card to win with is the king. If you win with the ace this is an obvious falsecard because East would have played the king if he'd had it. If you win with the queen West will know that you also hold the AK. By winning with the king West will be aware that you hold the ace, but the play is consistent with East holding the QJ and that may be enough to get a continuation.

When you want a card covered give the defenders value for money—play the highest card you can afford. When you want to slip a card through without it being covered—play the lowest that will do the job.

1.
```
            A 6 5
K 7 4              3 2
            Q J 10 9 8
```

2.
```
            A K J 3
Q 7 6 4            8 5 2
            10 9
```

1. With no outside entries back to hand, play the queen giving West some excuse for covering. West would be most unlikely to cover one of the lower cards.

2. If it is essential to make four tricks in this suit you will have to find the queen with West. If you play the ten West is sure to cover. Play the nine and you'll probably slip it through.

How would you tackle this hand at any form of scoring?

```
            ♠ A K
            ♥ Q 8 6
            ♦ A Q 8 4
            ♣ 8 5 3 2

            ♠ Q 8
            ♥ A K J 5
            ♦ 6 3 2
            ♣ A 9 7 4
```

South	North
1NT	3NT

The lead is the five of spades. One thing is clear: there is no time to establish the club suit because you would have to lose the lead twice. Meantime your opponents would have established three tricks in spades. Of course, if the diamond king is with West there will be no problem. To give yourself an extra chance that can't possibly cost, you should play a low diamond from dummy at trick two. This would be a reasonable play if you held, say, Jx. No doubt East should duck, even with Kx, but he will certainly be under pressure and will also be anxious to use his entries to establish West's suit. So your little piece of deception might see you home if the full hand were like this:

```
                    ♠ A K
                    ♥ Q 8 6
                    ♦ A Q 8 4
                    ♣ 8 5 3 2
♠ J 10 7 5 4                      ♠ 9 6 3 2
♥ 7 4 2                           ♥ 10 9 3
♦ J 10 5                          ♦ K 9 7
♣ K 6                             ♣ Q J 10
                    ♠ Q 8
                    ♥ A K J 5
                    ♦ 6 3 2
                    ♣ A 9 7 4
```

What is the best chance of not losing a trick from this holding when you have sufficient entries to both hands?

```
J 10 6 5 2

K
```

Yes, you lead to the bare king in the closed hand, but you should play the jack from dummy. If East holds the ace, but not the queen, you may persuade him that you are going to finesse for the queen—so he ducks and goes to bed with his ace.

A similar combination also offers a fine chance for deception. Again you want to get away with not losing a trick from this holding:

```
Q 10 6 3

K
```

The lead of the queen, or better still the ten, from dummy may be enough to create the impression that your own holding is anything but the blank king. If East holds the ace he is more likely to duck than if you play the low card.

Can you possibly restrict your losses to only one trick when playing this combination of cards?

```
9 7 6 4 2

Q J 10 8 3
```

Probably not. At least not legitimately. But you can try leading the queen. A gullible West might be tempted to play the king from Kx, fearful that otherwise the trick might be lost. There is also the chance that the same thing might happen, for different reasons, with West holding Ax. Of course, there is absolutely no excuse for the player holding Kx because declarer would have played quite differently with the AQ, but it costs nothing to try. The success rate is much higher than it should be.

Occasionally, a fairly drastic piece of deception is required if one is to have any hope of landing the spoils.

```
              ♠ J 8 6 2
              ♥ A K 10 9
              ♦ 9 2
              ♣ 10 9 3
♠ A 5                      ♠ K Q 10 7 4
♥ 8 7 3                    ♥ 5 4 2
♦ K 10 8 4 3               ♦ J 7 5
♣ Q 5 2                    ♣ 8 6
              ♠ 9 3
              ♥ Q J 6
              ♦ A Q 6
              ♣ A K J 7 4
```

South	North
1♣	1♥
2NT	3NT

The bidding might not please everyone, but that is how it happened at the table. West led the four of diamonds and declarer could see trouble lurking if the club finesse was wrong and West switched to a spade. So, instead of winning cheaply with the queen, he took East's jack with the ace! The ace of clubs and a heart to dummy heralded the moment of truth when the ten of clubs lost to West's queen. Lured into the belief that East held the queen of diamonds, West continued with a diamond to South's queen. Gratefully the declarer scored up +430. Had the declarer won the first trick with the queen of diamonds West would surely have switched to the ace of spades.

Declarer used a nice piece of deception on the following hand:

```
Pairs.         ♠ Q 7 4 2
               ♥ A J 9 4
               ♦ K J 9 3
               ♣ J
               ♠ 10 8 6 5 3
               ♥ 6
               ♦ A Q 7
               ♣ K Q 10 2
```

West	North	East	South
–	–	1♣	1♠
Pass	4♠	All Pass	

Against South's contract of four spades, West led a club to East's ace. East then switched to the king of hearts. Clearly the only problem was if the spades were 3-1 when there would be a big danger of losing three tricks in the suit. If they were 2-2 any order of play would suffice. In fact,

declarer called for dummy's queen of spades. Not only would this line succeed when West held the lone jack, it might also succeed if East made a mistake. When you see the full hand you'll appreciate the trap that East fell into.

```
              ♠ Q 7 4 2
              ♥ A J 9 4
              ♦ K J 9 3
              ♣ J
♠ A                        ♠ K J 9
♥ 8 7 5 3 2                ♥ K Q 10
♦ 10 5 4 2                 ♦ 8 6
♣ 7 5 4                    ♣ A 9 8 6 3
              ♠ 10 8 6 5 3
              ♥ 6
              ♦ A Q 7
              ♣ K Q 10 2
```

Yes, East covered the queen of spades with his king and when West's bare ace took the trick it was easy for declarer to go to dummy and lead a second spade towards his ten. He lost just one club and two spades.

Finally, a Machiavellian type of deception which is also an old chestnut. But invariably it works today just as it did half a century ago. I doubt if there are many experienced top class players who have failed to succeed with this coup at least two or three times in their bridge lives. Perhaps the reason it is so successful is that it is often difficult for the opponents to spot just what is going on until it is too late.

It is rubber bridge and you play the South cards in three no trumps, after the auction 1NT-3NT. The lead is the ten of spades. What is your plan?

```
              ♠ A 5 3
              ♥ J 10 5
              ♦ A Q J 6
              ♣ J 3 2
♠ 10 9 8 7                 ♠ 6 4 2
♥ A Q 7 3                  ♥ K 8 6 2
♦ 7 5 2                    ♦ 10 3
♣ K 9                      ♣ Q 8 6 5
              ♠ K Q J
              ♥ 9 4
              ♦ K 9 8 4
              ♣ A 10 7 4
```

The spade ten ran around to South's jack, declarer being quite content to confirm that he had this suit buttoned up. Then a diamond to dummy's jack was followed by the jack of hearts! This lost to West's queen and it didn't take West long to emerge with the king of clubs. After all, it looked like declarer was trying to establish his hearts! On the club king East played the six and South the seven. That was enough for West to continue the suit and declarer to score an exciting game.

"Ah, but that was rubber bridge," I can hear you say, "and it probably happened years ago." Correct—about ten years ago, to be precise. All right then, how about this hand from the 1992 U. S. Open Team Trials—the cream of American players in earnest combat. Could there be a better setting?

```
                  ♠ 10 6 5
                  ♥ A J 5 3 2
                  ♦ K 7
                  ♣ 7 5 2
   ♠ A J 7 2                    ♠ 9 8 4 3
   ♥ Q                          ♥ 10 9 8
   ♦ A 2                        ♦ J 10 9
   ♣ A K Q 9 8 6                ♣ J 4 3
                  ♠ K Q
                  ♥ K 7 6 4
                  ♦ Q 8 6 5 4 3
                  ♣ 10
```

In the Open Room the contract was two spades by West, making an over-trick for +140. In the Closed Room Jeff Meckstroth (West) opened with a strong club, diamond negative by East, doubled by South to show diamonds, and then only the black suits were bid until 3NT was reached.

The diamond king was led, won by the ace. With eight tricks on top, how do you suppose Meckstroth went about getting his ninth? Yes, the old chestnut, but it still worked like a charm. He played the heart queen at trick two! North took his ace and played his last diamond to South's queen. And South continued with . . . yes, a third diamond. 3NT made.

I think it was Charles Goren, the great American player, who said, "If you are going to tell a lie, don't stutter." That just about sums up the correct technique for all forms of deceptive play. I wouldn't mind betting that, when Meckstroth played the queen of hearts, he did it quickly, firmly, and with authority!

Safety Plays

Star Rating: ****

Safety Plays is a huge subject. Complete books have been devoted to them, yet there is almost always something more to be said. I shall concentrate on some of the more important examples.

No doubt most declarers think of a safety play as a means of guarding against a bad break in a particular suit. A kind of insurance policy that for a small premium will restrict the losses, and, indeed, this is very often the precise position with which a player is faced. However, there are many situations which come under the Safety Play umbrella which cost not one iota. No insurance to pay at all, just straightforward precaution plays that only demand correct handling. Look at the following:

1.   **West**   **East**

        ♥ K Q 10 6 3   ♥ A 9 4 2

Most players will know this one, since it is the easiest of plays to get right. The king is cashed first to guard against a possible ♥J875 in either hand.

2.   **West**   **East**

        ♥ K Q 8 7 3   ♥ A 9 6 2

Now, it is essential to play the ace first. If North has the four missing cards (♥J1054) nothing can be done about it, but if South has them, assuming plenty of spades back to hand, the suit can be collected without loss.

3.   **West**   **East**

        ♥ A Q 8 6   ♥ J 9 7 5 4 3

The jack should be played first from the East hand. If South has the singleton king or North has the three missing cards, the jack will do no harm. The advantage comes when South holds ♥K102. Now there will be no losers.

4.   **West**   **East**

        ♥ A 10 6 4 3   ♥ K 7 2

Most of the time nothing too dramatic would happen if you cashed the ace and king. With a normal 3-2 break (68 percent), you would lose just one trick. However, South might hold ♥QJxx. To guard against this possibility the king is followed by a small card to the ten when South plays low. If North holds ♥ QJxx there is nothing you can do about it.

5.   **West**   **East**

        ♥A K 10 5 4   ♥6 3 2

This is similar to the last example. Cash the ace first. Go to the East hand and lead low intending to play the ten unless South contributes an honor.

This might be a good moment to consider the different priorities facing a pairs player as opposed to a teams or rubber bridge player. Whereas the latter should always be primarily concerned with making the contract, even if this necessitates taking out an insurance policy which may cost a trick, the pairs player may not be able to afford such a luxury. The pairs player has to consider whether the contract is one that most of the room will reach, or is it a target that only a select few will equal? If the former, a safety play might turn an average plus into an average minus or worse; if the latter, it makes little difference when the safety play proves unnecessary, but collects most of the matchpoints when it turns out to be essential.

Consider the following:

       Dummy   **Declarer**

        ♥K 10 6 3   ♥A 9 8 5 4

Suppose that you are in 4♥ with this trump suit. You have lost two tricks but there are no more outside losers. With four cards outstanding they can only fall 2-2, 3-1 or 4-0. At rubber bridge or teams it is the 4-0 distribution that would demand the declarer's serious consideration. There is a certain safety play to guard against losing more than one trick in the suit. You play a low card from either hand and cover the card played by the next player. Suppose you play the four from hand, the next player plays the eight and dummy the ten. If this loses to the jack or queen the remaining cards will fall under the AK. This cautious approach may cost an extra trick (the outstanding trumps being 2-2 all the time) but that is peanuts to the teams player (possible cost 1IMP) or the rubber bridge player (possible cost 30 points) when the game can be safely underwritten.

The pairs player, however, may well calculate that most of the room will be in four hearts and, since a 4-0 break will only occur about 10 percent of the time, the premium is too expensive.

Before we leave the scene of nine cards missing the QJxx, consider these holdings:

1.   ♥A 9 2   ♥K 10 7 6 4 3
2.   ♥K 3   ♥A 10 9 8 7 6 2

1. This is similar to the previous example. If you wish to guarantee not to lose more than one trick in the suit, you play a low card (not an honor) from either hand and if the next player plays low, you cover. Say the three is led, the next player plays the five, and you call for the nine. North may win a cheap trick but the rest of the suit will present no problems and if North shows out on the nine you will have saved the day.

2. Again you are guarding against two losers in this suit. Maybe you are in a well-bid slam with no outside losers. Play the six and if the next player plays low, run it. This guarantees to hold your losses to just one trick when this is the layout:

♥ –

♥ K 3   ♥ A 10 9 8 7 6 2

♥ Q J 5 4

One everyday holding is something like this:

♥K 9 3   ♥A J 8 6 5

Suppose you can afford to lose one trick but not two. Your correct play is an ace and then small towards dummy, inserting the nine if LHO plays low. If either opponent holds ♥Q10xx you will lose only one trick. The key here is to play the top card first from the suit that contains the jack.

The same principle applies with nine cards missing Q10xx.

♥A 9 3 2   ♥K J 7 5 4

If you play the king first you will not lose more than one trick whatever the distribution of the outstanding cards. Should you make the mistake of playing the ace first, or playing low to the ace, you would lose two tricks when the suit is divided like this:

♥ –

♥A 9 3 2   ♥K J 7 5 4

♥Q 10 8 6

Another everyday situation is like this:

♥10 5 2   ♥A K 8 6 3

You play the ace and LHO follows with the jack. If you can afford to lose one trick but not two, your safety play is to follow with a small card towards dummy. You will be well rewarded when this is the layout:

♥Q 9 7 4

♥10 5 2   ♥A K 8 6 3

♥J

The ten will lose to the queen but North's remaining cards will be picked up when the five is led from dummy on the third round.

The next combination is also high on the frequency charts:

♥A Q 10 7 4   ♥9 6 5 2

If you need five tricks from this suit you will have to play for ♥Kx to be under the ♥AQ, but suppose you need only four. Now the correct play is to cash the ace and then lead towards the queen. The bonus is that you might drop a blank king over dummy resulting in no loss in the suit at all. More important, you avoid the hideous guess on the second round when the queen has just lost to the king. Do you play to drop the jack or do you finesse again? Better to avoid the problem and cash the ace first.

Although it is extremely helpful to be familiar with the common forms of safety play, they can be worked out at the table where other considerations can be taken into account. Once the underlying principles are understood the question of guarding against a bad break will arise automatically.

Obviously it is unwise to embark on a safety play if by doing so you endanger the contract in some way—allowing a ruff, for example. This hand from a match played many years ago illustrates the point:

♠ A K 5 4 3
♥ K 7 2
♦ 6 5 3
♣ K J

♠ J 10 9 7		♠ Q 9 8
♥ Q J 5		♥ 9 8
♦ 7 4		♦ A J 10 9 8
♣ 7 6 4 3		♣ A 10 9 8

♠ 6 2
♥ A 10 6 4 3
♦ K Q 2
♣ Q 5 2

In Room 1, South was the declarer in 3NT after East had bid diamonds. The diamond seven was led and declarer was allowed to win the trick. The hearts were cleared and West led another diamond. East cleared the suit and was then able to regain the lead with the ace of clubs to cash out for one down.

In Room 2, West also led the seven of diamonds, but against four hearts. East won and returned a diamond, and now it was South's big moment. He had recently come to grips with Safety Plays and recognized that by playing a small trump to the king and one back towards his hand he could guard against ♥QJxx with East. So on the second round of hearts it went two, nine, ten, jack. But then West put his partner in with the ace of clubs and ruffed the next diamond with the queen of trumps. One down, no swing!

This hand, from rubber bridge, might cause a problem especially if you have never seen this kind of position before:

```
            ♠ J 4
            ♥ 7 3
            ♦ A K J 7 6 4 2
            ♣ 6 4

            ♠ A 9 8 6
            ♥ A J 9 5
            ♦ 5 3
            ♣ A K 2
```

You, South, open one heart, North bids two diamonds, you rebid 2NT and North raises to three. West leads the queen of clubs which you win. You lead a diamond towards dummy, West plays the ten, and you . . .?

If you put on the jack the finesse was right.

The full hand:

```
            ♠ J 4
            ♥ 7 3
            ♦ A K J 7 6 4 2
            ♣ 6 4
♠ K 7                      ♠ Q 10 5 3 2
♥ 6 2                      ♥ K Q 10 8 4
♦ Q 10 9 8                 ♦ —
♣ Q J 9 7 5                ♣ 10 8 3
            ♠ A 9 8 6
            ♥ A J 9 5
            ♦ 5 3
            ♣ A K 2
```

Well, did you play dummy's jack of diamonds? If so, you have just put the contract on the floor. Unlucky, it's true, but the complete safety play is to play low from dummy in case East has diamond void. Perhaps it is worth mentioning that a "high flyer" in the West seat would follow with the ♦Q on the first round—giving you the maximum temptation to err!

Chapter 42

Counting

Star Rating: *****

Counting the hand is one of the most difficult tasks facing bridge players. It is also one of the most neglected. A beginner starts life by failing to count anything at all. When it comes to the last trick there is often an excited expectancy because no one is quite sure who is going to win it. Of course, all this uncertainty adds to the great aura of mystery, excitement and suspense that pervades the game, and in some ways it seems almost criminal to remove such obvious pleasure in flirting with the unknown. However, if progress is to be made, there are hurdles to be jumped and the first one the beginner tackles is the trump suit. Perhaps tired of coming to grief by taking an extra round for "lurkers," a conscious effort is made to count trumps. Not too exacting a task and one that quickly becomes routine.

From then on it gets a little harder. The points that a player holds, deduced initially from the bidding, should be next on the agenda. This is not too troublesome once you get used to it. Counting the points can be extremely profitable to declarer in situations like the following:

♠ J 10 5 2
♥ Q 3
♦ K J 6 2
♣ A 3 2

♠ A Q 9 8 6
♥ 8 6
♦ A 5 3
♣ K Q 4

West	North	East	South
Pass	Pass	Pass	1♠
Pass	3♠	Pass	4♠
All Pass			

West led the heart ace followed by the king. He then switched to the jack of clubs won by dummy's ace. Superficially, the contract appears to depend on one of two finesses. The spade king with East or the diamond queen with West. At trick four declarer took the spade finesse, but that lost to

West's king. Declarer won the club continuation and the spade ace drew the outstanding trumps. So, it was time for the second finesse—or was it?

Careful players who count points would have observed that West had already turned up with eleven points and, having passed originally, West was most unlikely to hold the queen of diamonds as well. Playing for doubleton queens with six cards missing is normally something to be avoided, like overpaying your taxes. However, the unlikely should always be preferred to the (almost) impossible and declarer had no illusions about his best chance. He cashed the ace and king of diamonds dropping the queen.

$$
\begin{array}{c}
\spadesuit\ J\ 10\ 5\ 2 \\
\heartsuit\ Q\ 3 \\
\diamondsuit\ K\ J\ 6\ 2 \\
\clubsuit\ A\ 3\ 2
\end{array}
$$

♠ K 4   ♠ 7 3
♥ A K 9 5   ♥ J 10 7 4 2
♦ 10 9 5 4   ♦ Q 7
♣ J 10 8   ♣ 9 7 6 5

♠ A Q 9 8 6
♥ 8 6
♦ A 5 3
♣ K Q 4

The full hand reveals how careful counting rescued this contract from the scrap heap labeled "Sorry, partner. All my finesses were wrong."

The last obstacle to be negotiated is more like a Grand National fence than a mere hurdle, or so it seems. Counting the distribution is the name of this particular game. Top class players tend to count everything so that at any given time they can usually tell if a hand is, say, 5-4-2-2 or 5-4-3-1, and which key cards that player holds.

So how important is this counting exercise? In truth there are many hands played where it does not matter much whether you count or not. Perhaps a shrewd guess would suffice. And, indeed, that is how many contestants play their bridge, even those heavily involved in tournaments. I've even heard some old-time internationals admit that they no longer count the hand. This strikes me as a very great pity for there is much satisfaction and enjoyment in being able to build up an accurate picture of the deal. Furthermore, it is frequently the only sure way to come up with the right answer.

Well, how difficult is it, and can you take any short cuts? The preliminary count starts during the auction and a player should get used to counting in multiples of thirteen. It is much easier to build a complete picture of the distribution, say 5-4-3-1, than to start by counting the cards, one by one, as they are played. That method would give a bottle of aspirin a headache.

♠ 7 6 4 2
♥ J 5
♦ K 8 4
♣ Q J 10 9

♠ A 5 3
♥ A K Q
♦ A Q 10 2
♣ A K 6

South	North
2♣	2♦
3NT	4NT
6NT	

South's rebid showed 25+ points and North's raise was quantitative—an invitation that South was delighted to accept. West led the king of spades.

You have eleven winners on top, with a great chance of making an extra trick in diamonds (if West has length in diamonds and spades he can be squeezed). The essential factor here is to get a count of the distribution—so there is no sitting this one out. A guess might not be good enough.

Since there is one losing spade, regardless of the distribution, we duck the first round, East following with the nine. West continues with the spade queen and East discards the two of hearts. So the first part of the jigsaw is that West started with five spades. Usually it is only necessary to count one of the defender's hands and since five of West's cards are now known, concentrate on him. You win trick two with the ace of spades and cash three hearts, everyone following. Then four rounds of clubs, discarding a spade. West follows to three clubs so you know he started with five spades, three clubs and at least three hearts, so he can hold no more than two diamonds.

The rest is simple. The ace of diamonds is followed by the king and then the ten of diamonds is finessed with complete confidence.

The full deal:

                ♠ 7 6 4 2
                ♥ J 5
                ♦ K 8 4
                ♣ Q J 10 9
♠ K Q J 10 8   ♠ 9
♥ 9 6 3   ♥ 10 8 7 4 2
♦ 7 3   ♦ J 9 6 5
♣ 8 4 2   ♣ 7 5 3
                ♠ A 5 3
                ♥ A K Q
                ♦ A Q 10 2
                ♣ A K 6

Sometimes there is just one tiny part of the jigsaw missing. You have counted carefully and know all the answers except for that one piece that would complete the picture. When this happens, go back over the bidding. So often there is a vital clue available that will solve your problem.

Consider this hand from a world championship match back in the mid-eighties with East/West vulnerable:

                ♠ 8 2
                ♥ Q J 6 3
                ♦ K Q 10 7 3
                ♣ A 6
♠ A Q 10 9 6 5   ♠ 7 4 3
♥ K 5   ♥ 10 9 8 2
♦ J 8 4   ♦ 5 2
♣ 5 4   ♣ 8 7 3 2
                ♠ K J
                ♥ A 7 4
                ♦ A 9 6
                ♣ K Q J 10 9

West	North	East	South
–	Pass	Pass	1♣
1♠	2♦	Pass	2♥
2♠	4♥	Pass	4NT
Pass	5♦	Pass	6NT
All Pass			

West found the good diamond lead against 6NT. With the benefit of seeing all four hands, it is easy to see that all finesses are out. The key to success—marked on the bidding—is to throw West in at trick eleven to lead away from the king of hearts. It is dummy to play and this is the end-game visualized:

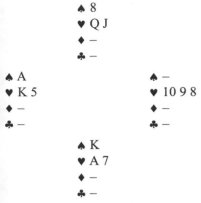

♠ 8
♥ Q J
♦ —
♣ —

♠ A   ♠ —
♥ K 5   ♥ 10 9 8
♦ —   ♦ —
♣ —   ♣ —

♠ K
♥ A 7
♦ —
♣ —

In fact this is exactly what declarer planned and I believe that most expert declarers would follow the same route. But West was still at the party and could tell where the hand was heading. So, planning to camouflage the hand, West discarded the five of hearts early, baring the king, and later the ten and queen of spades, leaving:

♠ 8
♥ Q J
♦ —
♣ —

♠ A 9   ♠ —
♥ K   ♥ 10 9 8
♦ —   ♦ —
♣ —   ♣ —

♠ K
♥ A 7
♦ —
♣ —

Declarer knew that West had started life with three diamonds and two clubs, and either two hearts and six spades or three hearts and five spades. West certainly did a good job in disguising the position and he was rewarded when declarer played a spade, hoping to make the last two tricks in hearts.

In this kind of dilemma the bidding will often indicate the answer, so let's go back and see. West was vulnerable, bid spades twice and only had an outside king to boost his assets. Surely this shrieks of a six-card suit. Indeed, from the comfort of your armchair the evidence is quite overwhelming.

On the next hand, declarer could not obtain an exact count, but, as so often happens, an inferential count was enough to put him on the winning line.

♠ J 9 3 2
♥ 9 7 3 2
♦ 4
♣ J 10 8 3

♠ A K 5
♥ —
♦ A K Q J 9 6 5
♣ A K 6

West	North	East	South
Pass	Pass	3♥	4♥
Pass	4♠	Pass	6♦
All Pass			

West led the heart king, East played the ace and South ruffed. On the AKQ of trumps East followed twice and then discarded a heart. Everyone followed to both the black aces. How should declarer continue?

It seems likely that East started with seven hearts because with an eight-card suit East might have opened four hearts. The lead of the king is also consistent with a holding of Kx. East has shown two diamonds, one spade and one club. So, if the inferential heart count is correct, there are just two cards unaccounted for in East's hand. They could include a black-suit queen, but the odds are heavily in favor of West holding them both. If South decides to cash the black kings he will be unlucky. The full hand:

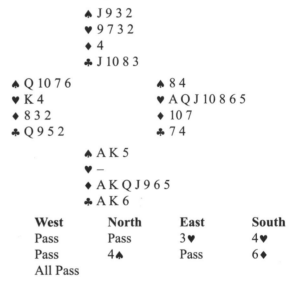

♠ J 9 3 2
♥ 9 7 3 2
♦ 4
♣ J 10 8 3

♠ Q 10 7 6   ♠ 8 4
♥ K 4   ♥ A Q J 10 8 6 5
♦ 8 3 2   ♦ 10 7
♣ Q 9 5 2   ♣ 7 4

♠ A K 5
♥ —
♦ A K Q J 9 6 5
♣ A K 6

West	North	East	South
Pass	Pass	3♥	4♥
Pass	4♠	Pass	6♦
All Pass			

In fact South decided that there was a better way of playing than to hope for a doubleton queen of spades or clubs. With West marked with length in the black suits an endplay seemed a much better bet, so he continued to cash his diamonds to reach this position:

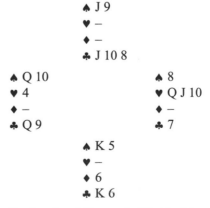

♠ J 9
♥ —
♦ —
♣ J 10 8

♠ Q 10   ♠ 8
♥ 4   ♥ Q J 10
♦ —   ♦ —
♣ Q 9   ♣ 7

♠ K 5
♥ —
♦ 6
♣ K 6

On the six of diamonds West had to part with his heart while dummy played the eight of clubs and East the ten of hearts. Declarer now had the choice of playing the king and another spade or king and another club. Either way West would take just one trick and concede the last two.

The last hand is something of a classic and appears in *Tiger Bridge Revisited*. Featuring the late Kenneth Konstam, world champion and sparkling dummy player, it is such a fine example of the need to count that it bears repetition.

```
        ♠ 7 4
        ♥ A 8
        ♦ Q 7 4
        ♣ A Q J 10 9 4

        ♠ A K 5 2
        ♥ K 5
        ♦ A K 10 9 6
        ♣ 7 2
```

West	North	East	South
			Konstam
–	–	3♠	3NT
Pass	7NT	All Pass	

Obviously North had great faith in Konnie. It was not misplaced.

The queen of hearts was led and won in dummy. Superficially, there seemed no way of avoiding the club finesse, but before committing himself Konstam played the ace and queen of diamonds. West discarded a heart on the second diamond and another heart when Konstam took the marked diamond finesse. The ace of spades was cashed and again

West discarded a heart. Now the king of hearts was cashed and East threw a spade. What's next?

If you've made up your mind, here is the full hand:

```
              ♠ 7 4
              ♥ A 8
              ♦ Q 7 4
              ♣ A Q J 10 9 4

  ♠ –                       ♠ Q J 10 9 8 6 3
  ♥ Q J 10 9 7 4 3 2        ♥ 6
  ♦ 8                       ♦ J 6 3 2
  ♣ 8 6 5 3                 ♣ K

              ♠ A K 5 2
              ♥ K 5
              ♦ A K 10 9 6
              ♣ 7 2
```

Konstam had a complete count of East's hand: seven spades, one heart, four diamonds and, therefore, one club. With four clubs marked in the West hand Konstam knew that he could not pick up the king if West held this card. Thus the only viable chance was to play for the singleton king! Renowned for his speed of play, Konstam hardly paused at all before leading a club to dummy's ace. When the king fell he spread his cards.

Was it imagination or did East keep his cards very close to his chest for the remainder of the round?! He need not have bothered. Good players count. They don't need to peek.

The Principle of Restricted Choice

Star Rating: ✱✱✱

In the early 1950's, Alan Truscott propounded the underlying Principle of Restricted Choice. Truscott's ideas were published in a magazine article, but it was left to Terence Reese to polish and explain it to a much wider readership. This he did through several of his books around that time. In particular, there is a chapter devoted to this principle in that great classic *The Expert Game,* a book which every ambitious player should read.

Those unfamiliar with the Principle of Restricted Choice (PRC) might consider the following problem to be a tough one:

K 10 8 6

A 9 5 4 3

South, the declarer, cannot afford to lose a trick in this suit, but when the ace is cashed, East follows with the jack. What next? Should South take a finesse, hoping that West started with Qxx, or play the king, hoping East started with the bare QJ?

With nine cards between the combined hands the *a priori* expectation after one round has been played is a 2-2 division. But in this case to play for the drop would be wrong. The two relevant holdings to consider are the bare jack and the queen jack. Holding the QJ alone, East would have a choice of cards to play on the first round and would play the queen some of the time—perhaps half the time. With the lone jack he would have no choice. Thus the fact that East played the jack affords the presumption that he had no option (if East had played the queen the same argument would apply) and declarer should finesse West for the queen. Surprisingly, perhaps, the odds are about 2-1 in favor of the finesse.

While this situation used to be regarded as something of a guess in days of yore, the finesse is more or less automatic in the modern game—assuming that there is no other pertinent piece of information available. The logic is simple enough. With a choice of plays, the player under the

microscope might select either one. This lends weight to the presumption that the player had no option.

Another frequent combination is this:

Dummy
A J 9 8 5

10 6 3 2

A first round finesse loses the king. When South plays the suit again West follows with a small card. Should declarer now finesse or play for the drop? The PRC is again relevant and the finesse is a firm favorite.

It is perhaps important to emphasize that the PRC gives a player a clear mathematical advantage (nearly 2-1 in favor) in the right circumstances. And the right circumstances are when two cards of equal rank could be played (e.g. the king or queen, the queen or jack, the jack or ten). Then the finesse against the remaining honor is the percentage play providing there is no more concrete evidence available. The next two hands illustrate this point.

♠ K 6 3
♥ A 9 6 4
♦ K 5
♣ 10 8 6 2

♠ Q 10 4 2
♥ K Q 2
♦ A 4
♣ K Q J 9

The popular contract was three no trumps by South. Whether the partnership bid all their suits or opted for a single 1♣-1♥-2NT-3NT, the opening lead was unaffected as the queen of diamonds was a fairly obvious choice. At trick two East wins the ace of clubs and knocks out declarer's last diamond. With only eight tricks on top, and no time to establish a spade winner, declarer has to rely on four tricks from hearts. But first he cashes the clubs. East discards two spades on the third and fourth rounds while West follows three times and then discards the nine of spades.

On the king and queen of hearts West follows with the five and seven and East with the three and jack. Declarer has now reached the critical point of the hand. Should he finesse dummy's nine of hearts or call for dummy's ace? Those declarers who were familiar with PRC had no doubts. They finessed and were well rewarded when the full hand was as follows:

```
              ♠ K 6 3
              ♥ A 9 6 4
              ♦ K 5
              ♣ 10 8 6 2
♠ A 9                        ♠ J 8 7 5
♥ 10 8 7 5                   ♥ J 3
♦ Q J 9 6                    ♦ 10 8 7 6 2
♣ 5 4 3                      ♣ A 7
              ♠ Q 10 4 2
              ♥ K Q 2
              ♦ A 4
              ♣ K Q J 9
```

Holding the J103 of hearts East might have chosen to follow with the ten on the second round. Without this card he would have no option thus the PRC leans heavily in favor of the finesse. This hand from a pairs contest may act as a warning for the unwary:

```
              ♠ A J 10
              ♥ 7 5
              ♦ K 7 3
              ♣ A 9 8 7 5

              ♠ K Q 9 8
              ♥ A 3
              ♦ A Q J 6
              ♣ K 10 3
```

West	North	East	South
2♥*	Pass	Pass	Dble
Pass	3♥	Pass	3♠
Pass	4♣	Pass	4NT
Pass	5♥	Pass	6NT

* Weak two, 5-9 points

Although six clubs would have been a better contract, South decided to go for gold. Six no trumps is not a good proposition but South liked his card play. The king of hearts was led and ducked, East following with the two. West continued with the queen of hearts, East playing the four. Declarer now started to cash his winners in spades and diamonds. West failed to follow to the second spade, but the diamonds broke 3-3. West's four discards were the J1086 of hearts, while East parted with the nine of hearts on the fourth diamond. When the club king was cashed, West played the two and East the jack. Declarer had to make up his mind whether to finesse in clubs or whether to play for the drop.

Without giving the matter much thought, declarer announced to the table that he knew all about the Principle of Restricted Choice and promptly took the club finesse, losing to East's queen! To add insult to injury, East then cashed the seven of spades for two down. This was the full deal:

```
              ♠ A J 10
              ♥ 7 5
              ♦ K 7 3
              ♣ A 9 8 7 5
♠ 5                          ♠ 7 6 4 3 2
♥ K Q J 10 8 6               ♥ 9 4 2
♦ 10 9 8                     ♦ 5 4 2
♣ 6 4 2                      ♣ Q J
              ♠ K Q 9 8
              ♥ A 3
              ♦ A Q J 6
              ♣ K 10 3
```

What this declarer had overlooked was a perfect count of the hand. East had shown five spades, three hearts and three diamonds so he had to have two clubs. When the jack of clubs was played on the first round the only possible holding for East that makes any sense is the bare QJ. Had South realized this instead of falling for an overwhelming desire to trot out his technical knowledge, he would have played the ace of clubs and then a very fortunate contract would have been landed. Note that West played well by discarding all his hearts. He knew his partner had three (the two followed by the four) and he wanted to make the play of the club suit as obscure as possible.

Perhaps the moral is this: however good the principle, the theories, the inferences and the mathematical odds, nothing compares with an exact count.

Squeezes

THE SIMPLE SQUEEZE

Star Rating: ***

If Ely Culbertson had invented the term "squeeze" I would have suspected a smidgen of suggestive innuendo. In fact, until recently I was under the impression that it was Culbertson who was responsible. But after a little research I find that it was Sidney Lenz, just as famous a character in his era, but perhaps not the provocative showman and impresario extraordinaire that was the hallmark of the irrepressible Ely.

The squeeze has had many names since it was first discovered in the early days of whist, but there is no doubt that Sidney Lenz's name is extremely apt. The implication is that you are being pushed into a corner with no room to move so that you are forced to capitulate, one way or another. Indeed, you are squeezed into submission.

Looked at another way, if you give a player two important tasks to do at the same time he simply won't be able to do both. Could you keep a dinner engagement at Antoine's in New Orleans at the same time as a similar engagement at Maxim's in Paris? Obviously not, and that is the sort of dilemma that faces a player who is being squeezed.

Unfortunately, the very term "squeeze" frightens many players from the arena. They have come to believe, or have been conditioned to believe, that such plays are only for experts and lesser mortals should not bother their heads about such esoteric gambits. The truth is far removed from this particular conception, for in reality a simple squeeze is much easier to execute than most low-level part scores.

Suppose you are South in six no trumps needing the remainder of the tricks to fulfill your contract. It is your lead and these are the cards that are left:

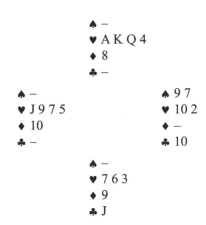

When you play the jack of clubs, West is like the person trying to be in New Orleans and Paris at the same time. How can he possibly hold on to the ten of diamonds, yet remain in control of the heart suit as well? Obviously it is impossible. He is squeezed!

Let's look at the full hand and see what might have gone wrong at an earlier stage had South been unfamiliar with the mechanics of a squeeze.

```
              ♠ 10 8
              ♥ A K Q 4
              ♦ A 8 5
              ♣ 9 6 5 3
♠ A 5 2                      ♠ 9 7 6 4 3
♥ J 9 8 5                    ♥ 10 2
♦ Q J 10 6 2                 ♦ 7 3
♣ 4                          ♣ 10 8 7 2
              ♠ K Q J
              ♥ 7 6 3
              ♦ K 9 4
              ♣ A K Q J
```

The lead is the queen of diamonds. Making a preliminary analysis, declarer would no doubt think "As soon as I've knocked out the ace of spades I'll have just eleven tricks on top so I'll need the hearts to break 3-3." Thus declarer wins the diamond lead, plays the king of spades to West's ace and wins the diamond continuation. Now, anxious to find out if the hearts do in fact divide evenly, he plays off the top three honors. Unlucky; the suit doesn't break and the endgame will look like this:

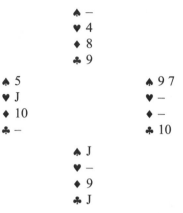

The jack of spades is cashed and is followed by the jack of clubs, but West is not bothered, and throws the jack of hearts without a care in the world. Dummy is dead and West is no longer under pressure. All West has to do is to keep the ten of diamonds and the slam is defeated.

So what went wrong? If a squeeze is going to operate you must have a link to both hands. If you break that link prematurely the squeeze is aborted. Declarer should have thought "If the hearts are breaking 3-3 now, they will also be breaking 3-3 later, so I had better not cut our communications." Of course, it is perfectly in order to take just two rounds of hearts, leaving the link to both hands intact, so that this could then be the end position:

```
              ♠ –
              ♥ Q 4
              ♦ –
              ♣ 9
♠ –                        ♠ 9 7
♥ J 9                      ♥ –
♦ 10                       ♦ –
♣ –                        ♣ 10
              ♠ –
              ♥ 7
              ♦ 9
              ♣ J
```

The lead of the jack of clubs still leaves West without resource.

So, you've discovered that you must have a link to the long suit and, of course, that one player needs to guard two suits. Another essential requirement is that there are no spare cards around for the defender who is being squeezed to discard. For example:

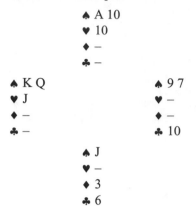

Diamonds are trumps and it is South to lead. When the three of diamonds is played, West can retire since there is no safe discard to make. Dummy is poised to take advantage of whichever card West chooses to abandon. If it is a spade, the ten of hearts is thrown, while if it is the jack of hearts, then the ten of spades is jettisoned. But suppose everyone had a small club—a trick that had not been lost earlier on—then this would be the position:

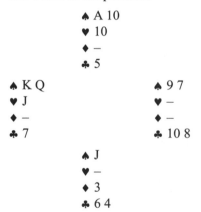

Now, when the three of diamonds is played, West can discard the seven of clubs and the squeeze fails. So, because of that spare card, declarer has dropped a trick, and will make only two out of the last four instead of three out of three. If that club trick had been lost earlier, then the squeeze would be watertight.

Not having superfluous cards around in the endgame means that when we are going to play for a squeeze we must lose what we can afford to lose early on. This is called rectifying the count, but don't let that name frighten you since the technique is simplicity itself.

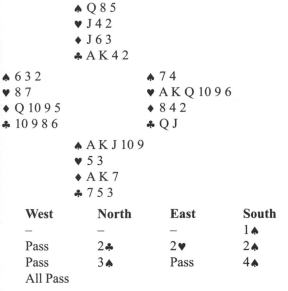

♠ Q 8 5
♥ J 4 2
♦ J 6 3
♣ A K 4 2

♠ 6 3 2   ♠ 7 4
♥ 8 7   ♥ A K Q 10 9 6
♦ Q 10 9 5   ♦ 8 4 2
♣ 10 9 8 6   ♣ Q J

♠ A K J 10 9
♥ 5 3
♦ A K 7
♣ 7 5 3

West	North	East	South
–	–	–	1♠
Pass	2♣	2♥	2♠
Pass	3♠	Pass	4♠
All Pass			

South plays in four spades after East has bid hearts on the first round. West leads the eight of hearts. East wins the first two hearts, but the third round is ruffed by South, West discarding the five of diamonds.

Superficially, since there are only nine tricks on top, South's prospects seem to depend on the clubs dividing 3-3 or the queen of diamonds being doubleton. In fact there is another live chance—that West holds four clubs plus the queen of diamonds. If so, West can be squeezed. In any case, trumps are drawn in three rounds and a low club played from both hands, East winning the queen.

Whatever the division of the clubs, you had to lose one sometime. In doing so now you have kept all your options open while at the same time rectifying the count for a squeeze should one exist (i.e. there will be no loose cards floating around in the endgame).

Let's say East switches to a diamond. Declarer wins the ace and continues with the king, but the queen does not appear. so the position at this point is as follows:

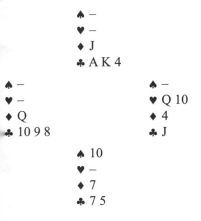

♠ –
♥ –
♦ J
♣ A K 4

♠ –   ♠ –
♥ –   ♥ Q 10
♦ Q   ♦ 4
♣ 10 9 8   ♣ J

♠ 10
♥ –
♦ 7
♣ 7 5

South plays the ten of spades. This is the squeeze card—the card that finally forces West into submission. You'll notice that all West's cards are busy—busy in the sense that he cannot spare any of them, yet West has to play one. If the queen of diamonds is thrown, dummy throws the four of clubs; if a club is thrown, dummy throws the jack of diamonds. In either case dummy will be high.

Let's try again, looking at the North/South cards only this time.

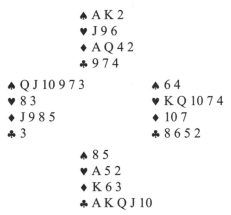

♠ A K 2
♥ J 9 6
♦ A Q 4 2
♣ 9 7 4

♠ 8 5
♥ A 5 2
♦ K 6 3
♣ A K Q J 10

South arrives in no trumps, leaving nothing unbid, and receives the lead of the queen of spades. At first glance it seems that the only realistic chance of success is a 3-3 diamond break which is, of course, against the odds. There is a remote chance of the ♥KQ being bare. But what about the two of spades? "Well, what about it? That's if you are being serious," I hear you saying. Yes, I am being serious, because if West by any chance has six spades the two may be a thorn in his side (it is called a menace card) when the final crunch comes. But if West is to be in trouble then he, and not East, will have to hold four diamonds. In any case, the plan is straightforward. You need to lose a trick to rectify the count and the only suit in which you can do this is the heart suit. So, you take the ace of spades and play a low heart from both hands. Time to see the full deal:

♠ A K 2
♥ J 9 6
♦ A Q 4 2
♣ 9 7 4

♠ Q J 10 9 7 3   ♠ 6 4
♥ 8 3   ♥ K Q 10 7 4
♦ J 9 8 5   ♦ 10 7
♣ 3   ♣ 8 6 5 2

♠ 8 5
♥ A 5 2
♦ K 6 3
♣ A K Q J 10

As you lead the six of hearts from the table, East will no doubt insert the ten, and after winning the trick continue with either the king of hearts or another spade. Let's say East returns West's suit, the king of spades winning in dummy. Declarer now cashes the ace of hearts and the five top clubs. This is the position before the last club is played:

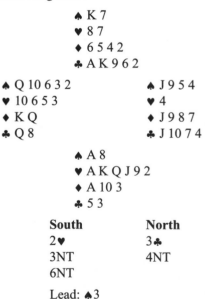

```
            ♠ 2
            ♥ —
            ♦ A Q 4 2
            ♣ —
♠ J                      ♠ —
♥ —                      ♥ K 7 4
♦ J 9 8 5                ♦ 10 7
♣ —                      ♣ —
            ♠ —
            ♥ 5
            ♦ K 6 3
            ♣ 10
```

When the ten of clubs is played (the squeeze card), West has an impossible discard. If West throws a diamond, dummy discards the two of spades. If West throws the jack of spades, dummy discards a diamond because the two of spades is now a winner.

I want to introduce a small technical point at this juncture. Let's go back to an earlier example:

```
            ♠ A 10
            ♥ 10
            ♦ —
            ♣ —
♠ K Q                    ♠ 9 7
♥ J                      ♥ —
♦ —                      ♦ —
♣ —                      ♣ 10
            ♠ J
            ♥ —
            ♦ 3
            ♣ 6
```

Diamonds are trumps and it is South to lead. When the three of diamonds is played West has to retire, but suppose we interchange the East and West cards so that this is the position:

```
            ♠ A 10
            ♥ 10
            ♦ —
            ♣ —
♠ 9 7                    ♠ K Q
♥ —                      ♥ J
♦ —                      ♦ —
♣ 10                     ♣ —
            ♠ J
            ♥ —
            ♦ 3
            ♣ 6
```

Now when the three of diamonds is played West has no problems. He discards the seven of spades, but dummy is squeezed in front of East and there is no third trick. East simply discards the same suit as dummy.

So let us alter this three-card ending yet again:

```
            ♠ A 10
            ♥ —
            ♦ —
            ♣ 6
♠ 9 7                    ♠ K Q
♥ —                      ♥ J
♦ —                      ♦ —
♣ 10                     ♣ —
            ♠ J
            ♥ 10
            ♦ 3
            ♣ —
```

Now, when the three of diamonds is played, West discards a spade, dummy a club and East . . . ? Yes, East is squeezed, unable to keep the master heart and a spade stopper.

In this particular example, forget the clubs. They are irrelevant. What matters are the major suits and we can immediately lay down this rule: in endings of this kind the squeeze will work against either opponent when the one-card menace or threat card (♥10) is in the same hand as the squeeze card (♦3) opposite the long menace (♠A10). But when the two vital holdings (♥10 and ♠A10) are in the same hand opposite the squeeze card (♦3), then the squeeze will only work if these cards are held by the hand (North) that has to play after the hand which is to be squeezed (West). Bearing this in mind, see what you make of the following hand:

```
            ♠ K 7
            ♥ 8 7
            ♦ 6 5 4 2
            ♣ A K 9 6 2
♠ Q 10 6 3 2             ♠ J 9 5 4
♥ 10 6 5 3              ♥ 4
♦ K Q                   ♦ J 9 8 7
♣ Q 8                   ♣ J 10 7 4
            ♠ A 8
            ♥ A K Q J 9 2
            ♦ A 10 3
            ♣ 5 3
```

South	North
2♥	3♣
3NT	4NT
6NT	

Lead: ♠3

Superficially, there appear to be only eleven tricks on top, and prospects look bleak. However, the likely club break is 4-2, so if the defender who has club length also controls the diamonds a squeeze should work. You don't mind which defender this is because the one-card menace (it is going to be the ♦10) will be in the same hand as the squeeze card (the last heart) which, in turn, will be opposite the suit with the long menace (clubs).

The plan is to duck a trick where you can afford it, in this case obviously a diamond, which will rectify the count. The rest should be plain sailing—you just cash your winners finishing in the South hand with these cards left:

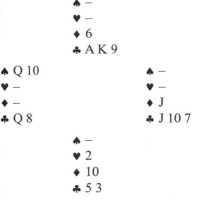

On the two of hearts West throws the ten of spades and dummy the six of diamonds, but what about East? The best thing East can do is to retire gracefully.

Sometimes a simple squeeze may be more attractive than a finesse.

```
        ♠ 6 4
        ♥ J 9 6 5 4 2
        ♦ 6 4 3
        ♣ A Q

        ♠ A K 5 2
        ♥ A K Q 3
        ♦ 7 5 2
        ♣ 9 3
```

West	North	East	South
Pass	Pass	Pass	1♥
2♦	4♥	All Pass	

West starts with three top diamonds, East discarding the eight of clubs on the third round. West now switches to the two of clubs.

It seems unlikely that West, who passed originally, has the king of clubs as well as the ♦AKQ, but players unfamiliar with squeeze technique may well come to the conclusion that they have no other chance and play the queen of clubs willy-nilly. If that is their decision then success is beyond recall, for this is the full hand:

```
        ♠ 6 4
        ♥ J 9 6 5 4 2
        ♦ 6 4 3
        ♣ A Q
♠ 8 3                   ♠ Q J 10 9 7
♥ 10 8 7                ♥ —
♦ A K Q 10 9            ♦ J 8
♣ 10 4 2                ♣ K J 8 7 6 5
        ♠ A K 5 2
        ♥ A K Q 3
        ♦ 7 5 2
        ♣ 9 3
```

The player well-versed in squeeze technique will recognize that the count has been rectified (he has lost the three tricks that he had to lose anyway) and he is just one trick short of the target. This is the perfect scenario for a squeeze, provided that one player can be entrusted to guard two suits. If you give the king of clubs to East then you must credit him with five spades also. Then East will be in sole command of the black suits and will be unable to withstand the pressure as you cash your winning hearts—all of them.

It is dummy to play and this is the position immediately before the last heart is played:

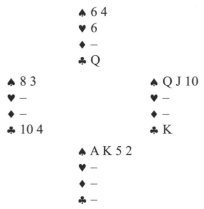

When declarer calls for the six of hearts (the squeeze card) East, who cannot possibly part with the king of clubs with the queen sitting in dummy, will throw a spade. Declarer also throws a spade but his ♠AK5 take the last three tricks.

You see what I mean about this sort of hand being easier to play than a part score? Nothing to count, nothing to do except play off your winners, just making sure that nobody throws away the king of clubs. The hand really plays itself once you have a small amount of basic knowledge.

Remember, even a lowly two, until thrown away, poses a threat to the opposition. All the time it is there they must retain a higher card to prevent the two becoming a master. How many times have you seen a declarer throw a small card from the dummy in the belief that it could not possibly be of use, when in reality it would have caused one of the defenders acute embarrassment?

To summarize, a simple squeeze will work against one opponent if the following conditions apply:

1. One opponent has sole control of two suits.

2. Declarer loses the tricks that have to be lost early in the game, reaching the position of having enough tricks to make the contract minus one. This is called rectifying the count (i.e. there are no unimportant cards around when the final crunch comes).

3. There must be direct communication to the long suit, or long menace as it is called (a master card plus others: Ax opposite x, for example). If a lone card (say a jack menacing a queen) is in the same hand as the long menace, the squeeze will only operate against the player who has to play before the hand containing the menaces.

4. If the single menace is in the same hand as the squeeze card (the card that turns the final screw), opposite the long menace, then the squeeze will work against either opponent.

THE DOUBLE SQUEEZE

Star Rating: ***

In the section on the simple squeeze I tried to show, in a straightforward way, that it was not a subject of which to be frightened. Indeed, in all basic situations the play is often relatively easy. The double squeeze, although it perhaps sounds more ponderous, is frequently no more difficult, but this time you intend to squeeze both your opponents.

Clubs are trumps and you need the last three tricks to fulfill your contract. It is South to play:

```
              ♠ J
              ♥ A 6
              ♦ –
              ♣ –
♠ Q                      ♠ –
♥ K J                    ♥ Q 10
♦ –                      ♦ Q
♣ –                      ♣ –
              ♠ –
              ♥ 5
              ♦ J
              ♣ 3
```

When the three of clubs is played West has to let a heart go, otherwise the jack of spades becomes a winner. Having done its work, you discard the jack of spades from dummy and now East is under pressure. To prevent your jack of diamonds from being promoted to winning rank, East also discards a heart. The ace and six of hearts take the last two tricks.

Of course, as with the simple squeeze, there should be no loose cards around in the endgame. Suppose you added a small diamond to each hand; now the squeeze would not

work. The end-position must be watertight.

The basis of the double squeeze is that if one opponent guards one suit and the other opponent guards another suit, then neither will be able to guard the third suit.

Spades are trumps. South is on lead, and needs the rest of the tricks.

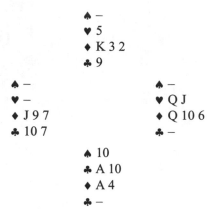

```
              ♠ –
              ♥ 5
              ♦ K 3 2
              ♣ 9
♠ –                      ♠ –
♥ –                      ♥ Q J
♦ J 9 7                  ♦ Q 10 6
♣ 10 7                   ♣ –
              ♠ 10
              ♣ A 10
              ♦ A 4
              ♣ –
```

South tries the ace of hearts but the suit fails to break, West discarding the seven of clubs. West is known to hold the ten of clubs and East the queen of hearts, and as declarer has all the tricks but one—the exact formula for a squeeze—and the single menace cards, the ♣9 and ♥10, are correctly placed, neither opponent will be able to guard the third suit—diamonds. Everything will happen automatically when the ten of spades is played. All declarer has to do is insure that neither opponent throws away the master card in clubs or hearts.

On the ten of spades West throws the seven of diamonds, dummy now parts with the nine of clubs and East . . . ? Having to retain the queen of hearts, East also throws a diamond. So dummy's three of diamonds takes the last trick.

The next hand was played in a pairs event.

This was the bidding at one table:

```
              ♠ 7 2
              ♥ 6 5 2
              ♦ A 3 2
              ♣ K Q 6
              ♠ 7 2
              ♥ A K Q 4
              ♦ K 8
              ♣ A J 10 9 8
```

South	North
1♣	1♠
2♥	3♦
3NT	4NT
6NT	

West leads the king of spades. North's bid of three diamonds was the fourth suit, and 4NT suggested the possibility of slam if South could find a little extra. Both players might have given up on slam earlier in the auction, but the final contract is by no means hopeless, the obvious chance being the 3-3 heart break. However, this was the full deal:

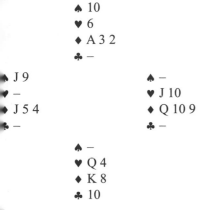

```
              ♠ A 10 8 6
              ♥ 6 5 2
              ♦ A 3 2
              ♣ K Q 6
♠ K Q J 9 4                  ♠ 5 3
♥ 9 3                        ♥ J 10 8 7
♦ J 5 4                      ♦ Q 10 9 7 6
♣ 7 5 3                      ♣ 4 2
              ♠ 7 2
              ♥ A K Q 4
              ♦ K 8
              ♣ A J 10 9 8
```

Fortunately for him, the declarer at this table was familiar with squeeze technique and he realized that to give himself an extra chance he must duck one round of spades, thereby rectifying the count. So West won the first trick with the king of spades and continued with the queen, won by dummy's ace. Declarer now cashed four clubs and the ace and king of hearts to arrive at this position:

```
              ♠ 10
              ♥ 6
              ♦ A 3 2
              ♣ –
♠ J 9                        ♠ –
♥ –                          ♥ J 10
♦ J 5 4                      ♦ Q 10 9
♣ –                          ♣ –
              ♠ –
              ♥ Q 4
              ♦ K 8
              ♣ 10
```

When the queen of hearts produced the nine of spades from West, declarer saw the perfect scenario for a double squeeze—West guarding spades, East guarding hearts and neither of them able to control diamonds.

The real crunch came when declarer played the ten of clubs. West had to discard a diamond, dummy parted with the now worthless spade, and East also had to part a diamond. The king, ace and three of diamonds took the last three tricks. Notice how easy it is for declarer once the key cards have been located: the jack of spades with West and the jack of hearts with East. All declarer has to do is to insure that West does not throw the jack of spades and East does not throw a heart. Apart from that there is no counting to do, no necessity to keep tabs on the diamond suit—the key middle suit which automatically becomes established no matter how small the supporting cards may be. Easy, isn't it, as soon as you see the light?

Let's try again.

```
              ♠ K 8 6
              ♥ A K 5
              ♦ 9 7 4 2
              ♣ K 6 3

              ♠ Q J 10 9 5 4
              ♥ J 6 3
              ♦ Q 6
              ♣ A 4
```

North	South
1NT	4♠

Without any technical refinements to help him out, South decided to try to clinch the rubber with a direct bid of four spades. When dummy went down, it was clear that there were only nine tricks. However, West started with the ♦AKJ, East discarding the eight of hearts on the third round and declarer ruffing. East won the ace of spades at trick four and returned the jack of clubs which was won by declarer's ace. On a second round of trumps everyone followed. What now?

If declarer thinks that West has length in hearts (and therefore the queen) there will be a simple red-suit squeeze against him. However, it is more likely that East has the heart length, in view of his shortage in diamonds and easy discard in hearts. This being the case, West will have to guard the diamonds (dummy's nine) and East the hearts (declarer's jack), and since three tricks have already been lost, the scene is set for a double squeeze. Neither side will be able to control the clubs when the pressure is applied.

The full hand:

```
              ♠ K 8 6
              ♥ A K 5
              ♦ 9 7 4 2
              ♣ K 6 3
♠ 7 2                        ♠ A 3
♥ 9 4                        ♥ Q 10 9 7 2
♦ A K J 10 3                 ♦ 8 5
♣ Q 8 5 2                    ♣ J 10 9 7
              ♠ Q J 10 9 5 4
              ♥ J 6 3
              ♦ Q 6
              ♣ A 4
```

It is necessary to cash the ace and king of hearts (the queen might drop) so that full pressure can be applied to West. Then the trumps are run to arrive at the following position:

♠ —
♥ —
♦ 9
♣ K 6

♠ —   ♠ —
♥ —   ♥ Q
♦ 10   ♦ —
♣ Q 8   ♣ 10 9

♠ 9
♥ J
♦ —
♣ 4

When the nine of spades is played West and East are squeezed in turn.

It does not always happen that both defenders are squeezed simultaneously. The process can come in two stages. First one opponent is squeezed in a simple squeeze position, then the other opponent gets the treatment.

Here is an example:

♠ A Q
♥ K Q 7 2
♦ J 6 4 3
♣ 5 4 2

♠ 4 3   ♠ K 6 2
♥ J 10 6 3   ♥ 9 8
♦ A K 5 2   ♦ Q 9 8 7
♣ K J 3   ♣ 10 8 7 6

♠ J 10 9 8 7 5
♥ A 5 4
♦ 10
♣ A Q 9

With no opposition bidding South became the declarer in four spades. West led the ace and king of diamonds. Declarer ruffed and tried the spade finesse. East won and switched to a club, South's queen losing to the king. West continued with a third diamond, ruffed by declarer who now played ♠A, ♥K, ♥A and ♠J to arrive at the following position:

♠ —
♥ Q 7
♦ J
♣ 5

♠ —   ♠ —
♥ J 10   ♥ —
♦ —   ♦ Q
♣ J 3   ♣ 10 8 7

♠ 10
♥ 5
♦ —
♣ A 9

Although declarer could not be sure, all the indications were that hearts were not going to break favorably, so he played his last spade. West could not part with a heart and discarded the club three. Backing his judgment, declarer now discarded the seven of hearts from dummy. At this point East had an easy club discard. However, when dummy was entered with the queen of hearts, East had to retain the diamond queen so he too had to bare his club honor. The ace and nine of clubs took the last two tricks.

I wonder if you can see (or even guess) what the thirteenth trick will be in this hand.

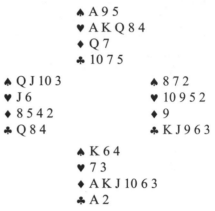

♠ A 9 5
♥ A K Q 8 4
♦ Q 7
♣ 10 7 5

♠ Q J 10 3   ♠ 8 7 2
♥ J 6   ♥ 10 9 5 2
♦ 8 5 4 2   ♦ 9
♣ Q 8 4   ♣ K J 9 6 3

♠ K 6 4
♥ 7 3
♦ A K J 10 6 3
♣ A 2

The contract is 7NT. West leads the spade queen and as you can see there is no soft option like the heart suit dividing kindly. So what is the plan, and which card do you think will become the thirteenth trick? The first trick is won in hand and when the hearts fail to break declarer runs the diamond suit to arrive at the following position:

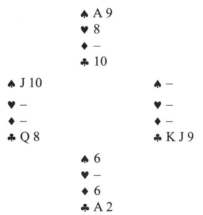

♠ A 9
♥ 8
♦ —
♣ 10

♠ J 10   ♠ —
♥ —   ♥ —
♦ —   ♦ —
♣ Q 8   ♣ K J 9

♠ 6
♥ —
♦ 6
♣ A 2

When the six of diamonds is played West has to throw a club, so dummy discards the nine of spades. So far, East has had no problem, and discards the nine of clubs. Now a spade to the ace squeezes East in hearts and clubs. Unable to throw a heart, East has to part with the jack of clubs, so the ace and two of clubs take the last two tricks.

Looking at the full hand you might be forgiven for overlooking the true merit of that ♣2, but the double squeeze is a powerful ally to have on your side.

THE TRIPLE OR PROGRESSIVE SQUEEZE
Star Rating: **

You have already seen that an opponent who is squeezed in two suits has to yield an additional trick. We now enter the area where we wish to obtain two additional tricks. For this to happen one opponent must guard three suits. What happens is that this opponent is initially squeezed out of one trick and then is squeezed again with the newly established trick. Of course, the cards have to lie favorably for the progressive squeeze to work.

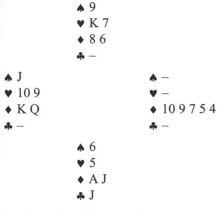

In this end-position, South, who is playing in no trumps, cashes the club jack and West has no safe discard. Let us say he decides to throw the spade jack. Now the spade nine is cashed and West is squeezed again in the red suits. One of the key factors for this type of squeeze to prove effective is that there must be two two-card menaces—one in either hand. Suppose, for example, South had cashed the diamond ace earlier. Now the position would be:

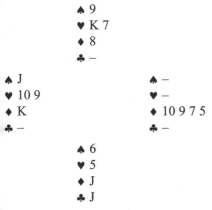

The jack of clubs is played and West can discard a heart. Dummy lets the diamond go but now when the seven of hearts is cashed West retains the jack of spades which takes the last trick. The hand which led to the five-card end position shown above was played in a pairs game with Neither Side Vulnerable.

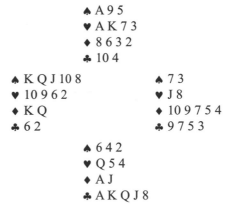

At one table South opened the bidding for one club, West bid one spade and North made a Sputnik double showing four hearts. When East passed South had an awkward rebid. He had plenty of points and a no trump game seemed a possibility, but obviously this could not be attempted unless North had a spade stop. So South tried the effect of two spades. West passed and North raised to three spades. North's idea was to show additional values and perhaps direct a no trump contract to his partner's hand in case he held something like ♠Qx. South converted to three no trumps which ended the bidding.

This was the full auction:

West	North	East	South
—	—	—	1♣
1♠	Dble	Pass	2♠
Pass	3♠	Pass	3NT
All Pass			

The king of spades was led and, with ten tricks on top, declarer's only problem was the number of overtricks. He made the routine play of ducking the first spade and winning the second. Then, before cashing all the clubs he took two hearts—the ace and the queen.

Here again is the five-card ending before the last club is cashed:

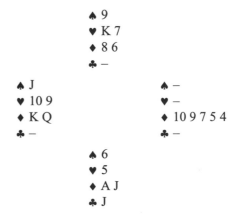

On the jack of hearts West discarded a heart—not that it mattered—and dummy parted with a diamond. Now dummy was entered with the king of hearts and the seven of hearts squeezed West in spades and diamonds. Declarer made twelve tricks.

The following hand from rubber bridge provided declarer with a chance to shine:

```
            ♠ 7 5 4 2
            ♥ Q 6 4
            ♦ A 7 4 2
            ♣ A J
♠ A K Q 10              ♠ 9 8 6
♥ 2                     ♥ A 5 3
♦ 10 9 6 5              ♦ Q J
♣ K Q 9 3              ♣ 8 7 6 5 4
            ♠ J 3
            ♥ K J 10 9 8 7
            ♦ K 8 3
            ♣ 10 2
```

At favorable vulnerability South took the opportunity of pre-empting with three hearts. West doubled for takeout, North raised to four hearts and East doubled for penalties. This was the auction:

West	North	East	South
–	–	–	3♥
Dble	4♥	Dble	All Pass

West leads three top spades. Declarer ruffs the third round and plays a heart to dummy's queen and East's ace. East switches to the queen of diamonds and it is apparent that declarer will have to pull something out of the bag if he is not to suffer a penalty. With only eight tricks on top a triple squeeze—to produce two extra tricks—seems the only hope.

The queen of diamonds is won by dummy's ace (the ♦K is needed as an entry to the South hand) and the trumps are run to produce this position:

```
            ♠ 7
            ♥ –
            ♦ 7 4
            ♣ A J
♠ 10                   ♠ –
♥ –                    ♥ –
♦ 10 9                 ♦ J
♣ K Q                 ♣ 8 7 6 5
            ♠ –
            ♥ 8
            ♦ K 8
            ♣ 10 2
```

When the eight of hearts is cashed West has three losing options.

There were some exciting exchanges at one table on the following hand:

```
            ♠ 5 3
            ♥ A 9 6 3
            ♦ A 8 3
            ♣ 6 5 4 2
♠ K 6 4 2              ♠ J 10 9 8 7
♥ 5                    ♥ 4 2
♦ Q J 10              ♦ 7 6 4 2
♣ A K Q J 10          ♣ 7 3
            ♠ A Q
            ♥ K Q J 10 8 7
            ♦ K 9 5
            ♣ 9 7
```

East/West bid to four spades after their opponents had got together in hearts, but rather than accept a small penalty South continued to five hearts—a delicate contract to say the least. Anyway, that was what West thought since he doubled to end the auction.

This was the full sequence:

West	North	East	South
–	–	Pass	1♥
Dble	3♥	Pass	4♥
Dble	Pass	4♠	5♥
Dble	All Pass		

West attacked in clubs and declarer trumped the third round. With only nine tricks immediately available, South saw that he had a mountain to climb. The king of spades was surely marked with West so there was no point in taking a finesse. However, a triple squeeze—yielding two tricks—was a possibility because West was already marked with club control and, on the bidding, might easily have the vital cards in diamonds as well.

So declarer cashed all his hearts and this was the position before the last heart was played:

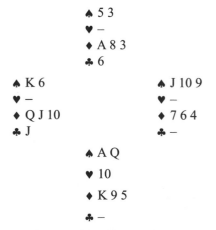

On the ten of hearts West thought it best to discard a diamond—in fact his choice was of no consequence—and now the king of diamonds was followed by the nine to dummy's ace. It was, of course, essential to unblock the diamonds so that dummy could win the third round which then squeezed West in the black suits. West did his best by blanking the king of spades, but declarer had no difficulty in reading the position and quickly played a spade to his ace to land an exhilarating contract.

This hand occurred at rubber bridge where over-enthusiasm led to South becoming declarer in six no trumps after East had opened the bidding at one spade:

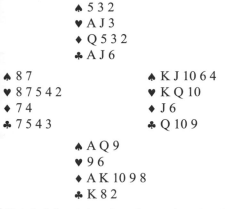

♠ 5 3 2
♥ A J 3
♦ Q 5 3 2
♣ A J 6

♠ 8 7
♥ 8 7 5 4 2
♦ 7 4
♣ 7 5 4 3

♠ K J 10 6 4
♥ K Q 10
♦ J 6
♣ Q 10 9

♠ A Q 9
♥ 9 6
♦ A K 10 9 8
♣ K 8 2

West led the eight of spades against South's contract of six no trumps and, even looking at all four hands, perhaps you can forgive declarer for failing to land the spoils (he went one down).

With just ten tricks on top prospects look daunting, especially since the club finesse is sure to be wrong. However, this is how declarer should have tackled the job. East's ten of spades is won by the queen and declarer now plans to put pressure on East by cashing his diamond winners. This is the position after the first five tricks:

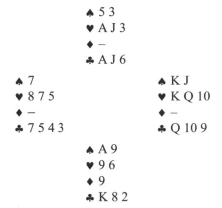

♠ 5 3
♥ A J 3
♦ —
♣ A J 6

♠ 7
♥ 8 7 5
♦ —
♣ 7 5 4 3

♠ K J
♥ K Q 10
♦ —
♣ Q 10 9

♠ A 9
♥ 9 6
♦ 9
♣ K 8 2

On the nine of diamonds dummy discards a spade, and East . . . ?

(a) If East discards a spade, the ace and nine of spades, dummy discarding the three of hearts, squeezes him in clubs and hearts. Say he now throws the ten of hearts, then the ace and another heart endplays him in clubs.

(b) If East discards a heart, then a heart is ducked in dummy. The probable spade return is won with the ace and now the ace and jack of hearts squeeze East in the black suits.

(c) If East discards a club, then three rounds apply unsustainable pressure in the majors. No doubt a heart would be thrown on the third club, in which case a heart is ducked as before.

Perhaps the moral is simple enough. If you are going to be a high-flyer then it pays to have a working knowledge of squeeze techniques.

Blocking Plays

Star Rating: ✸✸✸✸

Blocking plays—blocking the run of a suit—are often the only means of salvaging an otherwise doomed contract, so it pays to have a working knowledge of the techniques required. The common theme running through most of the following examples is that the operative player contributes a high card when in normal circumstances it would be usual to play low. This procedure is especially useful at no trumps.

1.   A 4

  K J 8 6 3   Q 7

          10 9 5 2

Against a no trump contract West leads the six, having overcalled in this suit. The standard lead holding KQJxx is the king, so the presumption is that East holds one of the top three honors. If declarer plays low from dummy the suit can be cleared at once. If the ace is played to the first trick the suit is blocked, which will be particularly effective if West has only one entry, and that entry can be knocked out immediately.

2.   6 5

  A 9 7 4 2   K J 10

          Q 8 3

Against a no trump contract West leads the four to East's king. East returns the jack, and to block the suit South should cover with the queen. You might wonder how South can differentiate between this example and the next. The solution lies in the spot card that is led. Assuming the lead to be the fourth highest, there is only one card lower than the four missing, so West is likely to have a five-card suit. Thus the only hope of preventing the suit being run at once is to block it.

3.   9 5

  A 10 7 6 4 2   K J

          Q 8 3

Against a no trump contract West leads the six to East's king, West having overcalled in the suit. When the jack is played next South blocks the suit by not covering. In this case both the four and the two are missing cards. If East has one of them there is nothing to be done, but if West has them both then refusal to cover effects an immediate blockage.

4.   9 4

  Q 7 2   A 10 8 5 3

          K J 6

Against a no trump contract West leads the two of a suit that his partner has bid and which he has supported. The ace wins and the five is returned. South can now block the suit by playing the king. This means that on regaining the lead the defense will not only have to unscramble their winners, but will also have to find an additional entry to enjoy the remainder of the suit.

5. (a)   Q 10 4

  8 2   A J 9 7 5

          K 6 3

Against a no trump contract West leads the eight of a suit that East has bid. To create a blockage declarer should play the queen. This gives East an unenviable choice. Ducking would give declarer two tricks in the suit. Alternatively if East wins he would have to wait for West to regain the lead to play the suit again. In this case a valuable tempo has been lost, for South still has to make the king before the suit is established.

5. (b)   K 9 3

  10 4   A J 8 7 6

          Q 5 2

This is a similar situation to 5 (a). The ten is led and when covered by the king East is faced with the same dilemma.

Time to look at some hands which all relate to the examples I have given.

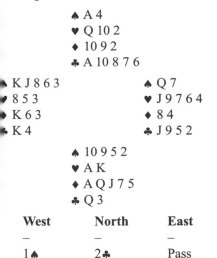

```
              ♠ A 4
              ♥ Q 10 2
              ♦ 10 9 2
              ♣ A 10 8 7 6
♠ K J 8 6 3              ♠ Q 7
♥ 8 5 3                 ♥ J 9 7 6 4
♦ K 6 3                 ♦ 8 4
♣ K 4                   ♣ J 9 5 2
              ♠ 10 9 5 2
              ♥ A K
              ♦ A Q J 7 5
              ♣ Q 3
```

West	North	East	South
–	–	–	1♦
1♠	2♣	Pass	2♠
Pass	3♠	Pass	3NT
All Pass			

The six of spades is led and, as is so often the case, everything depends on which card declarer plays from dummy to this trick. If declarer plays the four, the contract will be defeated. If declarer plays the ace, confident in the knowledge that this is standard blocking technique, at least game is made with four diamonds, three hearts and the two black aces.

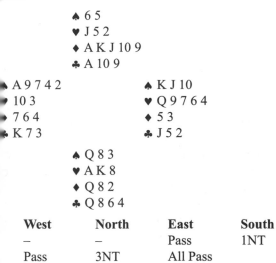

```
              ♠ 6 5
              ♥ J 5 2
              ♦ A K J 10 9
              ♣ A 10 9
♠ A 9 7 4 2             ♠ K J 10
♥ 10 3                 ♥ Q 9 7 6 4
♦ 7 6 4                ♦ 5 3
♣ K 7 3                ♣ J 5 2
              ♠ Q 8 3
              ♥ A K 8
              ♦ Q 8 2
              ♣ Q 8 6 4
```

West	North	East	South
–	–	Pass	1NT
Pass	3NT	All Pass	

West led the four of spades to East's king, and South's big decision came when East returned the jack of spades. Unquestionably the right play is the queen in an effort to block the suit. Assuming West's lead to be a genuine fourth highest, East must have three cards in the suit, and unless the third card is the ten there is no way to prevent the defense taking five tricks immediately.

Even having blocked the spade suit, declarer is not quite home. However, East cannot play hearts or clubs to advantage, so has to switch to a diamond. South wins in hand and now two club finesses land a rather fortunate game.

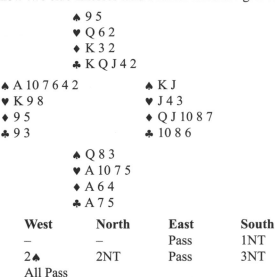

```
              ♠ 9 5
              ♥ Q 6 2
              ♦ K 3 2
              ♣ K Q J 4 2
♠ A 10 7 6 4 2         ♠ K J
♥ K 9 8               ♥ J 4 3
♦ 9 5                 ♦ Q J 10 8 7
♣ 9 3                 ♣ 10 8 6
              ♠ Q 8 3
              ♥ A 10 7 5
              ♦ A 6 4
              ♣ A 7 5
```

West	North	East	South
–	–	Pass	1NT
2♠	2NT	Pass	3NT
All Pass			

West leads the six of spades to East's king, and when the jack is continued South can see a glimmer of light. The four and two of spades are missing cards and, in view of the two spade overcall, are almost certainly with West. So the suit can be blocked, this time by simply refusing to cover. West studiously follows with the ten of spades, expecting East to read this as a signal for a heart switch. However, East woodenly plays the queen of diamonds and South's glimmer of light suddenly becomes as bright as the evening star. Declarer wins in dummy and cashes five clubs to produce this ending:

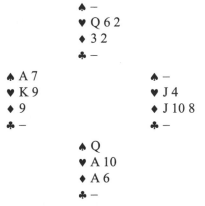

```
              ♠ –
              ♥ Q 6 2
              ♦ 3 2
              ♣ –
♠ A 7                  ♠ –
♥ K 9                 ♥ J 4
♦ 9                   ♦ J 10 8
♣ –                   ♣ –
              ♠ Q
              ♥ A 10
              ♦ A 6
              ♣ –
```

Since West is marked with the king of hearts on the bidding, declarer plays a diamond to the ace and exits with the queen of spades. West takes two spade tricks, but then has to concede the last two hearts.

North
♠ A K Q
♥ 9 4
♦ A J 10 9 6
♣ 9 6 2

West
♠ 10 6 4 3 2
♥ Q 7 2
♦ 7 5
♣ K 7 4

East
♠ 9 8 7
♥ A 10 8 5 3
♦ K 4 2
♣ Q 3

South
♠ J 5
♥ K J 6
♦ Q 8 3
♣ A 10 8 7 5

West	North	East	South
–	1♦	1♥	2♣
2♥	Pass	Pass	2NT
Pass	3NT	All Pass	

West leads the two of hearts to East's ace, East returning the five. If South does not go in with the king of hearts to block the suit, he will go down.

The bidding is the best indication of how the cards lie, although there is a second consideration. Defenders with AQxxx in this kind of situation often prefer to play the queen on the first round. All in all, the case for playing the king at trick two is a strong one.

Assuming that South has read the cards correctly and wins the second trick with the king of hearts, South can now safely take the losing diamond finesse. East plays a third heart to West's queen, at last unscrambling the suit, but East has no quick entry to take the setting tricks. Declarer makes one heart, four diamonds, three spades and a club. Now look at this one:

North
♠ Q
♥ Q 10 4
♦ A K Q 8 5 2
♣ J 7 6

West
♠ 7 6 5 4 2
♥ 8 2
♦ J 10 9 7
♣ A 9

East
♠ A J 9 3
♥ A J 9 7 5
♦ 6 4
♣ 4 3

South
♠ K 10 8
♥ K 6 3
♦ 3
♣ K Q 10 8 5 2

West	North	East	South
–	1♦	1♥	2♣
Pass	2♦	Pass	2NT
Pass	3NT	All Pass	

West leads the heart eight and now success rests on which card declarer plays from dummy. If familiar with blocking plays, South will call for the queen, leaving East with little option but to take the ace. East will have to switch and wait for West to regain the lead to play hearts once more. In the

meantime, declarer establishes the clubs and has no difficulty in getting home.

There is one last example I must include in this section. It illustrates how to handle the following combinations to lose only one trick when there are trumps left in both hands.

(a)	Jxx	**(b)**	Axx	**(c)**	Axxxx
	Axxx		Jxxx		xxx

With (a) and (b), unless there are obvious indications to the contrary, you must hope for one opponent to hold the blank KQ, K10 or Q10. With (c) you need the KQ alone. However, in each case there is the additional chance that an opponent holding Kx or Qx fails to unblock. The ace is played first, followed by a low card. Now, with trumps left in both hands and the side suits eliminated, the defender winning the second trick must concede a ruff and discard. Here are two final hands which illustrate this kind of blocking technique.

North
♠ 7 5 2
♥ K J 6 3
♦ J 5 4
♣ A Q 9

West
♠ A K J 10 6
♥ 5 2
♦ K 9 7 2
♣ 4 2

East
♠ Q 9 3
♥ 9 4
♦ Q 10
♣ 10 8 7 6 5 3

South
♠ 8 4
♥ A Q 10 8 7
♦ A 8 6 3
♣ K J

West	North	South	East
–	–	–	1♥
1♠	3♥	Pass	4♥
All Pass			

South ruffs the third round of spades, draws trumps, cashes the ace of diamonds and eliminates the clubs. Now a small diamond endplays East. Had East thrown the queen of diamonds under the ace, it would not have helped. When the suit is continued West can either win with the king, establishing dummy's jack, or duck with the same effect. The next hand was an exciting affair from a Paris tournament.

North
♠ K 10 8 7
♥ A 9 8 7 6
♦ A Q 10
♣ Q

West
♠ 5 3
♥ Q 10 3
♦ 8 6 4 2
♣ 10 9 8 7

East
♠ 4 2
♥ K J
♦ 7 5 3
♣ K J 6 5 4 2

South
♠ A Q J 9 6
♥ 7 4 2
♦ K J 9
♣ A 3

West	North	East	South
–	1♥	Pass	1♠
Pass	3♠	Pass	4♣
Pass	4♦	Pass	4NT
Pass	5♥	Pass	6♠
All Pass			

West led the ten of clubs to the queen, king and ace.

Declarer saw that he had a problem in the heart suit, and in order to camouflage the weakness he entered dummy with a trump and cashed the ace of hearts. There was a slight pause as East hesitated for a moment and then followed with the jack. The scene was now set for a rewarding endplay. A second trump, club ruff and three rounds of diamonds left these cards:

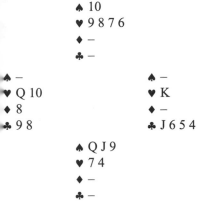

```
              ♠ 10
              ♥ 9 8 7 6
              ♦ –
              ♣ –
♠ –                        ♠ –
♥ Q 10                     ♥ K
♦ 8                        ♦ –
♣ 9 8                      ♣ J 6 5 4
              ♠ Q J 9
              ♥ 7 4
              ♦ –
              ♣ –
```

Declarer now exited with a heart and East was endplayed. He had to play a club so declarer discarded his last heart, ruffed in dummy and claimed his slam.

At some tables declarer signaled his intentions only too clearly by drawing trumps, eliminating diamonds and clubs and only then playing the ace and another heart. By this time East had recognized the strategy and had little difficulty in unblocking his king of hearts on the ace. When a second heart was played West was able to take command and cash his two heart winners for one down.

The lesson to be learned from this hand is that, if you are going in for this kind of blocking play, set the scene early—before your opponents are aware of your full intentions. They may—probably should—still do the right thing, but at least you have not issued a blueprint of your plans.

Unblocking Plays by Declarer

Star Rating: ****

Unlocking Plays cover a wide field and are likely to pop up at any moment. In the following five examples assume you are South, declarer in a no trump contract, and that there are no outside entries to dummy.

1.   ♥ K Q 6 5 4

♥ 2   ♥ J 10 7

        ♥ A 9 8 3

It is essential for South to retain the three until the fourth round in case the suit fails to break 2-2. The nine and the eight must be unblocked under the king and queen, then the three allows access to the remainder of the tricks.

2.   ♥ A 9 5 3

♥ J 10 8 7   ♥ K 4 2

        ♥ Q 6

The jack is led and run to East's king. With no outside entries to dummy, declarer will make only one trick unless he unblocks the queen.

3.   ♥ Q 6 3

♥ K J 9 8 2   ♥ 8 5

        ♥ A 10 4

The seven is led and a cheap trick can be won with the ten. However, if South badly needs an entry to the dummy, perhaps at a later stage, he must win with the ace and subsequently lead through West's king. It is worth noting that two tricks are won in either case—no more, no less—so there is no hardship in playing the ace on the first round when the only consideration is to insure an entry to the dummy.

4.   ♥ Q J 6

♥ K 10 8 4 2   ♥ 9 7

        ♥ A 5 3

The four is led. If South needs a certain entry to dummy, perhaps after unblocking a suit in which dummy has length,

then he must play low from dummy and win with the ace.

5.   ♥ A 5 4

♥ K Q J 10 9 7   ♥ 8 3

        ♥ 6 2

If South needs to unblock an offending high card from his own hand, he may hold off the first two rounds and then use the ace for this purpose. In this particular case there could be an outside entry to dummy, but still the unblocking play may be necessary.

Of course, unblocking plays are by no means restricted to no trumps. The following examples might occur when playing in a suit contract. Again you are South, the declarer.

6.   ♥ K 3

♥ A 10 9 7 5 2   ♥ 8 6

        ♥ Q J 4

The ace is led against this side suit. If South urgently requires entries to his own hand, he must jettison the king on the first round.

7.   ♥ A K Q

♥ 7 5 4   ♥ 3 2

        ♥ J 10 9 8 6

If South's only entry is via trumps, this side suit holding could be embarrassing. The solution is often to cash one or two of dummy's masters and then unblock the remaining honor(s) on declarer's long trumps.

8.   ♥ Q 10 5

        ♥ A K J

This looks an unlikely holding for an unblocking play, but suppose declarer has to use this suit to enter dummy, and wants dummy to have a high card remaining while he loses a trick to defender, so that defender will have to put dummy back on play. Then the solution is to cash the ace, overtake the jack with the queen and finally discard the king on the suit in which the defender is to be given the lead.

9.

      ♥ K 9 6

♥ —   ♥ 5 4 3

      ♥ A Q J 10 8 7 2

If this is the trump suit and some ruffing has to be done, yet three trump entries may be required to dummy—then three low cards must be preserved, and that includes the two, which will be the link to the six.

10.

      ♥ A K 7 4 2

♥ Q 10 6 5   ♥ J

      ♥ 9 8 3

South requires four tricks from this suit, losing just one, or three tricks, losing none with no outside entry to dummy. The ace is cashed and when East follows with the jack South unblocks the nine. Now a small card to the eight provides West with an option. If West wins with the ten, declarer can later lead the three and pick up the remainder of the suit. If West ducks on the second round, declarer will make only three tricks in the suit, but will not have lost one.

Time to look at some hands which are all related to the examples above:

      ♠ A 4
      ♥ Q 7 5
      ♦ K Q 6 5 4
      ♣ 10 9 6

♠ K Q J 8 3   ♠ 9 7 6
♥ 6 4 2   ♥ A K 8 3
♦ 2   ♦ J 10 7
♣ 8 4 3 2   ♣ J 7 5

      ♠ 10 5 2
      ♥ J 10 9
      ♦ A 9 8 3
      ♣ A K Q

South opens 1NT and then raises North's invitational 2NT to 3NT. West leads the king of spades and everything looks to be plain sailing, for are there not five diamonds, three clubs and one spade? Yes, there are nine tricks on top, but South must be careful to unblock the diamonds. The nine and eight must fall under the king and queen. Neglecting this simple unblocking play will find declarer locked out of dummy and unable to cash the ninth trick.

      ♠ A 9 5 3
      ♥ J 6 3
      ♦ 8 7 2
      ♣ 7 5 4

♠ J 10 8 7   ♠ K 4 2
♥ 8 5 4 2   ♥ Q 10 9 7
♦ 9 3   ♦ J 10 4
♣ A J 8   ♣ K 6 2

      ♠ Q 6
      ♥ A K
      ♦ A K Q 6 5
      ♣ Q 10 9 3

The bidding was uncomplicated. After a pass by East, South opened 2NT and North raised to 3NT. A heart lead would probably have defeated the contract, but West understandably elected to lead the jack of spades. Small from dummy, king from East and . . . ? Should South fail to unblock the queen, he will almost certainly find his task too great. If, however, South ditches his queen of spades on the first trick, the suit is unblocked so that a simple finesse can be taken against West's ten. Thus with five diamonds, two spades and two hearts South registers the game.

      ♠ 10 9 7
      ♥ Q 6 3
      ♦ Q 2
      ♣ Q J 10 6 3

♠ Q J 6 4   ♠ 8 2
♥ 8 5   ♥ 8 5
♦ A 7 6   ♦ K 9 8 5
♣ 7   ♣ 9 8 5 4 2

      ♠ A K 5 3
      ♥ A 10 4
      ♦ J 10 4 3
      ♣ A K

After three passes South bids one spade and then jumps to 3NT when North raises to two spades. The opposition do not enter the auction, so the final contract is 3NT by South.

West leads the seven of hearts, dummy plays low, East contributes the eight and South the . . . ? If declarer gleefully grabs a cheap trick with the ten, defeat is almost certain. More mature reflection will surely indicate that just two tricks will be won in this suit, whether South wins cheaply with the ten or extravagantly with the ace. But a vital consideration is to have an entry to dummy after unblocking the clubs, and this can only be achieved if the first trick is won by the ace. All the indications are that West holds the king of hearts, so after the ace of hearts and ace king of clubs a heart is led towards dummy's queen, and the defense is without further resource.

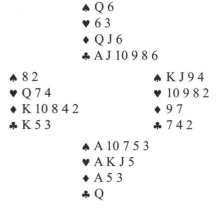

      ♠ Q 6
      ♥ 6 3
      ♦ Q J 6
      ♣ A J 10 9 8 6

♠ 8 2   ♠ K J 9 4
♥ Q 7 4   ♥ 10 9 8 2
♦ K 10 8 4 2   ♦ 9 7
♣ K 5 3   ♣ 7 4 2

      ♠ A 10 7 5 3
      ♥ A K J 5
      ♦ A 5 3
      ♣ Q

South opens one spade and then rebids two hearts over two clubs. North gives preference to two spades and then South jumps to 3NT which ends the auction.

West leads the four of diamonds, and however tempting it may be to play an honor from dummy, declarer must resist. South wins the first trick with the ace of diamonds, thereby unblocking the suit, plays the queen of clubs to dummy's ace and continues clubs. The queen and jack of diamonds form an entry to the established club winners and declarer is able to claim ten tricks.

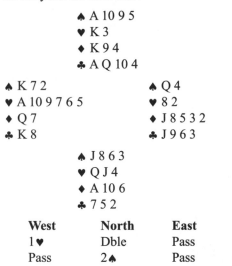

```
              ♠ A 5 4
              ♥ 8 3
              ♦ J 4 2
              ♣ A Q 6 5 3
♠ K Q J 10 9 7              ♠ 8 3
♥ 10 9 2                    ♥ Q J 7 5 4
♦ K Q 3                     ♦ 7 6 4
♣ 4                         ♣ J 10 5
              ♠ 6 2
              ♥ A K 6
              ♦ A 10 8 5
              ♣ K 9 8 7
```

South opened 1NT, West came in with two spades, and North bid 2NT. South, somewhat apprehensively, continued to 3NT.

The king of spades was led, and declarer's immediate anxiety was resolved when the ace of spades appeared in the dummy. However, there was another problem. Unless the clubs divided 2-2 the suit would be blocked, so declarer had to find some method of freeing them. This was achieved by ducking the first two spades and then discarding a club on the ace of spades. It would not have helped West to switch after the king of spades, as then the ace of spades would be an entry for the fifth club.

```
              ♠ A 10 9 5
              ♥ K 3
              ♦ K 9 4
              ♣ A Q 10 4
♠ K 7 2                     ♠ Q 4
♥ A 10 9 7 6 5             ♥ 8 2
♦ Q 7                       ♦ J 8 5 3 2
♣ K 8                       ♣ J 9 6 3
              ♠ J 8 6 3
              ♥ Q J 4
              ♦ A 10 6
              ♣ 7 5 2
```

West	North	East	South
1♥	Dble	Pass	1♠
Pass	2♠	Pass	4♠
All Pass			

Against the spade game West kicked off with the ace and another heart. Short of entries to hand, declarer jettisoned the king under the ace and was thus able to win the second trick in the closed hand. A spade to dummy's nine was won by the queen and at this early stage East had an unenviable choice of plays. The minor suits looked particularly unappe-

tizing, so East returned a spade to the jack, king and ace. A third spade was won by declarer's eight and declarer cashed the jack of hearts, discarding a small club from dummy, before taking the club finesse to leave:

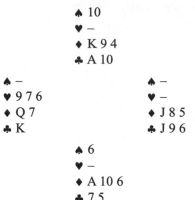

```
              ♠ 10
              ♥ —
              ♦ K 9 4
              ♣ A 10
♠ —                        ♠ —
♥ 9 7 6                    ♥ —
♦ Q 7                      ♦ J 8 5
♣ K                        ♣ J 9 6
              ♠ 6
              ♥ —
              ♦ A 10 6
              ♣ 7 5
```

It is a dummy to play, and the defense have two tricks. Declarer cashed the club ace and exited with the ten to East's jack—not that it mattered who won this trick. Either player would be endplayed and forced to open up the diamond suit. Although this was a pretty ending, declarer went about it the hard way. Discarding a diamond from dummy on the heart jack, not a club, would have given declarer three spades, two hearts, two diamonds, two clubs and a diamond ruff, ten tricks.

```
              ♠ Q 6 4
              ♥ 7 3
              ♦ A K Q
              ♣ 10 9 8 7 5
♠ A J 9 8 7                ♠ K 10 5 3
♥ 10 2                     ♥ 9 8 6 4
♦ 7 3                      ♦ 5 4 2
♣ A 6 4 3                  ♣ Q J
              ♠ 2
              ♥ A K Q J 5
              ♦ J 10 9 8 6
              ♣ K 2
```

West	North	East	South
–	–	Pass	1♥
1♠	2♣	2♠	3♦
Pass	4♦	Pass	4♥
All Pass			

The ace of spades was led and the suit continued, declarer ruffing the second round. The rest may look easy—draw trumps and cash the diamond winners for ten tricks—but unless declarer cashes one diamond before drawing two rounds of trumps he will go down. The correct play is to cash one heart and one diamond, return to hand with a trump and draw the outstanding trumps discarding (unblocking) the ace and king of diamonds from dummy. Now declarer can enjoy the rest of the diamond suit, just making his contract.

```
        ♠ 6 3
        ♥ Q J 10 3
        ♦ 9 7 5 3
        ♣ Q 10 5
♠ 8 5 4 2              ♠ 9 7
♥ K 8 6 4              ♥ 9 7 5 2
♦ 2                    ♦ A Q J 10
♣ 8 7 6 3             ♣ 9 4 2
        ♠ A K Q J 10
        ♥ A
        ♦ K 8 6 4
        ♣ A K J
```

After opening the bidding with two clubs, South arrived in four spades (150 for honors, partner!), although 3NT would have caused rather less hassle.

The two of diamonds was led to East's ace and the queen was returned, covered by the king and trumped by West, who now got off lead safely with a trump, leaving South the prospect of losing two more tricks in diamonds. However, having drawn trumps, declarer cashed the ace of hearts (the first unblock), the ace of clubs and overtook the jack of clubs with the queen. He now played the queen of hearts and when East played low declarer jettisoned the king of clubs for the second unblock. With nothing but clubs and hearts left, West had to put dummy back on play and thus South was able to discard both losing diamonds.

Sometimes you will need to pay particular attention to unblocking the trump suit.

For example, consider this hand:

```
        ♠ A K 4
        ♥ K 9 6
        ♦ J 3
        ♣ A 5 4 3 2
♠ Q J 10 9 7 6        ♠ 8 5 3
♥ –                   ♥ 5 4 3
♦ A Q 10 8 7 5        ♦ 9 6 2
♣ Q                   ♣ K J 10 8
        ♠ 2
        ♥ A Q J 10 8 7 2
        ♦ K 4
        ♣ 9 7 6
```

West	North	East	South
1♠	1NT	Pass	4♥
5♦	5♥	All Pass	

With only ten tricks on top, quite clearly, declarer has to establish one more trick, but at the same time South must also insure that East doesn't get on lead to push a diamond through. The first move is to duck the opening lead of the queen of spades leaving West on lead. Then, win the spade continuation and discard two clubs on the ace and king of spades. Next, cash the ace of clubs and ruff a low club high—making sure that you preserve three low hearts, and specifically the two, for entries to dummy. Then, the queen of hearts is overtaken by dummy's king, a second club is ruffed high, and the seven of hearts is overtaken by dummy's nine to ruff a third club high. This unblocking in trumps enables declarer to draw the last trump ending in dummy (the two to the six) and enjoy the established five of clubs, the eleventh trick.

Finally, consider the following hand where South's careful play left West with an insoluble problem:

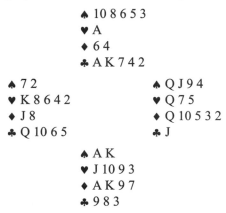

```
        ♠ 10 8 6 5 3
        ♥ A
        ♦ 6 4
        ♣ A K 7 4 2
♠ 7 2                 ♠ Q J 9 4
♥ K 8 6 4 2           ♥ Q 7 5
♦ J 8                 ♦ Q 10 5 3 2
♣ Q 10 6 5           ♣ J
        ♠ A K
        ♥ J 10 9 3
        ♦ A K 9 7
        ♣ 9 8 3
```

South opened the bidding with one diamond and rebid 1NT over his partner's one spade. North then tried three clubs, but South persisted with 3NT, which became the final contract.

West led the four of hearts and declarer started developing the club suit. On the ace of clubs East followed with the jack and South unblocked the nine. Now a low club to the eight gave West a problem. In fact, if West wins this trick declarer has an easy ride, as the marked club finesse yields four tricks in this suit alone. So West allowed the eight of clubs to win. Declarer now wisely abandoned clubs and turned his attention to establishing a second heart trick to make the contract.

If there is one thing a bridge player really enjoys above anything else it is a "heads I win, tails you lose" situation. Perhaps that is why South was so pleased with this hand.

47 Chapter

Assumption in Play

Star Rating: ****

A player frequently has to make an assumption about the lie of certain key cards. In the three cases that follow, even the greatest pessimist will find it difficult to place the critical card in an unassailable position. In each case declarer needs just one card to be correctly placed. As this is essential to success declarer makes the assumption that it is so placed.

1.

West	*East*
♠ Q 8 6 5 3	♠ A K J 10 7 2
♥ 9 5 3	♥ 7 4
♦ Q J	♦ A 6
♣ K Q 7	♣ J 10 5

East plays in four spades. To succeed the diamond king will have to be with North. Since there is no alternative, East assumes that North holds this card.

2.

West	*East*
♠ J 9 6 5	♠ 4 2
♥ A J 8 3	♥ Q 10 9 6 4 2
♦ J 10	♦ K Q
♣ J 10 8	♣ A K Q

West	**North**	**East**	**South**
–	–	1♥	Pass
2♥	2♠	4♥	All Pass

South leads the king of spades and follows with the three which is won by North's ten. North now cashes the ace of diamonds and then plays the ten of spades. Having no convenient discard, East ruffs with the ten of hearts which holds the trick, South discarding a diamond. It now becomes clear that South cannot have the king of hearts and so to succeed North must be credited with the bare king. East therefore makes this assumption and plays a heart to dummy's ace. The full hand:

♠ A Q 10 8 7
♥ K
♦ A 8 3
♣ 6 5 4 2

♠ J 9 6 5	♠ 4 2
♥ A J 8 3	♥ Q 10 9 6 4 2
♦ J 10	♦ K Q
♣ J 10 8	♣ A K Q

♠ K 3
♥ 7 5
♦ J 9 7 6 4 2
♣ 9 7 3

North's defense may have been a little naive. With three tricks in the bag he could reasonably hope for the king of trumps to be the setting trick—providing he didn't issue a blueprint of the defensive layout. A second diamond, or perhaps a club, at trick four might have had the desired effect, although no doubt East would have wondered why North hadn't played a third spade. This reflection might have led declarer to the winning play.

3.

♠ Q 10 8 3	♠ A J 9 7 4
♥ 8 7 5	♥ Q J
♦ K J 3	♦ A 9 6 5
♣ K Q 5	♣ A 6

West	**North**	**East**	**South**
–	–	–	Pass
Pass	Pass	1♠	Pass
3♠	Pass	4♠	All Pass

South leads the ace, king and a third heart, ruffed by the East. Dummy is entered with the king of clubs, South following with the jack, and the spade finesse loses to South who exits with the ten of clubs to East's ace. East plays one more round of trumps, and all follow. What now?

When the dummy went down, success seemed to depend on one of two finesses, the king of spades with North or the diamond queen with South. So should declarer take the diamond finesse? Let's look at the full hand:

```
              ♠ 5 2
              ♥ 10 9 3
              ♦ Q 7
              ♣ 9 8 7 4 3 2
♠ Q 10 8 3                    ♠ A J 9 7 4
♥ A J 8 3                     ♥ Q J
♦ J 10                        ♦ K Q
♣ J 10 8                      ♣ A K Q
              ♠ K 6
              ♥ A K 6 4 2
              ♦ 10 8 4 2
              ♣ J 10
```

Declarer has no doubt noted that South, who passed originally, has already turned up with eleven points, so there is no room for South to hold the queen of diamonds as well. With thirteen points he would have opened the bidding, so declarer assumes that North holds the queen of diamonds—and, either it has to be doubleton or South must have 10x. In fact the doubleton queen of diamonds is in no way inconsistent with the play so far—especially after a third round of clubs. Cashing the two top diamonds duly lands the contract.

The situation gets slightly more complex when there are more key cards involved. Consider South's problem on the following hand.

```
              ♠ K Q 8 2
              ♥ K 9 6 4
              ♦ J 4
              ♣ 8 7 6

              ♠ 6 5 4
              ♥ A J 10 7 5
              ♦ A Q 5 3
              ♣ Q
```

West	North	East	South
1NT *	Pass	Pass	2♥
Pass	3♥	Pass	4♥
All Pass			
* 12-14			

West leads the club ace followed by the king which is ruffed by declarer. The ace and king of hearts draw the outstanding trumps, West contributing the queen, and the lead is in dummy. How should declarer continue?

There are two critical cards involved at this stage—the ace of spades and the king of diamonds. Declarer will have no problem if West has the ace of spades, so for the moment he makes the assumption that the ace of spades is with East. What follows then is that if East holds the ace of spades, West must hold the king of diamonds to account for his opening bid.

The plan, therefore, is to ruff the third club back to hand at trick five and lead a low diamond. Here is the full hand:

```
              ♠ K Q 8 2
              ♥ K 9 6 4
              ♦ J 4
              ♣ 8 7 6
♠ 9 7 3                       ♠ A J 10
♥ Q 8                         ♥ 3 2
♦ K 10 6                      ♦ 9 8 7 2
♣ A K J 9 4                   ♣ 10 5 3 2
              ♠ 6 5 4
              ♥ A J 10 7 5
              ♦ A Q 5 3
              ♣ Q
```

West wins the king of diamonds and switches to a spade, but it is too late. The ace and queen of diamonds provide parking spaces for two of dummy's spades. One lesson to be learned here is this: if you can afford a key card to be wrong, assume it is wrong. The picture that then emerges may leave you with a viable alternative that is watertight.

The next hand features South with a critical decision at trick three:

```
              ♠ A J 9 8 5
              ♥ 10 7 4
              ♦ 10 9
              ♣ Q J 9

              ♠ K Q 10 7 3 2
              ♥ K J
              ♦ 7 6
              ♣ A 10 4
```

West	North	East	South
Pass	Pass	Pass	1♠
Pass	3♠	Pass	4♠
All Pass			

West led the diamond king and, after an encouraging signal from East, played a low diamond to the ace. East switched to the heart five and the moment of truth had arrived. Which heart should South play?

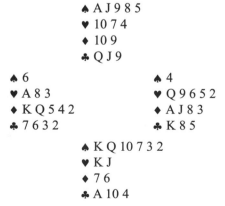

```
              ♠ A J 9 8 5
              ♥ 10 7 4
              ♦ 10 9
              ♣ Q J 9
♠ 6                           ♠ 4
♥ A 8 3                       ♥ Q 9 6 5 2
♦ K Q 5 4 2                   ♦ A J 8 3
♣ 7 6 3 2                     ♣ K 8 5
              ♠ K Q 10 7 3 2
              ♥ K J
              ♦ 7 6
              ♣ A 10 4
```

Whatever happens in hearts, the contract cannot be made unless East holds the club king. Therefore, it is necessary to assume that East holds this card. East has already turned up with the ace of diamonds, and with the heart ace as well East might have bid in third position. Thus West should be credited with the ace of hearts and declarer must insert the jack at trick three.

Swap the clubs around so that dummy has the A104 and declarer QJ9, and now it is right to play the heart king as West must be credited with the club king. Since West passed originally he is likely to hold ♥A, ♦KQ and ♣K.

It is particularly satisfying to embark on an apparent sacrifice and then find that with a little hopeful assumption you are actually in a making position:

                    ♠ A 10 8 4
                    ♥ 7 6 2
                    ♦ J 8 6
                    ♣ 9 5 4

                    ♠ K J 9 3 2
                    ♥ 10
                    ♦ A Q 7 3 2
                    ♣ Q J

West	North	East	South
–	–	–	1♠
2♥	2♠	4♥	4♠
All Pass			

West leads the two of clubs to East's ace. East returns the three of hearts and West wins with the jack. West cashes the king of clubs and continues with the ace of hearts which South ruffs. Time to pause for thought.

The play to the first four tricks suggests that West has five hearts and four clubs. What about diamonds and spades? For South to succeed East has to be credited with the king of diamonds, but that in itself is not enough—it must be precisely Kx so that there are no diamond losers. So declarer makes the hopeful assumption that East does in fact hold ♦Kx. Moving back to the West hand, that marks West with three diamonds. So, if West has five hearts, three diamonds and four clubs it follows that he can hold only one spade. Here is the full hand:

                    ♠ A 10 8 4
                    ♥ 7 6 2
                    ♦ J 8 6
                    ♣ 9 5 4

    ♠ 6   ♠ Q 7 5
    ♥ A Q J 5 4   ♥ K 9 8 3
    ♦ 10 5 4   ♦ K 9
    ♣ K 8 6 2   ♣ A 10 7 3

                    ♠ K J 9 3 2
                    ♥ 10
                    ♦ A Q 7 3 2
                    ♣ Q J

Having made the assumption about the diamonds, and as a result of that assumption the lie of the trumps, the rest was easy. A spade to dummy's ace was followed by the ten of spades which was allowed to run when East played low. Now the diamond finesse, the king of spades and the ace of diamonds permitted declarer to claim the remainder of the tricks.

Part VIII

CARD PLAY IN SUITS

by Brian Senior

Are you happy with your declarer play, confident you can get the best out of the cards, or are you all too often left with a vague feeling of disquiet after what looked to be a perfectly good contract has failed? Was it sheer bad luck that placed the crucial queen in the wrong hand or should you perhaps have succeeded anyway?

You may be surprised to learn that I am one who falls into the latter group, and I am glad to do so. I do not believe that there will ever be a perfect bridge player, one who never fails in a makeable contract, though we all know players who give the impression that they believe themselves to be perfect. The important thing is to be aware of your failings, to want to improve and to work to achieve that improvement. The smug few, who are content as they are, cannot improve, for they see no need to put in the necessary effort to do so. Truly, we are the lucky ones.

Bidding and defense are to some extent partnership activities and as such there is a limit to the improvement you can make on your own. As declarer, however, you are in sole charge, making this the easiest area of the game on which to work, and also perhaps the one most suited to learning from books.

The temptation is to rush out and buy a volume which explains the workings of exotic endplays and complex squeezes—the techniques of the "expert." Well, you will find both endplays and squeezes in this section, but you will also find a whole range of other more basic techniques. What you need is not only to know the various techniques but also to develop the judgment to know when to apply them.

Accordingly, while the exotic will make an occasional appearance, the problems in this book more than anything require clear thinking and looking ahead—in other words, good planning. Even a bad plan is likely to be an improvement on having no plan at all. Take this example:

```
              ♠ A K 9
              ♥ K Q 6 3 2
              ♦ 10 3
              ♣ J 5 3

              ♠ Q J 10 8 7 3
              ♥ 7 4
              ♦ A K 6 4
              ♣ 8
```

West	North	East	South
–	1♥	2♣	2♠
3♣	3♠	5♣	5♠
All Pass			

Contract: 5♠ by South. Opening lead: ♠2.

Partner's raise to 3♠ was perhaps a trifle aggressive on such a dull hand, but at first sight the contract looks easy. South has to lose to the heart and club aces, but his diamond losers can both be trumped in the dummy to give eleven tricks.

Are there any snags?

On any other lead it would probably be plain sailing, but West has hit on the best lead for his side. Suppose you win and play ace, king and ruff a diamond. There is no quick entry back to hand and, as soon as you give up the lead, the defense will waste no time in leading a second trump, removing dummy's last trump and leaving you with a diamond loser. Clearly your first plan will not succeed; is there an alternative?

If you cannot ruff both diamonds, the only hope is to set up dummy's heart suit for diamond discards. To retain your entries to dummy, you do not try to ruff a diamond, but instead win the spade lead in hand and lead a heart to the king. If this loses you continue with the queen and ruff a heart when you regain the lead; if it wins, play a diamond to hand to lead towards the second heart honor.

There is no guarantee of success, but there are several combinations of major suit distributions which will allow you to make eleven tricks. Try another example:

♠ 6
♥ 8 5 2
♦ 10 8 6 4 3 2
♣ J 7 3

♠ A K Q 10 4
♥ A 3
♦ K Q J 9 7
♣ 4

Contract: 5♦ by South. Opening lead: ♣A.

If West continues with the king of clubs, it is natural for declarer to ruff and play a trump, losing only to the missing aces. Suppose, however, that the opening lead is a heart. Now an immediate trump play would be fatal since declarer has three top losers—one heart, one diamond and one club—and can be defeated if he gives up the lead. Instead he must win the heart lead and play off his top spades, pitching dummy's losing hearts and only then, having reduced his losers to two, can he afford to lead a diamond.

It is clearly advantageous to know the correct way of playing various suit combinations in isolation, yet this should be only a guide. Rarely will you be playing a suit in isolation, usually the suit in question is only one part of the whole hand—and that is what you want to play correctly. For example:

♠ A K J 6 4   ♠ 10 9 8 5
♥ 7 6   ♥ A 4
♦ K 9 3   ♦ A Q J 10 7
♣ K 9 2   ♣ 8 4

Contract: 4♠ by West. Opening lead: ♥K.

Take the spade suit above. Even the most inexperienced player, muttering a rhyme about "eight ever, nine never," knows that the best play missing the queen to four is to play off the ace and king. Such rhymes have no part in the "thinking" player's game. He sees that, even if he loses to the ♠Q, he still has at least ten tricks, four spades, five diamonds, and one heart. He also sees four possible losers, one spade, one heart and two clubs. Is there a sure way to avoid the four losers?

Yes. Duck the heart lead, win the continuation, and run the ♠10. Even if the finesse fails you are safe as South can never gain the lead to attack clubs.

Similarly, it does no harm to know the percentage chance of a play succeeding. For most players, who have no desire to clutter their minds with tables of figures, it is sufficient to know that an even number of missing cards will tend to break unevenly, an odd number of cards as evenly as possible. So given a choice between a simple finesse in one suit (a 50 percent chance), and a 3-3 break in another, you would go for the finesse. Conversely, a 3-2 break would be more likely than the finesse.

The problems in this section will try to test your knowledge of a whole range of different play techniques, but most of all they will test your judgment and ability to make a sensible but sometimes flexible plan. Do not worry about overtricks, or indeed extra undertricks; your aim should always be to find the play most likely to fulfill your contract.

Do not expect to find chapters, with headings like "ducking plays" "endplays" and "finessing." There are no convenient labels when you play a contract in real life, neither will you find them here. There is, however, a general gradation of difficulty. Some of the early deals are quite straightforward while some of the later ones are pretty tough, at least in my judgment. You may make all the later contracts and fail in some of the early ones; that merely shows what my judgment is worth. Nevertheless, in principle the problems get tougher as you go along.

Below you will find an index which tells you which main techniques are needed in the play of each problem. If you want to improve a particular aspect of your play you can look up the appropriate heading and go through the relevant problems again.

This section is written in a question and answer format which leads you through the sort of steps you might take at the table. To get the most benefit from it, try to answer the questions before reading the answers.

Sixty Deals

DEAL ONE

Neither Side Vulnerable. Dealer South.

♠ K J 5
♥ A 10 6 3 2
♦ 9 7 4
♣ J 7

♠ A Q 10 7
♥ 8 7
♦ Q 5
♣ A K Q 8 2

West	North	East	South
–	–	–	1♣
Pass	1♥	2♦	2♠
Pass	3♠	Pass	4♠
All Pass			

Contract: 4♠ by South. Opening lead: ♦10.

East wins with the ♦K and plays the ♦A followed by the ♦J. Plan the play from here.

How many immediate winners do you have?
Unless the clubs break badly, ten—four spades, one heart and five clubs.

If clubs are 5-1, can you do anything about it?
No. If you try to ruff a club you are sure to get one of your existing club winners ruffed first.

Is there any other threat to the contract?
Yes. Suppose you ruff the third diamond and draw trumps. You will be all right if trumps are 3-3, but a 4-2 break will spell defeat.

Can anything be done to overcome a 4-2 trump break?
Yes, simply discard your losing heart on the third diamond. If East plays a fourth round you can ruff in dummy and preserve your own four card holding to draw the outstanding trumps. If East leads anything other than a fourth diamond you win, draw trumps and cash your winners.

The full deal:

♠ K J 5
♥ A 10 6 3 2
♦ 9 7 4
♣ J 7

♠ 9 8 4 3   ♠ 6 2
♥ Q J 5 4   ♥ K 9
♦ 10 6   ♦ A K J 8 3 2
♣ 9 6 3   ♣ 10 5 4

♠ A Q 10 7
♥ 8 7
♦ Q 5
♣ A K Q 8 2

Tip
Always try to keep trump control. Sometimes, as here, throwing a loser can prevent your long trump holding being forced.

DEAL TWO

Neither Side Vulnerable. Dealer West.

♠ K 9
♥ Q 10 9 8
♦ Q J 7 5 3 2
♣ 7

♠ A Q 10 8 7 6
♥ A 2
♦ A
♣ A 8 5 2

West	North	East	South
3♣	Pass	Pass	4♠
All Pass			

Contract: 4♠ by South. Opening lead: ♣Q.

East overtakes with the ♣K. How do you play?

How many winners have you?
You can be certain of at least five spade tricks plus the three aces. You have three clubs, one heart, and possibly a trump to lose, and must avoid at least two of these.

What's the best way of getting rid of some losers?
You can ruff club losers in dummy.

You need two ruffs; can anything go wrong?
Yes. On the bidding and play to trick one it looks as though East may have a singleton club. If you win the ace of clubs and ruff one with the nine, East may be able to over-ruff and return a trump, leaving you with two club losers and nowhere to get rid of them.

Is there a way to overcome this problem?
Yes. Take your first club ruff with the king. Come back to hand with the ace of diamonds and ruff another club with the nine. Even if East can over-ruff this, you have managed to get rid of two of your losing clubs. With only one club and one heart loser, you can afford to lose a spade trick.

The full deal:

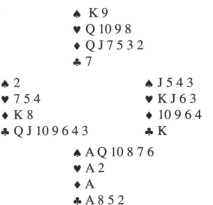

♠ K 9
♥ Q 10 9 8
♦ Q J 7 5 3 2
♣ 7

♠ 2   ♠ J 5 4 3
♥ 7 5 4   ♥ K J 6 3
♦ K 8   ♦ 10 9 6 4
♣ Q J 10 9 6 4 3 ♣ K

♠ A Q 10 8 7 6
♥ A 2
♦ A
♣ A 8 5 2

Tip

Count your losers as well as your winners. Sometimes, as here, you will see that you can afford an over-ruff, but only if it comes at the right time. By guaranteeing one winning ruff, you made certain that you could take a second ruff. It didn't matter now if there was an over-ruff as that would mean you had got rid of two of your potential losers on one trick.

DEAL THREE
Neither Side Vulnerable. Dealer South.

♠ A J 9 7 2
♥ A K 4
♦ J 8 3
♣ A 6

♠ K Q 10 8 6 3
♥ 7 5
♦ Q 9 4
♣ 8 3

West	North	East	South
–	–	–	2♠(*)
Pass	4♠	All Pass	

(*) 6-10

Contract: 4♠ by South. Opening lead: ♣K.

Over to you.

How many immediate tricks have you?
Nine; six spades, two hearts and one club. Unfortunately, the heart ruff is in the long trump hand, so does not produce an extra trick.

Where will the tenth trick be found?
It will have to come from the diamond suit, meaning that you will have to avoid losing a trick to the ten.

Is there any reason why you should finesse for the diamond ten one way rather than the other?
No. If you were to draw trumps and find them to be 1-1 then play three rounds of hearts and discover that they were 6-2, you would know that one defender had seven cards in the majors and the other three. Clearly the second hand would have more cards in the minors and therefore be more likely to hold any specific minor suit card.

So is this how you should play the hand; play the other suits first and hope to get a clue as to which defender is longer in diamonds then play him for the ten?
No. While there are many hands where that would be good technique, this is not one of them. You should play on the other suits first, but for a different reason.

Which is?
Suppose that you win the opening lead, draw trumps and play ace, king and ruff the heart. Now you exit with your small club. Whoever wins this trick is endplayed and forced to play to your advantage either by giving a ruff and discard or by leading a diamond. Either way, your problem is solved and you only lose two diamond tricks and one club.

The full deal:

♠ A J 9 7 2
♥ A K 4
♦ J 8 3
♣ A 6

♠ 4   ♠ 5
♥ Q 10 8 3   ♥ J 9 6 2
♦ K 10 5   ♦ A 7 6 2
♣ K Q K J 2   ♣ 10 9 7 5

♠ K Q 10 8 6 3
♥ 7 5
♦ Q 9 4
♣ 8 3

Tip

When you have an awkward guess, see if you can force the defense to solve your problem for you. Note that if you play this way you have no need of either the nine or eight of diamonds; the queen and jack are sufficient, whether in the same hand or, divided as here.

DEAL FOUR

Both Sides Vulnerable. Dealer South.

♠ A 10 7 4
♥ 5 4
♦ 8 6 3
♣ Q 8 6 4

♠ Q 3
♥ A K Q J 9 7
♦ A K 7
♣ 7 2

West	North	East	South
2♥	Pass	2NT	Pass
3♥	Pass	4♥	All Pass

Contract: 4♥ by South. Opening lead: ♦4.

East plays the ♦10. How do you play?

How many immediate tricks do you have?
Nine; six hearts, two diamonds and one spade.

Where might you find the tenth trick?
Clearly, it cannot come from diamonds, so that leaves clubs and spades. The obvious possibility is the club suit. If West has the ace and king of clubs you can lead twice towards the queen to establish your tenth trick. This will not come quickly enough to provide a discard for the diamond loser, but it will give you a discard for your second spade.

Is the club play likely to succeed?
Alas, no. It is very likely that West would have led a club had he held both the ace and king, rather than a potentially dangerous diamond lead from what looks to be something like Qxx(x)

So I have to try the spade suit?
Yes. If you had an entry to dummy you could effectively take two spade finesses, making your contract whenever either the king or jack was where you wanted it to be. But with no outside entry to dummy you have only one chance. The position of the king of spades is completely irrelevant, it is the jack which is the key. Win the opening lead, draw trumps and lead the ♠Q. Whether or not West plays the king, you duck. Win the next diamond and finesse the ♠10. If West has the jack, you will have your tenth trick.

The full deal:

♠ A 10 7 4
♥ 5 4
♦ 8 6 3
♣ Q 8 6 4

♠ K J 9   ♠ 8 6 5 2
♥ 10 8 6   ♥ 3 2
♦ Q 9 5 4   ♦ J 10 2
♣ A 10 3   ♣ K J 9 5

♠ Q 3
♥ A K Q J 9 7
♦ A K 7
♣ 7 2

Tip

Always take in to account not only what the defense did but also what they did not do. True, the spade play, needing only one key card to be well-placed, was always a better bet than a club play which required two well-placed cards, but West's failure to lead a top club confirmed that playing on clubs could not be successful.

DEAL FIVE

North/South Vulnerable. Dealer East.

♠ A K 10 4
♥ 8 7 4
♦ Q 10 9
♣ A J 4

♠ Q 9 7 6 3
♥ Q 3
♦ 6 3 2
♣ K 10 8

West	North	East	South
–	–	1♥	Pass
Pass	Dble	2♦	2♠
3♥	3♠	All Pass	

Contract: 3♠ by South. Opening lead: ♥K.

West continues with the ♥5, East wins with the ace and plays the ♥J.

How many immediate tricks do you have?
Assuming that you do not lose a spade, you have five spades and two clubs—seven in all.

Where will the other two tricks be found?
They will have to come, one from clubs and one from diamonds.

What should you do at trick three?
Despite the opening lead, it is fairly clear from the auction that hearts must be 5-3. Accordingly, to panic and ruff with the ♠Q would be a mistake, leaving you with an awkward guess when you come to draw trumps.

You ruff low, West following as expected, and play a spade to the ace and a spade back to the queen. They are 2-2, now what?
If you are to win a diamond trick, West must hold the jack, so lead a low diamond to the ten.

East wins the king and plays ace and another diamond to dummy's queen, West following each time. Now all you have to do is find the queen of clubs. Who has it?
If you have been counting the distribution of the opposing hands, you will know that East has turned up with five hearts, four diamonds and two spades and therefore has only two clubs to West's five.

Should you then play West for the club queen?
No. The distributional evidence may suggest that West is more likely to hold the queen, but the bidding provides a much stronger piece of evidence. Remember that West passed his partner's 1♥ opening so should not hold 6 HCPs. Since he has already turned up with the ♥K and ♦J, he will not hold another queen. Accordingly, play East for the missing ♣Q.

The full deal:

```
            ♠ A K 10 4
            ♥ 8 7 4
            ♦ Q 10 9
            ♣ A J 4
♠ 8 5                      ♠ J 2
♥ K 5 2                    ♥ A J 10 9 6
♦ J 5 4                    ♦ A K 8 7
♣ 9 6 5 3 2                ♣ Q 7
            ♠ Q 9 7 6 3
            ♥ Q 3
            ♦ 6 3 2
            ♣ K 10 8
```

Tip

Always listen to the bidding. Not only the bids which are made but also those which are not made can help you to get a picture of the opposing hands.

DEAL SIX

Both Sides Vulnerable. Dealer South.

```
            ♠ K Q 7 6 5
            ♥ K 9 4
            ♦ K 9 3 2
            ♣ 7

            ♠ A J 10 9 8
            ♥ 8 6 3
            ♦ 7
            ♣ A Q J 10
```

West	North	East	South
–	–	–	1♠
Pass	4♠	All Pass	

Contract: 4♠ by South. Opening lead: ♦Q.

Plan the play from here.

How many immediate winners do you have?
Only six; five spades and one club.

You need four more; where will you find them?
Three are easy, as you can either ruff three diamonds in hand or three clubs in dummy, bringing your total to nine. There are four possible sources of a tenth trick.

1. Play for East's ♦A to fall in three rounds.
2. Play for West to have the ♥A.
3. Play for East to hold the ♣K by taking a simple finesse.
4. Play for West to hold the ♣K by taking a ruffing finesse.

Which of these possibilities gives the best chance of success?
Line (1) is the poorest option. Not only are the odds against East having three or fewer diamonds, but to try this line means ducking the opening lead. If West can switch to a heart honor you will need the ♥A onside anyway.

Line (2) is a straightforward 50-50 shot, just as is the chance of a successful club guess, but it is inferior to either of the club plays because it gives no second chance.

Line (3) is better, as it succeeds when East holds the ♣K and the finesse succeeds, but even when the finesse fails you have the second chance of leading a heart to the king, giving you a total success rate of about 75 percent.

Line (4) is best of all, being virtually certain to succeed.

Why?
Suppose that you ruff the second diamond, draw trumps and play the ace and then the queen of clubs, throwing a heart from dummy if West does not cover. If the queen holds, you simply lead another club to repeat the finesse. But even if East wins the ♣K, what can he do to hurt you? Either he cashes the ♥A while he has the chance, but that is the last trick for the defense, or he exits passively in a minor. In the latter case, dummy's remaining hearts go on your jack and ten of clubs and you make the rest on a cross-ruff. By finessing into the hand which cannot effectively attack your

weak spot (hearts), you guarantee your contract irrespective of the success or failure of the finesse.

So that's it then; as long as you take the ruffing finesse in clubs you're bound to succeed?

Not quite. There is one more important play you must make. Although you know it will lose, you must play the ♦K at trick one. If you don't West might find a heart switch to defeat you.

The full deal:

```
              ♠ K Q 7 6 5
              ♥ K 9 4
              ♦ K 9 3 2
              ♣ 7
  ♠ 4 2                      ♠ 3
  ♥ Q J 2                    ♥ A 10 7 5
  ♦ Q J 10 4                 ♦ A 8 6 5
  ♣ K 8 6 4                  ♣ 9 5 3 2
              ♠ A J 10 9 8
              ♥ 8 6 3
              ♦ 7
              ♣ A Q J 10
```

Tip

When you have a two-way finesse, look to see if there is a dangerous opponent (one who could attack your weak spot if he gained the lead) and a safe opponent (one who could not). Sometimes, by finessing into the safe hand, you will greatly improve your chance of success even if the finesse loses.

DEAL SEVEN

Neither Side Vulnerable. Dealer South.

```
              ♠ A K 8 4
              ♥ A 10 8
              ♦ K 4
              ♣ A 9 7 6

              ♠ 6 2
              ♥ K Q J 7 3 2
              ♦ 10 6 2
              ♣ 4 3
```

West	North	East	South
–	–	–	2♥(*)
Pass	4♥	All Pass	
(*) 6-10			

Contract: 4♥ by South. Opening lead: ♣K.

Play on from here.

How many immediate winners do you have?

Nine; six trumps, one club and two spades.

Where will the tenth trick come from?

Either from finding the ace of diamonds onside or from ruffing the third diamond.

So how should you play?

Win the opening lead, cross to hand with a trump and play a diamond to the king. Whether or not that wins, you play diamonds each time you regain the lead and eventually get your ruff.

Is that a sure thing?

No, but it is how most players would tackle the hand.

Is there a better way?

Yes. The problem with playing this way is that if East has the ♦A and three trumps he will be able to play a trump each time you give up the lead and there will be none left in dummy to ruff the last diamond. By leading a round of trumps yourself you are doing the defender's job for him. The trouble is that dummy is too strong. Turn the ♦K into a smaller card and the right play would be easy to find; simply win the opening lead and play a small diamond immediately. Now it is impossible for the defense to prevent you getting your ruff.

The full deal:

```
              ♠ A K 8 4
              ♥ A 10 8
              ♦ K 4
              ♣ A 9 7 6
  ♠ Q 10 7 5 3               ♠ J 9
  ♥ 5                        ♥ 9 6 4
  ♦ 9 7 5 3                  ♦ A Q J 8
  ♣ K Q J                    ♣ 10 8 5 2
              ♠ 6 2
              ♥ K Q J 7 3 2
              ♦ 10 6 2
              ♣ 4 3
```

Tip

When you can see a sure line for your contract, take it. Don't be distracted by surplus high cards which offer a tempting combination of chances but which could lead to defeat if none of those chances come home.

DEAL EIGHT
North/South Vulnerable. Dealer South.

♠ 8 6 5 4
♥ J 7 2
♦ A K 4 3 2
♣ 5

♠ A Q 9 2
♥ A K Q 10 9 8 6
♦ 7
♣ A

West	North	East	South
–	–	–	2♥
4♦	4♥	Pass	4♠
Pass	6♥	All Pass	

Contract: 6♥ by South. Opening lead: ♦Q.

Over to you.

How many immediate winners do you have?
Eleven; seven trumps, two diamonds and two black aces.

Where will you find the twelfth trick?
From a successful spade finesse.

Apart from the spade finesse losing can anything go wrong?
Yes. On the bidding, it seems certain that East will be void in diamonds and can ruff the opening lead.

Can anything be done about this?
Yes. Play small from dummy at trick one and, if West continues diamonds, play low again. You can ruff the second diamond in hand, draw trumps ending in the dummy, and pitch two spades on the ace and king of diamonds before leading a spade to the queen.

The full deal:

♠ 8 6 5 4
♥ J 7 2
♦ A K 4 3 2
♣ 5

♠ 10
♥ 3
♦ Q J 10 9 8 6 5
♣ K J 3 2

♠ K J 7 3
♥ 5 4
♦ –
♣ Q 10 9 8 7 6 4

♠ A Q 9 2
♥ A K Q 10 9 8 6
♦ 7
♣ A

Tip

When you can see the tricks you need to fulfil your contract, take whatever steps you can to make sure that you don't lose any of them. Remember, it is the number of tricks you win that is important, not which tricks.

DEAL NINE
Both Sides Vulnerable. Dealer South.

♠ A Q 9
♥ K Q 6
♦ 7 4 3
♣ 10 9 6 5

♠ 8 3 2
♥ A 4 3
♦ A
♣ A K Q J 7 4

West	North	East	South
–	–	–	1♣
Pass	3♣	Pass	6♣
All Pass			

Contract: 6♣ by South. Opening lead: ♦Q.

What is your plan of action?

How many immediate tricks do you have?
Eleven; six trumps, three hearts, the ace of diamonds and the ace of spades.

Where might the twelfth trick come from?
Clearly, it has to come from the spade suit. The simple chance is to finesse the queen, hoping that West holds the king. An extra chance would be to find West with both the jack and ten of spades; you could first try leading a spade to the nine and, assuming that lost to the ten or jack, later finesse the queen.

Is that the best chance then?
No. The queen will be onside 50 percent of the time and the jack and ten about a quarter of the remainder – 62.5% in all. There is an alternative line which is a sure thing.

Win the opening lead, play a low club to the nine and ruff a diamond high. Cross back to dummy with a club to the ten and ruff the last diamond. Now draw the last trump, if there is one, and play three rounds of hearts, ending in hand. What you have done is eliminate all the defense's safe exit cards. If you now take a losing spade finesse, East will have to either give you a ruff and discard or play back a spade into dummy's holding.

So now I play a spade to the queen?
No. Now you lead a spade and just beat West's card as cheaply as possible. If you play the nine and East wins with the ten or jack his return gives you your twelfth trick. If West plays the ten or jack you cover with the queen. If East wins the king a spade return will trap the remaining minor honor, whoever has it.

The full deal:

```
              ♠ A Q 9
              ♥ K Q 6
              ♦ 7 4 3
              ♣ 10 9 6 5
♠ 10 7 6 5                    ♠ K J 4
♥ J 10 7 5                    ♥ 9 8 2
♦ Q J 10 9 7                  ♦ K 8 6 5
♣ –                          ♣ 8 3 2
              ♠ 8 3 2
              ♥ A 4 3
              ♦ A
              ♣ A K Q J 7 4
```

Tip

When deciding when to take an ace consider whether there is a chance of leaving the defenders with an awkward blockage. As this usually requires one opponent to have a long suit, remember the bidding which could give a clue whether such a blockage is plausible.

DEAL TEN

East/West Vulnerable. Dealer North.

```
              ♠ 10 7 6 3
              ♥ A 7 3
              ♦ A 4
              ♣ A Q 9 2

              ♠ A Q J
              ♥ 10 8 6
              ♦ 7
              ♣ K J 10 8 7 3
```

West	North	East	South
–	–	1NT(*)	Pass
3♣	Pass	4♣	Pass
5♣	All Pass		
(*) 12-14			

Contract: 5♣ by South. Opening lead: ♥4.

Plan the play.

How many immediate tricks do you have?
Nine; six trump tricks and three aces.

Where will you find the other two tricks you need?
From spades. Even losing to the king, you must make two out of the queen, jack and ten.

So, are there any problems?
Yes. Unfortunately, West has found the best opening lead for his side, threatening to establish two heart winners for the defense to go with their possible spade trick.

Can you still make your contract?
Of course, there is no problem if the spade finesse wins, but what if it loses?

If the hearts are 4-3, there is no chance as whether or not you win the first trick the defense will be able to establish and cash two heart tricks and one spade. What if they are 5-2? There are two possibilities. If East has five hearts, then ducking the first round will cut communications between the two defenders. Alternatively, if West has five hearts and East's doubleton consists of two honors, you can block the suit by rising with the ace at trick one. Ducking would allow East to win and return his second honor, forcing out the ace and leaving West to cash a second heart trick when he wins the ♠K.

So, should you win the ♥A or duck at trick one?
West's lead of the ♥4 is consistent with both four-two doubleton and honor to five. There are two reasons why it is correct to play the ace immediately and play for the blockage. Firstly, there are three possible combinations of honor to five against only one of exactly four-two doubleton, making the former more likely. Secondly, if East held ♥KQJ95 plus some diamond length and strength he might have overcalled.

No guarantees, but the best play is to take your ace immediately, draw trumps and take the spade finesse.

The full deal:

```
              ♠ 10 7 6 3
              ♥ A 7 3
              ♦ A 4
              ♣ A Q 9 2
♠ K 8 2                      ♠ 9 5 4
♥ J 9 5 4 2                  ♥ K Q
♦ K 8 6 2                    ♦ Q J 10 9 5 3
♣ 4                         ♣ 6 5
              ♠ A Q J
              ♥ 10 8 6
              ♦ 7
              ♣ K J 10 8 7 3
```

DEAL ELEVEN

East/West Vulnerable. Dealer South.

```
              ♠ 7 2
              ♥ 7 3 2
              ♥ K 10 7 4
              ♣ A 8 3 2

              ♠ A K J 10 9 8
              ♥ J 10 6
              ♦ A Q
              ♣ K 7
```

West	North	East	South
–	–	–	1♠
Pass	1NT	Pass	4♠
All Pass			

Contract: 4♠ by South. Opening lead: ♥A.

This is followed by the ♥KQ and a switch to the ♦5.

You have already lost three tricks, all you can afford. What other possible losers do you have?

Apart from a fairly unlikely ruff, only the queen of spades.

How can you play the spades to avoid a loser there?

There are three possible lines in the spade suit:

1. Cash the ace and king, hoping for a singleton or doubleton queen.
2. Cash the ace then cross to dummy and finesse the jack.
3. Use the ♦K and ♣A as entries to dummy to take two finesses.

So which line is best?

It is quite easy to see that (1) cannot be right. Assume for the moment that it is correct to cash the ace first. Now, should you finesse on the second round or cash the king? Finessing succeeds when East has queen to three, cashing the king when West has queen doubleton.

Any specific card is more likely to be one of three than one of two, by the odds of three to two, so the second round finesse must be better.

Lines (2) and (3) are exactly equal when spades break 3-2. Of the 4-1 breaks, line (2) gains when West has the bare queen. But line (3) gains whenever West has any of the other four singletons as it allows two finesses against East's queen to four while line (2) does not.

So what is the correct line of play?

Win the diamond switch in dummy and take a spade finesse. If that succeeds, cross to the ♣A to finesse a second time, then cash the ace and king.

The full deal:

```
              ♠ 7 2
              ♥ 7 3 2
              ♥ K 10 7 4
              ♣ A 8 3 2
♠ 6                        ♠ Q 5 4 3
♥ A K Q 8                  ♥ 9 5 4
♦ 6 5 3                    ♦ J 9 8 2
♣ J 9 6 5 4                ♣ Q 10
              ♠ A K J 10 9 8
              ♥ J 10 6
              ♦ A Q
              ♣ K 7
```

Tip

Learn how to play common suit combinations with the odds. Knowing the odds, follow them unless you have a good reason to do otherwise. Guessers have their successes but, in the long term, guesser is synonymous with loser.

Neither Side Vulnerable. Dealer South.

```
              ♠ Q 6 2
              ♥ K 10 4 2
              ♦ 10 8 6
              ♣ A K J

              ♠ A K 5
              ♥ A J 7 3
              ♦ 9 7 4
              ♣ Q 10 3
```

West	North	East	South
–	–	–	1NT
Pass	2♣	Pass	2♥
Pass	4♥	All Pass	

Contract: 4♥ by South. Opening lead: ♦K.

West continues with the ♦QJ overtaken by East with the ♦A. East now switches to the ♠J.

Again, you have lost all the tricks you can afford. What remaining problems do you have?
Only one; playing the trump suit without loss.

Do you have any clues where the queen might be?
No. It seems to be a complete guess.

Is there anything you could do to try to get a clue?
Not safely. Playing in no trumps, it is sometimes possible to cash your winners in other suits and hope to get a count on the hand before making the critical guess. In a suit contract, however, this risks having one of your winners ruffed.

So is it really a guess?
Assuming the hearts are 3-2, it really is a guess. You should cash either the ace or king, then finesse. This is better than cashing the ace and king because, as you have seen, the queen is more likely to be in queen to three than queen doubleton when there are five cards missing.

What if hearts are 4-1?
If there is a singleton queen, you have no problem, while if either defender has Q98x you have no chance because he can cover if you lead the ten or jack on the second round. The difference comes when somebody has a singleton eight or nine, leaving his partner with Q965 or Q865.

If there is a singleton eight or nine, can you play the suit for no loser?
Not if it is West who has the length. You cash the ace then lead the jack to the queen and king, but West has the nine and six sitting over your seven, so you must lose the fourth round of the suit.

*Suppose East has the length. You cash the king and lead the
ten to the queen and ace. That leaves you with the jack-
seven sitting over the nine-six. Cross back to hand with a
club and finesse the* ♥7.

So it is correct to play East for the ♥Q by cashing the king
then leading the ten. It is just as good as the alternative
when hearts are 3-2, but it gives you an extra chance when
the suit breaks 4-1.

The full deal:

```
              ♠ Q 6 2
              ♥ K 10 4 2
              ♦ 10 8 6
              ♣ A K J
  ♠ 9 7 4 3                    ♠ J 10 8
  ♥ 8                          ♥ Q 9 6 5
  ♦ K Q J                      ♦ A 5 3 2
  ♣ 9 6 5 4 2                  ♣ 8 7
              ♠ A K 5
              ♥ A J 7 3
              ♦ 9 7 4
              ♣ Q 10 3
```

Tip

Treasure your spot cards. If you examine them carefully,
you will sometimes find that they offer you an extra chance
if you use them wisely. The extra chance may not always be
a big one, but, every little bit helps. Ask any casino owner
the value of small percentages.

DEAL THIRTEEN

Both Sides Vulnerable. Dealer South.

```
              ♠ A 7 2
              ♥ 7 6 4 3
              ♦ 8 7
              ♣ 6 5 4 2

              ♠ K Q 6 5 4
              ♥ A 9
              ♦ A K 9
              ♣ A 9 3
```

West	North	East	South
–	–	–	2NT
Pass	3♣(*)	Pass	3♠
Pass	4♠	All Pass	
(*) 5-card Stayman			

Contract: 4♠ by South. Opening lead: ♥K.

Plan the play.

How many immediate winners do you have?
Seven; three spades, two diamonds, the ace of clubs and the
ace of hearts.

Which other three tricks can you hope to make?
A diamond ruff in the dummy plus your two long trumps.

Might there be any problems?
A 6-2 diamond break might mean that the diamond ruff
could not be taken without losing a trump trick. Also, if
trumps are 4-1, it might not be possible to make both of
your long trumps.

How can you overcome these problems?
A bad diamond break might be overcome by cashing the ace
and king of trumps before playing on diamonds. If the same
defender has a doubleton in both spades and diamonds he
will not be able to stop you from ruffing the third diamond.
Alternatively, if West has three spades and two diamonds
you need to play diamonds before spades so that you can
over-ruff in dummy. As for a possible 4-1 trump break; you
might be able to ruff twice in hand to make both small
trumps.

*So should you, or should you not, draw two rounds of
trump?*
The trouble with not drawing trumps is that you could go
down when the trumps break normally (3-2) if you run into
an over-ruff or trump promotion. So it must be best to take
two rounds of trumps to reduce this danger and to discover
the true position.

So you should win the ♥A *and play two top trump?*
No. If the trumps are 4-1 you will need to ruff two hearts in
hand and that not only requires two entries to dummy but
also involves giving up the lead, allowing the defense to
draw a third round of trumps. Correct play is to duck at trick
one so that you retain control, and win whatever West leads
next.

Does it matter which top trumps you play?
Yes. One of them must be the ace, leaving a low one in
dummy to take the diamond ruff. And the ace should win the
second round of trumps.

Why?
So that if trump do break badly you are in the right hand to
ruff a heart. You continue by playing three rounds of
diamonds, ruffing in dummy, and lead the last heart. If West
has the four trumps you will need him to also hold four
hearts and three diamonds so that he has to follow suit while
you take your ruffs. If it is East who has the long trumps you
are better placed. Assuming that everything has passed off
peacefully so far, East now has a choice of losing options
even if he is out of hearts. If he discards, you make your
remaining small trump, while if he ruffs you simply throw a
losing club and can draw his last trump when you regain the
lead.

Should you play the same way if trump are 3-2?
No. In that case you don't need to take any risks with the
heart break. Just take your diamond ruff, play a club to the
ace and draw trumps.

The full deal:

♠ A 7 2
♥ 7 6 4 3
♦ 8 7
♣ 6 5 4 2

♠ 8   ♠ J 10 9 3
♥ K Q J 8   ♥ 10 5 2
♦ J 10 6 3 2   ♦ Q 5 4
♣ Q 10 7   ♣ K J 8

♠ K Q 6 5 4
♥ A 9
♦ A K 9
♣ A 9 3

Tip

When a contract looks easy if trumps break evenly, see if there is any way you can overcome a bad break by making your small trumps by ruffing. Try to lose tricks when you can afford to do so, while you have control of the trump suit.

Deal Fourteen

Neither Side Vulnerable. Dealer South.

♠ K Q 10 6 3
♥ K 5 2
♦ J 4
♣ J 4 2

♠ A 4
♥ A Q J 10 8
♦ A 5 2
♣ 8 7 3

West	North	East	South
–	–	–	1♥
Pass	1♠	Pass	1NT
Pass	3♥	Pass	4♥
All Pass			

Contract: 4♥ by South. Opening lead: ♦K.

Plan the play from here.

How many immediate winners do you have?
Nine; five hearts, three spades and the ace of diamonds.

Which suit will provide the tenth trick?
A diamond ruff would provide an extra trick, but unfortunately this would involve ducking a round of diamonds and risking a club switch. A much better bet is the spade suit. If they break 3-3, you will have eleven tricks.

What if the spades do not break? Is there anything you can do to give yourself a chance?
You could ruff a spade to establish the fifth card as a trick.

How will you get to dummy to cash that spade trick?
You need to be a little careful. Win the opening lead to avoid the deadly club switch and draw just two rounds of trumps with the queen and the jack. If the hearts are 3-2, turn your attention to spades. Play the ace and king of spades then lead a low one and ruff high. Don't lead the queen on the third round because if this is ruffed you will not have established the suit. Now you can cross to dummy's ♥K, drawing the last trump in the process, and cash the two spade tricks for your contract.

What if hearts are 4-1?
Now there is no point in ruffing out the spades because you have no entry to dummy after drawing trumps. Instead you should just run the rest of your trumps then play in spades.

How should you play the spades?
If it is West who has the trump length, you should play spades from the top since there is no reason to suppose he will have length in both majors. If it is East who has the trump length, the decision is much closer. Cashing the ace then leading low to the ten will gain if West has jack to four or more but will lose when East holds jack doubleton or jack to three.

If East has four trumps to West's one, West has twelve non-trump cards to East's nine and so rates to be longer in any other suit, including spades. Probably the odds just favor a second round spade finesse, but it is very close.

The full deal:

♠ K Q 10 6 3
♥ K 5 2
♦ J 4
♣ J 4 2

♠ J 7 5 2   ♠ 9 8
♥ 7 3   ♥ 9 6 4
♦ K Q 10 7   ♦ 9 8 6 3
♣ A 9 5   ♣ K Q 10 6

♠ A 4
♥ A Q J 10 8
♦ A 5 2
♣ 8 7 3

Tip

Don't always assume that suits will divide favorably. Sometimes it may pay to delay the drawing of trumps until after you have established a side-suit. Particularly, as here, where the only entry to the established tricks is in the trump suit.

DEAL FIFTEEN
Neither Side Vulnerable. Dealer South

♠ Q 9 7 2
♥ 6 3
♦ 8 7 4 2
♣ A K Q

♠ K J
♥ A K Q J 9
♦ 3
♣ J 10 9 8 4

West	North	East	South
–	–	–	1♥
Pass	1♠	Pass	2♣
Pass	2♦	Pass	3♥
Pass	4♥	All Pass	

Contract: 4♥ by South. Opening lead: ♦Q.

West continues with the ♦6 to East's the king. What do you do?

How many immediate winners do you have?
Ten; five hearts and five clubs, assuming that neither defender has five hearts to the ten.

Should you ruff the second diamond?
There is no reason not to. If you discard, the defense will keep on with diamonds and you will have to ruff the next one.

Now what?
If hearts are 3-3 you can draw trumps, unblock the clubs and play a spade, making eleven tricks. If hearts are 4-2, this will not work because when you lead the spade the defense will win the ace and cash the rest of the diamonds.

What can you do if the hearts are 4-2?
By the time you discover the 4-2 break it will be too late to overcome it, unless you have already allowed for it. The problem is the club blockage, obliging you to use up a trump to return to hand after cashing dummy's winners.

How can you overcome the blockage?
Your own clubs are solid, so that you don't need dummy's high cards; you can afford to throw them away.

Cash one top club then play your four winning trumps, discarding the two remaining clubs on the third and fourth rounds. Now, whether hearts are 3-3 or 4-2, you can cash four more club tricks without worrying about how to get back to your hand.

The full deal:

♠ Q 9 7 2
♥ 6 3
♦ 8 7 4 2
♣ A K Q

♠ A 3   ♠ 10 8 6 5 4
♥ 7 5 4 2   ♥ 10 8
♦ Q J 9 6 5   ♦ A K 10
♣ 7 2   ♣ 6 5 3

♠ K J
♥ A K Q J 9
♦ 3
♣ J 10 9 8 4

Tip

When you can see that you have all the tricks you need to fulfil your contract, stop to consider what could go wrong. Sometimes, if you see the problem before you come to it, there is a way to overcome it.

DEAL SIXTEEN
Both Sides Vulnerable. Dealer South.

♠ 9 4
♥ 10 8 3
♦ A 9 5 4 2
♣ Q 6 3

♠ K 6
♥ A K Q J 9 5 2
♦ 6
♣ A 8 2

West	North	East	South
–	–	–	2♥
Pass	2NT	Pass	3♥
Pass	4♥	All Pass	

Contract: 4♥ by South. Opening lead: ♦Q.

Play on.

How many immediate winners do you have?
Nine; seven hearts and two minor suit aces.

Where will you find your tenth trick?
Either by leading to the king of spades and finding East with the ace or by leading to the club queen and finding West with the king.

That gives you two fifty-fifty chances, but is there another possibility you can try first?
Yes. If the diamonds are 4-3 and hearts 2-1, you can establish the fifth diamond if you are careful with your trump spots.

How should you play?

Win the ace of diamonds and ruff a diamond high. Lead the ♥9 to dummy's ten and ruff another diamond high. Now lead the ♥5 to the eight. If everyone has followed to three rounds of diamonds and hearts were 2-1, ruff another diamond high and play your carefully preserved ♥2 to dummy's three to cash the long diamond.

What if one of the red suits fails to break evenly?

When you cross to dummy for the last time, lead a spade to the king. Even if it loses you can hope to find the ♣K onside.

The full deal:

```
              ♠ 9 4
              ♥ 10 8 3
              ♦ A 9 5 4 2
              ♣ Q 6 3
♠ A J 10 8                ♠ Q 7 5 3 2
♥ 6 4                     ♥ 7
♦ Q J 10 8                ♦ K 7 3
♣ 10 5 4                  ♣ K J 9 7
              ♠ K 6
              ♥ A K Q J 9 5 2
              ♦ 6
              ♣ A 8 2
```

Tip

However good your prospects seem to be, always look for those little extra chances which can improve your prospects. Do this at trick one, before playing from dummy. If you leave it until after your main chances have let you down, it may be too late.

DEAL SEVENTEEN
North/South Vulnerable. Dealer South.

```
              ♠ 10 6 3 2
              ♥ K 10 3
              ♦ 9 7 2
              ♣ K 5 3

              ♠ A K
              ♥ A Q J 9 8 7
              ♦ A
              ♣ A Q 7 2
```

West	North	East	South
–	–	–	2♣
Pass	2♦	Pass	2♥
Pass	3♥	Pass	4♣
Pass	5♣	Pass	5NT
Pass	6♦	Pass	7♥
All Pass			

Contract: 7♥ by South. Opening lead: ♥6.

East discards the ♦3. Plan the play from here.

How many immediate winners do you have?

Twelve; six hearts, two spades, one diamond and three clubs.

Where will you find your thirteenth trick?

Perhaps from a 3-3 club break.

Can you find an extra chance?

Suppose that West had four or more clubs along with his four trumps. You could play clubs before drawing trumps and ruff the fourth round in dummy.

True. But that gives East eleven cards in spades and diamonds. He might have bid, particularly at this vulnerability. Is there a better chance?

Yes. Perhaps one defender, presumably East, has four or more cards in both black suits. Try this line. Win the opening lead, cash the ace and king of spades and lead a trump to dummy. Now ruff a spade and run the rest of your trumps. There is a small possibility that the queen-jack of spades will have fallen in three rounds. If it doesn't don't worry. Everyone is down to five cards. If the same player began with length in both black suits, he is now the only one who can guard either of them. Cash the ace of diamonds, leaving yourself with four clubs and dummy with three clubs and the ♠10. If you are in luck, East's last five cards have to be four clubs and a top spade—clearly impossible.

Congratulations. If a defender finds himself in this position you have squeezed him. Note the importance of ruffing a spade. Had you not done so, West could have kept a guard in that suit, allowing East to pitch his spades and hang on to the club stopper.

The full deal:

```
              ♠ 10 6 3 2
              ♥ K 10 3
              ♦ 9 7 2
              ♣ K 5 3
♠ J 8 4                   ♠ Q 9 7 5
♥ 6 5 4 2                 ♥ –
♦ K 10 6 4                ♦ Q J 8 5 3
♣ 9 4                     ♣ J 10 8 6
              ♠ A K
              ♥ A Q J 9 8 7
              ♦ A
              ♣ A Q 7 2
```

Tip

If you are one trick short of the number you require but have chances of another trick in two or more suits, don't despair. Perhaps one opponent will be trying to guard both suits and will find it impossible. Sometimes, as here, you will have to do a little preparatory work to improve the chance that only one opponent can cover each suit.

DEAL EIGHTEEN
East/West Vulnerable. Dealer South.

♠ J 9 8
♥ J 6
♦ K 9 8 6
♣ A Q J 10

♠ A K Q 10 7 6 3 2
♥ –
♦ A J 10 2
♣ 6

West	North	East	South
–	–	–	2♠
Pass	3♠	Pass	4♦
Pass	5♣	Pass	5♥
Pass	6♦	Pass	7♠
All Pass			

Contract: 7♠ by South. Opening lead: ♥A.

Plan the play.

How many immediate winners do you have?
Eleven; eight spades, one club and two diamonds.

You need two more tricks; where will you find them?
The obvious place is from diamonds, requiring a successful guess for the queen.

Any other possibilities?
There is the club suit. A ruffing finesse will work if East has the king, while a simple finesse followed by ace and a ruff could be right if West holds the king with only one or two small cards.

Playing on diamonds is slightly better than a 50 percent chance, either a singleton queen or a winning finesse. The ruffing club finesse is a straight 50 percent, while the simple finesse is significantly worse since it also requires West to be short in the suit. Which is the best play?
None of these. Or rather, none of these on its own. The best play is to combine two chances.

Which ones?
Ruff the opening lead and draw the missing trumps then cash the ace and king of diamonds. True, this is not the best play to bring in four diamond tricks, but there is a fair chance of dropping a singleton or doubleton queen and solving your problems immediately. The reason why this is better than taking a finesse is that it is less committal. If the queen does not fall, you can try a second chance. Play a club to the ace and take the ruffing club finesse. That is a fifty-fifty play, but by combining your chances you have added almost another 20 percent for the queen of diamonds dropping, making 70 percent in all. A lot better than relying on a finesse.

The full deal:

♠ J 9 8
♥ J 6
♦ K 9 8 6
♣ A Q J 10

♠ 5 4
♥ A K 9 8 3
♦ Q 3
♣ K 8 4 2

♠ –
♥ Q 10 7 5 4 2
♦ 7 5 4
♣ 9 7 5 3

♠ A K Q 10 7 6 3 2
♥ –
♦ A J 10 2
♣ 6

Tip
Rather than commit yourself to the single best chance of making your contract—here, a winning diamond guess – consider the possibility that combining two lesser chances might give a better overall chance of success.

DEAL NINETEEN
Both Sides Vulnerable. Dealer South.

♠ 8 7
♥ 10 2
♦ K J 10 8 3
♣ K 10 6 5

♠ 3
♥ A Q J 5 3
♦ A Q
♣ A 8 7 4 3

West	North	East	South
–	–	–	1♥
Pass	1NT	2♠	3♣
3♠	4♣	Pass	5♣
All Pass			

Contract: 5♣ by South. Opening lead: ♠Q.

West continues with the ♠2.

How many immediate winners do you have?
Nine; two clubs, five diamonds, a heart and a spade ruff.

Which suits will provide the other two tricks required?
There are two possibilities; a favorable club break and a successful heart finesse. Perhaps of more concern, however, is the number of potential losers you have.

How many losers might there be?
Four; two clubs and a heart plus the spade already lost.

You can only afford two losers in total. How good are your chances?
If you don't lose a club trick, either because they are 2-2 or East has a singleton honor and you guess well, you have no problem. The heart finesse is for an overtrick. If you have one club loser, you will have to avoid losing a heart, while if

you have two club losers you will be down whether or not there is a heart to lose.

How should you play?
You have no need to ruff anything, so it looks right to draw trumps.

Do you cash the ace or king first?
The ace. If East has all four trumps, you have two losers however you play. If West has four trumps, you can pick them up for one loser, but only by playing the ace and then low towards the king-ten.

When you cash the ♣A, East drops the jack. You lead a second round and West follows with the nine. Do you finesse or play the king?
Many self-styled experts will tell you to finesse, following the "principle of restricted choice." This states that if East had the bare jack he would have had no choice but to play it, while with the queen-jack doubleton he would have played the queen half the time. You should therefore assume that he does not have the queen when he plays the jack.

Although it looks strange at first sight, the principle of restricted choice is valid, but there is a much better argument on this deal in favor of playing the king.

What is it?
If you guess correctly, you are bound to succeed in your contract. The case to worry about is when you guess wrong. Say you finesse the ten and lose to doubleton queen-jack. Your contract is now dependent on the heart finesse—a fair bet on the auction, but no certainty.

Now try playing the ♣K and finding that West began with queen to three and so has a club trick to come.

What do you do if West has a club trick?
Play the ace and queen of diamonds, overtaking, and run the rest of the diamonds, discarding hearts from hand. West can ruff a diamond but if he does not you lead a club to his queen and he is in the same position. He is endplayed and must either lead a heart into your ace-queen or give a ruff and discard. Since three of your hearts went on the diamonds, either is fatal to the defense.

The full deal:

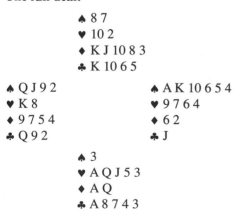

```
          ♠ 8 7
          ♥ 10 2
          ♦ K J 10 8 3
          ♣ K 10 6 5
♠ Q J 9 2              ♠ A K 10 6 5 4
♥ K 8                  ♥ 9 7 6 4
♦ 9 7 5 4              ♦ 6 2
♣ Q 9 2               ♣ J
          ♠ 3
          ♥ A Q J 5 3
          ♦ A Q
          ♣ A 8 7 4 3
```

Tip

Don't blindly follow rules or the odds. Remember to play the whole hand, not one suit in isolation. Sometimes you can afford a wrong guess, as long as the resulting loser is taken by the right defender.

DEAL TWENTY

North/South Vulnerable. Dealer South.

```
♠ A K 5 3 2
♥ 5
♦ K 8 7 3 2
♣ 8 6

♠ 8 6
♥ A K Q J 10 9 3
♦ A 4
♣ K 3
```

West	North	East	South
–	–	–	2♥
Pass	2♠	Pass	4♥
Pass	4♠(*)	Pass	5♣(*)
Pass	5♦(*)	Pass	6♥
All Pass			

(*) Cuebids

Contract: 6♥ by South. Opening lead: ♥8.

Plan the play.

How many immediate winners do you have?
Eleven; seven hearts, two spades and two diamonds.

Where might the twelfth trick come from?
There are three possibilities. You can hope to find East with the ace of clubs or ruff out one of dummy's suits to establish one or more long cards in it.

Can you combine two or more of these chances?
Yes, you can try setting up one of dummy's suits and if this fails fall back on the club play.

Does it matter which suit you try to establish, or is it a complete guess?
If you needed two extra tricks and therefore a 3-3 break, it would be a guess, but you need only one extra trick. Suppose you guess to play on spades. You draw trumps then play ace-king and ruff a spade. If they break 3-3, fine, if not you only have one more dummy entry so cannot both establish and cash the fifth spade.

Now try playing on diamonds instead of spades. Again you draw trumps then play ace-king and a third round. If they are 3-3, no problem.

What if diamonds are 4-2?
Again, no problem. Spades provide two entries to dummy. You cross to the ♠A and ruff another diamond then cross to the ♠K to cash the established trick.

And if the diamonds are 5-1?
By the time you discover this, it will be too late to switch your attention to spades. Play a club to the king and hope for the best.

The full deal:

```
                ♠ A K 5 3 2
                ♥ 5
                ♦ K 8 7 3 2
                ♣ 8 6
    ♠ J 9                      ♠ Q 10 7 4
    ♥ 8 6                      ♥ 7 4 2
    ♦ J 10 6 5                 ♦ Q 9
    ♣ A J 10 5 4               ♣ Q 9 7 2
                ♠ 8 6
                ♥ A K Q J 10 9 3
                ♦ A 4
                ♣ K 3
```

Tip

When planning to establish a long suit, always consider the entry situation. Sometimes, when you have a choice of suits to establish, whether in the same or different hands, a look at your entries will tell you which is the better option.

DEAL TWENTY-ONE

North/South Vulnerable. Dealer South.

```
                ♠ 8 6 3
                ♥ A Q 10 9
                ♦ K Q J 10
                ♣ 10 5

                ♠ A 7 4 2
                ♥ —
                ♦ A 9 8 7 6 5
                ♣ A K 4
```

West	North	East	South
–	–	–	1♦
Pass	1♥	Pass	1♠
Pass	4♦	Pass	6♦
All Pass			

Contract: 6♦ by South. Opening lead: ♣Q.

What is your plan from here?

How many immediate winners do you have?
Eleven; six diamonds, two clubs, a club ruff and the two major suit aces.

Which suit will provide the twelfth trick?
It will have to be hearts.

How might you play the heart suit?
The simple line is to use dummy's diamonds as entries to ruff two hearts and hope that the king falls in three rounds.

Is this likely to happen?
It is possible but not very likely.

Are there any other possibilities?
An endplay might be possible. Draw trumps, ruff out the clubs and play ace and another spade. If either defender wins with the doubleton king he will now have to either give a ruff and discard or lead a heart to give you a free finesse.

That is possible, but again unlikely. Even when a defender holds king doubleton, if he is awake he will unblock the king under the ace.

Try again.
If you had ♥AQJx, you could throw one spade on the queen and another on the jack and not care who had the ♥K. The ♥AQ109 is almost as good. Draw trumps and play the ace and queen of hearts, pitching a spade if East doesn't play the king. Whichever defender turns up with the ♥K, cross to dummy with a club ruff and lead the ♥10 for a second finesse again, if East plays low, you discard. As long as East has either the king or the jack of hearts, you will lose only one heart trick and get rid of all your spade losers in the process.

The full deal:

```
                ♠ 8 6 3
                ♥ A Q 10 9
                ♦ K Q J 10
                ♣ 10 5
    ♠ K J 9                    ♠ Q 10 5
    ♥ K 8 6 3                  ♥ J 7 5 4 2
    ♦ 3                        ♦ 4 2
    ♣ 9 8 6 3 2                ♣ Q J 7
                ♠ A 7 4 2
                ♥ —
                ♦ A 9 8 7 6 5
                ♣ A K 4
```

Tip

Rather than play for a missing honor to drop by ruffing out the suit consider the possibility of a ruffing finesse. Watch for combinations like AQ109, AJ109, QJ109, which allow for a double finesse to establish the trick required.

Deal Twenty-two

North/South Vulnerable. Dealer South.

♠ Q 10 9 4
♥ K 3 2
♦ 9 6 3
♣ 8 4 2

♠ A J
♥ A Q J 10 7 4
♦ A 7 2
♣ K 5

West	North	East	South
–	–	–	2♥
Pass	2NT	Pass	3♥
Pass	4♥	All Pass	

Contract: 4♥ by South. Opening lead: ♠7.

East plays the ♠5. How do you play?

How many immediate winners do you have?
Nine; six hearts, two spades and one diamond.

Where will you find the tenth trick?
There is only one dummy entry, so after taking the jack and ace of spades you cannot both establish and cash a third spade trick. It looks as though the only hope is that East has the ace of clubs.

That is only a fifty-fifty chance. Is there anything better?
There is, but only if you think of it before playing to trick one. When you avoid the loss of a spade trick you only get two winners. What if you give up a spade trick, doesn't that mean you can establish a third winner?

So how should you play?
Win the opening lead with the ace and cash two top hearts, leaving the king in dummy. Now play the ♠J and overtake with the queen, continuing the suit if this holds. When you regain the lead you can play a heart to the king and throw your losing diamonds on the ten and nine of spades.

Could anything go wrong?
Yes. First, trumps could be 4-0, in which case you will only be able to cash both spade tricks if the hand with the trumps also has four spades.

Should you still play the same way if hearts are 4-0?
No. You have only one dummy entry and, since it is unlikely that the same hand will have four cards in both majors, you should cash only one of the established spades then lead a club to the king. If you fail to do this, you may never get an opportunity to play for a well-placed ace of clubs.

Any other dangers?
If spades are 5-2, there is a possibility that one of your winners could get ruffed. If the ♣A is offside, you will then go down, but then you would have gone down however you played in that case, so have lost nothing.

The full deal:

♠ Q 10 9 4
♥ K 3 2
♦ 9 6 3
♣ 8 4 2

♠ 8 7 6
♥ 8 5
♦ Q 10 5
♣ A J 9 7 3

♠ K 5 3 2
♥ 9 6
♦ K J 8 4
♣ Q 10 6

♠ A J
♥ A Q J 10 7 4
♦ A 7 2
♣ K 5

Tip

Think through the play before playing to trick one. Grabbing what looks like a cheap trick could prove very expensive if it prevents you from following the best overall plan for success.

DEAL TWENTY-THREE

Neither Side Vulnerable. Dealer South.

♠ A Q J 8 6
♥ A Q
♦ 7 4 2
♣ 9 8 7

♠ K 10 7 3
♥ 7 3 2
♦ A Q J 10
♣ A J

West	North	East	South
–	–	–	1♠
Pass	4♣(*)	Pass	4♦
Pass	4♥	Pass	5♣
Pass	6♠	All Pass	

(*) Good raise to 4♠.

Contract: 6♠ by South. Opening lead: ♥4.

Plan the play.

How many immediate winners do you have?
Only eight; five trumps and three aces.

Where will you find the other four tricks?
There is a possibility of one extra heart trick from a successful finesse, three extra diamond tricks from a successful finesse, and a club ruff in hand.

So should you finesse the ♥Q at trick one?
No. A successful heart finesse may reduce the number of undertricks, but it will very rarely help you to make your contract. Meanwhile, a losing finesse will guarantee defeat.

Why is this?

It is easy to see how a losing heart finesse will spell defeat as you have an inescapable club loser. Suppose that the heart finesse wins, you are still dependent on the diamond finesse to make 6♠. But, if the diamond finesse works, you can throw the ♥Q on the fourth diamond.

So you rise with the ♥A, draw trumps and take the diamond finesse?

It's not quite that simple. You will need to take the diamond finesse at least twice and possibly three times. If you draw trumps then take the first finesse, the only way back to dummy to finesse again will be a third trump. If you want to finesse again you will have to use up your last trump to get back to dummy and will have none left for your club ruff.

So what is the correct sequence of plays?

Win the heart ace and take an immediate diamond finesse. If that wins you play a spade to dummy and repeat the finesse. Now draw the remaining trumps ending in dummy and take the diamond finesse again. Finally, throw the ♥Q on the fourth diamond and play ace and another club, eventually ruffing a club for your twelfth trick.

The full deal:

```
              ♠ A Q J 8 6
              ♥ A Q
              ♦ 7 4 2
              ♣ 9 8 7

♠ 9 4                      ♠ 5 2
♥ J 8 6 4                  ♥ K 10 9 5
♦ 9 3                      ♦ K 8 6 5
♣ Q 6 5 3 2                ♣ K 10 4

              ♠ K 10 7 3
              ♥ 7 3 2
              ♦ A Q J 10
              ♣ A J
```

Tip

Make sure that you have the communication to do everything you want to do. Where entries are at a premium, be careful not to waste any. That may mean, as here, that you cannot draw all of the trumps immediately but have to interweave the play.

Deal 24

Neither Side Vulnerable. Dealer South.

```
♠ Q 10 7
♥ A J 6 3
♦ J 4 2
♣ A 10 4

♠ A K J 9 5
♥ Q 4
♦ A 7 3
♣ 8 6 5
```

West	North	East	South
Pass	1NT	Pass	3♠
Pass	4♠	All Pass	

Contract: 4♠ by South. Opening lead: ♦6.

East plays the ♦Q. How do you play?

How many immediate winners do you have?

Eight; five spades and three aces.

Where can you find your other two tricks?

The queen and jack of hearts will provide one more trick even if you have to lose a trick to the king. It also looks as though West may have the ♦K, in which case leading up to the jack will establish another trick.

So everything looks very easy. Could anything go wrong?

Yes. There is something very suspicious about the diamond play. If West has led the ♦6, fourth highest, his holding must be either ♦K1086(5) or ♦K986(5)—he would have led the ten from ♦K1096(5). But that leaves East with ♦Q9(5) or ♦Q10(5). Normal play would be for East to finesse against dummy's jack, playing the nine and ten respectively.

So the ♦K is more likely to be with East than West and he is trying to mislead us?

Yes; unless he is a very weak player.

If there is no second diamond trick, is there any other hope?

Yes; you might be able to make three heart tricks.

How?

Leading the ♥Q from hand guarantees two winners but, assuming that West will cover with the king, no more. The correct play is cross to dummy with a spade and lead a low heart towards your queen. If East holds the king he either has to play it or never make it. If he plays the king, you will have three heart tricks and ten in all.

So this play guarantees the contract if East holds the ♥K?

No. If East has king to three or less he is trapped. If he ducks you can win the queen then play ace and another, ruffing out his king. But if East holds king to four hearts he can duck and let your queen win. Though you lose no heart trick, you may still have to lose two clubs and two diamonds.

Also, if trumps are 4-1, East can rise with the king from king doubleton or king to three and switch to a club. With the side entry knocked out, you will be unable to draw the last trump before cashing the fourth heart.

Nevertheless, the recommended play is your best hope of making the contract.

The full deal:

```
            ♠ Q 10 7
            ♥ A J 6 3
            ♦ J 4 2
            ♣ A 10 4
♠ 8 6 2                    ♠ 4 3
♥ 9 7 5 2                  ♥ K 10 8
♦ 6 5                      ♦ K Q 10 9 8
♣ K Q 3 2                  ♣ J 9 7
            ♠ A K J 9 5
            ♥ Q 4
            ♦ A 7 3
            ♣ 8 6 5
```

Tip

Don't take your eye off the ball just because you get what seems to be a favorable development. Always be suspicious of unusually favorable defensive plays. Make your plan as always and see if you can guard against not only bad breaks but also deception.

DEAL TWENTY-FIVE
Both Sides Vulnerable. Dealer South.

```
            ♠ –
            ♥ A K 7 6 4
            ♦ 6 4 2
            ♣ A 10 8 7 4

            ♠ A K Q J 10 9
            ♥ J 5 3
            ♦ A K Q 5
            ♣ –
```

West	North	East	South
–	–	–	2♠
Pass	3♥	Pass	3♠
Pass	4♣	Pass	4NT
Pass	5♥	Pass	5NT
Pass	6♦	Pass	7♠
All Pass			

Contract: 7♠ by South. Opening lead: ♣3.

What is your plan?

How many immediate winners do you have?
Twelve; six spades, three diamonds, two hearts and one club.

Where could you find the extra trick?
Either the jack of hearts, if the queen falls, or the long diamond.

Which is the more likely; the diamond break or the ♥Q to fall in two rounds?
Actually it is very close. A 3-3 break occurs a little over 35 percent of the time while a singleton or doubleton queen with five missing cards will occur approximately one time in three. So the break is fractionally better but neither is a very good bet.

So should you win the ace of clubs and pitch a heart from hand, relying on the 3-3 diamond break?
No. That is far too committal. What you should be looking for is a way to combine your chances. Even a singleton queen of hearts will be of no use to you once you throw a heart from hand.

How should you play?
Play a low club at trick one and ruff in hand. Draw all the trumps and now cash the ace and king of hearts. If the queen drops, you throw your low diamond on the ace of clubs and claim the remainder. If the ♥Q does not drop, throw the ♥J on the ace of clubs and hope that diamonds break.

You make your slam whenever diamonds are 3-3 or there is a singleton or doubleton queen of hearts. Is there any extra chance?
Yes. If the same defender started with queen to three hearts and four diamonds he will have been squeezed, needing his last four cards to be four diamonds and one heart—very difficult.

There are those who believe squeeze play to be something of which only experts are capable, yet here you may have squeezed an opponent without even thinking of the possibility, just by normal play. There were two crucial points in your "normal" play which make the squeeze possible; what were they?
First, it was essential to cash the last trump even though all the opposing trumps had been drawn. Suppose you had not done so. In the ending you would have had four diamonds plus a spade winner. With five cards left it would have been possible for a defender to keep four diamonds and the queen of hearts. Second, it was important to cash the ace-king of hearts before trying the diamonds. If you had cashed your diamond winners and found them to be 4-2, you could have tried hearts, but there would have been no squeeze. Why? Because you could no longer get back to your little diamond so when you cashed the ♣A the defender could afford to throw his diamond winner to keep the heart.

So when you are one trick short, needing all the remaining tricks, a squeeze may work quite automatically, but you must remember to cash all your winners and to keep communication open so you can reach both your possible length winners.

The full deal:

```
               ♠ —
               ♥ A K 7 6 4
               ♦ 6 4 2
               ♣ A 10 8 7 4
♠ 7 5 3 2                    ♠ 8 6 4
♥ 10 9                       ♥ Q 8 2
♦ J 3                        ♦ 10 9 8 7
♣ K J 6 3 2                  ♣ Q 9 5
               ♠ A K Q J 10 9
               ♥ J 5 3
               ♦ A K Q 5
               ♣ —
```

Tip

Try to combine your chances rather than commit yourself to only one possibility. Here, winning the ♣A prematurely commits you to a discard before you are ready to take it. Delay winning the club and you can try for the full range of winning options.

DEAL TWENTY-SIX
Both Sides Vulnerable. Dealer South.

```
               ♠ K J 8 6 3
               ♥ A 7 4 3
               ♦ 8 5 2
               ♣ 7

               ♠ A Q 10 9 7
               ♥ K 6
               ♦ A Q 10 4
               ♣ A 5
```

	West	North	East	South
–	–	–	–	1♠
Pass		3♠	Pass	6♠
All Pass				

Contract: 6♠ by South. Opening lead: ♣Q.

Plan the play.

How many immediate winners do you have?
Nine; five spades, two hearts and two minor suit aces.

Where might the extra tricks be found?
There are possibilities in all three side suits. There are two possible finesses in diamonds, while you can also ruff two hearts and one club. Unfortunately, the club ruff comes instead of a spade trick not as an extra trick.

So you will need an extra diamond trick; what are your chances?
Pretty good. Two finesses will bring home the contract whenever East holds either the king or jack.

Can you do any better than that?
Maybe. Suppose you didn't take the first diamond finesse until after you had eliminated clubs and hearts and drawn trumps. If the finesse lost, West would have to either lead back into your remaining diamonds or give you a ruff and discard.

So, how should you play?
Spades will need to be 2-1 for the endplay to work. Otherwise it will take three rounds to draw trumps plus two heart ruffs, leaving declarer with no trumps in one hand and so no ruff and discard threat.

Assuming spades are 2-1; win the opening lead and draw trumps, then play king and ace and ruff a heart, ruff a club and ruff a heart. The elimination is complete and you need only take a diamond finesse.

How will you take the finesse? Aren't you in the wrong hand?
Cross to dummy with a trump—but, of course, that is the last trump in declarer's hand so again there is no ruff and discard threat.

Could you have avoided this problem?
Yes. You must start the elimination earlier. Win the club, cash one top spade and play three rounds of hearts, ruffing the third round. Play a trump to dummy, ruff the last heart, ruff your club, and now you are where you want to be. Take a diamond finesse and West is endplayed if he wins.

And if spades are 3-0?
Now you will have to rely on one of the diamond finesses working as you have insufficient trumps for the elimination and endplay.

The full deal:

```
               ♠ K J 8 6 3
               ♥ A 7 4 3
               ♦ 8 5 2
               ♣ 7
♠ 5 2                        ♠ 4
♥ Q J 5 2                    ♥ 10 9 8
♦ K J 7                      ♦ 9 6 3
♣ Q J 10 4                   ♣ K 9 8 6 3 2
               ♠ A Q 10 9 7
               ♥ K 6
               ♦ A Q 10 4
               ♣ A 5
```

Tip

When planning an elimination and endplay, think the play through before you start and make sure you have the entries you need to end up in the right hand at the crucial moment.

Deal Twenty-seven

East/West Vulnerable. Dealer South.

```
♠ J 4
♥ 6 5 4 3
♦ K Q J 8 7
♣ 10 6

♠ 6 3 2
♥ A K Q 7 2
♦ A
♣ A 8 5 3
```

West	North	East	South
–	–	1♣	1♥
Pass	2♥	Pass	4♥
All Pass			

Contract: 4♥ by South. Opening lead: ♠10.

The lead is taken by East's ♠Q, who continues with the ace then the king of spades.

How many immediate winners do you have?
Assuming that hearts are not 4-0, which would surely spell defeat, eleven; five hearts, four diamonds, one club and the spade ruff.

So are there any problems?
No. Ruff the spade, draw trumps, unblock the ace of diamonds and cross to dummy to run the diamonds.

And how do you propose to get to dummy?
Ah. If the trumps are 2-2 there is no problem because you can lead the ♥2 to dummy, but a 3-1 break leaves you with no entry.

Is there any way to overcome this problem?
Just discard a club at trick three. You win the next trick, ruffing in hand if it is a fourth spade, draw trumps, unblock the diamond and cross to dummy. By keeping all four trumps in dummy you have guaranteed yourself an entry when you want one, after trumps have been drawn.

Doesn't this line risk going down when the hearts are 2-2 if East plays a fourth spade and West can ruff?
You need not worry about that as it would mean that East, who opened 1♣, also holds ace, king, queen to five spades. Surely he would then have bid 2♠ over 2♥?

The full deal:

```
              ♠ J 4
              ♥ 6 5 4 3
              ♦ K Q J 8 7
              ♣ 10 6
♠ 10 9 8 7 5              ♠ A K Q
♥ J 10 8                 ♥ 9
♦ 9 5 3                  ♦ 10 6 4 2
♣ 4 2                    ♣ K Q J 9 7
              ♠ 6 3 2
              ♥ A K Q 7 2
              ♦ A
              ♣ A 8 5 3
```

Tip

Don't play too quickly. Before making an obvious-looking play like ruffing the third spade, pause for a moment and check that you can afford to do so. You will have noticed that it is coming up time and again but, be careful of your communications. Always try to preserve your entries until you need them.

Deal Twenty-eight

East/West Vulnerable. Dealer South.

```
♠ A J
♥ A Q
♦ A Q 7
♣ 10 9 8 7 5 3

♠ K Q 3
♥ 10 4
♦ 9 8 2
♣ A K Q J 2
```

West	North	East	South
–	–	–	1♣
Pass	1♦	Pass	1NT
Pass	4♣	Pass	5♣
Pass	6♣	All Pass	

Contract: 6♣ by South. Opening lead: ♥3.

Plan the play.

How many immediate winners do you have?
Eleven; six clubs, three spades and two red aces.

What possibilities are there for a twelfth trick?
A winning finesse in either red suit would give you twelve tricks.

So what will you play at trick one?
The ♥Q.

It loses and back comes a spade. How do you play on?
Win in dummy, draw trumps and lead a diamond to the queen.

That also loses and you are one down. There was a 100 percent line available; what was it?
Look at the diamond spots. Had you held AQ9 opposite three small, you would have seen the possibility of an endplay. Effectively, that is exactly what you have here.

So how should you play?
Rise with the ace of hearts, draw trumps and play three rounds of spades, pitching the ♥Q. Ruff your losing heart, cross back to hand with a trump and lead a diamond, covering West's card. If East wins this trick he is endplayed.

As in an earlier deal, the ♥Q was a temptation. With ♥A2, you would surely have played correctly.

The full deal:

```
          ♠ A J
          ♥ A Q
          ♦ A Q 7
          ♣ 10 9 8 7 5 3
♠ 10 7 4 2              ♠ 9 8 6 5
♥ J 8 6 3 2            ♥ K 9 7 5
♦ J 6 3                ♦ K 10 5 4
♣ 6                    ♣ 4
          ♠ K Q 3
          ♥ 10 4
          ♦ 9 8 2
          ♣ A K Q J 2
```

Tip

Look carefully at your spot cards. Sometimes, suit combinations which appear to be quite different at first glance can actually be identical for practical purposes.

DEAL TWENTY-NINE

Both Sides Vulnerable. Dealer South.

```
          ♠ J 5 2
          ♥ 8
          ♦ K 9 6 3 2
          ♣ Q 8 4 3

          ♠ A K Q 10 6 4
          ♥ A 6 3 2
          ♦ 7
          ♣ 9 2
```

West	North	East	South
–	–	–	1♠
Dble	2♠	3♥	4♠
Dble	All Pass		

Contract: 4♠ doubled by South. Opening lead: ♣A.

West switches to the ♠3. Over to you.

How many immediate winners do you have?
Seven; six spades and the ace of hearts.

Where will you find three more tricks?
One in clubs or diamonds, and if the defense does not play another trump when it gains the lead, two tricks can come from ruffing hearts.

So should you take a heart ruff immediately?
No. If you do so you have no quick entry back to hand to take another ruff. When you lead a minor suit card from the dummy the defense will win and lead a second trump.

What should you do at trick three?
Lead your diamond. On the auction, West is heavy favorite to hold the ace of diamonds so you will establish the king as a trick.

West wins the ♦A and plays a second spade and East discards a low heart. This is bad news. You could ruff a heart and cash the ♦K, but that still leaves you with two losers. Is there any chance left?
Yes, a slim one. Instead of ruffing a heart, lead a club towards the queen. You know from the bidding and opening lead that West holds the king, so at worst you will swap your heart ruff for a club trick and go down one. The slim chance of making your contract is that West has ace-king to four clubs and East jack-ten-other. Now West has no defense. If he wins the ♣K and leads his last trump he stops you from ruffing any hearts, but you win in dummy and have the ♦K and ♣Q and, thanks to the fortunate lie, the ♣8 to cash. If West ducks the club your queen wins, you cash the ♦K and can arrange to ruff a heart with dummy's last trump.

The full deal:

```
          ♠ J 5 2
          ♥ 8
          ♦ K 9 6 3 2
          ♣ Q 8 4 3
♠ 8 7 3                ♠ 9
♥ Q 10 9              ♥ K J 7 5 4
♦ A Q J                ♦ 10 8 5 4
♣ A K 7 6              ♣ J 10 5
          ♠ A K Q 10 6 4
          ♥ A 6 3 2
          ♦ 7
          ♣ 9 2
```

Tip

Never give up. Always look to see if there is a plausible lie of the cards which gives you a chance of success and, if one exists, play for it.

DEAL THIRTY

Both Sides Vulnerable. Dealer South.

```
          ♠ A Q 10 4
          ♥ A 4 3
          ♦ 7 6 2
          ♣ K 7 4

          ♠ K J 9 8 7 6 3
          ♥ K Q 7
          ♦ A Q 8
          ♣ —
```

West	North	East	South
–	1NT	Pass	3♠
Pass	4♥	Pass	5♣
Pass	5♠	Pass	6♦
Pass	6♠	All Pass	

Contract: 6♠ by South. Opening lead: ♥J.

Plan the play.

How many immediate winners do you have?
Eleven; seven spades, three hearts and the ace of diamonds.

What will be your twelfth trick?
Hopefully, a second diamond.

The obvious way of making a second diamond trick is thanks to the successful finesse of the queen. Can you see anything better?
If you had the ♦AQ9 instead of the ♦AQ8, you could play to eliminate the other suits then lead a diamond and simply cover East's card to endplay West. The ♦8 is not quite good enough to guarantee an endplay because East can play any one of the nine, ten and jack to force you to play the queen. If that loses to the king, there are still two of the nine, ten and jack out – one to force out the ace and one to beat the eight.

So does that mean that there is no hope of an endplay?
No. An endplay could still work if East failed to go up with his nine, ten or jack as you could now play the eight. Also, if West had the ♦KJ, ♦KJ10, or ♦KJ109(x), West could be forced to win the first round. Nonetheless the odds are quite poor.

Is there any better chance?
Yes. There is the possibility of a quite different endplay.

Do you see what it is?
Win the heart lead in hand, play a spade to dummy and ruff a club. Win a second spade in dummy and ruff a second club then cash your remaining hearts, ending in dummy. Now lead the ♣K. If East plays low, discard the ♦8. When West wins the ace he is endplayed.

What if East plays the ace of clubs?
Then you ruff, play a spade to dummy and lead a low diamond, intending to play the eight. If West has to win, all well and good, if not, your last chance is the diamond finesse.

The full deal:

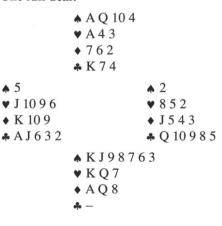

```
              ♠ A Q 10 4
              ♥ A 4 3
              ♦ 7 6 2
              ♣ K 7 4
♠ 5                        ♠ 2
♥ J 10 9 6                 ♥ 8 5 2
♦ K 10 9                   ♦ J 5 4 3
♣ A J 6 3 2                ♣ Q 10 9 8 5
              ♠ K J 9 8 7 6 3
              ♥ K Q 7
              ♦ A Q 8
              ♣ —
```

Tip

Although you have seen that holdings which look different can sometimes actually be identical, don't fall into the trap of thinking that similar holdings are necessarily identical. There is a whale of a difference between AQ9 and AQ8.

DEAL THIRTY-ONE
East/West Vulnerable. Dealer West.

```
              ♠ Q 7
              ♥ K J 10 7 4
              ♦ A 3 2
              ♣ A 9 6

              ♠ 8 5 3 2
              ♥ A Q 8 6
              ♦ Q 9 8
              ♣ K 2
```

West	North	East	South
1♠	Dble	Pass	3♥
Pass	4♥	All Pass.	

Contract: 4♥ by South. Opening lead: ♠ A.

West continues with the ♠K and then the jack. East pitches the ♣5 on the third round. Over to you.

How many immediate winners do you have?
Eight; five hearts, two clubs and the ace of diamonds.

Where will you find two more tricks?
You can ruff two spades in the dummy but, because this is with the long trump holding, it will only produce one extra trick. Alternatively, you can ruff a club in hand. The tenth trick will have to come from diamonds.

The easy play in diamonds is to lead low to the queen. Will this succeed?
It is possible but unlikely. On the auction, West figures to hold the ♦K.

So how will you make a second diamond trick?
With an endplay.

How should you play?
Start by ruffing the third spade high to avoid the risk of an over-ruff. You play three rounds of clubs, ruffing the third round and draw trumps. This takes three rounds, East following each time while West follows once then discards a club and a spade. You are left with:

```
              ♠ —
              ♥ K
              ♦ A 3 2
              ♣ —

              ♠ 8
              ♥ —
              ♦ Q 9 8
              ♣ —
```

What do you play next

It is important that when you drew trumps you ended in hand. Otherwise, if you lead a diamond to the eight, West can win cheaply and return a spade and must make a second diamond. If you cash your trump, he throws a diamond and has a spade and a diamond to come. If you are in the South hand, however, you can lead your spade. West plays the ♠10 and you discard a diamond. West must now lead away from ♦K.

The full deal:

```
                ♠ Q 7
                ♥ K J 10 7 4
                ♦ A 3 2
                ♣ A 9 6
♠ A K J 10 4                    ♠ 9 6
♥ 3                             ♥ 9 5 2
♦ K 6 4                         ♦ J 10 7 5
♣ Q 10 7 3                      ♣ J 8 5 4
                ♠ 8 5 3 2
                ♥ A Q 8 6
                ♦ Q 9 8
                ♣ K 2
```

Tip

Listen to the bidding and you will often get a clue as to the position of a missing high card. When it sounds badly placed, you may be able to force the defender to lead away from it.

DEAL THIRTY-TWO

North/South Vulnerable. Dealer South.

```
                ♠ A Q 8
                ♥ 8 7 6
                ♦ K Q 2
                ♣ Q 9 8 6

                ♠ 7 6 3 2
                ♥ A
                ♦ A 5
                ♣ A K J 10 7 3
```

West	North	East	South
–	–	–	1♣
Pass	3NT	Pass	4♣
Pass	4♠	Pass	6♣
All Pass			

Contract: 6♣ by South. Opening lead: ♥K.

Plan the play.

How many immediate winners do you have?
Eleven; six clubs, three diamonds and two major suit aces.

What do you hope will be your twelfth trick?
The queen of spades.

You could simply rely on the spade finesse, but is there anything you can do to improve your chances?
It would be quite easy to eliminate the other suits before playing on spades, setting up a possible endplay.

How would you go about this?
Win the heart lead, play a club to the dummy, ruff a heart and draw the remaining trump(s) then play three rounds of diamonds pitching a spade. Finally, ruff the last heart to get back to hand and lead a spade to the eight.

The trouble, as you have seen before, is that AQ8 is not a good enough holding to guarantee the endplay. Most of the time, you still require the king to be onside. As it is quite a poor chance, is there any alternative?
There is one other possibility. With only six cards outstanding, a doubleton with East is a distinct possibility. Rather than using the technique you have seen before of hoping to duck a spade to East, try for a different endplay. Cash the ♠A before ruffing the last heart, then lead a low spade to the queen. Now you make your contract whenever West holds the king but also when East holds the king doubleton as when he wins he has to give you a ruff and discard.

This is a better extra chance than trying to duck a spade to East against alert defenders because West can see the endplay coming and should always play a card higher than the eight.

The full deal:

```
                ♠ A Q 8
                ♥ 8 7 6
                ♦ K Q 2
                ♣ Q 9 8 6
♠ J 10 5 4                      ♠ K 9
♥ K Q J 5                       ♥ 10 9 4 3 2
♦ 9 7 6 3                       ♦ J 10 8 4
♣ 4                             ♣ 5 2
                ♠ 7 6 3 2
                ♥ A
                ♦ A 5
                ♣ A K J 10 7 3
```

Tip

Be flexible in your approach. Because you recognize that a familiar combination provides an extra chance, don't stop thinking. Perhaps there is something even better.

DEAL THIRTY-THREE
East/West Vulnerable. Dealer South.

```
♠ 8 6 5 4 2
♥ A Q 8
♦ 10 4 3 2
♣ J

♠ A J 10 9 7
♥ J
♦ Q 9
♣ A 10 8 5 4
```

West	North	East	South
–	–	–	1♠
Pass	4♠	All Pass	

Contract: 4♠ by South. Opening lead: ♥10.

How should you play?

How many immediate winners do you have?
Only the three aces.

How can you make the extra tricks you require?
By cross-ruffing and possibly establishing a long club trick.

Should you finesse at trick one?
It is tempting because if it works you will have a discard for one of your diamond losers. The trouble is that a losing finesse will guarantee defeat because East will quickly switch to diamonds. So you should rise with the ♥A.

What next?
Your main idea is to make seven of your small trumps by ruffing, but you do not want to risk being over-ruffed as you may then lose two trump tricks.

Since you need a total of seven ruffs, you cannot afford to play safe in trumps by taking a first round finesse to guard against ♠KQ3 with East. Should you then cash the ace of spades instead?
At first glance this looks quite attractive, preventing either defender from over-ruffing with a singleton honor. Plan the play, however. After a spade to the ace, you play ace and ruff a club, ruff a heart, ruff a club, ruff a heart, ruff a club. You are left with:

```
♠ 8
♥ –
♦ 10 4 3 2
♣ –

♠ J 10
♥ –
♦ Q 9
♣ 10
```

If clubs were 4-3, you need only give up a spade and two diamonds, but then you have a spade and a club to add to the eight tricks already won. But what if clubs were 5-2? You have no quick entry back to hand to ruff the last club. When you play a diamond, the hand with the remaining trump will win and draw dummy's last trump, leaving you one trick short.

Can you do anything to avoid this?
Yes. Delay playing the ace of spades by a couple of tricks. Win the first trick and play ace and ruff a club, then play a spade to the ace. This gives you an extra entry to hand for an extra club ruff. You continue as before but this time you can ruff all your club losers without having to give up the lead, so are safe even if the suit breaks 5-2.

The full deal:

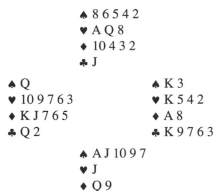

```
            ♠ 8 6 5 4 2
            ♥ A Q 8
            ♦ 10 4 3 2
            ♣ J
♠ Q                        ♠ K 3
♥ 10 9 7 6 3               ♥ K 5 4 2
♦ K J 7 6 5               ♦ A 8
♣ Q 2                     ♣ K 9 7 6 3
            ♠ A J 10 9 7
            ♥ J
            ♦ Q 9
            ♣ A 10 8 5 4
```

Tip

Don't assume an even break unless you have to. Make sure that your plan allows for a bad break in a side suit and preserve all the entries you might need to cover that eventuality.

DEAL THIRTY-FOUR
East/West Vulnerable. Dealer South.

```
♠ K Q 2
♥ A 7
♦ 10 8 4
♣ A J 6 4 2

♠ A J 10 9 7 3
♥ J 4
♦ A 7 3
♣ 7 3
```

West	North	East	South
–	–	–	1♠
Pass	2♣	Pass	2♠
Pass	4♠	All Pass	

Contract: 4♠ by South. Opening lead: ♥K.

Plan the play.

How many immediate winners do you have?
Nine; six spades and three aces.

Which suit will have to provide your tenth trick?
Clubs. There is no possibility in either red suit.

Will you win or duck the first trick?
Win. To duck would risk a diamond switch, establishing two more defensive winners before you have started on the clubs.

Having won the ♥A, should you now draw trumps?
No. You will need dummy's spades as entries to the clubs.

How should you set about the clubs?
It is tempting to cross to hand with a spade to lead a club towards the ace-jack, hoping to find West with the king and queen, but this is an illusion. Whenever the king-queen of clubs are not onside, this play reduces you to dependence on a 3-3 club break because whoever wins the first club can play a second spade, removing one of dummy's entries prematurely.

If, instead, you play clubs from dummy, you can arrange to ruff two rounds and establish a winner even on a 4-2 break—the most likely break, incidentally, when missing six cards.

So should you just play ace and another club at tricks two and three?
No. That again wastes a dummy entry and leaves you dependent on a 3-3 break. Duck a club at trick two. You can win a spade or diamond switch in hand, play ace and ruff a club high, cross to dummy with a high spade and ruff another club high if they are not yet established. Finally, you draw trumps ending in dummy and cash the long club trick. Only a 5-1 club or 4-0 spade break can defeat you.

The full deal:

```
              ♠ K Q 2
              ♥ A 7
              ♦ 10 8 4
              ♣ A J 6 4 2
♠ 8 5 4                      ♠ 6
♥ K Q 10 9                   ♥ 8 6 5 3 2
♦ Q J 6 2                    ♦ K 9 5
♣ K 9                        ♣ Q 10 8 5
              ♠ A J 10 9 7 3
              ♥ J 4
              ♦ A 7 3
              ♣ 7 3
```

Tip

When hoping to establish a long suit headed by the ace facing a small doubleton, it usually pays to duck the first round, preserving the ace as an entry to allow you to play the third round without having to use up an entry elsewhere.

DEAL THIRTY-FIVE
Both Sides Vulnerable. Dealer South.

```
              ♠ A 10 9
              ♥ A 5 3 2
              ♦ K 7 3
              ♣ 10 9 8

              ♠ K Q J 7 3
              ♥ 8
              ♦ A Q 5 2
              ♣ J 4 3
```

West	North	East	South
–	–	–	1♠
Pass	2NT	Pass	3♦
Pass	4♠	All Pass	

Contract: 4♠ by South. Opening lead: ♥Q.

How should you play?

How many immediate winners do you have?
Nine; five spades, three diamonds and the ace of hearts.

Where will you find your tenth trick?
Presumably from diamonds. A 3-3 break is the obvious route to success.

A 3-3 break occurs only a little over one time in three; can you find an extra chance?
You could play two rounds of trumps then three rounds of diamonds. If diamonds were 4-2 and the same hand had spade length and diamond length you could ruff the last diamond in dummy.

That is certainly an extra chance, but finding the same hand with the length in two suits is against the odds. There is something much better; can you see it?
If spades are 3-2, you can make ten tricks by a dummy reversal.

How do you play?
Win the heart lead and immediately ruff a heart. Play a spade to dummy and ruff the last heart. You have ruffed three times in hand and now cross to the ♦K to draw the last trump with dummy's ♠10 while you discard. You make three spade tricks in dummy, one heart, three heart ruffs in hand and three diamonds (or four if they break 3-3).

All this line requires is a 3-2 trump break; which is about a 70 percent chance.

What if spades are 4-1?
You will discover this when you play a spade to dummy for the second time. You are still all right as long as the hand with the long spades also has at least three diamonds. You could just continue with your plan and ruff the last heart, but it would be slightly better to try to cash three diamonds ending in dummy first. The advantage of this is that if the hand with the four spades has only three hearts he does not get an opportunity to discard a diamond when you ruff the fourth heart. Even with spades 4-1, you succeed when the long trump hand is at least 3-3 in the red suits.

The full deal:

　　　♠ A 10 9
　　　♥ A 5 3 2
　　　♦ K 7 3
　　　♣ 10 9 8

♠ 8 6 2　　　　　　　　♠ 5 4
♥ Q J 10 7　　　　　　♥ K 9 6 4
♦ 8 6　　　　　　　　　♦ J 10 9 4
♣ A Q 7 2　　　　　　　♣ K 6 5

　　　♠ K Q J 7 3
　　　♥ 8
　　　♦ A Q 5 2
　　　♣ J 4 3

Tip

When your shorter trump holding is strong and you have a side suit shortage with the long trump holding, consider the possibility of a dummy reversal, taking ruffs in the long hand and drawing trumps with the shorter holding.

DEAL THIRTY-SIX

Neither Side Vulnerable. Dealer South.

　　　♠ K J 7 3
　　　♥ 9 5
　　　♦ A Q 7
　　　♣ A 9 6 4

　　　♠ A Q 10 2
　　　♥ A Q
　　　♦ K J 10
　　　♣ K J 5 3

West	North	East	South
–	–	–	2NT
Pass	3♣	Pass	3♠
Pass	6♠	All Pass.	

Contract: 6♠ by South. Opening lead: ♦8.

How do you play?

How many immediate winners do you have?
Ten; four spades, one heart, three diamonds and two clubs.

Where will you find the two more required?
There are two possibilities; the club suit could provide either one or two extra tricks and there is also the heart finesse.

How should you begin?
By drawing trumps. You do not have any ruffing to do so should make sure that none of your high cards is ruffed.

It takes four rounds to draw trumps, West discarding two hearts and a diamond. What next?
The key to the hand seems to be the club suit because you will have to make at least one extra trick there if you are to succeed. However, there is a play available that will guarantee three tricks from this combination.

What is it?
Cash the king then lead low towards the ace-nine. If West plays low you put in the nine—either this wins or the suit has broken 3-2 and you have two tricks to cash when you regain the lead; if West plays an honor you win the ace and your jack and nine are at worst equals against the missing queen. And if West shows out you rise with the ace and lead back towards the jack.

Is that how to play the clubs on this deal?
You don't know yet because the correct play is different if you need four tricks from the suit and, you still don't know how many tricks you will need.

How will you find out?
By taking the heart finesse. If it wins, you have your eleventh trick and can follow the sure line explained above to produce a third club trick to give you your twelfth.

And if the heart finesse loses?
Now you need four club tricks and must play accordingly.

What is the correct play when four tricks are needed?
Most people start by cashing the ace, but this is an error. They cash the ace because they do not wish to lose to a singleton queen in the West hand. But if you look carefully at your clubs, you will see that if West has the bare queen you cannot make four tricks however you play, so this situation is irrelevant.

The correct play is to lead low from dummy, intending to finesse the jack on the first round. When clubs are 3-2, this is just as good as the alternative play, but the extra chance comes when it is East who has the bare queen. See the difference; if North still has the ace, you can pick up West's ten to four, while if you cashed the ace you cannot.

The full deal:

　　　♠ K J 7 3
　　　♥ 9 5
　　　♦ A Q 7
　　　♣ A 9 6 4

♠ 9　　　　　　　　　♠ 8 6 5 4
♥ J 8 7 6 4　　　　　♥ K 10 3 2
♦ 9 8 6　　　　　　　♦ 5 4 3 2
♣ Q 10 7 2　　　　　　♣ 8

　　　♠ A Q 10 2
　　　♥ A Q
　　　♦ K J 10
　　　♣ K J 5 3

Tip

It is a good thing to know how to play various suit combinations in isolation, but where the correct technique varies according to the number of tricks required, it may be necessary to do a little exploratory work first to discover which is the best approach on a particular deal. You rarely have the luxury of playing a suit in complete isolation.

Deal Thirty-seven

Both Sides Vulnerable. Dealer South.

♠ Q 10 9
♥ 7 4 3 2
♦ 8 6
♣ 9 8 6 2

♠ A J 4
♥ A Q J 10 9 6
♦ A Q
♣ 7 3

West	North	East	South
–	–	–	2♥
Pass	2NT	Pass	3♥
Pass	4♥	All Pass	

Contract: 4♥ by South. Opening lead: ♣A.

West continues with ♣K and ♣J overtaken by East's ♣Q.

How many many immediate winners do you have?
Only the three aces, but perhaps this is not a particularly useful question to ask on this deal.

All right. How many potential losers do you have?
Five; the two clubs already lost plus the kings in each of the other three suits.

You will need to keep your losers to only one of the three kings. Clearly the best way is to finesse against each of them. Since you have no immediate entry to dummy, it seems impossible to finesse in all three suits. What is the best way to force a dummy entry?
There are two possibilities. As long as you are careful to ruff the third club with a trump other than the six, you can play hearts from the top and eventually lead the six to dummy's seven. Alternatively, you can play on spades.

Which is the better choice?
Whichever suit you lead from hand, you increase the likelihood of having a loser in. You have to look at the overall likelihood of success of each of the proposed lines.

What if you play on hearts?
Cashing the ♥A means no heart loser whenever the king is singleton—a 26 percent chance. You will play two more rounds of hearts to get to dummy then take the spade finesse and then the diamond finesse, succeeding when either one works. One finesse out of two will work about three-quarters of the time so your 26 percent reduces to about 19.5 precent.

When the ♥K is not singleton, you will obviously have a heart loser, but will still be able to force an entry to dummy. This time, however, you will need both kings onside as you can afford no more losers. You will have a heart loser 74 percent of the time and both finesses will only succeed about one time in four, reducing the chance of success to 18.5 percent.

Your total success rate is therefore about 38 percent.

Is there any problem with this line?
There are two problems, one of which is easier to overcome than the other. The first one is that you need to take the spade finesse twice and still finish in dummy to take the diamond finesse. You must be very careful to lead the ♠Q for the first finesse and drop the ♠J under it. If you look at the suit carefully, you will see that if you play in any other way East can force you to win the second spade in hand and be unable to return to dummy to take the diamond finesse.

The second problem is more serious. When the ♥K is singleton, we have said that you need only one finesse out of two and you will make your contract. But suppose that you take the spade finesse and it wins. Now you repeat the finesse and West wins the king. You have no dummy entry left and could go down even with the ♦K onside.

A competent defender will always duck the first spade and if he does this smoothly you will have no way of knowing. As you do not, therefore, really have the chance to try both finesses, the true chance of success with this line is probably nearer to 33 percent.

What about the alternative line of giving up a spade to force an entry?
If you ruff the third club and play a spade to the nine, you will get a dummy entry on either the first or second round of spades but will lose a trick in the process. That means you will need both red suits to play for no losers.

You will take the heart finesse. When East has ♥K or ♥Kx, you will be able to re-enter dummy with the ♥7 to take the diamond finesse.

Is this better or worse than the first line of play?
East will have a singleton 39 percent of the time (a 2-1 break is a 78 percent chance) and it will be the king one time in three—13 percent. He will also be holding a doubleton 39 percent of the time and this will include the king two-thirds of the time (K8 or K5 but not 8-5)—26 percent.

So the hearts will behave 39 percent of the time, but then you still need the diamond finesse—50 percent chance—so your overall chance of success is only 19.5 percent.

So the first line, playing hearts from hand to force a dummy entry is the correct one?
Yes, but remember first not to ruff the third club with the ♥6, and, second, to be careful when you take the spade finesse.

The full deal:

```
              ♠ Q 10 9
              ♥ 7 4 3 2
              ♦ 8 6
              ♣ 9 8 6 2
♠ 8 6 5                      ♠ K 7 3 2
♥ 5                          ♥ K 8
♦ J 9 7 5 4 3                ♦ K 10 2
♣ A K J                      ♣ Q 10 5 4
              ♠ A J 4
              ♥ A Q J 10 9 6
              ♦ A Q
              ♣ 7 3
```

Tip

This is quite a complex hand, what with the care required in the spade suit and the possibility of the defensive duck in spades, yet I am sure that you got the basic line of play right. It looks obvious to play hearts first, and indeed the odds bear that out. Some other hands can be deceptive, and it is useful to be able to work out the relative chances of success of different lines of play. If you are going to do so, it is important to take into account all the factors, like the possibility of the defensive duck in this example.

DEAL THIRTY-EIGHT
Neither Side Vulnerable. Dealer South.

```
              ♠ J 6 2
              ♥ A K 7 3
              ♦ K J 7
              ♣ K 10 6

              ♠ 8 3
              ♥ 9
              ♦ A Q 10 8 5 3
              ♣ A J 3 2
```

West	North	East	South
–	–	–	1♦
Pass	1♥	1♠	2♦
Pass	2♠	Pass	3♣
Pass	5♦	All Pass	

Contract: 5♦ by South. Opening lead: ♠Q.

The ♠Q wins the first trick and West continues with the ♠7. East wins this trick with the ♠K and at trick three leads the ♠A. Plan the play from here.

How many immediate winners do you have?
Ten; six diamonds, two hearts and two clubs.

Which suit will provide your eleventh trick?
Clubs, with a successful guess for the queen.

Who will you play for the queen?
It is not clear. East is slightly more likely to hold the missing high cards because he bid, but he certainly doesn't need the ♣Q for his simple overcall. Against that, because he is shorter in spades, West figures to be longer in clubs and therefore more likely to hold the queen.

So what is the answer?
To delay the club guess as long as possible and hope to find a useful clue elsewhere. You can ruff the third spade high, as West looks likely to have a doubleton, then cash all your diamonds and the ace-king of hearts and hope to guess clubs in the ending.

Is there any way to improve on this?
Yes. If all you do is cash the top hearts, you will be guessing the heart distribution. Suppose instead that you ruff out the hearts. This will not give you any extra tricks, but it may enable you to get a complete count of the hand.

So the best play is?
Ruff the third spade high and play two top diamonds. On the second round, East pitches a spade. Now play ace-king and ruff a heart, a third diamond to dummy and ruff the last heart. However the hearts divide, you have an exact count. As it turns out, East only has two hearts so you know his shape to be precisely 6-2-1-4. If he has four clubs to West's two, East is twice as likely to hold the queen, quite apart from the fact that he overcalled, so play accordingly.

The full deal:

```
              ♠ J 6 2
              ♥ A K 7 3
              ♦ K J 7
              ♣ K 10 6
♠ Q 7                        ♠ A K 10 9 5 4
♥ 10 8 6 5 4 2               ♥ Q J
♦ 9 6 2                      ♦ 4
♣ 9 4                        ♣ Q 8 7 5
              ♠ 8 3
              ♥ 9
              ♦ A Q 10 8 5 3
              ♣ A J 3 2
```

Tip

When you have a two-way guess for a queen, delay your guess as long as possible. Perhaps you can find out which defender has the greater length in the key suit and is therefore more likely to hold the queen. Remember that if trying to get a count of another suit, it is more effective to play as many rounds of the suit as possible and force the defenders to follow suit if they can, rather than merely to run your trumps and watch their discards.

DEAL THIRTY-NINE
North/SouthVulnerable. Dealer South.

```
        ♠ J 8 5 4
        ♥ A 9 8 3
        ♦ A 4
        ♣ Q J 3

        ♠ A K 10 9 7 6
        ♥ 5
        ♦ K Q 6 2
        ♣ A 8
```

West	North	East	South
–	–	–	1♠
Pass	3♠	Pass	4♣
Pass	4♦	Pass	4♥
Pass	6♠	All Pass	

Contract: 6♠ by South. Opening lead: ♥K.

Plan the play.

How many immediate winners do you have?
Only seven; two spades, one heart, three diamonds and a club, but there are at least three extra spades and a diamond ruff available.

What is the only possible danger to your contract?
That West has all three missing trumps, giving him a trick there, and the club finesse also loses.

Is there any way to overcome such a lie of the cards?
Perhaps. There is no way to avoid the loss of a spade trick, but perhaps West can be thrown in with the queen at a time when he has nothing left but clubs.

What shape will you need West to be?
It doesn't matter exactly, but the endplay will not material-ize if West can ruff either red suit while he still has a card left in the other suit with which to get off lead. In practice, that is likely to mean that he needs to have at least three cards in each red suit.

How should you play?
You do not know yet that the endplay will be necessary, but entries to dummy are at a premium so you should ruff a heart at trick two, just in case. Now cash the ♠A. If West does not have all the spades, the play is easy, but what if he does? Cash your other top trump then lead a diamond to the ace, ruff another heart, and play king and queen of diamonds then the last diamond and ruff it.

Why play the ♦Q, running the risk of its being ruffed and West exiting with a heart?
This is balanced by the danger that West is 3-3-4-3. If you ruff the low diamond while retaining the queen, West will over-ruff your next heart play and exit with his last diamond to your queen, avoiding the endplay.

All right, so you play the ♦KQ and ruff the last diamond. Now what?
Ruff the last heart and exit with a spade. If everything has gone according to plan, West is left with nothing but clubs and has to lead away from his king.

The full deal:

```
                ♠ J 8 5 4
                ♥ A 9 8 3
                ♦ A 4
                ♣ Q J 3
  ♠ Q 3 2                      ♠ –
  ♥ K Q J 7                    ♥ 10 6 4 2
  ♦ 8 5 3                      ♦ J 10 9 7
  ♣ K 9 2                      ♣ 10 7 6 5 4
                ♠ A K 10 9 7 6
                ♥ 5
                ♦ K Q 6 2
                ♣ A 8
```

Tip

When a contract looks easy, check to see if there is any possible danger. If you discover one, try to find a way to overcome the danger. As always, do this before playing to trick one.

DEAL FORTY
East/West Game. Dealer South.

```
        ♠ Q 10 8
        ♥ 7 2
        ♦ A Q 10 9 4
        ♣ K 9 2

        ♠ A K J 7 3 2
        ♥ A 10
        ♦ J 8 6
        ♣ 8 3
```

West	North	East	South
–	–	–	1♠
Pass	2♦	2♥	2♠
Pass	4♠	All Pass	

Contract: 4♠ by South. Opening lead: ♥3.

East plays the ♥K. Over to you.

How many immediate winners do you have?
Eight; six spades and two red aces.

Where will you find the extra trick you need?
Though the ♣K is a possible trick, diamonds are a certainty to produce at least two extra tricks even if the finesse loses.

So you could draw trumps and take the diamond finesse. Can anything go wrong?
If the diamond finesse loses and East also has the ace of clubs, you could lose two clubs, a diamond and a heart.

Can you prevent this?
Yes. You can only lose two club tricks if West leads the suit. East can only cash the ace.

How can West gain the lead?
In hearts.

Can you prevent this?
Simply duck the opening lead, win the return and draw trumps. Now you can take the diamond finesse safe in the knowledge that even if it loses the dangerous hand cannot get in to attack your weak spot.

The full deal:

```
              ♠ Q 10 8
              ♥ 7 2
              ♦ A Q 10 9 4
              ♣ K 9 2
♠ 9 6 4                        ♠ 5
♥ Q 9 3                        ♥ K J 8 6 5 4
♦ 7 5                          ♦ K 3 2
♣ J 10 7 6 5                   ♣ A Q 4
              ♠ A K J 7 3 2
              ♥ A 10
              ♦ J 8 6
              ♣ 8 3
```

Tip

Don't play too quickly at trick one. It may be necessary to duck to cut communication between the defenders, thereby preventing them from attacking your potential weakness later in the play.

DEAL FORTY-ONE

East/West Vulnerable. Dealer North.

```
              ♠ A 10 6 3
              ♥ A K 10 9
              ♦ K J 6 4
              ♣ K 9 2

              ♠ K J 5
              ♥ J 7
              ♦ A Q 10 3 2
              ♣ Q 4 2
```

West	North	East	South
–	1♥	Pass	2♦
Pass	4♦	Pass	4♠
Pass	6♦	All Pass	

Contract: 6♦ by South. Opening lead: ♣A.

West continues with the ♣3. You ruff and draw trumps, which prove to be 2-2. What next?

How many immediate winners do you have?
Eleven; five diamonds, two ruffs and the ace and king of each major.

Where might you find your twelfth trick?
By finding either major suit queen. You can finesse either way in either suit or play to drop the queen.

Which is the best play?
One finesse is much as good as another; what you want is a way to combine your chances by trying to drop one queen and finessing for the other if that is unsuccessful.

What are the possible combinations?
There are a number of possibilities.

1. Cash the ace-king of spades, then finesse hearts either way.
2. Cash the ace-king of hearts, then finesse spades either way.
3. Cash the ace-king of hearts, then ruff a heart before guessing the spades.
4. Cash both ace-kings, then ruff a heart.
5. Cash both ace-kings, then take a ruffing heart finesse.

Which is best?
(1) Must be better than (2) because the queen is more likely to be doubleton with six cards missing than with seven. But (3) is better than either because it succeeds when either defender has the ♥Qx or ♥Qxx. (4) has the same chance in hearts as (3) but the chance in spades is inferior to that in (3)

Which leaves (3) and (5). Both lines include a finesse, which is a fifty-fifty proposition. The extra chances are:

(3)   ♥Qx   or   ♥Qxx
(5)   ♥Qx   or   ♠Qx

Best is line (3), cashing the ace-king of hearts and ruffing a heart before falling back on the spade guess. Queen to three with seven cards missing is a substantially better proposition than queen doubleton missing six cards (the odds are roughly 27 percent and 16 percent respectively.

One additional possibility is that if hearts prove to be 5-2 you will have a clue as to which defender is more likely to have the spade length so the finesse may not be quite a straight guess after all.

The full deal:

```
              ♠ A 10 6 3
              ♥ A K 10 9
              ♦ K J 6 4
              ♣ 8
♠ Q 8 7                        ♠ 9 4 2
♥ 6 5 3                        ♥ Q 8 4 2
♦ 7 5                          ♦ 9 8
♣ A J 9 6 3                    ♣ K 10 7 5
              ♠ K J 5
              ♥ J 7
              ♦ A Q 10 3 2
              ♣ Q 4 2
```

With a choice of several plays to find an extra trick, look for the line which gives the best combination of chances. A little work learning the odds for some of the most common breaks with different numbers of missing cards could be worthwhile.

Going back to the comparison between lines (3) and (5), the calculation was really quite straight forward once the basic percentages were known.

A 4-3 break occurs just a little over 62 percent of the time and common sense tells you that the queen will be with the three three-sevenths of the time; and three-sevenths of 62 percent is roughly 27 percent.

A 4-2 break occurs almost 49 percent of the time and the queen will be in the doubleton two times in six; and one-third of 49 percent is roughly 16 percent.

DEAL FORTY-TWO
East/West Vulnerable. Dealer South.

                    ♠ 9 6
                    ♥ A 2
                    ♦ A Q 10 6 3 2
                    ♣ Q 10 8

                    ♠ K 7 5
                    ♥ 7
                    ♦ 8 4
                    ♣ A K J 9 6 4 2

West	North	East	South
–	–	–	1♣
1♥	2♦	2♥	3♣
3♥	5♣	All Pass	

Contract: 5♣ by South. Opening lead: ♥K.

Plan the play.

How many immediate winners do you have?
Nine; seven clubs and two red aces.

Where might you find the other two tricks you require?
There are two possibilities. You can play to make the ♠K, then ruff your third spade or you can try to establish the diamonds.

Which is the better prospect?
Diamonds. You have three club entries to dummy so you should be able to establish diamonds even if they break 4-1. Playing spades requires East to have the ace or for the diamond finesse to win and, while the diamond finesse is a slight favorite on the auction, the spade is more likely to be offside.

But doesn't playing diamonds depend on the same thing? If the finesse loses you will still need the ♠A onside
That would be true if you took the diamond finesse, but what if you don't?

How can you avoid the finesse?
By ducking the opening lead. West cannot lead spades effectively. You win whatever he does lead in dummy and play the ♥A, throwing a diamond from hand. Now play ace and another diamond, ruffing, cross to dummy with a club and ruff another diamond. You can now cross to dummy again in trumps and, unless West's switch at trick two was to a club, even have the luxury of ruffing another diamond if necessary. If West did switch to a club, he removed one of your entries prematurely and you will need a 3-2 diamond break or possibly a bare honor.

With any luck, you have established the diamonds without allowing the dangerous hand (East) to gain the lead.

What if West did switch to a club and the diamonds are such that they cannot be established?
You will discover this when you play the second round of diamonds. There is still time to fall back on a favorable spade position. After ruffing the diamond, play a club to dummy and a spade to the king and keep your fingers crossed.

The full deal:

                    ♠ 9 6
                    ♥ A 2
                    ♦ A Q 10 6 3 2
                    ♣ Q 10 8

♠ A Q 8   ♠ J 10 4 3 2
♥ K Q 10 9 6 3   ♥ J 8 5 4
♦ J 7 5   ♦ K 9
♣ 5   ♣ 7 3

                    ♠ K 7 5
                    ♥ 7
                    ♦ 8 4
                    ♣ A K J 9 6 4 2

Tip

Look for ways to keep a dangerous opponent from gaining the lead when attempting to establish a side suit. Sometimes, an unusual duck elsewhere could be the key.

Deal Forty-three

East/West Vulnerable. Dealer South.

♠ Q 3
♥ 9 6 4
♦ A J 10 7 3
♣ 9 8 4

♠ 7
♥ A Q 2
♦ K Q 8 6 4
♣ A K Q 10

West	North	East	South
–	–	–	1♦
Pass	2♦	Pass	3♣
Pass	3♦	Pass	5♦
All Pass			

Contract: 5♦ by South. Opening lead: ♠A.

West continues with the ♠K. Over to you.

How many winners have you?
Ten; five diamonds, three clubs, one heart and a spade ruff.

What are the prospects for an eleventh trick?
Pretty good. The clubs may provide a fourth trick or the heart king may be onside.

There is something better. If you play clubs correctly, it may not matter whether you make three tricks or four from the suit. Can you see the possible ending?
Yes. Suppose that you draw trumps and cash two top clubs. Now cross to dummy with a trump and lead the third club. If East shows out you play the queen and then lead the ♣10 to West's jack and discard a heart from dummy. West is endplayed, forced to either lead a heart or give a ruff and discard.

If East follows to the third club, finesse the ten. Either this will win and you have your eleventh trick or it loses and West is endplayed as before.

So you ruff the second spade and lead a diamond. East discards a spade. Any problems?
If you draw the remaining trumps, cash two top clubs then cross to dummy with a diamond, you will not have a diamond left in hand, so the endplay will not work.

Can anything be done about this?
You will have to cash the two top clubs without drawing all the trumps. Draw a second round of trumps, cash the clubs and play a diamond to dummy, drawing the last trump as you go. Given West's failure to overcall, he probably does not have a five card major and hence will not have a singleton club, but if he has and can ruff one of your club winners, who cares? Is he not now endplayed? His return will give you one trick while the marked club finesse provides the other. 5♦ is unbeatable.

The full deal:

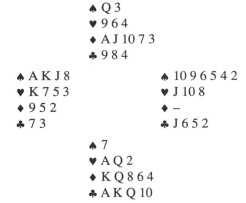

```
              ♠ Q 3
              ♥ 9 6 4
              ♦ A J 10 7 3
              ♣ 9 8 4
♠ A K J 8                  ♠ 10 9 6 5 4 2
♥ K 7 5 3                  ♥ J 10 8
♦ 9 5 2                    ♦ –
♣ 7 3                      ♣ J 6 5 2
              ♠ 7
              ♥ A Q 2
              ♦ K Q 8 6 4
              ♣ A K Q 10
```

Tip

Whether to play for a 3-3 break or take a third round finesse can often be a close decision. If you make the right preparations, sometimes you can afford to "guess" wrong as long as you lose the trick to the right opponent at the right time. Note that on the above deal if you were to swap dummy and declarer's heart holdings around, now it would be correct to play clubs from the top. If East has jack to four, this time he is the defender who can be endplayed.

Deal Forty-four

East/West Vulnerable. Dealer West.

♠ K 10 9 4
♥ A K 3
♦ A Q 8
♣ 9 7 5

♠ A Q J 7 6
♥ 7 6 2
♦ J 4 2
♣ K 3

West	North	East	South
1♣	Dble	Pass	4♠
All Pass			

Contract: 4♠ by South. Opening lead: ♥Q.

Plan the play.

How many immediate winners do you have?
Eight; five spades, two hearts and a diamond.

Where will you find two more tricks?
One is easy, as the queen and jack of diamonds guarantee a trick even if the finesse loses.

Will you you make your contract if the diamond finesse does lose?
No. On the auction it is clear that West has the ♣A and East would now switch to a club, leaving you with four losers. The bidding strongly suggests that the ♦K will be onside, however.

Assuming the ♦*K to be onside, as we need it to be, we are up to nine tricks. What about the tenth?*

While West may have king doubleton of diamonds, the best chance looks to be some kind of endplay against him.

What might you try?

It looks as though West has the queen and jack of hearts and possibly the ten, perhaps you should win the opening lead, draw trumps and play two more rounds of hearts to put West on lead.

That might work, but there is no guarantee that West will win the third round. If East can do so, you are likely to be defeated. What other possiblility is there?

After drawing trumps, you could take the diamond finesse, then play ace and another diamond.

But won't West get off lead with a heart?

So I must eliminate hearts before playing the third diamond.

How will you do this without risking East gaining the lead?

There is no sure way except by ducking the opening lead! Now you can win the next trick, draw trumps, unblocking hearts along the way, and play on diamonds as previously described. If West wins the king, he will have to either give a ruff and discard or lead a club.

The full deal:

```
              ♠ K 10 9 4
              ♥ A K 3
              ♦ A Q 8
              ♣ 9 7 5
♠ 5                        ♠ 8 3 2
♥ Q J 9 5                  ♥ 10 8 4
♦ K 10 6                   ♦ 9 7 5 3
♣ A Q J 4 2                ♣ 10 8 6
              ♠ A Q J 7 6
              ♥ 7 6 2
              ♦ J 4 2
              ♣ K 3
```

Tip

An endplay may come, as the name implies, near the end of the play, but the preparation to make it a success may have to come much earlier. Here, the very first card you played was crucial. It is vital to make your plan before playing to trick one.

Neither Side Vulnerable. Dealer South.

```
              ♠ A K
              ♥ 6 4 3 2
              ♦ A 7 5 2
              ♣ Q 6 4

              ♠ 10 4 3
              ♥ A 9 8 7
              ♦ 9
              ♣ A K J 7 2
```

West	North	East	South
–	–	–	1♣
Pass	1♦	Pass	1♥
Pass	4♥	All Pass	

Contract: 4♥ by South. Opening lead: ♦Q.

Plan the play.

How many immediate winners do you have?

Nine, assuming clubs are not 5-0; five clubs, two spades and two red aces.

Where will you find a tenth trick?

Either by ruffing a spade in the dummy or a diamond in hand.

Can anything go wrong?

Trumps could be 5-0, which would surely be fatal. Otherwise, the only danger is that one or more of your winners is ruffed by the defense.

How can you avoid this?

By drawing some trumps.

So you win the opening lead and play ace and another trump?

No. That would be very dangerous because trumps might be 4-1 and the defense could draw trumps and play their diamond winners.

The standard technique to keep control with ace to four opposite four low is to duck the first round then cash the ace when you regain the lead. Is that the right thing to do here?

No. Again, a 4-1 break could prove fatal. When you duck the heart, you are forced with a diamond. Now you cash the ♥A and get the bad news, so switch your attention to clubs. Eventually, somebody ruffs in, draws your last trump and cashes one or two diamonds.

So what should you do?

Win the opening lead, cash the ♥A, and start playing your winning clubs. Somebody will ruff in eventually but at worst has two more hearts to cash. That still leaves you with one trump in each hand and, as these can be made separately, you get back two tricks in return for the club that was ruffed. All you lose is three trump tricks.

The full deal:

```
              ♠ A K
              ♥ 6 4 3 2
              ♦ A 7 5 2
              ♣ Q 6 4
♠ Q 9 8 7 5               ♠ J 6 2
♥ 5                       ♥ K Q J 10
♦ Q J 10                  ♦ K 8 6 4 3
♣ 10 9 5 3                ♣ 8
              ♠ 10 4 3
              ♥ A 9 8 7
              ♦ 9
              ♣ A K J 7 2
```

Tip

It is vital to keep trump control. Even when you have identical trump holdings, the correct technique to use may vary according to the requirements of the rest of the hand. Be flexible.

DEAL FORTY-SIX

North/South Vulnerable. Dealer North.

```
              ♠ Q 6 4 2
              ♥ A Q
              ♦ A J 9 7 5
              ♣ A K
              ♠ 5
              ♥ K 9 7 6 4
              ♦ 6
              ♣ Q J 10 9 7 2
```

West	North	East	South
	2NT	Pass	3♥
Pass	3NT	Pass	4♣
Pass	4♥	All Pass	

Contract: 4♥ by South. Opening lead: ♠J.

West continues with the ♠10. Your play.

How many immediate winners do you have?
Eleven; three hearts, a spade ruff, one diamond and six club tricks

That is more tricks than you need. Can you see any problems?
There are awkward blockages in both hearts and clubs and your trumps have already been shortened. You are in danger of losing control.

What is the simple line of play?
Having ruffed the second spade, unblock the hearts and clubs, ruff a spade back to hand and cash the ♥K. If trumps are 3-3, they are now drawn and you can cash your club winners.

What if trumps are not 3-3?
On this line you will go down. Also, any line will surely fail if hearts are 5-1. You need a line which allows for a 4-2 heart break.

Can you find one?
The problem with the simple line was not that it established too many immediate losers or that you didn't have enough winners. In fact, you have an immediate winner to spare, but you lost trump control. After unblocking the hearts, you had to shorten your trumps to get back to hand. Suppose you didn't have to do that. The solution is quite simple once you think of it. Ruff the second spade, unblock the clubs, then play the ace of hearts and overtake the queen with the king. You have used two of your winners on the same trick, but you had one to spare so could afford to do so. Now just run the clubs. You lose two trumps, but that is all.

The full deal:

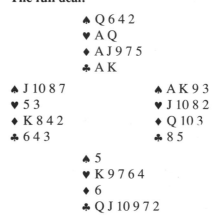

```
              ♠ Q 6 4 2
              ♥ A Q
              ♦ A J 9 7 5
              ♣ A K
♠ J 10 8 7                ♠ A K 9 3
♥ 5 3                     ♥ J 10 8 2
♦ K 8 4 2                 ♦ Q 10 3
♣ 6 4 3                   ♣ 8 5
              ♠ 5
              ♥ K 9 7 6 4
              ♦ 6
              ♣ Q J 10 9 7 2
```

Tip

Don't be too miserly to "waste" your high cards, even where doing so establishes extra tricks for the defense. If the "waste" allows you to keep control of the hand your investment will more than pay for itself.

DEAL FORTY-SEVEN
East/West Vulnerable. Dealer South.

♠ A K 10 8 7
♥ 6 3
♦ 9 8 4
♣ —

♠ Q 9
♥ A K Q J 8 5
♦ A
♣ A J 10 6

West	North	East	South
–	–	–	2♥
Pass	2♠	Pass	3♥
Pass	4♥	Pass	4NT
Pass	5♦	Pass	5NT
Pass	6♦	Pass	6♥
All Pass			

Contract: 6♥ by South. Opening lead: ♦K.

Plan the play.

How many immediate winners do you have?
Eleven, assuming hearts are not 5-0; three spades, six hearts and two aces.

Where might you find the extra trick?
A 3-3 spade break or doubleton jack would produce two extra tricks. Failing that, it may be possible to make a second club trick.

How will you play?
Say that you win the opening lead, draw trumps and play queen and another spade to dummy. When you cash the third spade the jack does not appear. You play a club to the ten but this loses to the queen and when East turns out to have the guarded king you are one down.

Is there something better?
The problem is that when the spades failed to behave you really wanted to take two club finesses but had no more entries. How about leading the ♠Q and overtaking, taking a club finesse and, on regaining the lead, playing the ♠9 to dummy's other top honor? Now if the spades are not good you can take a second club finesse.

The trouble with that is that the spades only come in when the jack is singleton or doubleton, heavily against the odds, and with only two spade tricks you not only need one of the club honors onside but also a 3-3 break. Remember the tip on the previous deal?
Of course! The right play after drawing trumps is to lead the ♠9 to dummy's ten. If that loses you can overtake the queen next time and have four spade tricks—all you need. If the spade finesse wins, play a club to your ten. You win the return and play the ♠Q to dummy's king. If the jack doesn't fall under the ace, you can take a second club finesse.

This line wins when the ♠J is doubleton, when the spades are 3-3, and when either club honor is onside.

The full deal:

♠ A K 10 8 7
♥ 6 3
♦ 9 8 4
♣ —

♠ 6 3   ♠ J 5 4 2
♥ 10 7 2   ♥ 9 4
♦ K Q J 7 5   ♦ 10 6 3 2
♣ Q 7 3   ♣ K 9 8

♠ Q 9
♥ A K Q J 8 5
♦ A
♣ A J 10 6

Tip

Be flexible. You should be willing to play normal suit combinations in unusual ways if it will help you with the rest of the hand.

DEAL FORTY-EIGHT
North/South Vulnerable. Dealer West.

♠ A Q J 5
♥ Q J 4
♦ K 4
♣ K 10 7 4

♠ 9 8 7 6 4 2
♥ —
♦ J 10 8 3
♣ A 9 3

West	North	East	South
4♥	Dble	Pass	4♠
All pass			

Contract: 4♠ by South. Opening lead: ♥A.

You ruff and then finesse the ♠Q, East wins with the king. Back comes a heart. What next?

How many immediate winners do you have?
Seven; the ruff already taken, two clubs and four more spades.

What are your potential sources of extra tricks?
You could increase your trump winners by one by ruffing both dummy's remaining heart losers, or you could discard on this trick and thereby establish a heart winner in the dummy. There is also the possibility of establishing extra tricks in either minor.

Should you discard on this heart return?
No. There is too great a danger that East will have both diamond honors and you will then certainly be down.

So you ruff the heart. What next?
Draw the last trump and ruff the third heart.

East turns up with the remaining trump and a third heart.

West pitches a heart on the trump. What do you play next?
It looks right to play on diamonds next because it will sometimes be possible to establish two tricks there to discard two clubs from dummy. Also, if it is possible to play diamonds for one loser you can then ruff two more and have ten tricks.

So which diamond do you lead from hand?
West may have the queen but is less likely to hold the ace for his four level opening, so you lead the jack and run it.

East wins the queen, cashes the ace and plays a third diamond. Do you play the eight or the ten?
A winning view gives you two discards for dummy's clubs, a losing view only one and, as you have already lost three tricks, you will then need some luck to succeed. It looks a guess, with East the slight favorite to hold the ♦9 since he is more likely to have length in the suit.

You could have avoided this guess. How?
Leading the ♦J was an error because you are always safe when West has the ♦Qx or the ♦Qxx even when you lead low to the king. Say the king loses to the ace. East will return a diamond as he cannot afford to open up the clubs. You play the ♦J and if it wins you are home, while if West wins with the queen he must either return a diamond into your ten-eight or open up the club suit. That last possibility does not guarantee your contract, but it greatly improves matters, picking up the suit when the honors are divided.

The real benefit comes when East has both diamond honors. Since you have not wasted your jack, he is powerless. You lead the second round through his queen and either he doesn't make it, or you make both the jack and ten.

The full deal:

```
              ♠ A Q J 5
              ♥ Q J 4
              ♦ K 4
              ♣ K 10 7 4

♠ 3                       ♠ K 10
♥ A K 10 9 7 6 2          ♥ 8 5 3
♦ 9 7 6                   ♦ A Q 5 2
♣ J 2                     ♣ Q 8 6 5

              ♠ 9 8 7 6 4 2
              ♥ –
              ♦ J 10 8 3
              ♣ A 9 3
```

Tip

Sometimes, you have no option but to guess, but whenever possible, you should try to avoid having to do so. By its very nature, a guess is a doubtful proposition; you will guess right some of the time, but you will also guess wrong at other times.

DEAL FORTY-NINE

Neither Side Vulnerable. Dealer West.

```
              ♠ Q J 9 4
              ♥ 10 7 4
              ♦ 10 8 3
              ♣ 6 5 2

              ♠ A K
              ♥ A K Q 9 8 6 3
              ♦ –
              ♣ A Q 8 7
```

West	North	East	South
5♦	Pass	Pass	6♥
All Pass			

Contract: 6♥ by South. Opening lead: ♦A.

Over to you.

How many immediate winners do you have?
Twelve; seven hearts, four spades and one club.

Are there any potential difficulties?
A 3-0 heart break, distinctly possible on the auction, would mean you had no obvious entry to the queen and jack of spades.

You ruff the opening lead and lay down the ♥A. Sure enough, West discards a diamond. What now?
You need to find a dummy entry. There is only one possibility; it must come from the trump suit.

How should you play?
Cash the ace and king of spades and lead a low heart to dummy's seven. East can win the jack but the ten provides you with the entry you need.

Giving up a heart trick reduced you to only eleven winners. You need to find a twelfth.
No problem. Having drawn the last trump with dummy's ten, throw two clubs on the spade winners and take the club finesse. This is not a certainty, but it is the only chance.

The full deal:

```
              ♠ Q J 9 4
              ♥ 10 7 4
              ♦ 10 8 3
              ♣ 6 5 2

♠ 8 7                     ♠ 10 6 5 3 2
♥ –                       ♥ J 5 2
♦ A K Q J 9 6 5 2         ♦ 7 4
♣ J 10 9                  ♣ K 4 3

              ♠ A K
              ♥ A K Q 9 8 6 3
              ♦ –
              ♣ A Q 8 7
```

Tip

If you cannot find a vital entry by normal play, try to create one by abnormal play. It goes against the grain to concede a trump loser with a holding like the one on this deal, but it gives you a chance which you wouldn't otherwise have.

Don't be afraid to do what has to be done.

DEAL FIFTY
Both Sides Vulnerable. Dealer South.

```
              ♠ K J 4
              ♥ J 9
              ♦ A J 8 7 5
              ♣ K 8 6

              ♠ A 6 5 3 2
              ♥ A 10 5
              ♦ K Q 2
              ♣ 7 4
```

West	North	East	South
–	–	–	1♠
Pass	2♦	Pass	3♦
Pass	3♠	Pass	4♠
All Pass			

Contract: 4♠ by South. Opening lead: ♥2.

East plays the ♥K. Over to you.

How many immediate winners do you have?
Eight; two spades, one heart and five diamonds.

Where will you find two more tricks?
After the lead you can establish a second heart trick by winning and returning the suit. The ace of clubs may be onside and you can also hope to make some of your long spades.

Perhaps, with a second defensive trick already established, this hand requires worrying about avoiding four losers rather than finding ten winners. What possible losers do you have?
One heart, one or two clubs depending on the position of the ace, plus possible trump losers.

Can you make the contract if trumps are 4-1?
Certainly not if East has queen-ten to four as he will have two trump tricks. If West has four it is possible but will require some good fortune elsewhere.

Perhaps it is best to find a new line which guarantees the contract on any 3-2 trump break and forget the 4-1 breaks.
All right. Any trump finesse has to be taken into the East hand anyway, which is good news as he cannot attack the club weakness. This just confirms that you should take the finesse rather than cash the ace and king.

But West has another potential entry, doesn't he?
Yes. The queen of hearts. If you take a losing spade finesse, East plays a heart to the queen and a club comes through.

How can you avoid this?
By ducking at trick one, giving up on the second heart trick. Win East's continuation and play a spade to the jack—you cannot afford to cash the ace first as then dummy could be forced to ruff a third heart with the ♠K if the spade finesse lost. You win any return, draw the last trump and run the diamonds.

What if West started with ♠Q10xx so when you cash the ♠K, East shows out? Do you still have a chance?
Yes, but you will need the ♣A onside and to be careful. If you now try to run the diamonds, West may ruff the third round and play his last trump. You win and lead a club but West wins and has a heart to cash for one down.

How can you avoid this?
When East shows out on the second spade, you must come to hand with a diamond and ruff your heart loser in dummy. Play a second diamond to hand and, if you have survived so far, you can cash the ♠A and play a third diamond. If West can ruff this you will need him to hold the ♣A, otherwise you continue diamonds until he does ruff, pitching clubs from hand.

The full deal:

```
              ♠ K J 4
              ♥ J 9
              ♦ A J 8 7 5
              ♣ K 8 6
♠ 8 7                         ♠ Q 10 9
♥ Q 6 4 2                     ♥ K 8 7 3
♦ 10 6 3                      ♦ 9 4
♣ J 9 5 2                     ♣ A Q 10 3
              ♠ A 6 5 3 2
              ♥ A 10 5
              ♦ K Q 2
              ♣ 7 4
```

Tip

Be careful to cut defensive communication whenever you can do so, thereby making it harder for them to attack your weak spots. On this deal, the heart duck meant that you might have to ruff a heart in dummy and so could not afford to cash the ♠A before finessing the jack. This might have led to avoidable defeat had East held the bare queen. Nonetheless, the heart duck was the right play because it guarded against a much more likely danger.

DEAL FIFTY-ONE

Both Sides Vulnerable. Dealer South.

```
        ♠ J 10 9 7
        ♥ 7 2
        ♦ A Q J 4
        ♣ J 10 7

        ♠ A K Q 8 6 4
        ♥ A K Q J
        ♦ 10 5
        ♣ K
```

West	North	East	South
–	–	–	2♣
Pass	2NT	Pass	3♠
Pass	4♦	Pass	4NT
Pass	5♦	Pass	6♠
All Pass			

Contract: 6♠ by South. Opening lead: ♥10.

Plan the play.

How many immediate winners do you have?
Eleven; six spades, four hearts and the ♦A.

Where might you find a twelfth trick?
The obvious source of an extra trick is the diamond finesse.

That is a fifty-fifty chance. Is there any alternative?
You could give up a club trick to the ace then take a ruffing finesse against the queen.

That is just another fifty-fifty finesse. Is there a way to combine the two chances of either the ♦K or the ♣Q being well placed?
No, but there is a quite different extra chance which can be combined with the main one of finding the ♦K onside.

What is that?
Win the opening lead and draw the outstanding trumps. Now cash the rest of your heart winners and discard two clubs from the dummy and play your king of clubs. If East has the ♣A he is endplayed, having to give a ruff and discard or lead into dummy's diamonds.

And if West wins the ♣A?
Then you take the diamond finesse. Instead of succeeding when one specific card (♦K) is well placed, you succeed when either one of two cards (♦K or ♣A) is where you want it to be—roughly a 75 percent chance.

The full deal:

```
              ♠ J 10 9 7
              ♥ 7 2
              ♦ A Q J 4
              ♣ J 10 7

   ♠ 3                      ♠ 5 2
   ♥ 10 9 8 4               ♥ 6 5 3
   ♦ 8 6 2                  ♦ K 9 7 3
   ♣ Q 9 5 4 3              ♣ A 8 6 2

              ♠ A K Q 8 6 4
              ♥ A K Q J
              ♦ 10 5
              ♣ K
```

Tip

Always look for ways to combine more than one chance as declarer. It may sometimes take a little seeking out, but it is surprising how often an opportunity exists for an endplay if you know where to look.

DEAL FIFTY-TWO

North/South Vulnerable. Dealer West.

```
        ♠ Q 5
        ♥ K Q 3 2
        ♦ A Q 7
        ♣ J 6 5 3

        ♠ A K 7 6 3 2
        ♥ A 5
        ♦ 9 6 3 2
        ♣ A
```

West	North	East	South
Pass	1NT	Pass	3♠
Pass	3NT	Pass	4♣
Pass	4♦	Pass	6♠
All Pass			

Contract: 6♠ by South. Opening lead: ♦J.

How do you play?

How many immediate winners do you have?
Eight; three top trumps, three hearts and two aces.

Where will you find the extra trick you need?
It is possible that you can ruff out the king and queen of clubs in three rounds, establishing the jack, but this unlikely. Almost certainly, you will need to make three long spades plus a second diamond trick.

What could go wrong?
East might have the ♦K, in which case you would have to guess to drop the doubleton king or to find West with jack-ten doubleton. Also, the spades could break badly.

What will you do at trick one?
Finesse the queen. The best chance is simply that West holds the king.

The ♦Q holds the trick. What next?

It must be right to play on trumps but, while a 3–2 breaks makes the contract easily, a 4-1 break requires you to make your small trumps by ruffing, and the obvious suit to ruff is clubs. You need to ruff three times and dummy has only three entries so you cannot afford to waste any.

So, how should you proceed?

Cash the ace of clubs, then play a spade to the queen and ruff a club. Cash a top spade and if everybody follows you can draw the last trump. If spades are 4-1 you cross to the ♦A and ruff a club then play ace, king and queen of hearts. If that all passes off peacefully, lead either a heart or a club off dummy. If West has the trump length you will have to guess which suit he cannot over-ruff, while if East has the length you cannot be beaten.

Why is that?

You have the ♠K7 and the ♦9 left and he has, say, the ♠J9 and a side card. If he discards you can ruff cheaply, while if he ruffs in you throw your losing diamond and his remaining trump falls under your king at trick thirteen.

The full deal:

```
              ♠ Q 5
              ♥ K Q 3 2
              ♦ A Q 7
              ♣ J 6 5 3
  ♠ 10                      ♠ J 9 8 4
  ♥ J 7 4                   ♥ 10 9 8 6
  ♦ K J 10 5                ♦ 8 4
  ♣ K 9 8 7 2               ♣ Q 10 4
              ♠ A K 7 6 3 2
              ♥ A 5
              ♦ 9 6 3 2
              ♣ A
```

Tip

Don't automatically assume that a key suit will break evenly, nor that an uneven break necessarily spells defeat. Superficially, a 4-1 spade break leaves you with one spade and one diamond as inescapable losers. By careful timing and good use of your entries, you managed to make both losers come on the same trick.

DEAL FIFTY-THREE

North/South Vulnerable. Dealer East.

```
              ♠ K 6 4
              ♥ K Q 8 6
              ♦ Q 9 7 2
              ♣ 9 5

              ♠ A 8 3
              ♥ A J 10 4
              ♦ A 8 4
              ♣ A 7 2
```

West	North	East	South
–	–	1♠	1NT
Pass	2♣	Pass	2♥
Pass	4♥	All Pass	

Contract: 4♥ by South. Opening lead: ♠7.

East plays the ♠9. Over to you.

How many immediate winners do you have?

Eight; four hearts, two spades and two minor suit aces.

Where might two more be found?

Diamonds can certainly be played for at least one more trick, however they lie, as long as you read the position correctly. Also, there is a club ruff to take.

What are the problems?

The main worry is that the defense is halfway towards establishing a spade winner for itself. You have an unavoidable club loser and, with ♦K marked with East for his opening bid, a real danger of two diamond losers.

You could get lucky and find East with a singleton or doubleton diamond, holding your losers to one. Is there any other hope?

Judging from the auction and the opening lead, spades are almost certainly 5-2 or conceivably 6-1. If you could somehow establish a second diamond trick on which to discard your spade loser you might be able to afford two diamond losers.

A 6-1 spade break looks like bad news because if you draw all the trumps you will be short of entries. Suppose spades are 5-2, what do you need to do?

If you are going to lose two diamond tricks, you cannot afford them both to be to East as he can establish and cash his spade winner. Also, if West wins the first diamond and East the second, he can cash his winners. What you need is for East to win the first diamond and West the second or for West to win both.

Is there a way to achieve this?

Yes, if West holds either the ten or jack of diamonds, though the play looks a little unnatural. You need to lead a low diamond from hand and play dummy's seven, losing to the ten or jack. East returns a spade and you win the king and lead the ♦Q to the king and ace. Now your ♦8 and ♦9 are equals against the remaining ten or jack and you can establish a trick on which to discard your spade loser. This only fails if East has all three diamond honors.

So how should you play?

Win the ♠A and immediately play a diamond to the seven. Assuming this loses to a minor honor (if it loses to the king you are almost home), win the spade continuation and play the ♦Q to the king and ace. Now draw two rounds of trumps, one top honor from each hand, and play the third diamond. Hopefully, you can win the return, draw the last trump and discard your last spade on the established diamonds.

Why not draw the last trump before setting up the diamond?

If you do this, you leave only one trump in each hand. West wins the third diamond and leads a club and your only quick dummy entry is by playing your last heart—but now you have no trump left to take the club ruff for the tenth trick.

The full deal:

```
              ♠ K 6 4
              ♥ K Q 8 6
              ♦ Q 9 7 2
              ♣ 9 5
♠ 7 2                        ♠ Q J 10 9 5
♥ 7 5 2                      ♥ 9 3
♦ 10 5 3                     ♦ K J 6
♣ J 10 6 4 3                 ♣ K Q 8
              ♠ A 8 3
              ♥ A J 10 4
              ♦ A 8 4
              ♣ A 7 2
```

Tip

When you have to establish a suit but cannot afford to let one opponent gain the lead, see if there is an unusual way of playing the suit which might achieve your goal. Always try to think flexibly and never overlook the bidding.

DEAL FIFTY-FOUR

North/South Vulnerable. Dealer South.

```
              ♠ Q 10 9 7 4 2
              ♥ —
              ♦ Q 9 8 4
              ♣ J 6 3

              ♠ 8
              ♥ A K Q 8 6 4 3
              ♦ A K J 7 3
              ♣ —
```

West	North	East	South
–	–	–	2♣
Dble	Pass	5♣	5♥
Dble	Pass	Pass	6♦
All Pass			

Contract: 6♦ by South. Opening lead: ♣A.

How do you plan to make your slam?

How many immediate winners do you have?

Eight; five diamonds and three hearts.

Where will you find your other four tricks?

From hearts. Perhaps they will break favorably and if not you can ruff them out.

What about the bidding; does it really seem likely that hearts will divide evenly?

No. Surely the only reason West can have for doubling 5♥ is that he has long hearts? Also, the opposition has bid up to the five level so must have distribution to compensate for their shortage of high cards.

So you will need to ruff hearts in dummy. What dangers might there be?

If West has heart length, there is a danger of an over-ruff in hearts.

Can you overcome that?

Probably. If hearts are 6–0 there is no hope, but with a 5-1 break you could take one low and one high ruff—as long as you don't cash any top hearts first.

So, does that solve all your problems?

There is one more worry; suppose diamonds are 4-0, that could lead to problems with entries.

Presumably, as West seems to be long in hearts and clubs, East would be the one with four diamonds if anyone. Does this suggest a solution?

The problem is that you are being forced at trick one so have only four trumps in hand. You cannot afford to ruff again so all your entries to hand must be found from within the trump suit. If you ruff a second heart high, you have the ♦KJ7 opposite the ♦9. When you lead the nine, East ducks and you have to lose a trump trick.

So you have to unblock the diamonds?
Yes. Be careful to preserve dummy's ♦4. Ruff the opening lead and ruff a heart with the nine. Now play the ♦8 to your ace and ruff a second heart with the queen. If diamonds prove to be 4-0, you can now lead the ♦4 to the seven, draw the remaining trumps and cash the hearts.

The full deal:

```
            ♠ Q 10 9 7 4 2
            ♥ –
            ♦ Q 9 8 4
            ♣ J 6 3
♠ K 6 3                    ♠ A J 5
♥ J 10 9 5 2               ♥ 7
♦ –                        ♦ 10 6 5 2
♣ A K Q 10 8               ♣ 9 7 5 4 2
            ♠ 8
            ♥ A K Q 8 6 4 3
            ♦ A K J 7 3
            ♣ –
```

Tip

Listen to the bidding and beware of distributional storms. When you suspect squally weather, take care to make a plan to allow for it.

DEAL FIFTY-FIVE

Neither Side Vulnerable. Dealer South.

```
            ♠ A 7 4
            ♥ A 2
            ♦ A 5 2
            ♣ A K Q 5 4

            ♠ Q 6 2
            ♥ K Q J 10 9 8
            ♦ Q 7 4
            ♣ 9
```

West	North	East	South
–	–	–	1♥
Pass	3♣	Pass	3♥
Pass	4NT(*)	Pass	5♦(**)
Pass	5♠(***)	Pass	7♥
All Pass			

(*)   Roman Keycard Blackwood
(**) One keycard
(***) Bid seven with the ♥Q

Contract: 7♥ by South. Opening lead: ♥3.

Plan the play.

How many immediate winners do you have?
Eleven; six hearts, three clubs and two aces.

Where might you find two more?
Perhaps by ruffing a club you can establish one more trick; otherwise, short of finding a very unlikely singleton king, you will need a squeeze.

What then is the natural line of play?
To draw trumps, then play four rounds of clubs, ruffing the fourth one. Now hope to squeeze an opponent who holds both the missing kings.

Will such a squeeze work?
No. There is a problem with entries. After drawing trumps and establishing the clubs you will be down to something like:

```
            ♠ A 7 4
            ♥ –
            ♦ A 5
            ♣ 5

            ♠ Q 6
            ♥ 10 9
            ♦ Q 7
            ♣ –
```

For the squeeze to work you would need to cash all your heart and club winners, leaving an opponent with only three cards left in which to keep two king doubletons. Here, you would need to cross to one of dummy's aces to cash the club and then find a way back to hand to cash your hearts. Whatever you try breaks up the squeeze.

Is there any other hope?
There is, but it requires quite a far-sighted play. The simple squeeze does not work, as you have seen, but a defender who is guarding all three suits can be squeezed in a different way. If you cash all six heart tricks, he will not be able to keep four clubs and two guarded kings.

So just run the trumps?
Not quite. Your menaces against him are the two queens and you will have no entry to them after cashing the last trump. The solution is a double Vienna Coup. Win the ♥A at trick one and cash the ♠A and ♦A before running the rest of the trumps and discarding dummy's small spades and diamonds. After eight tricks, you hope an opponent has to keep four clubs and both kings—clearly impossible. If he discards a club he gives two tricks immediately, while if he throws either king you can cash the established queen and squeeze him again between his clubs and the remaining king.

The full deal:

```
            ♠ A 7 4
            ♥ A 2
            ♦ A 5 2
            ♣ A K Q 5 4
♠ J 9 5 3                  ♠ K 10 8
♥ 6 4 3                    ♥ 7 5
♦ J 9 8                    ♦ K 10 6 3
♣ J 6 3                    ♣ 10 8 7 2
            ♠ Q 6 2
            ♥ K Q J 10 9 8
            ♦ Q 7 4
            ♣ 9
```

Tip

When planning a squeeze where your holding in one side suit is something like Ax(x) opposite Qx(x), it is often correct to cash the ace, unblocking the suit to allow your queen to be the threat against the opponent with the missing king. This play is called a Vienna Coup. The main thing is simply to be clear in your mind which of your cards are the threats against an opponent and make sure you have the communications to allow them to do their job.

DEAL FIFTY-SIX

North/SouthVulnerable. Dealer West.

```
♠ A J 9 3
♥ 5 3
♦ A 10 2
♣ Q 8 6 5

♠ K Q
♥ A K Q J 10 9
♦ 5 3
♣ K 9 2
```

West	North	East	South
2♦(*)	Pass	Pass	4♥
Pass	5♦	Pass	6♥
All Pass			

(*) Weak; 5–9 HCPs, six diamonds.

Contract: 6♥ by South. Opening lead: ♦K.

Plan the play.

How many immediate winners do you have?
Eleven; six hearts, four spades and the ace of diamonds, but there is an awkward blockage in spades so perhaps only ten.

Where will you find the extra tricks?
Knocking out the ♣A will provide a trick, as would over-coming the spade blockage or perhaps the ♠10 falling in three rounds.

What's your biggest difficulty?
The spade blockage and lack of an outside entry to dummy. If you cash the ♠KQ then lead a club to the queen, even if West holds the ace he will have a diamond to cash so it seems you must overtake the second spade and get rid of the diamond loser before playing on clubs.

If you draw trumps then play three rounds of spades, what do you then need to allow you to make your contract?
Either the ♠10 to fall, turning dummy's nine into a trick, or some good news in clubs—jack-ten doubleton with either hand or ace doubleton and guess which hand to lead from on the first round.

How likely is that?
The spade is possible though against the odds while a lucky club distribution is heavily against the odds.

Who is likely to hold the spade length and the ace of clubs?
On the bidding, both are likely to be with East.

Can you see a way to put pressure on East and give yourself a better chance?
Perhaps if you run your trumps he may suffer some kind of a squeeze. Anyway, since you only need to concede the lead once, you can certainly afford to cash five hearts, keeping one as a control card. Assuming that East is guarding both black suits, he is obliged to come down to four spades and ace to three clubs.

Why?
He must keep four spades or you can overtake the second spade and cash four spade tricks. If he keeps only two clubs, you can take three spade tricks and lead a club to your king then duck a club to his bare ace and make dummy's queen as your twelfth trick.

So East's last seven cards must be four spades and three clubs. What next?
As he cannot keep a diamond, you need no longer worry about diamond losers so can afford to cash your last trump. You have to throw a second club from dummy, leaving:

```
            ♠ A J 9 3
            ♥ –
            ♦ –
            ♣ Q 8
                        ♠ 10 8 7 6
immaterial              ♥ –
                        ♦ –
                        ♣ A 7 3
            ♠ K Q
            ♥ –
            ♦ 5
            ♣ K 9 2
```

with East still to discard. If he discards a spade, you can over-take the second spade and take your four spades then give up a club. If he comes down to ace doubleton club, cash your king and queen of spades then play the ♣K. If he wins, the ♣Q is a dummy entry, if he ducks you play a second club to his now bare ace and he must lead a spade to dummy.

The full deal:

```
            ♠ A J 9 3
            ♥ 5 3
            ♦ A 10 2
            ♣ Q 8 6 5
♠ 4 2                   ♠ 10 8 7 6 5
♥ 8 2                   ♥ 7 6 4
♦ K Q J 9 8 7           ♦ 6 4
♣ J 10 4                ♣ A 7 3
            ♠ K Q
            ♥ A K Q J 10 9
            ♦ 5 3
            ♣ K 9 2
```

Usually a squeeze forces a defender to discard a stopper/winner in a suit. Occasionally, as here, he may be squeezed out of his communication card to his partner's hand—but this can be just as effective if declarer needs to give up the lead to establish his tricks!

DEAL FIFTY-SEVEN

Neither Side Vulnerable. Dealer South.

> ♠ K J 8
> ♥ A K Q
> ♦ Q 7 6 2
> ♣ K 8 4
>
> ♠ Q 10 9 7 6 3
> ♥ 7
> ♦ A J 3
> ♣ A 5 2

West	North	East	South
–	–	–	1♠
Pass	2♦	Pass	2♠
Pass	4NT(*)	Pass	5♠(**)
Pass	6♠	All Pass	

(*) Roman Keycard Blackwood
(**) 2 keycards plus the ♠Q

Contract: 6♠ by South. Opening lead: ♥J.

Plan the play from here.

How many immediate winners do you have?
Six; three hearts, two clubs and a diamond.

Where will you find six extra tricks?
Knocking out the ♠A will provide five extra tricks, and the sixth will probably come from diamonds.

What is the obvious line of play?
To draw trumps as quickly as possible, throw a club and a diamond on the top hearts and take the diamond finesse.

What are the odds for this line of play?
As you are simply reliant on a finesse, it is a 50 percent chance.

Is there any alternative?
You could cash the three hearts immediately, throwing two diamonds from hand. Now play a diamond to the ace. You can negotiate two dummy entries in trumps to ruff diamonds twice as you draw trumps and use the ♣K as an entry to cash the ♦Q if the king has fallen.

That line is quite a bit more complicated, but is it better?
It succeeds when either defender has ♦K, ♦Kx or ♦Kxx. So you succeed on all 3-3 breaks—35.5 percent; on one-third of the 4-2 breaks—48.5 percent divided by 3 is approximately 16.2 percent; and one-sixth of the 5-1 breaks—14.5 percent divided by 6 is approximately 2.4 percent. That all adds up to 54.1 percent.

So is it a better line of play?
Yes, but only just. It is a little over 4 percent better than the simple finesse but runs the slight risk of a very bad break in one of the major suits, reducing the overall gain somewhat.

The full deal:

> ♠ K J 8
> ♥ A K Q
> ♦ Q 7 6 2
> ♣ K 8 4
>
> ♠ 5   ♠ A 4 2
> ♥ J 10 9 6 2   ♥ 8 5 4 3
> ♦ K 10 8   ♦ 9 5 4
> ♣ Q 10 6 3   ♣ J 9 7
>
> ♠ Q 10 9 7 6 3
> ♥ 7
> ♦ A J 3
> ♣ A 5 2

Tip

Know the odds for the most common divisions of missing cards and for finesses or combinations of finesses, so that you can compare the chances of different lines of play.

Deal 58

Neither Side Vulnerable. Dealer West.

> ♠ K 6 3
> ♥ J 4 2
> ♦ K J 8 6
> ♣ 7 5 3
>
> ♠ A 7 5
> ♥ A K Q 10 8
> ♦ A 7
> ♣ J 8 2

West	North	East	South
Pass	Pass	Pass	1♥
1♠	Dble(*)	Pass	2♠
Pass	3♥	Pass	4♥
All Pass			

(*) Takeout

Contract: 4♥ by South. Opening lead: ♣A.

This is followed by the ♣K, and the ♣4 to East's queen. East returns the ♠10. Over to you.

How many immediate winners do you have?
Nine; five hearts, two spades and two diamonds.

Which suit will provide your tenth trick?
Probably diamonds.

Who has the ♦Q?
Almost certainly East as West passed as dealer and has shown up with the ace-king of clubs and probably has the queen-jack of spades.

So how will you play the diamonds?
Assuming that trumps are not 5-1, you will be able to play ace, king and ruff a diamond, succeeding when East has queen to three.

Where will you win the spade switch?
In hand, retaining dummy's king as an entry to the hoped for diamond trick.

You draw trumps and they are 3-2, West discarding a spade on the third round. How do you like your chances?
They are not good. West has shown up with three clubs and two hearts and presumably has five spades for his overcall. In that case he can have at most three diamonds and you will not be able to ruff out East's queen.

Is there any hope?
If West holds ♦10 9(x), you could lead the jack on the third round, pinning the ten and establishing the eight.

There is one other possibility; what if West has ♦10x or ♦9x?
Then East has ♦Q10xxx or ♦Q9xxx. Ace, king and a third round is useless—but what if you win the third round of trumps in dummy and lead the ♦J on the first round? East must cover so you win the ace and lead back to the king, dropping West's nine or ten. Now your eight and six are equals against the remaining ten or nine and you can take a ruffing finesse.

Is this a sure thing?
No; it needs West to hold ♦10x or ♦9x. Also, you have a third round guess whether to play him for the doubleton or try to ruff out his ♦109x. Nonetheless, this is easily the best chance of setting up a third diamond trick.

The full deal:

```
              ♠ K 6 3
              ♥ J 4 2
              ♦ K J 8 6
              ♣ 7 5 3
♠ Q J 9 8 4                    ♠ 10 2
♥ 9 3                          ♥ 7 6 5
♦ 9 4                          ♦ Q 10 5 3 2
♣ A K 6 4                      ♣ Q 10 9
              ♠ A 7 5
              ♥ A K Q 10 8
              ♦ A 7
              ♣ J 8 2
```

Tip

Cherish your low cards. Here, it was the combined power of the eight, seven and six which provided you with the chance to play a suit in an unusual way.

DEAL FIFTY-NINE
North/South Vulnerable. Dealer West.

```
              ♠ A J 10 3
              ♥ A K 8 6 3
              ♦ Q
              ♣ K Q 5

              ♠ 7 5 4
              ♥ J 10 9 4
              ♦ 8 6 2
              ♣ A 8 2
```

West	North	East	South
1♦	Dble	Pass	1♥
2♦	3♥	Pass	4♥
All Pass			

Contract: 4♥ by South. Opening lead: ♦A.

West continues with the ♦K. You to play from here.

How many immediate winners do you have?
Six; two hearts, three clubs and a spade.

Where will the extra trick come from?
You will certainly make at least three more heart tricks, either by force or by ruffing. If the ♥Q drops you can make two extra hearts in hand plus two diamond ruffs to bring your total to ten. If there is a heart loser, you will still have two diamond ruffs but only one extra heart in hand and will need another trick from elsewhere—clearly from spades.

You ruff the second diamond and cash a top heart to which everyone follows small. What next?
There seems no reason to play West for the ♥Qxx, because with a singleton and some diamond support East might have scrapped up 2♦ over the double. Why not just lay down the second top heart?

Say you do that and West discards a diamond. What now?
You need to get to hand three times; once to ruff the last diamond and twice to take the spade finesses. The ace of clubs is one entry and the fourth round of hearts is another, but that leaves you with no heart in dummy to ruff the third diamond.

What this means is that you will only be able to lead spades from hand once, succeeding only when West holds either both missing honors or either honor doubleton. He is almost certain to hold at least one spade honor. Does this suggest an alternative line of play?
If you assume that West has at least one spade honor, then all you need is to make sure that you can take two spade finesses. It looks strange, but suppose that you lead a low trump on the second round instead of cashing the king. This may look peculiar but what can the defense do? If they play back a trump you win in hand and take a spade finesse and still have the ♣A as an entry to repeat the finesse. On a diamond return you can ruff high in dummy and lead a low heart back to hand. Again, you have two entries to lead spades and if West has a spade honor you are home.

The full deal:

                    ♠ A J 10 3
                    ♥ A K 8 6 3
                    ♦ Q
                    ♣ K Q 5
    ♠ K 9 6   ♠ Q 8 2
    ♥ 2   ♥ Q 7 5
    ♦ A K J 10 7 3   ♦ 9 5 4
    ♣ J 7 3   ♣ 10 9 6 4
                    ♠ 7 5 4
                    ♥ J 10 9 4
                    ♦ 8 6 2
                    ♣ A 8 2

Tip

Be willing to give up on the possibility of avoiding a loser in one suit if it will greatly improve your chances in another suit and in the whole hand.

DEAL SIXTY

Neither Side Vulnerable. Dealer South.

                    ♠ A J 3
                    ♥ A 6 4 2
                    ♦ K 8 3
                    ♣ J 9 2

                    ♠ K Q 7
                    ♥ K J 9 7 5
                    ♦ A 4
                    ♣ A K 8

West	North	East	South
–	–	–	2NT
Pass	3♣	Pass	3♥
Pass	6♥	All Pass	

Contract 6♥ by South. Opening lead: ♠8.

Plan the play.

How many immediate winners do you have?
Nine: three spades, two hearts, two diamonds and two clubs.

Where will you find three more tricks?
If hearts are 2-2 you will have three extra tricks. If there is a heart loser, you will need a third club trick. This could come from a double finesse against queen-ten, from dropping a doubleton queen, or perhaps an endplay after eliminating spades and diamonds.

Where will you win the first spade?
In hand. You might need entries to dummy.

What do you play at trick two?
A heart to the ace. There is no reason not to draw trumps.

East discards a diamond. Is there still a chance?
Yes, but a slim one. West has two natural tricks and the only way to reduce these to one is via an endplay.

What will you need for the endplay to succeed?
You will need to be able to eliminate all the side–suits before ducking a heart to West at trick eleven. That means West has to be precisely 3-4-3-3.

What about the clubs?
If West has to have exactly three clubs you cannot play to drop the queen, but must rely on the double finesse.

So your line of play is?
Lead the ♣J. Assuming this is covered, lead a spade to dummy and finesse against the ♣10. Now play three diamonds, ruffing the third, cash the remaining black winners and duck a heart. West is endplayed.

What if hearts are 3-1?
Now you will have cashed both top hearts. Ruff out the diamonds, cash your spade winners and exit with a heart. Whoever wins must lead a club so you succeed whenever you guess his holding—much better than the 25 percent chance of the double finesse.

The full deal:

                    ♠ A J 3
                    ♥ A 6 4 2
                    ♦ K 8 3
                    ♣ J 9 2
    ♠ 9 8 6   ♠ 10 5 4 2
    ♥ Q 10 8 3   ♥ –
    ♦ Q 10 2   ♦ J 9 7 6 5
    ♣ 7 5 3   ♣ Q 10 6 4
                    ♠ K Q 7
                    ♥ K J 9 7 5
                    ♦ A 4
                    ♣ A K 8

Tip

Sometimes a bad break makes it appear that a defender has two unavoidable trump tricks. Perhaps so, but see if there is any plausible distribution which will enable you to endplay him. Here, you needed a lot of luck, but perhaps after the terrible heart break you deserved some!

Part IX

CARD PLAY IN NO TRUMP
by Robert Berthe & Norbert Lébely

The intention of this section is to offer a unique approach to help sharpen the bridge player's skills as declarer in no trump contracts.

It is divided into two chapters, the first of which presents forty-eight deals, each of which enables you to discover some important technique applicable to the play. The emphasis is on methods by which you, as declarer, can reach the conclusions which will lead you to a successful play of the hand. We have not labeled the hands to indicate the particular maneuver illustrated, because we hope to teach you to discover for yourself the appropriate line of play.

To help you do this, we will offer the questions you must ask yourself as you plan the play of each hand and expect that these will help you to formulate a coherent plan. Each deal also concludes with a "Guiding Principle" which summarizes the technique presented.

The second chapter presents eighteen exercises pertaining to the methods discussed in the hands. These, as well as the deals in the first part, are arranged in an ascending order of complexity. Presumably,you will be an expert no trump declarer by the time the final exercise is reached.

On the following page there is an index of the various elements of playing no trump with a list of subjects and the hands in which these are relevant.

One last important detail should be mentioned. Declarer is, in these cases, being taught to insure the contract as if the hand is being played at rubber bridge or in a team match, rather than to make the maximum number of tricks, which would be more important in a pairs match.

Index of Play Techniques

Suppose you want information on a particular aspect of play techniques: simply refer to this section and you will immediately have a reference to the deals which relate to your individual problem.

For the explanatory deals in chapter 49 the reference is a number and for the exercises in chapter 50 the reference is a letter.

The crucial problem when playing no trumps is the dangerous opponent.
It is absolutely vital to prevent this adversary from gaining the lead for two main reasons:

1. He has an established suit: 1-8-12-21-27-38-45-A
2. Your guard in his partner's suit is exposed to a finesse: 11-28-34-40-G-J-R

There are various solutions to this problem:
1. The duck
>   Classic case: 1-11

>   Application of the Rules of 7 and 11: 1-8-10-11-16-28-33-34-38-39-40-45-
>   F-K-N

>   Special cases:
>   Bath Coup: 15
>   With KQxx: 34
>   With QJx opposite Axx: 44
>   Delayed-duck: 41
>   Deceptive duck: 23-P

You must nevertheless be aware that ducking may be fatal. It may be a question of:
>   Averting a dangerous switch: 18-24
>   Blocking the enemy suit: 30
>   Retaining a card of exit for a later throw-in: 42-O
>   Creating a second stopper: 5-40
>   Preserving a vulnerable holding: 12

2. Finessing into the correct hand: 27-G-J

3. Rejecting a finesse: 16-21-28-A

4. Avoidance: 45-R

5. Second hand high: 40-D

6. Stealing a tempo: 42

7. Choice of order in suit establishment: 16-19-32-38-Q

Communications problems must not be overlooked: 3-4-14-25-29-31-33-39-47-
    F-H-I-L-N

Suit establishment and safety-plays: 6-9-17-20-22-26-C-E-I-K

The race for suit-establishment: 2-7-13-B

Combined chances and probabilities: 35-48

Inferences from the bidding and opening lead: 11-38-42-44-B-D-O

Counting the hand: 37-43-M

Throw-in: 37-O

Psychological gambits: 24-36-46-P

49

Chapter

Forty-eight Deals

DEAL ONE

Both Sides Vulnerable. Dealer South.

- ♠ 8 7 4 3
- ♥ 4 3
- ♦ A Q 5
- ♣ K 10 8 7

- ♠ A K 6
- ♥ A 10 8
- ♦ K 9 3
- ♣ Q J 9 6

Lead: ♥5

South	West	North	East
1♣	Pass	1♠	Pass
1NT	Pass	2NT	Pass
3NT	All Pass		

How many winners do you have?
2 in spades, 1 in hearts, 3 in diamonds = 6 tricks.

Where will you find the three missing tricks?
In clubs, by knocking out the ace.

Each time you undertake a no trump contract you are confronted by a problem. What is it?
You have to ask yourself whether you should win the lead immediately or duck, and if the latter, how many times.

Why is this important?
Because it will determine the success or failure of many contracts. By holding up correctly, you will be cutting the communications between your opponents.

Consider the various distributions of the suit led:
In hearts there are eight cards missing:

1. If the hearts are 4-4, East/West will make only four tricks in any event: three hearts and the ace of clubs. Holding up will not have gained anything, but neither will it have cost.

2. If the hearts are 5-3, the length being presumably with West, and you are careful to duck twice, East, holding the ace of clubs, will be unable to give his partner the lead. The hold-up will thus have exhausted the communications between your two adversaries.

It must be pointed out that if West has the ace of clubs the contract is unmakable.

The full deal:

- ♠ 8 7 4 3
- ♥ 4 3
- ♦ A Q 5
- ♣ K 10 8 7

- ♠ Q 5 2
- ♥ K J 7 5 2
- ♦ 10 8 2
- ♣ 5 3

- ♠ J 10 9
- ♥ Q 9 6
- ♦ J 7 6 4
- ♣ A 4 2

- ♠ A K 6
- ♥ A 10 8
- ♦ K 9 3
- ♣ Q J 9 6

Tip

In no trump the technique known as the hold-up is fundamental, for if one of your opponents possesses an established suit it is essential that his partner should not be able to reach his hand.

For this purpose we advise you to employ the Rule of 7:

Whenever you possess only one guard in the suit led and envisage giving up the lead only once, count the number of cards you hold in that suit between your two hands, subtract the total from 7, and the answer will be the number of times you wiil be required to duck. Thus in the foregoing example, there were two hearts in dummy plus three in hand = 5; 7-5 = 2, therefore the Rule of 7 confirms that it was necessary to hold up twice.

DEAL TWO

Both Sides Vulnerable. Dealer South.

```
        ♠ K 3
        ♥ Q 5 2
        ♦ K J 9 8 7
        ♣ 6 5 4

        ♠ A 6 4
        ♥ A J
        ♦ 10 5 3
        ♣ A K Q J 10
```

Lead: ♠5

South	West	North	East
1♣	Pass	1♦	Pass
3NT	All Pass		

What is your winner count?
2 in spades, 1 in hearts, 5 in clubs = 8 tricks.

How will you establish the extra tricks?
In diamonds, if either the ace or queen is favorably placed and you guess correctly which one to play from dummy on the first round.

Is there the possibility of establishing a trick elsewhere? If so, what is it?
Yes, in hearts, if East has the king.

Can you succeed even if West has the king of hearts?
Of course; you need only play the ace followed by the jack without bothering about the position of the king.

Are you going to duck the first round of spades?
No. You must be careful to preserve the king of spades as an entry to the established queen of hearts. You have a second spade stopper and you have to give up the lead only once to your opponents. If you duck at Trick 1 the opponents will continue spades. Your only sure communication with the dummy will have evaporated prematurely and you will have to resort to the heart finesse, whereas the suggested line of play makes that finesse pointless.

So win the first trick with the ace of spades and continue with the ace and jack of hearts, thus making your contract 100 percent certain.

The full deal:

```
              ♠ K 3
              ♥ Q 5 2
              ♦ K J 9 8 7
              ♣ 6 5 4

♠ 10 8 7 5 2              ♥ Q J 9
♥ K 7 6 4                 ♥ 10 9 8 3
♦ A 2                     ♦ Q 6 4
♣ 9 8                     ♣ 7 3 2

              ♠ A 6 4
              ♥ A J
              ♦ 10 5 3
              ♣ A K Q J 10
```

Tip

Always count your certain tricks and ask yourself how many you have to establish. Do not make an automatic dash for your longest suit, for there may be a winning line of play against any distribution and any defense. Make a close study of your entry problems: lack of reflection at Trick 1 can often prove costly later.

DEAL THREE

Both Sides Vulnerable. Dealer East.

```
        ♠ 7 5 2
        ♥ 8 5 4
        ♦ 3 2
        ♣ K 7 6 5 3

        ♠ K 8 3
        ♥ A J 6
        ♦ A 9 7 4
        ♣ A 4 2
```

Lead: ♠6 East plays the jack

South	West	North	East
–	–	–	Pass
1NT	All Pass		

How many sure tricks do you have?
1 in spades (after the lead), 1 in hearts, 1 in diamonds, 2 in clubs = 5 certain tricks.

After winning the first spade with the king how will you set about finding the two extra tricks? What conditions must be satisfied?
From the club suit, and this must be divided 3-2.

What problem are you faced with?
Apart from the king of clubs the dummy has no other entry, and if you play ace, king and another club, you will certainly set up two tricks but you will not be in a position to benefit from them.

What technique must you apply?
You must duck a club in both hands, either on the first or second round of the suit. By proceeding thus, you will have maintained communications in your established suit.

The full deal:

```
              ♠ 7 5 2
              ♥ 8 5 4
              ♦ 3 2
              ♣ K 7 6 5 3

♠ A Q 10 6 4             ♠ J 9
♥ K 9 3                 ♥ Q 10 7 2
♦ 10 8 5                ♦ K Q J 6
♣ Q 10                  ♣ J 9 8

              ♠ K 8 3
              ♥ A J 6
              ♦ A 9 7 4
              ♣ A 4 2
```

Tip

This type of duck is a frequent ploy. While it is indispensable to compensate for the lack of entries, it may equally well be employed in order to verify the distribution of a particular suit without losing control. Thus with some holding like Kxx opposite Axxx, there is no question of establishing two immediate tricks for the defense. Perhaps the outstanding cards are 3-3; an initial duck in the suit will allow you to find out.

DEAL FOUR

Both Sides Vulnerable. Dealer North.

> ♠ K Q 3 2
> ♥ K 3
> ♦ A K 9 8 2
> ♣ 8 6
>
> ♠ A 4
> ♥ A 7 5 4 2
> ♦ 5
> ♣ Q J 10 9 2

Lead: ♠J

South	West	North	East
–	–	1♦	Pass
1♥	Pass	1♠	Pass
2NT	Pass	3NT	All Pass

Count your tricks before calling for dummy's first card.
3 in spades, 2 in hearts, 2 in diamonds = 7 tricks. You require two more.

Which suit will you elect to establish?
The defensive opening not being immediately threatening, your choice lies between hearts and clubs. Naturally you choose the club suit, for in order to satisfy your trick requirements it would be imperative that the hearts should break 3-3, which is only a 36 percent chance.

How many entries to your hand will you require?
You must foresee that the opposition will refuse the first round of clubs; consequently you will need two entries: one to remove the second top club (ace or king), and a second to allow you access to the established suit.

What are those two entries?
The ace of hearts and the ace of spades.

So which of dummy's cards do you contribute to Trick 1?
When you have a holding such like Ax opposite KQxx it is normal to begin with the ace, and then to play towards the two honors to avoid any blockage. However, you must certainly have realized that in the present example you must preserve the ace as an entry to your hand. Only by doing this will you be sure of establishing the club suit. You therefore take care to play the king on the opening lead. In this way you will be in hand when your opponents continue with spades and you will score ten tricks.

The full deal:

> ♠ K Q 3 2
> ♥ K 3
> ♦ A K 9 8 2
> ♣ 8 6
>
> ♠ J 10 9 8   ♠ 7 6 5
> ♥ J 6   ♥ Q 10 9 8
> ♦ Q 10 7 6   ♦ J 4 3
> ♣ A 7 3   ♣ K 5 4
>
> ♠ A 4
> ♥ A 7 5 4 2
> ♦ 5
> ♣ Q J 10 9 2

Tip

Whether you are playing in no trumps or in a suit contract, always exercise maximum care over the preservation of entries in the hand requiring suit establishment. You will frequently possess some holding such as Ax opposite Kx. If the opponents lead this suit, win with the honor which will subsequently play no further entry role. Train yourself to handle your entries correctly.

DEAL FIVE

Both Sides Vulnerable. Dealer South.

> ♠ A 8 2
> ♥ K 9 3
> ♦ J 4
> ♣ J 10 7 6 5
>
> ♠ K 4 3
> ♥ A 7 5
> ♦ A 10 3
> ♣ K Q 9 4

Lead: ♦6

South	West	North	East
1♣	Pass	3♣	Pass
3NT	All Pass		

How many sure tricks do you have?
2 in spades, 2 in hearts, 1 in diamonds = 5 certain tricks.

Where will the extra tricks come from?
The club suit naturally; all you have to do is to knock out the ace.

Which of dummy's cards do you play at Trick 1?
You have nothing to gain by playing the jack, for if West has led away from king-queen, your ten will take the first trick.

On the other hand what advantage will you derive from playing the four at Trick 1 in any event?
1. If East plays a small diamond your ten will win the trick.
2. If East produces a high honor, by winning with the ace you will have created a second stopper in the enemy suit.

For what precise reason is your contract assured?
Because you only need to abandon the lead once. The problem would be quite different had you been obliged to give up the lead twice.

The full deal:

```
            ♠ A 8 2
            ♥ K 9 3
            ♦ J 4
            ♣ J 10 7 6 5
♠ Q 9 7                    ♠ J 10 6 5
♥ J 6 4 2                  ♥ Q 10 8
♦ K 9 8 6 5               ♦ Q 7 2
♣ A                        ♣ 8 3 2
            ♠ K 4 3
            ♥ A 7 5
            ♦ A 10 3
            ♣ K Q 9 4
```

Tip

It would be extremely unwise to duck a queen or king with the following holdings:

Jxx	10x	xx
A10	AJx	AJ10

. . . where your intention is to give up the lead only once.

DEAL SIX

Neither Side Vulnerable. Dealer South.

```
            ♠ K 5 4
            ♥ A 7 6 2
            ♦ 7 4 3
            ♣ A 8 4

            ♠ A 6 3
            ♥ Q J 5 4
            ♦ A K 8
            ♣ K 7 2
```

Lead: ♠Q

South	West	North	East
1NT	Pass	3NT	All Pass

When the dummy goes down you have cause to congratulate partner for opting for the no trumps. You would have four certain losers in four hearts.

How many sure tricks do you have?
2 in spades, 1 in hearts, 2 in diamonds, 2 in clubs = 7 tricks. You have to find two more.

Which suit will furnish those tricks?
The only viable suit is hearts.

How will you play the suit?
1. If it breaks 3-2, you have only to worry about the position of the king and consequently you will make your contract with ease.
2. However, you will have realized that we are trying to increase your sense of foresight by asking this question, and so you should give some thought to a 4-1 division. After all, a 28 percent frequency is not negligible.

So, how will you set about it?
If West has four to the king you cannot avoid going down. On the other hand if it is East who has them you merely need to play twice towards your queen-jack.

You may also profit from a small additional chance. What is it?
Guard against a singleton king with West by cashing the ace first, the dummy has sufficient entries.

Are you going to duck the opening lead?
There is no point: you have two spade stoppers and you intend to give up the lead only once. Therefore:

(a) Ace of spades and four of hearts to the ace (the king does not appear).
(b) Small heart to your queen which holds, West discarding.
(c) Two of clubs to the ace.
(d) Small heart towards your jack; East cannot prevent you from making three heart tricks and thus your game.

The full deal:

```
            ♠ K 5 4
            ♥ A 7 6 2
            ♦ 7 4 3
            ♣ A 8 4
♠ Q J 10 8                 ♠ 9 7 2
♥ 3                        ♥ K 10 9 8
♦ J 9 5 2                  ♦ Q 10 6
♣ Q 6 5 3                  ♣ J 10 9
            ♠ A 6 3
            ♥ Q J 5 4
            ♦ A K 8
            ♣ K 7 2
```

Tip

Never rush blindly at a finesse which will not only fail to gain, but which runs the risk of costing a trick. Thus with:

QJx	QJxx
or	
Axxx	Axx

lead small towards dummy's honors.

DEAL SEVEN

North/South Vulnerable. Dealer East.

♠ Q 4 3
♥ K 8
♦ Q J 9 8 7
♣ Q J 2

♠ A 6 2
♥ A 3
♦ 10 5 4
♣ A K 10 7 3

Lead: ♥Q

South	West	North	East
–	–	–	Pass
1NT	Pass	3NT	All Pass

How many immediate tricks can you count?
1 in spades, 2 in hearts, 5 in clubs = 8 tricks. You need one more.

In which suit do you intend to find it?
It is very tempting to go for the diamonds, for you have only to dislodge the ace and king in order to find three tricks.

However, this line is doomed to failure. For what reason?
Your opponents have attacked a suit in which you have only two stoppers; the ace and king. They have nine cards in that suit and except in the highly improbable case of a 7-2 break with both the top diamonds with East or a blockage, they have no communications problems. If you set about establishing your longest suit, you will have to give up the lead twice at a time when you have only one heart stopper remaining. Clearly, the opponents will gather three or four heart tricks plus the ace and king of diamonds, for the lead has conferred upon them an undeniable advantage in suit-establishment.

Is there any hope of success? What is it?
Yes, you must hope that the king of spades is favorably placed (we won't insult you by asking you which opponent must have it).

So proceed with the play accordingly:
Win the opening lead with the ace of hearts and immediately play the two of spades towards the queen; West goes up with the king and continues with the four of hearts. Just take your seven other tricks: queen and ace of spades and five clubs.

This line of play was a mere 50 percent (favorable position of the king of spades), but there was no other winning line.

The full deal:

♠ Q 4 3
♥ K 8
♦ Q J 9 8 7
♣ Q J 2

♠ K 10 8   ♠ J 9 7 5
♥ Q J 9 7 4   ♥ 10 6 5 2
♦ K 6 2   ♦ A 3
♣ 9 5   ♣ 8 6 4

♠ A 6 2
♥ A 3
♦ 10 5 4
♣ A K 10 7 3

Tip

Always count the number of tricks you require carefully, and never embark automatically on an attractive looking suit without taking the time factor into consideration. Ask yourself whether your winners in the suit led are sufficient in number for you to give up the lead a certain number of times.

DEAL EIGHT

East/West Vulnerable. Dealer North.

♠ 10 9 5
♥ A 8 7 4 3
♦ 9 5
♣ Q 10 9

♠ A 8 4
♥ 5 2
♦ K Q J 10 6
♣ A K J

Lead: ♠6

South	West	North	East
–	–	Pass	Pass
1♦	Pass	1♥	Pass
1NT(*)	Pass	2♣(**)	Pass
2NT(***)	Pass	3NT	All Pass

(*)   15-18
(**) Crowhurst, a delayed Stayman bid
(***)Maximum, without three-card heart fit and ruffing-value

How many immediate tricks do you have?

1 in spades, 1 in hearts, 3 in clubs = 5 certain tricks and you can set up four diamonds by knocking out the ace. At Trick 1, East plays the jack of spades.

Will you duck the opening lead and if you do, how many times?

You will not have failed to bear in mind the Rule of 7. You possess 3+3 = 6 cards in spades: 7−6 = 1; you will therefore duck once only and win the second round of spades.

What in fact will happen if you duck the second round of spades?

If he has no entry or if the spades are 4-3 West will switch to a heart, a suit in which you only have one stopper. (Remember that the opponents know from the bidding that you have only two cards in hearts.) After taking the ace of spades you will establish the diamonds, hoping that the ace is not in the same hand as the long spades.

If the spades are 4-3, you will lose three spades and the ace of diamonds. East wins the second diamond and exits with a heart. Your contract is home with one spade, one heart, four diamonds and three clubs.

The full deal:

```
              ♠ 10 9 5
              ♥ A 8 7 4 3
              ♦ 9 5
              ♣ Q 10 9
♠ K Q 7 6 3               ♠ J 2
♥ Q J 10                  ♥ K 9 6
♦ 7 4                     ♦ A 8 3 2
♣ 8 7 2                   ♣ 6 5 4 3
              ♠ A 8 4
              ♥ 5 2
              ♦ K Q J 10 6
              ♣ A K J
```

Tip

Do not overlook the advantages of ducking and systematically apply the Rule of 7. In this way you will effectively counter any switch by the defense.

DEAL NINE

East/West Vulnerable. Dealer South.

```
              ♠ 9 3 2
              ♥ 8 5 3
              ♦ K J 5
              ♣ A Q 8 4

              ♠ K J 5
              ♥ A Q
              ♦ Q 8 7 2
              ♣ K J 10 2
```

Lead: ♥J

South	West	North	East
1NT	Pass	3NT	All Pass

Top tricks?

2 in hearts (the jack is covered by the king and ace and you have one further winner in the suit), 4 in clubs = 6 tricks. You need to find three more.

In which suit?

Diamonds naturally. If the suit should divide 3-3, you will make three tricks in it after removing the ace. If it breaks 4-2, the most probable division (48 percent), what precaution should you take?

Lead twice towards dummy's combined honor holding.

Why?

Imagine that West has Ax. If you maneuver correctly you will make three tricks, but if you play from dummy you will have sacrificed one of your honors to no good purpose.

Therefore, at Trick 2, play the two of diamonds towards the jack, which holds.

What now?

A club to your hand and a further diamond towards the table: West plays the ace and your objective has been attained.

The full deal:

```
              ♠ 9 3 2
              ♥ 8 5 3
              ♦ K J 5
              ♣ A Q 8 4
♠ A Q 8                  ♠ 10 7 6 4
♥ J 10 9 7 2             ♥ K 6 4
♦ A 4                    ♦ 10 9 6 3
♣ 9 5 3                  ♣ 7 6
              ♠ K J 5
              ♥ A Q
              ♦ Q 8 7 2
              ♣ K J 10 2
```

Tip

You will frequently be faced with combined honor holdings like:

QJxx

Kxx

Apply the principle of playing twice towards the two honors provided you have sufficient entries.

DEAL TEN

East/West Vulnerable. Dealer East.

- ♠ 10 9 8
- ♥ 10 9 4
- ♦ A K J 5
- ♣ J 10 2

- ♠ K Q J 5
- ♥ K Q J
- ♦ 9 4 2
- ♣ K Q 6

Lead: 7 (4th best)

South	West	North	East
–	–	–	Pass
1NT	Pass	3NT	All Pass

How many sure tricks?

In spite of the 26 points your trick-total is hardly impressive, and for the moment you are looking at only two certain tricks, in diamonds. (On this point, a reminder of that basic principle: never count potential winners as sure tricks.)

Where are you going to find the seven missing tricks?

In the three other suits, by knocking out their respective aces.

If the diamond length is with West as the lead shows, the contract seems to be in no danger. You have seven cards in this suit, headed by AK4 and the queen is probably right.

Now what card do you play from dummy at Trick 1: a top honor, the jack, or the five?

Before deciding, it might be well if we consider together the inferences of this fourth best lead. Originally, this conventional lead was created to help defenders, but declarer can also gather useful information from it. Let us take a closer look: you subtract the numerical value of the card led from 11 and the answer is the total number of cards higher than the lead possessed by the other three hands. Therefore deduct 7 from 11 and you obtain the answer 4. Now you hold ace, king, jack and nine which rank above the seven.

What inference do you draw from this very simple calculation?

East possesses no card higher than the seven. Consequently, it is not one of dummy's honors that you must select at Trick 1 but the five. East duly plays the six and you take the trick with the nine. Later you will finesse against West's queen and make four tricks in the suit. In this way you will simply give up three aces to the defense since you still retain three guards in the suit led initially. Thanks to your correct interpretation of the lead you will make the contract with an overtrick.

The full deal:

- ♠ 10 9 8
- ♥ 10 9 4
- ♦ A K J 5
- ♣ J 10 2

♠ A 2	♠ 7 6 4 3
♥ A 6 5	♥ 8 7 3 2
♦ Q 10 8 7 3	♦ 6
♣ A 9 4	♣ 8 7 5 3

- ♠ K Q J 5
- ♥ K Q J
- ♦ 9 4 2
- ♣ K Q 6

It is easy to check that good defense (refusal to allow you to slip through an early heart or club trick) will beat you if you play one of dummy's honors at Trick 1. In effect you will have to knock out West's three aces, but meanwhile the latter will have established two long diamonds.

Tip

Do not overlook the important information furnished by a lead of the fourth best, and refer systematically to the Rule of 11. However, bear in mind that the card led will furnish different information according to its numerical value:

1. A high card (6-8) will reveal the whereabouts of the outstanding honors in the suit, as in the example above.
2. A low card, a 2, 3 or a 4, with the lower cards visible in the latter two cases, will on the other hand give an indication of the distribution, for it will probably be from just a four-card suit.

DEAL ELEVEN

East/West Vulnerable. Dealer South.

- ♠ K 8
- ♥ 8 7 2
- ♦ A 10 3
- ♣ A J 10 9 6

- ♠ A 9 5
- ♥ K Q 5
- ♦ K 8 4 2
- ♣ Q 3 2

Lead: ♥6

South	West	North	East
1NT	Pass	3NT	All Pass

How many immediate tricks?

2 in spades, 1 in hearts (after the lead), 2 in diamonds, 1 in clubs = 6 tricks. Three more are required and these will be provided by the long club suit.

What inference do you draw from the lead? How many cards does East have higher than the six (fourth best)?
The Rule of 11 shows that he holds only one card higher than the six. It might be the ace, but in that case West would have led the top of his sequence J1096x. Therefore East's higher card will be the nine, ten or jack.

In fact, East contributes the jack. Now you have KQx opposite three small.

Where is the danger on this hand?
To enjoy the clubs you will take the club finesse. If West has the king all will be well, but if East has the king he will take it and play back a heart. If you have taken the first trick you will then be in danger of losing a club and four heart tricks.

Is there a better way?
Yes, you must duck the jack of hearts. One of two things will happen:

1. Either the hearts will divide 5-2 and West will be unable to regain the lead; or
2. East can return a heart and the suit will have broken 4-
3. You will then lose only three hearts and the king of clubs.

The full deal:

```
              ♠ K 8
              ♥ 8 7 2
              ♦ A 10 3
              ♣ A J 10 9 6
♠ Q 10 7                      ♠ J 6 4 3 2
♥ A 10 9 6 4                  ♥ J 3
♦ Q 9 5                       ♦ J 7 6
♣ 7 5                         ♣ K 8 4
              ♠ A 9 5
              ♥ K Q 5
              ♦ K 8 4 2
              ♣ Q 3 2
```

Tip

KQx is equivalent to an ace. You must duck with this honor holding whenever you fear that your right-hand opponent may gain the lead, for if this should prove to be the case, the prospect of retaining only Kx or Qx in the danger suit is scarcely a pleasant one.

East/West Vulnerable. Dealer South.

```
              ♠ A 7 5
              ♥ 8 7 2
              ♦ A K 8 3
              ♣ Q 9 3
              ♠ K 10 8
              ♥ K Q 5
              ♦ 10 2
              ♣ A J 10 8 5
```

Lead: ♥6

South	West	North	East
1NT	Pass	3NT	All Pass

How many immediate tricks?
2 in spades, 1 in hearts (after the lead), 2 in diamonds, 1 in clubs = 6 tricks. Three more are required and these will be provided by the club suit.

What inference do you draw from the lead?
Just as in Deal 11, West is marked with the ace of hearts and East plays the jack.

Do you duck the jack of hearts?
This was correct in Deal 11, but it would be wrong this time.

Why?
There is no danger of East gaining the lead to play a heart through your remaining doubleton honor because you can take the club finesse into the West hand.

If you duck the first heart, the defense will clear the suit and if West has the king of clubs he will cash two more heart winners after you have taken the club finesse and you will go down.

The full deal:

```
              ♠ A 7 5
              ♥ 8 7 2
              ♦ A K 8 3
              ♣ Q 9 3
♠ Q 9 4                       ♠ J 6 3 2
♥ A 10 9 6 4                  ♥ J 3
♦ 7 6 5                       ♦ Q J 9 4
♣ K 2                         ♣ 7 6 4
              ♠ K 10 8
              ♥ K Q 5
              ♦ 10 2
              ♣ A J 10 8 5
```

Tip

Whether you duck or not with KQx depends on who you fear getting the lead. If you cannot avoid allowing your right-hand opponent in, it is probably right to duck but if you can keep him off lead then win the trick immediately.

DEAL THIRTEEN

East/West Vulnerable. Dealer West.

　　　♠ K 10 4
　　　♥ A K 9 8 6
　　　♦ K 3
　　　♣ 10 5 2

　　　♠ J 9 2
　　　♥ 7 5 2
　　　♦ A Q J 10
　　　♣ K 9 8

Lead: ♣3

South	West	North	East
–	Pass	1♥	Pass
2♦	Pass	2♥	Pass
2NT	Pass	3NT	All Pass

East plays the queen of clubs; do you duck?
Obviously not, for you might fail to make a club trick at all. West probably has the ace and jack.

When you win with the king of clubs how many tricks do you have?
2 in hearts, 4 in diamonds, 1 in clubs = 7 certain tricks.

You have to establish two more. How will you do it?
1. A 3-2 heart break (68 percent) will furnish two tricks.
2. If West has the queen of spades (successive finesses if necessary), that suit will provide two tricks 50 percent of the time.

Which solution will you choose?
While the cultivation of percentage plays may normally constitute a sound habit, you must not forget that in no trump contracts, while it is essential to count your winners, you must not overlook those of the defense; in this example the defense has already set up three club tricks after the lead (West's three, the two being visible, has shown that the suit is fortunately divided 4-3). The defenders can take the ace of spades at any time. If you give up a heart trick to them to set up dummy's two long cards, they will rake in five tricks: three clubs plus the ace of spades plus a heart, and you will be defeated.

Therefore you must rely on the spade finesse.

So how do you proceed?
Play the jack of spades: East is forced to win with the ace and when he continues with a club West takes three clubs and exits with a heart. Naturally you win this trick.

How do you continue?
Play the king of diamonds, then three further rounds of the suit before taking another spade finesse.

The full deal:

　　　♠ K 10 4
　　　♥ A K 9 8 6
　　　♦ K 3
　　　♣ 10 5 2

♠ Q 6 5　　　　　　♠ A 8 7 3
♥ J 10 3　　　　　　♥ Q 4
♦ 6 4 2　　　　　　♦ 9 8 7 5
♣ A J 7 3　　　　　♣ Q 6 4

　　　♠ J 9 2
　　　♥ 7 5 2
　　　♦ A Q J 10
　　　♣ K 9 8

Tip

Do not be merely satisfied with counting those tricks which you require to establish; think about the defenders' tricks too. What is the point of setting up a ninth trick if meanwhile your opponents can run five?

DEAL FOURTEEN

East/West Vulnerable. Dealer North.

　　　♠ 9 4 3
　　　♥ 5
　　　♦ A K 10 9 8 7
　　　♣ A 9 4

　　　♠ A J 7 2
　　　♥ A K 7 3
　　　♦ Q
　　　♣ Q 7 5 3

Lead: ♥Q

South	West	North	East
–	–	1♦	Pass
1♥	Pass	2♦	Pass
3NT	All Pass		

Count your tricks.
1 in spades, 2 in hearts, 3 in diamonds, 1 in club = 7 tricks. You need two more.

Where from?
The diamonds, obviously.

What is the normal way of playing this suit?
You cash the queen, then cross to the table with the ace of clubs and lead your top diamonds.

However, have you noticed that the dummy will then be entryless? Therefore this line will fail if an opponent holds four or more diamonds to the jack.

What is the solution?
Overtake the queen of diamonds with the king and continue the suit until the jack appears. You may well have sacrificed a trick if the jack falls in three rounds, but if it does not, your ace of clubs will remain on the table as an entry to the established diamonds. You will have guaranteed nine tricks.

The full deal:

```
              ♠ 9 4 3
              ♥ 5
              ♦ A K 10 9 8 7
              ♣ A 9 4
♠ K 10 6 5                    ♠ Q 8
♥ Q J 10 9                    ♥ 8 6 4 2
♦ 4 3                         ♦ J 6 5 2
♣ K 6 2                       ♣ J 10 8
              ♠ A J 7 2
              ♥ A K 7 3
              ♦ Q
              ♣ Q 7 5 3
```

Tip

If you are short of entries do not yield to the temptation of false economy: if you have a bare honor opposite a suit containing all the intermediates, like AJ1098 facing K, overtake the king with the ace and give up a trick to the queen.

DEAL FIFTEEN

Both Sides Vulnerable. Dealer East.

```
              ♠ 8
              ♥ A 2
              ♦ 10 6 5 4
              ♣ A J 8 6 4 2

              ♠ A J 2
              ♥ Q J 6
              ♦ A K 3
              ♣ Q 10 9 3
```

Lead: ♠K

South	West	North	East
–	–	–	Pass
1NT	Pass	3NT	All Pass

How many tricks do you have?
1 in spades, 1 in hearts, 2 in diamonds, 1 in clubs = 5 tricks. You need four more.

Which suit will you set up?
The clubs, naturally, and you need only to capture or drop the king in order to establish sufficient tricks.

While it would therefore seem that the contract is in no danger the opening lead poses a problem. What is it?
East/West have nine spades between them. Suppose you win the first trick with the ace to preserve a guard in the suit with J2: if the guarded king of clubs is with East, the latter will return a spade and the contract will be in jeopardy.

What is the solution, then?
By refusing the first spade you will leave West on lead, thus preventing him from continuing with spades; should he insist, he will be playing into your AJ. You therefore apply the principle of ducking which has been effectively named the Bath Coup.

West gives you a suspicious glance and after a few moments' thought he switches to the seven of hearts.

What is your reaction? How should you reason it out?
Remember that four club tricks will suffice and that you do not require an extra trick in hearts.

Suppose you did try the heart finesse, what risk would you be running?
East might win the the king of hearts and return a spade before you had time to broach the clubs, and your Bath Coup at Trick 1 would have gained nothing. In fact you would go down an extra trick.

Consequently, do not be tempted by the heart finesse since your QJ still gives you a stopper in that suit.

Play the ace of hearts, then come to hand with the ace of diamonds to run the queen of clubs. The finesse fails, but your contract is assured.

Thus there were two traps on this hand, but doubtless you overcame them.

The full deal:

```
              ♠ 8
              ♥ A 2
              ♦ 10 6 5 4
              ♣ A J 8 6 4 2
♠ K Q 10 9 4                 ♠ 7 6 5 3
♥ 7 5 4                      ♥ K 10 9 8 3
♦ Q 9 7 2                    ♦ J 8
♣ 5                         ♣ K 7
              ♠ A J 2
              ♥ Q J 6
              ♦ A K 3
              ♣ Q 10 9 3
```

Tip

When you possess AJx in a suit and your left-hand opponent leads the king, you will gain a precious tempo by ducking. But be careful not to apply this technique blindly. The decision to duck or to win will depend on your chosen line of play.

DEAL SIXTEEN
Both Sides Vulnerable. Dealer South.

♠ K 6 3
♥ A 10 5
♦ A J 9
♣ J 10 8 3

♠ A 7
♥ K 9 6
♦ Q 10 6 2
♣ A Q 9 6

Lead: ♠4. East plays the ten

South	West	North	East
–	Pass	1♦	Pass
1NT	Pass	3NT	All Pass

Count up your sure tricks.
2 in spades, 2 in hearts, 1 in diamonds, 1 in clubs = 6 tricks.

You need to establish three extra tricks. If either the club or diamond finesses work you will make your contract without difficulty. However, you must have noticed that finesses rarely win in textbooks, so you must find a way of succeeding however the adverse cards are placed.

Will you duck the lead?
The Rule of 7 (amended) is equally valid when you have two stoppers, provided that a switch is not immediately imminent. Therefore duck at Trick 1. East continues with the jack to West's two and your ace.

Which suit do you play first, clubs or diamonds?
If the spades are 4-4, your order of play is of no great moment, but if they are 5-3, the length is certainly with West. You must therefore kill his potential entry by playing on clubs first. Later, you can take the diamond finesse in safety: either the communication between East/West will have been severed (spades 5-3), or the spades will be 4-4 and the opponents will make two spades and two minor-suit kings.

So, how do you continue?
You cannot afford to cross to dummy to take the club finesse since West might win with the king of clubs and return a heart, establishing a fifth trick for the defense when the king of diamonds is wrong. Simply lay down the ace and queen of clubs.

The full deal:

♠ K 6 3
♥ A 10 5
♦ A J 9
♣ J 10 8 3

♠ Q 9 8 4 2   ♠ J 10 5
♥ J 3 2   ♥ Q 8 7 4
♦ 7 5   ♦ K 8 4 3
♣ K 7 2   ♣ 5 4

♠ A 7
♥ K 9 6
♦ Q 10 6 2
♣ A Q 9 6

Tip

Apply the Rule of 7 when you hold two guards in the suit led, and do not fear a switch. Furthermore, you must exercise care over the order in which you embark on your suit establishment. Your main consideration is to kill the potential entry in the hand you consider to be dangerous while still retaining a stopper in the suit.

DEAL SEVENTEEN
Neither Side Vulnerable. Dealer South.

♠ A 7 6 4
♥ Q 9 2
♦ Q 5
♣ 6 5 4 2

♠ K 9 3
♥ A J 10 5
♦ A 3 2
♣ A K 8

Lead: ♦6

South	West	North	East
1♣	Pass	1♠	Pass
2NT	Pass	3NT	All Pass

How many top tricks?
2 spades, 1 hearts, 1 diamonds, 2 clubs = 6 tricks. You require three more.

What are your prospects?
The only viable suit is hearts, for it will be possible to set up three extra tricks if East has the king.

Do you play the five or the queen of diamonds at Trick 1?
The queen, naturally; you must hope that West has led away from the king, and you will gain nothing by playing the five, for East will insert an intermediate card forcing your ace. If the queen is ever to win a trick, it is now. The queen is covered by East's king.

Do you win immediately?
Since the success of the contract depends now on the favorable position of the king of hearts, there is no point in ducking.

How do you continue?
You cross to dummy with the ace of spades and play a heart.

Which card do you lead, the two, nine or queen?
You will not have failed to notice that you have no further communication with the table, so there is nothing to be gained by playing the two: you will not be able to repeat the finesse even if it wins. The queen seems to be the correct card to play since it will allow you to capture the king twice guarded.

However, what will happen if the king is three times guarded?
You will be unable to make four heart tricks since you will find yourself in one of the two following situations according to whether you have played the five or the ten from your hand, either:

92

AJ10

where you will be forced to win the next heart in your hand, East retaining the king still doubleton, or:

92

AJ5

when East will cover the nine with the king and retain 87 against your J5. There is only one correct card to play on broaching the hearts and that is the nine; you will contribute the 5 from your hand. That is followed by the queen for your ten, and finally the two towards your remaining tenace of AJ.

The full deal:

```
          ♠ A 7 6 4
          ♥ Q 9 2
          ♦ Q 5
          ♣ 6 5 4 2
♠ J 8                    ♠ Q 10 5 2
♥ 4 3                    ♥ K 8 7 6
♦ J 9 7 6 4              ♦ K 10 8
♣ Q 10 7 3               ♣ J 9
          ♠ K 9 3
          ♥ A J 10 5
          ♦ A 3 2
          ♣ A K 8
```

Tip

Certain suit-combinations require text book methods which should be almost automatic. Recourse to these is indispensable whenever you lack communication.

DEAL EIGHTEEN

East/West Vulnerable. Dealer South.

```
          ♠ J 3
          ♥ 7 5
          ♦ Q J 10 6 5
          ♣ A Q 10 3

          ♠ A 9 5
          ♥ A J 4
          ♦ A 9 3
          ♣ K J 5 2
```

Lead: ♥K. East plays the two

South	West	North	East
1NT	Pass	3NT	Pass

How many certain tricks do you have?
1 in spades, 1 in hearts, 1 in diamonds, 4 in clubs =7 tricks. You need two more.

Which suit will you establish?
The diamonds; you will take the diamond finesse and whether or not this succeeds you will have enough tricks.

Do you remember a technique already put to use, and if so, do you apply it in the present example?
It would seem that this is an appropriate moment to remind you of the Bath Coup, but what will happen if you leave West on lead at Trick 1?

On seeing his partner's discouraging two, West will realize that you began with AJx and he will undoubtedly switch to a spade. You will have to allow East to hold this trick and he will switch back to hearts while the king of diamonds is still out. Therefore you will not resort to the Bath Coup on this occasion, but win at once with the ace of hearts. Your Jx will constitute a secondary guard since only West can regain the lead in diamonds and he is not the dangerous opponent.

What now?
Cross to the table with a club and lead the queen of diamonds. When this holds you continue with the five on which East discards the seven of spades.

Do you take the ace or play the nine?
The ace, and then continue with the nine which West still does not capture. Do not forget to overtake with the ten and play another. There is no risk in setting up a tenth trick in diamonds since West cannot harm you.

The full deal:

```
            ♠ J 3
            ♥ 7 5
            ♦ Q J 10 6 5
            ♣ A Q 10 3
♠ 8 4 2                    ♠ K Q 10 7 6
♥ K Q 10 9 6               ♥ 8 3 2
♦ K 7 4 2                  ♦ 8
♣ 9                        ♣ 8 7 6 4
            ♠ A 9 5
            ♥ A J 4
            ♦ A 9 3
            ♣ K J 5 2
```

Tip

Never allow technical knowledge to cloud your judgment and do not yield to the temptation to duck if you fear a dangerous switch.

DEAL NINETEEN

East/West Vulnerable. Dealer South.

```
            ♠ A J 6 4 2
            ♥ 8 2
            ♦ K 5
            ♣ A 9 6 3

            ♠ 10 5
            ♥ A K 6
            ♦ Q J 10 7
            ♣ Q J 10 2
```

Lead: ♥Q

South	West	North	East
1NT	Pass	2♥(*)	Pass
2♠	Pass	3♣	Pass
3NT	All Pass		

(*) Transfer

Count your tricks.
1 in spades, 2 in hearts, 1 in clubs = 4 tricks. You need to set up five more.

Do you duck the opening lead?
Yes, because you're not afraid of a switch, quite the contrary, and you will be cutting communication if the hearts are 5-3.

Now examine the various prospects offered by each suit:
1. *Spades:* These are strictly limited since in order to set up three extra tricks here, you would have to find KQx with West, any other lie of the cards would be unfavorable.
2. *Diamonds:* You can establish three tricks by knocking out the ace.
3. *Clubs:* You can establish two or three tricks according to the position of the king.

What conclusion do you draw from the analysis of these combined holdings?
No suit alone can produce the five required tricks, so ask yourself the following questions:

1. Which suits will you choose?
2. Is the order in which you play them important?
3. Choice of suits: Clearly you must go for clubs and diamonds; they will provide five or even six tricks if the king of clubs is right.
4. Order of play: Let us recap briefly on the all-important problem at no trumps (both in defense and attack). West has led a suit in which you have five cards and two winners, and you will have to give up the lead once or twice according to the position of the king of clubs.

What will happen if you begin with the club finesse and it fails?
East will finish setting up his partner's suit, and you will be defeated if West has the ace of diamonds as well as the long hearts.

So what is the correct line?
You must begin with the diamonds to render West harmless, and take the club finesse later. One of two things will result from this:

1. It will win and you will make ten tricks.
2. It will fail, but nine tricks are assured because if West has five hearts he will be unable to regain the lead.

The full deal:

```
            ♠ A J 6 4 2
            ♥ 8 2
            ♦ K 5
            ♣ A 9 6 3
♠ K 3                      ♠ Q 9 8 7
♥ Q J 10 5 3               ♥ 9 7 4
♦ A 6 2                    ♦ 9 8 4 3
♣ 7 5 4                    ♣ K 8
            ♠ 10 5
            ♥ A K 6
            ♦ Q J 10 7
            ♣ Q J 10 2
```

Tip

When you require tricks from two suits and possess two stoppers in the suit led, you should begin with the suit in which the dangerous opponent has a potential entry.

DEAL TWENTY
Both Sides Vulnerable. Dealer North.

♠ A Q
♥ J 5 2
♦ 10 8 6 4 2
♣ K 7 6

♠ 6 5 3 2
♥ A Q 10 4
♦ A K
♣ A 8 5

Lead: ♠J

South	West	North	East
1NT	Pass	3NT	All Pass

How many winners do you have?
1 in spades, 1 in hearts, 2 in diamonds, 2 in clubs = 6 tricks.

You require three more, perhaps only two if the spade finesse succeeds. Therefore you put on dummy's queen which East "naturally" wins with the king, continuing with the eight of spades to dummy's ace.

Where will you find the three missing tricks and what must you hope for?
In hearts, provided that the king is with East.

Which heart breaks are favorable and why?
Singleton king, Kx, or Kxx with East. If East has four to the king you will not succeed against proper defense.

How do you handle this suit, then?
If it is divided 3-3 there will be no problem and you can lead dummy's jack, but if the king is doubleton, what will happen if you do begin with the jack? Well, East will simply cover and you will be forced to concede the fourth round to West.

What is the solution, then?
You must clearly be thrifty with your honors, since you do have another entry to the table. Play the two of hearts to the queen. When this holds, return to dummy with the king of clubs and play another small heart. When East's king appears you will make the four heart tricks which are essential for your contract.

The full deal:

♠ A Q
♥ J 5 2
♦ 10 8 6 4 2
♣ K 7 6

♠ J 10 9 7　　　　　♠ K 8 4
♥ 9 7 6 3　　　　　♥ K 8
♦ 9 7　　　　　　　♦ Q J 5 3
♣ 10 4 2　　　　　♣ Q J 9 3

♠ 6 5 3 2
♥ A Q 10 4
♦ A K
♣ A 8 5

Tip

If you have sufficient entries, do not play an honor towards the finesse on either of the first two rounds of the suit with holdings such as:

Qxx	Jxx
	or
AJ10x	AK10x

that is to say, whenever you are missing any of the vital intermediates (the nine in the two foregoing examples).

DEAL TWENTY-ONE
North/South Vulnerable. Dealer West.

♠ K Q 6
♥ 10 5 4
♦ J 8 6 3
♣ A 8 3

♠ A J 3
♥ Q J 9
♦ A Q 10 9
♣ K 5 2

Lead: ♥6

South	West	North	East
–	Pass	Pass	Pass
1NT	Pass	3NT	All Pass

First, count your certain tricks.
3 in spades, 1 in hearts (after the obvious continuation), 1 in diamonds, 2 in clubs = 7 tricks. You need two more.

Where will you look for the missing tricks?
In diamonds, obviously. If East has the king (50 percent) you will make ten tricks.

However, there is danger just around the corner. What is it?
West has led a heart, a suit in which you are weak. If the hearts are 4-3 (62 percent), East/West will take only three or four tricks (three hearts and possibly a diamond), but if they are 5-2, and the length presumably with West as the lead shows, then you are risking the loss of four heart tricks and the king of diamonds.

On the lead of the six of hearts, East plays the king and returns the two. West covers your queen with the ace and continues at Trick 3 with the three of hearts on which East discards the four of spades.

How are the hearts divided?
Unfortunately, 5-2, and West has two tricks all ready to cash.

You cross to dummy with a spade and put into operation your initial plan to establish the diamonds.

Which diamond do you play from dummy?
The jack. If East possesses the king he may well observe the rule of covering an honor with an honor thus saving you any

further worry. Perhaps he doesn't feel like making things easy for you since he contributes the two of diamonds without turning a hair.

What do you play from your hand?
Remember that West is the dangerous opponent for he has enough established hearts to defeat you. If he also has the king of diamonds you will not make the contract unless the king is singleton, so go up with your ace and enjoy West's discomfort when he reluctantly drops the bare king.

Can your play of the ace endanger the contract of 3NT?
In no way, since your prime objective is to make nine tricks and if the king of diamonds is with East you will give up a trick to him, thereby establishing the two tricks you require for your contract. East will have no way of reaching his partner. Should West have had the king of diamonds guarded there was no way of making the contract.

The full deal:

```
              ♠ K Q 6
              ♥ 10 5 4
              ♦ J 8 6 3
              ♣ A 8 3
♠ 10 8 2                      ♠ 9 7 5 4
♥ A 8 7 6 3                   ♥ K 2
♦ K                          ♦ 7 5 4 2
♣ J 7 6 4                    ♣ Q 10 9
              ♠ A J 3
              ♥ Q J 9
              ♦ A Q 10 9
              ♣ K 5 2
```

Tip

If one of your opponents is dangerous you must take all necessary precautions to avoid giving him the lead. One of these is the rejection of a finesse.

DEAL TWENTY-TWO
North/South Vulnerable. Dealer East.

```
              ♠ J 7 5 4
              ♥ K 9 6
              ♦ K J 2
              ♣ K 3 2

              ♠ A 6 3
              ♥ A 8
              ♦ A 9 7 5 4
              ♣ A 10 6
```

Lead: ♥Q

South	West	North	East
–	–	–	Pass
1NT	Pass	3NT	All Pass

How many immediate tricks do you have?
1 in spades, 2 in hearts, 2 in diamonds, 2 in clubs = 7 tricks.

How will you establish two extra tricks?
Obviously in diamonds, since your two hands has eight cards and you are missing only the queen and the ten.

Is it essential for you to capture the queen of diamonds?
Indeed no, only two extra tricks are required.

In such a case, then, what should you be thinking about?
A safety play, and in this case a textbook one: you must abandon the usual handling of the suit consisting of finessing against the queen in order to assure four tricks against any distribution, even Q10xx with East.

Are you conversant with this safety play?
You must first cash the honor accompanying the jack, then after re-entering your hand, play small towards Jx. Either:

1. West has Q10xx in which case the jack will win the trick.
2. East has Q10xx in which case the jack will force the queen and the ten will later be captured by finesse.

Is there any necessity for ducking the opening lead?
No, because you do not intend to give up the lead more than once, and a spade switch at Trick 2 might prove disastrous. Therefore, Trick 1: ace of hearts, Trick 2: diamond to the king, Trick 3: club to the ace followed by a small diamond towards Jx. West discards a spade. Then back to dummy to play the two of diamonds which will allow you to capture East's remaining 106.

The full deal:

```
              ♠ J 7 5 4
              ♥ K 9 6
              ♦ K J 2
              ♣ K 3 2
♠ Q 9 8 2                     ♠ K 10
♥ Q J 10 7 4                  ♥ 5 3 2
♦ 8                          ♦ Q 10 6 3
♣ J 7 5                      ♣ Q 9 8 4
              ♠ A 6 3
              ♥ A 8
              ♦ A 9 7 5 4
              ♣ A 10 6
```

Tip

Whenever your contract appears to be in no danger, adopt the most pessimistic outlook. Take out insurance by visualizing the worst possible distributions and take the safety play which is appropriate. Always be willing to abandon one trick for the sake of not losing more:

KJx

A9xxx

Play the king first, then small towards the jack.

AJxx	AJxxx
or	
K9xx	K9x

Play the ace first, then small towards K9. Play the 9 if East follows.

DEAL TWENTY-THREE
Neither Side Vulnerable. Dealer South.

♠ J 8 5
♥ Q 4 2
♦ K J 6 3
♣ Q 8 3

♠ A 6 3
♥ 9 7
♦ A Q 5
♣ A K 6 4 2

Lead: ♣J. East plays the seven

South	West	North	East
1NT	Pass	3NT	All Pass

How many certain winners?

1 in spades, 4 in diamonds, 3 in clubs = 8 tricks.

Is there any glimmer of a ninth?
In hearts and spades the prospects are not promising, and if you break either of these suits yourself you will be running the risk of immediate defeat. Only the club suit remains. If the clubs are 3-2 you will have five running club tricks, but West probably has four since he has led the suit.

If you win the first club and continue the suit, what will happen?
East will discard and doubtless give his partner a heart signal. You will lose a club and four or five hearts, for it is unlikely that West has both ace and king of this latter suit. You must therefore duck the jack of clubs as though you feared the suit.

Is it possible to cause West to go wrong (without being unethical, of course)?
When faced with situations like these, you should apply a simple but efficient technique against defenders who observe and interpret the small cards furnished by their partner. As declarer, you should make a habit of selecting the card which you yourself would play if you were defending: you signal if you wish partner to continue the suit, and discourage if not. In the present example you choose the four or the six of clubs. On seeing his partner's seven West will doubtless interpret this as an encouraging signal, and noting that the two is missing he will see no reason for changing his tack. Put yourself in his place: he remains on lead with the jack of clubs; what card would East play if he held ♣AK72? The 7, wouldn't he?

West will persist with another club simultaneously discovering the heart signal and his partner's consternation!

The full deal:

♠ J 8 5
♥ Q 4 2
♦ K J 6 3
♣ Q 8 3

♠ Q 10 9   ♠ K 7 4 2
♥ K 8 6   ♥ A J 10 5 3
♦ 9 7 2   ♦ 10 8 4
♣ J 10 9 5   ♣ 7

♠ A 6 3
♥ 9 7
♦ A Q 5
♣ A K 6 4 2

Tip

A knowledgeable declarer must cultivate the same signalling habits as a defender. There is little doubt that this technique will bring in many valuable points.

DEAL TWENTY-FOUR
Neither Side Vulnerable. Dealer South.

♠ 10 7 3
♥ A 6 5
♦ Q J 3
♣ A Q 7 2

♠ A 9 4
♥ Q 10 3
♦ A 10 9 8 2
♣ K 5

Lead: ♥2

South	West	North	East
1♦	Pass	2♣	Pass
2NT	Pass	3NT	All Pass

Winner count?
1 in spades, 1 in hearts, 1 in diamonds, 3 in clubs = 6 tricks.

You require three more tricks and you will have no difficulty in finding these in diamonds. If the finesse against the king is successful you will even set up four.

At first sight the contract poses no problems. Furthermore even the lead seems favorable. Nevertheless, you must be on your guard.

If you allow the opening lead to run to your hand and East produces the king, what may happen?
On seeing his partner's two, East will doubtless realize that West has only four hearts, and that this will not be sufficient to defeat your game; with a heart trick in the bag he may now find the dangerous spade switch and you could lose a heart, three spades and the king of diamonds.

How will you avoid this pitfall?
At bridge, greed is a reprehensible failing, and you should call for dummy's ace of hearts. Nothing can endanger your contract now, since you will play a diamond immediately and if West has the king, your queen of hearts will remain protected.

The full deal:

```
                ♠ 10 7 3
                ♥ A 6 5
                ♦ Q J 3
                ♣ A Q 7 2
♠ J 8 6 2                      ♠ K Q 5
♥ J 9 7 2                      ♥ K 8 4
♦ K 7 4                        ♦ 6 5
♣ 10 6                         ♣ J 9 8 4 3
                ♠ A 9 4
                ♥ Q 10 3
                ♦ A 10 9 8 2
                ♣ K 5
```

Tip

At teams or rubber bridge the understandable desire to realize the maximum number of tricks should never induce you to put the success of your contract at risk. Always opt for the 100 percent line if there is one.

DEAL 25

East/West Vulnerable. Dealer North.

```
                ♠ Q 7
                ♥ A 9 5
                ♦ A K 9 5 4
                ♣ 7 6 3

                ♠ A K 5
                ♥ 10 8 3 2
                ♦ 2
                ♣ A 9 8 5 4
```

Lead: ♠J

South	West	North	East
–	–	1♦	Pass
2♣	Pass	2♦	Pass
2NT	Pass	3NT	All Pass

How many top tricks do you have?
3 in spades, 1 in hearts, 2 in diamonds, 1 in clubs = 7 tricks.

Where do you expect to find the two missing tricks?
Even if there is a favorable 4-3 diamond break, that suit can only provide one long trick. On the other hand you have eight clubs between your two hands which will provide two extra tricks on a 3-2 break.

How many times will you have to give up the lead?
Twice. Now then, you have three stoppers in spades and two in diamonds. In hearts, your combined holding makes it impossible for the opponents to cash more than two tricks in the suit, and you are therefore under no threat in the race for suit-establishment.

Do you have sufficient entries?
At first glance yes, thanks to the ace and king of spades. However, if you began establishing the club suit by playing the ace you would be running the risk of losing not only your two long card tricks, but also the ace of spades if the defenders refused to play a third round of the suit.

What is the answer, then?
Duck twice in clubs in order to preserve an entry to your hand.

Trick 1: queen of spades, Trick 2: low club from both hands, Trick 3: ten of spades from West to your ace, Trick 4: low club from both hands again (East and West following).

There is only one club out now, and even if the defense does not play another round of spades, you will have nine tricks whatever they choose to switch to, and these will be made up of three spades, one heart, two diamonds and three clubs.

The full deal:

```
                ♠ Q 7
                ♥ A 9 5
                ♦ A K 9 5 4
                ♣ 7 6 3
♠ J 10 9 6 3                   ♠ 8 4 2
♥ Q 6                          ♥ K J 7 4
♦ J 8 3                        ♦ Q 10 7 6
♣ K Q J                        ♣ 10 2
                ♠ A K 5
                ♥ 10 8 3 2
                ♦ 2
                ♣ A 9 8 5 4
```

Tip

As a general rule, you should apply the ducking principle whenever the hand with length in the suit is lacking in entries.

DEAL TWENTY-SIX

Both Sides Vulnerable. Dealer East.

```
            ♠ 8 7 5 4
            ♥ A Q
            ♦ K 6 5 3 2
            ♣ Q 3

            ♠ A 6 3
            ♥ K 7
            ♦ A 8 4
            ♣ A J 6 5 2
```

Lead: ♦Q. East discards the ♥2

South	West	North	East
–	–	–	Pass
1NT	Pass	3NT	All Pass

How many tricks on top?
1 in spades, 2 in hearts, 2 in diamonds, 1 in club = 6 certain tricks.

Without the lead, revealing East's void, you would have sought to establish two long diamonds (3-2 break, 68 percent), and the club suit would have provided the ninth trick. As it is, your diamonds have turned out to be dangerous and you will have to bank on the club suit.

Do you know the correct technique with suits like: AQxxx opposite Jx or AJxxx opposite Qx?
In any event you can never make five tricks even if the finesse succeeds, for there are no intermediates.

How should you set about it, then?
You must play towards the doubleton honor (Jx or Qx).

Why?
If West has the doubleton king he will have to play it immediately and you will make four tricks. Of course this will work too, if the suit is 3-3.

The full deal:

```
            ♠ 8 7 5 4
            ♥ A Q
            ♦ K 6 5 3 2
            ♣ Q 3
♠ J 2                   ♠ K Q 10 9
♥ 10 9 4 3              ♥ J 8 6 5 2
♦ Q J 10 9 7           ♦ –
♣ K 8                   ♣ 10 9 7 4
            ♠ A 6 3
            ♥ K 7
            ♦ A 8 4
            ♣ A J 6 5 2
```

Tip

Experienced players are aware of and apply the technique required for the most common suit combinations. You should familiarize youself with the way each combination should be played.

DEAL TWENTY-SEVEN

Neither Side Vulnerable. Dealer West.

```
            ♠ K Q 6 5
            ♥ 8 3
            ♦ K 7
            ♣ A J 10 9 4

            ♠ A 3
            ♥ K 4 2
            ♦ A 8 6 5 2
            ♣ K 8 3
```

Lead: ♥9

South	West	North	East
–	Pass	1♣	2♥(*)
3♥(**)	Pass	3♠	Pass
3NT	All Pass		

(*) Mini pre-empt with six or more cards

(**) This cuebid after partner's minor-suit opening is primarily a demand to bid no trumps with a guard or half guard in the overcaller's suit. It would be preferable for North, holding Jx, Qx, or Jxx, to have the lead run up to him.

Trick total?
3 in spades, 1 in hearts (after the lead), 2 in diamonds, 2 in clubs = 8 tricks. One extra trick will be enough.

From which suit?
Clubs, naturally. If the finesse works, you will make three extra tricks.

At Trick 1, East overtakes the nine of hearts with the ten.

What maneuver is East attempting?
He is trying a defensive duck to maintain communications with his partner, who according to the bidding has a maximum of two hearts.

Do you take the king or do you duck too?
Resist the temptation to take your heart trick immediately and allow your right-hand opponent to hold the trick (the position of the ace is obvious). If you do take the king of hearts at Trick 1 you will be forced to guess the position of the queen of clubs. You have already realized that if you refuse the king of hearts now, your contract is safe.

Do you see how?
When you play the club suit you will proceed in such a way as to prevent East from gaining the lead. It will not matter if West can win the queen of clubs since he will no longer have a heart to play.

East continues with ace and another heart. You take your king while West and dummy discard spades.

What now?
Cross to dummy with the king of diamonds and play the jack of clubs which you run and which holds the trick. Continue with the four of clubs to your eight, West discarding, then cash the king. You will come to eleven tricks with no danger.

The full deal:

```
              ♠ K Q 6 5
              ♥ 8 3
              ♦ K 7
              ♣ A J 10 9 4
♠ J 9 8 7 2                    ♠ 10 4
♥ 9 5                          ♥ A Q J 10 7 6
♦ Q 10 9 4 3                   ♦ J
♣ 2                            ♣ Q 7 6 5
              ♠ A 3
              ♥ K 4 2
              ♦ A 8 6 5 2
              ♣ K 8 3
```

Tip

Duck according to the bidding, and orient your finesses so as to avoid giving the lead to the dangerous opponent.

Deal Twenty-eight

North/South Vulnerable. Dealer South.

```
♠ 6 4
♥ A 6 3
♦ 10 8 2
♣ A K 10 6 2

♠ K J 8
♥ K 8 5 4
♦ A K 7
♣ J 9 4
```

Lead: ♠7. East plays the nine

South	West	North	East
1♥	1♠	2♣	Pass
2NT	Pass	3NT	All Pass

What do you infer from the bidding and the lead?
West possesses at least five spades, and the Rule of 11 tells you that East has one card higher than the seven. Before proceeding, count your sure tricks:

1 in spades (after the lead), 2 in hearts, 2 in diamonds, 2 in clubs = 7 tricks, and two more are required.

Which suit will provide these?
The clubs. You hold AK10xx opposite J9x and when the queen has appeared, the two or three extra tricks will be yours.

East having played the nine of spades at Trick 1, what cards does West have in his suit?
AQ107x, the fifth card not being known.

Obviously you are forced to win the first trick with the jack of spades and you set about establishing the clubs.

How precisely?
The normal way is to test the suit by laying down the ace in order to guard against a singleton queen with East, and then return to hand in order to finesse against West.

But will you play like this?
Think now: you still have a spade guard in your hand, but only on condition that East does not gain the lead.

So how will you play the clubs?
Cash the ace and king and if you are lucky enough to drop the doubleton queen from East you can congratulate yourself on the accuracy of your analysis.

If the queen does not fall, what must you hope for?
That it is West who has it: certainly you will have sacrificed a trick, but remember that four club tricks are enough, and as West has no means of putting his partner in you will have brought home the contract.

(It must be pointed out that if East had the guarded queen of clubs, there is no way of making the contract but you would have played correctly.)

The full deal:

```
              ♠ 6 4
              ♥ A 6 3
              ♦ 10 8 2
              ♣ A K 10 6 2
♠ A Q 10 7 2                    ♠ 9 5 3
♥ Q 2                          ♥ J 10 9 7
♦ Q 6 3                        ♦ J 9 5 4
♣ 7 5 3                        ♣ Q 8
              ♠ K J 8
              ♥ K 8 5 4
              ♦ A K 7
              ♣ J 9 4
```

Tip

When one of your opponents is dangerous, you must be prepared to depart from normal practice in the handling of the suit to be established to prevent him from gaining the lead. The rejection of a finesse will sometimes cost a trick but will increase the probability of success of your contract, and at rubber bridge or teams it is essential.

DEAL TWENTY-NINE
Both Sides Vulnerable. Dealer North.

♠ 6 5
♥ K Q J 8 5
♦ 9 8
♣ Q 10 8 2

♠ A K J 4
♥ 10 9
♦ A Q 5 2
♣ A J 9

Lead: ♣5

South	West	North	East
–	–	Pass	Pass
1♦	Pass	1♥	Pass
2NT	Pass	3♣	Pass
3NT	All Pass		

How many sure tricks do you have?
2 in spades, 1 in diamonds, 2 in clubs (after the lead) = 5 tricks. You need to establish four tricks and clearly the heart suit will provide them. However, there is danger threatening.

What is it?
The opponent holding the ace of hearts will hold up to cut your communication with dummy.

But can you not be certain of reaching the table? How?
Yes, in clubs, provided you play neither the ten or the queen from dummy at Trick 1 and win with the ace!

Why?
You will remain with J9 in hand opposite Q108 and nothing will be able to prevent you from reaching the dummy.

You therefore win the ace of clubs and continue with the ten of hearts, followed by the nine, not forgetting to overtake with dummy's jack.

East takes with the ace of hearts and returns the jack of diamonds. Do you finesse against the king?
Certainly not, because if it fails you could lose three tricks in diamonds, the ace of hearts and the king of clubs. Remember that two diamond tricks are not essential for success. You go up with the ace of diamonds and continue with the jack of clubs.

Why do you not fear the king of clubs with East?
The Rule of 11 has revealed all: the five of clubs plus six higher ranking cards, all of which are visible to you. East will not regain the lead and the queen of diamonds is therefore protected.

Which card do you play on the jack of clubs?
The queen, then cash three heart winners. You will thus make two spades, four hearts, one diamond and two clubs.

Why did West not play the king of clubs on your jack?
He would have been giving you an extra trick.

The full deal:

♠ 6 5
♥ K Q J 8 5
♦ 9 8
♣ Q 10 8 2

♠ Q 8 7   ♠ 10 9 3 2
♥ 7 4   ♥ A 6 3 2
♦ K 7 6 4   ♦ J 10 3
♣ K 7 6 5   ♣ 4 3

♠ A K J 4
♥ 10 9
♦ A Q 5 2
♣ A J 9

Tip

Take care to preserve your communication with the hand containing a suit which can be established. If need be win a trick with an unnecessarily high card.

DEAL THIRTY
Both Sides Vulnerable. Dealer South.

♠ K 8 3
♥ K Q 6 3
♦ A 5
♣ K 8 7 2

♠ A Q 9
♥ J 2
♦ 10 9 7 3
♣ A Q 6 5

Lead: ♦6

South	West	North	East
1♣	Pass	1♥	Pass
1NT	Pass	3NT	All Pass

Sure trick total?
3 in spades, 1 in diamonds, 3 in clubs = 7 tricks.

The two missing tricks are easy to find: with KQxx opposite Jx in hearts you have only to knock out the ace.

Are you worried about the lead, and if so why?
If the suit breaks 4-3 you will lose at most three diamonds and the ace of hearts. However if the diamonds are 5-2, it would appear that you will only be successful if the hand containing the long diamonds does not have the ace of hearts as well. The solution which immediately springs to mind is to duck the opening lead.

Yet, is there no answer if West has both the ace of hearts and five diamonds?
To answer this question ask yourself first how many cards higher than the six East holds. One only (11-6 = 5 and you can see four of them).

Next try to picture West's precise diamond holding:
He cannot have KQJ6x otherwise he would have led the king. He has therefore led from a suit containing two honors and you can credit East with a doubleton honor. In the dangerous case where the diamonds are 5-2, three possible combinations exist: QJ86x opposite Kx; KJ86x opposite Qx or KQ86x opposite Jx.

Have these deductions put you on the right road?
You must block the enemy suit by going up with the ace of diamonds at Trick 1 even if this maneuver seems contrary to a normal reaction.

If East plays small he will later be on lead with his honor and unable to continue the suit, and if he chooses to unblock his honor card you will retain a second guard with 109x against West's KJxx. Whatever East decides to do you will make your contract, and if the diamonds do turn out to be ~3 your ploy will have cost nothing.

The full deal:

```
              ♠ K 8 3
              ♥ K Q 6 3
              ♦ A 5
              ♣ K 8 7 2
  ♠ 6 4                      ♠ J 10 7 5 2
  ♥ A 8                      ♥ 10 9 7 5 4
  ♦ K J 8 6 2                ♦ Q 4
  ♣ J 9 4 3                  ♣ 10
              ♠ A Q 9
              ♥ J 2
              ♦ 10 9 7 3
              ♣ A Q 6 5
```

Tip

One of the weapons available to declarer at no trumps is the blocking of the enemy suit. Consider the following holdings:

A10		AJ
	or	
9xxx		10xxx

If your left-hand opponent leads the seven go up with the ace immediately.

East/West Vulnerable. Dealer South.

```
              ♠ 8 7
              ♥ Q J 10 4
              ♦ A 6 3 2
              ♣ 7 6 5

              ♠ A K 5 4
              ♥ 2
              ♦ K Q 9 4
              ♣ A K 4 3
```

Lead: ♣10

South	West	North	East
1♦	Pass	1♥	Pass
1♠	Pass	2♦	Pass
3NT	All Pass		

How many sure tricks do you have?
2 in spades, 3 (or 4) in diamonds, 2 in clubs = 7 tricks.

Where will the two missing tricks come from?

The spade suit holds no hope; the eighth trick will come from diamonds if the suit divides 3-2 (68 percent); in clubs you could set up a long card if the suit breaks 3-3 (38 percent); however, West has led the ten, which could be from a doubleton or from length, and it is likely that this suit will break 4-2. In hearts you have QJ10, and so the ninth trick will come from that suit. However, you must reflect that communications are very thin.

How many entries are required in dummy?
Two are needed, one to play the second round of hearts and one to reach the established queen. It seems that only one exists: the ace of diamonds.

Can you see a solution? Do you not have a second entry to the table?
Yes, in diamonds, provided that you handle the suit with care. You will attack the suit by laying down the king and then the queen, and if both opponents follow, as you hope they will (a necessary hypothesis for the contract to succeed), the remaining diamond layout will be as follows:

```
              A6

              94
```

You will continue with the nine to the ace (first entry) and later the second entry will be the play of the four of diamonds to dummy's six.

Is it advisable to duck the opening lead?
You might consider ducking the ten of clubs, then if the opponents persist with the suit you will be able to verify whether it is breaking 3-3. But should West decide to abandon the club suit and switch to spades you would lose one club, two hearts and two spades, and you would be defeated. Consequently, take no risks, win the first trick with the ace of clubs and play the two of hearts to dummy's ten. As the full deal shows, the opponents can only take two clubs and two hearts.

The full deal:

```
              ♠ 8 7
              ♥ Q J 10 4
              ♦ A 6 3 2
              ♣ 7 6 5
♠ J 10 9 6              ♠ Q 3 2
♥ A 8 6 5              ♥ K 9 7 3
♦ J 8 7               ♦ 10 5
♣ 10 8                ♣ Q J 9 2
              ♠ A K 5 4
              ♥ 2
              ♦ K Q 9 4
              ♣ A K 4 3
```

Tip

A suit in which you have all the tricks should always be handled with care. Always take into consideration those entries which will be required for reaching your established winners in the other suits. For example, holding AKQ4 opposite J652, four entries are possible in the North hand if the outstanding cards are 3-2: play the ace-king to check the distribution, taking care to play the six and five, then the jack to the queen and finally the two to the four.

DEAL THIRTY-TWO

North/South Vulnerable. Dealer West.

```
              ♠ J 6 2
              ♥ A
              ♦ Q J 4 3
              ♣ K Q 9 8 7

              ♠ A 10 7 4
              ♥ K J 3
              ♦ A 2
              ♣ J 10 6 5
```

Lead: ♥6

South	West	North	East
–	Pass	1♣	Pass
1♠	Pass	2♣	Pass
3NT	All Pass		

Count your immediate tricks.

1 in spades, 2 in hearts, 1 in diamonds = 4 tricks. Your objective is to establish five more.

Which suits will provide the tricks?

1. The clubs will furnish four tricks with no problems;
2. In spades your chances are thin because the jack and ten are divided between your two hands and without the nine you have no genuine finesse position: East would have to have both honors;
3. In diamonds it is possible to set up a trick.

Therefore the clubs and diamonds will provide the extra tricks.

In which order will you tackle these suits?

It is tempting to set about your longest suit first, that is, clubs; however, West's heart attack has left you with only KJ to guard that suit.

What would happen if East should turn up with the ace of clubs?

He would play it immediately and quickly return a heart through your holding. Your jack would lose to the queen and West would lose no time in establishing his suit. If he has the guarded king of diamonds you will be defeated.

Any declarer with foresight should repress the desire to set up his best suit first and at Trick 2 should lead the queen of diamonds. West can win this trick if he likes, but will be unable to continue hearts without playing into your tenace. The clubs can now be set up without danger.

The full deal:

```
              ♠ J 6 2
              ♥ A
              ♦ Q J 4 3
              ♣ K Q 9 8 7
♠ K 8 5                ♠ Q 9 3
♥ Q 10 7 6 2          ♥ 9 8 5 4
♦ K 10 9 5            ♦ 8 7 6
♣ 4                   ♣ A 3 2
              ♠ A 10 7 4
              ♥ K J 3
              ♦ A 2
              ♣ J 10 6 5
```

Tip

Beginners are normally taught to play their best suits first, notably those where an ace has to be knocked out in preference to those where a king is missing. This rule, however, is subject to numerous exceptions because of the presence of one opponent who is more dangerous than the other. As you have just seen, it was not only essential to begin with the diamonds but also to take an aggressive finesse by leading the queen rather than resort to the textbook handling of cashing the ace first then playing small towards QJx. Two goals were reached:

1. Set up a quick diamond trick;
2. Avoid giving East the lead.

DEAL THIRTY-three
North/South Vulnerable. Dealer South.

♠ Q 7 6
♥ 9 3
♦ 8 6
♣ A Q 10 9 8 3

♠ A J 10
♥ A K 7 2
♦ K Q 5 3
♣ J 2

Lead: ♠5

South	West	North	East
1NT	Pass	3NT	All Pass

Count your certain tricks.
2 in spades (after the lead), 2 in hearts, 1 in clubs = 5 tricks.

Which suit will provide the extra tricks?
Clubs, of course. You may hope that the king is with West and lead the jack; if it holds, continue with a small one towards the table. If West has the doubleton or trebleton king you will make six tricks in the suit.

Imagine now that East has the king. Clearly, five club tricks will suffice, but is there not a danger?
If East is a good defender. he will not take his king of clubs immediately because it is in his interest to cut off your communication with the table. (An excellent defender should hold up even with Kx.)

What is the problem?
You will have to be able to reach the dummy.

How will you manage that?
Only one card will allow entry: the queen of spades.

What do you infer from the lead?
East holds no card higher than the five. (Rule of 11: 11-5 = 6 cards higher than the five and all these are visible.)

Which cards (a) from the dummy and (b) from your hand should be played at Trick 1?
1. The queen of spades should be preserved and you should, therefore, play small from the table;

2. Foreseeing the possibility of East holding the king of clubs two or three times guarded, or even king to four with West, it is essential to win the first trick with the ace of spades. If you retain Q7 opposite A10 you will deprive yourself of your entry to dummy, but if you leave yourself with Q7 opposite J10 you will be able to overtake your jack with the queen if West plays small. In any case the defenders will be helpless.

The full deal:

♠ Q 7 6
♥ 9 3
♦ 8 6
♣ A Q 10 9 8 3

♠ K 9 8 5 2   ♠ 4 3
♥ J 8 6 5   ♥ Q 10 4
♦ A 10 4   ♦ J 9 7 2
♣ 4   ♣ K 7 6 5

♠ A J 10
♥ A K 7 2
♦ K Q 5 3
♣ J 2

Tip

Beware of your natural instinct for economy when it is a question of preserving communication.

DEAL THIRTY-FOUR
Neither Side Vulnerable. Dealer South.

♠ A 8 2
♥ K 8 4 3
♦ 6
♣ A J 9 5 4

♠ K 7 5
♥ A Q 6
♦ K Q 7 3
♣ Q 10 3

Lead: ♦5

South	West	North	East
1NT	Pass	2♣	Pass
2♦	Pass	3NT	All Pass

Your sure trick count?
2 in spades, 3 in hearts, 1 in diamonds (after the lead), 1 in clubs = 7 tricks.

The club suit will obviously provide the extra tricks. You could even succeed if West holds four to the king thanks to your intermediates.

Do you duck the opening lead?
Apply the Rule of 11: 11-5 = 6, which tells you that North, East and South hold six cards higher than the five; since four of these are on view, East has the other two. If one of these is the ace, the contract will present no difficulty.

It is only after these preliminary reflections that you call for dummy's six. The nine appears on your right. Before playing automatically to Trick 1, think about the problem.

First of all, to what division of the outstanding cards should you pay particular attention?

The 5-3 break, since should the diamonds prove to be 4-4 you will lose at most four tricks. This first point having been settled, try to visualize precisely East/West's diamond holdings: East has played the nine at Trick 1, therefore his holding must be l09x.

Why?

With 98x he would have played the eight, the lower of two equivalents; with J9x he would have played the jack (the highest), and with A9x, the ace. Consequently, if the diamonds are 5-3, West has AJ85x and East 109x.

What will happen if you win the nine of diamonds?

If East has the king of clubs he will return the ten of diamonds and you will not be able to avoid defeat.

So what do you do?

Allow East to hold the nine of diamonds. East now continues with the ten of diamonds as foreseen.

Do you cover?

Once more, no, because if you do it will be West's turn to duck, and he will preserve a tenace position of AJ8 over your Q7, which will be sufficient to beat the contract. You must therefore duck twice, and your opponents will be powerless to realize more than four tricks.

The full deal:

```
                  ♠ A 8 2
                  ♥ K 8 4 3
                  ♦ 6
                  ♣ A J 9 5 4
     ♠ Q 6                      ♠ J 10 9 4 3
     ♥ 10 9 7 2                 ♥ J 5
     ♦ A J 8 5 2                ♦ 10 9 4
     ♣ 7 6                      ♣ K 8 2
                  ♠ K 7 5
                  ♥ A Q 6
                  ♦ K Q 7 3
                  ♣ Q 10 3
```

Tip

Inference drawn from the opening lead (Rule of 11) will guide you towards the winning line if it is necessary to duck the lead.

DEAL THIRTY-FIVE

Both Sides Vulnerable. Dealer West.

```
                  ♠ 7 2
                  ♥ A J 4 3
                  ♦ A 9 8
                  ♣ A 8 6 2

                  ♠ A 10
                  ♥ Q 10 9
                  ♦ K J 10 5 4
                  ♣ K 7 3
```

Lead: ♠K

South	West	North	East
–	Pass	1♣	Pass
1♦	1♠	Pass	Pass
3NT	All Pass		

Is there any point in ducking the king of spades?

Hardly, because you have only four cards in spades between your two hands. However, since you are not afraid of any switch, leave it until the second round. You will cut the communication between your opponents if the spades do turn out to be 7-2.

How many sure tricks do you have?

1 in spades, 1 in hearts, 2 in diamonds, 2 in clubs = 6 tricks.

How will you establish three more?

Either in diamonds, by "guessing" the position of the queen, or in hearts if the king is with West.

What are the risks?

You cannot afford to make any mistake. One false step (losing finesse) will be punished since both opponents are dangerous in this case. It is best to use an accepted technique.

What does this consist of?

Whenever you are faced with a crucial choice of finesse, try to combine your chances.

What does this signify in the present case?

Rather than stake everything on one of the two finesses, cash your two top diamonds. If the queen drops, your worries are over, and if it does not you fall back on the heart finesse. By playing in this way your chances are much better than 50 percent: singleton queen (6 percent) plus doubleton queen (28 percent) = 34+33 (50 percent of the remaining chances since that is the odds of the heart king being with West) = 67 percent.

Recap on the play:

Ace of spades, ace and king of diamonds, and on the second round West plays the queen. You now have nine tricks on top. It costs nothing now to play on West's susceptibilities by banging down the queen of hearts. If he has the king and hasn't yet recovered his composure he will perhaps make the mistake of covering, but in any event you put on the ace of hearts in order to cash your well-deserved nine tricks.

The full deal:

```
            ♠ 7 2
            ♥ A J 4 3
            ♦ A 9 8
            ♣ A 8 6 2
♠ K Q J 9 6              ♠ 8 5 4 3
♥ 5 2                   ♥ K 8 7 6
♦ Q 7                   ♦ 6 3 2
♣ J 9 5 4               ♣ Q 10
            ♠ A 10
            ♥ Q 10 9
            ♦ K J 10 5 4
            ♣ K 7 3
```

Tip

Whenever you are faced with a choice of several finesses without prior information (opponents' bidding or passes are frequent sources of excellent information), ask yourself first whether one opponent is more dangerous than the other. It is possible that the loss of the lead to either opponent would be dangerous and if such should be the case, you must seek to combine your chances. Try to capture a doubleton honor and if this does not work, fall back on a finesse in another suit.

DEAL THIRTY-SIX

Both Sides Vulnerable. Dealer South.

```
            ♠ 7 5
            ♥ 9 6
            ♦ J 10 9 8 6
            ♣ A K 5 2

            ♠ A Q 3
            ♥ Q 8 5
            ♦ A Q 7 3
            ♣ Q 10 8
```

Lead: ♠4. East plays the jack

South	West	North	East
1NT	Pass	3NT	All Pass

Count your tricks.
2 in spades (after the lead), 1 in diamonds, 3 in clubs = 6 tricks, and the diamonds will provide three or four more according to the position of the king.

Suppose the diamond finesse fails, what might happen?
West will realize that you still have the spade suit guarded with your ace and from his point of view the only chance of defeating the contract will be to switch to hearts in which case the defense will make at least five tricks (unless East has both the ace and king of hearts).

It is therefore desirable to induce West to continue with spades.

How will you manage that?
You must deceive this opponent by winning the opening lead with the ace of spades and not the queen. West will be convinced that his partner began with queen-jack and as soon as he wins with the king of diamonds he will hasten to play another small spade to his partner's presumed queen. Imagine his disappointment when you gather in this trick.

The full deal:

```
            ♠ 7 5
            ♥ 9 6
            ♦ J 10 9 8 6
            ♣ A K 5 2
♠ K 10 8 4 2            ♠ J 9 6
♥ K J 7 3              ♥ A 10 4 2
♦ K 4                 ♦ 5 2
♣ 9 6                 ♣ J 7 4 3
            ♠ A Q 3
            ♥ Q 8 5
            ♦ A Q 7 3
            ♣ Q 10 8
```

Tip

Good technique is generally sufficient to give you the best chance of making your contract, but in certain contexts a well-chosen ruse may be required.

DEAL THIRTY-SEVEN

North/South Vulnerable. Dealer East.

```
            ♠ A Q J
            ♥ K 8 6
            ♦ 6 5 2
            ♣ K 6 5 4

            ♠ K 7 6 3
            ♥ A Q 5 4
            ♦ A Q
            ♣ A Q 2
```

Lead: ♣J

South	West	North	East
–	–	–	Pass
2NT	Pass	6NT	All Pass

How many tricks can you count?
4 in spades, 3 in hearts, 1 in diamonds, 3 in clubs = 11 tricks.

Where will the twelfth trick come from?
1. In hearts or clubs if either suit breaks 3-3.
2. The diamond finesse if the king is favorably placed.

How will you begin: finesse or suit-break?
When you have only one trick to find and have a ten-ace holding, as in the diamond suit, always try to obtain a count of the adverse distribution, since in the endgame you will frequently be in a position to throw in one or other of your opponents, and he will then be obliged to open up the

crucial suit himself. Consequently you should delay the finesse until later.

How will you set about counting the hand?
You cash your winners and as soon as an opponent fails to follow, you will obtain information which will help you to construct the unseen hands.

Having won the opening lead in your hand, how do you continue?
Cash three rounds of spades, both defenders following three times, then come to hand with the ace of hearts. On the king of spades which follows both adversaries throw diamonds, as does dummy. On the third round of hearts you discover that West began with only two, since he now throws another diamond. Therefore no twelfth trick from hearts.

You now cash the queen of clubs, then play a small club to dummy's king. On this trick it is East who throws a diamond. So dummy's six of clubs is not good either. However, all is not lost. But ask yourself this question before resorting to the diamond finesse:

How many cards does each opponent have left and what are they?
You have cashed ten tricks and now are now holding the ♦AQ and a losing heart in hand, and dummy holds two small diamonds and a losing club.

How should you continue and why?
The East/West hands are an open book. West began originally with three spades, two hearts, four clubs and consequently four diamonds. East held three spades, four hearts, two clubs and four diamonds. West's remaining cards are two diamonds and a club, and East has two diamonds and a heart.

At this stage the contract is a laydown. Just play the six of clubs from the table, throwing the five of hearts from your hand. You will make the last two tricks whoever holds the king of diamonds. You must admit that the 100 percent guaranteed play is superior to the fifty-fifty chance.

The full deal:

```
              ♠ A Q J
              ♥ K 8 6
              ♦ 6 5 2
              ♣ K 6 5 4
♠ 10 8 2                    ♠ 9 5 4
♥ J 7                       ♥ 10 9 3 2
♦ K 9 4 3                   ♦ J 10 8 7
♣ J 10 9 7                  ♣ 8 3
              ♠ K 7 6 3
              ♥ A Q 5 4
              ♦ A Q
              ♣ A Q 2
```

Tip
Get yourself into the habit of counting the opponents' hands, and try to visualize the manner in which the play will unfold.

DEAL THIRTY-EIGHT
Both Sides Vulnerable. Dealer South.

```
              ♠ Q 10 9
              ♥ A 9
              ♦ A Q 8 3
              ♣ K 9 5 4

              ♠ A J 8 2
              ♥ K 8 4
              ♦ J 10 6
              ♣ A J 3
```

Lead: ♥7

South	West	North	East
1♣	Pass	1♦	Pass
1♠	Pass	3♣(*)	Pass
3NT	All Pass		

(*) Forcing

How many immediate tricks?
1 in spades, 2 in hearts, 1 in diamonds, 2 in clubs = 6 tricks. You have three more to find.

What inference do you draw from the lead? Who is the dangerous opponent?
The seven of hearts cannot be fourth best. As you can already see four cards higher than the seven this would have meant that West had led the seven from QJ107. Had West possessed this holding he would surely have led the queen. The lead is clearly "top of nothing," and you may reasonably locate QJ10 to any number of hearts on your right. It is East, therefore, who is the dangerous opponent.

In which suits will you establish your extra tricks?
In spades or in diamonds. Only one of these kings needs to be favorably placed for the contract to succeed, but if the finesse with which you begin fails you will have to try the other one.

Do you duck the opening lead?
Yes, it costs nothing and may be profitable if the hearts break 5-3 or 6-2.

East covers the nine with the ten, thus confirming your initial analysis, and continues with the five to dummy's ace.

Which suit will you play first?
It is essential to attend first to the dangerous opponent, that is, East. Since he can only regain the lead in diamonds, begin with that suit. Come to your hand with the ace of clubs and run the jack of diamonds. East takes it with the king and continues with a heart to your king. You can now cross to the table with a diamond and try the spade finesse. West wins this trick, but has no further heart.

The full deal:

          ♠ Q 10 9
          ♥ A 9
          ♦ A Q 8 3
          ♣ K 9 5 4

♠ K 6   ♠ 7 5 4 3
♥ 7 6 2   ♥ Q J 10 5 3
♦ 9 7 5 4   ♦ K 2
♣ Q 10 6 2   ♣ 8 7

          ♠ A J 8 2
          ♥ K 8 4
          ♦ J 10 6
          ♣ A J 3

Tip

The opening lead can bring vital information, and in most cases will allow declarer to pinpoint the dangerous adversary.

Deal Thirty-nine

Both Sides Vulnerable. Dealer South.

          ♠ K 7 4
          ♥ 7 5 3 2
          ♦ J 5 4
          ♣ 8 6 4

          ♠ A Q J
          ♥ A K 8
          ♦ K 9 2
          ♣ A Q J 2

Lead: ♦7. East plays the ace

South	West	North	East
2♣	Pass	2♦	Pass
2NT	Pass	3NT	All Pass

How many sure tricks do you have?
3 in spades, 2 in hearts, 1 in diamonds (after the lead), 1 in clubs = 7 certain tricks, and you have to find two more.

What possibilities do you have of realizing these extra tricks?
Your best chance is a successful finesse against the king of clubs.

As the cards lie, how many entries to dummy do you have for this finesse?
One only, the king of spades. It will allow the two extra tricks to be established if the king of clubs is well placed, but only if it is doubleton or trebleton. It will not suffice if the king is more than twice guarded.

Are you in a position to overcome this problem?
Yes, since you have the AQJ and the finesse can be repeated. However, to repeat the finesse you need a second entry on the table.

Can you see any way of creating one?
The Rule of 11 shows that West's ace of diamonds is the only card higher than the seven in East's hand. The queen is marked with West and therefore the jack is a potential entry.

On what condition?
That you contribute your king of diamonds at Trick 1. This astute unblock will create the extra entry without costing a trick, and you will then be able to finesse twice in clubs instead of only once. The full deal reveals the necessity for this maneuver.

The full deal:

          ♠ K 7 4
          ♥ 7 5 3 2
          ♦ J 5 4
          ♣ 8 6 4

♠ 8 3   ♠ 10 9 6 5 2
♥ J 9 6 4   ♥ Q 10
♦ Q 10 8 7 6   ♦ A 3
♣ 5 3   ♣ K 10 9 7

          ♠ A Q J
          ♥ A K 8
          ♦ K 9 2
          ♣ A Q J 2

Tip

Never yield to an automatic reflex when playing to a trick; always foresee the need to create the maximum number of entries required later for finessing and establishing your suit.

Deal Forty

North/South Vulnerable. Dealer North.

          ♠ Q 10 4
          ♥ A Q 6 5 2
          ♦ A Q 5
          ♣ 10 8

          ♠ K 8 2
          ♥ 4 3
          ♦ K J 4
          ♣ K Q J 9 6

Lead: ♠7

South	West	North	East
–	–	1♥	1♠
2♣	Pass	2♥	Pass
3NT	All Pass		

How many certain tricks can you count?
1 in spades (on the lead), 1 in hearts, 3 in diamonds = 5 tricks. You require four more.

Consider the various possibilities:
1. Hearts: even if West has king to three you do not have enough intermediates to make four tricks;
2. Clubs: this suit will provide them easily once the ace has been removed.

However, there is danger close to hand. What is it?
Suppose you play dummy's four on the opening lead: East
will put in the nine. If you duck this trick and East has the
ace of clubs, he will set up the spades and you will go down.
Similarly, if you win with the king and it is West who has
the ace of clubs he will continue with a small spade through
dummy's Q10 and again East will run enough tricks to
defeat you. If you put up the ten, East will cover with the
jack and wait patiently for West to lead another spade.

Is the problem insoluble?
Obviously not. You have an infallible solution: put up the
queen.

You know that East has AJ9xx from the lead and the
bidding; by selecting the queen you force him to win the
trick immediately. If he ducked he would be giving you a
second trick in the suit, and your remaining combination of
104 opposite K8 will prevent him from continuing profitably with the suit. He will lose timing and you will be ahead
in the race for suit-establishment.

The full deal:

```
                 ♠ Q 10 4
                 ♥ A Q 6 5 2
                 ♦ A Q 5
                 ♣ 10 8
  ♠ 7 3                        ♠ A J 9 6 5
  ♥ J 10 8                     ♥ K 9 7
  ♦ 10 7 3 2                   ♦ 9 8 6
  ♣ A 7 5 2                    ♣ 4 3
                 ♠ K 8 2
                 ♥ 4 3
                 ♦ K J 4
                 ♣ K Q J 9 6
```

Tip

Blocking the opponent's suit at Trick 1 may look impressive, but its success depended on finding precisely Q10x in
dummy. It is obvious that the contract would have presented
no difficulty if played from the correct side. Instead of a
premature leap to 3NT South should have made a cuebid of
two spades, inviting his partner to bid no trumps with a
stopper or partial stopper in the enemy suit. Even Qx alone
in the North hand would have been sufficient to insure two
stoppers with the lead coming from East.

DEAL FORTY-ONE
Both Sides Vulnerable. Dealer South.

```
          ♠ A 6 3
          ♥ 6 4
          ♦ A Q J 8
          ♣ Q 10 9 2

          ♠ K 9
          ♥ A Q 3
          ♦ 10 9 5 2
          ♣ K J 8 5
```

Lead: ♥J

South	West	North	East
1♣	Pass	1♦	Pass
1NT	Pass	3NT	All Pass

What is your winner count?
2 in spades, 2 in hearts (after the lead), 1 in diamonds = 5
tricks.

Where will you find four more tricks?
You must establish four winners in the minor suits, since
one of these suits alone will not be enough.

In which order will you play those suits?
Since West can only regain the lead in clubs, you must begin
with that suit. When an opponent wins the ace of clubs and
continues with a heart you can hold up and subsequently
take the diamond finesse into the safe hand.

On the jack of hearts East plays the king.

Do you take this trick?
With two guards in the enemy suit and two suits to exploit,
the hold-up would normally be correct, but in this case you
might well be embarrassed by a defensive switch.

What is it?
The spade switch, since you hold only five cards and two
stoppers in that suit. You would have to give up the lead in
clubs and then possibly lose to the king of diamonds, in
which case you would risk the loss of one heart, one club,
one diamond and two or three spades. So win at Trick 1 with
the ace of hearts and knock out the ace of clubs. West wins
the second round of clubs and continues with the ten of
hearts.

What do you do now?
At this stage you must absolutely duck just in case the hearts
are 5-3. This maneuver costs nothing if they should turn out
to be 4-4 after all. You win the third round of hearts, and
only now do you take the diamond finesse.

The full deal:

```
              ♠ A 6 3
              ♥ 6 4
              ♦ A Q J 8
              ♣ Q 10 9 2
♠ 7 4 2                      ♠ Q J 10 8 5
♥ J 10 9 7 5                 ♥ K 8 2
♦ 6 4 3                      ♦ K 7
♣ A 4                        ♣ 7 6 3
              ♠ K 9
              ♥ A Q 3
              ♦ 10 9 5 2
              ♣ K J 8 5
```

Tip

Whenever you have to establish more than one suit and fear a dangerous switch, you may have to win the first round of the enemy suit led and then duck later to cut communications between your adversaries. This technique has been aptly named the "delayed duck."

DEAL FORTY-YWO

East/West Vulnerable. Dealer West.

```
              ♠ 9
              ♥ K Q 7 6 3
              ♦ A K 5
              ♣ K Q 9 3

              ♠ A K 6 2
              ♥ J 5
              ♦ Q 6 2
              ♣ J 10 8 2
```

Lead: ♠Q

South	West	North	East
–	1♠	Dble	Pass
2NT	Pass	3♥	Pass
3NT	All Pass		

Preliminary analysis?
West has opened the bidding and your North/South combined point count is twenty-eight. Therefore West is marked with the outstanding twelve points.

How many tricks do you have?
2 in spades, 3 in diamonds = 5 tricks.

Which suits will provide the required four tricks?
1. Hearts, but this suit will only furnish four tricks with a 3-3 break, and remember that this division is only a 36 percent chance.
2. Clubs, but unfortunately only three tricks are possible from this suit and, consequently they alone will not suffice for the contract.

It seems reasonable to test the hearts first, but if they are not 3-3, you will lose a tempo in the race for suit-establishment: West will cash his two aces and at least three spades.

But are you not in a position to find the winning line?
The answer to this is that you must win a heart trick without West being able to capture one of your honor cards, and once this objective has been achieved, you switch immediately to clubs.

How do you proceed?
Win the opening lead with the king of spades (there is no point in ducking since you know that West has all the points), and present the five of hearts. West is helpless: if he goes up with the ace you will make four heart tricks (unless the ace is singleton), and you will not require a trick from the club suit; if West plays small, put on the king of hearts and turn your attention to the club suit.

The full deal:

```
              ♠ 9
              ♥ K Q 7 6 3
              ♦ A K 5
              ♣ K Q 9 3
♠ Q J 10 8 5                 ♠ 7 4 3
♥ A 10 8 2                   ♥ 9 4
♦ J 8                        ♦ 10 9 7 4 3
♣ A 7                        ♣ 6 5 4
              ♠ A K 6 2
              ♥ J 5
              ♦ Q 6 2
              ♣ J 10 8 2
```

Tip

Always take the adverse bidding into account when selecting your line of play. In this way you may be able to resort to an unusual maneuver which will improve the timing. When an opponent is placed on the horns of a dilemma to which no immediate response succeeds, the coup is called Morton's Fork.

DEAL FORTY-THREE

North/South Vulnerable. Dealer North.

```
              ♠ 9 3
              ♥ 7
              ♦ 8 6 2
              ♣ A K J 9 6 4 3

              ♠ A K Q 7
              ♥ A K Q
              ♦ A K Q J
              ♣ 10 5
```

Lead: ♥J

South	West	North	East
–	–	3♣	Pass
4NT	Pass	5♦	Pass
5NT	Pass	6♦	Pass
7NT	All Pass		

Top tricks?
3 in spades, 3 in hearts, 4 in diamonds, 2 in clubs = 12 tricks.

On what will the success of this grand slam depend?
In clubs you have nine cards missing the queen. You can either drop the queen by playing out your top clubs, or finesse against West.

What probabilities should guide you towards the correct line?
Cashing the ace and king, since there is a greater chance that the queen will be doubleton than trebleton.

When faced with a dilemma like this, what recourse have you to another technique?
Yes, a count of the hand. You cash your top winners in the side suits, hoping to gain valuable information about the adverse distribution.

Win the opening lead with the ace of hearts and cash the ace of clubs. West plays the two and East the eight. Had East shown out, you would have been able to claim.

You now come to hand with the ace of diamonds and play out your winners, keeping a close watch on the cards thrown by your opponents:

1. Both follow to two more rounds of hearts.
2. West follows to two rounds of diamonds and then discards a heart.
3. West follows to two rounds of spades, and discards a heart on the queen.

So, what are the two hands?
East's hand is an open book: he has five spades, three hearts, four diamonds and you have already seen one club. Consequently, the club finesse against West is marked.

The full deal:

```
              ♠ 9 3
              ♥ 7
              ♦ 8 6 2
              ♣ A K J 9 6 4 3
  ♠ J 6                      ♠ 10 8 5 4 2
  ♥ J 10 9 5 4 3            ♥ 8 6 2
  ♦ 10 5                    ♦ 9 7 4 3
  ♣ Q 7 2                   ♣ 8
              ♠ A K Q 7
              ♥ A K Q
              ♦ A K Q J
              ♣ 10 5
```

Tip

Whenever you are faced with a crucial choice between a finesse or suit-break, do not fail to try to count your opponents' hands first. They will be forced to discard while you are running your winners, and your final decision can be taken at a time when you are sure of doing the right thing.

DEAL FORTY-FOUR
Both Sides Vulnerable. Dealer South.

```
              ♠ Q J 4
              ♥ K 7
              ♦ J 10 8 5 3
              ♣ 8 5 2

              ♠ A 6 2
              ♥ A Q 10
              ♦ Q 9 6 2
              ♣ A Q J
```

Lead: ♠8

South	West	North	East
1♣	Pass	1♦	1♠
2NT	Pass	3NT	All Pass

Preliminary consideration?
East has bid one spade, a suit in which he doubtless holds at least five cards headed by K109, since West has led the eight (doubleton or singleton).

How many immediate winners do you have?
2 in spades (after the lead), 3 in hearts, 1 in clubs = 6 tricks.

Where do you expect to find the three missing tricks?
The club finesse is insufficient on its own, and you will have to find a trick from the diamond suit.

How many stoppers do you have in spades?
Two only. Now you have to knock out both the ace and king of diamonds and if both these honors are with East you will be defeated.

What must you assume?
That West holds at least one of them, since this hypothesis is essential for your success, and that he cannot continue with a spade to help establish his partner's suit. Suppose you instinctively put up one of dummy's honors on the opening lead.

If East covers with the king, what will you do?
You will duck. East will continue spades, and on winning this trick you will be able to set up your diamonds without interference. West will not have a spade to return and the defense will be helpless after your duck at Trick 1. This would seem to be the correct line of play. However, what if you are playing against a defender who doesn't automatically contribute "the card nearest his thumb" either?

What will he do?
He will refuse to cover the queen of spades, retaining a tenace position over dummy. As soon as you embark on the diamond suit West will rush in with his honor to preserve his partner's entry, and shoot back his second spade. Against this defense you will go down in comfort. So the apparently normal ploy of contributing one of dummy's honors at Trick 1 is unsatisfactory.

Is there any way out?

Of course: just play a small spade from both hands. West will continue spades, but will not have another one to play when he comes in with his diamond.

The full deal:

```
              ♠ Q J 4
              ♥ K 7
              ♦ J 10 8 5 3
              ♣ 8 5 2
♠ 8 3                      ♠ K 10 9 7 5
♥ J 8 6 5 4 3 2           ♥ 9
♦ K 4                     ♦ A 7
♣ 7 4                     ♣ K 10 9 6 3
              ♠ A 6 2
              ♥ A Q 10
              ♦ Q 9 6 2
              ♣ A Q J
```

Tip

Before playing hastily to the first trick, always consider carefully the play of the entire hand. Overcalls can provide valuable information.

DEAL FORTY-FIVE
Neither Side Vulnerable. Dealer South.

```
              ♠ A K 8 5
              ♥ 6 5 4
              ♦ 9 5 4
              ♣ A Q 8

              ♠ 7 6
              ♥ A 10 9
              ♦ A K 6 3 2
              ♣ K 7 5
```

Lead: ♥3

South	West	North	East
1♦	1♥	1♠	Pass
1NT	Pass	3NT	All Pass

Sure trick count?

2 spades, 1 heart, 2 diamonds and 3 clubs = 8 tricks. One more is needed.

Do you duck the opening lead? How many times?

Naturally, and taking account the Rule of 7, only duck once.

In which suit will you set up your extra trick?

The only chance lies in the diamond suit. If it breaks 3-2 (68 percent) two long cards can be established.

But what condition will be required for you to succeed?

East will have to hold the three diamonds; in this way West, the dangerous opponent, will be unable to regain the lead. Therefore after the initial duck at Trick 1 it would appear sufficient to cash the ace and king of diamonds in the hope that West has the doubleton.

Nevertheless, is there not a winning position when East has two diamonds and West three?

Yes, but then East would have to possess the queen doubleton precisely. By playing twice towards your ace and king you would insure the success of your contract by avoidance play.

You therefore duck the opening heart lead only once. After winning the heart continuation, cross to the table with a club and play a diamond towards your hand. (If you began with a top diamond from your hand East might well unblock the queen.) On the first round East plays the seven.

And you?

The ace.

How do you continue?

Cross to another club and play another diamond. This time East produces the queen.

Well?

Leave East in possession of this trick and your contract is assured.

The full deal:

```
              ♠ A K 8 5
              ♥ 6 5 4
              ♦ 9 5 4
              ♣ A Q 8
♠ Q 10 9                  ♠ J 4 3 2
♥ K Q 7 3 2              ♥ J 8
♦ J 10 8                 ♦ Q 7
♣ 10 6                   ♣ J 9 4 3 2
              ♠ 7 6
              ♥ A 10 9
              ♦ A K 6 3 2
              ♣ K 7 5
```

Tip

Avoidance plays frequently enhance the chances of success at no trumps and often, too, in trump contracts. The capacity to picture adverse distributions and the position of honor cards, and then to play accordingly, is the mark of a good player.

Had you held up the ace of hearts until the third round East could have seized the opportunity to discard the queen of diamonds.

DEAL FORTY-SIX
East/West Vulnerable. Dealer South.

♠ K 6 5 3
♥ Q 9
♦ K J 7
♣ A 10 4 3

♠ A Q
♥ A J 10
♦ 10 9 4 3 2
♣ K 6 5

Lead: ♥4. East plays the two

South	West	North	East
1♦	Pass	1♠	Pass
1NT	Pass	3NT	All Pass

Certain trick total?
3 in spades, 2 in hearts (after the lead), 2 in clubs = 7 tricks.

Which suit will provide the two missing tricks?
Diamonds, obviously.

How do you normally play such a suit?
You play towards the king-jack in the hope that the queen is favorably placed.

It would therefore seem that you should come to hand with a spade at Trick 2 and play a small diamond towards dummy's tenace, whereupon the contract will depend on the favorable position of the queen. If East has it he will return a heart through your hand and you will have to hope for a 4-4 heart break, losing two diamonds and two hearts. If the hearts are 5-3 you will duck East's heart return and hope he has the ace of diamonds as well.

Is there not a line of play offering a good chance of success even if East has the queen of diamonds and West the ace of diamonds and five hearts?
Yes, you must hope that your right-hand opponent will be taken in.

Suppose at Trick 2 you confidently play the seven of diamonds towards the closed hand. East will naturally think that you have the ace and it will be very difficult for him to rush in with the queen, for to do so might well be handing you the contract on a plate.

And what if the queen of diamonds is with West?
No problem, because he cannot harm you with a heart continuation without giving you another trick in the suit. He will have to switch and you will have all the time you require to knock out the ace of diamonds for three extra tricks, making ten in all.

The full deal:

♠ K 6 5 3
♥ Q 9
♦ K J 7
♣ A 10 4 3

♠ 10 8 7
♥ K 8 6 4 3
♦ A 5
♣ J 9 2

♠ J 9 4 2
♥ 7 5 2
♦ Q 8 6
♣ Q 8 7

♠ A Q
♥ A J 10
♦ 10 9 4 3 2
♣ K 6 5

Tip
You may be frequently forced to resort to unorthodox maneuvers to prevent an opponent from gaining the lead prematurely. If you act quickly, at the beginning of the hand, the defender in question may not have sufficient information to make the right play.

DEAL FORTY-SEVEN
North/South Vulnerable. Dealer North.

♠ 7 5
♥ 8 5 4 3
♦ A K Q 4 2
♣ 6 3

♠ A K 9
♥ A 10
♦ 10 9 8 5
♣ A Q 7 2

Lead: ♥K

South	West	North	East
–	–	Pass	Pass
1NT	Pass	2♣	Pass
2♦	Pass	3NT	All Pass

Immediate trick count?
2 in spades, 1 in hearts, 3 in diamonds, 1 in clubs = 7 tricks.

How do you envisage the success of the contract?
The diamond suit should yield five tricks. You have nine cards between the two hands including the three top honors and only a 4-0 break (9.5 percent) would appear to cause any difficulty. Should this be the case, your ninth trick could come from a successful club finesse. You should therefore, make this contract without too much difficulty.

In spite of all these favorable conditions, however, try to uncover the danger which threatens if you are not careful.
In diamonds you have AKQ42 opposite 10985, and dummy has no outside entry.

What will happen in the event of both 2-2 and 3-1 divisions?
If the diamonds are 2-2 there will be no problem; ace and king first, then small to the ten and back to the two winners on the table. If, on the other hand, an opponent holds ♦Jxx, you will have to play ace, king and queen, and you will then be cut off from the fifth diamond; the suit will be blocked.

Can you see a way of obviating this difficulty?
A first solution which comes to mind is that after discovering that an opponent has ♦Jxx you take advantage of being in the dummy to try the club finesse. However, a better chance is to seek to unblock the diamonds yourself, always provided that you are able to throw one of them on another suit. You would then release the fifth diamond without difficulty.

How will you do this?
On the enemy's heart suit, provided that it divides 4-3 or 5-2. When your opponent plays out his master hearts you will get rid of a diamond.

What must you do at Trick 1?
You must duck in order to verify whether East has a second heart. So you allow the king of hearts to hold the trick while East contributes the two. West continues with the queen of hearts which you take, East contributing the seven. Now you cash the ace and king of diamonds to test the suit and West discards a spade on the second round.

How do you continue?
Everything is in place; play the five of hearts from dummy and throw a diamond from your hand. It matters little whether West decides to take his two master hearts, since nothing can prevent you from getting at your two long diamonds. The four hands reveal that any other line was doomed to failure.

The full deal:

```
                  ♠ 7 5
                  ♥ 8 5 4 3
                  ♦ A K Q 4 2
                  ♣ 6 3
  ♠ J 6 2                      ♠ Q 10 8 4 3
  ♥ K Q J 9 6                  ♥ 7 2
  ♦ 7                          ♦ J 6 3
  ♣ K J 9 4                    ♣ 10 8 5
                  ♠ A K 9
                  ♥ A 10
                  ♦ 10 9 8 5
                  ♣ A Q 7 2
```

Tip

Pay careful attention to the potential role of small cards in the suits you intend to develop. Do not allow yourself to be caught unawares by a blockage in your main suit, and do all your planning at the beginning of the hand.

Had the hearts turned out to be 6-1, the club finesse (after discovering that the diamonds were 3-1) would have constituted your only chance.

DEAL FORTY-EIGHT

East/West Vulnerable. Dealer East.

```
                  ♠ A Q 5 4
                  ♥ 6 3
                  ♦ K Q J 6
                  ♣ 5 4 2

                  ♠ K 6 2
                  ♥ A K Q 10
                  ♦ A 5 3
                  ♣ A J 10
```

Lead: ♦10

South	West	North	East
–	–	–	Pass
2NT	Pass	3♣(*)	Pass
3♥	Pass	3♠	Pass
3NT	Pass	6NT(**)	All Pass

(*) Baron – asking for four-card suits in ascending order
(**) There cannot be two aces missing (21+12 = 33)

How many sure tricks do you have?
3 in spades, 3 in hearts, 4 in diamonds, 1 in club = 11 tricks. One more will bring home the contract.

Review the various options of establishing the extra trick:
1. In spades, if they break 3-3.
2. In hearts, by attempting a successful finesse of the ten rather than hoping to bring down the jack in two rounds.
3. In clubs, if the two missing honors (king and queen) are divided or both with East; simply take two successive finesses.

What are the respective chances of success for each of these maneuvers?
1. 3-3 spades break: 36 percent;
2. Single finesse: 50 percent.
3. A double finesse fails only 25 percent of the time, i.e. if both the missing honors are unfavorably placed. Consequently its chance of success is 75 percent.

Therefore except in the case of a clear indication to the contrary (information gleaned from the bidding, for example), select the line of play which offers the maximum chance of success.

Win the opening lead on the table and play the two of clubs to your ten; West wins with the queen and continues with the nine of diamonds which you take with the ace.

How do you continue? Can you attempt to improve your initial chance of 75 percent? In what way?
At this stage it is possible to keep various extra chances in hand without risk:

1. You will test the spade suit.
2. You will play the hearts from the top without finessing. If the jack falls you will not require another club finesse.

If the spades break 4-2 and the jack of hearts fails to appear, you will take another club finesse.

Let us recap on the different phases of the play:
1. At the very beginning, a small club to the ten and West's queen.
2. ♥AKQ, discarding a club from the table, but the jack does not fall.
3. King of spades, then ace and queen of spades to verify the division; West discards on the third round.
4. Three rounds of diamonds, South discarding the ten of hearts on the last one.
5. Small club towards your AJ. East plays the king which he has been forced to bare, for you have squeezed him! He could not abandon the ten of spades otherwise dummy's five would be high!

The full deal:

```
              ♠ A Q 5 4
              ♥ 6 3
              ♦ K Q J 6
              ♣ 5 4 2
♠ J 9                        ♠ 10 8 7 3
♥ J 8 5 2                    ♥ 9 7 4
♦ 10 9 8 7                   ♦ 4 2
♣ Q 9 3                      ♣ K 8 7 6
              ♠ K 6 2
              ♥ A K Q 10
              ♦ A 5 3
              ♣ A J 10
```

Tip

After the opening lead, get yourself into the habit of evaluating all your chances of success before opting for a particular line of play. In most cases it will be a simple matter of being aware of basic percentages such as those outlined here.

Eighteen Exercises

EXERCISE ONE

East/West Vulnerable. Dealer North.

> ♠ A Q 5
> ♥ 4 3 2
> ♦ Q 9 6 5 4
> ♣ Q 7
>
> ♠ K 6 4
> ♥ Q J 8
> ♦ A J 10 2
> ♣ A K 3

Lead: ♥6. East plays the king

South	West	North	East
–	–	Pass	Pass
1NT	Pass	3NT	All Pass

The opponents play three rounds of hearts, East discarding the two of clubs on the third round. You are in hand with the queen of hearts.

Questions

1. How many certain tricks do you have?

2. How do you give yourself the best chance? What must you hope for to bring home the contract?

Answers

1. You have 3 tricks in spades, 1 in hearts, 1 in diamonds, 3 in clubs = 8 tricks.

2. Above all you must prevent West from gaining the lead, for he has two tricks to cash. The choice is clear: if East has the king of diamonds you are in no danger; if, on the other hand, West has it, then the contract appears doomed unless it is bare. No doubt you have discovered the best line: cross to the table with a spade and lead the queen of diamonds

(you never know, East might cover it and it doesn't cost anything). East follows with the three, you go right up with the ace and West's king falls. He will doubtless regard you with suspicion in the future.

And if the king of diamonds is with East? You will certainly have lost a trick but the contract will be in no danger since East can do you no harm.

The full deal:

> ♠ A Q 5
> ♥ 4 3 2
> ♦ Q 9 6 5 4
> ♣ Q 7

♠ 8 7 3	♠ J 10 9 2
♥ A 9 7 6 5	♥ K 10
♦ K	♦ 8 7 3
♣ 10 6 5 4	♣ J 9 8 2

> ♠ K 6 4
> ♥ Q J 8
> ♦ A J 10 2
> ♣ A K 3

You may be in trouble against an expert West. Seeing his partner's king of hearts at Trick 1, West will realize that East cannot possibly have another entry, and when South covers the ten of hearts at Trick 2 West will duck, playing the seven. If you visualize the adverse hearts to be West: A976 and East: K105, you may think that you have no reason for not taking the diamond finesse, since you would expect to lose only a diamond and three hearts. If you suspect West of being capable of such deception you should refuse to be taken in and still play the ace of diamonds, because if you do assume the hearts to be 4-3 it may still only cost one trick, but not the contract, to refuse the finesse.

EXERCISE TWO
East/West Vulnerable. Dealer East.

♠ K Q 6
♥ 4 3
♦ Q 8 3
♣ A 6 5 4 2

♠ A J 10 3
♥ A 10 9
♦ K 10 2
♣ K 9 7

Lead: ♥2

South	West	North	East
–	–	–	Pass
1NT	Pass	3NT	All Pass

East plays the king of hearts at Trick 1 and, if you decide to duck, he will return the five.

Questions

1. Immediate trick total?

2. What inference do you draw from the lead, and do you duck?

3. Where will you find the extra tricks? (As always you must take the defense's tricks into consideration.)

Answers

1. You have 7 sure tricks: 4 in spades, 1 in hearts, 2 in clubs.

2. The hearts are most probably 4-4. Certainly, West may have false-carded on the opening lead, but East played back the five, which would be his lowest of three remaining cards.

Since you do not fear any switch (in fact you would rather like it), duck twice.

3. At first sight it would seem appropriate to play for a 3-2 club break (68 percent), but if you have taken the precaution of counting the tricks against you, you will find that they come to five: three hearts, one diamond, and a club voluntarily conceded. Since this line of play is doomed to failure, you must try to develop two diamond tricks by playing East for the jack (50 percent). At Trick 4 play the two of diamonds to the queen which holds (it does not matter where the ace is), and continue with the three towards your hand. You are lucky and West has to play the ace. Your contract is made with four spades, one heart, two diamonds and two clubs.

The full deal:

♠ 4 3
♥ 4 3
♦ Q 8 3
♣ A 6 5 4 2

♠ 9 5 4　　　　　♠ 8 7 2
♥ Q J 6 2　　　　♥ K 8 7 5
♦ A 7 5　　　　　♦ J 9 6 4
♣ Q 10 8　　　　♣ J 3

♠ A J 10 3
♥ A 10 9
♦ K 10 2
♣ K 9 7

EXERCISE THREE
Both Sides Vulnerable. Dealer West.

♠ J 7 6
♥ A 8 4
♦ Q J 5 4 3
♣ 6 2

♠ A Q
♥ K 10 7
♦ A 9 6 2
♣ A 10 8 4

Lead: ♠5

South	West	North	East
–	Pass	Pass	Pass
1NT	Pass	2NT	Pass
3NT	All Pass		

Questions

1. How many top tricks?

2. Which suit should you establish?

3. How will you play it?

Answers

1. 2 in spades, 2 in hearts, 1 in diamonds, 1 in clubs = 6 tricks. You need three more.

2. Diamonds: you have nine cards between the two hands and you should turn your immediate attention to these.

3. Remember that you need only three extra tricks and that you still have a spade stopper. You must therefore think of how to assure four diamond tricks against any adverse distribution. The missing cards are K1087. You should make a habit of visualizing all the cards held by the defenders.

Against any 2-2 or 3-1 division you will have no problem, consequently you should concentrate on the 4-0 break. There is only one way of dealing with the 4-0 division and that is to play the two of diamonds towards the queen. If West has the four diamonds you will lead twice towards dummy and he will be helpless; if it is East who has them he will win with the king and you will later be able to capture through his ten.

The full deal:

```
            ♠ A 8 4
            ♥ A 8 4
            ♦ Q J 5 4 3
            ♣ 6 2
♠ K 9 8 5 4              ♠ 10 3 2
♥ J 6 3 2               ♥ Q 9 5
♦ –                    ♦ K 10 8 7
♣ J 7 5 3              ♣ K Q 9
            ♠ A Q
            ♥ K 10 7
            ♦ A 9 6 2
            ♣ A 10 8 4
```

There are two contrasting attitudes which all good bridge players should adopt according to circumstances:

1.   Resolute optimism when faced with a desperate contract: "I need to find certain cards and distributions in this hand and I shall play accordingly."

2.   Basic pessimism when confronted by an apparently laydown contract: "What distribution (even the most outlandish) can endanger my contract? What steps can I reasonably take (without endangering the contract) to overcome the potential obstacle? If I can manage to obviate that danger I shall play accordingly."

Exercise Four

East/West Vulnerable. Dealer South.

```
            ♠ K 10 4
            ♥ Q 7 6
            ♦ A J 10 7
            ♣ Q 5 2

            ♠ Q 6 2
            ♥ K J 5
            ♦ K Q 9
            ♣ A J 10 6
```

Lead: ♠9

South	West	North	East
1NT	Pass	3NT	All Pass

Questions

1.   How many top tricks do you have?

2.   What inference do you draw from the lead?

3.   Which card do you play from dummy at Trick 1? Why?

4.   If you have played correctly at Trick 1, East has had to win; he now returns the nine of clubs; do you finesse? Justify your decision.

5.   What tricks will you set up?

Answers

1.   You have 6 tricks: 1 in spades (after the lead), 4 in diamonds, 1 in clubs. You require three more.

2.   The nine of spades is almost certainly a "lead for partner," and it would be logical to assume that East is marked with AJxxx.

3.   In that case, play the king of spades at Trick 1. It is a matter of both cutting communications between your opponents and preventing East from returning the suit at no cost to the defense.

4.   Since you must prevent West from regaining the lead (he would return another spade before you had knocked out the ace of hearts), you should assume that East's club switch, the nine, would tend to mark West with the king, and should therefore put up the ace.

5.   You now proceed to establish a heart trick. East wins the first round; if he returns a spade he will be giving you your ninth trick; he can only put West in with the king of clubs, and this will not harm you since your spade guard is still intact. Your contract will be made with an overtrick: one spade, two hearts, four diamonds and three clubs.

The recommended line of play would have failed had the ace of hearts and king of clubs been interchanged, but brilliant or illogical defense has to be accepted from time to time.

Drawing the correct inferences from the cards played by your opponents will enable you to benefit considerably in the long run.

The full deal:

```
            ♠ K 10 4
            ♥ Q 7 6
            ♦ A J 10 7
            ♣ Q 5 2
♠ 9 5                   ♠ A J 8 7 3
♥ 9 4 3 2              ♥ A 10 8
♦ 8 5 4               ♦ 6 3 2
♣ K 8 7 3             ♣ 9 4
            ♠ Q 6 2
            ♥ K J 5
            ♦ K Q 9
            ♣ A J 10 6
```

Exercise Five

North/South Vulnerable. Dealer South.

    ♠ A K 3
    ♥ A Q 5
    ♦ J 10 2
    ♣ A K 6 4

    ♠ Q 10 9
    ♥ K J 10
    ♦ A K 8 5 4
    ♣ 8 7

Lead: ♥9

South	West	North	East
1NT	Pass	6NT	All Pass

Questions

1. How many top tricks?

2. Only one suit can be established; what distribution do you have to consider?

3. Suppose your partner had bid seven no trumps, how would you play the diamonds?

Answers

1. You can count 3 in spades, 3 in hearts, 2 in diamonds, 2 in clubs = 10 tricks, and you require two more.

2. Only the diamond suit is viable. If you play the ace, then small towards J10 no 3-2 or 4-1 break can worry you, therefore your only consideration should be if one opponent holds all five outstanding diamonds: Q9763. Even though this distribution is extremely rare, you must not overlook the safety play for four tricks which is guaranteed.

3. In seven no trumps the safety-play is out of the question; five diamond tricks are required and you must play accordingly: East must have the queen either doubleton or two or three times guarded. You must take a first round finesse by running the jack. You must not test the suit by laying down the ace for East is more likely to have the queen to four than West the queen singleton.

To guard against 5-0 with either opponent, just play a small diamond towards J102: if West discards, East's nine will later be picked up by finesse, and if East discards, West not taking his queen on the first round, simply return to hand in another suit and lead another low diamond to dummy.

The full deal:

                    ♠ A K 3
                    ♥ A Q 5
                    ♦ J 10 2
                    ♣ A K 6 4
    ♠ J 6 2   ♠ 8 7 5 4
    ♥ 9 8 7 4   ♥ 6 3 2
    ♦ Q 9 7 6 3   ♦ —
    ♣ Q   ♣ J 10 9 5 3 2
                    ♠ Q 10 9
                    ♥ K J 10
                    ♦ A K 8 5 4
                    ♣ 8 7

This contract has a probability of success of about 45 percent, which is not very attractive since a grand slam should not be bid unless it is better than about 70 percent. Note that seven no trumps will not make as the cards lie.

Exercise Six

East/West Vulnerable. Dealer East.

    ♠ 8 6 3
    ♥ J 5 2
    ♦ A 10 9
    ♣ 7 6 5 4

    ♠ A Q J 4
    ♥ Q 10 3
    ♦ K Q J
    ♣ A K 9

Lead: ♥7

South	West	North	East
–	–	–	Pass
2NT	Pass	3NT	All Pass

East wins the heart lead with the ace and returns the suit.

Questions

1. Count your sure tricks.

2. Under what conditions will you succeed?

3. Which card will you play from your hand at Trick 1?

Answers

1. 1 in spades, 1 in hearts (after the lead and continuation), 3 in diamonds, 2 in clubs = 7 tricks.

2. The spade suit offers the best prospects: you can establish two tricks in the suit if East has the king, doubleton or trebleton. Why precisely Kx or Kxx? Quite simply because there is only one entry in dummy: the ace of diamonds.

At first sight it appears impossible to repeat the spade finesse and therefore prevail against Kxxx or longer with East; to overcome this obstacle it is necessary to play spades a second time from the North hand. How can you manage that?

3. The opening lead (seven of hearts) shows that East has only one card higher, the ace, which he has just played. Throw your queen under this and North's jack of hearts will provide the second entry. Your game will be made provided East has the king of spades however many times guarded, and on condition you pay attention to Trick 1.

The full deal:

```
                ♠ 8 6 3
                ♥ J 5 2
                ♦ A 10 9
                ♣ 7 6 5 4
♠ 10 9                        ♠ K 7 5 2
♥ K 9 8 7 4                   ♥ A 6
♦ 4 2                         ♦ 8 7 6 5 3
♣ J 8 3 2                     ♣ Q 10
                ♠ A Q J 4
                ♥ Q 10 3
                ♦ K Q J
                ♣ A K 9
```

Note that if you retain your queen of hearts in hand at Trick 1, West will always be able to prevent North's jack from becoming an entry.

EXERCISE SEVEN
North/South Vulnerable. Dealer West.

```
                ♠ 8 5
                ♥ K J 10 2
                ♦ A J 7 6
                ♣ A Q J

                ♠ K J 10
                ♥ A 9
                ♦ Q 10 5 3
                ♣ K 10 9 4
```

Lead: ♠7. East plays the six

South	West	North	East
–	2♠(*)	Dble	Pass
3NT	All Pass		

(*) Weak, 6-10 points

Questions

1. How many top tricks?

2. What is the danger? What suit will you play on?

3. How will you play that suit?

Answers

1. 1 in spades (after the lead), 2 in hearts, 1 in diamonds, 4 in clubs = 8 certain tricks.

2. The weak two spade opening and East's six of spades show that the ace and queen are marked with West. West's opening bid showing 6-10 points, he cannot have both the king of diamonds and the queen of hearts. If you take either the diamond or heart finesse against West and it falls, you will be defeated immediately.

Remember, you require only one extra trick, so set up a trick in hearts, taking care not to allow East to gain the lead. Play a heart from the dummy and put in the nine. If West wins with the queen the contract is assured. He will doubtless switch to a diamond, but you will rise with dummy's ace and claim your nine tricks.

3. Recap on the play: ten of spades at Trick 1, club to the queen, two of hearts to your nine which holds. Ace of hearts, small club to the ace (take care not to block the clubs), king of hearts. When the queen of hearts does not appear, overtake the jack of clubs with the king, cash the ten and take your ace of diamonds for nine tricks.

The full deal:

```
                ♠ 8 5
                ♥ K J 10 2
                ♦ A J 7 6
                ♣ A Q J
♠ A Q 9 7 4 3                 ♠ 6 2
♥ 6 5 4                       ♥ Q 8 7 3
♦ 9 2                         ♦ K 8 4
♣ 8 6                         ♣ 7 5 3 2
                ♠ K J 10
                ♥ A 9
                ♦ Q 10 5 3
                ♣ K 10 9 4
```

EXERCISE EIGHT
North/South Vulnerable. Dealer North.

```
                ♠ A Q 7 4 2
                ♥ K J 10
                ♦ A K 6
                ♣ K 3

                ♠ 6 5
                ♥ A 3
                ♦ 5 4 2
                ♣ Q J 10 9 8 6
```

Lead: ♥4

South	West	North	East
–	–	1♠	Pass
1NT	Pass	3NT	All Pass

Questions

1. Your winner count?

2. What suit will you establish?

3. What card will you play from dummy at Trick 1? Why?

Answers

1. 1 in spades, 2 in hearts, 2 in diamonds = 5 tricks. You require four more.

2. You will naturally establish clubs. They will furnish five tricks once the ace has gone. Obviously you will begin with the king and continue the suit until the ace appears.

3. At first sight the heart lead seems favorable since you no longer have to guess where the queen is. However, beware! You can bet that a careless declarer will play the ten in order to profit from the free finesse. What would be the danger in this play? The ten might be covered by the queen and South can say good-bye to the contract. He will be forced to win with the ace thereby killing the club suit for lack of a later entry.

Before yielding to his instinct of greed he would have done better to imagine how play would develop, and to this end preserve the only sure entry to his hand: the ace of hearts. Only one card is correct from dummy at Trick 1: the king of hearts (who cares if West has the queen?). The clubs will be established in comfort with the ace of hearts for entry.

You must admit that a goodly number of players do not take time to foresee how the play will go, and of these a large percentage would have defeated themselves in this cold contract.

The full deal:

```
              ♠ A Q 7 4 2
              ♥ K J 10
              ♦ A K 6
              ♣ K 3
♠ 10                        ♠ K J 9 8 3
♥ 9 6 5 4 2                 ♥ Q 8 7
♦ Q 8 3                     ♦ J 10 9 7
♣ A 7 5 4                   ♣ 2
              ♠ 6 5
              ♥ A 3
              ♦ 5 4 2
              ♣ Q J 10 9 8 6
```

Neither Side Vulnerable. Dealer South.

```
              ♠ 5 3 2
              ♥ A Q 7 4 3
              ♦ 9 8
              ♣ 7 6 4

              ♠ A Q 9
              ♥ 8 2
              ♦ A K 6 2
              ♣ A J 9 5
```

Lead: ♠7. East plays the ten

South	West	North	East
1♣	1♠	Pass	Pass
1NT	Pass	3♥	Pass
3NT	All Pass		

Questions

1. How many tricks do you have?

2. What conditions must be present for the contract to succeed?

3. How will you set about the hand?

Answers

1. 2 in spades (after the lead), 1 in hearts, 2 in diamonds, 1 in clubs = 6 sure tricks.

2. Only one suit is capable of furnishing three extra tricks: hearts. Unfortunately you have only AQxxx opposite two small and no outside entry. To establish three tricks the suit must divide 3-3 and the king lie with West. That gives you a mere half of 36 percent = 18 percent chance of success. It isn't much but there is nothing else to play for.

3. The opening lead is taken with the queen and you set about the hearts by playing the two towards dummy's three. If you put up the queen you would have no chance since there is no outside entry to the table. East wins with the nine and returns the six of spades.

You take this with the ace and continue hearts: the eight to West's ten and dummy's queen which holds; on the ace both opponents follow, and the rest of the hearts are good.

Bridge is a curious game: in this example you have to risk not making a heart trick at all (if East has the king), to make four.

The full deal:

```
              ♠ 5 3 2
              ♥ A Q 7 4 3
              ♦ 9 8
              ♣ 7 6 4
♠ K J 8 7 4              ♠ 10 6
♥ K 10 6                 ♥ J 9 5
♦ 5 3                    ♦ Q J 10 7 4
♣ Q 10 2                 ♣ K 8 3
              ♠ A Q 9
              ♥ 8 2
              ♦ A K 6 2
              ♣ A J 9 5
```

EXERCISE TEN

North/South Vulnerable. Dealer West.

```
              ♠ A K
              ♥ Q 3
              ♦ A 5 4
              ♣ A Q 10 9 8 2

              ♠ 9 5 3
              ♥ K 8 4
              ♦ Q 9 8 7 3
              ♣ K 7
```

Lead: ♥J

South	West	North	East
–	1♥	Dble	Pass
1NT	Pass	3NT	All Pass

Preliminary consideration:

Since North/South have 27 points between them, all the outstanding honor cards, with the exception perhaps of a jack, must be with the opening bidder.

Questions

1. How many top tricks do you have?

2. How many tricks do you require, and which suit will provide them?

3. What card do you play from dummy on the opening lead?

4. Can you make sure of the contract and if yes, how?

Answers

1. You have 2 in spades, 1 in hearts (after the lead), 1 in diamonds, 3 in clubs = 7 certain tricks.

2. Two more tricks are needed and you will look to the club suit for these.

3. West has a heart suit headed by AJ10 and by putting up the queen you will retain a second guard in the suit provided you keep East out of the lead.

4. If the clubs are 3-2 (68 percent) or the jack of clubs is bare, or West has Jxxx, success is assured, but what will happen if East has Jxxx? You will have to let your right-hand opponent in and his heart return will be fatal.

The solution is simple: after winning the queen of hearts at Trick 1, play the two of clubs of dummy and put in the seven from your hand. If West wins with the jack, the rest of the club suit is established and no return from him can harm you, and if West follows with a small club you will make six club tricks and East will not be able to play a heart through you.

The full deal:

```
              ♠ A K
              ♥ Q 3
              ♦ A 5 4
              ♣ A Q 10 9 8 2
♠ Q J 2                 ♠ 10 8 7 6 4
♥ A J 10 9 2            ♥ 7 6 5
♦ K J 10 6             ♦ 2
♣ 4                    ♣ J 6 5 3
              ♠ 9 5 3
              ♥ K 8 4
              ♦ Q 9 8 7 3
              ♣ K 7
```

EXERCISE ELEVEN

East/West Vulnerable. Dealer West.

```
              ♠ 6 3
              ♥ A 7 4 3
              ♦ K Q J
              ♣ A J 10 8

              ♠ A 10 9
              ♥ J 10 5
              ♦ A 10 4 3
              ♣ 9 5 2
```

Lead: ♠4

South	West	North	East
–	Pass	1♣	Pass
1NT	Pass	2NT	Pass
3NT	All Pass		

Questions

1. How many top tricks?

2. Where will the other tricks come from?

3. Do you duck the opening lead? If yes, how many times? (East will play the jack of spades at Trick 1, and continue with the two.)

4. How will you plan the rest of the play?

Answers

1. 1 in spades, 1 in hearts, 4 in diamonds, 1 in clubs = 7 sure tricks. You require two more.

2. The hearts are not very attractive for such a suit since Axxx opposite J10x will never bring in three tricks. In clubs, on the other hand, you have all the intermediates down to the eight. The jack and ten accompanying the ace, you will make three tricks 75 percent of the time.

3. The Rule of 7 would suggest that you should duck twice (7 − 5 = 2) and indeed this would be essential if the spades were breaking 5-3. However, there are further considerations on this deal. To take two finesses in the club suit you will need two entries to your hand. If you duck two spades and West switches to a red suit you will be in trouble. East's return of the two of spades suggests that he started with either two or four cards so either way you can afford to play the ace on the second round.

4. How do you handle the club suit? The success of your contract will depend on your answer to this question.

You may be inclined to begin with the nine from your hand but after the first finesse has lost to East you will be obliged to return to hand to take it again. If West began with four clubs to an honor you will be unable to capture it for lack of a further entry to your hand and the clubs will bring you only two tricks.

The correct way is to play the two to dummy's ten on the first round and later the nine to dummy's eight, thereby retaining the lead in your hand for a third finesse towards AJ.

The full deal:

```
              ♠ 6 3
              ♥ A 7 4 3
              ♦ K Q J
              ♣ A J 10 8
♠ K Q 7 4                 ♠ J 8 5 2
♥ K Q 9                   ♥ 8 6 2
♦ 5 2                     ♦ 9 8 7 6
♣ Q 7 6 3                 ♣ K 4
              ♠ A 10 9
              ♥ J 10 5
              ♦ A 10 4 3
              ♣ 9 5 2
```

Neither Side Vulnerable. Dealer South.

```
              ♠ K 4
              ♥ K Q 5 3
              ♥ A K J
              ♣ Q J 7 3

              ♠ A 9 3
              ♥ J 10 2
              ♦ Q 5 4 2
              ♣ 10 6 4
```

Lead: ♠Q

South	West	North	East
Pass	1♠	Dble	Pass
1NT	Pass	3NT	All Pass

Questions

1. How many top tricks?

2. Which suit will you establish?

3. Do you duck the opening lead? (Perhaps this question is not so simple as it appears if the defense is perfect.)

Answers

1. 2 in spades, 4 in diamonds = 6 tricks.

2. The three additional tricks will come from hearts, you just have to knock out the ace.

3. You hold two spade stoppers and intend to give up the lead only once (with the ace of hearts); the duck is therefore unnecessary, perhaps it is even harmful, since you will only make four diamond tricks by unblocking the AKJ. If the suit is 4-2 (48 percent) you will not be able to overtake the jack without sacrificing a trick.

See what will happen if you win the first trick with the king of spades, since you may well be inclined to do such in this situation: you unblock the diamonds and play a heart to the ten which holds, cash the queen of diamonds and then continue to establish the hearts. West wins the third round of hearts and plays on spades. You will have no entry to the table to cash your thirteenth heart. This solution is clearly unsatisfactory.

Now consider taking the lead with the ace of spades. You unblock the diamonds and play a heart to your ten. West cannot prevent you from reaching your hand to cash the queen of diamonds, and the king of spades remains on the table as access to the dummy's fourth heart.

If you had ducked the first round of spades, you could have said good-bye to your entry to the good heart.

The full deal:

                    ♠ K 4
                    ♥ K Q 5 3
                    ♦ A K J
                    ♣ Q J 7 3

♠ Q J 10 8 7   ♠ 6 5 2
♥ A 6 4   ♥ 9 8 7
♦ 9 6   ♦ 10 8 7 3
♣ A K 5   ♣ 9 8 2

                    ♠ A 9 3
                    ♥ J 10 2
                    ♦ Q 5 4 2
                    ♣ 10 6 4

As soon as the opening lead has been made you should consider any communication problems which might occur.

EXERCISE THIRTEEN

East/West Vulnerable. Dealer East.

                    ♠ Q 4 2
                    ♥ K Q 7
                    ♦ K Q 6
                    ♣ A 10 9 3

                    ♠ K J 10
                    ♥ A 9 8
                    ♦ A 10 8
                    ♣ K Q 6 5

Lead: ♠9

South	West	North	East
–	–	–	Pass
1NT	Pass	4NT	Pass
6NT	All Pass		

East wins the spade lead with the ace and continues with the six.

Questions

1. How many tricks do you have?

2. What is the only danger?

3. How will you overcome that obstacle?

4. Will your chosen technique be infallible?

Answers

1. You have 2 spades, 3 hearts, 3 diamonds and 3 clubs. That leaves you with one trick to find.

2. You can only establish the twelfth trick in clubs; if the suit breaks 3-2, no problem, but if it is 4-1 (28 percent) you will have to guess which opponent holds Jxxx.

3. Whenever you are faced with this kind of dilemma, there is a technique which should occur to you automatically: a count of the hand. You cash all your winners in the other three suits, for the discards furnished by your opponents will provide you with the solution.

4. A third round of spades reveals that West began with five, for East discards a diamond. Three rounds of hearts follow and again on the third round East discards a diamond. East's two major-suit doubletons reveal that West began with ten cards in spades and hearts. He therefore cannot have more than three cards in the minors. You now cash your diamond winners to find out the exact distribution. West follows twice but on the third round he discards the seven of spades. The composition of both hands in now known. West cannot have more than one club. Cash the ace in case West's singleton is the jack. No, he plays the four. Now lead the ten and run it if East fails to cover. The slam is yours.

The full deal:

                    ♠ Q 4 2
                    ♥ K Q 7
                    ♦ K Q 6
                    ♣ A 10 9 3

♠ 9 8 7 5 3   ♠ A 6
♥ J 6 5 4 2   ♥ 10 3
♦ J 3   ♦ 9 7 5 4 2
♣ 4   ♣ J 8 7 2

                    ♠ K J 10
                    ♥ A 9 8
                    ♦ A 10 8
                    ♣ K Q 6 5

Only one situation would leave you in doubt, and that is when both opponents followed to three rounds of spades, hearts and diamonds. Unless you were able to assess accurately from the manner in which each opponent followed suit the number of cards he began with, you would have no certain way of finding out if either began with four clubs.

EXERCISE FOURTEEN

Neither Side Vulnerable. Dealer East.

                    ♠ K J 2
                    ♥ Q J 10 6 3
                    ♦ 9 5
                    ♣ 10 7 2

                    ♠ A 9 5
                    ♥ 9 2
                    ♦ A K 10 4
                    ♣ A K 6 3

Lead: ♠7

South	West	North	East
–	–	–	Pass
1♣	Pass	1♥	Pass
2NT	Pass	3♣(*)	Pass
3NT	All Pass		

(*) Looking for three-card heart support

Questions

1. How many top tricks do you have?

2. Which suit will provide the extra tricks?

3. What inference do you draw from the lead? Which card should you play at Trick 1?

Answers

1. 2, possibly 3, in spades, 2 in diamonds, 2 in clubs = 6 tricks. Three more are required.

2. You must set up the hearts. However you must realize that your opponents, who are good defenders, will refuse to win the first round. They will be anxious to cut your communication and, consequently, you will require two more entries in the North hand: one to knock out the defense's second heart winner and one to reach the established tricks.

3. West has led the seven of spades (his fourth best); the Rule of 11 provides you with useful information: 11 - 7 = 4. There are four cards higher than the seven in the North, East and South hands. Well, they are all on view and it is easy to conclude that East has no card higher than the seven. Indeed, he plays the six on the opening lead.

Now remember that two entries are indispensable for the heart establishment. You should now know enough to play the correct card from your hand at Trick 1: not the nine of spades, as your instinct for economy tells you to, but the ace. Thus you will be able to reach the table twice, once by finessing the jack and later with the king.

The full deal:

```
              ♠ K J 2
              ♥ Q J 10 6 3
              ♦ 9 5
              ♣ 10 7 2

♠ Q 10 8 7 3              ♠ 6 4
♥ 8 4                     ♥ A K 7 5
♦ Q J 7 6                 ♦ 8 3 2
♣ 8 5                     ♣ Q J 9 4

              ♠ A 9 5
              ♥ 9 2
              ♦ A K 10 4
              ♣ A K 6 3
```

EXERCISE FIFTEEN

Both Sides Vulnerable. Dealer North.

```
              ♠ 7 6 3
              ♥ J 10 5
              ♦ A Q 8 6
              ♣ Q 4 2

              ♠ A K 5
              ♥ K 9 6
              ♦ K 4 3
              ♣ A 8 7 3
```

Lead: ♠10

South	West	North	East
–	–	Pass	1♠
1NT	Pass	3NT	All Pass

East overtakes the lead of the ten of spades with the jack.

Questions

1. How many tricks do you have initially?

2. What do you know about the position of the missing points?

3. Do you duck the opening lead?

4. How will you play if diamonds turn out to be 4-2?

Answers

1. 2 in spades, 3 in diamonds, 1 in club = 6 tricks.

2. Since you have 26 points between your two hands, the king of clubs, ace and queen of hearts and queen and jack of spades are marked with East.

3. The duck, whose main function is to cut communication between defenders, is pointless when all the honor strength lies in the same hand. It can even be fatal, for it can deprive declarer of the opportunity to put a defender on lead later in the play. Consequently, you win the spade at Trick 1, preserving the five as a potential exit card.

4. You must set up two heart tricks by finessing for the queen. A 3-3 diamond break will furnish the ninth trick.

At Trick 2 cross to the queen of diamonds and lead the jack of hearts: East goes in with the ace and returns the queen of spades; win with the king (West playing the four), and continue with two further rounds of diamonds. Unfortunately on the ace East discards the five of clubs. On the ten of hearts which follows East plays the queen and on your next heart he discards another club.

You now know the opener's hand: five spades, two hearts, two diamonds and four clubs; put him in with your remaining spade and he will have to yield the ninth trick by leading away from his king of clubs at Trick 12.

The full deal:

```
              ♠ 7 6 3
              ♥ J 10 5
              ♦ A Q 8 6
              ♣ Q 4 2
♠ 10 4                      ♠ Q J 9 8 2
♥ 8 7 4 3 2                 ♥ A Q
♦ J 10 5 3                  ♦ 9 7
♣ 10 9                      ♣ K J 6 5
              ♠ A K 5
              ♥ K 9 6
              ♦ K 4 3
              ♣ A 8 7 3
```

EXERCISE SIXTEEN
Neither Side Vulnerable. Dealer South.

```
              ♠ 6 4
              ♥ 8 4 2
              ♦ A 9 8 5 2
              ♣ A K Q

              ♠ A 9 5
              ♥ A J 5
              ♦ Q J 10 3
              ♣ J 10 3
```

Lead: ♥K

South	West	North	East
1♦	1♥	2♣(*)	Pass
2NT	Pass	3♦(**)	Pass
3NT	All Pass		

(*) Too strong for immediate diamond support
(**)Forcing

Preliminary consideration:

West has at least five hearts headed by the king-queen, therefore East has two at most. East is the only defender who can regain the lead (with the king of diamonds).

Questions

1. How many tricks do you have?

2. Which suit will you establish?

3. Do you duck the opening lead? (What is this coup called?)

4. If you decide to duck, is there not the danger of a switch?

5. What solution have you discovered?

6. Will your play succeed against perfect defense?

Answers

1. 1 in spades, 1 in hearts, 1 in diamonds, 3 in clubs = 6 tricks.

2. Obviously you will go for the diamonds.

3. If you win the opening lead immediately and the diamond finesse fails, your jack of hearts will be captured by finesse when East returns his partner's suit. You must therefore duck the opening lead. This is called the Bath Coup in this situation.

4. What will happen if you play the five on West's king? He will certainly not continue into your AJ, and he will almost certainly switch to a spade, a suit in which you have only five cards and a single stopper.

5. You must therefore not only duck the king of hearts, but induce West to continue with the suit. Have you found it? Just contribute your jack without hesitation. In this way you will mask the five of hearts and West will think that his partner has it. He will triumphantly set up his suit by playing another round and you will take your ace and run the queen of diamonds in peace. If East can win this trick you can sit back and enjoy West's discomfort as he waits in vain for the heart return.

6. The answer to this question is no, for really good defenders note their partners discards with the greatest care. If East/West are playing distributional signals throughout East's seven of hearts will be a clear indication to West that your heart holding is AJx and he will certainly find the deadly switch.

The full deal:

```
              ♠ 6 4
              ♥ 8 4 2
              ♦ A 9 8 5 2
              ♣ A K Q
♠ K Q 7                     ♠ J 10 8 3 2
♥ K Q 10 9 3                ♥ 7 6
♦ 7 6                       ♦ K 4
♣ 8 4 2                     ♣ 9 7 6 5
              ♠ A 9 5
              ♥ A J 5
              ♦ Q J 10 3
              ♣ J 10 3
```

EXERCISE SEVENTEEN

East/West Vulnerable. Dealer West.

♠ A 10 2
♥ A K
♦ A Q J 6 4
♣ J 9 5

♠ J 8 4
♥ J 7 5
♦ 3 2
♣ K Q 10 8 6

Lead: ♥4

South	West	North	East
–	Pass	1♦	Pass
1NT	Pass	3NT	All Pass

East plays the two of hearts at Trick 1, playing distributional signals.

Questions

1. How many top tricks?

2. Which suits will provide the extra tricks?

3. In which order will you play them?

Answers

1. 1 in spades, 2 in hearts, 1 in diamonds = 4 tricks. Five more are required.

2. The clubs will furnish four tricks, but since you do not have any entry to your hand, the defense will hold up twice and kill the suit. The diamonds are a possibility. If West has the doubleton king or even Kxxx you will establish three tricks. If he has Kxx you will make all five diamonds. You will obviously play twice from your hand towards AQJ.

The chance of making an extra trick from the spade suit is so thin that it is not worth considering.

3. After these preliminary analyses you play a club to your hand at Trick 2 and as foreseen nobody wants to take the ace. You now play a diamond to the jack which holds.

Return to hand with the king of clubs (East still cannot go in with the ace without setting up the rest of your clubs) and repeat the diamond finesse; now cash the ace of diamonds (East discards) and play another round to West. Your fifth diamond is now established as the ninth trick: one spade, two hearts, four diamonds and two clubs.

You will not have failed to notice that it would have been absurd to play a further round of clubs, since your hand was entryless.

The full deal:

```
              ♠ A 10 2
              ♥ A K
              ♦ A Q J 6 4
              ♣ J 9 5
♠ Q 9 7                      ♠ K 6 5 3
♥ Q 10 8 4 3                 ♥ 9 6 2
♦ K 10 7 5                   ♦ 9 8
♣ 4                          ♣ A 7 3 2
              ♠ J 8 4
              ♥ J 7 5
              ♦ 3 2
              ♣ K Q 10 8 6
```

EXERCISE EIGHTEEN

Neither Side Vulnerable. Dealer West.

♠ 9 3
♥ A K 6 4
♦ 9 5 3
♣ K Q J 2

♠ K J 5
♥ 5 3 2
♦ A J 4
♣ A 7 6 3

Lead: ♠7. East plays the queen

South	West	North	East
–	Pass	1♣	Pass
1♦	1♠	Pass	Pass
3NT	All Pass		

Questions

1. How many top tricks?

2. Do you duck East's queen of spades?

3. Which defender must you keep off lead?

4. Which suit will you set up?

5. What technique will you employ?

Answers

1. 1 in spades (after the lead), 2 in hearts, 1 in diamonds, 4 in clubs = 8 tricks. You require only one more.

2. You might think about ducking the queen of spades but this would only be effective if the spades were 6-2 and you were certain that only East could regain the lead. The 5-3 break is three times more likely (47 percent), and West, who clearly holds the ace of spades, only needs to duck once to maintain communication with his partner; if East gains the lead your position will be hopeless. Consequently, you must win with the king of spades at trick 1; you still retain a guard with your J5.

3. East is the dangerous opponent because if he regains the lead your ♠Jx will be captured by finesse.

4. The diamond suit is completely unattractive and your only hope of nine tricks lies in a 3-3 heart break. You must set up   the six of hearts.

5. However, since it is essential that East does not regain the lead, you must hope that West has ♥Qxx.

To make sure that he does not unblock that honor you must play twice towards the ace and king. If West plays the queen on either of your small heart leads, let him hold the trick.

The full deal:

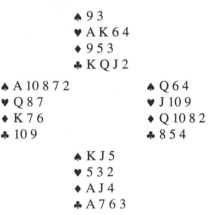

```
              ♠ 9 3
              ♥ A K 6 4
              ♦ 9 5 3
              ♣ K Q J 2
♠ A 10 8 7 2              ♠ Q 6 4
♥ Q 8 7                   ♥ J 10 9
♦ K 7 6                   ♦ Q 10 8 2
♣ 10 9                    ♣ 8 5 4
              ♠ K J 5
              ♥ 5 3 2
              ♦ A J 4
              ♣ A 7 6 3
```

Throughout this section it has been suggested that the defenders are leading fourth best. Here are one or two comments concerning the growing popularity of distributional leads (third and fifth).

> With five cards or three the lowest card is led: K 7 6 5 3
> With four cards the third highest is led: K 8 6 2

Instead of applying the Rule of 11 you apply:

> The Rule of 10 in the case of fifth highest;
> The Rule of 12 in the case of third highest.

Naturally the inferences are clear: the lead of a small card will be more frequently from a five-card suit, and a middle card will more probably be from four cards.

P LANNING THE D EFENSE
by Raymond Brock

Neither Side Vulnerable. Dealer North.

<pre>
                    ♠ Q J 10 8 7
                    ♥ 9 2
                    ♦ A Q 9 4
                    ♣ A 3
    ♠ A 5   ♠ 9 6 4 3
    ♥ K 8 3   ♥ A 7
    ♦ K J 7 5 2   ♦ 10 8 6
    ♣ Q J 2   ♣ K 10 9 8
                    ♠ K 2
                    ♥ Q J 10 6 5 4
                    ♦ 3
                    ♣ 7 6 5 4
</pre>

West	North	East	South
–	1♠	Pass	1NT
Pass	2♦	Pass	2♥
All Pass			

On the above hand, a young girl was West against Eddie Kantar and Alan Sontag, both former world champions.

West led a trump to her partner's ace, won the trump return and shifted to the queen of clubs. Kantar ducked the club, won the next and played a spade to his king and West's ace. West now put her partner in with a club, discarded a spade on the fourth club and received a spade ruff to put the contract two down. It is not often that Kantar takes less tricks than he apparently started with!

We play bridge for a variety of reasons, undoubtedly because it gives us pleasure, but the pleasure comes in a number of different ways—from winning, from taking delight in a wondrous bidding sequence or in a brilliant play, from a magic defense or simply just from throwing cards around at a social occasion with little concern for the outcome. But, in truth, we all like to do the best we can with our talents, given our limitations. Imagine the pleasure West must have felt with the result she achieved on that hand. She was probably hooked on the game for life.

Sometimes the simplest exercise of defense can bring down the high and mighty. We take great pleasure from seeing our gods reduced to mere mortals.

The following deal occurred in one of the Epson Worldwide Bridge Contests, in which the same hands are played simultaneously in clubs all over the world. The defensive play, by an average club player won the worldwide Best Played Hand award. South, the victim, was my wife, then Sally Horton, twice a world champion.

Neither Side Vulnerable. Dealer East.

```
                    ♠ K 8 7 5 4
                    ♥ K Q 8 4 2
                    ♦ –
                    ♣ A Q 2
    ♠ Q 9                           ♠ A 6 3
    ♥ A 6 3                         ♥ J 10 9
    ♦ K Q 8 5 3                     ♦ J 9 2
    ♣ 9 7 6                         ♣ K 8 5 4
                    ♠ J 10 2
                    ♥ 7 5
                    ♦ A 10 7 6 4
                    ♣ J 10 3
```

West	North	East	South
–	–	Pass	Pass
1♦	Dble	1NT	Pass
2♦	Pass	Pass	2♠
Pass	4♠	All Pass	

South's protective bid of two spades was aggressive but she deemed her diamond holding insufficient to do any real damage to two diamonds, so hoped to find a 4-3 spade fit. North, who should have made a second take-out double of two diamonds, was in a bit of a quandary over South's protection of two spades and decided to go for the game bonus.

West led a top diamond which went to declarer's ace. Declarer played a heart to the king and a low heart off the dummy to East's jack. Had this held the trick there would have been no story. Declarer would have ruffed the diamond return, ruffed a heart in hand and run the jack of spades, making her dubious contract because of the particularly favorable trump position. However, West had other ideas. She overtook her partner's jack of hearts with the ace and played another diamond. Declarer ruffed in dummy and still needed to ruff a heart in hand. "Knowing" that West would overruff if she ruffed low, she ruffed a heart with the jack of spades. This promoted a second trump trick for West's queen and, when the king of clubs was wrong, declarer had to go one down.

That deal showed my wife as the bamboozled expert. In 1991 she took part in the Macallan/Sunday Times Invitation Pairs Tournament in London, a last minute substitute for the American, Kerri Shuman. She played with Karen McCallum. The two had never played together before the event and, as the only women in the event, they were not expected to do well. However, their names were mostly to be found on the top half of the leader board and for a while they were lying second. In the following deal she was defending against the world number one, Robert Hamman, who was declarer in a modest two spades.

```
                    ♠ 6 5 3 2
                    ♥ 8 6
                    ♦ A 7 3
                    ♣ K 10 5 4
    ♠ A 8 4                          ♠ J 7
    ♥ K Q J 2                        ♥ 10 7 4 3
    ♦ 2                              ♦ Q J 10 6 4
    ♣ A J 8 7 3                      ♣ 9 2
                    ♠ K Q 10 9
                    ♥ A 9 5
                    ♦ K 9 8 5
                    ♣ Q 6
```

West kicked off with the two of diamonds, won by declarer with the king. The queen of clubs was won by the ace and West played the king of hearts which declarer (wrongly) won with the ace. He played a club to the king and ruffed a club, while East discarded a heart. Declarer then played a diamond towards the ace. West ruffed while East contributed the queen of diamonds, a suit-preference signal suggesting a heart entry. West now played the two of hearts to East's ten and received another diamond ruff. She then played the jack of clubs, enabling East to discard her last heart. When West got in with the ace of spades she played a third heart, allowing East to overruff the dummy. Two spades went one down whereas it had made eight or nine tricks at most other tables.

There are many great players who have argued that defense is the hardest part of the game but the one which gives them the most satisfaction for a job well done. The pleasure is greater because, as well as dealing with two opponents and solving the problem they and the hand pose, you also have to act as a nursemaid to partner. Partners can get in the way and ruin the best laid plans, so defense is not a game for the egoist but for the expert in communication.

Much pleasure is to be derived from a good defense and what is certainly true for most players is that their defense leaves the most room for improvement. Fortunately it is one of the areas where rapid strides can be made.

In this section I seek to illustrate various steps in defense including gathering evidence, what evidence and where from, making a plan, together with a number of techniques that might be considered. Although the hands are categorized to illustrate a particular topic, it is rare that they are to be considered solely under that heading; generally information is obtained from several sources, not just one.

SYSTEM AND CARDING

System

Unless marked to the contrary, please assume throughout this section that both partnerships are playing what has become a standard British system: weak (12-14) no trump, four-card majors (the higher ranking of two four-card suits is opened unless both majors, when one heart would be normal). Acol two bids. Where different methods are used, this will be annotated accordingly.

Leads, signals and discards

For any of the following chapters to be meaningful, there must be an agreement as to our style of leads, signals and discards. There are many different styles in common use at tournament level and they all have their adherents as well as their good and not so good points. In this section some of the deals are presented as they occurred and then whatever method was used at the table is left unchanged; however, many deals are presented as problems and for those we must have a common system of carding. The following is chosen because it is widely played and should be familiar to many readers.

Opening leads

Honor leads

Top of honor sequence (except trick one when the ace and queen ask for attitude while the king asks for count). Against no trumps the king asks for an unblock.

Small cards

Fourth highest from honors, second highest from small cards (including MUD).

Signals and discards

The first priority is to show distribution in the normal manner (i.e. high-low shows and even number). When an attitude is given, a high card encourages. Secondary carding is suit preference (i.e. from 753, first play to 3 to show an odd number, then choose between the 7 and 5 according to suit preference).

When it is clear that length is not important, signals and discards may be attitude or suit preference. Some situations when this applies are:

Against a suit contract when there is a singleton in dummy, suit preference is given; also when it is known that declarer has a singleton;

When a lead has set up a large number of tricks for declarer suit preference is given;

When partner may have led a singleton, suit preference is given;

Where there is clearly some urgency to cash winners and only one discard is available, a high card would ask partner to play that suit;

Some other rare situations like unusual card selection on lead (suit preference, or even attitude).

The Strategy of Defense

In this chapter we discuss the strategy of planning the defense, the steps we go through on every hand, whether it be slam, game or part score, in no trumps or a suit contract, whether it is our lead or partner's. In later chapters we will look at some specific situations, but this one is concerned with good advice which can and *should* be applied on every hand that you ever play.

Before we consider in detail what these steps should be we must define our objective. In tournament play, we concentrate heavily on preventing overtricks or in setting declarer as many tricks as possible. We are not going to assume that each hand is being played in a duplicate game. Here our objective is simply to defeat the contract.

Our intention is to turn every hand into a double-dummy problem or at least a partial one. This means that you have to try to reconstruct the invisible hands. You do this by gathering the evidence that is available from a number of sources: Step 1. Having a good picture of all four hands you can now form a plan to defeat the contract: Step 2. Once you have formed your plan you implement it: Step 3. As each hand progresses you gather more evidence and this may cause you to change your plan. This is a process which should continue throughout the hand, on every hand.

On occasions when you do not know enough about the other hands to form a coherent plan, you need to defend in a flexible and noncommittal manner that will either help you to discover the information you need or at least defer the critical decision until you have that information.

On every hand, you should go through three steps in planning the defense:

> **Gather the evidence**
>
> **Make a plan**
>
> **Implement the plan**

GATHER THE EVIDENCE
The evidence might be found in several areas:

1. The opponents' bidding
2. Your bidding (or lack of it)
3. The strength and distribution of your own hand
4. The sight of dummy
5. Partner's signals
6. Counting—points, distribution and tricks
7. Declarer's line of play

1. The opponents' bidding
There are several things you can learn from the opponents' bidding:

(a) Their general strength—are they minimum or maximum? This is important because there are only two (possibly three if you include deception) types of defense—active and passive.

Consider the following two bidding sequences:

(i)	West	North	East	South
	–	–	–	1NT
	Pass	3NT	All Pass	

On this sequence North/South could have any number of points between them, ranging from 24 to 32. North could have anything from 12 to 18 for his raise to game; South could have 12, 13 or 14.

Suppose West held:

> ♠ J 10 9
> ♥ 8 7 2
> ♦ K J 9 4
> ♣ Q 10 3

After this sequence it would be sensible for him to lead a diamond. If he gives away a trick it may well be declarer's tenth or eleventh anyway. However, it is the best chance to beat the contract. Maybe the full deal is:

                    ♠ K 8 2
                    ♥ A Q 3
                    ♦ Q 5
                    ♣ A J 9 8 4

♠ J 10 9   ♠ 5 4 3
♥ 8 7 2   ♥ 9 6 5
♦ K J 9 4   ♦ A 10 8 7 3
♣ Q 10 3   ♣ 6 5

                    ♠ A Q 7 6
                    ♥ K J 10 4
                    ♦ 6 2
                    ♣ K 7 2

(ii)	West	North	East	South
	–	–	–	1NT
	Pass	2NT	Pass	3NT
	All Pass			

After this sequence it is a different matter altogether. This time the opponents are known to be limited. North has at most 12 and South at most 14. It is probably not necessary to take the first five tricks; and, indeed, it may well be sufficient merely to avoid giving declarer anything. Perhaps the full deal is:

                    ♠ K 8 4
                    ♥ K J 10 3
                    ♦ A 7 6
                    ♣ 8 5 4

♠ J 10 9   ♠ 5 3 2
♥ 8 7 2   ♥ A Q 9
♦ K J 9 4   ♦ 10 8 5 2
♣ Q 10 3   ♣ K 9 2

                    ♠ A Q 7 6
                    ♥ 6 5 4
                    ♦ Q 3
                    ♣ A J 7 6

A diamond is the only lead to give declarer his contract. He wins the lead in hand and plays a heart to the ten and queen. Partner clears the diamonds and declarer knocks out the ace of hearts. The defense will make a couple of tricks in each red suit but then declarer will have nine tricks—four spades, two hearts, two diamonds and a club. Absolutely best for the defense is a club lead to the king and ace. Declarer can knock out the queen of hearts and East can switch to diamonds.

When declarer knocks out the ace of hearts, the defenders can cash diamonds ending up with East on lead and a club through will result in a three-trick defeat.

However, I am not suggesting a club lead—that is also much too dangerous. The lead that is most unlikely to give anything away is a spade. Although not quite so dynamic as a club, it does its job and there is no way for declarer to come to nine tricks.

Often it is not until dummy comes down that you can see whether or not your opponents have values in hand. After sequence (i) above, partner may make an aggressive lead, only to find that dummy is very minimal, for example:

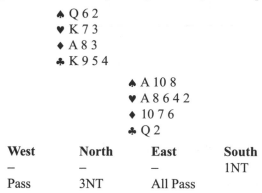

                    ♠ Q 6 2
                    ♥ K 7 3
                    ♦ A 8 3
                    ♣ K 9 5 4

                          ♠ A 10 8
                          ♥ A 8 6 4 2
                          ♦ 10 7 6
                          ♣ Q 2

West	North	East	South
–	–	–	1NT
Pass	3NT	All Pass	

Your partner leads the two of diamonds. Declarer plays low from dummy and wins your ten with his queen. He then plays a spade to dummy's queen, partner playing the three. Plan the defense.

Gather the evidence: Partner has made an aggressive opening lead in a four-card minor. It would be normal for him to prefer a major after the opponents have failed to use Stayman, so he probably does not have a four-card major. He may have chosen a diamond because he thought his opponents were unlimited, but you can see that dummy has overbid when he raised to 3NT and it is quite possible that they are too high. Declarer is probably 4-3-3-3 or 4-2-3-4.

Make a plan: You are obviously going to win the ace of spades, but then you must decide whether to switch to a heart or continue with diamonds. Were the 1NT opening to have been strong (15-17) it would have been clear to switch to a heart. You know that by continuing diamonds you can see at most four defensive tricks (two diamonds and two major-suit aces), so you must hope for miracles in the heart suit—perhaps declarer's hand is:

                    ♠ K J 5 4
                    ♥ Q 10
                    ♦ K Q 9
                    ♣ A 10 6 3

However, when the no trump is weak there is no need to be so aggressive because the combined values of the opponents are less, perhaps only 24 points, compared to the minimum of 27 if the no trump were strong. It is quite possible that declarer has only eight tricks anyway and it would be foolish to give him a ninth when his heart holding is Qxx.

Implement the plan: Return the seven of diamonds. The full deal:

```
              ♠ Q 6 2
              ♥ K 7 3
              ♦ A 8 3
              ♣ K 9 5 4
♠ 9 7 3                      ♠ A 10 8
♥ J 5                        ♥ A 8 6 4 2
♦ K J 5 2                    ♦ 10 7 6
♣ J 10 7 6                   ♣ Q 2
              ♠ K J 5 4
              ♥ Q 10 9
              ♦ Q 9 4
              ♣ A 8 3
```

If you switch to a heart, declarer cannot help but make two heart tricks for his contract. If you continue with diamonds he may play a heart to the ten for his ninth trick or he may try ducking a club, neither of which will work. Of course, it is quite possible that declarer will guess hearts correctly but there is nothing you can do about that.

If your partner discards a club on the fourth spade, you must be careful to unblock the queen of clubs or declarer would be able to force you to win the club trick and you will not be able to cash partner's long diamond, the fifth defensive trick.

(b) Their distribution—the extent to which their bidding gives this away varies tremendously

Some bridge players believe that the auction is about bidding what they think they can make, perhaps with an effort at deflecting the killing opening lead on the way. Those same players do not like to play many signals in defense on the grounds that it will help declarer.

Others try hard to describe their hands to each other as accurately as possible, both in the bidding and during the defense. They argue that they would prefer to bid to their best contract and beat every contract that is beatable; if they help their opposition along the way, so be it. There is no right or wrong style; it is a matter of philosophy.

By nature I tend towards the second school, but I am a great respecter of the first. However, the one thing that I do know is that when I am defending, particularly when I am on lead, I much prefer to be playing against the scientists.

Here is an example of too much bidding merely aiding the defending side:

```
              ♠ K Q J 8
              ♥ 8 7 6
              ♦ K J 10 7 6
              ♣ 6
              ♠ 4
              ♥ A K 4 3
              ♦ A Q 8 5 4
              ♣ 7 3 2
```

Table 1

West	North	East	South
–	–	–	1♠
Pass	4♠	All Pass	

West leads the five of hearts to your king, declarer playing the jack. Plan the defense.

Gather the evidence: You do not know very much about declarer's hand, but there seem to be fair chances of four defensive tricks.

Make a plan: The best chance seems to be to hope for two tricks in each red suit.

Implement the plan: Play the ace of hearts.

Table 2

West	North	East	South
–	–	–	1♠
Pass	2♦	Pass	3♦
Pass	4♠	All Pass	

Again, West leads the five of hearts to your king, declarer playing the jack. Plan the defense.

Gather the evidence: Declarer surely has three-card diamond support, so partner is marked with a void.

Make a plan: You can more or less guarantee the defeat of the contract by giving partner a diamond ruff. You cannot afford to play the ace and a low diamond because then partner will be ruffing a loser, but if you give partner a low diamond ruff now, you should later make the ace and queen.

Implement the plan: Play the eight of diamonds. The full deal:

```
              ♠ K Q J 8
              ♥ 8 7 6
              ♦ K J 10 7 6
              ♣ 6
♠ 10 7 5                     ♠ 4
♥ Q 10 9 5 2                 ♥ A K 4 3
♦ –                          ♦ A Q 8 5 4
♣ J 9 8 5 4                  ♣ 7 3 2
              ♠ A 9 6 3 2
              ♥ J
              ♦ 9 3 2
              ♣ A K Q 10
```

(c) Their weak points and their strong points
East/West Vulnerable. Dealer North.

```
              ♠ Q J 8 5 4
              ♥ 9 4
              ♦ K Q 2
              ♣ A 4 3
♠ A K 3 2
♥ A Q 10
♦ 6 5 4 3
♣ 7 2
```

West	North	East	South
–	1♠	Pass	2♣
Pass	2♠	Pass	3♣
Pass	3♦	Pass	5♣
All Pass			

You lead the king of spades against South's five clubs. Partner plays the six and declarer the nine. Plan the defense.

Gather the evidence: Declarer's three club bid was highly encouraging but non-forcing. After his partner moved on with three diamonds he liked his hand sufficiently to jump to five clubs. He must have a very good club suit and presumably no heart stopper or he would have tried for 3NT.

Make a plan: The plan is to cash your two heart tricks.

Implement the plan: Cash the ace of hearts, expecting to continue with the queen when partner plays an encouraging card.

The full deal:

```
              ♠ Q J 8 5 4
              ♥ 9 4
              ♦ K Q 2
              ♣ A 4 3
♠ A K 3 2                    ♠ 10 7 6
♥ A Q 10                     ♥ K J 7 6 3 2
♦ 6 5 4 3                    ♦ 8 7
♣ 7 2                        ♣ 9 8
              ♠ 9
              ♥ 8 5
              ♦ A J 10 9
              ♣ K Q J 10 6 5
```

Slam auctions often give away a great deal of information; in particular you should consider why your opponents have or have not used Blackwood.

Both Sides Vulnerable. Dealer North.

```
              ♠ K J 6
              ♥ J 8 6
              ♦ A Q
              ♣ A 8 5 4 2
                            ♠ A 10 8 7 2
                            ♥ 5 3
                            ♦ 7 4 2
                            ♣ J 9 3
```

West	North	East	South
–	1♣	Pass	1♦
Pass	1NT	Pass	2♥
Pass	2NT	Pass	3♥
Pass	4♥	Pass	6♥
All Pass			

West leads the king of clubs to dummy's ace. Dummy plays the six of spades. Plan the defense. Do you play the ace or a low card?

Gather the evidence: You know from the bidding that declarer has six diamonds and five hearts. Why has he not used Blackwood? Is it not more likely that he holds two clubs and a void spade than two singletons (and it is only wrong to duck the spade when he has the singleton queen).

Make a plan: You believe that declarer has a void spade and that you will present him with a trick in the suit if you go in with the ace. You must hope that you are going to come to one trick in clubs and one in trumps.

Implement the plan: Play a low spade. Declarer ruffs and eventually has to lose a trump and a club. The full deal:

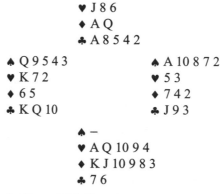

```
              ♠ K J 6
              ♥ J 8 6
              ♦ A Q
              ♣ A 8 5 4 2
♠ Q 9 5 4 3                  ♠ A 10 8 7 2
♥ K 7 2                      ♥ 5 3
♦ 6 5                        ♦ 7 4 2
♣ K Q 10                     ♣ J 9 3
              ♠ –
              ♥ A Q 10 9 4
              ♦ K J 10 9 8 3
              ♣ 7 6
```

2. Your bidding (or lack of it)

There are often some strong inferences to be made from partner's failure to bid, particularly when you know he has most of the defensive strength.

Neither Side Vulnerable. Dealer West.

```
              ♠ A K J 10
              ♥ 8 7 3
              ♦ Q 8 7
              ♣ 8 7 3
                            ♠ Q 6 5 3
                            ♥ 6 5 2
                            ♦ 9 4 2
                            ♣ 6 5 2
```

West	North	East	South
Pass	Pass	Pass	1♦
Pass	1♠	Pass	2NT
Pass	3NT	All Pass	

West leads the seven of spades. Declarer plays the jack from dummy and you win with the queen. Plan the defense.

Gather the evidence: Partner clearly has near opening values, say 10 points or so, but has passed twice, once as dealer and once when he failed to overcall. You are on lead for the one and only time.

Make a plan: Partner has chosen a passive lead when the opponents could be fairly strong and when he surely knows he holds most of your side's defensive tricks. The most likely reason for this is that he holds tenaces in all the other suits. Should you switch to a heart or a club? There is not much to go on, but if partner had a good four-card heart suit he may have chosen to overcall. He would never overcall two clubs with a four-card suit.

Implement the plan: Play the five of clubs. The full deal:

```
                ♠ A K J 10
                ♥ 8 7 3
                ♦ Q 8 7
                ♣ 8 7 3
    ♠ 9 7 4                    ♠ Q 6 5 3
    ♥ K 10 4                   ♥ 6 5 2
    ♦ K J 3                    ♦ 9 4 2
    ♣ K J 10 4                 ♣ 6 5 2
                ♠ 8 2
                ♥ A Q J 9
                ♦ A 10 6 5
                ♣ A Q 9
```

There is no guarantee that your defense will succeed but it is your best chance. It all depends on what declarer plays from hand on your club switch. As the cards lie he would succeed if he played the ace or the nine, but many players would play the queen. After all, why should he not take this finesse when he has so few entries to dummy? He does not know that your partner holds all the defensive strength. Looking at that dummy, it would be natural for you to switch to hearts or clubs whatever your hand.

3. The strength and distribution of your own hand

Whenever you hold either a very weak hand or a very strong defensive hand, you can make some accurate guesses about the other hands when you have seen the dummy.

```
                ♠ Q 10 6
                ♥ 9 8 5
                ♦ A K Q J 4
                ♣ A Q
                           ♠ A K 4
                           ♥ A K 6
                           ♦ 7 6 3 2
                           ♣ 8 7 3
```

West	North	East	South
–	1♦	Pass	1NT
Pass	3NT	All Pass	

Your partner leads the seven of spades. Declarer plays low from dummy and you win the king while declarer plays the nine. Plan the defense.

Gather the evidence: Here you can see all but eight points. Declarer will surely have most of them so there is little room for partner to have any high cards. Presumably declarer has the king of clubs, in which case he needs only the ten of diamonds or the jack of clubs to have nine tricks—one spade, five diamonds and three clubs.

Make a plan: The only chance is to take heart tricks now (three or more). It could be right to lead a low heart, hoping declarer will go wrong when he has Q10x. The trouble with this is that sometimes he will have Qx and be forced to do the right thing. If you knew how many hearts he held you would know what to do: if he had five you would play them from the top, if he had four you would play an honor and follow with a low one, hoping he might go wrong with Q10x.

Implement the plan: Play the king of hearts to obtain count. Continue with the ace of hearts if partner plays small, hoping he has five, or with a low heart if he plays high. The full deal:

```
                ♠ Q 10 6
                ♥ 9 8 5
                ♦ A K Q J 4
                ♣ A Q
    ♠ 8 7 5 3 2                ♠ A K 4
    ♥ 10 7 4 3 2               ♥ A K 6
    ♦ 8                        ♦ 7 6 3 2
    ♣ 4 2                      ♣ 8 7 3
                ♠ J 9
                ♥ Q J
                ♦ 10 9 5
                ♣ K J 10 9 6 5
```

4. Study the dummy

After your opening lead you should review your plan in the light of dummy.

East/West Vulnerable. Dealer West.

West holds:

```
                ♠ 7 4
                ♥ A K J 10 6 2
                ♦ 10 8
                ♣ A J 10
```

West	North	East	South
1♥	3♥(*)	Pass	3NT
All Pass			

(*) Asks for a heart stopper

Gather the evidence: North has suggested that his side might make game if South has a heart stopper. This bid is ideally based on nine tricks including a running suit, but at this vulnerability it could be semi-pre-emptive and based on slightly fewer tricks.

Make a plan: You don't expect partner to have many high cards and South surely has the queen of hearts, but you can do no better than lead a high heart—perhaps a look at dummy will help you decide. You are not optimistic, but the lead is noncommittal.

Implement the plan: Lead the king of hearts, asking partner to unblock.

Dummy is a disappointment since you cannot afford to give declarer a heart trick:

♠ A K
♥ 8 5
♦ A K Q J 9 7
♣ 7 4 2

Dummy plays the five of hearts, partner the seven and declarer the three.

Reconsider: If declarer wins a trick in his hand there are eight more tricks in dummy for his contract. What are your options? Partner's heart cannot be from a three-card holding—if he had Q97 he would have unblocked the queen. You could play partner for the king of clubs by switching to a club but you can do better than that. You can endplay the dummy by cashing a second heart and playing a spade or a diamond. East must have a club honor or declarer can always make his contract.

Implement the plan: Cash the ace of hearts and play a spade. When declarer cashes his winners he will squeeze his hand; when he eventually plays a club he will have come down to king doubleton and the queen of hearts and you will be able to take three club tricks. The full deal:

```
              ♠ A K
              ♥ 8 5
              ♦ A K Q J 9 7
              ♣ 7 4 2
♠ 7 4                      ♠ 10 8 5 3 2
♥ A K J 10 6 2             ♥ 7
♦ 10 8                     ♦ 6 4 3
♣ A J 10                   ♣ Q 8 6 3
              ♠ Q J 9 6
              ♥ Q 9 4 3
              ♦ 5 2
              ♣ K 9 5
```

5. Partner's signals

As the play develops you will gain more evidence from partner's signals.

Perhaps the most basic form of signalling is the distributional signal, for example to play high-low from a doubleton when partner leads a top honor against a suit contract.

Neither Side Vulnerable. Dealer North.

```
              ♠ A 7 4
              ♥ A 10 3
              ♦ Q J 3
              ♣ K Q 10 6
♠ 6 5                      ♠ 9 3
♥ J 7 6                    ♥ Q 9 5 4 2
♦ A K 7 6 2                ♦ 10 4
♣ 5 4 3                    ♣ A 9 8 7
              ♠ K Q J 10 8 2
              ♥ K 8
              ♦ 9 8 5
              ♣ J 2
```

West	North	East	South
–	1♣	Pass	1♠
Pass	1NT	Pass	4♠
All Pass			

Most Wests would choose to lead the ace of diamonds. If partner always followed suit with his lowest card, they would have to decide whether to give partner a diamond ruff or whether the lay-out of the red suits was:

```
              ♥ A 10 3
              ♦ Q 8 3
♥ J 7 6                    ♥ K 9 5 4 2
♦ A K 7 6 2                ♦ 10 5 4
              ♥ Q 8
              ♦ J 9
```

In this case a diamond continuation would merely set up a heart discard for declarer. Luckily, this particular guesswork is removed since even beginners are taught early to play high-low from a doubleton.

In other situations it is better to play suit-preference signals, that is a method whereby a high card asks partner to play the higher suit (usually excluding trumps) and a low card asks partner to switch to the lower suit. One situation in which such signals are very useful is when an honor is led against a suit contract and there is a singleton in the dummy. Here, generally speaking, other kinds of information are less useful.

Neither Side Vulnerable. Dealer West.

```
              ♠ A K 9 7 2
              ♥ 7
              ♥ 9 6 3
              ♣ A 6 5 4
                           ♠ 8 3
                           ♥ Q J 10 6 4 2
                           ♦ K J 10 7
                           ♣ 8
```

West	North	East	South
1♥	Dble	4♥	4♠
All Pass			

After an eccentric take-out double from North, South is declarer in four spades. Partner leads the ace of hearts. Plan the defense.

Gather the evidence: South may well have good distribution for his four spade bid. He probably does not have great length in spades since you can see seven of them and partner's bidding has not suggested extreme spade shortage (i.e. he did not press on to five hearts). He may have a second suit.

Make a plan: If declarer has a second suit of clubs it may be important to set up diamond tricks quickly and you wish to suggest to partner that he switch to a diamond now. Since dummy has a singleton heart, partner will be expecting you to give him a suit-preference signal.

Implement the plan: Play the queen of hearts, asking partner to switch to a diamond. The full deal:

```
              ♠ A K 9 7 2
              ♥ 7
              ♦ 9 6 3
              ♣ A 6 5 4
♠ 5 4                        ♠ 8 3
♥ A K 8 5 3                  ♥ Q J 10 6 4 2
♦ Q 8 5                      ♦ K J 10 7
♣ Q J 10                     ♣ 8
              ♠ Q J 10 6
              ♥ 9
              ♦ A 4 2
              ♣ K 9 7 3 2
```

Here you had a clear preference for partner to switch to a diamond so your signal was straightforward. Had you held no honor card in the minors, or indeed, equal holdings, you would have played a middle heart and left it to him to work out what to do.

The other major type of signal that we may use is the "attitude" signal. When using this method, a high card encourages partner to continue the suit that he has led and a low card discourages or shows no interest in the suit led. As was recommended earlier, an attitude signal should be given when partner leads an ace or a queen other than at trick one.

There are variations in these signalling methods and, indeed, other methods that you may wish to experiment with, but what is important is that you and your partner know what your methods are. I would suggest that you play distributional signals all the time until you are confident with them and then add other methods, but only in situations that are clearly defined and agreed.

6. Counting—points, distribution and tricks

(a) Counting points
Neither Side Vulnerable. Dealer East.

```
              ♠ 9 8 3
              ♥ J 8 6 5
              ♦ Q 9
              ♣ A K J 4
♠ 7 6
♥ Q 10 4 3
♦ A J 7 6 2
♣ 8 3
```

West	North	East	South
–	–	1NT	2♠
Pass	3♠	All Pass	

You lead the three of hearts which partner wins with the ace and declarer plays the two. Partner returns the seven to declarer's king. Declarer plays a club to dummy's king and the nine of spades, which holds, a spade to his queen and then the nine of hearts which you win, partner discarding the three of diamonds. Plan the defense.

Gather the evidence: If declarer has six spades the contract is unbeatable, so you must assume he has only five. What is his distribution in the minors? If he had three clubs he would have drawn the last trump before playing a heart, thus establishing the jack of hearts for a club discard. Therefore he is 3-5-3-2. Who has the king of diamonds? Partner has shown at most nine points, king of spades, ace of hearts, queen of clubs, and so he must have it to make up his 1NT opening.

Make a plan: In addition to the two heart tricks you already have, you must hope to take two diamonds. The fifth defensive trick will come when you play a third round of diamonds and partner overruffs the dummy. Partner's discard of the three of diamonds is consistent with this analysis.

Implement the plan: Play a low diamond to partner's king. The full deal:

```
              ♠ 9 8 3
              ♥ J 8 6 5
              ♦ Q 9
              ♣ A K J 4
♠ 7 6                        ♠ K 5 2
♥ Q 10 4 3                   ♥ A 7
♦ A J 7 6 2                  ♦ K 8 3
♣ 8 3                        ♣ Q 10 9 5 2
              ♠ A Q J 10 4
              ♥ K 9 2
              ♦ 10 5 4
              ♣ 7 6
```

(b) Counting distribution

♠ A 8 7
♥ J 7
♦ J 3
♣ K Q 10 9 3 2

                    ♠ K 2
                    ♥ Q 9 6
                    ♦ A Q 10 5
                    ♣ A 8 6 5

West	North	East	South
–	–	–	1NT
Pass	3NT	All Pass	

Partner leads the three of spades. Declarer plays low from dummy and your king wins the first trick, declarer playing the five. Plan the defense.

Gather the evidence: You can tell from the opening lead that both West and South have four spades. Partner would normally lead his longest suit against no trumps hence West has at most four hearts, leaving South with a minimum of four hearts. If West has no suit of longer than four cards he cannot have a void anywhere, therefore South cannot have three cards in clubs, nor normally will he have a singleton to open 1NT. Hence South's distribution is 4-4-3-2.

Make a plan: Superficially, it looks attractive to return a spade, hoping partner has the queen, thus removing declarer's entry to the club suit. However, this will not work if declarer has the queen of spades. Much better, you have just worked out that partner's distribution is 4-4-4-1 and there is an alternative line of defense which guarantees success.

Implement the plan: Switch to the ace and queen of diamonds. When you get in with a club you will have two more diamonds to cash. The full deal:

♠ A 8 7
♥ J 7
♦ J 3
♣ K Q 10 9 3 2

♠ J 9 4 3   ♠ K 2
♥ 10 9 8 2   ♥ Q 9 6
♦ 8 7 6 4   ♦ A Q 10 5
♣ 4   ♣ A 8 6 5

♠ Q 10 6 5
♥ A K 4 3
♦ K 9 2
♣ J 7

(c) Counting tricks
North/South Vulnerable. Dealer North.

♠ K 10 3
♥ 8 4
♦ A K Q J 6 5
♣ Q 10

                    ♠ A J 5 4
                    ♥ K 7 6
                    ♦ 10 9 3
                    ♣ K 7 3

West	North	East	South
–	1♦	Pass	1♥
Pass	3♦	Pass	3NT
All Pass			

Partner leads the five of clubs. Dummy plays the ten and declarer takes your king with his ace. Declarer plays a spade to dummy's king. Plan the defense.

Gather the evidence: Declarer surely has the queen of spades, in which case you can count his nine tricks—six diamonds, two clubs and one spade. You must take four tricks immediately.

Make a plan: The only chance to beat the contract is to take four tricks in hearts. This will need partner to hold AJ9x or AJ10x.

Implement the plan: Play the six of hearts. Partner wins and plays a low heart back to your king. You play a third round through declarer's tenace. If you play the king first, and then the seven, declarer will simply duck and you will not be able to take more than three tricks in the suit. The full deal:

♠ K 10 3
♥ 8 4
♦ A K Q J 6 5
♣ Q 10

♠ 8 7 6   ♠ A J 5 4
♥ A J 9 5   ♥ K 7 6
♦ 2   ♦ 10 9 3
♣ J 9 6 5 2   ♣ K 7 3

♠ Q 9 2
♥ Q 10 3 2
♦ 8 7 4
♣ A 8 4

7. Observing declarer's line of play

```
        ♠ Q J 6 2
        ♥ K Q 5 2
        ♦ A J
        ♣ Q 8 3
♠ K 8
♥ 9 8 3
♦ 6 4 2
♣ J 10 9 5 2
```

West	North	East	South
–	–	–	1♦
Pass	1♥	Pass	1♠
Pass	4♠	Pass	4NT
Pass	5♦	Pass	6♠
All Pass			

You lead the jack of clubs to the queen, king and ace. Declarer plays a diamond to the ace and runs the queen of spades to your king. Plan the defense.

Gather the evidence: Declarer is known to have at most nine points in his two longest suits. He probably has considerably more distribution than the minimum of five diamonds and four spades he has shown on the bidding.

Make a plan: If declarer had a losing club and the ace of hearts he would have cashed the ace of hearts, crossed to the ace of diamonds and discarded his club loser on a heart before taking the trump finesse; if he had a losing club and a void heart (unlikely given his use of Blackwood) he would have used his diamond entries to take a ruffing heart finesse before taking the trump finesse. The only trick we could have which might disappear is the ace of hearts.

Implement the plan: Play the eight of hearts. The full deal:

```
              ♠ Q J 6 2
              ♥ K Q 5 2
              ♦ A J
              ♣ Q 8 3
♠ K 8                    ♠ 7 3
♥ 9 8 3                  ♥ A J 10 7 4
♦ 6 4 2                  ♦ 7 5
♣ J 10 9 5 2            ♣ K 7 6 4
              ♠ A 10 9 5 4
              ♥ 6
              ♦ K Q 10 9 8 3
              ♣ A
```

Note declarer's shrewd play of the queen of clubs at trick one. This was a fine piece of deception that would have succeeded against many defenders.

North/South Vulnerable. Dealer East.

```
        ♠ K 6
        ♥ 8 7 4
        ♦ A J 4 2
        ♣ A K 4 2
♠ A 9
♥ J 9 6 5 2
♦ Q 6
♣ J 8 7 3
```

West	North	East	South
–	–	Pass	1NT
Pass	3NT	All Pass	

You lead the five of hearts to partner's queen and declarer's king. He now plays the queen, king and ace of clubs, while your partner follows twice and then discards the three of spades. Declarer cashes the ace of diamonds and plays a diamond to his ten and your queen. Plan the defense.

Gather the evidence: Declarer must have four diamonds, otherwise he has cut himself off from his long diamond trick since he doesn't know the king of spades is an entry. Partner's spade discard suggests a five-card suit, so declarer has four spades and he has shown up with three clubs exactly. Therefore he can only have two hearts.

Make a plan: You must continue hearts, knocking out declarer's ace. When you gain the lead with the ace of spades you will be able to cash three heart tricks.

Implement the plan: Play the two of hearts. The full deal:

```
              ♠ K 6
              ♥ 8 7 4
              ♦ A J 4 2
              ♣ A K 4 2
♠ A 9                    ♠ Q 10 5 4 3
♥ J 9 6 5 2              ♥ Q 10 3
♦ Q 6                    ♦ 8 7 3
♣ J 8 7 3              ♣ 10 6
              ♠ J 8 7 2
              ♥ A K
              ♦ K 10 9 5
              ♣ Q 9 5
```

MAKE A PLAN

You have seen a number of ways in which you can gather evidence. That was Step 1. Having obtained a good picture of the opponents' hands, you can now form a plan to defeat the contract—Step 2. There are several elements to consider when we are making a plan:

1. Assume the contract can be defeated
2. Play partner for the minimum
3. Technique
4. Flexibility

1. Assume the contract can be defeated

As stated earlier, the objective is to defeat the contract. (Having said that, some of the expert hands at the end of each chapter are concerned with taking as many tricks as possible.) If your aim is to defeat the contract you must always assume that it is possible to do so.

Neither Side Vulnerable. Dealer West.

```
             ♠ 8 6 2
             ♥ 9 5
             ♦ K J 10
             ♣ A Q J 7 4
♠ A Q 5
♥ A Q J 7 6
♦ Q 9 6
♣ 6 2
```

West	North	East	South
1♥	Pass	Pass	1♠
Pass	2♣	2♥	Pass
Pass	2♠	Pass	Pass
3♥	Pass	Pass	3♠
All Pass			

You lead the ace of hearts, partner following with the three and declarer with the four. Plan the defense.

Gather the evidence: Partner has few values since he passed one heart. You can expect an ace at most.

Make a plan: You cannot defeat the contract if partner has the king of spades (three spades and a heart), the ace of diamonds (two spades, a diamond and a heart) or the king of clubs (two spades, a heart and a club). If you are to assume you can beat the contract, you must play partner for the king of hearts so there is the possibility of three heart tricks to go with the two spades you already know about. You need to draw dummy's trumps and be on lead when you have done so.

Implement the plan: Lead the five of spades. When partner wins the king of hearts he will play a spade through declarer. The full deal:

```
             ♠ 8 6 2
             ♥ 9 5
             ♦ K J 10
             ♣ A Q J 7 4
♠ A Q 5            ♠ 4 3
♥ A Q J 7 6        ♥ K 8 3
♦ Q 9 6            ♦ 8 5 3 2
♣ 6 2             ♣ 10 9 8 3
             ♠ K J 10 9 7
             ♥ 10 4 2
             ♦ A 7 4
             ♣ K 5
```

2. Play partner for the minimum

This means you should play him for the most likely, e.g. you would play him for one card, say the king of spades, rather than another card *and* a specific suit length, say the queen of diamonds *and* four hearts.

Neither Side Vulnerable. Dealer West.

```
             ♠ Q 4
             ♥ K 7 5
             ♦ 4 3 2
             ♣ K Q 8 5 3
                        ♠ 6 5
                        ♥ 9 8 2
                        ♦ A Q J 10 7 5
                        ♣ A 10
```

West	North	East	South
Pass	Pass	3♦	3♠
Pass	4♠	All Pass	

Your partner leads the king of diamonds. You overtake with the ace and continue with the queen, South and West both following. Plan the defense.

Gather the evidence: Dummy is maximum in high cards but minimum in trump support.

Make a plan: It is possible that partner holds a slow heart trick and that four spades will go down if you defend passively—however, he will also need enough in clubs to prevent declarer running that suit; the other possibility is that partner holds a promotable trump trick, Jxx or 10xxx. Play partner for the minimum needed and go for the trump promotion, but remember to cash your outside winner(s) first.

Implement the plan: Cash the ace of clubs and then play a diamond. The full deal:

```
             ♠ Q 4
             ♥ K 7 5
             ♦ 4 3 2
             ♣ K Q 8 5 3
♠ J 9 2           ♠ 6 5
♥ 10 4 3          ♥ 9 8 2
♦ K 6            ♦ A Q J 10 7 5
♣ J 9 7 4 2       ♣ A 10
             ♠ A K 10 8 7 3
             ♥ A Q J 6
             ♦ 9 8
             ♣ 6
```

3. Technique

At a minimum you need a basic knowledge of the simpler techniques. Many of these are described in later chapters. To give you a taste of more advanced techniques, here is one which is covered in more detail in a later section.

North/South Vulnerable. Dealer West.

```
            ♠ 7 6 3
            ♥ A K 8 5
            ♦ K 6 3
            ♣ J 7 2
♠ K Q 10
♥ J 2
♦ Q J 8 5 4
♣ Q 9 3
```

West	North	East	South
Pass	Pass	Pass	1♠
Pass	2♣(*)	Pass	2♦(**)
Pass	3♠	Pass	4♠
All Pass			

(*) Drury, showing a maximum pass with three-card trump support

(**) Artificial, showing genuine opening values

You decide to lead the queen of diamonds against South's four spades. This runs around to declarer's ace, partner playing the seven. Declarer now plays a low trump. Plan the defense.

Gather the evidence: It looks as if your diamond lead has not been a great success. While it is possible that partner has failed to high/low with a 10 7 doubleton, it is more likely that he has a small doubleton or singleton seven.

Make a plan: If partner has a doubleton there is nothing you can do about it, but if he has a singleton you may be able to give him a ruff. When it comes to trump tricks, it does not really matter which trump you play on this round because they are effectively equal. However, if you are going to give partner a ruff, you must be the one on lead at trick three.

Implement the plan: Play the queen of spades. The full deal:

```
            ♠ 7 6 3
            ♥ A K 8 5
            ♦ K 6 3
            ♣ J 7 2
♠ K Q 10          ♠ A J
♥ J 2             ♥ 10 9 7 6 4 3
♦ Q J 8 5 4       ♦ 7
♣ Q 9 3           ♣ 10 8 6 4
            ♠ 9 8 5 4 2
            ♥ Q
            ♦ A 10 9 2
            ♣ A K 5
```

Had you played the ten of spades, partner would have had to win the jack and there would have been no defense. Since it was your queen that "swallowed" partner's jack, you could then give him a ruff with his ace.

This defensive play is called the Crocodile Coup because West had to "open his jaws and swallow up his partner's jack." It can occur in many guises.

4. Flexibility

"Don't put all your eggs in one basket" or "keep your options open" or "avoid guesswork" or "delay your decision for as long as possible" are all examples of flexibility, as it is used here.

Neither Side Vulnerable. Dealer South.

```
            ♠ 7 4
            ♥ J 10 6 5
            ♦ J 9 8 7
            ♣ 10 7 5
                  ♠ A 9
                  ♥ A Q 9 8 7
                  ♦ 6 4
                  ♣ 9 6 4 3
```

West	North	East	South
–	–	–	1♠
Pass	Pass	2♥	2♠
All Pass			

Your partner leads the king of hearts, followed by another heart to the ten and your queen, declarer following both times. Plan the defense.

Gather the evidence: You can count on two tricks in hearts and one in trumps. Thus partner needs at least two tricks in the minors and another trick from somewhere—perhaps a trump promotion—if you are to defeat the contract.

Make a plan: One problem is that you have no idea whether partner's outside tricks are in clubs or diamonds and it could be fatal to shift to the wrong suit. Since dummy has no entry there is no need to guess. You can afford to set up dummy's jack of hearts and await further information from partner.

Implement the plan: Play the ace of hearts. Declarer will ruff high while partner shows you attitude in the minors, in this instance discarding the ten of diamonds. Declarer continues with the king of spades, which you win with the ace to play a diamond. Partner cashes the ace and queen of diamonds and plays a third round of the suit which you will ruff with the nine of spades to promote partner's eight of trumps. The full deal:

```
        ♠ 7 4
        ♥ J 10 6 5
        ♦ J 9 8 7
        ♣ 10 7 5
♠ 8 3 2            ♠ A 9
♥ K 3             ♥ A Q 9 8 7
♦ A Q 10 5 3       ♦ 6 4
♣ J 8 2           ♣ 9 6 4 3
        ♠ K Q J 10 6 5
        ♥ 4 2
        ♦ K 2
        ♣ A K Q
```

Suppose instead that the full deal were:

```
        ♠ 7 4
        ♥ J 10 6 5
        ♦ J 9 8 7
        ♣ 10 7 5
♠ 8 3 2            ♠ A 9
♥ K 3             ♥ A Q 9 8 7
♦ Q 10 5 3 2       ♦ 6 4
♣ A Q J           ♣ 9 6 4 3
        ♠ K Q J 10 6 5
        ♥ 4 2
        ♦ A K
        ♣ K 8 2
```

Now partner would discard a low diamond on the queen of hearts and you would switch to a club.

It is important that your club switch should indicate to partner whether you hold an honor. On the hand you hold, partner must put you in with a trump for you to lead another club; had you held the king of clubs instead of the ace of spades, if would have been necessary to play three rounds of clubs ending in your hand and then a fourth club in the hope that it would promote a trump trick with partner holding, say, Jxx in spades.

You would switch to a low club if you held an honor. Without an honor you must switch to a higher card—often the second highest would be sufficient, but it is usually clearer to switch to the highest card. Here, if you switched to the six and declarer played the two, partner might think you had started with K986.

Sometimes you may not be able to invent a plan which will lead to the defeat of the contract, in which case you have to persuade declarer to go down. One of the more exciting and rewarding areas of the game is to paint a false picture of the hand so that declarer is bewitched into error. Techniques of this kind are known as deceptive plays, again a subject for a later section, but here is a sample:

Neither Side Vulnerable. Dealer North.

```
        ♠ A J 5
        ♥ Q 9
        ♦ A J 10 4 2
        ♣ K 10 7
                    ♠ 10 9 6 3
                    ♥ 10 7 2
                    ♦ 9 8
                    ♣ A 8 5 3
```

West	North	East	South
–	1♦	Pass	1♠
2♥	Dble(*)	Pass	3♥
Pass	3♠	Pass	4♠
All Pass			

(*) 15-18 balanced

Partner leads the ace of hearts. Plan the defense.

Gather the evidence: The bidding does not leave a great deal of strength for partner—a good heart suit and little else since South has shown at least near opening values. In any case, any club or diamond honors partner may have will be well placed for declarer, leaving two hearts and a club for the defense. The only possible weak spot is the trump suit.

Make a plan: If West holds any trump honor, then the contract will go down whatever you do, but if declarer's trump holding is more solid, maybe he can be given a false picture of the hand and therefore be persuaded to squander one of his honors.

Implement the plan: Play the ten of hearts at trick one, followed by the two at trick two. Everyone will think you have a doubleton. Partner will continue with a third heart, hoping you can overruff the dummy and that is what you hope declarer will think as well. Put yourself in declarer's shoes. Wouldn't you ruff with the jack of spades? The full deal:

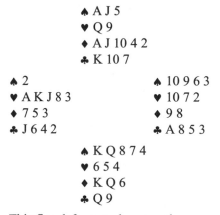

```
        ♠ A J 5
        ♥ Q 9
        ♦ A J 10 4 2
        ♣ K 10 7
♠ 2               ♠ 10 9 6 3
♥ A K J 8 3        ♥ 10 7 2
♦ 7 5 3           ♦ 9 8
♣ J 6 4 2         ♣ A 8 5 3
        ♠ K Q 8 7 4
        ♥ 6 5 4
        ♦ K Q 6
        ♣ Q 9
```

This fine defense and many others are also illustrated in the section of this book on signalling.

IMPLEMENT THE PLAN

You've gathered the data, Step 1, analyzed it and formed a plan, Step 2. Now you have to implement the plan, Step 3. What can go wrong? Well, it is *your* plan and you must never forget this because partner might have formed a different plan. When you know how to beat a contract, it is essential to insure that partner follows your plan and sometimes you may have to achieve this by deliberately deceiving him. At other times you must find some order of playing your cards to make it clear to partner what you need him to do. This theme can become quite complicated.

North/South Vulnerable. Dealer North.

```
              ♠ K 10 6 2
              ♥ J 7 3
              ♦ A Q
              ♣ K J 10 3
                              ♠ 9 8 5 3
                              ♥ A 5
                              ♦ J 9 6 5 3 2
                              ♣ A
```

West	North	East	South
–	1NT	Pass	3♥
Pass	4♥	All Pass	

Partner leads the seven of clubs to your ace. Plan the defense.

Gather the evidence: You expect your four tricks to be your two aces, partner's entry and a club ruff. Partner needs the ace of spades as his entry. The king of hearts would not serve since your ruff would then be with your natural trump trick. How are you going to make sure you take all your tricks?

Make a plan: If you return a spade, partner will surely play you for a doubleton spade. If you cash the ace of trumps and return a spade partner will play you for a singleton spade or why else would you cash the ace of trumps but to wake him up to something unusual. (For further explanation of this concept, see the section on "Unusual Play Calls For Unusual Action" in chapter 53) The answer must be to return a neutral card and only play a spade when you are in with the ace of trumps.

Implement the plan: Play the five of diamonds. The full deal:

```
              ♠ K 10 6 2
              ♥ J 7 3
              ♦ A Q
              ♣ K J 10 3
♠ A J 7 4                     ♠ 9 8 5 3
♥ 9 6                         ♥ A 5
♦ 10 7                        ♦ J 9 6 5 3 2
♣ 8 7 6 4 2                   ♣ A
              ♠ Q
              ♥ K Q 10 8 4 2
              ♦ K 8 4
              ♣ Q 9 5
```

Partner could hardly play you for a singleton diamond which would leave declarer with eight of them. But note the importance of the ace of trumps. On this deal it gave you the time to differentiate between a singleton club and a singleton or doubleton spade so that an attentive partner would know your plan.

Opening Leads

The opening lead is the first action in the defense. You will not, however, find lists of what card to lead from what holding; these abound in books of a bygone day. Instead discussion will concentrate on which suit should be led.

A simple question to start with: what do you lead against 2NT from:

> ♠ 8 4
> ♥ A K Q J 9
> ♦ 6 5 2
> ♣ Q 9 7

When I ask this question in my classes, there is much discussion about the "book" lead: should it be the ace or the king or should the jack be led to emphasize the solid suit. Those are the simple answers. There is also talk about the jack because it shows something in clubs, the lowest outside suit (suit preference). In truth, this is not likely to be of relevance this time—surely you will cash your hearts and then either cash partner's ace or just get off lead and let declarer get on with it.

Obviously this is a trick question. The correct answer is a question: "What was the bidding?" In fact, South opened one heart, a five-card suit, North responded one spade, South rebid 1NT which was raised to 2NT by North. Does this change your answer?

In the last chapter we developed a three-step strategy for defense: Step 1—gather the evidence, Step 2—make a plan, Step 3—implement that plan. These same three steps also apply when considering your opening lead.

GATHER THE EVIDENCE

This time, since it is only the first step in the play of the hand there are not as many places to look for evidence.

- The opponents' bidding
- Our bidding (or lack of it)
- The strength and distribution of our own hand

MAKE A PLAN

Again as before we have to:

- Assume that the contract can be beaten
- Play partner for the minimum
- Use technique
- Maintain flexibility

IMPLEMENT THE PLAN

- Don't let partner ruin it!

Now back to the problem with the best two pieces of advice I can offer you ringing in your ears:

LISTEN TO THE BIDDING

LOOK AT YOUR HAND

> ♠ 8 4
> ♥ A K Q J 9
> ♦ 6 5 2
> ♣ Q 9 7

Gather the evidence: It is probable that North has two hearts since with only one he may have chosen to investigate a suit contract rather than raise no trumps and with three hearts he would have supported South's known five-card suit. If dummy has two hearts and partner therefore has a singleton it is likely that declarer has 10xxxx. Why the ten? If partner has one, dummy two and declarer five cards in a suit, it is five chances to three that declarer has any specific card, in this case the ten. If you lead a high heart you will only make four tricks in the suit unless the ten drops.

Make a plan: The odds are against a heart lead being successful; some other suit must be chosen in the hope that partner can get in—if he doesn't they may have missed game—and switch to a heart. You consider a high spade and a high diamond.

Implement the plan: Lead the eight of spades because partner should not misunderstand your spade length, whereas he might misunderstand your diamond length given the spot cards you hold.

One of the rules taught to beginning bridge players is "Always return partner's suit." But actually you should return partner's suit only if it is right! The general rule is that if you lead a low card, fourth highest say, you expect partner to return the suit; if you lead a high spot card, unless conventional, you do not.

Sometimes partner's lack of action can be the clue you need.

Both Sides Vulnerable. Dealer North.

West holds:

♠ 9 5 4
♥ K 9 6 3 2
♦ 8 3
♣ 8 7 3

West	North	East	South
–	1♥	Pass	1NT
Pass	3NT	All Pass	

Gather the evidence: The opponents have bid confidently and yet partner must have fair values but didn't bid. Furthermore, you know that you cannot establish your own suit. There are those who would choose their shortest suit, arguing that that is more likely to be partner's length, but most would see it as a choice between their three-card suits—after all, even if you find partner with a five-card suit, if you have only a doubleton, declarer may have four cards over him; when you have a trebleton this is less likely. A spade looks attractive since neither North nor South is likely to hold four spades. However, on further consideration, neither is partner likely to hold a good four-card spade suit since he passed one heart with roughly opening values and, inferentially, short hearts.

Make a plan: You are more likely to find partner with minor-suit length, so you should lead your better minor.

Implement the plan: Lead the seven of clubs. The full deal:

```
                ♠ A J 10 3
                ♥ A Q J 7
                ♦ J 9 5
                ♣ A Q
  ♠ 9 5 4                   ♠ Q 8 2
  ♥ K 9 6 3 2               ♥ 10 5
  ♦ 8 3                     ♦ A 10 6
  ♣ 8 7 3                   ♣ K J 9 5 4
                ♠ K 7 6
                ♥ 8 4
                ♦ K Q 7 4 2
                ♣ 10 6 2
```

It is often difficult to decide whether or not to play for ruffs. What about this one?

East/West Vulnerable. Dealer South.

West holds:

♠ 5
♥ A 9 5
♦ K 7 4 2
♣ Q 9 5 4 2

West	North	East	South
–	–	–	1♥
Pass	2♦	Pass	2♥
Pass	3♥	Pass	4♥
All Pass			

Gather the evidence: The opponents have had a limited sequence to four hearts. Partner is likely to have about six or seven points.

Make a plan: It could be right to lead a club, hoping to set up some tricks there or to force declarer. However, it would need partner to hold good clubs, reducing his chance of high cards elsewhere which you need if you are to beat four hearts. Furthermore, since trumps break well a forcing game is unlikely to be successful. The singleton spade lead looks quite attractive—even if partner does not have the ace, you can hope to find him with two entries or with one entry and a cashing spade.

Implement the plan: Lead the five of spades. The full deal:

```
                ♠ Q 9 6 4
                ♥ K 7 3
                ♦ A J 6 5 3
                ♣ 6
  ♠ 5                       ♠ K J 8 7 2
  ♥ A 9 5                   ♥ 4
  ♦ K 7 4 2                 ♦ 10 9 8
  ♣ Q 9 5 4 2               ♣ A 10 7 3
                ♠ A 10 3
                ♥ Q J 10 8 6 2
                ♦ Q
                ♣ K J 8
```

When you see dummy it is clear that the only suit in which it is possible for partner to have a quick entry is clubs. If it were not clear, you would duck the first round of trumps in the hope that partner would be able to signal his entry card.

Players like to lead singletons, but often it is not the best defense. For it to be right you need both trump control and limited values so that partner has enough values to provide the necessary quick entries. When partner doesn't have what you want you run the risk of destroying his defensive values in the suit that you have led.

Is this one different?

East/West Vulnerable. Dealer South.

West holds:

♠ 8
♥ 8 5 3 2
♦ Q 6 5
♣ A K Q J 3

West	North	East	South
–	–	–	1♥
Pass	2♥	Pass	4♥
All Pass			

Gather the evidence: The opponents will have at least eight hearts between them. Their sequence is not limited, but in any case partner is unlikely to have more than three or four points.

Make a plan: You could lead your singleton spade, hoping partner had the ace, but you would still need two further defensive tricks. South's bidding suggests distributional values and his shortage is likely to be in clubs. If he has only five trumps he may well be embarrassed if you lead top clubs because he will have to ruff, which will reduce him to the same number of trumps as you. If he needs to lose another trick you will be able to cash more clubs if he has drawn all the trumps.

Implement the plan: Lead the ace of clubs. The full deal:

```
            ♠ Q J 3
            ♥ A J 6
            ♦ 10 3 2
            ♣ 10 9 6 5
♠ 8                      ♠ A 9 7 6 5
♥ 8 5 3 2                ♥ 9
♦ Q 6 5                  ♦ J 8 7 4
♣ A K Q J 3              ♣ 7 4 2
            ♠ K 10 4 2
            ♥ K Q 10 7 4
            ♦ A K 9
            ♣ 8
```

Notice that the ace of clubs was a flexible lead; you could either continue clubs to force declarer or switch to the spade, if that seemed best when you saw dummy. Here, even though East did hold the ace of spades, a spade lead will usually give the defense just three tricks—a spade, a spade ruff and a club. If, on the other hand, West leads two top clubs a careless declarer may go down. If he ruffs the second club and draws two rounds of trumps (discovering the bad news), he has no chance. Twist and turn as he might, declarer will lose another trick. His best line is to play on spades, but your partner wins the ace and, following your defense, continues with another club. The defense has two tricks while declarer has made four, but his trump fit is now 1-1 while you have two trumps and two master clubs. Declarer cannot draw your trumps and whatever he does you will eventually ruff a spade and play yet another club.

Declarer could have succeeded by playing spades before drawing trumps and continuing with spades until West shortens himself. Then dummy's three-card heart suit would be long enough to draw all the outstanding trumps. And yet another variation:

East/West Vulnerable. Dealer South.

West holds:

♠ 10 6
♥ 6
♦ J 9 8 5 3
♣ A K 6 5 3

West	North	East	South
–	–	–	1♠
Pass	4♠	All Pass	

Gather the evidence: Expecting that partner will have something, you can hope for two club tricks and a club ruff with partner holding another trick somewhere. Or you could play him for the ace of hearts or ace of trumps, in which case a heart ruff and your two club tricks would defeat the contract.

Make a plan: You can keep your options open by leading a top club, seeing dummy and getting a signal from partner. But if you then decide to switch to your heart, how will partner know for certain that it is a singleton?

Implement the plan: Lead the king of clubs. If partner plays low, follow with your heart. Partner should work out that you have deviated from your normal lead and are trying to convey an unusual message. The full deal:

```
            ♠ J 5 4 2
            ♥ K Q J 3
            ♦ A 7
            ♣ Q 8 2
♠ 10 6                   ♠ A 9
♥ 6                      ♥ 10 8 7 4 2
♦ J 9 8 5 3             ♦ 10 6 4
♣ A K 6 5 3             ♣ 10 7 4
            ♠ K Q 8 7 3
            ♥ A 9 5
            ♦ K Q 2
            ♣ J 9
```

Some expert pairs do have a conventional agreement that if they reverse their normal lead from ace-king, they are trying to indicate something unusual. This is usually a singleton, but there is no reason why the method shouldn't work with a void.

Sometimes you have a long, strong suit you would like to lead but, unfortunately, an opponent has bid it. What would you lead after this auction:

Neither Side Vulnerable. Dealer South.

West holds:

♠ A K 4
♥ 5 2
♦ K J 10 4 2
♣ J 9 3

West	North	East	South
–	–	–	1♣
Pass	1♠	Pass	3NT
All Pass			

Gather the evidence: South has at least four diamonds with 19 or 20 points; North has at least four spades with at least six points. Thus the opponents have at least 25 points, leaving partner with a maximum of three.

Make a plan: If partner has no more than three points you are unlikely to defeat 3NT by leading his suit even if you knew which it was. You must hope that South has only four diamonds, in which case partner doesn't need more than the doubleton nine. If you lead the jack you run the risk of blocking the suit if partner has 9x and declarer does the right thing.

Implement the plan: Lead the four of diamonds. The full deal:

♠ Q J 6 5 3
♥ Q J 10
♦ 7 6
♣ K 8 5

♠ A K 4	♠ 8 2
♥ 5 2	♥ 8 7 6 4 3
♦ K J 10 4 2	♦ 9 3
♣ J 9 3	♣ 7 6 4 2

♠ 10 9 7
♥ A K 9
♦ A Q 8 5
♣ A Q 10

You were lucky that the opponents reached the wrong game, but you had to be careful in order to take advantage of their misjudgment. If an opponent has bid your long suit this is not necessarily a reason for avoiding the lead, but it may affect your choice of which card to lead.

What would you lead after this sequence:

East/West Vulnerable. Dealer North.

West holds:

♠ Q 10 4 3
♥ K 8 5
♦ 7 5
♣ K J 8 6

West	North	East	South
–	1♦	Pass	1♠
Pass	2♠	Pass	2NT
Pass	3NT	All Pass	

Gather the evidence: Both your opponents' hands are limited, North by his two spade bid and South by 2NT. Also, you know the suits are not behaving well for declarer—you have four spades and your partner is likely to have four diamonds. Since declarer is known to have only four spades and it is unlikely that he has four hearts (he didn't respond one heart), his distribution is most likely to be 4-3-2-4 or even 4-2-2-5. Consequently, a club lead would be dangerous.

Make a plan: The major consideration when choosing your opening lead is whether you should be active or passive. On this occasion, with opponents limited and declarer's suits breaking badly, he will probably go down, provided you don't present him with a gratuitous trick on the opening lead. Although there can be no guarantee that a diamond is totally passive, it is more likely to be so than a heart.

Implement the plan: Lead the seven of diamonds. The full deal:

♠ A K 2
♥ A 7 4
♦ A 10 9 8 3
♣ 5 2

♠ Q 10 4 3	♠ 8 7
♥ K 8 5	♥ 10 9 3 2
♦ 7 5	♦ K Q 6 2
♣ K J 8 6	♣ 10 9 3

♠ J 9 6 5
♥ Q J 6
♦ J 4
♣ A Q 7 4

The opening lead in bridge is a little like the second service in tennis. You can try to serve an ace, but that risks losing the point immediately; on the other hand you can merely put the ball in play and hope to win the point later. Furthermore, although it may be reasonable to give up a trick to establish length winners when you have a five-card or longer suit, it is not so reasonable or so likely to be effective when your longest suit is only of four cards. Other situations where it is generally right to be passive are: at low levels and when the opponents' values are mostly in one hand and declarer will have to lead away from that hand quite often in the play, e.g. after a 2NT opener.

Is this hand different?

East/West Vulnerable. Dealer South.

West holds:

♠ J 10 9
♥ 10 9 5
♦ 7 6 4 3
♣ Q 7 3

West	North	East	South
–	–	–	1♦
Pass	1♥	Pass	1♠
Pass	3♦	Pass	3♥
Pass	3♠	Pass	3NT
All Pass			

Gather the evidence: Here the opponents have had a long and informative bidding sequence which suggests that, although limited, they have good values. Your lack of values tells you that partner has a fair hand, that spades and hearts break for declarer, and that the diamond suit will run. It sounds as though declarer has at least four diamonds, four spades and three hearts, therefore he has at most two clubs. Since he has bid no trumps, he probably has precisely two clubs. North has four hearts, three or four diamonds and three spades, thus much of the time he will also have a doubleton club. When he has three clubs his distribution will be 3-4-3-3 and he might have preferred to bid 2NT rather than three diamonds if he had a club stopper.

Make a plan: Do you have any doubt that, left to his own devices, declarer will make at least nine tricks? You need to be active. It sounds as if the opponents have only a single club stopper which you can knock out on the opening lead.

Implement the plan: Lead the three of clubs. The full deal:

♠ K 7 6
♥ A Q 4 3
♦ J 10 5 2
♣ 6 2

♠ J 10 9   ♠ Q 8 5
♥ 10 9 5   ♥ K 8 6
♦ 7 6 4 3   ♦ Q
♣ Q 7 3   ♣ K 10 9 8 5 4

♠ A 4 3 2
♥ J 7 2
♦ A K 9 8
♣ A J

Try this one:

North/South Vulnerable. Dealer South.

West holds:

♠ Q 9 5
♥ K 7 4
♦ K 10 4 2
♣ 9 6 4

West	North	East	South
–	–	–	1♥
Pass	1♠	Pass	2♣
Pass	2♦	Pass	3NT
All Pass			

Gather the evidence: Declarer almost certainly has a good holding in diamonds—after all, he did jump to 3NT. His bidding suggests five hearts, four clubs, three diamonds and hence a singleton spade.

Make a plan: Even if your partner has a helpful diamond holding, you may only be able to establish two or three tricks in the suit to go with your king of hearts. You decide that you need to be active since both hearts and clubs are breaking well for declarer. Declarer's weakness is in spades, his singleton, so you think it is the suit to attack even though it has been bid by dummy. Partner will have four or five of them. There is a danger that a low spade lead may block the suit, so try the queen which also has the advantage that it may trap a singleton jack in declarer's hand.

Implement the plan: Lead the queen of spades. The full deal:

♠ K J 6 3
♥ J 3
♦ J 7 5 3
♣ A J 3

♠ Q 9 5   ♠ A 8 7 4 2
♥ K 7 4   ♥ 10 8 5
♦ K 10 4 2   ♦ Q 8
♣ 9 6 4   ♣ 10 8 2

♠ 10
♥ A Q 9 6 2
♦ A 9 6
♣ K Q 7 5

Of course, your partner ducked the king of spades when declarer incorrectly covered your queen, so that when you won the king of hearts you could play the nine of spades for four tricks in the suit. Note that an initial low spade lead would have given declarer two stoppers in the suit.

Many people lead the fourth suit in this kind of auction without giving it a second thought. However, if you believe declarer has a singleton, it is very often a good idea to lead it. It attacks declarer's communications if nothing else but surprisingly often develop tricks by force. Here is another sequence where declarer is usually short in dummy's first bid suit:

West	North	East	South
–	1♠	Pass	2♣
Pass	2♦	Pass	3NT
All Pass			

Here you should assume South has good hearts. Obviously he may be bluffing, but if you spend your time worrying about that you will never get anywhere. Generally speaking, leading the unbid suit against a no trump contract is of exaggerated value. Occasionally, by not leading it you may find you let declarer get away with it when he has bid 3NT with Qxx, but not often, and not against good players.

Chapter 53

Partnership Co-operation

In this chapter we will look at the three basic types of signal—distributional (or count) signalling, attitude, and suit preference—then at unusual play that calls for unusual action.

DISTRIBUTIONAL SIGNALLING

In an earlier chapter you saw examples where it was important to tell partner about your distribution, in one case so that you could get a ruff. Against no trump contracts there is obviously no possibility of a ruff, but it can still be important to show partner how many cards you have in a suit.

Both Sides Vulnerable. Dealer South.

```
        ♠  8 7 2
        ♥  6 5 2
        ♦  10 2
        ♣  K Q J 10 8
                        ♠  J 6 3
                        ♥  10 8 3
                        ♦  Q 9 8 3
                        ♣  A 7 2
```

West	North	East	South
–	–	–	2NT
Pass	3NT	All Pass	

West leads the ten of spades against South's 3NT. Declarer wins with the king and plays a club to the king, partner playing the three. Plan the defense.

Gather the evidence: Since you can see the two of clubs, partner's three is clearly his lowest. Thus his distributional signal shows an odd number of cards in clubs.

Make a plan: If partner's club is a singleton there is nothing to be done since declarer will have four clubs, but if he has three cards then declarer will have only two and it is essential that you duck precisely one round.

Implement the plan: Play the two of clubs. The full deal:

```
                ♠  8 7 2
                ♥  6 5 2
                ♦  10 2
                ♣  K Q J 10 8
    ♠  Q 10 9 5              ♠  J 6 3
    ♥  K 7 4                ♥  10 8 3
    ♦  J 7 4                ♦  Q 9 8 3
    ♣  9 5 3               ♣  A 7 2
                ♠  A K 4
                ♥  A Q J 9
                ♦  A K 6 5
                ♣  6 4
```

If you had ducked two clubs, declarer would switch to hearts and eventually make two spades, three hearts, two diamonds and two clubs for his contract. However, if the hand were as below and East were to win the second club, declarer would have nine easy tricks. To avoid this West would play the nine of clubs and East, knowing that declarer had three clubs, would duck two rounds to limit him to two tricks in the suit.

```
                ♠  8 7 2
                ♥  6 5 2
                ♦  10 2
                ♣  K Q J 10 8
    ♠  Q 10 9 5 4            ♠  J 6 3
    ♥  K J 4               ♥  10 8 3
    ♦  J 7 4               ♦  Q 9 8 3
    ♣  9 3                ♣  A 7 2
                ♠  A K
                ♥  A Q 9 7
                ♦  A K 6 5
                ♣  6 5 4
```

The club spots are helpful here. When West plays the three in the first example, East knows it is either a singleton or from three cards; and when West plays the nine in the second example, East knows it is either a singleton or a doubleton. Had the lay-out of the club suit been:

$$\clubsuit \text{ K Q J 10 8}$$

♣ 6 5 4   ♣ A 7 2

$$\clubsuit \text{ 9 3}$$

and declarer had played the nine of clubs to the four and king, and then the queen of clubs from the dummy, it would have been impossible for East to tell whether his partner had 4 3 doubleton or 6 5 4. He would have had to guess. It is usually better to duck once too often than take the ace too early because it gives fewer tricks away when wrong.

"Third hand plays high" is a well-known adage, and good advice it is too . . . most of the time. However, the purpose of the third hand playing high is to force a high card from declarer's hand. If third hand's highest card is a lowly spot card, it is more useful to give partner a count.

Neither Side Vulnerable. Dealer South.

     ♠ K 10 7 6
     ♥ K J 9
     ♦ A 7 6
     ♣ Q J 4

♠ A 8 2
♥ 8 4 3
♦ K J 9 3 2
♣ A 8

West	North	East	South
–	–	–	1NT
Pass	3NT	All Pass	

You lead the three of diamonds against South's 3NT contract. This goes to dummy's six, partner's eight and declarer's ten. Declarer plays a club to the queen and then the jack of clubs which you win, partner playing the six followed by the seven. Plan the defense.

Gather the evidence: Partner has played the eight of diamonds at trick one, presumably from a doubleton.

Make a plan: If you play a second diamond, you will merely give declarer a third trick in the suit. There is room for partner to have a queen and if that is the queen of spades declarer may go wrong if you switch to that suit now.

Implement the plan: Switch to the two of spades. The full deal:

     ♠ K 10 7 6
     ♥ K J 9
     ♦ A 7 6
     ♣ Q J 4

♠ A 8 2   ♠ 9 5 3
♥ 8 4 3   ♥ 10 7 6 2
♦ K J 9 3 2   ♦ 8 5 4
♣ A 8   ♣ 9 7 6

     ♠ Q J 4
     ♥ A Q 5
     ♦ Q 10
     ♣ K 10 5 3 2

For once you are right to believe that it was your partner's fault. He should have played the four at trick one instead of the eight. Then you would have known that he had either a singleton or three cards in diamonds. You would have been able to play for the latter by leading your king of diamonds, hoping to squash declarer's queen.

ATTITUDE SIGNALLING

Experts disagree on whether distributional or attitude signals are most effective. The opponents of distributional signalling argue that it gives more useful information to declarer than it does to partner. It is true that an astute declarer can often take advantage of distributional information. However, it is also true that when we try to bid hands accurately we give away information to the opponents. Some players prefer to bid what they think they can make and tell nobody anything; others prefer to use more science. It is the same with defensive signalling. It is easier to defend accurately using distributional signals.

Generally speaking, partner will give you distributional information whether you like it or not. However, once the hand is in play, it is possible to elicit other kinds of information, for instance about attitude. Once the defense has begun, for example, you lead the ace and queen to ask for attitude and the king to ask for distribution.

East/West Vulnerable. Dealer South.

     ♠ Q 10 8 7
     ♥ A Q J 8
     ♦ J 7
     ♣ J 7 6

           ♠ 3
           ♥ K 7 6 3
           ♦ 9 6 3 2
           ♣ K Q 10 5

West	North	East	South
–	–	–	1♠
Pass	3♠	Pass	4♠
All Pass			

West leads the ten of hearts against four spades, the queen is played from dummy and you win with the king. Plan the defense.

Gather the evidence: There is a strong danger that declarer has five spade tricks, three hearts and two tricks in the minors.

Unless you hurry, declarer will be able to draw trumps and discard losers on the established hearts.

Make a plan: You need three tricks from the minors; perhaps three clubs or two clubs and a diamond. If declarer holds the ace of clubs he will duck when you lead an honor and you won't knows whether to continue. You can find out partner's "attitude" to clubs by switching to the queen. If partner encourages you, continue with clubs, otherwise you switch to a diamond.

Implement the plan: Play the queen of clubs. Declarer plays the eight and partner the two. Switch to a diamond and hope for two tricks. The full deal:

```
               ♠ Q 10 8 7
               ♥ K Q J 8
               ♦ J 7
               ♣ J 7 6
♠ 9 5 4                      ♠ 3
♥ 10 5                       ♥ A 7 6 3
♦ A Q 8 5 4                  ♦ 9 6 3 2
♣ 9 4 2                      ♣ K Q 10 5
               ♠ A K J 6 2
               ♥ 9 4 2
               ♦ K 10
               ♣ A 8 3
```

With a club holding of, say, AKQx, you would have switched to the king so that partner would have told you how many cards he held in the suit.

Both Sides Vulnerable. Dealer South.

```
               ♠ K 10 5 3
               ♥ K J 10 6 2
               ♦ 7 3 2
               ♣ A
♠ 8 7 2
♥ 7
♦ Q 10 9 6 4
♣ 8 7 3 2
```

West	North	East	South
–	–	–	1♠
Pass	4♠	All Pass	

Partner wins your heart lead with the ace, declarer playing the queen, and cashes the ace of diamonds, declarer playing the five. Plan the defense.

Gather the evidence: Partner is desperately looking to you for help with the defense. He doesn't know whether to try to cash minor-suit tricks or give you a heart ruff. He wants to know if you have a singleton heart.

Make a plan: You must tell partner you have a singleton heart by discouraging diamonds. Then partner can give you a heart ruff, you can lead a diamond to his king and he can give you another heart ruff for two down.

Implement the plan: Play the four of diamonds. The full deal:

```
               ♠ K 10 5 3
               ♥ K J 10 6 2
               ♦ 7 3 2
               ♣ A
♠ 8 7 2                      ♠ 4
♥ 7                          ♥ A 8 4 3
♦ Q 10 9 6 4                 ♦ A K 8
♣ 8 7 3 2                    ♣ J 10 9 5 4
               ♠ A Q J 9 6
               ♥ Q 9 5
               ♦ J 5
               ♣ K Q 6
```

Note that, from partner's point of view, your seven of hearts could have been singleton, doubleton or trebleton.

When partner leads an honor after you have led a short suit, he often wants to know your attitude to the suit led, i.e. whether you have a singleton or a doubleton. Attitude is not only governed by your holding in the suit, but also by what you want partner to do.

On opening lead you lead low (fourth) from honors and second from poor suits; later on in the hand you can take this concept a little further.

East/West Vulnerable. Dealer South.

```
               ♠ 5 2
               ♥ 10 6
               ♦ A Q J 9 8 3
               ♣ Q 7 4
               ♠ A J 8 6
               ♥ Q 7 2
               ♦ 10 7 5
               ♣ 9 8 5
```

West	North	East	South
–	–	–	1♣
Pass	1♦	Pass	1NT
Pass	3♦	Pass	3NT
All Pass			

Partner leads the four of hearts to your queen and declarer's king. Declarer now leads a low club which your partner takes with the ace and switches to the three of spades. You win with the ace. Plan the defense.

Gather the evidence: Declarer is threatening to make a large number of tricks. You can see six diamond tricks, at least one club and at least one heart. It is quite likely declarer has more tricks in clubs and that you need to take four tricks immediately. Partner also knows that. His three of spades is an attitude lead.

Make a pan: You should return partner's second suit. Had he held, for example, ♥A10843, he should have returned a high spade even from an honor. His three of spades tells you that you cannot beat the contract in hearts, but might be able to in spades.

Implement the plan: Play back the six of spades. The full deal:

```
              ♠ 5 2
              ♥ 10 6
              ♦ A Q J 9 8 3
              ♣ Q 7 4
♠ K 10 7 3                    ♠ A J 8 6
♥ J 9 8 4 3                   ♥ Q 7 2
♦ 6 2                         ♦ 10 7 5
♣ A 3                         ♣ 9 8 5
              ♠ Q 9 4
              ♥ A K 5
              ♦ K 4
              ♣ K J 10 6 2
```

SUIT-PREFERENCE SIGNALLING

The best known use of suit-preference signals is when giving partner a ruff.

East/West Vulnerable. Dealer North.

```
              ♠ K 4
              ♥ Q J 8
              ♦ K 10 8 4
              ♣ K Q 10 5
♠ J 7 2
♥ 2
♦ 9 7 3 2
♣ 9 7 6 3 2
```

West	North	East	South
–	1NT	Pass	3♠
Pass	3NT	Pass	4♠
All Pass			

You lead the two of hearts against South's four spades. Partner wins with the ace and declarer plays the ten. Partner returns the nine of hearts, declarer plays the king and you ruff. Plan the defense.

Gather the evidence: Partner has played back the highest outstanding heart.

Make a plan: Partner is asking you to return the higher of the two remaining side suits, i.e. a diamond.

Implement the plan: Play the seven of diamonds. Partner will win with the queen and continue hearts which you ruff to beat the contract by one trick. The full deal:

```
              ♠ K 4
              ♥ Q J 8
              ♦ K 10 8 4
              ♣ K Q 10 5
♠ J 7 2                       ♠ 9 3
♥ 2                           ♥ A 9 7 6 5 3
♦ 9 7 3 2                     ♦ A Q 6 5
♣ 9 7 6 3 2                   ♣ 8
              ♠ A Q 10 8 6 5
              ♥ K 10 4
              ♦ J
              ♣ A J 4
```

Note that without a suit-preference signal from partner you could not have been sure how to reach him.

Another good use of suit-preference signals is when selecting low spot cards. For example, suppose you hold 753 in a suit. On the first round you play the three to show an odd number, but on the next round you can choose between the seven or the five depending on where your outside preference lies.

North/South Vulnerable. Dealer South.

```
              ♠ Q 5
              ♥ K Q 4
              ♦ K Q J 6 2
              ♣ Q 10 7
♠ K 7
♥ J 7 3 2
♦ 10 5 4
♣ A K 4 3
```

West	North	East	South
–	–	–	1♠
Pass	2♦	Pass	2♠
Pass	3NT	Pass	4♠
All Pass			

Against South's four spades you lead the ace and king of clubs, partner following with the two and the six, while declarer plays the five and the eight. Plan the defense.

Gather the evidence: Declarer probably has seven spades for his bidding. If so, he has six spade tricks, one club and either red-suit ace would give him three tricks in that suit. It is critical to cash partner's red-suit ace.

Make a plan: Having already played the two of clubs to show an odd number, on the second round of the suit partner chose the lower—the six from J6 or 96. His preference, if any, should be for the lower red suit.

Implement the plan: Play the five of diamonds. The full deal:

```
              ♠ Q 5
              ♥ K Q 4
              ♦ K Q J 6 2
              ♣ Q 10 7
♠ K 7                      ♠ 4 3
♥ J 7 3 2                  ♥ 10 9 8 5
♦ 10 5 4                   ♦ A 9 8 7
♣ A K 4 3                  ♣ J 6 2
              ♠ A J 10 9 8 6 2
              ♥ A 6
              ♦ 3
              ♣ 9 8 5
```

There are two further points of interest. First, the lower card is deemed to be the "normal" one, showing either no preference or preference for the lower suit; thus the higher card sends a much stronger message. Second, it is not always so easy. Suppose declarer plays the eight and nine of clubs at tricks one and two. The issue is confused now since you don't know if partner has chosen the six from 6 5 or from J 6. You are reduced to guesswork. It shows just how advantageous it can be for declarer to falsecard.

Sometimes you cannot signal with small cards and then it is the honor cards that can carry a suit-preference message:

Both Sides Vulnerable. Dealer South.

```
              ♠ 4 3
              ♥ K J 10 6 5
              ♦ 8 4 2
              ♣ J 10 6
                           ♠ 8 6
                           ♥ A Q
                           ♦ 9 7 3
                           ♣ K Q 9 8 5 4
```

West	North	East	South
–	–	–	1♠
Pass	Pass	2♣	2♠
All Pass			

Your partner leads the ace of clubs followed by the two of clubs. Plan the defense.

Gather the evidence: You can see four defensive tricks in clubs and hearts and have to hope for two more from trumps and/or diamonds. A trump promotion is a possibility.

Make a plan: You are surely going to play three rounds of clubs—partner's two confirms a doubleton (with three he would play his highest on the second round). It is vital that if partner overruffs declarer he should return a heart. The only way that you can signal your heart preference is in the way that you play your club honors. Normally you would play the queen followed by the king, so this time play in reverse order and partner will know that your first honor was a suit-preference signal.

Implement the plan: Play the king of clubs and then the queen of clubs. Declarer ruffs with the queen as your partner discards the four of hearts. Declarer plays the ace and jack of spades. Your partner wins with the king and plays the two of hearts. You win the queen, cash the ace and play yet another club to promote partner's nine of spades. The full deal:

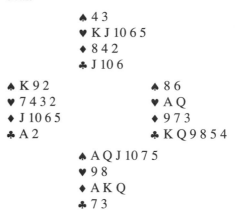

```
              ♠ 4 3
              ♥ K J 10 6 5
              ♦ 8 4 2
              ♣ J 10 6
♠ K 9 2                    ♠ 8 6
♥ 7 4 3 2                  ♥ A Q
♦ J 10 6 5                 ♦ 9 7 3
♣ A 2                      ♣ K Q 9 8 5 4
              ♠ A Q J 10 7 5
              ♥ 9 8
              ♦ A K Q
              ♣ 7 3
```

Note that this defense did not jeopardize your chances if partner held a diamond trick. He would have to come to it at the end in any case.

UNUSUAL PLAY CALLS FOR UNUSUAL ACTION

The following problem illustrates a common form of this type of signal.

Neither Side Vulnerable. Dealer South.

```
              ♠ J 7
              ♥ K J 7 3
              ♦ J 10 9 8
              ♣ A 5 4
♠ 9 8 4
♥ 8 2
♦ A 7 6 2
♣ J 8 7 2
```

West	North	East	South
–	–	–	1♥
Pass	3♥	Pass	4♥
All Pass			

You lead the eight of spades to partner's ace. He cashes the ace of trumps and plays the five of diamonds, declarer playing the king. Plan the defense.

Gather the evidence: What is going on? Partner is defending very strangely. Why has he cashed the ace of trumps?

Make a plan: It looks as if your four tricks are going to be three aces and a diamond ruff. Partner has defended in this way to make it clear that he has a singleton diamond. Had he returned a diamond immediately, you may well have ducked, playing for him to have a doubleton.

Implement the plan: Play the ace of diamonds. The full deal:

```
              ♠ J 7
              ♥ K J 7 3
              ♦ J 10 9 8
              ♣ A 5 4
♠ 9 8 4                      ♠ A 10 5 3 2
♥ 8 2                        ♥ A 6 5
♦ A 7 6 2                    ♦ 5
♣ J 8 7 2                    ♣ Q 10 6 3
              ♠ K Q 6
              ♥ Q 10 9 4
              ♦ K Q 4 3
              ♣ K 9
```

Indeed, if partner had returned the five of diamonds at trick two, you should have ducked, playing him for a doubleton. Often the solution to the problem of whether partner has a singleton or a doubleton is to ask what he would have done with the other holding.

Neither Side Vulnerable. Dealer South.

```
              ♠ A Q 10
              ♥ 8 7 2
              ♦ K J 8
              ♣ Q 10 8 4
♠ 8 4 2
♥ Q 9 6
♦ 6 4 3 2
♣ A 6 2
```

West	North	East	South
–	–	–	1NT
Pass	3NT	All Pass	

You lead the six of hearts. Partner wins with the king and continues with the ace, declarer following with the five and the jack. Plan the defense.

Gather the evidence: The problem is whether or not to unblock. Have you hit gold and found partner with AK1094, or does he just have AKx?

Make a plan: If partner wanted you to unblock he should have done something unusual to wake you up. Here he should have played his ace of hearts first, then the king.

Implement the plan: Play the six of hearts. The full deal:

```
              ♠ A Q 10
              ♥ 8 7 2
              ♦ K J 8
              ♣ Q 10 8 4
♠ 8 4 2                      ♠ 9 7 5 3
♥ Q 9 6                      ♥ A K 3
♦ 6 4 3 2                    ♦ 10 9 7
♣ A 6 2                      ♣ J 9 3
              ♠ K J 6
              ♥ J 10 5 4
              ♦ A Q 5
              ♣ K 7 5
```

Here is another example of an unusual card carrying an unexpected message:

East/West Vulnerable. Dealer East.

```
              ♠ 6 3 2
              ♥ Q J 10 9
              ♦ 8 7
              ♣ 6 4 3 2
♠ 4
♥ 8 7 3 2
♦ Q J 6 5
♣ K Q 9 7
```

West	North	East	South
–	–	2♠(*)	3NT
All Pass			

(*) Weak

You lead the four of spades to partner's king and declarer's ace. Declarer cashes the ace and king of diamonds, partner following with the nine and then discarding the five of spades. Declarer now leads the ten of diamonds to your jack, dummy discarding a club and partner the four of hearts. Plan the defense.

Gather the evidence: Partner has shown six spades for his vulnerable weak two bid (confirmed by his discard of the two—when he has to play an honor at trick one, the next card that he plays, whether it be following suit or a discard, should be the lowest from an even number), three hearts when he discards the three, and one diamond. Partner is 6-3-1-3 and therefore declarer has a 3-2-6-2 distribution. If declarer is very strong he may have nine tricks—two spades, four diamonds, two hearts and a club—unless you hurry.

Make a plan: You must switch to a club. It must be a top club to cater to declarer having ace-jack doubleton. Partner's clubs are bound to be headed by the jack or ten and you must be careful not to block the suit. If partner has both the jack and ten of clubs you must hope he rises to the occasion and unblocks both of them.

Implement the plan: Play the queen of clubs. No doubt declarer will win and knock out your last diamond stopper. Now when you play the king of clubs, partner should unblock his jack or ten. When you play honor cards in an unusual order it asks partner to unblock on the second honor. The full deal:

```
                    ♠ 6 3 2
                    ♥ Q J 10 9
                    ♦ 8 7
                    ♣ 6 4 3 2
   ♠ 4                              ♠ K J 10 8 7 5
   ♥ 8 7 3 2                        ♥ 6 5 4
   ♦ Q J 6 5                        ♦ 9
   ♣ K Q 9 7                        ♣ 10 8 5
                    ♠ A Q 9
                    ♥ A K
                    ♦ A K 10 4 3 2
                    ♣ A J
```

Now let's watch some experts at work. The following hand comes from some Mexican Trials and features Dr. George Rosenkranz, one of Mexico's finest players and a great bridge theorist.

Both Sides Vulnerable. Dealer South.

```
                    ♠ Q 10 7 5
                    ♥ 10 6
                    ♦ Q J 9 5
                    ♣ A 7 4
   ♠ A 4 2                          ♠ 9 8
   ♥ A Q 7 5 3                      ♥ K J 4 2
   ♦ 3                              ♦ 7 4 2
   ♣ J 10 8 6                       ♣ Q 5 3 2
                    ♠ K J 6 3
                    ♥ 9 8
                    ♦ A K 10 8 6
                    ♣ K 9
```

West	North	East	South
Rosenkranz		*Dubson*	
–	–	–	1♦
1♥	Dble(*)	Rdble(**)	1♠
3♥	3♠	Pass	4♠
Dble	All Pass		

(*) Negative
(**) One of the top three heart honors

On this deal Dr. Rosenkranz, West, was able to capitalize on one of his favorite conventions. Knowing of East's top heart honor, he could see a clear line of defense, so he risked a double. He started the defense off by leading his singleton diamond.

When in with the ace of spades, West confidently underled his heart honors to put his partner in for a ruff. East, who had played his seven of diamonds as a suit-preference signal at trick one, now made a great play. He knew that his partner must have the ace *and* queen of hearts in order to double and find this line of defense. East therefore won with the *jack* of hearts and played his four of diamonds back to give the ruff. West knew to put his partner in with the king of hearts for another ruff and a 500 penalty.

This hand was played at a recent Sunday Times/Macallan Tournament which is held in London every January.

Neither Side Vulnerable. Dealer East.

```
                    ♠ Q 8 4
                    ♥ Q J 10 4 3
                    ♦ K 7 3
                    ♣ K 9
   ♠ A J 10 3 2                     ♠ 6 5
   ♥ 8 6                            ♥ K 9 5 2
   ♦ J 8 6                          ♦ 10 9 5 2
   ♣ 8 7 3                          ♣ A Q J
                    ♠ K 9 7
                    ♥ A 7
                    ♦ A Q 4
                    ♣ 10 6 5 4 2
```

South was generally declarer in 3NT and West led the jack of spades to declarer's king. Declarer played ace and another heart which East won eventually and returned a spade. In with the ace of spades, it is crucial for West to switch to a club.

How can he know that is the right thing to do?

Many pairs got it wrong, but some managed. Berry Westra of the Netherlands held up his king of hearts until the fourth round, playing the two, five and nine to suggest club values. This was enough for his partner, Enri Leufkens, to find the right defense.

The Brazilian star, Gabriel Chagas, tried a different approach. He knew declarer's distribution from the bidding so he returned the nine of diamonds when in with the king of hearts. Thus his partner knew about all declarer's high cards and could work out that Chagas's clubs were strong.

Counting

Counting is really the keystone of the defense. Just as declarer should pause before playing from dummy at trick one, count his tricks, count his losers and form a plan, so should each defender get into the habit of counting—tricks, points and distribution. He should count during the bidding, at trick one and then on throughout the hand; every single hand, all the time, every time, even though on occasion it does not seem to matter and pays no dividend. The habit must become automatic.

There are three main things to count:

1. Tricks
2. Points
3. Distribution

COUNTING TRICKS

North/South Vulnerable. Dealer West.

```
♠ K Q 6
♥ A 3
♦ K 4
♣ A 10 9 5 3 2
              ♠ 10 9 8 7 2
              ♥ 2
              ♦ A 7 3 2
              ♣ K Q 8
```

West	North	East	South
2♥(*)	3♣	Pass	3NT
All Pass			
(*) weak			

Declarer takes the heart king in dummy and plays a low club. You win the queen as declarer plays the jack and your partner the four. Plan the defense.

Gather the evidence: Declarer surely has the ace of spades. If he has either ♠AJxx or the queen of diamonds, he is threatening to take nine tricks by way of four clubs, three spades, one heart and either a diamond or an extra spade.

Make a plan: The best chance to defeat the contract is to

find partner with queen to three or more diamonds. If that is the case you can establish two tricks in that suit to go with your two clubs and partner's one (at least) heart.

Implement the plan: Cash the ace of diamonds and continue with a low diamond. The full deal:

```
              ♠ K Q 6
              ♥ A 3
              ♦ K 4
              ♣ A 10 9 5 3 2
♠ 4                        ♠ 10 9 8 7 2
♥ K Q J 8 5                ♥ 2
♦ Q 10 8 5                 ♦ A 7 3 2
♣ 7 6 4                    ♣ K Q 8
              ♠ A J 5 3
              ♥ 10 9 7 6 4
              ♦ J 9 6
              ♣ J
```

Note that it might have been important to lead the ace of diamonds before playing a low one. If declarer had had the jack and ten and played the jack, partner might have covered with his queen, thus undoing your good work.

Both Sides Vulnerable. Dealer East.

```
♠ A 8 7 2
♥ K 9 6 3 2
♦ A 10 6 3
♣ —
              ♠ K J 9 4 3
              ♥ 7
              ♦ K 5
              ♣ A J 10 6 3
```

West	North	East	South
–	–	1♣	1♥
2♣	6♥	All Pass	

Against six hearts, your partner leads the eight of clubs and declarer discards a diamond from the dummy. Plan the defense.

Gather the evidence: Assuming that declarer has KQxx in clubs, if you win the ace of clubs you can count his 12 tricks: two aces, two high clubs, five trump tricks in hand plus one club ruff and two diamond ruffs in dummy.

Make a plan: Dummy has plenty of controls but not many tricks. If you duck the first club he only has 11 tricks: two aces, one high club, five trump tricks in hand plus three club ruffs in dummy.

Implement the plan: Play the ten of clubs. The full deal:

```
              ♠ A 8 7 2
              ♥ K 9 6 3 2
              ♦ A 10 6 3
              ♣ —
  ♠ Q 10 6              ♠ K J 9 4 3
  ♥ 5 4                 ♥ 7
  ♦ Q J 8 4             ♦ K 5
  ♣ 9 8 7 4             ♣ A J 10 6 3
              ♠ 5
              ♥ A Q J 10 8
              ♦ 9 7 2
              ♣ K Q 5 2
```

Neither Side Vulnerable. Dealer North.

```
              ♠ A K J 5
              ♥ Q 10
              ♦ Q 7 6 4 3
              ♣ J 7
  ♠ 7
  ♥ J 9 8 6 5 2
  ♦ 8 2
  ♣ A K Q 9
```

West	North	East	South
–	1♦	Pass	3NT
All Pass			

You lead the king of clubs, partner playing the two and declarer the eight. Plan the defense.

Gather the evidence: It looks as if partner has three small clubs and declarer four to the ten. The lead of the king asked partner to unblock an honor if he had it, so declarer must have the ten. It is extremely unlikely that declarer has only a doubleton club for his bidding as that would either leave him with at least one four-card major or five-card support for diamonds.

Make a plan: You have to cash one more top club to remove the jack from the dummy and then you need to find partner's entry. How do you decide where partner's entry is? If he has a diamond entry you don't have to worry since declarer will need to play the suit; if he has the queen of spades it will probably be too late; but if partner has the ace of hearts, it is easy to see that declarer could have nine tricks in spades and diamonds unless you switch to a heart now. Partner will no doubt try to help you with his signal on the

second club, but unless he plays the three or the eight, it will be unclear.

Implement the plan: Cash the queen of clubs (partner playing the five and declarer the eight) and switch to the six of hearts. The full deal:

```
              ♠ A K J 5
              ♥ Q 10
              ♦ Q 7 6 4 3
              ♣ J 7
  ♠ 7                  ♠ 10 9 8 4 3
  ♥ J 9 8 6 5 2        ♥ A 4
  ♦ 8 2                ♦ 10 9 5
  ♣ A K Q 9            ♣ 6 5 2
              ♠ Q 6 2
              ♥ K 7 3
              ♦ A K J
              ♣ 10 8 4 3
```

No doubt partner would do his best to signal to help you but it is difficult for him because of the size of his spot cards. On the king of clubs he was obliged to give you count with the two. On the queen of clubs he could choose between the six and the five—two cards when there are three suits. One could argue that declarer's long suit, diamonds, is out of the picture. Even so, the best partner could do was to play the five, suggesting either preference for hearts or no preference. As it is, he could easily have been dealt 542 of clubs when the five would have asked for a spade.

East/West Vulnerable. Dealer North.

```
              ♠ 6 3
              ♥ A 4 2
              ♦ Q J
              ♣ K Q J 10 9 8
  ♠ Q 9 5 4 2
  ♥ Q 7 6
  ♦ A 10 8 4
  ♣ A
```

West	North	East	South
–	1♣	Pass	2♣
2♠	3♣	Pass	3NT
All Pass			

You lead the four of spades and declarer wins partner's ten with his jack. Declarer plays a club which you win with the ace. Plan the defense.

Gather the evidence: Declarer must have the ace and king of spades, in which case you can count his nine tricks—five clubs, three spades and the ace of hearts.

Make a plan: The only way to beat the contract is to take four diamond tricks now, before declarer can get in to take his nine. You need partner to hold king to three or longer diamonds.

Implement the plan: Cash the ace of diamonds and play another one to partner's king. He can then continue diamonds and you will take four diamond tricks. The full deal:

```
              ♠ 6 3
              ♥ A 4 2
              ♦ Q J
              ♣ K Q J 10 9 8
♠ Q 9 5 4 2              ♠ 10 8 7
♥ Q 7 6                  ♥ K 10 9 8 5
♦ A 10 8 4              ♦ K 3 2
♣ A                      ♣ 5 3
              ♠ A K J
              ♥ J 3
              ♦ 9 7 6 5
              ♣ 7 6 4 2
```

East/West Vulnerable. Dealer South.

```
              ♠ A 5 4 2
              ♥ Q 8 3 2
              ♦ 10 5 2
              ♣ J 5

                        ♠ J 8 7
                        ♥ 9 7
                        ♦ Q 8 7
                        ♣ A 9 7 4 3
```

West	North	East	South
–	–	–	1♥
Pass	2♥	Pass	3♦
Pass	4♥	All Pass	

Partner leads the king of clubs and another club which declarer ruffs. Declarer cashes the ace and king of hearts, partner following, and then plays the king of spades, a spade to the ace and a third spade which your partner wins with the queen. He exits with the four of diamonds. Plan the defense.

Gather the evidence: You know that declarer is 3-5-4-1 and that you need two diamond tricks to beat four hearts.

Make a plan: If partner holds just Axx or Kxx in diamonds, you can never beat the contract; if partner holds AJx declarer will always go down. The critical holdings are KJx, when you must play the queen, and A9x, when you must play the eight. So is it even money? No. If partner held KJx he should have played the king—he is also counting, remember.

Implement the plan: Play the eight of diamonds. The full deal:

```
              ♠ A 5 4 2
              ♥ Q 8 3 2
              ♦ 10 5 2
              ♣ J 5
♠ Q 10 6                ♠ J 8 7
♥ 5 4                    ♥ 9 7
♦ A 9 4                  ♦ Q 8 6
♣ K Q 10 6 2            ♣ A 9 7 4 3
              ♠ K 9 3
              ♥ A K J 10 6
              ♦ K J 7 3
              ♣ 8
```

COUNTING POINTS

Neither Side Vulnerable. Dealer South.

```
              ♠ A K Q J 2
              ♥ 8 5 2
              ♦ Q J 10
              ♣ 10 4
♠ 10 7
♥ K 9 6
♦ K 5 3 2
♣ A K J 2
```

West	North	East	South
–	–	–	1♥
Pass	1♠	Pass	2♥
Pass	4♥	All Pass	

You lead the ace and king of clubs on which partner plays the three and seven, while declarer plays the six and queen. Plan the defense.

Gather the evidence: It looks as if partner has five clubs and declarer a doubleton. The points you can see, together with South's opening bid, leave partner room for very little—a queen at most. Such a queen could only be in hearts which would be unlikely to be of much use.

Make a plan: The way to preserve your diamond trick is to prevent declarer using dummy's spade suit. The way to do that is to lead a spade now.

Implement the plan: Play the ten of spades. When you win your king of hearts you can play another spade and declarer has no chance of making his contract because you have severed his communications. The full deal:

                    ♠ A K Q J 2
                    ♥ 8 5 2
                    ♦ Q J 10
                    ♣ 10 4

    ♠ 10 7   ♠ 9 8 4 3
    ♥ K 9 6   ♥ 4
    ♦ K 5 3 2   ♦ 7 6 4
    ♣ A K J 2   ♣ 9 8 7 5 3

                    ♠ 6 5
                    ♥ A Q J 10 7 3
                    ♦ A 9 8
                    ♣ Q 6

There are some hands, like the last one, where it is possible to work out declarer's probable line of play. Thus, here he would need tricks from dummy's spade suit after trumps have been drawn. By attacking spades before he has drawn trumps, you can restrict his winners in the suit. You can see that his alternative line—the diamond finesse—would not succeed and you do not need to worry about the lines of play that will fail anyway.

The following hand needs a different solution:

Both Sides Vulnerable. Dealer South.

                    ♠ 9 8 7
                    ♥ K 10 9 4
                    ♦ A Q J 4
                    ♣ J 5

    ♠ A K Q J 6 5
    ♥ A
    ♦ 9 7 6
    ♣ Q 6 2

West	North	East	South
–	–	–	1♥
2♠	4♥	All Pass	

You lead the ace of spades followed by the king, everyone following. Plan the defense.

Gather the evidence: It looks pretty hopeless. You can see 16 points in your own hand and 11 in dummy. Even if South has a minimum 12-count there is no room for partner to have more than a jack. Thus the "obvious" diamond switch will fail.

Make a plan: Your only hope is for partner to hold J8x or J8xx in trumps. If he does, you can play another spade. If he ruffs with the eight, declarer will have to overruff with the queen. When you get in with the ace of trumps you can play yet another spade and promote partner's jack. However, if you lead another top spade partner is likely to just discard something without giving the matter much thought.

Implement the plan: Play a low spade. This will force him to ruff and hopefully he will wake up sufficiently to ruff with the eight. The full deal:

                    ♠ 9 8 7
                    ♥ K 10 9 4
                    ♦ A Q J 4
                    ♣ J 5

    ♠ A K Q J 6 5   ♠ 10 2
    ♥ A   ♥ J 8 6
    ♦ 9 7 6   ♦ 8 3 2
    ♣ Q 6 2   ♣ 10 9 7 4 3

                    ♠ 4 3
                    ♥ Q 7 5 3 2
                    ♦ K 10 5
                    ♣ A K 8

North/South Vulnerable. Dealer South.

                    ♠ A 10 5
                    ♥ 7 5 2
                    ♦ K 3 2
                    ♣ J 10 6 4

                            ♠ J 9 8 2
                            ♥ A J 9 4
                            ♦ J 10 5
                            ♣ 5 3

West	North	East	South
–	–	–	1NT(*)
Pass	2♣	Pass	2♥
Pass	2NT	Pass	3NT
All Pass			

(*) 16–18

Your partner leads the six of spades to your eight and declarer's queen. Declarer now plays king, queen and another club, your partner winning the third as you discard a spade. Your partner continues with the seven of spades to the ten, jack and king. Declarer now plays a diamond to the king. Plan the rest of the defense.

Gather the evidence: Declarer has shown up with ten points in the black suits. To make up his 16-18 point range there are several possibilities: the king or queen of hearts with the ace and queen of diamonds, but that gives declarer six tricks in the black suits together with three diamond tricks, i.e. nine in all; he could have the king (and queen) of hearts with the ace of diamonds, but again this gives him nine tricks, six black tricks, two diamonds and at least one heart, and there is nothing the defense can do. You must dismiss these possibilities because you must assume the contract can be beaten. The third possibility is the king and queen of hearts together with the queen of diamonds which gives declarer six black tricks as before, one diamond trick and, unless you are careful, two hearts. Here there is something the defense can do. Partner has three spades and four clubs from the play, two hearts from the bidding, and, therefore, four diamonds.

Make a plan: You must unblock a diamond honor so that when declarer plays a heart from the table you can rise with the ace and play the other diamond honor through declarer, playing partner for A9xx in diamonds.

Implement the plan: Play the ten of diamonds. The full deal:

```
               ♠ A 10 5
               ♥ 7 5 2
               ♦ K 3 2
               ♣ J 10 6 4
♠ 7 6 3                      ♠ J 9 8 2
♥ 10 6                       ♥ A J 9 4
♦ A 9 7 4                    ♦ J 10 5
♣ A 8 7 2                    ♣ 5 3
               ♠ K Q 4
               ♥ K Q 8 3
               ♦ Q 8 6
               ♣ K Q 9
```

If you don't unblock diamonds, a clever declarer could get home by playing a heart to the king and exiting with the queen of diamonds.

East/West Vulnerable. Dealer South.

```
               ♠ K Q J 6
               ♥ 6 4
               ♦ A Q J 7 2
               ♣ K 5
♠ A 5 3
♥ A Q 10 7
♦ 8 6 5
♣ 10 9 8
```

West	North	East	South
–	–	–	Pass
Pass	1♦	Pass	1♥
Pass	1♠	Pass	1NT
Pass	2NT	Pass	3NT
All Pass			

You lead the ten of clubs which declarer wins in hand with the queen, partner playing the two. Declarer continues with the seven of spades. Plan the defense.

Gather the evidence: Declarer has nine or ten points, because with 11 he would have preferred to bid 2NT. Without the ace of clubs he would have played the king from dummy at trick one, so you can assume declarer has AQx, leaving him with one king and a jack, say, but which king?

Make a plan: Why is declarer playing in spades to give himself six tricks in the black suits when it would seem more natural to use one of his limited entries to take a diamond finesse? The answer is that he does not need to take a diamond finesse—because he holds the king himself.

If he has the king of diamonds, partner must have the king of hearts and you can take four heart tricks to beat the contract.

Implement the plan: Take the ace of spades and play a small heart to your partner's king. The full deal:

```
               ♠ K Q J 6
               ♥ 6 4
               ♦ A Q J 7 2
               ♣ K 5
♠ A 5 3                      ♠ 9 4 2
♥ A Q 10 7                   ♥ K 8 3
♦ 8 6 5                      ♦ 10 9
♣ 10 9 8                     ♣ J 7 4 3 2
               ♠ 10 8 7
               ♥ J 9 5 2
               ♦ K 4 3
               ♣ A Q 6
```

Note that even if partner did have the king of diamonds after all, nothing would be lost; declarer would have eight tricks and when partner won his king of diamonds you would have three heart tricks to take.

COUNTING DISTRIBUTION

North/South Vulnerable. Dealer West.

```
               ♠ 3
               ♥ A Q 6 3
               ♦ J 10 7 6 2
               ♣ Q 5 2
♠ 9 8 5 2
♥ J 10 9 8
♦ Q 9
♣ K 10 9
```

West	North	East	South
Pass	Pass	Pass	1♠
Pass	2♦	Pass	2NT
Pass	3NT	All Pass	

You lead the jack of hearts, which declarer wins in dummy with the ace, partner contributing the seven. Declarer now runs the jack of diamonds to your queen, partner playing the three. Plan the defense.

Gather the evidence: Partner has shown a doubleton heart and three diamonds. Declarer's bidding indicates at least a four-card spade suit, hence partner's distribution is 4-2-3-4 or 3-2-3-5.

Make a plan: Although it is safe enough to continue hearts, partner will not be able to clear the suit when he next gets the lead and you do not have the two entries necessary to establish the heart trick and to cash it. You know partner has length in clubs; perhaps you can establish his suit.

Implement the plan: Play the ten of clubs. The full deal:

```
              ♠ 3
              ♥ A Q 6 3
              ♦ J 10 7 6 2
              ♣ Q 5 2
♠ 9 8 5 2                    ♠ A Q 7 4
♥ J 10 9 8                   ♥ 7 5
♦ Q 9                        ♦ A 8 3
♣ K 10 9                     ♣ 8 7 6 3
              ♠ K J 10 6
              ♥ K 4 2
              ♦ K 5 4
              ♣ A J 4
```

When partner gets in with the ace of diamonds he can play another club to your king and you can clear the clubs. Declarer has eight tricks, but partner can get in with the ace of spades to cash his long club trick. (Declarer can thwart you by rising with the ace of clubs when partner plays the suit, but this is still your best chance of defeating the contract.)

North/South Vulnerable. Dealer South.

```
              ♠ Q 9 8
              ♥ A Q 7
              ♦ J 6
              ♣ Q 10 9 5 4
                            ♠ A 5 4 2
                            ♥ 6 5 3
                            ♦ A 10 7
                            ♣ K 8 2
```

West	North	East	South
–	–	–	1♠
Pass	2♣	Pass	2♥
Pass	3♠	Pass	4♠
All Pass			

Partner leads the eight of diamonds which you win with the ace, declarer playing the three. Plan the defense.

Gather the evidence: When declarer plays low from hand at trick one he is marked with the king and queen of diamonds and therefore has at least three diamonds to go with the five spades and four hearts he has already shown. He is most likely to be 5-4-3-1. If declarer has the ace of clubs and some holes in his heart suit the contract is surely unbeatable since partner's heart honors can be picked up.

Make a plan: You have to assume that partner has the ace of clubs. If this is the case you can assure the defeat of the contract by forcing declarer to ruff clubs. However, if you play a low club to partner's ace and he returns a club, declarer will surely play the ten from dummy and you will have to play your king. When you regain the lead with the ace of spades you will not be able to force declarer to ruff a second time.

Implement the plan: Play the king of clubs and another club. Declarer must ruff. When you get in with the ace of trumps you play another club. Again declarer must ruff and that will promote your long trump. The full deal:

```
              ♠ Q 9 8
              ♥ A Q 7
              ♦ J 6
              ♣ Q 10 9 5 4
♠ 6                         ♠ A 5 4 2
♥ 10 9 4                    ♥ 6 5 3
♦ 9 8 5 4 2                 ♦ A 10 7
♣ A J 7 6                   ♣ K 8 2
              ♠ K J 10 7 3
              ♥ K J 8 2
              ♦ K Q 3
              ♣ 3
```

It is surprising how often declarer can discover sufficient information about the distribution of the defenders' hands for a two-way guess for a queen to become an odds-on bet. It is also true that careful defenders can discover quite a lot about declarer's hand.

East/West Vulnerable. Dealer South.

```
              ♠ J 7 4
              ♥ J 7 6 4 2
              ♦ 8 3
              ♣ K Q 6
♠ K 8
♥ 10 5 3
♦ A 10 6 2
♣ A 10 9 5
```

West	North	East	South
–	–	–	1♣
Pass	1♥	Pass	1NT(*)
All Pass			
(*) 12–14			

You lead the two of diamonds which declarer wins with the nine, partner playing the four. Declarer now plays a club to the queen and the king of clubs on which partner discards the two of spades. Plan the defense.

Gather the evidence: Partner has shown an odd number of diamonds, presumably three, a singleton club and an odd number of spades, presumably five, by his discard of the two of spades.

Make a plan: It is highly probable, given the bidding and line of play, that declarer's distribution is 3-1-4-5. You must attack hearts.

Implement the plan: Play the three of hearts so that partner will know you have three hearts to an honor. If declarer has the bare king you wish partner to play the ace. The full deal:

```
                ♠ J 7 4
                ♥ J 7 6 4 2
                ♦ 8 3
                ♣ K Q 6
   ♠ K 8                    ♠ A 9 5 3 2
   ♥ 10 5 3                 ♥ K Q 9 8
   ♦ A 10 6 2               ♦ 7 5 4
   ♣ A 10 9 5               ♣ 4
                ♠ Q 10 6
                ♥ A
                ♦ K Q J 9
                ♣ J 8 7 3 2
```

It was a little unexpected for declarer to turn up with a singleton heart, but it is easy to see why he preferred to rebid 1NT rather than his five-card club suit.

Neither Side Vulnerable. Dealer South.

```
                ♠ J 6 3
                ♥ A Q 8 5
                ♦ K 8 6
                ♣ K 4 2

                         ♠ Q 10 9
                         ♥ K 6 2
                         ♦ A J 10 5 3
                         ♣ 6 3
```

West	North	East	South
–	–	–	1NT
Pass	2♣	Pass	2♠
Pass	3NT	All Pass	

Your partner leads the five of clubs which declarer wins with the seven. Declarer continues with the jack of hearts on which partner plays the three, dummy the five and you win the king. Plan the defense.

Gather the evidence: From the weak no trump opening and the points on view, you know that partner has between three and five points. Partner has led the five of clubs showing four, since you can see all the smaller cards; he followed with the lowest possible heart, showing three; and from South's response to Stayman it may be inferred that West has three spades. This leaves him with three diamonds. Declarer's most likely shape is 4-3-2-4.

Make a plan: It is likely that partner has an entry in one of the black suits. If you play a diamond now, declarer can win with the queen in hand but, when partner gains the lead, a diamond through will give you four more tricks for two down. If declarer wins with the king in dummy you know that you can drop declarer's queen when partner returns a diamond.

Implement the plan: Lead the jack of diamonds. The full deal:

```
                ♠ J 6 3
                ♥ A Q 8 5
                ♦ K 8 6
                ♣ K 4 2
   ♠ 8 7 4                  ♠ Q 10 9
   ♥ 7 4 3                  ♥ K 6 2
   ♦ 7 4 2                  ♦ A J 10 5 3
   ♣ A 10 8 5               ♣ 6 3
                ♠ A K 5 2
                ♥ J 10 9
                ♦ Q 5
                ♣ Q J 9 7
```

Note that declarer could (and should) have succeeded by knocking out partner's ace of clubs before playing hearts.

Now is as good a place as any to point out that just as you are fallible, although improving with these practice hands, so is declarer. Declarers do not always take the best line in a contract; they do overlook inferences which seem obvious in hindsight. Just because declarer misplays is no reason for you to misdefend. Sometimes, when you know that a contract is laydown, all you can do is give declarer the opportunity to go wrong and hope that he takes it.

Now let's look at some experts at work.

Since the liberalization of the Eastern bloc, there has been an explosion of bridge interest in those countries. The first hand comes from the Russian pairs championship and illustrates some fine play.

North/South Vulnerable. Dealer East.

```
                ♠ –
                ♥ 10 6 2
                ♦ A Q 8 7 3
                ♣ A K Q 9 3
   ♠ 9 8                    ♠ A K Q J 10 7 3
   ♥ A Q 9 8 7              ♥ K J
   ♦ 9 2                    ♦ J
   ♣ J 8 7 2                ♣ 10 6 4
                ♠ 6 5 4 2
                ♥ 5 4 3
                ♦ K 10 6 5 4
                ♣ 5
```

West	North	East	South
Ladyzhensky		*Bekesevitch*	
–	–	1♠	Pass
1NT	3♣(*)	4♠	5♦
All Pass			

(*) Clubs and diamonds

On this deal West started the ball rolling with an inspired opening lead. He felt sure that his side's defensive tricks would have to come from the majors and knew that there could not be sufficient tricks in spades to defeat the contract. Therefore, rather than lead his partner's suit, he kicked off with the ace of hearts—perhaps a small one would have been better, but this did give the defense a chance.

Now it was East's turn to be awake. He could see that if he simply played the jack of hearts, the defense could take no more than two heart tricks. In addition he could see the void spade in the dummy and therefore knew there could be no defensive trick in that suit. It was not hard to count declarer's possible losers and take his only chance—he played the king of hearts under the ace at trick one.

West now continued with the queen of hearts, dropping East's jack, and a third heart which East ruffed to defeat five diamonds.

The final deal comes from a major invitation pairs event with IMP scoring, which is held in the Netherlands every winter.

Neither Side Vulnerable. Dealer East.

```
              ♠ Q J 7 6
              ♥ J 8 7
              ♦ 9 5
              ♣ Q J 9 7
♠ 10 9 4 3              ♠ A 8
♥ 4                    ♥ K Q 6 5 3 2
♦ A Q 8 6 4            ♦ 2
♣ K 8 6               ♣ 5 4 3 2
              ♠ K 5 2
              ♥ A 10 9
              ♦ K J 10 7 3
              ♣ A 10
```

West	North	East	South
Westra	*Helness*	*Leufkens*	*Helgemo*
–	–	2♦(*)	2NT
Pass	3NT	All Pass	

(*) A weak two in either major

Against South's 3NT, West led the six of diamonds which ran around to declarer's seven. Declarer played the ace of clubs and ten of clubs which West won with the king. He now switched to the four of hearts to East's queen, which declarer ducked.

East could see that as soon as dummy's clubs were cashed declarer would get a perfect count of the hand. This would enable declarer to play spades successfully, by leading towards his supposed king in hand and later ducking a spade completely. To prevent declarer cashing his club winners at this stage, East found the fine play of the *king* of hearts.

South won in hand and played a spade to the queen and ace. East now failed to capitalize on his earlier good defense by continuing with a heart. This allowed declarer to make his game by squeezing West in spades and diamonds. Had East played a spade rather than a heart, declarer's communications would have been destroyed and he would have gone down.

This deal clearly helped the Norwegian North/South pair to win the event since the final margin was just 1 IMP.

Chapter 55

Communications

One of the most important aspects of card play is to maintain communications between the two hands that are playing together—i.e. either between the two defenders or between declarer and dummy. Communication plays in defense can be divided into two broad categories:

1. Keeping defensive communications open

2. Cutting declarer's communications

There is a common theme within these two headings: one side will seek to protect its entries while the other will seek to prevent their usefulness.

KEEPING DEFENSIVE COMMUNICATIONS OPEN

One of the most useful ways of keeping communications open is to duck winners. Let us start with a couple of very straightforward examples.

Neither Side Vulnerable. Dealer South.

```
              ♠ K 10 9
              ♥ K 7 4
              ♦ Q J 4
              ♣ A 7 6 5
♠ 8 7 2
♥ 6 5
♦ K 8 7 3 2
♣ J 9 3
```

West	North	East	South
–	–	–	1NT
Pass	3NT	All Pass	

You lead the three of diamonds against South's 3NT. Partner wins with the ace and returns the nine and declarer plays the ten. Plan the defense.

Gather the evidence: While it is quite possible that partner's original diamond holding was A9 doubleton, his play is also consistent with a three-card suit.

Make a plan: If you win the king of diamonds and play another, although the suit will be established you do not

have an entry with which to obtain the lead and cash your winners. It is true that if you duck this diamond and partner started with a doubleton, you may never make your king. However, if your partner thought that one more diamond winner would beat 3NT, he should not have returned the suit immediately.

Implement the plan: Play the two of diamonds, confirming that you began with a five-card suit. If partner has a third diamond, when he regains the lead he will play it and you will cash three winners. The full deal:

```
              ♠ K 10 9
              ♥ K 7 4
              ♦ Q J 4
              ♣ A 7 6 5
♠ 8 7 2              ♠ A 5 3
♥ 6 5                ♥ J 10 9 8 2
♦ K 8 7 3 2          ♦ A 9 5
♣ J 9 3              ♣ Q 2
              ♠ Q J 6 4
              ♥ A Q 3
              ♦ 10 6
              ♣ K 10 8 4
```

Ducking is an important way to keep communications open and can be just as important in suit contracts.

Both Sides Vulnerable. Dealer South.

```
              ♠ J 10 9 2
              ♥ K Q 6
              ♦ A 5
              ♣ K 9 4 3
                     ♠ 8 5
                     ♥ A 9 8 4 2
                     ♦ Q 9 7
                     ♣ Q 10 5
```

West	North	East	South
–	–	–	1NT
Pass	2♣	Pass	2♠
Pass	4♠	All Pass	

Your partner leads the ten of hearts against South's four spades. Plan the defense.

Gather the evidence: It is unlikely (or impossible depending on your opponents' system of responding to Stayman with both majors) that South holds a four-card heart suit, so partner's ten of hearts is probably top of a doubleton. Dummy is full weight for his bidding and there is no reason to suppose that the cards are lying badly for declarer.

Make a plan: If you win the ace of hearts and play another, even if partner gains the lead, say with a trump, he will not be able to put you in to give him a ruff.

Implement the plan: Play the two of hearts. The full deal:

```
              ♠ J 10 9 2
              ♥ K Q 6
              ♦ A 5
              ♣ K 9 4 3
♠ A 7 3                      ♠ 8 5
♥ 10 5                       ♥ A 9 8 4 2
♦ J 8 4 3 2                  ♦ Q 9 7
♣ J 8 2                      ♣ Q 10 5
              ♠ K Q 6 4
              ♥ J 7 3
              ♦ K 10 6
              ♣ A 7 6
```

This is a situation in which many expert pairs prefer to give an attitude signal. It is also a situation where you must try very hard to play smoothly. If you spend a long time deciding whether to win your ace, your partner will know you hold it and it would be unethical for him to act upon that information. He may feel honor bound to assume you don't have the ace and play a different suit when he is in with his trump trick.

The two previous examples have both been very straightforward. It is not always so easy.

Both Sides Vulnerable. Dealer South.

```
              ♠ K 10 6 5
              ♥ K J 9
              ♦ K
              ♣ J 10 7 4 3
                            ♠ J 8 2
                            ♥ A 10 6
                            ♦ A Q 10 7 2
                            ♣ 9 6
```

West	North	East	South
–	–	–	Pass
Pass	1♣	1♦	1♠
Pass	2♠	Pass	2NT
Pass	3♠	All Pass	

Your partner leads the six of diamonds and you take dummy's king with your ace. Plan the defense.

Gather the evidence: The two hands you can see each have 11 points and declarer is likely to have about the same number. Therefore, partner has about seven so the most you can expect is two tricks in the black suits (although there are some specific holdings where you might score three).

Make a plan: You need an extra trick from somewhere. If partner has the queen of hearts, you can establish two heart tricks. Declarer is threatening to set up some club tricks for heart discards so you must hurry.

Implement the plan: Switch to a low heart at trick two. The full deal:

```
              ♠ K 10 6 5
              ♥ K J 9
              ♦ K
              ♣ J 10 7 4 3
♠ Q 7                        ♠ J 8 2
♥ Q 7 5 3                    ♥ A 10 6
♦ 9 6 3                      ♦ A Q 10 7 2
♣ K 8 5 2                    ♣ 9 6
              ♠ A 9 4 3
              ♥ 8 4 2
              ♦ J 8 5 4
              ♣ A Q
```

It is not always just the ace that we need to preserve, sometimes the lower cards are just as precious.

Both Sides Vulnerable. Dealer North.

```
              ♠ K 7 4
              ♥ Q 2
              ♦ K Q J 10 9 4
              ♣ A Q
                            ♠ Q 5 2
                            ♥ A K J 7 6
                            ♦ 6
                            ♣ 7 6 3 2
```

West	North	East	South
–	1♦	1♥	1NT
Pass	3NT	All Pass	

Your partner leads the nine of hearts against South's 3NT and declarer plays the queen from dummy. Plan the defense.

Gather the evidence: It looks as if declarer has been optimistic about his heart stopper, but dummy has helped him nicely. If declarer has the ace of diamonds he surely has nine tricks and partner cannot have enough to beat the contract. Therefore you must hope that partner has the ace of diamonds.

Make a plan: If you take your top hearts now, when partner gets in with his ace of diamonds he won't have another heart to lead.

Implement the plan: Play the six of hearts. When partner gets in with the ace of diamonds he will play another heart and you can cash four winners. The full deal:

```
              ♠ K 7 4
              ♥ Q 2
              ♦ K Q J 10 9 4
              ♣ A Q
♠ 10 9 8 6                    ♠ Q 5 2
♥ 8 3                         ♥ A K J 7 6
♦ A 7 5                       ♦ 6
♣ 10 9 8 4                    ♣ 7 6 3 2
              ♠ A J 3
              ♥ 10 9 5 4
              ♦ 8 3 2
              ♣ K J 5
```

Another important reason to maintain communications between the two hands is to overcome blockages. Sometimes this is straightforward.

East/West Vulnerable. Dealer South.

```
              ♠ K J 10 6
              ♥ A Q 3 2
              ♦ A Q 10 3
              ♣ 10
                              ♠ 8 7 3 2
                              ♥ 9 5 4
                              ♦ K 5
                              ♣ A 8 4 3
```

West	North	East	South
–	–	–	1NT
Pass	2♣	Pass	2♦
Pass	3NT	All Pass	

Your partner leads the five of clubs against South's 3NT. You win with the ace as declarer plays the seven. You return the three, to declarer's nine and your partner's queen and partner cashes the king of clubs. Plan the defense.

Gather the evidence: Are you so pleased with your partner for making such a good lead that you have stopped thinking?

Make a plan: If you gaily play your four of clubs on this trick, what is going to happen next? Partner is going to play another club, the six, and you are going to have to win it with the eight and you will never enjoy partner's fifth club winner.

Implement the plan: Play the eight of clubs. The full deal:

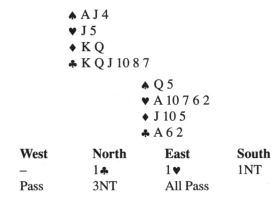

```
              ♠ K J 10 6
              ♥ A Q 3 2
              ♦ A Q 10 3
              ♣ 10
♠ 9 4                         ♠ 8 7 3 2
♥ 8 7 6                       ♥ 9 5 4
♦ 9 6 4                       ♦ K 5
♣ K Q 6 5 2                   ♣ A 8 4 3
              ♠ A Q 5
              ♥ K J 10
              ♦ J 8 7 2
              ♣ J 9 7
```

It would have been more difficult had your initial club holding been A873. Since returning the three would have blocked the suit, you would have had to return the eight at trick two and hope that partner did not go wrong.

The next hand is a little more difficult.

Neither Side Vulnerable. Dealer North.

```
              ♠ A J 4
              ♥ J 5
              ♦ K Q
              ♣ K Q J 10 8 7
                              ♠ Q 5
                              ♥ A 10 7 6 2
                              ♦ J 10 5
                              ♣ A 6 2
```

West	North	East	South
–	1♣	1♥	1NT
Pass	3NT	All Pass	

Partner leads the eight of hearts which you win with the ace and shift to the jack of diamonds. Partner wins the ace and returns the two. Plan the defense.

Gather the evidence: Declarer is soon going to have at least ten tricks via five clubs, three hearts, one spade and one diamond. You need three diamond tricks to go with the aces in hearts and clubs.

Make a plan: Partner has shown four diamonds and it is important not to block the suit or you won't be able to take the required three tricks.

Implement the plan: Play the ten of diamonds. The full deal:

```
              ♠ A J 4
              ♥ J 5
              ♦ K Q
              ♣ K Q J 10 8 7
♠ 10 9 8 6 3              ♠ Q 5
♥ 8 3                     ♥ A 10 7 6 2
♦ A 9 7 2                 ♦ J 10 5
♣ 9 4                     ♣ A 6 2
              ♠ K 7 2
              ♥ K Q 9 4
              ♦ 8 6 4 3
              ♣ 5 3
```

At least on this hand you had to think about the blockage problems. You began unblocking when you switched to the jack of diamonds, so you should still have been alert a trick later. Sometimes it is easy to let the critical moment pass you by. Of course, very occasionally a player can overreact: an international pair were somewhat embarrassed by their play of this heart suit:

```
              ♥   7
♥   A10865              ♥   KJ943
              ♥   Q2
```

Against 3NT, West led a heart to the king and the four was returned to declarer's queen. After careful thought West ducked, playing partner for K43 and declarer QJ97. Since West didn't have an entry he was optimistic that his partner did. Unfortunately declarer had nine tricks. Who was at fault, West for keeping communications open or East who played an honest card?

Well, we must blame East who should have deceived his partner into thinking he had four hearts by returning the three at trick two.

There can be many reasons for grabbing your only chance to be on lead.

North/South Vulnerable. Dealer West.

```
              ♠ K 3 2
              ♥ K Q J 10
              ♦ 8 7 3 2
              ♣ 8 7
                        ♠ 8 4
                        ♥ 9 8 5 4 2
                        ♦ 6 4
                        ♣ Q 9 6 2
```

West	North	East	South
1♣	Pass	Pass	2♠
Pass	3♠	All Pass	

Your partner leads the ace, king and queen of diamonds. Plan the defense.

Gather the evidence: Declarer probably has a good six-card spade suit along with the ace of hearts and king of clubs for his intermediate jump overcall in the balancing position.

Make a plan: If you discard now you will never gain the lead to play a club through declarer and in time he will discard club losers on dummy's hearts.

Implement the plan: Play the four of spades, ruffing partner's winner, and switch to a club. The full deal:

```
              ♠ K 3 2
              ♥ K Q J 10
              ♦ 8 7 3 2
              ♣ 8 7
♠ 9 7                    ♠ 8 4
♥ 7 3                    ♥ 9 8 5 4 2
♦ A K Q J                ♦ 6 4
♣ A J 10 4 3             ♣ Q 9 6 2
              ♠ A Q J 10 6 5
              ♥ A 6
              ♦ 10 9 5
              ♣ K 5
```

Here it was crucial that East get the lead to play a club, so he took his only opportunity by ruffing his partner's winner. However, West was unhelpful here. He should have played the jack of diamonds on the third round and then East would have ruffed automatically, thinking it a loser.

This hand was an example of needing to take the lead in order to play through declarer's unsupported honor. Another reason for such a play would be to preserve entries to the hand with the trick-taking potential.

Both Sides Vulnerable. Dealer East.

```
              ♠ K J 2
              ♥ Q J 9 4
              ♦ A K 5 3
              ♣ 6 4
                        ♠ 10 5 3
                        ♥ K 7 3
                        ♦ Q J 10 9
                        ♣ K 10 7
```

West	North	East	South
–	–	Pass	1NT
Pass	2♣	Pass	2♠
Pass	3NT	All Pass	

Partner leads the three of clubs and declarer wins your king with his ace. He plays a spade to dummy's jack, partner playing the four and, at trick three, he leads the queen of hearts. Plan the defense.

Gather the evidence: There is no room for partner to have much more than his known club suit and an ace.

Make a plan: If partner's ace is in clubs, declarer surely has nine tricks in the outside suits. Your best hope is that partner has the ace of hearts. If that is the case you must preserve his entry.

Implement the plan: Play the king of hearts and continue with the ten of clubs. The full deal:

```
              ♠ K J 2
              ♥ Q J 9 4
              ♦ A K 5 3
              ♣ 6 4
  ♠ 9 8 4                    ♠ 10 5 3
  ♥ A 6 5                    ♥ K 7 3
  ♦ 8 4                      ♦ Q J 10 9
  ♣ J 9 8 3 2                ♣ K 10 7
              ♠ A Q 7 6
              ♥ 10 8 2
              ♦ 7 6 2
              ♣ A Q 5
```

It would have been easier for you if declarer had ducked the first club—when he won the second you would have known he had the ace and queen. Furthermore, playing the queen of hearts from dummy was a good shot—you might well have ducked instinctively, thinking declarer was finessing.

CUTTING DECLARER'S COMMUNICATIONS

You have already seen some good reasons for the defenders to duck their winners, but declarer often has even more reason to try to lose his losers early. This is a very simple example:

Both Sides Vulnerable. Dealer South.

```
              ♠ 7 3 2
              ♥ 9 5
              ♦ 7 6
              ♣ A J 10 9 6 5
  ♠ J 10 9 6
  ♥ 8 7 2
  ♦ Q 10 5 4
  ♣ K 4
```

West	North	East	South
–	–	–	2NT
Pass	3NT	All Pass	

You lead the jack of spades, which holds, and continue with another spade to partner's queen and declarer's king. Declarer plays the seven of clubs. Plan the defense.

Gather the evidence: Dummy has a lot of tricks for his bidding. Surely declarer will make his contract easily if he can utilize dummy's clubs. If declarer has three or more clubs there is nothing to be done, so you must assume that he has a doubleton. If declarer had queen doubleton he would surely have started with the queen, so you assume he has a low doubleton.

Make a plan: If you play low on the club, declarer will play the nine. If your partner is more awake than you are, he will duck this, but a second club trick might be all declarer needs. If partner does not duck the club, later on you will have to play your king and declarer will make five tricks in the suit.

Implement the plan: Play the king of clubs. If declarer wins this he will be cut off from his suit once it is established. If he ducks, he may later finesse again and make no tricks in the suit. The full deal:

```
              ♠ 7 3 2
              ♥ 9 5
              ♦ 7 6
              ♣ A J 10 9 6 5
  ♠ J 10 9 6                 ♠ Q 8 5
  ♥ 8 7 2                    ♥ K 6 4 3
  ♦ Q 10 5 4                 ♦ J 9 8
  ♣ K 4                      ♣ Q 8 3
              ♠ A K 4
              ♥ A Q J 10
              ♦ A K 3 2
              ♣ 7 2
```

Note that it would be right for you to play the king of clubs even if you had three cards in the suit. No doubt declarer would duck but then would have to decide whether you had the king and queen or your partner had queen doubleton. He ought to get it right—but many would not—because if you had the king and queen you should have played low on the first club, thus allowing declarer a cheap second club trick but denying him the whole suit.

On occasion you will look silly when partner produces the bare queen and declarer makes the entire club suit without loss. However, this is unlikely and you should always take your best chance of beating the contract, even if it does risk giving declarer some gratuitous tricks.

This example of playing an honor to force declarer to play an honor prematurely is straightforward. It is a simple matter of forcing declarer to use an entry too early in the play for his own good. When it is a matter of forcing declarer to lose his timing in trumps it is much more difficult to spot the right moment.

Neither Side Vulnerable. Dealer North.

```
              ♠ A J 7 3
              ♥ –
              ♦ A K Q 7 6
              ♣ 9 8 6 3
  ♠ K 2
  ♥ A J 8 6 3
  ♦ 5
  ♣ K Q J 10 2
```

West	North	East	South
–	1♦	Pass	1♠
Dble	4♠	All Pass	

You lead the king of clubs against South's four spades and declarer wins with the ace, partner playing the four. Declarer now plays a low spade. Plan the defense.

Gather the evidence: If declarer has five trumps you can see that four spades is laydown—four trumps in hand, two ruffs in dummy, three diamonds and the ace of clubs—so you have to assume declarer has only four trumps. The fact that he is trying to draw trumps rather than play on a cross-ruff implies that he has some diamond length and wants to cash that suit.

Make a plan: It looks as if partner has a singleton club and, if declarer can duck a trump to him, he will be able to win the return, cash the ace of trumps and play winning diamonds until partner ruffs. You need to prevent declarer from drawing precisely two rounds of trumps.

Implement the plan: Play the king of spades. The full deal:

```
              ♠ A J 7 3
              ♥ —
              ♦ A K Q 7 6
              ♣ 9 8 6 3
♠ K 2                        ♠ Q 10 6
♥ A J 8 6 3                  ♥ K 9 5 4 2
♦ 5                          ♦ 10 9 4 3
♣ K Q J 10 2                 ♣ 4
              ♠ 9 8 5 4
              ♥ Q 10 7
              ♦ J 8 2
              ♣ A 7 5
```

If declarer ducks the king of spades, you will cash two club tricks which will go with partner's trump trick. If he wins the king of spades and plays another trump, partner will play a third round and declarer is one trick short.

Ducking is a useful tool that can be used to prevent declarer getting from one hand to another, just as you have seen it open communications between the two defending hands.

Neither Side Vulnerable. Dealer North.

```
              ♠ 4
              ♥ K J 8 7 2
              ♦ 8 5 4 2
              ♣ Q 8 2
                            ♠ 7 3 2
                            ♥ 6 5 3
                            ♦ J 7 3
                            ♣ A 10 9 6
```

West	North	East	South
–	Pass	Pass	2♣
Pass	2♦	Pass	2♠
Pass	3♥	Pass	4♠
All Pass			

Your partner leads ace, king and another diamond. Declarer ruffs the third round and draws three rounds of trumps,

partner following three times. Declarer now leads the king of clubs, partner playing the five. Plan the defense.

Gather the evidence: You know declarer has six spades and two diamonds, which leaves him with just five cards in clubs and hearts. If he also holds the jack of clubs, which looks likely for this play, what you do is only relevant if he has four clubs and the singleton ace of hearts.

Make a plan: If he has four clubs you must stop him getting to dummy to discard a losing club on the king of hearts.

Implement the plan: Play the six of clubs. The full deal:

```
              ♠ 4
              ♥ K J 8 7 2
              ♦ 8 5 4 2
              ♣ Q 8 2
♠ 9 8 5                      ♠ 7 3 2
♥ Q 10 9 4                   ♥ 6 5 3
♦ A K 10 9                   ♦ J 7 3
♣ 5 4                        ♣ A 10 9 6
              ♠ A K Q J 10 6
              ♥ A
              ♦ Q 6
              ♣ K J 7 3
```

When dummy comes down with a good source of tricks, it is important to start thinking about how best to neutralize it. One of the possibilities is to play the suit before declarer is ready to take full advantage. We saw an example in an earlier chapter. Here are some others:

Neither Side Vulnerable. Dealer West.

```
              ♠ 6 2
              ♥ Q 9 2
              ♦ 9 5 4 3
              ♣ A K J 10
♠ A 4
♥ A K J 7 4 3
♦ Q 7 6
♣ Q 5
```

West	North	East	South
1♥	Pass	Pass	1♠
2♥	2♠	Pass	3♠
All Pass			

You lead the ace and king of hearts, partner contributing the eight of hearts followed by the two of clubs. Plan the defense.

Gather the evidence: You are obviously going to give partner a heart ruff, but you have to decide which suit to ask him to return. He has told you he has five clubs and therefore declarer has just two clubs.

Make a plan: If partner returns a club after you have given him a ruff and you play another club when you get in with the ace of spades, declarer can never make more than two club tricks; if he tries to cash the jack of clubs you will ruff. Thus you will have all the time you need to make whatever diamonds you have coming to you—at least one.

Implement the plan: Play the three of hearts asking partner to ruff and return a club. The full deal:

```
              ♠ 6 2
              ♥ Q 9 2
              ♦ 9 5 4 3
              ♣ A K J 10
♠ A 4                        ♠ 9 7 5 3
♥ A K J 7 4 3                ♥ 8
♦ Q 7 6                      ♦ 10 8 2
♣ Q 5                        ♣ 9 8 7 3 2
              ♠ K Q J 10 8
              ♥ 10 6 5
              ♦ A K J
              ♣ 6 4
```

Note that had partner returned a diamond, declarer would have risen with the ace, knocked out your ace of spades and later discarded his diamond loser on one of dummy's clubs.

It is very easy to panic when dummy comes down with a good suit. It is tempting to switch from one suit to another in an attempt to cash or establish winners in the outside suits. This can be the right thing to do, but if dummy is short of entries it can work better to actually play dummy's suit while both defenders have trumps left, which may limit the number of tricks in the suit declarer can take, as in this hand.

Sometimes it is not tricks that declarer needs from dummy's good suit, but rather entries. Again, it can work well for the defense to give him his entry before he is ready to use it.

Neither Side Vulnerable. Dealer South.

```
              ♠ 3
              ♥ 10 9 5 3
              ♦ A Q J 10 9
              ♣ 8 6 2
♠ J 10 6
♥ J
♦ K 8 7
♣ A K Q 10 7 5
```

West	North	East	South
–	–	–	2♣
2♥	3♦	3♥	3♠
Pass	4♦	Pass	6♠
All Pass			

It looks as if your psych may well have kept your opponents out of their best contract, but it is important to stay awake. You lead the king of clubs, partner playing the four and declarer the three. Plan the defense.

Gather the evidence: It is clear that declarer has a singleton club so there can be no positive benefit from continuing the suit. Dummy's diamond suit is a serious threat.

Make a plan: If declarer has two or more diamonds, nothing can be done, but if he has a singleton the suit can be neutralized by a diamond switch now.

Implement the plan: Play the seven of diamonds. The full deal:

```
              ♠ 3
              ♥ 10 9 5 3
              ♦ A Q J 10 9
              ♣ 8 6 2
♠ J 10 6                     ♠ 8 7 5
♥ J                          ♥ Q 7 4
♦ K 8 7                      ♦ 6 4 3 2
♣ A K Q 10 7 5               ♣ J 9 4
              ♠ A K Q 9 4 2
              ♥ A K 8 6 2
              ♦ 5
              ♣ 3
```

Here the tricks available in dummy's diamond suit were not relevant; the entry was the key. He would have ruffed your club continuation and cashed the ace of hearts. When your jack dropped he would have crossed to the ace of diamonds and taken the heart finesse—the correct play according to the Principle of Restricted Choice. The diamond switch removed dummy's entry prematurely.

Another way to prevent declarer from utilizing the full potential of dummy's suit is to force him to use one of his entries prematurely so that he cannot establish and enjoy the suit.

Both Sides Vulnerable. Dealer South.

```
              ♠ 9 8
              ♥ 7 6
              ♦ K 10 6
              ♣ A K 10 7 6 2
                            ♠ 10 7
                            ♥ A J 4 2
                            ♦ 7 3 2
                            ♣ Q J 8 3
```

West	North	East	South
–	–	–	1♦
1♠	2♣	Pass	2♦
2♥	3♦	3♥	4♦
Pass	5♦	All Pass	

Your partner leads the king of hearts followed by the three of hearts to your ace. Plan the defense.

Gather the evidence: Partner's second heart in this situation should be showing you how many cards he has in the suit, i.e. he plays his original fourth highest (or second from three). Thus you can tell that he started with four hearts. He probably started with six spades since he bid twice with very few high-card values and he only has a four-card heart suit.

Make a plan: It does not matter how many spades West started with. Declarer's only chance of developing eleven tricks lie in dummy's club suit and your first priority must be to prevent that.

Implement the plan: Play a third heart, forcing dummy to ruff, depriving dummy of a later entry to cash the established club suit. The full deal:

```
            ♠ 9 8
            ♥ 7 6
            ♦ K 10 6
            ♣ A K 10 7 6 2
♠ K Q 6 5 3 2          ♠ 10 7
♥ K Q 5 3              ♥ A J 4 2
♦ 5                    ♦ 7 3 2
♣ 9 4                  ♣ Q J 8 3
            ♠ A J 4
            ♥ 10 9 8
            ♦ A Q J 9 8 4
            ♣ 5
```

Note that there was no rush to play a spade: if declarer had the ace of spades there was no need to switch to that suit. If partner had the ace, declarer could make no more than ten tricks after you returned a third heart, even if he had an extra diamond—seven diamonds, two clubs and a heart ruff.

Look at some full hands featuring the experts at work. The first example is from a tournament in Norway:

East/West Vulnerable. Dealer North.

```
            ♠ A K 5
            ♥ 10 6 4
            ♦ K 9 6 5 4
            ♣ J 4
♠ J 10 6              ♠ 8 2
♥ Q 8 7              ♥ K J 5 3
♦ Q 7 3 2            ♦ 10 8
♣ A 10 2             ♣ K 9 8 7 3
            ♠ Q 9 7 4 3
            ♥ A 9 2
            ♦ A J
            ♣ Q 6 5
```

West	North	East	South
Bjornskau		*Melstveit*	
–	1♦	Pass	1♠
Pass	1NT	2♣	3♣
Dble	3♠	Pass	4♠
All Pass			

Against South's four-spade contract, West led the jack of spades. Declarer won in dummy and led a diamond to the jack. Had West won this, declarer would have been home, making five spades, four diamonds and the ace of hearts. However, West ducked! Declarer could no longer make his contract because he could only make three diamond tricks. He tried to go for a club ruff, but the defense played another

trump each time they gained the lead.

It is unlikely that West could be certain that his play would succeed. However, it was quite clear that the defense had no chance if he won the diamond.

The next hand is from the semi-final of India's Modipon Cup.

Both Sides Vulnerable. Dealer West.

```
            ♠ J 10 9 8 3
            ♥ Q 5
            ♦ 10 6 5
            ♣ A 8 7
♠ 5 2                ♠ A 7 6 4
♥ 10 9 7 6 3         ♥ A 2
♦ 7 3                ♦ J 9 4
♣ K 9 6 5            ♣ Q J 4 2
            ♠ K Q
            ♥ K J 8 4
            ♦ A K Q 8 2
            ♣ 10 3
```

West	North	East	South
Padhye		*Desai*	
Pass	Pass	1NT	Dble
2♥	2♠	Pass	3NT
All Pass			

West led the ten of hearts to the five, two and declarer's jack. Declarer tested the diamonds and played off five rounds of the suit, discarding two spades from dummy. Declarer then played the king of spades which East won. East shifted to the two of clubs to West's king and West played another club which declarer also ducked. He was hoping that the defenders would play a third club on which he could discard the blocking queen of spades. However, East saw the trap and cashed the ace of hearts before exiting with a spade. Now West had to make a long heart at the end.

The final example contributed to the success of an Italian team in a recent Schiphol Tournament, held in the Netherlands.

East/West Vulnerable. Dealer West.

```
            ♠ K Q 10 4 2
            ♥ 7
            ♦ A J 8 4 2
            ♣ K Q
♠ J                  ♠ A 9 5
♥ Q 10 8 4 3         ♥ A K 5 2
♦ K Q 6 5            ♦ 10 7 3
♣ A 7 4              ♣ 8 6 5
            ♠ 8 7 6 3
            ♥ J 9 6
            ♦ 9
            ♣ J 10 9 3 2
```

West	North	East	South
Duboin		*Bocchi*	
1♥	2♥(*)	2♠(**)	4♠
Pass	Pass	Dble	All Pass

(*) Michaels, showing five spades and a five-card minor

(**) Raise to three hearts or better

West led a heart to his partner's ace and a heart was returned. Declarer ruffed in dummy and played the king of spades, which held, and the queen of spades. East won and returned a third spade. Declarer won and played the king and queen of clubs. West ducked both of these! Declarer now had to use up his only entry to cross to hand to give up a club and could no longer enjoy the suit. He went two down.

West, Giorgio Duboin of Italy, did well to duck his ace of clubs twice, but declarer should have played the suit earlier and then he could not have been beaten.

All About Trump

In this chapter we will be studying situations that can only occur when there is a trump suit: taking ruffs, drawing trumps, forcing declarer to ruff, trump control, withholding trumps and trump promotions.

TAKING RUFFS

Whenever you are defending a trump contract and have a singleton in a side suit you have to decide whether to look for ruffs in that suit. Sometimes the chance to look for ruffs does not come until you get the lead during the play of the hand. Usually, in this case, you are in a better position to know what to do because you can see dummy and have a better idea of what the hand is about. The same rules apply as when you are leading—there is no point in switching to a singleton unless there is a realistic chance of partner being able to give you your ruff and for that ruff to lead to the defeat of the contract. All too often a switch to a singleton does more harm than good. It can pick up partner's holding in the suit; it can alert declarer and cause him to find a winning line of play that he would not otherwise have done; it can establish too many winners for declarer. Our first example is straightforward:

East/West Vulnerable. Dealer West.

```
            ♠ A 10 7
            ♥ Q 7
            ♦ K Q J 10 6
            ♣ 8 7 3

                        ♠ Q 6 2
                        ♥ A 9 5 4 3
                        ♦ 2
                        ♣ J 10 5 4
```

West	North	East	South
1♥	Pass	4♥	4♠
All Pass			

Your partner leads the six of hearts which you win with the ace, declarer playing the ten. Plan the defense.

Gather the evidence: It appears that you have only one defensive heart trick and may have a spade trick. Partner needs at least two more tricks.

Make a plan: You could play your singleton diamond, hoping that partner has the ace. This plan will only work if partner has both minor-suit aces and in that case he may well have doubled four spades. Otherwise, if you switch to your singleton diamond, partner will win with the ace and give you a ruff, but declarer will win your return, draw trumps and discard any club losers on dummy's diamonds. If declarer has the ace of diamonds he will probably play you for a singleton diamond and pick up your trump trick and make an overtrick. It is far better to establish partner's club trick(s) first.

Implement the plan: Play the jack of clubs. The full deal:

```
            ♠ A 10 7
            ♥ Q 7
            ♦ K Q J 10 6
            ♣ 8 7 3

♠ 9                     ♠ Q 6 2
♥ K J 8 6 2             ♥ A 9 5 4 3
♦ A 9 8 7              ♦ 2
♣ K 9 2                ♣ J 10 5 4

            ♠ K J 8 5 4 3
            ♥ 10
            ♦ 5 4 3
            ♣ A Q 6
```

It is often important to choose the precise moment to take the ruff.

Neither Side Vulnerable. Dealer West.

♠ A 10 6 5
♥ A Q 10 6
♦ K Q
♣ 8 5 4

♠ 8 7
♥ K J 5 3
♦ 6
♣ A Q J 10 7 6

West	North	East	South
1♣	Dble	1♦	2♠
Pass	3♠	All Pass	

You lead the six of diamonds to the king and partner's ace, declarer playing the four. Partner switches to the nine of clubs, to the king and and your ace. You cash the queen of clubs and both follow. Plan the defense.

Gather the evidence: Partner did not know that he could have given you a diamond ruff at trick two—just as well since the contract could then have been made. There does not seem to be much prospect of further defensive tricks outside the spade suit, however there is just room for partner to hold the king of spades.

Make a plan: If partner has the king of spades he can ruff a club and then give you a diamond ruff.

Implement the plan: Play the six of clubs. The full deal:

♠ A 10 6 5
♥ A Q 10 6
♦ K Q
♣ 8 5 4

♠ 8 7   ♠ K 4
♥ K J 5 3   ♥ 9 8 4 2
♦ 6   ♦ A 8 7 5 3
♣ A Q J 10 7 6   ♣ 9 3

♠ Q J 9 3 2
♥ 7
♦ J 10 9 4 2
♣ K 2

Note that declarer could have succeeded had partner given you your diamond ruff right away. You would have had to exit with a trump or a heart. In either case, declarer can play both major-suit aces before ruffing a heart back to hand and discarding dummy's club losers on winning diamonds while East follows helplessly. It is often important to cash outside tricks before taking ruffs.

On this deal you were lucky that partner did not know whether or not you had a singleton. It is often not easy for him to tell, though we looked at some ways to help him work it out in Chapter 53.

DRAWING TRUMPS

When you have seen dummy, it may often seem to be a good idea to play trumps to prevent declarer from ruffing too many of your winners.

East/West Vulnerable. Dealer West.

♠ Q 8 5
♥ 8 7
♦ 7 6 2
♣ A Q 8 7 2

♠ J 10 9
♥ A Q 9 6 5
♦ A K J 10
♣ 3

West	North	East	South
1♥	Pass	Pass	1♠
Pass	2♠	All Pass	

You lead the king of diamonds against South's two spades, partner playing the five and declarer the eight.

Gather the evidence: It looks as if partner has four small diamonds. Partner's failure to raise hearts suggests that declarer may well have length there.

Make a plan: Your trump spots are so good that it seems unlikely that partner would be able to overruff the dummy, so it seems a good idea to play trumps before declarer can ruff any hearts in the dummy. You will just have to hope that partner can hold the club suit.

Implement the plan: Play the jack of spades. The full deal:

♠ Q 8 5
♥ 8 7
♦ 7 6 2
♣ A K 8 7 2

♠ J 10 9   ♠ 4 3
♥ A Q 9 6 5   ♥ J 2
♦ A K J 10   ♦ 9 5 4 3
♣ 3   ♣ Q J 9 5 4

♠ A K 7 6 2
♥ K 10 4 3
♦ Q 8
♣ 10 6

If declarer plays hearts you will continue with trumps; if declarer tries to set up dummy's clubs he will not fare any better.

It is often not sufficient to play just one or two rounds of trumps; if either hand has Axx it is often a good idea to duck the ace to insure that three rounds can be drawn.

East/West Vulnerable. Dealer South.

```
            ♠ Q 9 8 5
            ♥ A K 8 2
            ♦ A K 6
            ♣ 3 2
                        ♠ A 3 2
                        ♥ Q J 10 9 7 6
                        ♦ 10 9 4
                        ♣ 8 4
```

West	North	East	South
–	–	–	1♣
Pass	1♥	Pass	1♠
Pass	4♦	Pass	4♠
All Pass			

Partner leads the six of trumps against the spade game. Plan the defense.

Gather the evidence: Partner's trump lead suggests that he thinks the cards are lying badly for declarer and you have no reason to think otherwise. You know your heart values are lying over dummy and partner probably has a good club holding.

Make a plan: If you win the ace of spades and play another you will manage to draw two rounds of trumps. However, if partner gets the lead in clubs he will not have another trump to play and you cannot overruff dummy.

Implement the plan: Play the three of spades. The full deal:

```
            ♠ Q 9 8 5
            ♥ A K 8 2
            ♦ A K 6
            ♣ 3 2
♠ 7 6                   ♠ A 3 2
♥ 4 3                   ♥ Q J 10 9 7 6
♦ Q 8 7 5 3             ♦ 10 9 4
♣ K J 9 7               ♣ 8 4
            ♠ K J 10 4
            ♥ 10 5
            ♦ J 2
            ♣ A Q 10 6 5
```

When partner gets in with the king of clubs he will play another trump and now you will play the ace and a third round. Declarer will be a trick short, making four trumps, one club and two tricks in each red suit. Had you won the ace of trumps immediately and played another he would have been able to cross-ruff, increasing his number of trump winners to five.

When the need to draw declarer's trumps is urgent, you should do this even at the expense of a natural trump trick. This trick often comes back again with interest, particularly if you choose which trump to play with care.

Both Sides Vulnerable. Dealer West.

```
            ♠ 10 8 6 4
            ♥ K 8 6
            ♦ Q
            ♣ A 7 6 5 2
♠ J 9 2                 ♠ K
♥ Q J 10 9              ♥ A 7 5 3 2
♦ 6 2                   ♦ K 10 9 8 3
♣ K J 10 3             ♣ 9 4
            ♠ A Q 7 5 3
            ♥ 4
            ♦ A J 7 5 4
            ♣ Q 8
```

West	North	East	South
Wyszinski		*Chmurski*	
Pass	Pass	2♥(*)	2♠
Dble(**)	4♠	All Pass	

(*) Major/minor two-suiter, 5–10 HCP
(**) Pass or correct

West led the queen of hearts to the king and ace; East returned the king of spades to declarer's ace. Declarer played a club to the ace and ran the queen of diamonds. Now he exited with a club to his queen and West's king. Clearly it was necessary to play a trump to prevent a cross-ruff, but which one? West found the answer in the jack of spades. Thus when declarer ruffed in dummy with the ten and eight of spades, the nine was promoted and declarer went one down.

This deal won the Best Defense Award for the Polish pair Adam Wyszinski and Bartosz Chmurski at a Junior European Championship.

FORCING DECLARER TO RUFF

When you have four trumps it is often a good idea to lead your longest suit in the hope that you will be able to force declarer to ruff until he has fewer trumps than you do.

Neither Side Vulnerable. Dealer South.

```
            ♠ J 10 6
            ♥ Q 4 3
            ♦ A 7 5 3
            ♣ 6 5 2
♠ 8 2
♥ A 6 5 2
♦ K J 9 8 2
♣ 4 3
```

West	North	East	South
–	–	–	1♥
Pass	1NT	Pass	3♣
Pass	3♥	Pass	4♥
All Pass			

You lead the eight of diamonds against South's four hearts. Declarer wins with dummy's ace, partner playing the four and declarer the six. He now plays a heart to his jack. Plan the defense.

Gather the evidence: It looks as if declarer has a singleton diamond and probably either a 3-5-1-4 or 2-5-1-5 distribution, more likely the former as partner might have bid something with a six-card spade suit.

Make a plan: If you win the ace of trumps and continue diamonds, declarer will have to ruff and will now only have the same number of trumps as you. If he draws your trumps, when partner gets in with a black-suit winner you will be able to cash some diamonds.

Implement the plan: Win the ace of hearts and play another diamond. The full deal:

```
              ♠ J 10 6
              ♥ Q 4 3
              ♦ A 7 5 3
              ♣ 6 5 2
♠ 8 2                        ♠ A 9 7 4 3
♥ A 6 5 2                    ♥ 7
♦ K J 9 8 2                  ♦ Q 10 4
♣ 4 3                       ♣ J 10 9 8
              ♠ K Q 5
              ♥ K J 10 9 8
              ♦ 6
              ♣ A K Q 7
```

If declarer ruffs this diamond he is doomed. If he draws your trumps, you will be able to cash diamonds when partner gets in with the ace of spades; if declarer plays clubs instead you will ruff the third one and play another trump. What can declarer do now? If he draws trumps he will lose a club and a spade in the ending. If he ruffs his club in dummy while you discard a spade, what does he do next? Ruffing a diamond to hand and drawing trumps has the same two black-suit losers in the endgame. If instead he seeks to establish his spade tricks partner will win and give you a spade ruff.

If declarer does not ruff the second diamond, but rather discards his fourth club, he will succeed. He ruffs the next diamond, draws trumps and when he concedes the ace of spades to East, East has no more diamonds to play. It was a good idea for you to win the first round of trumps. Had you ducked a round, which is often good technique, declarer would have discovered the bad trump break and would have known that he had no chance if he ruffed the second diamond. As it was, he did not know trumps were breaking badly and was more likely to be careless.

Another reason for forcing declarer to ruff can be to kill the possibility of a discard.

Both Sides Vulnerable. Dealer East.

```
              ♠ 9 8
              ♥ K Q 10 6
              ♦ A 3 2
              ♣ Q 10 4 3
                            ♠ A 10 4 2
                            ♥ 9
                            ♦ 9 8
                            ♣ A K 9 7 6 5
```

West	North	East	South
–	–	1♣	1♥
Pass	4♥	All Pass	

Your partner leads the two of clubs to your king, declarer playing the jack. You decide to return the nine of clubs which partner ruffs. He obediently returns the seven of spades to your ace. Plan the defense.

Gather the evidence: The only possible place for a fourth defensive trick is in diamonds.

Make a plan: If declarer already has sufficient spade winners on which to discard dummy's diamond losers, there is nothing you can do about it. What you can do is make sure he cannot set up a club trick for a diamond discard.

Implement the plan: Play the seven of clubs. This will kill the potential trick in dummy. The full deal:

```
              ♠ 9 8
              ♥ K Q 10 6
              ♦ A 3 2
              ♣ Q 10 4 3
♠ J 7 6 3                    ♠ A 10 4 2
♥ 4 3                       ♥ 9
♦ K J 10 7 6 4              ♦ 9 8
♣ 2                        ♣ A K 9 7 6 5
              ♠ K Q 5
              ♥ A J 8 7 5 2
              ♦ Q 5
              ♣ J 8
```

When we can see no clear way to beat a contract but are sure that there are no outside winners that can disappear, it can sometimes be a good idea to break one of the "taboos" of the game and give a ruff and discard. This can be particularly successful if declarer's trump holding is a little tenuous.

North/South Vulnerable. Dealer South.

```
              ♠ K 9 8 3
              ♥ Q J 6
              ♦ A K 7 5
              ♣ J 8
                            ♠ A 10 7 2
                            ♥ 10 7 4 3
                            ♦ J 4
                            ♣ 6 5 2
```

West	North	East	South
–	–	–	1NT
Pass	2♣	Pass	2♠
Pass	4♠	All Pass	

Your partner leads ace, king and another heart against South's four spades, declarer following each time. Declarer wins the third heart, plays a spade to his queen and a spade back to dummy's king which you win with the ace. Plan the defense.

Gather the evidence: You can see 19 points and declarer has at least 12, giving partner a maximum of nine. You have seen most of these values already (ace and king of hearts), hence there is no room for partner to have the king of clubs. What else is there to play for but tricks in the trump suit?

Make a plan: At this stage of the play dummy has 98 of trumps, you have 107 and declarer has J6. If you return a small trump, he will win in dummy, cash the ace and king of clubs and ruff a club. He will then play a diamond to his queen (you assume this queen since the queen of clubs gives declarer ten tricks and you must always play to defeat the contract), draw your last trump discarding dummy's small diamond and dummy's last two cards will be winners—the ace and king of diamonds. If you return the ten of spades, declarer is no longer able to ruff a club but will draw trumps and squeeze your partner in the minors. When all else is known to fail, give a ruff and discard.

Implement the plan: Play the ten of hearts. The full deal:

```
              ♠ K 9 8 3
              ♥ Q J 6
              ♦ A K 7 5
              ♣ J 8
♠ 4                        ♠ A 10 7 2
♥ A K 5                    ♥ 10 7 4 3
♦ 10 9 8 3 2               ♦ J 4
♣ Q 10 7 3                 ♣ 6 5 2
              ♠ Q J 6 5
              ♥ 9 8 2
              ♦ Q 6
              ♣ A K 9 4
```

Declarer has no answer. Whichever hand ruffs the heart, you have promoted yourself a second trump trick.

TRUMP CONTROL

To have trump control you must have the highest outstanding trump, but that is not sufficient in itself. When you have trump control you can choose the moment to play that winner to best advantage and there is nothing declarer can do to stop you.

Both Sides Vulnerable. Dealer South.

```
              ♠ A K 8
              ♥ J 9 5
              ♦ 10 9 5
              ♣ K Q J 2
♠ 9 3
♥ A 7 6 2
♦ K Q 7 6 2
♣ 6 4
```

West	North	East	South
–	–	–	1♥
Pass	2♣	Pass	2♥
Pass	4♥	All Pass	

You lead the king of diamonds against South's four hearts. Partner overtakes with the ace and returns the jack and another diamond, declarer ruffing the third. Declarer plays a heart to his jack, partner following, and a heart to his queen, partner discarding the two of spades. Plan the defense.

Gather the evidence: South's bidding denies a diamond suit and the play has revealed a five-card heart suit only, hence declarer's distribution is known to be either 4-5-2-2 or 3-5-2-3. You can see 23 points and partner has played five; it therefore seems probable that declarer has all the outstanding high cards to make up his opening bid.

Make a plan: You are in the fortunate position of having trump control. You have the same number of trumps as declarer and you also have the ace. If you duck your ace of trumps for one more round, until dummy is void, and then play a fourth diamond, declarer will have to ruff, leaving himself out of trumps. When he plays off his black-suit winners you will ruff and cash your fifth diamond to beat four hearts by two tricks. Declarer will realize this and therefore start to cash his black-suit winners so that he loses just two trumps and two diamonds.

Implement the plan: Play the six of hearts. The full deal:

```
              ♠ A K 8
              ♥ J 9 5
              ♦ 10 9 5
              ♣ K Q J 2
♠ 9 3                      ♠ 10 6 5 4 2
♥ A 7 6 2                  ♥ 3
♦ K Q 7 6 2                ♦ A J 4
♣ 6 4                      ♣ 9 8 5 3
              ♠ Q J 7
              ♥ K Q 10 8 4
              ♦ 8 3
              ♣ A 10 7
```

The ace of trumps is the most powerful card in the pack and it is important not to play it prematurely.

East/West Vulnerable. Dealer South.

```
            ♠ Q 5
            ♥ 7
            ♦ A Q 7 2
            ♣ K 10 9 8 5 4
                        ♠ A 8
                        ♥ A 8 3
                        ♦ K J 6 5 3
                        ♣ Q J 3
```

West	North	East	South
–	–	–	1♠
Pass	2♣	Pass	2♠
Pass	3♦	Pass	3♠
Pass	4♠	All Pass	

Your partner leads the four of hearts against four spades and you win the ace and declarer plays the five. Plan the defense.

Gather the evidence: It sounds as if declarer has a very weak hand with at least six spades. Partner's lead looks as if it is from a five-card suit. Since declarer seems to have four hearts they are probably not very strong—he did not bid them. If partner has a reasonable heart holding, there is no room for him to have the ace of clubs, so that card will be with declarer.

Make a plan: You would like to play trumps to stop declarer ruffing hearts in the dummy, but if you play ace and another he will win, draw trumps, set up his clubs with one ruff and then get to dummy with the ace of diamonds to cash them. If you switch to a diamond to remove the dummy entry you give him an extra trick there and he will be able to ruff two hearts in the dummy for an overtrick. If you play a heart back he will be able to score two heart ruffs in the dummy, set up his clubs and then draw trumps—when you win the ace of spades you will not have any hearts left so again he will make an overtrick.

You are faced with the dilemma of Morton's Fork—damned if you do; damned if you don't—but there is a solution. Look at the effect of retaining trump control. Try playing a low spade and keeping the ace in your hand.

Implement the plan: Play the eight of spades. The full deal:

```
            ♠ Q 5
            ♥ 7
            ♦ A Q 7 2
            ♣ K 10 9 8 5 4
♠ 4 3 2                     ♠ A 8
♥ K J 9 4 2                 ♥ A 8 3
♦ 10 9 8                    ♦ K J 6 5 3
♣ 7 2                       ♣ Q J 3
            ♠ K J 10 9 7 6
            ♥ Q 10 6 5
            ♦ 4
            ♣ A 6
```

What can declarer do? His best shot is to win the trump in hand, ruff a heart, play a club to the ace, and take a diamond finesse. However, you can see that that will not work for him.

WITHHOLDING TRUMPS

We have been looking at examples of how important it can be to withhold the ace of trumps until the right moment. But it is not just the ace of trumps that you need to be careful about—withholding any trump can sometimes have a magical effect on disrupting declarer's timing and communications.

Both Sides Vulnerable. Dealer East.

```
            ♠ 8 6 3
            ♥ 10 5 4
            ♦ A K J 10 3
            ♣ A 4
♠ K 10 7
♥ A 6
♦ 9 6 5
♣ J 9 8 7 3
```

West	North	East	South
–	–	2♥(*)	2♠
Pass	4♠	All Pass	
(*) weak			

Against South's four spades you lead the ace of hearts followed by another heart. Partner wins with the queen and continues with the king of hearts, declarer ruffing with the jack of spades. Plan the defense.

Gather the evidence: Partner has played his hearts in such a way as to suggest no preference between the minors (he chose the queen from KQJ) so you cannot expect him to hold the king of clubs. You must look to the trump suit for an extra defensive trick.

Make a plan: You are in the lucky position of being able to see the certain defeat of the contract. If you overruff declarer will have no problems, but if you discard you will find that you have two natural trump tricks.

Implement the plan: Play the three of clubs. The full deal:

```
            ♠ 8 6 3
            ♥ 10 5 4
            ♦ A K J 10 3
            ♣ A 4
♠ K 10 7                    ♠ 2
♥ A 6                       ♥ K Q J 8 7 2
♦ 9 6 5                     ♦ 8 7 2
♣ J 9 8 7 3                 ♣ 10 6 5
            ♠ A Q J 9 5 4
            ♥ 9 3
            ♦ Q 4
            ♣ K Q 2
```

Sometimes it is a little more complicated.

East/West Vulnerable. Dealer South.

                ♠ 9 8 6 5
                ♥ K 10 9
                ♦ 8 5
                ♣ A J 9 2
                                ♠ J 7 2
                                ♥ Q J 7 4
                                ♦ J 9
                                ♣ K Q 10 3

West	North	East	South
–	–	–	1♥
Pass	2♥	Pass	3♦
Pass	4♥	All Pass	

Partner leads ace, king and another diamond, dummy ruffing with the ten of hearts. Plan the defense.

Gather the evidence: It was a rather pleasant surprise that partner held the two top diamonds. Given the known weakness of declarer's trump suit as well, he surely cannot have any losers in the black suits—and, even if he has, they are not going anywhere.

Make a plan: If you overruff with the jack, declarer will have a choice of how to play the trump suit later. He might play your partner for the queen by playing low to dummy's nine; or he might play to dummy's king and then run the nine, picking up your queen.

Implement the plan: Play the two of spades. By not overruffing you insure two trump tricks. A spade discard avoids any possibility of declarer picking up your trumps via a trump-reducing play in the endgame. The full deal:

                ♠ 9 8 6 5
                ♥ K 10 9
                ♦ 8 5
                ♣ A J 9 2
♠ 10 4 3   ♠ J 7 2
♥ 6   ♥ Q J 7 4
♦ A K 7 6 2   ♦ J 9
♣ 8 7 6 5   ♣ K Q 10 3
                ♠ A K Q
                ♥ A 8 5 3 2
                ♦ Q 10 4 3
                ♣ 4

TRUMP PROMOTIONS

You have already studied some kinds of trump promotion: when you forced declarer you promoted long trumps; when you refused to overruff you promoted trump honors. Now look at situations when what is nearly a trick, Qx or Jxx or 10xxx, can be promoted to full trick-taking status.

North/South Vulnerable. Dealer West.

                ♠ J 10 5 3
                ♥ 10 9 3
                ♦ A Q 10
                ♣ K 7 6
                                ♠ A K 4
                                ♥ 8 4
                                ♦ 8 6 5 2
                                ♣ A 8 3 2

West	North	East	South
Pass	Pass	1♣	1♥
Pass	2♣	Pass	2♥
All Pass			

West leads the queen of clubs, covered by the king and your ace. You cash the ace of spades, but partner discourages with the two so you play a club to his ten and he cashes the jack of clubs, everybody following. Partner now plays the seven of spades to your king. Plan the defense.

Gather the evidence: There are no outside tricks which can disappear—partner would have encouraged if he had the queen of spades; if he has the king of diamonds the finesse is right for declarer anyway.

Make a plan: The best chance is to promote partner's jack to three hearts into a trump trick.

Implement the plan: Play the thirteenth club. The full deal:

                ♠ J 10 5 3
                ♥ 10 9 3
                ♦ A Q 10
                ♣ K 7 6
♠ 8 7 2   ♠ A K 4
♥ J 6 5   ♥ 8 4
♦ K 9 4 3   ♦ 8 6 5 2
♣ Q J 10   ♣ A 8 3 2
                ♠ Q 9 6
                ♥ A K Q 7 2
                ♦ J 7
                ♣ 9 5 4

It is important to cash all your outside winners before trying for a trump promotion; if you fail to do this declarer may discard a loser instead of ruffing.

Both Sides Vulnerable. Dealer West.

```
            ♠ K 4
            ♥ K J 10 3
            ♦ 10 9 4
            ♣ K Q 8 7
♠ 10 9 3
♥ 8
♦ A K Q J 6 2
♣ J 9 2
```

West	North	East	South
3♦	Pass	Pass	3♥
Pass	4♥	All Pass	

You lead the queen of diamonds to which all follow. You then play the ace of diamonds and the king of diamonds, partner discarding the two of spades and five of clubs. Plan the defense.

Gather the evidence: Declarer presumably has both black-suit aces for his bidding, thus there is no room for a further defensive trick outside trumps.

Make a plan: Partner has indicated that you cannot take a trick in a black suit. Maybe a fourth round of diamonds will promote a trump trick.

Implement the plan: Play the jack of diamonds. The full deal:

```
            ♠ K 4
            ♥ K J 10 3
            ♦ 10 9 4
            ♣ K Q 8 7
♠ 10 9 3            ♠ J 8 6 5 2
♥ 8                ♥ Q 9 4
♦ A K Q J 6 2      ♦ 5
♣ J 9 2            ♣ 6 5 4 3
            ♠ A Q 7
            ♥ A 7 6 5 2
            ♦ 8 7 3
            ♣ A 10
```

If declarer discards from the dummy, partner can play the nine of hearts to force declarer's ace and guarantee a trump trick. If declarer ruffs with the jack or ten in dummy, partner simply discards and waits for his certain trump trick. Note that if you switched to a black suit declarer would be likely to pick up partner's trumps after your three-diamond opening.

So far all your trump promotions have involved forcing declarer to ruff in front of the defensive hand that holds the potential trump trick. Now look at a different situation where the defender with the weaker holding forces declarer to ruff with a higher trump than would otherwise be necessary, thus promoting a trump trick for his partner.

Neither Side Vulnerable. Dealer West.

```
            ♠ Q 5
            ♥ 7
            ♦ A J 9 8 3
            ♣ A Q 10 8 7
                        ♠ J 2
                        ♥ 10 2
                        ♦ 7 6 5 4
                        ♣ J 9 4 3 2
```

West	North	East	South
4♠	Pass	Pass	5♥
All Pass			

Your partner leads the ace and king of spades against South's five hearts, declarer following twice. He then plays a third spade, declarer discarding a diamond from the dummy. Plan the defense.

Gather the evidence: Dummy has an enormous hand on the bidding and only his fear of two losing spades stopped him bidding a slam. It is surely impossible that there are any more side losers. Partner clearly does not think so or he would not give the opposition a "ruff and discard."

Make a plan: There is a chance if partner's trump holding is as good as Jxx or 9xxx. If we ruff in with the ten of hearts declarer will have to overruff and this may promote a trump trick for partner.

Implement the plan: Play the ten of hearts. The full deal:

```
            ♠ Q 5
            ♥ 7
            ♦ A J 9 8 3
            ♣ A Q 10 8 7
♠ A K 10 9 7 6 4   ♠ J 2
♥ J 8 3            ♥ 10 2
♦ 2                ♦ 7 6 5 4
♣ K 6              ♣ J 9 4 3 2
            ♠ 8 3
            ♥ A K Q 9 6 5 4
            ♦ K Q 10
            ♣ 5
```

This particular type of trump promotion, where one defender ruffs in to force declarer to ruff high, is called an uppercut. That example was fairly easy; it can be much more difficult.

Let's look at the experts in action.

The first deal comes from the 1994 Generali Masters Individual, scored as matchpointed pairs, and shows that good signalling does not require a regular partnership. East was one of the leading American players, Kerri Sanborn (née Shuman) and West was Marijke van der Pas of the Netherlands.

Both Sides Vulnerable. Dealer West.

```
              ♠ 7 6 5
              ♥ Q 9 7
              ♦ Q 10 3
              ♣ K Q 6 4
♠ J 9 3                    ♠ A 2
♥ K 6 2                    ♥ A J 10 8 5 3
♦ A K 9 5 4                ♦ 8 6
♣ 8 5                      ♣ J 7 3
              ♠ K Q 10 8 4
              ♥ 4
              ♦ J 7 2
              ♣ A 10 9 2
```

West	North	East	South
v d Pas		*Sanborn*	
Pass	Pass	2♥	Pass
3♥	Pass	Pass	3♠
All Pass			

West led the ace, king and nine of diamonds. East ruffed and underled her ace of hearts to allow West to play another diamond. East ruffed with the ace of spades, which promoted a trick for West's jack. Two down was a fine score.

The following deal features one of Kerri Sanborn's regular partners, Karen McCallum. Together these two have won three world championships. This deal took place in a board-a-match event, which, although a teams event, has a scoring method much more like match points.

East/West Vulnerable. Dealer East.

```
              ♠ A K 10 3 2
              ♥ A 6 4 3
              ♦ 6 4
              ♣ 5 2
♠ 6 4                      ♠ Q J 7 5
♥ J 10 8                   ♥ 5 2
♦ A 9 3                    ♦ 10 8 7 2
♣ A Q 9 7 3                ♣ 10 8 4
              ♠ 9 8
              ♥ K Q 9 7
              ♦ K Q J 5
              ♣ K J 6
```

West	North	East	South
–	–	Pass	1NT
Pass	2♣	Pass	2♥
Pass	4♥	All Pass	

Without an attractive lead, West, Karen McCallum, started off with the jack of hearts which ran to declarer's king. Declarer cashed the queen of hearts, the ace and king of spades and ruffed a spade. West declined to overruff, instead discarding a club. Now declarer switched her attention to diamonds. West continued the good work by ducking the first, winning the second and exiting with the last trump, putting the lead in dummy. If declarer led a spade, East would make a spade and push through a club; as it was, declarer led a club which West won and exited with a diamond. The defense had to make two more tricks.

The next deal is from the 1992 Israeli Bridge Festival and shows how accurate defense can punish even a lowly one-level contract. East/West were Ophir and Ilan Herbst, who recently outgrew the Israeli Junior team, after being its spearhead for a number of years.

North/South Vulnerable. Dealer North.

```
              ♠ Q 9 8 3
              ♥ 9 8 3
              ♦ 9 7
              ♣ K J 6 3
♠ J 10 7 5                 ♠ A 6 4 2
♥ A 7 2                    ♥ K J 10
♦ J 8 6 5 2                ♦ A
♣ A                        ♣ 10 9 5 4 2
              ♠ K
              ♥ Q 6 5 4
              ♦ K Q 10 4 3
              ♣ Q 8 7
```

West	North	East	South
Ophir		*Ilan*	
–	Pass	1♣	1♦
Pass	Pass	Dble	All Pass

West kicked off with the ace of clubs and his brother played the two, a suit preference signal for a heart. Now came a heart to the king and the jack of hearts which declarer ducked. Now East played the ten of clubs for his partner to ruff. West cashed the ace of hearts, played the jack of spades to East's ace and received another club ruff. When East was in with the ace of diamonds, a fourth club promoted the jack of diamonds for an 800 penalty.

The final example features another pair of brothers, Jason and Justin Hackett, members of the British team that won the gold medal in the 1994 Junior European Championship and the 1995 World Junior Championship.

North/South Vulnerable. Dealer North.

```
                    ♠ Q J 5 4
                    ♥ A 10 7
                    ♦ A Q 9 7 2
                    ♣ 5
   ♠ 8 7 2                        ♠ K 10
   ♥ 6 5 4 2                      ♥ K Q 9
   ♦ K 4                          ♦ J 10 5
   ♣ A 8 7 6                      ♣ K J 4 3 2
                    ♠ A 9 6 3
                    ♥ J 8 3
                    ♦ 8 6 3
                    ♣ Q 10 9
```

West	North	East	South
Justin		*Jason*	
–	1♦	Pass	1♠
Pass	2♠	Pass	Pass
Dble	3♠	All Pass	

What a brave balancing bid from West! It pushed NS into a contract that had a (small) chance to go down. The five of hearts was led to the queen, a club went back to the ace and another heart was won with the king. East got off play with a heart which declarer won to play the queen of spades, covered by the king and ace. Now a diamond to the queen, ace of diamonds and another diamond.

West ruffed his partner's diamond winner and played the thirteenth heart to promote the ten of spades. One down. It is true that declarer could have succeeded by drawing a second round of trumps before exiting with a diamond, but that should not detract from the excellent defense.

Endplays

Chapter 57

One of the most advanced areas of declarer play is the endgame—including squeezes, endplays and throw-ins. Players are often frightened by these terms, but they shouldn't be, at least not when dealing with the simpler variety. Perhaps the most common type of endplay for declarer to implement is the elimination and throw-in. Here is a straightforward example:

```
              ♠ A K 8 7 2
              ♥ K 4
              ♦ Q 10 6
              ♣ A 10 7
♠ 4 3                        ♠ 9
♥ Q J 5 2                    ♥ 10 9 8 3
♦ K J 3 2                    ♦ 8 7 5
♣ J 6 2                      ♣ Q 9 8 4 3
              ♠ Q J 10 6 5
              ♥ A 7 6
              ♦ A 9 4
              ♣ K 5
```

West	North	East	South
–	–	–	1♠
Pass	2NT(*)	Pass	3♠
Pass	4♣	Pass	4♦
Pass	4NT	Pass	5♥
Pass	6♠	All Pass	

(*) Game forcing with four-card spade support

West leads a trump. Declarer draws trumps and eliminates hearts and clubs, cashing his winners and ruffing the losers in those suits. Declarer ends in dummy to run the diamond queen. If East covers there can be only one loser; if West wins he is endplayed either to lead another diamond, letting declarer score his ten, or give a ruff and discard. The slam is one hundred percent.

It can be difficult enough for declarer to spot these plays; what is even harder is for the defenders to spot them coming and do what is necessary to avoid them. It is also occasionally possible for the defenders to engineer such an endplay on declarer.

AVOIDING THE ENDPLAY/SQUEEZE

When declarer plays a hand in the normal but expert way, as in the hand above, there is often nothing to be done. However, it is important to make sure that there really is no avenue of escape before conceding defeat.

```
              ♠ K 8 2
              ♥ A Q 5 4
              ♦ K 7
              ♣ A Q 10 6
                            ♠ J 9 6
                            ♥ 6 2
                            ♦ Q 10 8 5 3
                            ♣ K J 7
```

West	North	East	South
–	–	–	1♥
Pass	2NT(*)	Pass	3♣
Pass	3♥	Pass	4♥
Pass	4NT	Pass	5♥
Pass	6♥	All Pass	

(*) Game forcing with four-card heart support

Your partner leads the five of spades which declarer wins with the ace, draws two rounds of trumps, partner following twice, plays a spade to the king and ruffs a spade in hand. He now plays a diamond to the king, a diamond back to his ace, partner playing the six and the two, and runs the nine of clubs to your jack. Plan the defense.

Gather the evidence: You are endplayed. Or are you? Declarer is known to have started with two spades, five hearts and, since partner has an even number of diamonds, presumably two diamonds (or he would have ruffed them in dummy), so he has four clubs.

Make a plan: If declarer has four clubs a ruff and discard cannot do him any good.

Implement the plan: Play the queen of diamonds. The full deal:

```
              ♠ K 8 2
              ♥ A Q 5 4
              ♦ K 7
              ♣ A Q 10 6
♠ Q 10 7 5 3              ♠ J 9 6
♥ 9 3                    ♥ 6 2
♦ J 9 6 2                ♦ Q 10 8 5 3
♣ 5 4                    ♣ K J 7
              ♠ A 4
              ♥ K J 10 8 7
              ♦ A 4
              ♣ 9 8 3 2
```

Try as he may, declarer cannot avoid losing a trick to your king of clubs.

Sometimes you need to be alert to avoid a throw-in.

```
              ♠ Q 8 7
              ♥ 7 6 2
              ♦ K Q 8 3
              ♣ 8 7 2
                         ♠ 9 5 2
                         ♥ Q 5 4 3
                         ♦ 10 4
                         ♣ J 10 6 5
```

West	North	East	South
–	–	–	1♦
Dble	3♦	All Pass	

Against South's three diamonds, your partner leads ace, king and another spade, declarer following three times. Having won the queen of spades, declarer cashes the ace and king of clubs in his hand, crosses to dummy's king of trumps and ruffs a club. He then cashes the ace of diamonds, plays a diamond to dummy's queen, partner discarding a club and plays a low heart. Plan the defense.

Gather the evidence: Declarer has shown up with three spades, five diamonds and two clubs. Therefore he has three hearts. As he is known to have a balanced hand he must have at least 15 points or he would have opened 1NT. He has already shown up with 12 points and so must have at least the king of hearts. You need to take three heart tricks to beat the contract.

Make a plan: If declarer's heart holding is better than just the king, it is hopeless, but if it is just the king you must still be careful. Declarer will not play the king on this round of the suit unless you force him to. He has heard the bidding and will expect your partner to hold the ace of hearts. If you play low, so will he and your partner will have to win this trick and lead away from his ace of hearts or give a ruff and discard.

Implement the plan: Play the queen of hearts. The full deal:

```
              ♠ Q 8 7
              ♥ 7 6 2
              ♦ K Q 8 3
              ♣ 8 7 2
♠ A K 10 6               ♠ 9 5 2
♥ A J 10                 ♥ Q 5 4 3
♦ J 9                    ♦ 10 4
♣ Q 9 4 3               ♣ J 10 6 5
              ♠ J 4 3
              ♥ K 9 8
              ♦ A 7 6 5 2
              ♣ A K
```

Usually it is the hand with all the high cards that must be careful to avoid the endplay.

```
              ♠ A 10 5 4
              ♥ Q 10 9 7
              ♦ K 10 2
              ♣ A 8
♠ K 7 6
♥ A K
♦ Q J 6 4
♣ K 4 3 2
```

West	North	East	South
1♣	Dble	2♣	2♥
All Pass			

You lead the queen of diamonds to the king and partner's ace, declarer playing the five. Partner continues with the seven of diamonds to declarer's eight and your jack. Plan the defense.

Gather the evidence: You can see four defensive tricks and you may make your black-suit kings if partner has the black jacks.

Make a plan: If partner does have the black jacks you must be careful not to be endplayed. If you continue with a third diamond now, what will you do when you are in with a trump?

Implement the plan: Cash the ace and king of hearts and continue with a diamond. The full deal:

```
              ♠ A 10 5 4
              ♥ Q 10 9 7
              ♦ K 10 2
              ♣ A 8
♠ K 7 6                  ♠ J 9 8 3
♥ A K                    ♥ 6 5
♦ Q J 6 4               ♦ A 7 3
♣ K 4 3 2               ♣ J 7 6 5
              ♠ Q 2
              ♥ J 8 4 3 2
              ♦ 9 8 5
              ♣ Q 10 9
```

The best declarer can do is to play the queen of clubs to your king and dummy's ace. However, when he plays another club, partner rises with the jack and plays a third club. You must come to a spade at the end.

It is always very difficult to discard correctly when declarer runs a long suit against you—even more so when holding what is called a "poisoned suit." This is one which neither defender can play without giving declarer a trick—like both the spade and the club suit in the hand above; equally neither defender can discard the suit without leaving declarer with a successful guess to make two tricks. The most common example is when the lay-out is:

```
                Ax
Kx                          Jx
               Q10
```

In the following deal, the defender's heart suit is distributed in this way, but they passed their defensive test with flying colors.

Both Sides Vulnerable. Dealer South.

```
                ♠ 2
                ♥ A 10 9 8 5
                ♦ K 7 6 4
                ♣ K J 4
♠ 10 5 4 3                  ♠ A Q J 9 8 7
♥ K 7 3                     ♥ J 2
♦ A J 9 8                   ♦ Q 10 3
♣ 3 2                       ♣ 10 8
                ♠ K 6
                ♥ Q 6 4
                ♦ 5 2
                ♣ A Q 9 7 6 5
```

West	North	East	South
Helness	*Perron*	*Chemla*	*Rohowsky*
–	–	–	1♣
Pass	1♥	2♠	Pass
3♠	Dble	Pass	3NT
All Pass			

Here the East/West barrage made it difficult for North/South and they arrived in the wrong game. Nevertheless, the defenders still had to be careful. West led the three of spades to the jack and declarer's king. Declarer cashed six rounds of clubs. This was then the position:

```
                ♠ –
                ♥ A 10 9 8
                ♦ K 7
                ♣ –
♠ 10 5 4                    ♠ A Q 9 8
♥ K 7                       ♥ J 2
♦ A                         ♦ –
♣ –                         ♣ –
                ♠ 6
                ♥ Q 6 4
                ♦ 5 2
                ♣ –
```

Declarer exited with a spade, but West won with the ten, cashed the ace of diamonds on which East threw a heart, and played a spade to East for one down.

The possibility of a squeeze is harder to spot than an endplay, but on general principles it is a good idea to try to disrupt declarer's communications.

North/South Vulnerable. Dealer North.

```
                ♠ K 8
                ♥ A K 9 5
                ♦ A Q 10 7
                ♣ 6 4 2
♠ 7 3 2
♥ 8 4 3
♦ 5 3
♣ A K Q 10 8
```

West	North	East	South
–	1♥	Pass	1♠
Pass	1NT	Pass	4♠
All Pass			

Against South's four spades, you start with three rounds of clubs, partner following twice and then discarding the two of hearts. Plan the defense.

Gather the evidence: Partner is known to have two clubs and probably at most two spades. His heart discard shows a five-card suit, so he has at least four diamonds. He is in danger of being squeezed unless you are careful.

Make a plan: Partner will not be caught in a simple squeeze, because he will be discarding after dummy; if he is to be squeezed there must be a threat in declarer's hand, presumably when he has three diamonds. It is important to destroy declarer's communications by switching to his singleton.

Implement the plan: Play the four of hearts. The full deal:

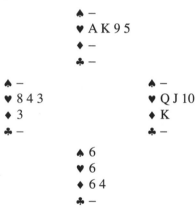

```
              ♠ K 8
              ♥ A K 9 5
              ♦ A Q 10 7
              ♣ 6 4 2
♠ 7 3 2                    ♠ 9 4
♥ 8 4 3                    ♥ Q J 10 7 2
♦ 5 3                      ♦ K J 9 8
♣ A K Q 10 8               ♣ 9 3
              ♠ A Q J 10 6 5
              ♥ 6
              ♦ 6 4 2
              ♣ J 7 5
```

Had you switched to a diamond, declarer would not have finessed since he would expect you to overcall with such a good club suit if you also had the king of diamonds. The end position would have been:

```
              ♠ –
              ♥ A K 9 5
              ♦ –
              ♣ –
♠ –                        ♠ –
♥ 8 4 3                    ♥ Q J 10
♦ 3                        ♦ K
♣ –                        ♣ –
              ♠ 6
              ♥ 6
              ♦ 6 4
              ♣ –
```

Your spot cards in the red suits are so small that when declarer cashes his last spade your partner will be squeezed in the red suits.

North/South Vulnerable. Dealer North.

```
              ♠ J 8 7
              ♥ 10 9 6
              ♦ A Q 10 7
              ♣ J 5 2
♠ 10 5 4
♥ J
♦ K J 4 3 2
♣ K Q 4 3
```

West	North	East	South
–	Pass	2♥(*)	2♠
Pass	3♠	Pass	4♠
All Pass			
(*) weak			

You lead your singleton heart against four spades. Partner wins the king, cashes the ace and plays back the seven, declarer contributing the two, three and four. Plan the defense.

Gather the evidence: It looks as if your partner has opened two hearts with a five-card suit, not unreasonable at this vulnerability. He has returned his middle card so has no preference between the minors.

Make a plan: You are in a position to count declarer's tricks: five spades, one heart, one club and at least two diamonds. If he has more than a singleton diamond he can always make three diamond tricks by way of two finesses. If he has a singleton diamond you need to switch to one now to avoid being squeezed in the minors.

Implement the plan: Play the three of diamonds. The full deal:

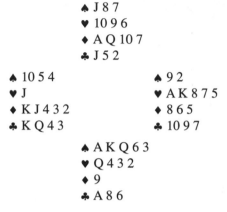

```
              ♠ J 8 7
              ♥ 10 9 6
              ♦ A Q 10 7
              ♣ J 5 2
♠ 10 5 4                   ♠ 9 2
♥ J                        ♥ A K 8 7 5
♦ K J 4 3 2                ♦ 8 6 5
♣ K Q 4 3                  ♣ 10 9 7
              ♠ A K Q 6 3
              ♥ Q 4 3 2
              ♦ 9
              ♣ A 8 6
```

SQUEEZES AND ENDPLAYS ON DECLARER

This can be one of the most satisfying of all plays—co-operation with partner to beat declarer at his own game.

Both Sides Vulnerable. Dealer South.

```
              ♠ Q J 9 4
              ♥ J 10 8 6
              ♦ 10
              ♣ Q 10 8 3
♠ K 10 6 2
♥ Q 9
♦ K Q 3
♣ K J 9 6
```

West	North	East	South
–	–	–	1♦
Pass	1♥	Pass	2NT
Pass	3NT	All Pass	

You lead the six of clubs. Dummy plays the ten, partner the two and declarer the four. The ten of diamonds is run to your queen and you continue with a small club to declarer's ace and partner's five. Declarer now plays the ace of diamonds and a small diamond to your queen—partner has followed with the two, the five and then the nine. Plan the defense.

Gather the evidence: Declarer's line of play indicates a six-card diamond suit and the points you can see together with 17 in the closed hand leave room for partner to have a king, which must be in hearts. Even if declarer has stretched and rebid 2NT with 16 points and partner has an ace, it is more likely to be in hearts than spades (partner's second club was the five and you know he has the seven).

Make a plan: You cannot play a spade as this will be declarer's ninth trick (four diamonds, two tricks each in clubs and spades and one heart). If declarer has three spades and two hearts you can afford to play the queen of hearts, but if he has two spades and three hearts this will be a disaster. How can you tell?

You must cash the king of clubs. There is no entry to the dummy so declarer cannot make use of his queen of clubs and it will force him to discard one of his diamond winners or to come down to two cards in each major. Now you *can* play the queen of hearts. Whatever declarer does, he cannot prevent partner gaining the lead to play a spade through.

Implement the plan: Cash the king of clubs: if declarer pitches a diamond, put him in dummy with a club and you must make two more tricks; if he pitches a major suit, you have to guess but it is most likely that he will have discarded from his three-card holding and then you can play the queen of hearts. The full deal:

```
              ♠ Q J 9 4
              ♥ J 10 8 6
              ♦ 10
              ♣ Q 10 8 3
♠ K 10 6 2              ♠ 7 5 3
♥ Q 9                   ♥ K 7 5 4
♦ K Q 3                 ♦ 9 5 2
♣ K J 9 6              ♣ 7 5 2
              ♠ A 8
              ♥ A 3 2
              ♦ A J 8 7 6 4
              ♣ A 4
```

When you were on lead with the king of diamonds, the position was:

```
              ♠ Q J
              ♥ J 10 8 6
              ♦ –
              ♣ Q 8
♠ K 10 6 2              ♠ 7 5 3
♥ Q 9                   ♥ K 7 5 4
♦ –                     ♦ –
♣ K J                  ♣ 7
              ♠ A 8
              ♥ A 3 2
              ♦ J 8 7
              ♣ –
```

Had you played the queen of hearts at this stage, declarer would have won with the ace and played a heart back. When you cashed the king of clubs declarer was sunk. If he had discarded a diamond winner you would simply have exited

with a club, putting him in dummy and forcing him to another nasty discard. Whatever he does he cannot possibly succeed.

East/West Vulnerable. Dealer East.

```
              ♠ A Q
              ♥ 8 6 4
              ♦ K Q 10 7 5 4 3
              ♣ 6
♠ 9 8 4 3
♥ Q 10
♦ A 9 6
♣ Q 10 9 3
```

West	North	East	South
–	–	Pass	1♣
Pass	1♦	Pass	1♠
Pass	3♦	Pass	3NT
All Pass			

You lead the unbid suit against South's 3NT, the queen of hearts. This runs to declarer's king, East playing the two. Declarer crosses to the ace of spades and plays a club to the jack and your queen. Plan the defense.

Gather the evidence: Declarer is threatening to take four clubs, at least one heart and probably three or four spades. It is possible that you have already set up four heart tricks with your opening lead, but it is more likely that declarer has a second heart stopper.

Make a plan: If partner's hearts are established there is no hurry to play one and if not they cannot be both set up and cashed for lack of entries. What you do want to do is tangle declarer's communications. The best way to do this is to remove his only dummy entry.

Implement the plan: Play the eight of spades. The full deal:

```
              ♠ A Q
              ♥ 8 6 4
              ♦ K Q 10 7 5 4 3
              ♣ 6
♠ 9 8 4 3              ♠ 7 6 5
♥ Q 10                 ♥ A 9 7 3 2
♦ A 9 6                ♦ J 8 2
♣ Q 10 9 3            ♣ 5 2
              ♠ K J 10 2
              ♥ K J 5
              ♦ –
              ♣ A K J 8 7 4
```

The best declarer can do is to win the spade in hand and clear the clubs. It looks as if he has four tricks in each black suit to go his heart trick, but look what happens when West cashes the ace of diamonds. Declarer must discard a black-suit winner. Now West exits with a spade and declarer has to lead away from his jack of hearts at trick twelve.

Our first expert deal came up in a European Junior Pairs event and won East/West a nomination for the Best Defended Hand of the Year.

Neither Side Vulnerable. Dealer East.

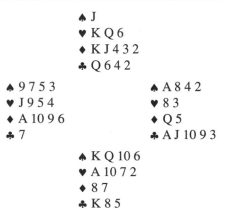

```
              ♠ J 5 4
              ♥ J 8 7 5 4
              ♦ –
              ♣ A 7 4 3 2
♠ 10                        ♠ Q 9 8 7 2
♥ A K                       ♥ 10 6 3 2
♦ 8 6 5 3 2                 ♦ Q J 4
♣ J 10 9 8 5                ♣ 6
              ♠ A K 6 3
              ♥ Q 9
              ♦ A K 10 9 7
              ♣ K Q
```

West	North	East	South
Berg	*Bruun*	*Johansson*	*Ron*
–	–	Pass	2NT
Pass	3♦	Pass	3♥
Pass	4♣	Pass	4NT
All Pass			

West led the jack of clubs to declarer's king. Declarer played back the nine of hearts which went to West's king and West continued with another club to declarer's queen, East discarding the nine of spades. The queen of hearts went to West's ace and he now switched to the ten of spades to South's king.

Declarer can now play ace, king and another diamond and whoever wins has to give dummy the lead. The defenders had other ideas, though, and they both unblocked diamonds to give declarer five tricks in the suit, but he could only manage nine tricks in total and was thus one down.

The following deal cropped up in the Vanderbilt, one of the major North American teams events, and features one of the best pairs in the world.

Neither Side Vulnerable. Dealer North.

```
              ♠ J
              ♥ K Q 6
              ♦ K J 4 3 2
              ♣ Q 6 4 2
♠ 9 7 5 3                   ♠ A 8 4 2
♥ J 9 5 4                   ♥ 8 3
♦ A 10 9 6                  ♦ Q 5
♣ 7                         ♣ A J 10 9 3
              ♠ K Q 10 6
              ♥ A 10 7 2
              ♦ 8 7
              ♣ K 8 5
```

West	North	East	South
Wolff		*Hamman*	
–	1♦	Pass	1♥
Pass	2♣	Pass	3NT
All Pass			

West led the seven of spades to his partner's ace and East returned a spade to declarer's king, dummy discarding a club. Declarer played a diamond to the jack and queen and East continued with another spade, dummy discarding a second club. Now declarer played a diamond to the king and another diamond, East discarding a spade and South a club. This was the position:

```
              ♠ –
              ♥ K Q 6
              ♦ 4 3
              ♣ Q 6
♠ 9                         ♠ –
♥ J 9 5 4                   ♥ 8 3
♦ A                         ♦ –
♣ 7                         ♣ A J 10 9 3
              ♠ 10
              ♥ A 10 7 2
              ♦ –
              ♣ K 8
```

West now played a club to dummy's queen and . . . East, the great Bob Hamman, ducked. Had he won and returned, say, a club, declarer would have cashed the ten of spades to squeeze West in the red suits. As it was West was under no pressure at all and declarer went one down. (He could have succeeded by cashing two top hearts and exiting with a diamond, but he preferred to play for hearts to break.)

The next deal also comes from a North American teams event where the scoring is like match-pointed pairs in that every trick is vital—all you have to do is score better than your opponents in the other room.

East/West Vulnerable. Dealer West.

```
              ♠ A 9 5
              ♥ K 8 7 5 4
              ♦ 8 2
              ♣ 9 8 3
♠ Q 6                       ♠ J 10 8 7 2
♥ Q 2                       ♥ J 10 6 3
♦ 10 9 7 5 4                ♦ K
♣ K Q J 5                   ♣ 10 7 2
              ♠ K 4 3
              ♥ A 9
              ♦ A Q J 6 3
              ♣ A 6 4
```

West	North	East	South
Lair	*Hamilton*	*Passell*	*Glubok*
Pass	Pass	Pass	1♦
Pass	1♥	Pass	2NT
Pass	3NT	All Pass	

West started off with king, queen and another club against South's no trump game. Declarer won, played a heart to the king, a diamond to the king and ace, the queen of diamonds to confirm the position and then ducked a diamond to West. He hoped that West would win, cash his long club and exit with a heart. The jack of diamonds would then squeeze East in the majors. West was awake, however, and refused to cash the club, simply exiting with a diamond. Declarer had to go one down.

The final deal sees Zia Mahmood in the unusual role (for him) of dummy. The star on this deal was West, Sidney Lazard, one of the great stalwarts of the game.

North/South Vulnerable. Dealer East.

```
                ♠ 10
                ♥ A
                ♦ A K Q 8 5 3
                ♣ Q 10 5 4 2
    ♠ A 8 4                   ♠ Q J 5 3 2
    ♥ J 10 9 7 2              ♥ 8 6 3
    ♦ 9 6                     ♦ 10 4
    ♣ 8 7 6                   ♣ K J 9
                ♠ K 9 7 6
                ♥ K Q 5 4
                ♦ J 7 2
                ♣ A 3
```

West	North	East	South
Lazard	*Zia*	*Kaplan*	*Rosenberg*
–	–	Pass	1♦
Pass	4NT	Pass	5♦
Pass	6♦	All Pass	

West did very well on this deal. First of all, he led the ace of spades, which, as you can see, was essential—on any other lead declarer can discard his spade loser on a heart. Then he switched to a club, thus preventing his partner being squeezed in the black suits. Declarer had to go one down.

West's heroic effort was not quite sufficient on this occasion as Zia's team went on to win this match, the Vanderbilt final, by 1 IMP.

PART XI

SIGNALLING

by Mark Horton

The aim of this section is to clarify the principles behind successful signalling in defense, using fairly standard general methods. In chess, a player who learns a long opening variation by rote without understanding the underlying ideas will soon be found out. The same principle applies in bridge where it is particularly important to understand the basic ideas involved before playing any particular method.

Since real life is more interesting than make believe, a large proportion of the deals in this section were actually played in major championships. Sometimes the carding methods of the players have been changed to those which are standard, but as you will see I am more concerned with principles than method.

Having said that I will recommend one or two specific treatments that many of the leading players have adopted to try to improve their defense and, in the final chapter, a number of alternative and additional methods are described.

Chapter 58

Laying Foundations

It was at the battle of Copenhagen that Nelson, on being instructed to disengage the enemy, put his telescope to his blind eye and said "I see no signal." Now while most bridge players have excellent eyesight it's remarkable how often they ask partner, "Didn't you see my signal?"

Why do things go wrong in defense? Perhaps the most common reason is that players get confused about which signal they are supposed to be giving or are trying to give.

In simple terms there are three basic signals which you may wish to give:

1. Count: when you tell partner how many cards you have in a suit.
2. Attitude: when you tell partner if you like their lead.
3. Suit Preference: when you try to tell partner which suit to switch to.

Before considering all three areas in depth, it is necessary to lay out some ground rules about leads.

Every defense starts with an opening lead. Accordingly, it is not sensible to get embroiled in a discussion on how best to signal to help the defense without at least knowing what our leading style is. Personally, I have nothing against third and fifth highest leads and I can even stomach the occasional session of attitude leads; however for the purposes of this book it makes sense to adopt the most popular leading style, covered by just about the best known defensive adage: "Fourth best of your longest and strongest."

While our basic leading method is going to be fourth best from good suits, in recent years most tournament players have modified the "fourth best" rule so that they lead the second highest card from bad suits, usually defined as a suit without an honor card. So, from Q753 we would lead the three but from 8-7-5-3, our choice would be the seven.

Similarly, we will choose to lead the middle card from three small cards rather than the old-fashioned top of nothing, so

from 8-7-5 lead the seven and not the eight. Certainly, it is true that partner might have some difficulty in distinguishing whether our lead of the seven is from 8-7-5 or from 8-7-5-3 but, in order to help him later in the play, with three small cards we will lead the middle card intending to play the highest card on the second round. This is a conventional arrangement commonly known as MUD—which sensibly stands for middle, up, down. To make the distinction between three and four small cards totally clear, with four small cards lead the second highest card and follow with the lowest, so that partner only has to decide whether you started with two cards or four.

All this may not strike the typical duplicate player as being very *avant garde*. That impression will not be altered by the statement that with two notable exceptions we will also adopt standard honor leads, so that most of the time we will lead the top of an honor sequence. However, the exceptions are much more up-market.

In the early days of bridge, players fell into two camps: those who led ace from ace-king and those who led king from ace-king. Whichever camp you belonged to, it was a fairly standard corollary that if you led these cards in the opposite way to your partnership agreement, then you were showing a doubleton.

Furthermore, depending on your style, until recently regardless of whether you would choose to lead the ace or king your partner would have to signal in the agreed partnership style. Traditionally, a high card from partner would encourage a continuation, while a low card would suggest no real interest in that suit, though some partnerships preferred to play count signals so that a high card usually showed an even number of cards while a low card suggested an odd number. You could choose which type of signal you gave but you couldn't do both.

Take a look at this deal which comes from the Women's Championship at the 1978 World Pairs Olympiad.

```
              ♠ 5
              ♥ Q 4
              ♦ K Q J 8 7 5 2
              ♣ A J 4
♠ A K 10 4 3 2          ♠ J 9 7 6
♥ 7 2                   ♥ K 10 8 6 5
♦ 10 4                  ♦ –
♣ 10 9 6                ♣ K 8 5 3
              ♠ Q 8
              ♥ A J 9 3
              ♦ A 9 6 3
              ♣ Q 7 2
```

It may be hard to believe but at a number of tables North/South came to rest in 3NT, and, even harder to believe, quite a few of them made it. How did this happen?

West led the ace of spades and East played an encouraging nine. Then, West had a problem because East would also play the nine of spades from Q9x. In both cases the defense could take the first six tricks but, if East had Q9x, West had to continue with a low spade while on the actual layout it was right to continue with the other top spade. Working on the assumption that South was more likely to have three spade than two, quite a few West players "guessed" wrong.

Of course, where the ace of spades was asking for count, West had no problem, for her partner's nine (unless a singleton) could only be from four cards or a doubleton. On the other hand, if East had held the jack, nine and six of spades then the play of the six would have told West that the queen of spades would not be dropping. Mind you, if East's spade holding had been Q96, then all the count signallers would have been able to do was congratulate South on an outrageous bid.

On balance, it seems that this was a situation where the count information was more beneficial than attitude, but inevitably there are occasions when the opposite would be the case.

Now wouldn't it be nice if West could choose the type of signal she wanted partner to give! Well, there is a surprisingly simple way of doing this. Using a mnemonic to help you remember, you can play A(ace) for Attitude and K(king) for Count.

It then becomes a question of deciding which piece of information you need to get from partner. Here one would probably come down on the side of a count signal and so lead the king.

I hope you are convinced that it's a good idea to adopt this leading method.

What happens if you are leading from a suit headed by the king-queen, as opposed to the ace-king? How can you get an attitude signal? The answer is to lead the queen. As long as partner remembers that this can be from king-queen as well as queen-jack you should have no problems.

Now let's take a look at a few specific examples of each type of signal:

```
              ♠ J 8 5
              ♥ A 10 9 6
              ♦ A K Q
              ♣ 10 7 3
♠ A K 7             ♠ Q 10 3
♥ 5 4               ♥ K 2
♦ 10 9 7 6 5        ♦ J 8 3 2
♣ 9 6 2            ♣ J 8 5 4
              ♠ 9 6 4 2
              ♥ Q J 8 7 3
              ♦ 4
              ♣ A K Q
```

After a simple bidding sequence: 1♥–3NT–4♥ you have to find an opening lead.

It was the late, great Barry Crane who said that "When God deals you the ace-king of a suit, you don't have a lead problem," and clearly you are going to start with a top spade.

How do you decide which signal to ask for?

As a general rule when you have more length in a suit there will be more chance of partner being short and hence able to ruff. On the other hand, if you are short you may well be facing length in partner's hand. Here it must be correct to find out if partner likes spades so the ace is the correct card, since it is asking for attitude.

With his holding East can afford to play the ten, insuring the defenders take their spade tricks after which the king of trumps will defeat the contract.

Of course, East's actual holding could have been Q32. He would then have to play the three and hope West noticed that the two was missing.

Now look at a situation where a count signal is required:

```
              ♠ 9 8 2
              ♥ A K 8 5 3
              ♦ 6
              ♣ J 8 5 3
```

You have to make the opening lead after this bidding sequence:

North	South
1♦	1♠
2♠	3♣
3♦	4NT
5♦	5♠
Pass	

You need to know how many hearts partner has and so the correct opening lead is the king of hearts.

Dummy comes down, and this is what you can see:

```
                    ♠ A Q J 10
                    ♥ J 2
                    ♦ K J 9 3 2
                    ♣ 7 6
   ♠ 9 8 2
   ♥ A K 8 5 3
   ♦ 6
   ♣ J 8 5 3
```

Partner plays the four of hearts and declarer follows with the ten. What do you try next?

A study of the cards tells you that partner must have either one, three or five hearts. Clearly the latter is a big favorite since South didn't bid hearts and he would be unlikely to use Blackwood with three losing hearts in his hand. You cannot take any more heart tricks and it's fairly obvious to switch to a diamond (especially so if you consider that the most likely reason for your opponents to stop at the five level after using Blackwood is that they are missing two aces). This enables you to get a ruff because the full deal turns out to be:

```
                    ♠ A Q J 10
                    ♥ J 2
                    ♦ K J 9 3 2
                    ♣ 7 6
   ♠ 9 8 2                        ♠ 6 4
   ♥ A K 8 5 3                    ♥ Q 9 7 6 4
   ♦ 6                            ♦ A 10 5
   ♣ J 8 5 3                      ♣ 10 4 2
                    ♠ K 7 5 3
                    ♥ 10
                    ♦ Q 8 7 4
                    ♣ A K Q 9
```

You may think this is pretty obvious, but when this hand came up in the Round Robin of the 1981 World Championship, five spades was allowed to make on two of the three occasions it was bid.

One thing should be made clear: every defensive signal is merely an aid for the defenders—it is not a substitute for clear thinking. You cannot afford to play as if you are in a strait jacket.

If you have read other books about signalling you may have noticed that some authors are enthusiastic about count signals, while other prefer attitude. Of course both methods are playable, but neither will be good enough on its own.

Here is a hand which has been used to illustrate the dangers of relying on count signals alone.

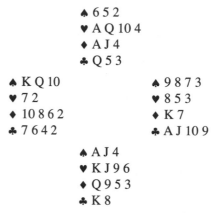

```
                    ♠ 6 5 2
                    ♥ A Q 10 4
                    ♦ A J 4
                    ♣ Q 5 3
   ♠ K Q 10                       ♠ 9 8 7 3
   ♥ 7 2                          ♥ 8 5 3
   ♦ 10 8 6 2                     ♦ K 7
   ♣ 7 6 4 2                      ♣ A J 10 9
                    ♠ A J 4
                    ♥ K J 9 6
                    ♦ Q 9 5 3
                    ♣ K 8
```

Against South's four heart contract West leads the king of spades and receives a count signal of the eight of spades from East. As you can see, it would be fatal for West to continue with a spade. Of course you would have had no problem because, on your opening lead of the queen of spades, partner's three of spades would have shown his lack of interest in the suit.

To summarize: I recommend that a lead of either the ace or queen should ask partner to give an attitude signal while a lead of a king asks for count. Before going on to examine the main types of signal in rather more detail, try the following lead quiz to make sure you understand the principles.

Quiz 37

In all the following hands you are West, what would you lead?

1.
♠ A K 7 4	West	North	East	South
♥ 5 2	–	–	–	2♥
♦ J 10 5	Pass	6♥	All Pass	
♣ 8 6 4 2				

2.
♠ A 7 2	West	North	East	South
♥ A Q J 9 3	–	–	–	1NT
♦ 6 5 2	Pass	3NT	All Pass	
♣ 7 4				

3.
♠ J 7 3	West	North	East	South
♥ K J 7 6 4	–	–	–	1NT
♦ 5 2	Pass	3NT	All Pass	
♣ A 8 6				

4.
♠ K J 4	West	North	East	South
♥ 9 7 5 4	–	–	–	1NT
♦ Q 6 2	Pass	3NT	All Pass	
♣ Q 6 5				

5.
♠ 4	West	North	East	South
♥ AK5	–	–	–	1♣
♦ KJ10973	1♦	2♥	Pass	3♣
♣ QJ4	Pass	3♥	Pass	3NT
	All Pass			

6.
♠ KQ83	West	North	East	South
♥ 4	–	–	–	1♥
♦ K10952	Pass	2♣	Pass	2♥
♣ 842	Pass	4♥	All Pass	

Answers to Quiz 37

1. The ♠K.

You are hoping to be able to cash two spade tricks. By getting a count signal from partner you should be able to judge whether to cash the ace of spades or switch to another suit.

2. The ♥A.

Since you have a sure entry in the ace of spades you can afford to have a look at dummy. If it contains just two hearts including the king you will be able to continue with a low heart at trick two. The standard lead of the queen would give declarer two heart stoppers if either hand held four hearts to the ten. The heart king is likely to be in the declarer's hand to give that hand the points to open 1NT.

3. The ♥6.

Fourth highest of your longest and strongest. With a good suit and a side entry this is the ideal time to attack.

4. The ♥7.

Second highest from a poor suit. Notice that if partner gets the lead early and if he knows that you have a poor suit he might switch to something more profitable.

5. The ♦K.

One of the exceptions that proves the rule. This is not the time to cash a high heart since you hope to use those as the entries to establish and cash your diamonds. It is clearly right to try to establish the diamonds, so lead one of those but choose the king just in case dummy has the singleton queen. Two diamond leads will clear the suit no matter where the ace and queen are located.

6. The ♠Q.

A good example of our recommended honor lead style. You are hoping the setting tricks will come from diamonds and spades, so lead the queen of spades to ask partner if he likes the suit.

Count Signals

OUT FOR THE COUNT

It is, obviously, important to be able to help your partner distinguish whether you have led from three or four small cards. In principle, count signals take this idea further by concentrating on distinguishing between holding an odd number and an even number of cards. The traditional way of giving count is to play high-low to show an even number of cards. Conversely, low-high shows an odd number of cards.

Here is an illustration of how the signals work:

High-Low

    ♠ A K 7 4   ♠ 9 2

Partner leads the king of spades, you play the nine of spades, which is the highest of your two cards, to show an even number.

Low-High

    ♠ A K 7 4   ♠ 9 5 2

Partner leads the king of spades, this time you play the two of spades, followed by a higher spade when he continues the suit.

Of course, if, for example, you show an even number of cards, there are times when partner will have to work out whether you have two, four or even six cards in the suit; however the two card differential usually makes it possible for partner to assess the distribution.

Let's look at some examples:

First put yourself in the West seat for the following deal with South playing in 3NT after a Staymanic sequence. You lead your fourth best heart, and when dummy appears this is what you can see:

        ♠ Q J 9 6
        ♥ Q J 5
        ♦ K J 10 2
        ♣ K 8

♠ K 2
♥ K 9 6 4 2
♦ 8 7
♣ J 5 4 2

South	North
1NT(*)	2♣(**)
2♦(***)	3NT
Pass	

(*)   12-14
(**) Stayman
(**) No four card major

Dummy's jack holds the trick while partner plays the three and declarer the seven. Declarer plays the queen of spades from the dummy, seven from partner, four from declarer and you take your king. What do you play next?

It is fairly clear that declarer has the ace of hearts, so another heart play from you figures to give him an extra trick with the queen of hearts, or does it?

No, not in this case.

Consider the layout of the heart suit carefully. You have five cards in the suit and dummy has three, so that leaves your partner and declarer with only five hearts between them. Playing standard count signals, your partner's three of hearts should indicate an odd number of cards in hearts, which must be either one or three. In this case it must be three because South has already denied holding four hearts in his response to North's Stayman inquiry. So, now you know that East has three hearts. That means that South must have started with only two. Therefore, South's heart ace is now singleton and, far from giving declarer a gratuitous trick, a heart continuation now will beat the contract if either defender can get the lead before declarer cashes nine tricks. So you play the two of hearts, so your partner knows that you started with a five card suit and therefore must be holding three winners in the suit if only you can get back in.

Look at the full deal:

```
              ♠ Q J 9 6
              ♥ Q J 5
              ♦ K J 10 2
              ♣ K 8
♠ K 2                      ♠ 8 7 5 3
♥ K 9 6 4 2                ♥ 10 8 3
♦ 8 7                      ♦ A 9 6
♣ J 5 4 2                  ♣ Q 6 3
              ♠ A 10 4
              ♥ A 7
              ♦ Q 5 4 3
              ♣ A 10 9 7
```

After winning the ace of hearts, South has three spade tricks, two hearts and two top clubs. There is no way he can arrive at nine tricks without playing diamonds, and when he does your partner will win the trick with the ace and play his third heart.

Notice also that if you were tempted to duck the king of spades you might have severely regretted it. Not because declarer could have seen through the back of your cards and dropped your singleton king, but by switching his attention to diamonds he would have made three diamonds and two tricks in every other suit.

Now, move over to the East seat for this deal from the 1992 World Teams Olympiad in Salsomaggiore, Italy.

West	North	East	South
–	–	–	1NT(*)
Pass	2♦(**)	Pass	2♥
Pass	3♦	Pass	3NT
All Pass			

(*) 12-14
(**) Transfer

Your partner leads the three of clubs to reveal this layout:

```
              ♠ A J 7
              ♥ J 10 9 8 6
              ♦ Q J 6 2
              ♣ A
                          ♠ 10 9 2
                          ♥ A 4 2
                          ♦ 9 4
                          ♣ 8 6 5 4 2
```

Can it possibly matter which club you play to this trick, given you only hold five small ones?

Yes, it is important to let partner know how many clubs you hold, therefore you should play the two of clubs, to show an odd number.

When declarer wins the first trick with the ace of clubs he plays the seven of clubs from hand. He continues with the queen of diamonds from dummy. Which card should you play?

The nine, beginning a high-low to show an even number of diamonds.

The queen of diamonds holds the trick, partner playing the seven, and declarer continues by playing dummy's two of diamonds to his king and your partner's ace. Partner returns the eight of diamonds while you discard a spade. Declarer wins this trick in dummy and plays the jack of hearts. What do you do now?

Of course, it is possible that declarer will misguess the heart suit if you play low smoothly, but you should go up with the ace to play a club because your partner's opening lead was presumably from a four card suit. You must hope that partner started with something like KJ93, in which case you will have three tricks to take in the suit provided that you can lead through declarer's queen.

Notice that with most other holdings partner might have led an honor or he would have been well placed to continue the suit himself when he got the lead with the ace of diamonds. If declarer sneaks through his king of hearts, he will have his nine tricks.

Let's look at the entire hand:

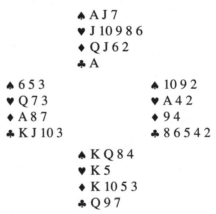

```
              ♠ A J 7
              ♥ J 10 9 8 6
              ♦ Q J 6 2
              ♣ A
♠ 6 5 3                    ♠ 10 9 2
♥ Q 7 3                    ♥ A 4 2
♦ A 8 7                    ♦ 9 4
♣ K J 10 3                 ♣ 8 6 5 4 2
              ♠ K Q 8 4
              ♥ K 5
              ♦ K 10 5 3
              ♣ Q 9 7
```

Rising with the ace of hearts and leading a club enables West to take three club tricks and beat the contract. On this particular deal the contract might have failed by two tricks if West had chosen to lead the jack of clubs at trick one since East would have been able to overtake the three of clubs on the fourth round of the suit to take a fourth club trick, while the lead of the three blocked the suit.

Now, what benefit did East derive from showing count on this deal? In absolute terms, not a lot. But consider the deal again from West's point of view:

♠ A J 7
♥ J 10 9 8 6
♦ Q J 6 2
♣ A

♠ 6 5 3
♥ Q 7 3
♦ A 8 7
♣ K J 10 3

When East played the two of clubs at trick one, West knew that he held either three or five clubs. When he won the ace of diamonds at trick three, he also knew that East probably had two diamonds. Consequently, West surmised that East probably had five clubs rather than three because South might not have opened 1NT with a 2-2-4-5 distribution. He also knew that with a minimum of three points missing there was a fair chance that East would have an entry somewhere to lead a club through.

However, having said that, West did not have enough information at his disposal to defend correctly with certainty. In particular, if East had held the queen of clubs it was quite possible that South would make nine tricks unless West continued with clubs right away. As it was West did well to decide that South was likely to hold the queen of clubs and exit passively with a diamond.

These two deals demonstrate that although giving count provides a lot of information to the defenders, which is frequently invaluable, it is not a panacea. However, if your partner can rely on you showing whether you have an even number or an odd number of cards in each suit as it is played, it will help him to build up a much clearer picture of the hand.

QUIZ 38

1.
	West	North	East	South
♠ A K J 5		–	1NT	Pass	4♥
♥ 6 3				
♦ A 6 4				
♣ 9 8 7 2				

As West, what would you lead?

2.
	West	North	East	South
♠ 4		–	–	–	1NT
♥ A K J 10 3				
♦ 8 2	Pass	2♣	Pass	2♠
♣ J 10 8 4 2	Pass	3♠	Pass	4♠
	All Pass			

What do you lead?

3.
	West	North	East	South
♠ 7 6 4 2		–	–	–	1♥
♥ 5				
♦ Q 7 5 3	Pass	2♥	Pass	4♥
♣ K Q 10 2	All Pass			

Your partner leads the king of spades. Which card do you play?

4.
	West	North	East	South
♠ 7 2		–	1♥	2♠(*)	3♥
♥ 6 4				
♦ A 10 9 6 3	Pass	4♥	All Pass	
♣ Q J 8 2				

(*) Weak?

Your partner leads the king of spades. Which card do you play?

5.
	West	North	East	South
♠ 9 4		–	–	–	1♥
♥ A 7 2				
♦ Q J 9 3	2♠(*)	3♥	Pass	4♥
♣ Q 10 6 4	All Pass			

(*) Weak

Your partner leads the king of spades and you see this dummy:

♠ Q 7
♥ Q J 5
♦ K 7 4 2
♣ 9 8 7 3

What do you play?

6.
	West	North	East	South
♠ 8 4		–	1NT	Pass	6♥
♥ 5 2				
♦ 8 7 6 4 2	All Pass			
♣ A K 8 3				

What do you lead?

7.
	West	North	East	South
♠ Q 8 7 4 2		–	–	–	1♦
♥ A 5				
♦ K 6	Pass	3♦	Pass	3NT
♣ 10 9 7 3	All Pass			

You lead the four of spades. Dummy appears with:

♠ J 10 5
♥ J 6 3
♦ Q J 10 7 3
♣ A 8

Declarer plays the jack of spades from dummy, and the king of spades from hand, partner following with the nine. Declarer crosses to dummy with a club and finesses the queen of diamonds. You win this trick with the king of diamonds. What next?

8.
	West	North	East	South
♠ K 10 9 7		–	–	–	2NT
♥ 9 4				
♦ A 10 3	Pass	3NT	All Pass	
♣ K 9 4 3				

Your partner leads the queen of clubs and you see this dummy:

♠ 6 4 2
♥ 7 5 3
♦ K Q J 7 5
♣ 6 5

Declarer wins the third club with the ace and plays the eight of diamonds to dummy's king, partner following with the two. How do you defend from here?

1. ♠K.

You would like to know how many spades partner has, so ask for count by leading the ♠K.

2. ♥K.

This is the same situation as in the first question.

3. ♠6.

Partner has asked you how many spades you have. With four small cards you play the second highest.

4. ♠7.

Partner has asked you to tell him how many spades you have—so play the seven of spades to show you have two. If partner had led the ace of spades asking you to encourage or discourage, your decision might well depend on whether or not you could over-ruff the dummy.

5. ♠9.

Partner has asked you to tell him how many spades you have and you have no reason to lie, so play the ♠9. Let's look at the full deal:

```
              ♠ Q 7
              ♥ Q J 5
              ♦ K 7 4 2
              ♣ 9 8 7 3
♠ A K J 6 5 3              ♠ 9 4
♥ 4 3                     ♥ A 7 2
♦ 10 5                    ♦ Q J 9 3
♣ J 5 2                   ♣ Q 10 6 4
              ♠ 10 8 2
              ♥ K 10 9 8 6
              ♦ A 8 6
              ♣ A K
```

When you play the nine of spades, partner knows that you have at most two spades, and, as a result he knows that declarer has at least three spades. His best chance of beating the contract is to try to keep declarer from ruffing his spade losers by switching to a trump, provided that you cooperate by ducking. Then, when South wins and plays a second spade, trying to set up the ruff, West should win and play a second round of trumps. You then take your ace and play a third round.

6. ♣K

By getting a count signal from partner you should be able to work out whether the ♣A will be the setting trick.

7. ♥A.

Partner's ♠9 must be from a doubleton (or even a singleton), so you should not be fooled by declarer's play of the ♠K, for he clearly has ♠AKx. The best chance is to find partner with a decent heart suit.

8. Duck.

If declarer continues with the ♦Q you should win the ace because you know that your partner has an odd number of diamonds. If he has a singleton, declarer has four and there is nothing you can do to stop him enjoying the suit; however if your partner has three diamonds then declarer only has two, so by winning the second round of the suit you can hold his diamond winners to just one since there looks to be no other entry to dummy.

Of course, if partner plays a card like the four on the first round you are not in such a good position on the second round because you have to guess whether he started with ♦42 or ♦964. You can be sure of holding declarer to just two winners in the suit by ducking the second round, or you can hope that your partner started with three and win the second round, but if it turns out that partner had a doubleton declarer will actually make four tricks in the suit.

KEEP ON COUNTING

It should be obvious that knowing how many cards each player holds in a particular situation will be valuable to the defenders. The most obvious situation is where the defense are cashing out to defeat the contract.

Consider this deal from the European Championships in Brighton back in 1987.

North/South Vulnerable. Dealer North.

```
              ♠ Q 6 3
              ♥ 5
              ♦ A Q 10 9 5
              ♣ A K J 4
```

West	North	East	South
Forrester	*Sverisson*	*Brock*	*Baldursson*
–	Pass	Pass	4♥
Dble	Pass	4♠	5♥
Dble	All Pass		

You hope you have three minor suit winners to beat the contract of 5♥ doubled. To find out how many tricks you can take in clubs you start with the ♣K, asking partner to signal his count.

When dummy comes down, this is what you can see:

```
              ♠ A 10 9 8
              ♥ 10 8 7
              ♦ K 7
              ♣ 9 8 3 2
♠ Q 6 3
♥ 5
♦ A Q 10 9 5
♣ A K J 4
```

Partner plays the ♣10 while declarer follows with the ♣7.

How many clubs does partner have?

An even number (assuming the ten isn't a singleton), either two or four.

If it's two, can you defeat the contract?

It will depend on the distribution of declarer's hand. At this vulnerability he must have a lot of tricks and partner may be void in hearts. Since partner bid 4♠, the possible shapes for declarer are: 2-9-1-1, 1-9-0-3 or 1-8-1-3.

What about 0-8-2-3? That would give East six spades and he might have opened with a weak two bid.

How do you continue the defense?

If declarer has either hand with three clubs there will be no problem unless he has a singleton king of spades in a 1-9-0-3 shape. However if South is 2-9-1-1 and partner has the spade king it is essential to switch to spades immediately. Since the latter case is more likely, it must be right to switch to spades immediately.

Take a look at the full hand:

```
              ♠ A 10 9 8
              ♥ 10 8 7
              ♦ K 7
              ♣ 9 8 3 2
♠ Q 6 3                      ♠ K J 5 2
♥ 5                          ♥ –
♦ A Q 10 9 5                 ♦ J 8 4 3 2
♣ A K J 4                    ♣ Q 10 6 5
              ♠ 7 4
              ♥ A K Q J 9 6 4 3 2
              ♦ 6
              ♣ 7
```

Tip
When making a signal, it is always sensible to make the message as clear as possible. In particular, when showing an even number with a four card suit, try to start your high/low by playing the second highest card.

As you can see it would be fatal to try to cash a second club as declarer can lead towards the ♦K and establish a discard for his losing spade. East made it very clear that he had an even number of clubs, rather than play the ♣6 which could have been from a three card holding.

Here is a simpler example from the same event, but this time from the women's section.

Both Sides Vulnerable. Dealer West.

```
              ♠ Q 7 6 4 2
              ♥ Q 2
              ♦ 5
              ♣ 9 8 5 3 2
```

West	North	East	South
S. Horton	*Møller*	*Landy*	*Kalkerup*
–	1♣	1♦	2♥
Pass	2NT	Pass	4♦(*)
Pass	4♠(**)	Dble	5♣
Pass	5♥	Pass	6♥
All Pass			

(*) Asking bid in diamonds
(**) The diamond ace

What are you going to lead against South's 6♥ contract?

Obviously partner has something in spades, either the ace or king, or perhaps even both.

However, declarer should not have two losing spades as she went on to slam, despite the double of four spades. Since North is known to hold the ace of diamonds and East overcalled in that suit, you decide to start with your singleton diamond.

This is what you see:

```
              ♠ J 9 8
              ♥ 3
              ♦ A Q 3 2
              ♣ K Q J 7 4
♠ Q 7 6 4 2
♥ Q 2
♦ 5
♣ 9 8 5 3 2
```

Declarer plays the ♦Q and partner wins with the king. She follows this with the ♠K and declarer follows with the ♠10.

It's always pleasant to take the first two tricks against a slam. Your partner is asking for a count signal in spades, so you play the ♠2. With no more spades to cash partner gives you a diamond ruff.

The full deal:

```
              ♠ J 9 8
              ♥ 3
              ♦ A Q 3 2
              ♣ K Q J 7 4
♠ Q 7 6 4 2                  ♠ A K 5 3
♥ Q 2                        ♥ 8 4
♦ 5                          ♦ K J 10 9 4
♣ 9 8 5 3 2                  ♣ 10 6
              ♠ 10
              ♥ A K J 10 9 7 6 5
              ♦ 8 7 6
              ♣ A
```

Tip
Always remember the bidding—especially when making your opening lead.

Your diamond lead started a fatal attack on declarer's communications. If West had been very brave, he could have set this contract more tricks but giving East an immediate ruff, suggesting the spade return by leading back the diamond jack and allowing East to make both of his trump tricks.

Put yourself in the East seat for the next example where you will need to draw some very subtle inferences.

North/South Vulnerable. Dealer South.

```
              ♠ Q 7 5 3
              ♥ Q 3 2
              ♦ K Q 5
              ♣ A J 10

                              ♠ K J 8 4
                              ♥ 9 6 4
                              ♦ J 10 9 4
                              ♣ K 6
```

West	North	East	South
–	–	–	1NT
Pass	2♣	Pass	2♦
Pass	3NT	All Pass	

Partner leads the ♥5. Declarer wins the first trick in hand with the ♥K and plays the ♣2 for the three, ten and your king.

You need four more defensive tricks. Where are they coming from?

Since you can see the three hearts lower than partner's lead, it is clear that partner can't have more than four hearts. The three of clubs shows an odd number and, since he would no doubt have led from a five card suit, it looks like partner has only three clubs. Declarer therefore has five.

If declarer has the ace of diamonds, he probably already has nine tricks. Even if partner has the ace of diamonds, it's well placed for declarer. All the evidence points to the need for an immediate attempt to cash out, and the only possible suit that can provide enough tricks is spades. So you switch to the four of spades. The full deal:

```
              ♠ Q 7 5 3
              ♥ Q 3 2
              ♦ K Q 5
              ♣ A J 10

    ♠ A 10 2                 ♠ K J 8 4
    ♥ 10 8 7 5               ♥ 9 6 4
    ♦ 7 6 2                  ♦ J 10 9 4
    ♣ 9 5 3                  ♣ K 6

              ♠ 9 6
              ♥ A K J
              ♦ A 8 3
              ♣ Q 8 7 4 2
```

Well worked out. Notice, however, that it would have been just a little bit easier for East if West had chosen to lead the eight of hearts rather than the five to indicate a poor suit.

Tip
Frequently the combination of lead information and count signal information will enable a defender to build up a picture of the whole hand.

Now put yourself in the East seat for the following exciting deal from the 1985 US Trials.

Both Sides Vulnerable. Dealer South.

```
              ♠ Q 6 2
              ♥ 10 9 8 7 4 2
              ♦ J 8 5
              ♣ 7

                              ♠ A J 9 5 4 3
                              ♥ A K 5
                              ♦ 10 9 2
                              ♣ 2
```

West	North	East	South
–	–	–	1♣
Pass	1♥	2♠	3♦
4♠	Pass	Pass	4NT(*)
Pass	5♦	Dble	All Pass
(*) Takeout			

West leads the ♠7 against South's contract of 5♦ doubled. Since your partner supported you fairly vigorously in the auction, you are confident that he has the ♠K so you play the jack of spades and declarer ruffs with the ♦6.

Declarer's next move is to cash the ♣A on which partner plays the ♣10. Next comes the ♣3, ♣8 from partner, ruffed with the ♦5 from dummy. How do you defend?

It is almost instinctive to overruff, but this would prove to be an expensive mistake. Have a look at the full deal and you will see what I mean.

```
                 ♠ Q 6 2
                 ♥ 10 9 8 7 4 2
                 ♦ J 8 5
                 ♣ 7
♠ K 10 8 7                        ♠ A J 9 5 4 3
♥ Q J 3                           ♥ A K 5
♦ 4 3                             ♦ 10 9 2
♣ K Q 10 8                        ♣ 2
                 ♠ –
                 ♥ 6
                 ♦ A K Q 7 6
                 ♣ A J 9 6 5 4 3
```

Let's suppose that you overruff and force declarer again by playing a low spade. Declarer then ruffs a second club with the ♦J, draws trumps in two rounds and concedes a club to your partner and eventually loses a heart to go down one.

Now suppose that you discard instead of over-ruffing the diamond. If declarer draws trumps in three rounds and concedes a club, your partner will be able to force out his last trump before declarer can establish his club suit. If, on the other hand, declarer ruffs a spade, ruffs a club with the jack of diamonds and then draws trump, he will have no trump left and your partner will still have a club winner, so your side will take the rest. In fact, the best declarer can do when you refuse to overruff is escape for three down; a penalty of 800.

How would count signals help you work all this out? Certainly, by playing the ♣10 followed by the ♣8 partner has shown you an even number of clubs, which really must be four because with nine clubs South would have insisted on playing in that suit. South is pretty well marked with a seven card club suit. It is inconceivable that South has fewer than five diamonds since he would hardly have offered North a choice by bidding 4NT with just 4-7 in the minors, and no doubt if South has six diamonds we will be struggling to beat five diamonds at all. So, in practical terms the combination of South's bidding and our partner's count signals have told us that South is probably 0-1-5-7.

Tip

Don't forget that it is important to give the count in declarer's suits as well as your own, so that both defenders can build up a picture of declarer's hand.

Now try this deal from The World Olympiad played in Miami in 1986.

Neither Side Vulnerable. Dealer North.

```
                 ♠ 9
                 ♥ Q 8 6 5 3
                 ♦ A 7 3
                 ♣ A Q 9 4
```

West	North	East	South
Fazli	*Meckstroth*	*Zia*	*Rodwell*
–	1♦(*)	Pass	1♥
Pass	1♠	Pass	2♣
Pass	3♥(**)	Pass	3NT
All Pass			

(*) Precision
(**) Shortage in hearts

What would you lead against South's 3NT contract?

You know that North is short in hearts so is likely to have either a 4-1-4-4 or 4-0-4-5 distribution. Although South bid the suit you decide to lead the ♥5, in preference to a club. When dummy is revealed, this is what you can see:

```
                 ♠ A 10 3 2
                 ♥ –
                 ♦ K Q 8 5
                 ♣ J 10 7 3 2
♠ 9
♥ Q 8 6 5 3
♦ A 7 3
♣ A Q 9 4
```

Partner produces the ♥A, while declarer discards the ♣2 from dummy and plays the ♥4 from hand.

Partner returns the ♥7 on which declarer plays the ♥J; you win the ♥Q while dummy discards the ♣3. Since the two of hearts is missing it looks as if declarer started with ♥KJ1094. You already have two heart tricks and you can see two aces. Where are you going to find the fifth defensive trick from?

Obviously you will get another trick from clubs if declarer plays them first, but aren't you worried that after knocking out the ace of diamonds declarer might have nine tricks without playing clubs at all? After all, partner has already produced the ♥A so you cannot rely on him making a further contribution. Can you see any way in which you might set up an extra trick for yourself?

Yes, if partner has a doubleton club. Switch to a low club now and when you regain the lead with the ♦A you will be able to cash the ♣A with profitable results.

You duly switch to ♣4 and declarer wins with the ♣10 in dummy, partner playing the ♣8. Declarer then continues with a diamond to the jack, partner following with the ♦2. Hoping partner's club was from a doubleton, you take the ♦A and lay down the ♣A. Here is the full deal:

```
              ♠ A 10 3 2
              ♥ –
              ♦ K Q 8 5
              ♣ J 10 7 3 2
♠ 9                        ♠ Q 8 6 5 4
♥ Q 8 6 5 3                ♥ A 7 2
♦ A 7 3                    ♦ 9 4 2
♣ A Q 9 4                  ♣ 8 5
              ♠ K J 7
              ♥ K J 10 9 4
              ♦ J 10 6
              ♣ K 6
```

Don't be disappointed if you got this hand wrong. It's a tough problem and at the table declarer was successful.

Notice, too, that if East had played the ♣5 rather than the eight, West would have known it was a singleton because if East has three small clubs then South's king would be singleton. Armed with that information, West might still have a chance of beating the contract.

Suppose, for example, that this was the actual deal:

```
              ♠ A 10 3 2
              ♥ –
              ♦ K Q 8 5
              ♣ J 10 7 3 2
♠ 9                        ♠ Q 8 7 6 5 4
♥ Q 8 6 5 3                ♥ A 7 2
♦ A 7 3                    ♦ 9 4 2
♣ A Q 9 4                  ♣ 5
              ♠ K J
              ♥ K J 10 9 4
              ♦ J 10 6
              ♣ K 8 6
```

On this layout West knows the club position after East plays the ♣5 on the first round of the suit, so there is no point in continuing the suit. So when declarer switches attention to diamonds West holds off until the third round and then exits with the ♥8. Declarer has only eight tricks available: two spades, two hearts, three diamonds and one club. If declarer takes an early spade finesse against East to set up an extra trick there he will no longer have communications to make both the extra spade trick and the long diamond.

Alternatively, if East were dealt four diamonds and five spades, declarer would only have two diamonds and ducking the first two rounds would also leave him a trick short.

Tip
Don't be afraid to lead a suit bid by the opponents against their no trump contract.

Now try another deal from the same championship. This time you are East:

Both Sides Vulnerable. Dealer West.

```
              ♠ K 9 8
              ♥ A 10 5
              ♦ A
              ♣ A K Q J 8 5
                           ♠ Q 4
                           ♥ K J 4
                           ♦ Q J 10 4 2
                           ♣ 10 7 2
```

West	North	East	South
Gwodzinsky	*Mitchell*	*Truscott*	*Kearse*
Pass	2♦(*)	Pass	2NT
Pass	3♣	3♦	3NT
Pass	6NT	All Pass	

(*) Strong and artificial

West leads the ♦6 against South's 6NT contract. Perforce, declarer wins the opening lead in dummy with the ace of diamonds, playing the five from hand. You play the ♦2 to show an odd number.

Declarer continues with the ♥5 from dummy. Having escaped any serious retribution for your somewhat risky intervention, you are hoping to defeat the contract. How do you plan your defense?

Declarer must have the ♦K for her 3NT bid. If she also has the ♠A and the ♥Q, twelve tricks are certain. You don't want to run the risk of declarer making all thirteen tricks, so you take the ♥K on which partner plays the ♥7, declarer following with the ♥2.

You continue with the ♦Q and declarer wins with the king, while partner plays the ♦8, the ♥10 being discarded from dummy.

Declarer now starts on the club suit, following to the first three rounds from hand, while partner follows once and then discards the ♦3 and the ♠2.

At this stage the following cards are left:

```
              ♠ K 9 8
              ♥ A
              ♦ –
              ♣ J 8 5
                           ♠ Q 4
                           ♥ J 4
                           ♦ J 10 4
                           ♣ –
```

What do you discard when declarer plays the jack of clubs from dummy?

You know partner started with three diamonds and one club. From her play in the major suits you deduce that she had five spades and four hearts. You also know she holds the ♥Q because declarer would have claimed twelve tricks by now if she had held that card. Since you only have two spades, you know it is essential that partner guards the spades, while you must guard both hearts and diamonds.

Partner knows you have five diamonds and three clubs but cannot know your major suit distribution. If partner plays you for three spades and discards two more, declarer will score twelve tricks and make her contract.

How can you prevent this?

By the time declarer has cashed all of North's clubs you are going to have to discard a spade, so you might as well discard one now to encourage partner to hold on to hers. More dramatic still, to beat the contract partner is going to need both the jack and ten of spades so you might as well make the position perfectly clear to your partner by discarding the queen of spades first. Here is the full deal:

```
            ♠ K 9 8
            ♥ A 10 5
            ♦ A
            ♣ A K Q J 8 5
♠ J 10 7 3 2              ♠ Q 4
♥ Q 9 7 3                ♥ K J 4
♦ 8 6 3                  ♦ Q J 10 4 2
♣ 3                      ♣ 10 7 2
            ♠ A 6 5
            ♥ 8 6 2
            ♦ K 9 7 5
            ♣ 9 6 4
```

On our next deal partner has the opportunity to make several signals.

Tip

Don't be afraid to lead a suit bid by the opponents against their no trump contract.

Neither Side Vulnerable. Dealer South.

```
            ♠ 8 6 3
            ♥ Q J
            ♦ 10 7 6 3
            ♣ A K J 7
♠ 7 2
♥ A 8 6 4 2
♦ Q J 9 2
♣ 9 3
```

West	North	East	South
–	–	–	1♠
Pass	2♣	Pass	2♠
Pass	3♠	All Pass	

You lead the ♦Q against South's 3♠ contract. Partner wins with the ♦A and returns the ♦5, declarer playing the ♦4 and then the ♦K. Who has the outstanding diamond?

Declarer has it, for with ♦A85 partner would have returned the ♦8 not the ♦5.

Declarer continues with the ♠A and then the king, East following with the jack and nine of spades. Clearly East held the ♠J109. Declarer plays the ♦8, which you win with the jack, partner discarding the nine of hearts. What are you going to play next?

Declarer has shown the ♠AKQ and the ♦K. If he had the ♥K, he would not have passed 3♠, so it's safe to play the ♥4.

Partner wins with the king and returns the ♥10 to your ace. You have taken four tricks and provided partner can ruff the next heart the contract will be down one.

Here is the full deal:

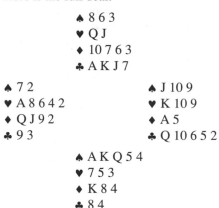

```
            ♠ 8 6 3
            ♥ Q J
            ♦ 10 7 6 3
            ♣ A K J 7
♠ 7 2                    ♠ J 10 9
♥ A 8 6 4 2             ♥ K 10 9
♦ Q J 9 2               ♦ A 5
♣ 9 3                   ♣ Q 10 6 5 2
            ♠ A K Q 5 4
            ♥ 7 5 3
            ♦ K 8 4
            ♣ 8 4
```

Tip

You should try to count declarer's points, as well as working out the shape of the hand.

60
Chapter
09

Attitude Signals

ALL ABOUT ATTITUDE

Of course, we all know players who find it difficult to hide their displeasure when partner leads the wrong suit. There can be no doubt that Groucho Marx's attitude signals, "Smile if you like my Lead" would simplify the game, even though they would make it much less challenging. However, since they are not allowed to make faces, most players agree to play their cards in one particular order to encourage partner to continue the suit, or in another order to suggest that partner switches to a different suit.

In standard methods, the mechanism is quite straightforward. The basic premise is that a high card is encouraging and a low one is discouraging. In traditional methods this would apply when partner has led the suit and also when you are discarding.

It's a good idea to signal with the most obvious card you can afford. For instance imagine the opponents are in four hearts after you have overcalled in spades. Your partner leads the ace of spades and your holding is:

♠ K Q J 10 9 3

Play the king of spades, making it clear you have a good sequence.

As with count signals, it is a good idea to agree that you will always play the highest of touching honors, which may allow partner to underlead his holding to good effect.

Now let's look at some examples of the attitude signal in action. Put yourself in the East seat for the following deal from the World Championships in Yokohama in 1991:

♠ 10
♥ A 8 4
♦ 6
♣ A K J 9 8 6 4 3

♠ K Q 9 8 7 6
♥ K 6
♦ A J 8 2
♣ 2

West	North	East	South
Caesar	*Arnolds*	*Moegel*	*Vriend*
–	1♣	1♠	Dble(*)
Pass	3♣	Pass	3NT
All Pass			

(*) Negative

Rather surprisingly perhaps partner leads the ♦K against South's 3NT contract, and this is what you can see. How do you plan your defense?

Obviously you need five tricks to defeat the contact, so where are they going to come from?

Partner must have a good suit of her own since she didn't lead your suit, so you are going to give an encouraging signal. How?

Of course, you could play the eight or even the jack to encourage, but you are going to make absolutely sure by overtaking the diamond king with the ace of diamonds and returning the jack of diamonds.

The full deal was:

```
              ♠ 10
              ♥ A 8 4
              ♦ 6
              ♣ A K J 9 8 6 4 3
♠ 4 2                        ♠ K Q 9 8 7 6
♥ Q J 5 3                    ♥ K 6
♦ K Q 10 9 7 3              ♦ A J 8 2
♣ 10                         ♣ 2
              ♠ A J 5 3
              ♥ 10 9 7 2
              ♦ 5 4
              ♣ Q 7 5
```

That was rather easy. Try your hand with this one from the World Junior Championship played in Nottingham, England in 1989:

```
              ♠ K
              ♥ K Q J 7
              ♦ A 6
              ♣ A 10 8 6 5 4
                            ♠ J 10 8 7 4
                            ♥ 5 2
                            ♦ K Q 7 3
                            ♣ 3 2
```

West	North	East	South
–	–	–	Pass
Pass	1♣	Pass	1NT
Pass	3NT	All Pass	

Partner leads the ♠5 against South's 3NT contract. What card are you going to play under North's king?

Once again you need five tricks to defeat the contract and spades seems the most likely source of tricks. You can tell from the lead of the five of spades that you can make at least three tricks in that suit. Partner's lead looks like his fourth best spade, so you know that partner must have one of the following holdings:

                    A Q 9 5

In which case you will get four spade tricks, provided you get the lead again before declarer has made nine.

                    Q 9 6 5

In which case you can set up three tricks in spades but your partner will need two entries to beat the contract, or

                    A 9 6 5

In which case you can set up three spades if partner continues the suit or four if he can put you in to lead a spade through declarer.

In all three cases you can afford to play the ♠J to encourage in spades, with the added bonus in the third case that partner will know that declarer has the ♠Q, because if you held both honors you would signal with the queen not the jack.

The full deal turned out to be:

```
              ♠ K
              ♥ K Q J 7
              ♦ A 6
              ♣ A 10 8 6 5 4
  ♠ Q 9 6 5                  ♠ J 10 8 7 4
  ♥ A 8 6 4                  ♥ 5 2
  ♦ J 8                      ♦ K Q 7 3
  ♣ Q J 9                    ♣ 3 2
              ♠ A 3 2
              ♥ 10 9 3
              ♦ 10 9 5 4 2
              ♣ K 7
```

Now try this deal from the 1987 Bermuda Bowl in Ocho Rios, Jamaica.

```
              ♠ K 6 2
              ♥ A 10 9
              ♦ J 7 4 3 2
              ♣ 8 2
                            ♠ Q 10 8 4
                            ♥ J 3
                            ♦ Q 8
                            ♣ 10 9 7 4 3
```

West	North	East	South
–	–	–	2NT(*)
Pass	3NT	All Pass	
(*) 19-20			

Partner leads the ♣A against South's 3NT contract. Which card should you play?

The combined point count of dummy and declarer's hands is 27-28, therefore partner can only have between 7-8 points in his hand. It seems most likely that he has the ace-king of clubs, and either the jack of clubs or the jack of spades.

You don't have any certain winners other than partner's opening lead, but you might have several clubs to cash. Therefore you should encourage partner to continue clubs, so play the ♣10.

The full deal was:

```
              ♠ K 6 2
              ♥ A 10 9
              ♦ J 7 4 3 2
              ♣ 8 2
  ♠ 9 7 5                    ♠ Q 10 8 4
  ♥ 7 6 5 4                  ♥ J 3
  ♦ 9 5                      ♦ Q 8
  ♣ A K J 6                  ♣ 10 9 7 4 3
              ♠ A J 3
              ♥ K Q 8 2
              ♦ A K 10 6
              ♣ Q 5
```

Now change seats and try the next example from the West seat:

```
              ♠ A
              ♥ K 7 4
              ♦ J 9 6 4 2
              ♣ A K 6 5
  ♠ K J 7 5 4 2
  ♥ 10 6
  ♦ Q 8 3
  ♣ 10 4
```

South	North
1NT(*)	3NT
Pass	
(*) 12-14	

You lead the ♠5 against South's 3NT contract and your partner plays the six while declarer plays the the nine. Declarer cashes the ace and king of diamonds and plays a third diamond, which you win with the queen while partner discards the nine of hearts. What do you do next?

First, what is going on in the spade suit? You have not seen the three yet, so it is possible that either partner or declarer has it. If partner has it presumably he is trying to encourage, so maybe he has ♠Q63 and you can cash the next five tricks. On the other hand, maybe declarer has it and he is trying to persuade you to continue spades. If declarer started with ♠Q93 that would leave partner with ♠1086 and in fact he was trying to discourage. How can you tell which?

The truth is that from the play in spades you can't tell. However what does partner's discard of the nine of hearts mean?

It is encouraging in hearts. Would partner encourage hearts if he had the queen of spades? No, probably not. So partner is telling you that he does not have the queen of spades and that he might have an entry in hearts. So you switch to the ten of hearts.

Here is the full deal:

```
              ♠ A
              ♥ K 7 4
              ♦ J 9 6 4 2
              ♣ A K 6 5
♠ K J 7 5 4 2              ♠ 10 8 6
♥ 10 6                    ♥ A J 9 8 2
♦ Q 8 3                   ♦ 10 7
♣ 10 4                    ♣ J 7 2
              ♠ Q 9 3
              ♥ Q 5 3
              ♦ A K 4
              ♣ Q 9 8 3
```

Obviously, partner takes the ace of hearts and switches back to spades. Is that so obvious?

No, but by this stage it was the only remaining chance. From the opening lead East could not tell that your spades were quite that good. Declarer could easily have had the ♠K, then if you had had the queen of hearts switching to it looked to be the only chance to beat the contract. However, when you led the ♥10, East knew that declarer had the queen of hearts and he could count 9 tricks for declarer if he didn't take the ace of hearts.

How?

Obviously declarer was known to have one heart trick, one spade trick, four diamond tricks and two clubs. If he held the king of spades, too, that would make nine, and if his spade honor was only the queen then he pretty well had to have the queen of clubs to make up his opening bid. So East took his ace and switched back to spades.

Our next example contains a subtle point which regular partnerships might find interesting:

```
              ♠ K J 9
              ♥ 8 7 2
              ♦ J 9 4 2
              ♣ J 5 2
                            ♠ 8 6
                            ♥ J 10 6 4
                            ♦ Q 7 3
                            ♣ Q 8 6 4
```

West	North	East	South
–	–	–	1♠
Pass	2♠	Pass	4♠
All Pass			

Partner leads the ♦A against South's 4♠ contract. Which card are you going to play?

It is unlikely partner has led from ace and a small diamond, so we should have at least two diamond tricks. The other tricks will probably have to come from either hearts or clubs.

To make this decision you have to try to visualize partner's probable diamond holding. He could hold ♦AKx or ♦AKxx (from ♦AKxxx, he would have led the king of diamonds to ask us for count). In either case you don't want partner to continue the suit because it will result in a diamond trick being established for declarer. Therefore you should play the three of diamonds to discourage partner from continuing the suit.

Suppose dummy's diamonds had been ♦J94, then you could have afforded to play the seven of diamonds to encourage partner to continue the suit.

Let's look at the full deal:

```
              ♠ K J 9
              ♥ 8 7 2
              ♦ J 9 4 2
              ♣ J 5 2
♠ 4 3                     ♠ 8 6
♥ 9 5 3                   ♥ J 10 6 4
♦ A K 6 5                 ♦ Q 7 3
♣ A 10 9 7               ♣ Q 8 6 4
              ♠ A Q 10 7 5 2
              ♥ A K Q
              ♦ 10 8
              ♣ K 3
```

As you can see, if partner plays out ace, king and another diamond, declarer will have an easy run, so it was important to get off to a good start by discouraging diamonds. However, the defense is not out of the woods yet. Obviously if partner switches to clubs it will be fatal, but he should be able to work out that there is no urgency to do so.

Now try your hand at the following quiz:

QUIZ 39

1.

♠ 8 3
♥ Q 9 6 2
♦ 7 5 2
♣ A K 7 4

	West	North	East	South
	–	–	–	1NT
	Pass	3NT	All Pass	

What do you lead?

2.

♠ 7 6 3
♥ A 5
♦ A Q 6
♣ K Q J 7 4

♠ Q 10 9 5 2
♥ 8 7 3
♦ K J 9
♣ 8 2

West	North	East	South
–	–	–	2♥
Pass	4♥	All Pass	

Partner leads the ♠A and this is the layout. What do you play?

3.

♠ A K Q 7
♥ K 8 4 3
♦ 9 6
♣ Q 8 4

♠ 8 2
♥ A 10
♦ Q J 8 7 4 2
♣ 9 7 3

West	North	East	South
–	–	2♦(*)	2♥
3♦	4♥	All Pass	

(*) Weak

West starts with the ♦A. Which card do you play?

4.

♠ Q J 10 9 5
♥ 7 4
♦ A Q
♣ 9 7 3 2

♠ A 8 7 4 2
♥ 8 3
♦ K 6
♣ A K 8 4

West	North	East	South
–	–	–	1♥
Pass	2♠	Pass	4♥
All Pass			

Partner leads the ♠6. Declarer drops the king under your ace. Now what?

ANSWERS TO QUIZ 39

1. ♣A.

You want to know if partner likes clubs, so lead the ace to ask for attitude. If he discourages by playing low there may still be time to find an effective switch.

2. ♠2.

You would like partner to switch to diamonds before the clubs are established. The obvious way to do this is to discourage in spades.

3. ♦Q.

The danger here is that if you discourage, partner may take it into his head to lead away from the ♣K before any losers go away on the spades. Therefore you should encourage partner to continue diamonds. Best is to play the ♦Q so partner can underlead the king for you to play a club through. Here is the full deal:

♠ A K Q 7
♥ K 8 4 3
♦ 9 6
♣ Q 8 4

♠ 9 6 5 4 3   ♠ 8 2
♥ 2   ♥ A 10
♦ A K 5   ♦ Q J 8 7 4 2
♣ K 10 6 5   ♣ 9 7 3

♠ J 10
♥ Q J 9 7 6 5
♦ 10 3
♣ A J 2

4. ♣A.

It is not clear whether partner or declarer has the missing spade. The way to find out is to ask partner if he likes clubs. If he encourages he can't have a singleton spade. However, if he discourages you should play the ♠8, knowing partner will ruff and at the same time suggesting he switch to a diamond.

MORE ON ATTITUDE

Put yourself in the West seat for the following hand:

    ♠ J 10 3 2
    ♥ A 6
    ♦ K Q J 10
    ♣ 9 6 2

♠ K 8
♥ J 10 8 5
♦ 8 5 4 3
♣ A Q 5

West	North	East	South
–	–	–	1♠
Pass	3♠	Pass	4♠
All Pass			

With both sides vulnerable, you look no further than the ♥J for your opening lead against South's 4♠ contract. Declarer plays the ace of hearts from dummy, while partner follows with the two. Declarer then leads the ♠J off the dummy, ♠4, ♠5 and you win with the king. How should you continue?

You have one trick in the bag and need three more. Partner's ♥2 was clearly discouraging, so you don't have a heart trick. You should be all right as long as partner has either the ♦A or the ♣K, provided you switch to the right suit now.

Let's consider alternative hands that declarer might hold, to see which is most likely. For example, he could have either:

(a)	♠ AQxxx	or	(b)	♠ AQxxx
	♥ Kx			♥ Kx
	♦ xxx			♦ Axx
	♣ KJx			♣ Jxx

Of course, there are other possibilities but, since aces are usually at a premium, declarer would be more likely to bid 4♠ with (b) rather than (a). So you should switch to the ♣A, which proves to be a success on the actual layout which was:

                ♠ J 10 3 2
                ♥ A 6
                ♦ K Q J 10
                ♣ 9 6 2

♠ K 8   ♠ 6 4
♥ J 10 8 5   ♥ Q 9 7 3 2
♦ 8 5 4 3   ♦ 9 6
♣ A Q 5   ♣ K J 7 4

                ♠ A Q 9 7 5
                ♥ K 4
                ♦ A 7 2
                ♣ 10 8 3

Tip
A low card is discouraging. It may suggest a switch but it does not carry any suit preference overtones.

Sometimes, it is important to remember that the opening lead itself is the first attitude signal you can make. This time put yourself in the East seat:

    ♠ K 9 8 2
    ♥ A J 4
    ♦ –
    ♣ A Q J 8 6 4

        ♠ A Q 6
        ♥ Q 10 9 6
        ♦ K 8 7 6 3 2
        ♣ –

This is what you can see when partner leads the ♦5 against 6♣ after the following bidding:

West	North	East	South
–	–	–	1♣
Pass	4NT	Pass	5♦
Pass	6♣	All Pass	

You may regard the North/South bidding as unsophisticated, but that won't help if you fail to defeat the contract. Declarer discards the two of spades from dummy, and if you play the ♦K declarer discards three losing spades on the diamond honors.

But if you worked out that partner's lead could not be fourth best and withheld your ♦K, the contract would be set. Even if partner was leading from ♦Q105, withholding your king was safe. Here is the full hand:

                ♠ K 9 8 2
                ♥ A J 4
                ♦ –
                ♣ A Q J 8 6 4

♠ 7 5 4 3   ♠ A Q 6
♥ 8 7 5 3   ♥ Q 10 9 6
♦ 9 5 4   ♦ K 8 7 6 3 2
♣ 9 3   ♣ –

                ♠ J 10
                ♥ K 2
                ♦ A Q J 10
                ♣ K 10 7 5 2

Tip
Don't forget the first signal may be transmitted by the opening lead.

The next example which comes from the European Championships played at Killarney in 1991 has a futuristic tone. As West, this is what you would see:

```
        ♠ 10 6
        ♥ 10 9 5
        ♦ 10 8 2
        ♣ K Q 7 6 5

♠ Q 9 3
♥ K Q 3 2
♦ K J 9 6 4
♣ 3
```

West	North	East	South
–	–	–	1♠(*)
Dble (**)	All Pass		

(*) 8-13, at least three spades
(**) 11-15, at least three spades or 16 plus points

You make the obvious opening lead of the ♣3. You are rather pleased with the appearance of dummy. Provided you defend carefully you should collect a useful penalty since partner is marked with a reasonable hand. Declarer plays the ♣K from dummy. Partner wins the ♣A, declarer following with the ♣10, and cashes the ♦A. You encourage with the ♦9 and partner continues with the ♦7. You win the ♦J and cash the ♦K, partner discarding the ♥8.

That's encouraging in hearts so you continue with the ♥K which holds the trick. You follow this with another heart to partner's ace. He returns the ♣J for you to ruff and you play the ♥3, hoping partner will be able to ruff. He does, while declarer follows helplessly with the ♥J. Partner now plays another club, which insures a trick for your ♠Q, and a penalty of 800 points. Here is the full deal:

```
            ♠ 10 6
            ♥ 10 9 5
            ♦ 10 8 2
            ♣ K Q 7 6 5
♠ Q 9 3                 ♠ 8 4 2
♥ K Q 3 2               ♥ A 8 6
♦ K J 9 6 4             ♦ A 7
♣ 3                     ♣ A J 9 5 2
            ♠ A K J 7 5
            ♥ J 7 4
            ♦ Q 5 3
            ♣ 10 8
```

Notice that your partner defended well. He knew that he could give you a club ruff immediately, but instead he concentrated on taking your outside winners first. Furthermore, with only three small trumps in his own hand it was important to establish a ruff in his hand rather than reduce your trump holding which was likely to be better. Notice that if East gave you a club ruff at trick two, regained the lead with the ♦A, say, and played another club for you to ruff, you would have scored a second trump trick but

declarer would have been able to discard one of his heart losers.

Tip
To extract the maximum penalty from a doubled contract always consider trying to cash your outside tricks before embarking on taking ruffs, which might allow declarer to throw a loser on a loser.

In the next example the attitude signal is of vital importance.

```
        ♠ K Q 6
        ♥ K J 6
        ♦ J 9 4 3 2
        ♣ A 5

♠ 8 7 3
♥ Q 7 3
♦ Q 8 5
♣ K Q 10 4
```

West	North	East	South
–	–	–	1NT
Pass	3NT	All Pass	

After this bidding, some players might lead a major suit, but there is no real reason not to lead a club and if you remember our preferred lead style you will select the ♣Q, asking if partner likes the suit.

Declarer wins with dummy's ♣A, following with the ♣7 from hand while your partner plays the ♣2. That suggests declarer has the ♣J, because with that card partner would have encouraged. You will need to find an entry to partner's hand to lead a club through. Declarer continues with the ace of diamonds, followed by the king and seven. On the third round you win the ♦Q while partner discards the ♥8.

That's encouraging in hearts so you switch to the ♥3. Partner wins with the ♥A and returns a club, enabling you to take three tricks in the suit to defeat the contract. Here is the full deal:

```
            ♠ K Q 6
            ♥ K J 6
            ♦ J 9 4 3 2
            ♣ A 5
♠ 8 7 3                 ♠ 10 5 4
♥ Q 7 3                 ♥ A 8 4 2
♦ Q 8 5                 ♦ 10 6
♣ K Q 10 4             ♣ 8 6 3 2
            ♠ A J 9 2
            ♥ 10 9 5
            ♦ A K 7
            ♣ J 9 7
```

Did you notice an interesting possibility here? Suppose East held ♥Q842 and West ♥A73. Now the discard of the ♥8 might cause declarer to go down two. However, when you switch to a heart declarer really ought to rise with dummy's king, because he knows he is staring defeat in the face if East can get the lead at all.

Tip

It may be necessary to make several attitude signals, both negative and positive, on the hand. Notice in particular East's decision to discourage on the lead of the ♣Q despite holding four cards in the suit. This is because your lead of the ♣Q principally asks you to encourage with a high card or excessive length, and on this hand you can assume that if partner has QJ10 he will continue anyway. Furthermore, you have the comfort of knowing that you have a certain outside entry to get the lead. The only time you might be wrong to discourage clubs would be if partner had QJ9xx and then he will be able to work out that it is right to continue as declarer will drop the ten under the ace.

The next example is a perfect illustration of when consideration of the hand as a whole should outweigh your feeling about the actual holding in the suit led.

```
        ♠ A J 5
        ♥ Q 9
        ♦ A J 10 4 2
        ♣ K 10 7
                        ♠ 10 9 6 3
                        ♥ 10 7 2
                        ♦ 9 8
                        ♣ A 8 5 3
```

West	North	East	South
–	1♦	Pass	1♠
2♥	Dble (*)	Pass	3♥
Pass	3♠	Pass	4♠
All Pass			

(*) 15-18 balanced

Partner leads the ace of hearts against South's 4♠ contract. How do you propose to defend? Where are you going to get the four tricks you need?

Clearly you hope for two in hearts and you can see the ace of clubs.

Given that North forced to game with his three heart bid you cannot expect a diamond trick. The best chance is to score a trump trick.

How can you do that?

There is no guarantee, but you could observe the effect of encouraging in hearts, playing high-low. Both partner and declarer will think you have a doubleton and declarer might ruff the third round high, thus promoting a trump trick for your ♠10963.

Here is the full deal:

```
              ♠ A J 5
              ♥ Q 9
              ♦ A J 10 4 2
              ♣ K 10 7
    ♠ 2                      ♠ 10 9 6 3
    ♥ A K J 8 3              ♥ 10 7 2
    ♦ 7 5 3                  ♦ 9 8
    ♣ J 6 4 2                ♣ A 8 5 3
              ♠ K Q 8 7 4
              ♥ 6 5 4
              ♦ K Q 6
              ♣ Q 9
```

Tip

Don't become a slave to your signalling method! Winning bridge players never stop thinking for themselves.

This example gives you a chance to match yourself against the world's best players in the Naturals versus Scientists match in London in 1992. This time you are back in the West seat holding:

```
        ♠ K J 7
        ♥ Q J 10 9 8
        ♦ A K J
        ♣ 5 3
```

and you witness the following exciting auction:

West	North	East	South
Rodwell	*Branco*	*Meckstroth*	*Chagas*
–	–	–	1♣
1♥	1♠	2♦(*)	3♣
3♥	Pass	Pass	3NT
Dble	All Pass		

(*) A full raise to 2♥

What is going on? You have 15 points and your partner must have 6-8, giving your side the majority of the points. Clearly declarer has a long club suit and excellent nerves! Anyway, your first decision is what are you going to lead?

Declarer surely has a heart stopper, either the ace or the king. It must be correct to have a look at dummy and find out if partner likes diamonds, so you should lead the ♦A. Dummy goes down and this is what you can see.

```
        ♠ A 5 4 3
        ♥ 7 3 2
        ♦ 9 5 3
        ♣ K 8 4
♠ K J 7
♥ Q J 10 9 8
♦ A K J
♣ 5 3
```

Dummy plays the ♦3, partner the ♦7 and declarer the ♦8. Now what?

With so many small diamonds missing, partner's card is clearly encouraging, so you continue with the ♦K and ♦J.

Good, for this was the full deal:

```
                 ♠ A 5 4 3
                 ♥ 7 3 2
                 ♦ 9 5 3
                 ♣ K 8 4
 ♠ K J 7                      ♠ Q 9 8 2
 ♥ Q J 10 9 8                 ♥ K 6 5
 ♦ A K J                      ♦ Q 7 6 4 2
 ♣ 5 3                        ♣ 10
                 ♠ 10 6
                 ♥ A 4
                 ♦ 10 8
                 ♣ A Q J 9 7 6 2
```

Suit Preference Signals

WHAT'S YOUR PREFERENCE?

Of all the standard signals, the ones that show suit preference are perhaps the most exciting. The basic idea is that by choosing to play either a high card or a low card you can indicate which specific suit you would like your partner to play.

However, before getting too involved in the mechanics of suit preference signals, it is important to remember that if a signal that you either give or receive can be interpreted as count or attitude then that interpretation should normally take precedence. It is rarely possible to give two messages with one play. A suit preference signal can only be made when the count or attitude position is known, or when the partnership have a special agreement, for instance when there is a singleton in dummy.

The most commonly played forms of suit preference signals are known as McKenny (British) or Lavinthal (American).

A high card shows strength in the highest remaining suit (trumps are usually excluded from the calculation) and a low card promises something in the lowest remaining suit.

One of the most common applications of the suit preference signal is when one or both of the defenders are ruffing. Let's look at an example from the Bermuda Bowl in Japan in 1991.

```
        ♠ A K 10 4 2
        ♥ K Q 9 5 2
        ♦ J 9
        ♣ 5
♠ 9 8
♥ 7
♦ 10 7 6 5 2
♣ J 8 6 4 2
```

West	North	East	South
–	–	–	1NT
Pass	2♦(*)	Pass	2♠
Pass	4♣(**)	Pass	4♠
All Pass			

(*) Game forcing Stayman
(**) Shortage

You make the obvious lead of your singleton heart against South's 4♠ contract. Partner wins the first trick with the ace of hearts and returns the ♥4, declarer playing the ♥3 and ♥J.

What next? Obviously you will ruff this trick but you need two more to defeat the contract. Where will you get them from?

If you are really lucky partner will have either the ace of clubs or the ace of diamonds, and, if you can choose the right one you should be able to get another heart ruff. Here partner's return of the ♥4 is a suit preference signal showing interest in the lower ranking suit (excluding trumps), which in this case is clubs. So you return a club and partner is able to give you another heart ruff.

The full deal:

```
               ♠ A K 10 4 2
               ♥ K Q 9 5 2
               ♦ J 9
               ♣ 5
♠ 9 8                        ♠ 6 5
♥ 7                          ♥ A 8 6 4
♦ 10 7 6 5 2                 ♦ K 8 3
♣ J 8 6 4 2                  ♣ A 10 9 7
               ♠ Q J 7 3
               ♥ J 10 3
               ♦ A Q 4
               ♣ K Q 3
```

As you can see, suit preference signals are particularly useful when you are giving your partner a ruff. Remember, a high card suggests that partner plays the highest side suit while a low card suggests that he plays the lowest remaining suit.

Sometimes a player will be able to give more than one signal on the same hand.

Look at this deal from the Cap Gemini Pandata Pairs played in The Hague in January, 1993.

```
            ♠ 7 5 3
            ♥ A 6 5 2
            ♦ K 9 5 4
            ♣ K 7
♠ A K 9 4 2
♥ 7 4
♦ 7
♣ J 9 6 5 4
```

West	North	East	South
Levy	*Rosenberg*	*Mouiel*	*Zia*
Pass	Pass	1♦	2♠(*)
Pass	3♠	Dble(**)	All Pass

(*) Weak jump overcall
(**) Takeout

You need five tricks to defeat 3♠, but in view of the bidding you are obviously hoping for more than that! East wins the diamond ace and returns the two of diamonds. Declarer plays the eight and ten from hand. Why did partner return the two of diamonds?

He is hoping you are going to ruff the diamond and he is indicating which suit is most likely to provide an entry for him to play another diamond back for you to ruff.

So which suit does he have his quick entry in?

If you remember what we said earlier, a club would spring to mind. So ruff the diamond and return a club. On your four of clubs declarer plays the king from dummy and the ten from hand. Partner wins with the ace and plays the jack of diamonds, which is covered by declarer's queen. Excellent!

Which card do you play after ruffing the diamond?

Think about it, and ask yourself, why did partner play such a high diamond for you to ruff, when he could have played a smaller one? Is he trying to indicate he has yet another entry to his hand?

When he returned the low diamond he was indicating he had a club entry, so a high diamond must mean he has an entry in hearts—the highest suit, excluding trumps. You should play the seven of hearts. Declarer goes up with the ace and plays a trump to his queen, on which partner discards the six of diamonds. You win this with your king and return your

remaining heart. If partner does have the king, he will take his trick and know to return another heart for you to ruff, because had you started with three hearts to the queen you would surely have led the two initially.

The full deal turns out to be:

```
            ♠ 7 5 3
            ♥ A 6 5 2
            ♦ K 9 5 4
            ♣ K 7
♠ A K 9 4 2        ♠ –
♥ 7 4              ♥ K J 10 9
♦ 7                ♦ A J 6 3 2
♣ J 9 6 5 4        ♣ A 8 3 2
            ♠ Q J 10 8 6
            ♥ Q 8 3
            ♦ Q 10 8
            ♣ Q 10
```

South could only take five tricks and thus suffered a penalty of –800.

Let's look at a situation where there is singleton in the dummy, and see how the defenders can help each other. Put yourself in the East seat:

```
            ♠ Q J 9 7 5 4 3
            ♥ A K J 3
            ♦ 8
            ♣ 4
                   ♠ A K 10 2
                   ♥ 6 2
                   ♦ J 10 6 3
                   ♣ K Q 7
```

West	North	East	South
–	1♠	Pass	2♥
3♣	4♣	4♠	5♦
Pass	5♥	All Pass	

Your partner, West, leads the six of spades. Clearly partner's lead is a singleton, so you will get one trick from spades. But where will the other two tricks come from? It looks as if they will have to come from the minor suits. But for the moment, it cannot be wrong to play the king of clubs. Declarer follows with the jack and partner plays the ten of clubs.

How do you continue?

In this situation partner knows you cannot be interested in how many clubs he holds. If he held the ace of diamonds you would expect him to play a low club. So how do you interpret his play of the ten of clubs? It is high card—therefore it is fairly safe to assume he wants a spade because he can over-ruff declarer!

```
            ♠ Q J 9 7 5 4 3
            ♥ A K J 3
            ♦ 8
            ♣ 4
♠ 6                        ♠ A K 10 2
♥ Q                        ♥ 6 2
♦ K Q 7                    ♦ J 10 6 3
♣ A 10 9 8 6 5 3 2         ♣ K Q 7
            ♠ 8
            ♥ 10 9 8 7 5 4
            ♦ A 9 5 4 2
            ♣ J
```

The next example highlights a common situation where you can give partner a ruff, but you have no immediate re-entry card.

```
            ♠ J 10 4
            ♥ A 5
            ♦ K J 7 3 2
            ♣ A 6 5

                        ♠ A 2
                        ♥ Q 10 6
                        ♦ 10 9 8
                        ♣ K 9 8 7 3
```

West	North	East	South
–	–	–	1♠
Pass	2♦	Pass	2♠
Pass	4♠	All Pass	

Partner leads the four of clubs against South's 4♠ contract. Declarer plays low from dummy and you take the king. That's the first trick for the defense. Three more are needed. Where are they to come from?

The ace of spades is sure to take a trick and you may be able to give partner a club ruff. Then you will need just one more trick, which is most likely to come from a red suit. For the moment you need to see if you can give partner a club ruff.

Which club do you return?

Although you don't have a certain trick in hearts, it must be correct to return the nine of clubs, suggesting that you prefer a heart switch to a diamond.

The full deal was:

```
            ♠ J 10 4
            ♥ A 5
            ♦ K J 7 3 2
            ♣ A 6 5
♠ 5 3                      ♠ A 2
♥ J 9 8 7 4 2              ♥ Q 10 6
♦ A 6 5 4                  ♦ 10 9 8
♣ 4                        ♣ K 9 8 7 3
            ♠ K Q 9 8 7 6
            ♥ K 3
            ♦ Q
            ♣ Q J 10 2
```

As you can see, nothing can go wrong if you ask for a heart. The defense are bound to take their two aces.

At the table East made the mistake of returning the ♣7 and West decided to underlead his ♦A, with disastrous consequences.

QUIZ 40

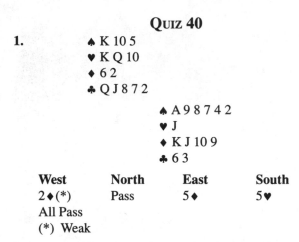

1.
```
            ♠ K 10 5
            ♥ K Q 10
            ♦ 6 2
            ♣ Q J 8 7 2

                        ♠ A 9 8 7 4 2
                        ♥ J
                        ♦ K J 10 9
                        ♣ 6 3
```

West	North	East	South
2♦(*)	Pass	5♦	5♥
All Pass			
(*) Weak			

Your partner leads the ♠6. You win with your ace of spades. What do you return?

2. This time you are West:

```
            ♠ K 7
            ♥ Q 9 7 4
            ♦ K J 5
            ♣ Q J 10 3
♠ 9 8 5 4 2
♥ 10 8 7 2
♦ 2
♣ 6 5 2
```

West	North	East	South
–	–	–	1♥
Pass	3♥	Pass	4♥
All Pass			

You lead the ♦2, partner wins with the ♦A and returns the ♦10. Your move.

3. Now stay in the West seat for the next problem:

```
            ♠ K Q 9 3
            ♥ A J 10 3
            ♦ 8 7 5 2
            ♣ 4
♠ 8 7 2
♥ 7 5
♦ 3
♣ A Q J 9 6 5 3
```

West	North	East	South
–	–	–	1♥
3♣(*)	4♥	All Pass	
(*) Weak			

You lead the ♦3. Partner wins the ♦A and returns the ♦10. Now what?

4. Stay in the West seat again:

```
            ♠ 4
            ♥ Q J 10 8 3 2
            ♦ K 10 7
            ♣ Q 7 2
♠ A Q 10 9 7 3
♥ 5
♦ 8 2
♣ 9 8 6 4
```

West	North	East	South
–	–	–	1♥
2♠(*)	4♥	4♠	6♥
All Pass			
(*) Weak			

You lead the ♠A. Partner plays the ♠K and declarer the ♠J. Now what?

5. This time test yourself in the East seat:

```
            ♠ K 10 9 7 3
            ♥ 8 2
            ♦ J 10 3
            ♣ 9 6 3
                        ♠ A Q
                        ♥ 7 3
                        ♦ K Q 9 7 4 2
                        ♣ 8 4 2
```

West	North	East	South
–	–	–	1♥
Pass	Pass	2♦	2♥
All Pass			

Partner leads the ♦A. You encourage with the ♦9 and partner continues with the ♦5. How do you direct the defense?

1. ♠9.

Partner's lead looks very much like a singleton because with a doubleton he would probably have led your suit—diamonds. Hoping that partner will ruff this trick, you return a high spade to suggest that partner underleads the ace of diamonds.

2. Ruff and return a spade, preferably the eight. Partner's ♦10 looks high, suggesting a spade rather than a club.

3. You ruff and should cash the ♣A. It looks as if partner has the ♠A. However you can be sure he doesn't have the ♣K, so you should take your ♣A in case it runs away when partner doesn't have the ♠A. Imagine declarer's hand is:

```
            ♠ A J
            ♥ Q 9 8 6 4
            ♦ K Q J 9
            ♣ K 10
```

He wins a spade return, cashes the ♠A and crosses to dummy with the ♥A. Then the clubs go away on the spades.

4. ♦8.

Partner must want a diamond very badly! Next time South might try using Blackwood.

5. Win the trick with the ♦K, then play the ♦Q. By playing your diamond honors in this order you are showing something good in spades. If your outside cards were in clubs you would win with the queen and continue with the diamond king.

THE RIGHT PREFERENCE

Now we are going to look at some more examples of the suit preference signal—and encounter some new ideas along the way.

Let's start with the following deal from the 1992 Epson Worldwide Bridge Contest.

```
              ♠ K J 7 3 2
              ♥ 5 3
              ♦ K 6 2
              ♣ K 8 7
♠ A
♥ A 10 9 8 2
♦ A J 9 7 5
♣ 9 3
```

West	North	East	South
–	–	Pass	1♣
1♥	1♠	Pass	2♣
2♦	3♣	Dble (*)	All Pass

(*) Competitive

With three certain tricks and a possible ruffing value you are happy to pass partner's competitive double. You make the obvious opening lead of the ♠A. Partner plays the ten of spades and declarer the four. What do you try next?

Obviously, partner has the spades well held (he can hardly have a doubleton, otherwise declarer would have five!). Of course partner is aware that by leading the ace of spades you are likely to be looking for a ruff, so the ten of spades might also be directing your attention towards the heart suit rather than the diamond suit. In any event, it is difficult to see how the contract can be defeated if he doesn't hold the king of hearts, or the ace of clubs. Therefore you should continue with the ace of hearts.

Partner plays the four and declarer the six of hearts. Under normal circumstances the four of hearts would be discouraging, but partner may only have the king-four in the suit. You should continue with the ten of hearts, to confirm you want a spade return from partner. Partner wins and returns the nine of spades. You ruff and the contract is now one down for certain.

The full deal:

```
              ♠ K J 7 3 2
              ♥ 5 3
              ♦ K 6 2
              ♣ K 8 7
♠ A                    ♠ Q 10 9 6 5
♥ A 10 9 8 2           ♥ K 4
♦ A J 9 7 5            ♦ 10 8 4
♣ 9 3                  ♣ J 6 4
              ♠ 8 4
              ♥ Q J 7 6
              ♦ Q 3
              ♣ A Q 10 5 2
```

Tip

When you lead an ace, partner will normally give you an attitude signal. However, on occasions, such as this one, where it was much more likely that you needed to know which of your two suits partner would like you to play, it can be right to make a suit-preference signal. Notice, too, that West was careful to continue with the ♥10 to confirm his interest in ruffing a spade.

Now let's look at two of the world's top players in action in the 1991 Bermuda Bowl in Yokohama:

```
              ♠ Q 10 5
              ♥ J 3
              ♦ K J 7 4
              ♣ A K Q 8
                        ♠ A K J 4
                        ♥ K 8 7 5
                        ♦ A Q 10 3
                        ♣ 6
```

West	North	East	South
Robson		*Forrester*	
–	–	–	Pass
Pass	1NT	Dble	2♣
Dble	All Pass		

Against two clubs doubled, Robson led the nine of diamonds, and Tony Forrester in the East seat could see the above layout.

Needing at least six tricks to defeat the contract, what were the prospects?

Very good! West had led a high diamond so Forrester knew he could give his partner a diamond ruff, but first he cashed the ♠K to make it clear he wanted a spade continuation. On this trick Robson played the ♠2.

Next he played the ♦A and the ♦3, ruffed by Robson, who returned the ♠9.

How did Forrester continue?

Since Robson had played the two of spades on the king he was known to hold an odd number of spades. Now by playing back his highest outstanding spade he was giving a suit preference signal for hearts.

Forrester cashed his remaining spade winner and played a heart to his partner's ace. He won the heart return and played his last diamond, enabling Robson to score the ♣J and record a score of +1100.

Here is the full deal:

```
              ♠ Q 10 5
              ♥ J 3
              ♦ K J 7 4
              ♣ A K Q 8
♠ 9 8 2                      ♠ A K J 4
♥ A 10 4 2                   ♥ K 8 7 5
♦ 9 8                        ♦ A Q 10 3
♣ J 5 4 2                    ♣ 6
              ♠ 7 6 3
              ♥ Q 9 6
              ♦ 6 5 2
              ♣ 10 9 7 3
```

Tip

You can indicate a lead to partner by cashing high cards before giving him a ruff. Once you have shown your length in a suit you can give a suit preference signal with the remaining cards.

Now put yourself in the West seat for the following deal from the 1993 Sunday Times/Macallan Pairs:

```
              ♠ Q J 7
              ♥ A Q J 7 6
              ♦ Q 8
              ♣ 8 7 4
♠ K 10 8 5 2
♥ 9 3
♦ A 7 4
♣ A 9 3
```

West	North	East	South
Rosenberg	*Rodwell*	*Zia*	*Meckstroth*
–	–	Pass	1♥
1♠	4♥	All Pass	

Against 4♥, since nothing else looked attractive, West began with the ♥3. Dummy plays the six, East the eight and declarer wins the trick with the ten of hearts. Declarer now plays the ♠9. West plays the king, dummy plays the seven while partner contributes the three.

It looks like declarer is trying to set up a spade trick before drawing trumps so that partner doesn't have a clear chance to signal which minor he would like you to play. But wait a minute, partner will surely realize that in this situation there is little to be gained from showing count. Perhaps he is following the principle of trying to tell you what you need to know, in which case his small spade is surely indicative of suggesting a club switch. West duly obliged and beat the contract.

The full deal was:

```
              ♠ Q J 7
              ♥ A Q J 7 6
              ♦ Q 8
              ♣ 8 7 4
♠ K 10 8 5 2                 ♠ 6 4 3
♥ 9 3                        ♥ 8
♦ A 7 4                      ♦ J 10 9 3
♣ A 9 3                      ♣ K J 10 5 2
              ♠ A 9
              ♥ K 10 5 4 2
              ♦ K 6 5 2
              ♣ Q 6
```

Notice that with his holding East would clearly play the ♠6 to suggest a diamond switch, while the ♠4 would be an attempt to give a natural signal. To illustrate how careful one must be in making this kind of signal, imagine the South hand to be:

```
              ♠ A 9
              ♥ K 10 5 4 2
              ♦ K 6 5
              ♣ K 6 5
```

A club now would give declarer the contract. East's cards would then be ♣QJ102 and he would play the four of spades on partner's king.

Tip

When your length in a suit is known or can be of no interest to partner it is sensible to use your cards to give a suit preference signal.

Now stay in the West seat for the next example:

```
              ♠ J 8 2
              ♥ A 9 5
              ♦ Q 10 9 6 5 3
              ♣ 10
♠ K 9 5 3
♥ K 6 4 3
♦ 4
♣ J 8 7 4
```

West	North	East	South
–	–	1♣	1♠
Dble	2♠	Pass	4♠
Dble	All Pass		

For once you have an obvious opening lead, the ♦4. You are pleased to see partner win the ♦A and return the ♦2 for you to ruff, declarer playing the ♦J and the ♦K.

What is your next move?

Partner has asked for a club by returning the ♦2. So do you play a club?

Well, if partner has the ♣A it cannot run away, but if declarer has it a club switch will be fatal now that the diamonds are set up.

What are you going to do?

A heart switch appears to be safe. As you have the guarded ♠K you can always play partner for the ♣A later.

Now look at the whole deal:

```
              ♠ J 8 2
              ♥ A 9 5
              ♦ Q 10 9 6 5 3
              ♣ 10
♠ K 9 5 3                    ♠ 7
♥ K 6 4 3                    ♥ Q 10 7
♦ 4                          ♦ A 8 7 2
♣ J 8 7 4                    ♣ K Q 5 3 2
              ♠ A Q 10 6 4
              ♥ J 8 2
              ♦ K J
              ♣ A 9 6
```

East might have returned a more neutral diamond (here that would be the seven), but he wanted to show West that he could underlead his hypothetical ♣A.

Tip

Never, never stop thinking for yourself, even when partner appears to have given a clear signal. This idea was emphasized by Berry Westra in his 1991 Bols Bridge Tip, "Don't follow your partner's signals blindly."

The next example has a familiar theme:

```
              ♠ A 10 6 2
              ♥ 9 6 2
              ♦ 4
              ♣ 10 6 5 4 3
♠ K 9 7 3
♥ A Q J 8 3
♦ 2
♣ A K 7
```

West	North	East	South
–	Pass	Pass	3NT(*)
Dble	Pass	Pass	Rdble
All Pass			

(*) A solid suit with a least one outside stopper

It's obvious that South has a solid diamond suit. His outside stopper could be anywhere so it must be right to retain the lead. If declarer has the king of hearts you will need to find an entry to your partner's hand. Since you would like to know how partner feels about clubs you start with the ace.

Partner plays the queen and declarer the eight. Is that a singleton queen or is partner indicating he likes the suit and has the jack?

If the queen of clubs is singleton it means declarer has ♣J 9 8 2. He must surely have at least eight diamonds and with such a wild distribution he would be unlikely to stand the double. You therefore continue with the seven of clubs. Partner wins and plays the ten of hearts. The full deal:

```
              ♠ A 10 6 2
              ♥ 9 6 2
              ♦ 4
              ♣ 10 6 5 4 3
♠ K 9 7 3                    ♠ Q J 8 5 4
♥ A Q J 8 3                  ♥ 10 7 4
♦ 2                          ♦ 10 7
♣ A K 7                      ♣ Q J 2
              ♠ –
              ♥ K 5
              ♦ A K Q J 9 8 6 5 3
              ♣ 9 8
```

Tip

By leading a top card it may be possible to keep the lead and determine the best defense after seeing dummy.

Now move over to the East seat for this deal from the European Mixed championships played in Ostend in 1992:

```
              ♠ A K 10 8 7 4
              ♥ 4 2
              ♦ 6 2
              ♣ 8 7 6
                            ♠ Q 9 6
                            ♥ 10 6 5 3
                            ♦ A 10 9 3
                            ♣ K Q
```

West	North	East	South
D'Fran'o	Saul	Sette	Quantin
–	–	–	1NT(*)
Pass	2♥(**)	Pass	2♠
Pass	3NT	All Pass	

(*) 15-17
(**) Transfer to spades

Against 3NT, your partner leads the ♣3. You play the ♣Q and declarer wins with the ace and advances the ♠J on which your partner plays the three and dummy the four. How do you defend?

One possibility would be to play the nine! This would work well if declarer started with only two spades and thought that your partner has started with queen to four spades, in which case he would take another finesse and the dummy would take no further part in the play. However, it is possible for declarer to hold three spades, in which case it would be foolish to duck, especially as we may already be in a position to defeat the contract.

Why is that?

Between your hand and dummy you can see 18 points, and declarer's maximum is 17, so West must have at least five. From his opening lead it looks like he must have the jack of clubs, which leaves him with at least four points in the red suits. If he has both red suit queens, declarer will be able to make nine tricks by rising with the king when you switch to a diamond, but otherwise partner must have a red king and you will beat the contract provided you switch to the right red suit.

So how do you continue?

Take the ♠Q and cash the king of clubs. Partner plays the ♣2.

What do you do next?

Partner's club two not only indicates that he started with five clubs but in this position he is giving you a clear suit preference signal, to switch to diamonds rather than hearts. So, you switch to the ♦10.

Here is the full deal:

```
              ♠ A K 10 8 7 4
              ♥ 4 2
              ♦ 6 2
              ♣ 8 7 6
♠ 3 2                        ♠ Q 9 6
♥ J 9 7                      ♥ 10 6 5 3
♦ K J 5                      ♦ A 10 9 3
♣ J 9 5 3 2                  ♣ K Q
              ♠ J 5
              ♥ A K Q 8
              ♦ Q 8 7 4
              ♣ A 10 4
```

Declarer finishes four down.

Tip

A defender can give a suit preference signal in a suit he has led when the defense is cashing tricks in that suit and count is not important. Notice in our example hand that if West's red suits were reversed he could afford to throw the ♣9 under your king, to indicate that he wanted a heart switch.

Let's look at a another similar example of the same thing. This time you are West:

```
              ♠ J 9 7 4 3
              ♥ Q 8
              ♦ Q 7 5
              ♣ K Q 2
♠ K 8 6
♥ 5 4 3 2
♦ J 10 3
♣ J 8 6
```

West	North	East	South
–	–	–	2♣
Pass	2♠	Pass	2NT
Pass	6NT	All Pass	

With nothing much to go on, you decide to lead what you hope will be a "safe" heart. Hoping not to confuse partner too much you choose the ♥4.

Declarer plays dummy's queen and the ten from his hand. Partner follows with the ♥7. Declarer then plays a spade from dummy to his queen, partner playing the ten. You take the queen with your king and play the ♦J. Why?

Clearly there is no future in hearts. With lots of high cards in dummy partner knows you don't need a count signal in spades, therefore his ten of spades should be a suit preference signal for diamonds. Here is the full deal:

```
              ♠ J 9 7 4 3
              ♥ Q 8
              ♦ Q 7 5
              ♣ K Q 2
♠ K 8 6                      ♠ 10 5 2
♥ 5 4 3 2                    ♥ 7
♦ J 10 3                     ♦ A 9 8 4 2
♣ J 8 6                      ♣ 10 7 5 4
              ♠ A Q
              ♥ A K J 10 9 6
              ♦ K 6
              ♣ A 9 3
```

Tip

When partner cannot possibly be interested in a count signal, consider following suit with either a high card or a low card to indicate which suit you would like partner to play.

Chapter 62

Additional Signals

Over the years a number of additional signals have been developed. A substantial selection of these are included in Chapter 64. However, among these developments there are two relatively recent additions to the signalling armory which have helped to improve significantly the standard of defense in tournament play. Happily both of these ideas fit in well with the general methods that have already been introduced.

The first of these is simply that you extend the use of suit preference signals into the trump suit.

SUIT PREFERENCE SIGNALS IN TRUMPS

For many years the mainstream view on signalling in trumps has been confined to the idea that you should play high-low in trumps to indicate a three card trump holding and a desire to ruff something. This is by no means a bad idea, but in my view extending suit preference signals into the trump suit is better. Consider the following example:

```
              ♠ 7 4 2
              ♥ 8 6 2
              ♦ 7 6 2
              ♣ 5 4 3 2
♠ 6                         ♠ 9 5 3
♥ Q J 10 9                  ♥ 7 5 4 3
♦ J 10 9 8                  ♦ 5 4
♣ J 10 9 8                  ♣ K Q 7 6
              ♠ A K Q J 10 8
              ♥ A K
              ♦ A K Q 3
              ♣ A
```

South surprises everybody by opening seven spades. As West, you lead the ♥Q, your partner follows with the five while declarer wins with the king. Three top trumps follow and you decide to let a couple of hearts go, hoping that partner has four. The ♥A comes next and partner plays the three.

The next trump presents you with a nasty problem—but not if you are playing suit preference signals in trumps. If your partner follows with the three, five and nine of trumps he is showing something in clubs so you can safely let yours go.

Now stay in the West seat for the following deal:

```
              ♠ J 5 2
              ♥ 9 8
              ♦ A Q J 10 7
              ♣ K 10 8
♠ A 4
♥ 7 6 2
♦ 9 5 4
♣ J 9 7 5 4
```

West	North	East	South
–	–	–	1♠
Pass	2♦	3♥	3♠
Pass	4♠	All Pass	

In accordance with our agreed leading style, you start off by leading the ♥6, second highest from three small. Declarer calls for the nine from dummy, partner plays the king and declarer the ace from his hand. The ♠K is played next. What do you do? Since you are not expecting to be able to give your partner a ruff there is no rush to take the ace, so you duck and partner plays the ♠3. Declarer continues with a spade which you have to win with your ace, partner contributing the ♠7.

What would you do next?

Partner's play of the ♥K suggests there is no future in that suit, and if you play suit preference signals in trumps partner's cards suggest a club switch rather than a diamond. So, you play the ♣5.

Here is the full deal:

```
              ♠ J 5 2
              ♥ 9 8
              ♦ A Q J 10 7
              ♣ K 10 8
♠ A 4                         ♠ 7 3
♥ 7 6 2                       ♥ K Q J 10 5 3
♦ 9 5 4                       ♦ 8 6
♣ J 9 7 5 4                   ♣ A Q 6
              ♠ K Q 10 9 8 6
              ♥ A 4
              ♦ K 3 2
              ♣ 3 2
```

Partner's excellent play in the heart suit would have probably been enough to persuade you to switch anyway and clubs looked to be a better option than diamonds. However the suit preference play in trumps confirmed your suspicions.

Let's look at another deal:

```
              ♠ K 8 7 4 2
              ♥ K 4
              ♦ Q 10 7
              ♣ Q 6 2
♠ A 10 6
♥ Q J 10 3 2
♦ 8 4
♣ K 4 3
```

West	North	East	South
–	–	–	1NT(*)
Pass	2♥(**)	Pass	2♠
Pass	2NT	Pass	3♠
Pass	4♠	All Pass	

(*) 12-14
(**) Transfer

You lead the queen of hearts against South's 4♠ contract. Declarer plays the ♥K from dummy and the eight from his own hand. Partner contributes the ♥5. Declarer then plays a low spade off the dummy to the three, jack and your ace. How would you continue?

You are fairly certain that from his play of the ♥5 partner has three. However, in this situation, since he cannot beat the ♥K on the initial lead, he might have decided to try to be helpful by playing his lowest heart to suggest a club switch.

Is there any other evidence to support the idea that partner would like a club switch?

Yes. If you play suit preference signals in trumps, unless partner has a singleton trump the ♠3 is low and also suggests a switch to clubs rather than diamonds. Accordingly, you switch to the three of clubs. Partner wins the ♣A, declarer playing the nine. Partner returns the ♣7, declarer contributes the jack and you win the king. Now what?

How many clubs does partner have? Partner could have almost any number, the return of the ♣7 could be from ♣A1087, ♣A10875, ♣A7 or ♣A75, so what are you going to do?

Return your last club. Why?

Just in case partner started with a doubleton. After all if partner has the ♦A or the ♦KJ the diamond trick will not run away, but if partner can ruff the club you have to return the suit now, before declarer draws trumps. The full deal is:

```
              ♠ K 8 7 4 2
              ♥ K 4
              ♦ Q 10 7
              ♣ Q 6 2
♠ A 10 6                      ♠ 9 3
♥ Q J 10 3 2                  ♥ 7 6 5
♦ 8 4                         ♦ K 9 6 5 3 2
♣ K 4 3                       ♣ A 7
              ♠ Q J 5
              ♥ A 9 8
              ♦ A J
              ♣ J 10 9 8 5
```

Notice that declarer chose his cards very carefully in the club suit in an attempt to obscure the true position. By concealing the five and playing the jack he made it difficult for you to know exactly how many clubs partner had, but unfortunately for him there was no risk for you in continuing the club suit.

Now if you turn back to Chapter 59 you will find this problem:

```
              ♠ J 10 3 2
              ♥ A 6
              ♦ K Q J 10
              ♣ 9 6 2
♠ K 8
♥ J 10 8 5
♦ 8 5 4 3
♣ A Q 5
```

West	North	East	South
–	–	–	1♠
Pass	3♠	Pass	4♠
All Pass			

You lead the heart jack against South's 4♠ contract which declarer wins in dummy while partner discourages. Declarer leads the ♠J off the dummy, partner contributes the four and you take the king. What do you do next?

When you looked at the hand before, you had to consider what South might have to bid on to 4♠, which led you to the conclusion that he was more likely to hold the ace of diamonds than the king of clubs. But this was by no means certain. Using suit preference signals in trumps you should be a lot more confident of finding partner with the king of clubs because he played the smallest outstanding trump on the first round.

The full deal was:

       ♠ J 10 3 2
       ♥ A 6
       ♦ K Q J 10
       ♣ 9 6 2

♠ K 8   ♠ 6 4
♥ J 10 8 5   ♥ Q 9 7 3 2
♦ 8 5 4 3   ♦ 9 6
♣ A Q 5   ♣ K J 7 4

       ♠ A Q 9 7 5
       ♥ K 4
       ♦ A 7 2
       ♣ 10 8 3

SMITH ECHOES

Consider the following situation:

       ♠ 8 4
       ♥ A K 5 3
       ♦ A 7 5 3
       ♣ Q 10 5

♠ A 10 7 3 2
♥ 10 8 6
♦ Q 4 2
♣ K 4

West	North	East	South
–	–	–	1NT
Pass	2♣	Pass	2♦
Pass	3NT	All Pass	

You lead the three of spades against South's 3NT contract. Partner plays the jack and declarer wins with the king. Declarer crosses to dummy with a top heart and runs the ♣10 to your king. How do you continue?

Now you face something of a dilemma, the full hand might be:

(a)   ♠ 8 4
       ♥ A K 5 3
       ♦ A 7 5 3
       ♣ Q 10 5

♠ A 10 7 3 2   ♠ J 9 5
♥ 10 8 6   ♥ Q 9 2
♦ Q 4 2   ♦ J 10 4
♣ K 4   ♣ 8 7 3 2

       ♠ K Q 6
       ♥ J 7 4
       ♦ K 9 8
       ♣ A J 9 6

In this case you have to defend passively. Declarer has only eight established tricks, one spade, two hearts, two top diamonds and three clubs. He could set up an extra trick in either hearts or diamonds, but not without your partner obtaining the lead to play a spade back through the queen.

Alternatively, the full hand might be:

(b)   ♠ 8 4
       ♥ A K 5 3
       ♦ A 7 5 3
       ♣ Q 10 5

♠ A 10 7 3 2   ♠ Q J 5
♥ 10 8 6   ♥ 9 7 2
♦ Q 4 2   ♦ J 10 4
♣ K 4   ♣ 8 7 3 2

       ♠ K 9 6
       ♥ Q J 4
       ♦ K 9 8
       ♣ A J 9 6

On this layout you need to continue spades immediately. A passive defense now would allow declarer to make ten tricks: one spade, four hearts, two diamonds and three clubs. How can you tell?

Frankly, playing standard methods you can't. In practice, you could guess that a less than skillful declarer might have made the mistake of winning the first trick with the queen if he held ♠KQ6, which might make you lean in favor of playing for the second scenario, but otherwise you face a total guess. Unless, of course, you have adopted the Smith signal.

This signal is remarkably simple, but extremely effective. Defending against a no-trump contract, you take the opportunity to make a Smith signal in the first suit played by declarer, in this example hearts. The idea is that if you like the suit led by your partner, you encourage a continuation by playing a high card in the first suit played by declarer.

Thus on the first of the example layouts (a) East should discourage a spade continuation by playing the two of hearts on the first round. In layout (b) holding the vitally important ♠Q, East should encourage a spade continuation by dropping the nine of hearts on the first round of the suit.

The same idea can also be applied by the opening leader, who can demand a continuation of his suit by playing a high card in the first suit led by declarer or suggest a relatively poor holding in the suit led by playing low. For example, consider the following situation:

```
              ♠ A 4
              ♥ A 10 5 3
              ♦ 7 5 3
              ♣ A J 7 2
                            ♠ 10 5 2
                            ♥ K 8 6
                            ♦ A 10 9 4
                            ♣ K 8 3
```

West	North	East	South
–	–	–	1NT
Pass	2♣	Pass	2♦
Pass	3NT	All Pass	

West leads the six of spades against South's 3NT contract. Declarer plays low from dummy and takes your ♠10 with the jack. At trick two, declarer leads the queen of hearts which runs to your king. How do you plan your defense?

First, you know that your partner has five spades. How?

Since South's response to Stayman denied a four card major, South can have at most three spades. Consequently, West must have five or six spades. However, since partner's fourth best spade was the six and there is only one card lower in the suit that you can see, he must have exactly five. You can envisage two possible layouts where you can beat the contract:

(c)
```
              ♠ A 4
              ♥ A 10 5 3
              ♦ 7 5 3
              ♣ A J 7 2
♠ K 10 7 6 3                 ♠ 10 5 2
♥ 9 7 2                      ♥ K 8 6
♦ J 8 6                      ♦ A 10 9 4
♣ 9 6                        ♣ K 8 3
              ♠ Q J 8
              ♥ Q J 4
              ♦ K Q 2
              ♣ Q 10 5 4
```

On this layout it is clearly right to continue spades. Then a third round when you next get the lead will enable partner to take three spade tricks to beat the contract.

Alternatively, the layout might be:

(d)
```
              ♠ A 4
              ♥ A 10 5 3
              ♦ 7 5 3
              ♣ A J 7 2
♠ Q 9 7 6 3                 ♠ 10 5 2
♥ 9 7 2                     ♥ K 8 6
♦ Q 8 6                     ♦ A 10 9 4
♣ 9 6                       ♣ K 8 3
              ♠ K J 8
              ♥ Q J 4
              ♦ K J 2
              ♣ Q 10 5 4
```

As you can see, a spade continuation now will do you no good at all. However, if you turn your attention to diamonds immediately you should still have time to establish that suit so that you will have five winners when you regain the lead with the ♣K.

How can you tell? Once again you can't without partner's cooperation. On layout (c) partner can see that if you have three spades you will be able to knock out the ace of spades and put him in to cash the spades when you next get the lead. Accordingly, he should encourage you to continue spades by making a Smith Echo with the nine of hearts when declarer leads the queen.

On the other hand, with (d) unless you have a four card spade suit (which you will be able to see for yourself) he knows that continuing spades is pointless. Therefore, with (d) he should discourage a spade continuation by playing the two of hearts on the first round of the suit.

Now look at the Smith signal in action in the 1993 Venice Cup in Santiago:

```
              ♠ K Q 8 3 2
              ♥ A
              ♦ K J 9 7
              ♣ Q 3 2
                            ♠ 10 7 6
                            ♥ 6 5 3
                            ♦ A 8 3
                            ♣ A J 7 5
```

West	North	East	South
Vogt	*Schulle*	*Nehmert*	*Meyers*
–	–	Pass	1NT(*)
Pass	2♦	Pass	2♠
Pass	3♠	Pass	3NT
All Pass			
(*) 10-12			

Your partner leads the ♥J. Declarer wins the ace in dummy and leads the ♦7. You play the ace. Why?

Because if you duck declarer may have nine tricks. If partner's hearts are poor, declarer may have five spade tricks, three hearts and a diamond. Declarer follows with the two of diamonds and partner with the five.

What are you going to do now?

Partner's low diamond suggests that her hearts are poor. With something like ♥KJ10xx clearly she would have made a Smith Echo. Accordingly, you switch to a club.

The full deal was:

```
              ♠ K Q 8 3 2
              ♥ A
              ♦ K J 9 7
              ♣ Q 3 2
♠ J 9 4                      ♠ 10 7 6
♥ J 10 9 8 2                 ♥ 6 5 3
♦ 10 5                       ♦ A 8 3
♣ K 10 9                     ♣ A J 7 5
              ♠ A 5
              ♥ K Q 7 4
              ♦ Q 6 4 2
              ♣ 8 6 4
```

This would be an easy hand for those players who use the method where the king and ten are strong leads against no-trumps because they would know there was no future in hearts when partner started with the jack.

Now have another look at a hand used earlier to illustrate the importance of counting:

```
              ♠ A J 7
              ♥ J 10 9 8 6
              ♦ Q J 6 2
              ♣ A
♠ 6 5 3                      ♠ 10 9 2
♥ Q 7 3                      ♥ A 4 2
♦ A 8 7                      ♦ 9 4
♣ K J 10 3                   ♣ 8 6 5 4 2
              ♠ K Q 8 4
              ♥ K 5
              ♦ K 10 5 3
              ♣ Q 9 7
```

West	North	East	South
–	–	–	1NT(*)
Pass	2♦ (**)	Pass	2♥
Pass	3♦	Pass	3NT
All Pass			

(*) 12-14
(**) Transfer

West leads the three of clubs against South's 3NT contract, East contributing the ♣2 under the ace to suggest an odd number of cards in the suit. After winning in dummy declarer sets about the diamond suit, West decides to duck one round and has to decide what to do after taking his ace on the second round.

When we first looked at this problem West did well to decide that South probably had the queen of clubs; after all East would have to play exactly the same way with either ♣Qxx or ♣Qxxxx. Now that you are playing Smith Echoes this is not the case any more. If East had the queen of clubs he should play high-low in diamonds, while in the actual example without the queen of clubs, East should play a low card on the first round of diamonds.

Notice how well Smith Echoes combine with distributional or count signals. Indeed, the Smith signal is so powerful that you can decide to do without encouraging and discouraging signals except in the most obvious situations (such as on the lead of an ace or queen) and for discards.

63

Chapter

Nobody Rings a Bell

In this chapter it is assumed that you are now familiar with suit preference signals in trumps and Smith Echoes, which in turn means that count signals will tend to take the upper hand in no-trump contracts. "Nobody rings a bell," the title of this chapter, indicates that in the problems that follow, all of which are real life situations, you will be given no further hint as to what is going on. You will have to decide for yourself what kind of signal you should be giving or what type of signal your partner has made to try to help you.

Let's start with the following deal from the 1993 Macallan/ London Sunday Times Tournament played in London. Put yourself in the East seat:

- ♠ Q 8 4
- ♥ Q J 10 4 3
- ♦ K 7 3
- ♣ K 9

		♠ 6 5	
		♥ K 9 5 2	
		♦ 10 9 5 2	
		♣ A Q J	

West	North	East	South
Sheehan	*Mouiel*	*Ata-Ullah*	*Levy*
–	Pass	Pass	1♣
1♠	2♥	Pass	2NT
Pass	3NT	Dble	All Pass

Not everyone would find your double, but it should concentrate your mind on the defense!

Partner leads the ♠J. Dummy plays the four, you the six and declarer wins with the king. Now he plays the ♥A on which partner plays ♥8, and then the ♥7, on which partner plays the ♥6.

How do you defend?

Partner's Smith Echo doesn't really help you much here. With only two spades in your hand there is no future in that suit; however it is convenient to know that your partner actually does hold the ace of spades. If you play back a spade after taking the king of hearts a club switch from him

will justify your bidding!

How can you make sure partner will play a club rather than a diamond?

By the order in which you play the small hearts before taking the king. If you play 9, 5, 2 in hearts before taking the king partner should know that you want a diamond switch, if you play 2, 5, 9, K, a club switch would be indicated. Note that your carding cannot really be confused as a Smith Echo because partner will know that you only have two spades when you play the five on the second round.

Here is the full deal:

		♠ Q 8 4	
		♥ Q J 10 4 3	
		♦ K 7 3	
		♣ K 9	

♠ A J 10 3 2		♠ 6 5
♥ 8 6		♥ K 9 5 2
♦ J 8 6		♦ 10 9 5 2
♣ 8 7 3		♣ A Q J

		♠ K 9 7	
		♥ A 7	
		♦ A Q 4	
		♣ 10 6 5 4 2	

On this deal the Dutch star, Berry Westra, held up hearts, as described and got the club switch from his partner, Leufkens.

Meanwhile, Gabriel Chagas solved the problem by switching to the ♦9. This would have worked badly if South had had ♦AQJx, but otherwise it was likely to put partner off playing the suit.

And what of Ata-Ullah?

He ducked two hearts, playing the two and five, won the third and played a spade to West's ace. Perhaps West should have got it right but his switch to the ♦J allowed the declarer to claim nine tricks.

Tip

When you are holding up a winner, you may be able to use the small cards as a suit preference signal. You may be able to direct partner's attention to one suit by denying honors in another.

Stay in the East seat for this deal from the 1987 World Championships in Ocho Rios, Jamaica:

```
        ♠ Q 8
        ♥ 9 4
        ♦ Q J 8 7 2
        ♣ A Q 10 3
                ♠ A 10 6 5 3
                ♥ Q 7 3
                ♦ A
                ♣ 9 8 6 5
```

West	North	East	South
–	–	–	1NT(*)
Pass	3NT	All Pass	

(*) 15-17

Partner leads the ♥6 against South's 3NT contract. Dummy contributes the four of hearts and declarer captures your queen with the king. Next he plays the ♦6 to the 3, J and your ace.

How do you continue?

It seems obvious to continue with a heart, because if partner has either ♥A10xxx or ♥AJxxx the contract will be down. However partner would have made a Smith Echo with either of these holdings. Partner's ♦3 suggests that there is no future in hearts so you should switch to spades. Down two!

Here is the full deal:

```
            ♠ Q 8
            ♥ 9 4
            ♦ Q J 8 7 2
            ♣ A Q 10 3
♠ K 9 7 2               ♠ A 10 6 5 3
♥ J 10 8 6 5           ♥ Q 7 3
♦ 10 4 3               ♦ A
♣ 4                    ♣ 9 8 6 5
            ♠ J 4
            ♥ A K 2
            ♦ K 9 6 5
            ♣ K J 7 2
```

Tip

The Smith Echo against no trumps is one of the best defensive conventions. A high/low in the first suit played by declarer says you like the opening lead, and a low/high suggests a switch.

Now move over to the West seat for this deal played in the 1990 Cap Gemini tournament in Amsterdam:

```
        ♠ 8 5
        ♥ A 6 3
        ♦ A J 10 9 4
        ♣ 9 7 5
♠ A 4 2
♥ J 5
♦ K 6 2
♣ A Q J 8 2
```

West	North	East	South
Kokish	*Forrester*	*Mittleman*	*Robson*
–	–	–	2♥(*)
Dble	3♦(**)	4♠	5♥
Dble	All Pass		

(*) Weak 2♥

(**) A raise to 3♥ with diamond values.

You decide to lead the ♠A.

Partner plays the ♠K, while declarer follows with the nine. How do you continue?

Clearly partner has the queen of spades and your only problem is to cash your winners in the correct order. No doubt partner has the ♣K, but you cannot be sure of his length in that suit. If partner has seven spades and four clubs then there probably is no defense. If partner has seven spades and three clubs, then you have to cash two club tricks. Since partner is far more likely to hold six spades, the simplest defense (and the winning one) is to continue with a spade.

Here is the full deal:

```
            ♠ 8 5
            ♥ A 6 3
            ♦ A J 10 9 4
            ♣ 9 7 5
♠ A 4 2                ♠ K Q J 10 7 3
♥ J 5                  ♥ 8 7
♦ K 6 2                ♦ 7
♣ A Q J 8 2            ♣ K 10 6 4
            ♠ 9 6
            ♥ K Q 10 9 4 2
            ♦ Q 8 5 3
            ♣ 3
```

Just in case you think this is too easy, at the table West convinced himself that partner was making a suit preference signal with the king of spades and switched to a diamond.

There were two good reasons why this was wrong. First the queen of spades would be the right card from East to suggest a diamond void, and then East might have bid 4♦ over 3♦ with a void and good spades.

Tip

Don't fall into the trap of ascribing an unnecessarily complex meaning to partner's signal.

Now stay in the West seat for the next hand:

```
        ♠ A Q 4
        ♥ J 9 2
        ♦ 10 7 6 5
        ♣ 8 6 5

♠ J 6 5 3
♥ K 4 3
♦ A Q J 9 4
♣ 2
```

West	North	East	South
–	–	–	1♥
2♦	2♥	3♣	3♥
All Pass			

You make the obvious lead of your singleton club. Partner wins the ace and returns the 4♣ for you to ruff. Declarer follows with the seven and jack.

How should you continue?

Clearly partner holds ♣AQ10943. From the return of the ♣4, he must be interested in diamonds.

So are you going to underlead your diamond ace?

No! If partner held the ♦K or a void, he would have returned the 3♣. It would appear he must have a singleton and you should therefore play the ace of diamonds. This is the full deal:

```
            ♠ A Q 4
            ♥ J 9 2
            ♦ 10 7 6 5
            ♣ 8 6 5

♠ J 6 5 3              ♠ 10 9 7 2
♥ K 4 3               ♥ 6 5
♦ A Q J 9 4           ♦ 3
♣ 2                   ♣ A Q 10 9 4 3

            ♠ K 8
            ♥ A Q 10 8 7
            ♦ K 8 2
            ♣ K J 7
```

Ace of diamonds, diamond ruff, club ruff, diamond ruff and a further club enables you to score your ♥K. Perhaps you should have doubled!

Tip

For the expert every card has a meaning and sometimes it can be very subtle. The application of logical principles should always enable you to decipher partner's intended message.

Now move back to the East seat:

```
        ♠ 5
        ♥ J 10 6 5
        ♦ A Q 5 4
        ♣ A Q 10 4

            ♠ A J 10 7 4
            ♥ 2
            ♦ K 8 3 2
            ♣ K J 3
```

West	North	East	South
Pass	1♦	1♠	3♥
Pass	4♥	Pass	4NT
Pass	5♥	Pass	6♥
All Pass			

Your partner leads the ♠6. You win the ace and return the ♥2. Declarer wins with the ♥K and plays the ♦J to the ace and a small diamond from dummy. What do you do now?

It looks as if declarer has a singleton diamond. What did partner play on the ♦J?

He played the ♦7. In that case you should play the ♦K!

Why?

Because with four small cards you should always give count starting with the second highest. If partner held ♦10976 he would have played the ♦9 under the jack.

The full deal:

```
            ♠ 5
            ♥ J 10 6 5
            ♦ A Q 5 4
            ♣ A Q 10 4

♠ 8 6 3 2             ♠ A J 10 7 4
♥ 8 7                ♥ 2
♦ 7 6                ♦ K 8 3 2
♣ 9 8 6 5 2          ♣ K J 3

            ♠ K Q 9
            ♥ A K Q 9 4 3
            ♦ J 10 9
            ♣ 7
```

If you fail to take your ♦K, declarer can discard his losing diamonds on the top spades and ruff a diamond to make his contract. Credit goes to the declarer for having the courage to adopt this deceptive line of play on the strength of your overcall. Unlucky for him that you were awake.

Tip

When giving a count signal whenever possible play or discard your second highest from four small cards.

Now try this deal from the 1993 Camrose Trials:

```
          ♠ K 7 5
          ♥ K J 9 3
          ♦ 9
          ♣ A 10 5 3 2
                        ♠ A Q J 10
                        ♥ 6 5 2
                        ♦ A 7 6 4
                        ♣ J 6
```

West	North	East	South
	Reardon		*Butland*
–	1♣	Dble	1♥
Pass	2♥	Pass	2♠(*)
Pass	4♥	All Pass	

(*) Asking for help in spades

West leads the ♠4 against South's 4♥ contract. You win with the ♠10 while declarer plays the five from dummy and three from hand.

How do you continue?

Partner may hold a doubleton spade in which case you could play ace and another, giving him a ruff. And the alternatives?

If partner has the ♦K you could return a low diamond. There is no doubt that declarer has a club fit with dummy, but there is room for partner to hold ♣Qxx or the ♣K; if that is the case, you could cash your winners and wait for the setting trick.

Given that your partner has had no opportunity to signal how can you decide? Well, partner did make a signal on the opening lead.

How did he do that?

After East's takeout double it would seem likely that West would have led a diamond from a suit headed by the queen rather than a spade from a possible three small. It would also be dangerous to lead away from the ♦K. It may turn out badly, but taking everything into consideration, a small diamond away from the ace seems the best possible way to defeat the contract and hope partner holds the king, and can win and return a spade through the king in dummy. The full deal:

```
          ♠ K 7 5
          ♥ K J 9 3
          ♦ 9
          ♣ A 10 5 3 2
♠ 9 4 2                 ♠ A Q J 10
♥ 8 7                   ♥ 6 5 2
♦ K 8 5 3 2             ♦ A 7 6 4
♣ 9 8 4                 ♣ J 6
          ♠ 8 6 3
          ♥ A Q 10 4
          ♦ Q J 10
          ♣ K Q 7
```

Remember that the first signal you make is with the opening lead.

Now try this hand from one of the North American majors, the Vanderbilt, played in Pasadena in 1992:

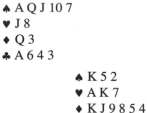

```
          ♠ A Q J 10 7
          ♥ J 8
          ♦ Q 3
          ♣ A 6 4 3
                        ♠ K 5 2
                        ♥ A K 7
                        ♦ K J 9 8 5 4
                        ♣ 10
```

West	North	East	South
Becker	*Mohan*	*Rubin*	*Goodman*
–	–	1♦	1♥
Pass	1♠	2♦	Pass
Pass	Dble	Pass	2♥
Pass	3♥	All Pass	

Your partner leads the ♦2 against South's 3♥ contract. Declarer plays the ♦Q from dummy and you cover with the king, and declarer plays the ace. He then plays a heart to the six, jack and your king. What next?

It looks as though the defense have four tricks, the ♠K, ♥AK, and a diamond (assuming declarer has at least a doubleton).

Can you see a fifth trick anywhere?

Yes, you could switch to your singleton club and after winning a subsequent trick play a low diamond to partner's ten to score a club ruff with your small trump.

The full deal:

```
          ♠ A Q J 10 7
          ♥ J 8
          ♦ Q 3
          ♣ A 6 4 3
♠ 9 8 6                 ♠ K 5 2
♥ 9 6                   ♥ A K 7
♦ 10 7 2               ♦ K J 9 8 5 4
♣ Q 9 8 5 2            ♣ 10
          ♠ 4 3
          ♥ Q 10 5 4 3 2
          ♦ A 6
          ♣ K J 7
```

Tip

Leading a low card in the suit bid by partner promises an honor which could be the ten.

Now stay in the East seat for this deal:

```
              ♠ A 7
              ♥ Q 10 9 8 7
              ♦ Q J 8
              ♣ 9 5 3
                              ♠ 10
                              ♥ A 6 4 3
                              ♦ K 9 7
                              ♣ 8 7 6 4 2
```

West	North	East	South
–	–	–	Pass
1NT(*)	Pass	Pass	2♠
Dble (**)	All Pass		

(*) 12-14
(**) Long or short in spades

West leads the ♣K asking for a count signal. As you have an odd number you play the ♣2. South plays the ♣10 and West continues with the ♣A.

Clearly partner has either ♣AK or ♣AKQ. In either case having shown length on the first round you can afford to make a suit preference signal now. To suggest you have cards in hearts play the ♣8.

South follows with the ♣J and West switches to the ♥J. You win with the ace and return the ♣4, hoping partner can ruff, which he does, and then he continues with the ♦A and a small diamond to your king, declarer playing the six followed by the ten.

The defense has already taken six tricks, but can you do any better? Declarer appears to have a 6-2-2-3 distribution. Therefore it cannot cost to play another club in the hope partner's remaining honor is the queen of trumps, thus insuring he makes an additional trump trick.

```
              ♠ A 7
              ♥ Q 10 9 8 7
              ♦ Q J 8
              ♣ 9 5 3
♠ Q 8 3 2                     ♠ 10
♥ J 2                         ♥ A 6 4 3
♦ A 5 4 3 2                   ♦ K 9 7
♣ A K                         ♣ 8 7 6 4 2
              ♠ K J 9 6 5 4
              ♥ K 5
              ♦ 10 6
              ♣ Q J 10
```

A passive defense at the end would allow declarer to escape for one down by playing the ♠J from hand and pinning East's ten.

A fourth club insures a trump trick no matter where or what declarer ruffs with.

Tip

After taking your outside tricks always consider attacking declarer's trump holding, even if this means that you are conceding a ruff and discard.

Now try this deal from the Venice Cup when it was contested in 1989 in Perth, Australia:

```
              ♠ A J 10 9 5
              ♥ 9 5
              ♦ J
              ♣ Q 9 7 6 3
♠ 8 6 4 3 2
♥ J 4 2
♦ Q 8 4
♣ A 2
```

West	North	East	South
Schippers	*Vogt*	*vd Pas*	*Schroeder*
–	Pass	3♦	4♥
5♦	5♥	Pass	6♥
Pass	Pass	Dble	All Pass
Zenkel	*Gielkens*	*von Arnim*	*Bakker*
–	Pass	3♦	4♥
5♦	5♥	Pass	6♥
All Pass			

The first problem you face is that of the opening lead. Let's suppose you decide to start with the ♣A, which was Schippers choice. The play to the first trick is ♣A, 3, 8, and K. Unless the ♣K is a false card from ♣KJ1054, there is no point in continuing with the suit.

If you decide to play partner for the king of spades (as West did here), you will be disappointed because the full deal looks like this:

```
              ♠ A J 10 9 5
              ♥ 9 5
              ♦ J
              ♣ Q 9 7 6 3
♠ 8 6 4 3 2                   ♠ Q 7
♥ J 4 2                       ♥ –
♦ Q 8 4                       ♦ A 10 7 6 5 3 2
♣ A 2                         ♣ J 10 8 5
              ♠ K
              ♥ A K Q J 10 8 7 6 3
              ♦ K 9
              ♣ K 4
```

Thanks to the fortunate position in spades declarer was able to discard both losing diamonds and make the slam.

Although East was unable to give West a suit preference signal on the ♣A, the decision to switch to a spade was clearly influenced by East's double which West obviously interpreted as a Lightner Double, which asks for an unusual lead (therefore not partner's suit) and is one of the most useful defensive bids ever invented.

At the other table where there was no double, Zenkel led a diamond. Von Arnim took the ace and switched to a club.

Tip

Be wary of doubling a slam which you cannot defeat in your own hand. Partner may interpret it as a Lightner Double. When your opponents bid a slam without using Blackwood, there may be two quick losers—if you can find them!

On the next deal you are West:

```
        ♠ 9 7 5 4
        ♥ A K 4
        ♦ J 2
        ♣ A K 3 2

♠ A 2
♥ 9 2
♦ Q 7 6 5
♣ J 10 9 8 4
```

West	North	East	South
–	–	–	2♥(*)
Pass	4♥	All Pass	

(*) A disciplined weak two bid

You decide to lead the ♠A to have a look at dummy. Your partner plays the eight and declarer the five.

Since the eight is encouraging, you continue with a spade.

Partner takes the king and returns the three for you to ruff. Declarer plays the ten and queen.

Clearly partner could not afford to play the jack of spades because that would establish dummy's nine, so nothing should be assumed from the return of the three. After ruffing what do you play next?

Partner must have either the ♦A or ♦K, and probably the ♣Q, otherwise declarer would have too many points for his bidding.

So are you going to switch to a diamond?

Yes, but wait a minute! If a low diamond is played, declarer will be able to squeeze West in the minors. So, perhaps a club is the right card to play?

No, this would give declarer the possibility of a double squeeze!

Suppose this was the full deal:

```
              ♠ 9 7 5 4
              ♥ A K 4
              ♦ J 2
              ♣ A K 3 2
♠ A 2                      ♠ K J 8 3
♥ 9 2                      ♥ 8 5
♦ Q 7 6 5                  ♦ K 9 8 4 3
♣ J 10 9 8 4               ♣ Q 6
              ♠ Q 10 5
              ♥ Q J 10 7 6 3
              ♦ A 10
              ♣ 7 5
```

If a club is played, declarer can reduce to this four card ending:

```
              ♠ 9
              ♥ –
              ♦ 2
              ♣ K 3
♠ –                        ♠ J
♥ –                        ♥ –
♦ Q 7                      ♦ K 9
♣ J 10                     ♣ Q
              ♠ –
              ♥ 7
              ♦ A 10
              ♣ 7
```

On the last trump West has to discard a diamond, while dummy throws a club, as does East. Then a club to king will squeeze East.

So, the contract cannot be defeated?

Yes, it can. Switch to the ♦Q and no one can be squeezed!

Tip

When you only need one more trick to defeat a contract don't forget to consider the possibility of declarer having a double squeeze available. The correct switch will often break up the position.

Stay in the West seat for this deal played in New York in 1992:

```
              ♠ Q 5 4 3
              ♥ 6 5 3
              ♦ K Q 9
              ♣ A Q 2
♠ K 9
♥ A Q 10 4 2
♦ A J 10 6
♣ 10 4
```

West	North	East	South
	Cohen		Zia
1♥	Dble	Pass	4♠
All Pass			

You decide to lead the ♣10 and dummy is revealed.

A takeout double would not be everyone's choice on the North hand, but your task is to defeat the contract, not to worry about the opponent's bidding.

Zia wins the opening lead in dummy with the queen and plays a spade to the ace, followed by a diamond. You rise with the ace, cash the king of trumps (partner following with the ten), and exit with a club. Declarer wins the ace, cashes the king and queen of diamonds, throwing hearts on both of them, and crosses to hand with a club to the king. He now leads a heart out of his hand, and this is what you can see:

```
              ♠ Q 5
              ♥ 6 5 3
              ♦ –
              ♣ –
♠ –
♥ A Q 10 4
♦ J
♣ –
```

Obviously declarer is down to ♠J87 and two hearts. Do you try for a crocodile coup, rising with the ace of hearts to swallow partner's king?

But, suppose declarer has ♥Kx?

The answer depends on which cards partner has played, particularly in diamonds. When declarer cashed the king and queen of diamonds, partner followed with the eight and seven. You should therefore go up with the ace of hearts.

```
              ♠ Q 5 4 3
              ♥ 6 5 3
              ♦ K Q 9
              ♣ A Q 2
♠ K 9              ♠ 10 2
♥ A Q 10 4 2       ♥ K
♦ A J 10 6         ♦ 8 7 4 3 2
♣ 10 4             ♣ J 9 7 5 3
              ♠ A J 8 7 6
              ♥ J 9 8 7
              ♦ 5
              ♣ K 8 6
```

Tip

It is possible to give a suit preference signal in a suit being played by declarer, especially where you have already shown your length or it is obvious to partner how many cards you hold.

Now try this one:

```
              ♠ A 10 6 5
              ♥ 8 7 3
              ♦ K Q J 3 2
              ♣ 8
♠ K J 9 8 7 2
♥ J 9 6
♦ 8 7
♣ A 5
```

West	North	East	South
–	–	–	1♣
2♠	3♦	3♠	4♣
Pass	4♦	Pass	4♠
Pass	5♦	Pass	6♣
All Pass			

Clearly South has a spade control so West elects to lead the ♦8. Partner plays the six and declarer wins with the ace. He then plays the ♣K. Now what is your plan?

From partner's play of the ♦6 it looks as if he has four diamonds (second highest from a bad suit).This is also consistent with South's failure to support the suit at any stage of the auction. Given that the raise in spades almost certainly promises three can you see how you can make life difficult for declarer?

Yes, take the ace of clubs and play another diamond now to kill the dummy. Declarer can take one discard on the ace of spades, but if he tries to take another on a top diamond you will be able to ruff. Hopefully, whatever he does you will get a heart trick later in the play.

Here is the full deal:

```
                  ♠ A 10 6 5
                  ♥ 8 7 3
                  ♦ K Q J 3 2
                  ♣ 8
♠ K J 9 8 7 2              ♠ Q 4 3
♥ J 9 6                    ♥ K 10 5
♦ 8 7                      ♦ 9 6 5 4
♣ A 5                      ♣ 10 7 3
                  ♠ –
                  ♥ A Q 4 3
                  ♦ A 10
                  ♣ K Q J 9 6 4 2
```

Tip

Counting out a hand using both the bidding and partner's signals as a guide is always a helpful procedure and sometimes it can lead to devastating conclusions.

Now try your luck with this deal from the Teams Olympiad played in Valkenberg in the Netherlands in 1980. You start with a lead problem:

```
                  ♠ A J 9 7
                  ♥ A J 8 7
                  ♦ A 7 6
                  ♣ 6 5
```

West	North	East	South
Flodqvist		*Sundelin*	
–	–	–	1NT
Pass	3NT	All Pass	

Against this sequence most players would elect to lead a major. Here West had to decide between hearts and spades. Should he prefer a spade because spades are stronger?

The famous English brothers, Bob and Jim Sharples had a theory that when faced with an equal choice between the majors a heart should be preferred, so they would have supported Flodqvist's choice of a heart. Indeed, Flodqvist reasoned that with three aces in his hand he could afford the ♥A. East contributed the ♥10 to the first trick and reading this as encouraging, Flodqvist continued with a low heart.

```
                  ♠ Q 6
                  ♥ 6 4 3
                  ♦ K Q 2
                  ♣ K 9 7 3 2
♠ A J 9 7                  ♠ J 4 3
♥ A J 8 7                  ♥ Q 10 2
♦ A 7 6                    ♦ 10 9 4 3
♣ 6 5                      ♣ 10 8 4
                  ♠ K 10 8 2
                  ♥ K 9 5
                  ♦ J 8 5
                  ♣ A Q J
```

Tip

With plenty of entries there may be an alternative to fourth best as the opening lead.

Now stay in the West seat for:

```
                  ♠ Q 10 6
                  ♥ 8 5 4 2
                  ♦ A Q
                  ♣ K Q 7 3
♠ 8 5 2
♥ A K J 6
♦ K 7
♣ J 8 6 4
```

West	North	East	South
–	–	–	Pass
Pass	1♣	Pass	1♠
Pass	1NT	Pass	3♠
Pass	4♠	All Pass	

West leads the ♥K to get count from partner, because it may be possible he is short and can get a heart ruff. East plays the ten of hearts and declarer the seven.

It seems clear that partner has a doubleton heart. You could play king, followed by ace and another heart, but that would be only three tricks. Where can an additional trick come from? It seems like partner needs one of the black aces to beat the contract, and if it is the ace of spades it is likely to be a singleton since South made a jump rebid in spades. Certainly, if you condense four top tricks into three by forcing partner to ruff you will not be very popular. So should you play a club, hoping for partner to have the ace of clubs, or a trump hoping for the ace of spades?

If you lead a club and declarer has the ace, he might be able to take a discard or two on the top clubs in dummy. If you lead a spade and partner has the ace of clubs and not the ace of spades it will not matter too much because declarer will not be able to take any discards on clubs without giving your partner the lead.

So, strange though it may seem, it must be right to switch to a trump since that will beat the contract whichever black ace partner has.

Here is the actual deal:

```
              ♠ Q 10 6
              ♥ 8 5 4 2
              ♦ A Q
              ♣ K Q 7 3
♠ 8 5 2                      ♠ A
♥ A K J 6                    ♥ 10 3
♦ K 7                        ♦ 10 8 6 5 4 2
♣ J 8 6 4                    ♣ 10 9 5 2
              ♠ K J 9 7 4 3
              ♥ Q 9 7
              ♦ J 9 3
              ♣ A
```

Tip

When considering the effect of alternative lines of defense, try to choose the one that gives you a second chance.

Alternative Methods

Over the years a number of special signals have been developed. Most of them fit into one of the categories we have already examined, but their more complex nature makes it convenient to group them together in a chapter. This list is by no means comprehensive, but you could easily meet opponents at the table employing any of these methods.

Let's start with something relatively simple:

THE SINGLETON SWITCH

Look at this deal from the Cap Gemini Pandata tournament played in The Hague in January 1993:

```
        ♠ 6 3
        ♥ K 9 4
        ♦ K J 5 3
        ♣ K 10 8 6
                        ♠ 10 8 4 2
                        ♥ J 6 3
                        ♦ 10
                        ♣ A J 9 5 2
```

West	North	East	South
Fallenius	*Westra*	*Nilsland*	*Leufkens*
1♠	Pass	3♠	Dble
4♠	4NT	Pass	5♦
All Pass			

Your partner leads the ♠K. Partner is asking for count, so you play the eight. Now West switches to the ♣4.

Fortunately, this is an easy problem. Since East/West have an agreement that the lead of the king followed by a switch may be a singleton, East therefore takes his ace and returns a club hoping partner can ruff.

Here is the full deal:

```
            ♠ 6 3
            ♥ K 9 4
            ♦ K J 5 3
            ♣ K 10 8 6
♠ A K Q J 9 5           ♠ 10 8 4 2
♥ 10 8 7                ♥ J 6 3
♦ Q 9 7                 ♦ 10
♣ 4                     ♣ A J 9 5 2
            ♠ 7
            ♥ A Q 5 2
            ♦ A 8 6 4 2
            ♣ Q 7 3
```

At another table, West started by leading his singleton club in the hope that after taking one club ruff he would be able to put his partner in with the ♠10 to get another. His confidence in his partner turned out to be sorely misplaced when East played the ♣9. Andrew Robson took every advantage as declarer. He won with the ♣Q, and got the trumps right. Then he played four rounds of hearts, discarding a spade from dummy before exiting with a spade. Whoever won the spade would be endplayed.

The idea that after cashing a king a switch is likely to be a singleton is not universally known but is quite effective.

The next example involves, perhaps, an even less well known idea.

WHEN DUMMY HAS A WORTHLESS HOLDING

Consider this deal from the European Women's Teams Championship played in Menton in 1993:

```
              ♠ 8 7 3
              ♥ Q 8 4 3 2
              ♦ 7
              ♣ 10 8 7 5
♠ A J 6 5
♥ J 9 6
♦ A J 6 3
♣ J 2
```

West	North	East	South
Zenkel	*Jakobs*	*von Arnim*	*Kristjans*
1NT(*)	Pass	Pass	Dble
Pass	2♦(**)	Pass	2♥
All Pass			

(*) 10-12
(**) Transfer

West began with the obvious lead of the ♣J. East won with the king and switched to the ♠2. Declarer played the ten and West won with the jack. West was well-placed now because she knew that her partner held the ♠K. How?

The partnership have a special agreement that when dummy has a worthless holding a switch to a low card guarantees the ace or king. Otherwise they lead second highest.

In practice, West returned the ♣2 to get a club ruff. East won and returned the ♣9. Declarer played the queen and West ruffed. What did East's nine mean?

It was confirming the king of spades and suggesting nothing of value in diamonds. West could see several ways of the contract going down three and decided to play a spade to her partner's king. East won and played the fourth club on which declarer discarded the ♠Q.

West ruffed and played the ♠A, forcing declarer to ruff with the ♥K. Declarer then played the ♦K, which West took with the ace to play her last spade. If declarer ruffed she would promote a trump trick for the defense, if not he loses that trick anyway. Either way she could not avoid going down three.

The full deal was:

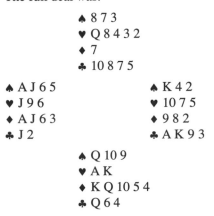

```
              ♠ 8 7 3
              ♥ Q 8 4 3 2
              ♦ 7
              ♣ 10 8 7 5
♠ A J 6 5              ♠ K 4 2
♥ J 9 6               ♥ 10 7 5
♦ A J 6 3             ♦ 9 8 2
♣ J 2                 ♣ A K 9 3
              ♠ Q 10 9
              ♥ A K
              ♦ K Q 10 5 4
              ♣ Q 6 4
```

Now look at another example from Deauville in 1974:

```
              ♠ A K Q 8 3
              ♥ A K 8
              ♦ J 7 6 3
              ♣ K
                      ♠ J 7 5 4
                      ♥ 10 9 7 2
                      ♦ A 10 5
                      ♣ 10 9
```

West	North	East	South
Flint	*Lebel*	*Sheehan*	*Mari*
–	1♠	Pass	1NT
Pass	3♦	Pass	3NT
All Pass			

West leads the ♥4 against 3NT by South. Declarer plays the ace from dummy. Partner has various possible holdings—♥Q654 or ♥J654. He may even have led from a three card suit. In any event it must be correct to show length, so you play the nine.

Declarer plays the ♥3 from hand and continues with the ♣K. Since you play Smith Echo it makes your play on the king of clubs difficult. You are not sure that you want to encourage partner to continue hearts or whether it is more important for him to know how many clubs you hold. Your club spots are so high he will no doubt be confused in any event. You elect to play the nine and hope for the best.

Partner wins and switches to the ♦2.

That's a surprise as you were expecting partner to duck. If partner doesn't have the queen of hearts he may have been worried that declarer had nine tricks via five spades, three hearts and a club.

His switch to a low diamond promises at least the king. What do you play? If declarer has ♦Qx it is unlikely the contract can be defeated so you therefore play the ♦10.

Suppose partner's diamonds were Q982? He would have led the nine instead of the two.

The full deal:

```
              ♠ A K Q 8 3
              ♥ A K 8
              ♦ J 7 6 3
              ♣ K
♠ 9 6 2               ♠ J 7 5 4
♥ J 6 4               ♥ 10 9 7 2
♦ K Q 4 2             ♦ A 10 5
♣ A 8 6               ♣ 10 9
              ♠ 10
              ♥ Q 5 3
              ♦ 9 8
              ♣ Q J 7 5 4 3 2
```

A lot has been written about giving signals in the trump suit. Playing suit-preference signals in trumps is by no means the only possibility.

Here is a more traditional approach:

GIVING COUNT IN TRUMPS (TRUMP ECHO)

Put yourself in the West seat for this deal:

```
            ♠ J 2
            ♥ 10 3
            ♦ Q 10 9 6 4
            ♣ J 8 5 3
♠ 8 4
♥ K 7 6 4 2
♦ 7 3
♣ A K 9 2
```

West	North	East	South
–	Pass	Pass	2♣
Pass	2♦	Pass	2♠
Pass	3♦	Pass	3♥
Pass	3NT	Pass	4♥
Pass	4♠	All Pass	

West has a fairly natural lead of the ♣K, asking partner to give count. Partner plays the seven and declarer the four.

Clearly East has either two, three or four clubs. Nothing else looks attractive, so it seems sensible to continue with the ♣A. Partner plays the six and declarer ruffs with the ♠5. He then plays the ♠7 to the jack and runs the ♥10 to West's king, partner playing the ♥5.

What do we know about the heart suit?

West knows his partner has a singleton heart because of the opposition's bidding (South has bid hearts twice, indicating five). The question now arises, do you give partner a ruff? The answer really depends on how many trumps he holds. If he holds three, it is right to do so and hope he has the ♦A. If he has four trumps, it is better to force declarer to ruff clubs. But how do you know for sure how many trumps he has?

One way is to give count in trumps.

If you have an odd number of trumps play high-low to indicate this. If you have an even number, do the reverse, play low-high. The idea of doing this the abnormal way around is simply so that the signaller is more likely to have a high trump left to ruff with.

Most players reserve this signal for times when a ruff is possible. If used indiscriminately declarer is often given too much information.

How does it work on this deal?

Well, suppose partner played the ten of spades under the jack, the full deal might look like this:

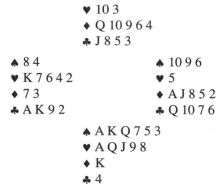

```
            ♠ J 2
            ♥ 10 3
            ♦ Q 10 9 6 4
            ♣ J 8 5 3
♠ 8 4                    ♠ 10 9 6
♥ K 7 6 4 2              ♥ 5
♦ 7 3                    ♦ A J 8 5 2
♣ A K 9 2               ♣ Q 10 7 6
            ♠ A K Q 7 5 3
            ♥ A Q J 9 8
            ♦ K
            ♣ 4
```

Declarer's known shape is to be 6-5-1-1, so the only chance of defeating the contract is to give partner a heart ruff and hope he has the ♦A. (Of course declarer didn't have to go down, but you won't win many bridge events if your opponents never make mistakes.)

On the actual hand partner plays the ♠3. The only hope now is to assume partner has four trumps (if declarer has a seven card suit the defense have no hope). The winning defense is, therefore, to force declarer with another club.

The actual deal is:

```
            ♠ J 2
            ♥ 10 3
            ♦ Q 10 9 6 4
            ♣ J 8 5 3
♠ 8 4                    ♠ 10 9 6 3
♥ K 7 6 4 2              ♥ 5
♦ 7 3                    ♦ J 8 5 2
♣ A K 9 2               ♣ Q 10 7 6
            ♠ A K Q 7 5
            ♥ A Q J 9 8
            ♦ A K
            ♣ 4
```

It was Mike Lawrence who suggested the possibility of giving count signals in the trump suit. They represent an interesting idea worthy of consideration.

REVOLVING DISCARDS

Next we look at an alternative to standard suit preference signals, the Revolving Discard:

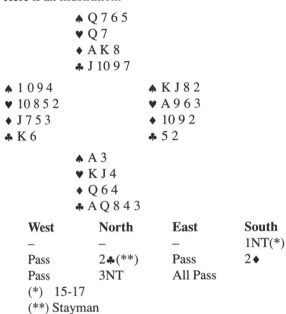

♠ 8 6 4 3
♥ A 7
♦ J 10 8 6 5
♣ A K

♠ A J 9 2
♥ 6 4
♦ Q 7 3
♣ J 10 9 4

West	North	East	South
–	–	–	1NT(*)
Pass	3NT	All Pass	
(*) 15-17			

As West you lead the ♣J against South's 3NT contract. Declarer wins with dummy's ♣K, East playing the ♣4, and continues with the jack of diamonds, on which partner discards the ♥J. When declarer plays low from hand you win with the queen. How should you continue?

You can already see seven tricks for declarer: the ♥A, four diamonds and the ♣AK. If partner has both black suit queens it would probably be best to continue with a club, hoping that declarer has ♥KQ alone (you know partner doesn't have the ♥Q from his discard of the ♥J).

However, if you are playing revolving discards, partner's play of the ♥J carries a special message. The way the convention works is that the discard of a high card asks for the next suit up (excluding trumps when playing in a suit contract). So the discard of a high spade would ask for a club, a high club for a diamond and so on.

It is possible to extend this by using low cards to ask for the next suit down, but you may decide it's better for them to retain their normal meaning.

In this case partner's card clearly asks for a spade, so you switch to the ♠2, which proves to be the only way to defeat the contract.

This is the full deal:

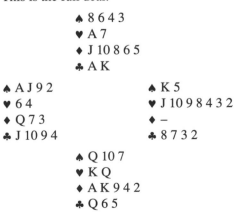

♠ 8 6 4 3
♥ A 7
♦ J 10 8 6 5
♣ A K

♠ A J 9 2   ♠ K 5
♥ 6 4   ♥ J 10 9 8 4 3 2
♦ Q 7 3   ♦ –
♣ J 10 9 4   ♣ 8 7 3 2

♠ Q 10 7
♥ K Q
♦ A K 9 4 2
♣ Q 6 5

REVERSE SIGNALS

A method which has gained in popularity in recent years is the "upside-down" or reverse signal.

When giving an attitude signal a high card is discouraging while a low one is encouraging. When giving count, high-low promises an odd number while low-high shows an even number.

The advantage lies in the fact that the defense does not have to worry about the possibility of a critical high card being wasted to give an encouraging signal.

Here is an illustration:

♠ Q 7 6 5
♥ Q 7
♦ A K 8
♣ J 10 9 7

♠ 1 0 9 4   ♠ K J 8 2
♥ 10 8 5 2   ♥ A 9 6 3
♦ J 7 5 3   ♦ 10 9 2
♣ K 6   ♣ 5 2

♠ A 3
♥ K J 4
♦ Q 6 4
♣ A Q 8 4 3

West	North	East	South
–	–	–	1NT(*)
Pass	2♣(**)	Pass	2♦
Pass	3NT	All Pass	
(*) 15-17			
(**) Stayman			

Hoping to strike it lucky, West started with the ♠10. The upside-down signaller can happily play the ♠2 to encourage a continuation and when West regains the lead with the ♣K he will continue spades and defeat the contract.

Of course, using normal signals East could not afford the ♠8 and will have to play the ♠2. If Smith Echoes are not in use, West is almost bound to switch when he regains the lead.

Now look at a deal which illustrates a situation where upside-down count signals work well:

♠ 6 4 3
♥ A 2
♦ 7 5 3
♣ K Q 10 9 8

♠ Q 10 7   ♠ J 8 5 2
♥ J 10 9 6   ♥ K 7 5
♦ Q 9 8   ♦ J 10 4
♣ A 6 2   ♣ J 7 3

♠ A K 9
♥ Q 8 4 3
♦ A K 6 2
♣ 5 4

West	North	East	South
Pass	Pass	Pass	1NT
Pass	3NT	All Pass	

West makes the obvious opening lead of the ♥J. East wins with the king and returns a heart, hoping to remove the entry from dummy's clubs. Declarer gets to his hand with a diamond and plays a club.

Playing upside-down signals East can afford to play the ♣J on the first round when West ducks. If West has only ♣Ax then there will be no defense and if West has ♣Axx he will know to take his ace on the second round.

Playing "normally" East would play the ♣3, and West could not be sure if it was from East's actual holding or from ♣J3 in which case it would be fatal to play the ace on the second round.

ODD-EVEN SIGNALS

Odd-even signals which were promoted by Benito Garozzo are also used frequently. The idea is basically simple:

An odd card (3, 5, 7 or 9) is encouraging while an even card (2, 4, 6, 8, or 10) is discouraging. It's usual to play that the discouraging cards have suit preference overtones.

Here is a deal that illustrates how they work:

```
              ♠ A K J 10 6
              ♥ 8
              ♦ J 6 3
              ♣ K 10 6 3
♠ Q 3                        ♠ 8 7 4 2
♥ A K 10 6 3                 ♥ J 5 4 2
♦ 10 9 4                     ♦ 8 7 5
♣ Q 8 4                      ♣ A 9
              ♠ 9 5
              ♥ Q 9 7
              ♦ A K Q 2
              ♣ J 7 5 2
```

West	North	East	South
–	–	–	1NT
Pass	2♥(*)	Pass	2♠
Pass	3NT	All Pass	

(*) Transfer

West leads the ♥A. When East discourages with the ♥2 West will probably be brave enough to switch to a club (remember the suit preference overtones) which will result in two down.

Remember you can only signal with the cards you are dealt and East's hearts might have been ♥9875. Then only the ♥8 would be discouraging and West might switch to a diamond with fatal consequences. Playing odd-even signals it is also sensible to have some arrangement as to what you do if you have all odd or all even cards.

PART XII

DECEPTION IN DEFENSE

by Barry Rigal

People get pleasures from bridge in vastly different ways. Some consider the bidding merely the prelude to the serious business of the play of the cards—and it is certainly true that there is little point in threading your way through the Scylla of 3NT and the Charybdis of four spades to a delicate contract of five clubs if you are going to go down by failing to count trumps.

Some people get their pleasure by simply playing well, that is to say, by not making mistakes. There are players I know who firmly believe that if they can accomplish the difficult task of not making errors, that is the highest level of the game; if they lose, at least it will be someone else's fault. I find this view a little impractical—even ignoring the fact that very few can aspire to playing error-free bridge. Having said that, it is arguable that you can succeed at every level of bridge by simply making the par bid and the par play. If you bid every game that should be bid, and succeed in every makeable contract you will be a fearsome opponent. But deception is not like that: the object of a deceptive play is to help to defeat the lay-down contract, and to succeed in the impossible one. In my opinion, the successful deceptive play is the one that yields the most pleasure, because in achieving your aim, you have thwarted fate; the fact that you may have embarrassed your friend or opponent at the same time may add to your pleasure—it certainly does to mine.

If that is the case for you too, then you may also feel, as I do, that deception in defense is in many ways the richest, most complex, dangerous, and ultimately satisfying area of the game. It is certainly arguable that deception in defense is more fun than declarer deception. The reason that it is more dangerous for a defender to try to deceive than it is for declarer is because of the existence of your partner. Some people view defense as one player issuing instructions and the other player obeying the command (that is, after all, what a "come-on" signal equates to). On the other hand, a lot of good defense involves situations where one defender cannot take control because he may not know what to do; instead he signals to his partner to let him take that decision based on full information. That is why deceptive defense can cause problems; when you feed a false message to partner you are usurping control from him, and playing a lone hand. If you get a bad result, for whatever reason, he will blame you—and he will be right to do so.

But deception as a defender is easier because the declarer is watching your cards and assuming they mean something, because defense is by its very nature a dialogue rather than a monologue. You know you have an eavesdropper, so you can deliberately send a false message, as long as it falls into the right ears. And deception as a defender is more satisfying because it is more risky.

Before looking at deception in detail I should like to point out that if declarer is not going to succeed in his contract, try to avoid complicating the issue! And deception for its own sake, when you have no clearly defined purpose in mind, is on balance not a great idea. It is not that such deception cannot or will not work; the problem is that it starts to break up partnership trust. The next time you reach a congruent position and play a true card your partner will have that nagging doubt at the back of his mind.

Let me give you an example: when defending a suit contract and your partner's lead at trick one is in a suit in which you have the king and jack, then it is frequently good technique to play the jack to discover who has the queen. Well, maybe not the first, but the second time that partner underleads an ace in this sort of position, won't you have a knot of tension as you make the correct technical play?

Having issued that warning, I invite you to step into the Garden of Delights.

Deception on Lead

FOURTH HIGHEST OR FIFTH?

If we assume that our partnership is playing a system of opening leads, which includes fourth highest from holdings that include an honor, then it is obviously possible to vary that in two ways. You can lead from a five card suit and pretend that you have only a four card suit—or you can try to make a four card suit look longer than it is. Neither of these ploys is guaranteed to achieve anything, but sometimes you can speculate with some accuracy that this kind of deception may be relevant.

Both Sides Vulnerable. Dealer West. Teams.

```
              ♠ A 4 2
              ♥ J 9 7 4
              ♦ K J 3
              ♣ K 7 4
♠ 10 5 3                    ♠ Q 9 8
♥ A 8 2                     ♥ 6 5 3
♦ A 8                       ♦ 10 7 5 4 2
♣ A 9 8 6 2                 ♣ 10 3
              ♠ K J 7 6
              ♥ K Q 10
              ♦ Q 9 6
              ♣ Q J 5
```

West	North	East	South
1♣	Pass	Pass	1NT
Pass	3NT	All Pass	

If you lead the six of clubs, then declarer is likely to knock out the ace of hearts, and then realize that the defense may well have five tricks if he concedes a trick to the ace of diamonds. Consequently, he may gamble on finding a 3-3 spade split with the queen well placed. All very unlikely but, on this layout, it will be his lucky day, not yours. However, the lead of the club two at trick one may well persuade him simply to knock out the side-suit aces, because he believes that you will only have one long club to cash. Of course, you will have to be careful to lead a small club when you are in with the ace of hearts so as not to reveal the position.

Sometimes the reverse position applies—it may be to your advantage to suggest a long suit when you do not have one. For example, if you change the defensive hands in the example above, it would not be absurd to lead the club six from:

```
        ♠ Q 5 3
        ♥ A 8 2
        ♦ A 8 3
        ♣ A 9 6 2
```

Who knows—if clubs are 4-3-3-3 around the table maybe declarer will be so worried about the club split that he will take an unnecessary spade finesse into your hand?

It is also worth noting that varying the choice of lead on both the above examples is a relatively safe strategy. As the hand on lead clearly has most of the defensive strength, there is much less chance of creating costly confusion for your partner.

Another example of this approach—on a very different kind of hand—decided the placing in the last round of a top American Pairs event.

Both Sides Vulnerable. Pairs.

```
              ♠ J 5
              ♥ A Q 10
              ♦ 7 2
              ♣ A J 10 8 4 2
♠ 10 4 3                    ♠ A 9 8 2
♥ K 6 4 3                   ♥ 7 5
♦ 10 6 4                    ♦ Q J 9 8 3
♣ Q 7 3                     ♣ 6 5
              ♠ K Q 7 6
              ♥ J 9 8 2
              ♦ A K 5
              ♣ K 9
```

Almost the entire field reached 3NT by South after a strong no trump opening bid, and received the lead of the heart three. Because they knew the lead was from a four card suit they figured that West was not especially distributional, and therefore at least as likely as East to hold the club queen. Thus they made 11 tricks without breathing hard.

A top-rank United States international was playing the contract of 3NT in front of the TV cameras (the major National United States tournaments have a Vu-graph and commentary for the spectators). He received the fourth highest lead of the four of hearts, and adroitly worked out that West's probable five card suit made East favorite to hold the club queen, so he ran the club jack from dummy. It was only an overtrick, but it made the difference between second place and fifth place.

Perhaps he should have been less trusting of his opponent, Zia Mahmood, who had deliberately selected a deceptive lead in the hopes of deflecting declarer from his normal play.

There is a follow up to this point, on a related but not identical matter. Generally, when you have lead from a five card suit you let partner know as soon as conveniently possible by disclosing your fifth highest card. But there are many occasions when this is not such a good idea. Sometimes it is a matter of technique—you may want to pass a suit preference message when the count is already implicitly known.

More typical is the idea that by concealing your low card you can lull declarer into a false sense of security. Again it may be easier to demonstrate this in a full hand.

East/West Vulnerable. Teams

```
                ♠ A J
                ♥ J 10
                ♦ A J 8 7 2
                ♣ Q J 7 4
♠ K 9 8 4 3                    ♠ Q 10
♥ A 8 4                        ♥ 7 6 5 3
♦ K 9                          ♦ 6 5 4 3
♣ 8 5 3                        ♣ 10 9 6
                ♠ 7 6 5 2
                ♥ K Q 9 2
                ♦ Q 10
                ♣ A K 2
```

Your opponents reach 3NT after a weak no trump opening by South, and you lead the four of spades. Your partner takes the jack with his queen and returns the ten of spades. If you helpfully signal with the three then declarer will appreciate that he may have five top losers if he knocks out the heart ace. He might then take the diamond finesse on the grounds that he will probably make his contract if you have the king of diamonds. He will survive even if East has both the diamond king and ace of hearts and make nine tricks without needing to test hearts.

But if you follow with the spade eight at trick two, declarer might try to knock out the ace of hearts rather than risk the diamond finesse, under the assumption that there are only

two remaining spade trick defenders can take.

Deception of this kind is not limited to leads *up* to declarer. Positions of the following kind occur a great deal more often than most people realize.

(a)   **(b)**

```
        8 5 2                              8 5 2
J 10 4          A K 6 3      6 4          A K J 10 3
        Q 9 7                              Q 9 7
```

(c)

```
        8 5 2
K 4            A J 10 6 3
        Q 9 7
```

You can make the life of a declarer at no trumps easy, or very difficult, as East on these three holdings. South's easy plays come if you switch to the ace or three in (a), the king in (b), and the ten or jack in (c). If declarer believes the spot cards in (a) he will know the suit is 4-3, so there is no merit in ducking his queen.

In (b) declarer will score his queen on the second or third round in some comfort, and, in the third instance, declarer may try to block the suit by ducking the first trick if you switch to the ten. So what is to be done?

Well, in the first example you could try switching to the six; if South believes you have a five-card suit he might try to block the suit as in example (c) by ducking. In (b) you might try the effect of the ten on the first round—again declarer might duck to block the suit. (Mind you when declarer's holding is queen-seven doubleton you had better have your excuses ready for your partner). In (c) the effect of leading the three might persuade declarer to rise with the queen, thinking that the suit was divided 4-3 as in example (a).

There are further variations of these falsecards which are not directly related. If declarer is known to have a guarded honor you can try to camouflage your holding even more subtly (again the play is at no trumps and you need to run your suit immediately to beat the contract).

The real holding		Pretending to be	
8 5 2		8 5 2	
10 4	A K J 6 3	K 4	A J 10 6 3
Q 9 7		Q 9 7	

The real holding		Pretending to be	
8 5 2		8 5 2	
J 4	A Q 10 6 3	A 4 (3)	Q J 10 6 (3)
K 9 7		K 9 7	

In the first example the switch to the jack gives the declarer an additional losing option. In the second you need to remain on lead so you must start with the ten, and continue with the queen so that you can cash out the suit if declarer guesses wrong on the second round too.

CODED LEADS PROMISING OR DENYING HIGHER HONORS

Many people these days find that an opening lead structure other than the top of a sequence works more efficiently. In particular the lead at no trumps of a king shows a very good suit and asks partner to unblock an honor if he has one (a holding such as AKJxx or KQ10xx might be suitable.) This system of leads also combines well with the "strong ten," whereby you lead the ten from jack-ten or ten-nine sequences only if you have a higher honor. The jack tends to deny a higher honor from jack-ten sequences, and one leads the nine from ten-nine sequences without a higher honor.

All this information can be very helpful to declarer too; consider the layout of these suits at no trumps

(a)		(b)	
	A Q 4		A Q 4
J 10 9 7 3	K 8 (2)	K **10** 9 7 3	J 8 (2)
	6 5 (2)		6 5 (2)

It is obvious that the coded leads (highlighted above) make life much easier for declarer. In the first example (a) he can duck the first round and take the ace on the second round. Either the king will fall or the suit will be blocked. However in (b) he can take the finesse with impunity.

However, this is not entirely one-way traffic; the reason for playing this system of leads is primarily because you believe that the information you give to partner is more valuable than the information presented to declarer. But sometimes when you hold a strong enough hand you cease to need to communicate with partner—you are going to be making all the decisions on a particular hand—and so you can make a deceptive lead within your own system. Sometimes you can predict declarer is more likely to be damaged by a false card than your partner.

The first book written on the play of the cards which has any relevance to the modern game was the work of Louis Watson. The following hand is taken from that book; since those days the false card found by Albert Morehead—a superb bridge writer and a fine player—has become more common; but it should still trip up the novice.

```
                    ♠ Q J 8 4
                    ♥ J 7 5
                    ♦ Q 7 3
                    ♣ 9 8 3
  ♠ A K 7 3                        ♠ 10 6 5 2
  ♥ 10 8 6                         ♥ 9 3
  ♦ 10 9 5                         ♦ K 4
  ♣ A Q 2                          ♣ J 10 7 6 4
                    ♠ 9
                    ♥ A K Q 4 2
                    ♦ A J 8 6 2
                    ♣ K 5
```

West	North	East	South
–	–	–	1♥
Pass	1NT	Pass	3♦
Pass	3♥	Pass	4♥
All Pass			

Morehead sat West and heard South show a game forcing two-suiter in the red suits, and drive to game in four hearts. He led the spade king and realized that the most he could hope for from his partner was one ace or king. The problem was that any honor in the red suits would now be likely to fall, as East could hardly hold more than a doubleton in either suit. Of course, partner might have the club king—but then the defense would only have two clubs to cash.

Morehead made the right initial assumption to play his partner for a top diamond, and then the right deceptive play of switching to the diamond nine! Put yourself in declarer's position. If this deceptive play had never occurred to you, would it not seem logical to you to cover the nine with dummy's queen, intending to use dummy's heart jack as an entry to repeat the finesse in diamonds to pick up the ten in East. Up went the diamond queen and down went the contract. Of course, if declarer had been left to his own devices he would have been forced to play diamonds for himself and the lack of entries to dummy would have compelled him to play East for the doubleton king, successfully.

In general, you should certainly think about trying these deceptive honor leads from a sequence when you have approximately opening bid values and the opponents have bid game. It is also the case that codified leads are fairly irrelevant against slams, where the extra information is more likely to be of use to declarer than partner.

You should also be aware of the caliber of your opposition before making a falsecard lead of this kind. If your partner is watching your cards, and your opponents do not, then falsecards are worse than pointless. Conversely, if your delicate attempts at passing information to your partner is the bridge equivalent of casting pearls before swine, feel free to let loose with falsecards at any opportunity, since there seems to be no real downside.

UNDERLEADING ACES AND OTHER THINGS

The practice of underleading aces is one of the most dangerous in the whole area of deception. When it works it can be the most satisfying of plays; when it fails it can be the most aggravating maneuver that your partner has ever seen!

Before you consider underleading an ace you should ask yourself a series of questions. And you need to get a positive response to at least some of them to consider the underlead.

1. (Against a slam): has dummy promised the king, or has declarer denied a control?

2. Is there a good reason for assuming neither dummy nor declarer has a singleton—in which case underleading the ace would be more likely to cost a trick than usual?

3. Has dummy shown a very strong hand, or the equivalent of a no trump overcall, or has declarer denied a stop?

4. Has declarer shown a weak hand and implicitly not a high card in the key suit?

5. Is it likely that your partner can read the position and will not do something embarrassing on the ace underlead?

Let us look at some auctions where an ace underlead is plausible; first of all the slam auction.

West	North	East	South
–	–	Pass	1♥
Pass	3♣	Pass	3♥
Pass	4♦	Pass	5♥
Pass	6♥	All Pass	

This is an easy one. South's jump to five hearts asks North to bid slam with a spade control, so the spade suit may be distributed like this:

```
          K 10 4
A 8 6 3           Q 9 2
          J 7 5
```

You see what I mean in the fifth question above? There is little point in leading a low spade if your partner is going to put in the nine when declarer misguesses! You want partner to be sufficiently clued-in to think you might underlead an ace if it seemed to be the right thing to do, but not to be wary of your leads in general on the grounds that you could underlead an ace at random.

Here are two hands where the underlead of an ace worked well. As you can see the opening leader has a measure of safety in the ace underlead, because the lead was from the AQJ holding—which restricts partner's opportunity for error.

Both Sides Vulnerable. Teams.

```
                ♠ J 9 7 6 5 4
                ♥ J 9 7 3
                ♦ 8
                ♣ 7 6
♠ A K 10 2                      ♠ 3
♥ K Q 8 4                       ♥ 6 5
♦ 3                             ♦ A K J 10 9 7 6
♣ K 8 4 2                       ♣ 10 5 3
                ♠ Q 8
                ♥ A 10 2
                ♦ Q 5 4 2
                ♣ A Q J 9
```

West	North	East	South
–	–	–	1♦(*)
Dble	1♠	Pass	1NT
Pass	2♠	3♦	All Pass

(*) Natural/strong no trump (2+ diamonds)

East finally got his diamond suit into action, despite South's best efforts, in this hand from the English trials. Other tables had reached the same contract with less of a struggle.

Most table led the spade queen against a diamond part score and declarer made ten tricks without raising a sweat. However, the lead of the club queen put East in a difficult position; perhaps his technically correct play is the king—but you can sympathize with the decision to duck, whereupon the defense took the ace of clubs and a ruff, and declarer has two more red suit losers for one down.

By contrast the next underlead was a little more dangerous because it was quite probable that declarer was stronger than dummy. The standard result on the hand at the World Championships in Albuquerque was for East-West to make nine tricks in spades, but this was not always the case.

```
                ♠ J 10 4
                ♥ A J 7 3
                ♦ A Q J
                ♣ K 6 4
♠ A K 9 5 3 2                   ♠ 7 6
♥ 9 4                          ♥ K Q 10 6 5
♦ 6 3                          ♦ K 7 2
♣ A J 9                        ♣ 8 7 5
                ♠ Q 8
                ♥ 8 2
                ♦ 10 9 8 5 4
                ♣ Q 10 3 2
```

West	North	East	South
–	–	Pass	Pass
1♠	Dble	1NT	Pass
2♠	All Pass		

Marinesa Letitzia, a United States World Champion, sat North. East-West finished in two spades (East having bid one no trump at his first turn), and Marinesa selected the diamond queen as her opening salvo!

Declarer ducked, and her partner contributed the ten. Now, obviously, the best defense (double-dummy) is to lead a small heart, but that is a lot easier looking at all four hands, and Marinesa pressed on with the diamond jack, and declarer ducked again. A discomfited declarer ruffed the diamond ace, and led a heart to the queen, and a club to the nine and king.

This was the ending:

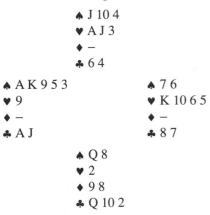

```
            ♠ J 10 4
            ♥ A J 3
            ♦ –
            ♣ 6 4
♠ A K 9 5 3           ♠ 7 6
♥ 9                   ♥ K 10 6 5
♦ –                   ♦ –
♣ A J                 ♣ 8 7
            ♠ Q 8
            ♥ 2
            ♦ 9 8
            ♣ Q 10 2
```

Marinesa led the ace of hearts and a small heart which her partner ruffed with the spade queen, and declarer discarded the jack of clubs. Now came the nine of diamonds, ruffed with the nine of spades and over-ruffed with the ten. A fourth round of hearts, ruffed with the eight of spades, provided declarer with the ultimate indignity of a third defensive uppercut for two down!

It is interesting how many times players who have underled an ace successfully try going to the well one more time, and frequently that is once too often—at least in theory.

The players generally reason that if declarer has got it wrong the first time he will do so next time too . . . and they are generally right!

East/West Vulnerable. Pairs.

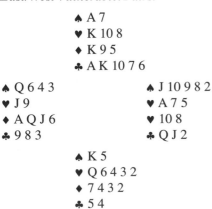

```
            ♠ A 7
            ♥ K 10 8
            ♦ K 9 5
            ♣ A K 10 7 6
♠ Q 6 4 3             ♠ J 10 9 8 2
♥ J 9                 ♥ A 7 5
♦ A Q J 6            ♥ 10 8
♣ 9 8 3              ♣ Q J 2
            ♠ K 5
            ♥ Q 6 4 3 2
            ♦ 7 4 3 2
            ♣ 5 4
```

West	North	East	South
–	–	–	2♥(!!)
Pass	4♥	All Pass	

If you have been brought up to believe that a weak two bid should be a sound six suit, the South opening may give you apoplexy; even the excuse of it being pairs, and your being non-vulnerable against vulnerable would cut no ice with me. But as you can see, the cards lie very invitingly for declarer.

However, the expert West on lead, Jeff Wolfson, unerringly selected the diamond queen as his opening salvo; with declarer very unlikely to hold the diamond king this has a lot going for it. Anyway, declarer not unreasonably ducked this, and Wolfson could have beaten the contract trivially by playing ace and a second diamond (and a spade switch would also have worked out fine); but not unreasonably he continued with the diamond jack—now declarer could have made his contract by playing the king—but he had not come this far to get the suit right!

You can also consider the underlead of an ace (at trick one, and in mid-hand) from AQx when dummy is likely to hold the king. Perhaps you can find this kind of layout.

```
            K 7 5 4
A Q 8 2            J 9 6
            10 3
```

If the queen holds, try a low one and see what happens.

The other deceptive form of underlead comes when you choose to underlead a sequence of honors, rather than to lead a card from that sequence. Typically this happens when your Left Hand Opponent has bid the suit in question and the contract finishes up in no trumps, so there is an implication that your partner may be able to contribute a card to help you out.

Here is a typical example, the defender in the West seat being Tim Seres of Australia.

```
            A 10 8 5
K Q J 7 2            9 6
            4 3
```

Tim led a low club at trick one when dummy had made its initial response in that suit and was not disappointed with the result when declarer played the eight from dummy.

A former team-mate of mine found a similar play when he had a hand with only one side entry, and decided to attack dummy's first bid suit in a contract of 3NT.

```
            K Q 7 4 3
J 10 9 8 5            A 6
            2
```

If he had led the jack initially then declarer would have worked out how dangerous the suit might be for the defense; but on a small card-lead it appears that you can play the queen from dummy. Even if this loses to the ace, as long as this exact position does not exist you can always duck the next round and prevent the defense from setting up four tricks in the suit.

Another position where you might consider an unnatural lead is through declarer's suit. A recently reported example of a successful underlead in dummy's suit featured the lead of the ten at trick one with this layout.

J 7 6 3

A K Q 10 8   9 4

5 2

In a similar vein you might consider an underlead of an ace-king-queen, or a non-standard honor lead in a suit implicitly bid by dummy with this sort of layout.

J 5 4 2

A K Q 9 3   10 8

7 6

Do not be afraid to look stupid in these positions; the good thing about the underlead is that it will give someone a story—you just hope it is your side and not the opposition!

There are other positions in which you may underlead a sequence of honors. Consider this layout at no trumps.

5 3

8 4   K Q 10 9 2

A J 7 6

If East is on lead and switches to a top honor, declarer gets his two tricks before the defense can take more than one trick. But if East switches to the ten, declarer may judge that his best play is to rise with the ace, as if he finesses he may set up three defensive winners. If the suit is blocked, with West holding a doubleton honor, then this would be the best play—but not here. Of course, East may get in again and try the nine the next time if he needs three quick tricks in the suit—to fool declarer twice in the same suit has an piquancy, but it helps to be bigger than the opponent you take for a ride in this way.

The American Internationals Jordan and Robinson showed a variant, in a position where, unusually, both halves of the defense played their part.

8 4

9 5 3   A K J 10 2

Q 7 6

When the Argentinian declarer reached 3NT (with nine top tricks outside the danger suit), Robinson led the three in his partner's suit—perhaps partly to suggest three cards, but also planting a seed of doubt in declarer's mind as to whether he had a top honor. Jordan won the ace to return the jack, and declarer elected to duck, hoping to block the suit. Again one can question declarer's play, but the fact remains

that if you give declarer a chance to err he will do so, sooner or later.

LEADING OR SWITCHING TO SHORTAGE

There are many occasions on opening lead where you would like to present declarer with a false description of your hand; there could be a whole host of reasons for wanting to do this—but in this section we are going to focus on simulating a lead from shortage, or not leading the standard card.

Again there are some reasons which are closer to technique (albeit fairly advance technique) for these plays. Sometimes you may want to lead low from a doubleton if you have an entryless hand and expect that leading the top of a doubleton may cause partner problems.

Say you are on lead to 3NT, with the only honor in your hand being in partner's suit; in either of these two following positions a low card might be right—but it helps if partner knows you might do this.

(a)   **(b)**

A K 9   A 10 5

J 2   Q 8 6 4 3   Q 2   J 9 6 4 3

10 7 5   K 8 7

Even if you have a slightly better hand it might be right to lead low from Qx in your partner's suit where your RHO has overcalled on no trump. Assuming your partner has enough entries, this one should work well.

10 9 5

Q 2   A 8 6 4 3

K J 7

The low card lead should save a trick and give timing to the defense.

One of the most typical plays is to pretend you have a singleton by underleading a king. The following hand was perpetrated against my team-mates in the final of a National event.

North/South Vulnerable.

      ♠ A 10
      ♥ A Q 7
      ♦ A K Q 2
      ♣ A K J 4

♠ K 3   ♠ 9 7 6 5 4 2
♥ J 10 9 8 6 5 4   ♥ –
♦ 7   ♦ J 10 6 3
♣ 9 7 2   ♣ 8 6 5

      ♠ Q J 8
      ♥ K 3 2
      ♦ 9 8 5 4
      ♣ Q 10 3

North-South seem destined to make six diamonds, and our team-mates duly reached that contract via a slightly rustic route; West opened three hearts, North doubled for takeout, and South bid four diamonds, raised to six diamonds. Unfortunately, the man on lead was a wily Polish player, with a name so complex that he was known to the whole world as "Zed," that being as close as anyone could get to pronouncing his name. Zed lead a low spade, and my team-mate reasonably enough was more worried about the spade ruff than about the 4-1 diamond split, so he rose with the ace.

There are many situations where the lead of dummy's first bid suit will discourage declarer from taking a finesse, or will persuade him to take a ruffing finesse later on. A couple of possible distributions of the key suit.

(a)   **(b)**

```
        A Q 10 9 4 2            A Q 10 9 4 2
   K 7 3          J 6     K 7 3            8 6 5
        8 5                    J
```

In the first example (a), declarer may be unwilling to finesse and lose the first two tricks; he may play for some alternative chance instead. In the second example (b), declarer is unlikely to play your partner for the king by taking a ruffing finesse, instead of trying to drop the king in three rounds. The lead of the seven caters to the chance that declarer may ruff one round before taking the finesse—then you will follow with what seems to be a doubleton.

Sometimes you simulate a singleton when you have in fact got an unusual trump holding; by faking a singleton you may achieve instant gratification (as in Zed's example) or you may persuade declarer away from his best play in the trump suit because of his fear of an impending ruff.

Two possible examples of the layout of the trump suit are as follows:

```
   A J 9 6 4        A 10 7 4
   K Q 3            Q J 9 6 2
   10 8 7 5 2       K 8 5 3
```

In the first instance declarer would make the standard safety play of leading up to dummy's jack, but if you appear to have a side-suit singleton declarer may be wary of trying the play. Similarly, if declarer thinks you are about to get a ruff he may play the second suit by laying down the ace and king, rather than playing the king and small to the ten.

The opportunity of representing yourself to have a singleton is not limited to trick one. The following hand came up in the final of the Brighton Teams.

North/South Vulnerable. Teams.

```
                  ♠ Q 4
                  ♥ K Q 10 7
                  ♦ Q 5 4
                  ♣ A Q 10 9
   ♠ 7 5 2                      ♠ K 9
   ♥ 2                          ♥ J 8 6 4
   ♦ K J 9 3 2                  ♦ A 10 8 7
   ♣ 8 7 5 3                    ♣ 6 4 2
                  ♠ A J 10 8 6 3
                  ♥ A 9 5 3
                  ♦ 6
                  ♣ K J
```

Neil Rosen, in the East seat for the eventual winners, heard his opponents explore for a slam, before coming to rest in five hearts. His partner led a diamond to the ace, and Rosen returned the spade nine. Declarer naturally rose with the ace, and could not recover from the bad heart split. (Even if you play the heart king and queen from dummy, another round of diamonds will insure a trump loser for your side.)

This next hand decided the Qualifiers for the Venice Cup (the Women's World championships) in Yokohama in 1991. Great Britain, as it turned out, actually needed a game swing on this hand to qualify—as you will see, the odds were stacked against them.

East/West Vulnerable. Teams.

```
                  ♠ 10 2
                  ♥ A K J 6
                  ♦ A J 9 4 3
                  ♣ 4 3
   ♠ J 9 6 3                    ♠ 8
   ♥ 5 4                        ♥ Q 10 9 8 3
   ♦ 8 7 2                      ♦ K 5
   ♣ 10 8 7 6                   ♣ A K Q J 9
                  ♠ A K Q 7 5 4
                  ♥ 7 3
                  ♦ A 10 6
                  ♣ 5 2
```

Where would you like to play the North-South cards? The Spanish played in five diamonds from the North seat, and the defense did their best by leading three rounds of clubs. To succeed, declarer must draw only two trumps and then ruff a spade, before crossing back to dummy by drawing the last trump; not difficult, you may say, but the Spanish declarer failed to get it right.

Pat Davies of Great Britain declared four spades from the South seat, after East had shown 10+ cards in hearts and clubs, and the defense also led three rounds of clubs, producing an easy +420. But how would Pat have played if the Spanish defender had cashed two clubs and switched to a diamond? If you believe East is 2-5-1-5 you might easily rise with the ace of diamonds and rely on the spade to behave. Fortunately, the defense only found this line in the post-mortem.

If you are defending a trump contract another layout which you can try to exploit is the following, in a suit bid by West:

```
              K J 5
A 10 8 6 2            Q 3
              9 7 4
```

Suppose that you are lead as East, and desperately need quick tricks in your partner's suit. Switch to the three and your partner will doubtless try to give you a ruff. On a good day declarer will finesse, hoping that your partner has no side entries; you can win the queen and hopefully put partner in via a side suit to give you your ruff.

As a general rule you could bear in mind that the dual principle of forcing declarer to take a premature decision in a side-suit, before he knows how trumps will behave. In addition, you should try to deceive declarer about length in a side suit to persuade him to get his play in the trump suit wrong. If you appear to have length in a side suit it would be natural for declarer to assume you were short in trumps, and vice versa. So you may be able to pull the wool over declarer's eyes by simulating a low length lead from a doubleton, or leading the eight or nine (which look like shortage) from an unbid five or six card suit.

Another opportunity for deceptive defense on opening lead can come when your partner has pre-empted, and you hold three cards to an honor. Let us look at this side-suit.

```
              K 6
Q 4 2                A J 10 8 7 3
              9 5
```

This does not look like such a dangerous suit from declarer's point of view, does it? Two quick losers but otherwise under control, one would think.

However, put yourself in the West seat; if your partner has opened a three level preempt in this suit, the lead of the queen followed by the two to the ace, will put declarer in a false position on the third round. He may ruff high unnecessarily, exposing himself to an additional trump loser.

Equally obviously this defense may give him a ruff and discard and let the contract make, so viewer discretion is advised—pick the moment to do this when you have no slow side-suit winners that may vanish to the ruff and discard.

You may think this unlikely to work in real life—however, this hand from the European championships in 1987 demonstrated that you can sometimes give declarer a problem in the easiest of contract.

Teams.

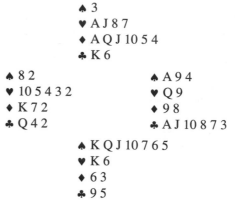

The auction was brief—North opened one diamond, Tjolpe Flodqvist for Sweden overcalled three clubs (intermediate) and South sensibly bid four spades. P-O Sundelin, with the pile of garbage in the West seat, led the club queen for two reasons: there was the deceptive element, and the possibility of remaining on lead at the end of trick one. It worked out spectacularly well. Flodqvist won the second round of clubs and led a third round, ruffed high by declarer, who some-what uncomfortably led a diamond to the queen, and a spade to his ten.

When no ace appeared, declarer had to decide whether Flodqvist had the doubleton or tripleton ace. If the former, he had to exit with a low spade, or the defense would get a trump promotion with a fourth round of clubs. Obviously, the winning line on the hand is to play a top spade, but I think declarer had the percentages on his side when he played a low spade from hand, thus generating a spectacularly unlikely second trump loser.

At a club where all conventions are prohibited, I was dummy when Richard Collins tried the following:

Board-a-Match.

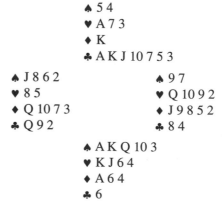

West	North	East	South
–	1♣	Pass	1♠
Pass	3♣	Pass	3♥
Pass	3♠	Pass	4NT
Pass	5♥	Pass	5NT
Pass	6NT	Pass	7NT
All Pass			

I am not proud of the three spade bid, and my 6NT bid (intending to show semi-solid clubs since with solid clubs I would have bid a grand slam) was also, as it transpired, capable of being misunderstood.

Having said that, Collins did his best to defeat what appeared to be an unsportingly lucky contract, when he led the club nine at trick one. He was listening to the auction, and knew dummy, with bad spades and nor great diamond stopper or heart support, should have the top clubs. Unfortunately for him, his reputation had gone before him, and my partner confidently finessed the clubs. A nice play by Jim Mason, and I am sure Richard would have been painfully pleased with the compliment.

The European Championships have proved an especially fertile breeding ground for deceptive play lately. Of course sometimes the seed falls on stony ground.

Teams.

```
              ♠ K 3
              ♥ K J 9 8 7 6 4
              ♦ Q 5
              ♣ 10 7
♠ 8 6 5 2                  ♠ A 9 7 4
♥ Q 10 3                   ♥ 5
♦ 10 7 3                   ♦ 8 6 4 2
♣ 6 5 3                    ♣ Q 9 4 2
              ♠ Q J 10
              ♥ A 2
              ♦ A K J 9
              ♣ A K J 8
```

When Poland played Israel, the Israeli player in the North seat reached six hearts, which is comfortable on any lead but the spade ace. However, Gawrys found the lead, and the Israeli declarer did not find the heart queen, and so went down one.

By contrast, Marek Szymanowski for Poland played 6NT from the South seat on a spade lead to the ace, and a diamond switch. He won in hand, and played off the ace and king of hearts; when no queen appeared he fell back on the club suit, running the ten, covered by the queen and king, and then successfully played the percentages by going back to dummy's diamond queen to play a club to the eight. "Nicely done" you may say, "but where is the deception?" Well, the point is that East could have saved the day by returning a club at trick two; declarer would not have finessed, knowing that he only needed the hearts to behave to make his contract, and by the time he misguesses the

hearts it would have been too late.

I include this final hand in this section on pretending to have shortage, more because I think it is of almost unparalleled elegance than because I think you will necessarily be able to use it yourself. The perpetrator of the smash-and-grab raid was Gabriel Chagas of Brazil, who has the deserved reputation of being one of the most resourceful declarers ever—together with an almost hypnotic ability to tempt his opponents into error. Look at all four hands before trying to work out how Chagas in the East seat managed to defeat four spades.

Teams.

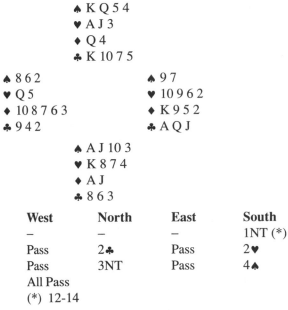

```
              ♠ K Q 5 4
              ♥ A J 3
              ♦ Q 4
              ♣ K 10 7 5
♠ 8 6 2                    ♠ 9 7
♥ Q 5                      ♥ 10 9 6 2
♦ 10 8 7 6 3               ♦ K 9 5 2
♣ 9 4 2                    ♣ A Q J
              ♠ A J 10 3
              ♥ K 8 7 4
              ♦ A J
              ♣ 8 6 3
```

West	North	East	South
–	–	–	1NT (*)
Pass	2♣	Pass	2♥
Pass	3NT	Pass	4♠
All Pass			
(*) 12-14			

West led the club two, which was conveniently ambiguous for the defense, and Chagas saw that whatever major suit honor his partner had was doomed. Deception therefore being necessary, he won the first trick with the club queen, cashed the club ace, and exited with the diamond nine! Naturally declarer won the ace, drew trumps and then took the guaranteed club finesse to dispose of his diamond loser, and Chagas produced the club jack and the diamond king to defeat the contract. It was not surprising that this sequence of plays won Chagas the award for the defense of the year.

MORE COUNT PROBLEMS

We have looked at some of the more blatant ways of confusing declarer about the defensive count in the early stages of the defense. There are, however, many facets to this kind of deception—for example where your intention is to deceive both declarer and partner, with the purest of intentions.

The sort of position I am envisaging comes when partner leads his suit against a no trump contract, and you win the first trick. Sometimes you need to deceive everyone to generate the best defense.

```
              ♠ 7 6 3
              ♥ Q J 7
              ♦ K J 8 5 4
              ♣ 10 9
♠ J 10 8 5              ♠ A Q 4 2
♥ 9 5 2                ♥ A 8 6
♦ 3 2                  ♦ Q 10 7
♣ 8 7 5 3              ♣ 6 4 2
              ♠ K 9
              ♥ K 10 4 3
              ♦ A 9 6
              ♣ A K Q J
```

After a straightforward auction (2NT - 3NT) your partner leads the jack spade, and you can see that there is no room for any other high card in his hand. If you return the spade two then declarer may work out that the defense have only four winners if he knocks out the heart ace. If you return the spade queen then declarer may postulate an original 5-3 split in spades, in which case he needs to take the diamond finesse, which will be the defense's fifth winner. You can, of course, see the converse to this; switch the diamond queen and the spade eight—so that your partner had found the same lead from:

```
              ♠ J 10 5
              ♥ 9 5 2
              ♦ Q 3 2
              ♣ 8 7 5 3
```

Your best defense is to win the first trick and to return the spade two. Now declarer will surely knock out the ace of hearts, and allow you to cash out for one down, instead of coming home by taking the diamond finesse.

Sometimes you want to pretend that you have three cards when you have four, for completely different reasons. Consider this hand in the contract of 3NT, at match-point pairs, where the overtricks are of paramount significance.

East/West Vulnerable. Pairs.

```
              ♠ A 10
              ♥ Q 2
              ♦ A J 10 8 7 2
              ♣ A 7 4
♠ J 6 4 3              ♠ 8 7 5
♥ J 10 8 4            ♥ A 9 5 3
♦ K 5                 ♦ 4 3
♣ J 8 5              ♣ Q 10 9 2
              ♠ K Q 9 2
              ♥ K 7 6
              ♦ Q 9 6
              ♣ K 6 3
```

When West leads the heart jack, to the queen and ace, you should pause before returning the automatic count card of the three. If you do that, declarer can see that there is no

point in ducking this trick. With hearts 4-4 or 6-2 he finishes up with the same number of tricks whether he ducks or not. By contrast, if you return the nine you give declarer a problem. If hearts are 5-3, a duck will allow declarer the chance to lose the diamond finesse into the safe hand. Given that some pairs will play the diamond slam, going down when the diamond finesse loses, he must be right to insure his contract by allowing the heart nine to hold. The extra trick will make a vast difference to your score on the board—everyone else makes at least twelve tricks.

Just as on the previous hand this theory applies in reverse; let us say that the heart suit is divided:

```
              Q 2
    J 10 8 5 4        A 9 3
              K 7 6
```

and it is you who has the diamond king; now you might be able to persuade declarer to rise with the heart king on the second round of the suit if you win the ace and return the three (simulating an original 4-4 split or a 6-2 split).

Sometimes it is partner whom you want to persuade not to duck at trick two. Look at the following hand.

North/South Vulnerable. Pairs.

```
              ♠ Q 10 4
              ♥ K J 10 7
              ♦ Q 5
              ♣ Q J 10 9
♠ A J 7 5              ♠ K 9 3
♥ 9 3 2                ♥ Q 8 6 5 4
♦ 9 4 3 2              ♦ J 8 7
♣ 5 2                 ♣ K 6
              ♠ 8 6 2
              ♥ A
              ♦ A K 10 6
              ♣ A 8 7 4 3
```

South opens one club, and rebids a 15-17 no trump, raised to three. Your partner leads a low spade against this contract and you take the ten with the king. Again it is automatic, but a tactical error, to return the spade nine. Your partner is likely to duck this trick to preserve communications, assuming you will get in fairly quickly and he can cash out the spades. Unfortunately, it will quite possibly be trick fourteen before your side gets the lead again, and you know it because all your honors are vulnerable. It must be right to persuade partner to win the second trick by returning the spade three; he will know that there is no point in ducking this.

Another variation on the same theme comes when you are encouraging partner to take his trick because you want him to switch to something else.

East/West Vulnerable. Pairs.

```
              ♠ Q 10
              ♥ Q 2
              ♦ Q 10 8 7 2
              ♣ A Q 8 7
♠ 8 3                         ♠ K J 9 7 5
♥ J 10 8 4                    ♥ A 9 5 3
♦ 9 5 4                       ♦ A 3
♣ 10 6 5 4                    ♣ 9 2
              ♠ A 6 4 2
              ♥ K 7 6
              ♦ K J 6
              ♣ K J 3
```

Your opposition reach their favorite contract of 3NT after a strong no trump opening, and the lead of the heart jack goes to the queen and ace. Try returning the nine of hearts.

If South ducks (hoping the suit is 5-3 and that your side will continue the suit), then it is up to your partner to realize that the suit is dead. If he is very sharp he may overtake and switch to a spade—which will make the difference between the contract succeeding and going down three.

One final wrinkle—this hardly qualifies as deception, more a tactical maneuver.

North/South Vulnerable. Pairs.

```
              ♠ J 6 3
              ♥ Q J 7
              ♦ K J 10 8 4
              ♣ Q 9
♠ 10 8 7 5                    ♠ 9 4 2
♥ K 9 6 5 2                   ♥ A 8
♦ 2                           ♦ A 7 5 3
♣ 8 5 3                       ♣ J 7 6 4
              ♠ A K Q
              ♥ 10 4 3
              ♦ Q 9 6
              ♣ A K 10 2
```

South opens on club and in response to North's one diamond bids 2NT to show 18-19 and North raises to 3NT. Your partner leads the heart five, playing standard fourth highest leads from good suits, and you win your ace. How do you persuade partner not to duck his heart king at trick two (in the hope that you have three hearts and an entry)?

The answer is very simple, if not entirely obvious; *don't play a heart back at trick two*. If you play a spade at trick two declarer will knock out the diamond ace, and now when you return a heart it will be too late for the hearts to set up, so your partner will have no choice but to win his heart king and hold declarer to ten tricks—rather than the eleven tricks that should result if you play a heart at trick two.

PREVENTING OVERKILL

Any play which temporarily misleads partner about your hand must technically qualify as deception—so prevention of overkill is a useful addition in one of the less discussed areas of the game. You may not even know what overkill is, but believe me, it is a most irritating experience. Almost without exception it occurs in defense to no trump contracts, when the defense have a complete suit to run. The critical moment generally arises at trick two of the defense, when one defender makes his correct systemic play, and creates ambiguity. Let us look at a couple of real life suit combinations which produced the overkill effect.

(a)

```
              ♠ A K J
              ♥ 7
              ♦ J 9 8 4 3 2
              ♣ K 9 7
♠ 8 7 5 3                     ♠ Q 9
♥ K 10 9 6 5                  ♥ A J 8 4 2
♦ 2                           ♦ 10 5
♣ 8 5 3                       ♣ A Q 6 4
              ♠ 10 6 4 2
              ♥ Q 3
              ♦ A K Q 6
              ♣ J 10 2
```

West led the six of hearts against 3NT; East won with the ace and returned the standard count card of the four. When South contributed the queen impassively, West thought the suit was divided

```
                    7
        K 10 9 6 5        A 4 2
             Q J 8 3
```

so he ducked—doubly embarrassing because it was not only a trick, it was declarer's ninth trick for his contract.

(b)

```
              ♠ 8 2
              ♥ A J 7
              ♦ K J 10 8 4
              ♣ Q 9
♠ K J 9 5                     ♠ A 10 7 6 4
♥ Q 9 6 5                     ♥ K 8 2
♦ 2                           ♦ 7 5 3
♣ 8 5 4 3                     ♣ J 7 6 4
              ♠ Q 3
              ♥ 10 4 3
              ♦ A Q 9 6
              ♣ A K 10 2
```

North raised a strong no trump to game, and West did well to lead a spade. East won the trick and returned the six; West took the queen with his king, and came to the conclusion that South had Q1073 and East A64, so he tried to put his partner in with a club for another spade play.

(Notice, West was playing South quite a compliment—it would be good deceptive play as South to play the queen in this position; the rule of eleven tells you that West has the king and jack so the cards are equivalent. Also note that if East had returned the ten it would have cleared up the problem, but blocked the suit.)

What went wrong? Well, the overkill phenomenon struck; East has such a good holding in his partner's suit that he could not convey it to his partner. His play at trick one was forced, and his natural count card did not do its proper job at the next turn. Let us try defending these hands again. If we can spot the danger of overkill, perhaps we can do something about it.

On hand (a) we hold five cards in the suit partner has led—so the possibility of overkill is a live one. At the end of trick one partner appears to have five cards in the suit; we have seen that the true card return of the four gave partner a problem—he could not distinguish between a three card holding and a five card holding. Why not pretend we have four cards in hearts by returning two? This solves all partner's problems; whether we have the jack or not, it cannot hurt to win the second trick and play the heart ten—result: happiness.

On hand (b) let us try the same thing, by returning the four, to simulate a four card suit. Partner will swallow the bait by pressing on with the suit at trick three, and the position will become plain.

Now that we have solved the problem with hindsight, let us see whether we can do a little forward planning.

Cover the West and South hands, and put yourself in the East seat to see if prevention is better than cure.

East/West Vulnerable. Teams.

```
              ♠ A K J 2
              ♥ 10 7 6 4
              ♦ 10
              ♣ K J 7 4
   ♠ 8 4 3                    ♠ 10 9 7 5
   ♥ K 8 2                    ♥ Q 9 5
   ♦ K 7 4 3 2                ♦ A Q 9 6
   ♣ 10 9                     ♣ 8 3
              ♠ Q 6
              ♥ A J 3
              ♦ J 8 5
              ♣ A Q 6 5 2
```

North uses Stayman and then finishes up in 3NT after his partner opens a weak no trump. West leads the diamond three and East can see the likelihood of a five card suit

opposite. But, whatever the length of your partner's suit, there is no need to make the standard "expert" play of the queen at trick one—if declarer wins the king it may be hard subsequently to convince West that East has this much in the suit.

Simply win trick one with the ace, and return the queen not the six. This has two bonuses; first, when partner takes the jack with the king you do not leave him guessing whether a heart shift is a good idea—as it would be if you had :

```
              ♠ 10 9 7 5
              ♥ A J 9 5
              ♦ A 6
              ♣ Q 8 6
```

And the second added bonus is that occasionally you may actually need to play the queen at trick two to unblock the suit, to allow you to cash your five tricks in diamonds, as in the above diagram.

What we are doing, in summary, is to misrepresent our remaining holding by one card (making three look like two, or four look like three) if we can see that the effect of doing this would be to allow partner to continue happily with the suit, and that playing our true card could create confusion (four cards looking like two, or three like one) which could be fatal to the defense.

I should emphasize at this point that in general it is a very bad idea to leave an ambiguity of one card. It is to avoid such ambiguity that some people lead third and fifth in their partner's suit. They also play low from three small in their partner's suit if they have not supported it to avoid confusion with a doubleton. But in our current examples the critical issue is that the one card confusion still allows partner to make the right play, whereas the two card confusion would not.

PREVENTING DECLARER FROM BLOCKING YOUR SUITS

We have looked at ways of misleading declarer and partner about the count in a critical suit, to get them to take tricks or duck them to suit our purposes. The same principle of misleading declarer also arises, relatively infrequently, when declarer has the power to block a suit, but does not or will not realize it unless you rub his nose in it.

Let us look at a single suit in isolation, and then at how this might fit into a whole hand.

```
                   7
   A 8 6 5 (4) 3        K Q 10 9
                 J (4) 2
```

I was faced with this problem in a televised match. Against a rather poorly bid three no trump contract my partner led the three, and it was clear from the leading methods that we played (low cards imply a good suit) that the suit could be run for at least five tricks as long as we did not block it. The embarrassing thing was that my partner could have had either five or six cards—hence the bracketed (four) above. If my partner had a five card suit I was confident that if I won the king or queen at trick one and returned the nine South would not think of playing the jack and we could unblock the suit happily. But if declarer had the doubleton jack this would be a spectacularly stupid way to block a previously unblocked suit. Never being afraid to look idiotic, I went for the falsecard route and all was well.

But the general point is more relevant than the specific holding: do not be overeager to cash your side's long suit; check that there are no potential problems with internal blockages.

The key give-away is when third hand has relative shortness and no low cards. It is at that point that deception becomes relevant.

```
              ♠ 9 7 6
              ♥ J 9 7 3
              ♦ A Q 8
              ♣ A 7 6
♠ 10 8 3 2               ♠ K Q J
♥ K                      ♥ A 8 6 5 4
♦ J 10 9 6 3             ♦ 7
♣ J 4 2                  ♣ 10 8 5 3
              ♠ A 5 4
              ♥ Q 10 2
              ♦ K 5 4 2
              ♣ K Q 9
```

After an unopposed auction 1♦ – 1♥–1NT–3NT, your partner leads the spade two and you can immediately appreciate that if your partner has four spades to the ace you can do anything you like in terms of the order you play your top spades and the contract still goes down; what you have to avoid, if partner has four spades to the ten, is declarer winning the first or second spade.

You could try the spade king at trick one and follow with the jack (which might cause partner problems if declarer for some reason wins trick one), but it looks better to play the jack at trick one followed by the queen.

Declarer will surely assume you have QJx, and play for his legitimate chance that you hold the ace and king of hearts, by ducking the second spade. But if you win trick one with the jack and follow up with the king, declarer may work out the potential blockage, and win the second spade to cross to table with a diamond and play the heart nine. (Note: this is good, and deceptive, declarer play, trying to persuade you to duck if you held ♥Axxx or ♥Kxxx, which would knock out your partner's entry while the spades are still blocked). As the cards lie, this line would actually be a legitimate way to make the contract.

Sometimes you can try to persuade declarer to unblock a suit which should be left blocked.

```
    7 5 4                        7 5 4
A 8 3        Q J 10 2    8 3 2        A Q J 10
    K 9 6                        K 9 6
```

As East you win the opening lead in a side-suit at no trumps and now need to cash four tricks in the above suit. It is a matter of personal taste how you persuade declarer that you have one holding and not the other.

I think with the first holding that to lead the ten, then the jack, might suggest AJ102, which would be ideal. With the second holding I would lead the queen and then the ten (which is what I would do if I were guileless with the first holding.)

A third regularly occurring position comes when you have attacked a suit like this at trick one in no trumps.

```
    Q 8 3                        Q 8 3
J 9 7 5 4    A 10 2    A J 9 5 4        10 7 2
    K 6                          K 6
```

Honest players in the first instance lead the five to the ten and king, and then continue with the jack—sometimes allowing declarers to duck the second round and block the suit. Put yourself in declarer's position and play the second example in the same way—maybe declarer will duck here, too.

One of the most elegant and unusual examples along these lines comes from an American Nationals:

North/South Vulnerable. Matchpoint Pairs.

```
              ♠ 6
              ♥ Q 10 9 6
              ♦ J 9 5 3
              ♣ 9 8 6 5
♠ A 9 5 3                ♠ Q 10 8 7
♥ A                      ♥ J 5 3 2
♦ K Q 8 4 2              ♦ 10 7
♣ A J 7                  ♣ 10 4 3
              ♠ K J 4 2
              ♥ K 8 7 4
              ♦ A 6
              ♣ K Q 2
```

The auction was short and not particularly sweet from South's perspective; he opened 1NT, and West either could not make a penalty double or decided that someone might run if he did double.

The lead of the diamond four went to the nine, ten and ace, and West won the heart ace at trick two to advance an innocent diamond eight; South's decision to duck should not be criticized too harshly; what happened in practice was that West cashed another three diamonds, squeezing South out of a heart and two spades. West unkindly exited with a low club, and declarer tested the hearts, then misguessed the spades and went down three.

SWITCHING TO UNSUPPORTED HONORS

Before looking at the deceptive element of switching to an unsupported honor, it may be worth emphasizing that such plays do not only deceive; sometimes these plays are also technically correct.

Sometimes it is easy to spot the position—sometimes very difficult. If the object is to reduce declarer's or dummy's trumps twice, by forcing him to ruff, then the switch to an honor may be positionally necessary. Let us look at essentially the same example, but from four different perspectives in the East seat.

	Easy			**Harder**	
	Q 10 4			J 9 4	
K 9 8 5 2		A 7 6 3	A 10 8 5 2		K 7 6 3
	J			Q	
	Difficult			**Tough**	
	Q			J	
K 8 6 4 3		A 10 5 2	Q 9 6 4 3		A 10 5 2
	J 9 7			K 9 7	

In the first "easy" example, the presence of the long suit in dummy makes the play of the ace easy, but, in the second example, the power of the closed hand strikes again, and it is not so simple to start with the king to pin the stiff queen. Likewise in the third and fourth examples it is necessary to underlead your ace as East to force dummy to ruff. The fourth example crosses into deceptiveness in that declarer can actually do something about the position if he guesses correctly.

The play of an unsupported honor is frequently made from shortage, looking for a ruff, or to kill a presumed singleton honor in declarer's hand. Sometimes, however, it is the only way to escape from an end-play, or to give declarer a guess as opposed to a sure thing. One example with a slight modification should show what I mean.

(a)
```
              ♠ A K J 2
              ♥ K 10 7
              ♦ A 10
              ♣ K J 7 4
  ♠ 8 7 3                    ♠ 10 9
  ♥ Q 9 4 2                  ♥ J 6 5
  ♦ K Q 7 4                  ♦ 9 6 5 3 2
  ♣ 10 9                     ♣ 8 5 3
              ♠ Q 6 5 4
              ♥ A 8 3
              ♦ J 8
              ♣ A Q 6 2
```

(b)
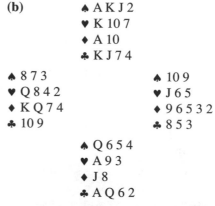
```
              ♠ A K J 2
              ♥ K 10 7
              ♦ A 10
              ♣ K J 7 4
  ♠ 8 7 3                    ♠ 10 9
  ♥ Q 8 4 2                  ♥ J 6 5
  ♦ K Q 7 4                  ♦ 9 6 5 3 2
  ♣ 10 9                     ♣ 8 5 3
              ♠ Q 6 5 4
              ♥ A 9 3
              ♦ J 8
              ♣ A Q 6 2
```

In both instances declarer plays six spades, which is a reasonable contract, but is endangered because of the mirror image of shapes of his hand and dummy. In (a) when declarer has drawn trumps and cashed off the clubs before throwing West in with a top diamond, West can beat the contract by force, by exiting with the heart queen. Now declarer cannot avoid a heart loser. Contrast this with what happens if West exits with the heart nine or a small card. In (b), West gets endplayed with a diamond honor again; this time he gives declarer a losing option by exiting with the queen, anything else being hopeless. Should declarer get it right? Probably. It depends whether he thinks West is good enough to exit with an unsupported honor in this position.

Similarly, as West, you may find yourself opening up this suit.

(a)
```
              J 9 5
  K 10 4              Q 8 3 2
              A 7 6
```

The only chance to get two tricks is to lead the king and hope for a misguess.

(b)
```
              J 9 5
  Q 10 4              A 9 3 2
              K 7 6
```

But beware. Your partner may not be enormously impressed with the deceptive switch to the queen on this layout!

If you are going to be able to switch to the honor in those positions, what happens when you are West in this position:

(c)
```
              J 9 5
  K Q 4              10 8 3 2
              A 7 6
```

I think a small card should work; declarer may assume you have Q104 or are just not good enough to underlead a king-queen.

Other suits where both East and West can present declarer with a losing option are the following:

(a)

```
        K 9 3
A J 7            10 6 4
        Q 8 5 2
```

(b)

```
        K 9 3
J 10 7            A 6 4
        Q 8 5 2
```

(c)

```
        K 9 3
J 7 4            A 10 6
        Q 8 5 2
```

The shift by West to the jack has a pretty fair chance of success in (a); however if East is on lead instead, the best he can do in this position would be to try the ten, pretending to be a man with J106.

In (b) West can shift to the jack or ten, depending on South's opinion of his skill. By contrast East would shift to a low card, and West must rise to the occasion by playing the jack not the ten.

In (c) West must lead the jack and East must lead the ten to give the defense a chance to get two tricks.

There are a number of more obscure positions where you need to shift to an honor. In a way, they all derive from the genuine technical position where East can "surround" the ten by leading the jack initially.

```
        10 4 2
K 9 8 3        A J 7
        Q 6 5
```

Now consider the following holdings; in each case you are East and need to run the suit in defense:

(a)

```
        10 4 2
A 9 8 3            Q J 7
        K 6 5
```

(b)

```
        10 4 2
Q 9 8 3            A J 7
        K 6 5
```

(c)

```
        10 4 2
A J 8 3            Q 9 7
        K 6 5
```

In all these examples, you start by leading a middle honor, and continuing with a small card if you are left on lead. Declarer has no clue as to what the right winning strategy is; compare what happens if you start with a small card when you have the ace, or if declarer knows your lead of the queen would promise the jack, and the lead of the jack would deny the queen!

Are these plays too difficult to find at the table? When this hand came up in a major pairs event, two different players in the East seat found the switch to the same unsupported honor.

Both Sides Vulnerable. Teams.

```
                ♠ 10 6 4
                ♥ 6
                ♦ K Q 9 5 3
                ♣ A Q 6 5
♠ A J 5 3                    ♠ Q 9 8
♥ A Q 10 8 5 3              ♥ J 2
♦ 4 2                       ♦ A 8
♣ J                         ♣ 9 8 7 4 3 2
                ♠ K 7 2
                ♥ K 9 7 4
                ♦ J 10 7 6
                ♣ K 10
```

South was declarer in both instance, in one case in the sensible contract of three diamonds, in the other case in the silly contract of 2NT.

Against three diamonds the opening lead was the club jack. Declarer won the king and played the diamond jack. Zia Mahmood in the East seat realized that if his side took their club ruff, declarer would hold his spade losers to one, by throwing spades on dummy's clubs. His only hope was the position shown: he switched to the spade queen, and declarer ducked, expecting Zia to have the queen jack of spades; now the defense have the choice of taking a club ruff or playing a second spade to get their fifth trick.

In 2NT you appear to be going two down—an insignificant loss since the par contract is your opponents taking nine tricks in hearts. However, the opening lead was a small heart, and South won his heart king. On the jack of diamonds West, Cezart Balicki of Poland, played the two (saying "I am happy for you to switch") and his partner Adam Zmudzinski duly won the second diamond to play the spade queen. Again declarer innocently ducked, and the roof fell in—he lost five hearts, four spades and the diamond ace for down five.

Sometimes you need to switch to an honor to simulate a different sort of sequence. Again let us postulate play in no trumps, and that you are East. If you know from the bidding that your partner's shape and high cards are limited, you may need to resort to desperate measures.

The real position		**Pretending to be**	
	J 9 3		J 9 3
Q 10 6 4	K 8 2	8 6 4	K Q 10 2
	A 7 5		A 7 5

If you switch to the king you force declarer to take an immediate position. If you play a small card the defense has no chance.

RUFFING PROBLEMS

It is normal practice to give partner the ruff he appears to want, when he leads from shortage. However, sometimes this is not a good idea especially if you know that he will not be able to over-ruff, which may simultaneously expose your delicate trump holding. This hand came up in the European Championships in Turku in 1989, and features a fine play by declarer as well as the defense.

Both Sides Vulnerable. Teams.

```
              ♠ A J 6 3
              ♥ K 6
              ♦ Q 8 5 3
              ♣ Q 6 5
  ♠ 8 5 4                    ♠ K
  ♥ Q 10 8 5 3               ♥ J 4 2
  ♦ 4 2                      ♦ A K 9 7 6
  ♣ 10 4 3                   ♣ A 8 7 2
              ♠ Q 10 9 7 2
              ♥ A 9 7
              ♦ J 10
              ♣ K J 9
```

North-South reached four spades after a nebulous diamond opening, and West led the diamond four. East intelligently observed that if he played a third round of diamonds West's inability to over-ruff declarer would clear up any guess for declarer in trumps, so he switched to a heart after two rounds of diamonds. Unfortunately declarer was alive to the possibility himself, and so he cautiously won the heart in dummy, and ruffed a diamond back to hand himself with the spade ten! Now West's failure to over-ruff made the position crystal-clear, and declarer duly dropped East's singleton king.

It is rarer, but not all that unusual, for the defense to be able to ruff once, but not to want to give a second ruff. To achieve success in this sort of position may require some fancy footwork—and arguably this hand belongs in the deceptive signalling rather than the leading category.

East/West Vulnerable. Dealer North. Matchpoint Pairs.

```
              ♠ 10 9 6 5
              ♥ K 10
              ♦ K Q J 3
              ♣ 9 8 6
  ♠ 3                        ♠ Q J 7
  ♥ 9 8 7 6 4 3 2            ♥ Q 5
  ♦ 8 5 4 2                  ♦ A 10 7
  ♣ 2                        ♣ A Q 10 4 3
              ♠ A K 8 4 2
              ♥ A J
              ♦ 9 6
              ♣ K J 7 5
```

West	North	East	South
–	Pass	1♣	1♠
Pass	3♦	Pass	4♠
All Pass			

North's jump to three diamonds showed the values for a raise to three spades and a good diamond suit, and West led his singleton club against four spades. East's dilemma is that he wants to give partner his club ruff, win the diamond ace, and play a fourth round of clubs. But West's failure to ruff with a high trump will then tip off South as to how to play trumps.

It must be better to try something devious. You have two options—though neither is guaranteed to succeed. You could cash the club ace, and then give your partner a ruff with the club ten. This is a suit preference for the higher suit, and your partner will dutifully play a heart; on a good day, declarer may sigh with relief and play trumps from the top.

Perhaps a less blatant way to defend is to lay down the diamond ace at trick two, and only then to give partner a ruff. Now there is no re-entry to your hand, and South has to work out why you "misdefended"—to me this looks less like an attempt to pull the wool over his eyes.

REFRAINING FROM THE CASH-OUT

This is a relatively simple concept which really only has one variation. Occasionally, it may be to your advantage not to cash the established long card in your partner's suit. It may tempt declarer into an indiscretion.

Both Sides Vulnerable. Pairs.

```
              ♠ A 9 8
              ♥ Q 8 5
              ♦ A J 3 2
              ♣ A 6 4
  ♠ Q 10 4 3                 ♠ K J 5 2
  ♥ 10 9 6 4                 ♥ J 7 3
  ♦ 9 4                      ♦ Q 8 5
  ♣ 7 3 2                    ♣ K 9 8
              ♠ 7 6
              ♥ A K 2
              ♦ K 10 7 6
              ♣ Q J 10 5
```

South opens a weak no trump, raised to 3NT, and West finds the spade lead. You have the opportunity for two fine defensive plays. To start with you win the first trick with the king and return the jack, simulating a three card suit, then exit with the spade five to dummy's ace. Declarer crosses to hand in hearts for the club finesse and you win and exit with a heart. Declarer could cash nine tricks now—but, playing matchpoints, wouldn't you be tempted to take the diamond finesse into the safe hand for an overtrick?

North/South Vulnerable. Teams.

```
              ♠ A 10 6
              ♥ Q 10 6
              ♦ A K 5 3
              ♣ J 5
♠ 9 5 3                     ♠ Q 8 7
♥ 9 8 7                     ♥ A K J 5
♦ 10 8 5 2                  ♦ Q 7
♣ 9 7 6                     ♣ 10 8 4 3
              ♠ K J 4 2
              ♥ 4 3 2
              ♦ J 9 4
              ♣ A K Q 2
```

South opens a 14-16 no trump, raised to three. Your partner finds his best lead for a decade, kicking off with the heart nine. You win and cash two more hearts only, giving declarer the impression that West has the long heart. (As the cards lie if you cash the last heart declarer will test diamonds before looking for the spade queen, making nine tricks trivially.) When you exit with a club, it would take a superhuman declarer to avoid taking a spade finesse into the safe hand, and the last heart will come as a rude surprise.

GIVING DECLARER A LOSING OPTION

Most people will give you credit for not being a complete fool—some of the time. Frequently, however, you can leave declarer unsure of whether your inferior play has been designed to generate an attractive, but losing, alternative—or whether you are truly stupid. If they play you for the latter possibility, it is the kind of insult that will carry its own reward with it—and they may not be so insulting the second time around.

For the first example you may care to put yourself in the East seat, and cover up the West and South hands.

Both Sides Vulnerable. Teams.

```
              ♠ J 10 6
              ♥ K Q 4
              ♦ J 8 4 3
              ♣ J 5 3
♠ K                         ♠ 7 4 3
♥ 10 9 8 6 3                ♥ A J 5 2
♦ 9 6 5                     ♦ 10 7 2
♣ 10 9 7 6                  ♣ Q 8 4
              ♠ A Q 9 8 5 2
              ♥ 7
              ♦ A K Q
              ♣ A K 2
```

West	North	East	South
–	Pass	Pass	2♣
Pass	2NT	Pass	3♠
Pass	4♠	Pass	6♠
All Pass			

Your partner leads the heart ten, to the king and your ace, as declarer follows with the seven. Dummy is satisfyingly bare—any thoughts as to where to go for honey?

Look at it this way: if declarer has solid spades, you are giving nothing away by playing a heart back—declarer always had at least one entry to dummy via the spade jack. But if declarer is missing a trump honor you can see that he may not be able to reach dummy; why not help him to take a losing finesse? If you look at the full hand you can see that left to his own devices declarer has little option but to lay down the spade ace, with what from your perspective would be regicidal consequences. So help him in a different direction.

Another sort of holding where you can assist declarer to self-destruct is the following:

```
        K 6 3
Q                    9 8 5 2
        A J 10 7 4
```

Again, if declarer is not given a helping hand he would probably get this trump suit right, by leading to the king before taking the finesse. But if East plays the suit first, by leading a small card, declarer may well take advantage of a not so free finesse. If he puts in the ten he creates a loser where the Fates had intended none.

In 1977, two young experts from Cambridge came face-to-face.

East/West Vulnerable. Pairs.

```
              ♠ A 7
              ♥ Q 6 5
              ♦ J 9 7 4 3
              ♣ K 7 3
♠ 6 3                       ♠ K Q 10 8
♥ K                         ♥ 9 7 4 3 2
♦ Q 10 8 5                  ♦ K 6 2
♣ Q J 9 8 4 2               ♣ 6
              ♠ J 9 5 4 2
              ♥ A J 10 8
              ♦ A
              ♣ A 10 5
```

West	North	East	South
–	–	Pass	1♠
Pass	1NT	Pass	2♥
Pass	2♠	All Pass	

Richard Granville in the South seat took a fairly restrained view, after his partner had been similarly pessimistic, so his side were already going to get a good matchpoint score. However, the play was all about overtricks. Graham Kirby led the club queen, and Granville won the ace, and played two rounds of spades. John Armstrong in the East seat took this trick and decided to shift to the diamond king (which would have been right if declarer had the singleton queen) and Granville took his ace, to play a club to the king, which Armstrong ruffed, to play a second diamond.

Declarer threw his losing club, and Kirby won his queen and played a third club, which Granville ruffed.

This was the ending:

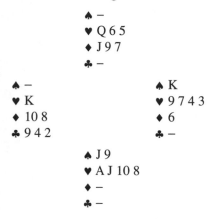

Granville exited with a third spade to Armstrong, who played a heart. After some thought Granville played the ace, and dropped the singleton king. The reason for this play was that he respected Armstrong as a defender enough to know that if John had had the heart king he would have cashed his spade winner when he was last on lead. If he had allowed himself to be endplayed, it was because it was to his advantage to be left to open up the hearts—hence he could not have the king.

Deception in Signalling

While it is relatively clear that deception on lead must involve play by the hand who is first to play to a trick, the difference between deceptive signalling and deception in following suit may not be clear. I have created a possibly artificial distinction by defining the signal as a card whose sole purpose is ostensibly to convey information to partner, as opposed to a play where you are simply following suit, or trying to win the trick.

FALSE COUNT

It is standard practice to tell your partner that you have a doubleton in a suit in which he leads the ace (from ace-king) by playing a high-low. This is not always the right defense if in practice you do not want partner to lead a third round of the suit. Let us look at some examples of why you should leave partner under the impression that you have three cards in the critical suit.

First, an obvious one! You have no trumps to ruff the third round of the suit. Unlikely, you say—well, this hand came up recently in the North American Swiss Teams Finals.

East/West Vulnerable. Teams.

```
              ♠ Q J 6
              ♥ K 9 5
              ♦ A J 5 3
              ♣ A J 8
♠ A K 9 4 2              ♠ 8 5
♥ 10 7 6 4              ♥ A Q J 3 2
♦ 8 6                  ♦ Q 10 9 7 4 2
♣ K 5                  ♣ —
              ♠ 10 7 3
              ♥ 8
              ♦ K
              ♣ Q 10 9 7 6 4 3 2
```

After a 1NT (15-17) no trump opening from the North, East overcalled two clubs to show hearts and a minor. There are no textbooks which tell you how to handle the South hand,

so South simply jumped to five clubs, doubled by West. This was the normal contract, although on a good day East/West might make five hearts.

On the lead of a top spade many Easts fell from grace and played the eight. West tried to give his partner a ruff, and declarer now had no problems in getting the trumps right, and discarding the heart loser on the diamond ace. Where East sensibly did not show his doubleton, West switched to a heart, and the defense then cashed a second spade and tried to cash another heart. I reckon that declarer should get the trumps right on the auction, to escape for down one—but can you see how declarer can clear up the problem (as the card lie) without having to guess? You know that East either has three spades, or no clubs; so ruff the second heat, overtake the diamond king with the ace, and play a third round of spades. When East discards it is clear he has a void in clubs.

On this next deal when you hold the West hand there is need for good defensive play. North plays in four spades doubled.

East/West Vulnerable. Pairs.

```
              ♠ K 10 7 5 3 2
              ♥ 10
              ♦ A K 10 9
              ♣ 10 4
♠ Q J 9                 ♠ 6
♥ A K Q J 8 4          ♥ 9 6 2
♦ 6 2                  ♦ Q 4 3
♣ 8 7                  ♣ A K 9 6 3 2
              ♠ A 8 4
              ♥ 7 5 3
              ♦ J 8 7 5
              ♣ Q J 5
```

West	North	East	South
–	–	Pass	Pass
1♥	1♠	2♣	2♠
3♥	3♠	4♥	Pass
Pass	4♠	Dble	All Pass

When East leads a top club against four spades, it can do no harm to discourage the suit, since you know that at best getting a ruff will break even; as you can see, if East goes ahead and gives his partner a ruff it will allow North to discard the heart loser. Of course, East might cash the second top club, in case West has a singleton club, but the position at the end of the second round of the suit should be clear. If partner has a doubleton and does not want a ruff, he has his reasons—don't try to overrule him!

There are a couple of other good reasons for not telling the truth with your initial signal. Let us look at why you should tell partner you like his opening lead, even when you are not mad about it.

First, there may be no better lead available; let us look at where we want to prevent partner making the "obvious" switch.

East/West Vulnerable.

```
              ♠ Q 9 6
              ♥ A J 5
              ♦ 6 5 3
              ♣ A 8 6 2
♠ A K 10 5 4                  ♠ 8 7 2
♥ 9 7                         ♥ 10 4 2
♦ K 10 8                      ♦ J 9
♣ Q 7 4                       ♣ J 10 9 5 3
              ♠ J 3
              ♥ K Q 8 6 3
              ♦ A Q 7 4 2
              ♣ K
```

Playing a five card major system South opens one heart, West overcalls one spade, North bids two spades to show at least a three heart invitation and South bids four hearts. When West leads a top spade your systemic play would be the two, but do you really want partner to play a diamond, which is his most probable switch if you discourage spades? You are better off encouraging a spade continuation (before the mice gct at it) and allowing partner to collect his diamond winners in the fullness of time.

Well, if it can be fun to deceive partner into doing the right thing, it is obviously more fun to bamboozle declarer into doing the wrong thing. What this generally involves is trying to persuade declarer that you are short enough in partner's suit that you are threatening a ruff or over-ruff.

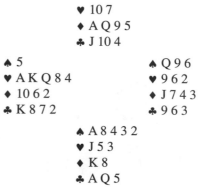

```
              ♠ K J 10 7
              ♥ 10 7
              ♦ A Q 9 5
              ♣ J 10 4
♠ 5                          ♠ Q 9 6
♥ A K Q 8 4                  ♥ 9 6 2
♦ 10 6 2                     ♦ J 7 4 3
♣ K 8 7 2                    ♣ 9 6 3
              ♠ A 8 4 3 2
              ♥ J 5 3
              ♦ K 8
              ♣ A Q 5
```

After South, your left-hand opponent opens one spade and your opponents reach game in that suit, despite your partner's two heart overcall. When your partner leads a top heart, much your best chance of defeating the contract is to signal a high-low in hearts to simulate a doubleton. If your partner leads three rounds of the suit, do you think declarer will be able to bring himself to ruff low? If he ruffs high then you have a trump trick and a club to come.

(Note that declarer has an elegant line to make if you tell the truth in hearts. Say your partner leads three rounds of hearts and declarer ruffs low; then he wins the spade king, cashes three rounds of diamonds finishing in dummy, discarding a club from hand, and then runs the spade jack. This line succeeds so long as West started with either one or two spades.)

The play of simulating a doubleton can generate remarkable results, even when you do not appear to have a vestige of a trump trick. Let us say that you make the same strong encouragement in hearts when the trump suit of spades is dealt as follows:

```
              K Q 10 9
J 5                     7 6
              A 8 4 3 2
```

Declarer ruffs the third heart high, notices your third heart with grave suspicion, and then has to find the spade jack to make his contract—and he may well assume that your defensive deception was based on holding trump length, like three trumps to the jack.

The European Championship is perhaps the best place to see top-class teams competing; there is a fortnight of bridge at which one can see the best players matching wits. On the following hand between France and Poland, the Poles came off best, when one player helped to promote his partner's trumps.

```
              ♠ A K 8 6 4 3
              ♥ 6 3
              ♦ Q 9 3
              ♣ 4 3
♠ 10 9 7 2                    ♠ 5
♥ A K J 2                     ♥ 8 5 4
♦ 7 6                         ♦ A 5 4 2
♣ 7 6 2                       ♣ K J 10 8 5
              ♠ Q J
              ♥ Q 10 9 7
              ♦ K J 10 8
              ♣ A Q 9
```

When South opened a 15-17 no trump North transferred into spades and bid four spades. Moszczynski (all the best Polish players have at least on Z in their name I thought—but maybe his partner, Julian Klukowski, has one in his middle name) lead the heart ace. Put yourself in Klukowski's shoes for a simple piece of mental arithmetic; partner has at least seven points in heart, you are looking at eight points, dummy has nine points and declarer has 15-17 points.

Partner, therefore, has at most a side-suit jack, and therefore, your club king is dead. Your best chance to get the setting trick (to go with your top three red winners) is to mislead everyone at the table into thinking you only have two hearts.

A third round of hearts may persuade declarer to ruff high in dummy—in which case you may get a trump trick or conceivably a trick with the diamond jack, to which you are not really entitled.

Of course, real life does not always work out equitably, but on this occasion the cards cooperated perfectly. Declarer had no reason to disbelieve the defense; he ruffed the third heart high in dummy, thereby generating a loser for himself, and going down one.

Sometimes, by contrast, you want to persuade declarer that there is no defensive ruff threatened, so that he misjudges how to deal with the trump suit.

```
              ♠ Q J 4
              ♥ Q 9 5
              ♦ K 6 5 4 3
              ♣ 9 4
♠ 6 2                         ♠ 10 7 5
♥ J 7 4                       ♥ 10 6 3 2
♦ Q 8 2                       ♦ A J 10 9
♣ Q J 10 7 5                  ♣ 8 3
              ♠ A K 9 8 3
              ♥ A K 8
              ♦ 7
              ♣ A K 6 2
```

Your opponents reach an excellent six spade contract, the club queen is led, and declarer sees that he can make either with the diamond king well placed or if something favorable happens in clubs. He wins the opening lead and plays a

diamond to the king and ace. You exit with a heart, and declarer wins in dummy and plays a club to his king. Now is the moment of truth; if you started high/low in clubs a declarer might come home by ruffing two clubs high in dummy and finessing the spade nine. However, if you simply followed up the line in clubs, declarer will surely ruff the third club low, and get over-ruffed.

There is also a relatively rare position where you can see that declarer at no trumps may have the problem of deciding how many rounds to hold up in partner's suit. Say West opens a weak two spades (systemically either a five or six card suit) and South finishes in 3NT. When partner leads the king, showing a suit with three honors, and asking you to give count—this is the layout:

```
              J 5
K Q 10 8 6           9 7 2
              A 4 3
```

If you show an odd number it is easy for declarer to hold up to the third round, but if you play high-low to show an even number it is unlikely that declarer will hold up twice.

Our final example is, I think, a rather difficult one to find; perhaps it is because your natural feeling of exasperation at partner's choice of opening lead might distract you from the best defense.

```
              ♠ Q 10 7 2
              ♥ K 10 4
              ♦ A K 9
              ♣ 10 4 3
♠ A K 3                       ♠ J 9 6
♥ J 4                         ♥ 9 6 2
♦ Q 6 2                       ♦ J 10 5 4 3
♣ K 8 7 6 2                   ♣ J 9
              ♠ 8 5 4
              ♥ A Q 7 5 3
              ♦ 8 7
              ♣ A Q 5
```

West	North	East	South
–	–	–	1♥
Pass	1♠	Pass	2♠
Pass	4♥	All Pass	

You may not agree with South's or North's rebid (as North I would rather rebid a forcing three hearts) but the net result is that you get to defend four hearts, and your partner leads the spade ace, thus clearing up a guess for declarer that he would no doubt have got wrong.

If you make the straightforward, honest, play of the six, then declarer will eventually play a spade to the queen and bring in the spades for two tricks. If you high/low in spades your partner will try to give you a ruff at trick three, and declarer will surely finesse the ten, hoping simply to find you with the club king, in which case the third club eventually goes on the spade queen. Not this time.

Sometimes a signal can blatantly give declarer a losing option—you may think that declarer was rather gullible given that the defenders here were one of the strongest pairs in the world, Bjorn Fallenius and Mats Nilsland of Sweden.

```
              ♠ A K 9
              ♥ A J 6
              ♦ A K 8 7 3
              ♣ 9 8
♠ 7 6 5                      ♠ Q 10 8 2
♥ K 10 8 7                   ♥ 9 5 3
♦ Q J 6 4 2                  ♦ 10 5
♣ 3                          ♣ K 7 5 2
              ♠ J 4 3
              ♥ Q 4 2
              ♦ 9
              ♣ A Q J 10 6 4
```

Both tables in a teams match reached six clubs, and both tables received the unhelpful lead of the five of spades, the defense playing third highest leads from either a three card suit or an even number.

The Swedish declarer played three rounds of diamonds at once, then took a heart finesse before playing on clubs. When he found the 4-1 split he cashed the heart ace, ruffed another diamond, went back to the spade ace, and ruffed a third diamond. He still had the spade ace and the club ace to come, for twelve tricks.

At the other table Bjorn Fallenius introduced a diversion at trick one when he followed with the ten—which was either discouraging or an odd number in their system. The French declarer took a trump finesse at once, then repeated it. When he found the 4-1 split he decided to assume the spade finesse was right, so he simply ran the spade jack, rather than take the heart finesse. The defense won and returned a spade. Declarer was left with insufficient entries to dummy to catch East's club honor by ruffing diamonds.

FALSE ATTITUDE

It is also sensible to lie about your attitude to discourage your partner's lead, when you can see that the obvious switch is the right defense.

```
              ♠ 10 7 4
              ♥ J 7
              ♦ A K 5
              ♣ K 9 7 5 3
♠ 5                          ♠ 9 8 6
♥ A K 10 8 4 2               ♥ 9 6
♦ 9 6 2                      ♦ J 10 7 4 3
♣ 8 4 2                      ♣ A Q 6
              ♠ A K Q J 3 2
              ♥ Q 5 3
              ♦ Q 8
              ♣ J 10
```

West	North	East	South
2♥	Pass	Pass	3♠
Pass	4♠	All Pass	

When West leads the heart king you can see that if you show two hearts your partner will lead three rounds of the suit, letting the contract make. Discourage hearts and with any luck partner will catch the club switch.

A variation on the same theme comes when you do like partner's lead—but can see that there are better defenses for him than continuing the suit.

Neither Side Vulnerable. Teams.

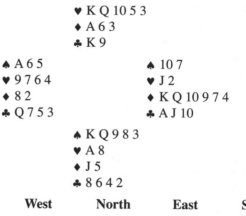

```
              ♠ J 4 2
              ♥ K Q 10 5 3
              ♦ A 6 3
              ♣ K 9
♠ A 6 5                      ♠ 10 7
♥ 9 7 6 4                    ♥ J 2
♦ 8 2                        ♦ K Q 10 9 7 4
♣ Q 7 5 3                    ♣ A J 10
              ♠ K Q 9 8 3
              ♥ A 8
              ♦ J 5
              ♣ 8 6 4 2
```

West	North	East	South
–	–	–	Pass
Pass	1♥	2♦	2♠
Pass	4♠	All Pass	

North's aggressive action opposite a passing partner, gives you a problem on defense. On the lead of the diamond eight declarer plays dummy's ace, and you can see that you need partner to get the lead via one of the majors, and shift to a club. If your partner shifts to a high club (denying an honor), then you will need to play him for a singleton diamond. If he shifts to a low club you will play your jack, hoping to get two club tricks and one diamond. So discourage at trick one by playing a low diamond, and hope partner does the right thing.

Another position where not enough thought is given to deception is when a side-suit is divided in such a way that at trick one you know that either your partner or declarer is void.

North/South Vulnerable. Teams.

```
              ♠ 10 7 6
              ♥ Q J 9 4
              ♦ J 9 5
              ♣ K J 3
♠ J 5 4                      ♠ 9
♥ K 10 8 2                   ♥ 7 6
♦ A 2                        ♦ K Q 10 7 6 4 3
♣ A 5 4 2                    ♣ Q 7 6
              ♠ A K Q 8 3 2
              ♥ A 5 3
              ♦ 8
              ♣ 10 9 8
```

West	North	East	South
–	–	3♦	3♠
Pass	4♠	All Pass	

On the lead of the diamond ace it is all too easy to fall into the trap of encouraging the opening lead—but you should work out that either declarer will ruff the next trick, or your encouragement will not mean much to a partner who began with a singleton. Dummy's hearts suggest that you might need to play clubs sooner rather than later—so it must be better to discourage the opening lead and hope for a club switch. (As a minor technical issue, if you wanted a heart switch, the diamond queen would shout for the higher suit here.)

FALSE SUIT PREFERENCE

It becomes more apparent the longer you play the game that the thing which divides the card players from the card pushers is the belief that every card means something. Therefore in defense you cannot afford to relax that much; it makes bridge harder, but a lot more enjoyable. Consequently, you will find that many players use an initial signal to be count or attitude, and a lot of subsequent signals to be suit preference. Let us look at the distribution of a typical suit.

```
              9 2
Q J 7 3               A K 10 8 5
              6 4
```

When West leads this (bid and supported) suit at trick one then East has a chance to signal count at trick one—his attitude is implicit because his side is just about to have won the trick. If West leads the jack at trick two then the size of East's card will carry a suit preference overtone.

Of course, the danger of sending a message to your allies is that the enemy are standing by to intercept your words, to use them to their best advantage. During the World War II, the Americans sent some of their messages in Navajo because there was no one on the Axis side who could interpret this language. Unfortunately, the powers that be have banned the bridge equivalent—encrypted signals—that

is signals that are only interpretable by the sending side, so every signal carries some form of government health warning that it may damage your side as well as help it.

Of course, getting the message to partner is frequently the priority, and it does not matter that the enemy understand. But that is not always the case. Let us look at two parallel examples, where the thinking bridge player will be able to work out that deception is necessary in one case, but potentially irrelevant or even harmful in the next.

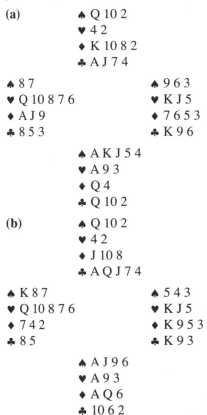

(a)
```
              ♠ Q 10 2
              ♥ 4 2
              ♦ K 10 8 2
              ♣ A J 7 4
♠ 8 7                        ♠ 9 6 3
♥ Q 10 8 7 6                 ♥ K J 5
♦ A J 9                      ♦ 7 6 5 3
♣ 8 5 3                      ♣ K 9 6
              ♠ A K J 5 4
              ♥ A 9 3
              ♦ Q 4
              ♣ Q 10 2
```

(b)
```
              ♠ Q 10 2
              ♥ 4 2
              ♦ J 10 8
              ♣ A Q J 7 4
♠ K 8 7                      ♠ 5 4 3
♥ Q 10 8 7 6                 ♥ K J 5
♦ 7 4 2                      ♦ K 9 5 3
♣ 8 5                        ♣ K 9 3
              ♠ A J 9 6
              ♥ A 9 3
              ♦ A Q 6
              ♣ 10 6 2
```

In both examples, South opens a strong no trump and is raised to game, and you lead the heart seven to your partner's king, ducked by declarer. When East returns the jack you can safely overtake, to drive out the ace.

In (a), you can see from your own high cards that there is a danger that declarer may succeed if partner wins his trick in a black suit, and switches to the other black suit. You can try to persuade your partner not to fall into that trap by showing an entry in the middle suit. Play the heart eight at trick three, which partner should be able to read as suit preference for the middle suit.

Example (b) is more difficult, but it looks as if declarer may have to guess whether to play on diamonds or spades for his nine tricks. If you are playing against someone you respect, I suggest playing a low heart at trick three. Now it is up to partner to make a good play; when he wins the second round of clubs (it looks routine to duck the first club in case declarer has only two) he should return the diamond nine, in itself a good deceptive play. He knows that if you had the spade ace, a sure immediate entry, you would probably have given true suit-preference; so you either have the diamond ace or the spade king; in either case, the diamond nine is the right card to play. If declarer still plays on diamonds not spades, you should be perversely pleased at the compliment he has paid your partnership.

There are many opportunities for deceptive suit preference based on the order in which you play your long suit; this was yet another example from the Minneapolis Nationals in 1994.

Neither Side Vulnerable. Teams.

```
                    ♠ 6 5 4
                    ♥ K J 9 8 6
                    ♦ 6 3
                    ♣ 9 8 6
     ♠ A 7                        ♠ Q J 10 9 8
     ♥ 7 5 2                      ♥ Q 10 3
     ♦ K 9 8 4                    ♦ 10 7 5 2
     ♣ Q 5 3 2                    ♣ 7
                    ♠ K 3 2
                    ♥ A 4
                    ♦ A Q J
                    ♣ A K J 10 4
```

South reached 3NT after East had pre-empted to show a bad hand with five or six spade. The defense led ace and a second spade, and Joanne Manfield took the opportunity to signal on the second round of spades with the eight, her lowest spade, to indicate an entry in the lowest suit. Once declarer (who clearly belonged to the chauvinistic group who believe women are genetically incapable of deceiving men at the bridge table) had swallowed the bait, he was dead.

Perhaps it would have been more cautious to play a heart to the king for a club finesse, but he simply played the heart ace and took the heart finesse at once to go down two. Of course, if East had shown a heart entry at trick two declarer can succeed by playing on the minor suits, rather than by playing on hearts.

Deception in Following Suit

In the previous chapter we have focused on positions in which our signals—ostensibly aimed at our partner—may be distorted either to deceive our partner or to deceive declarer. There are, however, many mores positions where our deception arises from the card with which we follow suit.

Here the card is not a signal *per se* (which to my mind at least implies a degree of choice in the card played), but rather we want generally to convey the impression that our card is forced, that we did not have a choice as to the card we played.

This chapter deals with perhaps the most significant of the areas in which deception may operate. Moreover, at least in part there are many single-suit combinations which recur with some frequency. If you can master and remember the ways to confuse declarer, and give him a losing option where none previously existed, then you are well on the road to becoming a tough opponent.

There is no simple way, as declarer, to overcome the deceptions outlined here. My strategy as declarer is a relatively straightforward one; when an opponent makes a play which I can see is potentially a false card, I try to work out whether in a similar position I would have been able to find the same deception. If I would not have managed it, I assume the card to be genuine. You might look at it this way; if the player in question has found a play you would not have considered, then:

(a) He is probably a better player than you and would beat you in the long run anyway.

(b) Maybe the play deserves to succeed.

(c) The price of knowledge has never been cheap.

THE MANDATORY FALSE CARDS
Giving Declarer a Losing Option
Of all the chapters in this section, this one is probably the most important; I guarantee that you will be able to find an opportunity to put some of these plays into practice, sooner

rather than later. Part of the problem with deception is that it is difficult to spot the tricky plays without having read them somewhere first. I am only scratching the surface here I know, but I hope that I have picked up on some of the most frequently occurring positions.

Put yourself in declarer's position in the South seat. How would you tackle these suits?

	A J 8 2			A K 8 2	
K 5		10 9 3	Q 5		10 9 3
	Q 7 6 4			J 7 6 4	

Your natural play is to finesse the jack and lay down the ace in the first example, and to play off the ace and king in the second case. But, if East drops a nine or ten at his first opportunity, then you have to weigh the chances of his holding the ten-nine doubleton—in which case your winning line is to cross back to hand and lead the honor from hand on the second round—which fails here, of course.

The general point is obvious; where you have a pair of touching intermediates, be alive to the possibility of sacrificing one of them. However, our next pair of cases have a similar, but slightly variant theme, involving declarer trying to establish a suit at no trumps.

	K 10 8 7 2			Q 10 8 7 2	
Q J 6 5		9 4	J 6 5		K 9 4
	A 3			A 3	

And another pair.

	K J 8 7 2			K J 8 7 2	
Q 6 5		10 9 4	Q 9 6 5		10 4
	A 3			A 3	

In the first case the only 4-2 split you can cope with for the one loser is to find the doubleton nine on your right, so in abstract your intention would be to lead ace and a small one to the ten. But, if East drops the nine in the first round, you have to contend with queen-nine or jack-nine doubleton, when the correct play would be to cash the king at the second trick. (We shall revisit this later.)

In the second case you appear to have a straight guess as to whether to play to the queen or the ten on the second round, but when the nine appears you play East for the jack-nine doubleton and try the queen. (What's that? East might drop the jack from jack-nine doubleton? We'll come to that later, too.) In the second pair of examples might the fall of the nine or ten distract you from finessing the jack? It shouldn't —but it might.

Some more examples of trying to persuade declarer to drop something that is not falling, come when declarer has a singleton trump in dummy.

```
         4                        4
J 10 3         A 5        9 6 3         A J 5
     K Q 9 8 7 6 2              K Q 10 8 7 2
```

In the first example, when declarer leads the four to his queen your best shot at getting two trump tricks is to contribute the ten or jack to persuade declarer to try to smother your jack-ten doubleton. In the second case, declarer would undoubtedly play a trump to the ten if you let him alone. But contribute the jack on the first round to tempt him into playing you for ace-jack doubleton. Of course, the need for this last play only arises when you need two tricks specifically from this suit. If you need three tricks, you would duck, in case declarer has Q109xxx. But the play is quite safe from AJ9.

More singletons in dummy.

```
         5                        5
K 4          J 10 3      A J 6          Q 9
     A Q 9 8 7 6 2              K 10 8 7 4 3 2
```

In the first example, suppose West is marked with the king, so South lays down the ace; East must falsecard by dropping ten or jack to create the required ambiguity. In the second case West has opened the bidding, so you know declarer is going to play him for the ace. Following with the queen gives declarer two losing options—of playing your partner for A6, or you for QJ.

Of course you then have a problem in this last example of what to do with Q93 or J93. I think it is best to follow with the nine at your first turn—and hope declarer plays you for a doubleton honor.

```
         5                        5
A 7 4          K J       J 10 6          A K
     Q 10 9 8 6 3 2              Q 9 8 7 4 3 2
```

In the first example, playing the king when the five is led from dummy gives declarer the chance to misguess on the second round. In the second case you need to give declarer an alternative to playing for the doubleton ace-king so West should play the jack at his first turn.

Our final group—very similar in nature.

```
         J                        J
A Q          10 9 4      A K          10 9 4
     K 8 7 6 5 3 2              Q 8 7 6 5 3 2
```

Clearly declarer has a chance to hold his losers to two, but if as East you follow with the nine or ten at your first turn you might nudge him in the wrong direction.

The cousins to these two are perhaps easier to spot; the falsecard is perhaps the natural instinctive play in any event—it just happens to create a losing option for declarer.

```
         5                        5
A Q          10 9 4      A K          10 9 4
     K J 8 7 6 3 2              Q J 8 7 6 3 2
```

When declarer makes his initial play from dummy, if you fail to play the nine or ten it leaves declarer no option but to try to drop the outstanding honor on the second round.

Sometimes you can generate remarkable results from very small cards, when declarer tries to read too much in to them—though one should beware of trusting one's opponents too far in international matches.

```
              ♠ Q 2
              ♥ Q 9 5 2
              ♦ J 9 6 5
              ♣ A 10 8
♠ A 9 7 3                 ♠ J 10 8 5
♥ K 6 4                   ♥ 10 8 3
♦ 8 7 2                   ♦ K 10
♣ 5 4 3                   ♣ K Q 9 7
              ♠ K 6 4
              ♥ A J 7
              ♦ A Q 4 3
              ♣ J 6 2
```

It looks normal, if slightly aggressive, to play in three no trumps, as indeed happened at both tables in the match between the Netherlands and Poland. Both Wests led a spade, won in dummy by the queen. The Dutch declarer made nine tricks in some comfort by taking diamond finesse and then laying down the ace of diamonds, dropping the king.

The Polish declarer took a slightly odd view when he led the diamond jack from dummy at trick two, to the king, ace and seven.

Now declarer took this card at face value—in which case his only chance would be the doubleton eight-seven of diamonds. He led the ace and jack of hearts from hand, with the West defender Wubbo de Boer ducking like a man who did not want to give him an entry to dummy for a diamond play. Eventually declarer got to dummy with the club ace to play the diamond nine, in an attempt to squash the eight— but the only thing that got squashed was his ego.

Another frequently occurring combination comes when declarer has to tackle:

```
        A J 9 5 4
Q 10 6            K 8 (2)
        7 3 (2)
```

Wherever the two in this suit is located, declarer figures to make the percentage play of a low card to the nine, intending to finesse the jack on the next round. But if West contributes an honor on the first round, declarer may be tempted to win the ace and play West for KQx.

(Of course the follow-up to that is that West should duck smoothly with KQx, expecting declarer to misguess; but maybe South will pay West the compliment of assuming he would play an honor from K10x . . .)

However the position does not have to be quite as straightforward as that; sometimes there are entry considerations to take account of as well. Look at this hand from a major pairs tournament in the United States.

Both Sides Vulnerable. Pairs.

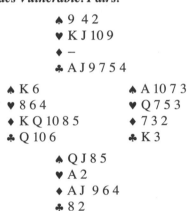

It is not easy for North-South to go plus on their cards—but one would certainly not think 3NT by South was necessarily where you wanted to finish.

Joanne Manfield and Danny Sprung were defending, and the opening lead of a heart was won by declarer in hand, to play a club toward dummy. Manfield hopped up with the queen, was allowed to hold the trick, and a second heart to East's queen for a diamond switch meant declarer had to get the clubs right by rising with the ace, to make the contract. When he misguessed, dummy was dead and the contract finished up down four.

Right, time for a new theme; this time out efforts are going to be directed to persuading declarer that we have shortage when in fact we have length, so that he generates an extra loser.

Three pairs of linked hands here; first the duck:

```
        A J 5              K J 5 2
4              K 10 8 3    4            A 10 8 3
        Q 9 7 6 2          Q 9 7 6
```

In both instances you are trying to deflect declarer from the winning line, of leading low to the jack, and then playing dummy's top card. In both cases you may succeed by dropping your eight on the first round. If you do, declarer may try to pin the ten-eight in the first instance by leading the queen from hand; and in the second example he may lead low back to the queen at the second trick.

Next pair; the falsecard on a losing trick:

```
        A 8 5 2            A K 9 2
4              J 9 6 3    4            Q 10 8 3
        K Q 10 7          J 7 6 5
```

In the first case, declarer will play the king followed by the ace unless you drop the nine, and get him to start worrying about that being a singleton. (Declarer may avoid this problem by tackling the suit by leading initially from dummy—then East cannot falsecard in total safety as West might have the singleton ten.) In the second example, declarer will surely play the ace and king—unless your eight persuades him to try and pin the ten-eight by crossing to hand to lead the jack.

And finally in this section, the falsecard on the winning trick:

```
        K J 9 2            A J 9 2
10 8 5 3       A    10 8 5 3        K
        Q 7 6 4          Q 7 6 4
```

It is fairly clear that declarer will lose the first trick in these suits to your partner's singleton honor. To give a chance to go wrong on the next round, drop the eight like a man with a singleton and hope declarer is watching your cards!

If we can do all of that with small cards, imagine how much fun we can have with honors that we do not need.

Well, to start with we can try to tempt declarer into an indiscreet finesse.

```
        A K 10 7 2        A K 9 7 3 2
Q 5            J 4    8 6            J 10 4
        9 8 6 3          Q 5
```

It does no harm to "split your honors" in the first case when declarer leads low from hand—who knows, it may tempt declarer into the "idiot's finesse" by crossing back to hand to dummy's ten? In the second case the odds may technically favor taking a finesse if a high card appears—but if you have any respect for East as a player, ignore this falsecard.

PLAYING THE HONOR FROM HONOR-TEN DOUBLETON

There are many positions where this is a possible play. Sometimes it is simply to create a losing option when declarer has a choice of cards to crash:

```
           4                          4 2
Q 7 6           K 10        Q 7 6           K 10
      A J 9 85 3 2                 A J 9 8 5 3
```

(No further entries to dummy)

In both these instances when declarer leads from dummy playing the king at your first turn would allow declarer to try to drop king-queen doubleton unsuccessfully. The same play works from queen-ten doubleton—but beware: if declarer has an eight card suit you may be clearing up a guess for him.

Sometimes dropping an honor allows declarer to finesse on the way back, under the assumption that you have a singleton.

```
          J 9 2                        J 9 2
7 4 3           K 10        7 4 3           Q 10
        A Q 8 6 5                   A K 8 6 5
```

Dropping the honor as East may persuade declarer to play low to the nine on the second round. Mind you, you have to be reasonably confident that declarer has both the missing top honors—otherwise the play risks throwing a trick—but, even so, declarer may still finesse into your ten.

More of the same, when declarer has a six-two fit and you have queen-ten.

```
        A K J 9 4 2                  K J 9 4 3 2
8 6 5           Q 10        8 6 5           Q 10
          7 3                          A 7
```

Perhaps declarer was going to finesse on the second round anyway, but you give him a different problem if you drop the queen on the first round. Don't drop the queen if declarer has a five-three fit; you give him a chance to play off a second honor to test of the suit is four-one and only then to finesse, with say KJ943 facing A72.

The lowly ten-eight doubleton has its part to play as well, in a little known falsecard. I first saw this in the European Championships in 1989—and I have been waiting since then for its reappearance!

```
            9 7 2
A K 5                 10 8
          Q J 6 4 3
```

Declarer simply led up to the queen-jack and held his losers to two. But if East had played the ten on the first round, might declarer have played low to the seven on the second round?

There are a couple of related themes where fooling from honor—ten-eight can bring unexpected rewards. These plays are pretty safe when dummy has the nine, although they sometimes give the optical illusion of wasting a card you cannot afford.

North/South Vulnerable. Teams.

```
                ♠ A Q 3
                ♥ 9 7 3
                ♦ K Q 10 5
                ♣ A Q 3
♠ 10 9 5 4                    ♠ 8 7
♥ Q 6                         ♥ K 10 8
♦ A 8 7                       ♦ J 6 3 2
♣ 10 6 2                      ♣ J 7 5 4
                ♠ K 6 2
                ♥ A J 5 4 2
                ♦ 9 6
                ♣ K 9 8
```

When South opens the bidding with one heart it excites North to some show of action before he subsides in four hearts. Your partner leads a stolid jack of spades, and you can see that some fireworks may be necessary to beat this contract. Declarer wins the ace as you follow with the eight, then plays a heart to the ten, jack and queen. Your partner plays a second spade, and when declarer wins this in hand he has a real problem. If you have the bare heart ten he cannot afford to lay down the heart ace now, or he will lose three trump tricks and the diamond ace. If he takes your card as honest he may lead a low heart from hand. You win your king, and lead a diamond to your partner's ace, and get a spade ruff for the setting trick.

And now for the acknowledged master holding when it comes to falsecards—there are probably at least twice as many good falsecards involving jack-nine combinations as I will quote here, almost all of them risk-free, which is always a bonus!

Imagine you are declarer as South, with the lead in dummy.

```
       10 8 5 3                      10 8 5
K                A J 9     3 2                A J 9
       Q 7 6 4 2                     K Q 7 6 4
```

Left to your own devices you would surely hold your losers to two in this suit in the first instance by leading low from dummy, and ducking when the nine appears (this is correct when West has a singleton ace or king, and wrong when East has ducked smoothly from AK9). But if East contributes the jack . . . And similarly in the second instance, you will play up to the king-queen twice, and not think any more about it, unless East drops the jack on the first round, when you may finesse the eight on the second round.

(In some cases East can afford the jack from the jack-nine, i.e., in positions such as the second example, if he knows his side need two tricks from the suit to beat the contract.)

This last position brings us on to two comparable situations.

(lead in dummy)	(lead in hand)
10 8 5 3	K 10 8 5
6 4 2 A J 9	A J 9 6 4 2
K Q 7	Q 7 3

Declarer will surely play these two suits for one loser if left to his own devices, but you have paid your entry fee and are entitled to contribute the jack on the first round. In the first case declarer may take a finesse of the ten-eight in the third round, and with the second holding declarer may finesse the seven on the second round.

Do you remember we were looking at this combination earlier?

	Q 10 8 7 5	
K 4 3 2		J 9
	A 6	

We have changed the defensive layout now; won't declarer lead to the eight on the second round if you drop the jack from this holding—or even perhaps from J93?

Again, the sight of a full hand may make the position clearer. Again the provenance is an American tournament.

	♠ A 6 4	
	♥ Q 7 5	
	♦ A 10 8 4 2	
	♣ 8 5	
♠ 7 3		♠ K Q 10 9 5
♥ J 9 4 2		♥ 10 3
♦ Q 7 6 5		♦ J 9
♣ J 9 4		♣ K Q 10 3
	♠ J 8 2	
	♥ A K 8 6	
	♦ K 3	
	♣ A 7 6 2	

West had a tough lead after a strong no trump was raised to three, and his selection of a fourth highest heart did not unduly discomfort declarer, who won in hand, and laid down the diamond king. When Lou Reich contributed the jack, it looked safe to declarer to play a diamond to the eight next. After all, if it lost it would presumably be to the queen. Alas for him, the defense could now get two diamond tricks, and declarer had only eight tricks.

If Reich had followed with the nine at his first turn might declarer still have gone wrong, playing him for a tricky 9x holding? Perhaps, but the *a posteriori* reasoning must be that, if he did not play him to have falsecarded with one holding, he would not play him to have falsecarded from another!

There are many situations where the trump holding of jack-nine generates some unusual play. For example Benito Garozzo, the Italian world champion, defeated a slam where the trump layout was as follows:

	8 7 6 5	
J 9		K 3
	A Q 10 4 2	

When the nine was led at trick one, even when the opening leader was Garozzo, declarer thought it was right to take two finesses. Note that if declarer has this nine card holding and tackles it himself by leading low to the queen, you can drop the jack with no risk. Perhaps he will now cross to dummy to repeat the finesse, in a suit you can ruff.

To close up this section, let me give you a couple of hands defended by two master players. First Martin Hoffman, perhaps the best card-player never to have made it to the Great Britain team. After West opened one diamond South became declarer in four hearts. Our hero was in the East seat.

Both Sides Vulnerable. Pairs.

	♠ A K Q 2	
	♥ A 10 8 3	
	♦ Q 8 2	
	♣ A 5	
♠ 9 4		♠ J 10 8 3
♥ K 2		♥ J 9 6
♦ A K J 9 7 6		♦ 10 3
♣ J 10 2		♣ 9 7 6 3
	♠ 7 6 5	
	♥ Q 7 5 4	
	♦ 5 4	
	♣ K Q 8 4	

West led two rounds of diamonds, and switched to the club jack. South won in dummy and tried to tempt Hoffman into shortening his trumps, by leading a third round of diamonds, but Hoffman discarded a club. Now declarer led the ace of hearts and a second heart; Hoffman contributed the jack on the second round, and declarer naturally played the queen. West could win the king and play a fourth round of diamonds, repromoting Hoffman's heart nine!

The final example comes from the London Sunday Times of 1990, regarded as the strongest invitation event in the World. In the West seat was Bobby Goldman, who with Paul Soloway, is, for more than fifteen years, among the best partnerships in American bridge.

Both Sides Vulnerable. Teams.

```
            ♠ A Q 2
            ♥ 8 3
            ♦ K Q 2
            ♣ Q 7 6 5 2
♠ J 9 8 4              ♠ 10 7 3
♥ 9 5 2               ♥ K Q J 7 6
♦ A J 7 6             ♦ 10 8 3
♣ J 9                 ♣ K 4
            ♠ K 6 5
            ♥ A 10 4
            ♦ 9 5 4
            ♣ A 10 8 3
```

After East had overcalled one heart, North-South propelled themselves in 3NT and Goldman led a heart, which declarer, Christian Mari of France, had to duck until the third round. Now it was essential to keep East off lead or he would cash his heart winners, so Mari played a spade to table and called for the club queen, which went king, ace, jack! Not unreasonably, Mari thought that he could cross to table again with a spade for the finesse of the club nine. However, Goldman won, and played a third spade. Now he had a spade winner to cash when he got in the diamond ace for the defense's fifth trick, a truly remarkable result.

Playing the Card You are Known to Hold

There are occasions when the play to date marks a defender with a certain card. Very often, playing this card at the first opportunity can create doubt in declarer's mind. This theme emerges frequently when declarer has taken a winning finesse, thus implicitly marking a card in one defender's hand.

```
            A J 4
Q 10 2              J 9 4
            K 9 5 3
```

Declarer tackles the suit by taking the finesse of the jack. When it holds, you are marked with the queen; so play it under the ace. Now declarer has to decide whether to finesse on the next round or not. If you follow with the ten, he has no guess because he knows you have the queen. Once you have seen it, it becomes obvious—now try the next suit.

```
            K 8 6 2
A 75                876
            Q 10 3
```

Declarer leads the two to his ten and the ace. You must drop the jack under the queen on the next round to give declarer a problem.

Sometimes it is not a question of an actual trick in the suit in question, rather of preventing declarer from getting a cross-ruff going efficiently. Let us look at this side-suit in a trump contract.

```
            9 4
J 7 2              K 10 5
            A Q 8 6 3
```

When declarer takes the finesse and then lays down the ace, then unless there is no further entry to dummy you know that your partner has the jack, or declarer would have repeated the finesse. So drop the king on the second round to leave declarer guessing whether to ruff the third round high or low.

We saw earlier that there were some shenanigans to the defense with a holding of honor-ten-eight. This elegant example combines some of those themes with the point about playing the known card.

North/South Vulnerable. Teams.

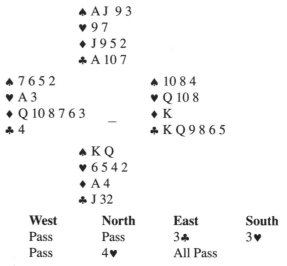

```
            ♠ A J 9 3
            ♥ 9 7
            ♦ J 9 5 2
            ♣ A 10 7
♠ 7 6 5 2              ♠ 10 8 4
♥ A 3                 ♥ Q 10 8
♦ Q 10 8 7 6 3        ♦ K
♣ 4                   ♣ K Q 9 8 6 5
            ♠ K Q
            ♥ 6 5 4 2
            ♦ A 4
            ♣ J 3 2
```

West	North	East	South
Pass	Pass	3♣	3♥
Pass	4♥	All Pass	

When your partner leads his club declarer can see that he has his work cut out for him. If he wins the ace and plays on spades he has little chance—so the best hope must be to find you with queen and another heart. He plays a heart to the jack (on which you contribute the ten) and your partner wins his ace, and optimistically switches to a diamond, to the nine, king and ace. Declarer lays down the heart king, on which you contribute the known card, the queen, and comes to the crossroads.

If he thinks you have the eight of hearts left—in which case he must be a very untrusting soul—he can succeed by playing out the top spades, overtaking the queen. The convenient fall of the ten allows him two discards for his losing clubs, but it fails when your partner is 5-3-4-1. As against that, if he believes you have two hearts, he simply plays a diamond towards dummy, to establish another sure discard for his club loser; this line fails of course, when you ruff your partner's winner (to avoid accidents) and cash your two club tricks.

There is a series of slightly less regularly occurring positions where an initial finesse has succeeded, and you need to preserve some ambiguity.

```
        K J 7 2                  K J 7 5 2
A Q 9 6          10 5 4   A Q 9 6          10 4
        8 3                      8 3
```

In the first example, where this is a side-suit in a trump contract, declarer leads to the king and exits with a low card; win the ace, the card you are known to hold, and declarer has no certainty that he can subsequently ruff the suit back to hand without fear of an over-ruff. In the second example, in no trumps, declarer leads low to the jack, and then comes back to hand to lead low again. Play the queen; this way declarer does not know the suit is 4-2. If you play the nine declarer will score his king and may then switch his attack because he knows the suit is not behaving.

A couple of more complex examples; in the first dummy has no outside entries.

```
            A Q 10 7 4
K J 9 6                        8
            5 3 2
```

Declarer leads low to the ten and then comes back to hand to lead up to dummy again. Play the jack and declarer will cover with the queen—getting only three tricks from the suit. If you duck, then declarer can work out the suit is 4-1. He ducks too, and later repeats the finesse to make four tricks.

On the following hand the defense have to find a good play, and West may find it more difficult than normal because the sight of dummy may depress his hopes of getting two tricks.

```
                ♠ K Q
                ♥ 6 3
                ♦ A K 9 5 2
                ♣ A Q 10 7
♠ 9 4                           ♠ J 10 8 7 3
♥ J 10 8 2                      ♥ Q 9 4
♦ 10 7 6                        ♦ Q J 8 4
♣ K J 9 2                       ♣ 3
                ♠ A 6 5 2
                ♥ A K 7 5
                ♦ 3
                ♣ 8 6 5 4
```

West	North	East	South
–	–	–	1♣
Pass	2♦	Pass	2♥
Pass	3♣	Pass	3NT
Pass	6♣	All Pass	

You lead the heart jack with high expectations of your trump suit, and are bitterly disappointed by the dummy. Declarer wins the ace of hearts and plays a club to the ten, on which your partner plays the three. Now declarer comes to the heart king and plays a spade to hand. When he plays a second club it is essential to follow with the jack. Why? Well you know what the trump position is but declarer has

to consider that East might have K93, in which case taking a second finesse would allow East to play a third trump—which would be fatal. If trumps are 3-2 declarer can rise with the club ace and cross-ruff in comfort to twelve tricks.

If declarer plays the club ace, the best he can do thereafter is to cash dummy's top spades, play ace king of diamonds and ruff a diamond, and lead the spade ace in this ending:

```
                ♠ –
                ♥ –
                ♦ 9 5
                ♣ Q 7
♠ –                             ♠ J 10
♥ 10 8                          ♥ 9
♦ –                             ♦ Q
♣ K 9                           ♣ –
                ♠ A 6
                ♥ 7
                ♦ –
                ♣ 8
```

If you ruff low, declarer can still succeed, but you throw a heart away (or ruff high and exit with a trump) and declarer must fail. Again, playing the club jack, the card you were inferentially known to hold, was critical.

Sometimes the card you are known to hold is not honor—this is, however, the only example I have seen where the significant card is as low as an eight.

Neither Side Vulnerable. Teams.

```
                ♠ Q 9 5 3
                ♥ 10 3
                ♦ Q 10
                ♣ K J 10 7 5
♠ 7 6 4 2                       ♠ J 8
♥ Q J                           ♥ K 8 4
♦ 9 7 6 5 2                     ♦ K 8 4 3
♣ 8 3                           ♣ A Q 4 2
                ♠ A K 10
                ♥ A 9 7 6 5 2
                ♦ A J
                ♣ 9 6
```

West	North	East	South
–	–	1NT	Dble
2♦	Dble (*)	Pass	2♥
Pass	3♣	Pass	3♥
All Pass			
(*) Values			

Against three hearts, your partner leads the club eight, and you obediently play three rounds of that suit; declarer ruffs the third round with the six, overruffed with the jack. Now partner plays the diamond seven (marking him with the five low diamonds) to dummy's ten.

At this point you need to do two good things to have a chance to beat the contract. First duck the diamond, to deny declarer an extra entry to dummy.

Secondly, when declarer crosses to table with the spade queen to lead a low heart, play the eight—remember, you are marked with this card; partner would have over-ruffed with it if he had it. Now declarer has to decide whether to play the nine or the ace; one is right if you began life with K84, the other if you began with KQ8—not so easy. If you had followed with the four then, since you are marked with the eight, declarer's only hope is that you began with K84 or Q84, as he cannot cope with KQ84.

(Yes, declarer might succeed if he makes his first trump play from hand—but nobody is perfect!)

PLAYING THE TOP OF A SEQUENCE OF HONORS

This is another section with a lot of meat in it; what we are looking at is a conscious decision to follow with a deceptively high card, and the purpose is to mislead any or all three of the other three people at the table—although dummy is a lower priority than declarer, it must be admitted.

Let us look at the opening trick where we are intending to deceive both partner and declarer—for the most part. Before we get on to deception let us look at a little-known defensive signal, which might be useful one day to you.

> 8 7 3
> Q 6 5   A K J 9 4
> 10 2

Partner finds a good lead in an unbid suit against 3NT, and you have to decide how to get him to unblock the queen; if you lead low at trick two declarer may turn up with an embarrassing queen-two! The answer is to win trick one with the ace, and then play the king—this being a request for an unblock.

Of course, another technical reason for playing ace then king is to show a doubleton; and a third possibility is that you may also have a suit-preference message to pass on.

But leaving aside the technical reasons for winning with the ace rather than the king, there is a common reason for making this play, which tends to be under-used. The aim is a mislead declarer about the location of the high cards—if you win the king you tend to pinpoint the remaining high cards in your partner's hand. Let us look at an example to see how much a slight false card can have a big effect.

East/West Vulnerable. Teams.

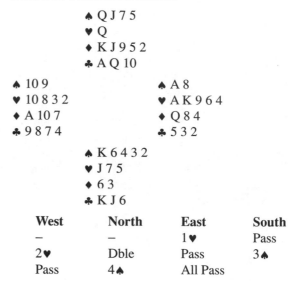

```
             ♠ Q J 7 5
             ♥ Q
             ♦ K J 9 5 2
             ♣ A Q 10
♠ 10 9                        ♠ A 8
♥ 10 8 3 2                    ♥ A K 9 6 4
♦ A 10 7                      ♦ Q 8 4
♣ 9 8 7 4                     ♣ 5 3 2
             ♠ K 6 4 3 2
             ♥ J 7 5
             ♦ 6 3
             ♣ K J 6
```

West	North	East	South
–	–	1♥	Pass
2♥	Dble	Pass	3♠
Pass	4♠	All Pass	

West leads the heart two and you can see that the only issue on the hand will be the diamond guess. If you win the heart king at trick one, South will discover you have the spade ace before negotiating diamonds—at which point it would be logical to assume West must have the diamond ace for him to have dredged up the initial response. But if you win the heart ace at trick one and play a club, the reverse logic will apply. South will not be able to construct an opening bid for you without the diamond ace, and he will surely therefore go wrong in diamonds.

An alternative reason for the ace-king falsecard is that you can set up a ruffing position for declarer. If a side-suit is divided along the following lines:

> J
> 9 6 4 3   A K 2
> Q 10 8 7 5

If you take your king when your partner leads this suit, declarer will have the successful option of ruffing out your ace-king, but if you win the first trick with the ace you give him the losing option of the ruffing finesse.

If you take your king when your partner leads this suit, declarer will have the successful option of ruffing out your ace-king, but if you win the first trick with the ace you give him the losing option of the ruffing finesse.

Why else should you win the first trick with the ace from the ace-king? Well maybe the suit is set out like this:

> 9 8 3   9 8 3
> J 7 5 2   A K 4   J 7 6 5   A K 4
> Q 10 6   Q 10 2

Our aim if we need three quick tricks from the suit is to win the ace and return a low card to put declarer to the guess. This is a suit combination which may lead to deceptive play by both declarer and the defense.

Declarer in the second example could discourage us from trying this maneuver by concealing the two—so we do not know if our partner has led from a five card suit—but he can do nothing deceptive in the first case. We know that partner has a four card suit when he leads the two, so the underlead at trick two should (errors and omissions excepting) be safe.

One of the most under used falsecards comes when partner leads a suit in which you have a pair of touching honors. It is normal practice to follow with the lower of the honors, which is helpful to both declarer and partner. Let us look at some suit layouts where the fact that partner is misled may be secondary to fooling declarer (though, having said that, it would be helpful for partner to know our tendencies here).

Let us look first at the king-queen.

```
      A J 7 2                       A J 7 2
10 8 6 4      K Q 5       9 7 6 4       K Q 5
       9 3                         10 3
```

If we win the queen at the first opportunity declarer may work out that we have KQx, and ruff out our other honor, but we certainly make life more difficult for him by playing the king initially. In the second case declarer may be lured into finessing twice if we win the first trick with the king.

Sometimes the effect of winning with the king from king-queen will be to discourage partner from continuing the suit. If this is the layout at no trumps:

```
              4
  J 7 5 2           K Q 3
         A 10 9 8 6
```

When partner leads the two, you know that declarer has a five-card suit. It may be worth considering playing the king at trick one to discourage partner from setting up declarer's suit.

What about the queen-jack?

(a) **(b)**

```
     A K 10 4                   K 10 8 4
8 6 5 2      Q J 7      A 6 5 2       Q J 7
       9 3                       9 3
```

It looks right in the first example to win the first trick with the queen to lure declarer into a second finesse; just hope partner does not feel obliged to discard all of his holdings too soon. In the second case we want to persuade declarer to get the second finesse wrong, and we boost our chances by the falsecard.

Of course it should go without saying that it is vital, if you are attempting these deceptive plays, that your partner is tuned in to the possibility that you could try a bit of skull-duggery. In the second example, your play might lead partner to rise with the ace prematurely on the second round of the suit, if he believes declarer has the jack; so if you are playing with a relatively inexperienced partner, this kind of falsecard may not be worth the effort.

Sometimes when partner has led from shortage you can disguise the fact with the queen-jack falsecard.

Say partner has led a singleton in a suit contract, and you have the trump ace.

Real-life		**Pretending to be**	
9 8 4		9 8 4	
3	Q J 7 5 2	J 7 5 3	Q 2
A K 10 6		A K 10 6	

You play the queen at trick one, then win your ace of trumps and continue with the two. Declarer has a tough problem.

Certainly the jack-ten has many moments. For example, consider these positions at trick one.

(a) **(b)**

```
     Q 9 7 3                    K 9 7 3
K 8 5 4      J 10 6     A 8 5 4       J 10 6
        A 2                       Q 2
```

With both these jack-ten holdings the sight of dummy may persuade us to play the jack.

Sometimes we can try to protect our jack-ten holding from further embarrassment after an indiscreet lead, by making a falsecard.

```
           Q 9 7 5
   3              J 10 6 4
         A K 8 2
```

When partner finds a bad moment to lead his singleton, declarer can easily pick up our holding for no loser. But maybe we can give South a nudge in the wrong direction by following with the jack at trick one, trying to persuade declarer that West has 10643. (Of course declarer may still go wrong if you play the ten. But if he is a creature of habit who starts his reasoning "East cannot have the jack-ten because . . ." then the falsecard must be the right strategy.)

There are other cases at trick one where we would like to lull declarer into a false sense of security.

```
            J 9 6
   5 4 2          K Q 10 7
           A 8 3
```

When partner leads the four (second from a bad suit), play the queen, and declarer may not try to dispose of one of his losers via a successful finesse in a side-suit, he may simply expect that the ten is onside for him, losing two tricks in this suit in the fullness of time. Sometimes the position is a little like signalling discouragement, when a switch is appropriate.

Let's look at the full hand where we manipulate our honors to get partner to do the right thing.

Teams.

```
                ♠ 10 9 3
                ♥ Q 3
                ♦ K Q 10 9 4
                ♣ K 10 5
♠ 6 2                        ♠ K Q J 8 5 4
♥ A 7 6                      ♥ 8 4
♦ 7 5 2                      ♦ 8 6
♣ J 9 7 3 2                  ♣ A Q 4
                ♠ A 7
                ♥ K J 10 9 5 2
                ♦ A J 3
                ♣ 8 6
```

North-South ignore the one spade opening and reach four hearts.

When partner leads the spade six you know that if he gets in again he may need to find the club switch to beat the contract. Make it easy for him by playing the spade king at trick one, to deny the queen. Now the club shift becomes trivial—maybe he should find it anyway, but there is no harm in being kind to partner.

PLAYING UNNECESSARILY HIGH

Let us have a look at some deceptive ways to win tricks on declarer's suits.

```
        K J 10 9 4
6 5 2                 A Q 8 7
        3
```

If declarer needs three tricks in this side suit to make his slam he will lead to the nine, and later on will take a ruffing finesse successfully. If we win the first trick with the ace we may persuade declarer to try to drop our partner's hypothetical Qxxx, by ruffing out the suit. No dice.

Why else should we win the ace when we could win the queen? Maybe we are defending a slam in another suit.

```
        K J 10 9 4
6                    A Q 8 7 5 2
        3
```

When partner leads the suit at trick one we may lull declarer into a false sense of security if we win the ace and return a low one. Declarer may discard, or ruff too low, whereas winning the queen might tip him off to the danger.

About fifteen years ago the English Bridge Union magazine published a hand from an unfeeling husband, comparing his wife to the Rueful Rabbit, who occasionally gets things right without knowing why. (The Rueful Rabbit is known to American players though Victor Mollo's writing.) This was the hand which had driven the husband to put pen to paper.

Teams.

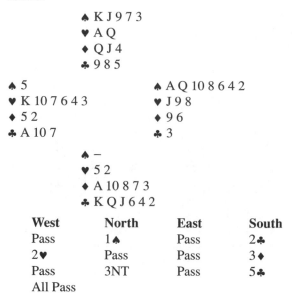

```
                ♠ K J 9 7 3
                ♥ A Q
                ♦ Q J 4
                ♣ 9 8 5
♠ 5                          ♠ A Q 10 8 6 4 2
♥ K 10 7 6 4 3               ♥ J 9 8
♦ 5 2                        ♦ 9 6
♣ A 10 7                     ♣ 3
                ♠ –
                ♥ 5 2
                ♦ A 10 8 7 3
                ♣ K Q J 6 4 2
```

West	North	East	South
Pass	1♠	Pass	2♣
2♥	Pass	Pass	3♦
Pass	3NT	Pass	5♣
All Pass			

When our narrator led his singleton spade South, the victim of the piece, naturally contributed the jack from dummy. East, as if it were the most natural thing in the world, played the ace, and declarer ruffed. The queen of clubs won the next trick, then West took his club ace on the next round of trumps and played the heart seven. I ask you: does it not look natural to take the ace and play the spade king to discard your heart loser? Now, West can ruff, and still has the diamond king to come for down one.

Sometimes the object is to persuade declarer to waste his entries or simply pure sadism, to build up his hopes and then dash them.

```
        Q 10 8 7 5
6 4 2                A K J
        9 3
```

Declarer, who is short of entries to hand, crosses to lead the nine in this suit. Win the king, so as to persuade declarer to make an unnecessary journey to repeat the finesse.

What about this trump suit?

```
        9 8 5
A K J                7 4
        Q 10 6 3 2
```

You lead a side suit and force declarer to ruff in hand, then, when declarer crosses to dummy to run the nine, you win the first trump with the king and force him again. Surely declarer will finesse in trumps again; now you draw trumps to run your suit; if you had won the first trick cheaply, declarer would have seen this coming and been more cautious.

If you can make this play with the AKJ, you can certainly do it with the AQx. Sometimes the right strategy with this holding (or even AQxx) in trumps is to hold up altogether, or win the first trick with the ace, to mislead declarer or to lull him to sleep prematurely.

Let us see a full hand.

```
                ♠ K 5
                ♥ 5 3
                ♦ K J 9 5 2
                ♣ A Q 10 7
♠ J 9 4                        ♠ 10 8 7 3
♥ J 10 9 8 2                   ♥ Q 7 6 4
♦ 6 3                          ♦ A Q 7
♣ K 8 2                        ♣ 9 3
                ♠ A Q 6 2
                ♥ A K
                ♦ 10 8 4
                ♣ J 6 5 4
```

It is not so easy to bid these hands to five clubs by North after a weak no trump from South; nonetheless when North-South come to rest in 3NT it seems as if declarer's normal line succeeds. As South you win the heart lead, lose the diamond finesse to East, and fall back on the clubs, which do behave. But what if East wins the first diamond with the ace, not the queen? Surely, declarer simply repeats the diamond finesse confidently? Oops.

Another example in a suit declarer is developing, possibly even in the trump suit.

```
           Q 10 4 3
5                     K J 7 2
           A 9 8 6
```

If declarer tackles this suit by leading to the ten then you will certainly only score one trick if you win the jack because declarer has a simple finesse against you. But if you win the king, will not declarer play your partner for a possible J752, and play to the ace on the second round?

It is usually easier, and more satisfying, to look at a full hand. In the 1990 World Team Championships in Geneva a variation of the king-jack position came up—nicely solved in defense by Ralph Katz.

Teams.

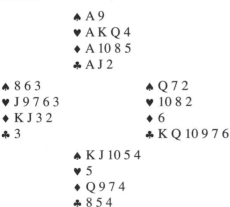

```
                ♠ A 9
                ♥ A K Q 4
                ♦ A 10 8 5
                ♣ A J 2
♠ 8 6 3                        ♠ Q 7 2
♥ J 9 7 6 3                    ♥ 10 8 2
♦ K J 3 2                      ♦ 6
♣ 3                            ♣ K Q 10 9 7 6
                ♠ K J 10 5 4
                ♥ 5
                ♦ Q 9 7 4
                ♣ 8 5 4
```

The Russian South reached six diamonds, East having shown clubs, and received a club lead. He won the ace to cash three rounds of hearts to discard his club losers, and then immediately played a diamond to the seven and king. When he ruffed the heart return he thought he knew the whole story. He would draw a second round of trumps with the ace, then play ace and king of spades, and run the jack of spades, East being 2-3-2-6.

Of course once he played a diamond to the ace he had a second loser in trumps; but if Katz had thoughtlessly won the first trump with the jack, declarer would have had no option but to finesse in diamonds, and subsequently, because of the entries, to play East successfully for the spade queen.

Try the same ploy with this variation for the spade queen.

```
           Q 10 4
5 3 2                 K J 7
           A 9 8 6
```

What about this one, if truly desperate measures are called for?

Declarer is known to hold only three cards in the suit, and dummy is entryless.

```
           A 10 9 8
7 6 2                 K J 4
           Q 5 3
```

Declarer runs the jack and you duck, then he plays the king and repeats the finesse, you hope.

SACRIFICE HONORS

There are many reasons to sacrifice an honor, sometimes it is to give declarer a losing option, when he has to decide if your honor is a singleton or not.

```
           A Q 10 8 4 3 2
K J                   9 5
           7 6
```

Declarer plays this suit to an entryless dummy in no trumps, and will have no problems if you play the jack. But he will probably duck your king, if you play it, to insure he can run suit.

An unlikely one I know, but perhaps, you can persuade declarer to take his eye off the ball and forget his safety plays with this entryless dummy.

```
           A K J 7 4 3 2
Q 10 9 8              –
           6 5
```

Declarer should duck the first round of this suit entirely to insure he can take six tricks from this suit—but if you play the queen at your first opportunity he might have a rush of blood to the head.

Let us have a look at a full hand where the sacrifice of an honor in an unusual position could sneak under declarer's guard.

```
              ♠ 9 8 3
              ♥ 4 3
              ♦ Q J 4
              ♣ A 10 7 5 3
♠ 10 6 2                    ♠ K Q J 5 4
♥ 10 8 7 6                  ♥ K 2
♦ 10 7                      ♦ A 9 8 6 5
♣ J 9 8 2                   ♣ 4
              ♠ A 7
              ♥ A Q J 9 5
              ♦ K 3 2
              ♣ K Q 6
```

West	North	East	South
–	Pass	1♠	Dble
Pass	2♣	Pass	2♥
Pass	2♠	Pass	3♣
Pass	3♦	Pass	3NT
All Pass			

You lead a spade against 3NT, and get a complete count of declarer's hand at once—his delayed club support implies that he must be 2-5-3-3. Your partner leads two rounds of spades, and declarer wins the second spade, cashes the king and queen of clubs, intending to run the clubs and pressurize East, then take a heart finesse and see what happens.

Is there anything you can do to stop him?

If you drop the club jack on the second round, apparently, declarer has suddenly acquired an extra entry to table. If he overtakes the queen to take another heart finesse, all of a sudden, his five club tricks are down to three. Even the king of hearts coming down in two rounds does not give him enough top tricks, and East is poised to cash out for one down as soon as a diamond is played.

Another good reason for dropping an honor prematurely comes about when a suit is behaving very favorably for declarer, and you want to persuade him otherwise.

Sometimes it may be simply a question of persuading declarer to waste precious entries; we have seen already that you can sacrifice the jack in this position.

```
        8 7 6 5
  J 4            K 3
        A Q 10 9 2
```

when declarer finesses. All these honors can go under the knife as well . . .

```
        A K Q 2            Q 10 6 5
  J 7 4        9 8 3   K 7 4        J 9 8
        10 6 5            A 3 2
```

In the first example, sacrifice the jack on the second round, to persuade declarer to play the third round to the ten; perhaps he will have problems getting back to dummy.

In the second case, if declarer plays the ace and a second round, play the jack whether declarer guesses the suit or not.

More of the same.

```
     A K 10 8 5            K J 9 3
  Q 6        J 7   Q 7 4        10 8 2
     9 4 3 2            A 6 5
```

If declarer is marked with four cards and lays down the ace in the first example you should follow with the jack, so that declarer has to cross to hand to take a finesse. In the second case, declarer lays down the ace from hand and plays to the jack, allowing you to follow with the ten, and misrepresent the suit to declarer.

Sometimes the play is massive deception.

```
        Q 7 4 3 2
  K J 9            8 6 5
        A 10
```

When declarer sets about this suit at no trumps, dropping the king under the ace may persuade him that the suit is 5-1 and he should turn his attentions elsewhere.

Sometimes we are looking at something more subtle than that.

```
              ♠ Q 10 8 3
              ♥ 4 3
              ♦ Q J 4
              ♣ K Q 9 5
♠ 6 2                      ♠ J 9 5 4
♥ J 8 7 6                  ♥ 2
♦ 10 7 2                   ♦ A 9 8 6 5
♣ 8 7 3 2                  ♣ J 10 4
              ♠ A K 7
              ♥ A K Q 10 9 5
              ♦ K 3
              ♣ A 6
```

Your partner's opening lead ability takes a vacation against six hearts, and he leads a spade to declarer's ace, rather than a diamond. Declarer cashes the ace, king and queen of hearts, then follows with the spade king. If you play a low spade, declarer (who now needs West to follow to at least three clubs) should next cash the three top clubs. With the highly favorable developments in that suit, declarer can next play the club nine, to discard his last diamond.

But if you drop the spade jack under the king, most normal declarers will assume your partner began with four spades, and will try to run that suit first for his discards (the right play if your partner is 4-4-3-2). This of course allows your partner to ruff in, and if he does not play a diamond now, you can always find another partner!

Sometimes third hand has the opportunity to follow with an honor to distract declarer from a winning route. The underlying concept is that, if declarer has a trump suit in which he might take a safety play—say:

A 8 4 3

K 10 5 2

you can discourage him as East (with QJ96) by dropping an honor in a side suit at trick one to simulate shortage. Then declarer is unlikely to risk the safety play—as, if West gets in with the doubleton queen or jack, declarer may lose out to a ruff as well.

You can go one step further than this; it is hard to beat the following maneuver for barefaced nerve. The defense was found by Liza Shaw, a British International champion, at the rubber bridge table.

♠ A K
♥ Q J 10 9
♦ 5 4
♣ A Q 10 8 7

♠ 9 8 7 6 2   ♠ 10 4 3
♥ 8 3 2   ♥ K 5
♦ Q J 9 6   ♦ 10 8 7 3 2
♣ 2   ♣ K 5 3

♠ Q J 5
♥ A 7 6 4
♦ A K
♣ J 9 6 4

West	North	East	South
–	–	Pass	1NT
Pass	2♣	Pass	2♥
Pass	4NT	Pass	5♥
Pass	6♥	All Pass	

West lead the club two, which declarer correctly assumed to be singleton. He therefore went up with the ace, and Liza deposited the king underneath it! Naturally, declarer now believed it was East who had the singleton club, and so he played the ace of hearts and a second heart, to avoid the risk of East getting a ruff from the doubleton trump. You can see the denouement of course. Liza won her heart king and gave her partner a club ruff.

Somewhere in the textbooks is the classic deception in the trump suit, in defense to a slam, of a holding like this:

A 10 4

J 3   Q 9 2

K 8 7 6 5

West led his long suit (in which East had a singleton) and declarer won in hand to lead a trump to the ace. When East dropped the queen under it, declarer knew enough to cross to hand for the safety play of leading up to the ten. Unluckily for him, West could win the jack, and gave his partner a ruff.

The 1975 Bermuda Bowl was won by a narrow margin by Italy over the United States. This hand provided most of their margin of victory. The Americans had played a sensible small slam—but the Italians had a major bidding accident to wind up in a terrible, but makeable Grand Slam of seven clubs.

♠ Q J 8
♥ A J 9 6 5
♦ K 8 2
♣ A Q

♠ 7 6 5 2   ♠ 4 3
♥ K 4 3 2   ♥ Q 10 8 7
♦ J 5 3   ♦ Q 10 6 4
♣ K 10   ♣ 7 5 4

♠ A K 10 9
♥ –
♦ A 9 7
♣ J 9 8 6 3 2

The West player had been confident that his club king would be a trick; he led a heart and declarer ruffed and played a club to the queen, then the club ace, finding the miraculous lie of the cards. But, if West had contributed the club king at trick two, declarer would probably take this at face value and he has a chance to make the contract if he believes this card is a singleton. If he simply were to draw trumps he would imagine he would have to lose a club trick—but he might succeed if East had four clubs and at least three spades.

He cashes the ace of hearts, three rounds of spades, two top diamonds and ruffs two more hearts. In this three card ending with the spade nine and the club jack-nine in hand, and the club queen and a heart and diamond in dummy, he ruffs his spade with the club queen and makes his last two trumps by a *coup en passant*.

♠ –
♥ J
♦ 8
♣ Q

(Projected)   (Projected)
♠ –   ♠ –
♥ K   ♥ –
♦ Q J   ♦ –
♣ –   ♣ 10 7 5

♠ 9
♥ –
♦ –
♣ J 9

As the cards lie, this line fails when East can ruff the third spade. Would the great Giorgio Belladonna have fallen for this deception? Almost certainly, yes—his comment after the event was that, if West had played the club king, America would have been champions.

Sometimes bridge themes are like city buses; you don't see them for a long time—and then two examples come on consecutive days, as happened in the 1989 European Championships. This was the first:

Teams.

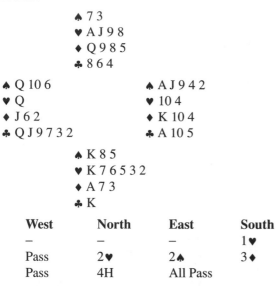

	♠ 7 3	
	♥ A J 9 8	
	♦ Q 9 8 5	
	♣ 8 6 4	
♠ Q 10 6		♠ A J 9 4 2
♥ Q		♥ 10 4
♦ J 6 2		♦ K 10 4
♣ Q J 9 7 3 2		♣ A 10 5
	♠ K 8 5	
	♥ K 7 6 5 3 2	
	♦ A 7 3	
	♣ K	

West	North	East	South
–	–	–	1♥
Pass	2♥	2♠	3♦
Pass	4H	All Pass	

The defense led the club queen (thus potentially avoiding a disaster in that suit) and East took his ace and exited with a second club. Declarer ruffed, played a heart to the ace, then a spade towards his king. East took his ace and played another club; declarer ruffed, led the spade king and ruffed a spade, and drew the last trump. This was the five card ending:

Teams.

	♠ –	
	♥ 8	
	♦ Q 9 8 5	
	♣ –	
♠ –		♠ J 9
♥ –		♥ –
♦ J 6 2		♦ K 10 4
♣ J 9		♣ –
	♠ –	
	♥ 7 6	
	♦ A 7 3	
	♣ –	

At this point declarer, who knew East to hold the diamond king from the auction, was well on his way to success; his intention was to lead the diamond three to the eight, to endplay East to lead a second diamond or give him a ruff and discard. However Nafiz Zorlu of Turkey in the West seat found the spectacular play of the diamond jack on this trick. Now declarer had to read whether this was the play of an unsupported honor, or from the jack-ten. In one case ducking the trick endplays West, in the other case the correct play is the queen from dummy. Perhaps justice was done

when declarer ducked allowing Zorlu to exit with a diamond for one down.

HOLDING UP ON A LOSING FINESSE

Let us go one step further than one of our earlier themes. If we can see some point in not winning a trick with the cheapest card possible, why win the trick at all?

As usual, there are some technical reasons for the hold-up as well as the deceptive aspect. Let us just look briefly at a couple of layouts where you may have reason to hold up. (Note the emphasis: if dummy has no side entries these hold-ups may be pointless or even costly. They are most effective when dummy has exactly one entry outside the suit.)

	K Q 10 9 2				A Q 10 9 2	
5 3		A J 8 4	5 3			K J 8 4
	7 6				7 6	

	A Q J 3 2	
10 3		K 9 8 4
	7 6	

East does not jeopardize his two tricks by ducking the first round of the suit, in any of our examples, but he does lose timing. Make up your mind whether dummy has 2+ entries, or no entries, in which case the duck costs timing, and maybe even a trick. If dummy has one entry, the duck will probably be right. And, for the purists, note that if declarer needs three tricks only from the third example and has one side-suit entry to dummy, he can duck the first round of the suit entirely as a safety play.

Having got the technical justification out of the way, let us look at why we might duck tricks. The most common reason is that we want to exhaust declarer's entries to dummy, or vice versa.

Some of these plays will become so automatic to you that you will not think of them necessarily as deceptive, but that is part of the story.

	A Q J 10 5				A Q J 10	
9 6 2		K 8 7	9 6 5			K 8 7 2
	4 3				4 3	

In both cases you can see that if dummy is entryless, then East saves at least one trick by ducking his king once. But wait a second; if it is right to duck with those North-South layouts, maybe it is worth investing a trick as East by ducking with a less rock-solid holding. Try these for size:

	A Q J 10 5				A Q J 10	
9 7 6 2		K 8	9 6 5			K 8 7
	4 3				4 3 2	

In the first case, we duck even though that would allow declarer to drop our honor on the next round, because we believe he is more likely to repeat the finesse. In the second case, we can duck twice, assuming declarer has enough entries to hand to take three finesses. Again, bear in mind that these plays are most effective if dummy has no side entries, or if you can see that declarer will waste valuable entries to hand repeating these finesses.

The following hand comes from the Spingold tournament in the United States, and features one of the United States' top players. The play concerned looks unnatural—but as long as you given the matter enough thought in advance, it should be logical enough.

Teams.

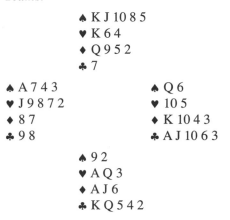

South played in 3NT, North having shown his spade suit on the way. West led a heart, which declarer took with the ace. When South ran the spade nine, Berkowitz in the East seat ducked—not an obvious play but, in theory and in practice, the winning move.

Why? Well, declarer surely has two or three small spades, and will repeat the finesse to your queen. If he has two spades you may (as in the real hand above) be able to cut him off from the spades altogether.

This is indeed what happened. Declarer naturally repeated the spade finesse and Berkowitz won the queen and returned a heart. Declarer finished up taking four tricks in the minors, three hearts, but only one spade trick, for one down.

(Note that it would also be the right play on this hand to duck in the East seat with Ax of spades (as opposed to Qx). In this instance it is more an entry destroying plan than deception, but the results could be equally successful.)

The logic behind holding up with distributions including the ace is in part to exhaust declarer when he has a doubleton. In both these two following cases you also do best to duck the first trick so long as dummy has no more than one entry.

	K J 10 9 2		K J 9 8 2	
8 7 5		A Q 4	Q 7 5	A 10 4
	6 3			6 3

In the first case, you should duck when declarer leads to the nine if dummy has one entry, otherwise take the trick (with the ace or queen depending on the rest of the of hand.) In the second case you should duck if declarer plays to the jack whatever the entry position (errors and omissions excepting).

The hand that follows incorporates a number of these themes, and in my opinion represents one of the great defenses in bridge history—because it is a sequence of fine plays to beat a contract which, most of the time, would probably succeed with overtricks.

Teams.

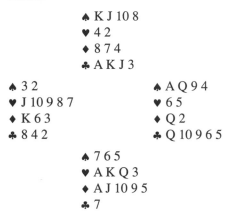

After North had bid both the black suits South jumped to 3NT, and West naturally led the heart jack. Declarer immediately played a spade to the jack—and with this section being all about deception you are doubtless trying to work out why East (a great player and journalist, Herman Filarski) should duck this trick. In fact that would be a very poor play; Filarski won and returned a heart, to destroy declarer's entries to hand. Declarer won the second heart, played a spade to the ten, and East ducked.

Declarer happily played a diamond on which Filarski played the queen (an entry disrupting play) and South took this to play a third, allowing Herman to cash two spade winners. This is the ending:

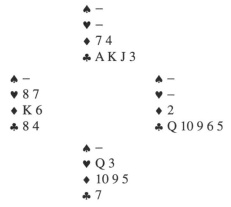

When Filarski led a diamond West kept up the good work by ducking, and now declarer cashed his last top heart, dummy throwing a diamond and East a club. Declarer now knew the defensive shape, so he cunningly played the club seven to the ace (on which East unblocked the ten), and the club three from dummy. But Filarski allowed his partner to win the eight and cash two winners for two down. North innocently inquired whether it would have been better to run the seven of clubs from hand in the four card ending—but Filarski had his answer ready—he would have ducked it.

The following examples show another common distribution, which you could easily encounter every session. As usual, South is declarer.

```
        K Q 10 2              10 8 6
J 5 3          A 9 4   A 7 4          J 5 3
        8 7 5                K Q 9 2
```

These distributions are to all intents and purposes identical, but it is a lot easier to duck the ace in the first example than in the second, where the honors are concealed. Of course, the point is that, if you win the ace at once, it is easy for declarer to finesse for the jack on the second round. If you duck the ace, declarer has to read the position very well.

Sometimes you have to steel yourself to a duck that appears highly unnatural; such as the following holdings.

```
         Q 5                   Q 5
10 9 2          K 7 6 3   10 2          K 8 6 3
         A J 8 4               A J 9 7 4
```

When declarer starts both suits by leading to the queen you have to duck in the first instance, in which case declarer will probably play your partner for Kxx, by ducking completely on the next trick, and subsequently laying down the ace. In the second example, declarer may finesse the nine on the way back if he has been convinced by a smooth duck from you.

Sometimes you need to duck an ace to preserve your entry to your own long suit. This example comes from the London Trophy, a contest designed primarily for non-experts. This hand graced the Final of an event at the end of the 1980s.

Aggregate Teams.

```
              ♠ Q 9 7 2
              ♥ A 6
              ♦ A J 9
              ♣ K Q J 2
♠ A 10 4                     ♠ 8 6 3
♥ 10 9 7 5 4                 ♥ K Q 3
♦ 10                         ♦ Q 8 7 2
♣ 9 8 4 3                    ♣ A 10 6
              ♠ K J 5
              ♥ J 8 2
              ♦ K 6 5 4 3
              ♣ 7 5
```

Mike Hill was occupying the West seat against 3NT (at the other table this contract had made comfortably from the North seat) and he made a good choice to lead the heart ten, not a small one, clearing up any ambiguity in the suit, His partner won the queen to return a small heart to the ace. Declarer rather forlornly played a spade to the king, and Hill ducked in perfect tempo—I was sitting behind him and I can vouch for it!

At this point declarer had to decide whether his left hand opponent had the spade ace and not the club ace—in which case he should play on clubs now—or whether Hill had defended so well. I have a lot of sympathy with him for getting it wrong and playing a club. Now the defense could untangle their winners and beat the contract by two tricks. But, if West wins the first spade, the hearts are blocked and all declarer has to do is guess the diamonds to make his contract—and he will probably get a count on the hand to succeed in doing that.

Now, try this one on for size! It won East the award for the best defense of the year in 1992, and he deserved it, too.

Teams.

```
              ♠ K Q 9 4
              ♥ K 7 6 3
              ♦ Q 8 5 2
              ♣ K
♠ 10 7 2                     ♠ A J 5
♥ 10 5                       ♥ Q J 9 4
♦ 9 3                        ♦ J 10 7 6
♣ Q J 10 9 7 2               ♣ 8 3
              ♠ 8 6 3
              ♥ A 8 2
              ♦ A K 4
              ♣ A 6 5 4
```

Imagine playing 3NT as South after a strong no trump and Stayman. You win the club lead and play a diamond to hand to try a spade to dummy's queen.

If East wins the ace and clears the clubs, you will test the diamonds, and eventually establish a spade trick without letting West get the lead. If East ducks, you may cross back to hand in diamonds to play a spade to the king, but if you win the next club you can still build a long spade without letting West get the lead. What happened at the table?

Declarer won the club lead, crossed to hand in diamonds and led a spade to the queen on which East, Mike Passell contributed the jack! Declarer assumed that East had jack-ten or ace-jack-ten, and he crossed to hand to play a spade to dummy's king. Passell won the ace and played a second club, and West now had the entry of the spade ten to cash out his clubs.

A quite different reason for holding up on a losing finesse comes when declarer's strategy depends on whether the finesse wins or loses. If it wins, he can perhaps afford a safety play in trumps for instance. If that is the case, then we can get some mileage out of a discreet duck.

Teams.

```
              ♠ A 10 2
              ♥ K 9 5 2
              ♦ A 3
              ♣ A Q 9 5
  ♠ 8 7                        ♠ K 5 4
  ♥ 8 7                        ♥ Q 10 4
  ♦ Q 10 7 5 2                 ♦ J 9 8 4
  ♣ 10 8 7 2                   ♣ J 6 4
              ♠ Q J 9 6 3
              ♥ A J 6 3
              ♦ K 6
              ♣ K 3
```

West	North	East	South
Pass	1♣	Pass	1♠
Pass	2NT	Pass	3♥
Pass	4♥	Pass	4NT
Pass	5♠	Pass	6♥
All Pass			

On the lead of the diamond five South takes some time to win the king, and then takes the spade finesse. It is not too hard to work out that the only reason for taking the danger-ous spade finesse before touching trumps is that South needs to know whether the spade finesse is working to judge how to play trumps.

Don't show him the spade loser; if you duck, South may think that he can afford the safety play in trumps of cashing the ace, and then leading low to the nine. Even if he has a trump loser, he "knows" there is no spade loser.

It is arguable that this final distribution falls more appropri-ately in the section of giving declarer a losing option rather than ducking an ace; whichever category you want to put it into, it is a useful one to have seen in print—you need to be able to defend in tempo to get the most out of it.

```
              Q 4
  J 10                     A 7 5
              K 9 8 6 3 2
```

Whether this is the trump suit or a suit at no trumps, declarer will presumably tackle it by leading to the queen. If you win the trick, declarer has only one distribution to play for to hold his losers to one—namely the jack-ten doubleton. Duck the trick, and declarer will probably play West for ace-ten doubleton.

PREVENTING THE BLOCKAGE

We have already seen a couple of examples where we were on lead and trying to persuade declarer not to block our suit, There are also a couple of positions where we have to know how to follow so as to persuade our opponent to untangle our suits for us. In this section tempo is also especially important. We must make these plays without betraying the fact that anything unusual is going on.

```
              9 7
  A 10 6 5 4 2              K J
              Q 8 3
```

You are East, defending 3NT after your partner has opened a weak two in this suit, and you know he has no side entry outside this suit. If this is the case, when partner leads a small card, try the jack at trick one—it will be almost impossible for declarer to duck this.

Two slight modifications on this.

```
        J 3                            J 3
A 10 6 5 4 2    K 9        A 9 6 5 4 2      K 10
        Q 8 7                          Q 8 7
```

In both these two cases you stand no chance of unscram-bling your suit if you play the king on the first trick, but if you follow with your intermediate card declarer will almost certainly misread the position. Obviously, you need to be confident that partner has no side entry to start attempting these plays—otherwise, in some instances, you may be throwing a trick or a tempo away. As I said earlier, it is also important to make these plays in tempo—otherwise you risk tipping off both declarer and your partner to the position. The point is that, while declarer (at his own risk) can take any advantage he likes from your hesitations, your partner doubtless will (and should) bend over backwards to avoid drawing any inferences from irregularities in your tempo. So if you reveal that you have an honor by a break before playing your card, he may feel obliged to defend on the basis that you do not.

It does not have to be the doubleton king that is potentially jamming the works; this next example is a fine play by Michel Lebel, playing with Michel Perron of France, from the 1989 European Championships.

```
              K 5
  A 10 9 8 4 3             Q 3
              J 7 6
```

Lebel was sitting East and his partner (who had shown a six-card suit with a weak hand in the auction) led the ten, promising a higher honor. Declarer ducked in dummy, and so did Lebel! One can hardly blame declarer for failing to read the position and playing the jack.

Virtually the same East-West holdings:

```
              J 5
  A 10 9 7 6 4             K 3
              Q 8 2
```

Duck the opening lead of the ten and you give South a headache.

PREVENTING DECLARER FROM DUCKING

Yet again it helps to know the basic rules of technique before exploring the elements of deception. First of all, let us look at when we should duck and what we should do to overcome declarer's wiles.

On all the following five holdings you are sitting East, defending a no trump contract at teams, and your partner is leading your suit. You have only one sure entry outside this suit in the first four examples and no entry in case five, but you need to set up your suit to beat the contract.

(a)   **(b)**

```
        7 4 3                         Q J 6
8 2              K Q 10 9 5   8 2            K 10 9 7 5
        A J 6                         A 4 3
```

In case (a) if you play the queen declarer can duck and kill the suit you must play the nine, and thus gain a tempo. In case (b) it is an error for declarer to play dummy's queen or jack; if he ducks he neutralizes the suit. But if he does err and you cover the jack (unless you have *two* entries, when covering is right) declarer can recover by ducking this trick.

(c)   **(d)**

```
        A J 6                         J 6 4
8 2              K 10 9 7 5   8 2            K Q 9 8 5
        Q 4 3                         A 10 3
```

(e)

```
        K 4 3
8 2              A Q 10 9 5
        J 7 6
```

Think of yourself as Adam in the Garden of Eden in example (c), (d) and (e). The snake in the form of a serpentine declarer may tempt you by playing dummy's jack or king respectively from dummy, but resist and play low, and you may reap a heavenly reward.

Those are the technical plays; now you need to focus on setting up your partner's suit and overcoming declarer's possible ducking strategy.

```
        A 5
10 8 7 6 3          K J 2
        Q 9 4
```

Consider this suit in a no trump contract; your partner (whom you know from the bidding to have a very weak hand) leads the six. Declarer plays low from the dummy, and if you make the natural play of the king you know that you will get exactly one trick from the suit. Try committing the heinous sin of finessing against partner, by playing the jack at trick one—now when declarer wins the queen (he will won't he?) you can clear the suit at your next turn by leading the king, and bingo! three winner. What if partner had the queen—then your play did not cost.

Of course this position arises in reverse when this is the layout:

```
        A 5
10 6 3            K J 8 7 2
        Q 9 4
```

When your partner leads your suit, and you have no quick entries, playing the jack preserves communication. But it helps to have your explanations ready for your partner if declarer has queen-nine doubleton.

More of the same:

```
        9 5
J 8 7 6 3          A Q 2
        K 10 4
```

If your partner, having very limited values, leads the six, then it costs nothing to put in the queen at your first turn. After all if partner has the king there is no harm done, and if declarer has the king you effectively prevent him from ducking. But do remember that this play is only relevant when partner has a weak hand.

Let us see two similar hands to get the point properly. In both cases you are defending 3NT, after South opens a weak no trump.

Teams.

```
                ♠ A K J
                ♥ 9 7
                ♦ J 10 4
                ♣ Q J 7 4 2
♠ 8 7 3                         ♠ 10 9 2
♥ J 8 6 4 2                     ♥ A Q 5
♦ K Q 7                         ♦ 9 6 5 3
♣ K 9                           ♣ 6 5 3
                ♠ Q 6 5 4
                ♥ K 10 3
                ♦ A 8 2
                ♣ A 10 8
```

Teams.

```
                ♠ K Q J
                ♥ 9 7
                ♦ J 10 2
                ♣ A J 7 4 2
♠ 8 7 3                         ♠ 10 9 2
♥ J 8 6 4 2                     ♥ A Q 5
♦ K 7 4                         ♦ Q 9 6 3
♣ 9 6                           ♣ K 5 3
                ♠ A 6 5 4
                ♥ K 10 3
                ♦ A 8 5
                ♣ Q 10 8
```

The first hand is a classic example of a little learning being a dangerous thing; if you play the heart queen at trick one, partner will win the club king and play you for the diamond ace rather than the heart ace. In contrast, the second hand is exactly the right moment to play the heart queen—if you do not the defense will surely fail, but declarer has no chance if you play the queen smoothly. The critical point is that if you trance before making the play, a hot declarer will read the position—it would be a shame to waste your chance for glory, wouldn't it?

DON'T GIVE THE WHOLE SHOW AWAY

There are two facets to this theme; the first relates to some specific suit combinations where your object is to leave declarer in doubt as to whether a suit is behaving favorably or not. The second part of the theme refers to the more general issue of not giving information away unnecessarily. Let us look at some suit combinations first, and see how declarer would tackle this suit to play it for only one loser.

```
        7 6 5 2
KQ                1 0 8 4
        A J 9 3
```

If you judge to follow the percentages by leading low from dummy and putting in the nine, your intention on the next round will be to play low to your jack. Not so fast; when East follows with the eight on the second round declarer can work out relatively simply that it is not physically possible for East to hold ♥K10x—his holding is 1084, 84, or K1084.

The only one of those that allows declarer to play the suit for one loser is the first one, so declarer drops the remaining honor. What can the defense do about this? It is relatively simple once you think about it; follows with the ten on the second round (if you prefer, you can think of this as a variation on playing the card you are known to hold) and now declarer can happily finesse on the second round.

That is a relatively common holding; this is a less frequently variation.

```
        6 5 2
A K                J 9 7
        Q 1 0 8 4 3
```

Declarer leads to his ten on the first round, forcing you to play the jack when he next leads the suit off dummy—the card you are known to hold.

Sometimes you need to protect partner's good play.

```
        A Q 1 0 8 6 5
J 9 2                K 4
        7 3
```

Declarer (who has no entry to dummy) leads a low card to dummy's ten, which holds the trick. Partner will not be impressed if you fail to play the jack on the second round,

because declarer's only real hope will be the actual layout. This is well illustrated by one of Terence Reese's imaginative themes from forty years ago.

Pairs.

```
                ♠ Q 10 2
                ♥ 9 5 3 2
                ♦ J 7 6
                ♣ A K Q
♠ K 7 4 3                       ♠ 8 5
♥ K 8 7                         ♥ J 6 4
♦ 10 5                          ♦ 9 8 4 3 2
♣ 10 8 7 2                      ♣ 9 6 4
                ♠ A J 9 6
                ♥ A Q 10
                ♦ A K Q
                ♣ J 5 3
```

Playing pairs, you reach 6NT on a club lead and win in dummy to run the spade ten, which holds the trick. You repeat the finesse but West wins the king and plays back another club. You win in dummy and, resigned to your fate, you try a heart to the ten. It holds the trick, so you cash all the spades and diamonds, and cross to table at trick eleven.

East's last two cards are the jack and six of hearts and, when you start to repeat the heart finesse, he must remember to play the jack so that West (who has reduced to the bare heart king and the master club ten) can get both of the last two tricks instead of neither of them! (It is pairs, and West figures that as the field will play in slam it is worth the risk of letting slam make to go for down two.)

Sometimes not giving the show away involves winning tricks early.

```
                ♠ 10 8 2
                ♥ J 6 2
                ♦ A Q J 10 6
                ♣ Q 10
♠ Q 3                           ♠ K J 9 7 5 4
♥ 5                             ♥ A 9 8 3
♦ 9 8 7 4 3                     ♦ 2
♣ J 9 7 6 2                     ♣ A 4
                ♠ A 6
                ♥ K Q 10 7 4
                ♦ K 5
                ♣ K 8 5 3
```

Your opponents reach four hearts after you open one spade, and your partner leads the spade queen, ducked, and a second spade. When declarer leads the heart queen it is natural but misguided to duck this trick; if you do, then declarer discovers the 4-1 heart split and has no problem in ruffing the next spade low, and drawing trumps for ten tricks.

But if you win the first heart and return a spade, it is probable that declarer will ruff this trick high, playing for trumps to be 3-2; unlucky.

On the other hand, it is probably more frequently the case that positions will arise where you should not win your tricks early. If you do, you let declarer test his chances in order.

```
          Q J 7 5 2
   9 8 4              K 10 6
          A 3
```

When declarer plays this suit at no trumps by leading the ace and a low card to dummy, it looks to be right to duck this trick.

If you take the trick, then declarer will regain the lead and can test the suit at his leisure, with a gain of tempo. If you duck this trick declarer may fear that either East or West has a four card suit, and will have two winners to cash if he plays a third round of the suit.

This may not sound critical, but let us see the theme in action in a full hand.

Teams.

```
                ♠ A 10 2
                ♥ Q J 8 5 2
                ♦ A 3
                ♣ A Q 5
   ♠ 9 8 7 6                    ♠ J 5 4
   ♥ 9 7 6                      ♥ A 10 4
   ♦ 10 2                       ♦ J 9 8 4
   ♣ 10 9 7 4                   ♣ J 8 6
                ♠ K Q 3
                ♥ K 3
                ♦ K Q 7 6 5
                ♣ K 3 2
```

Look how easy the play in 6NT is, on the lead of the spade nine. Declarer knocks out the heart ace, and does not need even to test the diamonds when the major suit behaves.

But it is not that easy if East ducks the first two heart tricks. If hearts are 4-2 then declarer goes down at once by playing a third round. A much better percentage play is to test the diamonds first. All well and good if they behave—if not, go back to hearts, hoping that they are 3-3 and that the man with the ace had the short diamonds. Declarer is doubly unlucky, to run into this distribution and this defense.

The purpose of signalling and discarding is to give useful information to your partner. If the only person who can benefit from a signal is declarer, there is no point in giving him a blueprint of your hand. Therefore, if you know that you who will have to take all the decisions, or you know that partner will not understand your delicate signal, then why bother to paint the picture?

In the European Championships played in Killarney in 1991, the winning British team generated a slam swing by very intelligent play at both tables.

Teams.

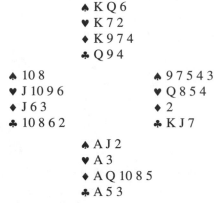

```
                ♠ K Q 6
                ♥ K 7 2
                ♦ K 9 7 4
                ♣ Q 9 4
   ♠ 10 8                       ♠ 9 7 5 4 3
   ♥ J 10 9 6                   ♥ Q 8 5 4
   ♦ J 6 3                      ♦ 2
   ♣ 10 8 6 2                   ♣ K J 7
                ♠ A J 2
                ♥ A 3
                ♦ A Q 10 8 5
                ♣ A 5 3
```

Both tables reached six diamonds from the South seat on the lead of the heart jack, and both declarers won the ace, drew trumps (East pitching two spades) and took the three top spades. Then they played a heart to king and another heart. The Czech East (who did not want to get endplayed if he won the heart queen) ducked and the British declarer, Andy Robson, ruffed the trick, and correctly decided that East had the club king. So he played a club to the nine (yes, West should have played the ten) and endplayed East to give him a ruff and discard or play a club for him.

At the other table where John Armstrong was East, the defense took a slightly different turn; when the third heart was led Armstrong rose with the queen (pretending to be a man who *did* want to be left on lead). Declarer duly ruffed the trick, and was persuaded by this play that John did not have the club king. So he laid down the club ace, and went down one.

TRUMP TRICKS

Promotions, uppercuts, and general fooling around)

The opportunity to ruff, and over-ruff, is hedged around with deceptive elements. Sometimes you can achieve interesting results by over-ruffing high. Look at this trump suit—we have seen it before in a slightly different context.

```
          Q 8 7 2
   4                  K J 6 3
          A 10 9 5
```

West leads a card in a suit in which North and East are void. If East over-trumps dummy's eight with the jack that will be his last trick in the suit. But if he over-ruffs with the king he may score the jack later if South lays down the ace, preparing for a finesse against West's jack.

A slight variation on that theme:

```
          J 8 7 2
   4                  Q 10 6 3
          A K 9 5
```

Whether East is over-ruffing dummy's eight, or following suit once West has switched to the four, he does best to play the queen. Either way declarer is likely to play West for the length.

Trump promotions and uppercuts are another tricky area. To understand them it is perhaps helpful to look at a few positions where the defense do best not to use their high trumps too soon.

When East leads a master card in a side suit in which West and North are void, West does best to discard rather than ruff in, when the trump suit is divided in the following ways.

```
        9 2                          9 2
Q 5           K 7 3        J 5             K 7 3
        A J 10 8 6 4              A Q 10 8 6 4
```

In either case, if West scores his queen (or jack) that is the last trump trick for the defense; in the first case discarding assures the defense of two tricks, in the second case declarer has the trumps to hold his losers to one. Note that in both cases, if East leads a losing plain card and South covers it, the defense does best to ruff in with the five, to force the over-ruff, leaving declarer an awkward guess on the next round. And of course that means it would probably be right as West to ruff low with king-five also.

Sometimes it is right not to over-ruff dummy to generate extra trump tricks, or to put declarer to the guess again. In the next two examples you are East, and declarer ruffs a card in dummy with a high trump in a suit in which you are also void.

```
        Q 2                          Q 2
A 9           K 8 3        10 4            K 8 3
        J 10 7 6 5 4              A J 9 7 6 5
```

When declarer ruffs with the queen you assure your side of the three tricks by not over-ruffing in case one. In the second example your chances of two tricks are much better if you do not over-ruff, since declarer may lead his nine next.

Two more positions where the defense maximize their chances by not over-ruffing; in each case dummy has ruffed with the ten, and you, as East, increase your chances of getting three and two tricks respectively by not winning the trick.

```
        K J 10 8 7 5              10 5
A 4 2         Q 9         4 2            Q 9 8 7
        6 3                        A K J 6 3
```

In the first example, declarer may take the finesse of the eight on the first or second round if you refrain from the over-ruff, and in the second case declarer may try and drop your partner's doubleton queen.

All sorts of strange things can happen if you refrain from taking your trump tricks at the first chance you get. Here you are defending four spades, and you lead a diamond in response to your partner's opening pre-empt.

```
               ♠ 10 8
               ♥ 9 6 4 2
               ♦ Q 10 9
               ♣ A 7 5 2
♠ K 4 3                        ♠ 5 2
♥ 10 5 3                       ♥ Q 7 2
♦ A 5                          ♦ K J 8 7 6 4
♣ J 9 8 6 3                    ♣ Q 10
               ♠ A Q J 9 7 6
               ♥ A K J
               ♦ 3 2
               ♣ K 4
```

When declarer ruffs the third diamond high you do not over-ruff, and when declarer crosses to table to run the spade eight you duck that too. Now is declarer's last chance to take the heart finesse—but I don't think he will, do you?

Sometimes the decision not to over-ruff can look like a quixotic rejection of a trick; but it can come back in the most surprising ways.

Pairs.

```
               ♠ A J 4 2
               ♥ 10 5 2
               ♦ A 3
               ♣ J 10 9 5
♠ K 7 3                        ♠ 8
♥ A 6                          ♥ K J 9 7 4 3
♦ Q J 9 7 5 2                  ♦ 8 4
♣ 7 2                          ♣ A 8 6 4
               ♠ Q 10 9 6 5
               ♥ Q 8
               ♦ K 10 6
               ♣ K Q 3
```

West	North	East	South
–	–	2♥	2♠
3♥	3♠	All Pass	

North-South appear to have done well to stop so low; on the sight of dummy you can see that desperate measures may be called for. Your partner signals encouragement on your opening lead of the heart ace, so you play a second round, and on the third round declarer ruffs with the spade nine, and you discard the club seven.

Now if declarer swallows the bait, and plays a spade to the ace and a second spade, you win your king and play a club to your partner for a club ruff.

An even more unusual opportunity presented itself to a French expert pair from thirty years ago.

```
            ♠ 7 6 4
            ♥ A Q J 10
            ♦ J 9 8 3
            ♣ 8 5
♠ K                    ♠ 10
♥ 9 7 6 5 3 2          ♥ K 8 4
♦ 7 4                  ♦ A K Q 10 6
♣ K J 6 2              ♣ Q 9 7 3
            ♠ A Q J 9 8 5 3 2
            ♥ –
            ♦ 5 2
            ♣ A 10 4
```

Pierre Jais opened one diamond in the third seat, but South brushed this aside by bidding four spades, and there the matter rested. On Dominique Pilon's lead of the diamond seven the defense played three rounds of the suit, and declarer ruffed with the jack. Pilon's decision not to over-ruff looks quixotic—but he could see that the trick should come back—and it did with interest!

Declarer naturally played the ace of clubs and a second club, allowing Jais to lead a fourth diamond. Declarer ruffed with the queen, and now Pilon had his trump trick back.

Sometimes your best chances of creating a trump trick is to appear to be creating one for your partner . . .

North/South Vulnerable. Teams.

```
            ♠ K Q 10 9 7
            ♥ J 10 6
            ♦ A J
            ♣ J 3 2
♠ 8 6 3 2              ♠ A 5 4
♥ –                    ♥ K 9 4
♦ Q 10 5              ♦ 9 8 6 4 2
♣ A K Q 10 7 4        ♣ 8 5
            ♠ J
            ♥ A Q 8 7 5 3 2
            ♦ K 7 3
            ♣ 9 6
```

West	North	East	South
–	–	Pass	1♥
3♣	3♠	Pass	4♥
All Pass			

At this vulnerability West's three club bid, though technically intermediate, could be anything.

Your partner elects to lead three top clubs against four

hearts (perhaps it would have been better to switch to a diamond in theory, although it would not work here) and on this trick you may find that ruffing with the heart nine (in an attempt) to appear like a person desperately promoting a trump for your partner) is your best move. You may be able to persuade declarer to lay down the heart ace now—if you do not ruff South is likely to play you for the heart king.

This final hand is another example of manipulating trumps in an unusual fashion, again from a standard American pairs event.

Let us consider it first of all as a declarer play problem, before seeing all four hands:

Both Sides Vulnerable. Pairs.

```
            ♠ Q
            ♥ A Q J 6 4
            ♦ K 8 7 3 2
            ♣ K 4

            ♠ J 7 4 2
            ♥ 8 3 2
            ♦ A 9
            ♣ 9 8 3 2
```

West	North	East	South
–	–	Pass	Pass
1♠	2♠	Pass	3♥
All Pass			

North's cuebid showed a two suiter with hearts and a minor.

West leads a top spade and switches to the club jack. You play the king, but East cashes the ace and queen, then exits with the spade ten which you ruff in dummy. You cross to the diamond ace and take a successful heart finesse, then play the diamond king, on which West follows with the queen, and ruff a diamond with the three, overruffed with the king. West exits with the spade king, which you ruff high in dummy, as East follows to reach this ending.

```
            ♠ –
            ♥ A 6
            ♦ 8 7
            ♣ –

            ♠ J
            ♥ 8
            ♦ –
            ♣ 9 8
```

It looks as if you have a complete count on the hand; West started life with a 5-2-2-4 shape, and you can ruff a diamond in hand, a club in dummy, and then take the heart ace and concede the last trick. So you confidently ruff a diamond to hand. Unlucky!

This was the full hand:

```
                    ♠ Q
                    ♥ A Q J 6 4
                    ♦ K 8 7 3 2
                    ♣ K 4
    ♠ A K 9 8 5                 ♠ 10 6 3
    ♥ K 10 5                    ♥ 9 7
    ♦ Q 6                       ♦ J 10 5 4
    ♣ J 10 7                    ♣ A Q 6 5
                    ♠ J 7 4 2
                    ♥ 8 3 2
                    ♦ A 9
                    ♣ 9 8 3 2
```

When you ruff the diamond West over-ruffs, and plays another spade, promoting her partner's heart nine for the setting trick.

Kitty Munson's decision to over-ruff with the "known" heart king made declarer's life impossible; if she had over-ruffed with her low trump, declarer would certainly have drawn a round of trumps in the four card ending, and given up a diamond for nine tricks.